Marketing Research
Methodological Foundations

Eighth Edition

Marketing Research
Methodological Foundations

Eighth Edition

Gilbert A. Churchill, Jr.
University of Wisconsin–Madison

Dawn Iacobucci
J.L. Kellogg Graduate School of Management
Northwestern University
and
University of Arizona

SOUTH-WESTERN
THOMSON LEARNING

Australia • Canada • Mexico • Singapore • Spain •
United Kingdom • United States

Marketing Research: Methodological Foundations, 8e
Gilbert A. Churchill, Jr. and Dawn Iacobucci

Publisher:
Michael P. Roche

Acquisitions Editor:
Mark Orr

Developmental Editor:
CJ Jasieniecki

Marketing Strategist:
Beverly Dunn

Project Manager:
Angela Williams Urquhart

Cover Image:
PhotoDisc © 2002.

Library of Congress Cataloging-in-
Publication Control Number

2001087534

ISBN: 0-030-33101-3

Dedication

To my wife and children;
and in memory of my grandmother, dad, mother, and our son, John.
GAC

Preface

Intended Market

This book is designed for the introductory sequence in marketing research and attempts to structure the discipline of marketing research for students.

The topic of marketing research is a complex one. It requires answers to a number of questions and a number of decisions about the technique or techniques to be used to solve a research problem. Without some overriding framework, students often become so overwhelmed by the bits and pieces that they fail to see the interrelationship of the parts to the whole. This distorted vision can be detrimental to both the aspiring manager and the aspiring researcher, for in a very real sense, marketing research is a series of trade-offs. Decisions made about one stage in the research process have consequences for the other stages. Managers must appreciate the subtle and pervasive interactions among the parts of the research process to be appropriately confident about a particular research result. Researchers also need to appreciate the interactions among the parts. The parts serve as "pegs" on which to hang knowledge accumulated about research methods, but researchers must avoid becoming enamored of the parts to the detriment of the whole.

This book attempts to serve both the aspiring manager and the aspiring researchers through its basic organization around the stages of the research process. The research process is a sequence of steps that must be completed when answering a research question. The six parts of the book parallel these specific stages:

1. Formulate the problem
2. Determine the research design
3. Design the data-collection method and forms
4. Design the sample and collect the data
5. Analyze and interpret the data
6. Prepare the research report

Moreover, the stages are broken into smaller parts, and a given stage is typically discussed in several chapters and appendices. Not only does this allow students to see the forest for the trees, but it also provides instructors a great deal of latitude about what is covered. An instructor's decision on what to cover will depend, of course, on the background, interests, and maturity of the students and on the time provided in the curriculum for marketing research. Because *Marketing Research: Methodological Foundations, Eighth Edition,* provides instructors great flexibility in the level of depth with which to cover any particular stage in the research process, it can be used in a variety of introductory marketing research course sequences: one- or two-quarter sequences or in semester courses. The first seven editions of the book have been used to advantage at both the undergraduate and graduate (and executive) levels by simply covering more material at a higher level of sophistication in the graduate courses.

Organization

Part 1, on formulating the problem, consists of three chapters. Chapter 1 provides an overview of marketing research, including the kinds of problems for which it is used, who is doing research, and how it is organized. It also discusses some of the career opportunities available in marketing research. Chapter 2 provides an overview of the various ways of gathering marketing intelligence. It emphasizes the increasingly important role played by decision support systems in providing business and competitive intelligence, and contrasts the information-system approaches to the project approach taken in the book. Chapter 3 overviews the research process in terms of the kinds of decisions to be made at each stage and then discusses in some detail the problem formulation stage of the research process.

Part 2 consists of two chapters and deals with the nature of the research design. It emphasizes ensuring that the research addresses the appropriate questions and treats them in an efficient manner. Chapter 4 overviews the roles of various research designs and also discusses two basic designs, the exploratory and the descriptive, at some length. Chapter 5 discusses the role and conceptual logic of experiments.

The four chapters in Part 3 delve into methods of data collection and design of data-collection forms. Chapter 6 focuses on secondary data as an information resource and includes a discussion of commercial marketing information services. The appendix to Chapter 6 discusses many of the prime sources of secondary data. Chapter 7 discusses the two main methods of data collection, observation and communication, and Chapter 8 covers the construction of questionnaires and observation data-collection forms. Chapter 9 explains the general topic of attitude measurement using scales and discusses some of the more common types of attitude scales. The important but often neglected topic of developing measures for marketing constructs of interest is discussed in the appendix to Chapter 9.

Part 4, which consists of three chapters, is concerned with the actual collection of data needed to answer questions. Chapter 10 discusses the various types of sampling plans that can be used to determine the population elements from which data should be collected. Chapter 11 treats the question of how many of these elements are needed, so that the problem can be answered with the required precision and confidence in the results. Chapter 12 discusses the many errors that can arise in completing this data collection task from a perspective that allows managers to better assess the quality of the information they receive from research.

Once data have been collected, emphasis in the research process logically turns to analysis, which amounts to searching for meaning in the collected information.

The search for meaning involves many questions and several steps. The five chapters and several appendices in Part 5 attempt to overview these steps and questions. Chapter 13 reviews the preliminary analysis steps of editing, coding, and tabulating the data. The appendix to Chapter 13 covers chi-square tests, contingency tables, and log linear models, all models of analysis useful for categorical data. The main questions that must be resolved before statistical examination of the data can begin are covered in Chapter 14. Next, Chapters 15, 16, and 17 review the statistical techniques most useful in the analysis of marketing data. Chapter 15 discusses the procedures appropriate for examining the differences among and between groups; Chapter 16 covers the assessment of association—namely, correlation and regression, including the application to conjoint analysis; and Chapter 17 examines the multivariate techniques of discriminant analysis, factor analysis, cluster analysis, and multidimensional scaling. The appendix to Chapter 17 introduces additional multivariate techniques: correspondence analysis, structural equations modeling, neural network models, and social networks.

Part 6 consists of one chapter and an epilogue. Chapter 18 discusses a critical part of the research process, the research report, which often becomes the standard by which the research effort is assessed. Chapter 18 discusses the criteria a research report should satisfy and the form it can follow to contribute positively to the research effort. This chapter also discusses some of the graphical means that can be used to communicate the important findings more forcefully. The epilogue ties together the elements of the research process by demonstrating in overview fashion their interrelationships.

Organizational Flexibility

The organization of the book around the stages in the research process produces several significant benefits. First, it demonstrates and continually reinforces how the "bits" of research technique fit into a larger whole. Students can see readily, for example, the relationship between statistics and marketing research, or where they might pursue additional study to become research specialists.

Second, the organization permits great flexibility. For example, instructors with only a single, brief, one-quarter introductory course in marketing research who are faced with the need to develop some appreciation for the basic questions addressed in research might choose to overview the research process at an elementary level. One way to accomplish this would be to omit Chapter 5 on causal research designs, Chapter 9 on attitude measurement, and Chapter 11 on sample size, and to cover only Chapter 13 from among the five analysis chapters. This approach would serve to present the process and at the same time to avoid some of the more technical questions of research design, measurement, and sampling, and the statistical analysis of the collected data.

On the other hand, instructors who wish to emphasize, say, the questions of analysis or measurement would have ample materials to do so. There is, for example, one database in the textbook itself and a number of other databases on disk that instructors can have students analyze using one of the standard statistical packages. The database in the book involves buying through catalogs. It is used to demonstrate everything from the coding of data to the most involved statistical techniques. The appendices to appropriate chapters contain sample computer output and discuss the interpretation of that output in light of the notions discussed in the chapter. These appendices provide students a direct connection between statistical concepts and the application of these concepts. The database is rich enough for students to perform their own analyses, thereby increasing their comfort level with the statistical techniques discussed. The specific portions of the book that should be used to produce this emphasis or several other emphases are discussed in the *Instructor's Manual*, which contains suggested outlines for organizing courses to achieve different emphases in different time frames.

Each part (except Part 6) concludes with cases that illustrate many of the major issues raised in the section. The cases present actual situations, although many of them have disguised names and locations to protect the identity of the sponsors. The cases afford students the opportunity to apply what they have learned by critically evaluating what others have done, thereby increasing their analytic skills.

Changes in the Eighth Edition

Compared to the last edition, this eighth edition contains some major changes. One change is an increased emphasis on the use of the Internet for marketing research. For example, we discuss research about the Internet and research using the Internet, we compare Web-based surveys to traditional techniques like mail surveys and phone interviews, and we provide Web sites for numerous references and resources in the text, including the secondary data sources enumerated in the appendix to Chapter 6. The Internet and phenomena in marketing like database marketing, relationship marketing, and one-to-one marketing have all spawned a booming industry on "data mining"—the analysis of very large databases—and this is a topic now introduced in Chapter 2, as it relates to decision support systems (DSSs) and management information systems (MISs).

Another change focuses on a major revision of the cases—more than 20 percent of the cases are new and another 20 percent have been revised. We also sought to heighten the international flavor of many of the examples and cases to reflect the increasingly multicultural interests of students and the compositions of marketing research classes. In several places, we also present material that is a little more advanced for the students with stronger analytical backgrounds or interests (for example, log linear and logit models in the appendix to Chapter 13, multivariate statistical developments in the appendix to Chapter 17). Instructors may not wish to cover the advanced materials with the entire class, but the material is available to challenge the students who seek more. The material on multidimensional scaling (MDS) has been moved into Chapter 17, which surveys multivariate statistical techniques, and the material on conjoint analysis has been integrated into the last section of Chapter 16, which covers multiple regression.

Readers will also be happy to know that a number of features incorporated in the fifth through seventh editions are being retained for this edition because they were so well received, including the video case and the extensive treatment of ethics in marketing research. The Thorndike Sports Video Case, which uses an original script and professional actors, is written in such a way as to allow the viewing of short segments that illustrate the points under discussion at a specific point in time.

There is a special icon at the end of the chapters that indicates the questions that might be asked after students view a segment of the video case. The video case should make for an interactive learning environment. This edition continues to present ethical scenarios that students need to address.

As part of the revision plan for the eighth edition, all of the chapters have been subjected to thorough scrutiny and rewrite. There has been a major updating of the examples and other pedagogy. For example, this edition contains more than 70 Research Realities, and 25 percent of them are new.

Special Features

As readers might suspect from the previous chapter descriptions, the level and difficulty of the material vary. Certain parts, such as the discussion of commercial information services in the secondary data chapter, are purely descriptive. Others, such as the concept of measurement, are by their nature abstract and, as such, are difficult for students not used to thinking in abstract terms. This range of difficulty, though, is characteristic of marketing research, and this book does not avoid topics simply because they are abstruse. Rather, the posture has been to include those topics that are vital to understanding the nature of the research process, while attempting to simplify complex ideas into their basic elements. Throughout, the emphasis is placed on conceptual understanding of the material rather than on mathematical niceties or discussion of interesting but unimportant tangents. The purpose here is to walk the middle ground between the two kinds of introductory textbooks currently available. One type discusses the concepts of marketing research without providing sufficient detail about some of the important, but perhaps more difficult, stages in the process. The other kind goes to the opposite extreme of discussing some technically difficult stages in great detail while omitting the basic structure of the process, and at other stages providing only cursory coverage of some of the more elementary, but critically important, methods. *Marketing Research: Methodological Foundations, Eighth Edition,* is designed to avoid such extremes by providing the student with a thorough treatment of the important concepts, both simple and complex.

The general approach employed throughout is not only to provide the student with the pros and cons of the various methods with which a research problem could be addressed, but also to develop an appreciation of why these advantages and disadvantages arise. The hope is that through this appreciation, students will be able to creatively apply and critically evaluate the procedures of marketing research.

This book contains a number of features designed to help students develop their creative and analytical marketing research skills. Some of the more important features follow.

- **Cases.** The cases at the end of each part are included to assist students in developing their evaluation and analytical skills. The cases are also useful in demonstrating the universal application of marketing research techniques. The methods of marketing research can be used not only by distributors of products, as is commonly assumed, but also to address other issues in the private and public sectors. The cases include such diverse entities or issues as the Big Brothers program, e-commerce, banking services, international data collection, and theater, among others. Moreover, raw data for 10 of the cases are available to allow students the opportunity to do their analyses to answer the questions posed, and in the process, develop their data analysis skills.

- **The Thorndike Video Case.** The video case allows for an interactive learning environment. Students can be shown segments of the video, and class discussion can then be structured to identify the issues and determine what should be done next. In this sense, the video case parallels the type of situation students are likely to encounter in the workplace. It also helps show how decisions made at one stage of the research process affect decisions made at later stages.

- **Ethical Dilemmas.** The ethical dilemmas present students with scenarios that arise when making marketing research choices. They are presented along with discussion of the technical choices, so that students can see not only the advantages and disadvantages of proceeding in particular ways but the social consequences of doing so as well.

- **Research Realities.** The Research Realities illustrate what is going on in the world of marketing research today, both in general and at specific companies.

- **Problems.** The problems at the end of each chapter allow students the opportunity to apply the concepts discussed in that chapter to very focused situations, thereby developing firsthand knowledge of the strengths and weaknesses of the various techniques.

- **NFO Coffee Study.** The questionnaire, coding form, and raw data from a study on ground coffee conducted by NFO are used to frame a number of application problems. These problems, which are denoted by a special section at the end of the chapters, allow students the opportunity to work with "live" data in honing their skills in translating research problems into data analysis issues and in interpreting computer output. Moreover, the database is rich enough for instructors to design their own application problems/exercises, thereby allowing even more opportunity for hands-on learning.

- **Exercises.** There are also exercises for each chapter in the *Instructor's Manual.* The exercises direct students to do small-scale projects using particular techniques. The exercises develop students' in-depth understanding of the techniques, including their proper application.

Supplements to the Textbook

- **Instructor's Manual.** The *Instructor's Manual* to the textbook completes a comprehensive teaching package. It includes a preface that offers suggestions on how the book and *Instructor's Manual* can be used most effectively. The preface is followed by suggested outlines on how to teach the course to achieve desired emphases within different time frames. Next are the chapter-by-chapter resource materials, which include the following for each chapter:

  1. Learning objectives
  2. List of key terms

3.   Detailed outline

4.   Lecture and discussion suggestions

5.   Suggested supplementary readings

6.   Answers to the application questions and/or problems in the book

7.   Student exercises and answers

8.   Suggested cases for the chapter

The individual chapter materials are followed by a section containing the analyses for the cases included in the book. A number of the cases ask students to perform their own analyses to answer the questions posed.

- **Data Disk.** The raw data for these cases are contained on a computer disk, which allows those who have statistical packages available on microcomputers to use them for analysis. Others may find it more convenient to upload the data from the disk onto the school's mainframe computer and to have students use the larger system for their analyses.

- **Transparency Masters.** There are 200 transparency masters that illustrate major points. Some of these transparency masters enlarge the more important figures or tables in the book to facilitate classroom discussion. Others are original to the *Instructor's Manual* to allow the instructor to discuss additional issues in class.

- **Text Bank.** The Test Bank contains more than 1,100 multiple-choice objective examination questions. Many of the questions are new for this edition.

- **Powerpoint CD-ROM.** The CD-ROM contains everything included in the *Instructor's Manual,* Test Bank, Transparency Masters, and Data Disk. These files allow the instructor access to this data which can be manipulated to suit the instructor's needs.

- **Computerized Test Bank.** Available in IBM 3.5, Windows, and Macintosh-compatible formats, the computerized version of the printed test bank enables instructors to preview and edit test questions, as well as add their own. The test and answer keys can also be printed in "scrambled" formats.

- **Video Collection.** In addition to the Thorndike Video Case that is incorporated throughout the text, there are other videos in the series. Companies ranging from Fossil watches to Hard Candy focus on the ideas and concepts presented throughout the text.

Acknowledgments

Writing a book is never the work of a single person, and when attempting to acknowledge the contributions of others, one always runs the risk of omitting some important contributions. Nonetheless, the attempt must be made, because this book has been helped immensely by the many helpful comments I have received along the way from users and interested colleagues. I especially wish to acknowledge those people who reviewed the manuscript for this or for one of the earlier editions of the book. While much of the credit for the strengths of the book is theirs, the blame for any weaknesses is strictly mine. Thank you one and all for your most perceptive and helpful comments.

My colleagues at the University of Wisconsin have my thanks for the intellectual stimulation they have always provided. Dr. B. Venkatesh, who is now with The Burke Institute, was particularly instrumental in getting the first edition off the ground. My discussions with him were important in determining the scope and structure of the book.

I wish to thank the many assistants at the University of Wisconsin who participated in typing one or more versions of the manuscript. A special thank you goes to Janet Christopher, who again did most of the typing on the eighth edition and who assumed responsibility for other activities as well. I also wish to thank students Tom Brown, Sara Evans, Margaret Friedman, Diana Haytko, Jacqueline Hitchon, Larry Hogue, Joseph Kuester, Jayashree Mahajan, Jennifer Markanen, Sara Pitterle, Kay Powers, and Frank Wadsworth for their help with many of the miscellaneous tasks on either this edition or one of the earlier editions. I would like to thank Mark Orr, acquisitions editor, and C.J. Jasieniecki, developmental editor, as well as the entire production staff who worked on this edition, for their professional effort. I also want to thank P.J. Ward of NFO for contributing the questionnaire, coding form, database, and the compatible problems and exercises using the database regarding coffee consumption that illustrate so nicely the statistical ideas discussed in the text. I am grateful to the literary executor of the late Sir Ronald A. Fisher, F.R.S., to Dr. Frank Yates, F.R.S., and to the Longman Group Ltd., London, for permission to reprint Table III from their book *Statistical Tables for Biological, Agricultural and Medical Research* (6th edition, 1974).

Finally, I owe a special debt of thanks to my wife, Helen, and our four children, Carol, Elizabeth, David, and Thomas. Their understanding, cooperation, and support through all eight editions of this book are sincerely appreciated.

Gilbert A. Churchill, Jr.
Madison, Wisconsin

I'd like to add my thanks, first and foremost to Gil Churchill, and also to Bill Schoof, for giving me this opportunity. Anyone who knows Gil will not be surprised by my comment that I couldn't have hoped for a more gracious and encouraging coauthor and mentor. I also thank the Marketing Department at Kellogg, Sidney Levy at the University of Arizona, my mom, and God, the Great Data Source.☺

Dawn Iacobucci
Evanston, Illinois

Reviewers

Mark I. Alpert
University of Texas–Austin

Robert L. Anderson
University of South Florida

Gary M. Armstrong
University of North Carolina

Frank J. Carmone, Jr.
Drexel University

Joseph Chasin
St. John's University

Imran S. Currim
University of California–Irvine

Michael R. Czinkota
Georgetown University

Albert J. DellaBitta
University of Rhode Island

John Dickinson
University of Windsor

James F. Engel
Eastern College

Peter Faynzilberg
Carnegie Mellon University

Claes Fornell
University of Michigan

Margot Griffin
California Lutheran University

Sachin Gupta
Northwestern University

James W. Harvey
George Mason University

Vince Howe
University of North
Carolina–Wilmington

Roy Howell
Texas Tech University

G. David Hughes
University of North Carolina

Dipak C. Jain
Northwestern University

Robert Krapfel
University of Maryland

Patrick Kurby
Rutgers University

H. Bruce Lammers
California State
University–Northridge

Peter La Placa
University of Connecticut

Charles L. Martin
Wichita State University

M. Dean Martin
Western Carolina University

Carlos W. Moore
Baylor University

Carl Obermiller
Seattle University

Christie H. Paksoy
University of North
Carolina–Charlotte

Kalyan Ramon
University of Florida

C.P. Rao
University of Arkansas

Arno Rethans
California State University–Chico

Kenneth J. Roering
University of Minnesota

Abhijit Roy
Plymouth State College

William Rudelius
University of Minnesota

Alan G. Sawyer
University of Florida

Randall L. Schultz
University of Texas–Dallas

Subrata K. Sen
Yale University

Allan D. Shocker
University of Minnesota

Seymour Sudman
University of Illinois

David Szymanski
Texas A&M University

Sandra Teel
University of South Carolina

Robert Thomas
Georgetown University

David J. Urban
Virginia Commonwealth
University

William G. Zikmund
Oklahoma State University

About the Authors

Gilbert A. Churchill, Jr., received his DBA from Indiana University in 1966 and joined the University of Wisconsin faculty in 1966. Professor Churchill was named Distinguished Marketing Educator by the American Marketing Association in 1986—only the second individual so honored. The lifetime achievement award recognizes and honors a living marketing educator for distinguished service and outstanding contributions in the field of marketing education. Professor Churchill was also awarded the Academy of Marketing Science's lifetime achievement award in 1993 for his significant scholarly contributions. In 1996, he received a Paul D. Converse Award, which is given to the most influential marketing scholars, as judged by a national jury drawn from universities, businesses, and government. Also in 1996, the Marketing Research Group of the American Marketing Association established the Gilbert A. Churchill, Jr., lifetime achievement award, which is to be given each year to a person judged to have made significant lifetime contributions to marketing research.

Professor Churchill is a past recipient of the William O'Dell Award for the outstanding article appearing in the *Journal of Marketing Research* during the year. He has also been a finalist for the award five other times. He was named Marketer of the Year by the South Central Wisconsin Chapter of the American Marketing Association in 1981. He is a member of the American Marketing Association and has served as consultant to a number of companies, including Oscar Mayer, Western Publishing Company, and Parker Pen.

Professor Churchill's articles have appeared in such publications as the *Journal of Marketing Research, Journal of Marketing, Journal of Consumer Research, Journal of Retailing, Journal of Business Research, Decision Sciences, Technometrics,* and *Organizational Behavior and Human Performance,* among others. He is coauthor of several books, including *Marketing: Creating Value for Customers,* 2nd ed. (Burr Ridge, IL: McGraw-Hill, 1998), *Sales Force Management: Planning, Implementation, and Control,* 6th ed. (Burr Ridge, IL: Irwin/McGraw-Hill, 2000), and *Salesforce Performance* (Lexington, MA: Lexington Books, 1984), and he is also the author of *Basic Marketing Research,* 4th ed. (Fort Worth, TX: Harcourt College Publishers, 2001) in addition to his coauthorship of *Marketing Research: Methodological Foundations,* 8th ed. (Fort Worth, TX: Harcourt College Publishers, 2002). He is a former editor of the *Journal of Marketing Research* and has served on the editorial boards of the *Journal of Marketing Research, Journal of Marketing, Journal of Business Research, Journal of Health Care Marketing,* and the *Asian Journal of Marketing.* Professor Churchill is a past recipient of the Lawrence J. Larson Excellence in Teaching Award.

Dawn Iacobucci (ya′kō-**boo**′chee) received her Ph.D. in Quantitative Psychology from the University of Illinois at Urbana-Champaign in 1987 and joined the Marketing Department at the J.L. Kellogg Graduate School of Management at Northwestern University in 1987. In fall 2001, Iacobucci joined the University of Arizona as Professor of Marketing and Psychology and head of the marketing department. She is currently editor of the *Journal of Consumer Psychology*. She edited the volumes *Kellogg on Marketing* and *Networks in Marketing* and coedited the *Handbook of Services Marketing and Management* with Teresa Swartz.

Professor Iacobucci's articles have appeared in such publications as the *Journal of Marketing Research, Journal of Marketing, Journal of Consumer Psychology, Harvard Business Review, Sloan Management Review, Journal of Interactive Marketing, Journal of Service Marketing, Psychometrika, Psychological Bulletin, Multivariate Behavioral Research,* and *Journal of Personality and Social Psychology,* among others. She teaches marketing research and services marketing courses to the Kellogg MBA students and analysis of variance and multivariate statistics seminars to the Northwestern doctoral students.

Brief Contents

Contents

Marketing Research, the Research Process, and Problem Definition

We begin with an overview, addressing two basic questions: what is marketing research and why is it important? Chapter 1 illustrates the enormous variety of problems that marketing research can be used to address and the types of business people who require a working knowledge of marketing research. These include marketing researchers and marketing managers, as well as consultants, entrepreneurs, financial analysts, Internet moguls, and the like—anybody who seeks an edge in understanding customers in competitive market environments. Chapter 2 discusses alternative ways of providing marketing intelligence, namely, projects designed to investigate specific issues, or ongoing data collection and analytical systems such as marketing information systems and decision support systems. Chapter 3 previews the research process that will form the backbone in structuring this book and discusses in detail the problem formulation stage of that process.

Marketing Research: A Pervasive Activity

Many people have a mistaken impression about marketing research. They believe it is simply asking consumers what they think or feel about a certain brand or an advertisement. Although marketing research does make use of consumer surveys, it involves much more than that. Consider the following examples.[1]

EXAMPLE   After watching countless hours of videotapes of consumers entering various retail outlets such as department stores, grocery stores, and banks, marketing researchers have advised against investing in elaborate store displays for the first 30 feet from the entrance, the so-called "decompression zone" in which shoppers are merely getting oriented to the store layout and are not inclined to pick up merchandise for purchase. Similarly, the researchers noted that most consumers are likely to veer right as they proceed into the store, not because most are right-handed, but because we drive on the right—British and Australian consumers veer left.[2]

EXAMPLE   Gillette develops new products (for example, Mach III razors) by watching consumers shave—not by standing in their bathrooms, but by watching video from microcameras that have been attached to razors that the consumers were using to shave. This closeup view shows clearly what the blades do to the whiskers and surrounding skin, enabling Gillette to create more effective shaving instruments, to make superior product claims, and to charge premium prices.[3]

EXAMPLE   When Wrigley found sales and market share for their Juicy Fruit gum declining, the company asked teens who were frequent gum-chewers to find pictures that reminded them of the gum and to write a short story about them. Marketing researchers studied each montage and noted a common theme of "sweet tasting." Advertising was created with the tagline "Gotta Have Sweet," which proved memorable, and sales rose 5 percent after the campaign.[4]

---

[1]Do not worry if some of the terms and data collection methods mentioned in the examples are unfamiliar, as they are described later in the book. The intent in the examples is simply to provide some flavor of the types of problems that marketing research is used to address and some of the approaches that are used.

[2]Kenneth Labich, "Attention Shoppers: This Man Is Watching You," *Fortune* (July 19, 1999), pp. 131–134.

[3]"Innovation Miniseries," *Industry Week* (July 19, 1999), p. 38.

[4]Jennifer Lach, "How Sweet It Is," *American Demographics* (March 2000), pp. s4–s21.

EXAMPLE   Many organizations are supplementing customer satisfaction surveys by deploying "secret shoppers" to conduct discreet tests of the moments-of-truth between customers and service providers. The secret shopper engages in a normal purchase transaction and reports back to the firm his or her experience answering questions such as: Was the merchandise easy to find and of high quality? Were the service people helpful? Could you get through to a knowledgeable person when calling the company's 800 customer service center number? Did the Web site function properly or were there dysfunctional links?[5]

EXAMPLE   In an attempt to speed up refueling and engender loyalty to its stations, Mobil Oil Company test-marketed an electronic key-chain wand called a Speedpass in St. Louis. Customers simply wave the device to activate the pump. The device automatically charges the gasoline purchase to the purchaser's designated credit card when refueling is complete, without the customer ever having to go inside the station or show the credit card. The Speedpass can be used only at Mobil stations.[6]

EXAMPLE   Researchers are intrigued with the potential of online chat rooms as a focus group forum. They cite large savings in travel expenses, because the participants can log in from all over the world. They also say that new products or advertisements can be shown online just as easily as in person, and they point out that the time-consuming and expensive step of transcribing focus group tapes is unnecessary, because the online focus group is already conducted in text, which may simply be downloaded and saved. Critics of online focus groups say that important cues and reactions like nonverbal body language are lost in the online environment, but supporters respond that they encourage online focus group participants to use emoticons, such as the smiley faces [:)], and note that soon, video capabilities will allow all participants to see each other, simulating more closely a traditional focus group.[7]

EXAMPLE   Dorothy Lane Market, in Dayton, Ohio, recently initiated a frequent-shopper program. Customers sign up for the discount program by providing some personal information, such as name and address, in exchange for a card, which the company uses to track buying habits. Price discounts go only to club members, and the company's direct-mail promotions are customized to reflect the individual's shopping habits. Not only are the store's customers happy that they don't have to clip coupons to save, Dorothy Lane is more profitable. Moreover, the card has helped to cut inventory and speed distribution. Because the card quickly reveals which products are selling and how fast, the stores are more likely to get just what they need, when they need it, from their suppliers.[8]

These examples simply scratch the surface regarding the scope of marketing research activities. This book will provide a better perspective on what marketing

---

[5]Bob Donath, "It's Time for You to Be a 'Mystery Inquirer,'" *Marketing News* (January 17, 2000), p. 6.

[6]Del Jones, "Mobil Speedpass Makes Gas a Point-at-Pump Purchase," *USA Today* (February 20, 1997), p. B1.

[7]James Heckman, "Turning the Focus Online," *Marketing News* (February 28, 2000), pp. 15–16.

[8]Calmetta Y. Coleman, "Finally, Supermarkets Find Ways to Increase Their Profit Margins," *The Wall Street Journal* (May 29, 1997), pp. A1, A6.

research is and how it can be used. For the moment, note that it involves more than asking individual consumers about their likes and dislikes. Although consumer surveys are an important marketing research tool, other methods are also used. The choice depends on the problem to be solved. The fundamental point is that marketing research is a pervasive activity that can take many forms because its basic purpose is to help managers make better decisions in any of their areas of responsibility.

Role of Marketing Research

Anyone planning a career in business should understand what marketing research can do. Every day, marketing managers are called upon to make decisions, sometimes minor, sometimes far-reaching, each of which will be better-informed and likely to produce better results with the intelligent use of marketing research. Effective decision making depends on quality input, and marketing research plays an essential role in translating data into useful information. Any business seeking an edge in attracting and retaining customers in competitive market environments turns to marketing. And in turn, marketing can create strategies to work toward these goals of attraction and retention, if the business understands its customers. This understanding comes through marketing research, both periodic projects directed toward specific problems at hand, and continuing, ongoing measurement of the marketplace.

Beyond marketing researchers and marketers, the success of one's career in many related fields would be enhanced by a working knowledge of marketing research. For example, much of management consulting is fundamentally marketing research. Entrepreneurs enhance their likelihood of staying in business by understanding their new and growing customer base. Financial analysts need to understand the perceptions of their consumer and business customers in order to sell their products. Those Internet service providers who invest the time to understand what their customers value will be around long after their less knowledgeable upstarts crash. People beyond traditional business boundaries also benefit from research. For example, land planners use marketing research to understand better the desires of their constituents—anything from shopping mall site location to where a new neighborhood park might be built. Politicians use marketing research to plan campaign strategies. As much as citizens protest negative ad campaigns, such ads continue because they are memorable and advertising agencies measure success in part through short-term memory measures. Clergy and congregations use marketing research to determine when to hold services, what genre of worship music to play, and how to serve the different segments in the congregation.

You may recall from your introductory course in marketing that the principal task of marketing is to create value for customers, where customer value is the difference between customer perceptions of the benefits they receive from purchasing and using products and services, and their perceptions of the costs they incur in exchange for them. Customers who are willing and able to make exchanges will do so when (1) the benefits of exchanges exceed the costs of exchanges, and (2) the products or services offer superior value compared to alternatives. In their attempts to create customer value, marketing managers generally focus their efforts on the elements of the marketing mix, or the four Ps—the product or service, its price, its placement or the channels in which it is distributed, and its promotion or communications mix.

The marketing manager's essential task is to develop a marketing strategy that involves combining the marketing mix elements in such a way that they complement each other and positively influence customers' value perceptions and behaviors. This task would be much simpler if all the elements that affect customers' perceptions of value were under the manager's control and if customer reaction to any contemplated change could be predicted with certainty. Usually, however, a number of factors affecting the success of the marketing effort, including economic, political and legal, social, natural, technological, and competitive environments, are beyond the marketing manager's control, and the behavior of individual customers is largely unpredictable.

Figure 1.1 summarizes the task of marketing management. Customers are the target because they are the focus of the firm's activities. Their satisfaction is achieved through simultaneous adjustments in the elements of the marketing mix, but the results of these adjustments are uncertain because the marketing task takes place within an uncontrollable environment (see Figure 1.2). Consequently, as director of the firm's marketing activities, the marketing manager has an urgent, continuous need for information—and marketing research is responsible for providing it. Marketing research is the firm's formal communication link with the customer and environment. It is the means by which the firm generates, transmits, and interprets information from the customer and environment about or relating to the success of the firm's marketing plans.

FIGURE 1.1   **The Task of Marketing Management**

Source: Gilbert A. Churchill, Jr. and J. Paul Peter, *Marketing: Creating Value for Customers*, 2nd ed. (Burr Ridge, IL: Irwin/McGraw Hill, 1998), p. 22.

FIGURE 1.2	**The Environments Affecting Marketing**

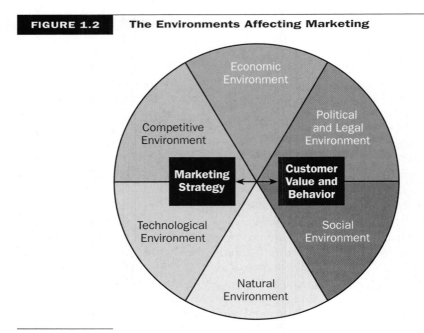

Source: Gilbert A. Churchill, Jr. and J. Paul Peter, *Marketing: Creating Value for Customers*, 2nd ed. (Burr Ridge, IL: Irwin/McGraw-Hill, 1998), p. 29.

The American Marketing Association's (AMA) definition of marketing research emphasizes its information-linkage role (ama.org):

> Marketing research is the function which links the consumer, customer, and public to the marketer through information—information used to identify and define marketing opportunities and problems; generate, refine, and evaluate marketing actions; monitor marketing performance; and improve our understanding of marketing as a process.

Note that this definition indicates that marketing research provides information to the marketer for use in at least four areas: (1) the generation of ideas for marketing action, including the identification of marketing problems and opportunities; (2) the evaluation of marketing actions; (3) the comparison of performance versus objectives; and (4) the development of general understanding of marketing phenomena and processes. Further, marketing research is involved with all phases of the information-management process, including: (1) the specification of what information is needed; (2) the collection and analysis of the information; and (3) the interpretation of that information with respect to the objectives that motivated the study in the first place.

A periodic survey (Table 1.1) conducted by the American Marketing Association details how many organizations use marketing research.[9] Much research, for

[9]Thomas C. Kinnear and Ann R. Root, *1994 Survey of Marketing Research* (Chicago: American Marketing Association, 1995). This survey is the ninth in a series begun in 1947.

TABLE 1.1	Research Activities of 587 Companies	
		% Engaged in Activity

A. Business/Economic and Corporate Research
1. Industry/market characteristics and trends — 92%
2. Acquisition/diversification studies — 50
3. Market share analyses — 85
4. Internal employee studies (morale, communications, and so on) — 72

B. Pricing
1. Cost analysis — 57%
2. Profit analysis — 55
3. Price elasticity — 56
4. Demand analysis
   a. market potential — 78
   b. sales potential — 75
   c. sales forecasts — 71
5. Competitive pricing analyses — 71

C. Product
1. Concept development and testing — 78%
2. Brand name generation and testing — 55
3. Test market — 55
4. Product testing of existing products — 63
5. Packaging design studies — 48
6. Competitive product studies — 54

D. Distribution
1. Plant/warehouse location studies — 25%
2. Channel performance studies — 39
3. Channel coverage studies — 31
4. Export and international studies — 32

E. Promotion
1. Motivation research — 56%
2. Media research — 70
3. Copy research — 68
4. Advertising effectiveness
   a. prior to marketplace airing — 67
   b. during marketplace airing — 66
5. Competitive advertising studies — 43
6. Public image studies — 65
7. Sales force compensation studies — 34
8. Sales force quota studies — 28
9. Sales force territory structure — 32
10. Studies of premiums, coupons, deals, etc. — 47

F. Buying Behavior
1. Brand preference — 78%
2. Brand attitudes — 76
3. Product satisfaction — 87
4. Purchase behavior — 80
5. Purchase intentions — 79
6. Brand awareness — 80
7. Segmentation studies — 84

Source: Thomas C. Kinnear and Ann R. Root, *1994 Survey of Marketing Research*, 1995, p. 49. Reprinted with permission from American Marketing Association, Chicago, IL 60606.

TABLE 1.2	Kinds of Questions Marketing Research Can Help Answer

A. Planning
1. Segmentation: What kinds of people buy our products? Where do they live? How much do they earn? How many of them are there?
2. Demand estimation: Are the markets for our products increasing or decreasing? Are there promising markets that we have not yet reached?
3. Environmental assessment: Are the channels of distribution for our products changing? What should our presence on the Internet be?

B. Problem Solving
1. Product
   a. In testing new products and product-line extensions, which product design is likely to be the most successful? What features do consumers value most?
   b. What kind of packaging should we use?
   c. What are the forecasts for the product? How might we re-energize its life cycle?
2. Price
   a. What price should we charge for our products?
   b. How sensitive to price changes are our target segments?
   c. Given the life-time value assessments of our segments, should we be discounting or charging a premium to our most-valued customers?
   d. As production costs decline, should we lower our prices or try to develop higher quality products?
   e. Do consumers use price as a cue to value, or a cue to quality, in our industry?
3. Place
   a. Where, and by whom, are our products being sold? Where, and by whom, should our products be sold?
   b. What kinds of incentives should we offer the trade to push our products?
   c. Are our relationships with our suppliers and distributors satisfactory and cooperative?
4. Promotion
   a. How much should we spend on promotion? How should it be allocated to products and to geographic areas?
   b. Which ad copy should we run in our markets? With what frequency and media expenditures?
   c. What combination of media—newspapers, radio, television, magazines, Internet ad banners—should we use?
   d. What is our consumer coupon redemption rate?

C. Control
1. What is our market share overall? In each geographic area? By each customer type?
2. Are customers satisfied with our products? How is our record for service? Are there many returns? Do levels of customer satisfaction vary with market? With segment?
3. Are our employees satisfied? Do they feel well-trained and empowered to assist our customers?
4. How does the public perceive our company? What is our reputation with the trade?

example, is done to measure consumer wants and needs. Other research assesses the impact of previous adjustments in the marketing mix or gauges the potential impact of new changes. Some research deals directly with the environment, such as studies of legal constraints on advertising and promotion and studies of social values, business policy, and business trends.

Another way of looking at the function of marketing research is to consider how management uses it. Some marketing research is used for planning, some for problem solving, and some for control. When used for planning, it deals largely with determining which marketing opportunities are viable and which are not promising for the firm. Also, when workable opportunities are uncovered, market-

TABLE 1.3	Marketing Research Questions about International Markets

- What is the nature of competition in the international market? Who are the major direct and indirect competitors? What are their characteristics?
- What are our firm's competitive strengths and weaknesses in reference to such factors as product quality, product lines, warranties, services, brands, packaging, distribution, sales force, customer service, advertising, prices, experience, technology, capital and human resources, and market share?
- What are the trade incentives and barriers in the country under consideration? What specific requirements (for example, import or export licenses) must be met to conduct international trade?
- Are we likely to encounter any prejudice against imports or exports among the country's customers? Its government?
- What are different governments doing specifically to encourage or discourage international trade? How difficult are the government regulations for our firm?
- How well-developed are the international mass communication media? Are the print and electronics media abroad efficient and effective?
- Are there adequate transportation and storage or warehouse facilities in the foreign market? What is the state of the retailing institutions?

See also Philip R. Cateora, *International Marketing*, 9th ed. (Burr Ridge, IL: Irwin, 1996); Johny K. Johansson, *Global Marketing: Foreign Entry, Local Marketing, and Global Management* (Burr Ridge, IL: Irwin, 1997), pp. 272–304, for discussion of the insights to be gained from and the problems involved in researching foreign markets.

ing research provides estimates of their size and scope, so that marketing management can better assess the resources needed to develop them. Problem-solving marketing research focuses on the short- or long-term decisions that the firm must make with respect to the elements of the marketing mix. Control-oriented marketing research helps management to isolate trouble spots and to keep abreast of current operations. The kinds of questions marketing research can address with regard to planning, problem solving, and control decisions are listed in Table 1.2.

It is important to highlight the key role of marketing research in the decision-making process. Marketing research is an essential element of marketing. Consider the following:

> "Market research is crucial to a corporation's marketing process." So says Herb Baum, President and CEO of Hasbro Inc. toy manufacturer. "I don't think anybody ought to be making marketing decisions without some form of research, because you can waste a lot of time and money. What it really does is it helps you understand your . . . customers."[10]

In addition, the communication link that marketing research serves between the firm and its customers and its environment is becoming increasingly critical and difficult as the world moves to a highly competitive global economy. Firms operating in the international arena often use marketing research to get a perspective on what it is like to do business in specific countries. Some of the questions that marketing research has been used to investigate in this capacity are listed in Table 1.3. Globalization of marketing research naturally follows the globalization of large,

[10]Michelle Wirth Fellman, "Marketing Research Is 'Critical,'" *Marketing Research* 11 (Fall 1999), pp. 4–5.

International Steps and Missteps Caused by Environmental Differences

Misstep Dutch building company Fomabo formed a strategic alliance with two Malaysian companies to build prefabricated housing in Malaysia. Following numerous bureaucratic delays in obtaining the proper licenses from regional authorities, the first group of houses was finally built. However, sales proved discouraging and the reasons were soon uncovered. The walls of the Fomabo houses were made of reinforced concrete, just like those in the Netherlands. Traditional Malaysian houses are made of wood, a feature that permits Malaysians to hang pictures and other objects on their walls. Hammering nails into concrete walls requires boring tools, an inconvenience that contributed to the general "feeling" of the new homes as less comfortable than traditional housing.

Step Domino's Pizza tried to enter the Japanese market even though Japanese consumers tend not to eat a lot of tomato-based foods, many have allergies to dairy products, and complex navigation is required to deliver pizza through the streets of Tokyo. Domino's should have conducted marketing research before attempting to enter Japan, but, better late than never, upon entering the marketing, they conducted some research and listened to their new customers. In reaction to the new consumer information, Domino's introduced sushi pizza toppings and created a street address database for their delivery scooters. What could have been another corporate export disaster tale was turned around to a highly successful overseas venture—by using marketing research.

Misstep Coca-Cola had little success in marketing a product in Chile. When the company attempted to in-

troduce a new grape-flavored drink, it soon discovered that the Chileans were not interested. Apparently, the Chileans prefer wine as their grape drink.

Step Increasingly, U.S.-based corporations are importing back to the U.S. the variations of cultural tastes and style they had accommodated in their successful exports. For example, Häagen-Dazs's caramel-milk ice cream, "*dulce de leche*," developed in Argentina, is a best-seller in many markets in the States. Nike's Brazilian soccer "boot," or its Kenyan running "mitten" (a shoe with a separate space for the big toe), and Levi's dark, stiff denim products favored in Japan have had successful sales in the U.S. following their international distribution. Marketing research on customer diversity and immigration have also supported the successful introduction of salsa, Thai food, and soccer-related products to U.S. market segments.

Misstep Chase and Sanborn met resistance when it tried to introduce its instant coffee in France. In the French home, the consumption of coffee plays a more significant role than in the English home. The preparation of coffee is a ritual in the life of the French consumer, and instant coffee is rejected because it is not "real" coffee.

Sources: David A Ricks, *Blunders in International Business* (Cambridge, MA: Blackwell, 1993), pp. 133–136; Tevfik Dalgic and Ruud Heijblom, "Educator Insights: International Marketing Blunders Revisited—Some Lessons for Managers," *Journal of International Marketing* 4, no. 1 (1996), pp. 81–91; Vijay Mahajan and Jerry Wind, "Rx for Marketing Research," *Marketing Research* 11, no. 3 (1999), pp. 7–13; David Leonhardt, "It Was a Hit in Buenos Aires—So Why Not Boise?" *Business Week* (September 7, 1998), pp. 56–58.

multinational clients, and just as products are adapted and tailored for local cultures and tastes, it is also important to recognize that for research too, what works in one environment does not necessarily work in another (see Research Realities 1.1). Marketing researchers point to international business as one of three key influences on changes in how they conduct their business—the other two factors being the Internet and one-to-one marketing:

The Internet, globalization, and one-to-one marketing are expected to be the primary influences on marketing research, says a survey of marketing research professionals. Interactive research and virtual reality are expected to flourish over the

TABLE 1.4	Factors Helping to Expand the Scope and Importance of Marketing Research

Management Recognizes the Importance of Marketing Research
1. There is a greater desire for knowledge-based decisions; managers are seeking to rely on empirically based knowledge for all management decisions.
2. Marketing researchers and management are partnering more closely; increasingly, research professionals are bringing their methodological expertise to dialog with business knowledge of management.
3. Marketing research is being designed more and more as an integral part of a knowledge center to address specific management needs, which allows improvement of decision making and the analysis of "what-if" scenarios.

Continuity in the Need for Information
1. There is an ongoing use of data; marketing research is expanding beyond single-event projects, implemented more as an ongoing process of knowledge acquisition.
2. Continuous evaluation and experimentation allow for adaptive experimentation and continuous improvement in decision making in changing business environments; even the marketing research is being regularly reviewed.

Technology
1. Databases are being developed on customers and prospects, and the databases are being augmented with user-friendly decision support systems.
2. Internet-based research can be used in creative research designs; at the least it can be fast and economical.

Globalization
Where appropriate, data are being collected from multiple countries for comparisons.

Adapted from Jerry Wind, "Start Your Engines: Gear Up for Challenges Ahead with Innovative Marketing Research Products and Services," *Marketing Research* 9 (Winter 1997), pp. 4–10.

Internet and future broadband electronic communications technologies. The globalization of business will drive more cross-cultural research, to recognize increasing diversity and changing demographic bases. And as companies build relationships with their customers as unique individuals, they will need marketing and marketing research like never before—just who is this customer and what does he or she want? "Marketing research in the 21st century may be barely recognizable by a 20th century researcher" and the marketing research industry will be under more pressure to attract top talent.[11]

We say more about the Internet later in this chapter and throughout the book, and we examine some one-to-one direct marketing and database marketing issues in the next chapter. See Table 1.4 for a summary of current marketplace phenomena that are impacting marketing research and increasing its applicability and importance.

Who Does Marketing Research?

Marketing research, as a significant business activity, owes its existence to the shift from a production-oriented to a consumption-oriented economy that occurred in this country at the end of World War II. However, some marketing research was

[11]Doss Struse, "Marketing Research's Top 25 Influences," *Marketing Research* 11 (Spring 2000), pp. 5–9.

conducted before the war, and the origins of formal marketing research predate the war by a good number of years:

> More by accident than foresight, N. W. Ayer & Son applied marketing research to marketing and advertising problems. In 1879, in attempting to fit a proposed advertising schedule to the needs of the Nichols-Shepard Company, manufacturers of agricultural machinery, the agency wired state officials and publishers throughout the country requesting information on expected grain production. As a result, the agency was able to construct a crude but formal market survey by states and counties. This attempt to construct a market survey is probably the first real instance of marketing research in the United States.[12]

There were even formal marketing research departments and marketing research firms before World War II.[13] However, marketing research really began to grow when firms found they could no longer sell all they could produce but rather had to gauge market needs and produce accordingly. Marketing research was called upon to estimate these needs. As consumer discretion became more important, there was a concurrent shift in the orientation of many firms. Marketing began to assume a more dominant role and production a less important one. The marketing concept emerged and along with it, a reorganization of the marketing effort. Many marketing research departments were born in these reorganizations. The growth of these departments was stimulated by a number of factors, including past successes, increased management sophistication, and the data revolution created by the invention of the computer. The success of firms with marketing research departments caused still other firms to establish departments.

Currently, the firm that does not have a formal marketing research department, or at least a person assigned specifically to the marketing research activity, is the exception rather than the rule (see Figure 1.3). Marketing research departments are prevalent among industrial and consumer manufacturing companies, but they also exist in other types of companies. Publishers and broadcasters, for example, do a good deal of research to generate statistics on market coverage to measure the size of the audience reached by the message and to provide a demographic profile of this audience. These data are then used to sell advertising space or time.

Financial service companies also use marketing research. Much of the research done by these departments involves forecasting, measurement of market potentials, determination of market characteristics, market share analyses, sales analyses, location analyses, and product mix studies.

Many advertising agencies have formal research departments. Much of the research conducted by these agencies involves such things as studying the effective-

---

[12]From Lawrence C. Lockley, "History and Development of Marketing Research," in Robert Ferber, ed., *Handbook of Marketing Research*, pp. 1–4. Copyright © 1974 by McGraw-Hill, 1974. Used with permission of McGraw-Hill Book Company.

[13]The Curtis Publishing Company is generally conceded to have formed the first formal marketing research department with the appointment of Charles Parlin as manager of the Commercial Research Division of the Advertising Department in 1911. The ACNielsen Company, the largest marketing research firm in the world, began operation in 1934. For a detailed treatment of the development of marketing research, see Robert Bartels, *The Development of Marketing Thought* (Homewood, IL: Irwin, 1962), pp. 106–124, or Jack J. Honomichl, *Marketing Research People: Their Behind-the-Scenes Stories* (Chicago: Crain Books, 1984), especially pp. 95–184.

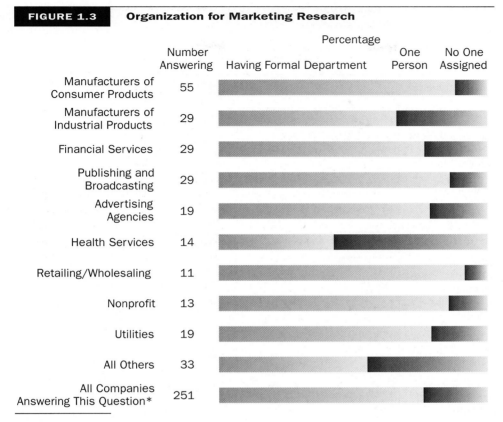

FIGURE 1.3   **Organization for Marketing Research**

	Number Answering	Percentage Having Formal Department	One Person	No One Assigned
Manufacturers of Consumer Products	55			
Manufacturers of Industrial Products	29			
Financial Services	29			
Publishing and Broadcasting	29			
Advertising Agencies	19			
Health Services	14			
Retailing/Wholesaling	11			
Nonprofit	13			
Utilities	19			
All Others	33			
All Companies Answering This Question*	251			

*Excludes marketing research and consulting firms.
Source: Thomas C. Kinnear and Ann R. Root, *1994 Survey of Marketing Research*, p. 7. Reprinted with permission from American Marketing Association, Chicago, IL 60606.

ness of alternative ad copy and optimizing the frequency of exposures of customers to ads. Many agencies also do marketing research for their clients, for example, measuring the market potential of the brand they are advertising, or the client firm's market share.

The enterprises included in the "all others" category shown in Figure 1.3, described earlier, include public utilities, transportation companies, and trade associations, among others. Public utilities and transportation companies provide their customers with statistics on area growth and market potential. Trade associations collect and disseminate operating data gathered from their members.

The entire spectrum of marketing research activity also includes specialized marketing research and consulting firms, government agencies, and universities. Most specialized research firms are small, but a few are quite large. Research Realities 1.2, for example, shows the revenues of the largest U.S. marketing research firms and the proportion of their revenues generated outside the United States. Some firms provide syndicated research; they collect certain information on a

RESEARCH REALITIES 1.2

The Top 20 U.S. Research Organizations

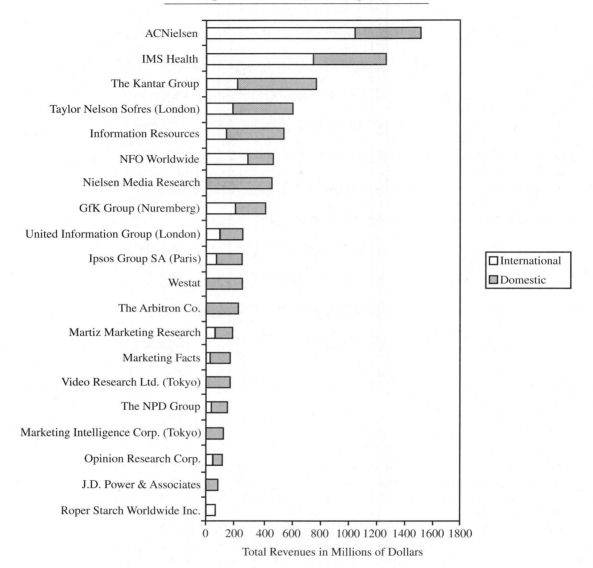

Total Revenues in Millions of Dollars

Source: Developed from the information in Jack Honomichl, "2000 Business Report on the Marketing Research Industry," *Marketing News* (August 14, 2000), p. H4. This report also describes the services provided by these research organizations.

regular basis, which they then sell to interested clients. The syndicated services include such operations as ACNielsen, which provides product movement data for grocery stores and drugstores, and the NPD Group, which operates a consumer panel. The syndicated services are distinguished by the fact that their research is not custom designed, except in the limited sense that the firm will perform special analyses for the client from the data it regularly collects. Other research firms, though, specialize in custom-designed research. Some of these provide only a field service; they collect data and return the data-collection instruments directly to the research sponsor. Some are limited-service firms that not only collect the data but also analyze them for the client. And some are full-service research suppliers that help the client in the design of the research as well as in collecting and analyzing data.

Government agencies provide much marketing information in the form of published statistics. In fact, the federal government is the largest producer of marketing facts through its various censuses and other publications.[14]

Much university-sponsored research of interest to marketers is produced by the marketing faculty or centers on business research found in business schools. Faculty research is often reported in marketing journals, whereas research centers often publish monographs (such as "white papers") on topics of interest.

Organization of Marketing Research

The organizational form of marketing research depends largely on the size and organizational structure of the individual company. In small firms, where one person often handles all the organization's research needs, there are few organizational questions other than determining to whom the research director will report. Most often, this will be the sales or marketing manager, although some marketing research managers report directly to the president or the executive vice president. Larger research units can take a variety of organizational forms, often one of these:

1. Organization by areas of application, for example, by product line, brand, market segment, and geographic area.

2. Organization by marketing function performed, for example, field sales analysis, advertising research, or product planning. An important new variant of this type of organization is the development in marketing research firms, advertising agencies, and manufacturers of centers, or groups of people, whose responsibilities focus on the Internet—both e-commerce and electronic forms of research, as described in Research Realities 1.3.

3. Organization by research technique or approach, for example, sales models, mathematical and/or statistical analysis, field interviewing, or questionnaire design.

Many firms with very large marketing research departments combine two or more of these organizational structures.

---

[14]Some government publications containing useful marketing information are reviewed in the appendix to Chapter 6.

RESEARCH REALITIES 1.3

Marketing Research, E-Commerce, and the Internet

Electronic marketing research takes one of two forms:

1. **Research on the Internet:** These studies use the Internet or other high-tech means to study any consumer or market behavior. The Internet becomes another modality for communicating with customers, like paper-pencil surveys, telephone interviews, and so on.

2. **Research about the Internet:** These studies focus on e-commerce or consumer and market behavior on the Internet as an end in itself. They often also use the Internet as a means of collecting data, for example, through e-mail contacts, Web-based surveys, or surreptitious observation and measurement of Web page visitations.

Electronic marketing research companies come in one of two forms:

1. **Full-service established marketing research firms** are extending their menu of services to include the Internet as another means of gathering information to enable their clients to answer questions about various consumer behavior. Most are also turning their attention to the Internet as an end to be studied—another class of customer behaviors to be understood. For example:

   A. **ACNielsen:** best known for media and retail measurement, formed a subsidiary, eRatings.com, as a global service to track audiences, advertis-

ing, and user activity on the Internet. Currently in five countries, with a three-year plan to extend to thirty, this group measures traffic to Web sites, audience exposure and response to banner advertising, and user demographics. ACNielsen also uses the medium in its e-Panel services, an electronic variant of its traditional ongoing consumer panels, which are used to assess reaction to new product concepts and movie trailers (previews), for example.

   B. **The NPD Group:** traditionally strong in consumer diaries, conducts both research about the Internet (for example, audience measurement, chats with Web site visitors, competitor site analysis, online purchase tracking, quick polls, and so on) and research for which the Internet is the means for studying other consumer behaviors (for example, online focus groups, mystery shoppers, and general surveys). SiteSelect is an NPD tool that randomly samples Web users to invite them to participate in a survey. The ongoing NPD Online Panel will occasionally be contacted via e-mail that an online NPD survey awaits them. NPD Online Focus Groups gather international participants in virtual rooms for speedy qualitative consumer insights.

   C. **Information Resources Inc.:** the powerhouse of consumer packaged goods data, combined with Media Metrix Inc. (described below) in

The organizational structure of the firm itself—particularly whether it is centralized or decentralized—also affects the organization of the marketing research function. With decentralized companies, the fundamental question is whether each division or operating unit should have its own marketing research department, whether a single department in central headquarters should serve all operating divisions, or whether there should be research departments at both levels. The primary advantages of a corporate-level location are greater coordination and control of corporate research activity, economy, increased capability from an information system perspective, and greater usefulness to corporate management in planning. The primary advantage of a division or group-level location is that it allows research personnel to acquire valuable knowledge about divisional markets, products, prac-

(continued)

e-SCAN, to let clients (for example, manufacturers of consumer packaged goods) measure the value of their online marketing investments. Clients can track known users of their brands to see which Web sites interest them, and in turn follow the Web site visitation data with subsequent purchase data (on- or off-line). Software is installed on the PCs of IRI's panel members who already use a ScanKey to record all their take-home purchases. The two sources of data are integrated to allow the Internet activities (sites visited, exposures to ads, surfing frequencies, and patterns) to be correlated with purchase data (volume, purchase cycles, promotional effectiveness, brand loyalty).

2. **Internet specialists** are newly formed or spun-off marketing research firms that concentrate their research efforts on the Internet and e-commerce. These firms use the Internet both as a means (research "on" the Internet) and as an end (research "about" the Internet) to studying customers and marketing. Examples follow:

   A. **Media Metrix Inc.** is the pioneer and leader in the field of Internet and other digital media measurement services. A panel of more than 50,000 individuals in homes and in the workplace is measured on which computer applications are open and which are in use, which Web pages are viewed on their browsers, which ads drew clicks, and so on. Results on frequencies of unique visitors can be reported per Internet or media industry, or per consumer usage segment.

   B. **i-tracks** specializes in Web-based surveys. Computer-assisted interviews allow clients to formulate quantitative surveys (such as rating scales) and qualitative surveys (such as open-ended questions), which can be speeded up and tailored for the survey-taker by programming skip patterns (for example, if yes, go to question 3; if no, go to question 4). Images, audio, and video can be presented. Surveys can be addressed to customers or employees for in-house assessments.

   C. **eMarketer** provides statistics and demographic data about Internet users, their usage patterns, advertising, electronic commerce and market size, growth, and geography. They offer well-designed reports on measured Internet activities and provide online weekly newsletters for business professionals.

   D. **Jupiter Communications** is a research, consulting, and publishing firm that focuses on consumer online behaviors and interactive technologies for business-to-business and business-to-consumer clients. They offer several analytical services, including using population measures and user demographics for both online and offline consumers to enhance market-size forecasts.

tices, and problems. Even though shifting between the corporate and divisional structures occurs quite frequently, the recent trend is toward a mixed arrangement in an attempt to secure the advantages of each.

For example, Kodak has a combination centralized/decentralized marketing research function. The people in the divisions work directly with managers of those business units. The centralized group is responsible for staying abreast of industry trends and changing technology, because changes here could affect numerous business units. Researchers assigned to corporate marketing research are also responsible for competitive analysis to ensure the most objective view. Finally, the centralized group serves as a quality control center for the research activity. Division-initiated projects are passed before this group for possible changes in method. One benefit of this review is that it provides better ways to approach specific tasks.

The Japanese are more likely to view research as a "line" function performed by all involved in the decision process rather than as a "staff" function performed by professional marketing researchers. Those involved in the decision team may play a role in gathering and interpreting information. For example, in developing its "Pro Mavica" professional still-video system, which, unlike conventional 35mm still cameras, records digital images on a two-inch-square floppy disk, Sony did extensive marketing research. This research involved a mail survey, personal and telephone interviews, and on-site tests to elicit user response to the product during its development. A unique aspect was that the Pro Mavica task force included both engineers and sales/marketing representatives from Sony's medical systems and broadcast units. In addition to working with their marketing peers, Sony's engineers gained insights from talking with prospects; they then incorporated user comments into product modifications.[15]

The most appropriate summary comment about the organization of the marketing research function is that this organization may be expected to be dynamic and ever-changing. It will depend on the relative importance of the marketing research function within the firm, on the scale and complexity of the research activities to be conducted, and on the firm's philosophy as to how marketing research should interface with the firm's decision making. The data indicate that large firms, for example, are likely to spend a larger proportion of the marketing budget on research than are small firms. As the firm's size and market position change, the emphasis and organization of the marketing research function must also change so that it is continually tailored to suit the firm's information needs.

One important change that has been occurring in marketing research in recent years is the transition from a specific-problem perspective to a total marketing intelligence perspective. This perspective is usually called a *marketing information system (MIS)* or *decision support system (DSS)*.[16] The emphasis in such systems is on diagnosing the information needs of each of the marketing decision makers so that these people have the kinds of information they need, when they need it, to make the kinds of decisions they must make. We shall have more to say on marketing intelligence systems in the next chapter.

Employment Opportunities in Marketing Research

It is important to acknowledge once more that consultants, entrepreneurs, Internet marketers, and many more types of business people will frequently find themselves conducting and using marketing research to enhance their business efforts. Thus, it is important that the reader whose heart is set on one of these career paths think creatively about how to incorporate marketing research into his or her corporate

---

[15]Michael Czinkota and Masaaki Kotabe, "Product Development the Japanese Way," *The Journal of Business Strategy* 11 (November/December 1990), p. 36.

[16]When discussing corporate information systems, MIS stands for management information system, and DSS refers to the structure of the decision support system for the whole company. Our interest is marketing intelligence, so we use the term MIS to refer to the marketing information system and DSS to refer to the structure of the information system to support marketing decision making. Some writers use MRIS to distinguish the marketing information system from MIS, the management information system.

responsibilities. In addition, it is important to be a knowledgeable and discerning consumer of marketing research. That is, whether one conducts the research or commissions it, it is important to be able to evaluate the quality of the research and its implications or caveats. It is true that CEOs may not be analyzing spreadsheets on a daily basis, but they do not forget that marketing research helps them understand their customers. Marketing research is the premier means to competitive advantages.

Having made the point that marketing research opportunities abound, in this section, we describe the traditional kinds of job opportunities that have marketing research as its central focus. Even with this narrower focus, it is difficult to generalize about the kinds of tasks a marketing researcher might perform. The responsibilities will depend upon the type, size, organizational structure, and philosophy of the firm with which the individual is employed. They will also depend upon whether the person works for a research supplier or for a consumer of research information.

The responsibilities of a marketing researcher could range from the simple tabulation of questionnaire responses to the management of a large research department. Research Realities 1.4 lists some common job titles and the functions typically performed by occupants of these positions. These job descriptions make clear that there are opportunities in marketing research for people with a variety of skills. One could find a career as a technical specialist, a statistician, or a research generalist managing others, such as a research director. The skills required to perform each job satisfactorily will, of course, vary.[17]

The typical entry-level position in consumer goods companies (for example, Kraft, General Motors, Procter & Gamble) is analyst, usually for a specific brand. While learning the characteristics and details of the industry, the analyst will receive on-the-job training from a research manager. The usual progression of responsibilities is to senior analyst, research supervisor, and research manager for a specific brand, after which time the researcher's responsibilities broaden to include a group of brands.

The typical entry-level position among research suppliers (such as ACNielsen, Information Resources, Market Facts, and NPD) is that of research trainee, a position which offers exposure to the types of studies in which the supplier specializes and procedures that are followed in completing them. Trainees may spend some time actually conducting interviews, coding completed data collection forms, or possibly even assisting with the analysis. The idea behind these simple tasks is to expose trainees to the processes that are followed in the firm so that when they become account representatives, they will be sufficiently familiar with the firm's capabilities to be able to develop intelligent responses, perhaps in the form of formal quotations, to client needs for research information. Research Realities 1.5 presents recent job listings, in both marketing research supplier and buyer firms, which gives some representation of the variety of employment possibilities.

---

[17]For discussions of the skills marketing researchers need and how the required skills are changing, see Richard Kitaeff, "Marketing Research Competencies," *Marketing Research: A Magazine of Management & Applications* 6 (Summer 1994), pp. 40–41; Kathie Julian and Sarah Coffer, "Kaleidoscope of Change," *Marketing Research: A Magazine of Management & Applications* 8 (Fall 1996), pp. 8–11.

RESEARCH REALITIES 1.4

Marketing Research Job Titles and Responsibilities

1. **Directors and Managers**

   A. **Research Director/Vice-President of Marketing Research:** This is the senior position in research. The director is responsible for the entire research program in the company. Accepts assignments from superiors, from clients, or may, on own initiative, develop and propose research undertakings to company executives. Employs personnel and executes general supervision of research department. Presents research findings to clients or to company executives.

   B. **Assistant Director of Research:** This position usually represents a defined "second in command," a senior staff member having responsibilities above those of other staff members.

2. **Analytically Skilled Methodologists**

   A. **Statistician/Data Processing Specialist:** Duties are usually those of an expert consultant on theory and application of statistical technique to specific research problems. Usually responsible for experimental design and data processing.

   B. **Qualitative Specialist:** Some firms have a person specifically assigned to oversee interview techniques and focus groups.

3. **Analysts**

   A. **Senior Analyst:** Usually found in larger research departments. Participates in planning research projects and directs execution of projects assigned. Operates with minimum supervision. Prepares or works with analysts in preparing questionnaires. Selects research techniques, makes analyses, and writes final report. Budgetary control over projects and primary responsibility for meeting time schedules rests with the senior analyst.

   B. **Analyst:** The analyst usually handles the bulk of the work required for execution of research projects. Often works under senior analyst's supervision. The analyst assists in questionnaire preparation, pretests them, and makes preliminary analyses of results. Most library research or work with company data is handled by the analyst.

   C. **Junior Analyst:** Working under rather close supervision, junior analysts handle routine assignments, for example, editing and coding of questionnaires, statistical calculations above the clerical level, and simpler forms of library research. A large portion of the junior analyst's time is spent on tasks assigned by superiors.

4. **Data Collection**

   A. **Field Work Director:** Usually only larger departments have a field work director, who hires, trains, and supervises field interviewers.

   B. **Full-Time Interviewer:** The interviewer conducts personal interviews and works under direct supervision of the field work director. Many companies outsource this function.

5. **Support Staff**

   A. **Tabulating and Clerical Help:** The routine, day-to-day work of the department is performed by these individuals.

   B. **Clerical Supervisor:** In larger departments, the central handling and processing of statistical data are the responsibilities of one or more clerical supervisors. Duties include work scheduling and responsibility for accuracy.

   C. **Librarian:** The librarian builds and maintains a library of reference sources adequate to the needs of the research department.

Source: Thomas C. Kinnear and Ann R. Root, *1994 Survey of Marketing Research*, 1995, p. 93. Reprinted with permission from American Marketing Association, Chicago, IL 60606.

In particular, there is a need for technically skilled marketing researchers—high-level data analysts and methodologists. Their skills are crucial to the excellence of a marketing research firm, and these talented people are in short supply. Usually these researchers have training from several of the following areas: probability and statistics, multivariate statistics and modeling, psychology, psychometric

A Sampling of Marketing Research Job Advertisements

1. **Blockbuster Inc.:** Rapid store growth, the launching of new business units, and a passion to understand our consumers has created several exciting opportunities in our worldwide headquarters.

   A. *Manager of E-Commerce Marketing Research:* Put your marketing research skills to work in the exciting world of online retailing. Be on the ground floor with the opportunity to design and manage the research function for blockbuster.com. Candidates for this position must have strong research skills, a creative outlook, and insatiable desire to understand the consumer.

   B. *Manager of Database Analysis:* Use your database analytical skills in this newly created position to provide valuable information about Blockbuster's different market tests and the home entertainment preferences of our consumers. Ideal candidates should have a strong working knowledge of database design, maintenance, and analysis. 5+ years experience is desired.

   C. *Sr. Marketing Research Analyst:* Your advertising sales or media research background is desired for this position. You are responsible for quantitative, qualitative, and secondary marketing research to support new business opportunities and advertising sales. 2+ years marketing research experience is desired.

   D. *Marketing Research Analyst:* Use your strong quantitative skills to complete important analyses of our different home entertainment offerings. In this position you will be responsible for preparing/presenting written analytical reports/summaries of findings. Knowledge of statistical software is desired.

2. **Washington Post:** In search of an experienced Research Manager with excellent research, communication, and people skills. The ideal candidate should have credentials in research analysis, project coordination and facilitation, and presentation writing. Three to five years of management and quantitative and qualitative research experience is strongly preferred. An understanding of statistical/analytical research tools is important to success in this position. The person in this position will act as consultant, mentor, and facilitator for three presentation writers and will assume quantitative and/or qualitative projects on his or her own. The Research Manager will assist the Research Department in communicating research more fully and completely to advertising sales, agencies, advertisers, News, Circulation, and other inside and outside audiences.

3. **The Gallup Organization:** Do you have a career commitment to cutting-edge, data-based Fortune 500 consulting? The Gallup Organization hires consultants to work with executives, implementing data-based management and client systems. Our work includes employee selection and development; and attitude, customer, and brand research. Offices in San Francisco; Toronto; Irvine, California; Miami; New York; and Detroit.

4. **NFO Research Inc.:** Insight is what NFO Research Inc. delivers. An NFO Worldwide company, we are an exciting, growing marketing information company and the world's leading provider of insight into the opinions, attitudes, and needs of consumers.

   A. *Marketing Project Director:* We'll rely on your expert communication ability and analytical problem-solving skills to coordinate and monitor all phases of marketing projects with Account Executives and our Marketing Manager.

   B. *Research Analyst:* Responsible for providing support to the Analytical Service Manager, you'll prepare data, assist with report writing, develop charts and graphs, and so on.

   C. *Assistant Analyst:* You'll provide support, including data preparation and charting, to a Research Analyst and the Analytical Service Manager. We'll rely on you to develop charts and graphs based on guidelines, format reports and presentations using templates, and maintain an analytical project schedule.

5. **ACNielsen**

   A. *Positions in Systems:* Senior Technical Analyst, Software Engineer and Senior Software Engineer, Project Manager and Senior Project Manager, Software Quality Assurance Analyst, Senior Business Analyst.

   B. *Positions in Operations:* Senior Software Engineer, Data Network Specialist, Manager of Contracts, Senior Statistical Analyst.

   C. *Positions in Finance:* Pricing Manager.

Excerpts taken from *Marketing News* (March 27, 2000), p. 22; (July 5, 1999), p. 16; (April 10, 2000), p. 23; acnielsen.com.

measurement, marketing research, sociology, consumer buying behavior, micro-economics, marketing management, and business communications. They stay current in methodologies by subscribing to academic journals, such as the *Journal of Marketing Research*, the *Journal of Consumer Psychology*, and the *Journal of the American Statistical Association*, and by attending professional development conferences such as the American Marketing Association's *Advanced Research Techniques Forum* and those sponsored by the Advertising Research Foundation. Without these talented professionals, a great deal of analytical software (for example, a statistical package) would be implemented by people with no understanding of models or consumers, which could yield erroneous results, which would be immediately detrimental to the research buyer, and ultimately would impact the marketing research supplier. "If we [marketing researchers] are to continue to grow as a business and a profession, we should recognize [these highly skilled methodologists] and nurture [their] growth" (p. 25).[18]

A successful marketing researcher needs human relations, communication, conceptual, and analytical skills. Marketing researchers must be able to interact effectively with others, because they rarely work in isolation. They should be able to communicate well both orally and in writing. If researchers cannot communicate the results and discuss what the results mean, it makes little difference what they know or how good the research is. They need to understand business in general and marketing processes in particular. When dealing with brand, advertising, sales, or other managers, they must understand the issues with which these managers contend and the types of mental models they use to make sense of the situations. Marketing researchers also should have some basic numerical and statistical skills, or at least they should be capable of developing those skills. They must be comfortable with numbers and the techniques of marketing research. Their growth as professionals and their advancement within their organization will depend on their use of these skills and their acquisition of other technical, management, and financial skills.

An increasingly common career path for those working in divisional structures is to switch from the research department to product or brand management. One advantage these people possess is that after working intimately with marketing intelligence, they often know as much or more about customers, the industry, and the competitors as anyone in the company with the same amount of experience. Researchers desiring this switch need more substantive knowledge about marketing phenomena and greater business acumen in general than those planning on staying in marketing research, although all researchers need a good foundation of business and marketing knowledge if they are going to succeed.

It is important to recognize that marketing research is a profession and that marketing researchers are professionals. Qualities of professionalism that have been applied to professions as varied as doctors, lawyers, accountants, and aeronautical engineers characterize marketing researchers as well. Marketing researchers report that they generally feel that they can do much of their work fairly autonomously, they enjoy a good variety in their work responsibilities, and generally

---

[18]William D. Neal, "The Marketing Research Methodologist: Demand Is Outstripping Our Supply of These Specialists," *Marketing Research* 10 (Spring 1998), pp. 21–25.

proceed without too much bureaucracy or rules, all of which contribute to their employment satisfaction and esprit de corps among marketing researchers.[19]

Successful marketing researchers tend to be proactive rather than reactive—they identify and lead the direction in which the individual studies and overall programs go rather than simply respond to explicit requests for information. Successful marketing researchers realize that marketing research is conducted for only one reason—to help make better marketing decisions.

Summary

This chapter presented an overview of the nature of marketing research, its usefulness in marketing decision making, the extent to which it is currently being used and by what types of companies, and the organization of the research function. By definition, marketing research is the function that links the consumer, customer, and public to the marketer through information, which is used to identify and define marketing opportunities and problems; to generate, refine, and evaluate marketing actions; to monitor marketing performance; and to improve understanding of marketing as a process.

Marketing research is indeed a pervasive activity. Marketing research departments exist in most large firms and among most types of companies. Marketing research has been employed in every domain of marketing management.

No one form of organization dominates the marketing research function. Rather, the research activity is typically organized to reflect the specific firm's unique needs. Two factors that bear heavily on this organization are the firm's size and the degree of centralization of its operations.

Job opportunities in marketing research are good and are getting better. There is a great deal of variety in the positions available and in the skills needed for them. Most positions require analytical, communication, and human relations skills. Marketing researchers must be comfortable working with numbers and statistical techniques and must be familiar with a great variety of marketing research methods and techniques.

Questions

1. What is marketing management's task? What is marketing research's task? What is the relation between the two tasks?
2. How is marketing research defined? What are the key elements of this definition?
3. Who does marketing research? What are the primary kinds of research done by each enterprise?
4. How would you explain the fact that production research began in the 1860s but that marketing research did not develop formally until the 1910s and did not experience real growth until after World War II?
5. What factors influence the internal organization of the marketing research department and its reporting location within the company?
6. In a large research department, who would be responsible for specifying the objective of a research project? For deciding on specific procedures to be followed? For designing the questionnaire? For analyzing the results? For reporting the results to top management?
7. What are the necessary skills for employment in a junior or entry-level marketing research position? Do the skills change as one changes job levels? If so, what new skills are necessary at these higher levels?

---

[19]Robert F. Lusch and Matthew O'Brien, "Fostering Professionalism," *Marketing Research* 9 (Spring 1997), pp. 25–31; Thomas E. Boyt, Robert F. Lusch, and Drue K. Schuler, "Fostering Esprit de Corps in Marketing," *Marketing Management* 6 (Spring 1997), pp. 21–27.

8.   How might your responsibilities vary if you conducted marketing research at the following:
- a marketing research firm
- an ad agency
- a large consumer packaged goods manufacturer
- an Internet startup company

Applications and Problems

1.   Discuss whether or not marketing research would be valuable for the organizations that follow. If you believe that marketing research would be valuable, describe in detail how it would be used to aid in decision making.
    a. A bank
    b. A multinational oil company
    c. A retail shoe store with only one outlet
    d. A Mercedes dealership in Lafayette, Louisiana
    e. A candidate for the U.S. Congress, representing a district in Chicago
    f. The Los Angeles Lakers
    g. A distributor of large-screen televisions, operating in Mexico City
    h. The English Department at your university
    i. A wheat farmer in Nebraska with 850 acres

2.   What do the two following research situations have in common?
    Situation I: The SprayIt Company marketed a successful insect repellent. The product was effective and a leader in the market. The product was available in blue aerosol cans with red caps. The instructions were clearly specified on the container in addition to a warning to keep the product away from children. Most of the company's range of products were also produced by competitors in similar containers. The chief executive officer (CEO) was worried because of declining sales and shrinking profit margins. Another issue that perturbed him was that companies such as his were being severely criticized by government and consumer groups for their use of aerosol cans. The CEO contacted the company's advertising agency and asked it to do the necessary research to find out what was happening.
    Situation II: This past April, the directors of a nearby university were considering expanding the business school because of increasing enrollment during the past 10 years. Their plans included constructing a new wing, hiring five new faculty members, and increasing the number of scholarships from 100 to 120. The funding for this ambitious project was to be provided by private sources, internally generated funds, and the state and federal governments. A previous research study completed five years earlier, using a sophisticated forecasting method, indicated that student enrollment would have peaked last year. Another study, conducted three years ago, indicated that universities could expect gradual declining enrollments during the next 10 years. The directors were concerned about the results of the later study and the talk it stimulated about budget cuts by the state and federal governments. A decision to conduct a third and final study was made to determine likely student enrollment.

3.   What do the two following research situations have in common?
    Situation I: The sales manager of CanAl, an aluminum can manufacturing company, was wondering whether the company's new cans, which would be on the market in two months, should be priced higher than the traditional products. He confidently commented to the vice president of marketing, "Nobody in the market is selling aluminum cans with screw-on tops; we can get a small portion of the market and yet make substantial profits." The product manager disagreed with this strategy. In fact, she was opposed to marketing these new cans. The cans might present problems in preserving the con-

tents. She thought, "Aluminum cans are recycled, so nobody is going to keep them as containers." There was little she could do formally because these cans were the president's own idea. She strongly recommended to the vice president that the cans should be priced in line with the other products. The vice president thought a marketing research study would resolve this issue.

Situation II: A large toy manufacturer was in the process of developing a tool kit for children from 5 to 10 years old. The tool kit included a small saw, screwdriver, hammer, chisel, and drill. This tool kit was different from the competitors', as it included an instruction manual, "101 Things to Do." The product manager was concerned about the safety of the kit and recommended the inclusion of a separate booklet for parents. The sales manager recommended that the tool kit be made available in a small case, as this would increase its marketability. The advertising manager recommended a special promotional campaign be launched to distinguish this tool kit from that of the competitors. The vice president thought that all the recommendations were worthwhile but the costs would increase drastically. She consulted the marketing research manager, who further recommended that a study be conducted.

4. Evaluate the research in the following example:

The HiFlyer Airline company was interested in altering the interior layout of its aircraft to suit the tastes and needs of an increasing segment of its market—business people. Management was considering reducing the number of seats and installing small tables to enable business people to work during long flights. Prior to the renovation, management decided to do some research to ensure that these changes would suit the needs of the passengers. To keep expenses to a minimum, the following strategy was employed:

The questionnaires were completed by passengers during a flight. Because they were easy to administer and collect, the questionnaires were distributed only on the short flights (those less than one hour). The study was conducted during the second and third weeks of December, because that was when flights were full. To increase the response rate, each flight attendant was responsible for a certain number of questionnaires. The management thought this was a good time to acquire as much information as possible, so the questionnaire included issues apart from the new seating arrangement. As a result, the questionnaire took 20 minutes to complete. After the study, management decided that the study would not be repeated, because the information was insightful enough.

5. Specify some useful sources of marketing research information for the following situation:

Dissatisfied with the availability of ingredients for his favorite dishes, Albert Lai would like to open his own retail ethnic grocery store. Based on the difficulty of finding many specialty ingredients, Albert realizes the need for a local wholesale distributor specializing in hard-to-find ethnic foodstuffs. He envisions carrying items commonly used in Asian and Middle-Eastern recipes.

With the help of a local accountant, Albert prepared a financial proposal that revealed the need for $150,000 in start-up capital for Lai's Asian Foods. The proposal was presented to a local bank for review by its commercial loan committee, and Albert subsequently received the following letter from the bank:

Dear Mr. Lai:

We have received and considered your request for start-up financing for your proposed business. While the basic idea is sound, we find that your sales projections are based solely on your own experience and do not include any hard documentation concerning the market potential for the products you propose to carry. Until such information is made available for our consideration, we have no choice but to reject your loan application.

Albert does not wish to give up on his business idea because he truly believes that there is a market for these ethnic food products. Given his extremely limited financial resources, where and how might he obtain the needed information? (Hint: First determine what types of information might be useful.)

6. Suppose that you have decided to pursue a career in the field of marketing research. In general, what types of courses should you take in order to help achieve your goal? Why? What types of part-time jobs, internships, and volunteer work would look good on your resume? Why?

Thorndike Sports Equipment Video Case

1. If you were interviewing for a position as a research analyst with Thorndike Sports Equipment, what company research would you do to prepare for the meeting with Thorndike's president?
2. Would Joyce Hernandez's position be described as marketing research? Explain.
3. Imagine that Luke, the president of Thorndike Sports, is boasting to you that the company is customer-driven because of the existence of an 800 telephone number. How would you respond to this statement?
4. What changes to the customer service department are necessary to make it an integral part of the research department?

2

Alternative Approaches to Marketing Intelligence

We stated in Chapter 1 that the fundamental purpose of marketing research is to help marketing managers and other business people make decisions they face each day in their areas of responsibility. As directors of their firms' marketing activities, marketing managers have an urgent need for information or marketing intelligence—they might need to know about the changes that could be expected in customer purchasing patterns, the types of marketing intermediaries that might evolve, which of several alternative product designs might be the most successful, the shape of a brand's demand curve, or any of a number of other issues that could affect the way they plan, solve problems, or evaluate and control the marketing effort. Marketing research is traditionally responsible for this intelligence function. As the formal link with the environment, marketing research generates, transmits, and interprets feedback regarding the success of the firm's marketing plans and the strategies and tactics employed to implement those plans.

Three main approaches are used to provide marketing intelligence: marketing research projects, marketing information systems (MISs), and decision support systems (DSSs). Projects are completed to address a specific, timely marketing question. MISs and DSSs are used for more continuous monitoring of consumer and market behavior. MISs are usually narrower in scope than DSSs and better for addressing narrow, well-defined, predictable issues; for example, scanner data from groceries may be checked by manufacturers to obtain hourly market shares, if so desired. DSSs are broader in scope than MISs, developed with much consideration of consumer behavior. Once developed, they are popular because they allow a manager to answer simple questions to a user-friendly interface. Then the computer takes the input to a model and produces some numbers and answers, such as sales forecasts for a new product launch.

In this chapter, we will describe each of these three approaches as clear and distinct from one another, though in practice, one often blends into another. For example, MISs were the forerunners of DSSs, and many contemporary systems have elements of each. Marketing research projects are used to help construct the modeling within a DSS and are used regularly to supplement it. Further, the increased popularity of large consumer databases (for example, from loyalty programs) is blending the continuity of the available data with its periodic use in projects.

The emphasis in this book is on marketing research projects. A project is comprised of steps to be taken to solve a specific problem faced by a marketing manager. The next chapter gives an overview of these steps, and the remainder of the book discusses each one in detail. In this chapter, we provide some appreciation for the differences between projects and the alternative schemes of MISs and DSSs and their complementary roles in providing marketing intelligence. First, the philosophical difference is explained. Then we discuss the essential nature of MISs and the components of DSSs. A critical element to any marketing research project, MIS, or DSS is the data set. Because these data sets are increasingly becoming huge, we will discuss issues of "data mining." Finally, the pervasiveness of data collection on consumer and market behavior regularly raises ethical issues such as privacy, which we also address.

Philosophical Difference—Periodic Projects and Continual Intelligence

The difference in perspective between a project approach to research and an emphasis on information systems was highlighted years ago in a useful analogy that compares a flash bulb and a candle:

> The difference between marketing research and marketing intelligence is like the difference between a flash bulb and a candle. Let's say you are dancing in the dark. Every 90 seconds you are allowed to set off a flash bulb. You can use those brief intervals of intense light to chart a course, but remember, everybody is moving, too. Hopefully, they'll accommodate themselves roughly to your predictions. You might get bumped and you may stumble every so often, but you can dance along.
> On the other hand, you can light a candle. It doesn't yield as much light but it's a steady light. You are continually aware of the movements of other bodies. You can adjust your own course to the courses of others. The intelligence system is a kind of candle. It's no great flash on the immediate state of things, but it provides continuous light as situations shift and change.[1]

Thoughtful marketing managers will recognize the value in conducting marketing research and will commission such projects recurrently. Myopic managers will devise a marketing research project only in times of crisis to be carried out with urgency, which often leads to an emphasis on data collection and analysis instead of the development of pertinent, actionable information. One suggestion for making research information more actionable is to think of management in terms of an ongoing process of decision making that requires a flow of regular input. Both MISs and DSSs represent ongoing efforts to provide pertinent decision-making information to marketing managers on a regular basis. Marketing research projects provide the regular input and can discretely fine-tune these more continuous systems.

Marketing Information Systems

The earliest attempts at providing a steady flow of information focused on the **marketing information system (MIS)**, which was defined as "a set of procedures and methods for the regular, planned collection, analysis, and presentation of

---

[1]Statement by Robert J. Williams, who was the creator of the first recognized MIS at the Mead Johnson division of the Edward Dalton Company. "Marketing Intelligence Systems: A DEW Line for Marketing Men," *Business Management* (January 1966), p. 32.

information for use in making marketing decisions."[2] The key word in the definition is "regular," since the emphasis in MISs is the establishment of systems that produce information needed for decision making on a recurring basis rather than relying on periodic research studies.

The design of MISs begins with a detailed analysis of the decision makers who will be using the system in order to secure an accurate, objective assessment of their decision-making responsibilities, capabilities, and styles. MIS analysts determine the types of decisions to be made and the types of information required to make those decisions. They examine the types of information the individual receives regularly and the special studies that are needed periodically. They seek feedback from the decision makers for improvements to the current information system. Given these specifications, systems designers then attempt to specify, get approval for, and subsequently generate a series of reports that would go to the various decision makers.

To complete these tasks, systems designers need to specify the data that would be input to the system, how that data could be secured and stored, how the data in separate data banks would be accessed and combined, and what the report formats would look like. Only after these analysis and design steps are completed can the system be constructed, which is essentially a programming task. Programmers write and document the programs, making data retrieval as efficient as possible in terms of use of computer time and memory. When all the procedures are debugged so that the system is operating correctly, it is put online. Once online, managers with authorized access ask for their reports. The information systems department issues a hard copy or, increasingly, managers simply access the reports directly through their company's intranet via the computer terminals on their desks.

When they were first proposed, MISs were held up as an information panacea. The reality, however, often fell short of the promise. The primary reasons are as much behavioral as technical. People tend to resist change, and with MISs, the changes are often substantial. Many decision makers are reluctant, for example, to disclose to others what factors they use (for example, using one's own intuition) and how they combine these factors when making a particular decision. (Some research in cognitive psychology suggests that even when decision makers have no motivation to withhold such information, they are frequently simply inaccurate in their implicit understanding of their own decision-making process.) Without accurate disclosure, it is next to impossible to design reports that will give these people the information they need in the form they need it.

Even when managers are willing to disclose their decision-making calculus and information needs, there are problems. Different managers emphasize different things and consequently have different data needs; few report formats can be optimal for different users. Either the developers have to design "compromise" reports that are satisfactory but not ideal for any single user, or they have to engage in the laborious task of programming to meet each user's needs.

---

[2]Peter D. Bennett, ed., *Dictionary of Marketing Terms*, 2nd ed. (Chicago: American Marketing Association, 1995), p. 167; also see Berend Wierenga and Gerrit H. van Bruggen, "The Integration of Marketing Problem-Solving Modes and Marketing Management Support Systems," *Journal of Marketing* 61 (July 1997), pp. 21–37.

Moreover, the costs and times required to establish such systems are often underestimated, due to underestimating the size of the task, changes in organizational structure or key personnel, and the electronic data processing systems they require. By the time these systems can be developed, the personnel for which they are designed often have different responsibilities, or the economic and competitive environments around which the systems are designed have changed. Thus, they are often obsolete soon after being put online, meaning that the whole process of analysis, design, development, and implementation has to begin anew.

Another fundamental problem with MISs is that the systems do not lend themselves to the solution for the kinds of problems managers typically face. Many of the activities performed by managers cannot be programmed, nor can they be performed routinely or delegated to someone else, because they involve personal choices. Because a manager's decision making is often ad hoc and addressed to unexpected events and choices, standardized reporting systems lack the necessary scope and flexibility to be useful. In addition, some decision making and planning are exploratory, so managers, even if they are willing to, may not be able to specify in advance what they want from programmers and model builders. As decision makers and their staffs learn more about a problem, their information needs and methods of analysis evolve. Furthermore, decision making often involves exceptions to rules and qualitative issues that are not easily programmed.

Decision Support Systems

As the problems with MISs became more apparent, the emphasis in supplying marketing intelligence on a more regular basis changed from the production of preformatted reports to a **decision support system (DSS)** mode. A DSS has been defined as "a coordinated collection of data, systems, tools, and techniques with supporting software and hardware by which an organization gathers and interprets relevant information from business and the environment and turns it into a basis for marketing decisions."[3]

As depicted in Figure 2.1, a DSS is comprised of data, model, and dialog systems that can be used interactively by managers. We discuss each system component in turn.

Data System of a DSS

The **data system** in a DSS includes the processes used to capture and the methods used to store data coming from marketing, finance, the sales force, and manufacturing, as well as information coming from any number of external or internal

---

[3]Bennett 1995, p. 77. For a general discussion of the design of business intelligence systems, see George M. Marakas, *Decision Support Systems in the 21st Century* (Upper Saddle River, NJ: Prentice Hall, 1998) and Won Jun Lee and Kun Chang Lee, "A Meta Decision Support System Approach to Coordinating Production/Marketing," *Decision Support Systems* 25 (April 1999), pp. 239–250.

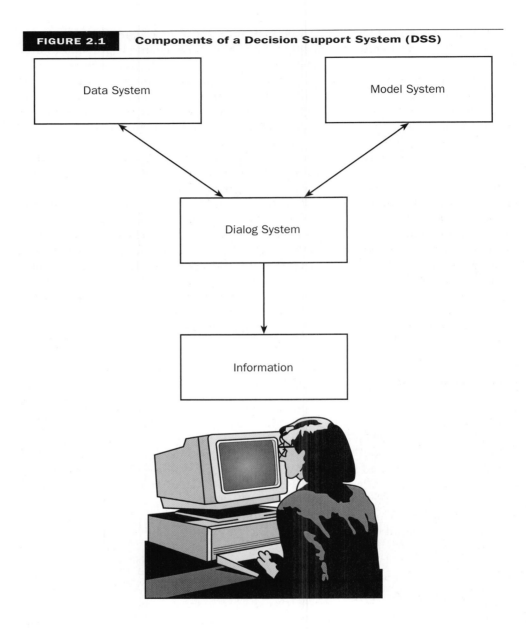

FIGURE 2.1   **Components of a Decision Support System (DSS)**

Data System

Model System

Dialog System

Information

sources. The typical data system will have different modules containing customer information, general economic and demographic information, competitor information, and industry information, including market trends.

The customer information module typically contains information on who buys and who uses the product, where they buy and use it, when, in what situations and quantities, and how often. It could also include information on how the purchase decision is made, the most important factors in making that decision, the influence of advertising or some sales promotion activity on the decision, the price paid, and so on. Marketing research projects would typically supply some of the information input to the customer information module of the data system. Other input might come from the purchase of syndicated commercial marketing information (as discussed in Chapter 6). In the section that follows on data mining, we shall see how several firms use their customer information databases.

The data module that contains general economic and demographic information attempts to capture some of the most relevant facts about what is happening in the external environment, for example, facts about national or international economic activity and trends, interest rates, unemployment, or changes in GNP. The demographic facts would concern changes in population, household composition, or any of the other factors that could potentially affect the future success of the firm. Much of this input would come from government data, primarily from the various censuses (discussed in more detail in Chapter 6).

Another data module could contain information on specific competitors. This information would address questions such as: Who are the competitors and what are their market shares? In which market niches do they operate? What is their percentage of sales by product? What are their distribution methods? Where are their production facilities located? How big are they? What are their goals? What are their unique capabilities?

The industry information and market trend data module would contain general information on what is happening in the industry, for example, financial information about margins, costs, research and development (R&D) activities, and capital expenditures. It could represent trends in manufacturing or technology, either with respect to raw materials or processes. The industry module could contain information on new technologies that might affect the production process or create new product substitution capabilities. It would also contain information on marketing trends, such as changing distribution or product consumption patterns.

A popular application of DSSs that incorporates many of these different data modules is the forecasting of sales for new products. Data input to these systems includes factors such as developmental resources (such as the number of R&D hours behind the prototype), concept testing (such as the percentage of consumers checking the "very likely" box on a scale of likelihood to purchase), prototype testing (such as the comparable percentages of consumers "very satisfied" with product usage), and marketplace promotion expenditures (such as the advertising budget allocated in millions of dollars).[4]

One important trend in the development of DSSs is the explosion in the past few years in databases that provide information on customers, competitors, industries, or general economic and demographic conditions. Several thousand databases can now be accessed online via computer, compared to fewer than 900 twenty years ago. Several hundred of these apply to the information needs of business. In addition, following the globalization of business, DSSs are increasingly becoming part of international competitive intelligence data systems. The insights that marketing managers can gather from commercially available databases are almost

---

[4]Morris A. Cohen, Jehoshua Eliashberg, and Teck H. Ho, "An Anatomy of a Decision-Support System for Developing and Launching Line Extensions," *Journal of Marketing Research* 34 (February 1997), pp. 117–129.

mind-boggling. They certainly dwarf the possibilities of even five years ago. (See the Appendix to Chapter 6 for an extensive list of sources of data.)

As the number of databases has expanded, so too has public concern with the issue of privacy, and if and how people's rights to privacy are being violated in the generation and sharing of these databases. We say more about privacy and ethics in the final section of this chapter. Beyond a sensitivity to such public concerns, however, an important criterion as to whether a particular piece of data should be included in the data bank is whether it is useful for marketing decision making. The basic task of a DSS is to capture relevant marketing data in reasonable detail and to organize that data in a truly accessible form. It is crucial that the database management capabilities built into the system can logically organize the data the same way a manager does.

Model System of a DSS

The model system includes all the routines that allow the user to manipulate the data to conduct the kind of analyses desired. Whenever managers look at data, they have a preconceived idea of how something works and, therefore, what is interesting and worthwhile in the data. These ideas are called **models.**[5] Most managers also want to manipulate data to gain a better understanding of a marketing issue. These manipulations are called **procedures.** The routines for manipulating the data may run the gamut from summing a set of numbers to conducting a complex statistical analysis to finding an optimization strategy using some kind of nonlinear programming routine. In the real world, "the most frequent operations are basic ones: segregating numbers into relevant groups, aggregating them, taking ratios, ranking them, picking out exceptional cases, plotting and making tables."[6]

The explosion in recent years in the number and size of the databases available has triggered a commensurate need for ways to analyze them efficiently. Analyzing these large databases has become known as **data mining,** which we discuss in the next section. For example, the huge quantities of scanner data that brand managers of consumer packaged goods receive every week require a great amount of time in order for even an astute analyst to provide simple summaries showing the major trends. In response, a number of firms have been developing expert systems, computer-based artificial intelligence (AI) systems that attempt to model how experts process information to solve the problem at hand. Figure 2.2 displays the type of output provided by The Partners, an expert system developed by Information Resources, Inc., for the analysis of this kind of scanner-generated data. The Partners can provide highlights of the performance of a brand and competitors' brands within minutes. It can sort through all the data and provide a comparison of current results with past results, by brand and by category as well as by markets,

[5]John D. C. Little and Michael N. Cassettari, *Decision Support Systems for Marketing Managers* (New York: American Management Association, 1984), p. 14. See also Efraim Turban and Jay E. Aronson, *Decision Support Systems and Intelligent Systems,* 5th ed. (Upper Saddle River, NJ: Prentice Hall, 1998).

[6]Little and Cassettari, *Decision Support Systems,* p. 15.

FIGURE 2.2   **Example Report Produced by the Expert System
The Partners**

SECRET's share has declined 0.7 points, from 11.1 to 10.4.

Among the components of SECRET, the top share gainer is SECRET STICK/SOLID (+0.7). The 2 products with the largest share loss are SECRET AEROSOL (−0.7) and SECRET ROLL-ON (−0.6).

Total US – Food's largest 3 share declines were posted in Boston, MA (−2.0), Los Angeles, CA (−1.3), and Detroit, MI (−1.2).

Among SECRET's major competitors, the 3 principal share gainers are MNEN LSpSt (+2.1), DEGREE (+0.9), and SUAVE (+0.5). The largest 3 share losses occurred for DRY IDEA (−1.5), BAN (−0.9), and SOFT & DRI (−0.9).

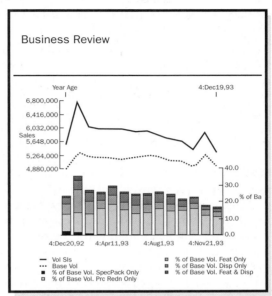

Sales Trend Review						
	Volume Share		Base Volume Share		Incrm Volume Share	
	Current	Change	Current	Change	Current	Change
SECRET	10.4	−0.7	9.7	−0.1	0.8	−0.6
SECRET STICK/SOLID	5.5	0.7	4.8	0.7	0.7	−0.0
SECRET AEROSOL	3.2	−0.7	3.1	−0.4	0.0	−0.4
SECRET ROLL-ON	1.8	−0.6	1.7	−0.4	0.1	−0.2
Competitors						
MNEN LSpSt	5.3	2.1	4.2	1.4	1.2	0.7
DEGREE	4.5	0.9	4.1	0.8	0.4	0.0
SUAVE	4.9	0.5	4.6	0.6	0.3	−0.0
DRY IDEA	2.6	−1.5	2.2	−1.0	0.3	−0.5
BAN	4.3	−0.9	4.0	−0.9	0.3	−0.0
SOFT & DRY	4.6	−0.9	4.1	−0.8	0.5	−0.1
Total US - Food	10.4	−0.7	9.7	−0.1	0.8	−0.6
Boston, MA	11.1	−2.0	9.5	−0.9	1.5	−1.1
Los Angeles, CA	8.8	−1.3	8.3	−1.4	0.5	0.1
Detroit, MI	9.2	−1.2	8.5	−1.3	0.6	0.1

Share Reference	DEODORANT/ANTI-PERSPIRANT		
Time	4 Wks Ending Dec 19, 93		
Comparison Period	4 Wks Ending Dec 20, 92		
Title	Business Review	08-29-1994	

regions, or key accounts. Moreover, as the figure indicates, the system can even produce a memo highlighting the major findings.[7]

Dialog System of a DSS—The Interface

The **dialog systems,** or language systems, are most important and differentiate DSSs from MISs. This interface permits managers who are not programmers themselves to explore the databases, using the system models to produce reports that satisfy their particular information needs. The reports can be tabular or graphical, and the report formats can be specified by individual managers. The interfaces are often menu-driven to facilitate user-friendliness, reduce errors, and increase usage. Instead of funneling their data requests through a team of programmers, managers can conduct their analyses themselves, which allows them to target the information they want rather than being overwhelmed with irrelevant data. Managers can ask a question and, on the basis of the answer, follow it with a subsequent question, and thus proceed interactively.

As the availability of online databases has increased, so too has the need for better dialog systems. The dialog systems are what put data at the managers' fingertips. That sounds simple enough, but it is a difficult task because of the large amounts of data that are available, the speed with which the data hit a company, and the fact that data come from various sources. To compound matters, the geographic boundaries used by the data suppliers differ from each other and most often from the firm's own geographic territories. Further, the services typically collect data on different time cycles. Some might provide it weekly; others might provide it twice a month, monthly, or even less often. The discrepancies must be reconciled in a meaningful way if the various data are going to be combined in a way that enables effective decision making.

A relatively new way to handle these problems is through distributed network computing. These systems rely on computers that are linked together. Because the computers are linked, users do not have to be concerned about where the information is stored in the network. More important, the systems used to access and manipulate the data use a common interface or server. Through that server, the analyst can enter data; query data; do spreadsheet analyses, plots, or statistical analyses; or even prepare reports, all through some very simple commands (see Figure 2.3). This structure is likely to continue because firms are finding that decentralization has other benefits, such as greater protection from hackers.

The Internet is also affecting the way businesses handle marketing intelligence. This global network was once limited to academicians and government employees sharing technological information, but it now extends to include computer servers at businesses and access providers. The Internet has grown explosively in terms of the number of users and the kinds of information available. The Internet now links people from more than 150 countries, with 100 million users in the U.S. alone. Its

---

[7]For general discussions of expert systems, see Luiz Moutinho, Bruce Curry, Fiona Davis, and Paulo Rita, *Computer Modeling and Expert Systems in Marketing* (New York: Routledge, 1994); Hugh J. Watson, George Houdeshel, and Rex Kelly Rainer, Jr., *Building Executive Information Systems and Other Decision Support Applications* (New York: Wiley, 1997).

FIGURE 2.3 Use of Dialog Systems with Common Server or Interface Using Simplified, Standardized Instructions to Perform Multiple Tasks

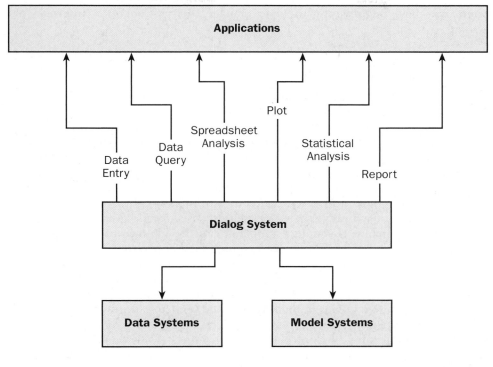

popularity is due in part to its easy access; all that is needed is a personal computer with the right software and modem or Ethernet hookup, plus a service provider, such as a commercial online service (America Online, for example).

Many Internet users browse the World Wide Web (WWW), a hypertext system that allows users to receive text, graphics, video, and sound. Hypertext is a method for linking and displaying text and graphics that permits users to click on particular words and images, thereby jumping to related documents or images. The Web's hypertext links may send users from the documents of one organization to those of another, perhaps in another part of the world. The number of Web sites has grown exponentially and is no longer estimable. Online penetration is approximately 40 percent in the U.S. (100 million individual users). Average weekly online time is 7.1 hours, just half of the time spent watching television (15.6 hours). Predominant online activities are exchanging e-mail (in which 96 percent of users engage at least once a month), using search engines (88 percent), and researching products and services (72 percent).[8] Many of the new Web sites contain information that belongs in companies' data systems, and the use of the Web to access

[8]Andrea Petersen, "Lost in the Maze," *The Wall Street Journal* (December 6, 1999), p. R6.

information on customers, competitors, industries, or general economic and demographic conditions will continue to grow rapidly.[9] Moreover, the search engines that have been designed to search the Web have proven to be so useful that many companies have begun using them to manage their intranets, or internal data systems.

Examples of DSSs

DSSs have long allowed managers to play "what-if" scenarios. Managers can simulate real-world conditions to learn about the relationships among different marketing actions and likely competitive response in a virtual marketplace, without the risk that such experimentation would cause in the real marketplace. Simulations can be programmed to be as complex and realistic as there are variables, data, experience, and assumptions to help support the interrelationships among the elements of the simulation. Input can include data and estimates on market characteristics (such as seasonality), customer preferences (such as attributes sought per segment, price sensitivity), customer loyalty (such as switching costs, trends over time), competitors' positions (such as consumers' judgments of their known product attributes, their prices and perceived prices), and competitors' access to customers (such as their distribution channels). Good simulations allow users to modify the input assumptions and parameters to see the range in possible outcomes, so as to make predictions with some degree of confidence. Shell Oil Products Co. recently used such a simulation and nixed plans to build unmanned service stations (that is, with self-service gas pumps only) because its analysis indicated that competitor reaction would be swift and sure, and any benefits due to the stations would be minor and short-term. Shell estimates that not investing in the self-serve stations saved them some $29 million.[10]

DSSs are increasingly relying on more sophisticated AI modeling and programming. Such systems still begin with the kind of information that marketing research projects can provide, including customers' historical behavior (for example, purchase transactions, reactions to past promotional efforts), and perceptual data (from surveys and internal databases). Banks use decision tree AI tools to analyze a database of loan applicants to predict who will pay back a loan and who will not. Such systems usually begin by making classifications on current customers for whom the outcome is known (that is, whether they paid back the loan or not). Decision tree analysis detects which customer characteristics are most diagnostic in distinguishing the good bets from the deadbeats. One bank found that home ownership enhances the likelihood of payback over rental status by a wide margin (defaults were 21.4 percent for home owners and 77.3 percent for renters). But there were differences even within these categories. For example, renters who had

---

[9]For discussions of how to develop an industry overview, for example, using the Internet, see Marydee Ojala, "Industry Overviews: Turning Industry Question Marks into Answers," *Online User* (July/August 1996), pp. 14–19. For a general discussion of doing marketing research online, see Reva Basch, "A Strategy for Market Research Online," *Online User* (May/June 1996), pp. 42–43.

[10]David J. Reibstein and Mark J. Chussil, "Virtual Competition," *Marketing Research* 9 (Winter 1997), pp. 44–51.

insurance defaulted less (51 percent) than their uninsured counterparts. Decision trees create rule-based procedures for the classification of the new loan applicant: *if* the loan applicant is a renter, for example, *then* default probability is 77.3 percent; *if* the loan applicant rents *and* the renter owns insurance, default probability drops to 51 percent. In developing the decision tree rules, the model iterates toward better prediction, and the iteration gives the appearance that the machine is "learning," hence the label "artificial intelligence."[11]

DSSs can be used for internal customers as well. Home Depot carries an extensive inventory in more than 400 retail outlets. Their stores have radio frequency–transmitted links to their centralized corporate data warehouse, which enables a real-time inventory and guides the store managers in placing orders. The firm estimates that the system saves it the costs of one administrative employee per store and gives the current employees more time to assist customers.[12]

Comparing DSSs, MISs, and Marketing Research Projects

In comparing DSSs and MISs, we note that both are concerned with improving information processing so that better marketing decisions can be made, yet they also differ in a number of ways:

1. DSSs tend to be aimed at the less well-structured, under-specified problems that managers face rather than at those problems that can be investigated using a relatively standard set of procedures and comparisons.

2. DSSs attempt to combine the use of models, analytical techniques, and procedures with the more traditional data access and retrieval functions.

3. DSSs specifically incorporate features that make them easy to use in an interactive mode by nontechnical people, including such things as menu-driven procedures for doing an analysis and graphical display of the results. Regardless of how the interaction is structured, DSSs respond to users' requests in "real time," that is, when the request is made so as to be timely in decision making.

4. DSSs emphasize flexibility and adaptability. They can accommodate different decision makers with diverse styles as well as changing environmental conditions.

In comparing DSSs and the traditional marketing research project approach, we note that the explosion in databases and DSSs has only increased the need for traditional marketing research projects and for understanding their strengths and weaknesses in gathering marketing intelligence. DSSs and projects are not competitive mechanisms for marketing intelligence, but are complementary and function best if they are well integrated.[13] For one thing, many of the project-oriented techniques discussed in this book are used to generate the information that goes into the databases that businesses use in their DSSs. Thus, the value of the insights gained from

---

[11]Barry de Ville, "Intelligent Tools for Marketing Research," *Marketing Research* 9 (Spring 1997), pp. 40–43.

[12]Norbert Turek, "Decision in to Action," *Informationweek* (October 26, 1998), pp. 85–90.

[13]Vijay Mahajan and Jerry Wind, "Rx for Marketing Research," *Marketing Research* 11 (Fall 1999), pp. 7–13.

these databases depends directly on the quality of the underlying data, and users must be able to assess that quality. In addition, although a DSS provides valuable input for broad strategic decisions, allows managers to stay in tune with what is happening in their external environments, and serves as an excellent early warning system, it sometimes does not provide enough information about what to do in specific instances. Examples include when the firm is faced with a new product introduction, a change in distribution channels, and the effectiveness of a new promotion campaign. When actionable information is required to address specific marketing problems or opportunities, the research project continues to play a major role.

In sum, both DSSs and marketing research projects are approaches to marketing intelligence that can be expected to remain important. In an increasingly competitive world, information is vital, and a company's ability to obtain and analyze information will largely determine the company's future. The light from both flash bulbs and candles is necessary.

Data Mining

Analyzing large databases has become known as **data mining,** and businesses hope it will allow them to boost sales and profits by better understanding their customers. The analysis of databases is not new—what is new and challenging is the extraordinary size of these databases.

The availability of huge databases began with scanner purchase data (discussed in Chapter 6). Estimates suggest that marketing managers in packaged goods companies are inundated with 100 to 1,000 times more bits of data than even a few years ago because of the adoption of scanner technology in their channels of distribution. Some data mining techniques also arose in response to "database marketing" or "direct marketing" (for example, by catalogue vendors or coupon distribution providers) in which a company is trying to form relationships with its individual customers, as marketing attempts to proceed from "mass" (one media message for all potential buyers) to "segments" (some targeting and positioning differences) to "one-to-one" marketing. In order to achieve such tailored market offerings, a company has to know a lot about its customers—hence the data contain many pieces of information on each of the company's many customers.

Traditionally, a company's database would have contained only current business information, but many now contain historical information as well. These "data warehouses" literally dwarf those available even a few years ago. For example, Wal-Mart has contracted with NCR Corporation to build a data warehouse with 24 terabytes (1 terabyte = 1,000 gigabytes) of data storage, which will make it the world's largest data warehouse. The system will provide information about each of Wal-Mart's over 3,000 stores in multiple countries. Wal-Mart plans to use the information to select products that need replenishment, analyze seasonal buying patterns, examine customer buying trends, select markdowns, and react to merchandise volume and movement.[14] See Research Realities 2.1 to gain a better understanding of the size of a number of different companies' customer information databases.

---

[14]"Sell-Through Is in the Details," *Discount Store News* (November 23, 1998), pp. S5–S7.

RESEARCH REALITIES 2.1

Size of Customer Information Databases

Fingerhut is the $2 billion mailer of 400 million catalogs a year to 65 million customers, approximately 10 million of whom are considered "active" customers. Fingerhut stores 1.5 terabytes of data representing transactions, demographics, and psychographics on these customers. A data mining expedition identified increased purchasing by households that had recently moved, and in response, Fingerhut created a special "mover's" catalog to address these special consumers' needs. They estimate their tailoring of their direct marketing efforts saves the company more than $3 million a year.

American Century Investments, a provider of mutual funds, stores 800 pieces of information for each of 25 million customers. Segmentation of their customers allows a more refined direct mailing effort, which tripled their customer response to a recent promotional effort.

Vermont Country Store sends out 3 million catalogs annually, for yearly sales around $50 million. More effective targeting based on a segmentation of their 10 years of accumulated marketing data enhanced recent sales of different target products from 2 to 12 percent.

Hallmark Cards assists its 15,000 store managers in "SKU (stock-keeping unit) optimization," the alloca-

tion of store square footage to its 40,000 products. It can determine which cards and gifts are selling on any given day at any given retail outlet.

First Union Corp. created a customer data repository that holds two years' worth of transactional information for each of its 16 million customers. The 27-terabyte relational database is mined to deliver optimally appropriate financial products to its customers.

Pillsbury's internal network allows its employees in over 70 countries access to data of several kinds, including consumer feedback that has been logged into a massive database (based on 3,500 calls a day to the 800 number printed on every Pillsbury product), manufacturing (testing equipment at new plants, statistics on production quality and packaging), and so on. Any employee, at a plant or at a sales call pitching new products to a grocer, can access the company's data.

Sources: Stewart Deck, "Mining Your Business," *Computerworld* (May 17, 1999), pp. 94–98; Jennifer Lach, "Data Mining Digs In," *American Demographics* 21 (July 1999), pp. 38–45; "Sell-Through is in the Details," *Discount Store News* (November 23, 1998), pp. S5–S7; Steward Deck, "Warehouse Expansion," *Computerworld* (April 19, 1999), p. 16; Roger O. Crockett, "A Digital Doughboy," *Business Week E.Biz* (April 3, 2000), pp. EB78–86.

In response to the increasingly massive data sets, firms have been working to create increasingly sophisticated data mining technologies (hardware and software) to analyze the data. Data mining uses *massively parallel processing (MPP)* and *symmetric multiprocessing (SMP)* supercomputer technologies (during which multiple data points and subroutines may be processing simultaneously, compared with old-fashioned "serial" processing, in which one datum is processed after another). These huge machines support "relational" database programs that can slice massive amounts of data into dozens of smaller, more manageable pools of information.

Sometimes these intensive approaches are applied to databases that are being analyzed with fairly traditional statistical techniques. For example, regression (see Chapter 16) is still a premier analytical tool, because many predictors can be used to capture complex consumer decision-making and market behavior—forecasting sales as a function of season, price, promotions, sales force, competitor factors, and delivery delays.[15] Other popular techniques of data mining include cluster analysis for segmentation and neural networks (see Chapter 17 for these multivariate

---

[15]Scott Shrake, "Regression Can Be a Good Thing," *Target Marketing* 22 (October 1999), p. 56.

statistical methods).[16] Businesses regularly use data mining analytical tools to mathematically model customers who respond to their promotional campaigns versus those who do not. The effects of direct mailing efforts, for example, are easily measured and compared as a function of customer information (demographics such as age, household size, income) and purchase behavior (past buying history, cross-sales).[17] Data mining can also be used to measure incremental business (additional traffic, sales, profits) that may be directly attributed to a recent promotion by deliberately withholding the promotional mailing from a "control" group (these "experimental" techniques are discussed in Chapter 5).[18]

In addition to standard techniques being applied to these huge data sets, marketing research methodologists are creating techniques and software especially for data mining analyses on large data sets. Sales of such customer management software are currently growing at five times the rate of the overall software market, as managers struggle to track every encounter with each customer, to facilitate call-center interactions between customers and customer service representatives, and to manage internal customers, for example, one's sales force.[19] Some of these relational database systems include NCR's Teradata system for Unix or Windows NT machines, IBM's Intelligent Miner, and SAS's Enterprise Miner.[20] Other software companies offer "content aggregator" services that synthesize multiple databases—company financial information, histories, executive profiles, and the like.[21]

As an illustration of a data mining exercise, Farmers Insurance used IBM's DecisionEdge software to look at the 200 pieces of information the company maintained on its database of 10 million automobile insurance policy owners. Think of a sports car owner and "you probably imagine a twenty-something single guy flaming down the highway in his hot rod." This profile fit many of its customers, but the data mining exercise identified another segment of sports car owner—married baby boomers with kids and more than one car. These customers produced fewer claims, yet had been paying the same sports-car surcharge. With this information in hand, Farmers could charge them less, providing greater value and customer satisfaction.[22] For additional examples of the kinds of consumer insights gained from data mining, see Research Realities 2.2.

There is no question that the explosion in databases, computer hardware and software for accessing those databases, and the World Wide Web are all changing the way marketing intelligence is obtained. Not only are more companies building DSSs, but those that have them are becoming more sophisticated in using them for general business and competitive intelligence. This, in turn, has produced

---

[16]Stewart Deck, "Mining Your Business," *Computerworld* (May 17, 1999), pp. 94–98.

[17]Patrick Hanrahan, "Mine Your Own Marketing Data," *Target Marketing* 23 (February 2000), p. 32.

[18]Robert Bibb, "Measuring Direct Mail Results," *Discount Merchandiser* 40 (January 2000), p. 94.

[19]Steve Hamm and Robert D. Hof, "An Eagle Eye on Customers," *Business Week* (February 21, 2000), pp. 67–76.

[20]Allan Holbrook, "Teradata Scales a Data Mountain," *InfoWorld* (February 14, 2000), pp. 81, 90; Beth Davis, "Data Mining Transformed," *Informationweek* (September 6, 1999), pp. 86–88.

[21]Hal Kirkwood, "A Global Business Information Newcomer: SkyMinder.com," *Online* 24 (March 2000), pp. 62–65.

[22]Jennifer Lach, "Data Mining Digs In," *American Demographics* (July 1999), pp. 38–45.

RESEARCH REALITIES 2.2

Consumer Insights Gained from Data Mining

Loyalty cards, such as those offered at supermarket retailers, offer consumers discounted prices and coupon incentives. In the past 10 years, more than 100 million loyalty cards and key tags have been issued: 30 percent of supermarket customers have them; of those, 70 percent use them. Companies know that all customers are not equal, and loyalty cards enable one-to-one marketing, customizing the shopping experience for households with different purchasing profiles (for example, sensitivities to price, value, brand, and quality). Loyalty cards and grocery purchases have yielded consumer insights and marketing actions such as these:

1. Of Diet Coke drinkers, 13% consume 83% of its volume. Taster's Choice is even more extreme—it generates 73% of its sales from only 4% of its customers.

2. Gillette used a direct marketing mailing campaign to send its razors and coupons to men and women who purchased competitors' razors.

3. Veryfine considered changing its fruit drink flavors but met with resistance when its most loyal users indicated that they did not even want the packaging to change.

4. Coca-Cola strengthened its relationship and power with retailers when it demonstrated that customers who purchased Coke as one of the items in their shopping carts were more profitable to the retailer (for the entire basket of purchases) than consumers who did not purchase Coke.

Federal Express data mines to obtain customer segments to pinpoint their desires for greater profitability. Customer service representatives are empowered to go to different lengths to satisfy customers who have been segmented as more and less profitable. This customer-relationship management effectively creates a profit-and-loss statement per customer and customer segment.

Rubbermaid data mines its warehouse to determine promotional effectiveness. It can model the likely sales resulting from a 25 percent reduction on prices with two-page ads compared to 40 percent price cuts with smaller ads. They also use their data for merchandise optimization and claim that this careful category management also enhances their relationships with their retailers, such as Wal-Mart, Pamida, and Ames.

Hotels regularly collect a great deal of information on their guests. They supplement guest history data with guest preferences, and can thereby provide better quality and customized service. Implementers of such data systems find greater customer satisfaction and loyalty, and increased revenue per customer.

Sources: Ann M. Raider, "Programs Make Results Out of Research," *Marketing News* 33 (June 21, 1999), p. 14; Paul C. Judge, "What've You Done for Us Lately?" *Business Week* (September 14, 1998), pp. 140–146; Clay Dickinson and Maite Tabernilla, "A New Customer Relationship Management Approach," *Lodging Hospitality* (May 15, 1999), pp. R11–R12.

---

some changes in the organization of the marketing intelligence function. One change has been the emergence of the position of chief information officer, or CIO.

The CIO's major role is to run the company's information and computer systems like a business.[23] The CIO serves as the liaison between the firm's top management and its information systems department. He or she has the responsibility for planning, coordinating, and controlling the use of the firm's information

---

[23]Jack J. Honomichl, "Why Marketing Information Should Have Top Executive Status," *Journal of Advertising Research* 34 (November/December 1994), pp. 61–66. For discussion of some of the problems facing CIOs, see Kaushik Shah, "Manager's Journal: The Perils of Techno Hype," *The Wall Street Journal* (March 25, 1996), p. 14A.

resources and is much more concerned with the firm's outlook than with the daily activities of the department. CIOs typically know more about the business in general than do the managers of the information systems department, who are often more technically knowledgeable. In many cases, the managers of the information systems department will report directly to the CIO. Information systems are not intended to be simply data warehouses—the management of information is ideally designed as an electronic library that allows all employees access to the "firm's collective wisdom."[24]

Privacy and Other Ethical Issues

As the number of databases has expanded, so too has public concern with the issue of privacy, and if and how people's rights to privacy are being violated in the generation and sharing of these databases. For example, motor vehicle bureaus sell information, including a driver's name, address, height, and weight, sometimes for relatively innocuous uses, such as targeted marketing lists (Sears, Roebuck & Co. has used state records on height and weight to pick prospects for its "Big and Tall" men's catalog, for example), other times to private investigators seeking to locate everyone from criminal defendants and witnesses, to fathers who are delinquent in child support. The generation and sales of Department of Motor Vehicle (DMV) data sets continues to be controversial; part of the Brady Handgun Act prohibited the release of such personal information. However, since the Supreme Court ruled this prohibition unconstitutional, DMV data will continue to be used and misused, at least for the near future.[25]

The sharing of financial data, personal information, and consumer purchases has generated much controversy. There is little doubt that as the ability to gather and organize individual-level data expands, so will the controversy regarding individual versus company rights. DoubleClick, the Internet advertising pioneer and the largest of the Web ad servers, has been targeted by privacy advocates for a variety of actions, including their nondisclosure of "cookie" file placements and surreptitious collection of data, their plan to merge lists of individual consumer identities with lists of their Web activities, and their unresponsiveness to critics.[26] For more information on cookies and related issues, see Research Realities 2.3.

There is concern about how the consumer purchasing and Web-surfing data will be used, including an electronic version of "redlining," a practice of crossing out certain members of a list (that is, a customer database) as being poor sales prospects (meaning unlikely to be profitable). Redlining was deemed unacceptable because it was based on stereotypes about people living in certain geographical locations. The electronic classification is presumably built on data profiles, but clearly has the potential for misuse, if managers make superstitious assumptions based on

---

[24]Robert Sutton, "Knowledge Management Is Not an Oxymoron," *Computerworld* (January 3, 2000), p. 28.

[25]Michael W. Miller, "Debate Mounts over Disclosure of Driver Data," *The Wall Street Journal* (August 25, 1992), p. B1. See also Diane K. Bowers, "Research Interests Protected in the Use of DMV Records," *Marketing Research: A Magazine of Management & Applications* 7 (Winter 1995), p. 45; John Gibeaut, "Keeping Federalism Alive," *ABA Journal* (January 1998), pp. 38–39.

[26]"Crisis Rx for DoubleClick," *Advertising Age* (February 28, 2000), p. 58; Ira Teinowitz and Jennifer Gilbert, "Marketers Address Web Concerns," *Advertising Age* (February 21, 2000), pp. 1, 60.

RESEARCH REALITIES 2.3

Web Threats to Privacy—The Cookie Monster

There is no question that the Web has the ability to be extremely nosy.

Web marketers can determine, without permission, your "domain," the portion of your e-mail address that follows the @ symbol. That can tell marketers you reached their site via a consumer service such as America Online or a corporate connection. Internet marketers can thus target specific domains for their ads.

More controversial are the whimsically dubbed "cookies," a technology that allows Web sites to track individual users. Prior to cookies, Web sites could tally requests for information made each day, but they could not tell whether one visitor made 100 requests or 100 unique visitors made one request each. With cookies, a Web site places a file on a visitor's computer that serves as a kind of tracking beacon. The site does not know your name or e-mail address, but it has your IP address and represents you as a distinct user. (Curious? Search your hard drive for a file called "cookies" and open it in a word-processing program to see who has served you a cookie. If you're concerned about privacy, delete the cookie files occasionally.)

Cookies feed some of the more dire privacy scenarios. With them, a Web magazine will see which articles you read; a merchant can tell not only which products you bought, but also which product descriptions you simply viewed. (Imagine a supermarket scanner that monitors everything you look at in a store.) Similarly, it not only knows which ads work; it also knows which don't.

Still, some of these fears are no doubt overblown. To begin, surfing is an anonymous activity, and cookies cannot automatically penetrate that shield. When you visit a Web site, the computer maintaining that site may know your domain, but it cannot know your identity, or even your e-mail address, unless you volunteer it. Of course, plenty of sites that sell products online require names, addresses, e-mail addresses, and credit-card information. Providing it, however, is your choice.

Access to cookie files may become limited in the near future, but not in response to consumers' concerns for privacy. Rather, companies are learning to protect their customers' information from competitors—if Mattel can see where you've surfed, so can Hasbro.

Sources: Thomas E. Weber, "Browsers Beware: The Web Is Watching," *The Wall Street Journal* (June 27, 1996), pp. B10, B12. See also Walter S. Mossberg, "Threats to Privacy On-Line Become More Worrisome," *The Wall Street Journal* (October 24, 1996), p. B1; Gautam Naik, "Do I Have Privacy On-Line?" *The Wall Street Journal* (December 9, 1996), p. R12; Kathryn Kranhold and Michael Moss "Keep Away From My Cookies, More Marketers Say," *The Wall Street Journal* (March 20, 2000), pp. B1, B6.

---

the Web sites you visit, the books you buy, your mortgage status, and the like. Current examples of data used to assist decisions include:

- Visa International managers watch a customer's behavior to spot fraud and identify people who may go bankrupt
- First Union Bank sorts customers into value segments on which customer service is based (for example, flexibility on credit card rates)
- Catalina Supermarkets offer free home delivery exclusively to its most profitable customers[27]

Companies planning on entering particular types of data in their data systems need to be sensitive to privacy issues.[28] Research Realities 2.4 offers a privacy checklist companies might use when developing their databases.

---

[27]Marcia Stepanek, "Weblining," *Business Week E.Biz* (April 3, 2000), pp. EB26–34.

[28]For general discussions of the privacy–database controversy, see Bruce Horowitz, "Marketers Tap Data We Once Called Our Own," *USA Today* (December 19, 1995), pp. 1A–2A; "How to Safeguard Your Privacy," *USA Today* (December 19, 1995), p. 48.

A Privacy Checklist

In the long run, ensuring a customer's privacy can improve a company's profitability. Privacy is really about earning the customer's trust, and trust is a central component of relationship marketing.

Anyone who uses personal information to target customers can stay on top of the privacy issue by writing a formal privacy policy. If you need to create a policy or review your old one, here are some basic guidelines:

1. **Remember "knowledge, notice, and no."** Tell your customers how you will use their personal information. If you plan to share the information with a third party, tell your customers and give them a chance to drop out of the database. Even if you don't sell your customer lists, tell them so. The practice of renting customer lists has become so widespread that a customer may assume you share your lists unless you explicitly tell them otherwise. The adaption of this policy to the sharing and selling of Internet data has been suggested as follows.

   a. Display your practices—companies must inform consumers how they gather and use information;
   b. Give people a choice—Web site users can opt in and choose to provide personal information, or they may opt out and choose not to do so;
   c. Show consumers the data—allow users to view and correct sensitive information, such as financial and medical data;
   d. Play fair or pay—it has been suggested that some agency such as the Federal Trade Commission (FTC) needs to enforce fair information practices.

2. **Exercise conscience and common sense**. So far, few legal restrictions apply to the gathering and use of personal information by the private sector. That's why privacy is more about "should" than "must." Clearly, some medical, financial, and lifestyle data are more sensitive than others. Apply a "sniff test" to any proposed reuse of your customer database. Would you be comfortable sending a member of your family the same offers that you propose to mail to your customers? If your company is identified as a sponsor of this mailing, would your 800-number be clogged with complaints?

Sources: Mary J. Culnan, "The Privacy Checklist," in Judith Waldrop, "The Business of Privacy," *American Demographics* 16 (October 1994), p. 55; Heather Green, et al., "Online Privacy: It's Time for Rules in Wonderland," *Business Week* (March 20, 2000), pp. 83–96.

Marketing Research—Ethics Beyond Privacy

Privacy is a particular concern with data mining and the existence of huge databases, and the issues are being exacerbated by the pervasiveness of the Internet. However, marketing researchers have long recognized that they must take care in conducting their business in a professional manner. In this final section, we discuss broader ethical issues beyond those of privacy and Internet databases.

Marketing researchers need to recognize that the effective practice of their profession depends a great deal on the goodwill of and participation by the public. In addition, while the current discussions in the media about privacy issues revolve primarily around the Internet (such as sharing of consumer data, Web site visits, and personal information), the marketing researcher is also affected by the American public's greater protectiveness of its privacy—it is more difficult and costly to approach, recruit, and survey participants. Thus, moral fairness and self-preservation dictate that marketing researchers develop a sense for ethical issues—good ethics is good business. Table 2.1 contains the marketing research code of ethics for the American Marketing Association.

TABLE 2.1	AMA Marketing Research Code of Ethics

The American Marketing Association, in furtherance of its central objective of the advancement of science in marketing and in recognition of its obligation to the public, has established these principles of ethical practice of marketing research for the guidance of its members. In an increasingly complex society, marketing management is more and more dependent upon marketing information intelligently and systematically obtained. The consumer is the source of much of this information. Seeking the cooperation of the consumer in the development of information, marketing management must acknowledge its obligation to protect the public from misrepresentation and exploitation under the guise of research.

Similarly, the research practitioner has an obligation to the discipline and to those who provide support for it—an obligation to adhere to basic and commonly accepted standards of scientific investigation as they apply to the domain of marketing research.

For Research Users, Practitioners, and Interviewers
1. No individual or organization will undertake any activity which is directly or indirectly represented to be marketing research, but which has as its real purpose the attempted sales of merchandise or services to some or all of the respondents interviewed in the course of the research.
2. If respondents have been led to believe, directly or indirectly, that they are participating in a marketing research survey and that their anonymity will be protected, their names shall not be made known to anyone outside the research organization or research department, or used for other than research purposes.

For Research Practitioners
1. There will be no intentional or deliberate misrepresentation of research methods or results. An adequate description of methods employed will be made available upon request to the sponsor of the research. Evidence that fieldwork has been completed according to specifications will, upon request, be made available to buyers of the research.
2. The identity of the survey sponsor and/or the ultimate client for whom a survey is being done will be held in confidence at all times, unless this identity is to be revealed as part of the research design. Research information shall be held in confidence by the research organization or department and not used for personal gain or made available to any outside party unless the client specifically authorizes such release.
3. A research organization shall not undertake marketing studies for competitive clients when such studies would jeopardize the confidential nature of client-agency relationships.

For Users of Marketing Research
1. A user of research shall not knowingly disseminate conclusions from a given research project or service that are inconsistent with or not warranted by the data.
2. To the extent that there is involved in a research project a unique design involving techniques, approaches, or concepts not commonly available to research practitioners, the prospective user of research shall not solicit such a design from one practitioner and deliver it to another for execution without the approval of the design originator.

For Field Interviewers
1. Research assignments and materials received, as well as information obtained from respondents, shall be held in confidence by the interviewer and revealed to no one except the research organization conducting the marketing study.
2. No information gained through a marketing research activity shall be used, directly or indirectly, for the personal gain or advantage of the interviewer.
3. Interviews shall be conducted in strict accordance with specifications and instructions received.
4. An interviewer shall not carry out two or more interviewing assignments simultaneously, unless authorized by all contractors or employers concerned.

Members of the American Marketing Association will be expected to conduct themselves in accordance with the provisions of this code in all of their marketing research activities.

Reprinted with permission from the American Marketing Association.

In particular, the marketing researcher can encounter ethical issues with three constituencies: (1) the research participants, (2) the client for whom the research is being conducted, and (3) the research team itself. We highlight some of the issues for each relationship in turn.

Research Participants

Regarding the research participants, there are two main issues: preserving the participants' anonymity and obtaining their consent to participate in the study. Maintaining their anonymity ensures that their identity is safe from invasions of privacy. Information obtained by marketing researchers can be extremely useful to other agents (for example, in compiling mailing lists of likely sales prospects), but unless consumers agree ahead of time to have their identities disclosed, such information should not be passed along. (Internet privacy critics refer to this as the ability to "opt in" or "opt out.")

Obtaining a respondent's "informed, expressed consent" is often straightforward; in a mall-intercept, for example, a consumer is confronted in a shopping mall and asked whether he or she would be willing to spend a few moments answering questions. The individual can agree or walk away. However, some common marketing research procedures exist that can involve consumers without their knowledge and therefore without their consent. **Participant observation** (discussed more in Chapter 7) is the name given to procedures in which the researcher participates in the activity of interest in order to observe people's behavior in their natural environment. A relevant example would be a marketer living among and traveling with a Harley-Davidson gang for six months to study the members' behaviors and consumption patterns. Minimal ethics require the researcher to reveal one's true identity and purpose once the data have been collected and to allow the people who have been observed to read the final report on their activities.

Observing people in public places (also discussed in Chapter 7) is less intrusive but common among marketing researchers; it is helpful to watch shoppers' reactions to new floor displays in a store. For many researchers, any activity or conversation occurring in a public place is fair game and arouses no ethical scruples. Strictly speaking, however, the research participants are being involved without their knowledge or consent, and their rights are being infringed.

Finally, in some field experiments, benefits are withheld from control groups (see Chapter 5). While this issue is perhaps more critical in medical testing, it can still affect the marketer (such as in studies on sales force management that deprive a control group of incentives).

Clients

Regarding the client, the marketing researcher must be careful to maintain confidentiality and technical and administrative integrity. Discretion and confidentiality are obligated in not revealing one client's affairs to another client who is a competitor, and in some circumstances, in not revealing the sponsor of the research to participants. Violations of research integrity can range from designing studies without due care through the unnecessary use of complex analytical procedures, to the deliberate fudging of data. It cannot be emphasized enough that in this stage of the profession's development, researchers must maintain the strictest technical integrity if they are to have credibility as professional experts. It is not only unethical but also shortsighted as a business to take advantage of the client's lack of expertise in research design and methodology, because where trust fails, funding eventually does also. Specific recommendations include choosing the simplest appropriate methodology, as opposed to unnecessarily sophisticated and costly techniques; expressing oneself in simple and generally accessible language rather than in intimidating jargon; making explicit mention of the limitations of the research; and refusing any project in which personal problems or conflicts will lead to inadequate performance. Administrative integrity covers issues such as refraining from passing on hidden charges to the client.

The Research Team

Finally, there are considerations regarding the research team itself. For example, when subordinates are acting according to instructions, the supervisor is partly responsible for their ethical conduct. Moreover, in addition to the official hierarchy, an unofficial sphere of influence exists that renders every team member partially responsible for the others' moral behavior. In particular, studies of organizational culture (such as in marketing research firms) show that actions of top management have been found to be the best predictor of perceived ethical problems for marketing researchers. The source of the boss's influence probably resides in subordinates' fear of reprisals for not conforming and in their acceptance of legitimate authority. As a consequence of the poor examples they see, marketing practitioners do not see themselves as being under pressure to improve their own ethics. See Research Realities 2.5 to get a better understanding of the kinds of ethical issues that confront marketing researchers.

RESEARCH REALITIES 2.5

Marketing Researchers' Own Perceptions of the Difficult Ethical Problems They Face

Ethical Issues to Which Practitioners Are Most Sensitive:	1. Maintaining their research integrity: for example, deliberately withholding information, falsifying figures, altering research results, misusing statistics, ignoring pertinent data.
	2. Treating outside clients fairly: for example, passing hidden charges to clients, overlooking violations of the project requirements when subcontracting parts of the project.
	3. Maintaining research confidentiality: for example, sharing information among subsidiaries in the same corporation, using background data developed in a previous project to reduce the cost of a current project.
Factors That Predict Sensitivity to Ethical Issues:	1. Organizational socialization (for example, "I know the rules associated with my job" and "I know what's considered appropriate behavior in my company").
	2. Ability to empathize (such as, "Generally, I find it easy to see things from the other person's perspective").

From John R. Sparks and Shelby D. Hunt, "Marketing Researcher Ethical Sensitivity: Conceptualization, Measurement, and Exploratory Investigation," *Journal of Marketing* 62 (April 1998), pp. 92–109.

Summary

This book takes a project-based approach to the provision of marketing intelligence. The difference between a project emphasis to research or the alternative MIS or DSS emphasis is that both of the latter rely on the continual monitoring of the firm's activities, its competitors, and its environment, whereas the former emphasizes the in-depth study of some specific problem or environmental condition.

An MIS was defined as a set of procedures and methods for the regular, planned collection, analysis, and presentation of information for use in making marketing decisions. The thrust in designing an MIS is the detailed analysis of each decision maker who might use the system in order to secure an accurate, objective assessment of each manager's decision-making responsibilities, capabilities, and style, and, most important, each manager's information needs. Given the specifications for information needs, system support people develop report formats and efficient systems for extracting and combining information from various data banks.

Although MISs did provide more regular marketing intelligence than had been true when firms relied on marketing research projects, such systems suffered from other problems. They required managers to disclose their decision-making processes, which many managers were reluctant to do. Further, the report formats were typically compromises that tried to satisfy the different styles of the different users. And the development time required for these systems often meant that they quickly became obsolete.

DSSs are replacing MISs in many companies. A DSS is a coordinated collection of data, systems, tools, and techniques with supporting software and hardware by which an organization gathers and interprets relevant information from business and the environment and turns it into a basis for marketing action. A DSS concentrates on the design of data systems, model systems, and dialog systems. The data systems include the processes used to capture and store information useful for marketing decision making. A marketing research project might be one input to a data system. The model system includes all the routines that allow users to manipulate data to conduct the kinds of analyses they desire.

The dialog systems are most important and most clearly differentiate DSSs from MISs. They allow managers to conduct their own analyses while they or one of their assistants sit at a computer terminal. This allows managers to analyze problems using their own personal insight into what might be happening in a given situation, relying on their intuition and experience rather than on a series of prespecified reports. This not only eliminates a lot of irrelevant data, but also saves time because managers can program the analysis themselves rather than waiting for the computer department to process their request for some specific information.

Data mining is the term used to describe the analysis of huge consumer databases—scanner purchase data, or investigations in database marketing or direct marketing—tasks for which companies can have hundreds of pieces of information on each of its millions of customers. Large databases require special storage and increasingly sophisticated hardware and software to enable massively parallel processing and symmetric multiprocessing. Sometimes traditional statistical techniques, such as regression or cluster analysis, may be applied to these huge data sets, but increasingly, special customer management software is used, especially for data mining. Information management is a challenge becoming recognized in the appointment of CIOs—chief information officers—whose guidance in the information assets of a firm should only increase in the future, particularly as the World Wide Web allows for greater access to more data.

In this chapter, we also considered a number of ethical issues that the marketing researcher must face, beginning with the acknowledgment of privacy issues in reaction to the explosion of the number and size of consumer information databases. Guidelines were offered to respect consumers' concerns for privacy, in which policy disclosure and consumer choice (for example, to "opt out") figure prominently. In addition, for the ideal purpose of professionalism and the pragmatic purpose of sustained business, marketing researchers are encouraged to consider additional ethical issues beyond privacy. These broader ethics concern the treatment of the research participants (such as preserving their anonymity and obtaining their consent), the research client (maintaining confidentiality among competing clients, not commissioning excessive analyses, charging fairly), and the research team itself (sharing responsibility for one another's behaviors and the importance of ethical leadership).

Questions

1. What is a marketing information system? How does a project emphasis to marketing research differ from an information systems emphasis?
2. What are the steps in MIS analysis? In developing an MIS system?
3. What are the main differences between an MIS and a DSS?
4. In a DSS, what is a data system? A model system? A dialog system? Which of these is most important? Why?
5. What is (are) the likely future approach(es) to marketing intelligence? Will there be a change in the relative importance of traditional research and MISs and DSSs?
6. What is data mining? How does it differ from traditional data analysis?
7. What are the central privacy issues of consumer data? How does the Internet impact these issues?
8. What classes of ethical issues does the marketing researcher face, beyond privacy?

Applications and Problems

1. You are responsible for deciding whether to adopt an MIS or a DSS for the following situations. Which system approach would you choose? Why?
   a. Production of profit and loss statements to estimate customer lifetime values for segments of video renters.
   b. Introduction of a new product line extension for Smucker's preserves and jellies.
   c. Determination of seasonal pricing schedules for Johnson outboard motors.
   d. Identification of the amount of time spent on hold by consumers on a toll-free, customer-service assistance telephone line.
2. Consider the industry of healthcare management, consulting, or financial investments. What specific capabilities of a DSS would enable greater customer satisfaction and profitability? What kinds of input should your company seek? Who should use the system, and to address what specific needs and questions?
3. You are the vice president of international marketing for a consumer packaged-goods company. In a recent board of directors meeting, it was decided that you would head the development of a competitive information system (CIS) for your organization. You have been asked to write a brief description of the types of data to be stored in the CIS along with possible uses of the data by employees within your company. Write a clear and concise paragraph describing your recommendations.
4. Imagine that you work for an airline. Your company has an extended database of customers' travel records. For the customers who are frequent flyer members, you also have personal data, both data that they have given freely (for example, when applying for membership) as well as data from other sources (such as Web surfing) that you can attach to your members' records because the identification information is clear. You and your data analyst have been mining this large data set to get ideas of travel packages that

you could offer that might interest these flyers. You notice that a good portion of your young, male business class flyers who report using their laptops in-flight are single. You consider offering a discount to travel destinations that specialize in singles. You think about sending notice of this promotion via e-mail. You also notice that a disproportionately large number of flights on which more than 5 percent of the seat occupants are children tend to be costly in terms of amenities, post-flight cleaning, and flight attendant time-spent, and these flights tended to generate relatively more customer complaints. You consider increasing fares for children. Do either of these issues raise privacy or ethical concerns?

3

The Research Process and Problem Formulation

Chapter 1 highlighted the many kinds of problems that marketing research can be used to solve. It emphasized that marketing research is the firm's communication link with the environment and that it can help the marketing manager in planning, problem solving, and control. Different companies use marketing research for different subsets of these activities.

A company's philosophy of how marketing research fits into its marketing plan determines its program strategy for marketing research. Some companies may use marketing research on a continuous basis to track sales or to monitor the firm's market share. Others may use marketing research only when a problem arises or an important decision—such as the launching of a new product—needs to be made. A program strategy specifies the types of studies that are to be conducted and their purposes. Research Realities 3.1, for example, outlines the types and purposes of the various studies that are conducted by Gillette Company in its constant endeavor to maintain its dominant share of the blade and razor market. The design of the individual studies themselves defines the firm's project strategy, for example, the use of personal interviews in the national consumer studies, mail questionnaires in the brand tracking studies, and telephone interviews when measuring brand awareness. In sum, project strategy deals with how a study should be conducted, whereas program strategy addresses the question of what types of studies the firm should conduct and for what purposes.

All research problems require their own special emphases and approaches. Because every marketing research problem is unique in some way, the research procedure typically is custom tailored. Nonetheless, there is a sequence of steps, called the **research process** (see Figure 3.1), that can be followed when designing the research project. This chapter reviews the research process and discusses the first step: formulating the problem.

Marketing Research—Sequence of Steps

I. Formulate Problem

One of the more valuable roles marketing research can play is helping to define the problem to be solved. Only when the problem is carefully and precisely defined can research be designed to provide pertinent information. Part of the process of problem definition includes specifying the objectives of the specific research projects that

Major Thrusts of Marketing Research at Gillette Company

Gillette is the global leader in male toiletries products. Its cutting-edge products are offered at premium prices. It is also among the most financially stable of firms. It has achieved these positions through a strong belief in marketing research and the development of innovative products, such as its MACH 3 razors, which outperform all other shaving instruments, and sells at a 2:1 ratio above the next razor, which is also a Gillette product. Gillette also creates special products for women, such as the Sensor Dazzlers. In recent years, Gillette has been introducing more than 20 new products per year, and approximately half of its sales come from brands that are no older than five years. What follows is a sample of the marketing research methods Gillette uses:

1. **Annual National Consumer Studies.** The objectives of these studies are to determine what brand of razor and blade was used for the respondents' last shave, to collect demographic data, and to examine consumer attitudes toward the various blade and razor manufacturers. These studies rely on personal interviews with national panels of men and women who are selected by using probability sampling methods.

2. **National Brand Tracking Studies.** These studies track the use of razors and blades to monitor brand loyalty and brand switching tendencies over time. Mail questionnaires are issued annually to panels of male and female shavers.

3. **Annual Brand Awareness Studies.** These studies are aimed at determining the "share of mind" Gillette products have. Telephone surveys employ aided and unaided recall of brand names and advertising campaigns.

4. **Consumer Use Tests.** The key objectives of the use-testing studies are to ensure that Gillette remains competitive, with products performing up to desired standards, and to substantiate claims in advertising and packaging. At least two consumer use tests are conducted each month by Gillette. In these tests, consumers are asked to use a single variation of a product for an extended period of time, at the end of which their evaluation of the product is obtained.

5. **Continuous Retail Audits.** These audits provide top management with monthly market share data, along with information regarding distribution, out-of-stock, and inventory levels of the various Gillette products. This information is purchased from the commercial information services providing syndicated retail audit data. The information is supplemented by special retail audits, which Gillette conducts itself, that look at product displays and the extent to which Gillette blades and razors are featured in retailer advertisements.

6. **Laboratory Research Studies.** These studies are designed to test the performance of existing Gillette products and to help in the design of new products. They include having people shave with Gillette and competitor products and measuring the results, as well as determining the number of whiskers on a man's face, how fast whiskers grow, and how many shaves a man can get from a single blade.

Source: Lawrence Ingrassia, "Gillette Holds Its Edge by Endlessly Searching for a Better Shave," *The Wall Street Journal* (December 10, 1992), pp. A1, A6; Barbara Carton, "To Make Gillette Bristle, Ask about the Razor's Edge," *The Wall Street Journal* (July 30, 1996), p. A1; Tara Rummell, "What's New at Gillette," *Global Cosmetic Industry* 165 (October 1999), pp. 16–18.

might be undertaken. Each project should have one or more objectives, and the next step in the process should not be taken until these goals can be explicitly stated.

II. Determine Research Design

The sources of information for a study and the research design go hand in hand. They both depend on how much is known about the problem. If relatively little is known about the phenomenon to be investigated, exploratory research is warranted. Exploratory research would begin with a review of **secondary data,** such as published

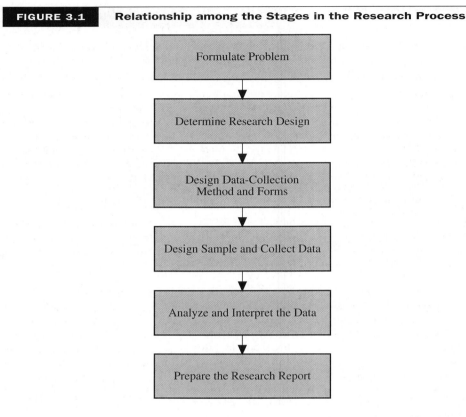

FIGURE 3.1   **Relationship among the Stages in the Research Process**

Formulate Problem

Determine Research Design

Design Data-Collection
Method and Forms

Design Sample and Collect Data

Analyze and Interpret the Data

Prepare the Research Report

data or syndicated data, or trade literature that discusses similar cases. Exploratory research may then involve interviewing knowledgeable people or conducting focus groups. One of the most important characteristics of exploratory research is its flexibility. Researchers know little about the problem at this point, so they must be ready to follow their experience and intuition about possible areas of investigation or tactics to adopt. If, on the other hand, the problem is precisely and unambiguously formulated, descriptive or causal research is needed. In these research designs, data collection is not flexible but is rigidly specified with respect to both the data-collection forms and the sample design to obtain precise results and conclusions, with implications that yield actionable results.

III. Design Data-Collection Method and Forms

Given the dynamic nature of business and customers, quite often the information needed to solve the problem cannot be found in the firm's own sales data or other internal records or in published documents, such as government census reports or industry sales trends. The research then must depend on **primary data,** which are collected specifically for the study. The research questions here are several: Should the data be collected by observation or questionnaire? Should the form be structured as a fixed set of alternative answers, or should the responses be open-ended? Should the purpose be made clear to the respondent, or should the study objectives be disguised? We elaborate upon additional questions throughout the book, but these should serve to illustrate the basic concerns of the research process.

IV. Design Sample and Collect Data

In designing the sample, the researcher must specify: (1) the sampling frame, (2) the sample selection process, and (3) the size of the sample. The sampling frame is the list of population elements from which the sample will be drawn. Although we often assume that the frame is implicit in the research problem and thus take it for granted, the assumption can be dangerous:

> Take the case of the manufacturer of dog food . . . who went out and did an intensive market study. He tested the demand for dog food; he tested the package size, the design, the whole advertising program. Then he launched the product with a big campaign, got the proper distribution channels, put it on the market and had tremendous sales. But two months later, the bottom dropped out—no follow-up sales. So he called in an expert, who took the dog food out to the local pound, put it in front of the dogs—and they would not touch it. For all the big marketing study, no one had tried the product on the dogs.[1]

As this classic example illustrates, the dog population was not part of the sampling frame, probably because it is people who buy dog food and not the dogs themselves. Nevertheless, the careless specification of population elements had dire consequences. Although the results may not be as severe, we need to realize that when we sample from, say, a phone book or a CD-ROM mailing list, we are not sampling from the population as a whole but only from people whose names appear in these sources.

The sample selection process requires that the form of the sample be specified. Will it be a probability sample, in which each population element has a known chance of being selected, or will it be a nonprobability sample? Will the probability sample be simple or complex? Will the nonprobability sample be one of convenience, judgment, or a quota system?

The decision on sample size involves determining how many people, households, business firms, or other entities must be studied to get sufficiently accurate and reliable answers that will allow a decision to be made regarding this problem without exceeding the time and money budgeted for the project.

Once the dimensions of the sample design are specified, data collection can commence. Data collection will require a field force of some type, although field methods will be largely dictated by the kinds of information to be obtained and the sampling requirements. The use of personnel to collect data raises a host of questions with respect to selection, training, and control of the field staff—questions that must be anticipated in designing the research.

V. Analyze and Interpret the Data

Researchers may amass a mountain of data, but these data are useless unless the findings are analyzed and the results interpreted in light of the problem at hand.

---

[1] Joseph R. Hochstim, "Practical Uses of Sampling Surveys in the Field of Labor Relations," *Proceedings of the Conference on Business Application of Statistical Sampling Methods* (Monticello, IL: The Bureau of Business Management, University of Illinois, 1950), pp. 181–182. As should be obvious from the example, researchers need to access both constituencies (dogs and dogs' purchasing agents) when assessing the appeal of a product like dog food. See Nancy J. Church, "Get the Dog's Opinion When Researching Dog Food," *Marketing News* (August 29, 1988), p. 41, for suggestions on how to go about this.

Data analysis generally involves several steps. First, the data-collection forms must be scanned to be sure that they are complete and consistent and that the instructions were followed. This process is called **editing.** Once the forms have been edited, they must be coded. **Coding** involves assigning numbers to each of the answers so that they can be analyzed. The final step in analyzing the data is **tabulation,** the orderly arrangement of data in a table or other summary format achieved by counting the frequency of responses to each question. It is common also to cross-classify the data against other variables. For example, researchers may have asked women if they liked a certain kind of new cosmetic. Their responses could be analyzed by age group, income level, and other characteristics.

The coding, editing, and tabulation functions are common to most research studies. The statistical tests applied to the data will be specific to the particular sampling procedures and data-collection instruments used in the research. These tests should be anticipated before data collection is begun, if possible, to assure that the data and analyses will be appropriate to the specified problem.

VI. Prepare the Research Report

The research report is the document submitted to management that summarizes the research results and conclusions. It is all that many executives will see of the research effort, and it becomes the standard by which that research is judged. Thus, it is imperative that the research report be clear and accurate, because no matter how well all previous steps have been completed, the project will be no more successful than the research report. Simply put, the research report is one of the most important factors affecting whether the research will be used and changes based on it implemented.

Additional Comments

Even though the preceding discussion should provide some understanding of the steps in the research process, each step is more complex than this introductory discussion suggests. Each involves numerous issues rather than a single decision or

---

ETHICAL DILEMMA 3.1

A manufacturer of bolts and screws approaches you and outlines the following problem: "My friend owns a hardware store, and you used a technique called multidimensional scaling to produce what I think he called a *perceptual map,* which positioned his operation in relation to his competitors and showed him where there was space in the market to expand his business. I don't understand the details of it, but I was very impressed with the map and I want you to do the same for me."

- What have you learned about the manufacturer's research problem?
- Is it likely that the development of a perceptual map will be useful to the manufacturer of bolts and screws?
- Is it ethical to agree to her proposal?

even a few decisions. Table 3.1 lists some of the typical questions that need to be resolved at each stage.

In addition, the stages have been presented as if one would proceed through them in a lockstep fashion when designing a research project. Nothing could be further from the truth. Rather, Figure 3.1 (shown earlier) could be drawn with a number of feedback loops suggesting a possible need to rethink and revise the various elements in the process as the study proceeds. The process would begin with problem formulation, but after that anything could happen. The problem might not be specified explicitly enough to allow the development of the research design, in which case the researcher would need to return to stage 1 to delineate the research objectives more clearly. Alternatively, the process may proceed smoothly to the design of the data-collection forms, the pretest of which may require a revision of the research objectives or the research design. Or the sample necessary to answer the problem as specified may be cost prohibitive, again requiring a revision of the earlier steps.

Once the data are collected, no revision of the procedure is possible. It is possible, though, to revise the earlier steps on the basis of the anticipated analysis. It is imperative, therefore, that the methods used to analyze the data are determined before the data are collected. Although it is difficult for beginning researchers to understand, the steps in the research process are highly interrelated. A decision made at one stage affects decisions at each of the other stages, and a revision of the procedure at any stage often requires modifications of procedures at each of the other stages. Unfortunately, it seems that this lesson is understood only by those who have experienced the frustrations and satisfactions of being involved in an actual research project.

All the steps in the research process are necessary and vital. It is true that errors can arise during any one of them, and it is dangerous to worry about one kind of error to the exclusion of others. The "total error" associated with a project cumulates the errors at each stage. For example, many beginning students of research argue for large sample sizes to reduce sampling error. What they fail to realize is that sample size is a decision made with respect to one subset of one stage in the process. Although the increase in sample size reduces sampling error, it can lead to an increase in the total error of the research effort, because other errors may increase more than proportionately with sample size. To keep the study within budget, the larger sample size may dictate fewer follow-ups with those who did not respond to the initial contact. The larger this nonresponse problem, the greater the question of whether the responses that are secured are representative of the selected sample. Response errors can also increase when the sample size is increased. The larger sample will typically mean the use of more interviewers if the study is being done by phone or in person. This raises a host of issues with respect to the selection and training of the interviewers so that they all handle the interviews in the same way. Otherwise, the different responses that are secured can be as much a function of the interviewers collecting the data as they are differences in respondents.

Thus, researchers frequently face a dilemma because of normal budget and time constraints. Should they select a large sample to minimize sampling error, or should they select a smaller sample, thereby ensuring better interviewer controls, more accurate responses, and a higher response rate among those contacted? In one study that investigated the incidence of sampling and nonsampling errors by

| TABLE 3.1 | Questions to Be Addressed at the Various Stages of the Research Process |

Stage in the Process	*Typical Questions*
Formulate Problem	• What is the purpose of the study? To solve a problem? To identify an opportunity? • Is additional background information necessary? • What information is needed to make the decision? • How will the information be used? • Should research be conducted?
Determine Research Design	• How much is already known? • Can a hypothesis be formulated? • What types of questions need to be answered? • What type of study will best address the research questions?
Determine Data-Collection Method and Forms	• Can existing data be used to advantage? • What is to be measured? How? • What is the source of the data? • Are there any cultural factors that need to be taken into account in designing the data-collection method? What are they? • Are there any legal restrictions on the collection methods? What are they? • Can objective answers be obtained by asking people? • How should people be questioned? • Should the questionnaires be administered in person, over the phone, through the mail, via fax, on the Internet, or through e-mail? • Should electronic or mechanical means be used to make the observations? • What specific behaviors should the observers record? • Should rating scales be used in the questionnaires?
Design Sample and Collect Data	• What is the target population? • Is a list of population elements available? • Is a sample necessary? • Is a probability sample desirable? • How large should the sample be? • How should the sample be selected? • Who will gather the data? • How long will the data gathering take? • How much supervision is needed? • What operational procedures will be followed? • What methods will be used to ensure the quality of the data collected?
Analyze and Interpret the Data	• Who will handle the editing of the data? • How will the data be coded? • Who will supervise the coding? • Will computer or hand tabulation be used? • What tabulations are called for? • What analysis techniques will be used?
Prepare the Research Report	• Who will read the report? • What is their technical level of sophistication? • Are managerial recommendations called for? • What will be the format of the written report? • Is an oral report necessary? • How should the oral report be structured?

comparing respondent replies against known data, the consistent finding was "that nonsampling error is the major contributor to total survey error, while random sampling error is minimal."[2] The fact that nonsampling error far outweighed sampling error led the authors to conclude that the "emphasis on methods to reduce random sampling error by emphasizing large samples may be misplaced."[3]

Finally, the stages in the research process serve to structure this book. The remainder of this chapter, for example, deals with stage 1, problem formulation, and each of the remaining stages warrants a special section in the book.

Problem Formulation

An old adage says, "A problem well defined is half-solved." This is especially true in marketing research, for it is only when the problem has been clearly defined and the objectives of the research precisely stated that research can be designed properly. "Properly" here means not only that the research will generate the kinds of answers needed but that it will do so efficiently.

Problem definition is being used in the broadest sense of the term here. It refers to those situations that might indeed represent real problems to the marketing decision maker as well as those situations that might be better described as opportunities. To understand the problem-definition stage of the process, it is helpful to have some appreciation of how problems and opportunities arise.

Marketing research problems or opportunities arise from three fundamental sources: (1) unanticipated change, (2) planned change, and (3) serendipity in the form of new ideas. Change in one form or another is by far the most important source.

One of the great sources of unanticipated change is the environment in which firms operate. Many elements in a firm's external environment can create problems or opportunities, including demographic, economic, technological, competitive, political, and legal changes that often can significantly affect the marketing function. How the firm responds to the new technology or to the new product introduced by a competitor or to the change in demographics or lifestyles largely determines whether the change turns out to be a problem or an opportunity. For example, Apple's Newton was the first hand-held digital assistant to the market, but Palm responded with its Pilot and soon dominated Apple. An example of a political or legal change is the deregulation of the financial services industry. Firms like Fidelity capitalized on this environmental change by introducing enhanced-services packages, including discount brokerage service. Unanticipated change can also arise within the firm's internal environment. The firm may be losing market share or its sales might not be as high as forecast. The firm may find itself losing key salespeople or its best distributors to competitors. In situations of unanticipated change,

---

[2]Henry Assael and John Keon, "Nonsampling vs. Sampling Errors in Survey Research," *Journal of Marketing* 46 (Spring 1982), p. 114. See also Judith T. Lessler and William D. Kalsbeek, *Nonsampling Error in Surveys* (New York: Wiley, 1992). We will say more about the various errors that can arise when conducting research when discussing each of the stages in the research process.

[3]Assael and Keon, "Nonsampling vs. Sampling Errors," p. 121.

a key issue is finding exactly what is happening and why. Marketing research plays a role in answering such questions.

Not all change is unanticipated; much of it is planned. Most firms want business to grow and contemplate various marketing actions for helping it do so, such as the introduction of new products, improved distribution, and more effective pricing and advertising strategies. Planned change is oriented more toward the future, whereas unanticipated change is oriented more toward the present and past. The basic question surrounding planned change is how the firm may bring about the desired change. The role of marketing research in this scenario involves investigating the feasibility of alternatives under consideration.

A third source of marketing problems or opportunities is serendipity, or chance ideas. The new idea might come from a customer in a complaint letter or by some other means. For example, Rubbermaid makes it a practice for its executives to read customer letters to find out how people like the company's products. These letters often lead to new product ideas. Tracking trends and interacting with consumers also yield ideas. For example, customers complain of time famine and the need for convenience, so Rubbermaid's larger products, such as closet storage units and outdoor tool sheds, are built to be assembled quickly and without tools. Strict attention to detail, including suggestions like this, has allowed the company to introduce hundreds of new products a year.[4] What is especially remarkable is that approximately one-third of their new products are developed from the ground up, yet the company claims a success rate of 80 to 90 percent. Marketing research plays an important role in the company's development process. Besides customers, other sources for good ideas are salespeople and their reports. Even comments from the trade might serve as the impetus for a decision problem, which research could pursue more rigorously.

Regardless of how decision problems or opportunities arise, most of them will require additional information for resolution. The manager must determine what information is necessary and how it can be obtained. Good communication between the manager (that is, the decision maker) and the marketing researchers is imperative. The decision makers need to understand what research can and cannot accomplish. The researchers need to understand the nature of the decision the managers face and what they hope to learn from research—the project objectives.

Researchers must avoid simply responding to requests for information. To do so is akin to allowing a patient who is seeing a doctor to make his or her own diagnosis, and, to cap it off, allowing the patient to prescribe the treatment as well. Rather, the researcher needs to work with the manager much like a patient works with a doctor; both need to be open in their communication as they translate symptoms into underlying causal factors.

Other Issues in Problem Formation

Sometimes marketers confuse problems with symptoms. A problem is a situation requiring some type of action, whereas a symptom is merely evidence that a problem

---

[4]Marshall Loeb, "How to Grow a New Product Every Day," *Fortune* (November 14, 1994), pp. 269–270; "Rubbermaid Mines for Profits," *Discount Store News* (March 22, 1999), pp. S3–S5; "Grand Masters of Marketing," *Marketing Management* 7 (Summer 1998), pp. 22–28.

exists. For example, Xerox became concerned a number of years ago that it was rapidly losing photocopier sales to Japanese competitors. That was the symptom. An investigation revealed that while Xerox was focusing on what features it could add to its copiers to make them more desirable, the problem was product quality. Customers wanted copiers that would break down less often.

Consultants face the issue of clarifying problem definitions, too; the clients think they know what is wrong and they hire the consultant to fix it. Often as not, the consultant must assess what is "really" wrong before they hope to fix the first symptom. Marketing researchers are the consultants in this case—they are the keepers and procurers of useful marketplace information.

There is a tendency to assume that managers have a clear understanding of the problems they face and that the only difficulty lies in communicating that understanding. This assumption is false. To many managers, the research problem is seen primarily as a lack of important facts. They count on preliminary research to clarify what they know and what they do not know; with the research, they will know more and can more confidently decide how to proceed, including by commissioning more research. Research results based on such a mode of operation most often turn out to be "interesting" but not very actionable.[5] A steady income of such exploratory research is important to the firm because it keeps the company close to the customer and helps to reduce levels of uncertainty in decisions throughout the organization. However, exploratory research is not particularly well-suited for addressing specific decision problems.

Even with a more precisely defined research question and impeccably executed research, both managers and researchers need to recognize that marketing research does not produce answers or strategies. It produces data—data that must be interpreted and converted into action plans by management. To be sure that the research reflects management's business priorities and concerns, managers must play an active role in communicating their information needs to researchers, and they need to stay in touch during the research process itself, to ensure that the research provides the information they truly need to help them make the decisions they face. Sometimes this means using their own intuition when interpreting the research findings, as Research Realities 3.2 demonstrates.

In other cases, managers need to get directly involved in the research process. For example, one factor that plays an important part in Japan's new-product development is that the Japanese consider marketing research to be a line function requiring involvement by all participants in the product development process rather than a staff function performed only by marketing researchers. One advantage of this perspective is a more hands-on approach that looks at the broader context and an emphasis on softer, less-formal data-collection methods. For example, Sony knows what appeals to children by watching them play video games. Their new entertainment robotics business created the "Aibo" dog-robot, and the first 2,500 produced sold in less than 20 minutes.[6]

---

[5]Diane H. Schmalensee and A. Dawn Lesh, "How to Make Research More Actionable," *Marketing Research* 10 (Spring 1999), pp. 23–36.

[6]Robert Triendl, "Sony Restructures to Embrace Digital Economy," *Research Technology Management* 42 (September/October 1999), pp. 4–5.

RESEARCH REALITIES 3.2

Managers as Active Participants in the Research Process

In the early days of pay-cable services, a television company was considering the establishment of a cultural cable channel as a logical extension of its business. A company executive commissioned a survey to determine the demand for such a channel, which would have carried a monthly fee similar to that charged by Home Box Office (HBO), the only existing pay-cable outlet at the time.

The survey appeared to give a green light to the project, indicating that 20 percent of all cable users would subscribe. But the executive, even though he could find no technical flaw in the questionnaire or the sampling technique, remained skeptical of the results. He remembered from his years of experience how focus group participants would often claim to be fans of public television but would rarely admit to watching *Dallas, Dynasty,* or other top-rated network shows. This phenomenon suggested to him that the survey data might not be realistic.

Pursuing his hunch, the executive hired another research firm to investigate the channel's potential. This firm knew that consumers have been known to tell "white lies" to an interviewer. They tend, for example, to exaggerate their involvement in socially desirable activities such as voting. Similarly, they are apt to overestimate their willingness to purchase attractive or glamorous new products or services. They may wish to please the interviewer, to appear open to new experiences, to appear financially capable of purchasing the offering, or—as in the case of the cable station—to appear intelligent and cultured. The new research team constructed its study to account for such tendencies.

Although the researchers asked many of the same questions that appeared in the first survey, they also included seemingly unrelated questions about respondents' recent participation in a range of activities, from attending the opera to going to the zoo to watching a ball game. Again, 20 percent said they were willing to pay for the cultural channel. But when respondents who had never before patronized cultural events were eliminated from the "yea sayers"— on the assumption that they were unlikely to undergo a sudden metamorphosis into highbrows—the research predicted that less than 1 percent of cable users were likely to subscribe. The company scrapped its plan for the station.

How did this cable executive avoid a calamity? First, his understanding of the market allowed him to recognize potential shortcomings in the initial research. Second, he was able to find a research company experienced in gauging consumers' real interest in new products. Obviously, had he commissioned the research only to support a decision he had already made, he would never have questioned the encouraging findings of the first study. His success underscores the importance of management's direct involvement in marketing research.

Source: Robert S. Duboff, "The Real Magic of Market Research," *Viewpoint* 17 (Summer 1988), pp. 19–20.

A proper understanding of the basic structure of decision problems can help researchers interact with management to better specify research issues. The simplest decision situations can be characterized by the following conditions:

1. A decision maker is operating in some environment in which there is a problem.

2. There are at least two courses of action, A_1 and A_2, that the decision maker can follow.

3. Once the decision maker chooses an action, at least two outcomes of that choice (O_1 and O_2) are possible, and one of them is preferred to the other.

4. There is a chance, but not an equal chance, that each course of action will lead to the desired outcome. If the chances are equal, the choice does not matter.

That is, a person faces a decision situation if he or she (1) has a problem, (2) has several good (but not equally good) ways of solving it, and (3) is unsure about which course of action to select. Research can assist in clarifying any of these characteristics of the decision situation. Let us briefly consider how.

The Decision Maker and the Environment

A critical element for the researcher in defining the problem is understanding the decision maker and the environment in which that person is operating: What is the background on the business? What factors have led to the manager's concerns with the issues? What information would help the decision maker in dealing with these issues? What would the decision maker do with the information?

If the decision maker's original posture will not change regardless of what is found, the research will be wasted. Surprisingly, research is sometimes simply "conscience money"; the research results are readily accepted when they are consistent with the decision the individual wants to make. When the research results conflict with the decision maker's original position, however, the results are questioned at best and discarded as being inaccurate at worst. The reason, of course, is that the individual's view of the decision problem is so strongly held that research will do little to change it. When this situation prevails, research will be a waste of the firm's resources. To avoid wasting resources because of the "I know better" or "don't bother me with the facts" traps, researchers need to assess the situation before doing the research, not after. This means determining the decision maker's objectives and finding out how the decision might change if certain results were found.

Often the task of determining how the management decision might change with research information is complicated by the fact that the researcher's contact is not the final decision maker but a liaison. Yet this determination must be made if the researcher is to design a cost-effective attack on the problem.

The researcher also needs to understand the environment in which the decision maker operates. What are the constraints on that person's actions? What are the resources at the decision maker's disposal? What is the time frame in which the manager is operating? It does little good to design a study, however accurate, that costs $50,000 and takes six months to complete when the decision maker needs the results within one month and has only $15,000 for the research. Obviously, some compromises must be made, and it is the researcher's responsibility to anticipate them by carefully examining the decision environment.

Researchers also need to be aware that the corporate culture can affect decision making and, consequently, research that supports that decision making. In some firms, the process by which decisions are made is dominant, whereas in other firms, the personality of management might be more important. At General Mills, for example, the emphasis is on research that evaluates alternatives, and their culture tries to force all information requests into action alternatives. Instead of focusing on the question "What proportion of potato chips are eaten at meals?" the emphasis would be on translating the question into "How can I advertise my potato chips for meal consumption?" or "Will a 'meal commercial' sell more chips than my present commercial?" To design the most effective research, researchers need to be aware of the general corporate culture regarding how decisions are made and what role research plays when making those decisions.

Alternative Courses of Action

Research can be properly designed only when the alternative courses of action being considered are known. The more obvious ones are typically given to the researcher by the decision maker, and the researcher's main task here is to determine whether the list of actions exhausts the alternatives. If the research is to be germane to all the alternatives, implicit options must be made explicit. Thus, it is important that the decision maker and the researcher work together to come up with a complete list of the alternative courses of action being considered.

As an example of the types of alternative courses of action available to a company, consider the Campbell Soup Company. As part of its ongoing research and its focus on keeping up with consumer and technological trends, the company's product managers team up with in-house and outside researchers to probe for openings in the market. In addition to Campbell's traditional family market, research teams have investigated the eating habits and flavor preferences of career women, Hispanics, consumers over age 55, and owners of microwave ovens. As for alternative courses of action, the company has considered lowering prices, advertising heavily, and positioning soup as a quick yet healthy snack food, for example, available through cappuccino-like dispensers at convenience stores.[7]

Researchers at times must be detectives to uncover the hidden agendas and alternatives lurking beneath the surface in any decision situation. If a critical piece of information remains undiscovered, even the most sophisticated research techniques cannot solve the problem. Attempting to impress the company president, researchers at Pillsbury discovered this fact belatedly—to their embarrassment:

> The late Bob Keith, then president of the Pillsbury Company, was once persuaded by Pillsbury's operations researchers to review one of his major marketing decisions using a formal decision model. He agreed to the outcomes, their values, and their probabilities, and chose the decision rule he felt most appropriate. The computer then calculated the expectations, compared them, and reported the alternative that should be chosen according to that rule. Mr. Keith disagreed, noting that another alternative was obviously the only correct choice—indeed, it was the choice that had been made not long before. "How can that be?" the researchers asked. "You accepted all the values and probabilities and chose the decision rule yourself. The rest is just arithmetic." "That's fine," Keith replied, "but you forgot to ask me about a few other things that were more important."[8]

Objectives of the Decision Maker

One of the more basic facts of decision making is that individuals differ in their attitudes toward risk, and these differences influence their choices. Some people are

---

[7]Judann Pollack, "Frozen Dinners Attack Appetites for Carryout," *Advertising Age* (September 2, 1996), p. 12; Mike Beirne, "Grocery Brands Reinvent Selves for Evolving Convenience Store Niche," *Brandweek* (October 11, 1999), p. 16.

[8] Charles Raymond, *The Art of Using Science in Marketing* (New York: Harper & Row, 1974), p. 17.

risk takers; they are willing to assume a good deal of risk for the chance of a big gain. Some are risk averse; they are willing to assume little risk, even when the size of the potential gain is large, if the chance of loss also exists. Some individuals simply walk a middle ground. A person's attitude toward risk is not always consistent. It changes with the situation and the magnitude of the potential consequences. Thus, a person may be a risk taker, even when the chances of things turning out badly are reasonably high, if that person feels secure and if the consequences of his or her actions would not be catastrophic. That same person may avoid risks if his or her position in the company is insecure or if the consequences would be disastrous if things were to turn out wrong. The researcher can often discover the decision maker's comfort with risk from intensive probing, using "what-if" hypothetical outcomes of the research.

It is also important to determine the decision maker's specific objectives. Despite what one might expect, the decision maker's objectives are rarely explicitly stated to the researcher, or they might not have been formulated accurately or precisely. For example, the decision maker might state that the firm wants customers to perceive their brand as "high quality," without elaborating upon that characterization. As a result, the study's objectives often must be extracted by the researcher. Indeed, a clarification of the goals might be among the most useful service provided to the decision maker.

The researcher must transform the vague platitudes ("high quality") into specific, operational objectives that the research can serve. One means of doing so consists of engaging the decision maker in a discussion to explore the possible solutions to the problem to see whether the firm would follow the prescribed course of action. If not, the conversation may probe further until the real objectives are revealed.

Once the objectives for the research are finally determined, they should be committed to writing. Doing so often produces additional clarity in communication and thinking. The decision maker and researcher should then agree formally on their written expression (by each initialing each statement of purpose) to prevent later misunderstandings. The formal endorsement of objectives also helps to ensure that the research will not treat symptoms, but the problem that produced the symptoms.

Consequences of Alternative Courses of Action

A great deal of marketing research is intended to determine the consequences of various courses of action. Many of the research examples highlighted in Chapter 1 deal with the effect of manipulating one of the elements in the marketing mix, which makes sense given that the marketing manager's task is to manipulate the elements of the mix to achieve customer satisfaction. What is a more natural marketing research activity than seeking answers to such questions as: What will be the change in sales produced by a change in the product's package? If we change the sales compensation plan, what will be the effect on the sales representatives' performance and on their attitudes toward the job and company? Which advertisement is likely to generate the most favorable customer response?

Researchers are primarily responsible for designing research that accurately assesses the outcomes of past or future contemplated marketing actions. In this capacity, they must gauge the actions against all the outcomes management deems relevant. Management, for example, may want to know the impact of the proposed

---

ETHICAL DILEMMA 3.2

The president of a small bank approaches you with plans to launch a special program of financial counseling and support for women and asks you to establish whether sufficient public interest exists to justify starting the program. No other bank in the city caters specifically to women, and you think that professional women, in particular, might be enthusiastic. If news of the plan leaks out, the president believes that competitors may try to preempt him, so he asks you to keep the bank's identity secret from respondents and to inquire only into general levels of interest in increased financial services for women. However, as you read through the literature that he has left on your desk, you notice that the bank is located in the most depressed area of the city, where women might be harassed and feel unsafe.

- Would it be unethical to research the general problem of how much demand exists for a women's banking program, when the bank in question will interpret the demand as encouragement to launch such a program itself?

- What might be the costs to the researcher in voicing misgivings about the suitability of this particular bank's launching of the program? Would you voice your misgivings?

- Does it violate respondents' rights if you do not reveal the identity of the research sponsor? If so, is it a serious violation in this case? Is there a conflict of interest here with respect to respondents' right to be informed versus the client's right to confidentiality?

---

change on sales and on consumer attitudes. If the research addresses only consumer attitudes, management will most assuredly ask for the relationship between attitudes and sales. Embarrassing questions of this nature can be avoided only if researchers painstakingly probe for all relevant outcomes before designing the research.

Decision Problem to Research Problem

A detailed understanding of the total decision situation should enable researchers working in consort with managers to translate the decision problem into a research problem. Suppose a new product is introduced and sales are below target. The decision problem faced by the marketing manager is what to do about the shortfall. Should the target be revised? Was the forecast too optimistic? Should the product be withdrawn? Should one of the other elements in the marketing mix, such as advertising, be altered? Suppose the manager suspects that the advertising campaign supporting the new product has been ineffective. The product manager might wish to have evidence that either confirmed or denied that suspicion before changing the advertising program. The research problem would then become the assessment of product awareness among potential customers.

Some illustrations of the distinctions between decision problems and research problems are found in Table 3.2. The decision problem involves what needs to be done. Research can provide the necessary information to make an informed

TABLE 3.2	Examples of the Relationship between Decision Problems and Research Problems

Decision Problems	Research Problems
1. Develop package for a new product	1. Evaluate effectiveness of alternative package designs
2. Increase market penetration by opening new stores	2. Evaluate prospective locations
3. Increase store traffic	3. Measure current image of the store
4. Increase amount of repeat purchasing behavior	4. Assess current amount of repeat purchasing behavior
5. Develop more equitable sales territories	5. Assess current and proposed territories with respect to their potential and workload
6. Allocate advertising budget geographically	6. Determine current level of market penetration in the respective areas
7. Introduce new product	7. Design a test market through which the likely acceptance of the new product can be assessed
8. Expand into other countries	8. Assess market potential for firm's products in each of the countries being considered
9. Select international distribution channels	9. Evaluate current channel structures and channel members in each of the countries being considered
10. Decide which merchandise will be made available for purchase over the Internet	10. Determine consumers' confidence in purchasing, unseen, different categories of products

choice, and the research problem essentially involves determining what information to provide and how that information can best be secured.

In making this determination, the researcher must make certain the real decision problem (not just the symptoms) is being addressed. Poor problem definition in many cases has led to poor research problem definition with unfortunate consequences, some more dire than others. The debacle with Coca-Cola Classic is well-known. What is perhaps less well known is that Miller did not invent Lite Beer. Rather, it was first developed by Meister Brau.[9] Taste tests indicated that people liked the beer, but when the product was introduced by Meister Brau, it failed. Meister Brau sold it to Miller, which defined the decision problem, and subsequently the research problem, as something more than having a preferred taste. Rather, Miller's research suggested that big beer drinkers tried to project macho images, and the very concept of a diet beer connoted "wimp." Miller's emphasis thus became one of changing the image of the brand through its use of famous sports personalities.

Sometimes the difficulty in problem definition involves cultural differences. A U.S. manager was trying to interest investors in Southeast Asia in a bagel restaurant franchise. The manager described the entire system, including the corporate support, local marketing, the menu, and products. After the four-hour meeting concluded, the investors politely thanked the presenter and voiced their first question, "What is a bagel?"[10] The manager had been focusing on solving implementation

[9]Wayne A. Lemburg, "Past AMA President Hardin, Head of Market Facts, Looks Back at the Early Days of Marketing Research," *Marketing News* (December 19, 1986), p. 9.

[10]Christopher Brady, "How to Integrate Your Company into the Global Market," *Foodservice Equipment & Supplies* 52 (October 1999), pp. 29–30.

RESEARCH REALITIES 3.3

Alternative Approaches to an Information Request and Their Likely Effects

I would like you to meet someone. Kevin is a research analyst who has been with The Minute Maid Company for a little more than two years now. He is well regarded by the marketing team he works with, especially in terms of his responsiveness to their research requests.

One morning, Kevin receives a phone call from the marketing manager on Minute Maid fruit punches. The marketing manager tells him that the R&D lab has been working on a new, improved flavor for Minute Maid fruit punch and that the lab has finally come up with one that he thinks is acceptable.

Before the manager authorizes full production of the new formula, he thinks it would be prudent to conduct a taste test to determine if consumers will react favorably to the new flavor. Actually, he is calling to find out how much product would be required for such a test. He adds that it is very important that this research be initiated quickly because a competitor, Tropicana, has just come out with a new, improved version of its product.

Kevin says OK, but before he designs the taste test, he needs more information. He needs to know if this formula change will impact both the chilled and frozen forms of the product. He also needs to know when the product will be available for the test. After getting those questions answered, Kevin decides to conduct personal interviews with 600 respondents in central mall facilities. Basically this will be a blind taste test.

Kevin next determines that he wants to use a triangular discrimination taste test to determine if respondents can detect differences between the products. That will be followed by a sequential monadic evaluation of each product to obtain additional diagnostic rating data and preference.

You might be saying to yourself that this design sounds pretty good—sequential approach so time and money are not wasted if the new flavor is not as good as everyone thinks; adequate sample sizes for both the chilled and frozen forms; and two phases for the evaluation, a triangle discrimination to see if respondents can detect differences and sequential monadic to obtain important diagnostic information to guide R&D and marketing.

Now let me introduce you to Joan. She has the same credentials as Kevin and is faced with the same initial phone call. The marketing manager asks her how much product she will need in order to conduct a taste test for him.

Joan responds that, before she can design any research, she needs a little more information. Sounds a lot like Kevin, right? Just listen. Joan is not sure what type of research is needed. She suggests a meeting with the manager to discuss the situation in more depth.

Joan begins to review the information she has been given by the marketing manager. She also begins to develop a list of key questions she wants to ask the marketing manager when they get together. First, she goes to her computer terminal and pulls up the most recent Nielsen Scantrack information she has on the Punches segment of the Juice and Juice Drink category. She wants to see if any change has occurred in the marketplace since the introduction of the new Tropicana Fruit Punch. She also checks to see if Minute Maid Fruit Punch has been affected by this introduction. Next, she checks on Nielsen household scanner panel information to see if there has been any change in key household purchase behavior—specifically, household penetration, buying rate, and loyalty rates for both Minute Maid and Tropicana. Finally, she reviews the historical project files to understand any prior research that has been conducted for the brand.

When Joan meets with the marketing manager, she asks the following questions:

1. Why are we considering a new formula? Tropicana doesn't seem to have hurt our franchise with the new flavor.

2. If we do use a new formula, what do we hope to accomplish? Do we expect to pull in new users or do we want to minimize the chances of our consumers shifting over to Tropicana?

3. How will we announce the new flavor? Will it be advertised or will we just use a notice on the package?

(continued)

4. Does the new formula perform the same in both chilled and frozen forms? Are the sensory profiles identical?

5. Can we obtain product from a regular production location? So often R&D's controls are much more stringent than those of our production plants. We would rather use product for this test that most closely resembles the product that consumers would be buying from grocery stores.

After getting answers to her questions, Joan then works out her research objectives and specific design. She also recommends a two-phased study, but her objectives are to determine Minute Maid users' response to the new flavor in terms of taste and overall preference and to determine competitive users' response to the new flavor versus the new Tropicana flavor.

Joan will also interview 600 respondents who are female heads of household, primary grocery shoppers, and between 18 and 60, and who have used Minute Maid fruit punch in the past month. Respondents in the first phase of the research must be regular, loyal users of Minute Maid. In the second phase, respondents must be users of the competitive product.

The research will involve personal, sequential, monadic, in-home placements over a two-week period. In the first phase, 300 respondents will evaluate Minute Maid's new formula versus the current formula to better understand how the current franchise will react to the formulation change. In the second phase, 300 respondents will compare the new Minute Maid formula to the new Tropicana formula to determine if the new flavor would attract competitive users. In both phases, half the sample will evaluate the chilled formula, while the other half will evaluate the frozen formula.

There are several clear differences between this research design and the first example, all dependent on the approach used to define the problem.

Kevin is what I would call a research order taker or research technician. He basically responded to the marketing manager's request for a taste test without considering the marketing situation that prompted the request.

His research design was sound, at least on the surface, given the information he had. He would have obtained answers to his questionnaire and those answers would probably be correct. Unfortunately, both he and the marketing manager would be wondering why the company was receiving so many consumer calls on the company's 800 number from longtime Minute Maid users complaining about the new flavor.

Joan, on the other hand, is an internal marketing consultant—a true marketing information professional. Her approach was to attempt to clearly understand the marketplace situation as well as potential marketing actions that could be taken based on this research.

Her research design was fundamentally sound as well, but it was more costly and time-consuming than that of Kevin. Why? Because she understood the risks involved as well as the potential gains that could accrue to the company based on this formula change.

In both instances, the marketing manager could make a decision based on the data obtained from a research study. The difference is that in one case, the manager might suspect marketing research because it failed to predict some Minute Maid users' negative response to the formula change, whereas in the other case, the manager may be more confident in using marketing research.

We marketing information professionals must strive to go beyond simple problem solving. We must insist on being internal marketing consultants. That is the only way we can be assured that our research designs, techniques, and statistical analyses will continue to be valid. It is the only way that marketing management will become more confident in its use of marketing research. It is the only way senior management can be assured that the company is receiving full value for its investment in resources and spending for marketing research.

Source: Personal correspondence with Larry P. Stanek, Vice President of Marketing Information, The Minute Maid Company.

issues, but neglected simple marketing research on the first customers—these investors.

How does one avoid the trap of researching the wrong decision problem? The main way is by refusing to respond to requests for information without developing a proper appreciation for the decision problem. The difference in response perspectives is highlighted in the Minute Maid example in Research Realities 3.3. There is an old saying: "If you do not know where you want to go, any road will get you there." It is the same in decision making. If you do not know what you want to accomplish, any alternative will be satisfactory. If the decision maker does not know what he or she wants to achieve, the research study will not accomplish it. Instead of preparing a research proposal outlining the methods to be used when a research request first comes in, researchers are well-advised to take the time to probe the situation carefully until they have acquired the necessary appreciation for: (1) the decision maker and the environment, (2) the alternative courses of action, (3) the decision maker's objectives, and (4) the consequences of alternative actions. As Figure 3.2 indicates, even marketing managers believe that researchers should take an active role in helping to define the decision problem and in specifying the information that will be useful for solving it.

Several mechanisms are available for making sure that the true decision problem will be addressed by the research. One way is to execute a "research request step," which requires that the decision maker and researcher have a meeting in which the decision maker describes the problem and the information that is needed. The researcher then drafts a statement describing his or her understanding of the problem. The statement should include, but is not limited to, the following items:

| **FIGURE 3.2** | **Percentage of Research Users Who Believe That Researchers "Absolutely Must" or "Preferably Should" Engage in the Activity** |

Activity

Consult at length with the executive requesting a study to make certain he or she understands the problem before conducting the research — 91%

Become familiar with management's objectives in a given area before beginning a marketing research project in that area — 95%

Help management define the problems to be studied — 72%

Question the soundness of the objectives that a member of marketing management may have for a problem being studied by the marketing research department — 55%

1. **Origin:** the events that led to a need for the decision to act; even though the events may not directly affect the research that is conducted, they help the researcher understand more thoroughly the nature of the research problem.

2. **Action:** the actions that are contemplated on the basis of the research.

3. **Information:** the questions that the decision maker needs to have answered in order to take one of the contemplated courses of action.

4. **Use:** a section that explains how each piece of information will be used to help make the action decision; supplying logical reasons for each piece of the research ensures that the questions make sense in light of the action to be taken.

5. **Targets and subgroups:** a section that describes from whom the information must be gathered; specifying the target groups helps the researcher design an appropriate sample for the research project.

6. **Logistics:** a section that gives approximate estimates of the time and money that are available to conduct the research; both of these factors will affect the techniques finally chosen.

This written statement should be submitted to the decision maker for approval. The approval should be formalized by having the decision maker initial and date the entire document to signal greater commitment than a verbal agreement.

Another way of ensuring that the true decision problem is addressed in the research is through the use of scenarios that attempt to anticipate the contents of the final report. Based on his or her understanding of the total decision situation, the researcher tries to anticipate what the final report could look like and prepares approximate templates. The researcher then confronts the decision maker with tough questions, such as, "If I come up with this cross-tabulation with these numbers in it, what would you do?" One of the biggest payoffs from this exercise is improved communication between researcher and manager as to the exact parameters of the study. For example, one large electronics company wished to determine the knowledge of and preferences for stereo components among young consumers. It was only after the researchers prepared mock tables showing preference by age and sex that the client's wishes became truly clear. Based on their prior discussions, the researchers specified the age breakdowns for the tables as 13 to 16 and 17 to 20. Only after presenting this scenario to the company's managers did the researchers learn that to the client, young meant children age 10 or older. The client further believed that preteens are very volatile, undergoing radical changes from year to year, especially as they approach puberty. Thus, not only was the contemplated research wrong from the standpoint of the age groups it would attempt to access, but the planned cross-tabulations were too gross to capture the client's basic concerns. Without the scenarios, the client's expectations may not have surfaced until the research was too far underway to change it.

The use of either a formal research request or hypothetical scenarios can help ensure that the purpose of the research is agreed on before the research is designed.

The Research Proposal

Once the purpose and scope of the research are agreed on, researchers can turn their attention to choosing the techniques that will be used to conduct the research. The techniques selected should also be communicated to the decision maker before the research begins. Typically this is done with a formal research proposal, which allows the researcher another opportunity to make sure that the research being contemplated will provide the information necessary to answer the decision maker's problem.

Research proposals can take many forms.[11] Some will be very long and detailed, running 20 pages or more. Others will be short and to the point. Much depends on the detail with which the various parts are described. Figure 3.3 contains a template that can be followed in preparing a research proposal. Again, the decision maker's approval for the plan should be sought and formalized by having him or her sign and date the proposal.

Research Realities 3.4 contains portions of an actual research plan (with some authorization and budget information removed) that was prepared by the research department at General Mills. Note the clearly stated criteria that will be used to interpret the results and the carefully crafted action standards, specifying what will be done depending on what the research results indicate. The effort expended by the marketing research department in translating information requests into specific, action-oriented statements like this helps account for the wide acceptance of and enthusiastic support for the research function at General Mills.

Is Marketing Research Justified?

The benefits of marketing research are many, but it is not without its drawbacks, and the question of whether the research costs are likely to exceed the research benefits always needs to be asked. There is no denying that the research process is often time-consuming and expensive. One might first ask, "Is there enough time to conduct a thoughtful research investigation?" In today's fast-paced marketplace, it might seem that the answer is frequently *no*. However, a negative answer neglects three important resources: (1) informal queries of in-house experts can be made quickly to yield at least preliminary insights; (2) secondary data, including syndicated databases, may be tapped instantaneously for detailed and comprehensive results; and (3) ongoing, continual data collection and mining efforts, which are increasingly pervasive across companies in the guise of customer relationship databases, can be accessed to understand customers' attitudes and behaviors. If the manager is pressed for time, therefore, and cannot conduct a new marketing research project, there is likely to already be relevant information around the organization.

One might then ask, "Is there a budget to conduct the requisite marketing research?" Myopic managers often look to marketing research as a luxury, a budget line some are quick to trim. We may of course be biased, but we would suggest an alternative question: "Will you have any budget to spend in the future if you do not understand your customers?"

---

[11]For suggestions on preparing proposals, see Ron Tepper, *How to Write Winning Proposals for Your Company or Client*, 2nd ed. (New York: Wiley, 1990); Robert T. Hamper, *Handbook for Writing Proposals* (Lincolnwood, IL: NTC Publishing Group, 1996); Herman Holtz, *The Consultant's Guide to Proposal Writing* (New York: Wiley, 1998).

FIGURE 3.3	Parts of a Typical Research Proposal, and an Example

---

Project Title:
Research on Your Consumers

by Bidding Marketing Research Firm

1

Marketing Problem

- Brief description of general problem; reason for conducting research
- Sum up preliminary discussions between researcher and manager; demonstrate knowledge of situation and particular information needs

2

Purpose of Research Project

- State goals and objectives, often with justification
- Describe scope of project (what will and will not be investigated)
- Spell out specific questions to be answered
- Address possible limitations due to time or budget constraints (to avoid later disagreement)

3

Data Sources and Methodology

- Describe the secondary data to be used
- Describe how the primary data will be gathered (for example, surveys, experiments)
- Keep methods descriptions nontechnical
- Describe sample and proposed size
- Include draft of questionnaire or outline for focus group moderator, and so on, if applicable

4

Time and Personnel

- Provide time estimates for each phase of the research
- Specify personnel required and their rates of pay
- Calculate nonpersonnel costs (such as supplies, printing, and mailing)

5

(continued)

Based on J. Paul Peter and James H. Donnelly, Jr., preface to *Marketing Management,* 8th ed. (Homewood, IL: Irwin, 2000), pp. 34–35

FIGURE 3.3   **(continued)**

Eau de Internet:
Selling Fragrances Online

by Marketing Researchers R Us

1

Marketing Opportunity

- $27 billion U.S. beauty market
- 45% U.S. population Internet access
- Related Internet site (fashion) up
  and running, possible profitable link?
- Manager concern that fragrances
  cannot be sampled electronically
  – Past research indicates trial is
    important
  – Image and brand are also
    important, can they dominate?

2

Purpose of Research Project

- Objective: to determine whether
  consumers will buy perfumes online
- Focus on women's attitudes (buying
  for self or gift), but not yet purchase
  behaviors
  – What concerns do women have
    regarding buying fragrances online?
  – What factors lower resistance to
    buying perfume online (brand,
    price, return policy?)
- Client desires results in 3 months;
  experience online continually
  evolving.

3

Data Sources and Methodology

- Secondary data: sales in beauty,
  perfumes, online fashion apparel
- Primary data: e-mail contact directed
  to Internet surveys
- Analysis: Mostly averages and cross-
  tabs
- Sample size goal of 300 women, given
  time constraints, segment those with
  Internet access, modify questions for
  gift purchases

4

Time and Personnel

- Preliminary phase, 3 weeks
- Survey pretesting and debugging,
  2 weeks
- Sample selection and solicitation,
  2 weeks
- Administer survey, follow-up, 1 week
- Analyses, 1 month
- Discuss required staff (and salaries)
- Other costs minimal (given format of
  electronic contact and survey
  execution)

5

RESEARCH REALITIES 3.4

A Sample Proposal at General Mills for Research on Protein Plus Cereal

1. **Problem and Background.** Protein Plus has performed below objectives in its test market. New product and copy alternatives are being readied for testing. Three alternative formulations—Hi Graham, Nut, and Cinnamon, which retain the basic identity of current Protein Plus, but which have been judged to be sufficiently different and of sufficient potential—have been developed for testing against the current formula.

2. **Decision Involved.** Which product formulations should be carried into the concept fulfillment test?

3. **Method and Design.** In-home product test will be conducted. Each of the four test products will be tested by a separate panel of 150 households. Each household will have purchased adult ready-to-eat (RTE) cereal within the past month and will be interested in the test product as measured by the selection of Protein Plus as one or more of their next 10 cereal packages they would like to buy. They will be exposed to Protein Plus in a booklet that will also contain an ad for several competitive products, such as Product 19, Special K, Nature Valley, and Grape Nuts. A Protein Plus ad will be constructed for each of the four test products, differing primarily in the kind of taste reassurance provided. Exposure to these various executions will be rotated so that each of the four test panels are matched on RTE cereal usage.

The study will be conducted in eight markets. Product will be packaged in current Protein Plus package flagged with the particular flavor reassurance for that product.

The criterion measure will be the homemakers' weighted post-study brand-share, adjusted to reflect the breadth of interest in the various Protein Plus communications strategies.

Rather than trust a random sampling procedure to represent the population at large, a quota will be established to ensure that the sample of people initially contacted for each panel will conform as closely as possible to the division of female heads of households under 45 (56 percent) and over 45 (44 percent) in the U.S. population.

4. **Criteria for Interpretation.** Each formulation generating a higher weighted homemaker share than standard will be considered for subsequent testing. If more than one formulation beats standard, each will be placed in a concept fulfillment test unless one is better than the other(s) at odds of 21 or more.

5. **Estimated Project Expense.** Within $6,500: $52,000.

6. **Individual who must finally approve recommended action:** _____

7. **Report to be delivered** by _____ if authorized by _____ and test materials shipped by _____.

Source: Used with permission of General Mills, Inc.

If conducted and interpreted properly, marketing research can be very illuminating and therefore worth the time and cost. However, if it is done incorrectly, it can be misleading and could possibly hurt more than help a company. Even when done correctly, in some situations, marketing research cannot provide answers a company seeks, or it poses risks that outweigh its possible advantages. The benefits of testing a new product, for example, must be weighed against the risk of tipping off a competitor, who can then rush into the market with a similar product at perhaps a better price. Moreover, when the product is truly innovative, it may be difficult for consumers to assess accurately how they would ultimately use it; the visionary company should not be discouraged by unenthusiastic reception, but use the consumer feedback to clarify the benefits to the users in advertising communications. The best strategy is to examine the potential benefits from the research and to make sure they exceed the anticipated costs, both financial and otherwise.

Choosing and Using a Research Supplier

Many business organizations today have formal marketing research departments. However, except for the very largest consumer products companies, many of these departments tend to be small—sometimes consisting of one person. In such cases, the firm's researcher may spend less time conducting actual research than supervising projects undertaken by research suppliers hired by the firm. Marketing managers in many large companies also use outside suppliers.

There are many advantages to using research suppliers. If the research workload tends to vary during the year, the firm may find it less expensive to hire suppliers to conduct specific projects when needed than to staff an entire in-house department that may sit idle between projects. Also, the skills required for various projects often differ. By hiring outside suppliers, the firm can match the project to the vendor with the greatest expertise in the particular area under investigation (for example, surveys and focus groups). In addition, hiring outside suppliers allows the sponsoring company to remain anonymous and to avoid problems that might arise with regard to internal politics.

Although it has become increasingly common to buy marketing research, many managers are uncertain as to how one selects a research supplier. Perhaps the first step is to decide when research is really necessary. There is no simple formula for assessing this need, but most managers turn to research when they are unsure about their own judgment and other information sources seem inadequate. Before contacting research suppliers, it is important for the manager to identify the most critical areas of uncertainty and the issues that would benefit most from research.

Once a manager has determined the most critical areas for research, he or she is ready to seek the right supplier for the job. The selection process is not easy, for there are thousands of qualified marketing research companies in the United States. Some are full-service "generalist" companies; others are specialists in qualitative research, advertising-copy testing, concept testing, and so on; and still others are services that only conduct interviews, process data, or work with statistics.

An excellent source that describes the larger and medium-sized providers is the *Marketing News* newsletter published by the American Marketing Association (cf. ama.org). Periodically, they also publish directories that highlight specialists—firms that focus on customer satisfaction measurement, focus groups, or international marketing research firms.[12] These directories are superior to a simple Internet search of "marketing research companies," because AMA is a long-established association and the newsletter objectively describes the different marketing research suppliers. Search engines find the providers, but the descriptions of the providers

---

[12]*Marketing News* (April 24, 2000; October 25, 1999).

are made up of their own sales pitches, making a comparison across suppliers more difficult.

Once the manager has formed a short list of candidate suppliers, their capabilities must be evaluated in light of the company's research needs. Sometimes a small-scale qualitative study may be most appropriate, and at other times, a large-scale quantitative research project would be optimal. It is essential that the vendor selected understands the firm's information needs and has the expertise required to conduct the research.

Experts suggest that managers should seek proposals from at least three companies. They also urge that the research user talk with the persons at the research supplier company who will be processing and analyzing the data, writing the report, supervising the interviewers, and making presentations to management.

Marketing research is still a bit of an art, not entirely a science. It benefits from heavy involvement of senior research professionals, who provide insights that come only from years of training and experience. A research firm's most important asset is the qualification of the research professionals who will be involved in the design, day-to-day supervision, and interpretation of the research.

The research user's responsibility is to communicate effectively with the prospective vendor and provide the necessary background and objectives for the study. It is also a good idea to ask about the supplier's quality-control standards. Most research firms are pleased when clients show concern about the quality of their work and will gladly explain their quality-control steps in the areas of fieldwork, coding, and data processing. Marketing research firms can also be the recipients of various awards for their excellence standards (for example, the Malcolm Baldrige Award).[13]

After reading the proposals and meeting key personnel, the manager should perform a comparative analysis. He or she should use the proposals to evaluate each vendor's understanding of the problem, how each will address it, and the cost and timing estimate of each. In making this evaluation, the manager needs to keep in mind that the value of the information is determined by its use, not its mere presence. Thus, the manager must be forthright in addressing how he or she would use the information provided by executing the various proposals.

Many firms have formal evaluation systems with specified criteria for evaluating suppliers. This is particularly true among those companies who use suppliers on a regular basis. Land O'Lakes, Inc., the dairy producer, for example, uses the criteria shown in Table 3.3 to evaluate the research suppliers it uses. The company has a formal set of written guidelines that it shares with potential research suppliers that spells out these criteria in more detail. Further, at the completion of each project, a research analyst, manager, or the research director evaluates the supplier on specified criteria. A comment section to explain the basis of the evaluations is provided. The firm applies as many of these criteria as it can when evaluating the proposals of new suppliers.

---

[13]Kevin T. Higgins, "Never-Ending Journey: Winning the Baldrige is Only the Start for Custom Research Inc. Partners," *Marketing Management* 6 (Spring 1997), pp. 4–7.

| TABLE 3.3 | Criteria Used by Land O'Lakes, Inc., to Evaluate Research Suppliers |

Criteria	*Description*
General Attitude and Responsiveness	enthusiastic, helpful, provides prompt replies on cost estimates, proposals, and so on
Marketing Insight	informative, understands study objectives, has ability to analyze data, provides recommendations
Fundamental Design	questionnaire is well designed, instructions are clear to consumers, and so on
Questionnaire Construction	format is sensible and easy to follow, order and wording of questions are clear, scales are suited to research questions
Tabulation Design	format is easy to understand, calculations are accurate
Day-to-Day Serving	responsive and informative on study progress, problems, and so on
Analysis	thorough, accurate, relates to objectives
Quality of Report Writing	concise, clear, accurate, provides executive summary
Presentation	well-planned, concise, materials are organized to enhance clear communication, presenter is verbally skilled to offer smooth presentation
Delivery Time	topline, tables, report
Cost	over, under, justified

Source: Courtesy of Stephen Lauring, Marketing Research Manager, Land O'Lakes, Inc.

Top suppliers will seem equally competent, so a manager must rely on his or her intuitive assessment regarding the soundness of the research design proposed, the supplier's responsiveness to the manager's specific questions, and the vendor's understanding of the subtler aspects of the marketing problem.

An increasingly popular way for firms to work with marketing research suppliers is to form long-term partnering relationships with a few select firms. In a typical collaborative partnership, the client and research firm work together on an ongoing basis on those projects for which the research firm has the necessary expertise, instead of the client relying on project-by-project bids to select suppliers for specific projects. In some situations, research firm staff may actually work at the client's premises on a regular basis. For example, many ACNielsen employees work directly at the offices of firms purchasing its scanner data, performing data analysis tasks that might have been done formerly by the client. The arrangements between firms and their research partners are often referred to as "preferred relationships," and may be captured by an informal understanding or formalized in a contract. The net result of partnering relationships is that both sides work with fewer companies, while the research firm becomes an additional resource that extends the client's information-gathering and analysis capabilities. Over time, the research firm becomes more familiar with the client's business and issues. This has allowed those in client firms to spend more time on managerial functions, including problem definition, design, interpretation, and recommendations, and less time on the nuts-and-bolts of a typical study.

Summary

A company's philosophy of how marketing research fits into its marketing plan determines its program strategy for marketing research. A program strategy specifies the types of studies that will be conducted and determines their purposes. The design of the individual studies defines the firm's project strategy.

Although each research problem imposes its own special requirements, a marketing research project can be viewed as a sequence of steps—the research process—that includes the following:

1. Formulate problem
2. Determine research design
3. Design data-collection method and forms
4. Design sample and collect data
5. Analyze and interpret the data
6. Prepare the research report

These steps are so highly interrelated that they can rarely be performed consecutively but rather require a good deal of iteration between and among the various steps. These steps organize the remainder of this book, with each section elaborating on a stage of the process. The stages also indicate the potential areas of expertise needed by the aspiring researcher.

The first stage in the research process is problem formulation. In defining the decision problem, the researcher and the manager need to be honest in their communications with each other. Decision problems or opportunities can arise from three sources: unplanned change; planned change; and serendipity, or chance ideas. The simplest decision problem is characterized by an individual, operating in an environment, who wants something, has alternative ways of pursuing it, and is in doubt about which course of action to take because the available options will not be equally efficient. The decision problem is what to do in this situation. To determine whether research can assist the decision maker in making the choice, it is necessary to translate the decision problem into a research problem that addresses the questions of what information to provide for the decision problem and how that information can best be secured.

It is absolutely imperative that the research address the "real" decision problem and not some visible, but incorrect, aspect of it. For this to happen, the researcher working on the problem must develop sufficient understanding of the decision maker and the environment, the alternative courses of action being considered, the decision maker's objectives (including the person's attitude toward risk), and the potential consequences of the alternative courses of action. One useful mechanism for ensuring that the actual decision problem will be addressed by the research is for the researcher to prepare a written statement of the problem after meeting with the decision maker. Another way is by preparing scenarios that anticipate the contents of the final report, including the planned cross-tabulations, and asking the decision maker what he or she would do with the results. In either case, it is useful to secure a signed agreement from the decision maker that the written statement correctly captures the situation. After such agreement is obtained, the researcher should prepare a research proposal, which describes the techniques that will be used to address the problem. The research proposal should include some perspective on how each stage in the research process will be handled, as well as the time and cost estimates.

Before proceeding with the research, the potential gains to be derived should always be specified explicitly and compared with the costs to ensure that the research is likely to be worthwhile.

Questions

1. What is the difference between a program strategy for research and a project strategy?
2. What is the research process?
3. What is the most serious error in research? Explain.
4. What are the sources of marketing problems or opportunities? Does a source change typically trigger a change in research emphasis? Explain.
5. What are the fundamental characteristics of decision problems?
6. What is involved in a research request step? What is included in the written statement?
7. What is involved in using scenarios to help define the decision problem?
8. What is the purpose of a research proposal? What goes into the various parts?
9. Why would firms want to use outside suppliers for their research? How should decision makers go about choosing an outside supplier for some research?

Applications and Problems

1. Given the following decision problems, identify the research problems:
   a. What pricing strategy to follow for a new product
   b. Whether to increase the level of advertising expenditures on print or online
   c. Whether to increase in-store promotion of existing products
   d. Whether to increase training for frontline service providers
   e. Whether to change the sales force compensation package
   f. Whether to change the combination of ticket price, entertainers, and security at the Indiana State Fair
   g. Whether to revise a bank's electronic payment service
2. Given the following research problems, identify corresponding decision problems for which they might provide useful information:
   a. Design a test market to assess the effect on sales volume of a particular discount scheme
   b. Evaluate inventory for retail and e-tail warehouses
   c. Evaluate the sales and market share of grocery stores in a metropolitan area
   d. Develop sales forecasts for a new product
   e. Assess the level of awareness of the benefits of a new generation of mobile phones
   f. Assess attitudes and opinions of customers toward existing theme restaurants
3. Briefly discuss the difference between a decision problem and a research problem.
4. In each of the following situations, identify the fundamental source of the marketing problem or opportunity, a decision problem arising from the marketing problem or opportunity, and a possible research problem.
   a. Cool Pool Supply is a manufacturer of swimming pool maintenance chemicals. Recently, a malfunction of the equipment that mixes anti-algae compound resulted in a batch of the product that not only inhibits algae growth but also causes the pool water to turn a beautiful shade of light blue (with no undesirable side effects).
   b. The MBA director of a local college recently extended offers to 20 promising students. Only 5 offers were accepted. In the past, acceptance rates have averaged 90 percent. A survey of nonacceptors conducted by the director revealed that the primary reason students declined the offer was their perception that the college's course requirements are too "restrictive."
   c. Chocoholic Candy Company has enjoyed great success in its small regional market. Management attributes much of this success to Chocoholic's unique distribution system, which ensures twice-weekly delivery of fresh product to retail outlets. The directors of the company have instructed management to expand Chocoholic's geographical market if it can be done without altering the twice-weekly delivery policy.

5. You are the marketing manager of a two-year-old Internet company. Recently you solicited proposals for an upcoming research project from three outside marketing research suppliers. You have the formal proposals in hand and must choose which supplier to use. In general, what criteria should you use in making your decision?

6. This chapter discussed the research problem and the problem formulation step in research design. Take a step back for a moment and consider the following question: In the absence of company problems, is there any need to conduct marketing research?

Thorndike Sports Equipment Video Case

1. What is the problem in Thorndike's racquetball division?

2. As research analyst for Thorndike, you have been assigned the project of solving "the Graph-Pro racquet problem." Outline the steps you would take in order to understand the scope of the problem. What types of research would you propose to Thorndike's president?

CASE 1.1
Big Brothers of Fairfax County

Big Brothers of America is a social-service program designed to meet the needs of boys ages 6 to 18 from single-parent homes. Most of the boys served by the program live with their mothers and rarely see or hear from their fathers. The purpose of the program is to give these boys the chance to establish a friendship with an interested adult male. Big Brothers of America was founded on the belief that an association with a responsible adult can help program participants become more responsible citizens and better adjusted young men.

The program was started in Cincinnati in 1903. Two years later, the organization was granted its first charter in New York state through the efforts of Mrs. Cornelius Vanderbilt. By the end of World War II, there were 30 Big Brothers agencies. Today there are more than 300 agencies across the United States, and more than 120,000 boys are matched with Big Brothers.

The Fairfax County chapter of Big Brothers of America was founded in Fairfax in 1966. In 1971, United Way of Fairfax County accepted the program as part of its umbrella organization and now provides about 85 percent of its funding. The remaining 15 percent is raised by the local Big Brothers agency.

Information about the Big Brothers program in Fairfax County reaches the public primarily through newspapers (feature stories and classified advertisements), radio, public service announcements, posters (on buses and in windows of local establishments), and word-of-mouth advertising. The need for volunteers is a key message emanating from these sources. The agency phone number is always included so that people wanting to know more about the program can call for information. Those calling in are given basic information over the telephone and are invited to attend one of the monthly orientation sessions organized by the Big Brothers program staff. At these meetings, men get the chance to talk to other volunteers and to find out what will be expected of them should they decide to join the program. At the end of the session, prospective volunteers are asked to complete two forms. One is an application form and the other is a questionnaire in which the person is asked to describe the type of boy he would prefer to be matched with, as well as his own interests.

The files on potential Little Brothers are then reviewed in an attempt to match boys with the volunteers. A match is made only if both partners agree. The agency stays in close contact with the pair and monitors its progress. The three counselors for the Big Brothers program serve as resources for the volunteer.

The majority of the inquiry calls received by the Fairfax County agency are from women who are interested in becoming Big Sisters (in the Big Brothers program) or from people desiring information on the Couples Program. Both programs are similar to the Big Brothers program and are administered by it. In fact, of 55 calls concerning a recent orientation meeting, only 5 were from males. Only three of the five callers actually attended the meeting, a typical response.

Although the informational campaigns and personal appeals thus seemed to have some effect, the results were also generally disappointing and did little to alleviate the shortage of volunteer Big Brothers. Currently, 250 boys are waiting to be matched with Big Brothers, and the shortage increases weekly.

Big Brothers of Fairfax County believed that a lack of awareness and accurate knowledge could be the cause of the shortage of volunteers. Are there men who would volunteer if only they were made aware of the program and its needs? Or is the difficulty a negative program image? Do people think of Little Brothers as problem children, boys who have been in trouble with the law or who have severe behavioral problems? Or could there be a misconception of the type of man who would make a good Big Brother? Do people have stereotypes with respect to the volunteers, for example, that the typical volunteer is a young, single, professional male?

QUESTIONS
1. What is (are) the marketing decision problem(s)?
2. What is (are) the marketing research problem(s)?
3. What types of information would be useful to answer these questions?
4. How would you go about securing this information?

CASE 1.2

Transitional Housing, Inc. (A)[1]

Transitional Housing, Inc. (THI) is a local nonprofit organization located in Madison, WI. THI provides assistance to homeless and very low income individuals and families in finding emergency shelter, food, employment, transitional housing, and affordable apartment housing. These services are provided through four basic THI programs (see Table 1.2.1 for details):

1. *The Drop-In Shelter:* An emergency drop-in shelter for men located at Grace Episcopal Church.

2. *The Transitional Housing Program:* Provides transitional living arrangements for families and single

men for six months or more depending on the needs of the individual/family and the unit.

3. *The Housing Opportunity Program:* Helps families in obtaining a lease.

4. *The Hospitality House:* A day shelter for homeless and very low income men, women, and children.

As part of its planning, the board of directors of THI was interested in determining ways to improve the organization's services. Their original idea was to conduct a survey of the organization's paid staff, volunteers, and guests (the homeless staying at THI or using its facilities or services) to determine which programs of THI they found particularly useful, which should be revised, and what other programs or services might be of more assistance to guests.

However, the analysis of THI's internal statistics and other published data indicated that THI needed

---

[1]The contributions of Monika Wingate to the development of this case are gratefully acknowledged.

TABLE 1.2.1	Programs Offered by Transitional Housing, Inc.

Drop-In Shelter
Located at the Grace Episcopal Church in the downtown area, the Drop-In Shelter (DIS) is a 46-person-capacity emergency drop-in shelter for men. Overflow capacity for 20 additional people is provided at St. John's Lutheran Church from October through April. The basic services provided at DIS are shelter, food, personal grooming supplies, and counseling. Medical and legal services are also provided once a week through volunteers. The shelter is open to all men who are not incapacitated by drugs or alcohol and agree to abide by the rules of DIS. Operating hours are from 8:00 P.M. to 8:00 A.M. seven days per week, 365 days per year. Both dinner and breakfast are provided for DIS guests through the support of approximately 1,200 volunteers (churches, community groups, and other interested individuals) who offer their help to DIS.

Transitional Housing Program
The Transitional Housing Program (THP) operates 15 traditional housing sites throughout Dane County. There are 20 family units and 39 single units. Residents of THP may stay in the units for a period of six months to "permanent," depending on the unit and the needs of the individual or family. Services provided to the residents of the THP include money management, employment counseling, case management, and referrals to agencies involved in providing services needed by the individual or family. DIS is often the first step in the process of single men getting involved in THP.

Housing Opportunity Program
The Housing Opportunity Program (HOP) is a service provided by THI that is designed to aid families in obtaining a lease in their own name and staying in the site on a permanent basis. THI leases apartments from area landlords and subleases the units to homeless families, who are referred to THI through area shelters. During this time, THI assumes responsibility for any unpaid rent or repairs that may accrue. Maintenance checks are performed monthly and outreach services are provided to families involved in the program.

Hospitality House
Hospitality House (HH), located on the near west side, is a day shelter and resource center for homeless and very low income men, women, and children. HH is generally regarded as a warm, safe place for the homeless to congregate, where services are provided but are not mandatory. The basic services provided at HH are assistance with finding employment and housing, help for obtaining benefits from other social service agencies, and mental health services. Telephones are available for the guests' use, and guests may also use HH as a mailing address while they are staying at DIS.

to narrow its focus. Specifically, internal information indicated the number of agencies serving the male homeless population was decreasing, and the number of homeless families was increasing. Moreover, THI was currently the only Madison shelter that served the male homeless population, and this community appeared to be underserved. In fact, the number of homeless men staying at THI's Drop-In Shelter had increased 89 percent, from 607 three years ago to 1,146 the past year. This was partly due to the closing of other Madison male shelters in the last three years. Finally, although the THI shelter has the capacity to serve 66 men per night, it was filled beyond capacity. During the winter, frequently more than 90 men were staying at the Drop-In Shelter on any given night, with many of them sleeping on the hallway floor.

Given this information, the board of directors decided to use the organization's limited resources to focus first on the Drop-In Shelter and the Hospitality House as it relates to the Drop-In Shelter. More specifically, the board asked for an evaluation of THI's current facilities and the services for the homeless as well as a determination of what future services and facilities it should try to provide.

QUESTIONS

1. What is the decision problem?

2. What is the research problem?

3. Discuss in general terms how you would address the board of directors' concerns. Specifically, who would you obtain information from and how would you access these people?

CASE 1.3
Hand-to-Hand against Palm (A)

An electronics and personal computing firm has been watching closely the success of the Palm Pilot and seeks to introduce a competitive device, beta-named "Organize My Life!" or OML for short. The OML marketing manager has gathered some intelligence on the Palm Inc. sales and believes that, for all its success, some potential markets are being underserved.

Handheld personal digital assistants (PDAs) were introduced unsuccessfully at first by Apple in 1993. Some analysts argue that the Newton, Apple's market offering, was not clearly positioned to the consumers; others argue that they were simply ahead of their time. 3Com's Palm Computing focused the PDA, limiting its functionality to calendars and appointments, contact directory information, and to-do lists, so as to convey its technological benefits more clearly to the potential user. In only five years, Palm achieved more than two-thirds of the global market to support this claim.[1] Over 5.5 million devices have been sold, and sales continue to show strong growth (sales are expected to reach 13 million in the next two years).

Competitors offer Internet access, including wireless variants, but the OML group has data that indicate only 17 percent of PDA users would pay extra for this feature—these users already have PC Internet access and view the PDA's access version as redundant, and worse, likely to be slow. OML is considering conducting research to investigate whether other features, like voice recognition capabilities, stereo quality sound systems for downloading music, video and digital photographic abilities, and global positioning mapping ("u r here") software would be valued.

In addition to seeking data on features, OML is considering the attractiveness of this technology to another segment. Its data indicate the typical Palm Pilot user is a male, in his early 40s, college-educated, and a white-collar professional with a relatively high income. OML is interested in serving the university student market. An important concern is that the typical student will have fewer discretionary funds than the current PDA purchaser profile. Thus, OML marketing discussions revolve around questions like these: What is the price point beyond which students would be less inclined to purchase this device? If the device were priced at, say, $299 or less, which features would be prohibitive to continue to offer? What are the students' priorities in terms of the functions and features they would like to see bundled into the PDA? Would the benefits sought depend on whether this device were targeted to undergraduates "in general" compared with engineering and computer science students and compared with MBA graduate students? How do we choose the features to offer and the segments to target?

QUESTIONS

1. What is the decision problem?

2. What is (are) the research problem(s)?

3. What recommendations would you make to the OML marketing manager to address the research problem(s)? That is, what data would you collect and how might those data be used to answer the research question(s) posed?

---

[1]See David Rynecki, "Is Palm's IPO Really the One to Catch?" *Fortune* (February 2, 2000), pp. 213–214.

CASE 1.4

E-Food and the Online Grocery Competition (A)

When everybody's busy, something's got to give. The relatively new service industry of online groceries (that is, grocery shopping online and the home delivery of the purchased items) has grown to address today's consumer demands of convenience and time savings. Perhaps the best-known provider in the industry is Peapod.com, an operation that began outside Chicago. Since its founding in 1989, it has expanded to nearly a dozen metropolitan markets, serving over 100,000 households. Other competitors sense the market potential, and many firms share space in the marketplace, including groceronline.com (which uses UPS and Federal Express rather than local delivery operators); or netgrocer.com (which covers towns and rural areas, with no annual fee and makes available merchandise such as books and CDs); as well as many as-yet-local providers.[1] Industry experts predict continued strong growth (though their numbers vary wildly; home food shopping is expected to grow to anywhere from $5 billion to $80 billion in the next three to five years).

These online grocery services provide virtual stores through which the electronic visitor navigates, as if pushing a shopping cart in a traditional grocer. The user clicks on items to purchase, which are placed in the user's cart. When complete, the user is "checked out," specifying a delivery date and time (paying a premium for narrower windows of delivery time precision, such as from 1 to 1:30 compared to 1 to 4 P.M.). Users pay annual dues and delivery costs proportionate to each shopping bill.

The software allows the user to store his or her preferences in a personal shopping list, which may be altered, adding or deleting items as deemed necessary with each e-visit. Across the various providers, the software also usually allows facile consumer comparison; for example, the SKUs in a particular category may be sorted by brand name, by price, by value (price per ounce, for example), by what is on "feature" (sale and point of purchase promotions), by various dietetic goals (such as "healthy," "low fat"), and so on. The user may write in "notes," to specify in more detail, for example, "Please pick up green (unripe) bananas, not yellow ones," or, "If Fancy Feast is out of beef, please get turkey instead," which instruct the professional shopper as to the user's particular preferences. Categories of items that can be purchased are continually expanding, from foods to drugstore items and other merchandise.

Most users are women, employed full-time, and married, with household incomes that exceed $100,000.

Online grocery providers tend to conduct the online business very well, if customers' satisfaction, repeat visits, and word-of-mouth are any indicators. That is, the software provided, the merchandise selected, the delivery reliability, and so on, are valued by the customer, with few complaints. However, home delivery of food is not a particularly profitable industry. One of the major paths to profit is in selling the data that result from the visitors' trips to the Web site.

Ashley Sims is an MBA student, taking her last term of classes, and thinking about starting up a local competitor online grocer. She's certain that by learning from the templates of the current providers in other markets, that she too can run the logistics of the business. However, she hopes that, given her contacts of computer experts, she can create a competitive advantage in the software setup, if she understands the consumers' mind-set as they travel through the e-grocery stores. She wants to know just what a user is thinking from the first click onto the Web site to the last "Done Shopping" click off the site. This knowledge would allow her to offer better advice to her software developers in terms of what features would facilitate the visitors' traversal of the grocery store. Data like these would help improve the system, and it would also lend great insight to the consumers' decision processes.

QUESTIONS

1. What is the decision problem?
2. What is (are) the research problem(s)?
3. Prepare a research proposal to submit to an online grocer on behalf of your research team.

CASE 1.5

Wisconsin Power & Light (A)[1]

Recent changes in the utility industry have led to a more deregulated and competitive environment. In response, Wisconsin Power & Light (WP&L) has been

---

[1] For more on the logistics concerns of such delivery systems, see "Upstarts," *Business Week E.Biz* (July 26, 1999), p. EB-46.

[1] The contributions of Kavita Maini and Paul Metz to the development of this case are gratefully acknowledged, as is the permission of Wisconsin Power & Light to use the material included.

shifting its focus from that of a product-driven company to one of a market- and information-driven company. Management has increasingly relied on information from marketing studies and has been incorporating the external data in their decision-making processes. WP&L's espousal of a market-sensitive mentality has helped to shape the company's overall business strategies. One current area of concern for WP&L involves environmental issues, so much so that one of the company's goals is "to be a responsible corporate citizen, promoting the social, economic, and environmental well-being of the communities that it serves."

WP&L, in an effort to realize its environmental goals, developed several programs for its residential, commercial, and industrial customers to foster the conservation of energy. The programs, which were classified under the BuySmart umbrella of WP&L's Demand-Side Management Programs, consisted of such specific programs as Appliance Rebates, Energy Analysis, Weatherization Help, and the Home Energy Improvement Loan (HEIL) program. All previous marketing research and information gathering focused primarily on issues from the customer's perspective, such as an evaluation of net program impacts in terms of energy and demand savings and an estimation of the levels of free ridership (individuals who would have undertaken the conservation actions promoted by the program, even if no program were in place). In addition, a study has been designed and is currently being conducted to evaluate and identify customer attitudes and opinions concerning the design, implementation, features, and delivery of the residential programs. Having examined the consumer perspective, WP&L's current goal is to focus on obtaining information from other participants in the programs, namely, employees and lenders.

The next task for the management of WP&L is a study of the HEIL program of the BuySmart umbrella. The HEIL program was designed to make low-interest-rate financing available to residential gas and electric WP&L customers for conservation and weatherization measures. The low-interest guaranteed loans are delivered through WP&L account representatives in conjunction with participating financial institutions and trade allies. The procedures for obtaining a loan begin with an energy "audit" of the interested customer's residence to determine the appropriate conservation measures. Once the customer decides on which measures to have installed, the WP&L representative assists in arranging the low-interest-rate financing through one of the participating local banking institutions. At the completion of the projects, WP&L representatives conduct an inspection of the work by checking a random sample of participants. Conservation measures eligible under the HEIL program include the installation of natural gas furnaces or boilers, automatic vent dampers, intermittent ignition devices, heat pumps, and heat pump water heaters. Eligible structural improvements include the addition of attic, wall, and basement insulation, storm windows and doors, sillbox insulation, window weather stripping, and caulking.

Purpose

The primary goal of the current study is to identify ways of improving the HEIL program from the lenders' point of view. Specifically, the following issues need to be addressed:

- Identify the lenders' motivation for participating in the program.
- Determine how lenders get their information regarding various changes/updates in the program.
- Identify how lenders promote the program.
- Assess the current program with respect to administrative and program features.
- Determine the type of credit analysis conducted by the lenders.
- Identify ways of minimizing the default rate from the lenders' point of view.
- Identify lenders' opinions of the overall program.
- Assess the lenders' commitment to the program.
- Identify if the reason for loan inactivity in some lending institutions is due to lack of a customer base.

QUESTION
1. Prepare a research request that will address WP&L's study objectives.

2

Determine Research Design

Part 2 deals with the general nature of designing research so that it addresses the appropriate questions efficiently. Chapter 4 provides an overview of the role of various research designs and also discusses two of the basic designs—the exploratory and the descriptive—at some length. Chapter 5 discusses the role of experiments in marketing research.

4

Research Design

The preceding chapters presented some of the kinds of problems that marketing research can help to solve. As you may have noticed, there can be great variation in the nature of the questions research might investigate. Some can be very specific: If we change the advertising mix, what might happen to sales? Others are much more general: Why have sales fallen below target? How do customers feel about the product? As you may have guessed, different formulations of a problem can lead to different research approaches to answer it.

This chapter introduces the notion of research design and discusses the basic types and their interrelations. It also reviews two of the design types—the exploratory and the descriptive—in some detail. The next chapter deals with the nature of causal or experimental designs.

Plan of Action

A **research design** is simply the framework or plan for a study, used as a guide in collecting and analyzing data. It is the blueprint that is followed in completing a study. It resembles the architect's blueprint for a house. Even though it is possible to build a house without a detailed blueprint, doing so will more than likely produce a final product that is different from what was originally envisioned by the buyer. Like an architect's blueprint for a house, it is the plan that is followed in completing a study. Even though it is possible to build a house without a detailed blueprint, doing so will more than likely produce a final product that is different from what the buyer envisioned. A certain room is too small; the traffic pattern is poor; some features really wanted are omitted; other less important details are included; and so on.

It is also possible to conduct research without a detailed blueprint. The research findings, too, will probably differ widely from what the consumer or user of the research wanted. "These results are interesting, but they do not solve the basic problem," is a common lament. Further, just as the house built without a blueprint is likely to cost more because of midstream alterations in construction, research conducted without a research design is likely to cost more than research properly executed using a research design.

Thus, a research design ensures that the study (1) will be relevant to the problem and (2) will use economical procedures. It would help the student learning research methods if there were a single procedure to follow in developing the framework or if there were a single framework to be learned. Unfortunately, this is not the case.

Rather, there are many research design frameworks, just as there are many unique house designs. Fortunately, though, just as house designs can be broken into basic types (for example, ranch, split-level, two-story), research designs can be classified into some basic types as well. One very useful classification is in terms of the fundamental objective of the research: exploratory, descriptive, or causal.[1]

Types of Research Design

The major emphasis in **exploratory research** is on the discovery of *ideas* and *insights*.[2] The soft-drink manufacturer faced with decreased sales might conduct an exploratory study to generate possible explanations.

The **descriptive research** study is typically concerned with determining the *frequency* with which something occurs or the relationship between two variables. The descriptive study is typically guided by an initial hypothesis. An investigation of the trends in the consumption of soft drinks with respect to such characteristics as age, sex, and geographic location would be a descriptive study.

A **causal research** design is concerned with determining *cause-and-effect* relationships. Causal studies typically take the form of experiments, because experiments are best suited to determine cause and effect. For instance, a soft-drink manufacturer may be interested in ascertaining the effectiveness of different advertising appeals. One way for the company to proceed would be to use different ads in different geographic areas and investigate which ad generated the highest sales. In effect, the company would perform an experiment, and if it was designed properly, the company would be in a position to conclude that one specific appeal caused the higher rate of sales.

Having stated the basic general purpose of each major type of research design, three important caveats are in order. First, although the suggested classification of design types is useful for gaining insight into the research process, the distinctions are not absolute. Any given study may serve several purposes. Nevertheless, certain types of research designs are better suited to some purposes than others. The crucial tenet of research is that *the design of the investigation should stem from the problem.* Each of these types is appropriate to specific kinds of problems.

Second, in the remainder of this chapter and in the next chapter, we shall discuss in more detail each of the design types. The emphasis will be on their *basic characteristics* and *generally fruitful approaches.* Whether or not the designs are useful in a given problem setting depends on how imaginatively they are applied. Architects can be taught basic design principles; whether they then design attractive, well-built houses depends on how they apply these principles. So it is with research. The general characteristics of each design can be taught. Whether they are productive in a given situation depends on how skillfully they are applied. There is no single best way to proceed, just as there is no single best floor plan for, say, a ranch-type house. It all depends on the specific problem to be solved. Research analysts, then, need an

---

[1]Claire Selltiz, Lawrence S. Wrightsman, and Stuart W. Cook, *Research Methods in Social Relations*, 3rd ed. (New York: Holt, Rinehart and Winston, 1976), pp. 90–91. See also Fred N. Kerlinger, *Foundations of Behavioral Research*, 3rd ed. (New York: Holt, Rinehart and Winston, 1986), pp. 347–390; Russell A. Jones, *Research Methods in the Social and Behavioral Sciences*, 2nd ed. (Sunderland, MA: Sinaver Associates, 1996); and Gerhard Lang and George D. Heiss, *A Practical Guide to Research Methods*, 6th ed. (Lanham, MD: University Press of America, 1998).

[2]The basic purposes are those suggested by Selltiz, Wrightsman, and Cook, *Research Methods*.

understanding of the basic designs so that they can modify them to suit specific purposes.

Third, the three basic designs can be looked at as stages in a continuous process. Figure 4.1 shows the interrelations. Exploratory or formulative studies are often seen as the initial step. When researchers begin an investigation, it stands to reason that they lack a great deal of knowledge about the problem. Consider, for example, the following problem: "Brand X's share of the disposable diaper market is slipping. Why?" This statement is too broad to serve as a guide for research. To narrow and refine it would logically be accomplished with exploratory research, in which the emphasis would be on finding possible explanations for the sales decrease. These tentative explanations, or hypotheses, would then serve as specific guides for descriptive or causal studies.

Suppose the tentative explanation that emerged was that "Brand X is an economy-priced diaper, originally designed to compete with low-cost store-brand diapers. Families with children have more money today than when the brand was first introduced and are willing to pay more for higher quality baby products. It stands to reason that our market share would decrease." The hypotheses that families with small children have more real income to spend and that a larger proportion of that money is going toward baby products could be examined in a descriptive study of trends in the baby products industry.

Suppose that the descriptive study did support the hypotheses. The company might then wish to determine whether parents were, in fact, willing to pay more for higher quality diapers and, if so, what features (such as better fit or greater absorbency) were most important to them. This might be accomplished partially through a test-marketing study, a causal design.

Each stage in the process thus represents the investigation of a more detailed statement of the problem. Although we have suggested that the sequence would be from exploratory to descriptive to causal research, alternative sequences might occur. The "families with small children have more money to spend on baby products" hypothesis might be so generally accepted that the sequence would go from exploratory directly to causal. The potential also exists for conducting research in the reverse direction. If a hypothesis is disproved by causal research (for example, the product bombs in the test market), the analyst may then decide that another descriptive study, or even another exploratory study, is needed. Also, not every research problem will begin with an exploratory study. It depends on how specific

| FIGURE 4.1 | **Relationships among Research Designs** |

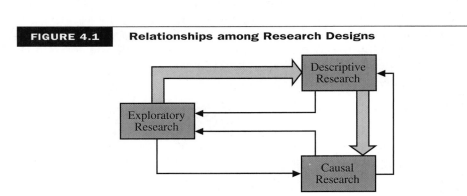

researchers can be in formulating the problem before them. A general, vague statement leads naturally to exploratory work, whereas a specific cause-effect hypothesis lends itself to experimental work.

Research Realities 4.1, for instance, lists some of the individual projects that were conducted by PepsiCo to support the conception and introduction of O'Grady's potato chips. In this instance, the examination of the potato chip category with respect to market shares and trends, the ideation sessions, and the focus groups to help develop meaningful ways to describe a thick potato chip could all be classified as exploratory research. The diary panel that was set up to measure trial and repeat purchase behavior would be considered descriptive, and the market simulation test and the test of the commercial would be considered causal.

Exploratory Research

As previously stated, the general objective in exploratory research is to gain insights and ideas. The exploratory study is particularly helpful in breaking broad, vague problem statements into smaller, more precise subproblem statements, it is hoped in the form of specific hypotheses. A **hypothesis** is a statement that specifies how two or more measurable variables are related.[3] A good hypothesis carries clear implications for testing stated relationships. In the early stages of research, we usually lack sufficient understanding of the problem to formulate a specific hypothesis. Further, there are often several tentative explanations for a given marketing phenomenon. For example: Sales are off because our price is too high; our dealers or sales representatives are not doing the job they should; our advertising is weak; and so on. Exploratory research can be used to establish priorities in studying these competing explanations. The priorities would be established because a particular hypothesis discovered in the exploratory study appears to be promising. They might also arise because the exploratory study generates information about the practical possibilities of researching specific, conjectural statements.

The exploratory study is also used to increase the analyst's familiarity with the problem. This is particularly true when the analyst is new to the problem arena (for example, a marketing research consultant going to work for a company for the first time).

The exploratory study may be used to clarify concepts. For instance, management is considering a change in service policy that will, it is hoped, result in improved dealer satisfaction. An exploratory study could be used to clarify the notion of dealer satisfaction and to develop a method by which dealer satisfaction could appropriately be measured.

When Congress discusses revising the tax code in order to make it "more fair" (so as to increase taxpayer compliance), a problem that often surfaces is how to determine what fairness in the tax code means. Is it tax enforcement that bothers people? Tax avoidance by other people? The way tax laws are written? Tax rates? That people believe their tax dollars are being poorly spent? Exploratory research would play a particularly important role in clarifying a concept such as this.

---

[3]See Kerlinger, *Foundations of Behavioral Research,* for a discussion of the criteria of good hypotheses and of the value of hypotheses in guiding research.

Research Supporting the Development and Introduction of O'Grady's Potato Chips

As a first step, Frito-Lay examined whether or not a consumer need existed for a different type of potato chip. An inventory was made of the potato chip product category. There were relatively few options available. Potato chips on the market were either flat or ridged, unflavored or cheese flavor or flavored with sour cream and onion. Yet Frito-Lay knew that consumers seek variety and often differentiate between products on a textural basis.

At the corporate level, a number of hurdle criteria were set: a $100-million-plus business, it had to add incremental volume, it had to have broad national appeal, and it had to be a unique, not easily replicated product.

To start with, new product ideas were developed through a number of sources. Ideation sessions were conducted with scientists, the marketing department, home economists, and consumers. Recipe books were collected, and the industry's packaged potato snack products were purchased from stores and studied for differentiation opportunities, for needs that weren't being filled.

Four distinct product ideas resulted from this exercise: a "better Pringles," which was dropped on judgment due to Pringles' lack of success; a "potato Frito," a thicker, processed chip that later became "crunch chips"; a super-crispy chip that became Ta-Tos; and a bite-sized, latticed chip—a small, thin, fragile O'Grady's forerunner. The ideas were exposed to consumers through product evaluation groups, which provided direction on product refinement and positioning issues. The results suggested that development should continue on all three, although the crunch chips and the Ta-Tos were the most well received at this stage. The O'Grady's product was deemphasized because consumers saw it as too light and thin.

Even though the Ta-Tos and crunch chips were well received and eventually went to test market, they did not fit with the business objective of being a new potato chip. Despite its consumer rejection, the lattice chip, which was to become O'Grady's, offered the most differentiable potato chip. O'Grady's was then taken from thin and crispy to the other end of the spectrum—thicker, heavier, and crunchier. The lattice cut gave it a unique appearance. The thickness gave it a unique texture (crunchiness) and taste (more potato taste). Home-use tests confirmed that the shift to thickness was positive, and focus group research was conducted to help develop meaningful, motivating ways of describing a thick potato chip. *Crunchy, hearty,* and *more potato taste* seemed to be most appealing.

From a market simulation test, the interest-generating ability of the concept and the fit of the product with the concept, as well as the trial and repeat and volume potential of the brand, were determined. Only two sizes and a plain flavor were tested. The results were positive, but they indicated that the product wouldn't surpass the corporate hurdle rate. So, an additional au gratin cheese flavor was developed and was selected using further home-use tests. At the same time, focus group copy development research led Frito-Lay to emphasize or embody simplicity, small-town values, implied wholesomeness, and heartiness. This commercial, opening with a potato plant, was found to be positively intrusive and memorable and to elicit positive consumer reactions with appropriate images being conveyed.

While in test market, a full range of research was conducted to monitor O'Grady's performance. An awareness and trial study was conducted. A diary panel was set up to measure trial, repeat, and depth of repeat. An image study was set up to make sure the desired positioning was conveyed. Finally, distribution checks helped monitor distribution and out-of-stock levels. These test market data allowed for fine-tuning of the national program and also provided standards against which to measure O'Grady's performance during expansion.

Source: Keynote talk by Norman Heller, President and Chief Executive Officer, PepsiCo Wines & Spirits International, at the Association of National Advertisers' New Product Marketing Workshop, October 16, 1984. For other examples of Frito-Lay's use of marketing research to understand its various product categories, see Robert Johnson, "In the Chips: At Frito-Lay, the Consumer Is an Obsession," *The Wall Street Journal* (March 22, 1991), p. B1; Chad Rubel, "Research Results Must Justify Brand Spending," *Marketing News* (February 26, 1996), p. 12; "Frito-Lay Profiles Salty Snack Consumers," *Supermarket News* (March 18, 1996), p. 39; "Anatomy of a Success Story," *Progressive Grocer* (July 1997), pp. 16–18; Emily Nelson, "Product Development Is Always Difficult: Consider the Frito Pie," *The Wall Street Journal* (October 25, 1999), pp. A1, A22.

In sum, an exploratory study is used for any or all of the following purposes:[4]

- Formulating a problem for more precise investigation or for developing hypotheses
- Establishing priorities for further research
- Gathering information about the practical problems of carrying out research on particular conjectural statements
- Increasing the analyst's familiarity with the problem
- Clarifying concepts

In general, exploratory research is appropriate to any problem about which little is known. Exploratory research then becomes the foundation for a good study.

Because knowledge is lacking when an inquiry is begun, exploratory studies are characterized by *flexibility* with respect to the methods used for gaining insight and developing hypotheses. Exploratory studies rarely use detailed questionnaires or involve probability sampling plans. Rather, investigators frequently change the research procedure as the vaguely defined initial problem is transformed into one with more precise meaning. Investigators follow where their noses lead them in an exploratory study. Ingenuity, judgment, and good luck inevitably play a part in leading to the one or two key hypotheses that, it is hoped, will account for the phenomenon.

Notwithstanding the flexibility, research experience has demonstrated that literature surveys, experience surveys, focus groups, and the analysis of selected cases are particularly productive in exploratory research. See Figure 4.2.

Literature Search

One of the quickest and cheapest ways to discover hypotheses is in the work of others, through a **literature search.** The search may involve conceptual literature, trade literature, or, quite often, published statistics.

The literature that is searched depends, naturally, on the problem being addressed. Miller Business Systems Inc. of Dallas, for example, routinely monitors trade literature to keep track of its competitors. The information on each competitor is

---

FIGURE 4.2   **Types of Exploratory Studies**

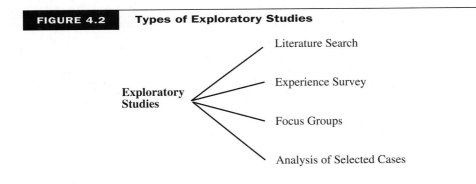

---

[4]Selltiz, Wrightsman, and Cook, *Research Methods,* p. 91.

entered into the "competitor profiles" that it keeps in its database. The company regularly scans these profiles for insights on what the competition might be doing. One such scan indicated that one competitor had hired nine furniture salesmen in a 10-day period. This was a tip-off to a probable push by the competitor in the office furniture market. With this early notice, Miller was able to schedule its salespeople to make extra calls on their accounts, thereby blunting the competitor's sales drive.[5]

Sometimes conceptual literature is more valuable than trade literature. For example, a search of conceptual literature would be warranted for a firm whose management believes that its field sales force is largely dissatisfied. The search would include works on psychology, sociology, and personnel, in addition to marketing journals. The focus would be on the factors determining employee satisfaction-dissatisfaction. The analyst would keep a keen eye out for those factors also found in the company's environment. The question of how to measure an employee's satisfaction would also be researched at the same time.

Suppose the problem is one that typically triggers much marketing research: "Sales are off. Why?" Exploratory insights into this problem could easily and cheaply be gained by analyzing published data and trade literature. Such an analysis would quickly indicate whether the problem was an industry problem or a firm problem. Very different research is in order if the firm's sales are down but (1) the company's market share is up, because industry sales are down farther; (2) the company's market share has remained stable; or (3) the company's market share has declined. The last situation would trigger an investigation of the firm's marketing-mix variables, whereas the first condition would suggest an analysis to determine why industry sales are off. The great danger in omitting exploratory research is obvious from the preceding example; without the analysis of secondary data as a guide, there is a great danger of researching the wrong "why."

A company's own internal data should be included in the literature examined in exploratory research, as Mosinee Paper Company found to its pleasant surprise. The company was contemplating dropping one of its products because of its dismal sales performance. Before doing so, though, the company tallied sales of the product by salesperson and found that only a single salesperson was selling that specific grade of industrial paper. On further investigation, Mosinee discovered how the buyers were using the paper—an application that had been known only to the one salesman and his customers. This information enabled management to educate its other salesmen as to the potential market for the paper and sales rose substantially.

It is important to remember that in a literature search, as in any exploratory research, the major emphasis is on the discovery of ideas and tentative explanations of the phenomenon and not on demonstrating which explanation is *the* explanation. The demonstration is better left to descriptive and causal research. Thus, the analyst must be alert to the hypotheses that can be derived from available material, both published material and the company's internal records.

---

[5]Steven P. Galante, "More Firms Quiz Customers for Clues about Competition," *The Wall Street Journal* (March 3, 1986), p. 17. See also Amanda Metcalfe and Helen West, "Striving to Be the Best—Understanding What the Customer Really Wants," *Marketing & Research Today* 24 (May 1996), pp. 131–140; Thomas L. L'egare, "Acting on Customer Feedback," *Marketing Research: A Magazine of Management & Applications* 8 (Spring 1996), pp. 46–51.

Experience Survey

The **experience survey,** sometimes called the *key informant survey,* attempts to tap the knowledge and experience of those familiar with the general subject being investigated. For example, a San Francisco builder focused on architects and designers when trying to get a handle on its competitors. The company asked these people to describe the traits of builders that tended to turn off buyers of expensive homes. Some of the answers included bad manners, workers who tracked dirt across carpets, and beat-up construction trucks, which buyers objected to having parked in their driveways. The company used these insights for a major repositioning of its business to the Bay Area's upper crust. The company bought a new truck, had its estimators don jackets and ties, and made sure its work crews were impeccably polite. For example, the crews began rolling protective runners over carpets before they set foot in clients' homes. In less than two years, the company's annual revenue more than quintupled.

In studies concerned with the marketing of a product, anyone who has any association with the marketing effort is a potential source of information. This would include the top executives of the company, sales manager, product manager, and sales representatives. It would also include wholesalers and retailers who handle the product as well as consumers who use the product. It might even include individuals who are not part of the chain of distribution but who might, nevertheless, possess some insight into the phenomenon. For example, a publisher of children's books investigating a sales decrease gained valuable insights by talking with librarians and schoolteachers. These discussions indicated that an increased use of library facilities, both public and school, coincided with the product's sales decline. These increases were, in turn, attributed to a very sizable increase in library holdings of children's books resulting from federal legislation that provided money for this purpose. Similarly, when designing the Louisville, a medium-duty conventional truck intended for beverage distribution, among other things, Ford Motor sought market information from fleet owners, mechanics, and drivers.[6]

Usually, a great many people know something about the general subject of any given problem. However, not all of them should be contacted.

> Research economy dictates that the respondents in an experience survey be carefully selected. The aim of the experience survey is to obtain insight into the relationships between variables rather than to get an accurate picture of current practices or a simple consensus as to best practices. One is looking for provocative ideas and useful insights, not for the statistics of the profession. Thus the respondents must be chosen because of the likelihood that they will offer the contributions sought. In other words, a *selected* sample of people working in the area is called for.[7]

One *does not,* therefore, use a probability sample in an experience survey. It is a waste of time to interview those who have little competence or little relevant experience. It is also a waste of time to interview those who cannot articulate their experience and

---

[6]Bob Deierlein, "A New Louisville Slugger," *Beverage World* 114 (June 1995), pp. 116–117.

[7]Selltiz, Wrightsman, and Cook, *Research Methods,* p. 94. See also Robert S. Weiss, *Learning from Strangers: The Art and Method of Qualitative Interview Studies* (New York: The Free Press, 1995).

knowledge. It is important, though, to include people with differing points of view. The following were all interviewed with varying degrees of success when the children's books sales decline was being researched: company executives, key people in the product group, sales representatives, managers of retail outlets in which the books were sold, teachers, and librarians.

The interviews were all unstructured and informal. The emphasis in each interview among those immediately concerned with the distribution of the product was "How do you explain the sales decrease? In your opinion, what is needed to reverse the downward slide?"[8] Most of the time in each interview was then devoted to exploring in detail the various rationales and proposed solutions. A number of sometimes conflicting hypotheses emerged. This provided the researchers with an opportunity to "bounce" some of the hypotheses off groups with differing vantage points and, in the process, get a feel for which of the hypotheses would be most fruitful to research. The interviews with librarians and teachers were divorced from the immediate problem. Here the emphasis was on discovering changes in children's reading habits.

The respondents were given a great deal of freedom in choosing the factors to be discussed. This is consistent with the notion that the emphasis in exploratory research is on developing tentative explanations and not on demonstrating the viability of a given explanation.

Focus Groups

Focus groups are another useful method for gathering ideas and insights. In a **focus group**, a small number of individuals are brought together in a room to sit and talk about some topic of interest to the focus group sponsor. The discussion is directed by a moderator. The moderator attempts to follow a rough outline of the issues under consideration, while at the same time making sure that the comments made by each person present are included in the group's discussion. Each individual is thereby exposed to the ideas of the others and submits his or her ideas to the group for consideration.

Focus groups are one of the more frequently used techniques in marketing research; they have proved to be productive for a variety of purposes, including the following:

1.   To generate hypotheses that can be further tested quantitatively
2.   To generate information helpful in structuring consumer questionnaires
3.   To provide overall background information on a product category
4.   To secure impressions on new product concepts

For example, in designing its Z3 roadster, BMW conducted focus groups in Japan, the United States, the United Kingdom, and Germany. The American influence is visible in the dual cupholders, the coinholder, and the third brake light.[9]

---

[8]Selltiz, Wrightsman, and Cook suggest that it is often useful in an exploratory study to orient questions toward "what works." That is, they recommend that questions be of the following form: "If (a given effect) is desired, what influences or what methods will, in your experience, be most likely to produce it?" (p. 95).

[9]Tim Neenan, "007's BMW Z3," *Ward's Auto World* 32 (March 1996), pp. 75–76.

Research Realities 4.2 discusses the insights Harley-Davidson gleaned from focus groups.

Although focus groups do vary in size, most consist of eight to twelve members. Smaller groups are too easily dominated by one or two members; with larger groups, frustration and boredom can set in, as individuals have to wait their turn to respond

---

RESEARCH REALITIES 4.2

Experience of Harley-Davidson with Focus Groups

After making a remarkable comeback in the 1980s, motorcycle manufacturer Harley-Davidson had buyers on two-year-long waiting lists all over the country. But that success placed the company in a familiar quandary: Should Harley expand and risk a market downturn, or should it stay the course, content with its good position in the industry?

"To invest or not to invest, that was the question," said Frank Cimermancic, Harley's director of business planning. "Dealers were begging us to build more motorcycles," he said. "But you have to understand our history. One of the things that caused past problems was a lack of quality, and that was the result of a too-rapid expansion. We did not want to relive that situation."

The company's dilemma was complicated by the fact that the market for heavyweight bikes was shrinking. "We were doing fine, but look at the market," Cimermancic said. "Maybe, we thought, we could reverse these trends and become an industry leader, something we hadn't been for a long time."

A new kind of customer seemed to hold the keys to market growth. White-collar motorcycle enthusiasts, or "Rubbies" (Rich Urban Bikers), started to shore up Harley sales in the middle '80s, adding to the company's success and image. But whether these Lenos and Forbeses were reliable, long-term customers was another question.

"Are those folks going to stay with us, or are they going to move on when the next fad comes along?" Cimermancic asked. "If we got the answer right, we could become a force in the industry. If we got it wrong, we would go right back to the early '80s. Nobody wanted to make the wrong decision and watch 20 percent of our employees walk away with their possessions in a cardboard box."

Harley also needed to know if it should market its products differently to different audiences. A core clientele of traditional "bikers" had kept Harley afloat during its leanest years, and they could not be alienated. "We had to understand the customer mindset," Cimermancic said. "Was there a universal appeal to owning a Harley?"

To find out, the company first invited focus groups made up of current owners, would-be owners, and owners of other brands to make cut-and-paste collages that expressed their feelings about Harley-Davidsons. Whether long-time Harley riders or fresh prospects, common themes emerged in the artwork: enjoyment, the great outdoors, freedom.

Harley-Davidson then mailed more than 16,000 surveys "with a typical battery of psychological, sociological, and demographic questions you typically see in studies," Cimermancic said, as well as subjective questions such as "Is Harley typified more by a brown bear or a lion?" The questionnaire got a 30 percent response rate, with no incentive for return.

From the responses, Harley identified seven core customer types: the Adventure-Loving Traditionalist, the Sensitive Pragmatist, the Stylish Status-Seeker, the Laid-back Camper, the Classy Capitalist, the Cool-headed Loner, and the Cocky Misfit. All of them appreciated Harley-Davidson products for the same reasons.

"Independence, freedom, and power were universal Harley appeals," Cimermancic said. "It didn't matter if you were the guy who swept the floor of the factory or if you were the CEO at that factory, the attraction to Harley-Davidson was very similar. We were surprised by a tremendous amount of loyalty across the board."

That loyalty meant the company could build and sell more motorcycles, without having to overextend itself. In 1990, Harley-Davidson expanded to build 62,800 bikes; last year, it built more than 105,000. Based on research, and the fact that names are again piling up on waiting lists, Harley expects its phenomenal growth to continue.

Source: Ian P. Murphy, "Aided by Research, Harley Goes Whole Hog," *Marketing News* 30 (December 2, 1996), pp. 16–17.

or get involved. Respondents are generally selected so that the groups are relatively homogeneous, minimizing both conflicts among group members on issues not relevant to the study objectives and differences in perceptions, experiences, and verbal skills. Differences that are too great with respect to any of these characteristics can intimidate some of the group participants and stifle discussion.

Most firms conducting focus groups use screening interviews to determine the individuals who will compose a particular group. One type they try to avoid is the individual who has participated before in a focus group, since some of these people tend to behave as "experts." Their presence can cause the group to behave in dysfunctional ways as they continually try to make their presence felt. Firms also try to avoid groups in which some of the participants are friends or relatives, because this tends to inhibit spontaneity in the discussion as the acquaintances begin talking to each other.

Given that the participants in any one group should be reasonably homogeneous, how can a firm ensure that it is getting a wide spectrum of insights? The key way is by having multiple groups. Not only can the characteristics of the participants vary across groups, but so can the issue outline. Ideas discovered in one group session can be introduced in subsequent group sessions for reaction. A typical project has four groups, but some may have up to twelve. The guiding criterion is whether the later groups are generating additional insight into the phenomenon under study. When they show diminishing returns, the groups are stopped.

The typical focus group session lasts from 1½ to 2 hours. Most focus groups are held at facilities designed especially for them, although they can be held at other places.[10] One advantage of these facilities is that they can incorporate the latest in technology because of the large number of groups held there. For example, video-conferencing technology can be used to link groups in different locations, allowing participants at the various locations to interact directly with one another.

The moderator in the focus group has a key role.[11] For one thing, the moderator typically translates the study objectives into a discussion guide that serves as an outline for the focus group session. To do so, he or she needs to understand the background of the problem and the most important information the client hopes to glean from the research process. The moderator also needs to understand the parameters of the groups in terms of their number, size, and composition, as well as how they might be structured to build on one another. Moreover, the moderator must lead the discussion so that all objectives of the study are met, and do so in such a way that *interaction* among the group members is stimulated and promoted. The moderator needs to make sure the discussion does not dissolve into nothing more than a set of concurrent interviews in which the participants take turns responding to

---

[10]David L. Morgan, *Planning Focus Groups* (Thousand Oaks, CA: Sage Publications, 1997).

[11]See Richard A. Krueger, *Focus Groups: A Practical Guide for Applied Research* (Thousand Oaks, CA: Sage Publications, 1994); Jane Farley Templeton, *The Focus Group: A Strategic Guide to Organizing, Conducting, and Analyzing the Focus Group Interview* (Thousand Oaks, CA: Sage Publications, 1994); Holly Edmunds, *The Focus Group Research Handbook* (Chicago: American Marketing Association, 1999) regarding the requirements for moderators and how to go about selecting them.

determined sets of questions. Moreover, he or she must do this while making sure the important issues on the discussion guide get addressed.[12]

This is an extremely delicate role. It requires someone who is intimately familiar with the purpose and objectives of the research and at the same time possesses good interpersonal communication skills. One important measure of a focus group's success is whether the participants talk to each other, rather than the moderator, about the items on the discussion guide.

Some of the key qualifications moderators must have are described in Table 4.1. Moderating an industrial focus group is even more difficult than moderating one involving a consumer product. A moderator for a consumer good typically knows something about the product or service at issue. After all, moderators are consumers, too. This is not so with many industrial goods. This means that the moderator's briefing for an industrial good has to be longer and more detailed. It also means that many of the group participants will know a great deal more about the product or service being discussed than the moderator. Directing group discussion under these conditions can be a taxing job indeed.

Moderators' responsibilities do not end when the group sessions end. Rather, they typically supervise the preparation of a transcript of each session and use the transcripts to develop a report for the client detailing the key insights the focus groups generated.

Sponsors can realize several advantages from the proper conduct of focus groups. For one thing, they allow for serendipity. Ideas can simply drop "out of the blue" during a focus group discussion. Further, the group setting allows them to be developed to their full significance, because it allows for snowballing. The comment by one individual can trigger a chain of responses from other participants. Often after a brief introductory warm-up period, respondents can "turn-on" to the discussion. They become sufficiently involved that they want to express their ideas and expose their feelings. Some feel more secure in the group environment than if they were being interviewed alone, since they soon realize that they can expose an idea without necessarily having to defend or elaborate on it. Consequently, responses are often more spontaneous and less conventional than they might be in a one-on-one interview.

Group interviews do offer certain benefits not obtainable with individual depth interviews, but they also have their weaknesses (see Table 4.2). Although group interviews are easy to set up, they are difficult to moderate and to interpret. It is easy to find evidence in one or more of the group discussions that supports almost any preconceived position. Because executives have the ability to observe the discussions through one-way mirrors or have the opportunity to listen to tape recordings of the sessions, focus groups seem more susceptible to executive and even researcher biases than do other data-collection techniques.

Seeing the session firsthand makes it easy to forget that the discussion, and consequently the results, are greatly influenced by the moderator and the specific

---

[12]See Richard A. Krueger, *Developing Questions for Focus Groups* (Thousand Oaks, CA: Sage Publications, 1997) for discussion of the techniques moderators use to get participants actively involved in the focus group interviews. See also Richard A. Krueger, *Moderating Focus Groups* (Thousand Oaks, CA: Sage Publications, 1997).

TABLE 4.1   **Seven Characteristics of Effective Focus Group Moderators**

Superior Listening Ability

It is essential that the moderator be able to listen to what the participants are saying. A moderator must not miss the participants' comments because of lack of attention or misunderstanding. The effective moderator knows how to paraphrase, to restate the comments of a participant when necessary, to ensure that the content of the comments is clear.

Excellent Short-Term Auditory Memory

The moderator must be able to remember comments that participants make early in a group, then correlate them with comments made later by the same or other participants. A participant might say that she rarely watches her weight, for example, then later indicate that she always drinks diet soft drinks. The moderator should remember the first comment and be able to relate it to the later one so that the reason for her diet soft drink consumption is clarified.

Well Organized

The best moderators see things in logical sequence from general to specific and keep similar topics organized together. A good moderator guide should be constructed logically, as should the final report. An effective moderator can keep track of all the details associated with managing the focus group process, so that nothing "falls through the cracks" that impacts negatively on the overall quality of the groups.

A Quick Learner

Moderators become intimately involved in a large number of different subject areas—and for only a very short time in each. An effective moderator is able to learn enough about a subject quickly in order to develop an effective moderator guide and conduct successful group sessions. Moderators normally have only a short period of time to study subject areas about which they will be conducting groups. Therefore, the most effective moderators can identify the key points in any topic area, then focus on them, so that they know enough to listen and/or probe for the nuances that make the difference between an extremely informative and an average group discussion.

High Energy Level

Focus groups can be very boring, both for the participants and for the client observers. When the tenor of a group gets very laid back and lifeless, it dramatically lowers the quality of the information that the participants generate. The best moderators find a way to inject energy and enthusiasm into the group so that both the participants and the observers are energized throughout the session. This ability tends to be most important during the second group of an evening (the eight to ten o'clock session), when observers and participants are frequently tired because of the late hour and can become listless if they are not motivated to keep their energy and interest levels high. The moderator must be able to keep his or her own energy level high so that the discussion can continue to be very productive to the end.

Personable

The most effective moderators are people who can develop an instant rapport with participants, so that the people become actively involved in the discussion in order to please the moderator. Participants who don't establish rapport with the moderator are much less likely to "open up" during the discussion, and the output from the group is not as good.

Well Above Average Intelligence

This is a vital characteristic of the effective moderator, because no one can plan for every contingency that may occur in a focus group session. The moderator must be able to think on his or her feet: to process the information that the group is generating, then determine what line of questioning will most effectively generate further information needed to achieve the research objectives.

Source: Thomas L. Greenbaum, *The Handbook of Focus Group Research,* 2nd ed. (Thousand Oaks, CA: Sage Publications, 1998), pp. 77–78.

TABLE 4.2	The Advantages/Disadvantages of Focus Groups versus Individual Depth Interviews

Advantages of Individual Depth Interviews versus Focus Groups
- They permit the interviewer to delve much deeper into a topic, because all the attention during the session is concentrated on one individual rather than a group of ten.
- They allow more candid discussion on the part of the interviewee, who might be intimidated to talk about a particular topic in a group of his or her peers. This is particularly the case for sensitive topics, such as personal-care products; financial behavior; or attitudes toward sex, religion, and politics.
- They eliminate negative group influences that can occur in a focus group. Because there is only one person being interviewed in the room, it is not possible for the individual's comments to be influenced by others.
- They are essential for certain situations where competitors would otherwise be placed in the same room. For example, it might be very difficult to do an effective focus group with managers from competing department stores or restaurants. Therefore, research with these people must be done on a one-to-one basis.

Limitations of Individual Depth Interviews versus Focus Groups
- They are typically much more expensive than groups, particularly when viewed on a per-interview basis. This is because the time of the moderator, which is the biggest cost in qualitative research, is the same for a two-hour focus group as it is for two hours of one-on-one interviews. Thus, for the same budget, the client gains input from significantly more people in a focus group.
- They generally do not get the same degree of client involvement as focus groups. It is difficult to convince most clients to sit through multiple hours of one-on-one interviews; this can be a problem if one of the objectives is to get the clients to view the research so they benefit firsthand from the information.
- They are physically exhausting for the moderator, so it is difficult to cover as much ground in one day as can be covered with groups. Most moderators will not do more than four or five interviews in a day, yet in two focus groups they can cover 20 people.
- Focus groups give the moderator the ability to leverage the dynamics of the group to obtain reactions that might not otherwise be generated in a one-on-one session.

Source: Adapted from Thomas L. Greenbaum, "Focus Groups vs. One-on-Ones: The Controversy Continues," *Marketing News* 25 (September 2, 1991), p. 16. Reprinted with permission of American Marketing Association.

direction he or she provides. Moderators possessing all the desired skills listed in Table 4.1 are extremely rare. One has to remember that the results are not representative of what would be found in the general population, and thus are *not* projectable. Further, the unstructured nature of the responses makes coding, tabulation, and analysis difficult. Focus groups should *not* be used, therefore, to develop head counts of the proportion of people who feel a particular way. Focus groups are better for *generating* ideas and insights than for systematically examining them.[13]

With the increasing tendency of companies to offer their products and services for sale worldwide, many U.S. companies are relying on foreign focus groups to research global markets. Firms considering doing so need to be aware of some of the more important differences between focus groups conducted in foreign countries and those held in the United States and Canada. See Research Realities 4.3.

[13]Wendy Sykes, "Validity and Reliability in Qualitative Market Research: A Review of the Literature," *Journal of the Market Research Society* 32 (July 1990), pp. 289–328; William J. McDonald, "Focus Group Research Dynamics and Reporting: An Examination of Research Objectives and Moderator Influences," *Journal of the Academy of Marketing Science* 21 (Spring 1993), pp. 161–168.

Major Differences between Focus Groups Held in Foreign Countries and Those Held in the United States and Canada

- **Time frame.** Although many U.S. companies are accustomed to developing a project on a Monday and having it completed by the end of the following week, this is almost impossible to do in foreign countries. Lead times tend to be much longer, with the Far East being particularly troublesome. If it takes two weeks to set up groups in the U.S., figure almost double that in most of Europe and even more than that for Asia.

- **Structure.** Eight to ten people in a group is a large number for most foreign groups, which often consist of four to six people. Further, the length of groups outside the U.S. can be up to four hours. Be very specific when arranging for international focus groups. Most foreign research organizations seem to adapt well to our format if properly informed and supervised.

- **Recruiting and recreating.** In general, the U.S. is much more rigid in adhering to specifications both in recruiting and rescreening. These processes must be monitored very carefully.

- **Approach.** Foreign moderators tend to be much less structured and authoritative, which can result in a great deal of down time during the sessions. Foreign moderators feel this is necessary to make group members feel comfortable with each other and build the rapport necessary to get the desired information. Also, they tend to use fewer writing exercises and external stimuli such as concept boards and photos. This must be considered when planning foreign sessions.

- **Project length.** Projects can take much longer to execute. In the U.S. we are accustomed to doing two, sometimes three or four, groups a day, but in many overseas markets, one group is the limit because of the time they are scheduled, the length of the sessions, or the demands of the moderators. Also, some moderators have a break in the middle of the group, which would be very unusual in the U.S. sessions.

- **Facilities.** The facility environment outside the U.S. and Canada is much like the setup here 20 years ago. For example, it is more common than not to watch a group in a residential setting on a television which is connected to the group room by cable. Further, many of the facilities overseas simply do not have the amenities, such as one-way mirrors, that we are accustomed to in the U.S.

- **Costs.** While varying considerably by region and country, it would not be unusual to pay almost twice as much per group for sessions conducted in Europe and almost three times as much for many areas in Asia.

Source: Thomas L. Greenbaum, "Understanding Focus Group Research Abroad," *Marketing News* 30 (June 30, 1996), pp. H14, H36.

Analysis of Selected Cases

The **analysis of selected cases** is sometimes referred to as the analysis of "insight-stimulating examples." By either label, the approach involves the *intensive study of selected cases* of the phenomenon under investigation. Examination of existing records, observation of the occurrence of the phenomenon, unstructured interviewing, or some other approach may be used. The focus may be on entities (individual people or institutions) or groups of entities (sales representatives or distributors in various regions).

The method is characterized by several features.[14] First, the researcher must be careful to record all relevant data, not just data that support any initial hypotheses

---

[14]These features are detailed further in Selltiz, Wrightsman, and Cook, *Research Methods,* pp. 98–99. See also Robert K. Yin, *Case Study Research: Design and Methods,* 2nd ed. (Thousand Oaks, CA: Sage Publications, 1994); Robert E. Stake, *The Art of Case Study Research* (Thousand Oaks, CA: Sage Publications, 1995).

he or she already formed. As with all forms of exploratory research, the goal is to gain insights, not to test explanations. By remaining neutral, it will be easier for the researcher to make the frequent changes in direction that are necessary as new information emerges. For example, he or she may first of all have to search for new cases or gather more data from previously contacted cases as the need arises. Second, the success of all forms of case analysis depends upon the researcher's ability to interpret the diverse mass of information that is eventually collected from one (or usually more) cases. The researcher must be able to sort through the data and see the "big picture," or insights that apply across multiple cases, not just details that apply only to individual cases. Third, as you may have guessed from the first two points, the data collection and analysis requirements of most forms of analysis of selected cases can be intense. In general, the researcher wants to obtain enough information to understand both the unique features of the case being studied and the features it has in common with other cases.

A case in point is a study aimed at improving the productivity of the sales force of a particular company. In this case, the investigator chose to study intensively several of the best salespeople and to compare them to several of the worst. While a comparison of their backgrounds and experience revealed little, the time spent making sales calls with them suggested the hypothesis that the sales people who checked the stock of retailers and pointed out items on which they were low seemed to most clearly differentiate the successful and poor representatives.

Some situations that are particularly productive of hypotheses are the following:

1. Cases reflecting changes and, in particular, abrupt changes. The adjustment of a market to the entrance of a new competitor can be quite revealing of the structure of an industry, for example.

2. Cases reflecting extremes of behavior. The example of the best and worst sales representatives was cited previously. Similarly, if one wanted to gain some idea of what factors account for the variation in company territory performance, one would be well advised to compare the best and worst territories, rather than looking at all territories.

3. Cases reflecting the order in which events occurred over time. For example, in the territory performance question, it may be that in one territory, sales are handled by a branch office where they were formerly handled by a manufacturer's agent, whereas in another, the sales branch office replaced an industrial distributor.

Which cases will be most valuable depends, of course, on the problem in question. It is generally true, though, that cases that display *sharp contrasts* or have *striking features* are most useful. This is because minute differences are usually difficult to discern. Thus, instead of trying to determine what distinguishes the average case from the slightly above-average case, we contrast the best and worst to magnify whatever differences may exist.

A frequently used example of the use of selected cases to develop insights is benchmarking. **Benchmarking** involves identifying one or more organizations that excel at carrying out some function and using their practices as a source of ideas for improvement. For example, L.L.Bean is noted for its excellent order fulfillment. During one spring, the company mailed 500,000 packages, with every order filled correctly. Even during the busy Christmas season, the company fills 99.9 percent of its orders correctly.[15] Therefore, other organizations have sought to improve their own order fulfillment by benchmarking L.L.Bean.

Organizations carry out benchmarking through such activities as reading about other organizations, visiting or calling them, and taking apart competing products to see how they are made. The process of benchmarking varies according to the information needs of the organization and the resources available.

Benchmarking is most useful for learning about existing rather than new products and about business practices, including ways of providing better value to customers. Benchmarked organizations are less likely to reveal information about new products or to disclose their strategies to competitors.

Xerox is widely credited with the first benchmarking project in the United States. In 1979, Xerox studied Japanese competitors to learn how they could sell midsize copiers for less than what it cost Xerox to make them. Today many companies, including AT&T, Eastman Kodak, and Motorola, use benchmarking as a standard research tool. Pittsburgh's Mellon Bank started benchmarking to improve the way it handled customer complaints about its credit card billing. Mellon benchmarked seven companies, including credit card operations, an airline, and a competing bank, by visiting three companies and phoning four. By applying what it learned, the bank cut its time to resolve a complaint from an average of 45 days to 25 days.[16]

ETHICAL DILEMMA 4.1

Prompted by an increasing incidence of homes for sale by owner, the president of a local real estate company asks you to undertake exploratory research to ascertain what kind of image realtors enjoy in the community. Unbeknownst to your current client, you undertook a similar research study for a competitor two years ago and, based on your findings, have formed specific hypotheses about why some homeowners are reluctant to sell their houses through realtors.

- Is it ethical to give information obtained while working for one client to another client who is a competitor? What should you *definitely* not tell your current client about the earlier project?

- Is it ethical to undertake a research project when you think that you already know what the findings will be? Can you generalize findings from two years ago to today?

- Should you help this company define its problem, and, if so, how?

---

[15]Otis Port, "Quality: Small and Midsize Companies Seize the Challenge—Not a Moment Too Soon," *Business Week* (November 30, 1992), pp. 66–72; "L.L.Bean Scores Efficiency Gains With Data Collection Upgrade," *Modern Materials Handling* 52 (December 1997), pp. 12–14.

[16]Jeremy Main, "How to Steal the Best Ideas Around," *Fortune* (October 19, 1992), pp. 102–106. See also Douglas Brownlie, "The Conduct of Marketing Audits," *Industrial Marketing Management* 25 (January 1996), pp. 11–22; Subra Balakrishnan, "Benefits of Customer and Competitive Orientations in Industrial Markets," *Industrial Marketing Management* 25 (July 1996), pp. 257–269; Lyndon Simkin and Sally Dibb, "Key Business Dilemmas and the Marketing Remit in Business-to-Business Marketing Services," *International Journal of Advertising* 17, no. 3 (1998), pp. 321–347.

Ethnographic methods, which increasingly are being used by marketers, provide another example of the selected case approach to develop insights. These procedures, which have been adapted from anthropology, involve the detached and prolonged observation of consumers' emotional responses, cognitions, and behaviors during their ordinary daily lives. Unlike anthropologists, though, who might live in the group being studied for months or years, ethnographers use a combination of direct observations, interviews, and video and audio recordings to make their observations more quickly. For example, ethnographers at Intel played a large part in the development of the "couch pad," a hand-held flat-screen display that shows Web pages related to TV programs. The ethnographer's inspiration came from watching real people watch Web TV and squabble over how much of the screen should be devoted to data from the Web. The hand-held display, which shows a Web page related to the TV program being viewed, allows one person to look at Web sites while another views TV.[17]

Descriptive Research

A great deal of marketing research can be considered descriptive research. Descriptive research is used when the purpose is as follows:

1. To describe the characteristics of certain groups. For example, based on information gathered from known users of our particular product, we might attempt to develop a profile of the "average user" with respect to income, gender, age, educational level, and so on.

2. To estimate the proportion of people in a specified population who behave in a certain way. We might be interested, say, in estimating the proportion of people within a specified radius of a proposed shopping complex who would shop at the center.

3. To make specific predictions. We might be interested in predicting the level of sales for each of the next five years so that we could plan for the hiring and training of new sales representatives.

Descriptive research encompasses an array of research objectives. The fact that a study is a descriptive study, however, does not mean that it is simply a fact-gathering expedition:

> Facts do not lead anywhere. Indeed, facts, as facts, are the commonest, cheapest, and most useless of all commodities. Anyone with a questionnaire can gather thousands of facts a day—and probably not find much real use for them. What makes facts practical and valuable is the glue of explanation and understanding, the framework of theory, the tie-rod of conjecture. Only when facts can be fleshed to a skeletal theory do they become meaningful in the solution of problems.[18]

---

[17]Dean Takahashi, "Doing Fieldwork in the High-Tech Jungle," *The Wall Street Journal* (October 27, 1998), pp. B1, B22. For discussion of the basics of the ethnographic methods, see Craig J. Thompson, "Interpreting Consumers: A Hermeneutical Framework for Deriving Marketing Insights from the Texts of Consumers' Consumption Stories," *Journal of Marketing Research* 34 (November 1997), pp. 438–455; Hy Mariampolski, "The Power of Ethnography," *Journal of the Market Research Society* 41 (January 1999), pp. 75–86.

[18]Robert Ferber, Donald F. Blankertz, and Sidney Hollander, Jr., *Marketing Research* (New York: The Ronald Press Co., 1964), p. 153. See also Thomas T. Semon, "Marketing Research Needs Basic Research," *Marketing News* (March 14, 1994), p. 12.

The researcher should not submit to the temptation of beginning a descriptive research study with the vague thought that the data collected should be interesting. A good descriptive study presupposes much prior knowledge about the phenomenon studied. It rests on one or more specific hypotheses. These conjectural statements guide the research in specific directions. In this respect, a descriptive study design is very different from an exploratory study design. Whereas an exploratory study is characterized by its flexibility, descriptive studies can be considered rigid. Descriptive studies require a *clear specification* of the *who, what, when, where, why,* and *how* of the research.

Consider a chain of food convenience stores planning to open a new outlet. The company wants to determine how people come to patronize the new outlet. Consider some of the questions that would need to be answered before data collection for this descriptive study could begin. Who is to be considered a patron? Anyone who enters the store? What if they do not buy anything but just participate in the grand-opening prize giveaway? Perhaps a patron should be defined as anyone who purchases anything from the store. Should patrons be defined on the basis of the family unit, or should they be defined as individuals, even though the individuals come from the same family? What characteristics of these patrons should be measured? Are we interested in their age and sex, or perhaps in where they live and how they came to know about our store? When shall we measure them—while they are shopping, or later? Should the study take place during the first weeks of operation of the store, or should the study be delayed until the situation has stabilized somewhat? Certainly, if we are interested in word-of-mouth influence, we must wait at least until that influence has a chance to operate. Where shall we measure the patrons? Should it be in the store, or immediately outside of the store, or should we attempt to contact them at home? Why do we want to measure them? Are we going to use these measurements to plan promotional strategy? In that case the emphasis might be on measuring how people become aware of the store. Or are we going to use them as a basis for locating other stores? In that case the emphasis might shift more to determining the trading area of the store. How shall we measure them? Shall we use a questionnaire, or shall we observe their purchasing behavior? If we use a questionnaire, what form will it take? Will it be highly structured? Will it be in the form of a scale? How will it be administered? By telephone? By mail? Perhaps by personal interview?

These questions are not the only ones that would be or should be asked. Certainly, some of the answers will be implicit in the hypothesis or hypotheses that guide the descriptive research. Others, though, will not be obvious. The researcher will be able to specify them only after some labored thought or even after a small pilot or exploratory study. In either case, the researcher is well advised to delay collecting that first item of information with which to test the hypotheses until clear judgments of the who, what, when, where, why, and how of descriptive research have been made.

The researcher should also delay data collection until a determination can be made on how the data are to be analyzed. Ideally, one would have a set of dummy tables developed before beginning the collection process. A **dummy table** is a table that is used to catalog the data collected. It is a statement of how the analysis will be structured and conducted. It is complete in all respects save for filling in the actual numbers; that is, it contains a title, headings, and specific categories for the variables making up the table. All that remains after collecting the data is to count the number of cases of each type. Table 4.3 illustrates a table that might be used by a women's specialty store investigating whether it is serving a particular age segment and whether this segment differs from that of its competitors.

Note that the table lists the particular age segments the proprietor wishes to compare. It is crucial that this specification of variables and categories be made before data collection begins. The statistical tests that will be used to uncover the relationship between age and store preference should also be specified before data collection begins. Inexperienced researchers often question the need for such hard, detailed decisions before collecting the data. They assume that delaying these decisions until after the data are collected will somehow make the decisions easier. Just the opposite is true, as any experienced researcher will attest:

> Most difficult for the beginning researcher to anticipate will be the analytical problems he may face after the data are gathered. He tends to believe that a wide variety of facts will be enough to solve anything. Only after struggling with sloppy, stubborn, and intractable facts, with data not adequate for the testing of hypotheses and with data that are interesting but incapable of supporting practical recommendations for action will he be fully aware that the big "mistakes" of research usually are made in the early stages. Each definition of a problem or problem variable will create different facts or findings, and a formulation once made serves to restrict the scope of analysis. No problem is definitively formulated until the researcher can specify how he will make his analysis and how the results will contribute to a practical solution.[19]

Once the data have been collected and analysis is begun, it is too late to lament, "If only we had collected information on that variable" or "If only we had measured the *Y* variable using a finer scale." Rectifying such mistakes at this time is next to impossible. Rather, the analyst must account for such contingencies when planning the study. Structuring the tables used to analyze the data makes such planning easier.

An alternative way of ensuring that the information collected in a descriptive study will address the objectives motivating it is to specify in advance the objective each question addresses, the reason the question is included, and the analysis in which the question will be used, although not going as far as laying out all the cross-classification tables. Although output planning like this is extremely valuable, there is added merit in specifying all anticipated dummy tables in advance. The dummy tables are particularly valuable in providing clues on how to phrase the individual questions and code the responses.

TABLE 4.3	Dummy Table: Store Preference by Age		
Age	*Prefer A*	*Prefer B*	*Prefer C*
Less than 30			
30–39			
40 or more			

---

[19]Ferber, Blankertz, and Hollander, *Marketing Research,* p. 171.

Figure 4.3 is an overview of the various types of descriptive studies. The basic division is between longitudinal and cross-sectional designs. The **cross-sectional study** is the most common and most familiar. It typically involves a sample of elements from the population of interest. Various characteristics of the elements or sample members are measured once. **Longitudinal studies,** on the other hand, involve panels. A **panel** is a fixed sample of elements. The elements may be stores, dealers, individuals, or other entities. The panel or sample remains relatively constant through time, although periodic additions are made to replace dropouts or to keep it representative. The sample members in a panel are measured repeatedly, as contrasted to the one-time measurement in a cross-sectional study. Both cross-sectional and longitudinal studies have weaknesses and strengths. Because they are both common, let us briefly review the principal advantages and disadvantages of each.

Longitudinal Analysis

True longitudinal studies rely on panel data and panel methods. As mentioned, a panel is a fixed sample of subjects that is measured repeatedly. There are two types of panels: true panels and omnibus panels. **True panels** rely on repeated measurements of the same variables. Nielsen maintains an international panel of households as a basis of its Homescan service. The panel households use a hand-held scanner to record every UPC-coded item they purchase. They simply pass the scanner across the UPCs on the packages of the purchased items when they return from shopping and then answer a programmed set of questions (such as regarding the store where purchased, price paid) by responding to a series of prompts from the machine. Similarly, National Purchase Diary (NPD) maintains a consumer panel of families who record their purchases in a paper diary when they return from shopping. The operations of these panels will be detailed when we discuss secondary sources of information in Chapter 6. The important point to note now is that each sample member is measured each time on the same characteristics—purchases.

In an **omnibus panel,** a sample of elements is still selected and maintained, but the information collected from the members varies. At one time, it may be attitudes about a new product. At another time, the panel members might be asked to evaluate alternative advertising copy. In each case, a sample might be selected from the larger group, which is, in turn, a sample of the population. The subsample might be drawn randomly. More than likely, though, participants with the desired characteristics will be chosen from a total panel. For example, the Parker Pen Company maintains a panel of 1,100 individuals who were chosen because they expressed some interest in writing instruments and, of course, because of their willingness to

---

FIGURE 4.3   **Classification of Descriptive Studies**

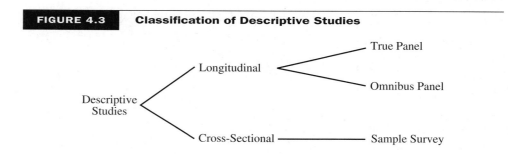

participate. Parker Pen uses selected members of this panel to evaluate new writing instruments. If the new instrument is a fountain pen, they often choose individuals who prefer fountain pens to test the products. Those chosen and the information sought varies from project to project.

Nickelodeon, the children's cable television network, uses a panel of children to help it evaluate its programming and magazine ideas. In an interesting twist, it uses online computer connections to gather their reactions. See Research Realities 4.4.

The distinction between the true panel and the omnibus panel is important. True longitudinal analysis, also called time series analysis, can be performed only on the first type of data, with repeated measurements of the same entities over time. We shall see why when we discuss the method of analysis unique to panel data—the turnover table. The turnover table can be used only when individuals and variables are held constant through time. This is not to deny the value of omnibus panels. Rather, the purpose is simply to erect a caution flag because in other respects (for example, sample design, information collection, and so forth), both types of panels have about the same advantages and disadvantages when compared to cross-sectional studies. Consequently, we shall treat both types together when discussing these general advantages.

Probably the single most important advantage of panel data is analytical. Suppose we are currently subscribing to the type of service that generates consumer purchase data from a panel of 1,000 families. Suppose further that we are interested in determining the effect of a recent package design for our Brand A and that our brand has two main competitors, B and C, and a number of other smaller competitors. Let us classify all these smaller, miscellaneous brands in a single catch-all category, labeled Brand D, and let us consider the performance of our brand at time t_1, before the change, and time t_2, after the package change.

We could perform several types of analyses on these data.[20] We could look at the proportion of those in the panel who bought our brand in period t_1. We could also calculate the proportion of those who bought our brand in period t_2. Suppose these calculations generated the data shown in Table 4.4. The table indicates that the package change was successful. Brand A's market share increased from 20 percent to 25 percent. Further, Brand A seemed to make its gains at the expense of its two major competitors, whose market shares decreased.

But that is not the whole story or even a completely accurate picture of the market changes that occurred. Look at what happens when, in assessing the effect of the package change, the identity of the sample members is maintained. Because we have repeated measures of the same individuals, we can count the number of families who bought Brand A in both periods, those who bought B or C or one of the miscellaneous brands in both periods, and those who switched brands between the two periods. Suppose that Table 4.5 resulted from these tabulations. This table, which is a **turnover table** (also called a **brand-switching matrix**), contains the same basic information as Table 4.4. That is, we see that 200 (or 20 percent) of the families bought Brand A in period t_1, and that 250 (or 25 percent) did so in period t_2.

---

[20]The classic book by Hans Zeisel, *Say It with Figures,* 5th ed. (New York: Harper & Row, 1968), pp. 200–239, has a highly readable version of the analyses that can be performed with panel data. See also Frank J. R. van de Pol, *Issues of Design and Analysis of Panels* (Amsterdam, The Netherlands: Sociometric Research Foundation, 1989); Steven E. Finkel, *Causal Analysis with Panel Data* (Thousand Oaks, CA: Sage Publications, 1995).

RESEARCH REALITIES 4.4

Use of an Online Computer Panel by Nickelodeon

After reading an article in a new magazine, a child pans it, calling the article "stupid." Another says: "It was boring." A third: "A lot of it was a little too weird for me." For market researchers, these sorts of spontaneous comments are priceless, but they're tough to obtain, because kids are often intimidated when they talk to adults. Now Nickelodeon, the children's cable television network, has gotten around that problem by setting up one of the first consumer product testing panels established over a computer network.

"It's a great tool because it gives a real sense of immediacy with the kids," says Michael Hainey, an editor of the *Nickelodeon Magazine* prototype that was skewered by the children. "We liked it because it was a sounding board for kids across the country." The children responded favorably to the magazine overall, Hainey says, but "We'll be rethinking" parts, such as a confusing table of contents and an article on a boy from North Dakota.

The children—75 of them between the ages of 8 and 12 in a dozen areas from Boston to Los Angeles—have been recruited for a two-year stint as participants in "Get hooked on Nick" by Nickelodeon's researchers. Nickelodeon wants to make sure that TV shows, often created by childless New Yorkers, will actually appeal to boys and girls of all races who are between the ages of 2 and 14 and who come from all over the country.

Other TV and movie people also are getting in touch with their fans on services such as CompuServ, Prodigy, and GEnie. Show publicists and directors sometimes go online to see how people reacted to a show that ran the night before. In other fields, computer software companies have been doing market research online in CompuServ forums for years, asking early testers to report problems as they find them.

But Nickelodeon seems to be the first network to formalize online research. The children that it selected all had computers and VCRs. Half are minorities, and half are girls. Family incomes in the group range from $20,000 to $120,000.

The children, who aren't paid, can go online and chat informally with each other or with Nickelodeon researchers three afternoons a week. Sometimes, they post jokes on a bulletin board or contribute a sentence to a fantasy story started by one child. When Nickelodeon wants reaction to a new show or to the magazine, it sends videos or a prototype to 20 kids and asks them to sign on to a special conference at a set time for one to two hours.

If a special research project comes up, the children are there. In one case, Nickelodeon sent 12 children videotapes of a new show called "The Tomorrow People" and then asked them their opinions. One conclusion: Many children didn't realize that action was shifting among several countries. Producers inserted graphics in the show to clarify the changes in location.

In December, when the network had just started the online project, it used the kids' group to decide whether to produce a special news show on Somalia. Researchers found that the children already understood the issues, and Nickelodeon dropped the idea.

Online isn't perfect, Nickelodeon researchers concede. "You'd prefer to see them in person," says Hainey. Online "tends to be a lot of monosyllabic typing." It also doesn't work for younger children, who reveal more by their body language than by their spoken or written words.

Therefore, Nickelodeon continues more traditional research, including analyzing Nielsen and Arbitron ratings, in-person focus groups, interviews at schools, and tracking letters and calls about shows. But the online group eliminates travel costs and lets people in New York get reaction in a few hours to questions such as preferred sneaker styles or what music children consider oldies—"Beatoven," one boy replied. It has already become "an unbelievable research resource to us," says Rande Price, manager of research.

Source: William M. Bulkeley, "Nickelodeon Sets Up Online Focus Group," *The Wall Street Journal* (March 29, 1993), p. B4. Reprinted by permission of Wall Street Journal, © Dow Jones & Company, Inc. All Rights Reserved Worldwide. See also Mark Lorando, "Kid Shows 'R' Us: Nickelodeon Rises in the Ratings by Paying More Attention to Children Than Their Parents," *The Times-Picayune* (March 23, 1998), p. D1.

| TABLE 4.4 | Number of Families in Panel Purchasing Each Brand | | |

Brand Purchased	During First Time Period, t_1	During Second Time Period, t_2
A	200	250
B	300	270
C	350	330
D	150	150
Total	1,000	1,000

| TABLE 4.5 | Number of Families in Panel Buying Each Brand in Each Period | | | | |

		During Second Time Period, t_2				
		Bought A	Bought B	Bought C	Bought D	Total
	Bought A	175	25	0	0	200
During First Time	Bought B	0	225	50	25	300
Period, t_1	Bought C	0	0	280	70	350
	Bought D	75	20	0	55	150
	Total	250	270	330	150	1,000

But Table 4.5 also shows that Brand A did not make its market share gains at the expense of Brands B and C, as originally suggested, but rather captured some of the families who previously bought one of the miscellaneous brands: 75 families switched from the catch-all category, Brand D, which they purchased during period t_1, to Brand A in period t_2. And, as a matter of fact, Brand A lost some of its previous users to Brand B during the period: 25 families switched from Brand A in period t_1 to Brand B in period t_2.

Table 4.5 also allows the calculation of brand loyalty. Consider Brand A, for example; 175, or 87.5 percent of the 200 who bought Brand A in period t_1, remained "loyal" to it (bought it again) in period t_2. By dividing each cell entry by the row or previous period totals, one can assess these brand loyalties and can also throw the basic changes that occurred in the market into bolder relief. Table 4.6, produced by such calculations, suggests, for example, that among the three major brands, Brand A elicited the greatest buying loyalty and Brand B the least. This is important to know because it indicates whether families like the brand when they do try it.[21]

[21]Table 4.6 can also be viewed as a transition matrix, because it depicts the brand-buying changes or transitions occurring from period to period. Knowing the proportion switching allows early prediction of the ultimate success of some new product or some change in market strategy. See, for example, Seymour Sudman and Robert Ferber, *Consumer Panels* (Chicago: American Marketing Association, 1979), pp. 19–27, which also provides an excellent review of the literature on such facets of consumer panels as their uses, sampling and sampling biases, data-collection methods, conditioning, data processing and file maintenance, costs of operating, and choosing a consumer panel service. See also Scott Menard, *Longitudinal Research* (Thousand Oaks, CA: Sage Publications, Inc., 1991).

TABLE 4.6	**Brand Loyalty and Brand-Switching Probabilities among Families in Panel**

		During Second Time Period, t_2				
		Bought A	*Bought B*	*Bought C*	*Bought D*	*Total*
During First Time Period, t_1	Bought A	.875	.125	.000	.000	1.000
	Bought B	.000	.750	.167	.083	1.000
	Bought C	.000	.000	.800	.200	1.000
	Bought D	.500	.133	.000	.367	1.000

Whether those who switched from one of the miscellaneous brands to Brand A were induced to do so by the package change is open to question for reasons that will be discussed in the next chapter. The point is that turnover or brand-switching analysis can be performed only when *repeated* measures are made over time, for the same variables for the same subjects. It is *not* appropriate for omnibus panel data, in which the variables being measured are constantly changing, nor is it appropriate for cross-sectional studies, even if successive cross-sectional samples are taken.

The turnover table can produce some special analysis advantages. For example, one can look at changes in individual entity behavior and attempt to relate them to a succession of marketing tactics—for example, advertising copy changes, package changes, price changes, and so on. Further, because the same subjects are measured before and after changes in marketing variables, small changes in the criterion variable are more easily identified than if separate studies were made using two or more independent samples. Variation of the criterion variable in the latter case may be due to changes in the composition of the sample. In sum, the turnover table is the heart of panel analysis and any analysis of true panel data that does not include a turnover table is overlooking the unique contribution that panels can make to the study of change.

Although the major advantage of a panel is analytical, panels also have some advantages in terms of the information collected in a study. This is particularly true with respect to classification information, such as income, education, age, and occupation. In many studies, there is a great deal of classification information that we would like to secure, as this allows more sophisticated analysis of the results. Unfortunately, cross-sectional studies are limited in this respect. Respondents being contacted for the first and only time typically do not stand still for lengthy, time-consuming interviews. The situation is different in panels because panel members are usually compensated for their participation; thus, the interviews can be longer and more exacting, or there can be several interviews. Also, the sponsoring firm can afford to spend more time and effort securing accurate classification information, because this information can be used in a number of studies.

Panel data are also believed to be more accurate than cross-sectional data, because panel data tend to be freer from the errors associated with reporting past behavior. Errors arise in reporting past behavior because humans tend to forget, partly because time has elapsed, but partly also for other reasons. In particular, research has shown that events and experiences are forgotten more readily if they are inconsistent with attitudes or beliefs that are important to the person or threaten the person's self-esteem. Because behavior is recorded as it occurs in a panel, less reliance is placed on a respondent's memory. When diaries are used to record purchases, the problems should be virtually eliminated because the respondent is instructed to record the purchases immediately upon returning home.

When other behaviors are of interest, respondents are asked to record those behaviors as they occur, thus minimizing the possibility that they will be forgotten or distorted when they are eventually asked about. Figure 4.4, for example, shows a page out of an Arbitron radio listening diary. These diaries, which are used to determine radio station listening audiences, are used by the stations to make programming decisions and by advertisers to figure out what to buy. Every person over the age of 12 in each of the participating households receives a new diary for each week he or she participates. A key advantage of the diary is that it is completely portable and can be filled out anywhere, which tends to increase its accuracy.

Errors also occur because the interviewer and the respondent have distinct personalities and different social roles. Very often respondents say what they think the interviewers *want* to hear or what they feel the interviewers *should* hear. The panel design helps reduce this interaction bias. First, respondents come to trust the interviewer to a greater degree because of repetitive contact. Second, more frequent contact creates rapport.

The main disadvantage of panels is that they are nonrepresentative. The agreement to participate involves a commitment on the part of the designated sample member. Some individuals refuse this commitment. They do not wish to be bothered with filling out consumer diaries or testing products or evaluating advertising copy or whatever else may be involved with the panel operation. Consumer panels that require households to keep a record of their purchases, for example, generally have cooperation rates of about 60 percent when participants are contacted in person and lower participation rates if telephone or mail is used for the initial contact.

The better ongoing panel operations select prospective participants systematically. The sponsoring organization attempts to generate and maintain panels that are representative of the total population of interest with respect to such characteristics as age, occupation, education, and so on. Quite often the organization will use quota samples so that the proportion of those in the sample with a particular characteristic (such as gender) equals the proportion in the population.[22]

All the research organization can do, though, is designate the families or respondents that are to be included in the sample. It cannot force individuals to participate, nor can it require continued participation from those who initially choose to cooperate. It often encourages participation by offering some premium or by paying panel members for their cooperation. Nevertheless, a significant percentage of individuals designated for inclusion refuse to cooperate initially or quickly drop from the panel. Depending on the type of cooperation needed, the refusal and attrition rates might run over 50 percent.

---

[22]Quota samples are explained in Chapter 10.

FIGURE 4.4   **Arbitron Radio Listening Diary**

THURSDAY

	Time		Station			Place			
	Start	**Stop**	Call letters or station name *Don't know? Use program name or dial setting.*	*Check (√) one*		*Check (√) one*			
				AM	**FM**	**At Home**	**In a Car**	**At Work**	**Other Place**
→ Early Morning (from 5 AM)									
→ Midday									
→ Late Afternoon									
→ Night (to 5 AM Friday)									

If you didn't hear a radio today, please check here. ☐

Source: © 1994 The Arbitron Company.

Of course, not all panel attrition is due to quitting. Some individuals move away and others die. In any case, the question arises whether the panel is then indeed representative of the population, since those designated to participate are not participating. Further, the payment of a reward for cooperation raises the question of whether particular types of people are attracted to such panels.

It is generally accepted, for example, that panel samples under-represent African Americans, persons with poor English-language skills, and those at the extremes of the socioeconomic spectrum.[23] Whether these types of nonrepresentativeness present problems depends on the purpose of the study and the particular variables of interest. It has also been argued that panels are nonrepresentative in other ways, including their attitudes and behaviors, although specific empirical evidence is sketchy.

In a series of studies investigating the "representativeness" of a continuing household panel, Market Facts compared survey results on specific issues when the data were gathered using their mail panel against the data gathered from randomly selected telephone samples. Research Realities 4.5 displays some of the findings with respect to selected product ownership, lifestyle, and leisure activity characteristics. As the sample of comparisons suggests, the evidence led Market Facts to conclude that "mail panel samples are likely to parallel the population in most, if not all, dimensions of leisure activity and lifestyle."[24] However, the series of studies also revealed instances of significant differences between the data that were generated by mail panel and data that were generated through telephone interviewing, leading the company to conclude that great caution must be exercised when using mail panels because of their potential to not be representative. The trouble with bias that is due to unrepresentativeness, of course, is that one never knows in advance whether it will affect the results, much less how.

Cross-Sectional Analysis

The cross-sectional study is the best known and most important type of descriptive design, as measured by the number of times it is used in comparison to other methods. The cross-sectional study has two distinguishing features. First, it provides a snapshot of the variables of interest at a single point in time, as contrasted to the longitudinal study, which provides a series of pictures that, when pieced together, provide a movie of the situation and the changes that are occurring. Second, the sample of elements is typically selected to be representative of some known universe. Therefore, a great deal of emphasis is placed on selecting sample members, usually with a probability sampling plan. That is one reason that the technique is often called a **sample survey.** The probability sampling plan allows the sampling error associated with the statistics generated from the sample, but used to describe the universe, to be determined. The "large" number of cases usually resulting from a sample survey also allows for cross-classification of the variables.

---

[23]"Mail Panels vs. General Samples: How Similar and How Different," *Research on Research* 59 (Chicago: Market Facts, Inc., undated).

[24]Ibid., p. 4.

RESEARCH REALITIES 4.5

Comparison of Responses of the Market Facts Mail Panel and a Randomly Selected Telephone Sample

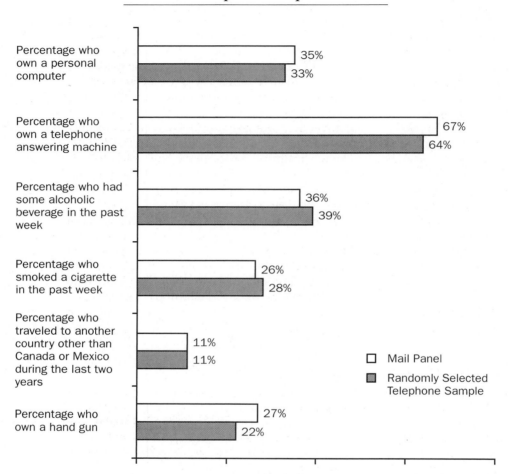

Source: "Mail Panels vs. General Samples: How Similar and How Different," *Research on Research* 59 (Chicago: Market Facts, Inc., undated).

The objective of cross-classification analysis is to establish categories so that classification in one category implies classification in one or more other categories. The method of cross-classification analysis will be detailed later, in the discussion of tabulation. For the moment, simply note that it involves counting the *simultaneous occurrence* of the variables of interest. For example, suppose that management believes that one's occupation is an important factor in determining the consumption of its product. Further, suppose that the proposition to be examined is that white-collar workers are more apt to use the product than blue-collar workers. This hypothesis could be examined in a cross-sectional study. Measurements would be taken from a representative sample of the population with respect to occupation and use of the product. In cross tabulation, researchers would count the number of cases that fell in each of the following classes:

- White-collar and use the product
- Blue-collar and use the product
- White-collar and do not use the product
- Blue-collar and do not use the product

That is, the emphasis would be on the relative frequency of occurrence of the joint phenomenon—white-collar occupation and user of the product. If the hypothesis is to be supported by the sample data, the proportion of white-collar workers using the product should exceed the proportion of blue-collar workers using the product.

As the chapters on analysis should illustrate, cross-classification analysis is a bread-and-butter technique that marketing researchers use to make sense out of survey data. One type of cross-classification analysis that is particularly effective for descriptive research arises when there is a series of "properly spaced" surveys, because this allows cohort analysis of the data. The **cohort**, which refers to the aggregate of individuals who *experience the same event within the same time interval*, serves as the basic unit of analysis in such studies. A very common analytic emphasis is on birth cohorts, or groups of people born within the same time interval. The potential usefulness of cohort analysis can be seen by looking at the age-based per capita soft-drink consumption data in Table 4.7. What do you think these 1979 data portend for the future of the soft-drink industry? A typical interpretation would suggest dire consequences as the large but young cohorts grow older and are replaced by smaller cohorts because of declining birthrates in the United States at the time. As a matter of fact, most people, on seeing these data, might be inclined to agree with the *Business Week* article at the time that stated, "By 1985, there will be four million fewer persons in the thirteen-to-twenty-four age group. And these four million persons would have consumed some 3.3 billion cans of soft drinks annually."[25]

A birth cohort analysis of soft-drink consumption data would focus on the changing consumption patterns of identifiable groups as they age—for example, all those born between 1940 and 1949. Table 4.8, for example, shows the percentage of

TABLE 4.7	Per Capita Consumption of Soft Drinks by Various Age Categories

Age	Per Capita Consumption, 1979
20–29	48 gallons
30–39	42 gallons
40–49	35 gallons
50+	24 gallons

Source: Joseph O. Rentz, Fred D. Reynolds, and Roy G. Stout, "Analyzing Changing Consumption Patterns with Cohort Analysis," *Journal of Marketing Research* 20 (February 1983), p. 12. Published by the American Marketing Association. For later statistics on the consumption of soft drinks, see Greg W. Prince, "The Beverage Market Index, 1999," *Beverage World* 118 (May 1999), pp. 58–70.

[25]"The Graying of the Soft Drink Industry," *Business Week* (May 23, 1977), p. 68.

TABLE 4.8	Consumption of Soft Drinks by Various Age Cohorts (Percentage Consuming on a Typical Day)				

Age	1950	1960	1969	1979	
8–19	52.9	62.6	73.2	81.0	
20–29	45.2	60.7	76.0	75.8	C8
30–39	33.9	46.6	67.7	71.4	C7
40–49	28.2	40.8	58.6	67.8	C6
50+	18.1	28.8	50.0	51.9	C5
		C1	C2	C3	C4

C1—cohort born prior to 1900   C5—cohort born 1931–1940
C2—cohort born 1901–1910   C6—cohort born 1940–1949
C3—cohort born 1911–1920   C7—cohort born 1950–1959
C4—cohort born 1921–1930   C8—cohort born 1960–1969

Source: Joseph O. Rentz, Fred D. Reynolds, and Roy G. Stout, "Analyzing Changing Consumption Patterns with Cohort Analysis," *Journal of Marketing Research* 20 (February 1983), p. 12. Published by the American Marketing Association.

people in each age cohort born between 1900 and 1969 who consume soft drinks on a typical day. Note that Table 4.8 is constructed so that the interval between any two surveys or measurement periods corresponds approximately to the age-class interval that is used to define the age cohorts used in the study (10 years in this case). Because of this, the consumption of the various age cohorts over time can be determined by reading down the diagonal. Consider Cohort C5, for example, which refers to all those born between 1931 and 1940. The C5 diagonal indicates that 52.9 percent of the people in this age group who were interviewed in 1950 consumed soft drinks on a typical day; by 1960 that percentage had increased to 60.7 percent, to 67.7 percent by 1969, and to 67.8 percent by 1979. A complete analysis of the cohort data in Table 4.8 that looks at the percentage of people consuming soft drinks and other data that show the amount consumed per capita suggests just the opposite conclusion of the *Business Week* article:

> Specifically, each succeeding cohort has increased its consumption and once the level is established consumption will remain relatively stable over the life course. Thus consumption in the cohort aged 20–29 will not decrease as the cohort ages. Further, total soft drink consumption would increase as the larger and younger cohorts (whose per capita consumption is high) replace the smaller and older cohorts (whose per capita consumption is lower).[26]

[26]Joseph O. Rentz, Fred D. Reynolds, and Roy G. Stout, "Analyzing Changing Consumption Patterns with Cohort Analysis," *Journal of Marketing Research* 20 (February 1983), p. 13. This article explains cohort analysis and uses it to analyze the effects of aging and cohort succession on consumption of a product class. See also Joseph O. Rentz and Fred D. Reynolds, "Forecasting the Effects of an Aging Population on Product Consumption: An Age-Period-Cohort Framework," *Journal of Marketing Research* 28 (August 1991), pp. 355–360. For general discussion of the use of cohort analysis in forecasting, see Joseph L. Bonnici and William B. Fredenberger, "Cohort Analysis—A Forecasting Tool," *Journal of Business Forecasting* 10 (Fall 1991), pp. 9–13. For another application, namely in understanding the postwar decline in savings in the United States, see Jagadeesh Gokhale, Laurence J. Kotlikoff, and John Sabellhaus, "Understanding the Postwar Decline in U.S. Saving: A Cohort Analysis," *Brookings Papers on Economic Activity,* no. 1 (1996), pp. 315–407.

ETHICAL DILEMMA 4.2

Marketing Research Insights was asked to carry out the data-collection and analysis procedures for a study designed by a consumer goods company. After studying the research purpose and design, a consultant for Marketing Research Insights concluded that the design was poorly conceived. First, he thought that the design was more complex than was necessary, inasmuch as some of the data could be obtained through secondary sources, precluding the necessity of much primary data collection. Second, the proposed choice of primary data collection would not produce the kinds of information sought by the company.

Although the consultant advised the company of his opinions, the company insisted on proceeding with the proposed design. Marketing Research Insights' management was reluctant to undertake the study, as it believed that the firm's reputation would be harmed if its name was associated with poor research.

- What decision would you make if you were a consultant for Marketing Research Insights?
- In general, should a researcher advance his or her opinion of a proposed design, or should the researcher remain silent and simply do the work?
- Is it ethical to remain silent in such situations?

By the mid-1990s, the adult population of the United States seemed to divide into six distinct cohorts, ranging in age from the Depression Cohort to Generation X.[27]

Not only does cross-classification analysis serve, then, as a basic analytic technique in descriptive research studies, but when there is a series of properly spaced surveys, cohort analysis, or a special form of cross-classification analysis, can be used to advantage.

The sample survey has several disadvantages, however. These include superficial analysis of the phenomenon, high cost, and the technical sophistication required to conduct survey research. Let us consider each disadvantage in turn.

One common criticism of survey data is that they typically do not penetrate very deeply below the surface, since breadth is often emphasized at the expense of depth. There is ordinarily an emphasis on the calculation of statistics that efficiently summarize the wide variety of data collected from the sometimes large cross section of subjects. Yet the very process of generating summary statistics to describe the phenomenon suggests that the eventual "average" might not accurately describe any individual entity making up the aggregate. The situation is much like that of "the guy who slept with his feet in the refrigerator and his head in the stove and who, on the average, was comfortable."

---

[27]See Geoffrey Meredith and Charles Schewe, "The Power of Cohorts," *American Demographics* 16 (December 1994), pp. 22–27, 30–31. For a discussion of some of the implications of these cohorts for marketers, see also Michael M. Phillips, "Selling by Evoking What Defines a Generation," *The Wall Street Journal* (August 13, 1996), pp. B1, B7.

Second, a survey is expensive in terms of time and money. It will often be months before a single hypothesis can be tested because of the necessary preliminaries so vital to survey research. The entire research process—from problem definition through developing the measuring instrument, designing the sample, collecting the data, and editing, coding, and tabulating the data—must be executed before an analyst can begin to examine the hypotheses that guide the study. As parts of the remainder of this book will show, each of these tasks can be formidable in its own right. Each can require large investments of time, energy, and money.

Survey research also requires a good deal of technical skill. The research analyst must either have the skills required at each stage of the process or have access to such skills in, say, the form of technical consultants. It is the rare individual indeed who has the technical sophistication both to develop an attitude scale and to design a complex probability sample.

Summary

A research design is the blueprint for a study that guides the collection and analysis of data. Just as different blueprints reflect differing degrees of detail, so research designs vary in their specificity. Some are very detailed and involve the investigation of specific "if-then" causal relationships, whereas others simply provide a picture of the overall situation. Figure 4.5 summarizes the important features of the different designs.

Exploratory research is basically "general picture" research. It is quite useful for becoming familiar with a phenomenon, for clarifying concepts, for developing but not testing "if-then" statements, and for establishing priorities for further research. Exploratory studies are characterized by their flexibility. The investigator's imagination and ingenuity will guide the pursuit, although literature searches, experience surveys, focus groups, and selected cases have proved to be useful for gaining insight into a phenomenon.

Descriptive studies are anything but flexible. Rather, they are rigid in requiring a precise specification of the who, what, when, where, why, and how of the research. Descriptive studies rest on one or more specific hypotheses. They are used when the research is intended to describe the characteristics of certain groups, to estimate the proportion of people who behave in a certain way, or to make predictions.

Descriptive studies are of two types: longitudinal and cross-sectional. Longitudinal studies rely on panel data. A panel is simply a fixed sample of individuals or some other entities from whom repeated measurements are taken. There are two different kinds of panels—panels in which the same measurements are taken in each measurement period (true panels) and those in which different measurements are taken in each measurement period (omnibus panels). The turnover table, a most informative method of analysis that is unique to panel data, is applicable only to panels in which the same variables are measured over time.

Cross-sectional studies, or sample surveys, rely on a sample of elements from the population of interest that are measured at a single point in time. A great deal of emphasis is placed on the scientific generation of the sample so that the members are representative of the population of interest. A typical sample survey involves summarizing and generalizing the data collected. The analysis of sample survey results rests heavily on the cross-classification table, which is used to report the joint occurrence of the variables of interest.

Cohort analysis is a special type of cross-classification analysis that can be used when there is a series of surveys and the spacing between them corresponds to a natural, or cohort, division of the population, where a cohort refers to the aggregate of individuals who experience the same event within the same time interval.

FIGURE 4.5   **Types of Research Designs**

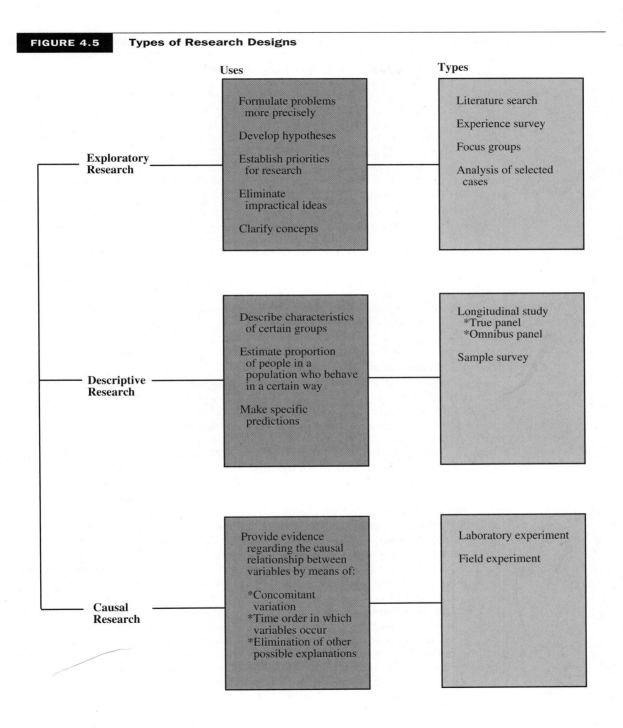

Questions

1. What is a research design? Is a research design necessary to conduct a study?
2. What are the different types of research designs? What is the basic purpose of each?
3. What is the crucial tenet of research?
4. What are the basic uses for exploratory research?
5. What is the key characteristic of exploratory research?
6. What are some of the more productive types of exploratory research? What are the characteristics of each type?
7. What are the basic uses of descriptive research?
8. What is the key characteristic of descriptive research?
9. What are the main types of descriptive studies, and what do their differences mean?
10. What are the basic types of panels, and of what importance are the differences that exist?
11. What is the turnover table? How is it read? What kinds of analyses does a turnover table allow that cannot be done with other types of studies?
12. What is the fundamental thrust of a sample survey? What are its advantages and disadvantages?
13. What are the basic types of cross-sectional studies? What are their relative advantages and disadvantages?
14. What is a cross-tabulation table? What is the objective of cross-classification analysis?
15. What is a cohort? What is cohort analysis?

Applications and Problems

1. Industrial Health Technologies, Ltd. (IHT), located on the East Coast, is a manufacturer of industrial respirators. The research and development (R&D) department recently designed a prototype respirator for the asbestos-abatement industry that is battery powered and would extend the operating life of current models from 8 to 30 hours without recharging. A similar model introduced by Deep Mine Safety Apparatus (DMSA) four months earlier was marginally successful. However, both IHT's and DMSA's models suffered from a technical flaw. It was found that use of the respirators for 30 hours without recharging required 18 hours of recharging to return the batteries to a state of full charge. Notwithstanding this technical flaw, IHT's management team, headed by Chuck Montford, was excited about R&D's efforts. Chuck and Carl Corydon, IHT's marketing manager, had decided to do a sample survey to gauge customer reaction to the new battery capability. A random sample of 100 asbestos-abatement firms was to be chosen from a list of East Coast federally licensed asbestos-abatement firms. Mail questionnaires were designed to determine respondents' attitudes and opinions toward this new respirator.

   In this situation, is the research design appropriate? If yes, why? If no, why not?

2. Emilie Malti, president of Jamaican Specialties, a specialty food marketing firm, was convinced that the target audience for her line of Caribbean conserves in mango, lime, passion fruit, and papaya consisted of women, ages 25 to 44, with household incomes of $30,000 and up. Jamaican Specialties's major competitor's (Pacific Flavor) market segment appeared to be more widely dispersed with respect to both age and income. Emilie and her marketing vice president, Ruth Marion, attributed this difference to the type of magazines in which Pacific Flavor advertised. Emilie and Ruth decided to conduct a study to determine the socioeconomic characteristics of their firm's market segment. They formed a panel of 800 women ages 18 and up. Mail questionnaires would be sent to all panel members. One month after receiving all questionnaires, the company would again send similar questionnaires to all panel members. In this situation, is the research design appropriate? If yes, why? If no, why not?

3.   Telephonic was a large supplier of residential telephones and related services in the southwestern United States. The R&D department of Telephonic recently designed a prototype with a memory function that can store the number of calls and the contents of the calls for a period of 48 hours. A similar model, introduced by Telephonic's competitor three months earlier, was marginally successful. However, both models suffered from a technical flaw. It was found that a call lasting more than 20 minutes would result in a loss of the dial tone for 90 seconds. This was mainly attributable to the activation of the memory function. Notwithstanding the flaw, management was excited about the efforts of the R&D department. They decided to do a field study to gauge consumer reaction to the memory capacity. A random sample of 1,000 respondents was to be chosen from three major metropolitan areas in the Southwest. The questionnaires were designed to uncover respondents' attitudes and opinions toward the new phone.

In this situation, is the research design appropriate? If yes, why? If no, why not?

4.   A medium-sized manufacturer of high-speed copiers and duplicators was introducing a new desktop model. The vice president of communications had to decide between two advertising programs for this product. He preferred advertising program gamma and was sure it would generate more sales than its counterpart, advertising program beta. The next day he was to meet with the senior vice president of marketing and planning to decide on an appropriate research design for a study that would aid in the final decision about which advertising program to implement.

What research design would you recommend? Justify your choice.

5.   Gettings & Gettings, a father-and-son insurance agency in Lafayette, Indiana, was concerned with improving its service. In particular, the firm wanted to assess whether customers were dissatisfied with current service and, if so, the nature of this dissatisfaction. What research design would you recommend? Justify your choice.

6.   Greg Martin is the owner of a pizza restaurant that caters to college students. Through informal conversations with his customers, Greg has begun to suspect that a video-rental store specifically targeting college students would do quite well in the local market. While his informal conversations with students have revealed an overall sense of dissatisfaction with existing rental outlets, he hasn't been able to isolate specific areas of concern. Thinking back to a marketing research course he took in school, Greg has decided that focus group research would be an appropriate method to gather information that might be useful in deciding whether to pursue further development of his idea (that is, developing a formal business plan, store policies, and so on).
    a. What is the decision problem and resulting research problem apparent in this situation?
    b. Who should Greg select as participants in the focus group?
    c. Where should the focus group session be conducted?
    d. Who should be the moderator of the focus group?
    e. Develop a discussion outline for the focus group.

7.   The Federal Reserve (the Fed) controls currency in the United States. Recently, the Fed has been considering some changes in the currency that circulates. One change involves paper money, which is currently all the same size and shape (no matter what the denomination of the bill). Some members of the Fed believe that money would be easier for consumers to handle if it came in different colors. For example, the one-dollar bill could remain green, the five-dollar bill could be printed on blue paper, the ten-dollar bill could be red, and so on. In addition, the Fed is considering changing the size of the bills, so that the five-dollar bill would be larger than the one, the ten would be larger than the five, and so on.

Before making these changes, the Fed believes that it might be useful to conduct some marketing research. Thus, Madison Marketing Research Inc. (MMR) is contacted by the Fed and asked to collect some information to help forecast whether these changes will be successful and popular with consumers. What research should Madison Marketing Research propose? Be specific when describing alternative research designs.

8. The leadership of the Boy Scouts of America (BSA) is concerned about several issues related to their membership. These issues include low retention rates among members (many scouts quit after only one or two years); high turnover rates among leaders; and declining membership in some regions (such as in large urban areas). Design a marketing research program to assist BSA in assessing and reversing these trends.

9. The Pen-Lite Company is a manufacturer of writing instruments such as fountain pens, ballpoint pens, soft-top pens, and mechanical pencils. Typically, these products have been retailed through small and large chains, drugstores, and grocery stores. The company recently diversified into the manufacture of disposable cigarette lighters. Distribution of this product was to be restricted to drugstores and grocery stores because management believed that its target market of low- and middle-income consumers would use these outlets. Your expertise is required to decide on an appropriate research design to determine if this would indeed be the case.

   What research design would you recommend? Justify your choice.

10. Airways Luggage is a producer of cloth-covered luggage, one of the primary advantages of which is its light weight. The company distributes its luggage through major department stores, mail-order houses, clothing retailers, and other retail outlets, such as stationery stores, leather-goods stores, and so on. The company advertises rather heavily, but it also supplements this promotional effort with a large field staff of sales representatives, numbering around 400. The numbers vary because one of the historical problems confronting Airways Luggage has been the large number of sales representatives' resignations. It is not unusual for 10 to 20 percent of the sales force to turn over every year. Because the cost of training a new person is estimated at $5,000 to $10,000, not including the lost sales that might result because of a personnel switch, Ms. Brooks, the sales manager, is rightly concerned. She has been concerned for some time and, therefore, has been conducting exit interviews with each departing sales representative. On the basis of these interviews, she has formulated the opinion that the major reason for this high turnover is general sales representatives' dissatisfaction with company policies, promotional opportunities, and pay. But top management has not been sympathetic to Ms. Brooks's pleas regarding the changes needed in these areas of corporate policy. Rather, it has tended to counter Ms. Brooks's pleas with arguments that too much of what she is suggesting is based on her gut reactions and little hard data. Top management desires more systematic evidence that job dissatisfaction in general and these dimensions of job dissatisfaction in particular are the real reasons for the high turnover before they would be willing to change things. Ms. Brooks has called on the Marketing Research Department in Airways Luggage to assist her in solving her problem.

   a. As a member of this department, identify the general hypothesis that would guide your research efforts.

   b. What type of research design would you recommend to Ms. Brooks? Justify your answer.

11. Fred Spears, director of advertising for *Competitive Farming*, is responsible for selling advertising space in the magazine. The magazine deals primarily with farming and the marketing of agricultural products and is distributed solely by subscription. Major advertisers are agricultural equipment manufacturers and production input suppliers, since the magazine is primarily directed at farmers, ranchers, and those persons employed in marketing agricultural products.

   Because the size and composition of the target audience for *Competitive Farming* are key concerns for prospective advertisers, Mr. Spears is interested in collecting more detailed data on the readership. Although he currently has total circulation figures, he believes that these understate the potential exposure of an advertisement in *Competitive Farming*. In particular, he thinks that for every subscriber to *Competitive Farming*, several others on the farm or employed within the various firms also read *Competitive Farming*. Fred wishes to determine how large this secondary audience is and also wishes to develop more detailed data on readers, such as degree of training in various areas, including pesticide handling, equipment repair, and commodity marketing. He believes that this detail would be helpful in influencing potential clients to commit their advertising dollars to *Competitive Farming*. Fred has asked you to assist him in solving his problems.

    a. Does Fred have a specific hypothesis? If yes, state the hypothesis.

    b. What type of research design would you recommend? Justify your answer.

12.   Investment Services, Inc. is a real estate developer headquartered in Florida but operating throughout the southeastern United States. One of the military bases located in one of the cities within Investment Services's market area recently closed, and the 40 housing units for military people located at the base were put up for public sale. The housing units, which were all duplexes, were somewhat run-down because the decision to phase out the base had been made some time ago. Only minimum maintenance was conducted after the fateful decision.

      Investment Services's management thinks that these units will command only a very low price at the public sale because of their dilapidated condition. The developers believe that because of this low price, the units could be repaired and sold at a nice profit.

      Before bidding on the contract, though, Investment Services's management is interested in determining what kind of demand there might be for these units. It has asked you to assist in determining this reaction. What kind of research design would you suggest? Why?

13.   The Wisconsin Ice Cream Co. of Mount Horeb, Wisconsin, a regional manufacturer of gourmet ice cream and frozen novelties, conducted a study in 2001 to assess how its brand of gourmet ice cream was faring in the market. Mail questionnaires were sent to a panel of 1,575 households. Wisconsin Ice Cream has three major competitors: Baumgardt's Food Co. of State College, Pennsylvania; Doug's Ice Cream of Michigan City, Indiana; and Guyer Foods of Charlevoix, Michigan. A similar study conducted in 2000 had indicated the following market shares: Wisconsin, 29.84% (470 families); Baumgardt's, 22.54% (355 families); Doug's, 26.03% (410 families); and Guyer's, 21.59% (340 families). The current study indicated that Wisconsin's market share had not changed during the one-year period. Results of the study indicated that Baumgardt's market share had decreased to 20% (315 families), Doug's market share had decreased to 20.32% (320 families), and Guyer's market share had increased to 29.84% (470 families). Wisconsin Ice Cream Co. managers decided that they had little to worry about.

      The 2001 study revealed some additional facts. Over the one-year period, 80 families had switched from Doug's and 50 families had switched from Guyer's to Wisconsin Ice Cream. Ten families had switched from Wisconsin and 15 families had switched from Doug's to Baumgardt's Ice Cream. Results also indicated that although none of Baumgardt's families had switched to Doug's Ice Cream, 40 of the Wisconsin and 5 of Guyer's families now purchased Doug's Ice Cream. It was revealed that Guyer's current customers comprise 80 families formerly purchasing Wisconsin Ice Cream, 65 families formerly purchasing Baumgardt's Ice Cream, and 40 families formerly purchasing Doug's Ice Cream.

    a. Do you think that Wisconsin's management team is accurate in analyzing the situation? Justify your answer.

    b. You are called on to do some analysis. From the preceding data, construct the brand-switching matrix. (Hint: Begin by filling in the row and column totals.)

    c. Indicate what this matrix reveals for each of the brands over the one-year period.

    d. Complete the brand loyalty and switching possibilities matrix on the next page.

    e. What can be said about the degree of brand loyalty for each of the four products?

		At Time t_2 (2001)				
		Bought Wisconsin	**Bought Baumgardt's**	**Bought Doug's**	**Bought Guyer's**	**Total**
	Bought Wisconsin					
	Bought Baumgardt's					
At Time t_1 (2000)	Bought Doug's					
	Bought Guyer's					
	Total					

14. Peppy Pet Company, a large manufacturer of pet food products, conducted a study in 2001 in order to assess how its brand of dog food was faring in the market. Questionnaires were mailed to a panel of 1,260 families with a dog. The Peppy Pet brand had three major competitors: Brand A, Brand B, and Brand C. A similar study conducted in 2000 had indicated the following market shares: Peppy Pet, 31.75% (400 families); Brand A, 25% (315 families); Brand B, 32.54% (410 families); and Brand C, 10.71% (135 families). The present study indicated that Peppy Pet's market share had not changed during the one-year period. However, Brand B increased its market share to 36.5% (460 families). This increase could be accounted for by a decrease in Brand A's and Brand C's market shares (Brand A now had a share of 22.23%, or 280 families; Brand C now had a share of 9.52%, or 120 families). The management of the Peppy Pet Company decided it had little to worry about.

The 2001 study also revealed some additional facts. Over the one-year period, 70 families from Brand A and 30 families from Brand C had switched to Peppy Pet. Five families from Brand B and 30 families from Brand C had switched to Brand A, while none of the Peppy Pet users had switched to Brand A. These facts further reassured management. Finally, 45 families switched from Brand B to Brand C, but none of the families using Peppy Pet or Brand A had switched to Brand C. Brand C's loyalty was estimated to be .556.

a. Do you think that the management of the Peppy Pet Company was accurate in its analysis of the situation? Justify your answer.

b. You are called upon to do some analysis. From the preceding data, construct the brand-switching matrix.

c. Indicate what this matrix reveals for each of the brands over the one-year period.

d. Complete the following table and compute brand loyalties.

e. What can be said about the degree of brand loyalty for each of the four products?

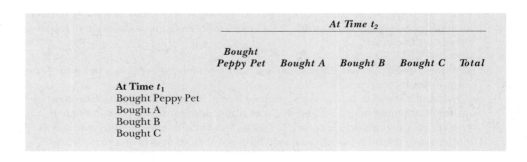

	At Time t_2				
	Bought Peppy Pet	**Bought A**	**Bought B**	**Bought C**	**Total**
At Time t_1					
Bought Peppy Pet					
Bought A					
Bought B					
Bought C					

15. The LoCalor Company is a medium-sized manufacturer of highly nutritional food products. The products have been marketed as diet foods with high nutritional content. Recently, the company was considering marketing these products as snack foods but was concerned about their present customers' reaction to the change in the products' images. The company has decided to assess customers' reaction by conducting a study using one of the established consumer panels.

   What type of panel would you recommend in the preceding situation? Why?

Thorndike Sports Equipment Video Case

1. Where should Ted look first for information on the kinds of racquets players desire?
2. If primary research is warranted, what projects would you propose to Luke Thorndike? What role would secondary research play in your primary research plans?
3. Looking at the primary research that you have decided is necessary in order to understand the problem in the racquetball division, how much will it cost Thorndike Sports Equipment to complete this project?
4. List three questions that you would ask retailers and/or players. Explain the rationale for asking these questions.
5. After informally speaking to a number of retailers and players, would you be able to provide solutions to the problem? Why or why not?
6. If the information gained from talking to these people cannot be used to solve the problem, is there still value in talking to these people?
7. As the researcher for Thorndike, you have been asked to construct a discussion guide for additional focus groups. Write up a discussion guide for the moderator to follow.
8. Should focus group participants be told the objective of the group? Why?
9. What are the benefits of doing qualitative research? How can findings from this type of research be used? What are the limitations of this type of research?
10. Ted has received valuable information from his focus group. Can he now reliably propose a solution to the racquet problem? Why or why not?
11. Ted mentions that he has videotaped the focus group sessions. What are some of the reasons for videotaping a focus group? What are some of the drawbacks to videotaping a focus group?
12. Is it ethical to videotape a group without telling participants that they are being taped? Is it ethical to make an audiotape of focus groups without telling the participants?

5

Causal Designs

Many times, the marketing manager has one or more specific *X-causes-Y* hypotheses that need to be examined: for example, a 5 percent increase in the price of the product will have no appreciable impact on the quantity demanded by customers, or redesigning the cereal package so that it is shorter and less likely to tip over will improve consumer attitudes toward the product. When the research question can be framed this explicitly, the researcher is dealing with a situation ripe for causal analysis. Descriptive research can be used for testing hypotheses. However, descriptive designs are not as satisfactory as experiments for establishing causality. The reasons require an understanding of the notion of causality, the types of evidence that establish causality, and the effect of extraneous variables in a research setting. In addition to explaining experimental design, this chapter deals with these concepts.

Concept of Causality

The concept of causality is complex, and a detailed discussion of it would take us too far afield. However, a few essentials will allow us to properly determine the role of the experiment in establishing the validity of an *X-causes-Y* statement.

The scientific notion of causality is very different from the commonsense, everyday notion.[1] First, the commonsense notion suggests that there is a single cause of an event. The everyday interpretation of the statement "*X* is the cause of *Y*" implies that *X* is indeed *the* cause. The scientific notion holds that *X* would be only one of a number of determining conditions.

Another difference between the commonsense and scientific notions of causality is that while the everyday interpretation implies a completely deterministic relationship, the scientific notion implies a probabilistic relationship. That is, the commonsense notion suggests that for *X* to be a cause of *Y*, *X* must always lead to *Y*. The scientific notion suggests that *X* can be a cause of *Y* if the occurrence of *X* makes the occurrence of *Y* more likely or more probable.

Finally, the scientific notion implies that we can *never prove* that *X* is a cause of *Y*. Rather, we always *infer* but never prove that a relationship exists. The inference is typically based on some observed data, perhaps acquired in a very controlled

---

[1]See Claire Selltiz, et al., *Research Methods in Social Relations*, rev. ed. (New York: Holt, Rinehart and Winston, 1959), pp. 80–82, for a brief but lucid discussion of the differences between the commonsense and scientific notions of causality. See also Earl R. Babbie, *The Practice of Social Research*, 8th ed. (Belmont, CA: Wadsworth Publishing, 1998).

experimental setting. Nevertheless, the scientific notion recognizes the fallibility of such procedures. This begs the question of what kinds of evidence can be used to support scientific inferences. There are three basic kinds of evidence: concomitant variation, time order of occurrence of variables, and elimination of other possible causal factors.[2]

Concomitant Variation

Consider the statement *"X is a cause of Y."* Evidence of concomitant variation as to the validity of this statement refers to the extent to which X and Y occur together or vary together in the way predicted by the hypothesis. Two cases can be distinguished—the qualitative and the quantitative.

Consider the qualitative case first. Suppose that the causal factor X was "dealer quality" and the effect factor Y was the company's market share. Now suppose that we were interested in examining the statement, "The success of our marketing efforts is highly dealer dependent. Where we have good dealers, we have good market penetration, and where we have poor dealers, we have unsatisfactory market penetration." Now, if X is to be considered a cause of Y, we should expect to find the following: In those territories where our good dealers are located, we would expect to have satisfactory market shares, and in those territories where our poor dealers are located, we would expect to have unsatisfactory market shares. However, if we found that the proportion of territories with unsatisfactory market shares was higher where the good dealers were located, we would conclude that the hypothesis was untenable.

Consider Table 5.1, in which the 100 dealers in each of the company's sales territories have been classified as good or poor. Suppose that the research department has also investigated the firm's market penetration in each sales territory and has categorized these market shares using some criteria supplied by management as being either satisfactory or unsatisfactory. This table provides evidence of concomitant variation. Where we find the presence of X, a good dealer, we also find the presence of Y, satisfactory market share, and where X is lacking, we are more likely to find a territory where our market share is unsatisfactory. Stating it another way, 67 percent of the good dealers are found in territories where our market share is satisfactory. However, only 25 percent of the poor dealers are located in territories where the market share is satisfactory.

Perfect evidence of concomitant variation would be provided, of course, if all good dealers were located in territories with satisfactory market shares and all poor

TABLE 5.1	Evidence of Concomitant Variation: Qualitative Case		
	Market Share—Y		
Dealer Quality—X	*Satisfactory*	*Unsatisfactory*	*Total*
Good	40 (67%)	20 (33%)	60 (100%)
Poor	10 (25%)	30 (75%)	40 (100%)

[2]Selltiz, et al., *Research Methods,* pp. 83–88.

TABLE 5.2	Evidence of Concomitant Variation between Marital Status and Candy Consumption

| | Candy Consumption—Y | | |
Marital Status—X	Eat Candy Regularly	Do Not Eat Candy Regularly	Total
Single	750 (75%)	249 (25%)	999 (100%)
Married	1,265 (63%)	745 (37%)	2,010 (100%)

Source: Adapted from *Say It with Figures,* 5th ed., rev. by Hans Zeisel, after Table 9–8 (p. 138). Copyright © 1968 by Harper & Row, Publishers, Inc. By permission of Harper & Row, Publishers, Inc.

dealers were located in territories with unsatisfactory market shares. The "pure" case will rarely be found in practice, as other causal factors will produce some deviation from a one-to-one correspondence between X and Y. So we search for the proportion of cases having X that also possess Y and compare that to the proportion of cases not having X that possess Y.

When the cause and effect factors can logically be considered continuous variables, the approach is similar. Now, though, the evidence should be consistent with regard to the amount of X in comparison to the amount of Y. Consider the relationship between advertising effort and sales. The firm's dollar expenditure on advertising is logically considered the cause, X, and sales the effect, Y. Further, the hypothesis would probably state that the higher the level of advertising expenditure, the greater the sales. Quantitative evidence of concomitant variation would be provided by finding evidence consistent with this hypothesis in that X was higher in those territories or in those years where Y was also greater. Again, the relationship could not be expected to be perfect, because that would deny the existence of other sales-determining factors. However, we would expect to find some positive relationship between the variables.

Suppose that an analysis of the relationship between X and Y provided supporting evidence of concomitant variation. What can we say? All we can say is that *the association makes the hypothesis more tenable; it does not prove it.*[3] Similarly, the absence of an association between X and Y cannot be taken in and of itself as evidence that there is no causal relationship between X and Y, because we are always inferring, rather than proving, that a causal relationship exists.

Consider first the case in which positive evidence of concomitant variation was provided. Table 5.2, which might be of interest to a candy manufacturer, suggests that candy consumption is affected by marital status.[4] Single people are more likely than married people to eat candy regularly. Seventy-five percent of the single people

[3]In Chapter 13 we will discuss the various conditions that can arise when looking at evidence of concomitant variation. For the moment, we simply wish to emphasize through example that association between X and Y does not mean there is causality between X and Y and that the absence of such association does not mean there is no causality.

[4]The example is adapted from Hans Zeisel, *Say It with Figures,* 5th ed., rev. (New York: Harper & Row, 1968), pp. 137–139. This classic book is recommended reading for all who are faced with the task of analyzing data.

TABLE 5.3	Candy Consumption by Age and Marital Status

	Up to 25 Years			25 Years and Over		
	Eat Candy Regularly	*Do Not Eat Candy Regularly*	*Total*	*Eat Candy Regularly*	*Do Not Eat Candy Regularly*	*Total*
Single	632 (79%)	167 (21%)	799 (100%)	120 (60%)	80 (40%)	200 (100%)
Married	407 (81%)	96 (19%)	503 (100%)	873 (58%)	634 (42%)	1,507 (100%)

Source: Adapted from *Say It with Figures,* 5th ed., rev. by Hans Zeisel, after Table 9–6 (p. 138). Copyright © 1968 by Harper & Row, Publishers, Inc. By permission of Harper & Row, Publishers, Inc.

TABLE 5.4	Lack of Evidence of Concomitant Variation between Age and Listening to Classical Music

	Listening to Classical Music—Y		
Age—X	*Listen*	*Do Not Listen*	*Total*
Below 40	390 (64%)	213 (36%)	603 (100%)
40 and Over	433 (64%)	243 (36%)	676 (100%)

Source: Adapted from *Say It with Figures,* 5th ed., rev. by Hans Zeisel, after Table 8–7 (p. 123). Copyright © 1968 by Harper & Row, Publishers, Inc. By permission of Harper & Row, Publishers, Inc.

in the sample ate candy regularly, whereas only 63 percent of the married people were regular consumers. Further, the evidence is not to be taken lightly, because it was obtained from a rather large sample of 3,009 cases. On the basis of this evidence, can we safely conclude that marriage causes a decrease in candy consumption? Or are there other possible explanations? What about the effects of age? Married people are usually older than single people, and perhaps older people eat less candy. Table 5.3 shows the relationship between candy consumption and marital status for different age segments of the population—up to 25 years, and 25 years and over. This is equivalent to holding the effects of age constant. As the table suggests, there is little difference in the candy-eating habits of married and single people: Up to 25 years of age, 79 percent of the singles and 81 percent of the marrieds eat candy regularly. For those over 25 years of age, 60 percent of the singles and 58 percent of the marrieds eat candy regularly. In effect, the data suggest that a person's candy consumption is unaffected by the individual's marital state. The original association suggested by Table 5.2 was spurious.

Consider now the case of the absence of initial evidence of concomitant variation and why that does not imply that there is no causation between X and Y. Table 5.4 implies that there is no relationship between a person's listening to classical music and the individual's age: In a sample of 1,279 cases, 64 percent of those under 40 and 64 percent of those over 40 listen to classical music.[5] For a record manufacturer

---

[5]The example is taken from Zeisel, *Say It with Figures,* pp. 123–125.

TABLE 5.5	**Listening to Classical Music by Age and Education**					
	College			*Below College*		
Age	*Listen*	*Do Not Listen*	*Total*	*Listen*	*Do Not Listen*	*Total*
Below 40	162 (73%)	62 (27%)	224 (100%)	228 (61%)	151 (39%)	379 (100%)
40 and Over	195 (78%)	56 (22%)	251 (100%)	238 (56%)	187 (44%)	425 (100%)

Source: Adapted from *Say It with Figures*, 5th ed., rev. by Hans Zeisel, after Table 8–8 (p. 124). Copyright © 1968 by Harper & Row, Publishers, Inc. By permission of Harper & Row, Publishers, Inc.

interested in delineating market segments, this is a finding of considerable import. It is also somewhat unexpected. Consider what happens, though, when educational level is also introduced as an additional explanatory variable. As Table 5.5 reveals, an association exists between age and listening to classical music. As college-educated people get older, they display a higher propensity to listen to classical music: 78 percent of those 40 and over listen, whereas only 73 percent of the under-40 respondents listen. The reverse situation occurs among those who do not have a college education: Whereas 61 percent of the under-40 age group listen to classical music, only 56 percent of the 40-and-over age group do so. The relationship between age and listening to classical music was originally obscured by the effect of education. When education was properly held constant, the relationship became visible.

The situations illustrated are not the only ones that can occur. A more complete picture will be presented in Chapter 13. For the moment, you should simply be aware that concomitant variation is one type of evidence that supports the existence of a causal relationship between X and Y. However, it is not the whole story. It may be that a causal relationship exists when there is no initial evidence of concomitant variation, or that no causal relationship exists when there is initial evidence.[6] Further evidence of the existence of a causal relationship can be provided by looking at the order of occurrence of variables and by eliminating other possible sources of explanation.

Time Order of Occurrence of Variables

The time order of variables' occurrence as evidence of a causal relationship between two variables is conceptually simple:

> One event cannot be considered the "cause" of another if it occurs *after* the other event. The occurrence of a causal factor may precede or may be simultaneous with the occurrence of an event; by definition, an effect cannot be produced by an event that occurs only after the effect has taken place. However, it is possible for each term in the relationship to be both a "cause" and an "effect" of the other term.[7]

---

[6]The medical literature provides a number of examples of these changes in conclusions in terms of what was once considered bad to eat or drink is now believed good and vice versa. See Philip E. Ross, "Lies, Damned Lies, and Medical Statistics," *Forbes* 156 (August 14, 1995), pp. 130–135.

[7]Selltiz, et al., *Research Methods*, p. 85.

Although conceptually simple, the application of this type of evidence to support causality requires an intimate understanding of the time sequence governing the phenomenon.

Consider the relationship between a firm's annual advertising expenditures and sales. This relationship is frequently used as evidence of the effect of advertising on sales for a given product. However, many companies follow a rule of thumb that uses past sales in allocating resources to advertising—for example, 2 percent of last year's sales. This practice begs the question of which way the relationship runs. Does advertising lead to higher sales, or do higher sales lead to an increased ad budget? An intimate understanding of the way the company establishes the ad budget should resolve the dilemma in this situation.

Elimination of Other Possible Causal Factors

The elimination of other possible causal factors is very much like the Sherlock Holmes approach to analysis. Just as Sherlock Holmes holds that "when you have eliminated the impossible, whatever remains, however improbable, must be the truth,"[8] this type of evidence of causality focuses on the elimination of possible explanations other than the one being studied. This may mean physically holding other factors constant, or it may mean "adjusting" the results to remove the effects of factors that do vary.

Take the situation of the divisional manager of a chain of supermarkets investigating the effects of end-of-aisle displays on apple sales. Suppose that the manager found that per-store sales of apples increased during the past week and that a number of stores were using end displays for apples. To reasonably conclude that the end displays were responsible for the sales increase, the manager would need to eliminate such explanatory variables as price, size of store, and apple type and quality. This might involve looking at apple sales for stores of approximately the same size, checking to see if the prices were the same in stores having an increase in sales and stores with no increase, and checking to determine if the type and quality of apples were consistent with those of the previous week.

The testing of new products illustrates the need for and the problems associated with trying to eliminate other possible causal factors in order to conclude that the result was attributable to the variable in question. When testing new products, manufacturers often wish to determine whether the product has any differential advantages in consumers' minds (for example, it is of superior quality or taste or has a desirable special feature). Yet when consumers are given a product to test, their responses can be affected by awareness of the manufacturer of the product. Respondents might rate the product higher or lower because of their attitudes toward the manufacturer, which makes it difficult to determine whether respondents indeed liked or disliked the product itself. To overcome such bias, letters rather than brand names are often used to label the products presented to respondents. That, in turn, raises the issue of whether the evaluations might be affected by the letters that are used. Research Realities 5.1 describes one of the more extensive investigations of whether respondents might systematically favor products identified by particular letters.

---

[8]Arthur Conan Doyle, "The Sign of the Four," in *The Complete Sherlock Holmes* (Garden City, NY: Garden City Publishing Company, Inc., 1938), p. 94.

Using Letters to Identify Products or Brands

To determine if some letters are perceived more favorably than others, Market Facts sent questionnaires to 4,000 households in its Consumer Mail Panel. Each subsample of 1,000 was balanced to be nationally representative with respect to geographic region, population density, age, and income. Approximately 3,000 questionnaires were returned.

The instructions given to the respondents were as follows:

When some people look at different letters of the alphabet, they may feel that certain letters have a more favorable meaning than other letters. For each letter shown below, please check the response that best describes how you feel about any meaning of the letter.

The 26 letters were then listed in one of four sequences:

1. Alphabetical order
2. Reverse alphabetical order
3. Random order:
   TJENXBFHZOGPACRWLQKDSIVYMU
4. Reverse random order

The responses available to the respondents were as follows:

Very Favorable	(200)
Somewhat Favorable	(100)
No Meaning	(0)
Somewhat Unfavorable	(−100)
Very Unfavorable	(−200)

The numbers in parentheses are the values assigned to the responses for the analysis of the data (and were not shown to the respondents).

Source: "Using Letters to Identify Products or Brands," *Research on Research*, no. 16 (Chicago: Market Facts, Inc., undated). Reprinted with permission.

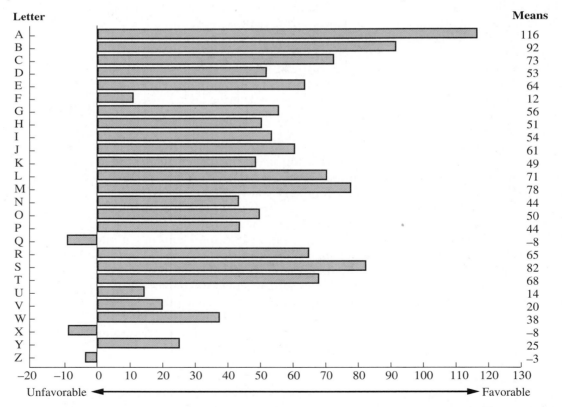

Letter	Means
A	116
B	92
C	73
D	53
E	64
F	12
G	56
H	51
I	54
J	61
K	49
L	71
M	78
N	44
O	50
P	44
Q	−8
R	65
S	82
T	68
U	14
V	20
W	38
X	−8
Y	25
Z	−3

Unfavorable ◄———————————► Favorable

The accompanying figure displays the average mean rating of each letter across the total sample. While not shown,

> there was a great deal of consistency in the rank order of the letters, although some minor differences exist among the versions. In particular, the top third of the letters are the same in all versions, as are the bottom third. Thus, it appears that the order in which the letters were presented had little effect on the ratings.
>
> With a few notable exceptions, letters near the beginning of the alphabet tended to be rated higher than those near the end. Letters A and B were rated the highest in all versions, and letters U through Z were among the lowest. However, the letters M and S (and, to a lesser extent, L, R, and T) were rated high, and letters F and Q were rated low in all versions.
>
> Because some letters were consistently perceived as being more favorable than others, care should be exercised in the selection of letters as brand labels. Choosing letters that are relatively similar with respect to their ratings may help to minimize bias caused by the product labels. Letters G through P (except L and M) were relatively homogeneous in their ratings. Of course, the letters used should not suggest or appear to be abbreviations for the actual brand names.[9]

Role of the Evidence

We shall see shortly that the controlled experiment provides all three types of evidence of causality. It allows us to check for concomitant variation and time order of occurrence of variables, secure in the fact that if the experiment has been designed correctly, many of the other possible explanations will have been eliminated. However, even in an experiment, not all other explanations will have *necessarily* been eliminated. There is also the possibility that in concluding that X caused Y, we may have neglected another factor that is associated with X and, in fact, caused Y. Alternatively, we may be wrong when we conclude that X did not cause Y, because we have neglected some condition under which X is indeed a determiner of Y.

The correct posture toward these three types of evidence is that they provide a reasonable basis for believing that X is, or is not, a cause of Y. We can never be absolutely sure, though, that the relationship has been conclusively demonstrated. Study replication along with knowledge of the problem are fundamental in increasing our confidence in the conclusion. The accumulation of studies pointing to a specific conclusion increases our confidence in its correctness. Similarly, an intimate knowledge of the phenomenon under investigation, in conjunction with a pattern of evidence, serves as a more reasonable basis for interpreting the results of research than does an examination of the evidence by one untrained in the subject matter of concern. Method knowledge is not a substitute for conceptual knowledge.

Experimentation

As mentioned, an **experiment** is capable of providing more convincing evidence of causal relationships than are exploratory or descriptive designs. This is why experiments are often called causal research. An experiment has greater ability to supply evidence of causality because of the *control* it affords investigators:

---

[9]"Using Letters to Identify Products or Brands," *Research on Research*, no. 16 (Chicago: Market Facts, Inc., undated).

> An *experiment* is taken to mean a scientific investigation in which an investigator manipulates and controls one or more independent variables and observes the dependent variable or variables for variation concomitant to the manipulation of the independent variables. An *experimental design,* then, is one in which the investigator *manipulates* at least one independent variable.[10]

Because investigators are able to control at least some manipulations of the presumed causal factor, they can be more confident that the relationships discovered are "true" relationships.

Both exploratory and descriptive designs are distinguished from **experimental designs** in that they are examples of *ex post facto* research. *Ex post facto* literally means "from what is done afterward." In *ex post facto* research, the criterion variable *Y* is observed. The analyst then attempts to find one or more causal variables, *X*s, which afford plausible explanations as to why *Y* occurred. This kind of retrospective analysis affords little control of the *X*s and therefore contains great potential that the occurrence of *Y* is attributable to some other *X*s than the ones being investigated. One is limited to supplying evidence of concomitant variation in *ex post facto* research. The lack of evidence about the time order of occurrence of variables and the systematic exclusion of other possible explanations of the phenomenon make such designs suspect for establishing causality.

Laboratory and Field Experiments

Two types of experiments can be distinguished—the laboratory experiment and the field experiment. Because each has its own advantages and disadvantages, research analysts need to be familiar with both.

A **laboratory experiment** is one in which an investigator creates a situation with the desired conditions and then manipulates some variables while controlling others. The investigator is consequently able to observe and measure the effect of the manipulation of the independent variables on the dependent variable or variables in a situation in which the effect of other relevant factors is minimized. A **field experiment** is a research study in a realistic or natural situation, although it, too, involves the manipulation of one or more independent variables under as carefully controlled conditions as the situation will permit.

The laboratory experiment is distinguished from the field experiment, then, primarily in terms of environment. The analyst creates a setting for a laboratory experiment, whereas a field experiment is conducted in a natural setting. The distinction is not always a clear one, because it is more one of degree than of kind, as both involve control and manipulation of one or more presumed causal factors. The degree of control and precision afforded by each type varies, however. A specially designed or artificial situation provides more control.

The distinction can perhaps best be made by seeing how each is used to investigate the effects of the same causal variable. Price is particularly interesting in this regard, as a number of laboratory and field experiments have investigated the effect

---

[10]Fred N. Kerlinger, *Foundations of Behavioral Research,* 3rd ed. (New York: Holt, Rinehart and Winston, 1986), p. 293. See also Geoffrey Keppel, *Design and Analysis: A Researcher's Handbook,* 3rd ed. (Englewood Cliffs, NJ: Prentice Hall, 1991); Geoffrey Keppel, *Design and Analysis,* 2nd ed. (New York: W. H. Freeman and Company, 1995).

of price on the quantity sold. The following investigation was designed to ascertain the closeness with which the price-demand estimates generated in a laboratory experiment correspond to the estimates generated in a field experiment.[11]

The laboratory experiment consisted of a set of simulated shopping trips. In each, subjects chose the brand they preferred to purchase from a full assortment of prepriced brands of cola and coffee. The relative prices of the different brands were changed for each of the eight simulated purchase trips for each subject. These price changes were communicated to each subject by index cards listing the available brands and their corresponding prices.[12] Each subject was free to switch brands to obtain the best product for the money. The trial purchase was not unlike an actual purchase in this respect. These simulated shopping trips were administered in the homes of a systematic sample of 135 homemakers in a small town in Illinois. The laboratory experiment followed a field experiment also designed to test the effect of price on the demand for different brands of cola and coffee.

The prices of the brands were also manipulated in the field experiment. The field experiment was conducted in two small towns in Illinois, 10 miles apart. The manipulations here, though, involved actual changes in price for the respective brands. Four supermarkets were used in all, two from each town. Two units in one town were designated as control stores, where the price of each brand was maintained at its regular level throughout the experiment. In the experimental town, the prices were systematically varied in the two stores during the experiment. Prices were marked on the package of each brand to be clearly visible but not conspicuous. After each price change, a cooling-off period was introduced to offset any surplus accumulated by consumers. The effect of the price change was monitored by recording weekly sales for each brand. This allowed brand market shares for each price condition to be determined. No displays, special containers, or other devices were used to draw consumer attention to the fact that the relative prices of the brands had been altered. All other controllable factors were also held as constant as possible.

Note the distinction between the two studies. In the field experiment, no attempt was made to set up special conditions. The situation was accepted as found, and manipulation of the experimental variable—price—was imposed in this natural environment. The laboratory experiment, on the other hand, was contrived. Subjects were told to behave as if they were actively shopping for the product. The prices of the respective brands were varied for each of these simulated shopping trips. Whereas the simulated shopping trips generated reasonably valid estimates of

[11]John R. Nevin, "Using Controlled Experiments to Estimate and Analyze Brand Demand," unpublished Ph.D. dissertation, University of Illinois, 1972. See also John R. Nevin, "Laboratory Experiments for Estimating Consumer Demand: A Validation Study," *Journal of Marketing Research* 11 (August 1974), pp. 261–268. For comparison of consumer choice processes in a laboratory versus an actual grocery store, see Raymond R. Burke, Barbara E. Kahn, and Leonard M. Lodish, "Comparing Dynamic Consumer Choice in Real and Computer-Simulated Environments," *Journal of Consumer Research* 19 (June 1992), pp. 71–82.

[12]The laboratory experiment also included a paired-preference experiment. The paired-preference experiment required each subject to make preference choices among all possible pairs of brands in a single-merchandise classification with each brand listed at its regular price. Subjects were also asked to indicate how much the price of the preferred brand would have to increase before they would switch to the original nonpreferred brand.

consumers' reactions to "real-life" (field experiment) price changes for brands of cola, they produced relatively invalid estimates for brands of coffee, because they tended to overstate the effects of the price changes.[13]

Internal and External Validity

Certain advantages and disadvantages result from the different procedure in the two types of experiments. The laboratory experiment typically has greater internal validity because of the greater control it affords. To the extent that we are successful in eliminating the effects of other factors that may obscure or confound the relationships under study, either by physically holding these other factors constant or by allowing for them statistically, we may conclude that the observed effect was due to the manipulation of the experimental variable. That is, we may conclude that the experiment is internally valid. **Internal validity** refers to our ability to attribute the effect that was observed to the experimental variable and not to other factors. In the pricing experiment, internal validity focused on the need to obtain data demonstrating that the variation in the criterion variable—brand demanded—was the result of exposure to the treatment or experimental variable—relative price of the brand—rather than other factors, such as advertising, display space, store traffic, and so on. These other factors were nonexistent in the simulated shopping trip.

Whereas the laboratory experiment is generally believed to be more internally valid, the field experiment is typically more externally valid.[14] **External validity** focuses on the problems of collecting data that demonstrate that the changes in the criterion variable observed in the experiment as a result of changes in the predictor variables can be expected to occur in other situations. Can the effect be generalized? Because laboratory experiments are more artificial than field experiments, it is questionable whether the results can be generalized to other populations and settings. In the simulated shopping trip, no real purchase takes place. Further, we may suppose that the experimenter's calling attention to the price may induce people to be more price conscious than they would be in a supermarket. They may attempt to act more "rationally" than they normally would. Further, those who agreed to participate in the laboratory experiment may not be representative of the larger population of shoppers, either because the location of the study was atypical or because those who willingly participate in such a study may be systematically different from those who decline to participate. This would seriously jeopardize the external validity of the findings.

The example in Research Realities 5.2 illustrates the difference between internal and external validity. Internal validity addresses the questions of whether the auto editor of the *Boston Globe* actually experienced a 25 percent increase in miles

---

[13]Nevin, "Laboratory Experiments," p. 266.

[14]For a general discussion of how the usefulness of experimental results is affected by the researcher's treatment of unmanipulated background factors in the experiment, see John G. Lynch, Jr., "On the External Validity of Experiments in Consumer Research," *Journal of Consumer Research* 9 (December 1982), pp. 225–244. For discussions of ways to enhance external validity, see Russell S. Winer, "Experimentation in the 21st Century: The Importance of External Validity," *Journal of the Academy of Marketing Science* 27 (Summer 1999), pp 349–358; John G. Lynch Jr., "Theory and External Validity," *Journal of the Academy of Marketing Science* 27 (Summer 1999), pp. 367–376.

Illustration of Internal and External Validity

Some technical breakthroughs sound too good to be true. With so many new devices and gadgets on the market that purport to save fuel, for example, it can be difficult to tell an effective product from a fraud.

The case of Tufoil, a popular motor-oil additive that's supposed to improve a car's gasoline mileage an average 10% to 20%, shows how difficult making a judgment can be.

. . . Tufoil's basic technology is a suspension of tiny particles of Teflon-like materials that reduces friction. Dudley Fuller and Glenn Rightmire, engineering professors at Columbia University, say the technology "shows promise." At the request of *The Wall Street Journal*, they read Tufoil's patent description and other technical documents.

. . . Tufoil has had rave reviews in several newspapers. In May, the *New York Times* cited testimonials from police departments and race-car drivers, and concluded: "Tufoil apparently does just what it says it does." The *Boston Globe's* auto editor wrote about a test he did on his own car.

"It worked!" wrote the editor. "We have good records on the car. We have kept track of every dime spent and every drop of gas put into it." With Tufoil in the crankcase, he said, the car got 12.5 miles to the gallon, compared with 10 before. Said the editor, "That's a 25% increase."

So it is. But tests performed by consumers, even those who are as expert as racers and auto editors, generally prove little. "There's a placebo effect," says William Haynes, an attorney for the Federal Trade Commission. "If you put a product in your car that you think will improve gas mileage, you may subconsciously change your driving habits."

Changes in temperature and humidity can alter a car's mileage significantly, too. "There are just so many variables" in such tests, Mr. Haynes says, that the only way to be certain is to test a product in a laboratory on a number of cars hooked to a dynamometer, an apparatus that measures engine power. Other authorities say dynamometer tests should be supplemented by tests on whole fleets of cars on the road, in which none of the drivers knows if the car has the product.

. . . This summer, the Energy Department finally ran limited dynamometer tests on Tufoil and other products, including three special motor oils made by major oil companies. Fuel economy improved 2.8% to 5% for Tufoil, 4.1% for Arco Graphite and 3.6% for Mobil 1; Exxon Uniflo made no difference. Mr. Reick believes the results for Tufoil were low because the car was a small four-cylinder Pontiac. But an Energy Department engineer involved in the tests says a 5% improvement is impressive for a lubricant.

Double-digit savings from additives don't make sense, other experts say. Peter Hutchins, who tests energy-saving devices for the Environmental Protection Agency, says only about 25% to 30% of the energy in a typical automobile engine is lost to friction. Thus, he reasons, "even if you eliminate all the friction in an engine—which is impossible—the best you could hope for is about a 25% improvement in fuel economy."

That's true for most cars, concedes Mr. Reick. But he insists Tufoil can work wonders in engines with acute friction caused by sticking piston rings and other problems.

Meanwhile, the Federal Trade Commission is complaining about some of Tufoil's advertising claims. The agency questions such language in Tufoil brochures as "average 10% to 20% better mileage," and "fully guaranteed and insured."

Though Mr. Reick bristles at the FTC criticisms, he also concedes he has "reservations" about some of the techniques being used to promote Tufoil. Indeed, if he could have his way, he would avoid the business end of Tufoil's operation: "I'd just stay in my lab in my garage and invent things."

Source: Paul Blustein, "Fuel-Saver Additive Gets Raves, but Claims Are Tougher to Prove," *The Wall Street Journal* (August 29, 1980), p. 15. Reprinted by permission of *The Wall Street Journal*, © Dow Jones & Company, Inc. 1980. All Rights Reserved Worldwide. For discussion of the controversy surrounding the claims of other devices for autos to save fuel and to reduce undesirable exhaust emissions, see Gregory A. Patterson, "Unusual Claims about Magnets Attract Suits," *The Wall Street Journal* (September 24, 1991), pp. B1–B2.

per gallon, and, if he did, whether the improvement could be attributed to using Tufoil in the crankcase. External validity refers to whether that result could be generalized to other drivers, other cars, and other situations.

The distinction between internal validity and external validity is an important one, in that the controls needed for each often conflict. A control or procedure required to establish internal validity will often jeopardize representativeness, and vice versa, for reasons that should become obvious from the discussion that follows of the various types of experimental designs and the account they take of extraneous influences. Both internal and external validity are matters of degree rather than all-or-nothing propositions.

Experimental Design

A common terminology will facilitate the discussion of the basic types of experimental design:[15]

> Let X refer to the exposure of an individual or group to an experimental treatment; an *experimental treatment* is the alternative whose effects are to be measured and compared. The experimental variables may be alternative prices, package designs, advertising themes, or any of a number of other variables. Certainly, the possible experimental treatments in marketing would include all the elements of the marketing mix.
>
> Let O refer to the process of observation or measurement of the test units. The *test units* are the individuals or other entities whose responses to the experimental treatments are being studied. The test units could be stores, dealers, sales representatives, consumers, or any of the many other entities that serve as objects for a firm's marketing efforts.

Further, let movement through time be represented by a horizontal arrangement of Xs and Os. Thus the symbolic arrangement

$$X \quad O_1 \quad O_2$$

would indicate that one or more test units were exposed to an experimental variable and that their response was then measured at two different points in time. Let a vertical arrangement of Xs and Os reflect simultaneous exposure or measurement of different test units. The symbolic arrangement

$$X_1 \quad O_1$$
$$X_2 \quad O_2$$

would then indicate that there are two different groups of test units; that each group of test units was exposed to a different experimental treatment but at the same time; and that the response of the two groups was also simultaneously measured.

[15]The basic symbolism follows the classic book by Donald T. Campbell and Julian C. Stanley, *Experimental and Quasi-Experimental Designs for Research* (Chicago: Rand McNally, 1966). It is also used by Seymour Banks, *Experimentation in Marketing* (New York: McGraw-Hill, 1965).

The promotions manager of a soft-drink company asks you to help her run an experiment to determine whether she should start advertising in cinemas showing "R," "X," and higher-rated movies. She explains that she has read a journal article indicating that viewers' responses to upbeat commercials are more favorable if the commercials follow very arousing film clips, and she believes that her soft-drink commercial will stimulate more sales of the drink in the cinema if it follows previews of very violent or erotic films, such as are shown before the main feature film.

- If you ran a laboratory experiment for this client, what kinds of manipulations would you use, and what are the ethical issues involved in their use?

- Is it feasible to run a field experiment, and would the ethical issues change if a field experiment were run rather than a laboratory experiment?

- If you found that increasing viewers' arousal levels did indeed make them more favorably disposed toward products advertised through upbeat commercials, what are the ultimate ethical implications for influencing television programming?

Extraneous Variables

We worry about experimental design because we want to be able to conclude that the observed response was due to our experimental manipulations. The key ingredient affecting our ability to do this is advance planning. In particular, we need to design the study so as to be able to rule out extraneous factors as possible causes. These extraneous factors fall into several categories.

HISTORY   The term **history** refers to the specific events, external to the experiment but occurring at the same time, that may affect the criterion or response variable. Suppose that a major appliance manufacturer was interested in investigating consumers' price sensitivity in regard to refrigerators. Suppose that the company conceived the following experiment to take place in Detroit.[16] Refrigerator sales at regular prices would be monitored for a four-week period. Then the price of all units would be cut 10 percent and these sales monitored for four weeks. The measure of price sensitivity would derive from comparing per-week sales at the lower price with per-week sales at the higher price. The experiment would be diagrammed as

$$O_1 \quad X \quad O_2$$

Now suppose that soon after the price reduction, the union contract with the auto industry expired, and there was a strike. What do you think would happen to refrigerator sales? Since major appliance purchases are usually postponable, it

---

[16]The experiment is admittedly poor. The issue was purposely presented this way to demonstrate the history effect more vividly.

could be expected that there would be fewer sales at the lower price than at the higher one. Would we therefore conclude that the demand curve for refrigerators is upward sloping—that is, the higher the price, the greater the number of units that could be sold? Obviously not, for we know that there were extenuating circumstances in the experiment that caused the observed aberration.

Unfortunately, the effects of history on a research conclusion are rarely so obvious. There are always a great many variables that can and do affect what we observe and whose effect is subtle and hidden. What we need is some way of isolating the effects of history, as we are rarely in a position to physically control it. This is particularly true in the field experiment, because laboratory experiments often give us some control in this regard.

MATURATION   Although similar to history, **maturation** specifically refers to changes occurring within the test units that are not due to the effect of the experimental variable but result from the passage of time. Thus, when the test units are people, maturation refers to the fact that people get older, become tired, or perhaps become hungry. Measured changes in attitude toward a product, for example, may occur simply because people have become older while using the product and not because of the reinforcement advertising to which they were exposed. Similarly, it may turn out that individuals who belong to a consumer panel changed their consumption of our brand over time not because of any changes in our marketing strategy but simply because of some change in them. They matured, so to speak, in that their tastes changed, or perhaps their marital status or family status changed.

Maturation effects are not limited to test units composed of people. Organizations also change. Dealers grow, become more successful, diversify, and so on. Stores change. Store traffic increases, its composition changes, the store's physical makeup decays; and then the store is perhaps renovated.

Of course, the type of maturation effect depends on the timing of the specific experiment in question. It would be hard to justify the argument that the people whose response was measured changed significantly as a result of, say, age maturation in an experiment that lasted a week. On the other hand, if the interview securing their responses lasted a couple of hours, they could very well have grown tired or have become hurried for some reason; for example, their spouses will be home from work in one-half hour and they have not yet started preparing dinner. Thus, their responses to the later questions may differ from those to the former simply because their own personal situation has changed, and for no other reason.

TESTING   The **testing effect,** which can be of two types, is concerned with the fact that the process of experimentation itself may affect the observed response. The *main testing effect* is the effect of a prior observation on a later observation. For example, students taking achievement and intelligence tests for the second time usually do better than those taking the tests for the first time, even though the second test is given without any information about the scores or items missed in the first one.[17] The first administration in and of itself is responsible for the improvement.

---

[17]Campbell and Stanley, *Experimental and Quasi-Experimental Designs,* p. 9.

In many situations, this main testing effect will manifest itself in respondents' desire to be consistent. Thus, in successive administrations of an attitude questionnaire, respondents reply in a consistent manner even though there has been some change in their attitudes. Alternatively, in a single administration, they answer later questions so that their replies parallel their replies to similar early questions as best they can recall them; that is, their responses to the latter part of the questionnaire are not made independently but are conditioned by their responses to the early questions.

The main testing effect may also be reactive; there are very few things in social science that can be measured in which the process of measurement does not itself change what is being measured. The very fact that persons report their attitudes to someone else may change those attitudes. Similarly, the very fact that a person is a member of a consumer panel that reports purchasing behavior may change that person's purchasing behavior.

There is also an *interactive testing effect*, which means that a prior measurement affects the test unit's response to the experimental variable. People who are asked to indicate their attitudes toward Chevrolet may become much more aware of the Chevrolet ads than those who are not queried. Yet if we are interested in the attitude impact of the ads, we are interested in their effect on the population as a whole and not simply on those individuals composing our sample.

The results of the two testing effects are different. The main effect manifests itself in the relation between observations and can be depicted as

$$\underset{\curvearrowleft}{} O_1 \quad X \quad O_2$$

That is, the process of measurement O_1 in turn affects the measurement O_1 or the latter measurement O_2. The interactive testing effect, on the other hand, can be diagrammed as

$$O_1 \quad X \quad O_2$$

That is, the process of measurement O_1 results in some change in the test unit's reaction to the experimental stimulus. The distinction is an important one, because the main testing effect usually exerts its greatest impact on the internal validity of an experiment, whereas the interactive testing effect most typically affects the external validity of a conclusion.

INSTRUMENT VARIATION   Any and all changes in measuring instruments that might account for differences in measurements are referred to as **instrument variation.** The change may occur in the instrument itself, or it may result from variations in its administration. When many observers or interviewers participate, significant instrument variation can occur because it is difficult indeed to ensure that all the interviewers will ask the same questions with the same voice inflections, with the same probes, with the same rapport, and so on. Thus, the recorded differences between the awareness level of, say, two respondents may not actually reflect a true difference in awareness but rather a difference that arose because each interviewer handled the interview slightly differently. Of course, the same thing can occur with interviews conducted by the same interviewer. It is highly unlikely that each situation will be handled in exactly the same way. Interviewers may become more adept at eliciting the desired responses, or they may become bored with the project and tired of interviewing. In either case, part of the difference in the reported scores will be due to the way each assignment is handled.

The measuring instrument may also undergo some modification during the course of an investigation. Modifications may be major or minor. If major (for example, a completely new set of attitude statements), the responses to each questionnaire would probably be analyzed separately. Sometimes, though, a minor modification is needed, such as a slight change in wording of a specific question that makes it more understandable without changing its meaning. Although slight, this kind of change could cause variations in the reported answers, and the analyst is well advised to be aware of this.

STATISTICAL REGRESSION   The tendency of extreme cases of a phenomenon to move closer to the average during the course of an experiment is called **statistical regression.** The test units may be extreme by happenstance, or they may have been specifically selected because of their extreme positions. For example, people may be chosen for investigation because they exhibit extreme behavior, say, in their alcohol consumption. Suppose a consumer panel is formed of these test units. It is likely that in subsequent monitoring, their *reported* alcohol intake would be closer to the average.

Alternatively, a cross-sectional study investigating the use of one brand of orange juice might reveal several families who used 10 cans in a week. This may be because they had house guests, and thus it would not be surprising that in a subsequent observation their orange juice consumption would be more typical.

There is always some variation in behavior, attitudes, knowledge, and so on, and it stands to reason that the most extreme cases of the phenomenon have the most room in which to vary. Statistical regression is concerned with the occurrence of this phenomenon.

SELECTION BIAS   Sometimes bias arises from the way in which test units are selected and assigned in an experiment. **Selection bias** is said to be present when there is no way of certifying that groups of test units were equivalent before being tested.

The following example typifies the problem of selection bias. "Many say the president has at least convinced them that the *X* (pick your topic) crisis is real or that the problems are more serious than they thought. In an Associated Press-NBC poll last week, 60 percent of those who heard the president's speech regarding *X* agreed that there is a worldwide crisis, while 40 percent of those who didn't hear the speech believe the crisis is real." The fallacy in the argument is that there is no way of determining if those who saw the president's speech had similar attitudes toward *X*, before viewing, to those who did not see it. What typically occurs is that exposure to some mass communication has been voluntary, and thus the exposed and unexposed groups inevitably possess a systematic difference on the factors determining the choice. Republicans listen to the speeches of Republican candidates; Democrats listen to those of Democratic candidates; those who have a favorable attitude toward a product pay more attention to the product's ads; and so on. If we are to conclude that exposure to the experimental stimulus (TV special, speech, ad, and so on) was responsible for the observed effect, we must somehow ensure that the comparison groups were equal before exposure.

The prior equality of comparison groups is established in two main ways: matching and randomization. Suppose there are 20 stores in total, 10 to be designated for an experimental group and 10 for a control group, and suppose that an experiment is designed to examine the effect of a special aisle display on sales of, say, ketchup. Now, we would certainly expect the sales of ketchup in any store to be associated with the store's traffic. We could, therefore, be far off in our conclusion if we somehow ended up with most of the large stores in one group and most of the small stores in the other group. To prevent this, we could consider matching the stores according to some external criterion, such as annual sales or square feet of floor space, and then assign one store from each matched pair to each group.

Alternatively, we could assign the 20 stores at random to each of the groups, using a table of random digits. In general, randomization is the preferred procedure in assuring the prior equality of the comparison groups.[18] First, it is hard to match test units on any but a few characteristics, so the test units may be equal in terms of the variables chosen but unequal in terms of others. In addition, if the matched characteristic is not an important determinant of the response, the researcher has wasted time and money in matching the test units. The general principle is as follows: "Whenever it is possible to do so, randomly assign subjects to experimental groups and conditions and randomly assign conditions and other factors to experimental groups."[19] Randomization does not play its usually productive role when the sample of test units is small, because randomization produces groups that are "equal on the average" only when the sample is large enough to allow the positive and negative deviations about the average to balance. With small samples, matching becomes a complement to, and not a substitute for, randomization, in that matched test units should then be randomly assigned to treatment conditions.[20]

EXPERIMENTAL MORTALITY   The loss of test units during the course of an experiment is called **experimental mortality.** It is a problem because there is no way of knowing if the test units that were lost would have responded to the experimental stimulus in the same way as those that were retained. One downside of online communication for medical researchers, for example, is that patients can share their experiences on electronic bulletin boards. By comparing notes, patients can determine if they are human guinea pigs getting placebos or experimental drugs that might cure them. Finding that they are getting placebos, some patients choose to drop out, raising serious problems for researchers trying to establish the effectiveness of new drugs or treatments.[21]

---

[18]See Kerlinger, *Foundations*, pp. 288–289, for a general discussion of the pros and cons associated with matching.

[19]Ibid., p. 288.

[20]Cook and Campbell suggest that "perhaps the best way of reducing the error due to differences between persons is to match *before* random assignment to treatments" with the best matching variables being those "that are most highly correlated with posttest scores." Thomas D. Cook and Donald T. Campbell, *Quasi-Experimentation: Design and Analysis Issues for Field Settings* (Chicago: Rand McNally College Publishing Company, 1979), p. 47.

[21]William M. Bulkeley, "Untested Treatments, Cures Find Stronghold on On-Line Services," *The Wall Street Journal* (February 27, 1995), pp. A1, A7.

Consider again the special aisle display and ketchup sales example. Suppose that during the course of the experiment, two managers of stores in the experimental group decided to use the display for another product. This would reduce the number of experimental stores to eight, and even though our major interest would be average store sales in the experimental group in comparison to average store sales in the control group, we would have no way of knowing if this average would have been higher or lower if the two dropout stores had continued participating. We *cannot* simply *assume* that their sales would have been like those in the other experimental stores. They might have been, but again they might have been vastly different. The problem with experimental mortality, as with all these other extraneous sources of variation, is not that they have indeed operated but rather that we *do not know whether or not they have operated* and whether or not they have affected the criterion variable. The key then becomes one of designing investigations so that this doubt can be eliminated.

Specific Designs

Three types of experimental designs are commonly distinguished: pre-experimental designs, true experimental designs, and quasi-experimental designs.[22] True experimental designs are the most effective in eliminating the doubt that can arise in interpreting research results, as they provide the most control over the various extraneous factors. Unfortunately, not all marketing problems allow the use of true experimental designs. An understanding of their features, though, should allow a more scientific interpretation of the results, with due allowance for the necessary caveats when pre-experimental or quasi-experimental designs are used.

Pre-experimental Designs

A pre-experimental design is distinguished by the fact that the researcher has very little control over both the *when* and the *to whom* of exposure to experimental stimuli and over the *when* and *to whom* of measurement.

THE ONE-SHOT CASE STUDY   A useful point of departure for discussing experiments is the one-shot case study. The one-shot case study can be diagrammed

$$X \quad O$$

A single group of test units is exposed to an experimental variable, and its response is observed once. There is no random allocation of test units in the group; rather, the group is self-selected or is selected arbitrarily by the experimenter. For example, we might interview a convenience sample of those who read a particular trade journal for their reaction to our product. The experimental stimulus here would be the ad.

---

[22]See Campbell and Stanley, *Experimental and Quasi-Experimental Designs,* for an extensive discussion of the three types.

The one-shot case study is of little value in establishing the validity of hypothesized causal relationships (the ad was responsible for creating a favorable attitude toward our product) because it provides too little control over the extraneous influences. It provides no basis for comparing what happened in the presence of X with what happened when X was absent. Yet the minimum demands of scientific inquiry require that such comparisons be made.

The one-shot case study is more appropriate for exploratory than conclusive research. It is appropriately used to suggest hypotheses; it is not appropriate for testing their validity.

THE ONE-GROUP PRETEST–POSTTEST DESIGN   The one-group pretest–posttest design is diagrammed as follows:

$$O_1 \quad X \quad O_2$$

It adds a pretest to the one-shot case study design. In effect, the convenience sample of designated respondents is interviewed for their attitudes toward our product before the ad is placed. They are also interviewed after the ad is run, and the effectiveness of the ad is taken as the difference (d) in their attitudes before and after exposure to the ad:

$$d = O_2 - O_1$$

Although widely used to argue the effectiveness of marketing strategies, the one-group pretest–posttest design's failure to control extraneous error nullifies its conclusions. Consider just some of the factors that might be responsible for the $O_2 - O_1$ difference, aside from the experimental variable X. First, history is uncontrolled. Other ads, trade journal articles, some firsthand experience with the product, or any of a host of other factors may have occurred simultaneously with the experiment that caused the attitude change observed in a particular respondent. The respondent's position may have changed. Because of a change in the individual's status, the respondent may have been more responsive to the product in question at O_2 than at O_1 (maturation). Both the interactive and main testing effects might be at work. Because respondents were interviewed to secure O_1, they paid more attention to the trade journal ad than the normal reader might (interactive testing effect), so the $O_2 - O_1$ difference cannot be generalized to the population of interest. In addition, respondents might attempt to appear consistent with their O_1 score (main testing effect). Perhaps the respondents' initial responses created an extreme attitude score in either a positive or negative direction; then statistical regression is likely to have occurred with the O_2 scores. Suppose there is some experimental mortality. Would the $O_2 - O_1$ difference have been larger or smaller if the lost participants were included? We do not know. Further, the sample was a convenience sample, and the result probably could not be generalized to the larger population. Even if the initial sample had been a probability sample, all the other extraneous sources of error could still have affected the results.

THE STATIC-GROUP COMPARISON   The static-group comparison is a design in which there are two groups, one that has experienced X and another that has not.

A key feature is that the groups have not been created by randomization. The static-group comparison is diagrammed

$$\text{EG:}\quad X\quad O_1$$
$$\text{CG:}\qquad\quad O_2$$

To continue with our previous example of the effectiveness of a particular ad, the static-group comparison would be conducted as follows: After the ad is run, interviews would be conducted among a sample of readers. Those who remembered seeing the ad would be considered the "experimental group," EG. Those who did not recall seeing the ad would be considered the "control group," CG. The attitudes of each group toward the product would be measured, and the effectiveness of the ad would be taken to be

$$d = O_1 - O_2$$

That is, the equation states the difference in attitudes between those seeing the ad and those not seeing it.

There are two fundamental sources of extraneous error in the static-group comparison. First, there is no way of ensuring that the groups were equivalent prior to the comparison. Those who have favorable attitudes toward a product often pay more attention to ads for the product than those who have unfavorable attitudes. It may be that the $O_1 - O_2$ difference reflects the initial attitude of the two groups and is not in any way attributable to the ad.

The second fundamental weakness of the static-group comparison involves its representativeness. It may be that the two groups were indeed equal at some previous time. Now, however, not all individuals contacted are willing to supply their attitudes toward the product. The design suffers experimental mortality as a result of this nonresponse, since the question of what the O_2 and O_1 scores would have been if all those designated to participate had indeed cooperated is unanswered.

True Experimental Designs

Randomization makes the data from true experimental designs more valid than data from any pre-experimental design. The true experimental design is distinguished by the fact that the experimenter can randomly assign treatments to randomly selected test units. In effect, the experimenter can control the *when* and *to whom* of exposure. The experimenter can also control the *when* and *to whom* of measurement. To distinguish the true experiment, let us denote a random assignment of test units to treatments by (R).

BEFORE–AFTER WITH CONTROL GROUP DESIGN   The before–after with control group design was considered an experimental ideal for a number of years. The design can be diagrammed

$$\text{EG:}\quad (R)\quad O_1\quad X\quad O_2$$
$$\text{CG:}\quad (R)\quad O_3\qquad\quad O_4$$

Although it diagrams quite simply, this design imposes a number of requirements on the researcher. First, the division of the test units is under the researcher's control. The researcher alone is able to decide which test units will receive the experimental stimulus and which will not. It is *not* up to the test units to self-select whether they will be members of the control or experimental groups, as they did in the preexperimental designs. Further, the experimenter cannot arbitrarily assign test units to the experimental and control groups. He or she must do this randomly. The experimenter may match the test units on some external criterion and then assign one member from each of the matched pairs to the experimental and control groups, but this final assignment is made randomly. Finally, each of the test units in both groups is measured before and after the introduction of the experimental stimulus.

Consider the problem faced by an in-house credit union in promoting the credit union idea among the company's workers. Suppose that the company is considering the effectiveness of a rather expensive brochure, "Know Your Credit Union," in creating awareness and understanding of the functioning of the credit union. Let the brochure be the experimental stimulus X. The use of the before–after with control group design to investigate the effectiveness of the brochure would proceed along the following lines:

First, a sample of the firm's employees would be selected at random. Second, one-half of these employees would be randomly assigned to the experimental group receiving the brochure, while the other half would form the control group. Third, each of the respondents selected for the sample would be measured, using some scale or questionnaire to ascertain the employee's knowledge of the credit union. Fourth, the brochure would be mailed to those respondents who were designated for the experimental group.[23] After the lapse of some appropriate time interval (say, one to two weeks), the knowledge scale or questionnaire would again be administered to each of the sample respondents.

Now consider this design in terms of the various sources of extraneous error. The difference O_4 minus O_3 reflects the effects of the extraneous influences. For instance, consider the possibility that during the course of the experiment there was a change in the bank prime lending rate and credit became more expensive. This history effect would be partially responsible for any differences in O_4 and O_3. However, it would also exert a similar influence on those belonging to the experimental group. Thus, if we were to consider the effect of the experimental variable to be E and the effect of these extraneous or uncontrolled sources of variation to be U, the impact of the experimental stimulus X could be secured as follows:

$$\frac{\begin{array}{rl} O_2 - O_1 & = E + U \\ O_4 - O_3 & = \quad U \end{array}}{(O_2 - O_1) - (O_4 - O_3) = E}$$

But note that this calculation applies to the following sources of extraneous variation: history, maturation, main testing effect, statistical regression, and instrument variation. All these influences should affect both groups approximately equally. Selection bias, of course, was eliminated by the random assignment of individuals to groups. The design can suffer from experimental mortality, however, if some of the employees designated for the study refuse to participate.

---

[23]The brochure would be mailed if that were the normal way of distributing it. If some other method of distribution were commonly used, the experimental procedure would also follow this mode of distribution.

Assuming that proper procedures were employed to eliminate experimental mortality, one can readily appreciate why this design was long considered ideal. But this changed with the discovery that the design may not control for the interactive testing effect. The pretest can make the experimental subjects respond to *X*, wholly or partially, because they have been sensitized. Yet the key question for credit union management is how employees in general, not just those pretested, respond to the brochure.

The situation in calculating the impact of the experimental stimulus then becomes

$$
\begin{array}{ll}
O_2 - O_1 & = E + U + I \\
O_4 - O_3 & = \phantom{E + {}} U \\
\hline
(O_2 - O_1) - (O_4 - O_3) & = E + I
\end{array}
$$

where *I* measures the interactive effect of testing. The analyst is unable to determine the impact of the experimental stimulus when the interactive effect of testing is present in the before–after with control group design. His or her calculation of the net difference provides a result, but this result has two components—a component due to the experimental stimulus and a component due to the interactive testing effect.

A classic example of the interactive testing effect occurred in a United Nations education campaign.[24] The study employed a sample of 2,000 individuals split into two equivalent groups of 1,000 each. Each member of the first group was interviewed to determine his or her knowledge of and attitudes toward the United Nations. This was followed by a publicity campaign of several months' duration, in turn followed by interviews with the second sample. A comparison of the two sets of scores produced practically no results; the members of the second sample were no better informed and did not have any more favorable attitudes than the first sample. The second sample was not even generally aware that the publicity campaign had been going on. In terms of the population of interest, the campaign was indeed a failure. Yet when the first sample was reinterviewed, there was a decided change in the members' attitudes toward and information known about the United Nations. They had been sensitized to watch for and pay more attention to United Nations publicity. The same kind of testing effect can operate in a before–after with control group design.

FOUR-GROUP SIX-STUDY DESIGN   In many research problems, the prior measurement is of such a nature that the test units are not sensitized to the experiment. In cases such as these, the before–after with control group design provides an estimate of the effect of the experimental variable. When an interactive testing effect is likely to be present, the four-group six-study design is a good choice.

The four-group six-study design can be diagrammed as

EG	I:	(R)	O_1	X	O_2
CG	I:	(R)	O_3		O_4
EG	II:	(R)		X	O_5
CG	II:	(R)			O_6

[24]S. A. Star and H. M. Hughes, "Report on an Educational Campaign: The Cincinnati Plan for the United Nations," *American Journal of Sociology* 40 (1949–1950), p. 389.

Consider again the problem of measuring the effect of the "Know Your Credit Union" brochure. The four-group six-study design would impose the following requirements on the researcher: First, a sample of the firm's employees would be selected at random. Second, the sample would be randomly divided into four groups. Those designated for the first experimental and control groups would be measured, using some appropriate instrument, for their knowledge of the credit union. The brochure would then be mailed to those designated as belonging to the first and second experimental groups. Then all four groups would be measured on their knowledge of the credit union. Thus, six measurements in all are made, as suggested by the name of the design.

One can readily appreciate the control afforded by the four-group six-study design. Selection bias is handled by the random assignment of test units to groups. The other extraneous sources of error are handled much as they were in the before–after with control group design—that is, by making the logical assumption that factors such as history, maturation, and so on should affect all groups. By thus looking at the "difference in differences," the impact of these extraneous factors should be netted out. Further, although there is a possible interactive testing effect with the first experimental group, there can be none with the second experimental group, because there is no prior measurement to sensitize the respondents. The lack of a prior measurement raises the question of how to calculate the effect of X in the second experimental and control groups. One thing that can be done is to estimate what the prior measurements would have been. The most logical estimate is one that takes account of the random assignment of the test units to groups, assuming that, except for sampling variations, the four groups were equal *a priori* in their knowledge of the credit union. Thus, the best estimate of the "before measurement" for the second experimental and control groups is the average of the before measurements actually taken; that is, $\frac{1}{2}(O_1 + O_3)$.

On substituting this estimate, the various differences between after and before measurements are as follows:

$$
\begin{array}{llll}
\text{EG} & \text{I:} & O_2 - O_1 & = E + U + I \\
\text{CG} & \text{I:} & O_4 - O_3 & = U \\
\text{EG} & \text{II:} & O_5 - \frac{1}{2}(O_1 + O_3) = E + U \\
\text{CG} & \text{II:} & O_6 - \frac{1}{2}(O_1 + O_3) = U
\end{array}
$$

What is the impact of the experimental stimulus? Clearly, it is determined by comparing the second experimental and control groups and is given specifically by the calculation

$$[O_5 - \tfrac{1}{2}(O_1 + O_3)] - [O_6 - \tfrac{1}{2}(O_1 + O_3)] = [E + U] - [U] = E$$

However, that is not the only estimated effect provided by the four-group six-study design. This design also allows the effect of the uncontrolled extraneous factors on the response to be estimated, and it provides for an estimate of the magnitude of the interactive testing effect. Two independent estimates of extraneous error are in fact provided, one by each of the control groups. An estimate of the size of the interactive testing effect is provided by comparing Experimental Groups I and II through the calculation

$$[O_2 - O_1] - [O_5 - \tfrac{1}{2}(O_1 + O_3)] = [E + U + I] - [E + U] = I$$

One need only look at the estimates of the various effects to appreciate why the four-group six-study design has become a conceptual ideal. Its practical application in marketing is somewhat limited, however, because the design is expensive in terms of time and money. Further, marketing samples are not always so large as to afford the luxury of dividing the samples of test units into four equal groups. If the group samples are small, it is unlikely that they will, in fact, be equal even if assigned randomly. Rather, the equality-of-groups assumption depends on the operation of the statistician's "law of large numbers." Nevertheless, the isolation of the various effects afforded by the four-group six-study design makes it a standard against which other designs may be compared.

AFTER-ONLY WITH CONTROL GROUP DESIGN   The careful reader will have observed that the researcher can estimate the impact of the experimental stimulus in the four-group six-study design simply by comparing Experimental Group II to Control Group II, which raises the question of why Experimental Group I and Control Group I are included. They are certainly *not* needed to generate an estimate of a "before measurement" for Experimental Group II and Control Group II, because regardless of what this measurement is, it cancels in the basic calculation of the effect of the experimental variable; that is,

$$[O_5 - \tfrac{1}{2}(O_1 + O_3)] - [O_6 - \tfrac{1}{2}(O_1 + O_3)] = O_5 - O_6$$

Thus, the before measurements are not needed to estimate the effect of the experimental stimulus. They do allow the researcher to study individual cases of change and to develop better methodology, because they enable study of the experimental variable under different conditions. If the researcher's sole interest is estimating the impact of the experimental variable, though, as is often the case, this estimate can be provided by studying the last two groups of the four-group six-study design in an after-only with control group design.

The after-only with control group design can be diagrammed as follows:

$$\text{EG:} \quad \text{(R)} \quad X \quad O_5$$
$$\text{CG:} \quad \text{(R)} \qquad\;\; O_6$$

where the observations have been subscripted with a 5 and 6 to indicate that these groups have not been pretested in the four-group six-study design. To use this design to investigate the effect of the "Know Your Credit Union" brochure, the researcher would again select a random sample of employees. One-half would be randomly assigned to the experimental group, and the other half would form the control group. Neither group would be premeasured, and the brochure would be mailed to all those in the experimental group. After some appropriate time lapse, both groups would be measured for their knowledge, and the estimated effect of the brochure would be provided by the difference O_5 minus O_6.

One can readily appreciate how the extraneous sources of error are eliminated in this experiment. The main extraneous factors are assumed to affect both groups, and thus their influence is eliminated by calculating the difference between O_5 and O_6. No interactive testing effect occurs since no pretest has taken place. The experimental test units should behave much like the larger population of employees, in that some might read the brochure carefully, some might read it casually, and some might simply throw it away without reading it. This is as it should be, and the results can therefore be generalized to the population of employees.

There are two very important caveats, though, with respect to the after-only with control group design. This design is very sensitive to problems of selection bias and experimental mortality. The prior equality of the groups is assumed because of the random assignment of test units to groups. Since no before measurement is made the assumption cannot be checked. It must be taken on faith, and this faith demands that the assignment of test units to groups was indeed random. Further, the design is highly sensitive to experimental mortality. There is simply no way of determining whether those who refuse to cooperate or who drop out of the experimental group are similar to those dropping out of the control group. Experimental mortality, if it exists, calls into question the foundation on which the after-only with control group design rests—namely, that the groups are equal save for the impact of the experimental stimulus.

Be aware that the after-only with control group design *does not allow* the investigation of individual cases of change. This can sometimes be of real concern. For example, the design would not allow credit union management to investigate the effect of the "Know Your Credit Union" brochure on those who already had a good working knowledge of the credit union versus those who had little awareness and knowledge. The design affords no way of determining an employee's prior knowledge. Both the before–after with control group design and the four-group six-study design are superior in this respect. However, if the individual cases of change are not of interest, the after-only with control group design is a viable one. As a matter of fact, it is probably the most frequently used experimental design in marketing research, because it possesses a number of sample-size, cost, and time advantages, involving as it does only two groups and two measurements.

Quasi-Experimental Designs

We have just seen that the true experimental design is distinguished by the control it affords the researcher. The researcher is able to determine who will be exposed to the experimental stimulus, when the exposure will occur, who will be measured, and where that measurement will take place. In some cases, the investigator simply will not have control of the *when* and *to whom* of exposure. The researcher will not be able to schedule the experimental stimuli or randomly assign test units to groups. If the researcher does have control of the *when* and *to whom* of measurement, though, a quasi-experimental design results.

There are a number of quasi-experimental designs, although we will discuss only the time-series experiment.[25] The discussion should indicate the emphasis in

---

[25]Campbell and Stanley, *Experimental and Quasi-Experimental Designs,* pp. 36–64, and Banks, *Experimentation in Marketing,* pp. 37–45; both present a number of useful quasi-experimental designs.

quasi-experimental designs. The time-series experiment was selected because it is uniquely suited to some types of marketing data that are routinely generated.

TIME-SERIES EXPERIMENT   The time-series experiment can be diagrammed as

$$O_1 \quad O_2 \quad O_3 \quad O_4 \quad X \quad O_5 \quad O_6 \quad O_7 \quad O_8$$

This diagram suggests that a group of test units is observed over time, that an experimental stimulus is introduced, and that the test units are again observed for their reaction. A change in the previous pattern of observations is taken as the effect of the experimental stimulus.

The time-series experiment demands that researchers have repeated access to the same test units. Further, although researchers cannot schedule the exposure of these test units to the experimental stimulus, they can control when the units will be measured. Panel data conform nicely, then, to the time-series experiment. Further, a number of panels supply marketing data routinely. This is why the time-series experiment is one of the most important quasi-experimental designs for the marketing researcher.

Of course, our interest when using the time-series experiment is in establishing that the observed effect is due to the experimental variable. This requires that we eliminate other plausible hypotheses for the occurrence of the phenomenon. Now, the time-series experiment bears some resemblance to the pre-experimental one-group pretest–posttest design. The resemblance is superficial, since the series of observations affords additional control. Consider some of the possible patterns of responses that may result, as illustrated in Figure 5.1.

Note first of all that the pattern of responses, rather than any single observation, is key in interpreting the data from a time-series experiment. Consider, say, the impact of a package change, *X*, on the firm's market share. On the basis of the plot of the data points in Figure 5.1, it would seem logical to conclude that the package change:

1. Exerted a positive impact in situation *A* (it raised the firm's market share).
2. Had a positive impact in situation *B* (it halted a decline in market share).
3. Had no long-run impact in situation *C* (sales in Period 5 seem to be borrowed from sales in Periods 6 and 7).
4. Had no impact in situation *D* (the firm's market share growth remained steady).
5. Had no impact in situation *E* (the observed fluctuation after the introduction of the experimental variable is no greater than what was previously observed).

Of course, we would be interested in testing for the statistical significance of any observed changes.

Consider now the additional control afforded by the time-series experiment versus the one-group pretest–posttest design in interpreting the after and before measurements. First, maturation can be partially ruled out as causing the difference in O_5 and O_4 because it is unlikely that it would operate only in this one instance. Rather, it would logically have an effect on a number of other observations. Instrument variation, statistical regression, and the main testing effect would be similarly avoided. Selection bias can be reduced by the random selection of test units. Experimental

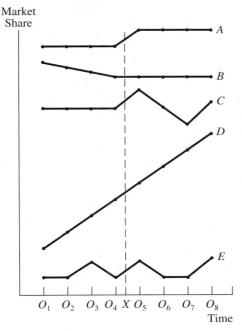

| FIGURE 5.1 | Some Possible Outcomes in a Time-Series Experiment When Introducing an Experimental Variable X |

mortality can, it is hoped, be controlled by paying some premium to maintain cooperation. Of course, we saw in Chapter 4 that the ability to solicit and maintain cooperation in panels presents some problems, and a panel may not completely control the problems of selection bias and experimental mortality. These conditions also occur in the one-group pretest–posttest pre-experimental design.

The failure to control history is the most fundamental weakness of the time-series experiment. Despite this, a carefully executed time-series experiment can provide some useful insight. If the careful examination of, say, consumer panel data before, during, and after introducing the experimental variable fails to turn up any unusual competitive reaction, and if researchers also record other environmental changes as they occur, the researchers are in a position to make a valid assessment of the effect of the experimental stimulus. Of course, researchers can never be as sure that the impact of history has been ruled out in a quasi-experimental design as they can in a true experimental design. However, a repeatable stimulus, such as a cents-off coupon program, will afford greater certainty, because the effect of history will not be the same each time.

Another weakness of the time-series experiment is that it may be influenced by the interactive testing effect. There may be some peculiarity in the experimental stimulus so that it affects only those sampling units subjected to repeated testing.

Experimental versus Nonexperimental Designs

By now you should appreciate that exploratory and descriptive designs are not particularly useful in establishing the existence of causal relationships. They simply do not provide the control necessary to infer that a causal relationship does indeed exist. Exploratory studies are less of a problem in this regard, since they are rarely used to make causal statements. Unfortunately, the same thing cannot be said about descriptive studies. Frequently, the evidence of a cross-sectional survey is employed to argue that X caused Y or the evidence from some time-series data is analyzed using, say, regression analysis to establish X as causing Y.

The error in such arguments can be appreciated by dissecting the typical descriptive study. A random sample of respondents is selected. The respondents are measured with respect to some effect or response variable Y. Next they are queried about the hypothesized causal factor X. If it is then found that those who possess X also possess Y and those who lack X also lack Y, the truth of the assertion that "X causes Y" is established. The research is *ex post facto*, because the researcher is starting with the observation of a dependent or criterion variable and is retrospectively searching for plausible explanations.[26]

A problem arises in descriptive studies with respect to all three types of evidence used to support causality. Concomitant variation is observed. However, there is no way of knowing that those who did and did not possess Y were at some prior time equivalent with respect to both Y and X. In the experiment, the researcher is able to establish this equivalence by the random assignment of test units to groups. The researcher also knows quite accurately who was exposed to X and does not have to rely on a respondent's memory. The analyst is thus able to determine whether Y occurs more frequently among the subjects who have been exposed to X than it does among those who have not.

The researcher is also better able to establish the time order of occurrence of variables in an experiment. The experimental and control groups are set up in such a way that it is reasonable to assume they did not differ in terms of the response variable before exposure to the experimental stimulus. With some experimental designs, the researcher actually measures the test units with respect to the criterion variable before exposing them to the experimental stimulus. In descriptive studies, the researcher simply has to assume that prior equality exists.

The descriptive study affords little control in eliminating other possible explanations. All the factors that affect experimental results also operate in descriptive research, but the analyst has no way of removing their effects. The analyst ends up in the awkward position of asserting it is this X and no other X that is causing Y. This assertion rests on a great deal of faith.

This is not to deny the important role descriptive designs play in marketing research. They are, after all, the dominant form. But the reader must be aware of the dangers of using descriptive designs to establish causal linkages between variables.

Experimentation in Marketing Research

Experiments in marketing were rare before 1960, but their growth since then has been steady. One of the most important growth areas has been in market testing, or test-marketing. Although some writers make a distinction between the terms, the

---

[26]Kerlinger, *Foundations*, pp. 347–360, has a particularly illuminating discussion of the problems of interpretation in *ex post facto* research.

essential feature of the **market test** is that "it is a controlled experiment, done in a limited but carefully selected part of the marketplace, whose aim is to predict the sales or profit consequences, either in absolute or relative terms, of one or more proposed marketing actions."[27] Very often the action in question is the marketing of a new product or service or an improved version of an old product or service. For example, Blockbuster Video in 1999 launched test marketing of CD-ROM rentals. At stores in Anchorage, Alaska, and Austin, Texas, Blockbuster began offering 10 computer games on CD-ROM to complement its rentals of movies and Nintendo and Sony PlayStation games. Consumers who rent the CD-ROMs get a coupon that they activate online, permitting them to play the game for three days. They keep the CD-ROM and may choose to renew the rental or buy the game.[28] As another example, consider Wendy's experience in developing the "Big Classic" hamburger, described in Research Realities 5.3.

RESEARCH REALITIES 5.3

Research Conducted by Wendy's for the "Big Classic" Hamburger

To find out what people want, Wendy's spent $1 million over nine months doing taste tests with 5,200 people in six cities. They tested:

- Nine different buns: some hard, some soft; with sesame seeds or poppy seeds; cold, toasted, or warmed; square or round; and even croissants.

- Forty special sauces, including steak sauce, hot sauce, mustard, and salad dressing.

- Three types of lettuce: chopped, shredded, and leaf.

- Two sizes of tomato slices.

- Four boxes in ten earth-tone colors.

The final product is a quarter-pound square beef patty topped with leaf lettuce, two tomato slices, raw onion rings, dill pickles, and extra dabs of ketchup and mayonnaise on a corn-dusted, hearth-baked kaiser bun. It comes in an almond-colored styrofoam box with a dome sculpted to resemble the bun's top. It can cost up to 10 cents more than the old burger, which is still on the menu.

A significant research finding was that the order of the condiments "makes a tremendous difference to consumers," said Denny Lynch, a spokesperson for Wendy's. "Which is why the Big Classic will taste different rightside up or upside down, depending on the way the toppings hit your taste buds."

Wendy's came up with a color code to help its employees remember the correct order: white, red, green, white, red, green (mayonnaise, ketchup, pickle, onion, tomato, lettuce).

Source: "Wendy's Discovers—Old Burger," *The Wisconsin State Journal* (September 19, 1986), p. 6. Reprinted with permission. For other tests being done by Wendy's, see "Marketing & Media: Wendy's Chain Is Testing Alternate Combo Meals," *The Wall Street Journal* (February 14, 1995), p. B12.

---

[27]Alvin R. Achenbaum, "Market Testing: Using the Marketplace as a Laboratory," in Robert Ferber, ed., *Handbook of Marketing Research* (New York: McGraw-Hill, 1974), pp. 4-31 to 4-54. See also "Some Methodological Issues in Product Testing," *Research on Research*, no. 41 (Chicago: Market Facts, Inc., undated); James F. Donues, "Marketplace Measurement: The Evolution of Market Testing," *Journal of Advertising Research* 27 (December 1987/January 1988), pp. RC-3–RC-5; Madhav N. Segal and J. S. Johar, "On Improving the Effectiveness of Test Marketing Decisions," *European Journal of Marketing* 26, no. 4 (1992), pp. 21–33.

[28]Omar L. Gallaga, "Blockbuster Video Tests Rentals of Desktop Computer Games," *Austin American Statesman* (April 26, 1999, downloaded from Dow Jones Publications Library at the Dow Jones Web site, www.dowjones.com, August 4, 1999).

ETHICAL DILEMMA 5.2

The regional sales manager for a large chain of men's clothing stores asks you to establish whether increasing his salespeople's commission will result in better sales performance. Specifically, he wants to know whether increasing the commission on limited lines of clothing will result in better sales on those lines along with the penalty of fewer sales on the remaining lines, and whether raising the commission on all lines will produce greater sales on all lines. Suppose that you think that the best way to investigate the issue is through a field experiment in which some salespeople receive increased commission on a single line, others receive increased commission across the board, and still others make up a control group whose members receive no increase in commission.

- Are there ethical problems inherent in such a design?
- Is the control group being deprived of any benefits?

Notwithstanding previous tests of the product concept, the product package, the advertising copy, and so on, the test market is still the final gauge of consumer acceptance of the product. ACNielsen data, for example, indicate that roughly three out of four products that have been test-marketed succeed, whereas four out of five that have not been test-marketed fail.[29]

An example of the benefits to be gained from test-marketing can be found in the experience of Pillsbury in developing its Oven Lovin' refrigerated cookie dough, which was packaged in resealable tubs. In focus groups, consumers raved about Oven Lovin', which was loaded with Hershey's chocolate chips, Reese's Pieces, and Brach's candies. Based on the rave reactions, the company omitted test-marketing and immediately rolled out the product, supporting it with heavy television advertising and some 200 million coupons. Sales took off like a rocket, rising from zero to almost $6 million a month. After three months, though, they began to crumble and were almost nonexistent two years later. Although consumers maintained they liked the product and resealable package, "many shoppers found they ended up baking the entire package at once—or gobbling up leftover raw dough instead of saving it—eliminating the need for the . . . package." In sum, the package provided a benefit consumers did not really need, particularly since it contained only 18 ounces of dough, compared with 20 ounces in a tube of Pillsbury Best dough, which was priced comparably.[30]

Test-marketing is not restricted to testing the sales potential of new products but has been used to examine the sales effectiveness of almost every element of the marketing mix. General Motors, for example, used its Cadillac car division to test market an alteration in its distribution strategy it was considering for all its car lines.

---

[29]"Test Marketing: What's in Store," *Sales and Marketing Management* 128 (March 15, 1982), pp. 57–85; "Pinning Down Costs of Product Introductions," *The Wall Street Journal* (November 26, 1990), p. B1.

[30]Kathleen Deveny, "Failure of Its Oven Lovin' Cookie Dough Shows Pillsbury Pitfalls of New Products," *The Wall Street Journal* (June 17, 1993), pp. B1, B8.

The Florida test involved keeping 1,200 new cars at a regional distribution center in Orlando for delivery to the state's 42 dealerships within 24 hours of an order. The approach was intended to whittle down the costly inventory that dealers have to maintain, improve manufacturing efficiency, and increase sales by allowing consumers to take quick possession of precisely the Cadillac model they want. GM and most other car makers have long been criticized for the waste associated with their typical practice of loading up dealership lots with an assortment of cars they think people will buy. This practice saddles dealers with high-cost inventory and does little to encourage just-in-time production practices at the factory level. Moreover, dealers often find themselves stuck with models that customers really do not want and short of the ones in demand.[31]

Market tests have also been employed to measure the sales effectiveness of new displays, the responsiveness of sales to shelf space changes, the impact of changes in retail prices on market shares, the price elasticity of demand for products, the effect of different commercials on sales of products, and the differential effects of price and advertising on demand.

Experimentation is not restricted to test-marketing. Rather, it can be used whenever the manager has some specific mix alternatives to consider (for example, package design A versus B) and when the researcher can control the conditions sufficiently to allow an adequate test of the alternatives. Experiments are often used, therefore, when testing product or package concepts and advertising copy, although they have also been used for a variety of other purposes.

Future and Problems of Experimentation

Although marketing experiments will continue to be used, particularly when the research problem is one of determining which is the best of an available set of limited marketing alternatives, experimentation is not without its problems. Test-marketing is a useful vehicle for illustrating these problems, because it has been characterized as a double-edged sword (although to a greater or lesser extent the problems are present in other types of experiments). As Larry Gibson, a former director of corporate marketing research for General Mills, commented about test-marketing: "It costs a mint, tells the competition what you're doing, takes forever, and is not always accurate. . . . For the moment, it's the only game in town."[32] Three of the more critical problems with experimentation in general and test-marketing in particular are cost, time, and control.

Cost

A major consideration in test-marketing has always been cost. First are the costs of the experiment itself with which to contend. These include the normal research costs associated with designing the data-collection instruments and the sample, as well as the wages paid to the field staff that collects the data. The direct research

---

[31]Gabriele Stern, "GM Expands Its Experiment to Improve Cadillac's Distribution, Cut Inefficiency," *The Wall Street Journal* (February 8, 1995), p. A12.

[32]"To Test or Not to Test Seldom the Question," *Advertising Age* 55 (February 20, 1984), pp. M10–M11.

costs are often substantial, and other costs must be borne as well. General Mills, for example, spent $28 million testing and refining its chain of Olive Garden restaurants.[33] Moreover, the test market should reflect the marketing strategy to be employed on the national scale if the results are to be useful, so the test also includes marketing costs for advertising, personal selling, displays, and so on.

With new-product introductions, there are also the costs associated with producing the merchandise. To produce the product on a small scale is typically inefficient. Yet to gear up immediately for large-scale production can be tremendously wasteful if the test-market indicates that the product is a failure.

Time

The time required for an adequate test-market can be substantial. For example, it took Procter & Gamble nine years to go national with Pampers disposable diapers after they were first introduced in Peoria, Illinois, and it took General Mills five years to test its Olive Garden restaurants.[34] One reason for extending the length of time for test markets is that empirical evidence indicates their accuracy increases directly with time. Experiments conducted over short periods do not allow for the cumulative effect of the marketing actions, for instance. Consequently, a year is often recommended as a minimum period before any kind of go–no-go decision is made to account for seasonal sales variations and repeat purchasing behavior. Experiments continued over long periods, however, are costly and raise additional problems of control and competitive reaction.

Time is of particular essence in today's faster-paced global environment, where competitive reaction can be so swift that many firms have committed themselves to speeding product introductions worldwide. For example, Procter & Gamble's test marketing of the Dryel home dry-cleaning kit and the Swiffer sweeper system each took less than a year and a half. Furthermore, the test markets were international— Columbus, Ohio, and Ireland for Dryel and Iowa and France for Swiffer. International testing enables the company to launch products globally, rather than waiting for U.S. success before moving overseas.[35]

Control

The problems associated with control manifest themselves in several ways. First, there are the control problems in the experiment itself. What specific test markets will be used? How will product distribution be organized in those markets? Can the firm elicit the necessary cooperation from wholesalers? From retailers? Can the test markets and control cities be matched sufficiently to rule out market characteristics as the primary determinant of the different sales results? Can the rest of the elements of the marketing strategy be controlled so as not to induce unwanted aberrations in the experimental setting? A common problem that firms have to overcome

---

[33]Annetta Miller and Karen Springen, "Egg Rolls for Peoria," *Newsweek* (October 12, 1992), pp. 59–60.

[34]Julie B. Solomon, "P&G Rolls Out New Items at Faster Pace, Turning Away from Long Marketing Testing," *The Wall Street Journal* (May 11, 1984), p. 25; Miller and Springen, "Egg Rolls." See also Dan Koeppel, "Will K-C Ever Get Once Overs Out of Missouri?" *Adweek's Marketing Week* (February 27, 1989), p. 62.

[35]Suzanne Vranica, "P&G Puts Two Cleaning Products on Its New Marketing Fast Track," *The Wall Street Journal* (May 18, 1996), p. B6.

when test-marketing products is the problem of too much control. Precisely because the product is being test-marketed, it receives more attention than it would ever receive on a national scale. In the test market, for example, store shelves may be better stocked, the sales force more diligent, and the advertising more prominent than would normally be the case. One reason given for the failure of Pringles potato chips, which was very successful in test market but bombed nationally, is that quality slipped when the project was mass produced on the necessarily larger scale.

Control problems are associated with competitive reaction, too. Although the firm might be able to coordinate its own marketing activities and even those of intermediaries in the distribution channel so as not to contaminate the experiment, it can exert little control over its competitors. Competitors can, and do, sabotage marketing experiments by cutting the prices of their own products, by gobbling up quantities of the test marketer's product (thereby creating a state of euphoria and false confidence on the part of the test marketer), and by other devious means. It has been called the most dangerous game in all of marketing because of the great opportunity it affords for misfires, as attested by the examples in Research Realities 5.4.

One could argue that the misfires reflected in Examples 5 and 8 in Research Realities 5.4 represent some of the fundamental reasons that firms test-market products. Indeed, it seems better to find out about product performance problems like these in test market rather than after a product is introduced nationally. Consider, for example, the losses in company prestige that would have resulted if the following problems had not been discovered in test markets:[36]

- Sunlight dishwashing liquid was confused with Minute Maid lemon juice by at least 33 adults and 45 children, who became ill after drinking it.

- When a large packaged-goods company set out to introduce a squirtable soft-drink concentrate for children, it held focus groups to monitor user reaction. In the sessions, children squirted the product neatly into cups. Once at home, however, few could resist the temptation to decorate their parents' floors and walls with the colorful liquid. After a flood of parental complaints, the product was withdrawn from development.

Other companies instead have been embarrassed when they have implemented faulty plans nationwide. A mid-1990s effort to merge television and computers flopped when NetTV was offered to the public at $3,000 for a 29-inch monitor coupled with a personal computer. Consumers couldn't figure out why they would want a computer in their living room, especially considering how frustrating a computer can be to operate.[37] Apple Computer's notorious mistake was introducing an early palmtop computer, the Newton, which failed miserably at one of its featured tasks: reading the user's handwriting. Newton quickly became the butt

---

[36]Lynn G. Reiling, "Consumers Misuse Mars Sampling for Sunlight Dishwashing Liquid," *Marketing News* 16 (September 3, 1982), pp. 1, 12; Problem 10 is discussed in Annetta Miller and Dody Tsiantor, "A Test for Market Research," *Newsweek* 110 (December 28, 1987), pp. 32–33.

[37]Lee Gomes, "It Sounded So Good . . . : The History of Consumer Electronics Is Littered with Failure," *The Wall Street Journal* (June 15, 1998), p. R22.

Examples of Test-Marketing Misfires

Example 1 When Campbell Soup first test-marketed Prego spaghetti sauce, Campbell marketers say they noticed a flurry of new Ragu ads and cents-off deals that they believe were designed to induce shoppers to load up on Ragu and to skew Prego's test results. They also claim that Ragu copied Prego when it developed Ragu Homestyle spaghetti sauce, which was thick, red, and flecked with oregano and basil, and which Ragu moved into national distribution before Prego.

Example 2 Procter & Gamble claims that competitors stole its patented process for Duncan Hines chocolate chip cookies when they saw how successful the product was in test market.

Example 3 A health and beauty aids firm developed a deodorant containing baking soda. A competitor spotted the product in test market, rolled out its own version of the deodorant nationally before the first firm completed its testing, and later successfully sued the product originator for copyright infringement when it launched its deodorant nationally.

Example 4 When Procter & Gamble introduced its Always brand sanitary napkin in test market in Minnesota, Kimberly-Clark Corporation and Johnson & Johnson countered with free products, lots of coupons, and big dealer discounts, which caused Always not to do as well as expected.

Example 5 A few years ago, Snell (Booz, Allen, and Hamilton's design and development division, which does product development work under contract) developed a temporary hair coloring that consumers used by inserting a block of solid hair dye into a special comb. "It went to market and it was a bust," the company's Mr. Schoenholz recalls. On hot days when people perspired, any hair dye excessively applied ran down their necks and foreheads. "It just didn't occur to us to look at this under conditions where people perspire," he says.

Example 6 Campbell Soup spent 18 months developing a blended fruit juice called Juiceworks. By the time the product reached the market, three competing brands were already on store shelves. Campbell dropped its product.

Example 7 Spurred by its incredible success with Fruit 'N Juice Bars, Dole worked hard to create a new fruity ice cream novelty product with the same type of appeal. Company officials expected that the product resulting from this development activity, Fruit and Cream Bars, which it test marketed in Orlando, Florida, would do slightly less well because it was more of an indulgence-type product. The test market results were so positive, however, that Dole became the number-one brand in the market within three months. The company consequently shortened the test market to six months. When it rolled out the product, though, the company unhappily found four unexpected entrants in the ice cream novelty category. Because of the intense competition, product sales fell short of expectations.

Example 8 Frito-Lay test-marketed its Max potato, corn, and tostado chips, which contained the Olestra fat substitute, in Grand Junction, Colorado; Eau Claire, Wisconsin; and Cedar Rapids, Iowa. A TV crew sampled the chips, got diarrhea, and then broadcast a report about it, creating lots of bad publicity for the chips.

Sources: Betsy Morris, "New Campbell Entry Sets Off a Big Spaghetti Sauce Battle," *The Wall Street Journal* (December 2, 1982), p. 31; Eleanor Johnson Tracy, "Testing Time for Test Marketing," *Fortune* 110 (October 29, 1984), pp. 75–76; Kevin Wiggins, "Simulated Test Marketing Winning Acceptance," *Marketing News* 19 (March 1, 1985), pp. 15, 19; Damon Darden, "Faced with More Competition, P&G Sees New Products as Crucial to Earning's Growth," *The Wall Street Journal* (September 13, 1983), pp. 37, 53; Roger Recklefs, "Success Comes Hard in the Tricky Business of Creating Products," *The Wall Street Journal* (August 23, 1978), pp. 1, 27; Annetta Miller and Dody Tsiantor, "A Test for Market Research," *Newsweek* 110 (December 28, 1987), pp. 32–33; Leslie Brennan, "Test Marketing Put to the Test," *Sales and Marketing Management* 138 (March 1987), pp. 65–68; Annetta Miller and Karen Springen, "Will Fake Fat Play in Peoria?" *Newsweek* (June 3, 1996), p. 50.

of jokes, and although Apple later improved the product, it sank under the weight of poor publicity.[38]

Examples 1 through 4 and 6 and 7, though in Research Realities 5.4, are of a different sort. By exposing the product to competitors through a test market, each of the firms lost much of its differential development advantage. The simple point is that the marketing manager contemplating a market test must weigh the costs of such a test against its anticipated benefits. Even though the market test may serve as the final yardstick for consumer acceptance of a product, perhaps more careful early product testing in the form of need-satisfaction studies and in-home product performance tests would indicate that the market test is not warranted in particular instances.

Types of Test Markets

Figure 5.2 shows some of the most commonly used **standard test markets.** A standard market is one in which companies sell the product through their normal distribution channels. The results are typically monitored by one of the standard distribution services discussed in the next chapter. An alternative to the standardized test market is the **controlled test market,** which is sometimes called the forced-distribution test market. In the controlled test market, the entire test program is conducted by an outside service. The service pays retailers for shelf space and

| FIGURE 5.2 | Some Popular Standard Test Markets |

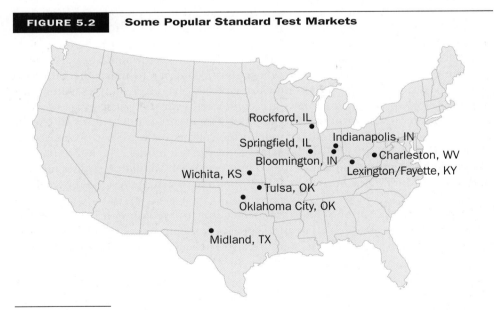

Source: Steve Lohr, "Test It in Tulsa, It'll Play in Peoria," *Chicago Tribune* (June 7, 1992), sec. 7, p. 1. See also Judith Waldrop, "Markets with Attitude," *American Demographics* (July 1994), pp. 22–33, for the "most typical" and "most surveyed" American cities.

[38]Jim Carlton, "Apple Drops Newton, an Idea Ahead of Its Time," *The Wall Street Journal* (March 2, 1998), p. B1.

therefore can guarantee distribution to those stores, which represent a predetermined percentage of the marketer's total food store sales volume. The service also positions the product in the best location in the store with the right number of shelf facings; it stocks the store shelves and coordinates any trade promotion programs. A number of firms operate controlled test markets, including Audits & Surveys and Burgoyne.

An increasingly popular variation of the controlled test market is the **electronic test market.** Electronic test markets differ from traditional controlled test markets in several ways. First, providers of the service recruit a panel of households in the test market area from which they secure a great deal of demographic information. People in these households are given identification cards, which they show when checking out at grocery stores. Everything they purchase is automatically recorded and associated with the household through scanners found in all supermarkets in the area. Second, suppliers of these services are capable of monitoring each household's television-viewing behavior. They thus can correlate exposure to test commercials with purchase behavior, which in turn allows users of the service to test not only consumer acceptance of a new or modified product but also various other parts of the marketing program. Research Realities 5.5 describes how the link between the demographic information of households and their purchase behavior can be used to advantage.

Another variation when test-marketing products is for firms to use a **simulated test market (STM)** as a prelude to a full-scale market test. Most STMs operate similarly. First, consumers are interviewed in shopping malls or sometimes in their homes. During the interview, they are exposed to the new product and are asked to rate its features. Then they are shown commercials for it and for competitors' products. In a simulated store environment, they are then given the opportunity to buy the product using seed money or cents-off coupons to make the purchase. Those not purchasing the test product are typically given free samples. After a use period, follow-up phone interviews are conducted with the participants to assess their reactions to the product and their repeat-purchase intentions. All the information is fed into a computer model, which has equations for the repeat purchase and market share likely to be achieved by the test model. The key to the simulation is the equations built into the computer model. Validation studies indicate that most STM models can come within 10 percent of actual sales in 80 percent of the cases.[39]

A prime advantage of STMs is the protection from competitors they provide. They are good for assessing trial- and repeat-purchasing behavior. They are faster and cheaper than full-scale tests and are also particularly good for spotting weak

---

[39]"Simulated Test Marketing Winning Acceptance," *Marketing News* 19 (March 1, 1985), pp. 15, 19; Allan D. Shocker and William G. Hall, "Pretest Market Models: A Critical Evaluation," *Journal of Product Innovation Management* 3 (September 1986), pp. 86–107; Kevin J. Clancy and Robert S. Shulman, "It's Better to Fly a New Product Simulator Than Crash the Real Thing," *Planning Review* 20 (July/August 1992), pp. 10–17; Christopher Power, "Will It Sell in Podunk? Hard to Say," *Business Week* (August 10, 1992), pp. 46–47; Raymond R. Burke, Bari A. Harlam, Barbara E. Kahn, and Leonard M. Lodish, "Comparing Dynamic Consumer Choice in Real and Computer-Simulated Environments," *Journal of Consumer Research* 19 (June 1992), pp. 71–82; Kevin J. Clancy, Robert S. Schulman, and Marianne Wolf, *Simulated Test Marketing: Technology for Launching Successful New Products* (New York: Lexington Books, 1994).

RESEARCH REALITIES 5.5

Use of an Electronic Test Market by Ocean Spray

In an attempt to be perceived more broadly, Ocean Spray developed a totally new fruit beverage, Mauna La'I Hawaiian Guava Drink. The product represented a significant departure for Ocean Spray, in that it was different in color, taste, and aroma from any other fruit drink on the market.

Concerned about how consumers might respond to the product, Ocean Spray decided to test market it using BehaviorScan's facilities in Eau Claire, Wisconsin, and Midland, Texas. Ocean Spray believed that the target market for Mauna La'I was similar to that for its cranberry drink: older children and adults with average education and income.

After six months in test market, initial trial for Mauna La'I was good, but the rate of repurchase was far below what was needed to be profitable. It did not appear that Mauna La'I would survive the test to go national. But on analyzing BehaviorScan's data more closely, Ocean Spray found a few surprises: (1) the buyer base was smaller than expected, but these consumers were buying the product more frequently than was projected; (2) the product was not selling to the target market—yuppies (young urban professionals) were buying the Mauna La'I.

After analyzing this pattern for nearly a year, Ocean Spray decided that it would be profitable to market the product as long as it was marketed towards the heavily beverage-consuming yuppies. Mauna La'I's media plan was altered to reach the more up-scale market, and the juice was rolled out nationally. After only three months in the national market, consumer demand was so high that Ocean Spray started to produce a 64-ounce size. John Tarsa, Ocean Spray's Manager of Marketing Research, believes that the use of an electronic test market was key to Mauna La'I's success. "In a traditional test market, we wouldn't be rolling with Mauna La'I at all, because our repeat number was no good. The electronic test market was instrumental in helping us decide what we needed to change to make it a success."

Source: Leslie Brennan, "Test Marketing Put to the Test," *Sales and Marketing Management* 138 (March 1987), p. 68. Electronic test markets are also used to test the effects of advertising strategy. See Leonard M. Lodish, Magid Abraham, Stuart Kalmenson, Jeanne Livelsberger, et al., "How TV Advertising Works: A Meta-Analysis of 389 Real World Split Cable T.V. Advertising Experiments," *Journal of Marketing Research* 32 (May 1995), pp. 125–139, for an integration of the findings.

---

products. The Achilles' heel of STMs is that they do not provide any information about the firm's ability to secure trade support for the product or about what competitive reaction is likely to be. Thus, they are more suited for evaluating product extensions than for examining the likely success of radically different new products.

Controlled test markets are more expensive than STMs but less costly than standard test markets. One reason they cost less is that the supplier secures distribution. The manufacturer does not need to use its own sales force to convince the trade that stocking the product is worthwhile. The manufacturer can rest assured that the new product will obtain the "right" level of store acceptance, will be positioned in the "correct" aisle in each store, will receive the "right" number of facings on the shelf, will have the "correct" everyday price, will not experience any out-of-stock problems, and will receive the planned level of trade promotion displays and price features.

The "perfect" implementation of the marketing plan also represents one of the weaknesses of the controlled test market. Acceptance or rejection of the new product by the trade is typically critical to any new product's success. When the manufacturer does not need to worry about this because the new product fits in nicely with the existing line for which the company already has distribution, the controlled test market works well.

However, the problem of over-control of the marketing effort still needs to be taken into account. The normal situation is going to involve out-of-stocks, poor aisle locations, inadequate displays, and less-than-perfect cooperation from the trade on pricing and promotions. When the manufacturer has sufficient experience to make these adjustments, the controlled test market provides a useful laboratory for testing acceptance of the product and for fine-tuning the marketing program. When the product is novel or represents a radical departure for the manufacturer, the question of trade support is much more problematic, and the controlled test is much less useful under these circumstances.

The traditional test market provides a more natural environment than either STMs or controlled test markets. The standard test market plays a more vital role when the following situations apply:

1.   It is important for the firm to test its ability to actually sell to the trade and get distribution for the product.

2.   The capital investment is substantial, and the firm needs a prolonged test market to accurately assess its capital needs or its technical ability to manufacture the product.

3.   The firm is entering new territory and needs to build its experience base so that it can play for real, but it wants to learn how to do so on a limited scale.

Choosing a Test Market Procedure

Those faced with the need to test-market a new product or to fine-tune another element of the marketing program need to choose which type of test market to use. One useful way to view that choice is to look at the alternatives as stages in a sequential process, with STMs preceding controlled test markets, which in turn come before standard test markets (see Figure 5.3). The sequence is not always as pictured, though. A very promising STM or controlled market test can cause a firm to skip one or more intermediate stages and perhaps move directly to national rollout.

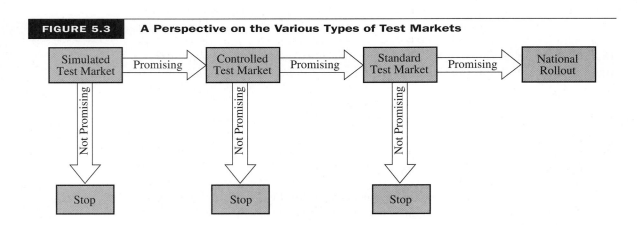

FIGURE 5.3   **A Perspective on the Various Types of Test Markets**

Summary

The emphasis in this chapter was on the third basic type of research design—causal design. The notion of causality was reviewed, and, according to the scientific interpretation of the statement "X causes Y," it was found that (1) we could never prove that X caused Y, and (2) if the inference that it did was supported by the evidence, X was one factor that made the occurrence of Y more probable, but it did not make it certain.

Three types of evidence support the establishment of causal linkages. Concomitant variation implies that X and Y must vary together in the way predicted by the hypothesis. The time order of occurrence of variables suggests that X must precede Y in time if indeed it is to be considered a cause of Y. The elimination of other factors requires the analyst to design the investigation so that the results do not lend themselves to a number of conflicting interpretations.

Experiments provide the most convincing evidence of the three types of causal linkages. An experiment is simply a scientific investigation, in which an investigator manipulates and controls one or more predictor variables and observes the response of a criterion variable. There are two general types of experiments: the laboratory experiment, in which an investigator creates an artificial situation for the manipulation of the predictor variables; and the field experiment, which allows these manipulations to take place in a natural setting. The greater control afforded by a laboratory experiment allows the more precise determination of the effect of the experimental stimulus. There is also, however, a greater danger of generalizing the results of a laboratory experiment because of its artificial nature.

In either type of experiment, the investigator has to be on guard against extraneous sources of error that may confound interpretation: history, maturation, testing (both main and interactive), instrument variation, statistical regression, selection bias, and experimental mortality. True experimental designs are particularly useful in controlling, or at least removing from the observed results, the impact of these errors. True experimental designs are distinguished from pre-experimental and quasi-experimental designs by the fact that they allow the investigator to decide which individuals are to be exposed to the experimental stimulus and to control when they are to be exposed.

Although experiments were rarely used in marketing before 1960, their growth since then has been steady. The market test to establish the sales potential of new products has become standard practice for some companies, and test-marketing is being used more and more to determine the effectiveness of contemplated changes of any elements of the marketing mix. Two increasingly popular variations when market-testing new products are the controlled test, in which the distribution of the product is guaranteed by the service provider, and the simulated test market (STM), in which reactions from users of the product are used in a series of equations to predict the repeat-purchase behavior and market share likely to be realized by the test product. Despite causal designs' growing use, descriptive designs are still the dominant form of marketing research investigations. This is partly due to tradition, but it also reflects the cost, time, and control problems associated with experimental research.

Questions

1. How do the scientific notions and commonsense notions of causality differ?
2. What types of evidence can be employed to support an inference of causality?
3. What is an experiment?
4. What is the distinction between a laboratory and a field experiment?
5. What is the difference between internal and external validity?

6. What are the basic extraneous variables that can affect the outcome of a research investigation?

7. What is the difference between the main testing effect and the interactive testing effect? Why is the distinction important?

8. What are the main ways of establishing the prior equality of groups? Which method is preferred, and why?

9. What are the distinctions between pre-experimental, true experimental, and quasi-experimental designs?

10. What are the basic types of pre-experimental designs?

11. What are the main types of true experimental designs? What are the key issues or problems associated with each of these designs?

12. How is the effect of the experimental stimulus determined in a before–after with control group design? In a four-group six-study design? In an after-only with control group design?

13. How does the true experimental, after-only with control group design differ from the pre-experimental, static-group comparison research design?

14. When would one want to employ a four-group six-study design instead of a before–after with control group design, and vice versa?

15. When would one want to employ a before–after with control group design or a four-group six-study design in lieu of an after-only with control group design, and vice versa?

16. What is the basic nature of the time-series experiment? How does the time-series experiment differ from the pre-experimental, one-group pretest–posttest design? What is the importance of this difference?

17. Compare descriptive research and true experimental design with respect to the ability of each to control or allow for extraneous factors.

18. How would you explain marketing's infrequent use of experimental research before 1960 and its steadily increasing use since then?

19. What is a test market? For what kinds of investigations can test markets be used? What are the problems associated with test markets?

20. What is the primary difference between a standard test market and a controlled test market?

21. How does an electronic test market work? What are its advantages compared to a traditional test market?

22. How does a simulated test market (STM) work? What are its main advantages and disadvantages compared to full market tests?

23. Under what conditions is a standard test market a better choice than either an STM or a controlled test market?

Applications and Problems

1. Charlie Sharp is the national sales manager of Hitech Inc. Charlie recently hypothesized that "Hitech's increase in sales is due to the new sales personnel that we recruited from the vocational school over the last several years. Sales of the new salespeople are up substantially, whereas sales for longer-term salespeople have not increased."

   Identify the causal factor X and the effect factor Y in the preceding statement.

2. To gather support for his conclusion, Charlie asked the research department of Hitech to investigate the sales of each of the company's salespeople. Using criteria supplied by management, the department categorized territory sales changes as *increased*

substantially, increased marginally, or *no increase.* Consider the following table, in which 260 sales personnel have been classified as *old* or *new:*

	Territory Sales Change			
Salesperson Assigned	*Increased Substantially*	*Increased Marginally*	*No Increase*	*Total*
New	75	30	5	110
Old	50	40	60	150

  a. Does this table provide evidence of concomitant variation? Justify your answer.

  b. What conclusions can be drawn about the relationship between X and Y on the basis of the preceding table?

3. Consider the following statement: "The increase in repeat-purchase frequency is due to retailers' decisions to stock our product in the gourmet food section of supermarkets during the last nine months. Repeat purchases from the gourmet section are up as much as 50 percent from our previous store location."

    Identify the causal factor X and the effect factor Y in the preceding statement.

4. The research department of the company in Question 3 investigated the change in repeat-purchase frequency for each store location. Using criteria supplied by management, the department categorized repeat-purchase frequency changes as *increased substantially, increased marginally,* or *no increase.* Consider the following table, in which 624 store locations have been classified as *old* or *gourmet:*

	Repeat-Purchase Frequency			
Store Location	*Increased Substantially*	*Increased Marginally*	*No Increase*	*Total*
Gourmet	180	72	12	264
Old	120	96	144	360

  a. Does this table provide evidence of concomitant variation? Justify your answer.

  b. What conclusions can be drawn about the relationship between X and Y on the basis of the preceding table?

5. Six months later, the research department in Question 4 investigated the situation once again. However, a new variable was considered in the analysis—namely, the size of the package. More specifically, they considered if repeat-purchase frequency was affected depending on whether the package was a 14- or 18-ounce size. The following table summarizes the research department's findings:

	14-Ounce Package			
Store Location	*Increased Substantially*	*Increased Marginally*	*No Increase*	*Total*
Gourmet	84	24	—	108
Old	65	19	—	84

Store Location	18-Ounce Package			
	Increased Substantially	Increased Marginally	No Increase	Total
Gourmet	6	12	6	24
Old	24	48	24	96

a. If the size of package is ignored, does this table provide evidence of concomitant variation between a change in repeat purchases and in-store location? Justify your answer.

b. If the size of package is considered, does the table provide evidence of concomitant variation between repeat purchases and in-store location? Justify your answer.

Several experimental designs are described in Questions 6 through 10. For each design, complete the following tasks:

(i)   Determine what type of design is being used. Explain.

(ii)   Diagrammatically represent the design.

(iii) Discuss the threats to internal and external validity for the design.

6. A leading manufacturer of frozen food products decided to test the effectiveness of an in-store display. Four large supermarkets, located near the company's main office, were selected for the experiment. The display was set up in two of the stores, and sales were monitored for a period of two weeks. The sales of the other two stores were also recorded, but no displays were used. Sales volume for the frozen food products increased 2 percent more in the stores that used the in-store displays than in the stores that did not use the displays.

7. A branch of Alcoholics Anonymous wanted to test consumer attitudes toward an anti-drinking advertisement. Two random samples of respondents in Piscataway, New Jersey, were selected for the experiment. Personal interviews relating to consumer attitudes toward alcoholism were conducted with both samples. One of the samples was shown the anti-drinking advertisement, and, following this, personal interviews were conducted with both samples in order to examine consumer attitudes toward alcoholism.

8. A manufacturer of a line of office equipment, based in Houston, Texas, marketed its products in the southwest United States. The region consisted of 30 geographic divisions, each headed by a divisional manager who had a staff of salespeople. The firm's management wanted to test the effectiveness of a new sales training program in which the sales personnel in five of the divisions typically participated. The divisional managers of these five divisions were instructed to monitor sales for each salesperson for each of the five months before and after the training program. The results were to be sent to the vice president of sales in Houston, who planned to compare them against sales changes in the other divisions.

9. A new manufacturer of women's cosmetics was planning to retail the firm's products through mail order. The firm's management was considering the use of direct-mail advertisements to stimulate sales of their products. Prior to committing themselves to advertising through direct mail, management conducted an experiment. A random sample of 1,000 housewives was selected from Memphis, Tennessee. The sample was divided into two groups, with each subject being randomly assigned to one of the two groups. Direct-mail advertisements were sent twice over a period of one month to respondents of one of the groups. Two weeks later, respondents of both groups were mailed the company's catalog of cosmetics. Sales to each group were monitored.

10. Milbar Corporation, a specialty hand-tool company located in Chagrin Falls, Ohio, was considering introducing a new style of snap ring pliers. Before it went ahead with

production of the pliers, Jack Bares, CEO, decided that the company should test the effectiveness of its sales promotion campaign. Jack chose four disparate cities in which to run the experiment. In two of the randomly chosen cities, Binghamton, New York, and Manderville, Louisiana, Milbar first questioned mechanics and parts people on their attitudes toward snap ring pliers. Next, Milbar ran the new pliers sales promotion campaign in the randomly chosen Binghamton and Medford, Oregon. Then Milbar went back to all four cities—Binghamton, Manderville, Medford, and Omaha, Nebraska—and measured mechanics' and parts people's attitudes toward the new and old snap ring pliers.

11. The product development team at Flameglo Log Company has been working on several modifications of Flameglo's highly successful line of fireplace logs. The most promising development is a new log that burns in several different colors. Based on favorable feedback from a few employees who have tested the product in their homes, management feels that the new log has the potential to become a major seller.

At a recent strategy meeting, the vice president of marketing suggested a test-marketing program before committing to introduction of the new log. He pointed out that a test market would be a good way to evaluate the effectiveness of two alternative advertising and promotional campaigns that have been proposed by Flameglo's ad agency. He feels that effectiveness should be evaluated in terms of the trial- and repeat-purchasing behavior engendered by each program. He also wants to gauge Flameglo's current distributors' acceptance of the new product.

The CEO of Flameglo, however, is not very enthusiastic about the idea of test-marketing. She is concerned that Flameglo's competitors could easily duplicate the new log; that the company is nearing the limit of its budgeted costs for developing the new log; and that the seasonal nature of log sales makes it imperative to reach a "go–no-go" decision on the new log by early April, only four months away.

The director of marketing research stated that she felt a test-marketing plan could be devised that would satisfy both the vice president of marketing and the CEO. She was instructed to submit a preliminary proposal at the next strategy meeting.

a. What information should be obtained from the test market in order to satisfy the vice president of marketing?

b. Under what constraints must the test-marketing plan operate in order to satisfy the CEO?

c. Given your answers to a and b above, what method of test-marketing should the director recommend? Why?

Thorndike Sports Equipment Video Case

1. After looking at the study constructed to test the effects of different strings, what do you think are the problems with this design?

2. Devise a study that overcomes the weaknesses you have identified in the previous question.

CASE 2.1

Rumstad Decorating Centers (A)

In 1929, Joseph Rumstad opened a small paint and wallpaper supply store in downtown Rockford, Illinois. For the next 45 years the store enjoyed consistent, although not spectacular, success. Sales and profits increased steadily but slowly as the original line of products was expanded to include unpainted furniture, mirrors, picture framing material, and other products to keep pace with the competition. In 1974, because of a declining neighborhood environment, Jack Rumstad, who had taken over management of the store from his father in 1970, decided to close the downtown store and open a new outlet on the far west side of the city. The west side was chosen because it was experiencing a boom in new

home construction. In 1996, a second store was opened on the east side of the city, and the name of the business was changed to Rumstad Decorating Centers. The east-side store was staffed with salesclerks but was basically managed by Rumstad himself from the west-side location. All ordering, billing, inventory control, and even the physical storage of excess inventory were concentrated at the west-side store.

In 1997, the east-side store was made an independent profit center. Rumstad personally took over the management of the outlet and hired a full-time manager for the west-side store. With the change in accounting procedures occasioned by this organiza-

---

TABLE 2.1.1   **Profit and Loss Statement for Rumstad Decorating Centers**

	East-Side Store		West-Side Store	
	1997	*1996*	*1997*	*1996*
Total sales	$114,461	$ 91,034	$ 87,703	$108,497
Cash sale discounts	4,347	2,971	4,165	2,930
Net sales	110,114	88,063	83,538	105,567
Beginning inventory	53,369	49,768	1,936	0
Purchases	64,654	56,528	163,740	59,366
Total	118,023	106,206	165,676	59,366
Ending inventory	51,955	53,369	115,554	1,936
Cost of sales	66,068	52,837	50,122	57,430
Gross profit or loss	44,046	35,226	33,416	48,137
Direct costs				
Salaries	24,068	19,836	24,549	26,583
Payroll taxes	2,025	1,814	1,764	2,060
Depreciation: furniture and fixtures	92	92	92	92
Freight	6	43	511	800
Store supplies	694	828	607	4,153
Accounting and legal expenses	439	433	439	433
Advertising	2,977	4,890	4,820	5,252
Yellow Pages	1,007	618	1,387	956
Convention and seminar expenses	0	33	83	216
Insurance	226	139	1,271	1,643
Office expense and supplies	4,466	4,393	5,327	5,010
Personal property tax	139	139	140	140
Rent	7,000	7,000	4,900	4,900
Utilities	2,246	1,651	2,746	2,359
Total direct costs	45,385	41,909	48,636	54,597
Profit or loss	(1,339)	(6,683)	(15,220)	(6,460)

tional change, it became possible to examine the profitability of each outlet separately.

Rumstad conducted such an examination early in 1998, using the profit and loss figures in Table 2.1.1, and became very concerned with what he discovered. Both stores had suffered losses for 1997, and, although he had anticipated incurring a loss during the first couple of years of operation of the east-side store, he was not at all prepared for a second successive loss at the west-side outlet. He blamed the 1996 loss on the disruptions caused by the change in organizational structure. Further, from 1996 to 1997, the east side had a 25 percent increase in net sales, a 25 percent increase in gross profits, and an 8 percent increase in total direct costs. Also, although the east-side store still showed a net loss, it was 80 percent less than the previous year's loss. The west-side store, on the other hand, had shown a 21 percent decrease in net sales, a 31 percent decrease in gross profit, an 11 percent decrease in direct costs, and a 136 percent increase in net loss. Rumstad is very concerned about the survival of the business and is particularly concerned with the west-side store. He has called you in as a research consultant to help him pinpoint what is happening so that he might take corrective action.

West-Side Store

The west-side store is located in the heart of the census tract with the highest per-capita income in the city. Most of the residents in the area are professional people or white-collar workers. The store is a freestanding unit located on a frontage road with the word "Rumstad" displayed across the front. Since Rumstad's transfer to the east-side store, there has been a succession of managers at the west-side store. The first one lasted for six months and the second and third for four months. The current manager, previously a salesclerk at the store for four years, has held the job for 10 months. Even though the products carried and the prices charged are the same in both stores, there is some difference in advertising emphasis. The west-side store does all its advertising in the *Shopper's World*, a weekly paper devoted exclusively to advertising, which is distributed free to all households in the community. Delivery is by and large door-to-door, although it is typical for a group of newspapers to be placed at the entrance to apartment buildings and for residents to pick up a copy if they so choose.

East-Side Store

The east-side store is located in a predominantly blue-collar area. Most of the residents in the immediate vicinity work for one of the machine-tool manufacturers that compose one of the basic industries in Rockford. The store is located in a small shopping center. It has a large window display area with a readily visible "Rumstad Decorating Center" sign above the store. The east-side store advertises periodically in the *Rockford Morning Star* in addition to its Yellow Pages advertising.

QUESTION

1. How would you proceed to answer Rumstad's problem?

CASE 2.2
Riverside County Humane Society (A)

The demands on the Riverside County Humane Society (RCHS) had increased rather dramatically over the past several years, while the tax dollars the society received to provide services had remained relatively unchanged. In an effort to halt further decline in the quality of its services and to provide better care for the pets at the center, the membership committee of the board of directors began making plans for a member/contributor drive. The organized drive was to be the first of its kind for the local chapter and the committee members wanted it to be as productive as possible.

As the plans began to evolve, the committee realized that the organization had only scattered bits and pieces of information about its current members. It did have a list of members and contributors for the last five years that had been compiled by the RCHS staff. In addition, it had access to the results of a survey done by a staff member several years earlier that focused on member usage of shelter facilities and their opinions of shelter services and programs. However, the organization had only sparse knowledge of the profile of its typical member and contributor, why they belonged or contributed, how long they had been associated with the Humane Society, how the services of the Humane Society could be improved, and so on. The committee members believed information on these issues was important to the conduct of a successful membership drive, and thus they commissioned some research to secure it.

One of the first things the researchers did was to contact other Humane Society chapters to determine what kinds of research they had done, particularly with respect to identifying the characteristics of their members. The researchers also interviewed key River-side County Humane Society staff members and several board members for their thoughts and ideas regarding RCHS membership. The researchers also held a focus group among members of the membership committee.

These research activities produced the following general ideas about membership and contributions:

1. The people who use the center's facilities are not necessarily the same people who would become members. Members love their own pets, take good care of them, and want other animals to be treated humanely.

2. Most contributors do not care about being a "member" because membership does not confer any rights or privileges, except a newsletter. Members are very different from contributors.

3. The female member of the household is probably making the decision regarding membership or contribution to the RCHS.

4. The majority of members in the RCHS are female and are at least 35 years old.

5. Many retired or elderly people contribute to or are members of the RCHS.

6. The average contribution is about $15 to $25.

7. People in the community have a generally positive perception of the RCHS.

8. An emotional appeal in a membership drive is likely to have the best chance for success.

9. Most people have heard about the RCHS primarily through education programs conducted by the society.

10. The greatest benefit associated with membership is the warm feeling that people get from belonging to the RCHS.

The research firm planned to select a sample of names from the current lists of members and contributors and to send them mail questionnaires to explore these ideas further.

QUESTIONS

1. What kind of research design is being used?

2. Is it a good choice?

3. Design a questionnaire that addresses the issues raised and that also gathers helpful demographic information on members and contributors.

CASE 2.3
HotStuff Computer Software (A)[1]

Simpson, Edwards and Associates has had considerable success with a computer software package that it designed to enable government agencies to manage their database systems. The firm is currently developing a second product, a more specialized version of its first endeavor. Called HotStuff, its latest computer software concept targets the firefighting industry. Researchers at Simpson, Edwards and Associates have a hunch that fire departments are a prime market for database software because of their extensive information-handling responsibilities—equipment inventories, building layouts, hazardous materials data, budget records, personnel files, and so on.

At this embryonic stage in the new product's development, the company is following the same game plan that helped it launch its previous success. Responsibilities have been broadly divided: Jean Edwards has assumed command of the production side and Craig Simpson has taken charge of marketing and promotion. Craig's first move was to reassemble the original team of staff members who had researched the market for government agency software. At their first orientation meeting, he submitted the following objectives for their deliberation:

1. Determine market potential.

2. Identify important product attributes.

3. Develop an effective promotional strategy.

4. Identify competitors in the market.

By the close of discussion, the group had decided that its first task would be exploratory research. Specifically, it decided to conduct experience surveys involving local fire chiefs, informal telephone interviews with state and national fire officials, and a literature search. Based on findings from the exploratory research effort, the group hoped to be able to pursue descriptive research to fulfill the four objectives.

Exploratory Research

The first finding to emerge from the exploratory research affected the target market for HotStuff. Fire departments are made up of two broad categories:

[1]The contributions of Jacqueline C. Hitchon to the development of this case are gratefully acknowledged.

municipal departments with full staffs of paid fire-fighters, and volunteer departments consisting of a paid chief and remaining members who may or may not be paid firefighters. The team quickly discovered that the two kinds of departments differ in two important ways. First, from the point of view of funding, municipal departments receive the majority of their funds from taxes, so the money is tightly controlled and tends to be earmarked for specific uses. Volunteer fire departments, on the other hand, rely heavily on donors and special events as sources of income, to the extent that fund-raising may account for more than 50 percent of their total receipts. Since money obtained through fund-raising is not technically part of the budget, it is not subject to budgetary controls per se.

The second key difference between municipal and volunteer departments concerned purchasing procedures. Local municipal departments tended to route all purchases through a central purchasing agent, who would then apply for approval from the data-processing center at city hall before acquiring computer hardware and software. Fire chiefs interviewed in volunteer departments, however, reported that they had sole authority to purchase any hardware or software required.

Telephone calls to out-of-state fire officials indicated that these differences were consistent across the nation. As a result, Simpson, Edwards and Associates decided to restrict its target market to volunteer fire departments.

A second finding uncovered in the exploratory research concerned the extent to which the needs of the target market were already being met. Inquiries within the state revealed that only a few volunteer departments had already purchased computers. Further, those with computers had not possessed them for long and were still in the process of automating manual databases. The general feeling among fire officials was that computerization would be an inevitable development in the industry in the near future. Indeed, four specialized software packages were already being advertised in fire prevention journals: Chief's Helper, Fire Organizer, Spread Systems, and JLT Software. Spread Systems differed from the others in that it consisted of separate programs, each of which sold individually and covered a particular information type, such as inventory records or hazardous materials. The strategy followed by Spread Systems allowed fire departments to reduce their expenditure on software because they could select only those programs that they needed. It was conjectured at Simpson, Edwards and

Associates that specific programs for specific functions may help overcome initial consumer caution toward spending several thousand dollars for computer software, because the expenditure would not be made all at one time. It was also believed that some makers of generic software packages that perform spreadsheet or database management analysis should be included in the list of competitors, although users of generic software packages needed some proficiency with computers to tailor these basic packages to their specific applications.

A third finding of interest from the exploratory research was that the term *volunteer* was offensive to departments officially classified as volunteer because they thought that it implied a lack of professionalism. In fact, their staffs were as well trained as members of municipal departments. This sentiment led the researchers to conclude that the label *volunteer* should not be used in the future promotion of HotStuff.

Based on what it learned from the exploratory research, Simpson, Edwards and Associates decided to conduct a more formal investigation to address the following objectives:

1. Determine the market potential for its new software by
   a. establishing the incidence of computer use and planned computer purchases in volunteer fire departments, and
   b. obtaining more information about volunteer fire departments' funding and authority structures.

2. Identify important product attributes—that is, the types of information that need to be handled by volunteer fire departments and that therefore need to be incorporated into the software.

3. Secure ideas for promotional strategy by
   a. determining which fire publications are read by the target market, and
   b. determining which association conventions are most well attended by the target market.

4. Identify competitors in the market by
   a. establishing which brands of software are currently used in volunteer fire departments, and
   b. establishing how satisfactory existing software packages are perceived to be.

Study Design

Simpson, Edwards and Associates' researchers believed that the best way to address these objectives was through a national survey of volunteer fire departments. They decided on a structured-disguised telephone survey using team members as interviewers. The state fire marshall informed the group that most volunteer fire departments were located in communities with populations under 25,000. Consequently, it was decided to sample towns with populations under 25,000 that were situated within a 20-mile radius of cities of at least 100,000 people. Volunteer fire departments within those towns could then be contacted by telephone by means of directory assistance. Two large cities were randomly selected from each state in the United States, excluding Alaska and Hawaii, and then a town located near each city was randomly selected. An atlas and the most recent *Current Population Reports* were used to identify cities and towns of the right specification.

A questionnaire was devised and pretested twice. The first pretest was conducted through personal interviews and was meant to test the questionnaire; the second pretest was performed by telephone and was meant to test the mode of administration. In each case, inquiries were directed to the fire chiefs as representatives of the departments. The actual survey was conducted between April 13 and April 24. It would have taken less time to administer the survey had there not been a national fire convention the week that the phone survey began. Because the national fire convention coincided with Easter week, many fire chiefs were not at their departments; because their children were not in school, they attended the convention with their families. Nonetheless, the interviewer team was able to increase the response rate to 85 percent by numerous callbacks.

QUESTIONS

1. Evaluate Simpson, Edwards and Associates' decision to focus on volunteer fire departments as its target market, based on the exploratory research.

2. Do you consider that exploratory research was productive in this case? Do you think that further useful insights could have been gained without significantly greater expenditure of resources? If so, what and how?

3. Comment on the differences between the four objectives as originally formulated and as reformulated after exploratory research.

4. Was the choice of phone interviews a good one?

CASE 2.4
Student Computer Lab (A)[1]

A major university served over 2,000 undergraduate and graduate students majoring in business administration. The large number of students enrolled in the Business School, coupled with increasing use of computer technology by faculty and students, created overwhelming demands on the Business School's computer center. In response, the Business School decided to upgrade its computer facilities.

Rod Stevenson, director of the Student Computer Center (SCC), opened an upgraded computer lab in the fall of 2001. The new lab offered specialized software required by student courses, both IBM-compatible and Macintosh (Mac) machines, and the latest technology in hardware and software.

Computer Lab Project

After operating for six months, Mr. Stevenson recognized potential problems with the new computer lab. Although the number of computers had doubled with the new lab, student suggestions and complaints indicated that the demand for computers at times exceeded the available resources. To address this problem, Mr. Stevenson established a task force to investigate the level of student satisfaction with the computer lab. The task force, made up of four graduate students, was established in January 2002. The task force aimed to help the computer lab identify student needs and to provide suggestions on how those needs could be most effectively met.

The first activity of the task force was to examine available information on the lab and its functions and resources. A layout of the lab is displayed in Figure 2.4.1. Students are divided into two rooms, one for Mac users and one for IBM-compatible users. The Mac room supported 18 computers, all loaded with the latest software. The IBM room had a total of 42 computers. Services offered by the computer lab included network and printer access. The lab usually had three to four lab monitors to collect money for printouts and answer students' questions. Lab hours were 8:00 A.M. to 9:30 P.M. on weekdays and 8:00 A.M. to 5:00 P.M. on Saturdays and Sundays.

After reviewing available information on the lab, the task force decided it needed to conduct some research before making recommendations on the services offered. Figure 2.4.2 displays a proposal written

---

[1]The contributions of Monika E. Wingate to the development of this case are gratefully acknowledged.

FIGURE 2.4.1   **Student Computer Lab**

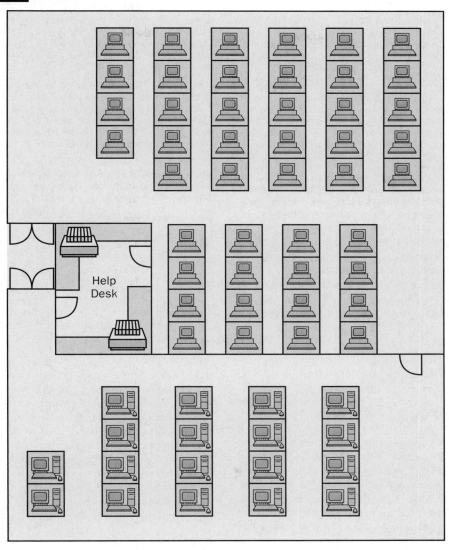

IBM compatible   Macintosh

Laser Printer

FIGURE 2.4.2   **Task Force Proposal**

DATE: February 1, 2002
TO: Rod Stevenson
FROM: Computer Center Improvement Task
                   Force
RE: COMPUTER LAB RESEARCH
                   PROPOSAL

Background: In 2001, the Business School opened a new student computer lab. Through suggestions and complaints, the SCC realizes that this lab has a resource allocation problem. Specifically, student demand for computers at times exceeds available resources. The aim of this research is to help the SCC identify student needs and to provide suggestions on how those needs can be most effectively met. The results of this research will be limited to the student computer lab. Other Business School computer facilities, such as the computer classrooms and the multimedia lab, are outside the scope of this project.

Objectives: The research objectives are as follows:

- Determine overall student satisfaction with the lab
- Identify current problem areas
- Collect student recommendations for improvements

Methodology: The research design is divided into two parts, exploratory research followed by descriptive research. The exploratory research would attempt to gain a better understanding of students' perceptions of the computer lab and to identify the issues that concern them. The student survey would aim to quantify the magnitude of these problems and to develop recommendations.

Focus Groups: The task force feels that focus groups would be the most appropriate method for exploratory research. Two sets of focus groups are recommended. One set will focus on students who use the computer lab, while the other will address the lab monitors who deal with student problems on a daily basis.

Student Survey: The focus group information would be used to develop questions for a subsequent survey. Since the population of interest is students enrolled in the Business School, this survey would be administered to students attending classes within the Business School, both graduates and undergraduates.

Time Schedule	Completed By
Focus Groups	March 11
Questionnaire Design	April 2
Pretest Questionnaire	April 9
Survey	April 23
Data Analysis	May 10

---

by the task force outlining the information to be obtained and the time frame for the research.

Focus Group Study

Mr. Stevenson received the proposal and approved it. He agreed with the task force's use of focus groups to gain a preliminary understanding of the students' attitudes. The focus groups would identify existing problems better than secondary research, although the process of collecting and analyzing the data would be more time consuming. After receiving approval, the task force posted information around the Business School to alert students that focus groups were being conducted. Free laser copies were offered as an incentive for participation. Students were selected based on their interest. The student focus group was held on March 10, 2002. Seven students participated; five were graduate students and two were undergraduate students. Transcripts are provided in Figure 2.4.3.

Because one of the responsibilities of the lab monitors is to assist students with questions and problems, separate focus groups were also conducted on March 9, 2002, and March 11, 2002, with eight lab monitors. Information from both the student and lab monitor focus groups was used as a guide to develop questions for the second phase, a student survey. Information from the focus groups was reduced to a list of key issues, which were then categorized. An exhaustive list of statements was devised to address potential user attitudes with respect to each issue. When the list was complete, statements were revised, combined, or eliminated to a set that succinctly covered the original key issue categories. The questionnaire was then pretested, and finally administered to a sample of students attending class in the Business School.

QUESTIONS

1. Did the moderator do an adequate job of getting the information needed by the SCC?

2. Do you think it was wise to include both graduate and undergraduate students in the group and both Mac and IBM users?

3. Analyze the focus group transcript thoroughly. Make a list of problems and ideas generated for the student computer lab.

4. What do you see as the benefits and limitations of the focus group findings? Do you think the task force plan for utilizing the focus groups is appropriate?

FIGURE 2.4.3   Student Focus Group Transcript

Moderator: I'm Robert from Professional Interviewing. I really appreciate your participation in this group session. As you can see, I am taping this session so I can review all of your comments. We are here tonight to talk about the computer lab at the Business School. As business students, you all have access to the lab for your class assignments. How do you think the computer lab is meeting your needs?

Lisa: I think that there is a problem with the lab because the folks that are using computers don't know about computers. That's been reflected in the fact that you go to one computer and you pick up a virus and these people don't know anything about viruses, they're transmitting them all over the place, nobody is scanning for viruses and there's something that could be easily put on the systems.

Oliver: I think there has to be training for the people who are watching the computers. They are ignorant. You ask them any question and they don't know. It's a computer lab and this computer doesn't seem to be doing the thing that it should be doing. Why? Why is this network different from the rest? How are we supposed to handle this network? They don't know.

Lisa: Not only that, they don't know any of the software.

Oliver: Absolutely!

Lisa: This is like I have Word at home and this is WordPerfect, "How do I do XYZ in WordPerfect?" They don't know. They say let me go check with John and it takes three of them.

Marion: And there are three of them!

Lisa: I know!

Oliver: There is always a big queue so you cannot get onto a Windows machine, you have to go to Pagemaker Plus if you need to make a presentation. You cannot go to these WordPerfect machines that have just keyboard entries. But there are very few computers and a lot of lines in the peak times and they are just not equipped to handle it. They have so many staff over there, five people, all of these people, but not one of them will help anyone.

Moderator: How about you, Jennifer, have you experienced this?

Jennifer: Yeah, I even had it today. I just don't have time to wait in line to get a computer. It's a half hour sometimes to go in and get one.

Lisa: And that's now. At the end of the semester it's worse.

Jennifer: Yeah, it gets worse.

Lisa: It takes an hour and there's no sign-up. There's no regular sign-up.

Mike: They truncated the hours the last two weeks of the semester.

Jennifer: You could take these four people and turn that into one educated person or take the four people and have one uneducated person there 24 hours a day. That would be nice. If all they're going to do is take your card and give you your copy, why do you have to have four of them? That's all they're doing. And studying.

Moderator: How about you, I didn't get your name?

Tammy: Tammy.

Moderator: Welcome, Tammy, how about you. What kind of things have you come across?

Tammy: What I'm hearing are a lot of the problems I've seen too. I just think there needs to be more computers in the lab and the hours need to be longer.

Mike: I don't think they need more computers. They just need to expand the hours and the computing labs.

Oliver: I had an idea where they don't need more computers. One suggestion I already put in the suggestion box, have people come with their own computers. Why does a grad student who is going to be here for two years, going to interface with technology when he leaves here, spend a thousand dollars and go buy his own system? They should do that. Have your own computer here, I'm saying it's a requirement. It's a requirement at a lot of universities that you come with your own system. Then you don't have to worry about it, you don't need to access to our labs. Now for undergraduates we still have similar problems but it would put less of a stress on the system.

Moderator: What would you suggest for people that would say, okay, I can get this computer system, but I have to get this software for this class, and this software for this class, and this software. That is a lot of money.

Oliver: Yeah, we can already jump into the network from home. All you need is the software.

Lisa: I don't think so.

Oliver: You can get in. I can check my mail and stuff.

Lisa: But not software.

(continued)

FIGURE 2.4.3   (continued)

Oliver:	Oh, software. I haven't tried and so I don't know.
Tammy:	Getting back to the machine. I'd love to have my own machine but I don't want to have it if I don't have to. As long as we have all these other computers, why not use what we've got?
Mike:	I can't afford it. If you want to buy a good computer, a decent printer, a decent monitor, you are still going to spend between $1,600 and $2,000.
Oliver:	I think while you're in school the school should support us with computers.
Mike:	I think one of the reasons there aren't enough computers is that people who aren't in the business school have access to come and use the lab. In the old building, they always checked your ID.
Tammy:	Yeah. Why don't we use the card machines? They were working, weren't they? They had the doors closed and you used a key card.
Oliver:	I think the old lab was better because they controlled people coming and going.
Mike:	Yeah. Gatekeeping.
Tammy:	They had hours when only graduate students could come in. I think that's something that should be started again because they have a lot more papers to type up.
Mike:	I don't see why this lab isn't 24 hours. I really don't. Why aren't the labs 24 hours?
Lisa:	Monitor problem, they need someone to monitor them, to work with them.
Jennifer:	Three people, 3 eight-hour shifts.
Mike:	They don't have a budget to increase their hours. They need to double the hours, like not having four monitors at one time.
Moderator:	There are peak hours and there are hours that there are a lot of open computers, where people don't generally come in. If there was a way to monitor those times and put a schedule up and people could come in and say that's a time when we could go there. Continually monitor that, what do you think about that?
Mike:	Every hour is a peak hour, particularly at the end of the semester.
Oliver:	I think it would be a good way of trying to smooth it out, because that's what you are trying to do. Have people go there when it's not so frequented. But then what about times like today? I happened to get out of class one-half hour early and went downstairs and utilized it. But if I hadn't signed up early, there were a million folks in there. There are some trade-offs, but I think it's a great idea to try and smooth it out. This morning there were four of us in there at 8:00 or 8:15 when it opened and I don't think anybody showed up until 10:00.
Mike:	One of the other problems in the lab right now, there are a lot of computers that are broken at one time.
Oliver:	Oh yeah!
Mike:	There are six of them right now that aren't working.
Oliver:	That's from people not knowing what they are doing. I was sitting down there on one of the old machines and there was a gentleman sitting next to me who couldn't figure out why it wouldn't work. He took his disk out and shut the computer off and it came back on and got a boot error. Then he got scared and he just left. He didn't go tell anyone. The monitors are looking from the other side, so they don't know there is anything wrong. Someone comes in, they just look around, and see that the computer is broken, or it's not booted up, and so on. That's why I am saying, it's the students themselves. People need to know how to work the system.
Ira:	I think there should be a small note pasted next to the computers saying the ways to handle each computer.
Marion:	Even a template for the word processing.
Ira:	Even a small hint for troubleshooting, please don't do this and do this.
Tammy:	I think an excellent model for this are the computer labs in the dorms. Those are run, the first time you use it, they scan everyone's ID to be sure you are a dorm resident, they know if it's the first time you are using it, they ask you to make sure you know how to use the software. They have a rack with every different kind of title and anything you need to use the software. They tell you exactly what's going to come up on the machine and what you have to do. I'm sure the Business School can get copies of it all and then just copy it.
Marion:	We have no reference guides for the software.
Tammy:	And then they have the guides there. The little orange books.
Moderator:	Are there any other concerns we haven't talked about?
Ira:	Is there any way the cost for a laser print can be reduced?
Tammy:	It kills me.

FIGURE 2.4.3   (continued)

Ira: It should be 7 cents. It is 6 cents in the library.

Tammy: You used to have the option to go to a dot matrix printer. They changed that this semester. The only way to go to the dot matrix was to go to an AT&T machine. Don't tell me someone is looking at cost.

Ira: I think the initial cost is pretty high, that is why they're keeping it at 10 cents.

Jennifer: If they are planning on getting more printers, I think they should have at least one or two individual print stations where you can grab your stuff. If you're working on your résumé and you want to print on bond paper or do envelopes, the people behind the desk won't let you do it because they don't know if other people are going to send it, they don't know what is going to come out.

Oliver: Or they waste your paper because they can't coordinate it.

Jennifer: So I think there should be some individual workstations.

Oliver: I have something to say and maybe I'm the only one with this problem. I always find that when I go there and I am working alone I have these groups creating a racket, so it's really frustrating. I'm working on a project, I need to think. I don't need this kind of heavy distraction, this loud talk. I go and work in groups too, we try to whisper. There should be some kind of discipline in the computer lab. I think I may be the only one being that sensitive, but I think there has to be silence maintained. It is a computer lab, it is a place for people working; if you're having a fun time go have it outside.

Moderator: How effective do you think their waiting lists system is?

Tammy: It sucks.

Ira: I didn't even know they had one.

Oliver: At the end of the last semester no one knew if the list was for the Mac side or the IBM side of the room.

Tammy: It would be better to set up a physical waiting list where there would be chairs or a bench or something like that.

Ira: Or like a number.

Tammy: Or six chairs in a row and you come down and sit down next to the computers and that means you are next to get on and then if you leave the next person can move down and then you can see that no one is getting in front of you.

Oliver: It worked pretty well for me. Every time I used the waiting list I had to wait for maybe a half hour and my name was called and I could get a computer. I have no complaints. This happened every time. There was no problem. I had no problems at all.

Mike: Until this time I didn't even know there was a waiting list. If there was an open computer I just would sit down.

Tammy: I found out the hard way, I went down and sat down and someone told me.

Jennifer: It's not very consistent. It's kind of whenever they feel like.

Moderator: Anything else?

Jennifer: I have one comment about the resources, since we are able to use the resources like e-mail and the Internet. The Internet's great but if you don't know any of the numbers to call out, it's kind of a useless thing. But there are books out there with the numbers that cost about $30 and if you keep one of the books as a reference copy at the desk for people to look at, I think it would be a great resource. I looked at the bookstore once and it's incredible the different things you can call up on it.

Tammy: Good point. I think they could put it down there with all the reference items.

Jennifer: I think they need more computers and longer hours. They're not meeting the demands.

Ira: At least the building hours.

Tammy: Match the library's hours. They're open 100 and some hours a week. Sunday night. They could close earlier on Friday and Saturday night (like 8 A.M. to 11 P.M.).

Jennifer: And do it during exams too—all of a sudden it's close to 5:00 and even Memorial Library is open later.

Moderator: We're close to wrapping up. Is there anything else?

Tammy: Oh, can I get templates? For the word processing, I don't know how to use them. You have to use control that, shift that.

Ira: They used to have them. Just photocopy them.

Moderator: Is there anything else? I want to thank all of you. Your concerns will definitely be evaluated and considered. I have some printout cards for all of you. I knew I said I would give you $5.00 on each card, but as it turned out there's $9.75 on each card.

CASE 2.5
Chestnut Ridge Country Club (A)[1]

The Chestnut Ridge Country Club has long maintained a distinguished reputation as one of the outstanding country clubs in the Elma, Tennessee, area. The club's golf facilities are said by some to be the finest in the state, and its dining and banquet facilities are highly regarded as well. This reputation is due in part to the commitment by the board of directors of Chestnut Ridge to offer the finest facilities of any club in the area. For example, several negative comments by club members regarding the dining facilities prompted the board to survey members to get their feelings and perceptions of the dining facilities and food offerings at the club. Based on the survey findings, the board of directors established a quality control committee to oversee the dining room and hired a new club manager.

Most recently, the board became concerned about the number of people seeking membership to Chestnut Ridge. Although no records are kept on the number of membership applications received each year, the board sensed that this figure was declining. They also believed that membership applications at the three competing country clubs in the area (namely, Alden, Chalet, and Lancaster) were not experiencing similar declines. Because Chestnut Ridge had other facilities, such as tennis courts and a pool, that were comparable to the facilities at these other clubs, the board was perplexed as to why membership applications would be falling at Chestnut Ridge.

To gain insight into the matter, the board of directors hired an outside research firm to conduct a study of the country clubs in Elma, Tennessee. The goals of the research were: (1) to outline areas in which Chestnut Ridge fared poorly in relation to other clubs in the area; (2) to determine people's overall perception of Chestnut Ridge; and (3) to provide recommendations for ways to increase membership applications at the club.

Research Method

The researchers met with the board of directors and key personnel at Chestnut Ridge to gain a better understanding of the goals of the research and the types of services and facilities offered at a country club. A literature search of published research relating to country clubs uncovered no studies. Based solely on

_____

[1]The contributions of David M. Szymanski to the development of this case are gratefully acknowledged.

their contact with individuals at Chestnut Ridge, therefore, the research team developed the survey contained in Figure 2.5.1. Because personal information regarding demographics and attitudes would be asked of those contacted, the researchers decided to use a mail questionnaire.

The researchers thought it would be useful to survey members from Alden, Chalet, and Lancaster country clubs in addition to those from Chestnut Ridge for two reasons: 1) members of these other clubs would be knowledgeable about the levels and types of services and facilities desired from a country club and 2) they had at one time represented potential members of Chestnut Ridge. Hence, their perceptions of Chestnut Ridge might reveal why they chose to belong to a different country club. No public documents were available that contained a listing of each club's members. Consequently, the researchers decided to contact each of the clubs personally to try to obtain a mailing list. Identifying themselves as being affiliated with an independent research firm conducting a study on country clubs in the Elma area, the researchers first spoke to the chairman of the board at Alden Country Club. The researchers told the chairman that they could not reveal the organization sponsoring the study but that the results of their study would not be made public. The chairman was not willing to provide the researchers with the mailing list. The chairman cited an obligation to respect the privacy of the club's members as his primary reason for turning down the research team's request.

The researchers then made the following proposal to the board chairman: In return for the mailing list, the researchers would provide the chairman a report on Alden members' perceptions of Alden Country Club. In addition, the mailing list would be destroyed as soon as the surveys were sent. The proposal seemed to please the chairman, for he agreed to give the researchers a listing of the members and their addresses in exchange for the report. The researchers told the chairman they must check with their sponsoring organization for approval of this arrangement.

The research team made similar proposals to the chairmen of the boards of directors of both the Chalet and Lancaster Country Clubs. In return for a mailing list of the club's members, they promised each chairman a report outlining that club's members' perceptions of their clubs, contingent on the research team securing approval from their sponsoring organization. Both chairmen agreed to supply the requested list of members.

The researchers subsequently met with the Chestnut Ridge board of directors. In their meeting, the

FIGURE 2.5.1	Questionnaire Used to Survey Alden, Chalet, and Lancaster Country Club Members

1. *Of which club are you currently a member?* _____
2. *How long have you been a member of this club?* _____
3. *How familiar are you with each of the following country clubs?*

Alden Country Club

_____ very familiar (I am a member or I have visited the club as a guest)
_____ somewhat familiar (I have heard about the club from others)
_____ unfamiliar

Chalet Country Club

_____ very familiar
_____ somewhat familiar
_____ unfamiliar

Chestnut Ridge Country Club

_____ very familiar
_____ somewhat familiar
_____ unfamiliar

Lancaster Country Club

_____ very familiar
_____ somewhat familiar
_____ unfamiliar

4. *The following is a list of factors that may be influential in the decision to join a country club. Please rate the factors according to their importance to you in joining your country club. Circle the appropriate response, where 1 = not at all important and 5 = extremely important.*

Golf facilities	1	2	3	4	5
Tennis facilities	1	2	3	4	5
Pool facilities	1	2	3	4	5
Dining facilities	1	2	3	4	5
Social events	1	2	3	4	5
Family activities	1	2	3	4	5
Number of friends who are members	1	2	3	4	5
Cordiality of members	1	2	3	4	5
Prestige	1	2	3	4	5
Location	1	2	3	4	5

5. *The following is a list of phrases pertaining to Alden Country Club. Please place an X in the space that best describes your impressions of Alden. The ends represent extremes; the center position is neutral.* Do so even if you are only vaguely familiar with Alden.

Club landscape is attractive.   :___:___:___:___:___:___: Club landscape is unattractive.

(continued)

FIGURE 2.5.1   (continued)

Clubhouse facilities are poor.   :___:___:___:___:___:___: Clubhouse facilities are excellent.

Locker room facilities are excellent.   :___:___:___:___:___:___: Locker room facilities are poor.

Club management is ineffective.   :___:___:___:___:___:___: Club management is effective.

Dining room atmosphere is pleasant.   :___:___:___:___:___:___: Dining room atmosphere is unpleasant.

Food prices are unreasonable.   :___:___:___:___:___:___: Food prices are reasonable.

Golf course is poorly maintained.   :___:___:___:___:___:___: Golf course is well maintained.

Golf course is challenging.   :___:___:___:___:___:___: Golf course is not challenging.

Membership rates are too high.   :___:___:___:___:___:___: Membership rates are too low.

6. *The following is a list of phrases pertaining to Chalet Country Club. Please place an X in the space that best describes your impressions of Chalet.* Do so even if you are only vaguely familiar with Chalet.

Club landscape is attractive.   :___:___:___:___:___:___: Club landscape is unattractive.

Clubhouse facilities are poor.   :___:___:___:___:___:___: Clubhouse facilities are excellent.

Locker room facilities are excellent.   :___:___:___:___:___:___: Locker room facilities are poor.

Club management is effective.   :___:___:___:___:___:___: Club management is ineffective.

Dining room atmosphere is pleasant.   :___:___:___:___:___:___: Dining room atmosphere is unpleasant.

Food prices are unreasonable.   :___:___:___:___:___:___: Food prices are reasonable.

Food quality is excellent.   :___:___:___:___:___:___: Food quality is poor.

Golf course is poorly maintained.   :___:___:___:___:___:___: Golf course is well maintained.

Golf course is challenging.   :___:___:___:___:___:___: Golf course is not challenging.

Tennis courts are in excellent condition.   :___:___:___:___:___:___: Tennis courts are in poor condition.

There are too many tennis courts.   :___:___:___:___:___:___: There are too few tennis courts.

Membership rates are too high.   :___:___:___:___:___:___: Membership rates are too low.

FIGURE 2.5.1   **(continued)**

7. *The following is a list of phrases pertaining to Chestnut Ridge Country Club. Please place an X in the space that best describes your impressions of Chestnut Ridge.* Do so even if you are only vaguely familiar with Chestnut Ridge.

Club landscape is attractive.	:___:___:___:___:___:___:	Club landscape is unattractive.
Clubhouse facilities are poor.	:___:___:___:___:___:___:	Clubhouse facilities are excellent.
Locker room facilities are excellent.	:___:___:___:___:___:___:	Locker room facilities are poor.
Club management is ineffective.	:___:___:___:___:___:___:	Club management is effective.
Dining room atmosphere is pleasant.	:___:___:___:___:___:___:	Dining room atmosphere is unpleasant.
Food prices are unreasonable.	:___:___:___:___:___:___:	Food prices are reasonable.
Food quality is excellent.	:___:___:___:___:___:___:	Food quality is poor.
Golf course is poorly maintained.	:___:___:___:___:___:___:	Golf course is well maintained.
Tennis courts are in poor condition.	:___:___:___:___:___:___:	Tennis courts are in excellent condition.
There are too many tennis courts.	:___:___:___:___:___:___:	There are too few tennis courts.
Swimming pool is in poor condition.	:___:___:___:___:___:___:	Swimming pool is in excellent condition.
Membership rates are too high.	:___:___:___:___:___:___:	Membership rates are too low.

8. *The following is a list of phrases pertaining to Lancaster Country Club. Please place an X in the space that best describes your impression of Lancaster.* Do so even if you are only vaguely familiar with Lancaster.

Club landscape is attractive.	:___:___:___:___:___:___:	Club landscape is unattractive.
Clubhouse facilities are poor.	:___:___:___:___:___:___:	Clubhouse facilities are excellent.
Locker room facilities are excellent.	:___:___:___:___:___:___:	Locker room facilities are poor.
Club management is ineffective.	:___:___:___:___:___:___:	Club management is effective.
Dining room atmosphere is pleasant.	:___:___:___:___:___:___:	Dining room atmosphere is unpleasant.
Food prices are unreasonable.	:___:___:___:___:___:___:	Food prices are reasonable.
Food quality is excellent.	:___:___:___:___:___:___:	Food quality is poor.
Golf course is poorly maintained.	:___:___:___:___:___:___:	Golf course is well maintained.

(continued)

FIGURE 2.5.1   (continued)

Tennis courts are in poor condition.	:___:___:___:___:___:___:	Tennis courts are in excellent condition.
There are too many tennis courts.	:___:___:___:___:___:___:	There are too few tennis courts.
Swimming pool is in poor condition.	:___:___:___:___:___:___:	Swimming pool is in excellent condition.
Membership rates are too high.	:___:___:___:___:___:___:	Membership rates are too low.

9. *Overall, how would you rate each of the country clubs? Circle the appropriate response, where 1 = poor and 5 = excellent.*

Alden	1	2	3	4	5
Chalet	1	2	3	4	5
Chestnut Ridge	1	2	3	4	5
Lancaster	1	2	3	4	5

10. *The following questions are designed to give a better understanding of the members of country clubs.*

Have you ever been a member of another club in the Elma area?
_____ yes   _____ no

Approximately what is the distance of your residence from your club in miles?
_____ 0–2 miles   _____ 3–5 miles   _____ 6–10 miles
_____ 10+ miles

Age: _____ 21–30   _____ 31–40   _____ 41–50
_____ 51–60   _____ 61 or over

Sex: _____ male   _____ female

Marital status: _____ married   _____ single   _____ widowed
_____ divorced

Number of dependents including yourself:
_____ 2 or less   _____ 3–4   _____ 5 or more

Total family income:
___ Less than $20,000
___ $20,000–$29,999
___ $30,000–$49,999
___ $50,000–$99,999
___ $100,000 or more
___ Do not know/Refuse to answer

Thank you for your cooperation!

TABLE 2.5.1 **Average Overall Ratings of Each Club by Club Membership of the Respondent**

| | Club Membership | | | |
Club Rated	Alden	Chalet	Lancaster	Composite Ratings Across All Members
Alden	4.57	3.64	3.34	3.85
Chalet	2.87	3.63	2.67	3.07
Chestnut Ridge	4.40	4.44	4.20	4.35
Lancaster	3.60	3.91	4.36	3.95

TABLE 2.5.2 **Average Ratings of the Respective Country Clubs across Dimensions**

| | Country Club | | | |
Dimension	Alden	Chalet	Chestnut Ridge	Lancaster
Club landscape	6.28	4.65	6.48	5.97
Clubhouse facilities	5.37	4.67	6.03	5.51
Locker room facilities	4.99	4.79	5.36	4.14
Club management	5.38	4.35	5.00	5.23
Dining room atmosphere	5.91	4.10	5.66	5.48
Food prices	5.42	4.78	4.46	4.79
Food quality	[a]	4.12	5.48	4.79
Golf course maintenance	6.17	5.01	6.43	5.89
Golf course challenge	5.14	5.01	[a]	4.77
Condition of tennis courts	[b]	5.10	4.52	5.08
Number of tennis courts	[b]	4.14	4.00	3.89
Swimming pool	[b]	[b]	4.66	5.35
Membership rates	4.49	3.97	5.00	4.91

[a]Question not asked.
[b]Not applicable.

researchers outlined the situation and asked for the board's approval to provide each of the clubs with a report in return for the mailing lists. The researchers emphasized that the report would contain no information regarding Chestnut Ridge nor information by which each of the other clubs could compare itself to any of the other clubs in the area, in contrast to the information to be provided to the Chestnut Ridge board of directors. The report would contain only a small portion of the overall study's results. After carefully considering the research team's arguments, the board of directors agreed to the proposal.

Membership Surveys

A review of the lists subsequently provided by each club showed Alden had 114 members, Chalet had 98 members, and Lancaster had 132 members. The researchers believed that 69 to 70 responses from each membership group would be adequate. Anticipating a 70 to 75 percent response rate because of the unusually high involvement and familiarity of each group with the subject matter, the research team decided to mail 85 to 90 surveys to each group. A simple random sample of members was chosen from each list. In all, 87 members from each country club were mailed a questionnaire (348 surveys in total). Sixty-three usable surveys were returned from each group (252 in total) for a response rate of 72 percent.

Summary results of the survey are presented in Tables 2.5.1, 2.5.2, and 2.5.3. Table 2.5.1 gives overall ratings of the country clubs, and Table 2.5.2 shows people's ratings of the various clubs on an array of dimensions. Table 2.5.3 is a breakdown of attitudes

TABLE 2.5.3	Attitudes toward Chestnut Ridge by Members of the Other Country Clubs		
Dimension	*Alden*	*Chalet*	*Lancaster*
Club landscape	6.54	6.54	6.36
Clubhouse facilities	6.08	6.03	5.98
Locker room facilities	5.66	5.35	5.07
Club management	4.97	5.15	4.78
Dining room atmosphere	5.86	5.70	5.41
Food prices	4.26	4.48	4.63
Food quality	5.52	5.75	5.18
Golf course maintenance	6.47	6.59	6.22
Condition of tennis courts	4.55	4.46	4.55
Number of tennis courts	4.00	4.02	3.98
Swimming pool	5.08	4.69	4.26
Membership rates	5.09	5.64	4.24

toward Chestnut Ridge by the three different membership groups: Alden, Chalet, and Lancaster. The data are average ratings of respondents. Table 2.5.1 scores are based on a five-point scale, where "1" is poor and "5" is excellent. Tables 2.5.2 and 2.5.3 are based on seven-point scales in which "1" represents an extremely negative rating and "7" an extremely positive rating.

QUESTIONS

1. What kind of research design is being used? Is it a good choice?

2. Do you think it was ethical for the researchers not to disclose the identity of the sponsoring organization? Do you think it was ethical for the chairmen to release the names of their members in return for a report that analyzes their members' perceptions toward their own club?

3. Overall, how does Chestnut Ridge compare to the other three country clubs (Alden, Chalet, and Lancaster)?

4. In what areas might Chestnut Ridge consider making improvements to attract additional members?

CASE 2.6

Hand-to-Hand against Palm (B)

The marketing manager for the "Organize My Life!" (OML) personal digital assistant (PDA) competitor to Palm Computing's Palm Pilot device is evaluating a number of proposals for research to be commissioned to investigate what kinds of features users of these devices might like to see in competitive and next-generation models (for example, sound, video, and so

on), and to understand the particular needs of the university student segment (such as price sensitivities, special needs of different groups of students, and so on). The manager is choosing from among three proposals, each of which has been presented by different members of the brand management team.

Proposal 1 advocates exploratory research. It argues that insufficient knowledge about the PDA category is known, so it would not be useful to go out and execute some large-scale survey. Rather, this proposal suggests that students come to a central point on campus (the campuses and the meeting places on each campus to be determined), at which place the students will be asked to do a "back-pack dump." In addition to the usual textbooks and notebooks, the researchers will see in a clear manner, using this observational technique, just what electronic equipment the student carries (for example, laptop computer, CD player, tape recorder, and so on), along with what kind of appointment book (such as electronic PDA or paper calendar) the student uses to keep track of homework assignments, friends and social events, and the like.

Proposal 2 recommends that since plenty of secondary data are available on the Palm Pilot and extant competitors, exploratory data would be a waste of time. If the OML team wants to know what the students want, the team should simply ask them. A survey has been designed which is comprised largely of lists of potential features for the OML PDA. The respondent would be asked to indicate the importance of each feature. For example, the features would be rated on a 10-point scale, where "0" means "I don't care about this; I would never use this feature," to "10," which means "This feature would be very important to me; I would use it several times a day." The list of features to be rated includes a calendar, to-do list, calculator, video games, hot sync capability, digital photography storage, infrared e-mailing ability, and so on. Pricing could be assessed similarly, for example, "How much would you be willing to pay for this PDA? <$100, $101 to $199, $200 to $299," and so on. The proponent of this research proposal reasons that the attributes that are most valued would appear as the features with the highest means on the rating scales, and that the OML developers would focus on offering the resulting combination of these important features.

Proposal 3 recommends a causal design. The idea would be to set up a "mock" store, featuring the OML with its list of attributes and price, side-by-side with the Palm and competitors (with the lists of their features and prices) and ask the student participants which PDA they would buy, how likely it is that they would buy the OML, and so on. The next group of students would see the OML with a different list of attributes and price point, with the competitors' information held constant, and they would be asked to make the same kind of choices. At the end, having cycled through different variations of the OML features, the team would know which properties were most attractive to the students, and the devices could be developed for market on this basis.

QUESTIONS

1. What are the trade-offs among the research designs being proposed? What information can each technique obtain that the others cannot?

2. Imagine role-playing as one of the OML team members and defending one of the three proposals. What strengths does your approach offer? What shortcomings must you acknowledge? What action could be taken as a result of obtaining the information in the form you seek it?

CASE 2.7
Bakhill Foods

Michelle Gill, the marketing manager for Bakhill Foods, was discussing the future advertising strategy for Bakhill Coffee with the firm's advertising agency when the discussion turned to magazine ads and the copy for those ads.

Gill had recently been to a conference on psychological perception. At that conference, it was pointed out that in spite of the old adage "you can't judge a book by its cover," we do just that in our interpersonal relations; an individual's initial perception of and reaction to another individual is affected by the physical attractiveness of the other person. Further, a fair summary statement of that research is "what is beautiful is good." The evidence cited at the conference supporting this proposition was impressive. What particularly impressed Gill, though, was that the positive attributes one associates with a physically attractive person do not depend on actual contact with that person. They arise when the judge is simply shown photographs of physically attractive and unattractive individuals but is otherwise unaware of subjects' traits.

Gill thought that this knowledge could be used to advantage in the advertising copy for Bakhill Coffee. She proposed that the product be shown with a physically attractive female. The advertising agency countered with the argument that it would be better to employ physically unattractive people in the ads to make the ads more believable and effective by making them less "romantic," since coffee is not a romantic product. Further, the agency suggested it might be better to employ males in the ads rather than females. After considerable discussion, the advertising agency proposed and conducted the following research to answer two questions: Should physically attractive or unattractive individuals be used in the ads? Should male or female models be employed?

The Design

Four different advertisements were prepared. The copy was the same in each ad; only the person holding the coffee was changed. The four ads included an attractive male, an attractive female, an unattractive male, and an unattractive female. The attractiveness of each model was determined by having a convenience sample of subjects view photographs of 20 different models (10 men and 10 women) and rate each model on a seven-point scale where "1" was unattractive and "7" was attractive. The male and female models with the highest and the lowest mean scores were then selected as the stimulus persons for the experiment.

A color ad with each of the four models and the planned copy was then developed. A sample of subjects for the experiment was developed by random sampling from the New York City telephone book. Contacted subjects were asked to participate in a marketing research experiment. The subjects were paid for their participation, and they were also reimbursed for their travel to the agency's headquarters.

On their arrival at the ad agency, the 96 recruits who had agreed to participate were randomly assigned to one of the advertisements. The 48 men and 48 women were first divided randomly into 12 groups of four persons each. One member of each group was then assigned to one of the four ads. Each saw one, and only one, test ad. However, three other "filler" ads were also used to disguise the particular ad of interest. The "fillers" were the same for each participant. Each participant was introduced to the experiment with the following instructions:

> We are interested in obtaining your opinions concerning particular test advertisements. You will be shown four ads, one at a time, and after each showing, you will be asked several questions about your reaction to the ad and the particular product depicted in the ad. You should note that this is not a contest to see which ad is better, so please do not compare the four ads in making your evaluations. Each ad should be judged by itself, without reference to the other ads.

After answering any questions, the experimenter presented the first ad. When the respondent had read the advertisement, it was taken away, and the experimenter then handed the respondent a copy of the data-collection sheet (Figure 2.7.1). After completion of this form, the experimenter presented the second ad, and the process was repeated. At no time were the participants allowed to look back at the advertisements once they had surrendered them to the researcher. To allow the respondents time to warm up to the task, the experimenter always placed the test ad third in the sequence of four.

The Scale

The items in the scale contained in Figure 2.7.1 were chosen in order to tap all three components (cognitive, affective, and conative) of attitude. *A priori*, it was

---

FIGURE 2.7.1   Sample Questionnaire for Bakhill Coffee Study

On each of the scales below, please check the space that you feel best describes the advertisement you just read.

Interesting	:__:__:__:__:__:__:	Dull
Unappealing	:__:__:__:__:__:__:	Appealing
Unbelievable	:__:__:__:__:__:__:	Believable
Impressive	:__:__:__:__:__:__:	Unimpressive
Attractive	:__:__:__:__:__:__:	Unattractive
Uninformative	:__:__:__:__:__:__:	Informative
Clear	:__:__:__:__:__:__:	Confusing
Not eye-catching	:__:__:__:__:__:__:	Eye-catching

What is your overall reaction to this advertisement?

Unfavorable	:__:__:__:__:__:__:	Favorable

With regard to the product itself, how do you feel this product compares to similar products put out by other manufacturers?

Distinctive	:__:__:__:__:__:__:	Ordinary

Would you like to try this product?

No — Definitely not	:__:__:__:__:__:__:	Yes — Definitely

Would you buy this product if you happened to see it in a store?

Yes — Definitely	:__:__:__:__:__:__:	No — Definitely not

Would you actively seek out this product in a store in order to purchase it?

No — Definitely not	:__:__:__:__:__:__:	Yes — Definitely

thought that the cognitive component would be measured by the terms *believable, informative,* and *clear;* that the affective or liking component would be effectively tapped by the terms *interesting, appealing, impressive, attractive,* and *eye-catching;* and that the conative component would be captured by the three behavioral-intention items at the bottom of the questionnaire.

These *a priori* expectations were not strictly confirmed. A basic item analysis suggested that the term *interesting* was not related to any of the three components, and it was dropped from the analysis.[1] Responses to the remaining items in each component were summed to produce a total score for each component. The analysis of these scale scores indicated the following:[2]

1. The attractive male model produced the highest cognition scores for the ad among females and males.

2. The attractive male model produced the highest affective scores among female subjects, whereas the attractive female model produced the highest affective scores among males.

3. The attractive male model produced the highest conative scores toward the product for female subjects, whereas the unattractive male model produced the highest conative scores among male subjects.

On the basis of these results, the advertising agency suggested that the attractive male model be employed in the advertisement.

QUESTIONS
1. What kind of design is being employed in this investigation?
2. Evaluate the design.

CASE 2.8
Internet Advertising and Your Brain (A)

Enough Internet startups have failed that they (or at least the venture capitalists) have finally come to recog-

nize that their business is no different from any other business, in that success depends on marketing—understanding one's customers, and hence, using marketing research. Imagine that your first job after business school is as the main marketing person for the six-month-old Internet company started by a friend of a friend.

This particular startup is a travel site that specializes in "extreme sports" (for example, skiing off cliffs, riding mountain bikes from great heights into large air bags, as well as the more "traditional" bungee jumping and skydiving). The target audience is the current profile of users, that is, men in their 20s (though the percentages of women and older thrill-seekers are growing). This group of customers is coincidentally also highly likely to be "wired"; thus, advertising on the Internet is expected to be effective at reaching this audience.

It is currently your responsibility as the Extreme Marketer to conduct tests to assess the effectiveness of your company's advertisements on the Internet. At the moment, you've created two variations of a banner ad inviting browsers to your Web site and you're trying to choose between the two—which is most likely to attract these guys to click onto your Web site to learn more about your vacation packages and then possibly purchase one?

One of the ad banners your creative staff has developed is depicted in vivid colors, with captivating graphics that attempt to illustrate the possible thrills, for example, a photo with a view of skiers at the top of a mountain shot from their delivery helicopter, or a photo of a skydiver in mid-air taken by a skydiving photographer. This ad format offers very little by way of informative content, such as details about the logistics of the trips, locations, lengths of stay, price, and so on. This ad is analogous to what is traditionally called the "beauty" shot in advertising production (a televised or still photo shot that shows the car or the jar of peanut butter without mentioning miles per gallon or caloric content). Thus, we will call this version of the possible banner ad "beauty."

Another banner ad has been prepared which appears somewhat less colorful and less pictorial in style, but which contains more detailed information about the extreme sports outings you are hoping to encourage the viewers to purchase. Given its greater information content, we'll call this version of the banner ad "info."

You could just run a little study at this point. You could purchase banner ad space on your usual business relationship Web sites, randomly assigning half of

---

[1] The rationale for and method of conducting an item analysis is explored more fully in Chapter 9 and its appendix.

[2] The analysis of this kind of data is elaborated in the appendix to Chapter 15.

those sites your beauty ad, and half your info ad. Then you would sit back and count over some duration (such as the next two weeks) the number of click-throughs you achieved with the one ad format versus the other, and conclude that the banner ad with the greater draw should be the one with which your firm proceeds.

However, you had done your homework and become aware of some secondary data from eye-tracking studies. These studies insert small cameras into PC screens that monitor where the PC user is looking. The results suggest that placing the banner ad on some locations on the screen may be more effective than others. For example, it is well-known that the brain processes whatever is in the right of a person's visual field in the left half of the brain, and stimuli in the left part of a person's visual field is processed in the right-brain hemisphere. Research conducted by physiological psychologists suggests that the left brain processes analytical features and verbal descriptions most effectively, whereas the right brain processes pictures and holistic impressions better.

The info ad is verbal and offers many facts that readers could use to analyze and assess their interest, and the beauty ad is mostly graphics and leaves a holistic impression of the thrill-seeking vacation. Thus, you're beginning to think that perhaps the info ad would be best understood and most persuasive if it were processed by a viewer's left brain, which would dictate placing it on the right side of a Web page. In contrast, the beauty ad might be better understood and more persuasive if it were processed by a viewer's right brain, which means placing the banner ad in the left side of the viewer's screen.

So now the Internet advertising study you've created is somewhat more complicated. There are two factors, rather than just one: the advertising type (beauty or info) and the banner placement (left or right). Your expectations are that the ad is most likely to be effective (measured for the moment by the number of click-throughs it achieves) if the beauty ad is placed to the left or the info ad is placed to the right. However, you create all possible combinations because, after all, your hypothesis about which ad should do better where is just a hypothesis. Thus, while each Web traveler sees only one ad, there are four ad variations: the beauty ad seen at the left, beauty at the right, info at the left, and info at the right. You buy your ad space at your usual supplier Web sites, and you randomly assign one of the four ads to each of those locations. You determine how long you will wait (for example, two weeks) before counting the results.

QUESTIONS

1. What kind of design has been described?

2. How might you improve upon what has been proposed?

3. What are the (null) hypotheses that will be tested using this design?

4. What method(s) will you use to analyze the resulting data that you obtain?

5. What strategic questions might supplement your approach to investigating these issues?

Design Data-Collection Method and Forms

Part 3 treats the third stage in the research process—designing the methods of data collection and the data-collection forms. Chapter 6 focuses on secondary data as an information resource, while the appendix to Chapter 6 describes the contents of some of the more useful sources of secondary information. Chapter 7 discusses observation and communication, the main methods of data collection. Chapter 8 deals with the construction of questionnaires and observational data-collection forms. Chapter 9 and its appendix discuss the general topic of attitude measurement using scales and reviews the many types of attitude scales.

6

Data Collection: Secondary Data

Once the research problem is defined and clearly specified, the research effort logically turns to data collection. The natural temptation for beginning researchers is to advocate some sort of survey among appropriate respondent groups. This should be a last, rather than a first, resort. "A good operating rule is to consider a survey akin to surgery—to be used only after other possibilities have been exhausted."[1] First attempts at data collection should logically focus on secondary data.

Secondary data are statistics that already exist; they had been gathered for a previous purpose, not for the immediate study at hand. **Primary data,** in contrast, are originated by the researcher for the purpose of the investigation at hand. The purpose, therefore, defines the distinction. For example, if General Electric Company collected information on the demographic characteristics of refrigerator purchasers to determine who buys the various sizes of refrigerators, this information would be primary data. If the company secured this same information from internal records gathered previously for other purposes (for example, warranty information) or from published statistics, the information would be considered secondary data.

Using Secondary Data

Beginning researchers are apt to underestimate the amount of secondary data available. Table 6.1, for example, lists some of the information on people and households that is available, even down to the refined level of small geographic areas, due to the government's population census. Not searching for the secondary data that are available on a topic is unfortunate, because secondary data possess important advantages over primary data. Further, because of the recent "information explosion," such an oversight will be even more consequential in the future.

Advantages of Secondary Data

The most significant advantages of secondary data are the cost and time economies they offer the researcher. If the required information is available as secondary data, the researcher simply needs to get online or go to the library, locate the appropriate

---

[1]Robert Ferber and P. J. Verdoorn, *Research Methods in Economics and Business* (New York: Macmillan, 1962), p. 208.

TABLE 6.1	Information Items Available from the Census of Population

100-Percent Component

Population
Household relationship
Sex
Race
Age
Marital status
Hispanic origin

Housing
Number of units in structure
Number of rooms in unit
Tenure—owned or rented
Vacancy characteristics
Value of owned unit or rent paid

Sample Component

Population
Education—enrollment and attainment
Place of birth, citizenship, and year of entry
Ancestry
Language spoken at home
Migration
Disability
Fertility
Veteran status
Employment and unemployment
Occupation, industry, and class of worker
Place of work and commuting to work
Work experience and income

Housing
Source of water, method of sewage disposal
Autos, light trucks, and vans
Kitchen facilities
Year structure built
Year moved into residence
Number of bedrooms
Farm residence
Shelter costs, including utilities
Condominium status
Plumbing
Telephone
Utilities and fuels

Note: Subjects covered in the 100-percent component will apply to all persons and housing units. Those covered by the sample component will apply to a portion of the population and housing units.

sources, and extract and record the information desired. Doing so should take no more than a few days and would involve little cost. If the information were to be collected in a field survey, the following steps would have to be executed:

1. Data-collection form designed and pretested
2. Field interview staff selected and trained
3. Sampling plan devised
4. Data gathered and checked for accuracy and omissions
5. Data coded and tabulated

As a conservative estimate, this process would take two to three months and could cost thousands of dollars, because it would include expenses and wages for field and office personnel. With secondary data, these expenses have been incurred by the original source of the information and do not need to be borne by the user. Expenses are shared by the users of commercial sources of secondary data, but even so, the user's costs will be much less than they would be if the firm collected the same information itself.

These time and cost economies prompt the general admonition: Do not bypass secondary data. Begin with secondary data, and only when the secondary data are exhausted or show diminishing returns, proceed to primary data. Sometimes secondary data may provide enough insight by themselves that there will be no need to collect primary data on the topic. This scenario will be particularly true when all the analyst needs is a ballpark estimate, which is often the case. For example, a common question that confronts marketing research analysts is, "What is the market potential for the product or service?" Are enough people or organizations interested in it to justify providing it? Research Realities 6.1 illustrates how secondary data were used to answer this question. In this case, a manufacturer of pet food used secondary data to assess the potential demand for a new product.

As the example indicates, it is often necessary to make some assumptions when using secondary data to use the data effectively (for example, the number of owners who were good prospects). The key is to make reasonable assumptions and to vary these assumptions in "what-if" scenarios to determine how sensitive a particular conclusion is to the variations of the assumptions. In the pet food example, "altering the assumption regarding the number of owners who were good prospects for the new product to include as few as one-tenth of the original number did not alter

---

RESEARCH REALITIES 6.1

Use of Secondary Data by a Manufacturer of Pet Foods to Assess the Potential Demand for a Dog Food That Included Both Moist Chunks and Hard, Dry Chunks

The question was, "Is there currently a significant number of persons who mix moist or canned dog food with dry dog food?" At this early stage in the exploration of this product concept, the firm did not want to expend funds for primary research. While an actual survey of pet owners would have yielded the best answer, such a survey would have required the expenditure of several thousand dollars. In addition, further development of the idea would have required a delay of several weeks to obtain the survey results. An effort to develop an acceptable first answer to the question of demand using secondary sources was initiated.

The firm identified the following information:

1. From published literature on veterinary medicine, the firm identified the amount (in ounces) of food required to feed a dog each day by type of food (dry, semimoist, moist), age, size, and type of dog.

2. From an existing survey conducted annually by the firm's advertising agency, the firm obtained information on

    a. the percentage of U.S. households owning dogs;

    b. the number, sizes, and types of dogs owned by each household in the survey;

    c. the type(s) of dog food fed to the dogs; and

    d. the frequency of use of various types of dog food.

It was assumed that dog owners who reported feeding their dogs two or more different types of dog food each day were good prospects for a product that provided premixed moist and dry food. Combining the information in the survey with the information from the literature on veterinary medicine and doing some simple multiplication produced a demand figure for the product concept. The demand exceeded 20 percent of the total volume of dog food sales, a figure sufficiently large to justify proceeding with product development and testing.

Source: David W. Stewart and Michael A. Kamins, *Secondary Research: Information Sources and Methods,* 2nd ed. (Thousand Oaks, CA: Sage, 1993), p. 129. Reprinted by permission of Sage.

the decision to proceed with the product. Under such circumstances, the value of additional information would be quite small."[2]

Even though it is rare that secondary data would completely solve the particular problem under study, secondary data typically will (1) help to clarify the problem under investigation; (2) suggest improved methods or data for investigating the problem; and/or (3) provide comparative benchmark data against which primary data can be more insightfully interpreted. For all of these reasons, let us reiterate: any good marketing research study should begin with secondary data.

Disadvantages of Secondary Data

Two problems commonly arise when secondary data are used: (1) they typically do not completely fit the problem; and (2) there may be problems with their accuracy.

PROBLEMS OF FIT   Because secondary data had been collected for someone else's purposes, it will be rare when they perfectly fit the problem as defined. The problems of fit are particularly acute in studies from different countries, because the various censuses are inconsistent in the information they collect, when they collect it, and how they present it. (Research Realities 6.2 discusses this problem further.) In some cases, the fit will be so poor as to render the data completely inappropriate. Secondary data may be ill-suited to problems for three reasons: (1) units of measurement; (2) class definitions; or (3) publication currency.

It is common for secondary data to be expressed in units different from those deemed most appropriate for the project. Size of retail establishment, for instance, can be expressed in terms of gross sales, profits, square feet, and number of employees. Consumer income can be expressed by individual, family, household, and spending unit. So it is with many variables, and a recurring source of frustration in using secondary data is that the source containing the information presents that information in units of measurement different from those needed.

Assuming that the units are consistent, we find that the classification boundaries presented are often different from those needed. For example, individuals in the census data are aggregated by age into the following categories: less than 18 years old, 18 to 24, 25 to 34, 35 to 44, and so on. If FirstHomeMortgage.com sought to learn more about potential home buyers who were "30-something," to tailor their services and position their Internet advertising banners, they would not be able to identify this age group cleanly. The firm could access data on people who were 25 to 34 and 35 to 44 years old. That imprecision may be acceptable for some purposes, but not others.[3]

---

[2]David W. Stewart and Michael A. Kamins, *Secondary Research: Information Sources and Methods*, 2nd ed. (Thousand Oaks, CA: Sage Publications, 1993), p. 130. See also Kathy Friedman, *Case Studies for Better Business Decisions* (Washington, DC: U.S. Department of Commerce, 1992); Richard E. Barrett, *Using the 1990 Census for Research* (Thousand Oaks, CA: Sage Publications, 1994) for discussion of the marketing-related information that is available from the federal and state governments and how that information can be used for such marketing tasks as estimating market potential, establishing sales quotas, allocating advertising budgets, locating retail outlets, and so on.

[3]The census survey has been modified also with regard to this issue of units of measurement on race or ethnicity. To recognize the increasing diversity of the U.S. population, the racial categories have been refined, offering more distinct options. In addition, citizens can state multiple affiliations so as to identify their ethnic origin more precisely. See William O'Hare, "Managing Multiple-Race Data," *American Demographics* (April 1998), pp. 42–44.

Inconsistencies in the Information Collected in Country Censuses

Language English-speaking countries, of course, present no language barriers to U.S. marketing researchers. And a number of nations offer bilingual census tabulations. Nations publishing census reports in English include the Scandinavian countries, Japan, South Korea, Taiwan, Singapore, and Thailand. Other countries offer only their native language. This is not too serious a problem if the language is French, Italian, Spanish, or Portuguese. Demographic terms in these languages are fairly close to English, and the format of the tables, along with a little guesswork, is often enough to let researchers find what they need. German, Hungarian, Polish, and languages using different alphabets, such as Russian, are much more difficult to decipher unless one has been trained in these languages.

Data Content What a researcher can get from a census depends on what is on the census form. The content is typically a mixture of traditional questions and some new items of interest to government bureaucrats and policy makers. These same forces, further modified by budget constraints, shape the form and content of the printed results.

European countries such as Switzerland and Germany print a good deal of information on noncitizens. Canada collects data on religion. Both of these topics are ignored in the U.S. censuses. What this suggests is that one cannot expect to find the same range of data topics from one country to the next; this can complicate a researcher's life enormously.

Consider income data, the lifeblood of most U.S. segmentation studies. Most nations do not include an income question in their censuses. Britain does not. Japan does not. Nor do France, Spain, and Italy. Among the few countries that have asked about income are Canada, Australia, New Zealand, Mexico, Sweden, and Finland.

Educational attainment can be used for socioeconomic status. However, educational systems vary enough among countries that comparisons can be fairly crude. Some countries report graduates of vocational-technical schools, while in this country education is reported simply by the number of years of school attended.

Data concerning marital status also varies from country to country. Ireland, for example, recognizes only three marital statuses: single, married, and widowed. Other countries tabulate the separated population, but sometimes lump it in with divorced or married populations. Latin American censuses often have "cohabitating" or "consensual union" as marital categories. Sweden cross-tabulates its cohabiting population by marital status. Although most countries gather data on marital status, few cross-tabulate it with household headship. Nor is headship often cross-tabulated by educational attainment.

Census Frequency The United States takes a census every 10 years, which is the typical frequency. Japan and Canada conduct their censuses every 5 years, but the mid-decade counts are not as complete as the ones done at the end of each decade. France takes a census irregularly; since the 1960s, the interval has been about 7 years. In what used to be West Germany, the most recent census was taken in 1987, but the previous one was in 1970, the same year of the last Dutch census.

Some northern and western European nations seem to be abandoning the census as a data collection tool. Instead, they hope to rely on population registers to account for births, deaths, and changes in marital status or place of residence. One result of this appears to be less hard-copy data. Assuming that government databases can be tapped for marketing research purposes, this would present no serious problem where research budgets are robust. However, government bureaucrats are not always friendly to marketing researchers.

Source: Donald B. Pittenger, "Gathering Foreign Demographics Is No Easy Task," *Marketing News* 24 (January 8, 1990), pp. 23, 25. Reprinted with permission of American Marketing Association.

Finally, secondary data quite often lack publication currency. The time from data collection to dissemination is often long, sometimes as much as two to three years, as, for example, with much government census data. Even though census data have great value while current, this value diminishes with time, given that many marketing decisions require current, rather than historical, information.

PROBLEMS OF ACCURACY   The accuracy of much secondary data is also questionable. As we discuss throughout this book, numerous sources of error are possible in the collection, analysis, and presentation of marketing information. When the researcher collects the information, the individual's firsthand experience should allow the assessment of the accuracy of the information and its bounds of error. These bounds can be critical for marketing decisions that are based on the information. When using secondary data, the researcher is not relieved from assessing accuracy, although the task is indeed more difficult.[4] The following criteria, though, should help the researcher judge the accuracy of any secondary data: the *source,* the *purpose of publication,* and *general evidence regarding quality.*

Consider the source first. Secondary data can be secured from either a primary source or a secondary source. A primary source is the source that originated the data. A secondary source is a source that, in turn, secured the data from an original source. *The Statistical Abstract of the United States,* which is published each year, contains a great deal of useful information for many research projects. The researcher using the *Statistical Abstract* would be using a secondary source of secondary data, because none of what is published in the *Statistical Abstract* originates there. Rather, all of it is compiled from other government and trade sources. The researcher who terminated the search for secondary data with the *Statistical Abstract* would violate the most fundamental rule in using secondary data—*always use the primary source of secondary data.*

There are two main reasons for this rule. First and foremost, the researcher will need to search for general evidence of quality (for example, the methods of data collection and analysis). The primary source will typically be the only source that describes the process of collection and analysis, and thus it is the only source by which this judgment can be made. Second, a primary source is usually more accurate and complete than a secondary source. Secondary sources typically do not include the caveats and qualifications included as disclaimers by the primary source.[5] Errors in transcription can also occur in copying the data from a primary source. Once made, transcription errors seem to hold on tenaciously, as the following example illustrates.

In 1901, Napoleon Lajoie produced the highest batting average ever attained in the American League when he batted .422 on 229 hits in 543 times at bat. In setting

---

[4]Herbert Jacob has a particularly helpful discussion on the various errors that are present in published data and what remedies are available to the analyst for treating these errors. See Herbert Jacob, *Using Published Data: Errors and Remedies* (Thousand Oaks, CA: Sage Publications, 1984). The problem of accuracy in secondary data seems to be getting worse as the ability to generate and capture data expands; see William M. Bulkeley, "Databases Are Plagued by Reign of Error," *The Wall Street Journal* (May 26, 1992), p. B6.

[5]See also William G. Zikmund, *Business Research Methods,* 5th ed. (Chicago: Dryden Press, 1996).

the type for the record book after that season, a printer correctly reported Lajoie's .422 average, but incorrectly reported his hits, giving him 220 instead of 229. A short time later, someone pointed out that 220 hits in 543 at bats yields a batting average of .405, and so Lajoie's reported average was changed. The error persisted for some 50 years until an energetic fan checked all the old box scores and discovered the facts.[6]

A second criterion by which the accuracy of secondary data can be assessed is the purpose of publication. Consider the examples in Research Realities 6.3. After reading them, do you believe any of the following: (a) pizza can be the mainstay in a healthy diet; (b) home handymen are an important group of innovators that marketers need to target in their communications; (c) Americans take their cars very seriously? Are your reactions any different if you are told: The survey in Example A was sponsored by either the American Heart Association or a pizza delivery franchise; the survey in Example B was sponsored by *Popular Mechanics* magazine; and the survey in Example C was sponsored by Bridgestone/Firestone, a tire manufacturer? Do you now have the same confidence in the objectivity of the results? Probably not, suggesting one can use the source as a criterion to evaluate the accuracy of

---

RESEARCH REALITIES 6.3

Using the Source to Evaluate the Accuracy of Secondary Data

A. The Food Pyramid Pizza Proxy   Dietitians agree that fruits and vegetables, and cereals and grains should comprise the largest shares of one's daily consumption in a healthy diet. Servings of dairy products and meats should be less, and fats and oils, minimal. In accordance with these guidelines, two-thirds of the dietitians we polled advocated a slice of pizza as the near-perfect food, citing the representation of nearly all food groups, in the approximate proportions recommended (for example, more bread than oils). Continued and increased consumption of pizza is encouraged.

B. Home Handymen   Home handymen play a significant role in millions of purchasing decisions, a new study finds. According to the study, 18 million "must-know" men affect what is bought by as many as 85 million other consumers. The study says that such men—independent do-it-yourselfers who have a compulsion

to know what makes things tick and enjoy fiddling with gadgets—are sought out for their advice by buyers of products in such areas as home improvement and electronics.

C. Americans and Their Cars   How strong are Americans' love affairs with their cars? A surprising 38 percent of the men surveyed recently by a Nashville research firm declared that they love their cars more than women. Nearly 8 percent of the women surveyed said that men who drove nice cars are more appealing, and roughly 15 percent of the respondents had even gone so far as to name their cars.

Sources: Example A: based on www.pizzafarm.org; Example B: "Just Ask the Man Who Has Taken One Apart," *The Wall Street Journal* (September 20, 1991), p. B1; Example C: "The 'Other Woman' May Be His Volvo," *The Wall Street Journal* (June 24, 1994), p. B1.

---

[6]*The Chicago Tribune* (September 19, 1960). If there had not been a cult of "baseball superfans whose passion is to dig up obscure facts about the erstwhile national pastime," the error might never have been discovered. See "You May Not Care but 'Nappie' Lajoie Batted .422 in 1901," *The Wall Street Journal* (September 13, 1974), p. 1.

secondary data. The objectivity of data are generally suspect when the findings are used as propaganda; that is, to promote sales or to advance the causes of a political party or special industry.[7]

This is not to say that data collected or sponsored by an interested party cannot be used by the researcher. Rather, it is simply to suggest that such data should be viewed most critically by the research user. A source that has no ax to grind but, rather, publishes secondary data as its primary function deserves confidence. If data publication is a source's *raison d'être*, high quality must be maintained to ensure its own long-term sustenance. Inaccurate data offer such a firm no competitive advantage, and its publication represents a potential loss of confidence and eventual demise. The success of any organization supplying data as its primary purpose depends on the long-term satisfaction of its users that the information supplied is indeed accurate.

The third criterion by which the accuracy of secondary data can be assessed is the general evidence of quality. One item of evidence here is the ability of the supplying organization to collect the data. The Internal Revenue Service, for example, has greater leverage in securing income data than does an independent marketing research firm. Related to this issue, though, is the question of whether the additional leverage introduces bias. Would a respondent be more likely to hedge in estimating his or her income in completing a tax return or in responding to a consumer survey? In addition, the user needs to ascertain how the data were collected. A primary source should provide a detailed description of how the data were collected, including definitions, data-collection forms, methods of sampling, and so forth. If it does not, researcher beware! Such omissions are usually indicative of sloppy methods.

When the details of data collection are provided, the user of secondary data should examine them thoroughly. Was the sampling plan sound? Was this type of data best collected through questionnaire or by observational methods? What about the quality of the field force? What kind of training was provided? What kinds of checks of the fieldwork were employed? What was the extent of nonresponse due to refusals, to subjects not at home, and by item? Are these statistics reported? Is the information presented in a well-organized manner? Are the tables properly labeled, and are the data within them internally consistent? Are the conclusions supported by the data? As these questions suggest, the user of secondary data must be familiar with the research process and the potential sources of error. The remainder of this book should provide much of the needed insight for evaluating secondary data. For the moment, though, let us examine some of the main sources of secondary data.

Types of Secondary Data

Secondary data can be classified in several ways. One of the most useful is by source: **internal data** are those found within the organization for whom the research is being conducted, whereas **external data** are those obtained from outside sources. The

---

[7]For other illustrations of how knowledge of the source provides insights into the accuracy of the data, see Jeff Bailey, "How Two Industries Created a Fresh Spin on the Dioxin Debate," *The Wall Street Journal* (February 20, 1992), pp. A1, A6; "Leading Researchers Invite Criticism—and They Get It," *Marketing News* 26 (June 22, 1992), p. 5; Cynthia Crossen, "How 'Tactical Research' Muddied Diaper Debate," *The Wall Street Journal* (May 17, 1994), pp. B1, B8.

ETHICAL DILEMMA 6.1

An independent marketing research firm was hired by a Los Angeles clothing designer to study the Denver ski resort market for upscale, après ski-wear. The manufacturer wanted to determine (1) whether sufficient market potential existed to warrant opening a retail store there, and (2) if so, where precisely the store should be located in the metropolitan area. The research firm went about the task by examining secondary data on the Denver market, particularly statistics published by the Census Bureau. In less than two months, the research firm was able to develop a well-documented recommendation as to what the clothing designer should do.

Approximately six months after completing this study, the firm was approached by an outdoor sporting goods designer and manufacturer to do a similar study concerning the location of a store through which it could more effectively serve its Denver customers.

• Is it ethical for the research firm to use the information it had collected in the first study to reduce its cost quote to the client in the second?

• Does it make any difference if the sporting goods firm also designs and distributes ski-wear?

• Would your answers change if some of the data were collected through personal interviews that the first client paid for?

external sources can be further classified into those that regularly publish statistics and make them available to the user at no charge (such as the United States government) and the commercial organizations that sell their services to various users (for example, Information Resources Inc., ACNielsen). In the remainder of this chapter, we will review some of the more important sources of commercialized statistics; Appendix 6A lists some of the main sources of published statistics. Together they represent some of the most commonly used sources of secondary data, the ones with which the researcher would typically commence the search. Figure 6.1 provides an overview of these sources.

Internal Secondary Data

Data that originate within the firm for which the research is being conducted are internal data. If they were collected for some other purpose, they are internal secondary data. The sales and cost data compiled in the normal accounting cycle represent promising internal secondary data for many research problems, such as evaluating past marketing strategy or assessing the firm's competitive position in the industry. It is less helpful in future-directed decisions, such as evaluating a new product or a new advertising campaign, except as a foundation for planning the research.

Generally, the single most productive source document is the sales invoice. From this, the following information can usually be extracted:

• Customer name and location
• Product(s) or service(s) sold

| FIGURE 6.1 | Types of Secondary Data |

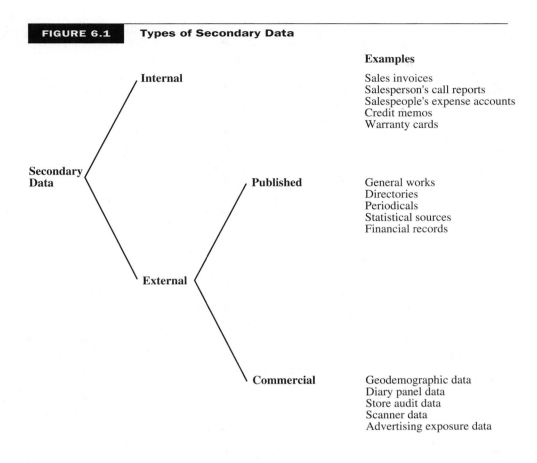

Examples

Internal
- Sales invoices
- Salesperson's call reports
- Salespeople's expense accounts
- Credit memos
- Warranty cards

Published
- General works
- Directories
- Periodicals
- Statistical sources
- Financial records

Commercial
- Geodemographic data
- Diary panel data
- Store audit data
- Scanner data
- Advertising exposure data

- Volume and dollar amount of the transaction
- Salesperson or agent responsible for the sale
- End use of product sold
- Location of customer facility where product is to be shipped and/or used
- Customer's industry, class of trade, and/or channel of distribution
- Terms of sale and applicable discount
- Freight paid or to be collected
- Shipment point for the order
- Transportation used in shipment

Loyalty programs, or membership clubs, are allowing companies to accumulate the details of each sale (as just listed) for each transaction over time with each customer. The marketing orientation is changing toward a longer-term relational database approach—a stored and continually updated sequence of sales invoice transactions. This additional compilation of information has enabled Gillette to increase market share, Veryfine to avoid disappointing consumers with undesirable product modifications, and Coca-Cola to strengthen its relationship with retailers.[8] Ideally, such detailed data also enable the firm to offer customized market offerings to the consumer, with the presumed goal of greater customer satisfaction. In reality, many companies are overwhelmed with the enormous size of the databases, and are only beginning to learn how to sort through the masses of information (see Research Realities 6.4).

Other internal documents provide more specialized input. Some of the more important of these are listed in Table 6.2. Most companies are likely to use only two or three of these sources of sales information in addition to the sales invoice. The selections depend on the company and the types of analyses used to plan and evaluate the marketing effort. Even something as simple as a product registration card can be used to advantage for marketing intelligence, as Research Realities 6.5 indicates.

Another useful but often overlooked source of internal secondary data is previous marketing research studies on related topics. Even though each study typically addresses a number of specific questions, most also involve only one or two key items that have been learned. Great synergy can result when these key items are studied and combined. Many marketing research and consulting firms, for example, Andersen Consulting, are building internal video libraries in which key personnel describe a study they had recently executed for a client. These video clips, which are cross-referenced by various keywords such as industry, segment, marketing issue, and study's purpose, can be accessed over the firm's intranet. Managers at these firms are convinced that such aggregations of knowledge are yielding a competitive advantage as its researchers are collectively moved further and more quickly up the learning curve, compared to their counterparts at competitor firms.

Two of the most important advantages associated with internal secondary data are their ready availability and low cost. Internal secondary data are the least costly of any type of marketing research, and, if maintained in an appropriate form, internal sales data can be used to analyze the company's sales performance by product, geographic location, customer, channel of distribution, and so on. Cost data allow the further determination of the profitability of these segments of the business.[9] The aspiring researcher should not bypass this information but should begin most studies with internal secondary data.

Searching for Published External Secondary Data

Such a wealth of external data exists that beginning researchers typically underestimate what is available. The statement that some relevant external secondary data is available on almost any problem a marketer might confront is not an exaggeration. The fundamental problem is not availability; it is identifying and accessing what is there. Even those researchers who do have an inkling of the amount of valuable secondary data are typically unsure of how to go about searching for it. Figure 6.2

---

[8]Ann M. Raider, "Programs Make Results Out of Research," *Marketing News* (June 21, 1999), p.14.

[9]See, for example, Charles H. Sevin, *Marketing Productivity Analysis* (New York: McGraw-Hill, 1965); Sanford R. Simon, *Managing Marketing Profitability* (New York: American Management Association, Inc., 1969), for two of the best treatments of sales and profitability analysis.

Data Mining

Data mining is the term applied to the exercise of digging through a lot of "coal"—seemingly uninteresting data—to find the golden nugget of useful marketing information. The analogy is continued when researchers speak of "drilling down" into the data. Database technology, statistics, and business acumen are all brought to bear in data mining. The phenomenon of making sense out of data is not new, but what is new is the enormous size of the databases on which the analytics are applied, due in part to the reduction in the expense of data storage technology (from $12 per megabyte 10 years ago to 20 cents today).

The databases are also extensive due to the pervasiveness of loyalty programs, which allow a company to accumulate a great deal of knowledge about consumer-purchase histories and expenditures, preferences, demographics, and so on. However, data mining assisted database and direct marketers even before loyalty programs; for example, if a magazine can communicate its readership profile clearly, it can generate more advertising revenue and do so more efficiently, facilitating the support of the magazine, and in turn, enhancing a more relevant fit of ads for the readers. As an example, Conde Nast, after analyzing its data on its 10 million subscribers across 17 magazines, noted a subscriber segment which owned Lexus automobiles and also had an affinity to Coach leather products. This ultimately resulted in a Lexus partnership with Coach leather interiors.

Data mining can enrich relationship management. The benefit to the company is the discovery and understanding of one's best (most profitable) customers, and an ability to experiment with market offerings (because it can track customers' sales responses to various promotions, for example). The benefit to business customers can be direct store delivery (for example, the replenishment of inventory as stock is electronically counted down) and the coordination of invoices and vendors. The benefit to end-user consumers is usually a product tailored more specifically to suit their particular needs.

For the portions of customer databases that are quantitative, sample sizes are typically huge, so most inferential statistics (for example, t-tests) are generally significant. Thus, analysts often rely on simple descriptive statistics (such as means and correlations). Regressions and predictions are also common, as are cluster analyses (discussed in Chapter 17, on multivariate analysis) to form customer segments. The goals of all these analyses are standard marketing fare: customer acquisition (responses to offers), retention (targeting valuable customers who may be tempted to leave to competitors), and even customer abandonment (identifying where to minimize service to costly customers, for example, young people with modest accounts at retail banks).

For the data on customers that are qualitative, such as click-stream data, stored e-mail communications, or histories of Web page traversals, analysts use "text-mining" techniques. These methods are comparable to standard descriptive statistics, but applied to alphabetic strings rather than numeric strings of data.

Recommendation technologies (RTs) such as those on books and CD e-tail vendors can be applied to quantitative or qualitative data and generally must be applied to large databases to be useful. These algorithms are the fastest-growing models among data mining tools. The models use "collaborative filtering," which is a form of cluster analysis to identify similar users, who, due to their similarity, help (collaborate) in creating overlapping lists of products that form the basis of the recommendations. For more information, see Chapter 17. For a comparison of data mining software vendors, see Peter R. Peacock, "Data Mining in Marketing: Part 2," *Marketing Management* 7 (Spring 1998b), p. 22, and visit cognos.com, datamincorp.com, ibm.com/bi, ncr.com, sas.com, splinfoware.com, spss.com, and torrent.com.

For more information on data mining, see Jo Bennett, "Database Technology: Vastly Improved," *Folio: The Magazine for Magazine Management* 28 (December 15, 1999), pp. 31–35; Maggie Biggs, "Resurgent Text-Mining Technology Can Greatly Increase Your Firm's 'Intelligence' Factor," *InfoWorld* 22 (January 10, 2000), p. 52; Michael Hess and Bob Mayer, "Test and Evaluate Your Way to Success," *Marketing News* (July 5, 1999), p. 12; Bob Moseley, "Conde Nast Goes Beyond Data-Basics," *Folio: The Magazine for Magazine Management* 28 (December 15, 1999), pp. 37–42; Peter R. Peacock, "Data Mining in Marketing: Part 1," *Marketing Management* 6 (Winter 1998a), pp. 9–18; Peter R. Peacock, "Data Mining in Marketing: Part 2," pp. 15–25; Raymond C. Pettit, "Data Mining: Race for Mission-Critical Info," *Marketing News* (January 3, 2000), p. 18; Barbara Depompa Reimers, "Getting Personal," *Informationweek* (January 3, 2000), pp. 51–55; Richard Shulman, "Something Old, Something New—Both Called DSD," *Supermarket Business* 54 (November 15, 1999), pp. 33–35.

TABLE 6.2	Some Useful Sources of Internal Secondary Data

Document	*Information Provided*
Cash register receipts	• Type (cash or credit) and dollar amount of transaction by department by salesperson
Salesperson's call reports	• Customers and prospects called on (company and individual seen; planned or unplanned calls) • Products discussed • Orders obtained • Customers' product needs and usage • Other significant information about customers • Distribution of salesperson's time among customer calls, travel, and office work • Sales-related activities: meetings, conventions, and so on
Salesperson's expense accounts	• Expenses by day by item (hotel, meals, travel, and so on)
Individual customer (and prospect) records	• Name and location and customer • Number of calls by company salesperson (agents) • Sales by company (in dollars and/or units, by product or service, by location of customer facility) • Customer's industry, class of trade, and/or trade channel • Estimated total annual usage of each product or service sold by the company • Estimated annual purchases from the company of each such product or service • Location (in terms of company sales territory)
Financial records	• Sales revenue (by product, geographic market, customer, class of trade, unit of sales organization, and so on) • Direct sales expenses (similarly classified) • Overhead sales costs (similarly classified) • Profits (similarly classified)
Credit memos	• Returns and allowances
Warranty cards	• Indirect measures of dealer sales • Customer service

provides some general guidelines that can be used to get started on a search of secondary data on a particular topic.[10]

STEP 1   Identify what you already know and what you wish to know about your topic, including relevant facts, names of researchers or organizations associated with the topic, and key papers and other publications with which you are already familiar.

STEP 2   Develop a list of key terms and names. These terms and names will provide access to secondary sources. Unless you have a very specific topic of interest, it is better to keep this initial list long and quite general.

STEP 3   You are ready to use the Internet or the library. It is useful to begin your search with several of the directories listed in Appendix 6A. Look at only the previous

---

[10]The figure and surrounding discussions are adapted from Stewart and Kamins, *Secondary Research*. See also Robert I. Berkman, *Find It Fast: How to Uncover Expert Information on Any Subject*, 4th ed. (New York: HarperCollins Publishers, 1997).

Targeting: It's in the Cards

When the Skil Corporation was launching a cordless power screwdriver, management was worried. It believed that the company had designed a useful product, but it wondered whether consumers would think the new tool was just a gimmick. Using information from product registration cards and follow-up interviews, Skil was quickly able to prove to itself that the screwdriver was not a fad.

The registration card research revealed something else, however. Although do-it-yourselfers were the primary market for the new product, a substantial portion of the purchasers were elderly people for whom the screwdriver's ease of operation was the chief advantage. "We hadn't realized the arthritis implications," says Skil's Ron Techter. In response, Skil began advertising in publications geared to older Americans.

Almost everyone has filled out a product registration card. As they slip the card into the mailbox, few consumers realize that they have just completed a questionnaire. Yet for National Demographics & Lifestyles (NDL), the information from product registration cards has been pure gold. NDL compiles information from these "mini-questionnaires" to feed its comprehensive database, which includes demographics and participation information covering 57 activities, interests, and lifestyles.

According to Jock Bickert, the company's founder, NDL data offer no special advantage at a national level, because a marketer can survey 1,500 or 2,000 consumers to obtain national projections. However, NDL's database is very powerful when one moves down to individual markets, neighborhoods, or even postal routes.

One company that has made effective use of NDL's data is Amana Appliance. One day, Bill Packard, domestic sales manager for an independent Amana Appliance distributor in Fort Lauderdale, was talking with Amana's manager of marketing services, Dave Collins. Collins mentioned that Amana could provide Packard with profiles of Amana purchasers from his territory for the past year and a half, based on NDL product registration cards. When the NDL profile arrived, Packard got an idea.

He took the information to the marketing director of a Boca Raton real estate developer who was trying to decide what brand of appliances to put into his $200,000 homes. Packard pointed out that the purchaser profile of high-end Amana products perfectly matched the developer's profile of potential customers. Initially skeptical, the marketing director polled 100 potential home buyers himself. These home-buyer profiles so closely matched Amana's that the developer decided to use Amana appliances in the kitchens.

"If you look at one of our completed questionnaires," says NDL's Jock Bickert, "you really begin to get a picture of the individual. You are able to say, 'This person is a likely candidate for these kinds of offers and promotions and appeals and is very unlikely for other kinds.' You can't do that if you are looking at demography alone."

Source: Wally Wood, "Targeting: It's in the Cards," *Marketing & Media Decisions* 23 (September 1988), pp. 121–122. See also Robert Bengen, "Teamwork: It's in the Bag," *Marketing Research: A Magazine of Management & Applications* 5 (Winter 1993), pp. 30–33, for discussion of how Samsonite uses warranty cards along with other information to improve its marketing.

two or three years of work in the area, using three or four general guides. Some directories and indexes use a specialized list of key terms or descriptors. Such indexes often have thesauri that identify these terms. Be sure that your list of terms and descriptors are consistent with those used in the thesauri.

Step 4   Compile the literature you have found. Is it relevant to your needs? Perhaps you are overwhelmed by information. Perhaps you have found little that is relevant. If so, rework your list of keywords and authors and expand your search to

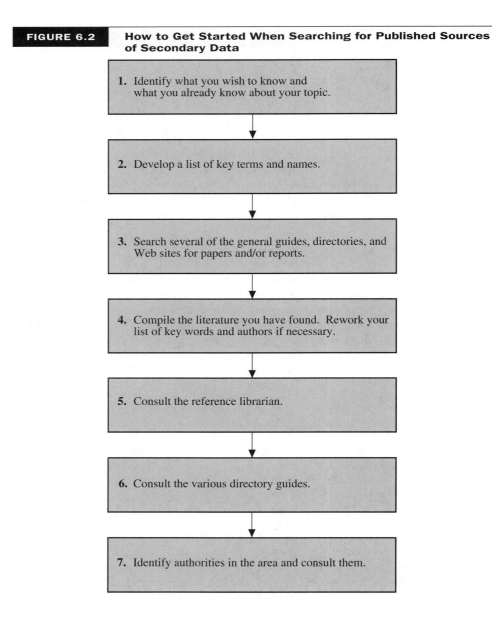

FIGURE 6.2   **How to Get Started When Searching for Published Sources of Secondary Data**

1. Identify what you wish to know and what you already know about your topic.

2. Develop a list of key terms and names.

3. Search several of the general guides, directories, and Web sites for papers and/or reports.

4. Compile the literature you have found. Rework your list of key words and authors if necessary.

5. Consult the reference librarian.

6. Consult the various directory guides.

7. Identify authorities in the area and consult them.

include a few more years and a few additional sources. Once again evaluate your findings. By the end of step 4, you should have a clear idea of the nature of the information you are seeking and sufficient background to use more specialized sources.

STEP 5   One very useful specialized source is a reference librarian. Reference librarians are specialists who have been trained to know the contents of many of the key information sources in a library and on the Web, as well as how to search those sources most effectively. It is a rare problem indeed for which a reference librarian cannot uncover some relevant information. Although the reference librarian can help you if you wish to consider a computer-assisted information search, the librarian will still need your help in the form of a carefully constructed list of keywords or topics. You need to remember that the reference librarian cannot be of much help until you can provide some rather specific details about what you want to know.

STEP 6   If you have had little success or your topic is highly specialized, consult one of the general guides to information listed in Appendix 6A. These are really directories of directories, which means that this level of search will be very general. You will first need to identify potentially useful primary directories, which will then lead you to other sources.

STEP 7   If you are unhappy with what you have found or are otherwise having trouble, and the reference librarian has not been able to identify sources, use an authority. Identify some individual or organization that might know something about the topic. The various Who's Who publications, Consultants and Consulting Organizations Directory, Encyclopedia of Associations, or Research Centers Directory should help you identify sources. The Bureau of the Census puts out a list of department specialists whom users can contact for information on any of the bureau's studies. These people are often quite knowledgeable about related studies in their areas of expertise. Faculty at universities, government officials, and business executives can also be useful sources of information.

Key General Sources of External Secondary Data

In addition to the key role played by reference librarians, other particularly important sources of external secondary data are associations, general guides to useful marketing information, and online computer searches.

ASSOCIATIONS   Most associations gather, and often publish, detailed information on such matters as industry shipments and sales, growth patterns, environmental factors affecting the industry, operating characteristics, and the like. Trade associations are often able to secure information from members that other research organizations cannot because of the working relationships that exist between the association and the firms that belong to it. Two useful sources for locating associations serving a particular industry are *Directories in Print* and the *Encyclopedia of Associations*, described in Appendix 6A.

GENERAL GUIDES TO BUSINESS INFORMATION   Other useful sources for locating information on a particular topic are the general guides to business information described in Appendix 6A. Table 6.3, for example, lists what the *Encyclopedia of Business Information Sources* has to say about data sources on the music industry. Aspiring researchers are also well-advised to acquaint themselves with the more important general sources of marketing information so that they know what statistics are available and where they can be found. Many important sources are described in Appendix 6A.

TABLE 6.3   **Sources of Data on the Music Industry**

Abstracts and Indexes
Music Index: A Subject-Author Guide to Over 300 Current International Periodicals. Harmonic Park Press. Monthly. $1,235.00/year. Annual cumulation. Supplement available. Guide to current periodicals.

Bibliographies
Information Sources in Music. Lewis Foreman, ed. Bowker-Saur. 1997. $100.00. Evaluates information sources in a wide range of music topics, including copyright, music publishing, reprographics, and the use of computers in music publishing.

Mix Bookshelf: Information Resources for Music Professionals. Cardinal Business Media, Inc. Semiannual. Free. An annotated catalog of about 600 publications relating to music, electronic music technology, musical instruments, and the music business.

Biographical Sources
Celebrity Register. The Gale Group. 1990. $99.00. 5th ed. Compiled by Celebrity Services International (Earl Blackwell). Contains profiles of 1,300 famous individuals in the performing arts, sports, politics, business, and other fields.

Contemporary Musicians: Profiles of the People in Music. Available from The Gale Group. 1998. $1817.00. 23 volumes in print. $79.00/volume.

Directories
Billboard's International Buyer's Guide of the Music-Record-Tape Industry. BPI Communications. Annual. $83.00. Record companies; music publishers; record and tape wholesalers; services and supplies for the music-record-tape-video industry; record and tape dealer accessories, fixtures, merchandising products; includes U.S. and over 65 countries. Formerly *Billboard's International Buyer's Guide of the Music Industry.*

MixPlus Music and Audio Resources for the U.S. and Canada. Cardinal Business Media Inc. Annual. $14.95 for each regional edition (East, West, Central). A professional directory for the recording and music businesses, listing concert promoters, rehearsal halls, consultants, record labels, recording studios, tape and disc mastering services, legal services, facility designers, music education programs, and other music and audio services.

Music Address Book: How to Reach Anyone Who's Anyone in the Music Business. Michael Levine. Harper & Collins Publishers, Inc. 1994. $14.00. 2nd ed.

Recording Industry Sourcebook. Cardinal Business Media, Inc. Annual. $79.95. Provides more than 12,000 listings in 57 categories of record/tape/compact disc labels, producers, distributors, managers, equipment suppliers, and others.

Handbooks and Manuals
All You Need to Know About the Music Business. Donald S. Passman. Simon & Schuster Trade. 1997. $27.00. 2nd expanded revised ed. Covers the practical and legal aspects of record contracts, music publishing, management agreements, touring, and other music business topics.

Entertainment Law. Robert Fremlin. West Group. Annual. $125.00. Includes supplement *Entertainment and Communication Law Series.*

Entertainment Law. Howard Siegel, ed. New York State Bar Assn. 1990. $60.00. Contains chapters by various authors on the legal aspects of television, motion pictures, theatre, music, phonograph records, and related topics.

Online Databases
PROMT: Predicasts Overview of Markets and Technology. The Gale Group. Companies, products, applied technologies and markets. U.S. and international literature coverage, 1972 to date. Daily updates. Inquire as to online cost and availability. Provides abstracts from more than 1,500 publications.

Periodicals and Newsletters
Entertainment Marketing Letter. EPM Communications, Inc. 22 times a year, $417.00/year. Newsletter. Covers the marketing of various entertainment products. Includes television broadcasting, videocassettes, celebrity tours and tie-ins, radio broadcasting, and the music business.

Stereo Review's Sound & Vision: Home Theater, Audio, Video, Multimedia, Movies, Music. Hachette Filipacchi Magazines, Inc. 10 times/year. $12.00/year. Popular magazine providing explanatory articles and critical reviews of equipment and media (CD-ROM, DVD, videocassettes, etc). Replaces *Stereo Review* and *Video Magazine.*

Statistics Sources
U.S. Industry and Trade Outlook. McGraw-Hill. Annual. $69.95. Produced by the International Trade Administration, U.S. Department of Commerce, in a "public-private" partnership with DRI/McGraw-Hill and Standard & Poor's. Provides basic data, outlook for the current year, and "Long-Term Prospects" (5-year projections) for a wide variety of products and services. Includes high technology industries. Formerly *U.S. Industrial Outlook.*

Trade/Professional Associations
American Society of Composers, Authors and Publishers. One Lincoln Plaza, New York, NY 10023. Phone (212) 621-6000.

National Association of Music Merchants. 5790 Arnada Dr., Carlsbad, Calif. 92008. Phone: (800) 767-6266 or (619) 438-8001.

Source: Taken from James Wov (ed.), *Encyclopedia of Business Information Sources,* 14th ed. (Detroit: Gale, 2000), pp. 587–588.

Online Computer Searches

Online computer searches are the state of the art, having become increasingly popular in the past 20 years for locating published information and data via computer-readable storage systems for databases. Many public and university libraries have invested in the equipment and personnel that are necessary to make database searching available to their patrons. There are now several thousand databases to pick from, with several hundred of them applying to business.

The operation of the online services involves three main components: a database producer, a database vendor, and a data user. The database producer collects the information and edits it according to the organization's criteria. The producer then puts it on tape or compact disc and sells it to the vendor. The vendor mounts the tape or disc on a computer, or perhaps sells the information on a CD-ROM. The vendor might combine or split the information to fit his or her own needs. Thus, the same database from different vendors might have different structures. The vendor pays a fee every time the database is used online and pays a fee for all citations from it.

The user pays when accessing the database whether he or she gets the information needed or not. The more information one gets, the more one pays. The user also pays for the use of the telephone lines, connection charges, and printing charges. Printing charges vary as a function of how much is printed and whether the printing occurs online or offline at a more convenient time, in which case the output is mailed to the user. In sum, the costs of using a database online include: (1) planning and executing the search; (2) telephone line charges; (3) connection charges; and (4) citation and printing charges. The big advantage of online searching is time savings. Some of the more well-known database vendors are ABI/Inform, CompuServ, DataStar, Dialog, Dun & Bradstreet, Lexis/Nexis, Ovid, and Questel. Some providers position themselves as assisting smaller businesses with sorting through the mountains of available data, for example, winstar.com.

Databases are typically defined by the type of information they contain. For example, bibliographic databases provide references to magazine or journal articles. They will list the name of the article, the author, the title of the journal, and the date of publication. They are also likely to include keywords that describe the contents of the article. Most bibliographic databases also provide an abstract or summary of the article. Some of the useful databases for marketers are those that contain the following:

- *Specific company or industry information:* The information in these databases comes primarily from reports filed with the Securities and Exchange Commission, stockholder reports, and stock market information. The databases cover financial, marketing, and product information, some company profiles, and the usual directory information, such as the name of the organization and its address and phone number. For example, both Moody's and Standard and Poor's provide both U.S. corporate descriptions as well as international corporate profiles. For Moody's U.S., see secure.telebase.com/smalloffice/bus_mus.htm; for global, www.smalloffice.telebase.com/bus_mint.htm. For Standard and Poor's North

American, see www.compustat.com/www/db/na_descr.htm, and for global, see www.compustat.com/www/db/gl_descr.htm. And of course, Internet search engines (such as Yahoo's business category at www.yahoo.com) are extremely useful in locating information about companies.

- *Mergers, affiliations, ownership information*: These databases typically list the institutions and people that own a stock by name, and the ownership changes, including the mergers and acquisitions, that have taken place in the recent past or are pending. Examples include Disclosure/Spectrum Ownership (www.dialogweb.com/topics/All/Business), the Insider Trading Monitor (library.dialog.com/bluesheets/html/bl0549.html) and World Trade Resources (www.worldtraderesources.com).

- *Company directory information*: Numerous directories are available that differ in the types of companies they cover (such as public or private), the size of the companies covered, and their geographic coverage. In addition to the name, address, and telephone number, many of the directories list the NAICS (formerly SIC) codes for the business. Examples include Dun's Business Locator (business.cd-rom-directory.com/cdprod1/cdhrec/002/296.shtml), and Standard and Poor's Corporate Register (www.dialogselect.com/sources/0526.html).

- *U.S. government contract information*: These databases are particularly useful to businesses dealing with the government. They contain information on whether a specific company has any government contracts and recent contract awards; an example is Commerce Business Daily (cbd.savvy.com).

- *Economic information*: These databases contain general economic and demographic information from U.S. census materials and from the private sector. Many of these databases contain forecasts of future economic activity; an example is Cendata (www.agnic.org/agdb/cendata.html).

- *General business information*: These databases cover companies, industries, people, and products. Increasingly these sources locate global, not just U.S., information. The sources are primarily trade and business-oriented journals, selected newspapers, and various reports. Examples are ABI/Inform (libraries and universities have access) and *Harvard Business Review* (www.hbsp.harvard.edu/products/hbr). Lexis/Nexis facilitates searches by organizing information into categories: news, business, statistics, general reference, and legal, which are further subcategorized; for example, the business category covers business news, financials, company comparisons, industry information, and so on.

- *Brand name/trade name information*: These databases contain information on specific products, including what competitors might be doing with respect to new-product introductions or expenditures on advertising, and which company owns a specific trademark; an example is Thomas Register Online (www.thomasregister.com).

- *People information*: These databases contain information on people who have been cited in the literature for their accomplishments in the arts, sciences, business, or other fields of endeavor. The data track people in the business world or inventors and the patents they hold. Examples include *American Men & Women of Science* (1998, 20th ed.) and Standard & Poor's Register—

TABLE 6.4	How to Conduct a Database Search

Step 1: Specify the information to be sought and develop a "search strategy," a set of words that will be entered into the computer for the actual search. If the database being searched is unfamiliar, it is often valuable to develop the search strategy with the help of a specialist familiar with the database.

Step 2: Log onto the database, either by loading the appropriate CD-ROM or by connecting to the database computer. The database computer will ask for identification to determine whether the searcher is an authorized user of the system. The user will reply by typing in a code. If it is accepted, the database computer will ask for the name of the database or file to be searched.

Step 3: Input the search strategy. When the search strategy has been entered, the computer will begin the search and will report the number of matches. If the number of matches is large, the user may wish to add further qualifications to the terms used in the search to find the specific information he or she needs.

Step 4: If the results are satisfactory, the user must decide the level of detail sought for each match made. The choices of published articles may include a simple bibliography, an annotated bibliography, a bibliography with abstracts, or the full text. The more detail the user wants, the more costly the search will be because of access and printing charges.

Biographical (New York: McGraw Hill, www.dialogselect.com/sources/0526. html).

As the preceding list indicates, companies use online databases to search for marketing data, economic trends, legislation, inventions, reports, speeches, journal articles, and many other types of information on a particular topic. Some especially useful guides to online databases are described in Appendix 6A. Table 6.4 explains how to conduct a database search.

In addition to using online databases, researchers can use the Internet to execute general searches of the World Wide Web to locate secondary data on a subject. To do so requires Web access through an access service provider and one or more search engines. Search engines are needed because the Internet contains well over 10 billion pages of documents that are not arranged for retrieval. Creators of search engines compile and index an electronic catalog of Web contents, then provide the software needed to search through the index for keywords or concepts specified by the user. The indices may be directory- or word-based or a combination of the two. The differences in perspective are described in Research Realities 6.6, which also contains the recommendations of a panel of experts as to how to search the Web using some of the more popular search engines.[11]

---

[11]As new search services are introduced, new comparisons are also reported; for example, Timothy Hanrahan, "The Internet: The Best Way to Search Online," in *The Wall Street Journal* (December 6, 1999), p. R25, characterizes about.com as well-organized and google.com as providing high-quality, relevant sites. *PC Magazine* cites www.northernlight.com as well-organized and indexing the most Web pages; see "Top 100 Web Sites" (February 8, 2000), pp. 93, 152. It also recommends www.deepcanyon.com as particularly useful for research in the computer industry and for Internet marketers (p. 150).

Searching the World Wide Web

THE START BUTTON

YAHOO!
http://www.yahoo.com

•

Yahoo! was cited repeatedly by members of our panel as the best all-around starting point for conducting research on the Web. Fans say it's the fastest way to find Web sites dedicated to any given subject.

But to get the most out of Yahoo, it's important to understand exactly how the site works. Unlike Alta Vista and other so-called search engines, which use computers to automatically index every word at a Web site, Yahoo is a true directory. The sites it catalogs have been sorted by Yahoo's staff into subject categories, subcategories, and subsubcategories.

That is, you can click your way down through successive levels of subjects to find sites that interest you. For instance, choosing the category "Business and Economy" calls up a new set of selections, including "Employment," "Finance and Investment," and "Real Estate."

Here's where the directory versus search engine difference comes in. Suppose you need to find the Web site for General Motors Corp. quickly, but you aren't sure of the address. If you type "General Motors" into Yahoo's search box, the site comes back immediately with a category that lists all of GM's sites. But searching on the same phrase at a search engine would call up a list of Web pages that merely contain the words "General Motors," forcing a user to sift through dozens of pages before finding the actual GM corporate site.

One caveat: Because the Web is constantly changing, Yahoo's listings are not always completely up to date. Do not be surprised if it turns out that a site listed in the directory has disappeared.

DESPERATELY SEEKING SOMETHING

ALTAVISTA	**INFOSEEK**
http://altavista.digital.com	*http://www.infoseek.com*
EXCITE	**LYCOS**
http://www.excite.com	*http://www.lycos.com*
HOTBOT	
http://www.hotbot.com	

•

Where Yahoo's directory-style guide is speedy, search engines are thorough—almost unbelievably so. And for that reason, nearly all of our experts said they keep at least one of these massive indexes in their arsenal of Web tools.

Generally, the time to enlist a search engine is when searches at a directory have not panned out, when you are seeking something that may not be directly related to a Web site's topic, or you just want to cast as wide a net as possible.

Favorite search engines varied among our group. But all of them operate on the same basic premise: Instead of categorizing complete sites the way Yahoo does, search engines operate by indexing individual words or groups of words found on the pages at Web sites. Think of a catalog that would index every word found in all the books of a library's collection.

As a result, search engines turn up word matches in the most unlikely places. Search for "General Motors" at Infoseek, for example, and you'll soon stumble upon the Web site for the Vancouver Canucks hockey team. Why? The pages contain multiple references to the Canucks' home arena: General Motors Place.

That kind of find may be serendipitous. Or, more likely, it may be completely irrelevant to the task at hand. Searching at one of these indexes may turn up tens of thousands of Web pages, requiring you to slog through page after page of results before locating something useful.

When all else fails, read the instructions: The relevance of the findings and the efficiency of the search can be enhanced greatly if you actually read through the "help" pages at the search engine you are using. All of these sites offer advanced search commands that can significantly narrow your results. For instance, at most sites, typing in two words would call up a list of pages that contain either word. But placing the two words within quotation marks will force the search engine to look for the words as one phrase (such as "jet ski").

For more information, see Thomas E. Weber, "Watching the Web: Experts Pick Their Most Useful Sites," *The Wall Street Journal* (August 28, 1997), p. B26.

ETHICAL DILEMMA 6.2

In early March, a marketing manager for a tax consultancy stumbled onto an important piece of competitive intelligence while visiting a local printer near the company's plant. While waiting to speak with the salesperson who handled the company's account, the manager noticed some glossy advertising proofs for one of its competitor's products. The ad highlighted a new customer satisfaction guarantee. When he mentioned the guarantee to the printer, he was told that it was part of a new advertising campaign. The marketing manager called a meeting of the company's own management on his return to headquarters. As a result of that meeting, the company initiated a pre-emptive customer satisfaction guarantee campaign of its own that effectively neutralized the competitor's strategy.

- Did the marketing manager act ethically in reporting the information back to his own company?

- Would your judgment be different if the proofs were in a folder and the marketing manager somewhat casually but inadvertently opened the folder while standing there? What if he did so on purpose after noticing that the folder pertained to the competitor?

- Should information like this be entered into the firm's DSS?

Standardized Marketing Information Services

The many standardized marketing information services that are available are another important source of secondary data for the marketing researcher. These services are available at some cost to the user and in this respect are a more expensive source of secondary data than published information. However, they are also typically much less expensive than primary data, because purchasers of these data share the costs incurred by the supplier in collecting, editing, coding, and tabulating them. Because it must be suitable for a number of users, though, what is collected and how the data are gathered must be uniform. Thus, the data may not always ideally fit the needs of the user, which is their main disadvantage over primary data.

This section reviews some of the main types and sources of standardized marketing information service data.

Profiling Customers

Market segmentation is common among businesses seeking to improve their marketing efforts. Effective segmentation demands that firms classify their customers into relatively homogeneous groups. That enables them to tailor marketing programs to each group. A common segmentation base for firms selling industrial goods takes into account the industry designation or designations of its customers, most typically by means of the North American Industry Classification System (NAICS) codes. The NAICS codes comprise a system developed by the U.S. Census Bureau for organizing the reporting of business information, such as employment, value added in manufacturing, capital expenditures, and total sales. Each major industry in the United States is assigned a number, indicating the group to which it belongs. The types of businesses making up each industry are further identified by additional digits. The NAICS codes are replacing the Standard Industrial Classification (SIC) codes. Figure 6.3 displays the categorization for marketing consultants.

One of the commercial services that is especially popular among industrial goods and service suppliers is Dun's Business Locator, an index on CD-ROM that provides basic data on over 10 million U.S. businesses, including the industry code of each establishment (business.cd-rom-directory.com/cdprod1/cdhrec/002/296.shtml). These records allow sales management to construct business-to-business sales prospect files, define sales territories and measure territory potentials, and isolate potential new customers with particular characteristics. They allow advertising management to select prospects by size and location; to analyze market prospects and select the media to reach them; to build, maintain, and structure current mailing lists; to generate sales leads qualified by size, location, and quality; and to locate new markets for testing. Finally, they allow marketing research to assess market potential by territory; to measure market penetration in terms of numbers of prospects and numbers of customers; and to make comparative analyses of overall performance by districts and sales territories and in individual industries.

Firms selling consumer goods can ill afford to target individual customers, because no single customer is likely to buy much of any product or service. Rather, firms need to target groups of customers. Their ability to do this has increased substantially since the 1970 census, which was the first electronic census. Since that time, the Census Bureau has made available computer files of the facts that have been gathered which make the data usable from personal computers. Having the data available in electronic form allows their tabulation by arbitrary geographic boundaries, and an entire industry has developed since 1970 to take advantage of this capability. The "geodemographers," as they are most typically called, combine census data with their own survey data or data that they gather from administrative records, such as motor vehicle registrations or credit transactions, to produce customized products for their clients.

For example: R. L. Polk has a product for retailers called the Vehicle Origin Survey (www.stratmap.com/dat_cons.htm and www.polk.com). Polk gathers license-plate numbers from cars parked in shopping centers and matches them against Polk's National Vehicle Registration Database to find out where these retail customers live. The shopping center can then use plots of its customers' residences to determine its trading area.[12] Moreover, the locations can be computer matched with the Census Bureau's demographics for the area using its files, thereby providing a demographic profile of the people who shop there.

Geodemographic Data

Mapping software, at its most sophisticated called a geographic information system (GIS), combines various kinds of demographic data with geographic information on maps. The user can draw a map showing average income levels of a county, then zoom in closer to look at particular towns in more detail. Most GIS programs on the market can show information as detailed as a single block; some programs can show individual buildings. Seeing the information on a map can be more useful than

---

[12] *Where & Who (Are the Customers)* (Detroit: R. L. Polk & Co., undated).

FIGURE 6.3	Partial Analysis of North American Industry Classification System (NAICS) Codes for Marketing Consultants

11 Agriculture, forestry, fishing		
21–22 Mining, Utilities		
23 Construction	**54.11** Legal Services	
31–45 Manufacturing, Wholesale and Retail Trade	**54.12** Accounting, Tax Preparation	
48–49 Transportation	**54.13** Architectural, Engineering	
51 Information	**54.14** Specialized Design Services	**54.16.1.1** Administrative Management and General Management Consulting
52–53 Finance, Insurance, Real Estate	**54.15** Computer System Design	**54.16.1.2** Human Resources and Executive Search Consulting
54 **Professional, Scientific and Technical Services**	**54.16** **Management, Scientific, Technical Consulting Services**	**54.16.1.3** **Marketing Consulting Service**
55 Management of Companies and Enterprises	**54.17** Scientific Research and Development	**54.16.1.4** Process, Physical Distribution, Logistics Consulting
61 Educational Services	**54.18** Advertising and Related Services	**54.16.1.8** Other Management Consulting
62 Health Care, Social Assistance		**54.16.2** Environmental Consulting Services
71 Arts, Entertainment, Recreation		
72 Hospitality, Food Services		
92 Public Administration		

merely reading tables of numbers. At PepsiCo, a GIS enabled marketers to analyze traffic patterns and consumer demographics to identify the best sites for new Taco Bell and Pizza Hut restaurants.[13] Programs designed specifically for use as GISs include Maptitude (Caliper Corporation; see www.caliper.com/maptovu.htm) and MapInfo (see www.mapinfo.com).

Geodemographers also regularly update the census data through statistical extrapolation. The data can consequently be used with much more confidence during the years between the censuses. Another value-added feature that has contributed to the success of the industry has been its cluster analyses of the census data to derive "homogeneous groups" that describe the American population. For example, Claritas, Inc. (the pioneer and a leader in the industry) used over 500 demographic variables in its PRIZM (Potential Ratings for Zip Markets) system when classifying residential neighborhoods. This system breaks the 250,000 neighborhood areas in the United States into 40 types based on consumer behavior and lifestyle. Each of the types has a fancy name that theoretically describes the type of people living there, such as Urban Gold Coast, Shotguns and Pickups, Pools and Patios, and so on. Figure 6.4, for example, describes the Towns and Gowns cluster. Claritas, Inc. or the other suppliers will do a customized analysis for whatever geographic boundaries a client specifies (see www.stratmap.com/dat_cons.htm). Alternatively, a client can send an electronic list of the zip code addresses of their customer database, and the geodemographer will attach the cluster codes. Figure 6.5 shows one type of map that can be produced by these services.[14]

Measuring Product Sales and Market Share

A critical need in today's increasingly competitive environment is for firms to have an accurate assessment of their status in the marketplace. A common yardstick for that assessment is sales and market share. Firms selling industrial goods or services typically track their own sales and market shares through analyses of their sales invoices. They also obtain feedback from the sales department in terms of how they did in various product or system proposal competitions. An alternative source that companies use to measure their market share is one of the online bibliographic data sources discussed previously. Many times, a search of an appropriate database will turn up published studies containing product, company, and market information, including market-share statistics.

---

[13]Eric Schine, "Computer Maps Pop Up All Over the Map," *Business Week* (July 26, 1993), pp. 75–76.

[14]For discussion of some of the marketing insights made possible by the availability of geodemographic data, see Michael Weiss, *The Clustered World* (Ithaca, NY: American Demographic Books, 1999); Diane Crispell, *The Insider's Guide to Demographic Know How* (Burr Ridge, IL: Irwin Professional Publishing, 1992). Most issues of the monthly journal *American Demographics* contain a feature column called "The Grid" which uses such data to map phenomena as varied as where new or used car buyers live (January 2000 issue); where there exists high consumer demand for green goods (April 1999); local baby booms (May 1999); organic farming (August 1999); orthopedic surgeons (September 1999); and so on. Another useful keyword is TIGER, for Topologically Integrated Geographic Encoding and Referencing, the Census Bureau's database. Modeling techniques for using these data are continually being improved; see Daniel S. Putler, Kirthi Kalyanam, and James S. Hodges, "A Bayesian Approach for Estimating Target Market Potential with Limited Geodemographic Information," *Journal of Marketing Research* 33 (May 1996), pp. 134–149.

| FIGURE 6.4 | Sample Cluster Profile from the Potential Ratings for Zip Markets System |

The **Towns and Gowns** cluster describes most of our college towns and university campus neighborhoods. With a typical mix of half locals (Towns) and half students (Gowns), it is wholly unique, with thousands of penniless 18- to 24-year-old kids, plus highly educated professionals, all with a taste for prestige products beyond their evident means.

Predominant Characteristics

- Households (%U.S): 1,290,200 (1.4%)
- Population (%U.S.): 3,542,500
- Demographic Caption: College Town Singles
- Ethnic Diversity: Dominant White, High Asian
- Family Type: Singles
- Predominant Age Ranges: Under 24, 25–34
- Education: College Graduates
- Employment Level: White-Collar/Service
- Housing Type: Renters/Multi-Unit 10+
- Density Centile: 58 (1 = Sparse, 99 = Dense)

More Likely To:

Lifestyle	Products and Services
Go to college football games	Have a personal education loan
Play racquetball	Use an ATM card
Go skiing	Own a Honda
Play billiards/pool	Buy 3+ pairs of jeans annually
Use cigarette rolling paper	Drink Coca-Cola Classic
Use a charter/tour bus	Eat Kraft Macaroni and Cheese
Radio/TV	**Print**
Listen to CHR/rock radio	Read Self
Watch VH1	Read newspaper comics section
Watch Jeopardy	Read Rolling Stone
Listen to variety radio	Read GQ
Watch The Simpsons	

Source: Claritas, Inc.

Manufacturers of consumer goods also monitor their sales by account through the examination of sales invoices. For them, though, that is only part of the equation to determine how they are doing. Using factory shipments as a sales barometer neglects the filling or depleting of distribution pipelines that may be occurring. The other part of the equation involves the measurement of sales to final consumers. Historically, such measurements have been handled several ways, including the use of diary panels of households and the measurement of sales at the store level.

FIGURE 6.5 Sample Geodemographic Map

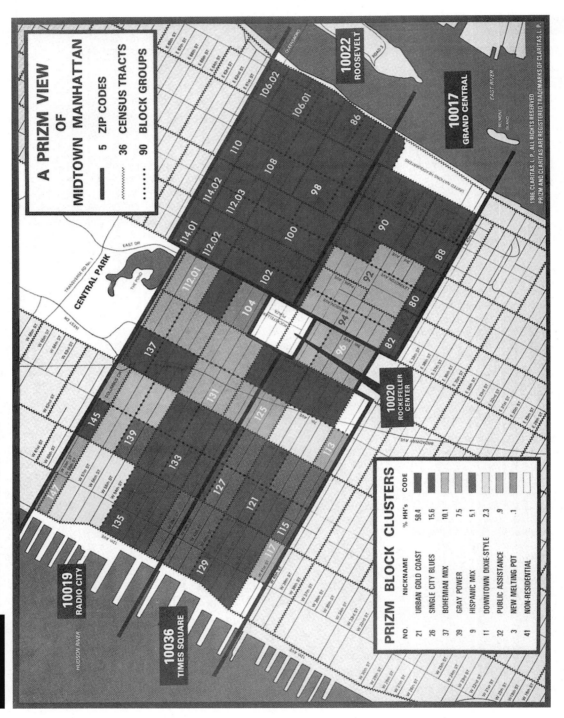

A PRIZM VIEW
OF
MIDTOWN MANHATTAN

5	ZIP CODES
36	CENSUS TRACTS
90	BLOCK GROUPS

PRIZM BLOCK CLUSTERS

NO.	NICKNAME	% HH's	CODE
21	URBAN GOLD COAST	58.4	
26	SINGLE CITY BLUES	15.6	
37	BOHEMIAN MIX	10.1	
39	GRAY POWER	7.5	
9	HISPANIC MIX	5.1	
11	DOWNTOWN DIXIE-STYLE	2.3	
32	PUBLIC ASSISTANCE	.9	
3	NEW MELTING POT	.1	
41	NON-RESIDENTIAL		

10022 ROOSEVELT

10017 GRAND CENTRAL

10020 ROCKEFELLER CENTER

10019 RADIO CITY

10036 TIMES SQUARE

DIARY PANELS   The NPD Group, the largest national paper diary panel in the United States, samples quarterly from its panel of more than half a million households, which report their purchases and consumption using a preprinted diary to document their monthly purchases in approximately 50 product categories (for example, there are 4,000 food products alone). Figure 6.6 illustrates the sample diary for Toys & Games/Hobby & Craft Purchases. Note that the diary asks for considerable detail about the toy purchased, including the price paid, store where purchased, age and sex of both the recipient and the purchaser, as well as other specific characteristics of the purchase.

The households composing NPD are geographically dispersed but demographically balanced so they can be projected to total U.S. purchasing. Panel members

FIGURE 6.6   Sample Page from The NPD Group, Inc., Diary

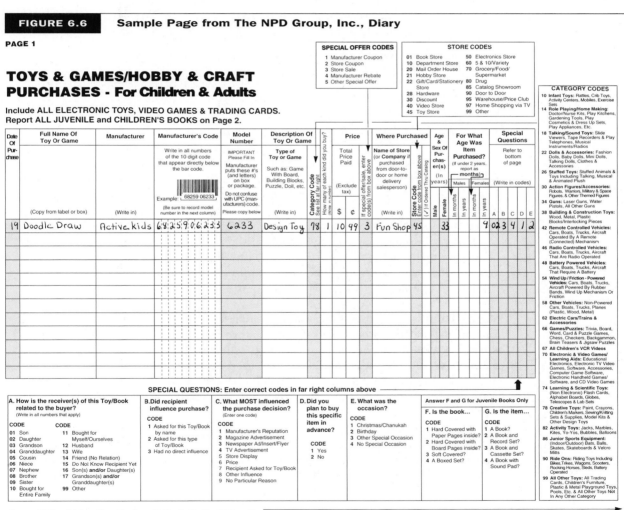

Source: Courtesy of The NPD Group, Inc., Port Washington, NY.

are recruited quarterly and are added to the active panel after they have satisfactorily met NPD's reporting standards. Households are recruited so that the composition of the panel mirrors the population of the United States. The panel is balanced with respect to size, age of female head of household, household income, and geography. Panel members are compensated for their participation with gifts, and households are dropped from the panel at their request or if they fail to return three of their last six diaries.

The diaries are returned to NPD monthly, the purchase histories are aggregated, and reports are prepared. Using these reports, the subscribing company is able to assess (among other things) the following:

- Size of the market, proportion of households buying over time, and amount purchased per buyer
- Manufacturer and brand shares over time
- Brand loyalty and brand-switching behavior
- Frequency of purchase and amount purchased per transaction
- Influence of price and special price deals, as well as average price paid
- Characteristics of heavy buyers
- Impact of a new manufacturer or brand on the established brands
- Effect of a change in advertising or distribution strategy[15]

For example, analysis of the NPD Toy Market Index shows that holiday season retail sales of toys are fairly stable over the past five years (approximately $5.6 billion), and that most of these purchases are made by "mom." If the toy category is electronic (such as video games) or the purchase is made online, the numbers skew somewhat less dramatically toward women being the major purchaser: 80 percent of retail toy purchases are made by women whereas 65 percent of Internet toy purchases are made by women. For the purchases of video games in particular, 65 percent of retail purchases and 59 percent of online video game purchases are made by women.

STORE AUDITS   Another historically popular way of measuring sales to ultimate customers is at the store level, using either store audits or scanners. Scanners reflect the new way of measuring sales; store audits reflect the old. However, as pervasive as scanners seem to be, store audits are still used in some types of stores that do not use scanners, primarily because the products they sell do not lend themselves to scanner processing or because the stores have not made the investment in scanner equipment.

The basic concept of a store audit is a simple inventory. The research firm sends field workers, called auditors, to a select group of retail stores at fixed intervals. On each visit, the auditor takes a complete inventory of all products designated for the audit. The auditor also notes the merchandise moving into the store by checking

---

[15]See *Insights* (New York: NPD Research, Inc., undated, and www.npd.com) for discussion of these and other analyses using diary-panel data.

wholesale invoices, warehouse withdrawal records, and direct shipments from manufacturers. Sales to consumers are then determined by the following calculation:

$$\text{Sales} = \text{Beginning inventory} + \text{Net purchases (from wholesalers and manufacturers)} - \text{Ending inventory}$$

The store audit was pioneered by ACNielsen and served as the backbone of the Nielsen Retail Index for many years. The method is still used to measure sales and to gather other information for small, independent grocery stores, convenience stores, and liquor stores. The company takes the auditing records and generates the following information for each of the brands for each of the products audited:

- Sales to consumers
- Purchases by retailers
- Retail inventories
- Out-of-stock stores
- Prices
- Special factory packs
- Dealer support (displays, local advertising, coupon redemption)

Subscribers to ACNielsen receive data broken down by competitor, geographic area, or store type. ACNielsen will also provide special reports to clients for a fee. These special reports include such information as the effect of shelf facings on sales, the sales impact of different promotional strategies, premiums, or prices, or the analysis of sales by client-specified geographic areas. The stores pinpointed for inclusion in the panel are contacted personally to secure their cooperation. Further, the stores are compensated for their cooperation on a per-audit basis.

SCANNERS   Since the late 1970s, ACNielsen has been replacing its Retail Index service with its SCANTRACK service. The SCANTRACK service emerged from the revolutionary development in the grocery industry brought about by the installation of scanning equipment to read Universal Product Codes (UPCs). UPCs are 11-digit numbers imprinted on each product sold in a supermarket. The first digit, called the number system character, indicates the type of product it is (such as grocery or drug). The next five digits identify the manufacturer, and the last five a particular product of the manufacturer, be it a different size, variety, or flavor. See Figure 6.7.

Every product has a unique 11-digit code. As the product with its bar code is pulled across the scanner, the scanner identifies the 11-digit number, looks up the price in the attached computer, and immediately prints the description and price of the item on the cash register receipt. At the same time, the computer can keep track of the movement of every item that is scanned.

Scanners are now so pervasive that the majority of information supplied today is based on scanning data. Using either a sample of stores to represent a channel or a census of all stores to represent a retail organization, scanning data are available across multiple outlets, including grocery, mass merchant, drug, selected warehouse

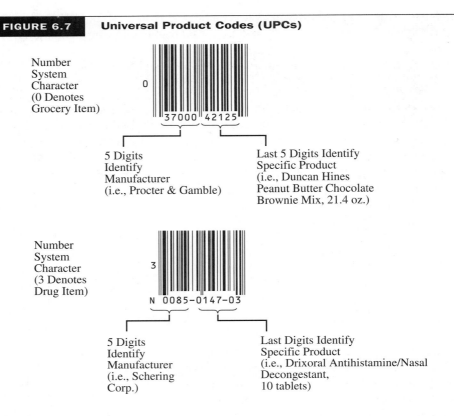

FIGURE 6.7   Universal Product Codes (UPCs)

Number System Character (0 Denotes Grocery Item)

0

37000 42125

5 Digits Identify Manufacturer (i.e., Procter & Gamble)

Last 5 Digits Identify Specific Product (i.e., Duncan Hines Peanut Butter Chocolate Brownie Mix, 21.4 oz.)

Number System Character (3 Denotes Drug Item)

3

N 0085-0147-03

5 Digits Identify Manufacturer (i.e., Schering Corp.)

Last Digits Identify Specific Product (i.e., Drixoral Antihistamine/Nasal Decongestant, 10 tablets)

club, and selected convenience stores. Where scanning is available, units and the price at which sold are collected from a retailer's system. ACNielsen takes these data and matches the UPC to a description to make the information analytically useful (for example, share of category, regular versus low fat).

Additionally, other marketing mix data are combined with this information into what are called "single-source data," which means that one marketing research supplier is the source of product sales data that have been combined with television and local newspaper advertising exposure data, coupon usage, and so on. These factors are collected to help explain the "causes" of sales fluctuations. They include:

- Display information—stores are audited and items on display are recorded
- Feature information—features are collected and coded to identify items being advertised
- Price decreases—the system identifies decreases via comparisons to historical prices

See the excerpt from some scanner data in Table 6.5.

By combining the retail sales and marketing mix factors, the effectiveness of various marketing actions can be assessed, for example, by estimating what "base"

| TABLE 6.5 | Sample Scanner Data |

"Scanner data" are the grocery- and retail-scanned purchases made by consumers. They typically store variables such as store number, brand purchased, quantity purchased, number of ounces or size purchased, whether any of the brands in the category were on sale or otherwise featured (for example, end-of-aisle displays), whether a coupon was used, and so on. Any random grocery shopper's purchases are captured in scanner data. Scanner panel data are those that further integrate a household's purchases with additional information such as its family's demographics, what television stations it had been playing at different times during the past week, and so on. These additional data are known only for the participating panel members. These families agree to participate, which involves their presenting a special membership card to be scanned to flag their data in the database for later analyses, in exchange for moderate compensation.

In this data set, the variables are interpreted as follows:

X_1 = observation number
X_2 = household identification number
X_3 = brand bought during this purchase
X_4 = brand bought last purchase
X_5 = price per ounce of brand A
X_6 = price per ounce of brand B
X_7 = price per ounce of brand C
X_8 = price per ounce of brand D
X_9 = 1 if brand bought was advertised on television last week
X_{10} = 1 if brand bought was on display or otherwise featured in the grocer
X_{11} = 1 if a coupon was used to buy the brand
X_{12} = number of total purchases by this household through the duration of this data set

X_1	X_2	X_3	X_4	X_5	X_6	X_7	X_8	X_9	X_{10}	X_{11}	X_{12}
109	2212251	A	—	.53	.59	.62	.51	1	0	0	5
110	2212251	C	A	.63	.51	.66	.50	0	0	0	5
111	2212251	B	C	.57	.60	.56	.45	0	1	0	5
112	2212251	A	B	.55	.54	.42	.41	1	0	0	5
113	2212251	A	A	.56	.54	.56	.49	0	0	0	5
114	4412319	D	—	.55	.53	.51	.48	0	0	0	9
115	4412319	B	D	.53	.55	.52	.50	0	1	0	9
116	4412319	C	B	.44	.50	.46	.51	0	0	0	9
117	4412319	B	C	.61	.40	.65	.50	0	1	0	9
118	4412319	C	B	.54	.59	.60	.51	0	1	0	9
119	4412319	C	C	.56	.56	.46	.50	0	0	0	9
120	4412319	B	C	.56	.54	.41	.49	0	1	0	9
121	4412319	A	B	.55	.55	.52	.48	1	0	0	9
122	4412319	C	A	.55	.54	.71	.50	0	0	0	9
123	4142957	C	—	.55	.53	.45	.50	0	1	1	4
124	4142957	B	C	.53	.53	.52	.50	0	1	0	4
125	4142957	C	B	.54	.50	.55	.51	0	0	1	4
126	4142957	B	C	.51	.51	.53	.49	0	1	1	4
127	5281115	B	—	.55	.50	.64	.48	0	1	0	5
128	5281115	A	B	.49	.54	.46	.45	1	0	0	5
129	5281115	B	A	.60	.48	.61	.52	0	1	0	5
130	5281115	B	B	.56	.52	.42	.50	0	1	1	5
131	5281115	B	B	.55	.52	.56	.50	0	0	0	5
132	2143377	A	—	.53	.52	.51	.51	1	0	1	7
133	2143377	C	A	.52	.51	.42	.52	0	1	1	7
134	2143377	B	C	.55	.50	.46	.48	0	0	0	7
135	2143377	C	B	.50	.54	.51	.47	0	1	0	7
136	2143377	B	C	.51	.50	.62	.44	0	1	1	7
137	2143377	A	B	.55	.50	.56	.45	0	0	1	7
138	2143377	A	A	.56	.50	.61	.48	0	0	1	7
139	3301329	A	—	.56	.55	.62	.51	1	0	0	3
140	3301329	A	A	.54	.54	.66	.50	0	0	1	3
141	3301329	A	A	.55	.53	.61	.51	1	0	0	3

sales would have been without the presence of the action. The data allow clients to evaluate the effectiveness of short-term promotions, to evaluate pricing changes, to follow new-product introductions, and to monitor unexpected events such as product recalls and shortages.

Scanners' effects on the collection of sales and market share data have been profound. Research Realities 6.7 provides an example. Scanners also provide an ability to link purchase behavior with demographic information. Before the advent of scanners, the link was made using diaries. A problem with diaries is that their accuracy depends on the conscientiousness of those in the panel to record their purchases as they occur. Scanner data are not subject to such recording biases. Several firms have developed systems to take advantage of this fact, including Information Resources and ACNielsen. A key feature of the new systems is the ability to link television-viewing behavior with product-purchasing behavior to produce single-source data.

The basics of single-source research are straightforward. As an example, consider the operation of the Information Resources BehaviorScan system. Across all of the markets in which BehaviorScan operates, a panel of more than 55,000 households have been recruited by Information Resources to present identification cards at each of the grocery or drugstores every time their members make a purchase. Almost all the supermarkets and drugstores in each area are provided scanners by Information Resources.[16] Each household member presents his or her identification card when checking out. The card is scanned along with the purchases, allowing Information Resources to relate a family's purchases by brand, size, and price to the family's demographic characteristics and the household's known exposure to coupons, newspaper ads, free samples, and point-of-purchase displays.

Information Resources also is able to direct different TV advertising spots to different households through the "black boxes" that have been attached to the television sets in each test household, in cooperation with the cable television systems serving the markets. Doing so allows Information Resources to monitor the buying reactions to different advertisements or to the same advertisement in different types of households (for example, whether the buying reactions to a particular ad are the same or different among past users and nonusers of the product). This targetable-TV capability allows Information Resources to balance the panel of members for each ad test within each market according to the criteria the sponsor chooses (such as past purchasers of the product), thereby minimizing the problem of having comparable experimental and control groups.

ACNielsen's system is designed to measure natural consumer behavior rather than test the effects of different promotions or advertising. Its Homescan Service maintains a panel of 52,000 participating households whose purchases are measured through an electronic wand they are asked to pass over the UPCs on products brought into the house. Because the Homescan Panel does not depend on retailer cooperation or retailer scanning abilities, it is not outlet-dependent and provides a

---

[16]Information Resources Inc. now also offers BehaviorScan for testing in mass merchandisers, such as Wal-Mart, Kmart, and Target, in addition to grocery stores and drugstores. See *Testing Services* (Chicago: Information Resources, undated, and www.infores.com).

An Example of the Impact of Scanners

HARTSDALE, NY—TVT Records President Steve Gottlieb spends his Wednesday mornings hunched over a computer screen, studying numbers that tell him whether he's having a good week. Most music industry executives are doing the same thing, since that's the day SoundScan transmits data showing how many albums Alanis Morissette, Stone Temple Pilots, and other artists have sold.

SoundScan, a company that didn't exist at the dawn of the 1990s, in five years has transformed the record business simply by providing an accurate accounting of how the product is selling.

Information provided by SoundScan has changed the way music is marketed, rerouted concert tours and leveled the playing field between major record companies and independents.

SoundScan's leaders, Michael Fine and Michael Shalett, formed a partnership in the late 1980s to set up focus groups of music consumers. Fine had a background in political polling and Shalett in radio and record promotion. They decided to compete with Billboard, the music industry's chief trade paper, which was trying to establish a computerized system for tracking music sales to make its record charts more accurate.

For all the money at stake, compiling the weekly Top 40 list was unscientific. Trade publications would ask selected record stores to phone in reports of their top sellers. It was susceptible to manipulation—a store owner might be persuaded to inflate the sales of a certain disc in return for, say, tickets to a hot concert.

SoundScan signed major retail chains like Musicland, TransWorld, and Camelot to exclusive deals letting the company keep track of sales through bar codes. The system went online in January 1991.

It took until the middle of that year to establish a market. But when Sony became the first major record company to sign up for SoundScan's service, most of the others quickly followed suit. So did artist managers, concert promoters, and the ABC Radio Network. Bill-board abandoned its own efforts and began basing its charts on SoundScan's data.

Suddenly, the industry had a comprehensive record of what was selling and where. Not only could it tell how many discs Madonna really sold, it could also see if opera was hot in Omaha or alternative rock big in Albuquerque.

SoundScan showed that many discs sell the most copies in their first week of release, with only the true hits growing in sales as time went on. It's the sort of information that guides advertising and marketing decisions; many record stores now host events on the release date of a much-awaited album. Record companies tend to show more patience in supporting new artists if SoundScan data show these musicians are making an impact, said Geoff Mayfield, Billboard's charts director.

Artists such as Sheryl Crow, Hootie & the Blowfish, and Morissette may not have been a success in the pre-SoundScan era, he said.

Large record companies, no longer able to manipulate charts to help their artists, now face tougher competition from nimble independent labels like Tommy Boy, he said.

Marketers use SoundScan's information in very specific ways. Concert promoters are able to see where an artist is doing well and are using that information in scheduling tours.

SoundScan measures sales in close to 13,000 music outlets in the United States, representing between 85 percent and 90 percent of the total music sold, Shalett said.

Many independent stores are missing from SoundScan's count. Mayfield's heard his share of gripes from industry officials who see this as a crucial weakness; they believe their discs are selling big in the stores not counted. He discounts most complaints as sour grapes.

For more information, see David Bauder, "Tracking Sales by Computer Transforms Music Industry," *Wisconsin State Journal* (May 28, 1996), p. 5B.

total market perspective regarding sales of a product. The electronic unit then queries panel members with respect to where the purchase was made; age and sex of the shopper; price paid; and deal type, if any, among other things. The information from each household is downloaded once a week to ACNielsen's computer simply by transmitting the data over the telephone.[17] Some of the other types of analyses that are possible with SCANTRACK's National Household Panel Reports are described in Table 6.6.

The impact of single-source measurement on the conduct of marketing activities has been and promises to be so profound that it may "ultimately rival the importance of the microscope to scientists," according to a report by J. Walter Thompson USA.[18]

A Campbell Soup Company single-source experiment with its V-8 juice shows how the system works. Using an index of 100 for the average household's V-8 consumption, Campbell found that demographically similar TV audiences can consume vastly different amounts of V-8. In early 1987, for example, *General Hospital* had a below-average V-8 consumption rate of 80 index, while *Guiding Light* had an above-average 120 index. The results were surprising, because *General Hospital* actually had a slightly higher percentage of women 25 to 54 years old—the demographic groups most predisposed to buy V-8—and so would ordinarily have been expected to be a better advertising forum to reach V-8 drinkers.[19]

Although single-source measurement offers the opportunity for new market insights, firms subscribing to these services need to prepare themselves for the incredible amounts of data these services produce. Without proper planning, firms can drown in these data. That is why decision support and expert systems for analyzing data are becoming increasingly important in marketing research.

Measuring Advertising Exposure and Effectiveness

Another area in which a great deal of commercial information is available for marketers relates to the assessment of exposure to and effectiveness of advertising. Most suppliers of industrial goods advertise most heavily in trade publications. To sell space more effectively, the various trade publications typically sponsor readership studies, which they then make available to potential advertisers. Suppliers of con-

---

[17]ACNielsen Household Panel (Schaumburg, IL: ACNielsen, undated, and www.acnielsen.com). For a specific example of the use of Homescan, see "Using the Numbers," *Progressive Grocer* 75 (May 1996), pp. 117–123.

[18]"Study Predicts Bigger Impact by Single-Source Data," *Marketing News* 22 (February 1, 1988), p. 13. See also John Phillip Jones, "Single-Source Begins to Fulfill Its Promise," *Journal of Advertising Research* 35 (May/June 1995), pp. 9–16.

[19]Joanne Lipman, "Single-Source Ad Research Heralds Detailed Look at Household Habits," *The Wall Street Journal* (February 16, 1988), p. 35. Such data have allowed large-scale assessments of advertising (Andrew Roberts, "How Successful Are TV Ads?" *Marketing Week* [London, March 5, 1998], pp. 44–45); and the effects of sales promotions (John Philip Jones, "Point of View: STAS and BehaviorScan—Yet Another View," *Journal of Advertising Research* [March/April 1998], pp. 51–53). For other examples of analyses that single-source measurement systems allow, see David J. Curry, *The New Marketing Research Systems* (New York: Wiley, 1992).

TABLE 6.6   Types of Analyses Possible Using ACNielsen's Homescan Service, SCANTRACK

Type	Purpose	Key Measures
Market Overview/ Trend Analysis	To provide a general overview of consumer purchasing for a particular product category, its major segments, and major brands. Measures are compared between brands and over time to identify changes and developments in the marketplace. Data can be analyzed for any time period, can be looked at across or within outlet types, or can be looked at for specific consumer groups (for example, heavy buyers, microwave owners, and so on).	Volume and market share Percentage of households purchasing category (penetration) Volume per buyer (buying rate) Volume per purchase Purchase occasion per buyer (frequency) Pricing (total, deal, nondeal) Percentage of volume on deal (coupon vs. store special) Distribution of volume by outlet (for example, grocery, drug, club warehouse, and so on)
Demographic Analysis	To target advertising and promotional efforts most effectively by determining the demographic profile of particular buyer groups (for example, brand buyers, heavy buyers, frequent commercial viewers). By evaluating the absolute sales importance of one demographic segment versus another, along with the importance of each demographic segment relative to the general population, the overall profile of each buyer group can be identified.	Across all demographic characteristics, the following measures are produced: Distribution of buyers Distribution of volume Market share (within demo group) Percentage of volume on deal (within demo group) Buyer index (distribution of buyers— distribution of population) Volume index (distribution of volume— distribution of population)
Loyalty/Combination Purchase Analyis	To understand the extent to which buyers are loyal to a brand or store; to determine the competitive set in which brands or stores operate; and to identify size/flavor/form preference. The report also looks at the importance of price and dealing when buyers purchase competitive items.	Percentage of brand buyers purchasing competitive items Percentage of brand volume accounted for by buyers who purchase competitive brands Percentage of competitive brand volume purchased on deal by Brand A buyers Brand A buyers' total category volume (distribution) Interaction index—index of Brand A's interaction with competitive brands versus expectations
Brand-Shifting Analysis	To identify the sources of growth or decline in a brand's sales. By looking at changes from period to period on a household-by-household basis, we can see if volume changes were attributed to consumers switching to/from other brands, increasing/decreasing their overall category purchasing, and/or entering/leaving the market.	Brand-shifting volume Increased/decreased category purchasing New/lost category buyers Percentage of shifting gains/loss Gain/loss index Interaction index
Trial and Repeat Analysis	Trial measures consumer interest in a new product by evaluating the percentage of households making at least one purchase of the product. Trial also measures the ability of a marketing plan to translate interest into purchasing. Repeat purchasing evaluates product satisfaction by determining the percentage of triers repurchasing the brand—the ability of a product to deliver on its promise.	Cumulative trial Cumulative repeat Depth of repeat Package rate (volume on trial, on repeat) Percentage volume on deal (total on trial vs. on repeat) Market share (total from trial vs. from repeat)

Source: ACNielsen.

sumer goods and services also have access to media-sponsored readership studies. In addition, a number of services have evolved to measure consumer exposure to the various media.

TELEVISION AND RADIO   The Nielsen Television Index is probably the most generally familiar commercial information service. Even the most casual television watcher has probably heard of the Nielsen ratings and the impact they have on which TV shows are canceled by the networks and which are allowed to continue. The index itself is designed to provide estimates of the size and nature of the audience for individual television programs. For a long time, the basic data were gathered through the use of audimeter instruments, which are electronic devices attached to the television sets in cooperating households. Each audimeter was connected to a central computer, which recorded when the set was on and to what channel it was tuned. Data was also gathered through written diaries used on occasion to determine who was watching TV when the audimeter indicated the set was on. In the late 1980s, Nielsen started measuring TV audiences through the use of people meters. These devices attempt to measure not only the channel to which a set is tuned, but who in the household is watching. Each member of the family has his or her own viewing number. Whoever turns on the set, sits down to watch, or changes the channel is supposed to enter his or her number into the people meter. All this information is transmitted immediately to the central computer for processing.

Through the data provided by these basic records, Nielsen develops estimates of the number and percentage of all TV households viewing a given TV show. Nielsen also breaks down these aggregate ratings by 10 socioeconomic and demographic characteristics, including territory, education of head of household, county size, time zones, household income, age of woman of house, color TV ownership, occupation of head of house, presence of children, and household size. These classifications assist the network in selling advertising on particular programs, while they assist the advertiser in choosing programs to sponsor that reach households with the desired characteristics.[20]

Advertisers buying radio time are also interested in the size and demographic composition of the audiences they will be reaching. Radio-listening statistics are

---

[20]Greater detail about the Nielsen television rating can be found in The Nielsen Ratings in *Perspective* (Northbrook, IL: ACNielsen Company, undated, and www.acnielsen.com). For discussion of the controversy surrounding the use of people meters for TV audience measurement, see J. Ronald Milavsky, "How Good Is the A.C. Nielsen People-Meter System? A Review of the Report by the Committee on Nationwide Television Audience Measurement," *Public Opinion Quarterly* 56 (Spring 1992), pp. 102–115; Elizabeth Jensen, "Networks Blame Faulty Ratings for Drop in Viewership," *The Wall Street Journal* (November 22, 1996), pp. A1, A8; Chuck Ross, "P&G Cuts Local TV Ads, Slams Nielsen Diaries," *Advertising Age* (February 8, 1999), pp. 3, 74. Nielsen is experimenting with a passive meter system in which viewers would be identified through computer-image recognition technology. For discussion of the opportunities and problems with this system, see Steve McClellan, "New Nielsen System Is Turning Heads," *Broadcasting* 122 (May 18, 1992), p. 8; Barry Cook, "Commercial Television: Dead or Alive? A Status Report on Nielsen's Passive People Meter," *Journal of Advertising Research* 35 (March/April 1995), pp. RC5–RC10. Interactive television technology, such as that offered by Wink Communications, will allow for even more precise tracking measurement on consumer responses to the medium (see Yochi J. Dreazen, "Investors Bat Eyes at TV Pioneer Wink," *The Wall Street Journal* [July 21, 1999], p. B8).

typically gathered using diaries that are placed in a panel of households. Arbitron, for example, generates telephone numbers randomly to ensure that it is reaching households with unlisted numbers. Those household members who agree to participate when called are sent diaries, in which they are asked to record their radio-listening behavior for a short period. Most radio markets are rated only once or twice a year, although some of the larger ones are rated four times a year. The April/May survey is conducted in every Arbitron market and consequently is known as the "sweeps" period. Radio ratings typically are broken down by audience age and sex and focus more on individual than household behavior, in contrast to television ratings.

PRINT MEDIA   Several services measure exposure and readership to print media. For example, the Roper Starch Readership Service measures the reading of advertisements in magazines and newspapers. They maintain the world's largest database of some tens of thousands of print advertisements in more than 1,000 issues of consumer and farm magazines, business publications, and newspapers, which are assessed each year, using over 50,000 personal interviews in more than 35 countries. The Starch surveys employ the "recognition method" to assess a particular ad's effectiveness. With the magazine open, the respondent is asked to indicate whether he or she has read each ad. Three degrees of reading are recorded:

1. Noted—a person who remembered seeing any part of the advertisement in that particular issue
2. Associated—a person who not only "noted" the advertisement but also saw or read some part of it that clearly indicates the brand or advertiser
3. Read most—a person who read 50 percent or more of the written material in the ad[21]

During the course of the interview, data are also collected on the observation and reading of the component parts of each ad, such as the headlines, subheadings, pictures, copy blocks, and so forth.

Interviewing begins a short time after the issue of the magazine is placed on sale. For weekly and biweekly consumer magazines, interviewing begins three to six days after the on-sale date and continues for one to two weeks. For monthly magazines, interviewing begins two weeks after the on-sale date and continues for two weeks.

The interviews are conducted by a trained staff of field interviewers, who have the responsibility of selecting those to be interviewed, since a quota sample is employed. Each interviewer must locate within a particular area an assigned number of readers who are 18 years of age and over, with various occupations, family sizes, and marital and economic statuses. The quotas are determined so that different characteristics will be represented in the sample in proportion to their representation in the population. Readers are included in the sample when they conform to

---

[21] *The Starch Readership Report: Methodology and Use* (Mantaroneck, NY: Starch INRA Hooper, undated; also see www.roper.com).

the specified demographic characteristics and when they reply in the affirmative when asked if they had read the particular magazine issue in question. The size of the sample varies by publication. Most Starch studies are based on a minimum of 100 issue readers.

Starch readership reports are compiled issue by issue and include three features: (1) labeled issue, (2) summary report, and (3) adnorm tables. The target ads in each issue are labeled to indicate overall readership level as well as the noting or reading of the major components of the ads. The summary report lists all the ads that were measured in the issue. The ads are arranged by product category and show the percentages for the three degrees of ad readership: noted, associated, and read most, allowing the comparison of the readership of each ad versus the other target ads in the issue. The adnorm tables enable one to compare the readership of an ad in a given issue with the norm for ads of the same size and color that are for the same product category for that publication.

Starch readership data allow advertisers to compare their ads with competitors' ads, current ads with previous ads, current ads against competitors' previous ads, and current ads against Starch adnorm tables. This process can be effective in assessing changes in theme, copy, layout, use of color, and so on.[22]

MULTIMEDIA SERVICES   The Simmons Media/Marketing Service uses a national probability sample of more than 19,000 respondents and serves as a comprehensive data source allowing the cross-referencing of product usage and media exposure. Four different interviews are conducted with each respondent so that magazine, television, newspaper, and radio can all be covered by the Simmons Service. Information is reported for total adults and for men and women separately.[23]

The service conducts personal interviews to obtain measures of respondent readership of individual magazines and newspapers. Self-administered questionnaires are used to gather product purchase and usage information for over 800 product categories, which remain relatively fixed from year to year. Television-viewing behavior is ascertained by means of a personal viewing diary, while radio-listening behavior is gathered through telephone and personal interviews.

A probability sample is used in selecting respondents for the study. All households receive a premium for participating, and a minimum of six calls are made in the attempt to interview previously unavailable respondents. A large number of demographic characteristics are gathered from each respondent included in the study, which permits firms to identify the heavy purchasers of various products. Historically, Simmons had made the data available in printed form, but now makes it available on

---

[22]The measurement of newspaper and magazine circulation is notoriously difficult. For example, some indices do not count the distribution of complimentary papers, for example, *USA Today* in hotels. Advertising agencies also complain that the indices are not provided frequently enough to be timely and relevant—often only twice a year (see Matthew Rose, "Circulation Counting Stirs Debate," *The Wall Street Journal* [December 13, 1999], p. B25). The Starch Reports, or those by comparable providers, such as First Magazine Marketing Reader Panels in the U.K. (www.fmm.co.uk), can provide more customized and tailored consumer data.

[23]*Simmons Research: Your Key to Opportunity* (New York: Simmons Market Research Bureau, Inc., undated, and see www.smrb.com).

CD-ROM. Table 6.7, for example, displays a small portion of the information provided by Simmons regarding the relationship between computer use and a household's demographic characteristics. By also taking into account the purchasers' media habits, the firms are better able to segment and target the most promising groups.

Simmons determines magazine readership using the "through-the-book" or editorial interest method. In the through-the-book method, respondents are screened to determine which magazines they might have read during the past six months. They are then shown actual issues of magazines stripped of confusing material (for identification purposes), such as advertising pages and recurring columns and features. Nine feature articles unique to the issue are exhibited, and an indirect approach—asking respondents to select the articles they personally find especially interesting—is employed. At the end, a qualifying question is asked: "Now that you have been through this magazine, could you tell me whether this is the first time you happened to look into this particular issue, or have you looked into it before?" Respondents must affirm prior exposure to the issue to qualify as readers. Expressions of doubt or uncertainty would disqualify them. Simmons provides databases of usage and preference for some 865 product lines, but its focus is on media, covering 150 variables on magazine readership, cable-viewing habits, radio-listening patterns, and so forth.

Mediamark Research also makes available information on exposure to various media and household consumption of a number of products and services. Its annual survey of 20,000 adult respondents covers more than 250 magazines, newspapers, radio stations, and television channels and over 450 products and services.[24] Information is gathered from respondents by two methods. First, a personal interview is used to collect demographics and data pertaining to media exposure. Magazine readership is measured by a "recent reading" method that asks respondents to sort a deck of magazine logo cards according to whether they (1) are sure they have read; (2) are not sure they have read; and (3) are sure they have not read a given magazine within the previous six months.

Newspaper readership is measured using a "yesterday reading" technique in which respondents are asked which of the daily newspapers on the list of papers that circulate in the area were read or looked into within the previous seven days. For Sunday and weekend papers, a four-week time span is used. Radio listening is determined through a "yesterday" recall technique in which respondents are shown a list of five time periods and are asked how much time was spent listening to a radio during each time period on the previous day. They are then asked what stations were listened to. Television audience data are collected in a similar manner.

On completion of the interview, interviewers leave a questionnaire booklet with respondents. The booklet, which covers personal and household usage of approximately 3,500 product categories and services and 5,700 brands, is personally picked up by the interviewer after a short time period. The 20,000 respondents for the Mediamark reports are selected using probability sampling methods.

---

[24]More detail about Mediamark's operations and the types of analyses allowed by the media exposure and product-uses databases can be found in the company's publications (*Knowledge Is Power, How Syndicated Consumer Research Helps Improve the Odds*), or at www.mediamark.com.

TABLE 6.7   Sample Output from Simmons Media/Marketing Service

	TOTAL U.S. '000	INTERACTIVE COMPUTER SERVICES USE OR SUBSCRIBE A '000	B % DOWN	C % ACROSS	D INDX	PERSONAL COMPUTER: TOTAL OWN AT HOME/ USE AT WORK A '000	B % DOWN	C % ACROSS	D INDX	OWN AT HOME A '000	B % DOWN	C % ACROSS	D INDX	PERSONALLY USE AT WORK A '000	B % DOWN	C % ACROSS	D INDX
TOTAL ADULTS	187747	9973	100.0	5.3	100	58794	100.0	31.3	100	41392	100.0	22.0	100	35896	100.0	19.1	100
MALES	90070	5178	51.9	5.7	108	28652	48.7	31.8	102	20931	50.6	23.2	105	16917	47.1	18.8	98
FEMALES	97676	4795	48.1	4.9	92	30142	51.3	30.9	99	20462	49.4	20.9	95	18980	52.9	19.4	102
PRINCIPAL SHOPPERS	115901	5596	56.1	4.8	91	33828	57.5	29.2	93	22997	55.6	19.8	90	21535	60.0	18.6	97
18 - 24	23951	1407	14.1	5.9	111	7535	12.8	31.5	100	5652	13.7	23.6	107	3680	10.3	15.4	80
25 - 34	41492	2466	24.7	5.9	112	13864	23.6	33.4	107	7931	19.2	19.1	87	9545	26.6	23.0	120
35 - 44	40678	3112	31.2	7.6	144	16372	27.8	40.2	129	11910	28.8	29.3	133	10649	29.7	26.2	137
45 - 54	29045	2124	21.3	7.3	138	11628	19.8	40.0	128	8691	21.0	29.9	136	7395	20.6	25.5	133
55 - 64	21263	656	6.6	3.1	58	5684	9.7	26.7	85	4041	9.8	19.0	86	3281	9.1	15.4	81
65 OR OLDER	31318	*208	2.1	0.7	13	3712	6.3	11.9	38	3168	7.7	10.1	46	1347	3.8	4.3	22
18 - 34	65443	3873	38.8	5.9	111	21399	36.4	32.7	104	13582	32.8	20.8	94	13225	36.8	20.2	106
18 - 49	122143	8176	82.0	6.7	126	44653	75.9	36.6	117	30601	73.9	25.1	114	28109	78.3	23.0	120
25 - 54	111215	7702	77.2	6.9	130	41864	71.2	37.6	120	28532	68.9	25.7	116	27589	76.9	24.8	130
35 - 49	56701	4304	43.2	7.6	143	23254	39.6	41.0	131	17019	41.1	30.0	136	14884	41.5	26.3	137
50 OR OLDER	65603	1797	18.0	2.7	52	14141	24.1	21.6	69	10791	26.1	16.4	75	7787	21.7	11.9	62
GRADUATED COLLEGE	37353	4261	42.7	11.4	215	19396	33.0	51.9	166	14460	34.9	38.7	176	12998	36.2	34.8	182
ATTENDED COLLEGE	39301	3243	32.5	8.3	155	15170	25.8	38.6	123	10506	25.4	26.7	121	9358	26.1	23.8	125
GRADUATED HIGH SCHOOL	73139	2112	21.2	2.9	54	18834	32.0	25.8	82	12486	30.2	17.1	77	11037	30.7	15.1	79
DID NOT GRADUATE HIGH SCHOOL	37954	*357	3.6	0.9	18	5395	9.2	14.2	45	3940	9.5	10.4	47	2504	7.0	6.6	35
EMPLOYED MALES	62041	4359	43.7	7.0	132	22896	38.9	36.9	118	16191	39.1	26.1	118	14722	41.0	23.7	124
EMPLOYED FEMALES	53100	4197	42.1	7.9	149	22405	38.1	42.2	135	13920	33.6	26.2	119	16125	44.9	30.4	159
EMPLOYED FULL-TIME	99735	7571	75.9	7.6	143	39145	66.6	39.2	125	25452	61.5	25.5	116	27601	76.9	27.7	145
EMPLOYED PART-TIME	15406	985	9.9	6.4	120	6156	10.5	40.0	128	4659	11.3	30.2	137	3247	9.0	21.1	110
NOT EMPLOYED	72606	1417	14.2	2.0	37	13494	23.0	18.6	59	11281	27.3	15.5	70	5049	14.1	7.0	36
PROFESSIONAL/MANAGER	32308	3716	37.3	11.5	217	17275	29.4	53.5	171	12245	29.6	37.9	172	12575	35.0	38.9	204
TECHNICAL/CLERICAL/ SALES	35568	3752	37.6	10.5	199	15754	26.8	44.3	141	9646	23.3	27.1	123	11142	31.0	31.3	164
PRECISION/CRAFT	12562	*430	4.3	3.4	65	3640	6.2	29.0	93	2537	6.1	20.2	92	2156	6.0	17.2	90
OTHER EMPLOYED	34704	658	6.6	1.9	36	8631	14.7	24.9	79	5684	13.7	16.4	74	4974	13.9	14.3	75
SINGLE	41125	2448	24.5	6.0	112	12533	21.3	30.5	97	8489	20.5	20.6	94	6954	19.4	16.9	88
MARRIED	111354	6208	62.3	5.6	105	39317	66.9	35.3	113	28638	69.2	25.7	117	24221	67.5	21.8	114
DIVORCED/SEPARATED/ WIDOWED	35268	1317	13.2	3.7	70	6944	11.8	19.7	63	4266	10.3	12.1	55	4721	13.2	13.4	70
PARENTS	61860	4511	45.2	7.3	137	23819	40.5	38.5	123	16839	40.7	27.2	123	14792	41.2	23.9	125

	Total ('000)	'000	%	%	Index	'000	%	%	Index	'000	%	%	Index	'000	%	%	Index
WHITE	159985	8666	86.9	5.4	102	52721	89.7	33.0	105	37324	90.2	23.3	106	32329	90.1	20.2	106
BLACK	21570	882	8.8	4.1	77	4266	7.3	19.8	63	2605	6.3	12.1	55	2732	7.6	12.7	66
OTHER	6191	*426	4.3	6.9	130	1808	3.1	29.2	93	1463	3.5	23.6	107	836	2.3	13.5	71
NORTHEAST-CENSUS	38611	1966	19.7	5.1	96	11922	20.3	30.9	99	8163	19.7	21.1	99	7272	20.3	18.8	99
MIDWEST	45021	2576	25.8	5.7	108	15610	26.6	34.7	111	10468	25.3	23.3	105	9944	27.7	22.1	116
SOUTH	65246	3721	37.3	5.7	107	18893	32.1	29.0	92	13309	32.2	20.4	93	11449	31.9	17.5	92
WEST	38869	1710	17.2	4.4	83	12368	21.0	31.8	102	9453	22.8	24.3	110	7231	20.1	18.6	97
COUNTY SIZE A	76945	4369	43.8	5.7	107	24542	41.7	31.9	102	17476	42.2	22.7	103	14688	40.9	19.1	100
COUNTY SIZE B	55516	3229	32.4	5.8	110	18012	30.6	32.4	104	12638	30.5	22.8	103	11308	31.5	20.4	107
COUNTY SIZE C	27293	1190	11.9	4.4	82	8752	14.9	32.1	82	6254	15.1	22.9	102	5303	14.8	19.4	102
COUNTY SIZE D	27993	1184	11.9	4.2	80	7488	12.7	26.7	80	5025	12.1	17.9	85	4597	12.8	16.4	86
METRO CENTRAL CITY	58084	2824	28.3	4.9	92	17115	29.1	29.5	94	12005	29.0	20.7	94	10374	28.9	17.9	93
METRO SUBURBAN	88940	5638	56.5	6.3	119	30126	51.2	33.9	108	21543	52.0	24.2	108	18334	51.1	20.6	108
NON-METRO	40722	1512	15.2	3.7	70	11553	19.6	28.4	70	7845	19.0	19.3	91	7188	20.0	17.7	92
TOP 5 ADI'S	42410	2098	21.0	4.9	93	13209	22.5	31.1	93	9165	22.1	21.6	98	7848	21.9	18.5	97
TOP 10 ADI'S	59256	3183	31.9	5.4	101	18943	32.2	32.0	101	13219	31.9	22.3	101	11365	31.7	19.2	100
TOP 20 ADI'S	81977	4730	47.4	5.8	109	26089	44.4	31.8	109	18500	44.7	22.6	102	15985	44.5	19.5	102
HSHLD. INC. $75,000 OR MORE	26297	2967	29.7	11.3	212	12811	21.8	48.7	189	10029	24.2	38.1	156	7919	22.1	30.1	157
$60,000 OR MORE	43694	4393	44.1	10.1	189	20680	35.2	47.3	181	15855	38.3	36.3	151	13037	36.3	29.8	156
$50,000 OR MORE	61638	5922	59.4	9.6	181	28313	48.2	45.9	165	21123	51.0	34.3	147	17876	49.8	29.0	152
$40,000 OR MORE	83714	7345	73.6	8.8	165	36288	61.7	43.3	144	26594	64.2	31.8	138	22835	63.6	27.3	143
$30,000 OR MORE	110173	8431	84.5	7.7	144	45042	76.6	40.9	131	32011	77.3	29.1	131	28400	79.1	25.8	135
$30,000 - $39,999	26459	1087	10.9	4.1	77	8753	14.9	33.1	77	5417	13.1	20.5	106	5565	15.5	21.0	110
$20,000 - $29,999	28910	841	8.4	2.9	55	6755	11.5	23.4	55	4530	10.9	15.7	75	3770	10.5	13.0	68
$10,000 - $19,999	29666	424	4.3	1.4	27	4575	7.8	15.4	27	3052	7.4	10.3	49	2555	7.1	8.6	45
UNDER $10,000	18998	**277	2.8	1.5	27	2423	4.1	12.8	27	1800	4.3	9.5	41	1171	3.3	6.2	32
HOUSEHOLD OF 1 PERSON	23989	626	6.3	2.6	49	4499	7.7	18.8	49	2458	5.9	10.2	60	3083	8.6	12.9	67
2 PEOPLE	61625	2525	25.3	4.1	77	17399	29.6	28.2	77	11972	28.9	19.4	90	11261	31.4	18.3	96
3 OR 4 PEOPLE	75459	5268	52.8	7.0	131	27736	47.2	36.8	131	20306	49.1	26.9	117	16349	45.5	21.7	113
5 OR MORE PEOPLE	26674	1554	15.6	5.8	110	9161	15.6	34.3	110	6657	16.1	25.0	110	5203	14.5	19.5	102
NO CHILD IN HSHLD	113318	4693	47.1	4.1	78	31278	53.2	27.6	78	21714	52.5	19.2	88	19495	54.3	17.2	90
CHILD(REN) UNDER 2 YEARS	13676	657	6.6	4.8	90	4461	7.6	32.6	90	2760	6.7	20.2	104	2659	7.4	19.4	102
2 - 5 YEARS	27475	1493	15.0	5.4	102	8887	15.1	32.3	102	5954	14.4	21.7	103	5544	15.4	20.2	106
6 - 11 YEARS	35656	2595	26.0	7.3	137	12916	22.0	36.2	137	9451	22.8	26.5	116	7798	21.7	21.9	114
12 - 17 YEARS	34050	2769	27.8	8.1	153	13431	22.8	39.4	153	10183	24.6	29.9	126	7627	21.2	22.4	117
RESIDENCE OWNED	129490	7682	77.0	5.9	112	44189	75.2	34.1	112	31867	77.0	24.6	109	27007	75.2	20.9	109
VALUE: $70,000 OR MORE	80885	6351	63.7	7.9	148	32555	55.4	40.2	148	24353	58.8	30.1	129	19684	54.8	24.3	127
VALUE: UNDER $70,000	48605	1331	13.3	2.7	52	11633	19.8	23.9	52	7515	18.2	15.5	76	7323	20.4	15.1	79
RESIDENCE RENTED	52590	1781	17.9	3.4	64	12694	21.6	24.1	64	8111	19.6	15.4	77	7786	21.7	14.8	77

*PROJECTION RELATIVELY UNSTABLE BECAUSE OF SAMPLE BASE—USE WITH CAUTION
**NUMBER OF CASES TOO SMALL FOR RELIABILITY—SHOWN FOR CONSISTENCY ONLY

Source: *1994 Study of Media & Markets* (New York: Simmons Market Research Bureau, Inc., 1994), p. 187.

The difference in the procedures used by Simmons and Mediamark to measure media exposure, particularly magazine readership, can create a real dilemma for advertisers attempting to buy media space. Both firms interview approximately 20,000 people for each study, but the figures reported by them can be very different. In general, it seems that Mediamark's figures of readership are about 10 percent higher for weeklies and 35 percent higher for monthlies, but that can vary dramatically by publication.[25]

Customized Measurements

It is true that some industries are more likely than others to compile databases on their vendors and customers, to which the marketing researcher may refer as secondary data for a preliminary understanding of the marketplace before conducting primary research. For example, consumer packaged goods have access to scanner data, as described in this chapter, which yield information about one's own product and one's competitors, and the marketing mix environment for both. Similarly, data are plentiful in the pharmaceuticals industry, for example, physicians' scripts. In contrast, for many business and services marketing questions, secondary data can be minimal, and primary marketing research dominant. Accordingly, it may be advantageous to seek the assistance of a marketing research firm that conducts customized research, not standardized or specialized services analyzing secondary data.

MAIL PANELS   To discuss all the suppliers of customized marketing information would take us too far afield, but we do want to discuss mail panels to give readers a sense of their operation. Although they are not a true source of secondary data (because the data collected using them are specifically designed to meet the client's needs), the studies are sufficiently standardized and have enough features in common to warrant their inclusion here.

NFO Research Inc. is one of the major independent research firms specializing in custom-designed consumer surveys using mail panels. NFO maintains representative panels drawn from a sampling frame of more than 550,000 U.S. households and more than 100,000 in Europe. These panels represent over one million consumers who have agreed to cooperate without compensation in completing self-administered questionnaires on a variety of subjects. The topics may include specific product usage; reaction to the product or advertising supporting it; reaction to a product package; attitude toward or awareness of some issue, product, service, or ad; and so on.

The national panel is dissolved and rebuilt every two years so that it matches current family population characteristics with respect to income, population density, age of homemaker, and family size for the continental United States and each of the nine geographic divisions in the census.

---

[25]Jeff Gremillion, "Reader Research Rumble," *Mediaweek* 6 (September 16, 1996), pp. 4–5; Jane Beresford, "A House of Cards," *Mediaweek* 6 (July 8, 1996), p. 13.

A current demographic profile is maintained for each family in the data bank. Included are such characteristics as size of family, education, age of family members, presence and number of children by sex, occupation of the principal wage earner, race, and so on. This information is used to generate highly refined population segments. If the user's needs require it, NFO can offer the client panels composed exclusively of mothers of infants, teenagers, elderly people, dog and cat owners, professional workers, mobile home residents, multiple car owners, or other specialized types. Each of these panels can be balanced to match specific quotas dictated by the client.[26]

The Consumer Mail Panel (CMP), operated as part of Market Facts Inc., also represents a sample of households that have agreed to respond to mail questionnaires and product tests. Samples of persons for each product test or use are drawn from over 655,000 households in the CMP pool. The pool is representative of the geographical divisions in the United States and Canada and is broken down, within these divisions, according to census data on total household income, population density and degree of urbanization, and age of panel member.

According to CMP, its mail panel is ideally suited for experimental studies because the samples are matched. In particular, CMP is believed to be particularly valuable when

1. large samples are required at low cost because the size of the subgroups is large or many subgroups are to be analyzed;

2. large numbers of households must be screened to find eligible respondents; and

3. continuing records are to be kept by respondents to report such data as products purchased, how products are used, TV programs viewed, magazines read, and so on.

CMP has recorded a number of other characteristics with respect to each participating household that allow for cross tabulation of the client's criterion variable against such things as place of residence (state, county, and standard metropolitan area), marital status, occupation and employment status, household size, age, sex, home ownership, type of dwelling, and ownership of pets, dishwashers, washing machines, dryers, other selected appliances, and automobiles.[27]

Summary

When confronted by a new problem, the researcher's first attempts at data collection should logically focus on secondary data. Secondary data are statistics that already exist, in contrast to primary data, which are collected for the purpose at hand. Secondary data possess

---

[26]More detailed information about the mail panel can be found in the company's publication *NFO* (Toledo, OH: NFO Research, Inc., undated) and at www.nfow.com.

[27]More detail about the Market Facts mail panel can be found in the company's publications: *Why Consumer Mail Panel Is the Superior Option, Data Collection and Analysis for Reducing Business Decision Risks*, and *Consumer Mail Panel Reference Guide*. Also visit www.marketfacts.com/products/us/cmp2.html.

significant cost and time advantages, and it is only when their pursuit shows diminishing returns and the problem is not yet resolved that the researcher should proceed to primary data. The problem will typically not be resolved completely with secondary data, because secondary data rarely suit the problem perfectly. There are usually problems of appropriateness, because units of measurement, class definitions, and publication currency may be different from those required. Nevertheless, diligent pursuit of secondary data still typically offers the researcher a great deal of insight into the problem, information required to resolve it, and ways in which the information can be obtained. Sometimes secondary data will completely eliminate any need to collect primary data.

Secondary data can be found in either primary or secondary sources. A primary source is the source that originated the data, whereas a secondary source is a source that secured the data from an original source. The primary source should always be used. Further, the researcher should make some judgment about the quality and accuracy of secondary data by examining the purpose of publication, the ability of the organization to collect the data, and general evidence of careful work in its presentation and collection. Researchers should also become familiar with how to conduct an online computer search of existing databases or a general Web search; these modes of inquiry promise to become even more important in the future.

Secondary data include internal company data, published external secondary data, and data supplied by commercial marketing information services. Internal sales and cost data are the most inexpensive source of marketing information and can be used to gain perspective on research problems. Such a wealth of published external secondary data is available that it is easy to overlook it, and the researcher is well advised to follow the process listed in Figure 6.2 (or some variation of it) when locating secondary data. Further, aspiring researchers should carefully examine the sources described in Appendix 6A so that their contents are familiar.

Standardized marketing information services can be an important adjunct to the researcher's data-collection efforts. These services offer economies of scale because they serve a number of clients for a variety of purposes, and thus they are able to spread their costs of operation among clients. If they are suitable for the clients' needs, they offer substantial time and cost advantages in the collection of primary data. Some common uses of the standardized marketing databases are to profile customers, to measure product sales and market share, and to measure advertising exposure and effectiveness.

Questions

1. What is the difference between primary and secondary data?
   a. What are the advantages and disadvantages of secondary data?
   b. What criteria can be employed to judge the accuracy of secondary data?
   c. What is the difference between a primary source and a secondary source of secondary data? Which is preferred? Why?
   d. What distinguishes internal secondary data from external secondary data?
   e. How would you search for secondary data on a particular topic?
   f. How would you perform an online computer search? What types of information would you hope to find?
   g. What is the basic operation of a store audit?
   h. Describe how a type of business can be more successfully identified using Dun's Business Locator.
   i. If you were a product manager for Smooth-n-Creamy frozen yogurt and you needed up-to-date market share information by small geographical sectors, would you prefer NPD data or Nielsen data? Why?

    j. For what types of studies would you prefer NPD consumer diary data rather than BehaviorScan consumption data? Vice versa?

    k. What is the advantage of using single-source data?

    l. How are Starch scores determined?

    m. What is the basis for the Nielsen television ratings?

    n. How do the multimedia services operate?

    o. For what types of studies would you use mail panels?

Applications and Problems

1. List some major secondary sources of information for the following situations:

    a. The marketing research manager of a national soft-drink manufacturer has to prepare a comprehensive report on the soft-drink industry.

    b. Mr. Baker has several ideas for instant cake mixes and is considering entering this industry. He needs to find the necessary background information to assess its potential.

    c. Ms. Smith wishes to make the tee-off times at the golf course she manages available to schedule online. She needs to collect information on the golf business and Internet penetration in her town.

    d. Mr. Wabit has heard that the profit margins in the fur business are high. The fur industry has always intrigued him, and he decides to do some research to determine if the claim is true.

    e. A recent graduate hears that condominiums are once again a good investment. She decides to collect some information on the condominium market.

2. Assume that you are interested in opening a fast-food Mexican restaurant in St. Louis, Missouri. You are unsure of its acceptance by consumers and are considering doing a marketing research study to evaluate their attitudes and opinions. In your search for information you find the following studies:

    Study A was recently conducted by a research agency for a well-known fast-food chain. To secure a copy of this study, you would be required to pay the agency $350. The study evaluated consumers' attitudes toward fast food in general based on a sample of 500 stay-at-home moms for the cities of Springfield, Illinois; St. Louis and Kansas City, Missouri; and Topeka, Kansas. The findings indicated that respondents did not view fast food favorably. The major reason for the unfavorable attitude was the low nutritional value of the food.

    Study B was completed by a group of students as a requirement for an MBA marketing course. This study would not cost anything; it is available in your university library. The study evaluated consumers' attitudes toward various ethnic fast foods. The respondents consisted of a convenience sample of 200 students from St. Louis. The findings indicated a favorable attitude toward two ethnic fast foods, Italian and Mexican. Based on these results, one of the students planned to open a pizza parlor in 1999, but instead accepted a job as sales representative for General Foods Corporation.

    a. Critically evaluate the two sources of data.

    b. Which do you consider to be better? Why?

    c. Assume that you decide it will be profitable to become a franchisee in fast food. Identify five specific secondary sources of data and evaluate the data.

3. For many years, Home Decorating Products had been a leading producer of paint and painting-related equipment, such as brushes, rollers, turpentine, and so on. The company is now considering adding wallpaper, to its line. At least initially, it did not intend to actually manufacture the wallpaper, but rather planned to subcontract the manufacturing. Home Decorating Products would assume the distribution and marketing

functions. Before adding wallpaper to its product line, however, Home Decorating secured secondary data assessing the size of the wallpaper market. One mail survey made
by a trade association showed that, on the average, families in the United States wallpapered two rooms in their homes each year. Among these families, 60 percent did the
task themselves. Another survey, which had also been done by mail but by one of the
major home magazines, found that 70 percent of the subscribers answering the questionnaire had wallpapered one complete wall or more during the last twelve months.
Among this 70 percent of the families, 80 percent had done the wallpapering themselves. Home Decorating Products thus has two sets of secondary data on the same
problem, but the data are not consistent.

Discuss the data in terms of the criteria one would use to determine which set, if either, is correct. Assume that you are forced to make the determination on the basis of
the information in front of you. Which would you choose?

4. Assume that your school is interested in developing a marketing plan to boost sagging
attendance at major athletic events, particularly home football games. As an initial step
in developing the new marketing plan, the athletic department has decided that it
needs demographic and lifestyle profiles of people who currently attend games on a regular (season-ticket) basis. Fortunately, the ticket office maintains a listing of all season-
ticket purchasers (including names and addresses) from year to year. What potential
sources of internal secondary data might the athletic department first investigate before
considering the collection of primary data?

5. Several scenarios follow. In each case, a need exists for standardized marketing information. Recommend a service that could provide the required information. Explain
your choices.

a. As part of its advertising-sales strategy, radio station KMJC wants to stress that its programming appeals to young adults between the ages of 19 and 25. The advertising
salespeople need "numbers" to back up this claim.

b. Fresh Express brand managers have developed a unique coupon and television campaign for its self-contained bags of salads. The company needs to know the following
in order to evaluate the campaign:
   (i) Are people more likely to use the coupon if they have also seen the television ad?
   (ii) What is the median size of the household using the coupon?
   (iii) What is the proportion of new purchasers to past purchasers among the users of
        the coupon?

c. A national manufacturer of a pain remedy is considering a package change to a
childproof container specifically targeted to households with young children. The
change will necessitate a 10 percent price increase. The manufacturer wants to know
if its target market (parents with children under eight years of age) will perceive the
price increase as justified since the new package is childproof.

d. DLH Advertising Agency assured one of its clients that, despite the $300,000 cost of
placing a half-page ad in one issue of a national magazine, the actual cost of the ad
per reader would be less than two cents. DLH is preparing a report to the client and
needs data to back its assurance.

e. Polybuild Software, Inc. is introducing a software package that will make long-range
forecasts of contaminant buildup levels in plants that manufacture polyester fibers.
Polybuild needs a current listing of potential customers, organized by plant sales volume, to prioritize sales calls for the new package.

f. WestTowne Shopping Center wants to know the demographic characteristics of its
patrons. However, the mall's retail tenants recently voted to ban marketing research
interviews in or around the mall area, due to numerous customer complaints about
harassment by interviewers. Where might the mall obtain the desired information?

A P P E N D I X   6 A

Secondary Data[1]

So much published secondary data is available that it is impossible to mention all of it in a single appendix. For this reason, only a representative cross section of the available material is presented.[2] These secondary sources are organized into sections according to the type of information they contain. We begin with a discussion of perhaps the most comprehensive source, governmental secondary data.

Census Data and Other Government Publications

The Bureau of the Census of the United States Department of Commerce is the largest gatherer of statistical information in the country. The original census was the Census of Population, which was required by the Constitution to serve as a basis for apportioning representation in the House of Representatives. The first censuses were merely head counts. Not only has the Census of Population been expanded, but the whole census machinery has also been enlarged. At this point there are nearly two dozen different population and economic industry censuses, all of which are of interest to the marketing researcher. Table 6.1, shown earlier, lists some of the most useful data on population and housing that are available in the Census of Population, for example. Table 6A.1 lists some of the most useful data that are collected in the various industry censuses that are described in this appendix.

Census data are of generally high quality. Further, they are quite often available on the detailed level that the researcher needs. When not available in this form, researchers can purchase, for a nominal fee, the electronic files to create their own tabulations from the Bureau of the Census. Alternatively, researchers can contract with one of the private companies that market census-related products for information on a particular issue, which allows researchers to obtain information tailored to specific needs, and to do so quickly. Further, many of the private providers update the census data at a detailed geographic level for the between-census years.

There are two major drawbacks to the use of census data: (1) censuses are not taken every year—most of the economic census data are gathered every 5 years, in the years ending in "2" and "7," and the population census data are gathered every 10 years; and (2) the delay from time of collection to time of publication is quite substantial, often two years or more. This last weakness, however necessary because of the massive editing, coding, and tabulation tasks involved, may render the data obsolete for certain research problems. The first difficulty requires that researchers supplement the census data with current data. Unfortunately, current data are rarely available in the detail researchers desire, particularly for classifications by small geographic areas, unless one takes advantage of the services of a private provider with update capability.

---

[1]The wonderful assistance of Eunice Graupner, Reference and Bibliographic Instruction Librarian in the University of Wisconsin School of Business Library, in revising this appendix is gratefully acknowledged.

[2]For more detailed treatment, see David W. Stewart and Michael A. Kamins, *Secondary Research: Information Sources and Methods*, 2nd ed. (Beverly Hills, CA: Sage Publications, 1993).

TABLE 6A.1	Information Available from Economic Industry Censuses

Major Data Items	Retail	Wholesale	Construction	Manufacturers	Minerals
Number of Establishments and Firms					
All establishments	X		X		
Establishments with payroll	X	X	X	X	X
Establishments by legal form of organization	X	X	X	X	X
Firms	X	X		X	X
Single-unit and multi-unit firms	X	X		X	X
Concentration by major firms	X	X		X	
Employment					
All employees	X	X	X	X	X
Production (construction) workers			X	X	X
Employment size of establishments	X	X	X	X	X
Employment size of firms	X	X			
Production (construction) worker hours			X	X	X
Payrolls					
All employees, entire year	X	X	X	X	X
Production (construction) workers			X	X	X
Supplemental labor costs, legally required and voluntary	X	X	X	X	X
Sales Receipts, or Value of Shipments					
All establishments	X		X	X	X
Establishments with payroll	X	X	X		
By product or line or type of construction	X	X	X	X	X
By class of customer	X	X			
By size of establishments	X	X	X	X	X
By size of firm	X	X			
Operating Expenses					
Total	X	X			
Cost of materials, etc.	X	X	X	X	X
Specific materials consumed (quantity and cost)	X	X		X	X
Cost of fuels	X	X	X	X	X
Electric energy consumed (quantity and cost)	X	X		X	X
Contract work		X	X	X	X
Products bought and sold				X	X
Advertising	X	X			
Rental payments, total	X	X	X	X	X
Building and structures	X	X	X	X	X
Machinery and equipment	X	X	X	X	X
Communications services	X	X	X	X	X
Purchased repairs	X	X	X	X	
Capital Expenditures					
Total	X	X	X	X	X
New, total	X	X	X	X	X
Buildings/equipment	X	X	X	X	X
Used, total	X	X	X	X	X
Buildings/equipment				X	X

The federal government also collects and publishes a great deal of statistical information in addition to the censuses. Some of this material is designed to supplement the various censuses and is gathered and published for this purpose (for example, Current Population Reports), whereas other data are generated in the normal course of operations, such as collecting taxes, social security payments, claims for unemployment benefits, and so forth.

Given that overview, a description of the most relevant industry censuses follow; they are listed alphabetically. They are available from the U.S. Bureau of the Census: Government Printing Office, or www.census.gov, including www.census.gov/econ/www/econ_cen.html:

- Census of Agriculture (govinfo.kerr.orst.edu/ag-stateis.html): offers detailed breakdowns by state and county on the number of farms, farm types, acreage, land-use practices, employment, livestock produced and products raised, and value of products. It is supplemented by the annual publications *Agriculture Statistics and Commodity Yearbook* and bulletins issued by the Department of Agriculture.

- Census of Construction Industries (www.census.gov/const/www/cci/frames. html): covers establishments primarily engaged in contract construction, construction for sale, or subdividing real estate property into lots. Statistics are provided for such things as value of inventories, total assets, and employment by state.

- Census of Finance, Insurance and Real Estate (www.census.gov/econ/www/se0100.html): collects statistics on commercial banks, savings institutions, credit unions, life insurance providers, hospital and medical service planners, fire, marine and casualty insurance providers, and real estate land subdividers and developers. Information includes location, revenue, and payroll.

- Census of Government (www.census.gov/prod/www/abs/govern.html): presents information on the general characteristics of state and local governments, including employment, size of payroll, amount of indebtedness, and operating revenues and costs.

- Census of Manufacturers (www.census.gov/prod/www/abs/97ecmani.html): categorizes some 450 types of manufacturing establishments and contains detailed industry and geographic statistics for such items as the number of establishments, quantity of output, value added in manufacture, capital expenditures, employment, wages, inventories, sales by customer class, and energy consumption. The *Annual Survey of Manufacturers* covers the years between publications of the census, and *Current Industrial Reports* contains the monthly and annual production figures for some commodities.

- Census of Mineral Industries (www.census.gov): offers detailed geographic breakdowns for some 50 mineral industries on such matters as the number of establishments, production, value of shipments, capital expenditures, cost of supplies, employment, and payroll. Data are supplemented annually by *The Minerals Yearbook*, published by the Bureau of Mines of the Department of the Interior.

- Census of Retail Trade (www.census.gov/econ/www/retmenu.html): classifies retail stores by type of business, presenting statistics on such items as the number of stores, total sales, employment, and payroll. The statistics are broken down by small geographic areas, such as counties, cities, and standard metropolitan statistical areas. Current data pertaining to some of the information can be found in *Monthly Retail Trade*.

- Census of Service Industries (www.census.gov): provides data on receipts, employment, type of business (for example, hotels), and number of units by small geographic areas. Current data can be found in *Monthly Selected Services Receipts*.
- Census of Transportation, Communications and Utilities (www.census.gov/econ/www/se0400.html): covers passenger travel, truck and bus inventory and use, and the transport of commodities by the various classes of carriers, telephone and telegraph communications, and electric, gas, steam, water and sanitary services. Indices cover expenses, revenues, and output measures per state.
- Census of Wholesale Trade (www.census.gov/econ/www/retmenu.html): classifies wholesalers into over 150 business groups and contains statistics on the functions they perform, sales volume, warehouse space, expenses, and so forth. It presents these statistics for counties, cities, and standard metropolitan statistical areas. Current data can be found in *Monthly Wholesale Trade*.

Useful companion resources include:

> *Guide to Industrial Statistics* (Washington, DC: U.S. Bureau of the Census, www.census.gov/prod/www/abs/manu-min.html): a guide to the Census Bureau's programs relating to industry, including the types of statistics gathered and where these statistics are published.
>
> *Census Catalog and Guide* (U.S. Bureau of the Census, Washington, DC: Government Printing Office): an annual, cumulative publication describing all products (reports, maps, microfiche, computer files, and online accessible items) that the Census Bureau has issued since 1980, including information about how to order the information. Also included is an appendix that includes, among other things, a directory of telephone numbers of Census Bureau specialists by area of expertise.
>
> *"Ferret" (Federal Electronic Research, Review, and Extraction Tool):* a compilation of census data and data from the Bureau of Labor Statistics and the National Center for Health Statistics as described and accessed at www.fedstats.gov/toolkit.html.

The censuses just listed describe industry data. The two that follow describe data on individuals, consumers, and potential markets. They are published decennially for the years ending in "0":

- Census of Housing (www.census.gov/hhes/www/housing.html): first taken in 1940 in conjunction with the Census of Population, lists such items as type of structure, size, building condition, occupancy, water and sewage facilities, monthly rent, average value, and equipment, including stoves, dishwashers, air conditioners, and so on. For large metropolitan areas, it provides detailed statistics by city block. The periods between publications of the Census of Housing are covered by the bureau's annual *American Housing Survey*.

- Census of Population (www.census.gov/population/www/estimate/popest. html): reports the population by geographic region. It also provides detailed breakdowns on such characteristics as sex, marital status, age, education, race, national origin, family size, employment and unemployment, income, and other demographic characteristics. The *Current Population Reports* annually update the census, making use of the latest information on migrations, birth and death rates, and so forth.

Related sources include:

> *County and City Databook* (U.S. Bureau of Census, Washington, DC: Government Printing Office): Published once every five years, the *Databook* serves as a convenient source of statistics gathered in the various censuses tabulated on a city and county basis. Included are statistics on population, education, employment, income, housing, banking, manufacturing output and capital expenditures, retail and wholesale sales, and mineral and agricultural output, among others.
>
> *County Business Patterns* (U.S. Department of Commerce, Washington, DC: Government Printing Office): This annual publication contains statistics on a number of businesses by type and their employments and payrolls broken down by county. These data are often quite useful in industrial market-potential studies.

Useful companion resources include:

> *The 1990 Census of Population and Housing: User's Guide,* which provides information about how the data were collected and the scope of every subject, discusses how to locate all the statistics for a given geographical area, and provides a glossary of terms used in the census. An index to the summary data is also available.
>
> *Factfinder for the Nation* (U.S. Bureau of the Census, Washington, DC: Government Printing Office): Issued irregularly, this series of publications describes the range of Census Bureau materials that are available on a variety of subjects and suggests some of their uses. A few of the subjects included are population statistics, housing statistics, statistics on race and ethnicity, and availability of census records about individuals.

Let us now turn to secondary sources other than censuses, some governmental, some from private agencies. The secondary data sources we describe in the remainder of this appendix are classified according to whether they provide the following:

- Industry information
- Company information
- Market and consumer information
- General economic and statistical information
- General guides to business information
- Indexes and specialized directories

Industry Information

Almanac of Business and Industrial Financial Ratios (Englewood Cliffs, NJ: Prentice-Hall or www.wsdinc.com/pgs_bks/t15090.shtml): This publication contains the number of establishments, sales, and selected operating ratios for various industries (such as food stores). The figures are derived from tax return data supplied by the Internal Revenue Service and are reported for 12 categories, based on assets, within each industry. The data thus allow the comparison of a particular company's financial ratios with competitors of similar size.

Commodity Yearbook (New York: Knight-Ridder Financial/Commodity Research Bureau, www.investorsoftware.com/products/7498.htm): This annual publication contains data on prices, production, exports, stocks, and other aspects for approximately 100 individual commodities.

Industry Norms and Key Business Ratios (Murray Hill, NJ: Dun & Bradstreet, www.dnb.com/prods_svcs/allprods.htm): This annual publication provides industry norm statistics for over 800 types of businesses.

Inside U.S. Business: A Concise Encyclopedia of Leading Industries (New York: McGraw Hill, 1994): Twenty-five major industries are discussed in detail, along with a description of top companies, recent trends, and key issues.

KR (Knight-Ridder) Information Ondisc: Business & Industry (Beachwood, OH: Responsive Database Services, Inc., www.business-cd-rom-directory.com/cdprod1/cdhrec/002/055.shtml): Updated monthly, this database provides access to over 600 business journals and trade publications. All articles have extensive abstracts and over 60 percent contain the full text as well.

Manufacturing USA: Industry Analyses, Statistics, and Leading Companies (Detroit: Gale Research): provides comprehensive information on more than 450 manufacturing industries. (Also see *Service Industries USA,* listed later.)

Moody's Industry Review (New York: Moody's Investors Service, www.moodys.com): provides financial information on more than 135 industry groups and compares the performance of top companies within each industry.

North American Industry Classification System[3] Manual (Springfield, VA: Office of Management and Budget, National Technical Information Service, 1997, and see www.census.gov/epcd/www/naics.html): provides the basic system used for classifying industries into 20 major divisions. The system is used for federal economic statistics classified by industry.

---

[3]The NAICS is replacing the former SIC (Standard Industrial Classification) codes to reflect the changing economic base, particularly to reflect more detail in the growing services sectors. For example, the former SIC category of "Services" is refined into seven new categories: Information; Professional, Scientific, and Technical; Administrative Support, Waste Management and Remediation; Education; Health Care and Social Assistance; Arts, Entertainment, and Recreation; and Other Services. Examples of particular industries newly recognized by the NAICS system are software, convenience stores, pet supply stores, HMOs, and casinos. Tables indicating correspondence between the former SIC codes and the new NAICS are also provided.

Predicast's Basebook (Foster City, CA: Information Access Co.): Arranged by industry classification, this publication provides a wide array of statistical information on U.S. business sectors.

RMA Annual Statement Studies (Philadelphia: Robert Morris Associates, www.rmahq.org, spokpl.lib.wa.us/marion/aat-2118): This volume provides composite financial data on over 400 manufacturers, wholesalers, retailers, service providers, and agricultural endeavors.

Service Industries USA: Industry Analyses, Statistics, and Leading Organizations (Detroit: Gale Research): provides comprehensive information on 150 service industries. (Also see *Manufacturing USA,* listed previously.)

Standard & Poor's Industry Surveys (New York: Standard & Poor's Corporation, www.standardpoor.com): Organized by broad industry headings, this quarterly publication consists of detailed articles as well as charts and graphs depicting trends in 52 areas.

U.S. Industry Profiles: The Leading 100 (Detroit: Gale Research): The top U.S. industries are described along with an industry outlook, the names of relevant associations, trade journals, statistical sources, and other sources of information.

Worldcasts (Foster City, CA: Information Access Co.): Published quarterly, Worldcasts provides worldwide forecast information for regions and products. Forecast data are drawn from over 800 publications.

Company Information

As an overview, first consider *How to Find Information About Companies* (Washington, DC: Washington Researchers, 14th ed., 1998), a useful guide to locating information about specific companies. Also see its companion, *How to Find Information about Foreign and Global Companies.*

Directory of Corporate Affiliations Library (Wilmette, IL: National Register Publishing): An annual publication which provides a description of the companies that own more than 117,000 U.S. and international corporations.

Fortune Directory (New York: Time, Inc., www.fortune.com): Published annually by the editors of *Fortune* magazine, this directory provides information on sales, assets, profits, invested capital, and employees for the 500 largest industrial corporations in the United States.

Hoover's Handbook of American Business (Austin, TX: Hoover's Business Press): profiles over 700 of the largest and fastest-growing companies in the United States. A useful "List-Lover's Compendium" is also included.

Million Dollar Directory (New York: Dun & Bradstreet): Published annually, this reference source lists the offices, products, sales, and number of employees for United States companies with assets of at least $500,000.

Moody's Manuals (New York: Moody's Investors Service, www.moodys.com): Published annually, these manuals contain balance sheets and income statements for individual companies and governmental units.

Notable Corporate Chronologies (New York: Gale Research, 2nd ed., 1998): compiles company histories for over 1,150 corporations worldwide and includes article citations for further reading.

Standard & Poor's Corporate Records (New York: Standard & Poor's Corp., www.standardpoor.com): provides current financial statistics, news items, and background information on approximately 12,000 publicly traded companies.

Standard & Poor's Register of Corporations, Directors and Executives (New York: Standard & Poor's Corp., www.standardpoor.com): This annual publication lists officers, products, sales, addresses, telephone numbers, and employees for more than 56,000 United States and Canadian public companies.

Thomas Food Industry Register (New York: Thomas Publishing Co.): provides detailed information on more than 40,000 food-related companies.

Thomas Register of American Manufacturers and *Thomas Register Catalog File* (New York: Thomas Publishing Co.): Published annually in paper and CD-ROM format, this multivolume publication lists the specific manufacturers of individual products and provides information on their addresses, branch offices, and subsidiaries.

Value Line Investment Survey (New York: Value Line Publishing): This quarterly publication provides current information on 1,700 publicly traded companies. Although written with investors in mind, it offers concise yet comprehensive company information.

Market and Consumer Information

A useful overview guide is *Data Sources for Business and Market Analysis*, 4th ed. (Metuchen, NJ: Scarecrow Press, 1994), an annotated guide to original statistical sources arranged by source of information rather than by topic.

A Guide to Consumer Markets (New York: The Conference Board): Issued annually, this publication contains data on the behavior of consumers in the marketplace. It includes statistics on population, employment, income, expenditure, and prices.

Aging America—Trends and Projections (U.S. Senate Special Committee on Aging and the American Association of Retired Persons, Washington, DC: Government Printing Office): This chartbook describes the sustained growth in America's elderly population expected during the next 30 years. Graphs and tables cover such areas as demographics, employment, health, and income.

Editor and Publisher Market Guide (New York: Editor and Publisher Magazine): Published annually, this guide contains data on some 265 metropolitan statistical areas, including location, population, number of households, principal industries, retail sales and outlets, and climate.

Marketing Economics Guide (New York: Marketing Economics Institute): This annual publication provides detailed operating information on 1,500 retailing centers throughout the country on a regional, state, county, and city basis. It contains information on population, percent of households by income class, disposable income, total retail sales, and retail sales by store group.

Rand McNally Commercial Atlas and Marketing Guide (Chicago: Rand McNally Company): This annual atlas contains marketing data and maps for some 100,000 cities and towns in the United States. Included is information on such matters as population, auto registrations, and retail trade.

Sales and Marketing Management Survey of Buying Power (New York: Sales and Marketing Management): Published annually, this survey contains market data for states, a number of counties, cities, and standard metropolitan statistical areas. Included are statistics on population, retail sales, and household income, and a combined index of buying power for each reported geographic area.

General Economic and Statistical Information

Economic Indicators (Council of Economic Advisers, Washington, DC: Government Printing Office): This monthly publication contains charts and tables of general economic data, such as gross national product, personal consumption expenditures, and other series important in measuring general economic activity. An annual supplement presenting historical and descriptive material on the sources, uses, and limitations of the data is also issued.

Economic Report of the President (U.S. Government, Washington, DC: Government Printing Office): This publication results from the president's annual address to Congress about the general economic well-being of the country. The end of the report contains summary statistical tables using data collected elsewhere.

The Economic Policy Institute (www.epinet.org): a nonprofit, nonpartisan think tank that conducts research and provides its findings and observations on the economy, including labor markets and globalization, the government, and public policy.

Federal Reserve Bulletin (Washington, DC: Federal Reserve System Board of Governors): Published monthly, this publication is an important source of financial data, including statistics on banking activity, interest rates, savings, the index of industrial production, an index of department store sales, prices, and international trade and finance.

The Handbook of Basic Economic Statistics (Washington, DC: Economic Statistics Bureau of Washington, DC): This monthly publication provides a compilation of more than 1,800 statistical series related to the national economy condensed from the volumes of information released by the federal government.

Handbook of Cyclical Indicators (Washington, DC: U.S. Department of Commerce): This monthly publication contains at least 70 indicators of business activity designed to serve as a key to general economic conditions.

Monthly Labor Review (U.S. Bureau of Labor Statistics, Washington, DC: Government Printing Office): This monthly publication contains statistics on employment and unemployment, labor turnover, earnings and hours worked, wholesale and retail prices, and work stoppages.

Statistical Abstract of the United States (U.S. Bureau of the Census, Washington, DC: Government Printing Office): This annual publication reproduces more than 1,500 tables originally published elsewhere that cover such areas as the economic, demographic, social, and political structure of the United States. The publication is intended to serve as a convenient statistical reference and as a guide to more detailed statistics. The latter function is fulfilled through references to the original sources in the introductory comments to each section, the table footnotes, and a bibliography of sources. The *Statistical Abstract* is one of the more important general sources for the marketing researcher, since it contains data on many social, economic, and political aspects of life in the United States. Thus, it is a source with which many researchers begin the search for external secondary data.

- Also see: *Historical Statistics of the United States* (U.S. Bureau of the Census, Washington, DC: Government Printing Office): This volume was prepared by the Bureau of the Census to supplement the *Statistical Abstract*. One problem a user of *Statistical Abstract* data faces is that figures cannot be compared at various points in time because of the changes in definitions and classifications occasioned by a dynamic economy. *Historical Statistics* contains annual data on some 12,500 different series, using consistent definitions and going back to the inception of the series.

- Also see: *State and Metropolitan Area Databook* (U.S. Department of Commerce, Washington, DC: Government Printing Office): This book is a *Statistical Abstract* supplement put out by the Department of Commerce. It contains information on population, housing, government, manufacturing, retail and wholesale trade, and selected services by state and standard metropolitan statistical areas.

Statistics of Income (Internal Revenue Service, Washington, DC: Government Printing Office): This annual publication is prepared from federal income tax returns of corporations and individuals. There are different publications for each type of tax report—one for corporations, one for sole proprietorships and partnerships, and one for individuals. The *Corporate Income Tax Return* volume, for example, contains balance sheet and income statement statistics compiled from corporate tax returns and broken down by major industry, asset size, and so on.

Survey of Current Business (U.S. Bureau of Economic Analysis, Washington, DC: Government Printing Office): This monthly publication provides a comprehensive statistical summary of the national income and product accounts of the United States. Some 2,600 different statistical series are reported, covering such topics as general business indicators, commodity prices, construction and real estate activity, personal consumption expenditures by major type, foreign transactions, income and employment by industry, transportation and communications activity, and so on. Most of the statistical series present data on the last four years.

- Also refer to *Business Statistics* (U.S. Department of Commerce, Washington, DC: Government Printing Office): Published every two years, this publication provides a historical record of the data series appearing monthly in the Survey of Current Business.
- And see *A User's Guide to BEA Information* (U.S. Bureau of Economic Analysis, Washington, DC: Government Printing Office): This booklet provides a directory for Bureau of Economic Analysis publications, computer files, and other information sources.

General Guides to Business Information

American Marketing Association Bibliography Series (Chicago: American Marketing Association, www.ama.org/pubs/catalog/big.asp): Issued periodically, each of the publications provides an in-depth annotated bibliography of a topic of interest in marketing.

Business Information: How to Find It, How to Use It, 2nd ed., edited by Michael R. Lavin (Phoenix, AZ: Oryx Press, 1992): A general guide to searching for business information, this book provides useful information for the development of search strategies.

Business Information Sources, 3rd ed., edited by Lorna M. Daniells (Berkeley: University of California Press, 1993): A guide to the basic sources of business information organized by subject area.

Encyclopedia of Business Information Sources, 14th ed. (Detroit: Gale Research, 2000): A guide to the information available on various subjects, including basic statistical sources, associations, periodicals, directories, handbooks, and general literature.

The Federal Database Finder (Chevy Case, MD: Information USA Inc.): This useful resource provides a directory of over 4,200 no-cost and fee-based databases and data files that are available through the federal government.

Guide to American Directories, 14th ed., edited by Bernard Klein (Coral Springs, FL: Todd Publications, 1994): This guide provides information on directories published in the United States, categorized under 300 technical, mercantile, industrial, scientific, and professional headings.

A Handbook on the Use of Government Statistics (Charlottesville, VA: Taylor Murphy Institute): This publication is designed to assist the businessperson with the use of government statistics. A series of brief case descriptions are presented.

Statistics Sources, 23rd ed., Paul Wasserman, et al., eds. (Detroit: Gale Research, 1999): A guide to federal, state, and private sources of statistics on a wide variety of subjects.

Indexes

ABI/Inform (Ann Arbor, MI: UMI): This business database indexes 800 scholarly, trade, and popular business journals. The full text of some articles is available.

American Statistics Index (Washington, DC: Congressional Information Service): Published annually and updated monthly, the publication is intended to serve as a comprehensive index of statistical data available to the public from any agency of the federal government.

Business Index (Foster City, CA: Information Access Company): The *Business Index* is a microform index to over 460 business periodicals, *The Wall Street Journal, Barrons,* the *New York Times,* and business information from more than 1,100 general and legal periodicals.

Business Periodicals Index (Bronx, NY: The H. W. Wilson Company): The *Business Periodicals Index* is a general purpose business index published monthly (with quarterly and annual compilations) and is composed of subject entries covering approximately 350 business periodicals.

The Information Catalog (New York: FIND/SVP): *The Information Catalog* is a bimonthly publication of FIND/SVP, a business information and research firm. This resource contains overviews of reports, directories, and reference works that may be of interest to businesses. The reports had been produced by FIND/SVP and other research companies, publishers, and brokerage firms.

Statistical Reference Index (Washington, DC: Congressional Information Service): Published monthly (with annual cumulations), this publication is intended to serve as a selective guide to U.S. statistical publications from private organizations and state government sources.

The Wall Street Journal Index (Princeton, NJ: Dow Jones Books): This publication provides a monthly subject index of information appearing in *The Journal* for general news and corporate news.

Academic Indexes

Communications Abstracts (Thousand Oaks, CA: Sage Publications, Inc.): *Communications Abstracts* provides an index to communications-related articles, books, and reports. It is issued quarterly and covers such topics as marketing, advertising, and mass communication.

Dissertation Abstracts International (Ann Arbor, MI: University Microfilms International): Issued monthly, this publication contains descriptions of doctoral dissertations from nearly 500 participating institutions in North America and around the world. The approximately 35,000 annual entries are divided into three divisions: the humanities and social sciences, the sciences and engineering, and European abstracts.

Journal of Marketing, "Marketing Literature Review" (Chicago: American Marketing Association): Each quarterly issue of the *Journal of Marketing* includes a "Marketing Literature Review" section that indexes a selection of article abstracts related to marketing from the business literature. Abstracts are drawn from over 125 business journals; entries are indexed under marketing subject headings.

Social Sciences Citation Index (Philadelphia: Institute for Scientific Information): Published three times yearly, with annual cumulations, this publication indexes all articles in about 1,400 social science periodicals and selected articles in approximately 3,300 periodicals in other academic disciplines.

International and Cross-Cultural Information

*American Marketing Association International Membership Directory &
Marketing Services Guide* (Chicago: American Marketing Association):
This directory, produced annually, is an international directory of AMA
members and member companies as well as a guide to providers of
marketing services.

Business America: This biweekly publication of the Department of
Commerce (Washington, DC: Government Printing Office,
www.doc.gov) contains marketing reports and economic analyses per
country.

Business Organizations, Agencies, and Publications Directory (Detroit: Gale
Research): This directory serves as a guide to approximately 30,000
organizations, agencies, and publications related to foreign and
domestic business, trade, and industry.

Country Information Kits (Washington, DC: Overseas Private Investment
Corporation, www.opic.gov): This publication provides helpful
background information on over a dozen developing and emerging
countries and worldwide regions.

Foreign Trade of the U.S. Statistics (Washington, DC: Bernan Assoc., 1999;
edited by the Chief Economist of the U.S. Population Census): A guide
to the published and unpublished sources of foreign trade statistics.

Hispanic and Asian Marketing Communication Research, Inc.
(www.hamcr.com): This publication presents studies that profile the
Latin American and Asian consumer.

*Greenbook 1999–2000: International Directory of Marketing Research Companies
and Services* (1999–2000; New York: American Marketing Association,
New York Chapter): This annual publication provides an alphabetic
listing of domestic and international marketing research companies. A
geographic listing is also provided, along with an index of principal
personnel.

International Financial Statistics (Washington, DC: International Monetary
Fund, www.imf.org): Statistics presented include exchange and interest
rates, and banking and government finance indexes.

Organization for Economic Cooperation and Development (Washington, DC:
OECD, www.oecd.org): This publication presents statistics on the
24-member OECD countries on production, market demand,
employment, and wages.

Predicast's F&S Index Plus Text (New York: Information Access Co.,
business.cd-rom-directory.com/cdprod1/cdhrec/006/788.shtml): This
international database provides citations, abstracts, and some full-text
articles from over 2,400 business and trade publications.

Stat-USA.gov: Internet service offered by the Department of Commerce;
tracks export statistics.

United Nations Statistical Yearbook (New York: United Nations): This annual
United Nations publication contains statistics on a wide range of foreign
and domestic activities, including forestry, transportation,
manufacturing, consumption, and education.

World Almanac and Book of Facts (New York: Newspaper Enterprise Association): Issued annually, this publication serves as a well-indexed handbook on a wide variety of subjects. Included are industrial, financial, religious, social, and political statistics.

World Association of Research Professionals (www.esomar.nl): This association offers detailed information on marketing research firms worldwide— perfect if you need to partner abroad, for example, for global studies of customer satisfaction.

World Factbook (Washington, DC: Government Printing Office): This annual CIA publication provides data on demography, economy, and so on per country.

Specialized Directories

Two good overview resources are:

Gale Directory of Databases (Detroit: Gale Research): Published twice a year, this comprehensive guide describes more than 11,500 databases, 3,700 database producers, and 2,100 online services.

Information Industry Directory (Detroit: Gale Research): This directory lists and describes over 4,000 producers and vendors of electronic information.

Additional resources include:

American Business Locations Directory (Detroit: Gale Research): This unique directory provides 150,000 site locations for 1,000 of the largest American corporations. Sites include manufacturing plants, branch offices, R&D centers, and subsidiaries.

Consultants and Consulting Organizations Directory, 21st ed. (Detroit: Gale Research, 1999): This directory lists approximately 24,000 firms and individuals who are active in consulting and describes their services and fields of interest.

Directories in Print, 18th ed. (Detroit: Gale Research, 1999): This directory is a descriptive guide to over 15,000 print and nonprint directories and includes a valuable keyword index.

Directory of American Research and Technology, 32nd ed. (New York: Bowker, 1998): This directory is a guide to R&D capabilities of more than 11,000 industrial organizations in the United States. It contains an alphabetical listing of the organizations, addresses of facilities, sizes of staff, and fields of research.

Encyclopedia of Associations (Detroit: Gale Research): Published annually, this directory lists the active trade, business, and professional associations, and briefly describes their activities and lists their publications.

Findex, The Directory of Market Research Reports, Studies and Surveys (Bethesda, MD: Cambridge Information Group): This publication indexes and provides abstracts to more than 10,000 marketing research reports produced by top U.S. and international research firms.

Hoover's Masterlist of Major U.S. Companies (Austin, TX: Hoover's Business Press): This annual volume gives brief histories and key statistics for the largest U.S. companies.

Standard Directory of Advertisers (Wilmette, IL: National Register Publishing): This annual directory lists over 25,000 companies with allotments for advertising campaigns of more than $75,000. Included are individual listings containing information on type of business, address, key personnel, advertising agency relationship, products advertised, media utilized, and so on. The directory is published in two editions, one sorted by product classification and one by geographic location.

Standard Directory of Advertising Agencies (Wilmette, IL: National Register Publishing): This annual directory lists approximately 10,000 advertising agencies and provides such information as personnel by title, key accounts, addresses, and telephone numbers.

7

Data Collection: Primary Data

In Chapter 6, we saw that secondary data represent fast and inexpensive research information; the researcher who gives secondary data only a cursory look is being reckless. However, it is also the case that rarely will secondary data provide a complete solution to a research problem. For example, the units of measurement employed to report the data may be wrong; the data will be somewhat dated by the time of their publication; the data may not be sufficiently complete; and so on. When these conditions occur, the researcher logically turns to primary data.

This chapter is the first of three dealing with primary data: it is an introduction to primary data. Chapter 8 describes issues surrounding the data-collection forms used to obtain primary data, and Chapter 9 says more about how to measure consumer attitudes and behaviors. The current chapter is divided into four parts: part 1 discusses the types of primary data generally obtained from customers; part 2 discusses communication and observation techniques and the suitability of each method for securing the different kinds of primary data; part 3 elaborates on communication methods, discussing the types of questionnaires and modalities of administration; and part 4 does the same for observational methods.

Types of Primary Data

Demographic/Socioeconomic Characteristics

One type of primary data of great interest to marketers is a consumer's demographic and socioeconomic characteristics, such as age, education, occupation, marital status, gender, income, or social class. These variables are used to cross-classify the collected data to help make sense of the consumers' responses. Suppose we are interested in people's attitudes toward ecology and pollution. We might suspect, test, and find that attitudes toward green marketing are related to the respondents' level of education. Similarly, marketers frequently ask whether the consumption of particular products (for example, SUVs, disposable diapers, vacation golf packages) are related to a person's (or family's) age, education, income, and so on. Demographic variables may seem simple (that is, that they would not capture nuances of consumer preferences), so it may seem risky to make such generalizations about people. However, consider two stable examples of the usefulness of demographics in predicting consumer preferences and behaviors: (1) 18- to 49-year-old men tend to be interested in sports, and it is this segment that makes sports TV programming highly profitable; (2) most of the disposable income in the U.S. comes from people 40 years old and older.[1] Such demographic information (for example, age and gender) and socioeconomic characteristics (such as wealth and discretionary funds) are often used to delineate market segments.[2]

Demographic and socioeconomic characteristics represent attributes of people. Some of these attributes, such as a respondent's age, gender, and level of formal education, can be readily verified. Some, such as social class, can only be approximated because they are relative and not absolute measures of a person's standing in society.[3] Income represents an intermediate degree of difficulty in verifiability; that is, although a person's income is an actual quantity, ascertaining the amount sometimes proves to be difficult.

Psychological/Lifestyle Characteristics

Another type of primary data of interest to marketers is the customer's psychological and lifestyle characteristics in the form of personality traits, activities, interests, and values. Personality refers to the normal patterns of behavior exhibited by an individual. It represents the attributes, traits, and mannerisms that distinguish one person from another. We often characterize people by the personality traits they display, for example, aggressiveness, dominance, friendliness, or sociability. Marketers are interested in personality because the traits people possess seem to be important in affecting the way consumers and others in the marketing process behave. The argument is often advanced, for example, that personality can affect a consumer's choice of stores or products (a consumer concerned with animal testing may purchase body lotions only at the Body Shop, for example) or an individual's response to an in-store advertisement or point-of-purchase display (which may appeal to consumers who are more "impulsive" or who are "variety seekers"), just as it is believed, say, that extroversion or empathy make for successful salespeople. Personality alone does not perfectly predict consumption behavior, but it helps, so personality variables remain dear to the hearts of marketing researchers. Personality is typically measured by one of the standard personality inventories that has been developed by psychologists.[4]

Lifestyle or psychographic analysis rests on the premise that the firm can plan more effective strategies to reach its target market if it knows more about those customers in terms of how they live, what interests them, and what they like. For example, Frito-Lay conducted research that identified two broad categories of snackers, which it called Compromisers and Indulgers. The Compromisers are typically

---

[1]Terry Lefton, "Ups and Downs: 18–49 Men," *Brandweek* (May 10, 1999), pp. S12–S14; Carol M. Morgan and Doran J. Levy, "Where the Bucks Are," *Brandweek* (November 30, 1998), pp. 20–28.

[2]See Art Weinstein, *Market Segmentation* (Thousand Oaks, CA: Sage, 1994); Harry Webber, *Divide and Conquer: Target Your Customers through Market Segmentation* (New York: Wiley, 1998). For an application to churchgoers, see Eric Felten, "Data Diving," *The Wall Street Journal* (April 28, 2000), p. W17.

[3]See Douglas B. Holt, "Does Cultural Capital Structure American Consumption?" *Journal of Consumer Research* 25 (June 1998), pp. 1–25; Linda P. Morton, "Segmenting Publics by Social Classes," *Public Relations Quarterly* 44 (Summer 1999), pp. 45–46.

[4]Two collections that are especially relevant to marketers and consumer behavior researchers are: Gordon C. Bruner II and Paul J. Hensel, *Marketing Scales Handbook: A Compilation of Multi-Item Measures* (Chicago: AMA, 1994) and William O. Bearden and Richard G. Netemeyer, *Handbook of Marketing Scales*, 2nd ed. (Thousand Oaks, CA: Sage, 1999).

TABLE 7.1	Lifestyle Dimensions		
	Activities	*Interests*	*Opinions*
	Work	Family	Themselves
	Hobbies	Home	Social issues
	Social events	Job	Politics
	Vacation	Community	Business
	Entertainment	Recreation	Economics
	Club membership	Fashion	Education
	Community	Food	Products
	Shopping	Media	Future
	Sports	Achievements	Culture

Source: Adapted from Joseph T. Plummer, "The Concept and Application of Life Style Segmentation," *Journal of Marketing* 38 (January 1974), p. 34. Published by the American Marketing Association.

female and are relatively likely to exercise, read health and fitness magazines, be concerned about nutrition, and read product labels. Frito-Lay appeals to this group with its Baked Lay's potato chip, a reduced-fat snack. Frito-Lay's traditional potato chips are targeted to the other psychographic category, the Indulgers, who are mostly male, are in their late teens and early twenties, snack heavily, feel unconcerned about what they eat, and hesitate to sacrifice taste for a reduction in fat.[5]

The thrust in psychographic research has been to develop a number of statements that reflect a person's activities, interests, and opinions (AIO) and consumption behavior. The statements might include such things as "I like to watch football games on television," "I like stamp collecting," "I am very interested in national politics." Subjects are asked to respond to a great many statements.[6] For example, the NPD Group taps its ongoing panel of 65,000 to 250,000 consumers monthly with multipage surveys on category-specific purchase behaviors (such as apparel, food, and sporting goods) as well as "omnibus" trends and lifestyle patterns. Table 7.1 contains the list of characteristics that are assessed with AIO inventories. The goal is to identify groups of consumers who have similar lifestyle profiles and therefore are likely to behave similarly toward the product or service. Research Realities 7.1 provides descriptions of travelers who share the goal of visiting friends or relatives, but who differ in family composition (that is, children or not), length of trip (short or long), and the activities they seek (such as visiting beaches or theme parks). Only after being armed with such segment descriptions can the marketer determine which groups may be deemed attractive to target. Further, segment descriptions usually lend insight into attributes that would be appealing in advertising (for example, show pictures of children at theme parks, or couples on beaches).

---

[5]"Frito-Lay Profiles Salty Snack Consumers," *Supermarket News* (March 18, 1996), p. 39.

[6]One of the more popular lists is the 300-question inventory that appears in William D. Wells and Douglas Tigert, "Activities, Interests, and Opinions," *Journal of Advertising Research* 11 (August 1971), pp. 27–35. See Qimei Chen and William D. Wells, "Attitude Toward the Site," *Journal of Advertising Research* (September/October 1999), pp. 27–37, for a recent application to Web site evaluation. For evidence regarding the reliability and validity of psychographic inventories, see Thabet A. Edris and A. Meidan, "On the Reliability of Psychographic Research: Encouraging Signs for Measurement Accuracy and Methodology in Consumer Research," *European Journal of Marketing* 24, no. 3 (1990), pp. 23–41.

RESEARCH REALITIES 7.1

Lifestyle Descriptions and Qualities Sought by People Traveling to Visit Friends and Family in Australia

Beach Relaxation (38%)   Major reason for trip is pleasure travel. Visiting friends and family is important along with taking advantage of warm weather and beaches. Tend to be repeat visitors, staying with friends and relatives, or in recreation vehicle parks.

Active Beach Resort (15%)   Tend to be younger, traveling with children, coming longer distances. Seek weather as predominate feature. They'll visit theme parks, beaches, and other family attractions. These young families stay in suites or apartments, or with friends and relatives. This group incurs the greatest overall expenditures.

Active Nature Lovers (16%)   Seek good weather, then visiting friends and family and the Great Barrier Reef. Likely to have traveled greater distances (for example, from Europe), and therefore spend the most on transportation. They stay the longest, often with friends and relatives.

Inactives (31%)   Visiting friends and relatives is the only major activity planned; likely to have traveled shorter distances, staying the shortest duration. They spend the least.

Source: Gianna Moscardo, et al., "Developing a Typology for Understanding Visiting Friends and Relatives Markets," *Journal of Travel Research* (February 2000), pp. 251–259.

One problem that marketers experienced when using psychographics or AIO inventories was that the categories of users distinguished for one product would be different from the categories identified for another product. Thus, each product required new data collection and analysis. It was also impossible to create demographic descriptions of various groups that would be useful when developing marketing strategies for new products. The purpose of value and lifestyle research (VALS) is to avoid these problems by creating a more general psychographic framework that can be used for a variety of products.[7] Table 7.2, for example, shows six international segments that have been identified from applying values surveys to teenagers.

Attitudes/Opinions

Some authors distinguish between attitudes and opinions, and others use the terms interchangeably. Typically, the term *attitude* is used to refer to an individual's "preference, inclination, views, or feelings toward some phenomenon," whereas *opinions*

---

[7]The original VALS was a typology of the American population developed to provide a model of societal values; see Arnold Mitchell, *The Nine American Lifestyles* (New York: Macmillan, 1983). It has been supplanted in the United States by VALS2, which is more focused on predicting consumer behavior. SRI International runs the proprietary VALS2; see www.sri.com. Another value-based classification scheme is the List of Values (LOV); for example, see Lynn R. Kahle, Sharon E. Beatty, and Pamela Homer, "Alternative Measurement Approaches to Consumer Values: The List of Values (LOV) and Values and Life Style (VALS)," *Journal of Consumer Research* 13 (December 1986), pp. 405–409; Wagner A. Kamakura and Thomas P. Novak, "Value-System Segmentation: Exploring the Meaning of LOV," *Journal of Consumer Research* 19 (June 1992), pp. 199–132; Lynn R. Kahle, Gregory Rose, and Aviv Shoham, "Findings of LOV Throughout the World, and Other Evidence of Cross-National Consumer Psychographics," *Journal of EuroMarketing* 8 (1999), pp. 1–13.

TABLE 7.2		Segments Identified Using Values Surveys among Teens Worldwide			
Segment	*%*	*Key Countries*	*Enjoy*	*Worry About*	*Own/Wear/Do*
Thrills & chills (sensations)	18	Germany, U.K., Lithuania, Greece, Netherlands, South Africa, U.S.	going out to eat, going to a bar, drinking, smoking cigarettes, going to a party, going on a date, dancing; have most online access	finding love, unplanned pregnancy, own attractiveness	fast food, acne medication, perfume, would dye hair, would like tattoo or nose ring; do NOT have a job or attend church
Upholders (family, tradition)	16	Vietnam, Indonesia, Taiwan, China, Italy, Peru, Venezuela, Puerto Rico, India, Philippines, Singapore	reading books, spending time with family and visiting relatives; have least online access	not living up to others' expectations; believe the world will improve in their lifetime	do NOT have jobs to earn money, eat fast food, wear deodorant, wear tattoos or nose rings, carry guns; girls do NOT wear makeup
Quiet achievers (success, anonymity)	15	Thailand, China, Hong Kong, Ukraine, Korea, Lithuania, Russia, Peru	studying, listening to music, visiting museums; do NOT enjoy going to parties or drinking wine/beer	not living up to others' expecta-tions; believe the world will improve in their lifetime; do NOT worry about fin-ishing education, pregnancy, AIDS, or drugs	do NOT have jobs, or backpacks, blue jeans or athletic shoes; girls do NOT wear makeup
Resigned (low expectations)	14	Denmark, Sweden, Korea, Japan, U.K., Norway, Germany, Belgium, France, Netherlands, Spain, Argentina, Canada, Turkey, Taiwan	do NOT enjoy doing something artistic/creative, attending opera, play or ballet, or visiting relatives	do NOT worry about going to college, the economy, rain forest, global warming, living up to others' expectations	have or would dye hair; do NOT care about access to new technology
Boot-strappers (achievement, individualism)	14	Nigeria, Mexico, U.S., India, Chile, Puerto Rico, South Africa, Venezuela, Colombia	spending time with family and visiting relatives	do NOT worry about not having friends or being lonely; believe education is good preparation for future and that they will have a good life	attend religious services; do NOT receive allowances
World savers (environment)	12	Hungary, Brazil, Phillippines, Venezuela, Spain, Colombia, Belgium, Argentina, Russia, Singapore, France, Poland, Ukraine, Italy, South Africa, Mexico, U.K.	attending opera, plays, and ballet, doing something artistic/creative (such as taking photos), going camping/hiking, going to a bar, dancing	racism, poverty for others, environment, AIDS, war, terrorism, being able to have children, finding love	would NOT carry gun

For more information, see Elissa Moses, *The $100 Billion Allowance: Accessing the Global Teen Market* (New York: Wiley 2000), pp. 80–103.

are "verbal expressions" of those attitudes. Because attitudes are typically secured from respondents by questioning (that is, requiring a verbal expression), we shall not make a distinction, but will treat the terms *attitudes* and *opinions* interchangeably as representing a person's ideas, convictions, or liking with respect to a specific object or idea.

Attitude is one of the more pervasive notions in marketing, because it is generally thought that attitudes are related to behavior. When consumers like a product, they will be more inclined to buy it than when they do not like it, and when they like one brand more than another, they will tend to buy the preferred brand. Attitudes thus may be said to be the forerunners of behavior.

Accordingly, marketers are often interested in people's attitudes toward the product itself (for example, "Do you like soft drinks?"), their overall attitudes with respect to specific brands (for example, "Coke, Pepsi, or 7-Up?"), and their attitudes toward specific aspects or features possessed by several brands (such as "diet, caffeine-free, cherry?"). Attitude is so important in behavioral science, and particularly in marketing, that Chapter 9 is devoted to various types of instruments used to measure it.

Awareness/Knowledge

As used in marketing research, awareness/knowledge refers to what respondents do and do not know about some object or phenomenon. For instance, a problem of considerable importance is the effectiveness of ads in such media as TV, radio, magazine, billboard, and Web banners. One measure of effectiveness is the product awareness generated by the ad, using one of the three approaches described in Table 7.3. All three tests of memory (unaided recall, aided recall, and recognition) are aimed at assessing the respondent's awareness of and knowledge about the ad. They are assumed by advertisers to reflect differences in the extent to which consumers have cognitively processed, in depth and detail or just superficially, the ad, the brand name, the featured attributes, and so on. It is thought that consumers have retained more knowledge from the ad when they state the brand in an unaided recall test (for example, "What products and brands do you remember seeing ads for?") compared to a recall test where they have been given hints (such as "Do you remember recently seeing ads for PCs?"), and that both of these show superior knowledge and retention over simple recognition ("Do you remember seeing this ad for Dell?").[8]

---

[8]Asher Koriat, Morris Goldsmith, and Ainat Pansky, "Toward a Psychology of Memory Accuracy," *Annual Review of Psychology* 51 (2000), pp. 481–537; Myra A. Fernandes and Morris Moscovitch, "Divided Attention and Memory," *Journal of Experimental Psychology: General* 129, no. 2 (June 2000), pp. 155–176; Terri E. Cameron and William E. Hockley, "The Revelation Effect for Item and Associative Recognition," *Memory and Cognition* 28, no. 2 (March 2000), pp. 176–183; William P. Wallace, Christine P. Malone, and Alison D. Spoo, "Implicit Word Activation During Prerecognition Processing," *Psychonomic Bulletin and Review* 7, no. 1 (March 2000), pp. 149–157; Luigi Castelli and Cristina Zogmaister, "The Role of Familiarity in Implicit Memory Effects," *European Journal of Social Psychology* 30 (March/April 2000), pp. 223–234; Jeffrey N. Rouder, Roger Ratcliff, and Gail McKoon, "A Neural Network Model of Implicit Memory for Object Recognition," *Psychological Science* 11 (January 2000), pp. 13–19; Stephen J. Hellebusch, "Survey May Not Measure True Awareness," *Marketing News* (September 27, 1999), p. 28; Rolf Reber, P. Winkielman, and Norbert Schwarz, "Effects of Perceptual Fluency on Affective Judgments," *Psychological Science* 29, no. 1 (1998), pp. 45–48; Daniel L. Schacter, "Implicit Memory: History and Current Status," *Journal of Experimental Psychology: Learning, Memory and Cognition* 13, no. 3 (1987), pp. 501–518.

TABLE 7.3	Approaches Used to Measure Awareness

Unaided recall: Without being given any clues, consumers are asked to recall what advertisements they have seen recently. Prompting is not used because, presumably, even if prompting for the general category were used (such as for soups), respondents would have a tendency to remember more advertisements in that product category.

Aided recall: Consumers are prompted, typically in the form of questions about advertisements in a specific product category. Alternatively, respondents might be given a list showing the names or trademarks of advertisers that appeared recently (in the ad format being tested, such as on radio or Web), along with names or trademarks that did not appear, and would be asked to check those to which they were exposed.

Recognition: Actual advertisements are shown or described to consumers, who are asked whether or not they remember seeing each one.

One of the common indices used to measure the short-term success and impact of an ad is "day-after recall" (or DAR), which is a phone survey, as the name implies, made the day following the airing of a new ad (such as the day after the Super Bowl). The DAR scores are compared to the ad agency's databank of such indices to project sales, by using other recent ads that had achieved similar DAR scores as benchmarks.

Increasingly, psychologists and advertising researchers are exploring the idea that consumers do not have to explicitly remember an ad for that ad to nevertheless have an impact on their behavior. For example, after airing an ad for Reebok, the researcher might choose to use "implicit" or indirect tests of memory. Rather than asking, "Do you remember any recent ads for athletic shoes or Reeboks?" the researcher might instead ask consumers to list brand names of sneakers, their choice set of sporting shoes, shoes affiliated with athlete spokepersons, and so on, to assess the number of times the Reebok brand name appears. Researchers have even asked questions as oblique as, "Name all the brands of any kind of product that start with R" to see how often Reebok would appear, along with names such as Reese's, Rolex, and Ramada. The assumption in these tests is that if Reebok appears disproportionately more than it should (based on market shares), the ad was successful in bring the Reebok brand name to mind.

In addition to ad testing, memory measures are used to assess awareness of products. Marketing researchers are often interested in determining whether the respondent is aware of the product and its features, its price and where it may be purchased, its brand name and country of origin (for example, American-made, or made in Taiwan), and whether the customer connects the brand to the competitive advantages claimed in recent advertising. In general, awareness questions help the marketer assess consumers' knowledge of any element of the consumer experience—advertisements, products, retail stores, and so on.

Intentions

A person's intentions refer to the individual's anticipated or planned future behavior. Marketers are interested in people's intentions primarily with regard to purchasing behavior. One of the better known studies concerning purchase intentions is that conducted by the Survey Research Center at the University of Michigan (see www.isr.umich.edu/src). The center regularly conducts surveys for the Federal

Reserve Board to determine the general financial condition of consumers and their outlook with respect to the state of the economy in the near future. The center phones a sample of 500 households monthly, asking 50 core questions about consumer confidence and buying intentions for big-ticket items such as appliances, automobiles, and homes during the next few months. The responses are then analyzed and used as one indicator of future economic activity. In marketing, intentions are often gathered by asking respondents to indicate which of the following best describes their plans with respect to a new product or service:

- Definitely would buy
- Probably would buy
- Undecided
- Probably would not buy
- Definitely would not buy

The number of people who answer that they definitely would buy or probably would buy are often combined into a "top box" to indicate likely reaction to the new product or service.

It is true that behavioral intentions do not predict behavior perfectly; a disparity often exists between what people say they are going to do and what they actually do. For example, in one study, consumers were told of a new pricing option for a service to which they already subscribed. They were asked to indicate how likely they were to buy the service when it became available. Only 45 percent of those indicating that they definitely would buy the service (the "top box") did so within the first three months of its availability. Further, some of the respondents who indicated that they would not buy it actually did so.[9]

While the prediction of behaviors by intentions is not perfect, sometimes behavioral data are too expensive, difficult, or even impossible to obtain. For example, if Doritos were to create a new spicy salsa-flavor chip as a line extension, by definition no purchase data would exist because the snack food would not have been available yet for purchase. If the marketer had data on a household's purchases of regular Doritos and salsa and spicy foods, perhaps an inference could be drawn to predict consumption of the new salsa chip (this inference requires assumptions, of course). In the absence of even these behavioral data, consumer judgments of their intentions are as close to actual behaviors as marketers can get. To help compensate for the imperfect prediction, those organizations that collect purchase intentions data often adjust the data for the bias that intentions data are likely to contain (based on their past experience).

Purchase intentions are most often used when studying the purchase of commodities requiring large outlays, such as an automobile for a family, or plant and equipment for a business. The general assumption is that the larger the dollar expenditure, the more preplanning necessary and the greater the correlation between anticipated and actual behavior.

---

[9]Albert C. Bemmaor, "Predicting Behavior from Intention-to-Buy Measures: The Parametric Case," *Journal of Marketing Research* 32 (May 1995), pp. 176–191; William J. Infosino, "Forecasting New Product Sales from Likelihood of Purchase Ratings," *Marketing Science* 5 (Fall 1986), p. 375.

Motivation

The concept of motivation seems to contain more semantic confusion than most terms in the behavioral sciences. Some writers insist that motives are different from drives and use the latter term primarily to characterize the basic physiological needs (that is, hunger, thirst, shelter, and sex). Others distinguish between needs and wants, stating that needs are the basic motivating forces which translate themselves into more immediate wants which satisfy these needs (for example, hunger needs give rise to wanting a good steak dinner).

For our purposes, a motive may refer to a need, a want, a drive, an urge, a wish, a desire, an impulse, or any inner state that directs or channels behavior toward goals. A marketing researcher's interest in motives typically involves determining why people behave as they do. Several reasons explain this interest. First, it is believed that motives tend to be more stable than particular behaviors; therefore, motives offer a better basis for predicting future behavior than does past behavior. Second, if we understand the motives behind a person's behavior, we understand the behavior better and, in turn, are in a better position to influence future behavior, or at least provide offerings consistent with that anticipated behavior.

Behavior

Behavior concerns what customers have done or are doing. Usually in marketing, this means purchase and usage behavior. Behavior is a physical activity that takes place under specific circumstances, at a particular time, and involves one or more participants. The focus on behavior, then, involves a description of the activity with respect to the various components. The marketing researcher investigating behavior is well advised to use Table 7.4 as a checklist in designing data-collection instruments so that the key behavioral dimensions of interest are secured. There are many facets to each dimension, and the researcher has to make a conscious inclusion or omission decision about each facet. Consider the "where," for example. The "where of purchase" may be specified according to the kind of store, the location of the store by broad geographic area or specific address, the size of the store, or the name of the store. The study of behavior involves the development of a description of the purchase or use activity, either past or current, with respect to some or all of the characteristics contained in Table 7.4.

Behavior data are becoming increasingly available through various technologies (for example, scanners and the Web) and increasingly important to marketers, such as in building relationships with customers. Perhaps the most prevalent of behavioral data are scanner data—SKUs and other marketing information (such as price or

TABLE 7.4	Behavior Checklist	
	Purchase Behavior	*Use Behavior*
What and how much		
Who		
When		
Where		
How		

coupon use) captured at purchase, stored in massive data banks, integrated with such other marketing variables as advertising exposure, to enable the marketing researcher to conduct sophisticated analyses of behavior in the marketplace. For the past 10 to 20 years, scanner data have made a great impact for consumer packaged goods marketers, but marketers responsible for pharmaceuticals, financial products, and a variety of other goods and services will also have access to these numerous data as scanners and other technologies become more pervasive. Scanner data were discussed more fully in Chapter 6. A different technology that yields similar behavior data is the Web and all it entails, including the production of personal profile data, click-stream trails, and records of response to Web advertising.[10] A revolution is occurring regarding data access. The marketer talented at analyzing these data sets will derive great insights (this book will give you many means to do so!).

Basic Means of Obtaining Primary Data

The researcher attempting to collect primary data has a number of choices to make among the means that will be used. Figure 7.1 presents an overview of these choices. The primary decision is whether to employ communication or observation techniques. Communication involves questioning respondents to obtain the desired information using a data-collection instrument called a questionnaire or survey. The questions may be oral or written, and the responses may also be given in either form. Observation does not involve questioning. Rather, facts or behaviors are recorded. The observer may be a person or persons, or the data may be gathered using some mechanical device. For example, a researcher interested in the brands of canned vegetables a family buys might conduct a pantry audit in which the shelves are checked to see which brands the family has on hand.

We say more about the methods and decisions associated with each in the sections that follow. For now, we note that communication and observation each has its own advantages and disadvantages, which we discuss next. Generally, the strengths and weaknesses of these methods can be classified according to several dimensions: (1) versatility (that is, what can you do with the technique?); (2) business logistics (for example, how much will a study cost, how quickly will we see the results, and what do response rates look like?); and (3) data quality (are the responses objective and accurate?). The communication method of data collection has the *general* advantages of versatility, speed, and lower cost, whereas observational data are *typically* more objective and accurate.

Versatility

Versatility refers to a technique's ability to collect information on the many types of primary data of interest to marketers. A respondent's demographic/socioeconomic characteristics and lifestyle, the individual's attitudes and opinions, awareness and knowledge, intentions, the motivation underlying the individual's actions, and even the person's behavior may all be ascertained by the communication method. All we

---

[10]Shira Levine, "Clicking on the Customer," *America's Network* 104 (April 1, 2000), pp. 86–92.

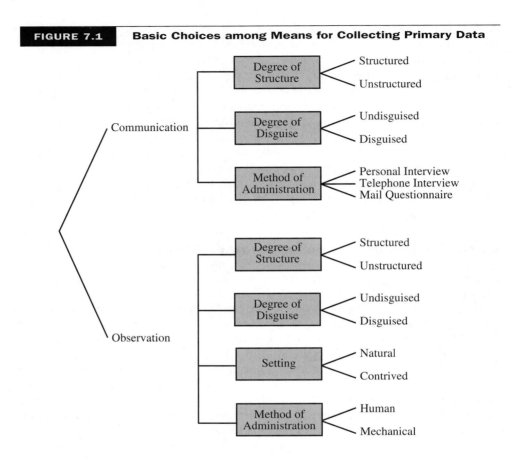

FIGURE 7.1   **Basic Choices among Means for Collecting Primary Data**

need to do is ask (although problems of accuracy of the replies may result, an issue we will discuss later).

Not so with observation. Observation is limited in scope to information about behavior and certain demographic/socioeconomic characteristics. Among behaviors, note that we are limited to observing present behavior; we cannot observe a person's past behavior, nor can we observe the person's intentions as to future behavior. If we are interested in any of these other things, we must ask. Among demographic/socioeconomic characteristics, some can be readily observed (for example, gender). Others can be observed but with less accuracy. A person's age and income, for example, might be inferred by closely examining the individual, including the person's mode of dress and purchasing behavior. Clearly, though, both of these observations can be subject to errors.

The other basic types of primary data cannot be measured by observation. We simply cannot observe an attitude or opinion, a person's awareness or knowledge, or motivation. Certainly, we can attempt to make some inferences about these variables on the basis of the individual's observed behavior. For instance, if a person is observed purchasing a can of a new flavor of Progresso soup, we might infer that the person has a favorable attitude toward Progresso. There is a real question, though, as to the correctness of the inference. A great deal of controversy exists over whether attitudes precede behavior or behavior precedes attitude formation. Perhaps the latter explanation is correct, and the person, in fact, has no particular attitudes toward Progresso as a brand but just thought he or she would try it. The individual may not even have been aware of that brand previously but just saw it for the first time on the shelf. Generalizing from observed behavior to states of mind is clearly risky, and researchers need to recognize this. Questioning clearly encompasses a much broader base of primary data.

Speed and Cost

The speed and cost advantages of the communication method are closely intertwined (time is money!). Assuming that the data lend themselves to either method, communication is often a faster means of data collection than observation, because it provides a greater degree of control over data-gathering activities. Researchers are not forced to wait for events to occur with the communication method, as they are with the observation method. In some cases, it is impossible to predict the occurrence of the event precisely enough to observe it. For other behaviors, the time interval can be substantial. For instance, an observer checking for the brand purchased most frequently in one of several appliance categories might have to wait a long time to make any observations at all. Much of the time the observer would be idle. Such idleness is expensive, given that the worker will probably be compensated on an hourly rather than a per-contact basis. Events of long duration also cause difficulty; an observational approach to study the relative influence of a husband or wife in the purchase of an automobile, for example, would be prohibitive in terms of both time and money.

There are always exceptions—instances when observation is faster and costs less than communication, such as in the purchase of consumer packaged goods. Scanners allow many more purchases to be recorded and at less cost than if purchasers were questioned about what they bought.

ETHICAL DILEMMA 7.1

A national department store chain with a relatively sophisticated image is planning to open a store in an area inhabited by wealthy professionals. The marketing research director of the company wants a detailed profile of the residents' characteristics and lifestyles to tailor the new store to the tastes of this lucrative new market. He suggests that you, a member of his staff, contribute to the research effort by spending a month observing the residents going about their daily affairs, such as eating in restaurants, attending church, shopping in other stores, socializing with one another, and so on. You are then to prepare a report on what types of expenditures support their lifestyles.

- Are there ethical problems involved in observing people in public places? Do the ethical problems become more serious if you socialize with your subjects?
- Who has ethical responsibility for your behavior: The marketing research director? You? Both?

Objectivity and Accuracy

Balanced against these disadvantages of limited scope, time, and cost are the objectivity and accuracy of the observational method. Data that can be secured by either communication or observation typically will be more accurate by observation because this method is independent of the respondent's unwillingness or inability to provide the information desired. For example, respondents are often reluctant to cooperate whenever their replies would be embarrassing or would in some way place them in an unfavorable light. Since observation allows the recording of behavior as it occurs, it does not depend on the respondent's memory or mood in reporting what occurred.

Observation typically produces more-objective data than does communication. The interview represents a social interaction situation. Thus, the replies of the person being questioned are conditioned by the individual's perceptions of the interviewer. The same is true of the interviewer, although the interviewer's selection and training affords the researcher a greater degree of control over these perceptions than those of the interviewee.

With observation, though, the consumer's perceptions play less of a role. Sometimes people are not even aware that they are being observed, thus removing the opportunity for them to tell the interviewer what they think the interviewer wants to hear or to give socially acceptable responses. The problems of objectivity are concentrated in the observer's methods, which makes the task easier. The observer's selection, training, and control, and not the consumer's perceptions of the field worker, become the crucial elements.

Communication Methods

Choosing the communication method of data collection implies several decisions. For example, should we administer questionnaires by mail, over the telephone, in person at a shopping mall, or by using fax, e-mail, or the Web? Should the purpose of the study be disguised or remain undisguised? Should the answers be open-ended, or should the respondent be asked to choose from a limited set of alternatives? These decisions are interdependent; a decision about method of administration, say, has implications regarding the degree of structure that must be imposed on the questionnaire.

Figure 7.1 on page 268 summarizes the decisions that a researcher must make when collecting data, including issues of structure and disguise. **Structure** is the degree of standardization imposed on the questionnaire. In a highly structured questionnaire, the questions to be asked and the responses permitted the respondents are completely predetermined (for example, "Circle a number from 1 to 7"). In a highly unstructured questionnaire, the questions to be asked are only loosely predetermined, and respondents are free to answer in their own words (such as, "Tell me how your family feels about Philadelphia Cream Cheese"). A questionnaire in which the questions are fixed but the responses are open-ended would represent an intermediate degree of structure.

Disguise is the amount of knowledge about the purpose of a study communicated to a respondent. An undisguised questionnaire makes the purpose of the research obvious by the questions posed, whereas a disguised questionnaire attempts to hide the purpose of the study. For example, if Ford wished to determine its customers' satisfaction, they might worry that a cover letter from Ford and questions all about Ford cars and trucks would bias the respondents' answers favorably toward Ford, since the survey's purpose is clear. If Ford wished for more objective data, they might forgo letterhead, or go through an outside marketing research agency, and ask their drivers about Ford, GM, and Honda cars. In this scenario, the target of the research is less clear, and it would be expected that the customer will answer more truthfully.

Structured–Undisguised Questionnaires

Structured–undisguised questionnaires are most commonly used in marketing research. Questions are presented with exactly the same wording, and in exactly the same order, to all respondents. The reason for standardizing questions is to ensure that all respondents are replying to the same question. If one interviewer asks, "Do you drink orange juice?" and another asks, "Does your family use frozen orange juice?" the replies would not be comparable.

In the typical structured–undisguised questionnaire, the responses as well as the questions are standardized. Consider the following question regarding a person's attitude toward pollution and the need for more government legislation controlling it, and note the fixed-alternative responses.

Do you feel the United States needs more or less antipollution legislation?

☐   Needs more

☐   Needs less

☐   Neither more nor less

☐   No opinion

No claim is made that this is a good question, but it is certainly an example of a structured–undisguised question. The question's purpose is clear: it deals with the respondent's attitudes toward antipollution legislation. The question is structured because respondents are limited to one of four stated replies.

The greatest advantages of structured–undisguised questions are that they are simple to administer and easy to tabulate and analyze. Respondents should have little difficulty replying. Their responses should be reliable in that if they were asked the question again, they would respond in a similar fashion (assuming, of course, that their attitudes have not changed in the meantime).

The fixed-alternative question is reliable for several reasons. First, the frame of reference is often obvious from the alternatives. For example, consider the question, "How much do you watch television?" If no alternatives are supplied, one respondent might say "every day," another might say "regularly," and still another might respond with the number of hours per day. These responses would be more difficult to interpret than an alternative form that included the response categories "every day," "at least three times a week," "at least once a week," and "less than once a week." Providing alternative responses also often helps to make the question clear. The question, "What is your marital status?" is more confusing than is the question, "Are you married, single, widowed, or divorced?" Providing the dimensions in which to frame the reply helps ensure the reliability of the question.

The reliability of fixed-alternative questions can be associated with loss of validity, if the answers do not accurately reflect the true state of affairs. Fixed alternatives may force a response to a question on which the subject does not have an opinion. This is particularly true if the "no opinion" category is not provided as an alternative. Even when it is provided, there is often a tendency to keep the number of "no opinions" at a minimum. Thus, the interviewer presses the respondent for a reply, which the person gives. Whether or not it accurately reflects the individual's attitude is another matter.

Alternatively, it may be that the respondent has an opinion, but none of the response categories allows the accurate expression of that attitude. The previous example about pollution makes no allowance for distinguishing among those who feel that we definitely need a great deal more antipollution legislation ("true" environmentalists) versus those who feel not as strongly that something more should be done to clean up our air and water, and more legislation prohibiting pollution may be one answer.

Fixed-alternative responses may also lower validity when the response categories themselves introduce bias, as when an "appropriate" response is omitted because of an oversight or when insufficient prior research produces response categories that are inappropriate. The provision of an "other" category may help, but it does not eliminate this bias altogether, because respondents are generally reluctant to respond in the "other" category. In using a fixed-alternative question, one must be reasonably certain that the alternatives adequately cover the range of probable replies.

Fixed-alternative questions are most productive when possible replies are well known, clear-cut, and limited in number. Thus, they seem to work best when securing factual information (age, education, home ownership, and so on) and when eliciting expressions of opinion about issues on which people hold clear-cut opinions (for example, strongly agree to strongly disagree). They are frequently used to collect data on attitudes, intentions, awareness, demographic and socioeconomic characteristics, and behavior. (Questions for obtaining data on motivations are discussed later in this chapter.)

Consumer research can be structured in ways other than rating scales. New technology is being explored in testing advertisements, whereby consumers watch ads and turn knobs and dials continuously through the ad to depict moments during which the ad made them feel happy or sad, or interested versus disinterested. Usually the ad is then replayed and the consumers are asked to explain their highest and lowest dial registers. Researchers find that an overall rating of an ad tends to correlate with the peak emotional experience during the ad, and the final moments in the ad. The validity and long-term viability of the method is still being determined, however; skeptics would argue that the impact of an ad is more of a gestalt, overall impression and that it might even take time to affect the consumer, and therefore the moment-by-moment judgments during the ad may not be predictive of eventual attitudes toward the ad or the brand or purchase behavior.[11]

---

[11]Hans Baumgartner, Mita Sujan, and Dan Padgett, "Patterns of Affective Reactions to Advertisements: The Integration of Moment-to-Moment Responses into Overall Judgments," *Journal of Marketing Research* 34 (May 1997), pp. 219–232.

Unstructured–Undisguised Questionnaires

In unstructured–undisguised questionnaires, the purpose of the study is clear but responses to the questions are open-ended. Consider the following question: "How do you feel about pollution and the need for more antipollution legislation?" The initial question is constant. With it the interviewer attempts to get the respondent to talk freely about his or her attitudes toward pollution. After presenting this initial question, the interview becomes very unstructured as the interviewer probes more deeply (hence, interviews are often called "depth interviews"),[12] and the respondent's subsequent answers determine the direction the interviewer takes next, and so forth. The interviewer may attempt to follow a rough outline, but the order and the specific framing of the questions will vary from interview to interview, as will the specific content resulting from each interview.

The freedom permitted the interviewer in conducting these depth interviews reveals the major advantages and disadvantages of the method. Proponents of interviews and most qualitative techniques (for example, observational methods, described later in the chapter) say these methods enable the researcher to obtain deeper, richer, "thicker" descriptions than, say, surveys with fixed-alternative responses. By not constraining the respondent to a fixed set of replies and by careful probing, an experienced interviewer should be able to derive a more accurate picture of the respondent's true position on some issue, particularly for sensitive matters in which there is social pressure to conform and to offer a "socially acceptable" response. Note the caveats—"experienced interviewer" and "careful probing"; depth interviews require highly skilled interviewers. They are hard to find and expensive when found. Further, the lack of structure allows the interviewer to influence the result; that is, the interviewer's judgment about when to probe and how to word the probes can affect the response. Good depth interviews often take a long time to complete (an hour or more), which makes it difficult to secure the cooperation of respondents. It also means that a study using depth interviews is likely to involve fewer respondents, or will require a greater number of interviewers. The more interviewers there are, the greater the likelihood that the variation in responses will be partly interviewer-induced because of differences in administering the questionnaire.[13] The interview can also be problematic to analyze. The services of one or more skilled psychologists are typically required to interpret the responses. These people's services do not come cheaply. Further, the psychologist's own background and frame of reference will affect the interpretation. This subjectivity raises questions about both the reliability and validity of the results. It also causes difficulty in determining what the correct interpretation is and presents problems when tabulating the replies.

---

[12]Andrea Fontana and James H. Frey, "Interviewing: The Art of Science," in Norman K. Denzin and Yvonna S. Lincoln, eds., *Collecting and Interpreting Qualitative Materials* (Thousand Oaks, CA: Sage, 1998), pp. 47–78.

[13]Another source of possible interviewer bias is the interviewer and respondent match on demographics such as gender or ethnicity; usually the matching is unnecessary unless the topic is culturally sensitive; see Cynthia Webster, "Hispanic and Anglo Interviewer and Respondent Ethnicity and Gender," *Journal of Marketing Research* 33 (February 1996), pp. 62–72.

Coding open-ended questions can be challenging, and it is nearly always more time-consuming than entering rating scale data and computing means. However, the information obtained from consumers "in their own words" through interviews and open-ended questions on surveys can also be extremely rewarding and insightful. Further, some of the problems with coding open-ended questions may be changing with new technology. Researchers are increasingly feeding respondents' answers into computers programmed to recognize a large vocabulary of words in their search for regularities in the replies. Consumers' responses are usually first broken into "thought units." For example, if a consumer is asked, "Tell me about the last time you had poor service at a restaurant," and answers, "Well, the service was slow and the waiter was rude," the sentence would be parsed into "service was slow" and "waiter was rude," because they express different qualities and would need to be coded differently. Computer analysis can quickly rank each word that respondents use by the frequency of usage and then can print out sentences containing the keywords. The detailed analysis of these sentences allows researchers to pick up on recurring themes.[14] Although these systems automate the coding of unstructured interviews, they leave interpretation to the individual analyst. Nevertheless, the systems can achieve in hours what a human review might take weeks to accomplish.

The depth interview is probably best suited to exploratory research. Exploratory research is conducted when less is known about consumers' reactions. Interviews and other unstructured methods allow the flexibility to pursue whatever the consumers wish to talk about—topics that the marketing researcher is unlikely to anticipate fully enough to write questions for a survey.

A currently popular use of the depth interview is called *laddering* studies, in which the emphasis is on discovering the relationship between product attributes and consumer benefits and values, or means-end chains. The ladder metaphor implies that the researcher is going deeper and deeper, from abstract goals to more specific means of achieving those goals. In one study, consumers first identified values important to them such as good health, family security, happiness, and so forth. Each of those goals, in turn, is sought through different routes. Good health, for example, is thought to be achieved in a number of ways, including relaxation, exercise, low-sugar diets, low-cholesterol diets, and cleanliness. These intermediary goals are achieved by even more specific means. For example, relaxation is achieved through the use of products as diverse as red wine and hot tubs. Low-sugar diets are achieved through eating dietetic foodstuffs, and low cholesterol through eating fish and chicken. Cleanliness was said to be achieved through use of dishwashers, which kill germs; soaps and deodorants, which make one feel clean; and even bottled

---

[14]Formally, the procedure is known as content analysis; for example, see Robert P. Weber, *Basic Content Analysis*, 2nd ed. (Thousand Oaks, CA: Sage, 1990); Matthew B. Miles and A. Michael Huberman, *Qualitative Data Analysis*, 2nd ed. (Thousand Oaks, CA: Sage, 1994). For examples, see David W. Stewart and Girish N. Punj, "Effects of Using a Nonverbal (Musical) Cue on Recall and Playback of Television Advertising," *Journal of Business Research* 42, no. 1 (May 1998), pp. 39–51. Also see Thomas J. Richards and Lyn Richards, "Using Computers in Qualitative Research," in Norman K. Denzin and Yvonna S. Lincoln, eds., *Collecting and Interpreting Qualitative Materials* (Thousand Oaks, CA: Sage, 1998), pp. 211–245.

water, which contains no sediment.[15] These value chains are then often reflected in advertising appeals, for example, "These disposable paper towels do not pick up the bacteria that kitchen cloths do, and keep your family safer from germs," and "The purity of this bottled water helps to keep your body clean and healthy."

Unstructured–Disguised Questionnaires

Unstructured–disguised questionnaires lie at the heart of what has become known as motivation research. A researcher needs only limited experience with surveys to realize that many areas of inquiry are not amenable to exploration by direct questions. Many important motives and reasons for choice are of a kind that consumers will not describe because a truthful description would be damaging to their egos. Other motives they cannot describe, either because they do not have the words to make their meaning clear or because their motives exist below the level of awareness. Very often such motives are of paramount importance in consumer behavior. Attempting to inquire into them with direct questions often yields replies that are either useless or misleading.

Researchers have circumvented the respondents' reluctance to discuss their feelings by developing techniques that are largely independent of the respondents' self-awareness and willingness to reveal themselves. The main thrust in these projective methods has been that of concealing the topic of inquiry by using a disguised stimulus. Though the stimulus is typically standardized, participants are allowed to respond to it in a very unstructured form. The basic assumption in "projective" methods is that an individual's reaction to a relatively unstructured stimulus is indicative of the person's basic perceptions of the phenomenon. Reactions to clear stimuli (such as a picture of a brand of toothpaste) tend to show more uniformity (though respondents can differ in whether they like or dislike the brand), whereas reactions to an ambiguous stimulus (for example, a picture of a man seated at an office desk) allows, even requires, respondents to project their needs, motives, and values; the respondent chooses his or her own interpretation, description, and evaluation of the ambiguous stimulus.[16]

In general terms, a projective technique involves the use of a vague stimulus that an individual is asked to describe, expand on, or build a story or structure

---

[15]Thomas J. Reynolds and Johnathan Gutman, "Laddering Theory, Method, Analysis and Interpretation," *Journal of Advertising Research* 26 (February/March 1988), pp. 11–31; Fred Langerak, Ed Peelen, and Ed Nijssen, "A Laddering Approach to the Use of Methods and Techniques to Reduce the Cycle Time of New-to-the-Firm Products," *Journal of Product Innovation Management* 16 (March 1999), pp. 173–182; Frenkel ter Hofstede, Anke Audenaert, Jan-Benedict E. M. Steenkamp, and Michael Wedel, "An Investigation into the Association Pattern Technique as a Quantitative Approach to Measuring Means-End Chains," *International Journal of Research in Marketing* 15 (February 1998), pp. 37–50; Jeffrey F. Durgee, Gina Colarelli O'Connor, and Robert W. Veryzer, "Observations: Translating Values into Product Wants," *Journal of Advertising Research* 36 (November/December 1996), pp. 90–100.

[16]Fred N. Kerlinger, *Foundations of Behavioral Research*, 4th ed. (New York: Holt, Rinehart and Winston, 1999). See also W. G. Klopfer and E. S. Taulkie, "Projective Tests," in M. R. Rosenzweig and L. W. Porter, eds., *Annual Review of Psychology* (Palo Alto, CA: Annual Reviews, 1976), pp. 543–567; Sidney J. Levy, *Brands, Consumers, Symbols, and Research* (Thousand Oaks, CA: Sage, 1999); Paul E. Meehl, "The Dynamics of 'Structured' Personality Tests," *Journal of Clinical Psychology* 56, no. 3 (March 2000), pp. 367–373; Marvin Leibowitz, *Interpreting Projective Drawings* (Philadelphia: Brunner/Mazel, 1999); R. W. Kamphaus, Martha D. Petoskey, and Ellen W. Rowe, "Current Trends in Psychological Testing of Children," *Professional Psychology: Research and Practice* 31, no. 2 (April 2000), pp. 155–164.

around. Although almost any stimulus can serve, three common types of projective methods are word association, sentence completion, and storytelling.

Word Association   With word association projective methods, consumers respond to a list of words, reacting to them with the first word that comes to mind. The test words are interspersed throughout the list with some neutral, or less central, words to conceal the purpose of the study. In a study on pollution, the list of keywords might be *traffic, lakes, smokestacks,* and *city,* mixed in with words such as *margarine, blue jeans,* and *government.*

The responses to each of the keywords are recorded verbatim and analyzed. The key analysis is the examination of the content of the responses; that is, what themes may we derive from these respondents' word choices? While the analysis of the responses is subjective, some common responses will often emerge. These common responses, when classified and grouped, are then used to reveal patterns of interest, underlying motivations, or stereotypes. It is often possible to categorize the associations as favorable–unfavorable, pleasant–unpleasant, modern–old-fashioned, and so forth, depending on the research question. For example, for each of the following words, very often only two or three descriptor words emerge (try it among your friends!): McDonald's, Sears, Exxon, Coca-Cola, Microsoft, Madonna, Michael Jordan, Michael Jackson, Chicago, Mexico, Japan, lawyers, accountants, marketers, and consultants. This list also illustrates the flexibility of the method—one can obtain consumer perceptions of firms and brand equity, celebrity endorsers, tourist destinations, career objectives, and so forth. When a word elicits a greater variety of associations across respondents, it is thought that the stimulus may be less familiar (for example, lacrosse, Swedish Royal family) or more complex (for example, Reagan, carbohydrates, Supreme Court), or for whatever other reasons yields greater individual differences.

The word association responses are also judged in three more objective, easily measured ways:

- By the frequency with which any word is given as a response
- By the amount of time that elapses before a response is given
- By the number of respondents who do not respond at all to a test word after a reasonable period of time

The amount of time that elapses before a response is given to a test word is carefully determined. A stopwatch may be used, or the word associations may be easily conducted on PCs, during which reaction times can be recorded to the millisecond by the computer's internal clock. (Purists would say that a computer-administered word association test will not be as rich and informative as one administered by a trained psychologist who can also lend insight by interpreting the nonverbal cues, such as body language.) Respondents who hesitate (operationally defined as taking longer than three seconds to reply) are judged to be sufficiently emotionally involved in the word that they do not provide their immediate reaction but an acceptable response. If they do not respond at all, their emotional involvement is judged to be so high as to block a response. An individual's pattern of responses, along with the details of the response to each question, are then used to assess the person's attitudes or feelings on the subject.

Sentence Completion   This method requires the respondent to complete a number of sentences. Respondents are instructed to reply with the first thoughts that come to mind. The responses are recorded verbatim and then analyzed.

Once again, while the analysis of qualitative responses is subjective, sometimes the results are nevertheless clear and there would be good agreement in their interpretation. For example, imagine one person completing sentences about the environment as follows:

> People who are concerned about ecology *care about the future.*
> A person who does not use our lakes for recreation is *being thoughtful about the ecosystem.*
> When I think of living in a city, I *can't help but think of the smog over LA.*

Compare those response to these of another person:

> People who are concerned about ecology *are just tree-huggers who want to run up my taxes.*
> A person who does not use our lakes for recreation is *a person who doesn't enjoy water sports.*
> When I think of living in a city, I *think about cruising my car downtown on Saturday night*!

Presumably, these two respondents could easily be characterized as belonging to segments of consumers who are more and less ecologically concerned.

Sometimes the disguised nature of sentence completion questions can shed light on a topic that a more direct rating scale might not. For example, when consumers are asked, "Do you think it is important to give blood?" most say yes, due to pressures for social desirability and conformity. And we might indeed be convinced that a person regularly gives blood who completes sentences like: "I always give blood during blood drives at work, unless . . . *I'm sick,*" and "People who don't give blood . . . *are pretty selfish, in my opinion.*" Contrast the values of that person with someone who completed the sentences as follows: "I always give blood during blood drives at work, unless . . . *I'm in a hurry,*" and "People who don't give blood . . . *just don't like needles.*" From this person's sentences, a picture emerges of someone who will resist donating blood in the presence of only minor hurdles, suggesting that their actual compliance will be low.

One advantage of sentence completion over word association projective methods is that there are simply more words to provide respondents with a more directed stimulus. Just enough direction should be given to evoke some association with the concept of interest. The researcher needs to be careful not to convey the purpose of the study or provoke the "socially accepted" response. Obviously, skill is needed to develop a good sentence completion or word association test.

A particular form of association tests that is gaining some popularity is to have consumers draw metaphors and analogies in the sentence completions (that is, "An *X* is like a *Y* . . ."). For example, one recent study took place in a competitive HMO market in a major U.S. city. Participants were asked to talk about their HMO and their perceptions of the other HMO brands. Then they were asked to draw comparisons between the HMOs and brands of cars. One consumer said, "[HMO A] is a Cadillac . . . If I were to get into an accident, the car would absorb most of my injuries, [HMO A] would absorb my financial aspects. [HMO B] is a GMC or Chevy truck . . . it has the cushion in case I ever did need it . . . a truck might be pretty big but . . . it's not as much metal to take care of you. You can be injured a lot worse." Again, the responses are open, and it may seem that the interpretation would be subjective, but the consumers help interpret their own metaphors when they say, "HMO A is like a Lincoln Town Car *in that it* is comfortable, nice, all-American," or "HMO A is like a Lexus or Infiniti *in providing* a very good product, and very good service." In comparison, in this study, HMO B was likened to a station wagon (that is, low-key transportation, not flashy), Ford Escort (comparably small and inexpensive), and Hyundai (unproven, unfamiliar, comparably small). It is not the case that these researchers cared about the cars, per se, but that the cars metaphor allowed consumers to talk about their HMOs in unrestricted and creative ways.[17]

Storytelling   The storytelling approach often relies on pictorial material, such as cartoons, photographs, or drawings. These pictorial devices are descendants of the psychologists' Thematic Apperception Test (TAT), which in turn descended from the famous Rorschach ink blot tests. The TAT consists of a copyrighted series of pictures about which the participant is asked to tell stories. Some of the pictures are of ordinary events and some of unusual events; in some of the pictures the persons or objects are clearly represented, and in others they are relatively obscure. A respondent's interpretation of these pictures or events is used to interpret the individual's personality; for example, whether the person is impulsive or shows intellectual control in interpreting the stimulus, whether the subject is creative or unimaginative, and so on.

When used in a marketing situation, the same pattern is followed. Respondents are shown a picture and asked to tell a story about the picture. However, the responses are used to assess attitudes toward the consumer behavior phenomenon rather than to interpret the subject's personality.[18]

With respect to the environmental pollution example, the stimulus might be a picture of a city, and the respondent might be asked to describe what it would be like to live there. The analysis of the individual's response would then focus on the emphasis given to pollution in its various forms. If no mention were made of traffic congestion, dirty air, noise, and so on, the person would be classified as displaying little concern for pollution and its control.

Note that the various projectile methods differ somewhat in their degree of structure of the stimulus. The word association and sentence completion methods

---

[17]Russell Lacey, "Dimensions of the Ideal HMO Brand," *Marketing Health Services* 20 (Spring 2000), pp. 32–35. For more on sentence completion, see Richard Rasulis, David Schuldberg, and Michael Murtagh, "Computer-Administered Testing with the Rotter Incomplete Sentences Blank," *Computers in Human Behavior* 12, no. 4 (Winter 1996), pp. 497–513; Karen Turnbow and Richard H. Dana, "The Effects of Stem Length and Directions on Sentence Completion Test Responses," *Journal of Personality Assessment* 45, no. 1 (February 1981), pp. 27–32.

[18]Sidney J. Levy, "Interpreting Consumer Mythology: Structural Approach to Consumer Behavior Focuses on Story Telling," *Marketing Management* 2 (1994), pp. 4–14; Teresa Fagulha, "The Once-Upon-A-Time Test," in Richard Henry Dana, ed., *Handbook of Cross-Cultural and Multicultural Personality Assessment* (Mahwah, NJ: Erlbaum), pp. 515–536.

involve presenting the stimuli to the respondent in the same sequence and in this sense are structured. They are unstructured as far as the response is concerned, as is the storytelling method. Respondents are free to interpret and respond to the stimuli in terms of their own perceptions and words, and that is why these methods are categorized as disguised–unstructured techniques.

The unstructured nature of the projective methods produces many of the same difficulties encountered with the undisguised–unstructured methods of data collection. The greater standardization of the stimulus is a distinct advantage, but the challenge in making sense of the replies remains. The final interpretation of what was said often reflects the interpreter's frame of reference as much as it does the respondent's. Different interpreters often reach different conclusions about the same response. This raises havoc with the editing, coding, and tabulation of replies and suggests that projective methods are also more suited for exploratory research than for descriptive or causal research.

Structured–Disguised Questionnaires

Structured–disguised questionnaires are the least used in marketing research. They were developed in an attempt to secure the advantages of disguise in revealing subconscious motives and attitudes along with the advantages in coding and tabulation common to structured approaches. The arguments supporting the structured-disguised approach typically rest on some proposition regarding the role of attitude in the person's mental and psychological makeup.

One proposition holds that an individual's knowledge, perception, and memory are conditioned by the person's attitudes. Thus, in order to secure information about people's attitudes when a direct question would produce a biased answer, we can simply ask them what they know. Presumably, greater knowledge reflects the strength and direction of an attitude. Democratic voters could be expected to know more about Democratic candidates and the Democratic platform than those intending to vote Republican, for example. This argument is consistent with what we know about the operation of selective cognitive processes—that individuals tend to selectively expose themselves, selectively perceive, and selectively retain ideas, arguments, events, and phenomena that are consistent with their own beliefs. Conversely, people tend to avoid, see differently, and forget situations and items that are inconsistent with their preconceived beliefs.

This proposition suggests that one way of avoiding the socially acceptable response in securing a respondent's attitude toward pollution and the need for antipollution legislation would be to ask the person what he or she knows rather than how he or she feels. Thus, the researcher might frame such questions as the following: "What is the status of the antipollution legislation listed below?" A number of bills would be listed, some actual and some hypothetical. The respondent would be asked to check the box that best describes the current status of the legislation; such as, "In committee," "Passed by the House but not the Senate," "Vetoed by the president," and so on. Respondents' attitudes toward the need for more legislation would then be assessed by the accuracy of their responses.

The main advantages of this approach emerge in analysis. Responses are easily coded and tabulated and an objective measure of knowledge quickly derived. However, do we wish to infer that a high level of awareness of the legislative status is indicative of a favorable or an unfavorable attitude toward the need for more

---

ETHICAL DILEMMA 7.2

Pharmaceutical Supply Company derives its major source of revenue from physician-prescribed drugs. Until recently, Pharmaceutical Supply had maintained a dominant position in the market. A new competitor had entered the market, however, and was quickly gaining market share.

In response to competitive pressure, Pharmaceutical Supply's management decided that it needed to conduct an extensive study concerning physician decision making with regard to selection of drugs. Janice Rowland, the marketing research director, decided that the best way to gather this information was through the use of personal and telephone interviews. Ms. Rowland directed the interviewers to represent themselves as employees of a fictitious marketing research agency, as she believed that a biased response would result if the physicians were aware that Pharmaceutical Supply was conducting the study. In addition, the interviewers were instructed to tell the physicians that the research was being conducted for their own purpose and not for a particular client.

Was Ms. Rowland's decision to withhold the sponsor's true name and purpose a good one?

- Do the physicians have a right to know who is conducting the research?
- It has been argued that use of such deception prevents a respondent from making a rational choice about whether or not she or he wishes to participate in a study. Comment on this.
- What kind of results might have been obtained if the physicians knew the true sponsor of the study?
- What are the consequences for the research profession of using this form of deception?

---

antipollution legislation? That is, whether this measure of knowledge can also be interpreted as a measure of the person's attitude relies on an assumption about the consumer's cognitive system.

Questionnaires Classified by Method of Administration

Questionnaires can also be classified by the method that will be used to administer them. The main methods are personal interview, telephone, mail, fax, e-mail, and Web surveys.

A personal interview implies a direct, face-to-face conversation between the interviewer and the respondent or interviewee. The interviewer asks the questions and records the respondent's answers, either while the interview is in progress or immediately afterward. The interview can take place in a home or an office or usually at a central location like a shopping mall, where shoppers are stopped (or intercepted, hence the term *mall intercept*) and asked to participate.

The telephone interview means that this conversation occurs over the phone.

The normal administration of a mail questionnaire involves mailing the questionnaires to designated respondents with an accompanying cover letter. The respondents complete the questionnaire at their leisure and mail their replies back to the research organization.

Faxed surveys operate just like mail questionnaires, except of course that they are faxed to and from the recipients. Fax surveys work much better for business-to-business research because most consumers do not have fax machines at home.

E-mail surveys are one of two types:

- The questions of the market research study are embedded in the text of the e-mail itself
- The questions in the survey are in an e-mail attachment file

Each has its pros and cons: Replying to embedded e-mail surveys is extremely quick. Alternatively, the attachment is likely to look more professional than the flat embedded text, and it can allow for hyperlinking, skip-patterns, artwork, and so on. However, it is one more step to open an attachment, and any additional steps that add to the hurdle of completing a survey means that response rates will drop off. Web surveys resemble the attachment files in that hypertext and graphics can improve both the appearance and quality control of the survey, as well as enhance the inherent appeal by, for example, requesting consumer reactions to vivid depictions of an ad or product.

The preceding descriptions suggest the most common or "pure" methods of administration. A number of variations are possible. Questionnaires for a "mail" administration may simply be attached to products or printed in magazines and newspapers. Similarly, questionnaires in a personal interview may be self-administered, perhaps in the interviewer's presence, to provide an opportunity for the respondents to seek clarification on points of confusion from the interviewer. Alternatively, the respondents might complete the questionnaire in private for later pickup by a representative of the research organization, in which case the interaction would be less like a personal interview. Another possibility is for the interviewer to hand the designated respondent the questionnaire personally but then have the respondent complete it in private and mail it directly to the research organization. In this case, the personal interview is indistinguishable from the mail questionnaire method.

Often the different modalities are mixed to enhance sample cooperation; for example, a business manager may receive a letter, e-mail, or phone call asking for his or her help in the study, and after this prenotification, the survey is faxed to the manager at his or her place of business. Web surveys are either initiated by sending an e-mail to the sample of potential respondents, asking them to visit a certain World Wide Web address to complete the survey form, or by a cooperative relationship with another Internet vendor in placing a banner on its site. The user then just clicks through to the survey.

Each of these methods of communication possesses some advantages and disadvantages. When discussing the pros and cons, the pure cases logically serve as a frame of reference. When a modified administration is used, the general advantages and disadvantages may no longer hold. They may also cease to hold in specific situations, in which case a general advantage may become a disadvantage, and vice versa. The advantages and disadvantages also may not apply when dealing with different countries with different cultures.

For example, telephone interviews are commonly conducted in the U.S., and they are frequent also in the Netherlands, Germany, and the United Kingdom (U.K.). They are rare in Japan, where it is not culturally acceptable to answer questions from "strangers" over the telephone; for different reasons (the unreliability of the communications networks), phone surveys are exceedingly rare in Mexico, Argentina, and Hungary. Door-to-door interviewing is illegal in Saudi Arabia, legal but prohibitively expensive in the U.S., and more common in Switzerland and the U.K. Finally, good mailing lists are critical to the success and frequent use of mail surveys in the U.S. and also in Sweden, where the government routinely publishes lists of every Swedish household, making mail studies very feasible there.[19]

The specific problem and culture, then, will actually dictate the benefits and weaknesses that are associated with each method. Nevertheless, a general discussion of advantages and disadvantages serves to highlight the various issues that need to be considered in deciding on the manner in which the data will be collected. Sampling control, information control, and administrative control are definite points to consider when comparing the methods.

Sampling Control

Sampling control concerns the researcher's ability to direct the inquiry to a designated respondent and to get the desired cooperation from that respondent.

Directing the Inquiry　The direction of the inquiry is guided by the sampling frame—that is, by the list of population elements from which the sample will be drawn. With the telephone method, for example, one or more phone books typically serve as the sampling frame. Respondents are selected by some random method from the phone books serving the areas in which the study is to be done. Phone book sampling frames are inadequate in at least two important respects: they do not include those who do not have telephones and they do not include those who have unlisted numbers.

Regarding phone ownership, in the U.S., almost 95 percent of households have phones, yet there is some variation by regions and by other demographic factors. In other countries, such as the U.K., phone penetration nearly resembles that in the States, but worldwide, phone access is generally lower (for example, it is 20 percent in Russia).[20] Table 7.5 summarizes the evidence regarding the demographic factors affecting phone ownership in the U.S. The differences in phone ownership by various demographic factors can bias the results of a telephone survey. The proportion

---

[19]Jeffrey Pope, *How Cultural Differences Affect Multi-Country Research* (Minneapolis, MN: Custom Research, Inc., 1991); V. Kumar, *International Marketing Research* (Upper Saddle River, NJ: Prentice Hall, 2000).

[20]Andrew Beutmueller, "Stepping Out," *Communications International* (April 2000), pp. 44–47; Iain Noble, Nick Moon, and Dominic McVey, "Bringing It All Back Home . . . Using RDD Telephone Methods for Large-Scale Social Policy and Opinion Research in the UK," *Journal of the Market Research Society* 41 (April 1998), pp. 93–120.

TABLE 7.5	**Summary of Studies of Demographic Factors Related to Telephone Ownership**

1. Telephone coverage tends to be greater in urban areas than in rural areas, although in countries with very high overall telephone penetration (such as in the United States, Canada, United Kingdom, France, Denmark, and Norway), the difference is rather small.
2. In the United States, coverage is lower in the South. Similar regional differences prevail in some other countries (for example, Ireland and Israel), but regional categorizations are country specific and are hard to compare cross-nationally.
3. In the United States, coverage is lower among nonwhites. No racial information was available from other countries.
4. Telephone coverage is always lower among those with lower incomes, the unemployed, those in manual or low-prestige occupations, and the less educated.
5. Telephone coverage is consistently lower for renters and people who live in apartments or trailers rather than in single-family homes.
6. Households without telephones tend to be headed by younger people, unmarried people, and frequently men.
7. Nontelephone households tend to be either smaller than average or larger than average.

Based on Tom W. Smith, "Phone Home? An Analysis of Household Telephone Ownership," *International Journal of Public Opinion Research* 2 (Winter 1990), p. 386.

of households with telephones increases each year, however, so bias resulting from the exclusion of nontelephone households should diminish in the future. For example, differences between rural and urban response rates are likely to diminish with satellite services and mobile or cellular phones (given that these technologies do not require infrastructures that may be absent in some rural locations).

Regarding unlisted numbers, a household's phone number may not appear in a directory for two reasons: First, phone book sampling frames do not include the segment of the population that has requested an unlisted telephone number, which has been growing steadily and now represents approximately a third of the 87.1 million U.S. telephone households. The problem is particularly acute in urban areas in general, and certain urban areas in particular. Figure 7.2, for example, shows the 10 metropolitan areas in the United States with the highest proportion of unlisted numbers. In addition, phone book publishers simply cannot keep pace with the proliferation of new phone numbers that were assigned after a current directory was published. Studies that rely on phone book sampling frames under-represent mobile households. Specifically, anywhere from 12 percent to 15 percent of the residential numbers in a typical telephone directory are disconnected when called, thus reducing the number of listed telephone households to roughly 56 million. A comparison of unlisted versus listed households indicates that unlisted households are younger, more likely to live in urban areas, nonwhite, more mobile, and are either very high or very low income versus listed households.[21]

Some researchers attempt to overcome the sampling bias of unlisted numbers by using random digit dialing (RDD). RDD entails the random generation of numbers to be called and often the automatic dialing of those calls as well. The calls are

[21]J. Michael Brick, Joseph Waksberg, Dale Kulp, and Amy Starer, "Bias in List-Assisted Telephone Samples," *Public Opinion Quarterly* 59 (Summer 1995), pp. 218–235; also see Survey Sampling, Inc., at ssisamples.com for statistics on listed and unlisted phone numbers, and their sampling solutions.

FIGURE 7.2   **Ten Metro Areas with the Highest Proportion of Unlisted Telephone Numbers***

*All are coincidentally in California.
For more information, see Survey Sampling, Inc. at ssisamples.com (Summer 2000).

typically handled through one central interviewing facility. This procedure allows geographically wide coverage. One problem with the random generation of phone numbers is that it can increase survey costs, because approximately 34,000 area-code–prefix combinations are in use in the continental United States. When the last four digits are generated randomly, approximately 340 million possible phone numbers can be called. However, there are fewer working residential telephone numbers in the United States; calling random telephone numbers will result in residential contacts only about one-fourth of the time. An alternative scheme to random digit dialing is plus-one sampling, in which a probability sample of phone numbers is selected from the telephone directory and a single, randomly determined digit is added to each selected number. One test comparing RDD to white pages of telephone listings found slightly better response rates for white-page calls, but thankfully, no significant differences in demographic or other self-reported profile data between the RDD and white-page samples.[22]

For mail questionnaires, one or more mailing lists typically serve as the sampling frame. The quality of these lists determines the sampling biases. If the list is a reasonably good one, the bias can be small. For example, some firms have established panels of consumers that can be used to answer mail questionnaires and that are representative of the population in many important respects. In addition, some

---

[22]Richard Pothoff, "Some Generalizations of the Mitofsky-Waksberg Technique of Random Digit Dialing," *Journal of the American Statistical Association* 82 (June 1987), pp. 409–418; David H. Wilson, Gary J. Starr, Anne W. Taylor, and Eleonora Dal Grande, "Random Digit Dialing and Electronic White Pages Samples Compared," *Australian and New Zealand Journal of Public Health* 23 (December 1999), pp. 627–633.

mailing lists that may be ideally suited for certain types of studies can be purchased. Business-to-business marketing research is usually easier in this regard—the mailing list and lists of phone and fax numbers are more stable than those for consumers, and businesses are fewer in number.

Suppose you run a direct-mail business that specializes in selling mono-grammed baby bibs. For a fee at any given time, you can obtain a mailing list containing the names and addresses of up to one million pregnant women. And, if it should suit your purposes, the list can be limited to women whose babies are expected in a certain month or who are expecting their first child. Mothers-to-be are a prime potential for relationship marketing, because "not only is she likely to buy, but she must buy" maternity clothes and skin creams during pregnancy, and baby clothes, toys, formula, and so forth, upon arrival of the newborn. Lists are ultimately derived from hospital records and therefore are highly reliable. In addition, many firms continue to develop the marketing relationship by sending their representatives to deliver bedside drop-offs of gift packs, trial sizes of relevant products, and redeemable coupons at stores such as Mothercare.[23]

Sometimes the list is internally generated. Spurred on by technical advances, a number of firms are developing greater capabilities to target questionnaires or other mailings to specific households. For example, American Express, with its image-processing technology, now is able to select all its cardholders who made purchases from golf pro-shops, who traveled more than once to Europe, who attended symphony concerts, or who made some other specific purchase using their American Express card. Relationship and database marketing are giving marketers many opportunities to cross-sell to customers. These databases are continually updated, so they also serve as an excellent sampling frame to survey current customers.

The quality of the mailing list determines the sampling control in a mail study. If there is an accurate, applicable, and readily available list of population elements, the mail questionnaire allows a wide and representative sample, since it costs no more to send a questionnaire across the country than it does to send one across town. Even ignoring costs, it is sometimes the only way of contacting the relevant population, such as busy executives who will not sit still for an arranged personal or telephone interview but may respond to a mail questionnaire. The key is addressing the questionnaire to a specific respondent rather than to a title or position.

It is also critical to target well—response rates will be greater for surveys on topics that the recipient cares about. Targeting is more efficient than simply increasing the sample size. That increases mailing costs, and fewer complete surveys will be obtained from a mass, uncustomized effort. It is estimated that the average U.S. consumer receives some 543 unsolicited mailings per year (compared with 83, 41, and 63 for Germany, the U.K., and France, respectively); direct mailing is a $1.5 trillion market in the U.S., employing 8.7 million people.[24]

Regarding newer technologies, fax surveys operate like phone surveys in their sampling frames. Either phone or fax may be used for research on businesses, but

---

[23]Lisa A. Yorgey, "Reaching Expectant and New Mums," *Target Marketing* 23 (March 2000), pp. 60–63.

[24]All those who think unsolicited mail is a bother, however, can contact the Direct Marketing Association (see www.the-dma.org), a trade group of over 4,600 direct-mail marketing firms (commercial and non-profit, U.S. and 53 nations abroad), and that organization will remove the name from every member's list.

phones are much more successful than faxes for consumer research. E-mail-administered questionnaires are similar to mail questionnaires when it comes to sampling control. The sample, of course, is limited to those who own or have access to a computer and an e-mail account. However, if an accurate, applicable, and readily available list of e-mail addresses exists, e-mail allows a geographically dispersed sample to be used. For many populations of interest, though, generating a list of relevant e-mail addresses is difficult. While the gap is closing, people who use e-mail and the Internet are still more affluent and better educated than the general population, and many, many marketers are in the business of selling their wares to the general population.

It is conceptually difficult, but practically possible to achieve sampling control for the administration of questions using personal interviews. For some select populations (for example, doctors, architects, or businesses), a list of population elements from which a sample can be drawn may be readily available in association or trade directories. For studies focused on consumers in which in-house interviews are to be conducted, however, few lists are available, and those available are typically badly out of date. What is often done for consumer research sampling households is to use area sampling procedures. (The general approach is discussed in a later chapter devoted to sampling issues.) For now, simply be aware that it involves the substitution of areas (for example, zip codes) and dwelling units (apartment buildings) instead of people as the sampling units. The substitution offers the advantage of accurate, current lists of sampling units, in the form of maps, over the generally inaccurate or unavailable lists of people. There remains the problem of ensuring that the field interviewer contacted the right household and person, but the personal interview does afford some sampling control in directing the questionnaire to specific sample units.

A popular alternative for conducting personal interviews among consumers is to use mall intercepts. The technique involves exactly what the name implies: interviewers intercept or stop those passing by in a mall and ask if they would be willing to participate in a research study.[25] Those who agree are typically taken to the firm's interviewing facility that has been set up in the mall (such as a small, rented office), where the interview is conducted. With shopping mall intercepts, two issues affect the ability to direct the inquiry to a randomly determined respondent. First, although a great many people do shop at malls, almost one in four people does not. Moreover, only those who visit the particular mall in question have a chance of being included in the study. Second, a person's chances of being asked to participate depend on the likelihood of that person being in the mall. That, in turn, depends on the frequency with which he or she shops there and the time spent in the mall. Thus, in analyses, replies may be weighted by the reciprocal of the number of visits made to the mall in a set amount of time.[26]

---

[25]For general discussions of the mall intercept as a data-collection technique, see Alan J. Bush, Ronald F. Bush, and Henry C. K. Chen, "Method of Administration Effects in Mall Intercept Interviews," *Journal of the Market Research Society* 33 (October 1991), pp. 309–319.

[26]The weighting technique was suggested by Seymour Sudman, "Improving the Quality of Shopping Center Sampling," *Journal of Marketing Research* 17 (November 1980), pp. 423–431. For empirical assessments of the usefulness of the weighting, see Clifford Nowell and Linda P. Stanley, "Length-Biased Sampling in Mall Intercept Surveys," *Journal of Marketing Research* 28 (November 1991), pp. 475–479. For information on the relationship between mall shopping behavior and various demographic characteristics, see Abhik Roy, "Correlates of Mall Visit Frequency," *Journal of Retailing* 70 (Summer 1994), pp. 139–161.

Getting Cooperation   Directing the survey to a specific respondent is one thing; getting a response from that individual is quite another. In this respect, the personal interview affords the most sample control. With a personal interview, the respondent's identity is known, and thus there is little opportunity for anyone else to reply. The problem of nonresponse as a result of refusals to participate is also typically lower with personal interviews than with either telephone interviews or mail-administered questionnaires. Sometimes a problem occurs with potential respondents not being at home but this can often be handled by coming back at more appropriate times. Usually the principle holds that the more personal the appeal, the more difficult it is for a respondent to say no: malls are face-to-face and phone solicitations are person-to-person. Mail is the least personal, most anonymous channel, and many mail surveys end up in recycling bins, unless the topic is inherently interesting to the consumer, or perhaps if some incentive is offered to complete the survey. We say more about these factors later.

Telephone methods suffer from "not-at-homes" or "no-answers." In one very large study involving more than 259,000 telephone calls, it was found that over 34 percent of the calls resulted in a no-answer, a situation that may get worse with the increased popularity of such telephone devices as the answering machine and caller ID. However, call screening (that is, through answering machines or caller ID services) has not disabled telephone interviewing as much as one might have thought. While approximately 25 percent of U.S. households have caller ID, and 65 percent own answering machines, research firms generally can still get through to talk to a live consumer. Doing so simply requires persistence; more contact must be attempted.[27] Fortunately, calling back is much simpler and more economical than following up personal interviews. The relatively low expense of a telephone contact allows a number of follow-up calls to secure a needed response, whereas the high cost of field contact restricts the number of follow-ups that can be made in studies employing personal interviews.

As Table 7.6 also indicates, the probability of making contact with an eligible respondent on the first call was less than one in ten. In phone surveys, there are also known biases in the over-representation of larger households; that is, with more people in the house, there is simply a greater chance that someone will be home to pick up the phone and answer the survey.[28] Making sure the intended respondent replies is somewhat more difficult with telephone interviews than with personal interviews; often, researchers want the "male or female head of the household" to answer the questions, and not just any household member.

Mail questionnaires afford the researcher little control in securing a response from the intended respondent. The researcher can simply direct the questionnaire

---

[27]Roger A. Kerin and Robert A. Peterson, "Scheduling Telephone Interviews," *Journal of Advertising Research* 23 (April/May 1983), pp. 41–47; Peter Tuckel and Trish Shukers, "The Answering Machine Dilemma," *Marketing Research* 9 (Fall 1997), pp. 4–9; Michael W. Link and Robert W. Oldendick, "Call Screening: Is It Really a Problem for Survey Research?" *Public Opinion Quarterly* 63 (Winter 1999), pp. 577–589.

[28]Researchers suggest inversely weighting responses as a function of household size; see Andrew Gelman and Thomas C. Little, "Improving on Probability Weighting for Household Size," *Public Opinion Quarterly* 62 (Fall 1998), pp. 398–404.

| TABLE 7.6 | **Results of First Dialing Attempts** | |

Result	*Number of Dialings*	*Probability of Occurrence*
No answer	89,829	.347
No eligible person	75,285	.291
Out-of-service	52,632	.203
At home	25,465	.098
Business	10,578	.041
Busy	5,299	.020
Refusal	3,707	.014 (.146)*
Completion	21,758	.084 (.854)*
Total	284,553	1.000

*Probability of occurrence given eligible individual is at home.
Based on Roger A. Kerin and Robert A. Peterson, "Scheduling Telephone Interviews," *Journal of Advertising Research* 23 (April/May 1983), p. 44.

to the designated respondent and offer the individual some incentive for cooperating.[29] However, the researcher cannot control that cooperation. Many persons refuse to respond. Often only those most interested in the survey topic will respond. Some people are incapable of responding because they are illiterate; it is hardly any wonder that people who have difficulty with everyday tasks such as reading job notices or getting a driver's license would not respond to a mail questionnaire. Whatever the reason, the nonresponse may cause a bias of indeterminate direction and magnitude.

E-mail- or Web-administered questionnaires are somewhat better in these respects. For one thing, literacy is not a problem because those owning and using computers are typically better educated. Moreover, there is much less likelihood that someone other than the intended respondents will reply, given that the questionnaires reside in personal e-mail accounts. Although fax surveys provide less control in terms of who responds, they too are less subject to literacy problems because those who have access to and use fax machines are typically better educated.

Generally, regardless of the method of survey administration, marketing researchers have noted the steady decline in sample cooperation. It has been suggested that higher compensations may be required to obtain responses. Greater incentives would drive up costs of research or tempt researchers to be frugal on sample size. Yet one consistent finding is that potential respondents are more likely to participate in the study if the research topic is inherently interesting to them—intrinsic interest exceeds extrinsic incentives in raising response rates. Enhanced databases may enable greater tailoring so that consumers are contacted only on

[29]See Paul L. Erdos, *Professional Mail Surveys* (Malabar, FL: Kreiger, 1983); Donald A. Dillman, "The Design and Administration of Mail Surveys," *Annual Review of Sociology* 17 (1991), pp. 225–249; or Pamela L. Alreck and Robert B. Settle, *The Survey Research Handbook,* 2nd ed. (Chicago: Irwin, 1995), for a discussion of the problem of sample control in mail surveys and what can be done to overcome respondent resistance.

topics relevant to them, and not en masse. Other solutions will continue to evolve. For example, it has been suggested that for e-commerce, filling out a survey may become part of the cost of an online service provider. Even so, the captured audience is self-selected on intrinsic interests (in venturing to the particular Web site), so they might not perceive the cost of filling out a survey as particularly high. Other implications may be that more contact attempts may be required before locating willing respondents. Finally, statistical solutions are also evolving; it has been suggested that to compensate for nonrespondents, post-survey adjustments of the data may be required.[30]

Information Control

Just as we had compared communication and observation techniques on the versatility of the methods, that is, the kinds of data one might obtain, the differing methods of communication-based data collection (person, phone, and fax) also vary in the type of questions that can be asked, and the amount and accuracy of the information that can be obtained from respondents.

The personal interview can be conducted using almost any form of questionnaire: structured or unstructured, disguised or undisguised. The interaction allows the interviewer to present pictures or examples of advertisements, lists of words, scales, and so on, as stimuli to which the respondents would react. The consumer can taste new flavors of Pepperidge Farm cookies, or smell new line extensions of Michael Jordan colognes. Visual aids can be used with mail questionnaires, but the use of the telephone rules out much.

Personal interviews allow the use of open-ended questions that require extensive probes. Written questionnaires using mail, e-mail, or fax do not lend themselves to such questions. Telephone interviews can incorporate open-ended questions, but not nearly to the same extent as in-person interviews, mostly because phone surveys need to be brief, so as not to be discontinued by an increasingly bored or irritated respondent midway through the survey.

Personal interviews also allow the automatic, contingent sequencing of questions; for example, if the answer to question 4 is positive, the interviewer may be instructed to proceed to ask questions 5 and 6, whereas if the answer had been negative, the interviewer asks questions 7 and 8. Automatic sequencing is also possible with telephone interviews, especially when the interviewer is reading from a computer screen and the question skipping is preprogrammed. Skipping questions is not advised for mail questionnaires, e-mail, or fax because respondents will get confused and make errors. Web surveys can easily be programmed to contain skip

---

[30]Seymour Sudman and Edward Blair, "Sampling in the 21st Century," *Journal of the Academy of Marketing Science* 27 (Spring 1999), pp. 269–277; Tracy L. Tuten, Michael Bosnjak, and Wolfgang Bandilla, "Banner-Advertised Web Surveys," *Marketing Research* 11 (Spring 2000), pp. 16–21. In business-to-business surveys also, the content of the survey is the clearest determinant of response rates and data quality. Day of week that the survey is sent had little effect; see Thomas V. Greer, Nuchai Chuchinprakam, and Sudhindra Seshadri, "Likelihood of Participating in Mail Survey Research," *Industrial Marketing Management* 29 (March 2000), pp. 97–119.

patterns. There is also a greater danger of "sequence bias" with mail, e-mail, and faxed questionnaires than with questionnaires administered in person or over the phone. That is, respondents can see the whole questionnaire, and thus their replies to any single question may not be independently arrived at but may be conditioned by their previous responses. For example, if you present a print ad on page one, and on page three ask memory questions about the ad and the brand featured and its attributes, the respondent could, and likely would, flip back to page one, fill in your questions dutifully, but in so doing, destroy the validity of those questions for recall.

On the other hand, mail, e-mail, Web, or fax questionnaires allow respondents to work at their own pace. This may produce more thoughtful responses than would be obtained in personal or telephone interviews, where a certain urgency is associated with giving a response. A thought-out response, however, is no guarantee of an appropriate reply. If the question is ambiguous, self-administered surveys offer no opportunity for clarification.

The anonymity associated with a mailed questionnaire does afford people an opportunity to be more frank on certain sensitive issues (such as sexual behavior). Because replies to e-mail can often be traced to the sender, there is less anonymity with e-mail than with mail or faxed questionnaires. The jury is not officially in, but early reports suggest respondents feel a great deal of anonymity when answering Web surveys, and so again may answer questions more truthfully.

Both personal and telephone interviews can cause interviewer bias because of the respondent's perception of the interviewer or because different interviewers ask questions and probe in different ways. This kind of bias does not occur for mail, e-mail, or faxed questionnaires. Both of these biases also can be controlled relatively easily in telephone surveys. There are fewer interviewer actions to which the respondent can react, and a supervisor can be present during telephone interviews to ensure that they are being conducted consistently. It is typically more difficult, though, to establish rapport over the phone than in person. The respondent in a telephone interview often demands more information about the purposes of the study, the credentials of the interviewer and research organization, and so on.

With regard to length of questionnaire or amount of information to be collected, the rule of thumb is that long questionnaires can be handled best by personal interview, next best by written formats (mail, Web, fax, e-mail), and least well by telephone interview. So much depends on the topic of inquiry, the form of the questionnaire, and the approach used to secure cooperation that this advice should be interpreted carefully.

As with so many matters, computers are changing the way surveys are conducted. They were first used in the early 1970s to assist with telephone interviews. The early systems linked mainframe computers or minicomputers to cathode-ray tube terminals (CRTs). Their essential function was to present on the terminal the questions that normally would have been on a paper questionnaire. Interviewers would read the questions as they came up on the screen and would enter respondents' answers directly on the keyboard. The early systems generated such substantial savings in time and resources that they spawned a virtual revolution in data collection. Partly because of the advantages that accrue with computer administration of questionnaires, telephone interviews have become the most popular data-collection technique.

Currently, there are two essential applications of computer-aided interviewing (CAI) software:

1. Telephone surveys in which each interviewer has a personal computer from which to ask questions (see Table 7.7 for more on Computerized Adaptive Telephone Interviewing, or CATI)

2. In-person interviews in which the interviewer transports a portable laptop computer to the interview site and uses it to interview the respondent, or places the computer in front of the respondent and lets the respondent answer questions as they appear on the screen

One of the most important advantages of computer-assisted interviewing is the information control it allows. First, the computer displays each question exactly as

---

TABLE 7.7   **Common Features in Computerized Adaptive Telephone Interviewing (CATI) Software**

Questionnaire writing system: This system helps the researcher create a computer-administered questionnaire. The software capabilities generally include the construction of complex skip patterns and logic branches, in which different answers to a question direct respondents to different parts of the questionnaire; randomization of questions and answer alternatives; construction of long lists; insertion of previous answers into the text of the current question; and consistency checks.

Call management system: This system serves two functions: (1) it builds the sample database by manually typing in the sample or by transferring the sample from an existing database; (2) it controls the flow of sample to the interviewing stations. It ensures that call-backs are made when scheduled, that busy numbers are redialed after a preset delay, that time zones are recognized, and that no part of the sample is overworked.

Quota control system: This system allows quota cells to be defined (for example, the number of women in Atlanta, the number of men in New York City) and quota limits to be placed on the cells. The system tracks the quota while interviewing is in progress, closing out completed cells. In conjunction with the call management system, it prevents a sample corresponding to a closed cell from being sent to the interviewing stations.

Call disposition monitoring system: This system tracks each call attempt by its disposition (no answer, busy, immediate refusal, failed to qualify, call-back, complete, and so on), thereby tracking interviewing progress. It is also used to calculate the incidence of qualified respondents so that it can be compared with the incidence that was assumed in constructing the cost quotation for the study.

Interviewer system: In addition to displaying the questionnaire for the interviewer system, CATI systems may determine which call to attempt next, provide call history information for the call before it is placed, dial the telephone number, automatically reschedule a "no answer" for another attempt, automatically determine when "busy" numbers are to be redialed, aid in scheduling call-backs, assist with assigning the call disposition codes, and increment the quota count for completed interviews. These features can eliminate most of the standard paperwork for the interviewer.

Reporting system: A valuable aspect of a CATI system is its ability to generate accurate and timely reports, including quota reports, call disposition reports, incidence reports, top-line reports of respondent data, and interviewer productivity reports. Automatic reporting increases supervisor productivity and the overall quality of the data collection. Less time is spent compiling reports and more time is spent on their interpretation and supervising the interviewing. Reports also give the study director and analysts an indication of whether the study is progressing according to plan.

Analysis capabilities: Some CATI systems also include an integrated cross-tabulation and statistics package which allow analyses to be performed with a minimum of spec writing and retyping of text for annotating tables.

Source: Based on Joseph Curry, "Computer-Assisted Telephone Interviewing: Technology and Organizational Management" (Ketchum, ID: Sawtooth Software, 1987), pp. 7–9. For general overviews of the effect of CATI systems, see William E. Saris, *Computer-Assisted Interviewing* (Thousand Oaks, CA: Sage, 1991). For an annotated bibliography, see Edith D. deLeeuw and Joop J. Hox, "Computer-Assisted Data Collection Data Quality and Costs: An Annotated Bibliography," *The Survey Statistician* 32 (1995), pp. 5–10.

the researcher intended (and had programmed). It will show only the questions and information that the respondent should see. Further, it will display the next question only when an acceptable answer to the current one is entered on the keyboard. For example, if a respondent says that he or she bought a brand that is not available in that particular locale, the computer can be programmed to reject the answer, which greatly simplifies skipping or branching procedures. The interviewer does not have to grapple with selecting the next question given the response to the current one; the computer does this automatically. This saves considerable time and confusion in administering the questionnaire and permits a more natural flow to the interview. It also ensures that there will be no variation in the sequence in which the questions are asked. Information control also manifests itself in the following:

1.   *Personalization of the questions.* During the course of the interview, the computer sorts all previous responses (such as name of spouse, cars owned, supermarket patronized) and can then customize the wording of subsequent questions—for example, "When your wife, Ann, shops at the Acme, does she usually use the Fiat or the Buick?" Such personalized questions can enhance rapport and thus provide for higher-quality interviews.

2.   *Customized questionnaires.* Key information elicited early in the interview can be used to customize the questionnaire for each respondent. For example, only product attributes previously acknowledged by respondents as determinants of their decisions would be used to measure their brand perceptions, rather than using a more exhaustive list of attributes common to all respondents.

In addition to the enhanced branching abilities and personalization of the questionnaires that they allow, computer-assisted interviews often produce increased accuracy in the results. As was stated previously for Web surveys (but not for e-mails), the evidence suggests that people are more truthful when responding to a computer than to an interviewer or even when completing a self-administered, paper-and-pencil questionnaire. They seem to think that the computer is less judgmental and provides them greater anonymity.

Computer-assisted interviewing also speeds the data collection and processing tasks. The preliminary tabulations of the answers are available at a moment's notice, because the replies are already stored in memory. One does not have the typical two- to three-week delay caused by coding and data entry that happens when questionnaires are completed by hand.

Even though computers have had a profound effect on interviewing techniques, they are not a panacea. There are limits to what the machines can do. They cannot win over respondents with social chitchat or explain questions that are misunderstood. Unless the interviewees are good typists, the computers can't elicit lengthy responses. Computers are incapable of recognizing fuzzy or superficial answers and they cannot prod respondents to elaborate or answer other follow-up questions. The computer systems that ask questions by phone with mechanical voices have raised the ire of some people who consider unsolicited, randomly dialed calls an invasion of privacy; luckily these surveys seem to have declined in usage. E-mail or Web administration can be used only among those likely to own or have access to a PC. These techniques can be quite useful in industrial marketing surveys, because most business people have access to PCs and faxes, but they are more limited in general consumer surveys unless the product or service at issue involves a population likely to own such technologies (for example, consumer reaction to a new software program, or fax feature).

Administrative Control

One of the greatest advantages of Internet surveys is that they provide the marketing researcher the quickest turnaround. Half of e-mail surveys are typically completed and returned the same day they were sent. It can take two weeks to achieve that same response rate using the postal service. Telephone surveys, Web surveys, and faxes offer the next-quickest ways of obtaining information. Regarding phone surveys, a number of calls can be made from a central exchange in a short period, perhaps 15 to 20 per hour per interviewer if the questionnaire is short. By comparison, an in-home personal interview affords no such time economies, because of dead time between each interview while the interviewer travels to the next respondent. (If the researcher wishes to speed up the replies secured with in-home personal interviews or phone interviews, the number of interviewers must be increased, which raises costs and interviewer variation.)

While the mail questionnaire represents a standardized stimulus and thus allows little variation in administration, it also affords little speed control. It often takes a couple of weeks to secure the bulk of the replies, at which time a follow-up mailing is often begun. The followup will also involve a time lapse of several weeks for the questionnaires to reach the respondents, be completed, and be returned. Depending on the number of follow-up mailings required, the total time needed to conduct a good mail study can often be substantial. Of course, with mail or other self-administered questionnaires, the time required to secure a great many replies with a very large sample is little different from the time necessary for a small sample. This is not so with personal and telephone interviews, where there is a direct relationship between the number of interviews and the time required to complete them.

In-home personal interviews tend to be the most expensive per completed contact (followed by phone surveys), and the e-mail and Web questionnaires tend to be the cheapest (followed by mail interviews), but the topic and procedures of the study can change the relative cost picture dramatically. For example, the per-contact cost of the mail questionnaire is generally low. However, if nonresponse is substantial, the cost per return may be quite high. Faxing can be expensive if many of the destination recipients are long-distance. For the most part, though, the telephone, mall, and in-home personal interview methods require progressively larger field staffs. The larger the field staff, the greater the problems of control. Good quality control costs money, and that is why the personal interview in the home is typically the most expensive data-collection method.

Table 7.8 presents the results of several studies that compared the turnaround times, response rates, and costs of a variety of methods of administering questionnaires. The table shows response rates for "traditional" research methods (mail, phone, mall, door-to-door) as well as some newer techniques (fax, e-mail, Web). Note the differences in response rates and in turnaround times and cost, and also

TABLE 7.8	**Comparing Methods of Administering Questionnaires**

The following table shows the comparisons among traditional techniques (door-to-door, mall, phone, mail) to newer, electronic techniques (fax, e-mail, Web) in terms of response notes, completion times, and costs.

	Technique						
	Door-to-Door	*Mall*	*Phone*	*Mail*	*Fax*	*E-mail**	*Web*
Response rates	15%	29%	75%	35–63%	25%	8–37%	26%
% bad addresses				0–19%	41%	19–20%	24%
Response time in days (mean)				13–18	9	4–6	7
Days (median)				12	12	2	5
# Days to receive 45% responses				13		1	
# Days to receive 80% responses				28		9	
Fixed costs				$59	$57	$57	$57
Unit cost				$1.56	$0.56	$0.01	$0.01
Variable costs (200 surveys sent)				$312	$112	$2	$2
Total cost				$371	$169	$59	$59

*Response rates for e-mail surveys that are embedded in the text of the e-mail tend to run 20 to 25%. When the recipient must open an attached file, response rates dropped to 8%. No differences were found in the content of the responses, but attached surveys were considered more attractive and easier to fill out.

Source: The indices in this table were compiled from the following sources: *Respondent Cooperation and Industry Image Survey* (Port Jefferson, NY: The Council for Marketing and Opinion Research, 1996); Rick Weible and John Wallace, "Cyber Research: The Impact of the Internet on Data Collection," *Marketing Research* 10 (Fall 1998), pp. 18–24; Duane P. Bachmann, John Elfrink, and Gary Vazzana, "E-mail and Snail Mail Face Off in Rematch," *Marketing Research* 11 (Spring 2000), pp. 10–15; also see Alan C. B. Tse, "Comparing the Response Rate, Response Speed and Response Quality of Two Methods of Sending Questionnaires," *Journal of the Market Research Society* 40 (October 1998), pp. 353–361; Curt J. Dommeyer and Elanor Moriarty, "Comparing Two Forms of an E-Mail Survey: Embedded vs. Attached," *International Journal of Market Research* 42 (Winter 2000), pp. 39–50.

between e-mail surveys in which the surveys had been embedded versus those contained in an attached file. As suggested previously, the attachment requires more effort (that is, opening the file) than checking off responses and returning an e-mail, and sure enough, response rates are lower for the attachments.

Each method of data collection has its uses, and none is superior in all situations.[31] The research problem as finally defined will often suggest one approach over the others, but the researcher should recognize that the approaches often can be used most productively in combination. For example, a trial product may be sent by regular mail or picked up at a mall, with a phone or Web survey following up to assess the consumer's reaction.

Many researchers worry that Internet samples are still peculiar, in part due to differential access to e-mail and the Web. Indeed, even as that chasm tightens, there may still be self-selection biases. Worse, the novelty of an e-mail or Web survey is starting to wear off, and response rates are beginning to plummet. Nevertheless, at least for the near future, due to the fact that e-mail surveys (embedded and attached) and Web surveys are so quick and so cheap (no real costs other than labor), and the quality of

[31]For general references on conducting telephone, mail, or personal interview surveys, see James H. Frey and Sabine Martens Oishi, *How to Conduct Interviews by Telephone and in Person* (Thousand Oaks, CA: Sage, 1995); Thomas W. Mangione, *Mail Surveys* (Thousand Oaks, CA: Sage, 1995).

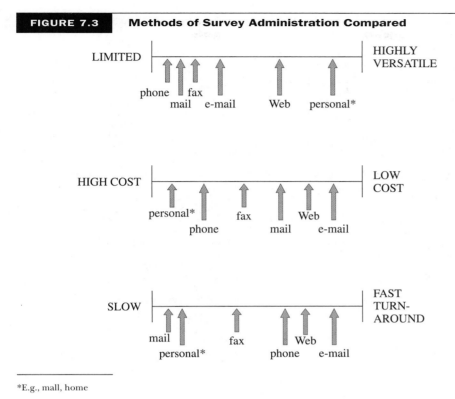

FIGURE 7.3   Methods of Survey Administration Compared

*E.g., mall, home

the data is consistently being compared equitably to standard techniques, e-mail and Web surveys are here to stay. Software is available that facilitates writing online surveys and capturing their results.[32]

Figure 7.3 summarizes the logistics comparisons between these major methods of administering questionnaires. Table 7.9 elaborates on the overall strengths and weaknesses of these methods.

Methods of Observation

Observation is a fact of everyday life. We are constantly observing other people and events as a means of securing information about the world around us. Admittedly, some people make more productive use of those observations than others. Consider the story of William Benton, one of the cofounders of the Benton and Boles advertising agency,[33] concerning his walk along a street in Chicago during a hot day in 1929.

---

[32]Diane K. Bowers, "FAQs on Online Research," *Marketing Research* 10 (Spring 1999), pp. 45–48; Dana James, "Precision Decision," *Marketing News* (September 27, 1999), pp. 23–25. Online surveys may even help maintain relationships with channel partners; see Tricia Campbell, "High-Speed Surveys," *Sales and Marketing Management* 152 (February 2000), pp. 30–32. For a review of providers of software to write Web surveys, see Nelson King, "What Are They Thinking," *PC Magazine* (February 8, 2000), pp. 163–178.

[33]Now D'Arcy, Masius, Benton & Bowles (see www.dmbb.com).

| TABLE 7.9 | Primary Communication Methods of Data Collection: Advantages (+) and Disadvantages (−) |

Personal Interview (At Home or Mall)
Sampling control
+ High response rates; best for getting response from specific, identified person
− Generally narrow distribution, difficult to identify sampling frame
Information control
+ Allows use of any type of question; sequencing of questions is easily changed; allows probing using open-ended questions; allows clarification of ambiguous questions; permits easy use of visuals and other sensory stimuli; mall interview needs to be shorter than at-home interview
− Subject to interviewer bias; interviewer supervision difficult to maintain (though easier in mall than at home)
Administrative control
− Generally most expensive method (at home even more than at mall); relatively slow (though mall is quicker)

Written Formats (Mail, Fax, Web, E-mail)
Sampling control
+ May be only method able to reach certain respondents; sampling frame easily developed when mailing lists are available; wide distribution possible
− Low response rates; little control in securing response from specific individual; cannot control respondent's speed of survey completion
Information control
+ Not subject to interviewer bias; respondents work at their own pace; ensures anonymity; best for personal, sensitive questions
− Researcher cannot explain ambiguous questions; does not allow probing; difficult to change sequence of questions; respondents can view entire questionnaire as they respond
Administrative control
+ Generally least expensive; very short response time for e-mail
− Long response time for mail

Telephone
Sampling control
+ Relatively strong response rates; wide distribution possible
− Difficult to establish representative sampling frame due to unlisted numbers
Information control
+ Less interviewer bias than in person, and interviewer supervision is stronger; sequence of questions is easily changed
− Cannot use visual aids; more difficult to establish rapport over the phone than in person
Administrative control
+ Relatively low cost; quick turnaround; little difficulty and cost in handling call-backs; allows easy use of computer support
− Interview must be brief

Since it was hot, most of the windows were open, so he could hear the radios in the apartments he passed. What he mainly heard were the voices of the actors in *Amos and Andy,* one of the leading comedy programs at that time. Struck by this, Benton retraced his steps, this time counting the radios he could hear. He counted 23 of them in all, and found that 21 were tuned to *Amos and Andy.* Rushing back to his advertising firm, Benton suggested that they advertise one of their clients' products, Pepsodent toothpaste, on *Amos and Andy.* The sales of Pepsodent took off like a rocket, all because of Benton's first audience survey of radio listeners.[34]

Observation is also a tool of scientific inquiry. When used for that purpose, however, the observations are more systematically planned and recorded so that

---

[34]Edward Cornish, "Telecommunications: What's Coming," paper delivered at the American Marketing Association's 1982 Annual Conference held in San Francisco, CA, June 14–17.

they relate to the specific phenomenon of interest. Although planned, they do not have to be sophisticated to be effective. For example, researchers watched consumers buy dog food. They found that adults bought the dog food, but that senior citizens and children bought dog treats. They learned that the elderly want to treat their pets as one might treat children, and that children may not appreciate the responsibility of feeding the dog, but they can understand giving the dog a treat, just as a child wants a cookie. Unfortunately for these no-longer-flexible adults and the vertically challenged children, the treats were usually stocked on the top-most shelf. These researchers' cameras "witnessed one elderly woman using a box of aluminum foil to knock down her brand of dog biscuits." When the retail grocer moved the treats to where children and older people could reach more easily, sales soared overnight.[35]

Observation offers the researcher a number of possible approaches. Like communication methods, observational data may be gathered employing structured or unstructured methods that are either disguised or undisguised. Further, as Figure 7.1 shows (on page 268), the observations may be made in a contrived or a natural setting and may be secured by a human or mechanical observer.

Structured–Unstructured Observation

The distinction here is analogous to that for communication methods. Structured observation applies when the problem has been defined precisely enough to permit a clear specification of the behaviors that will be observed and the categories that will be used to record and analyze the observations. Unstructured observation is used for studies in which the formulation of the problem is not specific; a great deal of flexibility is allowed the observers in terms of what they note and record. For example, by peering from catwalks built above the stores, researchers for Marsh Supermarkets discovered to their dismay that people shopped heavily the periphery of the store—the produce, dairy, and meat sections—but often bypassed the central dry-goods section that accounted for the bulk of the store space.[36]

To distinguish between structured and unstructured observation, consider a study investigating the amount of deliberation and search that goes into a soup purchase. On the one hand, the observers could be instructed to stand at one end of a supermarket aisle and record each sample customer's deliberation and search. This might produce the following record: "Purchaser first paused in front of the Campbell's brand. He looked at the price on the shelf, then picked up a can of Campbell's, glanced at its picture and its list of ingredients, and set it back down again. He then checked the label and price for Progresso. He set that back down again, and after a slight pause, picked up a different flavor can of Campbell's than he originally looked at, placed it in his cart, and moved down the aisle." On the other hand, observers might simply be told to record the first soup can examined, the total number of cans picked up by any customer, and the time in seconds that the customer spent in front of the soup shelves by checking the appropriate boxes in the observation form. The second situation represents more structure than the first.

---

[35]Paco Underhill, *Why We Buy: The Science of Shopping* (New York: Touchstone, 2000), p. 18.

[36]Michael J. McCarthy, "James Bond Hits the Supermarket: Stores Snoop on Shoppers' Habits to Boost Sales," *The Wall Street Journal* (August 25, 1993), pp. B1, B5.

To use the more structured approach, it would have been necessary to previously decide precisely what was to be observed and the specific categories and units that would be used to record the observations. These decisions presuppose specific hypotheses (for example, based on secondary data, managerial experience as account manager, or even intelligent guesswork), and the structured approach is again more appropriate for descriptive and causal studies. The unstructured approach would be useful in generating insights into the relevant dimensions of deliberation and search behavior. It would not be appropriate, however, for testing hypotheses about this kind of behavior, because of the many different kinds of behaviors that could be recorded and the difficulty of coding and quantifying the data in a consistent manner.

One way to develop consistency in coding is to use multiple coders who are extremely well trained. This technique is used, for example, in observational studies examining the patterns of interactions between married couples in making selections of large household expenditures at electronics and appliances stores, such as the purchase of a large-screen TV or a washer and dryer. The observers record verbatim the verbal exchanges between the couple when making the choice. The coders then assess which party initiated the selection, the response of the other party, and the content and tone of the communication, including the occurrence of any unpleasant consequences, such as arguments. The aim of such studies is to determine which party dominates the purchase choice in a given category and whether both parties appear to be satisfied.

The advantages and disadvantages of structure in observation are similar to those in communication. Structuring the observation reduces the potential for bias and increases the reliability of observations. However, the reduction in bias may be accompanied by a loss of validity, since the number of seconds spent in deliberation or the number of cans of soup picked up and examined may not represent the complete story of deliberation and search. What about the effort spent simply looking at what is available but not picking anything up, or the discussion between husband and wife about which TV set to select? A well-trained, highly qualified observer might be able to interpret these kinds of behavior and relate them in a meaningful way to search and deliberation.

Although the marketing manager's observations can be valuable for self-edification purposes, for the serious data-collection effort, as with any marketing research, it is probably best to hire an expert (for example, a marketing researcher trained in anthropology), to minimize the biases that a brand manager is likely to have that the objective, neutral party would not. Much like the interview communication technique, most of what you pay for in hiring marketing research experts is not their time nor even the logistics of sending them to the field to observe. Their added value comes from their training, their experience, and their ability to look at the same event that anyone else can look at, but to discern what is really going on. Their talents in making inferences about consumer behavior and the interpretations they offer are what yields insight from observational analyses. They are trained to minimize their own biases, but indeed, they are human, and some will slip in. The alternative is to use some nonhuman mechanical device to make observations. However, (a) some human decisions still are made (such as where to place the camera in the store), and (b) a machine cannot offer any interpretation.

Unstructured observation is well-suited for exploratory research—just what does the customer do? For example, researchers wanted to see how women used body lotion. They thought direct observation might be too intrusive, so they video-taped the product use in action. They found two groups of women: one group "slapped on the lotion, rubbing it briskly into their skin." The other group "caressed their skin as they applied it." Querying the women, the researchers found that the first group saw the lotion as a restorative for dry skin. The second group sought the benefit of imparting softness and moisture to their skin.[37]

Structured observation can be quite precise as a follow-up method of inquiry. For example, State Farm Insurance began with secondary data and its compilation of accident reports, and created the list of the "10 Most Dangerous Intersections." They then sent researchers to those sites to try to piece together possible suggestions and solutions to the troublesome spots. Their work helped promote road safety and contributed to enhancing State Farm's perception in consumers' eyes that it is a premier automobile insurer.[38]

Disguised–Undisguised Observation

Disguise in observational methods refers to whether or not the consumers know they are being observed. In the search and deliberation study, observers may assume a position well out of the way so shoppers are not aware that their behavior is being observed. In some cases, the disguise is accomplished by observers becoming part of the situation, with the other participants unaware of this role. For example, some firms use paid observers disguised as shoppers, that is, "mystery shoppers," to evaluate sales service and the attitudes and courtesy of the employees. Hilton Hotels supplement guest and employee surveys with reports from secret shoppers to diagnose which features of the customer experience at the hotel (for example, the check-in process or the cleanliness of the bathrooms) should be high priority for redesign and improvement.[39]

The observer's presence is disguised, of course, to control the tendency for people to behave differently when they know their actions are being watched. Several issues can be raised about the disguised observation, though. First, it is often very difficult to disguise an observation completely. Second, identifying oneself as a research worker often increases one's ability to secure other relevant information, such as background data. Third, it raises the issue of under what circumstances disguised observation is ethical.[40]

Disguised observations may be made directly or indirectly. An observer stationed at the checkout counter counting the number of cans of each brand of soup being purchased would be engaged in direct observation. However, an observer

[37]Bill Abrams, *The Observational Research Handbook: Understanding How Consumers Live with Your Product* (Chicago: AMA and NTC, 2000), p. 105.

[38]Faith Russell, "Dangerous Intersections," *Marketing News* (February 28, 2000), p. 18.

[39]Dieter Huckestein and Robert Duboff, "Hilton Hotels," *Cornell Hotel and Restaurant Administration Quarterly* (August 1999), pp. 28–38; Paula Kephart, "The Spy in Aisle 3," *American Demographics* 18 (May 1996), pp. 16, 19.

[40]Patricia A. Adler and Peter Adler, "Observational Techniques," in Norman K. Denzin and Yvonna S. Lincoln, eds., *Collecting and Interpreting Qualitative Materials* (Thousand Oaks, CA: Sage, 1998), pp. 79–109.

who counted inventory on hand by brand at the end of each day and adjusted the results for additions to inventory would be engaged in indirect observation. The key is that instead of observing the behavior itself, the researcher is observing the effects or results of that behavior.

There are many types of indirect observation.[41] One could, for example, estimate measures of share of market for the various brands of soup by conducting pantry audits. In a pantry audit, respondents' homes would be visited and permission would be sought to examine the pantry inventory and determine the presence and amount of various brands of soups. Although one would typically not incur the expense of an audit for a single product, the audit could be used to advantage to assess consumption of a prespecified set of products. For example, recently marketing researchers have taken the philosophy that part of understanding how consumers use a particular product (for example, peanut butter) can be determined by the other products they buy and use with it (such as jelly, chocolate, bananas, and crackers). The inventory of kitchen cabinets and refrigerators would demonstrate clearly the co-ownership of complementary products.

Pantries are not the only focus for an audit: researchers have inventoried or photographed the contents of consumers' refrigerators, their medicine cabinets, their closets, and their garages. Photos of a medicine cabinet will indicate not only what products it contains, and what brands and sizes, but also their arrangement—that which is stored front and center is probably used most frequently.

Researchers for *Gourmet* magazine have moved right into their readers' homes to "look into their cabinets," "pore over their Visa bills," or "snip labels out of their clothes." *Gourmet* is especially trying to understand its younger readers—readers who are affluent, knowledgeable about food trends, and know hot restaurants and fine wines. A sample of readers were given disposable cameras and asked to take photos of cherished household belongings. Knowing what customers treasure can yield insight into cross-selling opportunities, or even subtle messages in ads to appeal to this target group by indicating an understanding of their values.[42]

Observation methods are proving to be especially useful for marketers to learn about tastes and preferences of different ethnic groups. Rather than creating a survey that might not be in the respondent's first language, or worrying about translations and back-translations, researchers can simply watch what these consumers do, or they can go to their households and snoop around their kitchens (with permission, of course!). For example, consumer packaged goods manufacturers from General Mills to Procter & Gamble are testing bilingual packaging and are asking Hispanic and Asian women what they serve their families. These inquiries are highly motivating because these segments are under-served, and any relevant product offerings are hugely successful; for example, when Frito-Lay extended its Doritos snack chip line to include Salsa Verde and Flamin' Hot Sabrositos, targeting Hispanic consumers, sales were hugely successful, topping $100 million within one year after the new flavor introductions. In a pantry audit of Hispanic households, one is more

---

[41]For insight into some of the many ingenious ways that have been developed to make indirect measurements by observation, see Eugene J. Webb, Donald T. Campbell, and Richard D. Swartz, eds., *Unobtrusive Measures* (Thousand Oaks, CA: Sage, 1999).

[42]Tony Case, "Getting Personal," *Brandweek* 41 (March 6, 2000), pp. M52–M54.

likely to find eggs, fish and other seafood, and beef than in non-Hispanic households, and less likely to find sugars and sweets. They also inventory more because Hispanic families do not eat out as frequently as non-Hispanic households.[43]

Over the years, many innovative, indirect measures of behavior have been used:

- A car dealer in Chicago checked the position of the radio dial of each car brought in for service. The dealer then used this as a proxy for share of listening audience in deciding upon the stations on which to advertise.

- The number of different fingerprints on a page has been used to assess the readership of various ads in a magazine, and the age and condition of the cars in the parking lot has been used to gauge the affluence of the group patronizing the outlet.

- Scuff marks on museum floor tile have long been used as a means of measuring the popularity of the display.

- Consumers have been watched through one-way mirrors trying to assemble a PC from right out of the box to surfing on the Net (and no, they don't tend to read the instructions).

For more examples of observational techniques in marketing research, see Research Realities 7.2.

Observation is often more useful than surveys in sorting fact from fiction with respect to behaviors, particularly "desirable" behaviors. For example, most people would not want to acknowledge that they spend more on cat food than on baby food, but consumers can be observed doing so. In another study, asking parents whether the color of a new toy would matter, the parents uniformly said no. At the end of the study, as a token of their participation, the parents were offered a toy to take home to their child, and all the parents clamored for the purple and blue toys.

Observation can be helpful in designing store layout and operations. For example, to try to understand why a new frozen baby food was underperforming relative to expectations, a researcher hung out where that product was sold and noticed that children got finicky in the frozen-food sections because they were cold, so mothers would rush down that aisle. The researcher was able to persuade managers to place smaller freezer units in the regular (warmer climate) baby-food aisles. Sales were then quite successful. Or consider that over 90 percent of furniture shoppers are couples, and potential purchases are most likely if one of the parties is in the store at least ten minutes. The woman may be looking over the "fluffed pillows and floral duvets," but if the spouse pulls her away, the sale is lost. As a result, some furniture stores are being retrofit with entertainment centers where sports fans can watch live events via cable.[44]

Videotaping is an especially useful technology for marketing research observations. Sometimes it is used in conjunction with mall intercept interviews by the marketing researcher conducting the ethnography. For example, grocery shoppers videotaped purchasing beef have been engaged in conversation to see whether they

[43]Roberta Bernstein, "Food for Thought," *American Demographics* 22 (May 2000), pp. 39–42.

[44]Joshua Macht, "The New Market Research," *Inc* 20 (July 1998), pp. 86–94.

RESEARCH REALITIES 7.2

Additional Examples of Observational and Ethnographical Marketing Research

1. Researchers can evaluate the "servicescape," the atmosphere and "feeling" a store radiates. Such qualitative observations can be informative to management about the image that is portrayed in preparation for repositioning a chain or a local provider. In a complementary manner, researchers can assess customers' expectations and desires using interviews and then use observational techniques to see if any retailers are currently providing the service sought. For example, in a study of women shopping for bridal gowns and related paraphernalia, researchers found that some women expected to use the bridal salon retailers as "clearinghouses." In interviews, such customers would say, "I like brides' magazines . . . What I did is look in there and got a good idea of what I wanted and went from there . . . I would look at the magazine and pick out what I wanted and then take it to the stores and say, 'I want this right here.'" For this segment, a bridal salon that had good channel access to dress lines and offered a businesslike, efficient setting would be optimal.

   Other brides sought other attributes, such as convenience. For them, they hoped the bridal salon would be a "one-stop shop" where they could also purchase tuxedos, bridal party dresses, flowers, and other accoutrements. Bridal salons may position themselves differentially to these segments, some emphasizing quality, and others value, each seeking the satisfaction of their targeted segments.

2. Other qualitative researchers have conducted content analysis of ads running during actual televised shows to determine whether they were story-like in structure or had some other format; for example, did they provide information to the viewer on the product benefits in more of a lecture, or a cognitive argument form? Story elements include scenes, actors, goals, outcomes, and a temporal dimension (beginning, middle, and end). The idea is that a story is engaging. Thus, a viewer might relate better to its richness, find it memorable and more persuasive, and in turn like the brand more. For example, an AT&T ad depicts a businessman traveling alone who feels better after he calls his wife from the airfone while on board. Presumably this vignette enhances a consumer's positive feeling toward airfones: the moral of the ad's story was that using an airfone could help the traveler achieve the goal of staying in touch with his family and overcoming homesickness. If the story engaged viewers, they might "relate" to the story and be persuaded that the phone could be beneficial to them as well.

3. Qualitative data (interviews, focus groups, and observations) have also been instrumental to marketers interested in enhancing consumers' perceptions of destinations and the brand equity of locations, for example, for consumer tourism or to attract businesses. Researchers studying perceptions of Scotland found that the country's core industries were incorrectly perceived to be whisky, wool, and salmon, when in fact, information technology (IT) is its greatest export. Ad copies were tested for consumer reaction: themes of tenacity played well (especially to the Japanese consumers), and an ad that emphasized Scotland's spirit with bright and dramatic tartan colors played especially well to younger, rebellious consumers. (The author notes that the project's name, "Galore," comes from the fact that *galore* is supposedly one of only two words to come out of Gaelic to enter into the English language. She notes the other word is *whisky*.)

Sources: Cele Otnes, "Friend of the Bride" in John F. Sherry Jr., ed., *Servicescapes: The Concept of Place in Contemporary Markets* (Chicago: AMA, 1998), pp. 229–257; Jennifer Edson Escalas, "Advertising Narratives," in Barbara B. Stern, ed., *Representing Consumers: Voices, Views and Visions* (New York: Routledge, 1998), pp. 267–289; Kate Hamilton, "Project Galore: Qualitative Research and Leveraging Scotland's Brand Equity," *Journal of Advertising Research* 40 (April 2000), pp. 107–111.

ETHICAL DILEMMA 7.3

A leading manufacturer of breakfast cereals was interested in learning more about the kinds of processes that consumers go through when deciding to buy a particular brand of cereal. To gather this information, an observational study was conducted in the major food chains of several large cities. The observers were instructed to assume a position well out of the shoppers' way, because it was thought that the individuals would change their behavior if they were aware they were being observed.

- Is it ethical to observe another person's behavior systematically without that person's knowledge? What if the behavior had been more private in nature? What if the behavior had been recorded on videotape?
- Does use of this method of data collection invade an individual's privacy?
- Even if no harm is done to the individual, is harm done to society?
- Does the use of such a method add to the concern over "Big Brotherism"?
- Can you suggest alternative methods for gathering the same information?

---

comment on the product's fat content, or their knowledge of how to prepare a particular cut. Observational techniques can be a useful tool in redesigning and selling hi-tech products to business customers also. For example, Hewlett-Packard's medical products division sent their researchers to watch surgeons operate. They noticed that monitors portraying electronic video of scalpel movement were often blocked by other staff members walking between the physician and the monitor, so H-P created a surgical helmet that casts images nearly holographically, in front of a surgeon's eyes.[45]

Natural Setting–Contrived Setting Observation

Observations may be obtained either in natural or contrived settings. The former may be completely natural, or there may be an induced experimental manipulation. When observing a customer comparing soups, for example, we may simply choose to study the amount of search and deliberation that normally go into the purchase of soups. Alternatively, we may introduce some point-of-purchase display materials to measure their effectiveness. One measure of effectiveness might be the amount of search and deliberation they stimulate for the particular brand being promoted. Both of these studies could take place in a supermarket, which would be the natural setting. Alternatively, we could bring a group of people into a controlled environment, where they could engage in some simulated shopping behavior. We might have established a soup display in this controlled environment and study the degree of each participant's deliberation and search as he or she proceeds to make the purchase choices.

An increasingly popular method for assessing customer reactions in a controlled environment is computer simulations, even virtual reality, which enable

---

[45]Bob Becker, "Take Direct Route When Data-Gathering," *Marketing News* 33 (September 27, 1999), pp. 29, 31; Kendra Parker, "How Do You Like Your Beef?" *American Demographics* 22 (January 2000), pp. 35–37.

marketers to display potential new products or product displays without going to the expense of physically building them. The technology originally relied on users wearing special goggles and gloves to see and manipulate objects. The advantage was that the objects appeared in three dimensions, as if they were actually there. For example, General Motors used virtual reality technology to test consumers' reactions to the view from the front seat of a new car.[46]

The technology has also been used in consumer shopping experiments. For example, Research Realities 7.3 describes the use of Visionary Shopper, a system that uses a video display, instead of goggles and gloves, to simulate a retail environment. Such machine-run interviews are self-administered, so there would be no interviewer bias and greater consistency across interviews. These multimedia, interactive interviews are vivid and multisensory and are often intrinsically interesting and fun for the respondent; thus, data quality is thought to be good and response rates can be relatively high. This technique has been used for a variety of testing applications, for example, to simulate grocery store shelf-facings when setting up the real thing would be cumbersome and time-consuming or to use when an actual prototype of a new product would be expensive, such as in testing many children's electronic games. These multimedia interviews often strike clients of marketing researchers as having high face validity (they seem "believable"), which should therefore enhance forecasting consumer reactions to new product concepts. Qualitative marketing research, particularly in the form of interviews and observation, is used frequently in testing new product development, especially for truly innovative products where consumers may need help articulating their needs and desires.[47]

The advantage of the laboratory environment is that we are better able to control extraneous influences that might affect the interpretation of what happened, thus creating greater internal validity. For example, shoppers in a natural setting might see a friend shopping and stop to chat a while about their kids, while standing in front of the display of soups, deliberating over which to buy. If we were measuring the time spent in deliberation, this interruption could raise havoc with the accuracy of the measurement. The disadvantage of the laboratory setting is that the contrived setting itself may cause differences in behavior and thus raise real questions about the external validity (generalizability) of the findings.

A contrived setting also tends to speed the data-collection process, result in lower-cost research, and allow the use of more objective measurements. Hilton's "Vacation Stations" lend age-appropriate toys to children and families staying at the participating hotels in North and South America. Toy Tips and the Toy Research Institute can observe the children to garner information on which toys will be the most popular during upcoming holiday seasons.[48] Another advantage of the con-

---

[46]Phil Guarisco, "How GM Targets 'Mature' Market Niche," *Advertising Age* 64 (January 11, 1993), p. 26.

[47]Betsy Stewart, "Multimedia Market Research," *Marketing Research* 11 (Fall 1999), pp. 14–18; Glen L. Urban, et al., "Information Acceleration: Validation and Lessons from the Field," *Journal of Marketing Research* 34 (February 1997), pp. 143–153; Fareena Sultan and Gloria Barczak, "Turning Marketing Research High-Tech," *Marketing Management* 8 (Winter 1999), pp. 25–29.

[48]Glenn Withiam, "Hilton's Vacation Station Conducts Toy Research," *Cornell Hotel and Restaurant Administration Quarterly* 40 (December 1999), p. 15.

RESEARCH REALITIES 7.3

Use of Visionary Shopper to Examine Shopping Behavior

Visionary Shopper, which displays 3-D color images of a simulated retail shelf, replicates different price and promotion conditions to approximate actual store shopping.

Visionary Shopper has done away with the helmet and other equipment to concentrate the action on a video display, as shown in the photo. The screen displays very sharp, 3-D color images of a simulated retail shelf stocked with a complete set of products in a category, arranged as they would be in a grocery store. Prices are shown on shelf cards below the brands and promotions are highlighted by shelf markers.

Using track-ball and touch-screen interfaces, consumers can "walk down" an aisle of a store to the product category and observe the brands on the shelf. Touch a product and it zooms off the shelf to cover most of the screen. The consumer then can examine the fronts and backs of package labels while the screen displays its price and other characteristics.

Another touch or click puts the product back on the shelf or into a shopping basket, indicating purchase.

The system tests marketing and product variables using a test vs. control design under the simulated VR conditions. Test variables may include price points, temporary shelf price reductions, special displays, shelf sets, package design and copy, line extensions— virtually any existing condition that can be changed at the shelf or any new condition that may be desired. The technology also lends itself to product concept testing because it shows a product in the context of competitive products right on the shelf.

The system currently is installed at mall locations geographically dispersed through the United States, although the company will install the system anywhere temporarily for special projects. Shoppers are recruited in the typical way and asked to participate in a 20-minute session using the system. Additional questions can be displayed on the screen as needed. In effect, the system compresses multiple shopping trips into one sitting.

Source: Laurence N. Gold, "Virtual Reality Now a Research Reality," *Marketing Research: A Magazine of Management & Applications* 5 (Fall 1993), pp. 50–51. Reprinted by permission of Raymond R. Burke.

trived setting is that the researcher does not need to wait for events to occur but can instruct the participants to engage in the needed kind of behavior. This means that a great many observations can be made in a short period of time; perhaps an entire study can be completed in a couple of days or a week. This can substantially reduce costs. As the Hilton toys example illustrates, observational techniques can be especially useful in studying consumer behavior in children. For more examples, see Research Realities 7.4.

Human–Mechanical Observation

Much scientific observation is in the field, with researchers taking notes on the observations they make. One or more individuals are trained to systematically observe a phenomenon and to record on the observational form the specific events that took place. Researchers commonly use tools such as written field notes, first making their observational impressions on-site, and later reflecting their theoretical and summary thoughts off-site. While much field research is still of this pencil-and-paper variety, electrical or mechanical observation also has its place in marketing research. While some technologies (such as tape recorders) have been used for a long time, the development of new and less-expensive technologies is expanding the role and importance of electrical/mechanical observation. Increasingly, ethnographic researchers rely on technology to assist them, particularly as various tools—such as tape and video recorders—get smaller in size, which means they are lighter for the researcher to carry and less intrusive during the research and interactions with the consumers at the field site. Audio- and videotapes are becoming *de rigeur*. Field researchers also bring laptops with them and rely later on computer transcriptions. Researchers who want to understand the fuller lives and contexts of consumers and their uses of brands sometimes ask those consumers to choose representative artifacts or photographs to express their individualities (for example, "This tie is special to me because I wore it at my first job interview," or "I know this vase is chipped, but it was my grandmother's, from the old country, and it always adds warmth to the flowers I pick up at the market," or "This picture shows me and my kid brother on our trip to Vegas—our first trip without our parents—it was cool that the hotel treated us like adults").[49]

Some of the earliest uses of electrical/mechanical observation focused on copy research and involved the galvanometer, tachistoscope, and eye camera. The galvanometer is used to measure the emotional arousal induced by an exposure to specific advertising copy. It belongs to the class of instruments that measure autonomic reactions, or reactions that are not under an individual's voluntary control. Because these responses are not controlled, it is not possible for individuals to mask or hide their "true" reactions to a stimulus. The galvanometer records changes in the electrical resistance of the skin associated with the minute degree of sweating that accompanies emotional arousal. For example, a person could be fitted with small electrodes to monitor electrical resistance and then shown different advertising

---

[49]Russell W. Belk, "Multimedia Approaches to Qualitative Data," in Barbara B. Stern, ed., *Representing Consumers: Voices, Views and Visions* (New York: Routledge, 1998), pp. 308–338; Christina Hughes, "From Field Notes to Dissertation," in Norman K. Denzin and Yvonna S. Lincoln, eds., *Collecting and Interpreting Qualitative Materials* (Thousand Oaks, CA: Sage, 1998), pp. 35–46.

RESEARCH REALITIES 7.4

Using Observational Primary Data Collection Techniques to Study Children as Consumers

1. Ethnography involves observation techniques, depth interviews, and perhaps audio- and video-taping technology to record people, typically in their natural settings. It is a technique that is gaining ground and credibility in marketing research. For example, General Mills has researchers watching children and their eating habits. To allow children to eat on the run, while simultaneously assuring mothers that they were providing healthy food snacks, General Mills created "Go-Gurt," a yogurt packaged in a tube, so that it could be eaten "on the go," without a spoon.

2. Researchers find that, like us adults, children have less free playtime—toy manufacturers find themselves competing with the Internet, children's time with their friends, TV shows, and soccer practice. Today's kids are sophisticated, having outgrown dolls and action figures by age 8, instead preferring complex software. It is simply difficult to capture their attention and advertise toys to them. It is equally challenging to cut through the clutter to capture parents' attention. Parents trust brand names (such as Hot Wheels, Barbie, Crayola) and if they perceive a toy to be of high quality, price is not an issue (for example, Lego's $200 Mindstorms robot-building toys sold much better than had been projected). Marketing researchers have found it to be much more effective to get children to try toys (and then parents to buy toys) through demo testing and sampling the products and brands. Researchers then observe the children in play, noting what toys are popular, what features might be troublesome, and so forth. Observational research provides feedback about the products, which the researchers expected, but it also functions as a sales vehicle, because it turns out that these play sessions generate big word-of-mouth among the pint-size consumers.

3. Observational techniques can be used on older children also. For example, MTV tries to understand the youth market, to be on the leading edge in trend-setting. It's easier to project an image of "cool" if the music station knows what teens care about. MTV researchers regularly reconnaissance young teen consumers' CD collections, their closets, and the music clubs they frequent. All these venues give the adult researchers insights into youth values, enabling them to design more relevant programming and to advertise in a way that communicates more authentically to these rather affluent young people. Teens are a substantial segment, spending a good $150 billion.

4. Some marketing researchers seek to capture teens surfing the Internet (for example, through online focus groups and surveys) to collect product-specific information from teens as well as general information about their interests and life issues. Some researchers are so aggressively pursuing these young Internet users that policies and guidelines are already being established to protect young people. For example, in accordance with the Children's Online Privacy Protection Act, researchers are required to obtain a parent's permission prior to the child's participation in the research.

Michelle Wirth Fellman, "Breaking Tradition," *Marketing Research* 11 (Fall 1999), pp. 20–24; T. L. Stanley and Becky Ebenkamp, "In Search of the Magic Formula," *Brandweek* 41 (February 14, 2000), pp. 28–34; Margaret Littman, "How Marketers Track Underage Consumers," *Marketing News* 34 (May 8, 2000), pp. 4, 7; Lisa Holton, "The Surfer in the Family," *American Demographics* 22 (April 2000), pp. 34–36; Sally Beatty and Carol Hymowitz, "How MTV Stays Tuned in to Teens," *The Wall Street Journal* (March 21, 2000), pp. B1, B4; Denise Lavoie, "Agency Aims to Get Inside Teenagers' Minds," *Marketing News* 33 (September 27, 1999), p. 8.

copy. The strength of the current induced would then be used to infer the subject's interest or attitude toward the copy.[50]

The tachistoscope is a device that provides the researcher timing control over a visual stimulus. The exposure interval may range from less than one-hundredth of a second to several seconds. After each exposure, respondents are asked to describe everything they saw and what it meant. By systematically varying the exposure, the researcher is able to measure how quickly and accurately a particular stimulus (such as an ad) can be perceived and interpreted. Note, though, that the use of a verbal reply implies that the tachistoscope is not a mechanical observer but rather a mechanical means of presenting stimuli. Today, PCs can mimic the effect of these machines, showing an ad or product picture, however briefly, and then recording anything the researcher wants—reaction times, ratings, and so on.

The eye camera is employed to study eye movements while a respondent reads advertising copy. Eye cameras are positioned to strike the cornea of the subject's eye, and eye movements are traced on videotape and analyzed by computer. Alternatively, tiny video cameras can be clipped to a respondent's eyeglasses to yield a visual record as that person reads an advertisement. Watching where people look allows the marketer detailed study of consumer behavior, answering questions such as: Where did the individual look first? How long did the person linger on any particular place? Did the consumer read the whole ad or just part of it? Following eye paths has also been used to analyze package designs, billboards, and displays in the aisles of supermarkets.[51] Similar technology can also measure pupil dilation, which is assumed to indicate a person's interest in the stimulus being viewed. Pupilometrics have been used to evaluate color schemes in packaging and optimal advertisement placement in magazines.

Two methods of mechanical observation that are used to provide useful supplementary information in telephone interviews—response latency and voice pitch analysis—owe their popularity to mechanical/electronic recorders and the computer's ability to diagnose what is recorded. Response latency is the amount of time a respondent deliberates before answering a question. Since response time seems to be directly related to the respondent's uncertainty in the answer, it assists in assessing the individual's strength of preference when choosing among alternatives. Thus, it provides an unobtrusive measure of, for example, brand preference or ambiguity experienced by a respondent in answering a particular question. Once a survey question appears on the computer screen, two methods are used to measure response time: (1) a stopwatch function internal to the PC gets reset to zero and

---

[50]A review of 118 studies on involuntary responses to advertising found that pupil dilation, skin moisture, and heart rate are the most commonly used. See Paul J. Watson and Robert J. Gatchel, "Autonomic Measures of Advertising," *Journal of Advertising Research* 19 (June 1979), pp. 15–26; Priscilla A. LaBarbera and Joel D. Tucciarone, "GSR Reconsidered: A Behavior-Based Approach to Evaluating and Improving the Sales Potency of Advertising," *Journal of Advertising Research* 35 (September/October 1995), pp. 33–53.

[51]Lee S. Weinblatt, "The Evolution of Technology in Pre-Testing," *Marketing Research* (Spring 1994), pp. 42–45; Rik Pieters, Edward Rosbergen, and Michel Wedel, "Visual Attention to Repeated Print Advertising," *Journal of Marketing Research* 36 (November 1999), pp. 424–438; Arthur F. Kramer, Sowon Hahn, David E. Irwin, and Jan Theeuwes, "Age Differences in the Control of Looking Behavior," *Psychological Science* 11 (May 2000), pp. 210–217.

counts time until the respondent enters a response into the keyboard; or (2) a voice-activated electronic function in the PC is automatically triggered at the onset of the respondent's voice and stopped when the voice stops. A digital readout indicates response latency to the interviewer for each consumer and each question. Such a system has several advantages. First, the method provides an accurate response latency measure without respondents being aware that this dimension of behavior is being recorded. Second, because the time is measured by an automatic device, the technique does not make the interviewer's task any more difficult, nor does it appreciably lengthen the interview.[52]

Voice pitch analysis relies on the same basic premise as the galvanometer: participants experience a number of involuntary physiological reactions, such as changes in blood pressure, rate of perspiration, or heart rate, when emotionally aroused by external or internal stimuli. Voice pitch analysis examines changes in the relative vibration frequency of the human voice that accompany emotional arousal. All individuals function at a certain physiological pace, called the baseline. The baseline in voice analysis is established by engaging the respondent in unemotional conversation, which is recorded. Deviations from the baseline level indicate that the respondent has reacted to the stimulus question. These deviations can be assessed by special audio-adapted computer equipment that can measure the abnormal frequencies in the voice caused by changes in the nervous system, changes that may not be discernible to the human ear. A net reaction score can be generated by comparing the abnormal frequency produced by the stimulus to the person's normal frequency. The greater the difference, the greater the emotional intensity of the consumer's reaction is said to be.

Voice pitch analysis has at least two advantages over other physiological reaction techniques. First, these techniques measure the intensity but not the direction of feeling. With voice pitch analysis, the "recording of the physical phenomenon (voice pitch) occurs simultaneously with the subject's conscious interpretation of the attitude (verbal response); the direction (positive or negative) of the attitude is ascertained from the subject's self-report, while the intensity of the emotion is measured at the same time by mechanical means."[53] Second, whereas the measurement of blood pressure, pulse rate, psychogalvanic response, or other physiological reactions requires subjects to be connected to the equipment, voice pitch analysis allows a much more natural interaction between researcher and participant. This tends to make it less time consuming and expensive to use.

[52]Robert C. Grass, Wallace H. Wallace, and Samuel Zuckerkandel, "Response Latency in Industrial Advertising Research," *Journal of Advertising Research* 20 (December 1980), pp. 63–65. For general discussions of the use of response latency measures, see John N. Bassili and Joseph F. Fletcher, "Response-Time Measurement in Survey Research," *Public Opinion Quarterly* 55 (Fall 1991), pp. 331–346; I. Koch and J. Hoffmann, "Patterns, Chunks, and Hierarchies in Serial Reaction-Time Tasks," *Psychological Research* 63 (2000), pp. 22–35.

[53]Nancy Nischwonger and Claude R. Martin, "On Using Voice Analysis in Marketing Research," *Journal of Marketing Research* 18 (August 1981), pp. 350–355; Dirk Michaelis, Matthias Froehlich, and Hans Werner Strube, "Selection and Combination of Acoustic Features for the Description of Pathologic Voices," *Journal of the Acoustical Society of America* 103, no. 3 (March 1998), pp. 1628–1639.

ETHICAL DILEMMA 7.4

You are running a laboratory experiment for the promotion manager of a soft drink company. The promotion manager has read a journal article indicating that viewers' responses to upbeat commercials are more favorable if the commercials follow very arousing film clips, and he is interested in testing this proposition with respect to his firm's commercials. To establish whether film clips that induce high levels of arousal result in more extreme evaluations of ensuing commercials than film clips that do not, you are pretesting film clips for their capacity to arouse. To do this, you are recording respondents' blood pressure levels as they watch various film clips. The equipment is not very intrusive, consisting of a finger cuff attached to a recording device. You are satisfied that the procedure does not threaten the subjects' physical safety in any way. In addition, you have made the participants familiar with the equipment, with the result that they are relaxed and comfortable and absorbed in the film clips. On getting up to leave at the end of the session, one person turns to you and asks, "Is my blood pressure normal then?"

- Is it ethical to give respondents information about their physiological responses that they can interpret as an informed comment on the state of their health?

- What might be the result if you do not tell that person the function of the equipment?

Perhaps most exotic of all, marketing researchers are exploring the use of high-tech headsets based on electroencephalogram (EEG) technology developed at NASA to monitor astronauts' alertness. The purpose is to assess whether a consumer finds an ad arousing or interesting. Five times per second, electrodes monitor the electrical impulses emitted by the brain as the consumer is exposed to various stimuli. Research on brain waves is only in its infancy, but thus far the evidence suggests that the two hemispheres of the brain respond differently to specific stimuli, with the right hemisphere responding more to emotional stimuli and the left to rational stimuli.[54] Critics argue that the technique is too new to have benchmarking data to interpret ad copy–testing results and further argue that it remains to be seen whether researchers can translate such physiological measures into attitudes toward ads and brands (whether they can correlate with purchase behaviors and Web ad click-throughs, for example). However, supporters exploring these techniques argue that brain waves will indicate more objectively than consumers' self-reports which ads, and which elements of ads, they find more interesting than others. In addition, they argue that consumers may shade answers on a survey, for example, to

---

[54]Michael L. Rothschild and Yong J. Hyun, "Predicting Memory for Components of TV Commercials from EEG," *Journal of Consumer Research* 16 (March 1990), pp. 472–478; Rebecca Gardyn, "What's on Your Mind?" *American Demographics* (April 2000), pp. 31–33; Jennifer Gilbert, "Capita Taps Brain Waves to Study Web Ads' Potency," *Advertising Age* (February 14, 2000), p. 55; Joan Meyers-Levy and Christie L. Nordhielm, *Gender-Based Difference in Decision Making: Implications for Marketers* (Boston: Harvard Business School, Neuroscience Primer, August 1998).

appear in a more socially desirable light, but they cannot mask their emotions as indicated by brain waves.

Summary

Marketing researchers who cannot find secondary data to answer their marketing questions turn to primary data collection. The types of primary data of interest to marketing researchers include demographic and socioeconomic characteristics, psychological and lifestyle characteristics, attitudes and opinions, awareness and knowledge, intentions, motivation, and behavior of individuals and groups.

Communication and observation are the two basic means of obtaining primary data. Communication involves the direct questioning of respondents, whereas observation entails the systematic checking of appropriate facts or actions. Observation can be used to secure behavioral data and some demographic or socioeconomic and lifestyle characteristics, and it has the advantage of objectivity over communication methods. However, observation is not as useful for measuring those things that are not directly observable, such as attitudes, awareness, knowledge, intentions, or motivation. When these constructs are of interest, communication methods must be used.

Communication methods may be classified by their degree of structure, disguise, and method of administration. A structured questionnaire has a well-defined sequence and standardized response categories. It is most productively used for testing specific hypotheses, as would occur in descriptive or causal research. When the research is exploratory, unstructured questionnaires can be used. In an unstructured questionnaire, the response categories are not predetermined; the respondents are allowed to answer in their own terms.

The disguised questionnaire attempts to hide the purpose of the research from the respondent. This goal is particularly important when respondents may be tempted to give socially accepted responses on sensitive issues, rather than reporting their true opinion.

Questionnaires can be administered by personal interviews in the home or a mall or some other convenient facility, over the phone, using paper-and-pencil questionnaires by mail or fax, or by using computer-administered surveys on e-mail or the Web. Each approach has advantages and disadvantages, and the approaches vary in terms of the control they offer the researcher with respect to sample, information, and administration. The methods are not mutually exclusive and can often be used productively in combination. Observation methods can also be classified by several criteria, including degree of structure and disguise, the naturalness of the setting, and whether human or mechanical devices are employed to secure the data.

Most observations in marketing research are obtained in a completely natural setting, although certain types of observations are regularly obtained in contrived or laboratory settings using electrical or mechanical equipment. The laboratory setting allows greater control of extraneous influences and thus may be more internally valid, although less externally valid. Electrical and mechanical measuring instruments permit more objective, reliable measurements by eliminating possible human observers' biases—for example, selective attention. However, they also eliminate the human observer's integrative powers, which usually contribute to the overall interpretation and understanding of the observed data.

Questions

1. What types of primary data interest marketing researchers most? How are they distinguished?
2. What are the general advantages and disadvantages associated with obtaining information by questioning or by observation? Which method provides more control over the sample?

3. What is a disguised questionnaire? What is a structured questionnaire?

4. What are the advantages and disadvantages of structured–undisguised questionnaires? Of unstructured–undisguised questionnaires?

5. What is the rationale for employing unstructured–disguised stimuli? What is a word association test? A sentence completion test? A storytelling test?

6. What operating principle or assumption underlies the use of structured–disguised questionnaires? What are the advantages and disadvantages associated with structured–disguised questionnaires?

7. How do personally administered questionnaires, telephone surveys, mail, fax, e-mail or Web surveys differ with respect to the following?
   a. sampling control
   b. information control
   c. administrative control

8. How can observational methods be classified? What are the key distinctions among the various types?

9. What principle underlies the use of a galvanometer? What is a tachistoscope? What is an eye camera? What is an optical scanner?

10. What does response latency assess? How is it measured?

11. What is voice pitch analysis? What does it measure?

Applications and Problems

1. Should the communication or observational method be used in the following situations? Justify your choice. Also specify the degree of structure and disguise that should be used.

   a. The Metal Products Division of Geni Ltd. devised a special metal container to store plastic garbage bags. Plastic bags posed household problems, as they gave off unpleasant odors, looked disorderly, and provided a breeding place for insects. The container overcame these problems, as it had a bag-support apparatus that held the bag open for filling and sealed the bag when the lid was closed. In addition, the storage area held at least four full bags. The product was priced at $53.81 and was sold through hardware stores. The company has done little advertising and has relied on in-store promotion and displays. The divisional manager was wondering about the effectiveness of these displays. She has called on you to do the necessary research.

   b. Cardworth is a national manufacturer and distributor of greeting cards. The company recently began distributing a lower-priced line of cards that was made possible by using recycled paper. Quality differences between the higher- and lower-priced cards did not seem to be noticeable to laypeople. The company followed a policy of printing its name and the price on the back of each card. The initial acceptance of the new line of cards convinced the vice president of production that the company should use recycled paper for all their cards and increase its profit margin from 12.3 percent to 14.9 percent. The sales manager has strongly opposed this move and commented, "You know, consumers are concerned about the quality of greeting cards; a price difference of five cents on a card does not matter." The vice president has called on you to undertake the study.

2. Which survey method (mail, telephone, personal interview in the home or in a mall, fax, e-mail, or Web) would you use for the following situations? Justify your choice.

   a. Administration of a questionnaire to determine the number of people who listened to the "100 Top Country Tunes in 2002," a program that aired on December 31, 2002.

   b. Administration of a questionnaire to determine the number of households having an individual with mental health problems and a history of such problems in the family.

   c. Administration of a questionnaire by a national manufacturer of microwave ovens that will test people's attitudes and opinions toward a new model.

    d. Administration of a questionnaire by a local dry cleaner who wants to determine customers' satisfaction with a recent discount scheme.

    e. Administration of a questionnaire by the management of a small hotel that wants to assess customers' opinions of its service.

3.   Several objectives for marketing research projects follow. For each objective, specify the type(s) of primary data that would be of use along with a possible method of data collection.

    a. Assess "people flow" patterns inside a shopping mall.

    b. Gauge the effectiveness of a new advertisement.

    c. Gauge a salesperson's potential for success.

    d. Segment a market.

    e. Identify the shopper types that patronize a particular store.

    f. Discover how people feel about a new package design.

4.   Consider each of the following research projects. In each case, identify weak areas and describe how the research might have been improved to better attain its objectives. Be specific.

    a. A local bank was interested in determining how it might better serve the needs of low-income households. It inserted a four-page survey into the monthly statement-of-account mailings of all account holders with less than $500 in their accounts. The survey was structured and undisguised; 1,200 surveys were mailed and 98 were completed and returned.

    b. The Lee-Casey Lawn and Garden Company, which recently began business in a small midwestern city, has developed a special liquid fertilizer for a certain type of shrubbery. Lee-Casey is interested in determining whether there is a market for the product among homeowners, but it is unsure whether that particular type of shrubbery is popular in that area. In order to find out, Lee-Casey conducted a telephone survey of homeowners in the area. They were eventually able to reach about 75 percent of the homeowners; of these, 85 percent participated in the survey.

    c. A new business clothing shop is to open in a few months. The owners are unsure whether the new shop should be located in a shopping mall or at a downtown location. Since they think it would be best to simply ask shoppers for their preferences as to location, the owners contracted a local marketing research company to conduct a study. Using a structured, undisguised questionnaire format and the mall intercept method of administration, the research company was able to report to the owners of the new business clothing shop that most people prefer to shop for clothes in a shopping mall.

    d. Quick-Stop, Inc., recently opened a new convenience store in Northglenn, Colorado. The store is open every day from 7:00 A.M. to 11:00 P.M. In order to better plan the location of other units in the Denver metro area, management is interested in determining the trading area from which this store draws its customers. How would you determine this information by questionnaire method? By observation method? Which method would be preferred? Be sure to specify in your answer how you would define "trading area."

Thorndike Sports Equipment Video Case

Thorndike Sports Equipment has decided to introduce three new racquets: a lightweight, a standard weight, and a heavyweight. The company wants to introduce these racquets with descriptive names that will tell the customer which weight category the racquet belongs to without simply using light, standard, and heavy as descriptors. Design a research study that will provide customer information on appropriate names for these new racquets. Your research plan can be a multiple-stage project, but you must provide estimated costs associated with your research proposal.

8

Data-Collection Forms

In the previous chapter, the various types of questionnaires and observation forms and their methods of administration were discussed. The general advantages and disadvantages of using communication and observational methods, as well as the pros and cons associated with the many specific types of questionnaire or observational methods, were also dealt with. This chapter builds on that discussion. It reviews the procedures one should follow in developing a questionnaire or observational data-collection form.

Questionnaire Design

Although much progress has been made, designing questionnaires is still an art and not a science. Much of the progress has come from such admonitions as "avoid leading questions" or "avoid ambiguous questions." It is much easier to embrace the admonitions than it is to develop questions that are indeed not leading or ambiguous. Nevertheless, Figure 8.1 offers a method that the beginning researcher can use to develop questionnaires. More experienced researchers would be expected to develop their own patterns, although the steps listed in Figure 8.1[1] would still be part of that pattern.

The stages of development are presented here in sequence, but researchers will rarely be so fortunate as to develop a questionnaire in step-by-step fashion. A more typical development will involve some iteration and looping. The researcher finds that the possible wordings of a response do not secure the content decided on or that the content is not completely consistent with the information desired. This discovery, of course, requires a loop back to an earlier stage to make the necessary changes. Researchers should not be surprised, then, if they find themselves working back and forth among some of the stages. That is natural.

Researchers should also be warned not to take the stages too literally. They are presented as a guide or a checklist. With questionnaires, the proof of the pudding is very much in the eating. Does the questionnaire produce accurate data of the kind needed? Blind adherence to procedure is no substitute for creativity in approach, nor is it any substitute for a pretest (Step 9 of Figure 8.1) with which one

---

[1]This procedure is adapted from one suggested by Arthur Kornhauser and Paul B. Sheatsley, "Questionnaire Construction and Interview Procedure," in Claire Selltiz, Lawrence S. Wrightsman, and Stuart W. Cook, *Research Methods in Social Relations,* 3rd ed. (New York: Holt, Rinehart and Winston, 1976), pp. 541–573. See also Arlene Fink, *How to Design Surveys* (Thousand Oaks, CA: Sage Publications, 1995).

FIGURE 8.1   **Procedure for Developing a Questionnaire**

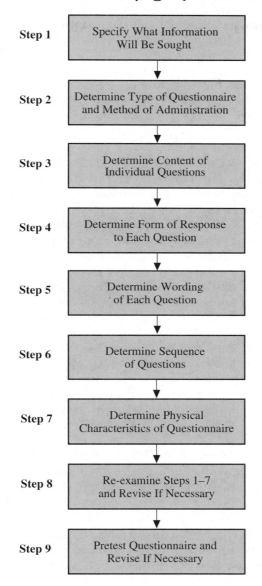

Step 1	Specify What Information Will Be Sought
Step 2	Determine Type of Questionnaire and Method of Administration
Step 3	Determine Content of Individual Questions
Step 4	Determine Form of Response to Each Question
Step 5	Determine Wording of Each Question
Step 6	Determine Sequence of Questions
Step 7	Determine Physical Characteristics of Questionnaire
Step 8	Re-examine Steps 1–7 and Revise If Necessary
Step 9	Pretest Questionnaire and Revise If Necessary

can discover whether the typical respondent indeed understands each question and is able and willing to supply the information sought.

Information Sought

Deciding what information will be sought is easy to the extent that researchers have been meticulous and precise at earlier stages in the research process. By the same token, if researchers have been sloppy and careless, the decision will prove to be difficult. Both descriptive and causal research demand sufficient prior knowledge to allow the framing of specific hypotheses for investigation, which then guide the research. The hypotheses also guide the questionnaire. They determine what information will be sought and from whom, because they specify what relationships will be investigated. If researchers have heeded the earlier admonition to establish "dummy tables" to structure the data analysis, their job of determining what information is to be collected is essentially complete. Researchers must collect information on the variables specified in the dummy tables in order to investigate these hypotheses. Further, researchers must collect this information from the right people and in the right units. The hypotheses, then, will not only be a guide to what information will be sought but in large part will also determine the type of question and form of response used to collect it.

This is not meant to deny that the preparation of the questionnaire itself may suggest further hypotheses and other relationships that might be investigated at slight additional effort and cost. A most important warning is in order here. If the new hypothesis is indeed vital to understanding the phenomenon, by all means include it and use it to advantage when designing the questionnaire. On the other hand (and we are repeating ourselves), if it simply represents one of those potentially "interesting findings" but is not vital to the research effort, forget it. The inclusion of "interesting but not vital" items simply lengthens the questionnaire, causes problems in administration and analysis, and often increases nonresponse.

The exploratory research effort is, of course, aimed at the discovery of ideas and insights and not at their systematic investigation. The questionnaire for an exploratory study is, therefore, loosely structured, with only a rough idea of the kind of information that might be sought. This is particularly true at the earliest stages of exploratory research. It is also true, but to a lesser extent, at the later stages of exploratory research, when the emphasis is on determining the priorities that should be given to various hypotheses in guiding future research.

Type of Questionnaire and Method of Administration

After specifying the basic information that will be sought, the researcher needs to specify how it will be gathered. The *how* requires decisions about the structure and disguise to be used in the questionnaire and whether it will be administered by mail, telephone, or personal interviews. We saw in the preceding chapter that these decisions are not independent. If the researcher decides on a disguised–unstructured questionnaire using a picture stimulus storytelling format, this precludes straight telephone administration and raises serious questions about a mail administration of the instrument. Similarly, mail administration is not recommended for unstructured–undisguised questionnaires with open-ended questions, particularly if they should have probes.

The type of data to be collected will have an important effect, of course, on the method of data collection. For example, the San Francisco research firm King, Brown & Partners had a client that wanted to know what proportion of Internet users had various multimedia plug-ins (for example, Shockwave or Acrobat for downloading and playing multimedia files). From experience, King, Brown & Partners knew that one-third or more users don't accurately know which plug-ins they have, especially when it comes to such detailed information as which version of the

---

ETHICAL DILEMMA 8.1

As a new researcher for a large research supplier, you are told to design an attitude and usage questionnaire for a new customer, an appliance manufacturer. Before starting this project, your supervisor mentions that a similar study was completed 12 months ago and may provide some useful background information. Because you have no experience in durable consumer goods, you decide to use this previous report as a good source of secondary information.

After finding a copy of the previous study's final report, you discover that the report was completed for a competing appliance company. However, the report provides valuable background and competitive information. Because a questionnaire was developed and used successfully for this project, you decide to take a copy of the questionnaire and update it for the current client.

- Is it ethical for researchers to use questionnaires developed and paid for by prior clients on competitive client projects?

- Instead of using the questionnaire, would it have been legitimate to use the previous report as a source of secondary information to provide background information for the current project?

- Would the preceding situation be different if the prior research had been completed for a long-term, contract client?

---

plug-in. It would have been a waste of time to call or write to computer users and pose such questions. Rather, the researchers set up an online survey that was structured to help the users answer accurately. They created a kind of multimedia test, in which they used a variety of plug-in file formats to display images. For each image, users who downloaded the survey were asked whether they could see the image. If they clicked yes, the researchers knew, by the format used to create the image, precisely what plug-in they were using. This methodology let respondents provide data without knowing the technical details.[2]

Another influence on the data collection method is the culture of the country where the study is being done. (See Research Realities 8.1.) A researcher investigating the relationship between some behavior and a series of demographic characteristics in the United States (for example, how dishwasher ownership is related to income, age, family size, and so on) could use mail, telephone, or in-home or mall personal interviews to gather the data. The methods would not be equally attractive because of cost and other considerations, but they all could be used. On the other hand, a researcher interested in measuring attitudes could not use all the methods, although which ones could or could not be used would depend largely on previous decisions about structure and disguise. A decision to use a lengthy attitude scale, for example, would preclude a telephone administration, although it would allow the collection of data by either mail or personal interview. An open-ended questionnaire

---

[2]Chris Grecco and Hal King, "Of Browsers and Plug-Ins: Researching Web Surfers' Technological Capabilities," *Quirk's Marketing Research Review* (July 1999), pp 58–62.

RESEARCH REALITIES 8.1

How Cultural Differences Affect Marketing Research in Different Countries

Willingness to Cooperate Compared with people around the world, Americans tend to be unusually helpful and friendly, which is reflected in their general willingness to cooperate in marketing research surveys. Quite often, Americans will answer the questions of a total stranger (in the research industry, we call them "interviewers") about almost any subject—up to and including one's sex life. And Americans will agree to be interviewed anywhere: over the telephone, in a shopping mall, or at their place of business.

This climate of assumed cooperation can spoil Americans for doing research elsewhere in the world. Individual consumers in many other countries are less ready to answer any questions from an interviewer, let alone delicate or personal ones. Business people in many parts of the world have a more closed attitude than Americans about taking part in surveys.

In Korea, for example, business people are reluctant to answer any survey questions about their company—it is considered disloyal to divulge any type of information to "outsiders." And most Japanese business people are hesitant to take part in surveys during business hours—taking time away from your work for a survey is like "stealing" from your employer.

Differences in Research Costs The cost of doing exactly the same research can vary dramatically from country to country. Japan is generally regarded as the most expensive research market in the world; projects there usually cost several times what the same study would cost in the United States.

But even within a single region, such as the European community, costs can vary dramatically from country to country. ESOMAR, the European Society for Opinion and Marketing Research (the European equivalent of a combined American Marketing Association and Advertising Research Foundation), periodically studies differences in research costs from country to country within Europe. Below are examples of some of the cost differences ESOMAR found in its most recent study.

Examples of European Union Research Cost Indices

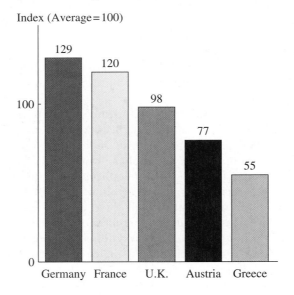

Index (Average = 100)

Germany	129
France	120
U.K.	98
Austria	77
Greece	55

Source: Jeffrey Pope, *How Cultural Differences Affect Multi-County Research* (Minneapolis, MN: Custom Research, Inc., 1991).

on attitudes would raise serious questions about mail administration. Thus, the researcher must specify precisely what primary data are needed, how these data might be collected, what degree of structure and disguise will be used, and how the questionnaire will be administered.

Figure 8.2 offers an example. The primary data at issue are the use of caffeinated ground coffee and attitudes toward various brands. The questions are all very structured and undisguised. The questionnaire is to be administered by mail, using part of the NFO (National Family Opinion, Inc.) panel. Note the ease with which most of the responses could be tabulated.

Individual Question Content

The researcher's previous decisions regarding information needed, the structure and disguise to be imposed on its collection, and the method for administering the questionnaire will largely control the decisions regarding individual question content. But the researcher can and should ask some additional questions.[3]

IS THE QUESTION NECESSARY?   Suppose that an issue is important. The researcher then needs to ask whether the point has been adequately covered by other questions. If not, a new question is in order. The question should be framed to secure an answer with the required detail but not with more detail than needed. Very often in marketing, for example, we employ the concept of stage in the life cycle to explore family consumption behavior. Stage in the life cycle is a composite variable in which the various stages are defined in terms of marital status, presence of children, and the ages of the children. The presence of children is important because it indicates a dependency relationship, particularly if the youngest child is under 6, representing one type of responsibility, or is over 6 but under 17, representing another type of responsibility for the parents. In a study using stage in the life cycle as a variable, there is no need to ask the age of each child. Rather, all that is needed is one question aimed at securing the age of the youngest child if there are any children. Once again the role of the hypotheses and dummy tables is obvious when designing the questionnaire.

ARE SEVERAL QUESTIONS NEEDED INSTEAD OF ONE?   There will often be situations in which several questions are needed instead of one. Consider the question, "Why do you use Crest?" One respondent may reply, "To reduce cavities," while another may reply, "Because our dentist recommended it." Obviously two different frames of reference are being employed to answer this question. The first respondent is replying in terms of why he is using it now, whereas the second is replying in terms of how she started using it. It would be better to break this one question down

---

[3]These questions were suggested by Kornhauser and Sheatsley, "Questionnaire Construction." For a systematic treatment of questionnaire construction, see the classic work by Stanley L. Payne, *The Art of Asking Questions* (Princeton, NJ: Princeton University Press, 1951). Other good general sources are Seymour Sudman and Norman M. Bradburn, *Asking Questions: A Practical Guide to Questionnaire Design* (San Francisco: Jossey-Bass, 1982); William Foddy, *Constructing Questions for Interviews and Questionnaires* (New York: Cambridge University Press, 1993); Arlene Fink, *How to Ask Survey Questions* (Thousand Oaks, CA: Sage Publications, 1995).

FIGURE 8.2   **Mail Questionnaire for Caffeinated Ground Coffee Study**

1. *What type of coffeemaker do you usually use to prepare your ground coffee at home?* (CHECK *ONE* BOX)

    1□ Automatic drip
    2□ Electric percolator
    3□ Stove top percolator
    4□ Stove top dripolator
    □ Other (Specify): _____

2. a. *Check all the brands of regular ground coffee that you have ever used at home.* (CHECK *ALL* THAT APPLY)
   b. *Check the one brand you use most often.* (CHECK *ONE* BOX)
   c. *Check all the brands you currently have on hand.* (CHECK *ALL* THAT APPLY)
   d. *Check the one brand you will probably buy next.* (CHECK *ONE* BOX)
   e. *For each brand please indicate how much you like the brand overall on a scale of 1 to 10 with "1" meaning dislike it extremely and "10" meaning like it extremely. Rate each brand, whether you have used the brand or not.*

	"A" Ever Used	"B" Use Most Often	"C" Have On Hand	"D" Will Buy Next	Brand Rating "1" Dislike It Extremely ◀ − − − − − − − − ▶ "10" Like It Extremely
Folgers	1□	1□	1□	1□	01□ 02□ 03□ 04□ 05□ 06□ 07□ 08□ 09□ 10□
Hills Brothers ..	2□	2□	2□	2□	01□ 02□ 03□ 04□ 05□ 06□ 07□ 08□ 09□ 10□
Maxwell House Regular	3□	3□	3□	3□	01□ 02□ 03□ 04□ 05□ 06□ 07□ 08□ 09□ 10□
Maxwell House Master Blend	4□	4□	4□	4□	01□ 02□ 03□ 04□ 05□ 06□ 07□ 08□ 09□ 10□
Yuban	5□	5□	5□	5□	01□ 02□ 03□ 04□ 05□ 06□ 07□ 08□ 09□ 10□
Other (Specify):____	6□	6□	6□	6□	01□ 02□ 03□ 04□ 05□ 06□ 07□ 08□ 09□ 10□

3. *What do you usually add to the coffee you drink?* (CHECK *ALL* THAT APPLY)

    1□ Nothing (I drink it black)
    2□ A dairy creamer, like milk, cream, or half-and-half
    3□ A non-dairy creamer, powdered or liquid
    4□ Sugar
    5□ Artificial sweetener
    □ Something else (Specify): _____

4. *Are you the principal coffee purchaser for your household?*

    1□ Yes
    2□ No

FIGURE 8.2   (continued)

5. *Please indicate how important it is to you that a ground coffee have each of the following character-istics.* (CHECK *ONE* BOX FOR *EACH* CHARACTERISTIC)

	Not At All Important									Extremely Important
Rich taste	01☐	02☐	03☐	04☐	05☐	06☐	07☐	08☐	09☐	10☐
Always fresh	01☐	02☐	03☐	04☐	05☐	06☐	07☐	08☐	09☐	10☐
Gets the day off to a good start	01☐	02☐	03☐	04☐	05☐	06☐	07☐	08☐	09☐	10☐
Full-bodied taste	01☐	02☐	03☐	04☐	05☐	06☐	07☐	08☐	09☐	10☐
Rich aroma in the cup	01☐	02☐	03☐	04☐	05☐	06☐	07☐	08☐	09☐	10☐

	Not At All Important									Extremely Important
Good value for the money	01☐	02☐	03☐	04☐	05☐	06☐	07☐	08☐	09☐	10☐
The best coffee to drink in the morning	01☐	02☐	03☐	04☐	05☐	06☐	07☐	08☐	09☐	10☐
Rich aroma in the can/bag	01☐	02☐	03☐	04☐	05☐	06☐	07☐	08☐	09☐	10☐
Smooth taste	01☐	02☐	03☐	04☐	05☐	06☐	07☐	08☐	09☐	10☐
Highest quality coffee	01☐	02☐	03☐	04☐	05☐	06☐	07☐	08☐	09☐	10☐

	Not At All Important									Extremely Important
Premium brand	01☐	02☐	03☐	04☐	05☐	06☐	07☐	08☐	09☐	10☐
Not bitter	01☐	02☐	03☐	04☐	05☐	06☐	07☐	08☐	09☐	10☐
The coffee that brightens my day the most	01☐	02☐	03☐	04☐	05☐	06☐	07☐	08☐	09☐	10☐
Costs more than the other brands	01☐	02☐	03☐	04☐	05☐	06☐	07☐	08☐	09☐	10☐
Strong taste	01☐	02☐	03☐	04☐	05☐	06☐	07☐	08☐	09☐	10☐

	Not At All Important									Extremely Important
Has no aftertaste	01☐	02☐	03☐	04☐	05☐	06☐	07☐	08☐	09☐	10☐
Economy brand	01☐	02☐	03☐	04☐	05☐	06☐	07☐	08☐	09☐	10☐
Rich aroma while brewing	01☐	02☐	03☐	04☐	05☐	06☐	07☐	08☐	09☐	10☐
The best ground coffee available	01☐	02☐	03☐	04☐	05☐	06☐	07☐	08☐	09☐	10☐
Enjoy drinking with a meal	01☐	02☐	03☐	04☐	05☐	06☐	07☐	08☐	09☐	10☐
Costs less than other brands	01☐	02☐	03☐	04☐	05☐	06☐	07☐	08☐	09☐	10☐

6. *On a scale of 0 to 10 with "0" meaning does not describe at all and "10" meaning describes completely, please indicate how well the following statements describe each of the coffee brands listed below. Rate each brand, whether you have used the brand or not. Please write in the number which indicates your answer on the lines provided.*

(continued)

FIGURE 8.2   **(continued)**

	Folgers	Hills Brothers	Maxwell House Regular	Maxwell House Master Blend	Yuban
Rich taste	____	____	____	____	____
Always fresh	____	____	____	____	____
Gets the day off to a good start	____	____	____	____	____
Full-bodied taste	____	____	____	____	____
Rich aroma in the cup	____	____	____	____	____

	Folgers	Hills Brothers	Maxwell House Regular	Maxwell House Master Blend	Yuban
Good value for the money	____	____	____	____	____
The best coffee to drink in the morning ..	____	____	____	____	____
Rich aroma in the can/bag	____	____	____	____	____
Smooth taste	____	____	____	____	____
Highest quality coffee	____	____	____	____	____

	Folgers	Hills Brothers	Maxwell House Regular	Maxwell House Master Blend	Yuban
Premium brand	____	____	____	____	____
Not bitter	____	____	____	____	____
The coffee that brightens my day the most	____	____	____	____	____
Costs more than the other brands	____	____	____	____	____
Strong taste	____	____	____	____	____

	Folgers	Hills Brothers	Maxwell House Regular	Maxwell House Master Blend	Yuban
Has no aftertaste	____	____	____	____	____
Economy brand	____	____	____	____	____
Rich aroma while brewing	____	____	____	____	____
The best ground coffee available	____	____	____	____	____
Enjoy drinking with a meal	____	____	____	____	____
Costs less than other brands	____	____	____	____	____

7. *Please indicate your sex and age.*

    1☐ Male

    2☐ Female   Age:_____

into separate questions that reflect the possible frames of reference that could be used; for example:

☐   How did you first happen to use Crest?

☐   What is your primary reason for using it?

DO RESPONDENTS HAVE THE NECESSARY INFORMATION?   The researcher should carefully examine each issue to ascertain whether the typical respondent can be expected to have the information sought. Respondents will give answers. Whether the answers mean anything is another matter, however. In one public opinion survey, the following question was asked:[4]

Which of the following statements most closely coincides with your opinion of the Metallic Metals Act?

☐   It would be a good move on the part of the United States.

☐   It would be a good thing, but should be left to the individual states.

☐   It is all right for foreign countries, but should not be required here.

☐   It is of no value at all.

☐   No opinion.

The proportion of respondents checking each alternative was, respectively, 21.4 percent, 58.6 percent, 15.7 percent, 4.3 percent, and 0.3 percent. The second alternative captures the prevailing sentiment. Right? Wrong! There was no Metallic Metals Act, and the point of this classic example is that *most questions will get answers, but the real concern is whether the answers mean anything.*[5] For the answers to mean anything, the questions need to mean something to the respondent. This means that, first, the respondent needs to be informed with respect to the issue addressed by the question, and, second, the respondent must remember the information.

---

[4]Sam Gill, "How Do You Stand on Sin?" *Tide* 21 (March 14, 1947), p. 72.

[5]In a subsequent replication of the study on the Metallic Metals Act almost 40 years later, 64 percent of those interviewed had a definite opinion on the nonexistent act. See Daniel T. Seymour, "Numbers Don't Lie—Do They?" *Business Horizons* 27 (November/December 1984), pp. 36–37. A number of other examples in the literature report findings of people having opinions about totally fictional issues like the Metallic Metals Act. See, for example, George F. Bishop, Robert W. Oldendick, Alfred J. Tuchfarber, and S. E. Bennett, "Pseudo-Opinions on Public Affairs," *Public Opinion Quarterly* 44 (Summer 1980), pp. 198–209; Herbert Schuman and Stanley Presser, "Public Opinion and Public Ignorance: The Fine Line between Attitudes and Nonattitudes," *American Journal of Sociology* 85 (March 1980), pp. 1214–1225; Del I. Hawkins and Kenneth A. Coney, "Uninformed Response Error in Survey Research," *Journal of Marketing Research* 18 (August 1981), pp. 370–374; Kenneth C. Schneider, "Uninformed Response Rates in Survey Research: New Evidence," *Journal of Business Research* 13 (August 1985), pp. 153–162; George F. Bishop, Alfred J. Tuchfarber, and Robert W. Oldendick, "Opinions on Fictitious Issues: The Pressure to Answer Survey Questions," *Public Opinion Quarterly* 50 (Summer 1986), pp. 240–250; Arthur Sterngold, Rex H. Warland, and Robert O. Herrmann, "Do Surveys Overstate Public Concern?" *Public Opinion Quarterly* 58 (Summer 1994), pp. 255–263. The phenomenon is not unique to opinions. It also applies when measuring brand awareness, where it has been observed that the more plausible sounding a brand name, the more likely consumers are to claim they are aware of it even though it does not exist. See "'Spurious Awareness' Alters Brand Tests," *The Wall Street Journal* (September 13, 1984), p. 29. See also Eric R. A. N. Smith and Peverill Squire, "The Effects of Prestige Names in Question Wording," *Public Opinion Quarterly* 54 (Spring 1990), pp. 97–116.

Consider the question, "How much does your family spend on groceries in a typical week?" Unless the respondent does the grocery shopping or the family operates with a fairly strict budget, he or she is unlikely to know. In a situation like this, it might be helpful to ask "filter questions" before this question to determine if the individual is indeed likely to have this information. An example filter question might be, "Who does the grocery shopping in your family?" It is not unusual, for example, to use filter questions of the sort, "Do you have an opinion on . . . ?" before asking about the specific issue in question in opinion surveys. The empirical evidence indicates that providing a filter like this will typically increase the proportion responding "no opinion" by 20 to 25 percentage points.[6]

Not only should the individual have the information sought, but he or she should remember it. Our ability to remember various events is influenced by the event itself and its importance, the length of time since the event, and the presence or absence of stimuli that assist in recalling it. Important events are more easily remembered than unimportant events. Although many older adults might be able to remember who shot President John F. Kennedy, the year in which the assassination occurred, or what happened to the assassin, or might be able to recall the first car they ever owned, many of them will be unable to recall the amount of television or the particular shows they watched last Wednesday evening, or the first brand of mouthwash they ever used, when they switched to their current brand, or why they switched. The switching and use information might be very important to a brand manager for mouthwashes, but it is unimportant to most individuals, a condition we have to continually keep in mind when designing questionnaires. We need to put ourselves in the shoes of the respondent, not those of the product manager, when deciding whether the information is important enough for the individual to remember it.

We also need to recognize that an individual's ability to remember an event is influenced by how long ago it happened. While we might recall the television programs we watched last evening, we might have much greater difficulty remembering those we watched last week on the same evening and might find it all but impossible to recall our viewing pattern of a month ago. The moral of this is that if the event could be considered relatively unimportant to most individuals, we should ask about very recent occurrences of it.[7]

---

[6]Herbert Schuman and Stanley Presser, "The Assessment of 'No Opinions' in Attitude Surveys," in Karl F. Schnessler, ed., *Sociological Methodology, 1979* (San Francisco: Jossey-Bass, 1979), pp. 241–275. See also George F. Bishop, Robert W. Oldendick, and Alfred J. Tuchfarber, "Effects of Filter Questions in Public Opinion Surveys," *Public Opinion Quarterly* 47 (Winter 1983), pp. 528–546; Otis Dudley Duncan and Magnus Stenbeck, "No Opinion or Not Sure?" *Public Opinion Quarterly* 52 (Winter 1988), pp. 513–525; Kenneth C. Schneider and James C. Johnson, "Link between Response-Inducing Strategies and Uninformed Response," *Marketing Intelligence and Planning* 12, no. 1 (1994), pp. 29–36; Barbel Knauper, "Filter Questions and Question Interpretation: Presuppositions at Work," *Public Opinion Quarterly* 62 (Spring 1998), pp. 70–78.

[7]Bruce Buchanan and Donald G. Morrison, "Sampling Properties of Rate Questions with Implications for Survey Research," *Marketing Science* 6 (Summer 1987), pp. 286–298. See also Scot Burton and Edward Blair, "Task Conditions, Response Formulation Processes, and Response Accuracy for Behavioral Frequency Questions in Surveys," *Public Opinion Quarterly* 54 (Spring 1991), pp. 50–79; Richard Nadeau and Richard G. Niemi, "Educated Guesses: The Process of Answering Factual Knowledge Questions in Surveys," *Public Opinion Quarterly* 59 (Fall 1995), pp. 323–346; Geeta Menon, "Are the Parts Better than the Whole? The Effects of Decompositional Questions on Judgments of Frequent Behaviors," *Journal of Marketing Research* 34 (August 1997), pp. 335–346.

For more important events, two effects operating in opposite directions affect a respondent's ability to provide accurate answers about events that happened in some specified time period (for example, how many times the person has seen a doctor in the last six months). These are telescoping error and recall loss. **Telescoping error** refers to the fact that most people remember an event as having occurred more recently than in fact is the case. **Recall loss** means that they forget an event happened at all. The extent of the two sources of error on the accuracy of the reported information depends on the length of the reference period. For long periods, the telescoping effect is smaller while the recall loss effect is larger. For short periods, the reverse is true. "Thus, for short reference periods, the telescoping error may outweigh the recall loss, while for long periods the reverse will apply; in between there will be a length of reference periods at which the two effects counterbalance each other."[8] Unfortunately, no single reference period can be used to frame questions for all events, because what is optimal depends on the importance of the event to those involved.

A third factor that affects our ability to remember is the stimulus we are given. As we saw in the preceding chapter, there is a definite increase in retention when a respondent's memory is jogged using a recognition measure rather than an aided recall measure, and the aided recall measure, in turn, produces more "remembering" than an unaided recall measure.

WILL RESPONDENTS GIVE THE INFORMATION?   Even though respondents have the information, there is always a question of whether they will share it. Eastern Europeans are wonderful in this regard.

> [U]nlike blasé Western consumers, people in Eastern Europe are more than willing to answer questions. After years of directives from the top, people are flattered to be asked their opinions, even if they're just being asked about the taste of a toothpaste or the feel of a shaving cream. Gallup's Mr. Manchin [a regional vice-president] recounts how an old lady in Hungary thanked the interviewer at the end of an hour-long session. "It was such a wonderful experience to have a chance to talk to you for so long," she said. "How much do I pay you?"[9]

Researchers in many other parts of the world are not as fortunate and sometimes encounter situations in which respondents have the necessary information but they will not give it. Their willingness, in turn, seems to be a function of the amount of work involved in producing an answer, their ability to articulate an answer, and the sensitivity of the issue.

---

[8]Graham Kalton and Howard Schuman, "The Effect of the Question on Survey Responses: A Review," *Journal of the Royal Statistical Society, Series A*, 145 (Part 1, 1982), pp. 44–45. See also William A. Cook, "Telescoping and Memory's Other Tricks," *Journal of Advertising Research* 27 (February/March 1987), pp. RC5–RC8; Norman M. Bradburn, Lance J. Rip, and Steven K. Shevell, "Answering Autobiographical Questions: The Impact of Memory and Inference on Surveys," *Science* 236 (April 10, 1987), pp. 157–161; McKee J. McClendon, "Acquiescence and Recency Response Order Effects in Interview Surveys," *Sociological Methodology and Research* 20 (August 1991), pp. 60–103.

[9]Lee Valeriano Lourdes, "Marketing: Western Firms Poll Eastern Europeans to Discern Tastes of Nascent Consumers," *The Wall Street Journal* (April 27, 1992), p. B1.

Even though a purchasing agent may be able to determine to the penny how much the company spent on cleaning compound last year or the relative amount spent on each brand bought, the agent is unlikely to take the time to look up these data to reply to an unsolicited questionnaire. Questionnaire developers need to be constantly mindful of the amount of effort it might take respondents to give the information sought. When the effort is excessive, they may have to settle for approximate answers, or they may be better off omitting the issue completely, since these types of questions tend to irritate respondents and damage their cooperation with the rest of the survey.

When respondents are unable to articulate their answers on an issue, they are likely to ignore it and also refuse to cooperate with the other parts of the survey. Such issues should be avoided, or else the researcher should use a good deal of creative energy designing a mechanism that allows respondents to articulate their views. Although respondents might not be able to express their preferences in furniture styles, for example, they should be able to indicate the style they like best when shown pictures, prototypes, hardware samples, and fabric swatches. La-Z-Boy used this approach when it invited a panel of consumers to evaluate a line of new products, including fabrics and styles. The consumers liked all the fabrics except for two plaid designs, which they rated as not soft enough. La-Z-Boy dropped one of the patterns and asked the manufacturer to modify the other one to make it softer.[10]

General Motors also used pictures to determine preferences for grille designs when they found that respondents could not articulate their likes and dislikes. Similarly, J.C. Penney used pictures of its displays of women's clothing along with pictures of the displays of four of its competitors to determine its positioning in the market.[11]

When an issue is embarrassing or otherwise threatening to respondents, they are likely to refuse to cooperate. Such issues should be avoided whenever possible. If that is impossible because the issue is essential to the study, the researcher needs to pay close attention to how the issue is addressed, particularly with respect to question location and question phrasing.

In general, it is better to address sensitive issues later rather than earlier in the survey.[12] Most surveys will produce some initial mistrust in respondents. One has to overcome this skepticism and establish rapport. This is made easier when respondents have the opportunity to warm to the task by answering nonthreatening questions early in the interview, particularly questions that establish the legitimacy of the project.

---

[10]Stella M. Hopkins, "Furniture Makers Start Asking Customers What They Want," *Charlotte (NC) Observer* (October 12, 1998) (downloaded from Dow Jones Publications Library, Dow Jones Web site, www.dowjones.com, August 16, 1999).

[11]Harper W. Boyd, Jr., Ralph Westfall, and Stanley F. Staasch, *Marketing Research: Text and Cases*, 6th ed. (Homewood, IL: Richard D. Irwin, 1985), p. 272; Gail Tom, Michelle Dragics, and Christi Holderegger, "Using Visual Presentation to Assess Store Positioning: A Case Study of J.C. Penney," *Marketing Research: A Magazine of Management & Applications* 3 (September 1991), pp. 48–52.

[12]Question sequence will be discussed more fully later in the chapter.

When sensitive questions must be asked, it helps to consider ways to make them less threatening. Some helpful techniques in this regard include the following:[13]

1. Hide the question in a group of other, more innocuous, questions.

2. State that the behavior or attitude is not unusual before asking the specific questions of the respondent (for example, "Recent studies show that one of every four households has trouble meeting monthly financial obligations"). This technique, known as the use of counterbiasing statements, makes it easier for the respondent to admit the potentially embarrassing behavior.

3. Phrase the question in terms of others and how they might feel or act (such as, "Do you think most people cheat on their income tax? Why?"). Respondents might readily reveal their attitudes toward cheating when preparing income tax forms when asked about other people, but they might be very reluctant to do so if they were asked outright if *they* ever cheat on their taxes and why.

4. State the response in terms of a number of categories that the respondent may simply check. Instead of asking women for their age, for example, one could simply hand them a card with the age categories

    A: 20–29   B: 30–39   C: 40–49   D: 50–59   E: 60+

    and ask them to respond with the appropriate letter.

5. Use the **randomized response model,** which has the respondent answer one of several paired questions. The particular question is selected at random—for example, by having the respondent draw colored balls from an urn. The respondent is instructed to answer Question A if the ball is, say, blue, and Question B if the ball is red. The interviewer is unaware of the question being answered by the respondent, because he or she never sees the color of the ball drawn. Under these conditions the respondent is less likely to refuse to answer or to distort the answer he or she provides. A study to investigate the incidence of shoplifting might pair the sensitive question, "Have you ever shoplifted?" with the innocuous question, "Is your birthday in January?" The incidence of shoplifting can still be estimated by using an appropriate statistical model, because the percentage of respondents answering each question is controlled by the proportion of red and blue balls in the urn. Suppose, for example, that there are five red and five blue balls in the urn; thus, the probability that the respondent will answer Question A, "Have you ever shoplifted?" is one-half. Further, the proportion of people whose birthdays fall in January is also known to be .05 from census data. Suppose that the proportion who answered "yes" to either Question A or B is .20. Using the standard laws of probability, we could

---

[13]For general treatments on how to handle sensitive questions, see Kent H. Marquis, et al., *Response Errors in Sensitive Topic Surveys: Estimates, Effects, and Correction Options* (Santa Monica, CA: Rand Corporation, 1981); Claire M. Renzetti and Raymond M. Lee, eds., *Researching Sensitive Topics* (Thousand Oaks, CA: Sage Publications, 1992); Raymond M. Lee, *Doing Research on Sensitive Topics* (Thousand Oaks, CA: Sage Publications, 1993); Roger Tourangeau and John Smith, "Asking Sensitive Questions: The Impact of Data Collection Mode, Question Format, and Question Context," *Public Opinion Quarterly* 60 (Summer 1996), pp. 275–304.

then estimate the proportion of the people in the sample who were responding "yes" to the sensitive question by using the formula

$$\lambda = p\pi_S + (1 - p)\pi_A$$

where

λ = the total proportion of "yes" responses to both questions,
p = the probability that the sensitive question is selected,
$1 - p$ = the probability that the innocuous question is selected,
π_S = the proportion of "yes" responses to the sensitive question, and
π_A = the proportion of "yes" responses to the innocuous question.[14]

Substituting the appropriate quantities indicates that

$$.20 = .50\pi_S + .50(.05)$$
$$\text{and } \pi_S = .35$$

or that 35 percent of the respondents had shoplifted. Note, though, that the researcher cannot use the randomized response technique to determine specifically which respondents have shoplifted. This would preclude any opportunity to determine, for example, if shoplifting behavior was associated with any particular demographic characteristics.

Form of Response

Once the content of the individual questions is determined, the researcher needs to decide on the particular form of the response. Will the question be open-ended or fixed-alternative? If fixed-alternative, will it be a multichotomy, a dichotomy, or perhaps a scale?

---

[14]James E. Reinmuth and Michael D. Geurts, "The Collection of Sensitive Information Using a Two-Stage Randomized Response Model," *Journal of Marketing Research* 12 (November 1975), pp. 402–407. For an elementary overview of the randomized response model, see Cathy Campbell and Brian L. Joiner, "How to Get the Answer Without Being Sure You've Asked the Question," *American Statistician* 26 (December 1973), pp. 229–231. For reviews and examples of its use, see D. G. Horvitz, B. G. Greenberg, and J. R. Abernathy, "Randomized Response: A Data Gathering Device for Sensitive Questions," *International Statistical Review* (August 1976), pp. 181–195; Paul E. Tracy and James Alan Fox, "The Validity of Randomized Response for Sensitive Measurements," *American Sociological Review* 46 (April 1981), pp. 187–200; Brian K. Burton and Janet P. Near, "Estimating the Incidence of Wrongdoing and Whistle-Blowing," *Journal of Business Ethics* 14 (January 1995), pp. 17–30. For discussion of randomization devices and methodologies for self-administered and telephone interview applications of the randomized response method, see Donald E. Stem, Jr., and R. Kirk Steinhorst, "Telephone Interview and Mail Questionnaire Applications of the Randomized Response Model," *Journal of the American Statistical Association* 79 (September 1984), pp. 555–564; Jamshid C. Hosseini and Robert L. Armacost, "Randomized Responses: A Better Way to Obtain Sensitive Information," *Business Horizons* 33 (May/June 1990), pp. 82–86. For general treatments, see James Alan Fox and Paul E. Tracy, *Randomizing Response: A Method for Sensitive Surveys* (Thousand Oaks, CA: Sage Publications, 1986); Arijit Chaudhuri and Rahul Mukerjee, *Randomized Response: Theory and Techniques* (New York: Marcel Dekker, Inc., 1987); U. N. Umesh and Robert A. Peterson, "A Critical Evaluation of the Randomized Response Model: Applications, Validations, and Research Agenda," *Sociological Methods and Research* 20 (August 1991), pp. 104–138.

OPEN-ENDED QUESTIONS   Respondents are free to reply to **open-ended questions** in their own words rather than being limited to choosing from a set of alternatives. The following are examples:

How old are you? _____
Do you think laws limiting the amount of interest businesses can charge consumers are needed? _____
Can you name three sponsors of the Monday night football games? _____
Do you intend to purchase an automobile this year? _____
Why did you purchase a Magnavox brand color TV? _____
Do you own a VCR? _____
How many long-distance telephone calls do you make in a typical week? _____

These questions span the gamut of the types of primary data that could be collected from demographic characteristics through attitudes, intentions, and behavior. The open-ended question is indeed a versatile device.

Open-ended questions are often used to begin a questionnaire. The general feeling is that it is best to proceed from the general to the specific in constructing questionnaires. So an opening question like, "When you think of television sets, which brands come to mind?" gives some insight into the respondent's frame of reference and could be most helpful in interpreting the individual's replies to later questions. The open-ended question is also often used to probe for additional information. The probes "Why?" "Why do you feel that way?" and "Please explain" are often used to seek elaboration of a respondent's reply.

MULTICHOTOMOUS QUESTIONS   The **multichotomous question** is a fixed-alternative question; respondents are asked to choose the alternative that most closely corresponds to their position on the subject. Table 8.1, for example, presents some of the preceding open-ended questions as multichotomous questions. Respondents would be instructed to check the box or boxes that apply.

The examples in Table 8.1 illustrate some of the difficulties encountered in using multiple-choice questions. None of the alternatives in the interest-ceiling legislation question, for example, may correctly capture the respondent's true feeling on the issue. The individual's opinion may be more complex, for one thing. He or she may believe that interest-ceiling legislation is needed, assuming that a number of provisos or contingent possibilities can be satisfied (for example, that business firms will not reduce the amount of credit available to customers nor shorten the length of the repayment period). If these conditions cannot be satisfied, the respondent may feel just the opposite. The multiple-choice question does not permit individuals to elaborate on their true position but requires them to condense their complex attitude into a single statement. Of course, a well-designed series of multiple-choice questions could allow for such elaborations. An exhaustive coverage of the potential qualifiers would also substantially increase the length of the questionnaire.

The interest-ceiling legislation question also illustrates a general problem in question design: Should respondents be provided with a "don't know" or "no opinion" option? There is no question that if a respondent truly does not know an answer or has no opinion on an issue that he or she should be allowed to state that

TABLE 8.1	Examples of Multichotomous Questions

Age	*Television Purchase*
How old are you?	*Why did you purchase a Magnavox brand color TV?*
☐ Less than 20	☐ Price was lower than other alternatives
☐ 20–29	☐ Feel it represents the highest quality
☐ 30–39	☐ Availability of local service
☐ 40–49	☐ Availability of a service contract
☐ 50–59	☐ Picture is better
☐ 60 or over	☐ Warranty was better
	☐ Other
Interest-Ceiling Legislation	*Telephone-Use Behavior*
Do you think laws limiting the amount of interest businesses can charge consumers are needed?	*How many long-distance telephone calls do you make in a typical week?*
☐ Definitely needed	☐ Less than 5
☐ Probably needed	☐ 5–10
☐ Probably not needed	☐ More than 10
☐ Definitely not needed	
☐ No opinion	

when responding. However, the issue is whether that option should be *explicitly* provided the respondent in the form of a "don't know" or "no opinion" category by asking a filter question such as "Do you have an opinion on . . . ?" The arguments regarding the provision of a neutral point or category revolve around data accuracy versus respondent cooperation. Those suggesting that a neutral point, or "no opinion" answer, should not be provided argue that most respondents are not likely to be exactly neutral on an issue. Instead of providing them an easy way out, it is much better to have them think about the issue so that they can frame their preference, however slight it may be; that is certainly better than allowing the researcher to infer the majority opinion using only the responses from those taking a stand on the issue. Those who argue for including a neutral or "no opinion" category among the responses are inclined to suggest that forcing a respondent to make a choice when his or her preference is fuzzy or nonexistent simply introduces response error into the results. Further, it makes it harder for respondents to answer and may turn them off to the whole survey. The jury is still out about which form better captures respondents' true position on an issue, although there is no question that the two alternatives can produce widely differing proportions of the number of respondents holding a neutral view, potentially in the range of 10 to 50 percent.[15] For

---

[15]Kalton and Schuman, "The Effect of the Question on Survey Responses: A Review," pp. 51–52. See also Duncan and Stenbeck, "No Opinion or Not Sure?" pp. 513–525; Gail S. Poe, et al., "Don't Know Box in Factual Questions in a Mail Questionnaire: Effects on Level and Quality of Response," *Public Opinion Quarterly* 52 (Summer 1988), pp. 212–222; Mikael Gilljam and Donald Granberg, "Should We Take Don't Know for an Answer," *Public Opinion Quarterly* 57 (Fall 1993), pp. 348–357; Howard Schuman and Stanley Presser, *Questions and Answers in Attitude Surveys: Experiments on Question Form, Wording, and Context* (Thousand Oaks, CA: Sage Publications, Inc., 1996).

A financial institution has developed a new type of savings bond. The marketing director of this institution has requested that a local research supply company design a questionnaire that will help quantify target consumers' interest in this new bond. However, the marketing director is concerned about the possibility that competitors will hear about the new product concept because of the survey. He requests that the questionnaire be written in such a way that the true purpose of the study is masked.

To mask the actual purpose of the study, the questionnaire primarily asks respondents for details of their holiday plans and budgets. Because respondents are asked questions about their finances only after being asked multiple vacation-related questions, it is hoped that respondents will assume the information is for a travel company. Moreover, the marketing director of the financial institution asks that interviewers tell respondents that the information is being gathered for a travel-related company.

- Discuss the implications of deceiving respondents on a questionnaire in this way.
- If the interviewers had not been told to explicitly tell respondents that the information was for a travel-related corporation, would the deception be acceptable?
- Are there ways of acquiring this type of information without resorting to deception while still protecting the institution's new product idea?
- Discuss the validity issues associated with respondents knowing the purpose of the survey as they are completing it.

example, Research Realities 8.2 reports the results of one study that used both four-point and five-point purchase intention scales. The scales were the same except for the provision of the neutral category in the five-point scale. The general conclusion emerging is that if one used only the extreme points (that is, definitely will buy/definitely will not buy) for evaluating a new product or idea, *either* scale could be used. On the other hand, the researcher who wanted to use two categories as the percentage likely to buy the product (definitely will buy or probably will buy) would find a difference in the two scales, with the four-point scale providing more positive responses than the five-point scale.[16]

---

[16]"Measuring Purchase Intent," *Research on Research,* no. 2 (Chicago: Market Facts, Inc., undated). See also Gregory J. Spagna, "Questionnaires: Which Approach Do You Use?" *Journal of Advertising Research* 24 (February/March 1984), pp. 67–70; George F. Bishop, "Experiments with the Middle Response Alternative in Survey Questions," *Public Opinion Quarterly* 51 (Summer 1987), pp. 220–232; Raphael Gillet, "The Top-Box Paradox," *Marketing Research: A Magazine of Management & Applications* 3 (September 1991), pp. 37–39; H. H. Friedman and T. Amoo, "Multiple Biases in Rating Scale Construction," *Journal of International Marketing and Marketing Research* 24 (October 1999), pp. 115–126.

RESEARCH REALITIES 8.2

A Comparison of the Use of Four-Point versus Five-Point Scales to Measure Purchase Intent

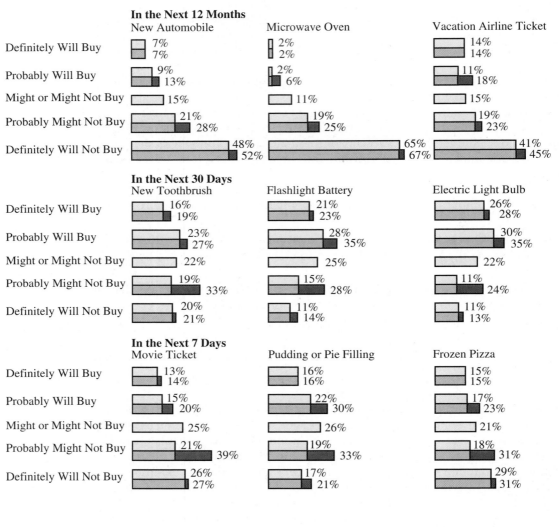

In the Next 12 Months

	New Automobile	Microwave Oven	Vacation Airline Ticket
Definitely Will Buy	7% / 7%	2% / 2%	14% / 14%
Probably Will Buy	9% / 13%	2% / 6%	11% / 18%
Might or Might Not Buy	15%	11%	15%
Probably Might Not Buy	21% / 28%	19% / 25%	19% / 23%
Definitely Will Not Buy	48% / 52%	65% / 67%	41% / 45%

In the Next 30 Days

	New Toothbrush	Flashlight Battery	Electric Light Bulb
Definitely Will Buy	16% / 19%	21% / 23%	26% / 28%
Probably Will Buy	23% / 27%	28% / 35%	30% / 35%
Might or Might Not Buy	22%	25%	22%
Probably Might Not Buy	19% / 33%	15% / 28%	11% / 24%
Definitely Will Not Buy	20% / 21%	11% / 14%	11% / 13%

In the Next 7 Days

	Movie Ticket	Pudding or Pie Filling	Frozen Pizza
Definitely Will Buy	13% / 14%	16% / 16%	15% / 15%
Probably Will Buy	15% / 20%	22% / 30%	17% / 23%
Might or Might Not Buy	25%	26%	21%
Probably Might Not Buy	21% / 39%	19% / 33%	18% / 31%
Definitely Will Not Buy	26% / 27%	17% / 21%	29% / 31%

5-point

4-point   Difference between 5-point and 4-point

Source: "Measuring Purchase Intent," *Research on Research*, no. 2 (Chicago: Market Facts, Inc., undated). Reprinted with permission.

The TV-set purchase question (Table 8.1) illustrates a number of problems associated with multiple-choice questions. First, the list of reasons cited for purchasing a Magnavox color TV may not exhaust the reasons that could have been used by the respondent. The person may have purchased a Magnavox out of loyalty to a friend who owns the local Magnavox distributorship or because she or he really practices the "buy locally" admonition advanced by many small town chambers of commerce. The "other" response category attempts to solve this problem. A great many respondents checking the "other" category, though, will render the study useless. Thus, the burden is on the researcher to make the list of alternatives in a multiple-choice question exhaustive. This may entail extensive prior research into the phenomenon that is to serve as the subject of a multiple-choice question.

Unless the respondent is instructed to check all alternatives that apply, or is to rank the alternatives in order of importance, the multiple-choice question also demands that the alternatives be mutually exclusive. The income categories shown below violate this principle:

☐ $10,000–$20,000
☐ $20,000–$30,000

A respondent with an income of $20,000 would not know which alternative to check. A legitimate response with respect to the color TV purchase question might include several of the alternatives listed. The respondent thought the picture, warranty, and price were all more attractive on the Magnavox than they were on other makes. Thus, the instructions would necessarily have to be "Check the most important reason," "Check all those reasons that apply," or "Rank all the reasons that apply from most important to least important."

A third difficulty with the TV purchase question is its great number of alternative responses. The list should be exhaustive, yet the alternative statements an individual can simultaneously process appears to be limited. In one early study, the researchers presented each respondent with a card with six alternative statements. After each respondent had made his or her choice, the card was immediately replaced with another. On the second card, two of the six statements had been changed, and one statement from the original list was omitted. Yet only one-half of the respondents "could identify the changes and a mere handful located the omission."[17] The meaning of all this is that in designing multiple-choice questions, the researcher should remain cognizant of human beings' limited data-processing capabilities. Perhaps a series of questions is more appropriate than one question. If there are a great many alternatives to a single question, they should be shown to respondents using cards and not simply read to them.

The fourth weakness of the TV purchase question is that it is susceptible to a potential order bias. The responses are likely to be affected by the order in which

---

[17]Hadley Cantril and Edreta Fried, *Gauging Public Opinion* (Princeton, NJ: Princeton University Press, 1944), chap. 1, as reported in Payne, *The Art of Asking Questions*, p. 93. For a discussion of how to take account of people's information-processing abilities when designing questionnaires, see Seymour Sudman, Norman M. Bradburn, and Norbert Schwarz, *Thinking About Answers: The Application of Cognitive Process to Survey Methodology* (San Francisco, CA: Jossey-Bass, 1996).

the alternatives are presented. Research Realities 8.3, for example, shows how the distribution of responses to the same behaviors was affected by the order in which the alternatives were listed on two versions of a mailed questionnaire. That the three questions produced statistically significant differences in the distributions of replies is especially noteworthy because order bias is least likely to occur in mail questionnaires because respondents can see all the response categories. In point of fact, response order bias is typically much greater in telephone surveys or interviews in which the structured responses are read to the respondents. The recommended procedure for combating this order bias is to prepare several forms of the questionnaire, or several cards, if cards are used to list the alternatives. The order in which the alternatives are listed is then altered from form to form. If each alternative appears once at the extremes of the list, once in the middle, and once somewhere in between, the researcher can feel reasonably comfortable that the possible effects of position bias have been neutralized.

The long-distance telephone call example in Table 8.1 illustrates another problem with multiple-choice questions when they are used to get at the frequency of various behaviors. The range of the categories used in the question seems to cue respondents about how they should reply. That is, the response scale categories themselves affect subjects' reports of the frequency with which they engage in the behavior. A scale with the following three categories would likely produce a different picture of the frequency with which these same respondents make long-distance telephone calls than the one shown in Table 8.1:

☐   Less than 10
☐   10–20
☐   More than 20

It seems that respondents make judgments about the researcher's knowledge or expectations from the categories and then respond accordingly. Specifically, they seem reluctant to report behaviors that are unusual in the context of the response scale—namely, those that constitute the extreme categories.[18] A general strategy for combating this tendency is to use open-ended answer formats when obtaining data on behavioral frequencies.

DICHOTOMOUS QUESTIONS   The **dichotomous question** is also a fixed-alternative question but one in which there are only two alternatives listed; for example:

Do you think laws limiting the amount of interest businesses can charge consumers are needed?

☐   Yes
☐   No

---

[18]Norbert Schwarz, et al., "Response Scales: Effect of Category Range on Reported Behavior and Comparative Judgments," *Public Opinion Quarterly* 49 (Fall 1985), pp. 388–395; Norbert Schwarz, et al., "The Range of Response Alternatives May Determine the Meaning of the Question: Further Evidence on Information Functions of Response Alternatives," *Social Cognition* 6, no. 2 (1988), pp. 107–117; Eric A. Greenleaf, "Measuring Extreme Response Style," *Public Opinion Quarterly* 56 (Fall 1992), pp. 328–351.

RESEARCH REALITIES 8.3

How the Order in Which the Alternatives Are Listed Affects the Distribution of Replies

[Compared to a year ago] the amount of time spent watching television by my household is . . .

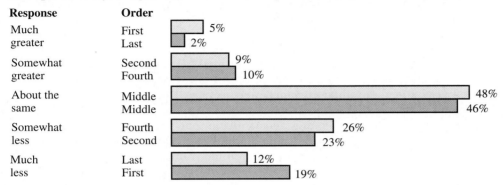

Response	Order	
Much greater	First / Last	5% / 2%
Somewhat greater	Second / Fourth	9% / 10%
About the same	Middle / Middle	48% / 46%
Somewhat less	Fourth / Second	26% / 23%
Much less	Last / First	12% / 19%

[Compared to a year ago] my household eats out at restaurants . . .

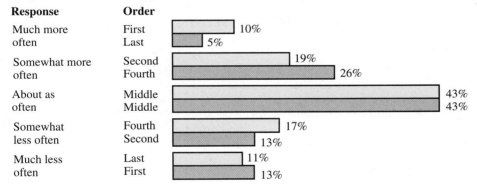

Response	Order	
Much more often	First / Last	10% / 5%
Somewhat more often	Second / Fourth	19% / 26%
About as often	Middle / Middle	43% / 43%
Somewhat less often	Fourth / Second	17% / 13%
Much less often	Last / First	11% / 13%

Most home repair or improvement projects completed in my home during the past have been completed by . . . [Base: Those completing a project.]

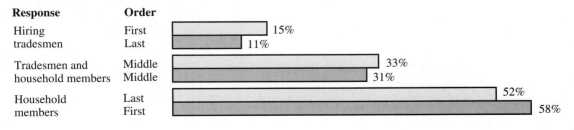

Response	Order	
Hiring tradesmen	First / Last	15% / 11%
Tradesmen and household members	Middle / Middle	33% / 31%
Household members	Last / First	52% / 58%

Source: "An Examination of Order Bias," *Research on Research*, no. 1 (Chicago: Market Facts, Inc., undated). Reprinted by permission.

Do you intend to purchase an automobile this year?

☐   Yes

☐   No

We have already seen how the first of these questions could also be handled as a multiple-choice question. The second could also be given a multichotomous structure. Instead of simply presenting the yes-no alternatives, the list could be framed as "Definitely intend to buy," "Probably will buy," "Probably will not buy," "Definitely intend not to buy," and "Undecided." Dichotomous questions can often be framed as multichotomous questions, and vice versa. (The two possess similar advantages and disadvantages, which were reviewed earlier when discussing structured questions. They will not be repeated here.) The dichotomous question offers the ultimate in ease of coding and tabulation, and this probably accounts for its being the most commonly used type of question in communication studies.

One special problem with the dichotomous question is that the response can depend on how the question is framed. This is true, of course, of all questions, but with the dichotomous question it represents a special problem. Consider two alternative questions:

Do you think that gasoline will be more expensive or less expensive next year than it is now?

☐   More expensive

☐   Less expensive

Do you think that gasoline will be less expensive or more expensive next year than it is now?

☐   Less expensive

☐   More expensive

Now, the questions appear identical, and certainly we might want to expand each to include categories for "No opinion" and "About the same." The fact remains, though, that the two questions will elicit different responses.[19] The simple switching of the positions of "More expensive" or "Less expensive" can affect the response an individual gives. Which, then, is the correct wording?

One generally accepted procedure for combating this order bias is to employ a **split ballot.** One phrasing is used on one-half of the questionnaires, and the alternative phrasing is employed on the other one-half of the questionnaires. The averaged percentages from the two forms should then cancel out any biases.

---

[19] Two of the best discussions of this are to be found in Payne, *The Art of Asking Questions,* and Howard Schuman and Stanley Presser, *Questions and Answers in Attitude Surveys* (Orlando: Academic Press, 1981), especially pp. 56–77. See also Michaela Wanke, Norbert Schwarz, and Elizabeth Noelle-Neumann, "Asking Comparative Questions: The Impact of the Direction of Comparison," *Public Opinion Quarterly* 59 (Fall 1995), pp. 347–372; Donald A. Dillman, et al., "Effects of Category Order on Answers in Mail and Telephone Surveys," *Rural Sociology* (Winter 1995), pp. 674–687.

SCALES   Another type of fixed-alternative question is the question that employs a scale to capture the response. For instance, when inquiring about VCR use, the following question might be asked:

How often do you tape programs for later viewing with your VCR?
☐   Never
☐   Occasionally
☐   Sometimes
☐   Often

In this form, the question is a multichotomous question. However, the responses also represent a scale of use. The scale nature of the question would be more obvious perhaps if the following form were used to secure the replies:

Never	Occasionally	Sometimes	Often

The advantage of this scheme is that the descriptors could be presented at the top of the page, and types of programs could be listed along the left margin (for example, films, sporting events, network specials, and so on). The respondent would then be instructed to designate the frequency with which the VCR is used to record each type. The instruction would only need to be given once at the beginning, and thus a great deal of information could be secured from the respondent in a short period of time.

Decide on Question Wording

Step 5 in the questionnaire development process involves the phrasing of each question. This is a critical task, because poor phrasing of a question can cause respondents to refuse to answer it (even though they agreed to cooperate in the study) or to answer incorrectly, either on purpose or because of misunderstanding. The first condition, known as **item nonresponse,** can create a great many problems during data analysis. The second condition produces measurement error, in that the recorded or obtained score does not equal the respondent's true score on the issue.[20]

Experienced researchers know that the phrasing of a question can directly affect the responses to it. One humorous anecdote in this regard involves two priests, a Dominican and a Jesuit, who are discussing whether it is a sin to smoke and pray at the same time. "After failing to reach a conclusion, each goes off to consult his respective superior. The next week they meet again. The Dominican says, 'Well, what did your superior say?' The Jesuit responds, 'He said it was all right.' 'That's funny,' the Dominican replied, 'my superior said it was a sin.' Jesuit: 'What did you

---

[20]The notion of measurement error is defined more formally in Appendix 9A. For a review of the literature on the quality of questionnaire data, including item omission, see Robert A. Peterson and Roger A. Kerin, "The Quality of Self-Report Data: Review and Synthesis," in Ben Enis and Kenneth Roering, eds., *Annual Review of Marketing 1981* (Chicago: American Marketing Association, 1981), pp. 5–20; see also Floyd Jackson Fowler, Jr., "How Unclear Terms Affect Survey Data," *Public Opinion Quarterly* 56 (Summer 1992), pp. 218–231.

ask him?' Reply: 'I asked him if it was all right to smoke while praying.' 'Oh,' says the Jesuit, 'I asked my superior if it was all right to pray while smoking.'"[21]

Even though it is recognized, then, that the wording of questions can affect the answers obtained, it is sometimes hard to develop good phrasings of questions, because there are few basic principles researchers can rely on when framing questions. Instead, the literature is replete with rules of thumb. While the rules of thumb are often easier to state than to practice, researchers need to be aware of the admonitions that surround the wording of questions.

USE SIMPLE WORDS   A "vocabulary problem" confronts most researchers. Because they are more highly educated than the typical questionnaire respondent, researchers are prone to use words familiar to them but not understood by many respondents. This is a difficult problem, because it is not easy to dismiss what one knows and put oneself in the respondent's shoes when trying to assess his or her vocabulary. A significant proportion of the population, for example, does not understand the word *Caucasian*, although most researchers do, and a very serious problem in designing questionnaires to survey Hispanics is in developing an unambiguous ethnic identifier.[22] The researcher needs to be constantly aware that the average person in the United States has a high school, not a college, education and that many people have difficulty in coping with usual tasks, such as making change, reading job notices, or completing a driver's application blank. A basic admonition is to keep the words simple. When there is a choice between more difficult and simpler wording, it is best to choose simplicity. There is always great potential for respondents to misunderstand what they are being asked even when simple words are used. Research Realities 8.4, for example, lists some problem words identified by Payne more than 40 years ago and explains why these words can cause difficulty. Payne identified more than 80 such words, which is one very important reason (and there are many) that those charged with the task of designing questionnaires would be well advised to read Payne's classic book.[23]

AVOID AMBIGUOUS WORDS AND QUESTIONS   Not only should the words used be simple, but they also should be unambiguous. The same is true for the questions. Consider again the multichotomous question below:

How often do you tape programs for later viewing with your VCR?

☐   Never

☐   Occasionally

☐   Sometimes

☐   Often

---

[21]Sudman and Bradburn, *Asking Questions*, p. 1.

[22]Gonzola R. Soruco, "Sampling and Nonsampling Errors in Hispanic Population Telephone Surveys," *Applied Marketing Research* 29 (Summer 1989), pp. 11–15; Patricia Braus, "What Does 'Hispanic' Mean?" *American Demographics* 15 (June 1993), pp. 46–49, 58.

[23]Payne, *The Art of Asking Questions*.

Some Multi-Meaning Problem Words Researchers Should Use with Caution

about   Among other uses, "about" is sometimes intended to mean somewhere near in the sense that both 48 percent and 52 percent are "about" half. It is also used to mean nearly or almost, in the sense that 48 percent is "about" half while 52 percent is "over" half. This small difference in interpretation may make a slight difference in the way various respondents answer certain questions.

all   Here is the first mention of a "dead giveaway" word, a term you will see frequently from here on.

Your own experience with true-false tests has probably demonstrated to you that it is safe to count almost every all-inclusive statement as false. That is, you have learned in such tests that it is safe to follow the idea that "all statements containing 'all' are false, including this one." Some people have the same negative reaction to opinion questions which hinge upon all-inclusive or all-exclusive words. They may be generally in agreement with a proposition, but nevertheless hesitate to accept the extreme idea of *all, always, each, every, never, nobody, only, none,* or *sure.*
Would you say that all cats have four legs?
Is the mayor doing all he can for the city?

It is correct, of course, to use an all-inclusive word if it correctly states the alternative. But you will usually find that such a word produces an overstatement. Most people may go along with the idea, accepting it as a form of literary license, but the purists and quibblers may either refuse to give an opinion or may even choose the other side in protest.

always   This is another dead giveaway word.
Do you always observe traffic signs?
Is your boss always friendly?

and   This simple conjunction in some contexts may be taken either as separating two alternatives or as connecting two parts of a single alternative.
Is there much rivalry among the boys who sell soda pop and crackerjack?
Some people will answer in terms of rivalry between two groups—those who sell pop and those who sell crackerjack. Others will take it as rivalry within the single group comprising both pop and crackerjack salesmen.

any   The trouble with this word is a bit difficult to explain. It's something like that optical illusion of the shifting stairsteps, which you sometimes seem to see from underneath and sometimes seem to see from above but which you aren't able to see both ways at the same time. The trouble with "any" is that it may mean "every," "some," or "one only" in the same sentence or question, depending on the way you look at it.

See whether you can get both the "every" and "only one" illusions from this question and notice the difference in meaning that results:
Do you think any word is better than the one we are discussing?
You could think, "Yes, I think just any old word (every word) is better." On the other hand, you might think, "Yes, I believe it would be possible to find a better word."

Another difficulty with "any" is that when used in either the "every" or the "not any" context it becomes as much a dead giveaway word as are "every" and "none."

bad   In itself the word "bad" is not at all bad for question wording. It conveys the meaning desired and is satisfactory as an alternative in a "good or bad" two-way question.

Experience seems to indicate, however, that people are generally less willing to criticize than they are to praise. Since it is difficult to get them to state their negative views, sometimes the critical side needs to be softened. For example, after asking, *What things are good about your job?*, it might seem perfectly natural to ask, *What things are bad about it?* But if we want to lean over backwards to get as many criticisms as we can, we may be wise not to apply the "bad" stigma but to ask, *What things are not so good about it?*

could   No fault is found with the word itself, but we are well advised to remember that it should not be confused with "should" or "might."

ever   This word tends to be a dead giveaway in a very special sense. "Ever" is such a long time and so inclusive that it makes it seem plausible that some unimpressive things may have happened.

(continued)

RESEARCH REALITIES 8.4

(continued)

Have you ever listened to the Song Plugger radio program?

"Yes—I suppose I must have at some time or other."

go "Go" is given more space in the index of *The American Thesaurus of Slang* than any other word—a total of about 12½ columns.

When did you last go to town?

If the respondent takes this literally, it is a good question, but the "go to town" phrase has more than a dozen different slang meanings, including a couple that might get your face slapped.

heard Sometimes these words are used in a very general sense *(Have you heard of . . . ?)* to include learning about not only through hearing but also through reading, seeing, etc. Unfortunately, however, some respondents apparently take such words literally. They don't say that they've heard when they've only seen, for instance. In one study, only half as many people said that they had "heard or read" anything about patents as reported having attended a patents exposition. Evidently, they considered whatever they learned from attendance as separate from hearing or reading.

less This word is usually used as an alternative to "more," where it may cause a minor problem. The phrase "more or less" has a special meaning all its own in which some respondents do not see an alternative. Thus, they may simply answer "yes, more or less" to a question like:

Compared with a year ago, are you more or less happy in your job?

The easy solution to this problem is to break up the "more or less" expression by introducing an extra word or so to reverse the two:

Compared with a year ago, are you more happy or less happy in your job?

Compared with a year ago, are you less happy or more happy in your job?

like This word is on the problem list only because it is sometimes used to introduce an example. The problem with bringing an example into a question is that the respondent's attention may be directed toward the particular example and away from the general issue which it is meant only to illustrate. The use of examples may sometimes be necessary, but the possible hazard should always be kept in mind. The choice of an example can affect the answers to the question—in fact, it may materially change the question, as in these two examples:

Do you think that leafy vegetables like spinach should be in the daily diet?

Do you think that leafy vegetables like lettuce should be in the daily diet?

you The dictionary distinguishes only two or three meanings of "you"—the second person singular and plural and the substitution for the impersonal "one"—"How do you get there?" in place of "How does one get there?" In most questions "you" gives no trouble whatever, it being clear that we are asking the opinion of the second person singular. However, and here is the problem, the word sometimes may have a collective meaning as in a question asked of radio repairmen:

How many radio sets did you repair last month?

This question seemed to work all right until one repairman in a large shop countered with, "Who do you mean, me or the whole shop?"

Much as we might want to, therefore, we can't give "you" an unqualified recommendation. Sometimes "you" needs the emphasis of "you yourself" and sometimes it just isn't the word to use, as in the above situation where the entire shop was meant.

Source: Stanley L. Payne, *The Art of Asking Questions.* Copyright 1951, Princeton University Press. © 1979 renewed by Princeton University Press. Excerpts, pp. 158–176, reprinted with permission of Princeton University Press.

For all practical purposes, the replies to this question would be worthless. The words *occasionally, sometimes,* and *often* are ambiguous. To one respondent, the word *often* might mean "almost every day." To another it might mean, "Yes, I use it when I have the specific need. This happens about once a week." The words *occasionally* and *sometimes* could also be interpreted differently by different respondents.[24] Thus, although the question would get answers, it would generate little real understanding of the frequency of use of the VCR to tape programs.

A much better strategy would be to provide concrete alternatives for the respondent, rather than the preceding ambiguous options. The alternatives might read, for example:

☐ Never use
☐ Use approximately once a month
☐ Use approximately once a week
☐ Use almost every day

Whether these would be the appropriate categories depends on the purpose of the study. The important thing is that the researcher has provided a consistent frame of reference for each respondent. Respondents are no longer free to superimpose their own definitions on the response categories.

An alternative way to avoid ambiguity in response categories when asking about the frequency of some behavior is to ask about the most recent instance of the phenomenon. The question might be framed in the following way, for example:

Did you tape any programs with your VCR in the last two days?
☐ Yes
☐ No
☐ Can't recall

The proportion responding *yes* would then be used to infer the frequency with which the VCR was used, and the follow-up question "For what purpose?" (among all those responding yes) would give insight as to how respondents are using it. Some respondents who normally use their VCR might not have used it the last two days, but the opposite would be true for others. The same would be true with respect to purposes for which it was used. There might be some variation in comparison to what individuals normally do, but the variation should cancel out if a large enough sample of respondents was used. Thus, the aggregate sample should provide a good indication of the proportion of times the VCR is used and the proportion of times it is used to tape various types of programs. The researcher, in effect, relies on the sample to provide insight into the frequency of occurrence of the

---

[24]For empirical evidence of what happens with vague quantifiers, see Nora Cate Schaeffer, "Hardly Ever or Constantly? Group Comparisons Using Vague Quantifiers," *Public Opinion Quarterly* 55 (Fall 1991), pp. 395–423; George D. Gaskell, Colm A. O'Muircheartaigh, and Daniel B. Wright, "Survey Questions about the Frequency of Vaguely Defined Events: The Effects of Response Alternatives," *Public Opinion Quarterly* 58 (Summer 1994), pp. 241–254.

phenomenon, rather than a specific question that may contain ambiguous alternatives. It is important that the sample be large enough in this instance so that the proportions can be estimated with the appropriate degree of confidence.

AVOID LEADING QUESTIONS   A **leading question** is one framed to give the respondent a clue about how he or she should answer. Consider the question:

Do you feel that limiting taxes by law is an effective way to stop the government from picking your pocket every payday?

☐   Yes

☐   No

☐   Undecided

This was one of three questions in an unsolicited questionnaire that the author received as part of a study sponsored by the National Tax Limitation Committee. The committee intended to make the results of the poll available to members of Congress and to state legislators. Given the implied purpose, it is probably not surprising to see the leading words "picking your pocket" being used in this question, or the leading word "gouge" being used in another question. What is especially unfortunate is that it is unlikely the questions themselves accompanied the report to Congress. Rather, it is more likely that the report suggested that some high percentage (for example, 90 percent of those surveyed) favored laws that limited taxes. Conclusion: Congress should pay attention to the wishes of the people and pass such laws.

One sees instances of this phenomenon every day in the newspaper. While not seeing the questionnaire, the public is treated to a discussion of the results of this or that study concerning how the American people feel on issues. Yet the wording of a question makes a difference and it is important for researchers to realize that.[25] If one truly wants an accurate picture of the situation, one needs to avoid leading the respondent. Research Realities 8.5 contains some examples of leading questions.

AVOID IMPLICIT ALTERNATIVES   An **implicit alternative** is one that is not expressed in the options. Consider the two following questions, which were used in two random samples of full-time homemakers to investigate their attitudes toward having a job outside the home.[26]

☐   ***Would you like to have a job, if this were possible?***

☐   ***Would you prefer to have a job, or do you prefer to do just your housework?***

---

[25]For examples, see Tom Smith, "That Which We Call Welfare by Any Other Name Would Smell Sweeter: An Analysis of the Impact of Question Wording on Response Patterns," *Public Opinion Quarterly* 51 (Spring 1987), pp. 75–83; Stephen Budiansky, et al., "The Numbers Racket: How Polls and Statistics Lie," *U.S. News & World Report* (July 11, 1988), pp. 44–47; Warren Mitofsky, "Mr. Perot, You're No Pollster," *The New York Times* (March 27, 1993), p. 15; G. Evans Witt, "Say What You Mean," *American Demographics* 21 (February 1999), p. 23.

[26]E. Noelle-Neumann, "Wanted: Rules for Wording Structured Questionnaires," *Public Opinion Quarterly* 34 (Summer 1970), p. 200. See also Philip Gendall and Janet Hoek, "A Question of Wording," *Marketing Bulletin* 1 (May 1990), pp. 25–36.

RESEARCH REALITIES 8.5

Some Examples of Leading Questions

When Levi Strauss & Co. asked students which clothes would be most popular this year, 90 percent said Levi's 501 jeans. They were the only jeans on the list.

A survey for Black Flag said: "A roach disk . . . poisons a roach slowly. The dying roach returns to the nest and after it dies is eaten by other roaches. In turn these roaches become poisoned and die. How effective do you think this type of product would be in killing roaches?" Not surprisingly, 79 percent said effective.

A Gallup poll sponsored by the disposable-diaper industry asked: "It is estimated that disposable diapers account for less than 2 percent of the trash in today's landfills. In contrast, beverage containers, third-class mail, and yard waste are estimated to account for about 21 percent of the trash in landfills. Given this, in your opinion, would it be fair to ban disposable diapers?" Eighty-four percent said no.

Source: Cynthia Crossen, "Studies Galore Support Products and Positions, But Are They Reliable," *The Wall Street Journal* (November 14, 1991), p. A1.

Even though the two questions appear to be very similar, they produced dramatically different responses. For the first version, 19 percent indicated they would not like to have a job, whereas for the second, 68 percent suggested they would prefer not to have one, over three and one-half times as many. The difference in the two questions is that version 2 makes explicit the alternative implied in version 1.

As a general rule, one should avoid implicit alternatives unless there is a special reason for including them. Further, because the order in which the alternatives appear can affect the responses, one should rotate the order of the options in samples of questionnaires.

AVOID IMPLICIT ASSUMPTIONS   Questions are frequently framed so that there is an **implied assumption** about what will happen as a consequence. The question "Are you in favor of placing price controls on crude oil?" will elicit different responses from individuals, depending on their views of what that might produce in the way of rationing, long lines at the pumps, and so forth. A better way to state the question is to make explicit the consequence(s). Thus, the question would be altered to ask, "Are you in favor of placing price controls on crude oil if it would produce gas rationing?"

Figure 8.3 shows what can happen when the consequences are explicitly stated in a question. Version B makes the implied consequence in version A explicit; the only way the seat belt law could be effective is if there were some penalty for not complying with it. Yet, when there was no explicit statement about what would happen if a person did not comply with the proposed law, 73 percent were in favor of it. When people faced the prospect of a fine for noncompliance, only 50 percent favored a mandatory seat belt law.

AVOID GENERALIZATIONS AND ESTIMATES   Questions should always be asked in specific rather than general terms. Consider the question, "How many salespeople did you see last year?" which might be asked of a purchasing agent. To answer the

---

FIGURE 8.3   **Illustration of What Can Happen When an Implied Assumption Is Made Explicit**

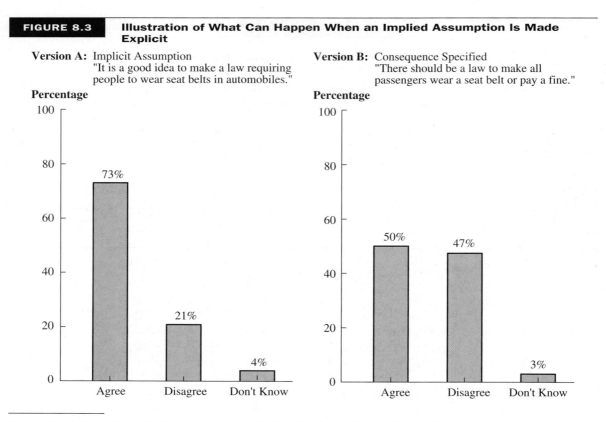

Version A: Implicit Assumption
"It is a good idea to make a law requiring people to wear seat belts in automobiles."

Version B: Consequence Specified
"There should be a law to make all passengers wear a seat belt or pay a fine."

Source: Albert J. Ungar, "Projectable Surveys: Separating Useful Data from Illusions," *Business Marketing* 71 (December 1986), p. 90.

---

question, the agent would probably estimate how many salespeople call in a typical week and would multiply this estimate by 52. This burden should not be placed on the agent. Rather, a more accurate estimate would be obtained if the purchasing agent were asked, "How many representatives called last week?" and the researcher multiplied the answer provided by 52.

AVOID DOUBLE-BARRELED QUESTIONS   A **double-barreled question** is one that calls for two responses and thereby creates confusion for the respondent. The question, "What is your evaluation of the price and convenience offered by catalog showrooms?" is asking respondents to react to two separate attributes by which such showrooms could be described. The respondent might think that the prices are attractive but the location is not, for example, and thereby is placed in a dilemma about how to respond. The problem is particularly acute if the individual must choose an answer from a fixed set of alternatives. One can and should avoid double-barreled questions by splitting the initial question into two separate questions. A useful indicator that two questions might be needed is the use of the word *and* in the initial wording of the question.

Decide on Question Sequence

Once the form of response and specific wording for each question have been decided, the researcher is ready to begin putting them together into a questionnaire. The researcher needs to recognize immediately that the order in which the questions are presented can be crucial to the success of the research effort. Again, there are no hard-and-fast principles but only rules of thumb to guide the researcher in this activity.

USE SIMPLE, INTERESTING OPENING QUESTIONS   The first questions asked the respondent are crucial. If respondents cannot answer them easily, find them uninteresting, or find them suspicious or threatening in any way, they may refuse to complete the remainder of the questionnaire. Thus, it is essential that the first few questions be simple, interesting, and in no way threatening to respondents. Questions that ask respondents for their opinion on some issue are often good openers, as most people like to think that their opinion is important. Sometimes it is helpful to use such an opener even when responses to it will not be analyzed, since opinion questions are often productive in relaxing respondents and getting them to talk freely.

USE FUNNEL APPROACH   The **funnel approach** to question sequencing gets its name from its shape, starting with broad questions and progressively narrowing down the scope. If respondents are to be asked, "What improvements are needed in the company's service policy?" and also "How do you like the quality of service?" the first question needs to be asked before the second. Otherwise, quality of service will be emphasized disproportionately in the responses simply because it is fresh in the respondents' minds.

There should also be some logical order to the questions.[27] This means that sudden changes in topics and jumping around from topic to topic should be avoided. Transitional devices are sometimes necessary to smooth the flow when a change in subject matter occurs. Sometimes the simple insertion of appropriate filter questions will serve this purpose well, although the insertion of a brief explanation is the most commonly used bridge when a change in subject matter occurs.

DESIGN BRANCHING QUESTIONS WITH CARE   **Branching questions** are used to direct respondents to different places in the questionnaire, based on their response to the question at hand. Thus, for example, a respondent replying yes to the question of whether he or she bought a new car within the last six months would be directed to one place in the questionnaire where he or she might then be asked for specific details surrounding the purchase, whereas someone responding no to the same question would be directed elsewhere. Branching questions are used to

---

[27]Jon A. Korsnik and Duane F. Alwin, "An Evaluation of a Cognitive Theory of Response-Order Effects in Survey Measurement," *Public Opinion Quarterly* 51 (Summer 1987), pp. 201–219; McKee J. McClendon and David J. O'Brien, "Question-Order Effects on the Determinants of Subjective Well-Being," *Public Opinion Quarterly* 52 (Fall 1988), pp. 351–364; Norbert Schwarz, "What Respondents Learn from Questionnaires: The Survey Interview and the Logic of Conversation," *International Statistical Review* 63 (1995), pp. 153–177; Frederick O. Lorenz, John Saltiel, and Danny R. Hoyt, "Question Order and Fair Play: Evidence of Even-Handedness in Rural Surveys," *Rural Sociology* 60 (Winter 1995), pp. 641–653.

reduce the number of alternatives that are needed in individual questions while simultaneously ensuring that the information needed is secured from those capable of supplying it. Those for whom a question is irrelevant are simply directed around it. Branching questions and directions are much easier to develop for surveys administered by telephone or in person, especially for those administered through computer-assisted interviewing, than for those sent through the mail. With mail questionnaires, the number of branching questions needs to be kept to an absolute minimum so that respondents do not become confused when responding or refuse to cooperate because the task becomes too difficult.

Although they can be used more liberally with telephone and personal interview surveys, branching questions still need to be designed with care, since evidence indicates that branching instructions increase the rate of item nonresponse for items immediately following the branch.[28]

When using branching questions, it is generally good practice to (1) develop a flow chart of the logical possibilities and then prepare the branching questions and instructions to follow the flow chart; (2) place the question being branched to as close as possible to the question causing the branching to minimize the amount of page flipping that is necessary; and (3) order the branching questions so that respondents cannot anticipate what additional information is required.[29] This last point suggests that the questionnaire should first ask, for example, whether the respondent owns any of the following small appliances before beginning to ask for the brand name, the store where purchased, and so on, for each appliance to which the respondent replied yes. Otherwise, respondents will quickly recognize that yes answers to the ownership question lead to a number of other questions and that it is less taxing to say no in the first place.

ASK FOR CLASSIFICATION INFORMATION LAST   The typical questionnaire contains two types of information: basic information and classification information. Basic information refers to the subject of the study (for example, intentions or attitudes of respondents). Classification information refers to the other data that we collect to classify respondents in order to extract more information about the phenomenon of interest. For instance, we might be interested in determining if a respondent's attitudes toward the need for interest-ceiling legislation are in any way affected by the person's income. Income here would be a classification variable. Demographic/socioeconomic characteristics of respondents are often used as classification variables for understanding the results.

The proper questionnaire sequence is to present questions securing basic information first and those seeking classification information last. There is a logical reason for this. The basic information is most critical. Without it, there is no study. Thus, the researcher should not risk alienating the respondent by asking a number of personal questions before getting to the heart of the study, since it is not unusual for personal characteristics to alienate respondents most. Respondents who readily offer their attitudes toward the energy crisis may balk when asked for their income. An early question

[28]Donald J. Messmer and Daniel J. Seymour, "The Effects of Branching on Item Nonresponse," *Public Opinion Quarterly* 46 (Summer 1982), pp. 270–277.

[29]Sudman and Bradburn, *Asking Questions*, pp. 223–227.

aimed at determining their income may affect the whole tenor of the interview or other communication. It is best to avoid this possibility by placing the classification information at the end.

PLACE DIFFICULT OR SENSITIVE QUESTIONS LATE IN THE QUESTIONNAIRE   The basic information itself can also present some sequence problems. Some of the questions can be sensitive. Early questions should not be, for the reasons previously mentioned. If respondents feel threatened, they will turn off to the questionnaire. Thus, the sensitive questions should be relegated to the body of the questionnaire and intertwined and hidden among some not-so-sensitive ones. Once respondents have become involved in the study, they are less likely to react negatively or be turned off completely when delicate questions are posed. For example, one study investigating the impact of time and memory factors on response in surveys found that response bias becomes smaller as the interview progresses and that aided recall has no effect at the start of an interview but has a large effect late in the interview.[30]

Determine Physical Characteristics

The physical characteristics of the questionnaire can affect not only the accuracy of the replies that are obtained,[31] but also how respondents react to it and the ease with which the replies can be processed. In determining the physical format of the questionnaire, a researcher wants to do those things that help the respondent accept the questionnaire and that facilitate handling and control by the researcher.

SECURING ACCEPTANCE OF THE QUESTIONNAIRE   The physical appearance of the questionnaire can influence respondents' cooperation. This is particularly true with mail questionnaires, but it applies as well to questionnaires administered by personal interviews. If the questionnaire looks sloppy, for whatever reason, respondents are likely to think that the study is unimportant and refuse to cooperate, despite words to the contrary about its importance. If the study is important (and why conduct it if it is not?), make the questionnaire reflect that importance. This means that good-quality paper should be used for the questionnaires. It also means that the questionnaires should be printed, not mimeographed or otherwise photocopied.

The introduction to the research can also affect acceptance of the questionnaire. With mail questionnaires, the cover letter serves to introduce the study. It is very important that the cover letter convinces the designated respondent to cooperate. Good cover letters are rarely written in a hurry; rather, they usually

---

[30]Seymour Sudman and Norman M. Bradburn, "Effects of Time and Memory Factors on Response in Surveys," *Journal of the American Statistical Association* 68 (December 1973), pp. 805–815. See also David Mingay and Michael T. Greenwell, "Memory Bias and Response-Order Effects," *Journal of Official Statistics* 5, no. 3 (1989), pp. 253-263.

[31]For examples, see Charles S. Mayer and Cindy Piper, "A Note on the Importance of Layout in Self-Administered Questionnaires," *Journal of Marketing Research* 19 (August 1982), pp. 390–391; Marie Elena Sanchez, "Effects of Questionnaire Design on the Quality of Survey Data," *Public Opinion Quarterly* 56 (Summer 1992), pp. 206–217.

require a series of painstaking rewrites to get the wording just right. Research Realities 8.6 lists important content considerations in the construction of cover letters.[32] With personal and telephone interviews, the introduction to the research is necessarily shorter. Nonetheless, the introduction needs to convince respondents about the importance of the research and the importance of their participation. Typically, this means describing how they can benefit from it, the fact that their replies will be confidential, and the incentive, if any, that they will receive for participating.

It is a good idea to include the name of the sponsoring organization and the name of the project on the first page or on the cover if the questionnaire is in book form. Both of these lend credibility to the study. However, since awareness of the sponsoring firm can often induce bias in respondents' answers, many firms use fictitious names for the sponsoring organization. This also helps eliminate phone calls or other inquiries from respondents asking for the results of the study.

FACILITATE HANDLING AND CONTROL   Several things that facilitate handling and control by the researcher also contribute to acceptance of the questionnaire by

---

RESEARCH REALITIES 8.6

Sample Cover Letter for a Mail Questionnaire

Panel A: Contents

1. Personal communication
2. Asking a favor
3. Importance of the research project and its purpose
4. Importance of the recipient
5. Importance of the replies in general
6. Importance of the replies when the reader is not qualified to answer most questions
7. How the recipient may benefit from this research
8. Completing the questionnaire will take only a short time
9. The questionnaire can be answered easily
10. A stamped reply envelope is enclosed
11. How recipient was selected

12. Answers are anonymous or confidential
13. Offer to send report on results of survey
14. Note of urgency
15. Appreciation of sender
16. Importance of sender
17. Importance of the sender's organization
18. Description and purpose of incentive
19. Avoiding bias
20. Style
21. Format and appearance
22. Brevity

Source: Paul L. Erdos, *Professional Mail Surveys*, rev. ed. (Melbourne, FL: Robert E. Krieger Publishing Co., Inc., 1983), pp. 102–103. Reprinted with permission.

---

[32]Each of the parts listed in Research Realities 8.6 is discussed in detail in Paul L. Erdos, *Professional Mail Surveys* (Melbourne, FL: Robert E. Krieger Publishing Co., 1983), pp. 101–117. See also Linda B. Bourque and Eve P. Fiedler, *How to Conduct Self-Administered and Mail Surveys* (Thousand Oaks, CA: Sage Publications, 1995).

RESEARCH REALITIES 8.6

Panel B: Sample*

PROFESSIONAL MAIL SURVEYS COMPANY——— 17
7432 East Court Avenue
Elveron, California   90101
(213) 991-5550

(Date)

1 —Dear Mr. Smythe:

2 ——— Will you do us a favor?

3 — We are conducting a nationwide survey among executives and managers in the metalworking industries. The purpose of this research is to find out the opinion of yourself and other experts on the advantages and disadvantages of using three new steel products. Your —— 1
5 — answers will enable steel manufacturers to be aware of the requirements of the users and the opinions of nonusers of these items, and this —— 3 in turn will help them to design the products you need.

5 — Your name appeared in a scientifically selected random sample. ——— 11
Your answers are very important to the accuracy of our research,
6 — whether or not your company is a user of one or more of the products described.

9 ——— It will take only a short time to answer the simple questions on the enclosed questionnaire and to return it in the stamped reply envelope.— 10

12 — Of course all answers are confidential and will be used only in combination with those of other metalworking executives and managers —— 4 from all over the United States.

3 —
13 —— If you are interested in receiving a report on the findings of this research, just write your name and address at the end of this questionnaire, or if you prefer, request the results of the Survey on Steel Products in a separate letter. We will be glad to send you a complimentary report when ready.

14 —— Please return the completed questionnaire at your earliest convenience. Thank you for your help.

Sincerely,

15

James B Jones ——— 1

James B. Jones
Director —— 16

18 — P.S. The enclosed dollar bill is just a token of appreciation.

respondents. These include such things as questionnaire size and layout and question sequencing.

Questionnaire size is important.[33] Smaller questionnaires are better than larger ones if (and this is a big if) they do not appear crowded. Smaller questionnaires seem easier to complete; they appear to take less time and are less likely to cause respondents to refuse to participate. They are easier to carry in the field and are easier to sort, count, and file in the office than larger questionnaires. If, on the other hand, smaller size is gained at the expense of an open appearance, these advantages are lost. A crowded questionnaire has a bad appearance, leads to errors in data collection, and results in shorter and less informative replies. For both self-administered and interviewer-administered questionnaires, for example, researchers have found that the more lines or space left for recording the response to open-ended questions, the more extensive the reply.

While postcard size probably represents the lower limit, letter size probably represents the upper limit to the size of an individual page in a questionnaire. When the questions will not all fit on the front and back of one sheet, multiple sheets need to be used. When this happens, the questionnaire should be made into a booklet rather than stapling or paper clipping the pages together. This not only facilitates handling but also reinforces an image of quality.

Numbering the questions also facilitates handling and promotes respondent cooperation. This is particularly true when branching questions are employed. Without numbered questions, instructions about how to proceed (for example, "If the answer to Question 2 is yes, please go to Question 5") cannot be used. Even with numbered questions, though, it is helpful if the respondent can be directed by arrows to the appropriate next question after a branching question. Another technique researchers have found useful with branch-type questions is the use of color-coding on the questionnaire, where the next question to which the respondent is directed matches the color of the space in which the answer to the branching or filter question was recorded.

Numbering the questions makes it easier to edit, code, and tabulate the responses.[34] If the questionnaires themselves are numbered, it is easier to keep track of the questionnaires and to determine which ones, if any, are lost. It also makes it easier to monitor interviewer performance and to detect interviewer biases, if any. The research director will be able to develop a log that lists which questionnaires were assigned to which interviewers. Mail questionnaires are an exception to the principle that the questionnaires themselves should be numbered. Respondents often interpret an assigned number on a mail questionnaire as a mechanism by which their responses can be identified. The accompanying loss in anonymity is

---

[33]A. Regula Herzog and Jerald G. Bachman, "Effects of Questionnaire Length on Response Quality," *Public Opinion Quarterly* 45 (Winter 1981), pp. 549–559; David Jobber, "An Examination of the Effects of Questionnaire Factors on Response to an Industrial Mail Survey," *International Journal of Research in Marketing* 6 (December 1989), pp. 129–140; Andrew G. Bean and Michale J. Rozkowski, "The Long and Short of It," *Marketing Research: A Magazine of Management & Applications* 7 (Winter 1995), pp. 21–26.

[34]These elementary steps, which are involved in the processing of all questionnaires, are discussed in Chapter 13.

threatening to many of them, and they refuse to cooperate or otherwise distort their answers.

Re-examination and Revision of the Questionnaire

A researcher should not expect that the first draft will result in a usable questionnaire. Rather, re-examination and revision are the order of the day in questionnaire construction. Each question should be reviewed to ensure that the question is not confusing or ambiguous, potentially offensive to the respondent, leading or bias inducing, and also that it is easy to answer. How can one tell? An extremely critical attitude and good common sense should help. The researcher should examine each word in each question. The literature on question phrasing is replete with examples of how some seemingly innocuous questions produce response problems.[35] When a potential problem is discovered, the question should be revised. After examining each question—and each word in each question—for its potential meanings and implications, the researcher might test the questionnaire in some role-playing situations, using others working on the project as subjects. This role playing should reveal some of the most serious shortcomings and should lead to further revision of the instrument.

Pretesting the Questionnaire

The real test of a questionnaire is how it performs under actual conditions of data collection. For this assessment, the questionnaire **pretest** is vital. The questionnaire pretest serves the same role in questionnaire design that test marketing serves in new-product development. Even though the product concept, different advertising appeals, alternative packages, and so on, may all have been tested previously in the product development process, test marketing is the first place where they all come together. Test marketing provides the real test of customer reactions to the product and the accompanying marketing program. Similarly, the pretest provides the real test of the questionnaire and the mode of administration.

A number of interesting examples have been published of unintended implications from questions that could have been avoided with an adequate pretest of the questionnaire. In one lifestyle study, for example, the following question was asked: "How would you like to be living two years from now?" While the question was intended to get at hoped-for lifestyles, a large group of the respondents simply replied yes. In another study, a question about brands of deodorant was used on a self-administered questionnaire. It was only when a number of replies came back with the written response "AirWick" that the researchers realized that putting the word

---

[35]Payne's book is particularly good in this regard. Chapter 13, for example, is devoted to the development of a passable question. When one considers that an entire chapter can be devoted to the development of one passable question (not a great question, mind you), one can appreciate the need for re-examining each question under a microscope for its potential implications. A condensed treatment of the things to be avoided in a question is to be found in Lyndon O. Brown and Leland L. Beik, *Marketing Research and Analysis*, 4th ed. (New York: Ronald, 1969), pp. 242–262. See also Sudman and Bradburn, *Asking Questions*, which has recommendations specific to the type of question being asked (for example, opinions versus demographic characteristics), and Floyd J. Fowler, Jr., *Improving Survey Questions* (Thousand Oaks, CA: Sage Publications, 1995).

ETHICAL DILEMMA 8.3

A candy manufacturer tells you that he wants to raise the price of his gourmet chocolates and he needs you to establish the maximum price increase that shoppers will stand. He suggests that you interview patrons of gourmet candy shops without informing them of the sponsor or purpose of the research, describe the candy to them in general terms, and suggest prices that they might find acceptable, starting with the highest price.

- Is it ethical to ask people questions when their answer may be detrimental to their self-interest?

- Is it ethical not to reveal the purpose or sponsor of the research? If you did reveal the purpose of the research, would survey respondents give the same answer as otherwise?

---

personal in front of *deodorant* would have eliminated the confusion caused by the question.[36] *Data collection should never begin without an adequate pretest of the instrument.*

The pretest can be used to assess both individual questions and their sequence.[37] It is best if there are two pretests. The first pretest should be done by personal interview, regardless of the actual mode of administration that will be used. An interviewer can watch to see if people actually remember data requested of them, if some questions seem confusing, or if some questions produce respondent resistance or hesitancy for one reason or another. The pretest interviews should be conducted by the firm's most experienced interviewers among respondents similar to those who will be used in the actual study.

The personal interview pretest should reveal some questions in which the wording could be improved or the sequence changed. If the changes are major, the revised questionnaire should again be pretested employing personal interviews. If the changes are minor, the questionnaire can be pretested a second time using mail, telephone, or personal interviews, whichever method is going to be used for the full-scale study. This time, though, less-experienced interviewers should also be used in order to determine if typical interviewers will have any special problems with the questionnaire. The purpose of the second pretest is to uncover problems unique to the mode of administration.

---

[36]Linda Kirby, "Bloopers," *Newspaper Research Council* (January/February 1989), p. 1.

[37]Shelby D. Hunt, Richard D. Sparkman, Jr., and James B. Wilcox, "The Pretest in Survey Research: Issues and Preliminary Findings," *Journal of Marketing Research* 19 (May 1982), pp. 265–275; Ruth N. Bolton, Randall G. Chapman, and John M. Zych, "Pretesting Alternative Survey Administration Design," *Applied Marketing Research* 30, no. 3 (1990), pp. 8–13; Lois Oksenberg, Charles Cannell, and Graham Kalton, "New Strategies of Pretesting Survey Questions," *Journal of Official Statistics* 7, no. 3 (1991), pp. 349–365; Nina Reynolds, Adamantios Diamantopoulus, and Bodo Schlegelmilch, "Pretesting in Questionnaire Design: A Review of the Literature and Suggestions for Further Research," *Journal of the Market Research Society* 35 (April 1993), pp. 171–182.

Finally, the responses that result from the pretest should be coded and tabulated. The code book to be used when processing the questionnaires needs to be determined.[38] We have previously discussed the need for the preparation of dummy tables before developing the questionnaire. The tabulation of pretest responses can check on our conceptualization of the problem and the data and method of analysis necessary to answer it:

> [T]he tables will confirm the need for various sets of data. If we have no place to put the responses to a question, either the data are superfluous or we omitted some contemplated analysis. If some part of a table remains empty, we may have omitted a necessary question. Trial tabulations show us, as no previous method can, that all data collected will be put to use, and that we will obtain all necessary data.[39]

The researcher who avoids a questionnaire pretest and tabulation of replies is either naive or a fool. The pretest is the most inexpensive insurance the researcher can buy to ensure the success of the questionnaire and the research project. A careful pretest, along with proper attention to the do's and don'ts presented in this chapter and summarized in Table 8.2, should make the questionnaire development process successful.

Observational Forms

Generally, fewer problems occur in constructing observational forms than questionnaires, because the researcher is no longer concerned with the fact that the question and the way it is asked will affect the response. Through proper training of observers, the researcher can create the necessary expertise so that the data-collection instrument is handled consistently. Alternatively, the researcher may simply use a mechanical device to measure the behavior of interest and secure complete consistency in measurement. This is not to imply that observational forms offer no problems of construction. Rather, the researcher needs to make very explicit decisions about what is to be observed and the categories and units that will be used to record this behavior. Figure 8.4, which is the observation form used by a bank to evaluate the service provided by its employees having extensive customer contact, shows how detailed some of these decisions can be. In this case, the observers acted as shoppers.

The statement that "One needs to determine what is to be observed before one can make a scientific observation" seems trite indeed. Yet this is exactly the case. Almost any event can be described in a number of ways. When we watch someone making a cigarette purchase, we might report that (1) the person purchased one package of cigarettes; (2) the woman purchased one package of cigarettes; (3) the woman purchased a package of Tareyton cigarettes; (4) the woman purchased a

---

[38]See Chapter 13 for discussion of how to code data, which should be decided before the final questionnaires are administered.

[39]Brown and Beik, *Marketing Research and Analysis*, pp. 265–266.

TABLE 8.2	Some Do's and Don'ts When Preparing Questionnaires

Step 1: Specify What Information Will Be Sought

1. Make sure that you have a clear understanding of the issue and what it is that you want to know (expect to learn). Frame your research questions, but refrain from writing questions for the questionnaire at this time.
2. Make a list of your research questions. Review them periodically as you are working on the questionnaire.
3. Use the "dummy tables" that were set up to guide the data analysis to suggest questions for the questionnaire.
4. Conduct a search for existing questions on the issue.
5. Revise existing questions on the issue, and prepare new questions that address the issues you plan to research.

Step 2: Determine Type of Questionnaire and Method of Administration

1. Use the type of data to be collected as a basis for deciding on the type of questionnaire.
2. Use degree of structure and disguise as well as cost factors to determine the method of administration.
3. Compare the special capabilities and limitations of each method of administration and the value of the data collected from each with the needs of the survey.

Step 3: Determine Content of Individual Questions

1. For each research question ask yourself, "Why do I want to know this?" Answer it in terms of how it will help your research. "It would be interesting to know" is not an acceptable answer.
2. Make sure each question is specific and addresses only one important issue.
3. Ask yourself whether the question applies to all respondents; it should, or provision should be made for skipping it.
4. Split questions that can be answered from different frames of reference into multiple questions, one corresponding to each frame of reference.
5. Ask yourself whether respondents will be informed about and can remember the issue that the question is dealing with.

6. Make sure the time period of the question is related to the importance of the topic. Consider using aided-recall techniques like diaries, records, or bounded recall.
7. Avoid questions that require excessive effort, that have hard-to-articulate answers, and that deal with embarrassing or threatening issues.
8. If threatening questions are necessary,
   a. hide the questions among more innocuous ones.
   b. make use of a counterbiasing statement.
   c. phrase the question in terms of others and how they might feel or act.
   d. ask respondents if they have ever engaged in the undesirable activity, and then ask if they are presently engaging in such an activity.
   e. use categories or ranges rather than specific numbers.
   f. use the randomized response model.

Step 4: Determine Form of Response to Each Question

1. Determine which type of question—open-ended, dichotomous, or multichotomous—provides data that fit the information needs of the project.
2. Use structured questions whenever possible.
3. Use open-ended questions that require short answers to begin a questionnaire.
4. Try to convert open-ended questions to closed (fixed) response questions to reduce respondent workload and coding effort for descriptive and causal studies.
5. If open-ended questions are necessary, make the questions sufficiently directed to give respondents a frame of reference when answering.
6. When using dichotomous questions, state the negative or alternative side in detail.
7. Provide for "don't know," "no opinion," and "both" answers.
8. Be aware that there may be a middle ground.
9. Be sensitive to the mildness or harshness of the alternatives.
10. When using multichotomous questions, be sure that the choices are exhaustive and mutually exclusive, and if combinations are possible, include them.

package of Tareyton 100's; (5) the woman, after asking for and finding that the store was out of Virginia Slims, purchased a package of Tareyton 100's; and so on.

A great many additional variations are possible (for example, the type, name, or location of the store where this behavior occurred). In order for this observation to be productive for scientific inquiry, we must predetermine which aspects of this behavior are relevant. The decision about what to observe requires that the researcher specify the following:

- Who should be observed? Anyone entering the store? Anyone making a purchase? Anyone making a cigarette purchase?

TABLE 8.2   (continued)

11. Be sure that the range of alternatives is clear and that all reasonable alternative answers are included.
12. If the possible responses are very numerous, consider using more than one question to reduce the potential for information overload.
13. When using dichotomous or multichotomous questions, consider the use of a split ballot procedure to reduce order bias.
14. Clearly indicate if items are to be ranked or if only one item on the list is to be chosen.

Step 5: Determine Wording of Each Question
1. Use simple words.
2. Avoid ambiguous words and questions.
3. Avoid leading questions.
4. Avoid implicit alternatives.
5. Avoid implicit assumptions.
6. Avoid generalizations and estimates.
7. Use simple sentences, and avoid compound sentences.
8. Change long, dependent clauses to words or short phrases.
9. Avoid double-barreled questions.
10. Make sure each question is as specific as possible.

Step 6: Determine Question Sequence
1. Use simple, interesting questions for openers.
2. Use the funnel approach, first asking broad questions and then narrowing them down.
3. Ask difficult or sensitive questions late in the questionnaire when rapport is better.
4. Follow chronological order when collecting historical information.
5. Complete questions about one topic before moving on to the next.
6. Prepare a flow chart whenever filter questions are being considered.
7. Ask filter questions before asking detailed questions.
8. Ask demographic questions last so that if respondent refuses, the other data are still usable.

Step 7: Determine Physical Characteristics of Questionnaire
1. Make sure that the questionnaire looks professional and is relatively easy to answer.
2. Use quality paper and print; do not photocopy the questionnaire.
3. Attempt to make the questionnaire as short as possible while avoiding a crowded appearance.
4. Use a booklet format for ease of analysis and to prevent lost pages.
5. List the name of the organization conducting the survey on the first page.
6. Number the questions to ease data processing.
7. If the respondent must skip more than one question, use a "go to."
8. If the respondent must skip an entire section, consider color coding the sections.
9. State how the responses are to be reported, such as a check mark, number, circle, and so on.

Step 8: Re-examine Steps 1–7 and Revise If Necessary
1. Examine each word of every question to ensure the question is not confusing, ambiguous, offensive, or leading.
2. Get peer evaluations of the draft questionnaire.

Step 9: Pretest Questionnaire and Revise If Necessary
1. Pretest the questionnaire first by personal interviews among respondents similar to those to be used in the actual study.
2. Obtain comments from the interviewers and respondents to discover any problems with the questionnaire, and revise it if necessary. When the revisions are substantial, repeat steps 1 and 2 of the pretest.
3. Pretest the questionnaire by mail or telephone to uncover problems unique to the mode of administration.
4. Code and tabulate the pretest responses in dummy tables to determine if questions are providing adequate information.
5. Eliminate questions that do not provide adequate information, and revise questions that cause problems.

- What aspects of the purchase should be reported? Which brand they purchased? Which brand they asked for first? Whether the purchase was of king size or regular cigarettes? What about the purchaser? Is the person's sex to be recorded? Is the individual's age to be estimated? Does it make any difference if the person was alone or in a group?

- When should the observation be made? On what day of the week? At what time of the day? Should day and time be reported? Should the observation be recorded only after a purchase occurs or should a customer approaching a salesclerk also be recorded, even if it does not result in a sale?

- Where should the observation be made? In what kind of store? How should the store be selected? How should it be noted on the observational form—by type, by location, by name? Should vending-machine purchases also be noted?

The careful reader will note that these are the same kinds of who, what, when, and where decisions that need to be made in selecting the research design. The "why" and "how" are also implicit. The research problem should dictate the why of the observation, whereas the how involves choosing the observation device or form that will be used. A paper-and-pencil form should be very simple to use. It should parallel the logical sequence of the purchase act (for example, a male approaches the clerk, asks for a package of cigarettes, and so on, if these behaviors are relevant) and should permit the recording of observations by a simple check mark if possible. Again, careful attention to detail, exacting examination of the preliminary form, and an adequate pretest should return handsome dividends with respect to the quality of the observations made.

| FIGURE 8.4 | Form Used by Observer Acting as Shopper to Evaluate Service Provided by Bank Employees |

Bank _____

Date _____ Time _____ Shopper's Name _____

Nature of Transaction: ☐ Personal   ☐ Telephone

    Details _____

            _____

            _____

            _____

- -

A. For Personal Transactions:

    Bank Employee's Name _____

How was name obtained?
  ☐ Employee had name tag
  ☐ Name plate on counter or desk
  ☐ Employee gave name
  ☐ Shopper had to ask for name
  ☐ Name provided by other employee
  ☐ Other _____

FIGURE 8.4   (continued)

B. For Telephone Transactions:

   Bank Employee's Name _____

How was name obtained?   ☐ Employee gave name upon answering the telephone
                            ☐ Name provided by other employee
                            ☐ Shopper had to ask for name
                            ☐ Employee gave name during conversation
                            ☐ Other _____

C. Customer Relations Skills	Yes	No	Does Not Apply
1. Did the employee notice and greet you immediately?	☐	☐	☐
2. Did the employee speak pleasantly and smile?	☐	☐	☐
3. Did the employee answer the telephone promptly?	☐	☐	☐
4. Did the employee find out your name?	☐	☐	☐
5. Did the employee use your name during the transaction?	☐	☐	☐
6. Did the employee ask you to be seated?	☐	☐	☐
7. Was the employee helpful?	☐	☐	☐
8. Was the employee's desk or work area neat and uncluttered?	☐	☐	☐
9. Did the employee show a genuine interest in you as a customer?	☐	☐	☐
10. Did the employee thank you for coming in?	☐	☐	☐
11. Did the employee enthusiastically support the bank and its services?	☐	☐	☐
12. Did the employee handle any interruptions effectively? (phone calls, etc.)	☐	☐	☐

Comment on any positive or negative details of the transaction that you found particularly noticeable.

_____

_____

_____

_____

_____

(continued)

FIGURE 8.4   **(continued)**

D. Sales Skills	Yes	No	Does Not Apply
1. Did the employee determine if you had any accounts with this bank?	☐	☐	☐
2. Did the employee use "open-ended" questions in obtaining information about you?	☐	☐	☐
3. Did the employee listen to what you had to say?	☐	☐	☐
4. Did the employee sell you on the bank services by showing you what the service could do for you?	☐	☐	☐
5. Did the employee ask you to open the service which you inquired about?	☐	☐	☐
6. Did the employee ask you to bank with this particular bank?	☐	☐	☐
7. Did the employee ask you to contact him/her when visiting the bank?	☐	☐	☐
8. Did the employee ask you if you had any questions or if you understood the service at the end of the transaction?	☐	☐	☐
9. Did the employee give you brochures about other services?	☐	☐	☐
10. Did the employee give you his/her calling card?	☐	☐	☐
11. Did the employee indicate that you might be contacted by telephone, engraved card, or letter as a means of follow-up?	☐	☐	☐
12. Did the employee ask you to open or use other services? Check the following if they were mentioned.	☐	☐	☐

☐ savings account
☐ checking account
☐ automatic savings
☐ Mastercharge
☐ Master Checking
☐ safe deposit box
☐ loan services
☐ trust services
☐ automatic loan payment
☐ bank hours
☐ other_____

| FIGURE 8.4 | (continued) |

Comment on the overall effectiveness of the employee's sales skills.

_____

_____

_____

_____

_____

Source: Courtesy of Neil M. Ford.

ETHICAL DILEMMA 8.4

As you supervise the sending out of a mail survey from a client's place of business, you notice some numbers printed on the inside of the return envelopes. You point out to the client that the cover letter promises survey respondents anonymity, which is not consistent with a policy of coding the return envelopes. She replies that she needs to identify those respondents who have not replied so that she can send a follow-up mailing. She also suggests the information might be useful in the future in identifying those who might react favorably to a sales call for the product.

- Is it ethical to promise anonymity and then not adhere to your promise?
- Is it healthy for the marketing research profession if legitimate research becomes associated with subsequent sales tactics?

Summary

A researcher wishing to collect primary data will need to tackle the task of designing the data-collection device sooner or later. Most typically this will mean designing a questionnaire, although it may mean framing an observational form.

Questionnaire design is still very much of an art rather than a science, and there are many admonitions of things to avoid when doing the designing. Nevertheless, a nine-step procedure (Figure 8.1, page 315) was offered as a guide. This guide indicates that researchers need to ask and answer some specific questions when designing questionnaires, including: What information will be sought? What type of questionnaire will be used? How will that questionnaire be administered? What will be the content of the individual questions? What will be the form of response—dichotomous, multichotomous, or open-ended—to each question? How will each question be phrased? How will the questions be sequenced? What will the questionnaire look like physically?

Researchers should not be surprised to find themselves repeating the various steps when designing a questionnaire. Further, although the temptation is sometimes great, one should never omit a pretest of the questionnaire. Regardless of how good it looks in the abstract, the pretest provides the real test of the questionnaire and its mode of administration. Actually, at least two pretests should be conducted. The first should use personal interviews, and after all the troublesome spots have been smoothed over, a second pretest using the normal mode of administration should be conducted. The data collected in the pretest should then be subjected to the analyses planned for the full data set, as this will reveal serious omissions or other shortcomings while it is still possible to correct these deficiencies.

Observational forms generally present fewer problems of construction than questionnaires, because the researcher no longer needs to be concerned with the fact that the question and the way it is asked will affect the response. Observational forms do, however, require a precise statement of who or what is to be observed, what actions or characteristics are relevant, and when and where the observations will be made.

Questions

1. What role do the research hypotheses play in determining the information that will be sought?
2. Suppose you were interested in determining the proportion of men in a geographic area who use hair sprays. How could the necessary information be obtained by open-ended question, by multiple-choice question, and by dichotomous question? Which would be preferable?
3. How does the method of administration of a questionnaire affect the type of question to be employed?
4. What criteria can a researcher use to determine whether a specific question should be included in a questionnaire?
5. What is telescoping error? What does it suggest about the period to be used when asking respondents to recall past events?
6. What are some recommended ways by which one can ask for sensitive information?
7. What is an open-ended question? A multichotomous question? A dichotomous question? What are some of the key things researchers must be careful to avoid in framing multichotomous and dichotomous questions?
8. What is a split ballot, and why is it employed?
9. What is an ambiguous question? A leading question? A question with implicit alternatives? A question with implied assumptions? A double-barreled question?
10. What is the proper sequence when asking for basic information and classification information?
11. What is the funnel approach to question sequencing?
12. What is a branching question? Why are such questions used?
13. Where should one ask for sensitive information in the questionnaire?
14. How can the physical features of a questionnaire affect its acceptance by respondents? Its handling and control by the researcher?
15. What is the overriding principle guiding questionnaire construction?
16. What decisions must the researcher make when developing an observational form for data collection?

Applications and Problems

1. Evaluate the following questions:
   a. *Which of the following magazines do you read regularly?*
      _____ Time
      _____ Newsweek
      _____ Business Week

   b. *Are you a frequent purchaser of Birds Eye frozen vegetables?*

      _____ Yes   _____ No

   c. *Do you agree that the government should impose import restrictions?*

      _____ Strongly agree

      _____ Agree

      _____ Neither agree nor disagree

      _____ Disagree

      _____ Strongly disagree

   d. *How often do you buy detergent?*

      _____ Once a week

      _____ Once in two weeks

      _____ Once in three weeks

      _____ Once a month

   e. *Rank the following in order of preference:*

      _____ Kellogg's Corn Flakes

      _____ Quaker's Life

      _____ Post Bran Flakes

      _____ Kellogg's Bran Flakes

      _____ Instant Quaker Oat Meal

      _____ Post Rice Krinkles

   f. *Where do you usually purchase your school supplies?*

   g. *When you are watching television, do you also watch most of the advertisements?*

   h. *Which of the following brands of tea are most similar?*

      _____ Lipton's Orange Pekoe

      _____ Turnings Orange Pekoe

      _____ Bigelow Orange Pekoe

      _____ Salada Orange Pekoe

   i. *Do you think that the present policy of cutting taxes and reducing government spending should be continued?*

      _____ Yes   _____ No

   j. *In a seven-day week, how often do you eat breakfast?*

      _____ Every day of the week

      _____ 5–6 times a week

      _____ 2–4 times a week

      _____ Once a week

      _____ Never

2. Make the necessary corrections to the preceding questions.

3. Evaluate the following multichotomous questions. Would dichotomous or open-ended questions be more appropriate?

   a. *Which one of the following reasons is most important in your choice of stereo equipment?*

      _____ Price

      _____ In-store service

      _____ Brand name

      _____ Level of distortion

      _____ Guarantee/warranty

   b. *Please indicate your education level.*

      _____ Less than high school

      _____ Some high school

      _____ High school graduate

      _____ Technical or vocational school

      _____ Some college

_____ College graduate
_____ Some graduate or professional school

c. *Which of the following reflects your views toward the issues raised by ecologists?*
_____ Have received attention
_____ Have not received attention
_____ Should receive more attention
_____ Should receive less attention

d. *Which of the following statements do you most strongly agree with?*
_____ American Airlines has better service than Northwest Airlines
_____ Northwest Airlines has better service than United Airlines
_____ United Airlines has better service than American Airlines
_____ United Airlines has better service than Northwest Airlines
_____ Northwest Airlines has better service than American Airlines
_____ American Airlines has better service than United Airlines

4. Evaluate the following open-ended questions. Rephrase them as multichotomous or dichotomous questions if you think it would be appropriate.
   a. *Do you go to the movies often?*
   b. *Approximately how much do you spend per week on groceries?*
   c. *What brands of cheese did you purchase during the last week?*

5. Discuss how each of the following respondent groups would influence the development of the questionnaire form.
   a. Medical doctors
   b. Welfare recipients
   c. Air Force commanders
   d. Cuban refugees

6. Your employer, a commercial marketing research firm, has contracted you to perform a study whose objective is the investigation of usage patterns and brand preferences for infant diapers among migrant farm workers in the southeastern United States. You have been assigned to develop a suitable questionnaire and method of administration to collect the desired information. What potential problems might arise in the design and administration due to the nature of the population in question? List these problems and provide solutions. What method of administration would you recommend?

7. Campus Cookery, the local burger spot, has asked you to comment on some of the questions that have been developed for a survey they are conducting on a new sandwich offering. What is wrong (if anything) with each of the following questions?
   a. *Why haven't you tried our new sandwich at Campus Cookery?*
   b. *Don't you think that Campus Cookery's products are of the highest quality?*
   c. *Would you say that our new sandwich tastes good, is priced correctly, is attractive, and is healthy?*
      ☐ Yes   ☐ No
   d. *Have you tried our new sandwich at Campus Cookery?*

Very Infrequently	Infrequently	Average	Very Frequently
_____	_____	_____	_____

8. Analyze the following questions. What (if anything) is wrong with each question?
   a. *How do you like the flavor of this high-quality, top-bean coffee?*
   b. *What do you think of the taste and texture of this Danish Treat coffee cake?*
   c. *We are conducting a study for Guess watches. What do you think of the quality of Guess watches?*
   d. *How far do you live from the closest mall?*
   e. *Who in your family shops for clothes?*
   f. *Where do you buy most of your clothes?*

9. A small brokerage firm was concerned with the declining number of customers and decided to do a quick survey. The major objective was to find out the reasons for patronizing a particular brokerage firm and to find out the importance of customer service. The following questionnaire was to be administered by telephone. Evaluate the questionnaire.

Good Afternoon Sir/Madam:

We are doing a survey on attitudes toward brokerage firms. Could you please answer the following questions? Thank you.

1. *Have you invested any money in the stock market?*
   ____ Yes   ____ No

   If respondent replies *yes*, continue; otherwise terminate interview.

2. *Do you manage your own investments or do you go to a brokerage firm?*
   ____ Manage own investments   ____ Go to a brokerage firm

   If respondent replies "go to a brokerage firm," continue; otherwise, terminate interview.

3. *How satisfied are you with your brokerage firm?*

Very Satisfied	Satisfied	Neither Satisfied nor Dissatisfied	Dissatisfied	Very Dissatisfied
____	____	____	____	____

4. *How important is personal service to you?*

Very Important	Important	Not Particularly Important	Not at All Important
____	____	____	____

5. *Which of the following reasons is the most important in patronizing a particular firm?*
   ____ the commission charged by the firm
   ____ the personal service
   ____ the return on investment
   ____ the investment counseling

6. *Approximately how long have you been investing through the brokerage firm you are currently using?*
   ____ about 3 months   ____ about 9 months
   ____ about 6 months   ____ about 1 year or more

7. *How much capital do you have invested?*
   ____ $500–$750   ____ $1,000–$1,500
   ____ $750–$1,000   ____ $1,500 or more

Good-bye and thank you for your cooperation.

---

10. Suppose that the Nuclear Regulatory Commission is considering a proposal made by a California utility company to build a nuclear reactor in a small town located in southern California. According to the proposal, the new reactor could provide energy for a good portion of southern California at considerable savings over conventional sources of energy. Ultimately, substantial savings would be passed along to the consumer, according to the utility company. Opponents of the project, primarily antinuclear groups and environmental organizations, claim that such a project would needlessly put

people who reside in the area, as well as the environment, at risk while the utility company makes a handsome profit. The proponents respond that no other suitable site can be found in southern California and that the benefits of less-expensive energy sources far outweigh any potential risks associated with the project—particularly for individuals and families at or below the poverty line. Both sides, citing statistics from various public opinion polls, claim to have public opinion on their side.

a. Write a question for a public opinion survey that is likely to produce results in favor of building the nuclear reactor (that is, results that support the utility's position).

b. Write a question for a public opinion survey that is likely to produce results showing that most people are not in favor of building the new nuclear facility (that is, results that support the opposition's viewpoint).

c. Write an appropriate survey question that attempts to accurately measure public opinion about whether the nuclear reactor should be built.

Thorndike Sports Equipment Video Case

1. Ted needs help writing questions for his questionnaire. What questions would you suggest are necessary?

2. What are the advantages of using closed-ended questions? List some drawbacks.

3. What are the advantages of open-ended questions? What are the disadvantages?

9

Attitude Measurement

Attitude is one of the most pervasive notions in all of marketing. It plays a pivotal role in the major models describing consumer behavior, as well as in many, if not most, investigations of consumer behavior that do not rely on a formal integrated model.[1] Attitude plays this central role mainly because it is believed to strongly influence behavior. Many marketers believe that attitudes *directly affect* purchase decisions and that their purchase and use experiences, in turn, *directly affect* their subsequent attitudes toward the product or service. Academic researchers, therefore, use attitude as an important explanatory variable in creating models of behavior.

Practitioners are also interested in people's attitudes and use them for a variety of purposes. One major use is assessing the company's reputation, both overall respect to specific aspects of its operations, according to one study. Research Realities 9.1, for example, lists the American companies, according to one study, with the best overall reputations and also the top five with respect to their emotional appeal, social responsibility, products and services, workplace environment, vision and leadership, and financial performance.

Researchers and practitioners share some common problems as well as a common interest in attitude. For one thing, although attitude is one of the most widely used ideas in all of social psychology, it is also one of the most inconsistently used concepts. There are a variety of interpretations, but there does seem to be substantial agreement about the following:

1. Attitude represents a predisposition to respond to an object, not actual behavior toward the object. Attitude thus possesses the quality of readiness.

2. Attitude is persistent over time. It can change, to be sure, but alteration of an attitude that is strongly held requires substantial pressure.

3. Attitude is a latent variable that produces consistency in behavior, either verbal or physical.

4. Attitude has a directional quality. It connotes a preference regarding the outcomes involving the object, evaluations of the object, or positive/neutral/ negative feelings for the object.[2]

---

[1] See, for example, James F. Engel, Roger D. Blackwell, and Paul Miniard, *Consumer Behavior*, 8th ed. (Fort Worth, TX: The Dryden Press, 1996).

[2] Adapted from the introduction by Gene F. Summers, ed., *Attitude Measurement* (Chicago: Rand McNally, 1970), p. 370. See also J. Paul Peter and Jerry C. Olson, *Consumer Behavior and Marketing Strategy*, 5th ed. (Burr Ridge, IL: Irwin/McGraw-Hill 1999). One reason for the many definitions of attitude is the age-old scientific problem of going from construct to operational definition, a problem that is reviewed in Appendix 9A.

RESEARCH REALITIES 9.1

The Best Corporate Reputations in America in Order of Rank

Overall

1. Johnson & Johnson	11. Dell	21. FedEx
2. Coca-Cola	12. General Electric	22. Procter & Gamble
3. Hewlett-Packard	13. Lucent	23. Nike
4. Intel	14. Anheuser-Busch	24. McDonald's
5. Ben & Jerry's	15. Microsoft	25. Southwest Airlines
6. Wal-Mart	16. amazon.com	26. America Online
7. Xerox	17. IBM	27. DaimlerChrysler
8. Home Depot	18. Sony	28. Toyota
9. Gateway	19. Yahoo!	29. Sears
10. Disney	20. AT&T	30. Boeing

In Terms Of

Emotional Appeal	Social Responsibility	Products and Services
1. Johnson & Johnson	1. Ben & Jerry's	1. Johnson & Johnson
2. Coca-Cola	2. amazon.com	2. Intel
3. Hewlett-Packard	3. Johnson & Johnson	3. Hewlett-Packard
4. Ben & Jerry's	4. Wal-Mart	4. Xerox
5. Xerox	5. Xerox	5. Ben & Jerry's

Workplace Environment	Vision and Leadership	Financial Performance
1. Johnson & Johnson	1. Microsoft	1. Microsoft
2. Lucent	2. Intel	2. Wal-Mart
3. Ben & Jerry's	3. Anheuser-Busch	3. Coca-Cola
4. Hewlett-Packard	4. Coca-Cola	4. Johnson & Johnson
5. Intel	5. Dell	5. Intel

For more information, see Ronald Alsop, "The Best Corporate Reputations in America," *The Wall Street Journal* (September 23, 1999), pp. B1, B20.

These consistencies led to our definition of attitude in Chapter 7 as *representing a person's ideas, convictions, or liking with regard to a specific object or idea.*

Scales of Measurement

To properly address the subject of attitude measurement, it is necessary to define measurement and to briefly review the types of scales that can be used to measure attitudes. Incidentally, *scale* is used in two different contexts when discussing measurement. One use refers to the "level" of measurement. The other to the "particular scale or type" of instrument used. We take up the level of measurement issues first.

Measurement consists of "rules for assigning numbers to objects in such a way as to represent quantities of attributes."[3] Note two things about the definition: First,

---

[3]Peter D. Bennett, ed., *Dictionary of Marketing Terms,* 2nd ed. (Chicago: American Marketing Association, 1995), p. 173.

it indicates that we measure the attributes of objects and not the objects themselves. We do not measure a person, for example, but may choose to measure the individual's income, social class, education, height, weight, or attitudes, all of which are attributes of this person. Second, the definition is broad in that it does not specify how the numbers are to be assigned. In this sense, the rule is too simplistic and conveys a false sense of security, because there is a great temptation to read more meaning into the numbers than they actually contain. We often incorrectly attribute all the properties of the scale of numbers to the assigned numerals.

Consider the properties of the scale of numbers. Take the numbers 1, 2, 3, and 4. Now let the number "1" stand for one object, "2" for two objects, and so on. The scale of numbers possesses several properties. For example, we can say that "2" is larger than "1" and "3" is larger than "2," and so on. Also, we can say that the interval between "1" and "2" is the same size as the interval between "3" and "4," which is the same as that between "2" and "3," and so on. We can say still further that "3" is three times greater than "1," while "4" is four times greater than "1" and two times greater than "2," and so on.

However, when we assign numerals to attributes of objects, these relations do not necessarily hold. Rather, we have to determine which properties of the scale of numbers actually apply. "This problem has nothing to do with determining the properties of the number; rather, we must determine the *properties of the attribute itself,* and then be sure that the numerals are assigned so that the *numerals properly reflect the properties of the attribute*" (emphasis added).[4] Consider the different types of scales on which attributes can be measured—namely, nominal, ordinal, interval, and ratio.[5] Table 9.1 summarizes some of the more important features of these scales, which are elaborated in the following sections.

Nominal Scale

One of the simplest properties of the scale of numbers is *identity*. A person's social security number is a **nominal scale,** as are the numbers on football jerseys, lockers, and so on. These numbers simply *identify* the individual assigned the number. Similarly, if in a given market segmentation study males are coded "1" and females "2," we have again made use of a nominal scale. The individuals are uniquely identified as male or female. All we need to determine an individual's sex is to know whether the person is coded as a "1" or as a "2." Note further that there is nothing implied by the numerals other than identification of the sex of the person. Females, although they bear a higher number, are not necessarily "superior" to males, or "more" than males, or twice as many as males as the numbers 2 and 1 indicate, or vice versa. We could just as easily reverse our coding procedure so that each female is a "1" and each male a "2."

---

[4]Wendell R. Garner and C. D. Creelman, "Problems and Methods of Psychological Scaling," in Harry Helson and William Bevan, eds., *Contemporary Approaches to Psychology* (New York: Van Nostrand, 1967), p. 3. The following discussion relies heavily on this excellent article. See also Earl R. Babbie, *The Practice of Social Research,* 8th ed. (Belmont, CA: Wadsworth Publishing Company, 1998).

[5]Our classification follows that of Stanley S. Stevens, "Mathematics, Measurement and Psychophysics," in Stanley S. Stevens, ed., *Handbook of Experimental Psychology* (New York: John Wiley, 1951), the most accepted classification in the social sciences.

TABLE 9.1	Scales of Measurement		

Scale	Basic Comparisons[a]	Typical Examples	Measures of Average[b]
Nominal	Identity	Male–female User–nonuser Occupations Uniform numbers	Mode
Ordinal	Order	Preference for brands Social class Hardness of minerals Graded quality of lumber	Median
Interval	Comparison of intervals	Temperature scale Grade point average Attitude toward brands	Mean
Ratio	Comparison of absolute magnitudes	Units sold Number of purchasers Probability of purchase Weight	Geometric mean Harmonic mean

[a]All the comparisons applicable to a given scale are permissible with all scales above it in the table. For example, the ratio scale allows the comparison of intervals and the investigation of order and identity, in addition to the comparison of absolute magnitudes.
[b]The measures of average applicable to a given scale are also appropriate for all scales below it in the table; that is, the mode is also a meaningful measure of the average when measurement is on an ordinal, interval, or ratio scale.

The reason we could reverse our codes is that the only property conveyed by the numbers is identity. With a nominal scale, the only permissible operation is counting. Thus, the mode is the only legitimate measure of central tendency. It does not make sense in a sample consisting of 60 men and 40 women to say that the average sex is 1.4, given males were coded "1" and females "2" $[0.6(1) + 0.4(2)]$. All we can say is that there were more males in the sample than females, or that 60 percent of the sample was male.

Ordinal Scale

A second property of the scale of numbers is that of *order*. Thus, we could say that the number "2" was greater than the number "1," and that "3" was greater than both "2" and "1," and that "4" was greater than all three of these numbers. The numbers 1, 2, 3, and 4 are ordered, and the larger the number, the greater the property. Note that the **ordinal scale** implies identity, since the same number would be used for all objects that are the same. An example would be the assignment of the number "1" to denote freshmen, "2" to denote sophomores, "3," juniors, and "4," seniors. Note that we could have just as well used the numbers "10" for freshmen, "20" for sophomores, "25" for juniors, and "30" for seniors. This assignment would still indicate the class level of each person and the *relative standing* of two persons when compared in terms of who is farther along in the academic program. Note further that this is all that is conveyed by an ordinal scale. The difference in rank says nothing about the difference in academic achievement between two ranks. This is perhaps easier to see if we talk about the three top people in a graduating class. The fact that one person was ranked number one while the second was ranked number two tells us nothing about the difference in academic achievement between the two. Nor can we say that the difference in academic achievement between the first- and second-ranked people equals the difference between the second- and third-ranked people, even though the difference between "1" and "2" equals the difference between "2" and "3."

As suggested, we can transform an ordinal scale in any way that we wish as long as we maintain the basic ordering of the objects. The ordinal scale is thus said to allow any monotonic positive transformation of the assigned numerals, because the differences in numerals are void of meaning other than order.

Again, whether we can use the ordinal scale to assign numerals to objects depends on the attribute in question. The attribute itself must possess the ordinal property to allow ordinal scaling that is meaningful.

With ordinal scales, both the median and mode are permissible or meaningful measures of average. Thus, if 20 people ranked Product A, for example, first in comparison with Products B and C, while 10 ranked it second and 5 ranked it third, we could say that (1) the average rank of Product A as judged by the median response was one (with 35 subjects, the median is given by the eighteenth response when ranked from lowest to highest), and that (2) the modal rank was also one.

Interval Scale

A third property of the scale of numbers is that the *intervals* between the numbers are meaningful in the sense that the numbers tell us how far apart the objects are with respect to the attribute. This means that the *differences* can be compared. The difference between "1" and "2" is equal to the difference between "2" and "3." Further, the difference between "2" and "4" is twice the difference that exists between "1" and "2."

One classic example of an **interval scale** is the temperature scale, as it indicates what we can and cannot say when we have measured an attribute on an interval scale. Suppose that the low temperature for the day was 40°F and the high was 80°F. Can we say that the high temperature was twice as hot (that is, represented twice the heat) as the low temperature? The answer is an unequivocal no. To see the folly in claiming 80°F is twice as warm as 40°F, one simply needs to convert these temperatures to their centigrade equivalents where $C = (5F - 160)/9$. Now we see that the low was 4.4°C and the high was 26.6°C, a much different ratio between low and high than was indicated by the Fahrenheit scale.

The example serves to illustrate that we cannot compare the absolute magnitude of numbers when measurement is made on the basis of an interval scale. The reason is that in an interval scale, the zero point is established arbitrarily.[6] This means that any positive linear transformation of the form $y = a + bx$, where b is positive, x is the original number, and y is the transformed number, will preserve the properties of the scale.

What, then, can we say when measurement is made on an interval scale? First, we can say that 80°F is warmer than 40°F. Second, given a third temperature, we *can compare the intervals;* that is, we can say the difference in "heat" between 80°F and

---

[6]The zero point on the Fahrenheit scale was originally established by mixing equal weights of snow and salt.

120°F is the same as the difference between 40°F and 80°F, and that the difference between 40°F and 120°F is twice the difference between 40°F and 80°F. To see that this conclusion is legitimate, we can simply resort to the centigrade equivalents; 120°F represents 48.8°C, and the difference between 4.4°C (40°F) and 26.6°C (80°F) is the same as that between 26.6°C (80°F) and 48.8°C (120°F)—namely, 22.2°. Further, the difference of 44.4°C between 4.4°C and 48.8°C is twice as large as that between 4.4°C and 26.6°C, as it was when the Fahrenheit scale was used. The comparison of intervals is legitimate with an interval scale because the relationships among the differences hold regardless of the particular constants chosen for a and b when transforming an interval set of numbers. With an interval scale, the mean, median, and mode are all meaningful measures of average.

Ratio Scale

The **ratio scale** differs from an interval scale in that it possesses a *natural* or *absolute* zero, one for which there is universal agreement about its location. Height and weight are obvious examples.

With a ratio scale, the comparison of the *absolute magnitude* of the numbers is legitimate. Thus, a person weighing 200 pounds is said to be twice as heavy as one weighing 100 pounds, and a person weighing 300 pounds is three times as heavy. Further, we have already seen that the more powerful scales include the properties possessed by the less powerful ones. This means that with a ratio scale we can compare intervals, rank objects according to magnitude, or use the numbers to identify the objects.

Ratio scales only allow the proportionate transformation of the scale values and not the addition of an arbitrary constant as do interval scales. A proportionate transformation is of the form $y = bx$, where x again represents the original values and y the transformed values and b is some positive constant. The conversion of feet to inches ($b = 12$) is an obvious example. All the relationships among the objects are preserved whether the comparison is made in feet or inches.

The geometric mean as well as the more usual arithmetic mean, median, and mode are meaningful measures of average when attributes are measured on a ratio scale.

Scaling of Psychological Attributes

The attribute determines the most powerful scale that can be used to measure the characteristic. That is always the way it is in measurement. The characteristic and its qualities set the upper limit for the assignment of numerals to objects. Because of the procedures used in generating the instrument, it is always possible to end up with what we might call a less powerful measure of the attribute (for example, a nominal rather than an ordinal scale). However, we can never exceed the basic nature of the attribute with our measure; for example, we can never generate an interval scale for an attribute that is only ordinal in nature. Thus, it is critical to know something about the attribute itself before we assign numbers to it using some measurement procedure. For instance, few psychological constructs can reasonably be assumed to have a natural or absolute zero:

For example, what would an absolute zero of intelligence be? Or what is the absolute zero of attitude toward the Republican Party? There can be neutrality of feeling, and neutral position is often used as the zero point on the scale, but it does not represent an absolute lack of the attitude.[7]

The problem is no less real in marketing. Many of our constructs, borrowed from psychology and sociology, possess no more than interval measurement and some even less. We have to be very careful in conceptualizing the construct or characteristic so as not to delude ourselves or mislead others with our measures and (more importantly) *with our interpretation of those measures.*

Further, the procedure used in constructing the scale determines the type of scale actually generated. The more powerful scales allow stronger comparisons and conclusions to be made. Thus, we can make certain types of comparisons that allow particular conclusions when measurement is on a ratio scale, for example, that we cannot make when measurement is on an interval, an ordinal, or a nominal scale. There is a great temptation to *assume* that our measures have the properties of the ratio or at least the interval scale. Whether they do in fact is another question, and the simple condition that the attributes of the objects have been assigned numbers should not delude us. Rather, we should critically ask: What is the basic nature of the attribute? Have we captured this basic nature by our measurement procedure?

Moreover, although ratio scales allow stronger comparisons, they are also more demanding on subjects. For example, Figure 9.1 uses the issue of a respondent's preferences for six different soft drinks to illustrate how questions about this issue might be framed to secure reactions on a nominal, an ordinal, an interval, and a ratio scale. Readers are encouraged to complete the exercise in light of their own preferences. Did you find it more difficult to complete the "more powerful" scales at the bottom of the figure than the nominal scale at the top? Thus, while we might like to capture a respondent's reaction on a ratio scale, there is often a question as to whether our measurement procedure will allow it.

Attitude-Scaling Procedures

Attitudes have been measured, in a number of ways, including self reports, observation of overt behavior, indirect techniques, performance of "objective" tasks, and physiological reactions.[8] By far the most common approach has been **self reports,** in which people are asked directly for their beliefs or feelings toward an object, activity, or class of objects. A number of self-report scales and scaling methods have been devised to secure these feelings. The main types will be reviewed in the next section. For the moment we will consider very briefly the other approaches to attitude determination.

---

[7]Garner and Creelman, "Problems and Methods," p. 4.

[8]This classification of approaches is taken from Stuart W. Cook and Claire Selltiz, "A Multiple Indicator Approach to Attitude Measurement," *Psychological Bulletin* 62 (1964), pp. 36–55. See also Dagmar Krebs and Peter Schmidt, eds., *New Directions in Attitude Measurement* (Berlin: Walter de Gruyter, 1993).

FIGURE 9.1	Assessing a Respondent's Liking of Soft Drinks with Nominal, Ordinal, Interval, and Ratio Scales

Nominal Scale

Which of the soft drinks on the following list do you like? Check all that apply.

____ Coke
____ Dr Pepper
____ Mountain Dew
____ Pepsi
____ Seven Up
____ Sprite

Ordinal Scale

Please rank the soft drinks on the following list according to your degree of liking for each, assigning your most preferred drink rank = 1 and your least preferred drink rank = 6.

____ Coke
____ Dr Pepper
____ Mountain Dew
____ Pepsi
____ Seven Up
____ Sprite

Interval Scale

Please indicate your degree of liking of each of the soft drinks on the following list by checking the appropriate position on the scale.

	Dislike a Lot	Dislike	Like	Like a Lot
Coke	____	____	____	____
Dr Pepper	____	____	____	____
Mountain Dew	____	____	____	____
Pepsi	____	____	____	____
Seven Up	____	____	____	____
Sprite	____	____	____	____

Ratio Scale

Please divide 100 points among each of the following soft drinks according to your degree of liking for each.

____ Coke
____ Dr Pepper
____ Mountain Dew
____ Pepsi
____ Seven Up
____ Sprite
 100

OBSERVATION OF BEHAVIOR   The observation approach to attitude determination rests on the presumption that a subject's behavior is conditioned by his or her attitudes and, thus, that we can use the observed behavior to infer these attitudes. Thus, observers inferred that consumers are not looking for a low-fat meal when they enter McDonald's from the fact that its McLean Deluxe hamburger was a marketing flop in spite of the $50 million the company spent to launch the product.[9] What is sometimes done when using behavior observation to infer something about attitudes is to create an artificial situation and see how the individual behaves. For example, to assess a person's attitude toward antipollution legislation, the subject might be asked to sign a "strong" petition prohibiting pollution. The individual's attitude toward pollution would be inferred on the basis of whether or not he or she signed. Alternatively, subjects might be thrust into a group discussing the issue of pollution and their behavior observed. Did the persons oppose or support antipollution legislation in the discussion?

INDIRECT TECHNIQUES   The indirect techniques of attitude assessment use some unstructured or partially structured stimuli, as discussed in Chapter 7, such as word association tests, sentence completion tests, storytelling, and so on. Because the arguments concerning the use of these devices were detailed previously, they will not be repeated here.

PERFORMANCE OF "OBJECTIVE" TASK   These approaches rest on the presumption that a subject's **performance of objective tasks** will depend on the person's attitude. Thus, to assess a person's pollution posture, we might ask him or her to memorize a number of facts about the extent of pollution, the magnitude of the cleanup task, and pending antipollution legislation. This material would reflect both sides of the issue. The researcher would then attempt to determine what facts the person assimilated. The assumption is that subjects would be more apt to remember those arguments that are most consistent with their own position.

PHYSIOLOGICAL REACTIONS   The physiological reaction approach to attitude measurement was also detailed in Chapter 7. Here, through electrical or mechanical means, such as the galvanic skin response technique, the researcher monitors the subject's response to the controlled introduction of some stimuli. One problem that arises in using these measures to assess attitude is that the individual's physiological response provides only an indication of the intensity of the individual's feelings and not whether they are negative or positive.

MULTIPLE MEASURES   Although self-report techniques for attitude assessment are the most widely used in marketing research studies because they are easy to administer, one should be aware of these other approaches, particularly when one is attempting to establish the validity of a self-report measure. They can provide useful insight into how the method of measurement, and not the differences in the basic attitudes

---

[9]Hugh Graham, "Annals of Marketing: Don't Go Changin'," *Globe and Mail* (September 25, 1998) (downloaded from Dow Jones Publications Library at the Dow Jones Web site, www.dowjones.com, August 10, 1999).

of subjects, caused the scores to vary. This is consistent with the notion of using multiple indicators to establish the convergent and discriminant validity of a measure.[10]

Self-Report Attitude Scales

Given that attitude is one of the most pervasive concepts in all of social psychology, it should not prove surprising to find that many methods have been advanced to measure it. Although the self-report technique is common to many of the methods, they still differ in terms of the way the scales are constructed and used. In this section, we shall review some of these self-report scales, particularly those that have novel features or have been used extensively in marketing studies. The discussion should give you an appreciation of the main types and their construction and use. Incidentally, in following the arguments, you will find it helpful to distinguish between how a scale is constructed and how it is used.

Equal-Appearing Intervals

Suppose that one of the banks in town is interested in comparing its image to the images of its competitors and has developed a list of statements that can be employed to describe each bank. Now suppose that, when presented with a list of characteristics, a respondent describes Bank A, the sponsor of the research, as having convenient hours and a convenient location but generally discourteous service and higher service charges on personal checking accounts. Does this respondent have a favorable or unfavorable attitude toward Bank A? Suppose that the respondent describes Bank B as just the opposite. To which bank is the individual more favorably disposed? We cannot say without knowing what the individual statements imply about the person's overall attitude. It is the purpose of **equal-appearing interval** scaling to develop values for the statements (characteristics) so that we can assess a person's attitude toward Bank A or any other bank by analyzing the statements with which the individual describes each bank.[11]

SCALE CONSTRUCTION   The general procedure for constructing a scale using equal-appearing intervals is first to generate a large number of statements concerning the psychological object of interest. The statements are then edited to remove obviously ambiguous, irrelevant, and awkward statements, as well as statements that

---

[10]The arguments are elaborated in Cook and Selltiz, "A Multiple Indicator Approach." The ideas of convergent and discriminant validity are discussed in Appendix 9A. Evidence of the convergent validity of a measure is provided by the extent to which it correlates highly with other measures designed to assess the same construct. Evidence of the discriminant validity of a measure is indicated by low correlations between the measure of interest and other measures that are supposedly not measuring the same variable or construct.

[11]The equal-appearing interval technique was developed by L. L. Thurstone and E. J. Chave, *The Measurement of Attitude* (Chicago: University of Chicago Press, 1929). The procedure provided an alternative to the paired comparison method of determining statement scale values when the number of statements was large. The paired comparison method, which was also devised by Thurstone, was a forerunner of much modern-day psychological measurement. See L. L. Thurstone, "A Law of Comparative Judgement," *Psychological Review* 34 (1927), pp. 273–286, and "Psychological Analysis," *American Journal of Psychology* 38 (1927), pp. 368–389.

are matters of fact rather than opinion. A relatively large sample of judges is then asked to sort the statements by their degree of favorableness, and a scale value is determined for each statement by the frequency with which the statement is placed in each of the piles. The statements are then screened on the basis of two criteria: the scale values and the dispersion in judgments exhibited by the subjects. A final scale is formed from those statements that span the range of scale values and that display relatively good interjudge reliability. Let us illustrate the procedure using our bank example.

The first task would be to generate a large number of statements. These statements could be generated from a search of the literature, discussions with knowledgeable people, personal experience, or in any of the other ways one uses to develop insight into a phenomenon. The important thing at this stage is that the statements be as exhaustive as possible; that is, they reflect all the attributes of the object that may lead to formation of attitudes about it. Thus, we would want to incorporate statements about a bank's level of service, convenience, interest paid on savings accounts, interest required on loans, and so on.[12] Further, it is often productive at this stage to include several statements that apply to the same attribute but that are worded differently. The following would be examples.

1.   The bank offers courteous service.

2.   The bank has a convenient location.

3.   The bank has convenient hours.

4.   The bank offers low interest rates on loans.

5.   The bank pays low interest on its savings accounts.

•

•

•

m.   The bank's service is friendly.

Ideally, *m* would be in the neighborhood of 100 to 200, and each statement would be presented on a separate card.

After editing the statements, a large sample of subjects would be recruited as judges.[13] Each judge would be instructed to sort the statements into one of 11 piles based on the "degree of favorableness" of the statement. Note this. The judges are not asked whether they agree or disagree with a statement, but rather they are asked

---

[12]For a list of some of the attributes of a bank one might want to inquire about, see Neil M. Ford, *How to Measure Your Bank's Personality* (Chicago: Bank Marketing Association, 1973); See also Sid C. Dudley, Gary F. Young, and Richard L. Powers, "A Study of Factors Affecting Individuals' Banking Preferences," *Journal of Professional Services Marketing* 1 (1985), pp. 163–168; R. Kenneth Teas and John Wong, "Measurement of Customer Perceptions of the Retail Bank Delivery System," *Journal of Professional Services Marketing* 7, no. 1 (1991), pp. 147–167.

[13]When developing the techniques, Thurstone and Chave used 300 judges. Edwards summarizes a number of studies, however, in which fewer judges have been used to produce reliable scales. See Allen L. Edwards, *Techniques of Attitude Scale Construction* (New York: Appleton-Century-Crofts, 1957), pp. 94–95. The serious student of attitude measurement would be well advised to read Edwards's good little book.

| FIGURE 9.2 | **Thurstone Equal-Appearing Interval Continuum** |

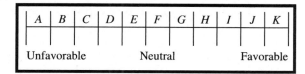

| TABLE 9.2 | **Equal-Appearing Interval Sort of the Statements into Categories** |

					Sorting Categories								
Statement	A 1	B 2	C 3	D 4	E 5	F 6	G 7	H 8	I 9	J 10	K 11	Scale Value	Q Value
1	0	8	10	30	60	60	14	12	6	0	0	5.4	1.7
2	0	0	0	0	0	6	16	28	44	66	40	9.6	1.8
3	0	0	0	0	10	10	14	32	84	34	16	8.9	1.5
4	0	0	8	16	36	58	48	24	10	0	0	6.2	2.0

to evaluate the statement on its own merits. For example, they would be asked to place (1) those statements that seem to express the *most unfavorable* things one could say about the object in the *A* pile of Figure 9.2; (2) those statements that express the *most favorable* things one could say in the *K* pile; and (3) those statements that are neither positive nor negative in the *F* pile. Those statements that express some intermediate level of favorableness or unfavorableness would, of course, be placed in one of the other piles. The piles are most typically formed by arranging a set of cards with letters on them in front of the judge. Only the two end points and the middle position are anchored with word descriptions in addition to the letter. The presumption is that each judge will perceive the categories as representing equal increments of favorableness, and thus the name *equal-appearing intervals.*

Suppose that 200 judges sorted the *m* statements according to their favorableness and that Table 9.2 contains the resulting distribution for the first four statements. The right-hand columns of the table contain the scale and *Q* values for each statement. The scale value represents the "average" value of the statement, given the scores assigned each sorting category. The scale values locate each statement on the favorability continuum in Figure 9.2. The median is typically used as the measure of average. The *Q* value is the interquartile range, which provides a measure of spread or dispersion in where each statement is placed.

The scale values and measures of dispersion are used to select a subset of statements to serve as the final instrument. Typically, the researcher selects 20 to 22 statements that span the scale of favorableness; that is, some of the statements in the final list would have low scale values, some intermediate values, and some high values. Ideally, the scale values would be equally spaced. One can see from the limited example that several, if not many, of the initial statements will have approximately equal scale values. How does one then choose among them? This is where the interquartile range enters. We would like to have items in our final scale that are likely to be interpreted consistently by those responding. Thus, we do not want to include a statement that could be agreed to by those with both positive and negative attitudes toward the object. Large values of Q indicate that, at least in our judgment sample, there was wide disagreement among the judges as to the degree of favorableness expressed in the statement, and, therefore, the statement is ambiguous. Given that two statements have approximately equal values, we choose the one that has the smallest Q. In sum, the scale and Q values serve as filters for reducing the total stimuli to a more manageable number.

SCALE USE   Assume that some 20 to 22 statements have been selected from the larger list of m statements using the procedure detailed previously. The statements are randomly placed in the final instrument so that there is no order to the scale values. The instrument is then ready to be administered to one or more samples of subjects whose attitudes we are interested in assessing.

When the instrument is administered, subjects are asked to indicate those statements with which *they agree.* For example, subjects would be asked to select those statements from the total list that reflect their feelings toward Bank A. A subject's attitude score is considered to be the average of the scale scores for the statements with which the person agrees. Thus, if the subject agreed with three statements with the scale scores 8.2, 8.7, and 9.8, the person's attitude score would be 8.9. Since the scale value 6 represents a neutral attitude, the conclusion would be that the subject had a favorable attitude toward Bank A.

Several criticisms have been leveled at the method of scoring. One centers on subjects' being asked to select only those statements with which they agree and *not* being asked to respond to each of the statements. This makes it possible for two subjects who respond quite differently to have the same attitude score. Thus, a subject agreeing with statements with scale scores 4, 6, and 8 would have the same attitude score as another person who only agreed with the statement having a scale score of 6. But do they, in fact, have the same attitude? There is still considerable controversy on this point.

Another frequent criticism is that the method does not allow subjects to express the intensity of their feelings. For example, a subject could feel quite strongly that the bank had very convenient hours or he might feel that although basically convenient, the hours could be improved. In either case, all that the subject would be able to do would be to indicate that he agrees with the statement. Yet, are not the two attitudes basically different?

As you might suspect, the equal-appearing interval scale is time consuming to construct. Once constructed, though, it is very easy to administer and is easy for respondents to complete. It can further be used to assess attitudes toward a variety of objects (for example, each bank in town). The technique can also be employed to scale other characteristics besides attitude, such as the amount of perceived puffery in each of a series of advertising claims or the consistency in the favorableness of various adjectives across groups of people.[14] The effort involved in its construction and the limited diagnostic information it provides have tended to limit its use in

---

[14]Used in this way, the method is helpful in developing anchors for scales that are perceived by respondents to be equally spaced.

FIGURE 9.3	Example of Likert Summated Rating Form				
	Strongly Disagree	**Disagree**	**Neither Agree Nor Disagree**	**Agree**	**Strongly Agree**
1. The bank offers courteous service.	____	____	____	____	____
2. The bank has a convenient location.	____	____	____	____	____
3. The bank has convenient hours.	____	____	____	____	____
4. The bank offers low interest rate loans.	____	____	____	____	____

assessing attitudes. The evidence indicates, for example, that it is used less than the other self-report techniques for assessing attitudes. Nonetheless, its other potential uses still make the equal-interval technique a valuable component in the marketing researcher's measurement arsenal.

Summated Ratings

The Likert method of **summated ratings** overcomes the previous criticisms about scoring and allowing an expression of intensity of feeling.[15] The method is both constructed and used in a slightly different way than equal-appearing intervals.

SCALE CONSTRUCTION   The basic format of the scale for the summated ratings method is the same in both construction and use. Subjects are asked to indicate their degree of agreement or disagreement *with each and every statement* in a series by checking the appropriate cell. Figure 9.3 serves as an example. Again, the researcher attempts to develop a great many statements that reflect qualities of things about the object that possibly influence a person's attitude toward it. In this respect, the procedure is no different from that used in the method of equal-appearing intervals. The method is quite different, though, in terms of the judgment sample and what is asked of the subjects.

It is often argued that those judging the statements need not represent the population on which an equal-appearing interval scale will be used, because the judges are asked only to indicate the degree of favorableness of each statement.[16] With a Likert scale, there is no question that the screening sample should be representative of the larger group, because of both the different task assigned the subjects and the method by which the total set of statements is reduced to a smaller, more consistent subset. It must be pointed out that a screening sample has not always been used in the published marketing applications of the summated rating scale. This is unfortunate, because omitting refinement of a scale is likely to result in a more ambiguous, less reliable, less valid instrument.

Once again, assume that there are 200 subjects in the screening sample. First, each statement is classified *a priori* as favorable or unfavorable. Subjects are then

---

[15]The scale was first proposed by Rensis Likert, "A Technique for the Measurement of Attitudes," *Archives of Psychology*, no. 140 (1932).

[16]Some empirical evidence tends to refute this argument. Even though the judges are supposed to evaluate each statement on its own merits, a judge's own attitudes may tend to influence his or her placement of the statements. Edwards, *Techniques*, pp. 106–116, summarizes these studies.

asked to indicate their degree of agreement or disagreement with each statement with respect to a specific bank (or banks) by placing a checkmark in the appropiate category.[17] The various degrees of agreement are assigned scale values, although the particular values differ from researcher to researcher. Sometimes the values -2, -1, 0, 1, 2 are employed, whereas the values 1, 2, 3, 4, 5 are preferred by other researchers for the respective response categories. It makes no difference in the conclusions we can draw, since the decision is completely arbitrary. Suppose that we decide to use the values 1 through 5. Now, a subject could be considered to feel positively about the bank if he or she either agreed with a favorable statement or disagreed with an unfavorable statement. Therefore, it is necessary to reverse the scaling with negative statements. Thus, a *strongly agree* response to a favorable statement and a *strongly disagree* response to an unfavorable statement would both receive scores of 5.

A total attitude score can be calculated for each subject using the same scoring procedure. The distribution of total scores is then used to refine the original list of m statements. The procedure, known as item analysis, rests on the proposition that there should be consistency in the response pattern of any individual. If the individual has a very favorable attitude toward the object, he or she should basically agree with the favorable statements and disagree with the unfavorable ones and vice versa. If we should happen to have a statement that generates a very mixed response, we would tend to question it on the grounds that it must be ambiguous or at the very least not discriminating of attitude. A parallel example would be the problem $2 + 2 = 4$ for a college math course. The problem tells us little about a person's math ability because both poor and good students could be expected to answer the problem correctly. Thus, the problem would be unsuitable for scaling college students on their math ability.

The same argument holds for attitude scales. We do not want to clutter up the scale with irrelevant statements but rather wish to include only those statements that discriminate among subjects with respect to their attitude. Although you embrace the premise, you may be wondering about the procedure. After all, did we not just say that those with a "very favorable" attitude could be expected to respond favorably to positive statements? How does one determine who has a favorable or unfavorable attitude, though? After all, aren't we developing the scale so that we can measure a person's attitude, and thus aren't we engaged in circular reasoning of "using a person's basic attitude to select statements by which that attitude can be measured"? You would be right, of course. Yet there is a way out of the circle. The trick is to assume that the total score generated by the response to all m statements serves as a proxy for the person's true attitude. One can then relate each statement in turn to this total score to ascertain which statements are nondiscriminating.

One can relate individual statement scores to total scores by several methods. The most conceptually appealing approach calculates the product-moment correlation of each item with the total score.[18] Those items that have the highest correla-

---

[17] Paul E. Spector, "Choosing Response Categories for Summated Rating Scales," *Journal of Applied Psychology* 61 (June 1976), pp. 374–375, contains a list of typical category descriptors and their numerical values.

[18] Jum C. Nunnally and Ira H. Bernstein, *Psychometric Theory*, 3rd ed. (New York: McGraw-Hill, 1994), Chaps. 6–8, have a rather compelling argument as to why correlation coefficients should be used to refine scales. The correlation coefficient is discussed in Chapter 16.

| TABLE 9.3 | Difference in Means for One Statement for the Two Groups with the Most Favorable and the Least Favorable Attitudes |

Response Category	Scale Value x	High Group f	fx	Low Group f	fx
Strongly agree	5	28	140	2	10
Agree	4	14	56	6	24
Neither agree nor disagree	3	6	18	18	54
Disagree	2	2	4	20	40
Strongly disagree	1	0	0	4	4
Sums		50	218	50	132

$$\bar{x}_H = \frac{2.18}{50} = 4.36, \qquad \bar{x}_L = \frac{132}{50} = 2.64, \qquad d = \bar{x}_H - \bar{x}_L = 4.36 - 2.64 = 1.72$$

tion with the total are the best. Those with correlations near zero are suspect and should be eliminated. By ranking the correlations, one can use this method to devise a final scale of any length desired. One simply selects those 25, 50, or however many statements having the highest correlations with the total score, although there usually is some attempt to include negative as well as positive statements.

An alternative way of performing an item analysis involves the division of subjects into some arbitrarily defined groups. For example, those subjects with the top 25 percent of all total scores would be considered to have the most favorable attitudes, whereas those with the lowest 25 percent of all total scores would be considered to have the least favorable attitudes. If the item is a good one, it would seem reasonable that after correcting for the scoring direction, the mean score for each statement for the favorable attitude group should exceed the mean score for the unfavorable attitude group. The statements can then be ranked according to their difference in mean scores. Those with mean differences near zero are poor statements and should be eliminated. Sometimes the researcher will go one step farther and test for the statistical significance of the difference in mean scores for the two groups, in which case only those statements that show a statistically significant difference would be retained.[19] Table 9.3 displays a comparison of means, without testing for the statistical significance of the difference, for a sample statement "The bank has a convenient location," and assumed responses for the 50 subjects with the most favorable and the 50 subjects with the least favorable attitudes. The calculation indicates that the statement is a discriminating one, because the difference in mean scores is indeed positive.

SCALE USE   One advantage of the Likert scale of summated ratings is that directions for its use are the same as the directions employed to generate scores by which to screen statements. The statements remaining after purification of the original list are randomly ordered on the scale form so as to mix positive and negative ones, and subjects are asked to indicate their degree of agreement with each statement. Subjects generally find it easy to respond, because the response categories do allow the

---

[19] The statistical test would be the t test for the difference in two means described in Chapter 15.

expression of the intensity of the feeling. The subject's total score is generated as the simple sum of the scores on each statement.[20]

A problem of interpretation arises with the summated rating scale that did not exist with the equal-appearing interval scale. With the latter, a score of 9.2, say, represented a favorable attitude toward Bank A, but what does a score of 78 on a 20-item Likert scale indicate? Because the maximum is $20 \times 5 = 100$, can we assume that the person's attitude toward the bank is favorable? We cannot, since the raw scores assume meaning only when we compare them to some standard. This problem is not unique to psychological scaling but arises every day of our lives in a variety of ways. We are always making judgments on the basis of comparisons with some standard. Most typically, the standard is established through our experiences and rarely is rigorously defined. Thus, when we say "The man sure is tall," we are in effect saying that on the basis of the experience we have, the man is taller than average.

In psychological scaling, this is formalized somewhat by clearly specifying the standard. Very often the standard is taken as the average score for all subjects, although averages are also computed for certain predefined subgroups. The procedure is called developing norms. Comparisons can then be made against the norms to determine whether the person has a positive or negative attitude toward the object. Norms are not, of course, necessary for comparing subjects to determine which person has the more favorable attitude. Here one can simply compare the subjects' raw scores. Nor are norms necessary when attempting to determine whether an individual's attitude has changed over time or whether a person likes one object better than another. One can simply compare the later and earlier scores or the difference in scores for the two objects.

Semantic Differential

The **semantic differential** scale grew out of some research at the University of Illinois designed to investigate the underlying structure of words.[21] The technique has been adapted, however, to measure attitudes.

The original semantic differential scale consisted of a great many bipolar adjectives, which were employed to secure people's reactions to the objects of interest. It was found that the reactions to the bipolar scales tended to be correlated and that three basic uncorrelated dimensions could be found to account for most of the variation in ratings: an *evaluation* dimension represented by such adjective pairs as good–bad, sweet–sour, helpful–unhelpful; a *potency* dimension represented by bipolar items, such as powerful–powerless, strong–weak, deep–shallow; and an *activity*

---

[20]For an example, see William C. Lundstrom and Lawrence M. Lamont, "The Development of a Scale to Measure Consumer Discontent," *Journal of Marketing Research* 13 (November 1976), pp. 373–381, which reports the procedures used and the results obtained in the development of a Likert scale to measure consumer discontent. For a generalizable procedure on how to go about constructing scales, see Gilbert A. Churchill, Jr., "A Paradigm for Developing Better Measures of Marketing Constructs," *Journal of Marketing Research* 16 (February 1979), pp. 64–73. See also Paul E. Spector, *Summated Rating Scale Construction* (Thousand Oaks, CA: Sage Publications, Inc., 1992); Howard Schuman and Stanley Presser, *Questions and Answers in Attitude Surveys* (Thousand Oaks, CA: Sage Publications, 1996).

[21]Charles E. Osgood, George J. Suci, and Percy H. Tannenbaum, *The Measurement of Meaning* (Champaign, IL: University of Illinois Press, 1957).

FIGURE 9.4   **Example of Semantic Differential Scaling Form**

Service is discourteous	:__:__:__:__:__:__:	Service is courteous
Location is convenient	:__:__:__:__:__:__:	Location is inconvenient
Hours are inconvenient	:__:__:__:__:__:__:	Hours are convenient
Loan interest rates are high	:__:__:__:__:__:__:	Loan interest rates are low

---

dimension captured by adjective pairs, such as fast–slow, alive–dead, noisy–quiet. The same three dimensions tended to emerge regardless of the object being evaluated.[22] Thus, the general thrust in using the semantic differential technique to form scales has been to select an appropriate sample of adjective pairs so that a score could be generated for the object for each of the evaluation, potency, and activity dimensions. The object could then be compared to other objects using these scores.

The approach in marketing has been somewhat different from the general thrust. First, instead of applying the *basic* adjective pairs to the objects of interest, marketers have generated items of their own. These items have not always been antonyms, nor have they been single words. Rather, marketers have used phrases to anchor the ends of the scale, and some of these phrases have been attributes possessed by the product. Since a negative amount of the attribute is often a meaningless notion, lack of the attribute has been used as one end of the scale and a great deal of the attribute as the other.[23]

Second, instead of attempting to generate evaluation, potency, and activity scores, marketers have been more interested in developing profiles for the brands, stores, companies, or whatever is being compared, as well as total scores by which the objects could be compared. In this respect, the use of the semantic differential approach in marketing studies has tended to follow the Likert approach to scale construction rather than the semantic differential tradition. Unfortunately, marketers have often failed to engage in the recommended scale purification procedures that should accompany this switch in emphasis, thus raising questions about the validity of the resulting semantic differential scales.[24]

Let us again use the bank attitude scaling problem to illustrate the semantic differential method. First, a researcher would generate a large list of bipolar adjectives or phrases. Figure 9.4 parallels Figure 9.3 in terms of the attributes used to describe the bank, but it is arranged in a semantic differential format. All we have done in Figure 9.4 is to try to express the characteristics that could be used to describe a

---

[22]See David R. Heise, "The Semantic Differential and Attitude Research," in Summers, ed., *Attitude Measurement*, pp. 235–253, for an overview of the many studies in which the three dimensions were found. Factor analysis is the basic procedure employed to reduce a number of bipolar adjective pairs to basic dimensions. The rudiments of factor analysis are presented in Chapter 17.

[23]Much of the impetus for these practices seems to have been provided by W. A. Mindak, "Fitting the Semantic Differential to the Marketing Problem," *Journal of Marketing* 25 (April 1961), pp. 28–33.

[24]After a sample of subjects uses the scale to evaluate an attitude object, the scale should be purified in the same manner as was the summated rating scale. The total score for each subject would be calculated and the ambiguous or nondiscriminating items eliminated by calculating item to total correlations or by looking at the mean scores by item of the high and low total scores. Although this is rarely done with semantic differential scales, it is an important step in ensuring that the scale is really measuring what it was designed to measure.

FIGURE 9.5	Contrasting Profiles of Banks A and B

Service is discourteous   : —— : —— : —— : —— : —— : —— : —— :   Service is courteous

Location is inconvenient   : —— : —— : —— : —— : —— : —— : —— :   Location is convenient

Hours are inconvenient   : —— : —— : —— : —— : —— : —— : —— :   Hours are convenient

Loan interest rates are high   : —— : —— : —— : —— : —— : —— : —— :   Loan interest rates are low

—— Bank A
- - - - Bank B

bank, and thus serve as a basis for attitude formation, in terms of positive and negative statements. Note that the negative phrase sometimes appears at the left side of the scale and other times at the right. This is done to prevent a respondent with a positive attitude from simply checking either the right- or left-hand sides without even bothering to read the descriptions.

The scale would then be administered to a sample of subjects. Each respondent would be asked to read each set of bipolar phrases and to check the cell that best described her feelings toward the object. The end positions are usually defined for the respondent in the instructions as being *very closely descriptive* of the object, the center position as being *neutral,* and the intermediate positions as *slightly descriptive* and *quite closely descriptive.* Thus, for example, if the subject thought that Bank A's service was courteous but only moderately so, she would check the sixth position reading from left to right.

The subject could be asked to evaluate two or more banks using the same scale.[25] When several banks are rated, the different profiles can be compared. Figure 9.5, for example (which is sometimes referred to as a **snake diagram** because of its shape), illustrates that Bank A is perceived as having more courteous service and a more convenient location and as offering lower interest rates on loans, but also as having more inconvenient hours than Bank B. Note that in constructing these profiles, the customary practice of placing all positive descriptors on the right, to facilitate communication, has been followed. The plotted values simply represent the average score of all subjects on each descriptor. Although the mean is most often used, there is some controversy about whether the seven scale increments can be treated as an interval scale. If not, as critics contend, then the median scores should

---

[25]The most popular form of the semantic differential scale places the objects being evaluated at the top and the descriptors used for the evaluation along the sides as the rows. One somewhat popular variation lists the descriptors at the top and the objects being evaluated along the side. For an empirical comparison of the two approaches, see Eugene D. Jaffe and Israel D. Nebenzahl, "Alternative Questionnaire Formats for Country Image Studies," *Journal of Marketing Research* 21 (November 1984), pp. 463–471. See also Linda L. Golden, Gerald Albaum, and Mary Zimmer, "The Numerical Comparative Scale: An Economical Format for Retail Image Measurement," *Journal of Retailing* 63 (Winter 1987), pp. 393–410; Ron Garland, "A Comparison of Three Forms of the Semantic Differential," *Marketing Bulletin* 1 (May 1990), pp. 19–24.

be used to develop the profiles. In either case, the plotted profiles readily communicate the perceived positions of Banks A and B by the sample respondents.

When a total score by which objects can be compared is desired (for example, which alternative package design is preferred by customers), the score is generated by summing the scores for the individual descriptors. The individual items may be scored $-3, -2, -1, 0, 1, 2, 3$, or $1, 2, 3, 4, 5, 6, 7$. Again, even though the decision is arbitrary because of the arbitrary nature of the zero point, these scores are simply summed in the same way as they were in the Likert procedure. It is unfortunate that few marketing studies employ a screening sample with semantic differential scales by which an original sample of items could be refined. Although not extremely important in an item-by-item profile comparison, the lack of a rudimentary item analysis is critical when comparing total scores to determine which subject had the most favorable attitude or which object was evaluated most favorably by a given subject. The total scores may be meaningless if the items used in generating the scores are inappropriate, as they very well can be when simply created but not analyzed for their internal consistency of meaning. The argument and the procedure for accomplishing an item analysis here parallel those for the Likert scale.

Perhaps it is the ease with which semantic differential scales can be developed, or the ease with which the findings can be communicated, or accumulated experience of their value that accounts for the semantic differential scale's great popularity in marketing. The technique does allow subjects to express the intensity of their feelings toward company, product, package, advertisement, or whatever. When combined with proper item analysis techniques, the semantic differential seems to offer the marketing researcher a most valuable research tool.

Stapel Scale

A modification of the semantic differential scale that has received some attention in marketing literature is the **Stapel scale.** It differs from the semantic differential scale in that (1) adjectives or descriptive phrases are tested separately instead of simultaneously as bipolar pairs; (2) points on the scale are identified by number; and (3) there are 10 scale positions rather than 7. Figure 9.6 casts the same four attributes previously used to measure attitudes toward banks in a Stapel scale format. Respondents are told to rate how accurately each statement describes the object of interest (Bank A, for example). Instructions such as the following are given to respondents:

> You would select a *plus* number for words that you think describe (Bank A) accurately. The more accurately you think the word describes it, the larger the *plus*

FIGURE 9.6   Example of a Stapel Scale

	−5	−4	−3	−2	−1	+1	+2	+3	+4	+5
Service is courteous	☐	☐	☐	☐	☐	☐	☐	☐	☐	☐
Location is convenient	☐	☐	☐	☐	☐	☐	☐	☐	☐	☐
Hours are convenient	☐	☐	☐	☐	☐	☐	☐	☐	☐	☐
Loan interest rates are high	☐	☐	☐	☐	☐	☐	☐	☐	☐	☐

number you would choose. You would select a *minus* number for words you think do not describe it accurately. The less accurately you think a word describes it, the larger the *minus* number you would choose. Therefore, you can select any number from +5, for words that you think are very accurate, all the way to −5, for words that you think are very inaccurate.[26]

The advantage claimed for the Stapel scale is that it frees the researcher from the need to develop bipolar adjectives for the many items affecting attitudes, which can indeed be a formidable task. Despite this advantage, the Stapel scale has not been as warmly embraced as the semantic differential form, judging by the number of published marketing studies using each.[27] One problem with using it is that many of the descriptors used to evaluate an object can be phrased one of three ways—positively, negatively, or neutrally—and the phrasing chosen seems to affect the results as well as subjects' ability to respond.[28] Nevertheless, it is a useful addition to the researcher's equipment arsenal, and it does lend itself to administration by telephone.[29]

It should be pointed out that a total score on both the semantic differential and Stapel scales is like a total score on a Likert scale. The score 48, for example, is meaningless by itself but takes on meaning when compared to some norm or other score. There is a good deal of controversy about whether semantic differential, Stapel, or even Likert-generated total scores represent interval scaling or, in actuality, reflect ordinal scaling. While the controversy rages, marketers have been inclined to assume the posture of many psychological scaling specialists, who assume interval scaling of their constructs not because they believe that they have necessarily measured them on an interval scale but because interval scaling allows more powerful methods of analysis to be brought to bear. The persistence of this posture in psychological scaling attests to its general fruitfulness, and it seems reasonable that marketers have also found the assumption of interval scaling productive if not entirely correct. There is also a logical justification for this assumption:

> By assuming interval measurement where only ordinal measurement exists, some measurement errors will occur. The result of errors generally is the attenuation of relations among variables. That is, one's apparent results will be more attenuated

[26]Irving Crespi, "Use of a Scaling Technique in Surveys," *Journal of Marketing* 25 (July 1961), p. 71. For an example of the use of a Stapel scale, see Mark E. Slama and Armen Tashchian, "Validating the S-O-R Paradigm for Consumer Involvement with a Convenience Good," *Journal of the Academy of Marketing Science* 15 (Spring 1987), pp. 36–45.

[27]One study that compared the performance of the Stapel scale to the semantic differential found basically no difference between the results produced by, or respondents' ability to use, each. See Del I. Hawkins, Gerald Albaum, and Roger Best, "Stapel Scale or Semantic Differential in Marketing Research," *Journal of Marketing Research* 11 (August 1974), pp. 318–322. See also Grahame R. Dowling, "Measuring Corporate Images: A Review of Alternative Approaches," *Journal of Business Research* 17 (August 1988), pp. 27–34.

[28]Michael J. Etzel, Terrell G. Williams, John C. Rogers, and Douglas J. Lincoln, "The Comparability of Three Stapel Scale Forms in a Marketing Setting," in Ronald F. Bush and Shelby D. Hunt, eds., *Marketing Theory: Philosophy of Science Perspectives* (Chicago: American Marketing Association, 1982), pp. 303–306.

[29]Gregory D. Upah and Steven C. Cosmas, "The Use of Telephone Dials as Attitude Scales," *Journal of the Academy of Marketing Science* (Fall 1980), pp. 416–426; Barbara Loken, et al., "The Use of 0-10 Scales in Telephone Surveys," *Journal of the Market Research Society* 29 (July 1987), pp. 353–362.

ETHICAL DILEMMA 9.1

An independent researcher was hired by a national chain of department stores to develop a scale by which the chain could measure the image of each of its stores. The researcher thought that the best way to do this was through a semantic differential scale. Since she was interested in establishing her credentials as an expert on store-image research, however, she decided to also develop items for a Likert scale and to administer both of the scales to designated participants. She realized that this might induce greater respondent fatigue and perhaps lower-quality responses, but she was willing to take the chance because she knew that the client would not sanction or pay for administering the second survey to an independent sample of respondents.

- Is it ethical for the researcher to accept the risk of lowering the quality of the data addressing the client's issue so that she can further her own goals and career?

- What if the data collected by the two instruments provided stronger evidence that store image had indeed been measured adequately than that collected through the sole use of the semantic differential scale?

- Would it make any difference if there was a reasonable chance that the Likert format would produce a better instrument for measuring retail image than a semantic differential format?

than they are in reality. Thus it is unlikely that the decision to assume interval measurement when it does not exist will lead to the spurious overestimation of results.[30]

Further, from a statistical point of view, the assumption of intervality often makes sense. Statistical tests of significance, for example, "do not care from where the numbers come." The key criterion in choosing a statistical test is that the assumptions underlying the use of a particular statistical test must be satisfied.[31] It is not necessary, therefore, to be *overly* concerned about the level of measurement from a *statistical* point of view. What we must be careful about is the *interpretation* of the results (for example, arguing that a person with a score of 80 has twice as favorable an attitude toward an object as a person with a score of 40 unless the measurement scale is ratio).

---

[30]George W. Bohrnstedt, "Reliability and Validity Assessment in Attitude Measurement," in Summers, ed., *Attitude Measurement,* pp. 81–82.

[31]Evidence demonstrates, for example, that there is little difference in results when ordinal data are analyzed by procedures appropriate to interval data. See Sanford Labovitz, "Some Observations on Measurement and Statistics," *Social Forces* 46 (1967), pp. 151–160; Sanford Labovitz, "The Assignment of Numbers to Rank Order Categories," *American Sociological Review* 35 (1970), pp. 515–524; John Gaito, "Measurement Scales and Statistics: Resurgence of an Old Misconception," *Psychological Bulletin* 87 (1980), pp. 564–567. We will have more to say on the relationship between scales of measurements and statistical techniques in Chapter 14.

Rating Scales

The previous discussion dealt with some of the main scaling methods that have been used to measure attitudes. The treatment was by no means exhaustive. Particularly conspicuous by its absence was a discussion of the importance of the various attributes to the individual. That is, in each scaling method discussed, we attempted to determine the individual's perceptions of Bank A. This may not be enough. Even though the individual believes that the bank has convenient hours, the person may not value this attribute, and, therefore, it may not affect her attitude toward the bank. On the other hand, suppose the individual values location convenience; if she perceives the bank as being inconveniently located, this will have a negative, and perhaps a strong negative, effect on her feeling toward the bank. To capture the differing emphases people place on specific attributes, researchers often try to measure their importance. Research Realities 9.2, for example, depicts the importance of various attributes to people who are shopping for microwave ovens, console color televisions, and portable video cameras or camcorders.

Admittedly, a good deal of controversy exists about how the importance of various attributes should be incorporated in determining a person's attitude toward an object. The controversy involves some very complex arguments as to how one determines which attributes are salient (that is, used in forming an attitude) and how they should be measured. For example, when asked about importance directly, many respondents usually believe that most, if not all, of the characteristics that are listed are more than moderately important. Researchers have attempted to get around this measurement problem in a number of ways, including changing the type of scale (for example, asking respondents how concerned they are about each attribute rather than how important each attribute is to them)[32] and by determining attribute importance indirectly rather than through self reports.[33] We shall not delve into the controversy. Rather, we shall simply use importance values to focus a discussion of general types of rating scales. Some of these scales were employed previously, but now we wish to describe the basic rating scales in one place, using importance values as a vehicle to make the differences between them more vivid. Knowledge of the basic types should facilitate the development of special scales for particular purposes.

One feature is common to all rating scales: "The rater places the person or object being rated at some point along a continuum or in one of an ordered series of

---

[32]For empirical comparisons involving various forms of self-report scales of attribute importance, see "Measuring the Importance of Attributes," *Research on Research*, no. 28 (Chicago: Market Facts, Inc., undated); "The Use of Concern Scales as an Alternative to Importance Ratings," *Research on Research*, no. 44 (Chicago: Market Facts, Inc., undated); "An Analysis of Importance Ratings," *Research on Research*, no. 60 (Chicago: Market Facts, Inc., undated).

[33]Three indirect ways are through conjoint analysis, information display boards, or statistical derivation of them for groups of respondents. For examples of these approaches, see Roger M. Heeler, Chike Okechuku, and Stan Reid, "Attribute Importance: Contrasting Measurements," *Journal of Marketing Research* 16 (February 1979), pp. 60–63; Scott A. Neslin, "Linking Product Features to Perceptions: Self-Stated versus Statistically Revealed Importance Weights," *Journal of Marketing Research* 18 (February 1981), pp. 80–86; Steven A. Sinclair and Edward C. Stalling, "How to Identify Differences between Market Segments with Attribute Analysis," *Industrial Marketing Management* 19 (February 1990), pp. 31–40; Gordon A. Wyner and Hillary Owen, "What Is Important?" *Marketing Research: A Magazine of Management & Applications* 5 (Summer 1993), pp. 48–50.

RESEARCH REALITIES 9.2

Most Important Considerations When Shopping for Selected Appliances

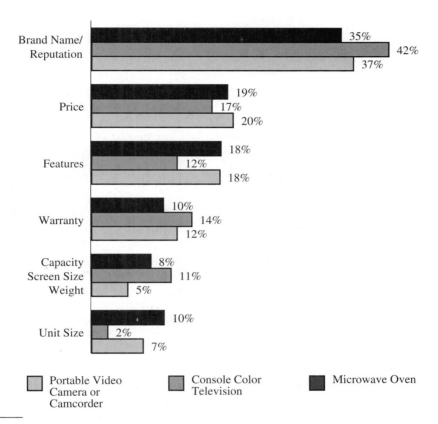

Portable Video Camera or Camcorder   Console Color Television   Microwave Oven

Source: Margaret Steele, "Major Appliances—The Top Shopping Consideration," *TeleNation Reports* (Fall 1987), p. 1. Published by Market Facts, Inc. Reprinted with permission.

categories; a numerical value is attached to the point or the category."[34] The scales differ, though, in the fineness of the distinctions they allow and in the procedures involved in assigning objects to positions. Three of the most common rating scales are the graphic, the itemized, and the comparative.[35]

Graphic

When using **graphic rating scales,** individuals indicate their rating by placing a check at the appropriate point on a line that runs from one extreme of the attribute to the

---

[34]Claire Selltiz, Lawrence S. Wrightsman, and Stuart W. Cook, *Research Methods in Social Relations,* 3rd ed. (New York: Holt, Rinehart and Winston, 1976), pp. 403–404.

[35]Ibid., pp. 404–406.

FIGURE 9.7	Graphic Rating Scale

Please evaluate each attribute in terms of how important the attribute is to you personally by placing an "X" at the position on the horizontal line that most reflects your feelings.

Attribute	Not Important	Very Important
Courteous service	_____	
Convenient location	_____	
Convenient hours	_____	
Low interest rate loans	_____	

other. Many variations are possible. The line may be vertical or horizontal. It may be unmarked or marked; if marked, the divisions may be few or many, as in the case of a thermometer scale, so called because it looks like a thermometer. Figure 9.7 is an example of a horizontal, end-anchored-only, graphic rating scale. Each individual would be instructed to indicate the importance of the attribute by checking the appropriate position on the scale. The importance value would then be inferred by measuring the length of the line from the left origin to the marked position.

One of the great advantages of graphic rating scales is the ease with which they can be constructed and used. They provide an opportunity to make fine distinctions and are limited in this regard only by the discrimination abilities of the rater, although some evidence suggests they are not reliable as itemized rating scales.[36]

For their most effective use, the researcher is well advised to avoid end statements that are so extreme that they are unlikely to be used and to place descriptive statements as close as possible to their numerical points on the scale.[37]

Itemized

The **itemized rating scale** is similar to the graphic in that individuals make their judgments independently—that is, without the benefit of direct comparison. The itemized rating scale is distinguished by the fact that the rater must select from a limited number of categories. In general, five to nine categories work well, because they permit fine distinctions and yet seem to be readily understood by respondents, although 10 or more can be used.[38] There are a number of possible variations with itemized scales. Figure 9.8, for example, depicts three different forms of itemized rating scales that have been used to measure customer satisfaction. Note that the categories are ordered in terms of their scale positions. Note further that in some cases the categories have verbal descriptions attached, and in other cases they do

---

[36]A. O. Gregg, "Some Problems Concerning the Use of Rating Scales for Visual Assessment," *Journal of the Market Research Society* 8 (January 1980), pp. 29–43; Linda Weiser Friedman, "Comparison of Itemized vs. Graphic Rating Scales: A Validity Approach," *Journal of the Market Research Society* 28 (July 1986), pp. 285–289.

[37]Selltiz, Wrightsman, and Cook, *Research Methods*, p. 204.

[38]Eli P. Cox III, "The Optimal Number of Response Alternatives for a Scale: A Review," *Journal of Marketing Research* 17 (November 1980), pp. 407–422. For discussion of the use of number of scale points specifically with respect to customer satisfaction measurement, see the special section "Scales: A Weighty Debate," *Marketing Research: A Magazine of Management & Applications* 6 (Fall 1994), pp. 6–33.

FIGURE 9.8 Three Different Forms of Itemized Rating Scales Used to Measure Satisfaction

Measure	Description
Delighted–Terrible Scale	*How do you feel about _____ ?*
	I feel:

7	6	5	4	3	2	1

| Delighted | Pleased | Mostly Satisfied | Mixed (About Equally Satisfied and Dissatisfied) | Mostly Dissatisfied | Unhappy | Terrible |

A = Neutral (neither satisfied nor dissatisfied)
B = I never thought about it

Percentage Scale

Overall, how satisfied have you been with this _____ ?

100%	90	80	70	60	50	40	30	20	10	0%
Completely Satisfied										Not at All Satisfied

Need Satisfaction–Dissatisfaction

To what extent does this _____ meet your needs at this time?

Extremely Well: ___: ___: ___: ___: ___: ___: ___ : Extremely Poorly
(7)   (1)

Source: Adapted from Robert A. Westbrook, "A Rating Scale for Measuring Product/Service Satisfaction," *Journal of Marketing* 44 (Fall 1980), p. 69. Published by the American Marketing Association.

FIGURE 9.9   **Itemized Rating Scale**

Please evaluate each attribute in terms of how important the attribute is to you personally by placing an "X" in the appropriate box.

Attribute	Not Important	Somewhat Important	Fairly Important	Very Important
Courteous service	☐	☐	☐	☐
Convenient location	☐	☐	☐	☐
Convenient hours	☐	☐	☐	☐
Low interest rate loans	☐	☐	☐	☐

---

not. Category descriptions are not absolutely necessary in itemized rating scales, although their presence and nature do seem to affect the responses.[39] When they are used, it is important to ensure that the descriptors mean similar things to those responding.[40] When they are not used, it is tempting to conclude that a graphic rating scale is being used. That is an erroneous conclusion, however. The distinguishing feature of an itemized scale is that the possible response categories are limited in number. Thus, a set of faces varying systematically in terms of whether they are frowning or smiling used to capture a person's satisfaction or preference (appropriately called a faces scale) would be considered an itemized scale, even when no descriptions are attached to the face categories.

A Likert statement serves as an example of a five-point itemized rating scale, whereas a semantic differential adjective pair is an example of a seven-point scale. Figure 9.9 is an itemized rating scale used to ascertain importance values; this four-point scale has the descriptor labels attached to the categories.

The itemized rating scale is also easy to construct and use, and although it does not permit the fine distinctions possible with the graphic rating scale, the clear definition of categories generally produces more reliable ratings.

Comparative

Unlike graphic and itemized scales, **comparative rating scales** involve relative judgments because raters make their judgments of each attribute with direct reference to the other attributes being evaluated.

---

[39] Albert R. Wildt and Michael B. Mazis, "Determinants of Scale Response: Label versus Position," *Journal of Marketing Research* 15 (May 1978), pp. 261–267; H. H. Friedman and J. R. Liefer, "Label versus Position in Rating Scales," *Journal of the Academy of Marketing Science* (Spring 1981), pp. 88–92; Norbert Schwarz, et al., "Rating Scales: Numeric Values May Change the Meanings of Scale Labels," *Public Opinion Quarterly* 55 (Winter 1991), pp. 570–582; Colm O'Muircheartaigh, George D. Gaskell, and Daniel B. Wright, "Weighing Anchors: Verbal and Numeric Labels for Response Scales," *Journal of Official Statistics* 11 (1995), pp. 295–307.

[40] For lists of category descriptors and their numerical values, see James H. Myers and W. Gregory Warner, "Selected Properties of Selected Evaluation Adjectives," *Journal of Marketing Research* 5 (November 1968), pp. 409–412; Spector, "Choosing Response Categories for Summated Rating Scales"; Robert A. Mittelstaedt, "Semantic Properties of Selected Adjectives: Other Evidence," *Journal of Marketing Research* 8 (May 1971), pp. 236–237; Melvin R. Crask and Richard J. Fox, "An Exploration of the Interval Properties of Three Commonly Used Marketing Research Scales: A Magnitude Estimation Approach," *Journal of the Market Research Society* 29 (July 1987), pp. 317–339.

FIGURE 9.10	Comparative Rating Scale

Please divide 100 points between the two following attributes in terms of each attribute's relative importance to you.

Courteous service   _____

Convenient location   _____

An example of a comparative rating scale used for securing importance values is the constant sum scaling method. In the **constant sum method,** the individual is instructed to divide some given sum among two or more attributes on the basis of their importance to him or her. Thus, in Figure 9.10, if the subject assigned 50 points to courteous service and 50 points to convenient location, the attributes would be judged to be equally important; if the individual assigned 80 to courteous service and 20 to convenient location, courteous service would be considered to be four times as important.[41] Note the difference in emphasis with this method. All judgments are now made in comparison to some other alternative, and all possible pairs of the m stimuli would be presented to the individual for rating.

Comparison of two attributes is not mandatory in the constant sum method, although it is the most common. The individual could also be asked to divide 100 points among three or more attributes; again all possible combinations would be presented to the individual for judgment.

Although comparative scales require more judgments from the individual than either graphic or itemized scales, they do tend to eliminate **halo effects** that so often manifest themselves in scaling. Halo effects occur when there is carryover from one judgment to another.[42]

The great temptation in securing importance values by either the graphic or itemized scaling methods is for the individual to indicate that all, or nearly all, of the attributes are important. Yet empirical research indicates that when individuals are confronted by decisions that are complex because many alternatives or attributes are involved, they tend to simplify the decision by reducing the number of alternatives or attributes they actually consider. This is consistent with the notion that only certain attributes are salient when forming attitudes. The comparative scaling methods do allow more insight into the relative ranking, if not the absolute importance, of the attributes to each individual.

---

[41]By considering all possible pairs of attributes in combination, one is able to construct scale values to reflect the importance ratings of each attribute to each individual. See Joy P. Guilford, *Psychometric Methods,* 2nd ed. (New York: McGraw-Hill, 1954), pp. 214–220, or Warren S. Torgerson, *Theory and Methods of Scaling* (New York: John Wiley, 1958), pp. 104–116, for a discussion of the procedure. Another comparative rating scale method is that of magnitude estimation, in which respondents are asked to judge directly the "magnitude" of each stimulus versus a reference stimulus. For a general treatment of magnitude scaling, see Milton Lodge, *Magnitude Scaling: Quantitative Measurement of Opinions* (Thousand Oaks, CA: Sage Publications, 1981). For specific examples of its use, see Crask and Fox, "An Exploration of the Interval Properties"; Bruno Neibecker, "The Validity of Computer-Controlled Magnitude Scaling to Measure Emotional Impact of Stimuli," *Journal of Marketing Research* 21 (August 1984), pp. 325–331; Noel Mark Noel and Nessim Hanna, "Benchmarking Consumer Perceptions of Product Quality with Price: An Exploration," *Psychology & Marketing* 13 (September 1996), pp. 591–604.

[42]See Lance Leuthesser, Chiranjeev S. Kohli, and Katrin P. Harich, "Brand Equity: The Halo Effect Measure," *European Journal of Marketing* 29, no. 4 (1995), pp. 57–66, for discussion of the halo effect when measuring brand equity.

TABLE 9.4	Impact of Selected Measure Characteristics on Reliability Estimates

Measure Characteristic	*Conclusion*
Number of items in final scale	The hypothesis that a positive relationship exists between the number of items used in the scales and the reliability of the measure is supported.
Difficulty of items	The hypothesis that a negative relationship exists between the difficulty of the items and the reliability of the measure is not supported.
Reverse scoring	The hypothesis that scales with reverse-scored items will have lower reliability than scales without them is not supported.
Type of scale	No *a priori* prediction was made that one of the scale types is superior, and no relationship was found between scale types and the reliability of the measure.
Number of scale points	The hypothesis that a positive relationship exists between the number of scale points over the normal range and the reliability of the measure is supported.
Type of labels	No *a priori* prediction was made that numerical and verbal labels are superior to verbal labels only, or vice versa, and no relationship was found between type of labels and the reliability of the measure.
Extent of scale points description	The hypothesis that scales for which all points are labeled have higher reliability than scales for which only polar points are labeled is not supported.
Respondent uncertainty or ignorance	The hypothesis that scales with neutral points have higher reliability than forced-choice scales is not supported.

Source: Adapted from Gilbert A. Churchill, Jr., and J. Paul Peter, "Research Design Effects on the Reliability of Rating Scales: A Meta-Analysis," *Journal of Marketing Research* 21 (November 1984), pp. 365–366. Published by the American Marketing Association.

Which Scale to Use

For some readers, the discussion in this chapter might beg the question of which scale they should use when faced with a problem of measuring attitudes. When making the choice among scale types, number of scale points to use, whether or not to reverse some of the items, and so on, readers might find comfort in the findings of a very extensive study of the marketing measurement literature that examined these questions and more with respect to their effect on the reliability of measures. Reviewing the marketing literature over a 20-year period, the study examined measures for which at least two indicants of their quality were reported, and then quantitatively assessed the effect of a measure's features on its reliability.[43] **Reliability** assesses the issue of the similarity of results provided by independent but comparable measures of the same object, trait, or construct; it is an important indicator of a measure's quality because it determines the impact of inconsistencies in measurement on the results. Reliability is a necessary, but not a sufficient, condition for ensuring the validity of a measure.[44]

Table 9.4 reports the study's findings with respect to some of the major questions surrounding the construction of attitude scales. The general conclusion emerging from the table is that many of the choices do not seem to materially affect the quality of the measure that results. The exceptions are the number of items and the number of scale points. For both of these characteristics, the reliability of the measure increases as they increase. For the other characteristics, though, no choices are superior in all instances. Many of the choices are and will probably remain in the domain

---

[43]Gilbert A. Churchill, Jr., and J. Paul Peter, "Research Design Effects on the Reliability of Rating Scales: A Meta-Analysis," *Journal of Marketing Research* 21 (November 1984), pp. 360–375.

[44]The issue of reliability and its relationship to the validity of a measure are discussed in Appendix 9A.

of researcher judgment, including the choice among semantic differential, Likert, or other rating scales. All the scales have proved to be useful at one time or another. All rightly belong in the researcher's measurement tool kit.

The nature of the problem and the planned mode of administration will affect the final choice. So will the characteristics of the respondents, their commitment to the task, and their experience and ability to respond.[45] In some cultures, graphic rating scales may be unknown, and respondents with low levels of education may not even be able to conceptualize a continuous scale from extreme dissatisfaction to extreme satisfaction, say, that is divided into equal increments of satisfaction. In other cultures, such as Eastern Europe, the use of these scales may be a very new experience for most research participants, and interviewers may need to spend considerable time explaining the scale. In still other situations, it might be necessary to develop new scales. For example, the "sad-to-happy faces" scale that works in the United States does not work in Africa; rather, their culture requires some different-looking faces to depict the various stages of happiness. See Figure 9.11.

ETHICAL DILEMMA 9.2

The Samuelson Research Firm was contacted by Larkin Electronics, a manufacturer of small electronic radio parts, to conduct a survey of Larkin's employees. The purpose of the research was to determine the state of worker morale and the importance of certain employee grievances so that Larkin's management could gauge the strength of its position in collective bargaining with the employee union. Samuelson Research agreed to conduct the study.

- What are the consequences for the employees if they participate in such a survey?

- Is this research detrimental to the employee's immediate self-interest?

- Do researchers have the right to ask questions concerning this issue?

- Does this research undercut the position of labor's representatives, inasmuch as they have no corresponding way of gauging the intensity of management's opinions?

- If you were director of the research, what kind of questions might you ask of Larkin's management?

- Would you have agreed to conduct such a survey?

- In general, should a researcher be concerned with the uses of the research that he or she conducts or its effects on the research participants?

---

[45]John R. Hauser and Steven M. Shugan, "Intensity Measures of Consumer Preference," *Operations Research* 28 (March–April 1980), pp. 278–320; Duane F. Alwin and Jon A. Krosnick, "The Reliability of Survey Attitude Measurement: The Influence of Question and Respondent Attributes," *Sociological Methodology and Research* 20 (August 1991), pp. 139–181; James G. Helgeson and Michael L. Ursic, "The Role of Affective and Cognitive Decision-Making Processes during Questionnaire Completion," *Psychology & Marketing* 11 (September/October 1994), pp. 493–510; Rajendar K. Garg, "The Influence of Positive and Negative Wording and Issue Involvement on Responses to Likert Scales in Marketing Research," *Journal of the Market Research Society* 38 (July 1996), pp. 235–246.

| FIGURE 9.11 | Examples of "Sad-to-Happy Faces" Scales That Work in the United States versus Those That Work in Africa |

Source: The African faces can be found in C. K. Corder, "Problems and Pitfalls in Conducting Marketing Research in Africa," in Betsy Gelb, ed., *Marketing Expansion in a Shrinking World,* Proceedings of American Marketing Association Business Conference (Chicago: American Marketing Association, 1978), pp. 86–90. Reprinted with permission of American Marketing Association.

Summary

This chapter reviewed the methods suggested for measuring attitudes, which were defined as representations of the person's ideas of, or liking for, a specific object or idea. Typically, marketers are concerned with such objects as companies, brands, advertisements, packages, and the like.

Measurement was defined as the assignment of numbers to objects to represent quantities of attributes. Measurement can occur on either a nominal, ordinal, interval, or ratio scale. The properties of these scales were distinguished, and it was pointed out that a controversy exists over whether the measurement of attitudes has been accomplished with ordinal or interval scales. The scales certainly are not ratio, since the origin is not natural, and they are definitely something more than nominal, because they possess more than the identity property. The debate focuses on whether the differences in scores convey meaning other than relative ranking of individuals. The prevailing posture in marketing seems to agree with that of the psychologists—that many of the scales are interval.

Historically, attitudes have been measured by observing behavior, by indirect questioning, by the performance of objective tasks, and by physiological reactions, although direct assessment by means of self-report devices has been the most common. The main self-report techniques were reviewed, including the methods of equal-appearing intervals, summated ratings, semantic differential, Stapel scale, and Q-sort.

As typically constructed, these scales attempt to measure what individuals believe and like about specific objects. Many would argue that simply measuring beliefs about the attributes possessed by the object is not sufficient if we want to assess a person's attitude toward the object. Rather, we must somehow ascertain the importance of the various attributes to the individual. The methods for securing importance values—the graphic, itemized, or comparative rating scales—were thus reviewed. The itemized scale is most commonly used, but there is a good deal of controversy about which rating scale can more accurately measure an individual's importance values.

The empirical evidence indicates that none of the attitude scaling devices is superior in all instances. Each one has its place. Nor is there one single optimal number of scale positions or single optimal condition for other measure characteristics. The nature of the problem, the characteristics of the respondents, and the planned mode of administration will and should affect the choice of which technique should be used in a particular instance and what features the scale should possess.

Questions

1. What is an attitude?
2. What is measurement? What are the scales of measurement, and what information is provided by each?
3. What is a Thurstone equal-appearing interval scale?
4. In an equal-appearing interval scale, what is the scale value for a statement?
5. How does one construct a Likert summated rating scale?
6. How are subjects scaled with a Likert scale? What must be done to give meaning to the scales?
7. What is a semantic differential scale? How is a person's overall attitude assessed with a semantic differential scale?
8. How does a Stapel scale differ from a semantic differential scale? Which is more commonly used?
9. What is the task assigned subjects and what is the thrust or emphasis of Q-sort methodology?
10. What is a graphic rating scale? An itemized scale? A constant sum scale?

Applications and Problems

1. Identify the type of scale (nominal, ordinal, interval, or ratio) being used in each of the following questions. Justify your answer.

   a. *During which season of the year were you born?*

   _____ Winter _____ Spring _____ Summer _____ Fall

   b. *What is your total household income?*_____

   c. *Which are your three most preferred brands of cigarettes? Rank them from 1 to 3 according to your preference, with 1 as most preferred.*

_____ Marlboro	_____ Salem
_____ Kent	_____ Kool
_____ Benson and Hedges	_____ Vantage

   d. *How much time do you spend traveling to school every day?*

_____ Under 5 minutes	_____ 16–20 minutes
_____ 5–10 minutes	_____ 30 minutes and over
_____ 11–15 minutes	

   e. *How satisfied are you with* Newsweek *magazine?*

_____ very satisfied	_____ dissatisfied
_____ satisfied	_____ very dissatisfied
_____ neither satisfied nor dissatisfied	

   f. *On an average, how many cigarettes do you smoke in a day?*

_____ over 1 pack	_____ less than 1/2 pack
_____ 1/2 to 1 pack	

   g. *Which one of the following courses have you taken?*

_____ marketing research	_____ sales management
_____ advertising management	_____ consumer behavior

   h. *What is the level of education for the head of the household?*

_____ some high school	_____ some college
_____ high school graduate	_____ college graduate and/or graduate work

2. The analysis for each of the preceding questions is given below. Is the analysis appropriate for the scale used?

   a. About 50 percent of the sample were born in the fall, 25 percent of the sample were born in the spring, and the remaining 25 percent were born in the winter. It can be concluded that the fall is twice as popular as the spring and the summer seasons.

   b. The average income is $25,000. There are twice as many individuals with an income of less than $9,999 than individuals with an income of $40,000 and over.

   c. Marlboro is the most preferred brand. The mean preference is 3.52.

   d. The median time spent traveling to school is 8.5 minutes. Three times as many respondents travel fewer than 5 minutes than respondents traveling 16–20 minutes.

   e. The average satisfaction score is 4.5, which seems to indicate a high level of satisfaction with *Newsweek* magazine.

   f. Ten percent of the respondents smoke less than 1/2 pack of cigarettes a day, whereas three times as many respondents smoke over one pack of cigarettes a day.

   g. Sales management is the most frequently taken course because the median is 3.2.

   h. The responses indicate that 40 percent of the sample have some high school education, 25 percent of the sample are high school graduates, 20 percent have some college education, and 10 percent are college graduates. The mean education level is 2.6.

3. a. Assume that a manufacturer of a line of packaged meat products wanted to evaluate customer attitudes towards the brand. A panel of 500 regular consumers of the brand responded to a questionnaire that was sent to them and that included several attitude scales. The questionnaire produced the following results:

   (i) The average score for the sample on a 20-item Likert scale was 105.

   (ii) The average score for the sample on a 20-item semantic differential scale was 106.

(iii) The average score for the sample on a 15-item Stapel scale was 52.

The vice president has asked you to indicate whether these customers have a favorable or unfavorable attitude towards the brand. What would you tell him? Please be specific.

b. Following your initial report, the vice president has provided you with more information. The following memo is given to you: "The company has been using the same attitude measures over the past eight years. The results of the previous studies are as follows:

	Likert	Semantic Differential	Stapel
1994	86	95	43
1995	93	95	48
1996	97	98	51
1997	104	101	55
1998	110	122	62
1999	106	112	57
2000	104	106	53
2001	105	106	52

We realize that there may not be any connection between attitude and behavior, but it must be pointed out that sales peaked in 1998 and since then have been gradually declining." With this information, do your results change? Can anything more be said about customer attitudes?

4. A leading manufacturer of electric guitars routinely attempts to measure consumer attitudes toward its products, generally by asking a consumer to examine a product and then to complete a brief questionnaire about several of the product's attributes. Over the years, the research manager for the company has decided that scale items related to five attributes have high correlations with total scale scores. The attributes are tone quality, appearance, durability, price, and ease of playing. The following scale is thus used to assess attitudes toward a product:

	Strongly Disagree	Disagree	Neither Agree nor Disagree	Agree	Strongly Agree
1. Tone quality is good.	___	___	___	___	_X_
2. The guitar is attractive.	___	___	___	_X_	___
3. The design is durable.	___	___	___	_X_	___
4. The price is appropriate.	___	_X_	___	___	___
5. The guitar is easy to play.	___	___	___	___	_X_
	(1)	(2)	(3)	(4)	(5)

a. Suppose that a consumer has examined a guitar and provided the responses shown in the preceding table. Determine the total score. Would you say that the consumer has a favorable attitude toward the guitar?

b. The particular model of guitar that the respondent examined has been available for five years. The average total scores using this scale for each of these years are as follows:

First year	18
Second year	17
Third year	18
Fourth year	16
Fifth year	17

Would you conclude that the consumer has a favorable attitude toward the guitar?

c. Assume that the respondent had also completed a comparative rating scale by dividing 100 points between the five attributes according to their importance to her. How could this information be useful in assessing the respondent's attitude toward the electric guitar?

d. Following are the results of the comparative rating task completed by the respondent:

Tone quality	10
Appearance	25
Durability	10
Price	40
Ease of playing	15

What can you now conclude about the respondent's attitude toward the guitar?

APPENDIX   9A

Psychological Measurement

A problem that marketers have in common with scientists is how to go about measuring the variables in which they have an interest. For example, marketers are well aware of the fact that consumers' spending can be affected by their general feelings as to "how good things are." But how do you measure this general affective state? *American Demographics* considered productivity and technology, leisure, consumer attitudes, social and physical environment, income, and employment opportunities in developing its "Well-Being Index," which it uses in comparing areas and preparing forecasts.[1] The measurement problem is particularly acute when the variables represent psychological notions (for example, attitudes).

The essence of the measurement problem is captured in Figure 9A.1.[2] The basic researcher or scientist uses theories in an attempt to explain phenomena. These theories or models consist of constructs (denoted by the circles with Cs in them), linkages among and between the constructs or concepts invented by scientists (single lines connecting the Cs), and data that connect the constructs with the empirical world (double lines). The single lines in Figure 9A.1 represent **constitutive** or **conceptual definitions,** in that a given construct is defined in terms of other constructs in the set. The definition may take the form of an equation that precisely expresses the interrelationship of the construct to the other constructs, such as the equation in mechanics that suggests that force equals mass times acceleration. Alternatively, the relationship may be only imprecisely stated, which is typically the case in the social sciences.

The double lines in Figure 9A.1 represent operational definitions. An **operational definition** describes how the construct is to be measured. It specifies the activities that the researcher must complete in order to assign a value to the construct

[1]Elia Kacapyr, "Money Isn't Everything," *American Demographics* 18 (July 1996), pp. 10–11; Elia Kacapyr, "The Well-Being Index," *American Demographics* 18 (February 1996), pp. 32–35, 43.

[2]Figure 9A.1 and the discussion surrounding it are adapted from the classic book by Warren S. Torgerson, *Theory and Methods of Scaling* (New York: John Wiley, 1958), pp. 1–11.

| **FIGURE 9A.1** | **Schematic Diagram Illustrating the Structure of Science and the Problem of Measurement** |

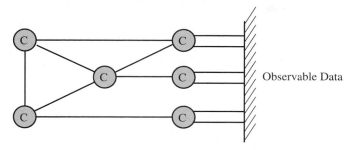

(for example, sum the scores on the 10 Likert-type statements to generate a total score). In essence, the operational definition tells the investigator what to do and how to measure the concept. Table 9A.1, for example, shows how consumer sentiment toward marketing was assessed in one large study using Market Facts' mail panel. The measurement assessed respondents' reactions to product quality, product prices, advertising, and retailing and personal selling support. Conceptual definitions logically precede operational definitions and guide their development, for we must specify what a construct is before we can develop rules for assessing its magnitude.

The role of scientific inquiry is to establish the relationships that exist among the constructs of the model. Some of the constructs must be related to observable data if scientists are to accomplish their task. Otherwise, the model will be circular, with given unobservable constructs being defined in terms of other unobservable constructs. Because a circular model cannot be supported or refuted by empirical data, it is not legitimately considered a theory. Rather, a theory or system of explanation rests on the condition that at least some of the constructs can be operationalized sufficiently to allow their measurement. Recall that measurement is defined as "rules for assigning numbers to objects to represent quantities of attributes." The rigor with which these rules are defined and the skill with which they are implemented determine whether the construct has been captured by the measure.

You would undoubtedly scoff at the following measurement procedure. John has blue eyes and Bill has brown eyes and, therefore, John is taller than Bill. You might reply that "the color of a person's eyes has nothing to do with the person's height and, therefore, you have not in fact measured their height, if that is indeed your purpose. Further, if you wanted to see who was taller, the best procedure would be to measure them with a yardstick or to stand them side by side and compare their heights." You would be right on both counts. If I measured both John and Bill by asking them how tall they were, you would have probably voiced less objection to my procedure, unless I concluded that John was taller if Bill was definitely the bigger man on observation of the two together. Now the interesting thing about most psychological constructs is that we cannot rely on visual comparisons to either confirm or refute a measure. We cannot see an attitude, a personality characteristic, a person's knowledge about or awareness of a particular product, or other psychological characteristics, such as intelligence, mental anxiety, or whatever. These characteristics are all part of the consumer's "black box." Their magnitude must be inferred

TABLE 9A.1	**Illustration of Operational Definitions**

Concept	Measurement[a]
	Sum of responses to following items, each measured on five-point disagree-agree scale:
Product Quality	The quality of most products I buy today is as good as can be expected. I am satisfied with most of the products I buy. Most products I buy wear out too quickly. (R) Products are not made as well as they used to be. (R) Too many of the products I buy are defective in some way. (R) The companies that make products I buy don't care enough about how well they perform. (R) The quality of products I buy has consistently improved over the years.
Price of Products	Most products I buy are overpriced. (R) Business could charge lower prices and still be profitable. (R) Most prices are reasonable considering the high cost of doing business. Competition between companies keeps prices reasonable. Companies are unjustified in charging the prices they charge. (R) Most prices are fair. In general, I am satisfied with the prices I pay.
Advertising for Products	Most advertising provides consumers with essential information. Most advertising is annoying. (R) Most advertising makes false claims. (R) If most advertising were eliminated, consumers would be better off. (R) I enjoy most ads. Advertising should be more closely regulated. Most advertising is intended to deceive rather than to inform consumers. (R)
Retailing or Selling	Most retail stores serve their customers well. Because of the way retailers treat me, most of my shopping is unpleasant. (R) I find most retail salespeople to be very helpful. Most retail stores provide an adequate selection of merchandise. In general, most middlemen make excessive profits. (R) When I need assistance in a store, I am usually *not* able to get it. (R) Most retailers provide adequate service.

[a]An (R) indicates scoring of the item needs to be reversed so that higher scores indicate more positive attitudes.
Source: Developed from the information in John F. Gaski and Michael J. Etzel, "The Index of Consumer Sentiment Toward Marketing," *Journal of Marketing* 50 (July 1986), pp. 71–81.

from our measurements. Since we cannot resort to a visual check on the accuracy of our measures, we must rely on assessing the procedures employed to derive the measure. Eye color is certainly not height, but have we captured the sales representatives' satisfaction with their job if we directly ask them how satisfied they are? Probably not, for reasons that will become obvious later.

Note that the problem of establishing operational definitions for constructs (measuring the constructs) is not unique to the researcher interested in scientific explanation. The practitioner shares this concern. A manufacturer, for example, interested in assessing customer reactions to a new product, needs to know that the company is in fact measuring consumer attitudes toward the new product and that the accuracy of the data is not being influenced by the interviewers asking the questions or by one of the many other factors with which the research must contend. The ability to make these assessments relies heavily on an understanding of measurement, measurement error, and the concepts of reliability and validity. Understanding these ideas is the task to which we now turn.

Variations in Measured Scores

Recall that the definition of measurement states that it is the attributes of objects we measure and not the objects themselves. Now, measurement, particularly psychological measurement, always takes place in a rather complex situation in which a great many factors affect the attribute or characteristic being measured, including the process of measurement itself. For example, whenever energy prices suddenly soar, often a public outcry arises, accompanied by accusations that the oil companies are deliberately creating strategies to manipulate prices. Consider that we are interested in measuring people's attitudes toward the oil companies after a recent spike in prices. Suppose further that one of the procedures described in the chapter was used to develop an attitude scale to measure these feelings and that the scale was administered to a sample of respondents. A high score means that the respondent believed the oil companies had little to do with precipitating the crisis, whereas a low score indicates just the opposite and, therefore, reflects a poor attitude toward the petroleum producers. Suppose that Mary had a score of 75 and Jane had a score of 40 on the instrument and that the minimum and maximum scores possible were 25 and 100. Conclusion: Mary has a much more favorable attitude toward the oil companies than does Jane. Ideally, yes; practically, maybe. It depends on the quality of the measurement. Consider some of the potential sources of differences in these two scores of 75 and 40.[3]

1. *True differences in the characteristic that one is attempting to measure.* In the ideal situation, the difference in scores would reflect true differences in the attitudes of Mary and Jane and nothing else. This situation will rarely, if ever, occur. Rather, the difference will also reflect the factors that follow.

2. *True differences in other relatively stable characteristics of the individual that affect the score.* Not only does a person's position on an issue affect the score, but other characteristics can also be expected to have an effect. For example, Research Realities 9A.1 illustrates the impact culture has on people's response styles. Perhaps the difference between Mary's and Jane's scores is simply due to the greater willingness of Jane to express her negative feelings. Mary, by contrast, follows the adage, "If you can't say something nice, don't say anything at all." Her cooperation in the study has been requested and so she responds, but not truthfully.

---

[3]These differences are adapted from Claire Selltiz, Lawrence L. Wrightsman, and Stuart W. Cook, *Research Methods in Social Relations*, 3rd ed. (New York: Holt, Rinehart and Winston, 1976), pp. 164–168. See also Duane F. Alwin and David J. Jackson, "Measurement Models for Response Errors in Surveys: Issues and Applications," in Karl F. Schuessler, ed., *Sociological Methodology 1980* (San Francisco: Jossey-Bass, 1979), pp. 69–119; Frank E. Saal, Ronald G. Downey, and Mary Anne Lakey, "Rating the Ratings: Assessing the Psychometric Quality of Ratings Data," *Psychological Bulletin* 88 (September 1980), pp. 413–428; Ellen J. Wentland and Kent W. Smith, *Survey Responses: An Evaluation of Their Validity* (San Diego, CA: Academic Press, 1993).

RESEARCH REALITIES 9A.1

Impact of Culture on Response Styles

One of the most important and dramatic ways culture impacts multicountry research is in the different ways people in various countries respond to survey questions and use questionnaire scales. In a carefully controlled experiment, Custom Research, Inc. (CRI) explored the use of different kinds of scales in new product research. The result: *We found extraordinary differences from country to country in the way respondents use common survey scales.* For example: Survey respondents in the Philippines and Italy are four times more likely than respondents in Hong Kong or Japan to use the "top box" of a buying intent scale.

And these differences are clearly the result of culture, not economic levels. Japan and the United States, two of the most affluent countries in the world, are dramatically different on these measures. These differences must be understood and taken into account in analyzing multicountry studies. In the CRI experiment across 18 countries, here are a few of the differences we found on use of the buying intent scale:

Examples of Buying Intent Indices

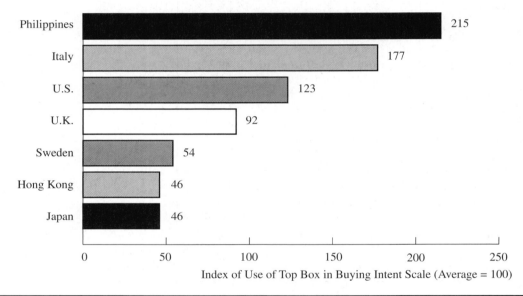

Index of Use of Top Box in Buying Intent Scale (Average = 100)

3. *Differences caused by transient personal factors.* A person's mood, state of health, fatigue, and so on, may all affect the individual's responses. Yet these factors are temporary and can vary. Thus, if Jane had just returned from an IRS audit of her tax return, her responses may be decidedly different than if she were interviewed after receiving a sizable tax refund.

4. *Differences caused by situational factors.* The situation surrounding the measurement also can affect the score. Mary's score might be different if her husband were there while the scale was being administered. Incidentally, this problem is the bane of researchers studying the decision-making process of married couples. When the husband is asked for the respective roles of husband and wife in purchasing a new automobile, for instance, one set of responses is secured;

RESEARCH REALITIES 9A.1

(continued)

But the effect of cultural differences on scale use is even more complex: Differences even exist within the same country from one scale to another.

That is illustrated by comparing the example below, showing use of the uniqueness scale, with the previous example on buying intent. Italians are less bullish in their use of the uniqueness scale, while respondents in the United Kingdom are more aggressive in using the uniqueness scale than in stating buying intent.

This means there is no single, simple way to adjust for country-to-country differences. It requires experience across countries and a thorough understanding of how each scale is used differently country by country.

Source: Jeffrey Pope, *How Cultural Differences Affect Multi-Country Research* (Minneapolis, MN: Custom Research, Inc., 1991).

Examples of Uniqueness Indices

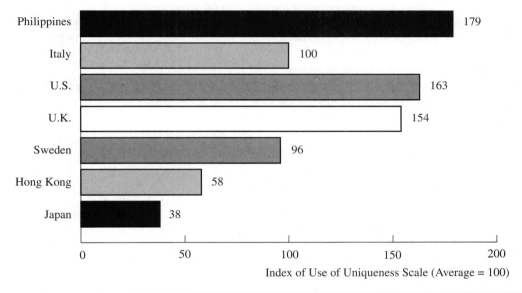

Index of Use of Uniqueness Scale (Average = 100)

when the wife is asked, the responses are different; when the two are asked together, still a third set is obtained. Which is correct? It is hard to say, but the fact remains that the situation surrounding a measurement can affect the scores that are obtained.

5.   *Differences because of variations in administration.* Much measurement in marketing involves the use of questionnaires administered by phone or in person. Because interviewers can vary in the way they ask questions, the responses also may vary as a function of the interviewer. The same interviewer may even handle two interviews differently enough to trigger a variance in recorded answers, although the respondents do not really differ on the characteristic.

6.   *Differences resulting from sampling of items.* When we measure any construct, we tap only a sample of items relevant to the characteristic being measured. Thus,

our attitude scale for the petroleum companies will contain only a sample of all the items or statements that we could possibly have included. If we added, deleted, or changed the wording of some items, we would undoubtedly change the absolute score achieved by Mary and Jane and could conceivably even change their relative scores so that Jane came out with the more positive attitude. Thus, we must constantly be aware that our measurement represents a narrow conception of the construct and that the resulting score will vary as a function of the items included to capture the construct. A man's height can serve as an indicator of his "size," but so can his weight, the size of his waistline, his chest size, and so on. We certainly could expect to have a better measure of a man's size if we included all these items. So it is with psychological measurements. Other things being equal, a one-item scale is a less adequate sample of the universe of items relevant to a characteristic than is a 25-item scale.

7. *Differences caused by lack of clarity of the measuring instrument.* Sometimes a difference in response to a questionnaire or an item on a scale may represent differences in interpretation of an ambiguous or complex question rather than any fundamental differences in the characteristic one is attempting to measure. One of the researcher's main tasks is to generate items or questions that mean the same thing to all respondents so that the observed differences in scores are not caused by differences in interpretation.

8. *Differences caused by mechanical factors.* Such things as a lack of space to record the responses, inadvertent check marks in the wrong box, and improper interpretation of a hard-to-read answer can all affect the scores that are assigned.

Classification and Assessment of Error

As mentioned, the ideal in measurement is to generate a score that reflects true differences in the characteristic one is attempting to measure and nothing else. What we in fact obtain, though, is something else. A measurement, call it X_O, for what is observed can be written as a function of several components:

$$X_O = X_T + X_S + X_R$$

where
X_T represents the true score of the characteristic being measured,
X_S represents systematic error, and
X_R represents random error.

The total error of a measurement is given, of course, by the sum of X_S and X_R; it is important to note that it has two components. **Systematic error** is also known as constant error, because it affects the measurement in a constant way. An example would be the measurement of a man's height with a poorly calibrated wooden yardstick. Differences in other stable characteristics of the individual, which affect the person's score, are a source of systematic error. **Random error** is not constant error but, rather, is due to transient aspects of the person or measurement situation. A random error manifests itself in the lack of consistency of repeated or equivalent measurements when the measurements are made on the same object or person. An example would be the use of an elastic ruler to measure a man's height. It is unlikely that on two successive measurements the observer would stretch the elastic ruler to the same degree of tautness, and, therefore, the two measures would not agree although the man's height had not changed. Differences resulting from transient personal factors are an example of this type of error in psychological measurement.

The distinction between systematic error and random error is critical because of the way the validity of a measure is assessed. **Validity** is synonymous with accuracy or correctness. The validity of a measuring instrument is defined as "the extent to which differences in scores on it reflect true differences among individuals on the characteristic we seek to measure, rather than constant or random errors."[4] When a measurement is valid, $X_O = X_T$, since there is no error. The problem is to develop measures in which the score we observe and record actually represents the true score of the object on the characteristic we are attempting to measure. This is much harder to do than to say. It is not accomplished by simply making up a set of questions or statements to measure the construct (for example, a person's attitude toward the petroleum companies' precipitation of the energy crisis). Rather, the burden is on the researcher to establish that the measure accurately captures the characteristic of interest. This relationship between measured score and true score is never established unequivocally but is always inferred. The bases for the inference are two: (1) direct assessment employing validity, and (2) indirect assessment via reliability.[5] Let us consider each of these sources of evidence in turn.

Predictive Validity

As mentioned, a measuring instrument is valid to the extent that differences in scores among objects reflect the objects' true differences on the characteristic that the instrument tries to measure. We normally do not know the true score of an object with respect to a given characteristic. If we did know it, there would be no need to measure the object on that characteristic. What we do, therefore, is infer the validity of the measure by looking for evidence of three types of its validity: predictive, content, and construct.

Predictive validity focuses on the usefulness of the measuring instrument as a predictor of some other characteristic or behavior of the individual; it is also sometimes called criterion-related validity. **Predictive validity** is ascertained by how well the measure predicts the criterion, be it another characteristic or a specific behavior. An example would be the Graduate Management Admissions Test. The fact that this test is required by most of the major schools of business attests to its predictive validity; it has proved to be useful in predicting how well a student with a particular score on the exam will do in an accredited MBA program. The test score is used to

[4]Selltiz, Wrightsman, and Cook, *Research Methods,* p. 169.

[5]For detailed discussion of the conceptual relationships that should exist among the various indicants of reliability and validity and an empirical assessment of the evidence, see J. Paul Peter and Gilbert A. Churchill, Jr., "The Relationship among Research Design Choices and Psychometric Properties of Rating Scales: A Meta-Analysis," Journal of Marketing Research 23 (February 1986), pp. 1–10. See also Mark S. Litwin, *How to Measure Survey Reliability and Validity* (Thousand Oaks, CA: Sage Publications, 1995).

predict the criterion of performance. An example of an attitude scale might be the use of scores that sales representatives achieved on an instrument designed to assess their job satisfaction to predict who might quit. The attitude score would again be used to predict a behavior—the likelihood of quitting. Both of these examples illustrate predictive validity in the true sense of the word—that is, use of the score to predict some future occurrence. There is, however, another type of predictive validity—concurrent validity. **Concurrent validity** is concerned with the relationship between the predictor variable and the criterion variable when both are assessed at the same point in time. For example, a pregnancy test administered to women to ascertain whether they are pregnant provides an example of concurrent validity. The interest here is not in forecasting whether the woman will become pregnant in the future but in determining if she is pregnant now.

Predictive validity is determined strictly by the correlation between the two measures; if the correlation is high, the measure is said to have predictive validity. "Thus if we found that accuracy in horseshoe pitching correlated highly with success in college, horseshoe pitching would be a valid measure for predicting success in college."[6] This is not meant to imply that sound theory and common sense are not useful in selecting predictor instruments for investigation, but after the investigations are done, the entire proof of the pudding is in the correlations.

Predictive validity is relatively easy to assess. It requires, to be sure, a reasonably valid measure of the criterion with which the scores on the measuring instrument are to be compared. Given that such scores are available (for example, the grades the student actually achieves in an MBA program, the sales representatives' quitting or not), all that the researcher needs to do is to establish the degree of relationship, usually in the form of some kind of correlation coefficient, between the scores on the measuring instrument and the criterion variable. Although easy to assess, predictive validity is rarely the most important kind of validity. We are often concerned with "what the measure in fact measures" rather than simply whether it predicts accurately or not.

Content Validity

Content validity focuses on the adequacy with which the domain of the characteristic is captured by the measure. Consider, for example, the characteristic "spelling ability." Suppose that the following list of words was used to assess an individual's spelling ability: strike, shortstop, foul, inning, catcher, pitcher, ball, umpire, bullpen, dugout. Now, you would probably take issue with this spelling test. Further, the basis for your objection probably would be that all the words relate to the sport of baseball. Therefore, you could argue that an individual who is basically a very poor speller could do well on this test simply because he or she is a baseball enthusiast. You would be right, of course. A person with a basic capacity for spelling but with little interest in baseball might, in fact, do worse on this spelling test than another person with less native ability but a good deal more interest in baseball. The test could be said to lack content validity, because it does not properly sample the domain of all possible words that could be used but is very selective in its emphasis.

---

[6]Jum C. Nunnally and Ira H. Bernstein, *Psychometric Theory*, 3rd ed. (New York: McGraw-Hill, 1994), p. 95.

The preceding example illustrates how content validity is assessed, although not how it is established. Content validity is sometimes known as "face validity" because it is assessed by examining the measure with an eye toward ascertaining the domain being sampled. If the included domain is decidedly different from the domain of the variable as conceived, the measure is said to lack content validity. Theoretically, to capture a person's spelling ability, we should administer all words in the English language. The person who spelled the greatest number of these words correctly would be said to have the most spelling ability. This is a completely unrealistic procedure. It would take much of a person's lifetime to complete. Therefore, we resort to sampling the domain of the characteristic by constructing spelling tests that consist of samples of all the possible words that could be used. Different samplings of items can produce different comparative performances by individuals. We need to recognize that whether we have assessed the true characteristic depends on how well we have sampled the domain of the characteristic. This is not only true for spelling ability, but also holds for psychological characteristics in which we have an interest.

How can we ensure that our measure will possess content validity? We can never guarantee it because it is partly a matter of judgment. We may feel quite comfortable with the items included in a measure, for example, while a critic may argue that we have failed to sample from some relevant domain of the characteristic. Although we can never guarantee the content validity of a measure, we can severely diminish the objections of the critics. The key to content validity lies in the *procedures* that are used to develop the instrument.

One of the most critical elements in generating a content-valid instrument is conceptually defining the domain of the characteristic. The researcher has to specify what the variable is and what it is not. The task of definition is expedited by examining the literature to determine how the variable has been defined and used. Because it is unlikely that all the definitions will agree, the researcher must specify which elements in the definition underlie his or her use of the term. The researcher's next step is to formulate a large collection of items that broadly represent the variable as defined. The researcher needs to be quite careful to include items from all the relevant dimensions of the variable. Again, a literature search may be productive in indicating the various dimensions or strata of a variable. At this stage, the researcher may wish to include items with slightly different shades of meaning, since the original list of items will be refined to produce the final measure.

The collection of items must be large so that after refinement the measure still contains enough items to adequately sample each of the variable's domains. In the example cited previously, a measure of a sales representative's job satisfaction would need to include items about each of the components of the job (duties, fellow workers, top management, sales supervisor, customers, pay, and promotion opportunities) if it is to be content valid. The process of refinement, the essence of which is the internal consistency exhibited by the items within the test, is statistical in nature.

Construct Validity

Construct validity is most directly concerned with the question of what the instrument is, in fact, measuring. What construct, concept, or trait underlies the performance or score achieved on that test? Does the measure of attitude measure attitude or some other underlying characteristic of the individual that affects his or her score? Construct validity lies at the very heart of scientific progress. Scientists need constructs with which to communicate. So do you and I. Thus, in marketing we speak of people's socioeconomic class, their personality, their attitudes, and so on. These are all constructs that we use as we try to explain marketing behavior. And although vital, they are also not observable. We can observe behavior related to these constructs, but we cannot observe the constructs themselves. Rather, we operationally define the constructs in terms of a set of observables. When we agree on the operational definitions, precision in communication is advanced. Instead of saying that what is measured by these 75 items is the person's brand loyalty, we can speak of the idea of brand loyalty.

While the measurement of constructs is vital to scientific progress, construct validity is the most difficult type of validity to establish.[7] Research Realities 9A.2, for example, discusses the problems encountered historically when measuring the construct "discretionary income" and a proposed new measure. We need to ensure, through the plans and procedures used in constructing the instrument, that we have adequately sampled the domain of the construct and that there is internal consistency among the items of the domain. The assumption about the internal consistency of a set of items is that "if a set of items is really measuring some underlying trait or attitude, then the underlying trait causes the covariation among the items. The higher the correlations, the better the items are measuring the same underlying construct."[8] We saw that internal consistency was also at issue in determining content validity, and, as a matter of fact, negative evidence of the content validity of a measure also provides negative evidence about its construct validity. A measure possessing construct validity must be internally consistent insofar as the construct is internally consistent. On the other hand, it is not true that a consistent measure is a construct-valid measure. "To the extent that the elements of . . . a domain show . . . consistency, it can be said that *some* construct may be employed to account for the data, but it is by no means sure that it is legitimate to employ the construct name which motivated the research. In other words, consistency is a *necessary* but not *sufficient* condition for construct validity."[9]

Given that the domain of the construct has been specified, a set of items relevant to the breadth of the domain has been generated, the items have been refined, and the remaining items have been shown to be internally consistent, the remaining step is to see how well the measure relates to measures of other constructs to which the construct is theoretically related. Does it behave as expected? Does it fit

---

[7]See Gilbert A. Churchill, Jr., "A Paradigm for Developing Better Measures of Marketing Constructs," *Journal of Marketing Research* 16 (February 1979), pp. 64–73, for a procedure that can be used to construct scales having construct validity. See J. Paul Peter, "Construct Validity: A Review of Basic Issues and Marketing Practices," *Journal of Marketing Research* 18 (May 1981), pp. 133–145, for an in-depth discussion of the notion of construct validity. See also Robert F. DeVellis, *Scale Development: Theory and Applications* (Thousand Oaks, CA: Sage Publications, 1991).

[8]George W. Bohrnstedt, "Reliability and Validity Assessment in Attitude Measurement," in Gene F. Summers, ed., *Attitude Measurement* (Chicago: Rand McNally, 1970), p. 93. See also George W. Bohrnstedt, "Measurement," in Peter H. Rossi, James D. Wright, and Andy B. Anderson, eds., *Handbook of Survey Research* (Orlando: Academic Press Inc., 1983), pp. 69–121.

[9]Nunnally and Bernstein, *Psychometric Theory*, p. 103.

Measuring the Construct "Discretionary Income"

Along with sex and age, family income is among the most often collected and most effective predictors of consumer behavior. Virtually all marketing research instruments include an income question, and the answers to that question are used in many ways. Income describes consumers, segments markets, predicts or explains purchases, and provides reasons for purchasing pattern changes.

Although family income is a useful predictor, it is far from complete. Consumers with low incomes sometimes behave like consumers with high incomes and vice versa. Among the many reasons for such contradictions is that consumers differ greatly in their financial obligations and in their ability to manage the funds they have. When two families have exactly the same income, the amount remaining after the essentials have been purchased may leave one family relatively well off and the other relatively poor. Families with more "discretionary" income have more opportunity to purchase extras or luxury and convenience items, or to put the money away for future use. Knowledge of discretionary income, therefore, would be of considerable value in marketing research.

Despite its obvious benefits, the discretionary income concept has not been used much over the years. One author ascribed this neglect to the fact that consumers cannot determine and report their discretionary income objectively and precisely. Other scholars have cited the generally ambiguous way in which consumers employ economic ideas. They have been especially bothered by the fact that what is "discretionary" and what is "essential" are to some degree a matter of individual taste.

One way to avoid such problems is to use a psychological approach in determining discretionary income. Instead of trying to get consumers to provide hard, objective economic data, the psychological approach focuses on an entirely subjective variable: how people think about what they have.

Our measure of subjective discretionary income (SDI) was created from three items already present on the DDB Needham advertising agency Life-style Questionnaire:

1. No matter how fast our income goes up, we never seem to get ahead.

2. We have more to spend on extras than most of our neighbors do.

3. Our family income is high enough to satisfy nearly all our important desires.

The statements are answered on a 6-point scale with definitely disagree (1) and definitely agree (6) as the anchor points. When the responses to the three items are summed, with the first item being reverse coded, the result is a score with a range from 3 to 18. Respondents who score high on this scale are indicating that they have enough money to buy what they think they need and then some. Respondents who score low are saying that they have a tough time simply making ends meet.

Each item taps an important aspect of the SDI construct. The first item measures an aspect of SDI very close to perceived economic well-being and also probably related closely to ability to manage money. The second item speaks of "extras" in relation to neighbors, an important reference group. The third item pertains to feelings of having enough income for things that are considered to be important but are still termed "desires." This item gets at the very essence of what "discretionary" means.

Source: Thomas C. O'Guinn and William D. Wells, "Subjective Discretionary Income," *Marketing Research: A Magazine of Management & Applications* 1 (March 1989), pp. 32–41. For estimates of the amount of discretionary income U.S. households have, see Thomas G. Exter, *The Official Guide to American Incomes: The Demographics of Who Does and Who Doesn't Have Money,* 2nd ed. (Ithaca, NY: New Strategist Publications & Consulting, 1996).

the theory or model relating this construct to other constructs? The diagram showing the relationships among a set of constructs is often referred to as the *nomological net*. Determining if the construct behaves as expected with respect to the other constructs to which it is theoretically related is consequently referred to as *establishing its nomological validity*.

For example, consider Figure 9A.2, which depicts the relationship between the constructs "job satisfaction" and "job turnover." Suppose that we had developed the measure X to assess a sales representative's job satisfaction. Now, the construct validity of the measure could be assessed by ascertaining the relationship between job satisfaction as measured by X and company turnover as measured by Y. Those companies in which the X scores are low, indicating less job satisfaction, should experience more turnover than those with high scores. If they do not, one would question the construct validity of the job satisfaction measure. In other words, the construct validity of a measure is assessed by whether the measure confirms or denies the hypotheses predicted from the theory based on the constructs. Is the evidence consistent with the hypothesized linkages among the constructs as captured in a model like Figure 9A.2? The fallacy, of course, is that the failure of the hypothesized relationship to obtain among the observables may be due to a lack of construct validity or incorrect theory. We often try to establish the construct validity of a measure, therefore, by relating it to a number of other constructs rather than simply one, and we also try to use those theories and hypotheses that are sufficiently well founded to inspire confidence in their probable correctness.

If the trait or construct exists, it is also true that it should be measurable by several different methods. Otherwise the trait could be considered to be nothing more than an artifact of the measurement procedure. Moreover, the methods should be independent insofar as possible. If they are all measuring the same construct, though, the measures should be highly correlated, which provides evidence of their **convergent validity.** Discriminant validity is also required to establish the construct validity of a measure. **Discriminant validity** requires that a measure does

---

FIGURE 9A.2   **Diagram Relating the Constructs "Job Satisfaction" and "Job Turnover"**

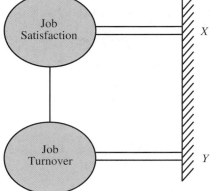

not correlate too highly with measures from which it is supposed to differ.[10] If the correlations are too high, this suggests that the measure is not actually capturing a distinct or isolated trait.

Indirect Assessment through Reliability

The similarity of results provided by independent but comparable measures of the same object, trait, or construct is called **reliability.** It is distinguished from validity in that validity is represented in the agreement between two attempts to measure the same trait through *maximally different* methods, whereas reliability is the agreement between two efforts to measure the same trait through *maximally similar* methods.[11] If a measure were valid, there would be little need to worry about its reliability. If a measure is valid, it reflects the characteristic that it is supposed to measure and is not distorted by other factors, either systematic or transitory.

Evaluating the reliability of any measuring instrument consists of determining how much of the variation in scores is due to inconsistencies in measurement.[12] The reliability of the instrument should be established before it is used for a substantive study and not after.

Before discussing how this evidence is generated, one point needs emphasis. Reliability involves determining the consistency of independent or comparable measures of the same object, group, or situation. To the extent that a measure is reliable, it is not influenced by transitory factors. In other words, the more reliable the measure, the lower is X_R in the equation for observed scores. Note what this implies. A measure could be reliable and still not be valid, since even if X_R equals zero, $X_O = X_T + X_S$. The converse is, of course, not true. If the measure is valid, $X_O = X_T$, because the measure is simply reflecting true scores without error. Thus, it is often said that (1) if a measure is valid, it is reliable; (2) if it is not reliable, it cannot be valid, since at a very minimum $X_O = X_T + X_R$; and (3) if it is reliable, then it may or may not be valid, because reliability does not account for systematic error. In other words, although lack of reliability provides negative evidence of the validity of a

---

[10]One convenient way of establishing the convergent and discriminant validity of a measure is through the multitrait-multimethod matrix of Campbell and Fiske. See Donald T. Campbell and Donald W. Fiske, "Convergent and Discriminant Validation by the Multitrait-Multimethod Matrix," *Psychological Bulletin* 56 (1959), pp. 81–105. See also Neal Schmitt, Bryan W. Coyle, and Bruce B. Saari, "A Review and Critique of Analyses of Multitrait-Multimethod Matrices," *Multivariate Behavioral Research* 12 (October 1977), pp. 447–478; Joseph A. Cote and M. Ronald Buckley, "Estimating Trait, Method, and Error Variance: Generalizing Across to Construct Validation Studies," *Journal of Marketing Research* 24 (August 1987), pp. 315–318. For examples of its use, see Ronald E. Goldsmith and Janelle Emmert, "Measuring Product Category Involvement: A Multitrait-Multimethod Study," *Journal of Business Research* 23 (December 1991), pp. 363–371; Chesy Ofir and Srinivas K. Reddy, "Measurement Errors in Probability Judgments," *Management Science* 42 (September 1996), pp. 1308–1325.

[11]Campbell and Fiske, "Convergent and Discriminant Validation," p. 83.

[12]See J. Paul Peter, "Reliability: A Review of Psychometric Basics and Recent Marketing Practices," *Journal of Marketing Research* 16 (February 1979), pp. 6–17, for a detailed treatment of the issue of reliability in measurement. See Gilbert A. Churchill, Jr., and J. Paul Peter, "Research Design Effects on the Reliability of Rating Scales: A Meta-Analysis," *Journal of Marketing Research* 21 (February 1984), pp. 360–375, for an empirical assessment of the factors that seem to affect the reliability of rating scales.

TABLE 9A.2	Relative Frequency with Which Various Psychometric Properties of Measures Are Investigated

Reliability	95%
Convergent validity	25
Discriminant validity	17
Construct validity	83

Source: Developed from the information in J. Paul Peter and Gilbert A. Churchill, Jr., "The Relationship among Research Design Choices and Psychometric Properties of Rating Scales: A Meta-Analysis," *Journal of Marketing Research* 23 (February 1986), pp. 1–10.

measure, the mere presence of reliability does not mean that the measure is valid. Reliability is a necessary, but not a sufficient, condition for validity. Reliability is more easily measured than validity, though, and this accounts for the emphasis on it over the years. Table 9A.2 indicates that even among studies in which a major thrust is the assessment of the psychometric quality of the measures, reliability is the most frequently investigated property.

Stability

One of the more popular ways of establishing the reliability of a measure is to measure the same objects or individuals at two different points in time and to correlate the obtained scores. Assuming that the objects or individuals have not changed in the interim, the two scores should correlate perfectly. To the extent that they do not, random disturbances were operating in either one or both of the test situations to produce random error in the measurement. The procedure is known as test–retest reliability assessment.

One of the critical decisions the researcher must face in determining the **stability** of a measure is how long to wait between successive administrations of the instrument. Suppose that the researcher's instrument is an attitude scale. If the researcher waits too long, the person's attitude may change, thus producing a low correlation between the two scores. On the other hand, a short wait is likely to produce test bias—people may remember how they responded the first time and be more consistent in their responses than is warranted by their attitudes. To handle this problem, many researchers will use alternate forms for the two administrations. Instead of putting all the items in one form, the researcher generates two instruments that are as identical as possible in content. That is, each form should contain items from the same domains, and each domain of content should receive approximately the same emphasis in each form. Ideally, there would be a one-to-one correspondence between items on each of the two forms so that the means and standard deviations of the two forms would be identical and the intercorrelations among the items would be the same in both versions.[13] Even though it is next to impossible to achieve the ideal, it is possible to construct forms that are roughly parallel, and the

[13]Bohrnstedt, "Reliability and Validity," p. 85.

parallel forms can be correlated across time as the measure of test–retest reliability. The recommended time interval between administrations is two weeks.[14]

Equivalence

The basic assumption in constructing an attitude scale is that when several items are summed into a single attitude score, the items are measuring the same underlying attitude. Each item can, in one sense, be considered a measure of the attitude, and the items should be consistent (or equivalent) in what they indicate about the attitude. The **equivalence** measure of reliability focuses on the internal consistency or internal homogeneity of the set of items forming the scale.

The earliest measure of the internal consistency of a set of items was the split-half reliability of the scale. In assessing split-half reliability, the total set of items is divided into two equivalent halves; the total scores for the two halves are correlated, and this is taken as the measure of reliability of the instrument. Sometimes the division of items is made randomly, whereas at other times the even items are assumed to form one-half and the odd the other half of the instrument. The total score on the even items is then correlated with the total score obtained from the odd items.

Pointed criticism has been directed at split-half reliability as the measure of a scale's internal consistency. The criticism focuses on the necessarily arbitrary division of the items into equivalent halves. Each of the many possible divisions can produce different correlations between the two forms or different reliabilities. Which division is correct or, alternatively, what is then the reliability of the instrument? For example, a 10-item scale has 126 possible splits or 126 possible reliability coefficients.[15]

A more appropriate way to assess the internal homogeneity of a set of items is to look at all the items simultaneously, using coefficient alpha. One reason is that coefficient alpha has a direct relationship to the most accepted and conceptually appealing measurement model, the **domain sampling model.** The domain sampling model holds that the purpose of any particular measurement is to estimate the score that would be obtained if *all* the items in the domain were used. The score that any subject would obtain over the whole sample domain is the person's true score, X_T.

In practice, one typically does not use all the items that could be used, but only a sample of them. To the extent that the sample of items correlates with true scores, it is good. According to the domain sampling model, then, a primary source of measurement error is the inadequate sampling of the domain of relevant items.

Basic to the domain sampling model is the concept of a very large correlation matrix showing all correlations among the items in the domain. No single item is likely to provide a perfect representation of the concept, just as no single word can be used to test for differences in subjects' spelling abilities and no single question can measure a person's intelligence.

---

[14]Nunnally and Bernstein in *Psychometric Theory*, pp. 252–255, argue strongly against using straight test-retest reliability and in favor of alternate forms reliability.

[15]In general, for a scale with $2n$ items, the total number of possible splits of the items into two halves is $(2n)!/2(n!)(n!)$. See Bohrnstedt, "Reliability and Validity," p. 86.

The average correlation among the items in this large matrix, $\bar{r}$, indicates the extent to which some common core is present in the items. The dispersion of correlations about the average indicates the extent to which items vary in sharing the common core. The key assumption in the domain sampling model is that all items, *if they belong to the domain of the concept,* have an equal amount of common core. This statement implies that the average correlation in each column of the hypothetical matrix is the same, and in turn equals the average correlation in the whole matrix. That is, if all the items in a measure are drawn from the domain of a single construct, responses to those items should be highly intercorrelated. Low inter-item correlations, in contrast, indicate that some items are not drawn from the appropriate domain and are producing error and unreliability.

Coefficient alpha provides a summary measure of the intercorrelations that exist among a set of items. Alpha is calculated as:[16]

$$\alpha = \left(\frac{k}{k-1} \right) \left(1 - \frac{\sum\limits_{i=1}^{k} \sigma_i^2}{\sigma_t^2} \right)$$

where

k = number of items in the scale,

σ_i^2 = variance of scores on item i across subjects, and

σ_t^2 = variance of total scores across subjects where the total score for each respondent represents the sum of the individual item scores.

Coefficient alpha routinely should be calculated to assess the quality of measure. It is pregnant with meaning because the *square root* of coefficient alpha is the *estimated correlation of the k-item test with errorless true scores.*

If alpha is low, what should the analyst do? If the item pool is sufficiently large, this outcome suggests that some items do not share equally in the common core and should be eliminated. The easiest way to find them is to calculate the correlation of each item with the total score and to plot these correlations by decreasing order of magnitude. Items with correlations near zero would be eliminated. Further, items that produce a substantial or sudden drop in the item-to-total correlations would also be deleted.

If the construct had, say, five identifiable dimensions or components, coefficient alpha would be calculated for each dimension. The item-to-total correlations used to delete items would also be based on the items in the component and the total score for that dimension.

The preceding discussion dealt with the equivalence of reliability when applied to a *single* instrument. An alternative equivalence measure is used when different observers or different instruments measure the same individuals or objects at the same point in time. Do these methods produce consistent results? Are they equivalent as measured by the correlations among the total scores? An example would be

---

[16]See Nunnally and Bernstein, *Psychometric Theory,* pp. 209–292, for the rationale behind coefficient alpha and more detailed discussion of the formula for computing it. For discussion of its use in marketing and psychology, see Robert A. Peterson, "A Meta-Analysis of Cronbach's Coefficient Alpha," *Journal of Consumer Research* 21 (September 1994), pp. 381–391.

a beauty contest. Do the judges, using the established criteria of beauty, talent, poise, and so on, rank the contestants in the same order in terms of winner, first runner-up, second runner-up, and so on? The reliability of the measure is greater to the extent that the judges agree.[17] This type of equivalence is the basis of convergent validation when the measures are independent.

Developing Measures

As a beginning researcher, one can easily become confused about how one goes about developing measures of marketing constructs. How does one contend with the basic issues of reliability and validity, and how does one choose among the various coefficients that can be computed? Figure 9A.3 diagrams a sequence of steps that can be followed to develop valid measures of marketing constructs.[18]

Step 1 in the process involves specifying the domain of the construct that is to be measured. Consider, for example, measuring customer satisfaction with a recently purchased space heater. What attributes of the product and the purchase should be measured to accurately assess the family's satisfaction? Certainly one would want to be reasonably exhaustive in the list of product features to be included, incorporating such facets as cost, durability, quality, operating performance, and aesthetic features. But what about purchaser's reaction to the sales assistance received? What about the family members' reactions to subsequent advertising for a competitor's product offering the same features at lower cost? Or what about the family's reactions to news of some negative environmental effects resulting from use of the product? To detail which of these factors should be included or how customer satisfaction should be operationalized is beyond the scope of this book. Obviously, however, researchers need to be very careful about specifying what is to be included in the domain of the construct being measured and what is to be excluded.

Step 2 in the process is to generate items that capture the domain as specified. Those techniques that are typically productive in exploratory research, including literature searches, experience surveys, and insight-stimulating examples, are generally productive here. The literature should indicate how the variable has been defined previously and how many dimensions or components it has. The search for ways to measure customer satisfaction would include product brochures, articles in trade magazines and newspapers, or results of product tests, such as those published by *Consumer Reports*. The experience survey might include discussions with people in the product group responsible for the product, sales representatives,

---

[17]For a general discussion of the measurement of interjudge reliability, see William D. Perreault, Jr., and Laurence E. Leigh, "Reliability of Nominal Data Based on Qualitative Judgments," *Journal of Marketing Research* 26 (May 1989), pp. 135–148; Marie Adele Hughes and Dennis E. Garrett, "Intercoder Reliability Estimation Approaches in Marketing: A Generalizability Theory Framework for Quantitative Data," *Journal of Marketing Research* 27 (May 1990), pp. 185–195. See also Roland T. Rust and Bruce Cooil, "Reliability Measures for Qualitative Data: Theory and Implications," *Journal of Marketing Research* 31 (February 1994), pp. 1–14.

[18]The procedure is adapted from Gilbert A. Churchill, Jr., "A Paradigm for Developing Better Measures of Marketing Constructs," *Journal of Marketing Research* 16 (February 1979), pp. 64–73.

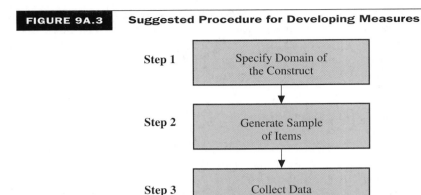

FIGURE 9A.3   **Suggested Procedure for Developing Measures**

Step 1 — Specify Domain of the Construct

Step 2 — Generate Sample of Items

Step 3 — Collect Data

Step 4 — Purify Measure

Step 5 — Assess Validity

Source: Adapted from the procedure suggested by Gilbert A. Churchill, Jr., "A Paradigm for Developing Better Measures of Marketing Constructs," *Journal of Marketing Research* 16 (February 1979), p. 66.

dealers, persons in marketing research, consumers, and outsiders who have a special expertise in heating equipment. The insight-stimulating examples could involve a comparison of competitors' products or a detailed examination of some particularly vehement complaints in unsolicited letters about the performance of the product. Examples that reveal sharp contrasts or have striking features would be most productive. Focus groups also could be used to advantage at the item-generation state.

Another potential source of items involves having respondents focus on the interactions that were crucial or critical in shaping their reactions to the phenomenon. For example, the following questions were asked of all respondents in an attempt to identify the features of service encounters that make them satisfactory or unsatisfactory:[19]

- Think of a time when, as a customer, you had a particularly *satisfying (dissatisfying)* interaction with an employee of an airline, hotel, or restaurant.

- When did the incident happen?

[19]Mary Jo Bitner, Bernard H. Booms, and Mary Stanfield Tetreault, "The Service Encounter: Diagnosing Favorable and Unfavorable Incidents," *Journal of Marketing* 54 (January 1990), pp. 71–84. See also Mary Jo Bitner, Bernard H. Booms, and Lois A. Mohr, "Critical Service Encounters: The Employee's Viewpoint," *Journal of Marketing* 58 (October 1994), pp. 95–106.

- What specific circumstances led up to this situation?
- Exactly what did the employee say or do?
- What resulted that made you feel the interaction was *satisfying (dissatisfying)?*

Note the emphasis of having respondents describe a specific instance in which a good or poor service interaction occurred. A similar procedure could be used among a sample of purchasers of the space heater to generate items.

Step 3 involves collecting data about the concept from a relevant sample of the target population—for example, all those who have purchased a space heater within the last six months.

Step 4 uses the data collection in step 3 to purify the original set of items. The purification involves eliminating items that seemed to create confusion among respondents and items that do not discriminate between subjects with fundamentally different positions on the construct. The fundamental criterion that is used to eliminate items is how each item goes together with the other items. If all the items in a measure are drawn from the domain of a single construct, responses to those items should be highly correlated. If they are not, that is an indication that some of the items are not drawn from the appropriate domain and are producing error and unreliability, and they should be eliminated. Several of the equivalence reliability coefficients mentioned earlier can be used to make this assessment, as can other statistical techniques.[20]

Step 5 in the process involves determining the validity of the purified measure. Primarily, this involves assessing its convergent, discriminant, and construct validity, because its content validity will have largely been addressed in steps 1 through 4. The assessment of its construct validity involves determining whether it behaves as expected, which in turn involves determining its predictive validity.

Applications and Problems

1. Discuss the idea that a particular measure could be reliable and still not be valid. In your discussion, distinguish between reliability and validity.
2. Discuss the use of IQ tests (or similar tests, such as the Graduate Management Admissions Test) in measuring intelligence, an often-used construct. In particular, do you believe that these tests adequately measure a person's abilities? If not, what traits, abilities, or types of intelligence do the tests fail to measure?
3. You have developed a questionnaire designed to measure attitudes toward a set of television ads for a new snack-food product. The respondents, as a group, will view the ads on a television set and then complete the questionnaire. Due to logistical circumstances beyond your control, you must split your sample of respondents into three groups and collect data on three separate days. What steps might you take in an effort to minimize possible variance in scores caused by the three separate administrations?
4. Many areas of marketing research rely heavily on measures of psychological constructs. What characteristics inherent in these constructs make them so difficult to measure? What tools can the marketing researcher bring to bear when evaluating the "correctness" of his or her measure? In other words, what things can we do that allow us to

---

[20]See Churchill, "A Paradigm," for detailed discussion of which coefficients should be used and the rationale for their use.

state with some degree of confidence that we are indeed measuring the construct of interest?

5.   You are the national sales manager for Perry Pharmaceutical, Inc. You have been concerned with trying to determine the most important characteristics a salesperson must possess to be successful. Much of the current research suggests that salesperson adaptiveness is a key component of success. You would like to determine if this is indeed the case. To assess this, you need to develop a scale to measure salesperson adaptiveness, collect data with your sales force, and then compare the results to each individual's sales record. At this time, you are asked only to develop a scale to measure salesperson adaptiveness. What kinds of questions would you include? Are there general areas that you think must be measured with a number of different questions?

CASE 3.1

Suchomel Chemical Company

Suchomel Chemical Company was an old-line chemical company that was still managed and directed by its founder, Jeff Suchomel, and his wife, Carol. Jeff served as president and Carol as chief research chemist. The company, which was located in Savannah, Georgia, manufactured a number of products that were used by consumers in and around their homes. The products included waxes, polishes, tile grout, tile cement, spray cleaners for windows and other surfaces, aerosol room sprays, and insecticides. The company distributed its products regionally. It had a particularly strong consumer following in the northern Florida and southern Georgia areas.

The company not only had managed to maintain but had increased its market share in several of its key lines in the past half-dozen years in spite of increased competition from the national brands. Suchomel Chemical had done this largely through product innovation, particularly innovation that emphasized modest product alterations rather than new technologies or dramatically new products. Jeff and Carol both believed that the company should stick to the things it knew best rather than try to be all things to all people and in the process spread the company's resources too thin, particularly given its regional nature. One innovation the company was now considering was a new scent for its insect spray, which was rubbed or sprayed on a person's body. The new scent had undergone extensive testing both in the laboratory and in the field. The tests indicated that it repelled insects, particularly mosquitoes, as well as or even better than the two leading national brands. The company was particularly concerned about what to call it as it considered the introduction of the new brand.

The Insecticide Market

The insecticide market had become a somewhat tricky one to figure out over the past several years. Although growth had occurred in the purchase of insecticides in general, much of it had occurred in the tank liquid market. The household spray market had decreased slightly during the same time span. Suchomel Chemical had not suffered from the general sales decline, however, but had managed to increase its sales of spray insecticides slightly over the past three years. The company was hoping that the new scent formulation might allow it to make even greater market share gains.

The company's past experience in the industry led it to believe that the name that was given to the new product would be a very important element in the product's success, because there seemed to be some complex interactions between purchase and usage characteristics among repellent users. Most purchases were made by married women for their families. Yet repeat purchase was dependent on support by the husband that the product worked well. Therefore, the name must appeal to both the buyer and the end user, but the two people are not typically together at the time of purchase. To complicate matters further, past research indicated that a product with a name that appeals to both purchaser and end user will be rejected if the product's name and scent do not match. In sum, naming a product like this that is used on a person's body is a complex task.

Research Alternatives

The company followed its typical procedures in developing possible names for the new product. First, it asked those who had been involved in the product's development to suggest names. It also scheduled some informal brainstorming sessions among potential customers. Subjects in the brainstorming sessions were simply asked to throw out all the names they could possibly think of with respect to what a spray insecticide could or should be called. A panel of executives, mostly those from the product group but a few from corporate management as well, then went through the names and reduced the large list down to a more manageable subset based on their personal reactions to the names and subsequent discussion about what the names connoted to them. The subset of names was then submitted to the corporate legal staff, who checked them for possible copyright infringement. Those that survived this check were discussed again by the panel, and a list of 20 possible names was generated. Those in the product group were charged with the responsibility of developing a research design by which the final name could be chosen.

The people in the product group charged with the name test were considering two different alternatives for finding out which name was preferred. Both alternatives involved personal interviews at shopping malls. More specifically, the group was planning to conduct a set of interviews at one randomly determined mall in each of the cities of Atlanta, Savannah, Tallahassee, and Orlando. Each set of interviews would involve 100 respondents. The target respondents were married females, ages 21 to 54, who purchased the product category during the past year. Likely looking respondents were to be approached at random and asked if they used any insect spray at all over the past year and then asked their age. Those that qualified would be asked to complete the insecticide-naming exercise using one of the two alternatives being considered.

Alternative 1 involved a sort of the 20 tentative names by the respondents. The sort would be conducted in the following way: First, respondents would be asked to sort the 20 names into two groups based on their appropriateness for an insect repellent. Group 1 was to consist of the 10 best names and Group 2 the 10 worst. Next, respondents would be asked to select the four best from Group 1 and the four worst from Group 2. Then they would be asked to pick the one best from the subset of the four best and the one worst from the subset of the four worst. Finally, all respondents would be asked why they picked the specific names they did as the best and the worst.

Alternative 2 also had several stages. All respondents would first be asked to rate each of the 20 names on a seven-point semantic differential scale with end anchors "Extremely inappropriate name for an insect repellent" and "Extremely appropriate name for an insect repellent." After completing this rating task, they would be asked to spray the back of their hands or arm with the product. They would then be asked to repeat the rating task using a similar scale, but this time it was one in which the polar descriptors referred to the appropriateness of the name with respect to the specific scent. Next, they would be asked to indicate their interest in buying the product by again checking one of the seven positions on a scale that ranged from "Definitely would not buy it" to "Definitely would buy it." Finally, each respondent would be asked why she selected each of the names she did as being most appropriate for insect repellents in general and the specific scent in particular.

QUESTIONS

1. Evaluate each of the two methods being considered for collecting the data. Which would you recommend and why?

2. How would you use the data from each method to decide what the brand name should be?

3. Do you think that personal interviews in shopping malls are a useful way to collect these data? If not, what would you recommend as an alternative?

CASE 3.2
Wisconsin Power & Light (B)[1]

In response to the current consumer trend toward increased environmental sensitivity, Wisconsin Power & Light (WP&L) adopted several high-visibility environmental initiatives. These environmental programs fell under the BuySmart umbrella of WP&L's Demand-Side Management Programs and were intended to foster the conservation of energy among WP&L's residential, commercial, and industrial customers. Examples of specific programs include: Appliance Rebates, Energy Analysis, Weatherization Help, and the Home Energy Improvement Loan (HEIL) program. All previous marketing research and information gathering focused primarily on issues from the customers' perspective, such as an evaluation of net program impacts in terms of energy and demand savings, and an estimation of the levels of free ridership (individuals who would have undertaken the conservation actions promoted by the program, even if no program were in place). In addition, a study has been designed and is currently being conducted to evaluate and identify customer attitudes and opinions concerning the design, implementation, features, and delivery of the residential programs. Having examined the consumer perspective, WP&L's next objective is to focus on obtaining information from other participants in the programs, namely employees and lenders.

WP&L's first step in shifting the focus of its research is to undertake a study of the HEIL program of the BuySmart umbrella. The HEIL program, introduced four years ago, was designed to make low-interest-rate financing available to residential gas and electric WP&L customers for conservation and weatherization measures. The low-interest guaranteed loans are delivered through WP&L account representatives in conjunction with participating financial institutions and trade allies. The procedures for obtaining a loan

---

[1]The contributions of Kavita Maini and Paul Metz to the development of this case are gratefully acknowledged, as is the permission of Wisconsin Power & Light to use the material included.

begin with an energy audit of the interested customer's residence to determine the appropriate conservation measures. Once the customer decides on which measures to have installed, the WP&L representative assists in arranging low-interest-rate financing through one of the participating local banking institutions. At the completion of the projects, WP&L representatives conduct an inspection of the work by checking a random sample of participants. Conservation measures eligible under the HEIL program include the installation of natural gas furnaces/boilers, automatic vent dampers, intermittent ignition devices, heat pumps, and heat pump water heaters. Eligible structural improvements include the addition of attic/wall/basement insulation, storm windows and doors, sillbox insulation, window weather stripping, and caulking.

Purpose

The primary goal of the current study is to identify ways of improving the HEIL program from the lenders' point of view. Specifically, the following issues need to be addressed:

- Identify the lenders' motivation for participating in the program.
- Determine how lenders get their information regarding various changes/updates in the program.
- Identify how lenders promote the program.
- Assess the current program with respect to administrative and program features.
- Determine the type of credit analysis conducted by the lenders.
- Identify ways of minimizing the default rate from the lenders' point of view.
- Assess the lenders' commitment to the program.
- Identify lenders' opinions of the overall program.
- Identify if the reason for loan inactivity in some lending institutions is due to lack of a customer base.

Methodology

WP&L decided to use a telephone survey of participating lending institutions to collect the data for its study. WP&L referenced two lists of lending institutions, which were supplied by its resident marketing staff, in order to select the sample for the survey. A total of 124 participating lending institutions were identified with the lists. However, it was found that one of the lists was shorter than the other by 15 names. Specifically, the names of some of the branches of major banks were not enumerated on one of the lists. Nevertheless, all 124 institutions, including the 15 discrepant ones, were included in the pool of names from which the sample was drawn.

The sample pool was classified into three groups based on loan activity in the 2001 calendar year. The groups fell out as follows:

Group	Number of Lenders	Loan Activity, 2001
1	44	0 loans
2	40	1 to 7 loans
3	40	8 to 54 loans

The rationale for the classification strategy was to allow analysis of key variables by three key groups: no loan activity, "light" loan activity, and "heavy" loan activity. The delineation between "light" and "heavy" activity was determined by the median number of loans issued by "active" participants.

The final sample for the survey consisted of 20 randomly chosen institutions from Groups 2 and 3, and 10 from Group 1. The samples of 20 lenders from both Groups 2 and 3 were identified by selecting every other listed respondent after a randomly determined starting point in each list. The 40 institutions selected from among Groups 2 and 3 formed the sample base in which WP&L was most interested (this was because each of these 40 institutions demonstrated loan activity in the past year). The sample size ($n = 40$) was based on judgment. The 10 randomly selected institutions from Group 1 were chosen primarily to explore the hypothesized reasons for zero-loan activity. These 10 zero-loan lenders received a shortened version of the telephone survey that focused only on their lack of activity.

All the districts within WP&L's service territory were notified two weeks in advance that a survey would be conducted. The survey was pretested and modified before final administration. All interviewing was conducted over a one-week period by a project manager and research assistant, both employees of WP&L's marketing department.

QUESTIONS

1. Given the project's objectives, describe the best way to proceed in terms of data collection. Provide support for your conclusion.

2. What kind of sample was used by Wisconsin Power & Light in its research effort? What advantages did WP&L gain by using the sampling method they used? What were the disadvantages? Suggest possible sampling alternatives that WP&L could have used.

CASE 3.3

E-Food and the Online Grocery Competition (B)

Ashley Sims is the MBA student who is considering starting her own grocery online. Two weeks ago, she ran a focus group consisting of 12 of her classmates, some of whom use an online grocer, and some of whom do not. She kept the moderator questions broad, just trying to get a sense of what e-visitors are looking for in their online grocery trips. Figure 3.3.1 contains a sampling of the verbata from that focus group.

Those data indicate variance on satisfaction with the current system, and even for loyal users, different levels of satisfaction with different features of the system. While people seem generally happy, there is clearly room for improvement in elements of online grocery shopping.

In addition, Sims is trying to think long-term, knowing that she wants one arm of her business to focus on grocery delivery, and one arm of her business to grow into a profitable consumer research business, offering in-depth insight into the consumer-decision processes for grocery shopping and online shopping more generally. Sims figures additional research will be required to understand how to set priorities in potentially improving the software, and the broader questions of how to understand the consumer's behavior and infer the thought processes underlying that behavior.

Sims used this textbook in her own marketing research class, so she knows there are many research methodologies to choose from. She is fresh off of her experience running the focus group that yielded the data in Figure 3.3.1. While it was fun and she thinks she learned a lot, she doubts that she could run another focus group that could be shaped to address these fairly specific concerns. She's thought about doing a survey—just asking people, "Do you care about brands?" or "Are you price sensitive?" and so on. However, she doubts that people would admit to being overly influenced by brand or price, even though their purchases may indicate that they are. She's also rejected an observational technique—a friend had suggested that she sit down next to a person who is about to do an online grocery run and just watch what they do and take notes. She's afraid that her presence would be off-putting and the person doing the grocery shopping might behave differently from how they normally would (for example, maybe buy asparagus rather than M&M's).

Ashley's computer-geeky friend tells her that every mouse click gets stored into a user file and that she should look at what people actually do rather than what they say. Sims is intrigued by this but understandably is having difficulty in obtaining such data from current online grocery providers. She decides to invest in having a programmer create a smaller-scale simulation of an online grocer. She will ask participants to pretend they are grocery shopping online. She'll strip off each user file and analyze the click-stream data. She might run a survey, too, but with the click-streams, she'll know just what people did, not just what they say they would do.

FIGURE 3.3.1	Sampling of Verbatim Accounts from Focus Group on Online Grocery Trips

- "It's great! I don't need a car!" (Current user)
- "It's difficult to just browse, like if I'm not sure what I'm in the mood for." (Had tried online shopping but is no longer a user)
- "I can't touch the fruits. I can't read the side of the box on cereals." (Current user)
- "They chose my vegetables better than I would have!" (Current user)
- "I wish they could pick up my dry cleaning too." (Not a user, intends to begin)
- "It's kind of expensive. There's a big annual fee, a delivery charge each time, and you know you've got to tip the delivery guy." (Current user)
- "This is terrific—I don't like to shop for food even if I had the time, which I certainly do not." (Current user)
- "I guess it's okay. Thing is, there's a <name of local grocery> on my way home from work, so that's just as convenient. For me." (Non-user, does not intend to begin)
- "Don't I get any, you know, frequent flyer points things?" (Non-user, getting used to the concept)

FIGURE 3.4.1   (continued)

11. *Please indicate the source(s) of any advertisements you have seen or heard.*

	Have Not Seen/Heard	Shopper's World	Rockford Morning Star	Radio	TV	Other	Don't Recall
Emerson	____	____	____	____	____	____	____
Rumstad	____	____	____	____	____	____	____
Wallpaper Shop	____	____	____	____	____	____	____

12. *Do you know which of the following items are available in these stores? If so, check the item(s) that apply.*

	Don't Know	Paint	Paneling	Carpeting	Draperies	Other
Emerson	____	____	____	____	____	____
Rumstad	____	____	____	____	____	____
Wallpaper Shop	____	____	____	____	____	____

13. *Which name brands of paint, if any, do you associate with the following stores?*

	Benjamin Moore	Dutch Boy	Glidden	Pittsburgh	Do Not Associate Any Listed
Emerson	____	____	____	____	____
Rumstad	____	____	____	____	____
Wallpaper Shop	____	____	____	____	____

14. *Have you ever visited any of these west side stores?*

	Never	Within Last Year	1–5 Yrs. Ago	More than 5 Yrs. Ago
Emerson	____	____	____	____
Rumstad	____	____	____	____
Wallpaper Shop	____	____	____	____

Section II

If you have visited or have knowledge of *one or more* of the stores listed below, please indicate the extent to which you agree or disagree with the following statements for each store(s). For instance, if you have knowledge of only one store, please answer each question for that particular store. If you have not visited or have no knowledge of any of these stores, omit this section and proceed to Section III.

(continued)

FIGURE 3.4.1   **(continued)**

	Strongly Agree	Agree	Neither Agree nor Disagree	Disagree	Strongly Disagree

15. The location of the store is convenient.

Emerson
Rumstad
Wallpaper Shop

16. The sales personnel are knowledgeable.

Emerson
Rumstad
Wallpaper Shop

17. The store lacks additional services **(e.g., matching paint, decorator services, etc.).**

Emerson
Rumstad
Wallpaper Shop

18. The store carries good-quality products.

Emerson
Rumstad
Wallpaper Shop

19. The prices are reasonable in relation to the quality of the products.

Emerson
Rumstad
Wallpaper Shop

20. The store hours are inconvenient.

Emerson
Rumstad
Wallpaper Shop

Section III

1. Your sex: ____ Male   ____ Female

2. Your age: ____ Under 25   ____ 25–29 years   ____ 30–39 years
____ 40–54 years   ____ 55 or over

FIGURE 3.4.1   (continued)

3. *How long have you lived in Rockford?*
   ____ Less than 1 year   ____ 1–3 years   ____ 4 or more years

4. *Do you:* ____ Own a home or condominium   ____ Rent a house
   ____ Rent an apartment   ____ Other

5. *When was the last time you painted or remodeled your residence?*
   ____ Never   ____ Within past year   ____ 1–5 years ago
   ____ More than 5 years ago

6. *Approximately how many times have you received the weekly* **Shopper's World** *in the past 3 months?*
   ____ Never   ____ 1–5 times   ____ 6–12 times

7. *Do you read or page through the* **Shopper's World?**
   ____ Do not receive it   ____ Never   ____ Less than ½ the time
   ____ About ½ the time   ____ More than ½ the time

---

excluded because they were outside the specified area. Blocks within each of the 10 remaining wards were enumerated, and five blocks were randomly selected from each ward. An initial starting point for each block was determined, and the questionnaires were then administered by the Parrett field staff at every sixth house on the block. All interviews were conducted on Saturday and Sunday. If no one was at home or if the respondent refused to cooperate, the next house on the block was substituted; no one was at home at 39 households, and 18 others refused to participate. The field work was completed within one weekend and produced a total sample of 123 responses.

QUESTIONS

1. Evaluate the questionnaire. Do you think the questionnaire adequately addresses the concerns raised by Rumstad?

2. How would you suggest the data collected be analyzed to best solve Rumstad's problem?

3. Do you think personal administration of the questionnaires was called for in this study, or would you suggest an alternative scheme? Why or why not?

CASE 3.5
Premium Pizza Inc.[1]

The 1980s saw a sharp increase in the use of promotions (coupons, cents-off deals marked on the package, free gifts, and so on) because of their manifest success at increasing short-term purchase behavior. In fact, sales promotion is now estimated to account for over one-half of the typical promotion budget, while advertising accounts for less than half. In many industries, however, the initial benefit of increased sales has resulted in long-term escalation of competition. As firms are forced to "fight fire with fire," special offer follows special offer in a never-ending spiral of promotional deals.

The fast-food industry has been one of the most strongly affected by this trend. Pizzas come two for the price of one; burgers are promoted in the context of a double-deal involving cuddly toys for the kids; tacos are reduced in price some days, but not others. It is within this fiercely competitive, erratic environment that Premium Pizza Corporation has grown from a small local chain into an extensive midwestern

---

[1]The contributions of Jacqueline C. Hitchon to this case are gratefully acknowledged.

network with national aspirations. Over the past few years, Jim Battaglia, vice president of marketing, has introduced a number of promotional offers, and Premium Pizza parlors have continued to flourish. Nevertheless, as the company contemplates further expansion, Jim is concerned that he knows very little about how his customers respond to his promotional deals. He believes that he needs a long-term strategy aimed at maximizing the effectiveness of dollars spent on promotions. And, as a first step, he thinks that it is important to assess the effectiveness of his existing offers.

SPECIFIC OBJECTIVES

In the past, Jim has favored the use of five types of coupons, and he now wishes to determine their independent appeal, together with their relation to several identifiable characteristics of fast-food consumers. The five promotional concepts are listed in Table 3.5.1. The consumer characteristics that Jim's experience tells him warrant investigation include number of children living at home, age of youngest child, propensity to eat fast food, propensity to eat Premium Pizza in particular, preference for slices over pies, propensity to use coupons, and occupation.

The specific objectives of the research study can therefore be summarized as follows:

1. To evaluate the independent appeal of the five promotional deals to determine which deals are most preferred.

2. To gain insight into the reasons that certain deals are preferred.

3. To examine the relationships between the appeal of each promotional concept and various consumer characteristics.

TABLE 3.5.1	**Five Promotional Concepts**
Coupon A	Get a medium soft drink for 5 cents with the purchase of any slice.
Coupon B	Buy a slice and get a second slice of comparable value free.
Coupon C	Save 50 cents on the purchase of any slice and receive one free trip to the salad bar.
Coupon D	Buy a slice and a large soft drink and get a second slice free.
Coupon E	Get a single-topping slice for only 99 cents.

PROPOSED METHODOLOGY

After much discussion, Jim's research team finally decided that the desired information could best be gathered by means of personal interviews, using a combination of open-ended and closed questions. A medium-sized shopping mall on the outskirts of a metropolitan area in the Midwest was selected as the research site. Shoppers were intercepted by professional interviewers while walking in the mall and asked to participate in a survey requiring five minutes of their time.

The sampling procedure employed a convenience sample in which interviewers were instructed to approach anyone passing by, providing that they met certain criteria (see Figure 3.5.1). In sum, the sample of respondents was restricted to adult men and women between the ages of 18 and 49 who had both purchased lunch, dinner, or carryout food at a fast-food restaurant in the past seven days and had eaten restaurant pizza within the last 30 days, either at a restaurant or delivered to the home. In addition, interviewers were warned not to exercise any bias during the selection process, as they would do, for example, if they approached only those people who looked particularly agreeable or attractive. Finally, interviewers were asked to obtain as close as possible to a 50–50 split of male and female participants.

The questionnaire was organized into three sections (see Figure 3.5.2). The first section contained the screening questions aimed at ensuring that respondents qualified for the sample. In the second section, respondents were asked to evaluate on 10-point scales the appeal of each of the five promotional concepts based on two factors: perceived value and likelihood of use. After they had evaluated a concept, interviewees were asked to give reasons for their likelihood-of-use rating. The third and final section consisted of the questions on consumer characteristics that Jim believed to be pertinent.

The questionnaire was to be completed by the interviewer based on the respondent's comments. In other words, the interviewer read the questions aloud and wrote down the answer given in each case by the interviewee. It was decided to show respondents an example of each coupon before they rated it. For this purpose, enlarged photographs of each coupon were produced. It was also thought necessary to depict the 10-point scales that consumers should use to evaluate the promotional offer. Coupons and scales were therefore assembled in a booklet so that, as the interviewer showed each double-page spread, the respondent

FIGURE 3.5.1	Interviewer Instructions

Below are suggestions for addressing each question. Please read all the instructions before you begin questioning people.

Interviewer Instructions
Approach shoppers who appear to be between 18 and 49 years of age. Since we would like equal numbers of respondents in each age category and a 50 percent male-female ratio, please do not select respondents based on their appeal to you. The interview should take approximately five minutes. When reading questions, read answer choices *if indicated.*

Question 1:   Terminate any respondent who has not eaten lunch or dinner from any fast-food restaurant in the last seven days.

Question 2:   Terminate any respondent who has not eaten pizza within the last 30 days. This includes carry-out, drive-thru, or dining in.

Question 3:   Terminate respondent if not between 18 and 49 years of age. If between 18 and 49, circle the appropriate number answer. For this question, please read the question and the answer choices.

After completing questions 1 through 3, hand respondent the coupon booklet. *Make sure that the booklet and the response sheets are the same color.* Also check to see that the coupon booklet number indicated on the upper right-hand corner of the response sheet matches the coupon book number.

Question 4:   Ask the respondent to open the coupon booklet and read the first coupon concept. Read the first section of Question 4 showing the respondent that the scales are provided on the page above the coupon concept. Enter his or her answer in the box provided.

                Read the second section of the question and enter respondent's answer in the second box provided.

                When asking the respondent, "Why did you respond as you did for use," please record the first reason mentioned and use the lines provided to probe and clarify the reasons.

This set of instructions applies to Questions 5 through 8. Periodically remind the respondent to look at the scales provided on the page above the coupon concept that he or she is looking at.

Question 9:   Enter number of children living at home. If none, enter the number zero and proceed to Question 11.

Question 10:   Enter age of *youngest* child living at home in the box provided.

Question 11:   Read the question and each answer slowly. Circle the number corresponding to the appropriate answer.

Question 12:   Read the question and each answer slowly. Circle the number corresponding to the appropriate answer. If answer is never, proceed to Question 14. Otherwise, continue to Question 13.

Question 13:   Circle the number corresponding to the appropriate answer. Do not read answer choices.

Question 14:   Circle the number corresponding to the appropriate answer. Do not read answer choices.

Question 15:   Read the question and each answer slowly. Circle the number corresponding to the appropriate answer.

Question 16:   Read the question and each answer slowly. Circle the number corresponding to the appropriate answer.

Question 17:   If an explanation is requested for occupation, please tell respondent that we are looking for a broad category or title. "No occupation" is not an acceptable answer. If this should happen, please probe to see if the person is a student, homemaker, retired, unemployed, etc.

At the end of the questionnaire, you are asked to indicate whether the respondent was male or female. Please circle the appropriate answer. This is not a question for the respondent.

FIGURE 3.5.2   Questionnaire

Response Number   _____
Coupon Book #   _____

(Approach shoppers who appear to be between the ages of 18 and 49 and say . . .)

Hi, I'm _____ from Midwest Research Services. Many companies like to know your preferences and opinions about new products and promotions. If you have about 5 minutes, I'd like to have your opinions in this marketing research study.

(If refused, terminate)

1. *Have you eaten lunch or dinner in, or carried food away from, a fast-food restaurant in the last seven days?*

   . . . **(must answer yes to continue)**

2. *Have you eaten restaurant pizza within the last 30 days, either at the restaurant or by having it delivered?*

   . . . **(must answer yes to continue)**

3. *Which age group are you in?* **(read answers, circle number)**
   1 18–24   2 25–34   3 35–49   4 Other — Terminate interview

I am now going to show you five different coupon concepts and ask you three questions for each. Please respond to each coupon independently of the others. Look at the next coupon only when I ask you to.

4. *Please read the first coupon concept. Using a ten-point scale as shown on the page above, how would you rate this concept if one represents very poor value and ten represents very good value?*

   [ ] enter value

   *Looking at the second scale, how would you rate this concept if one represents definitely would **not** use and ten represents definitely would use?*

   [ ] enter value

   *Why did you respond as you did for use?*_____
   _____
   _____

5. *Please turn the page and read the next coupon concept. Ignoring the last coupon and using the same scale, how would you rate this concept in terms of value?*

   [ ] enter value

   Referring to the second scale, how would you rate this concept in terms of your level of use?

   [ ] enter value

   *Why did you respond as you did for use?*_____
   _____
   _____

FIGURE 3.5.2 (continued)

6. *Please turn the page and read the next coupon concept. Ignoring the last coupon and using the same scale, how would you rate this concept in terms of value?*

enter value

Referring to the second scale, how would you rate this concept in terms of your level of use?

enter value

*Why did you respond as you did for use?*_____
_____
_____

7. *Please turn the page and read the next coupon concept. Ignoring the last coupon and using the same scale, how would you rate this concept in terms of value?*

enter value

Referring to the second scale, how would you rate this concept in terms of your level of use?

enter value

*Why did you respond as you did for use?*_____
_____
_____

8. *Please turn the page and read the next coupon concept. Ignoring the last coupon and using the same scale, how would you rate this concept in terms of value?*

enter value

Referring to the second scale, how would you rate this concept in terms of your level of use?

enter value

*Why did you respond as you did for use?*_____
_____
_____

Thank you. The following questions will help us classify the preceding information.

9. *How many children do you have living at home?*
If answer is none, proceed to question 11.

enter number
none = 0

10. *What is the age of your youngest child?*

11. *How often do you eat fast food for lunch or dinner?*
(read answers, circle number) 1 Once per month or less
2 Two to three times per month
3 Once or twice a week
4 More than twice a week

(continued)

FIGURE 3.5.2 (continued)

12. *How often do you eat at Premium Pizza?*
    (read answers, circle number) 1 Never visited Premium Pizza
    2 Once per month or less
    3 Two to three times per month
    4 Once a week or more
    If answer is never, proceed to question 14.

13. *Do you* **yourself** *usually buy whole pies or slices at Premium Pizza?*
    1 whole pies
    2 slices
    (circle one)

14. *Have you used fast-food or restaurant coupons in the last 30 days?*
    1 yes
    2 no
    (circle one)

15. *Have you ever used coupons for Premium Pizzas?*
    (read answers, circle number) 1 Never
    2 I sometimes use them when I have them.
    3 I always use them when I have them.

16. *What is your marital status:*
    (read answers, circle number) 1 Single
    2 Married
    3 Divorced, separated, widowed

17. *What is your occupation?*_____

This is *not* **a question for the respondent.**
Please circle appropriate answer — respondent was: 1 male
    2 female
    (circle number)

Thank you for your participation — **Terminate interview at this time.**

---

would see the scales on the top page and the coupon in question on the bottom page (see Figure 3.5.3).

Because the researcher wished to counterbalance the order in which the coupons were viewed and rated, the five coupons were organized into booklets of six different sequences. Each sequence was subsequently bound in one of six distinctly colored binders. A total of 96 questionnaires were then printed in six different colors to match the binder. In this way, there were 16 questionnaires of each color, and the color of the respondent's questionnaire indicated the sequence that he or she had seen.

The questionnaire and procedure were pretested at a mall similar to the target mall and were found to be satisfactory.

QUESTIONS

1. Is the choice of mall intercept interviews an appropriate data-collection method given the research objectives?

2. Do you think that there are any specific criteria that the choice of shopping mall should satisfy?

FIGURE 3.5.3   **Stimuli**

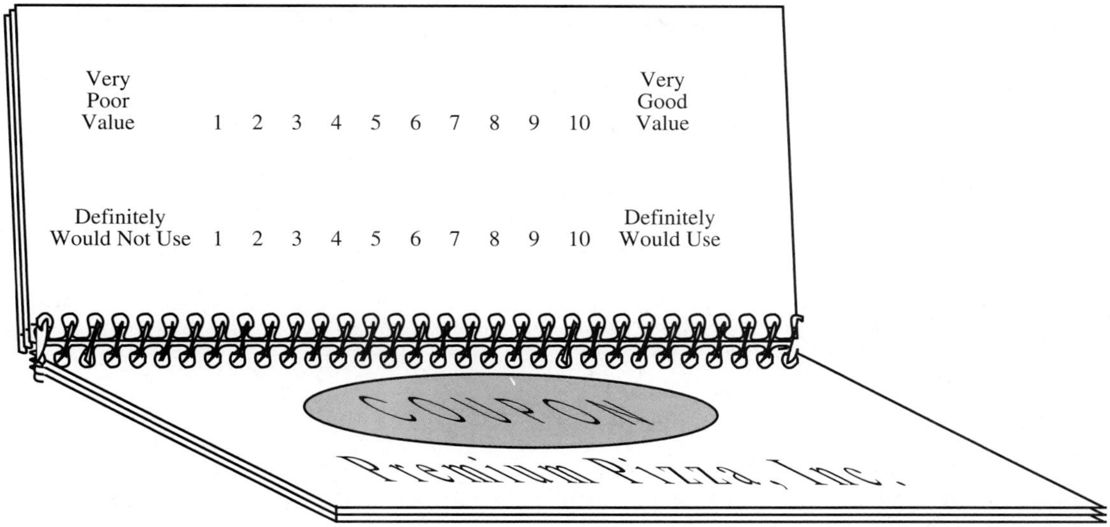

| Very Poor Value | 1 2 3 4 5 6 7 8 9 10 | Very Good Value |

| Definitely Would Not Use | 1 2 3 4 5 6 7 8 9 10 | Definitely Would Use |

COUPON

Premium Pizza, Inc.

3. Evaluate the instructions to interviewers (Figure 3.5.1).

4. Evaluate the questionnaire (Figure 3.5.2).

5. Do you think that it is worthwhile to present the coupons in a binder, separate from the questionnaire? Why or why not?

6. Do you consider it advisable to rotate the order of presentation of coupons? Why or why not?

CASE 3.6

School of Business[1]

The School of Business, one unit in a public university enrolling over 40,000 students, has approximately 2,100 students in its bachelor's, master's, and doctorate programs, emphasizing such areas of business as accounting, finance, information and operations management, marketing, and management. Because the School of Business must serve a diverse student population on limited resources, it feels it is important to measure accurately students' satisfaction with the school's programs and services.

Accurate measurement of student satisfaction will enable the school to target improvement efforts to those areas of greatest concern to students, whether that be by major, support services, or some other aspect of their educational experience. The school feels that improving its service to its customers (students) will result in more satisfied alumni, better community relations, additional applicants, and increased corporate involvement. Because graduate and undergraduate students are believed to have different expectations and needs, the school plans to investigate the satisfaction of these two groups separately.

In a previous survey of graduating seniors using open-ended questions, three primary areas of concern were identified: the faculty, classes/curriculum, and resources. Resources consisted of five specific areas: Undergraduate Advising Services, the Learning Center, Computer Facilities, the Library, and the Career Services Office. The research team for this project developed five-point Likert-scale questions to measure students' satisfaction in each of these areas. In addition, demographic questions were included to determine whether satisfaction with the school was a function of a student's grade point average, major, job status upon graduation, or gender. Previous surveys used by the School of Business and other published satisfaction scales provided examples of questions and question formats. Figure 3.6.1 shows the questionnaire that was used.

---

[1]The contributions of Sara L. Pitterle to the development of this case are gratefully acknowledged.

FIGURE 3.6.1   Survey of Graduating Business Students

In your opinion, what are the greatest strengths and weaknesses of the Business School?

Strengths:

Weaknesses:

Classes/Curriculum

Please indicate the extent to which you agree with the following statements.

	Strongly Agree (1)	Agree (2)	Neither Agree/Dis. (3)	Disagree (4)	Strongly Disagree (5)				
I was satisfied with the quality of classes I took within my major.						1	2	3	4	5
I was able to take enough electives within my major.						1	2	3	4	5
"Lecture-Driven" vs. "Project" or "Group" class formats are most useful for learning.						1	2	3	4	5
The Business School taught too much theory and not enough about real-life applications.						1	2	3	4	5
Creative problem solving was encouraged in my classes.						1	2	3	4	5
My classes were too large.						1	2	3	4	5
I was challenged by my coursework.						1	2	3	4	5
There were not enough group projects in my classes.						1	2	3	4	5
More night courses should be offered.						1	2	3	4	5
Overall, the material presented in my classes was current.						1	2	3	4	5

Faculty

My professors are concerned about my future success.						1	2	3	4	5
Overall, the Business School professors are good teachers.						1	2	3	4	5
The Business School places too much emphasis on research and not enough on teaching.						1	2	3	4	5
Overall, my professors were accessible outside of class.						1	2	3	4	5
The Business School takes my comments on professor evaluation forms seriously.						1	2	3	4	5
Overall, my professors provided adequate office hours during the term.						1	2	3	4	5
Overall, my professors encouraged students to raise relevant questions during class.						1	2	3	4	5
My professors tested memorization skills on exams more than ability to apply concepts.						1	2	3	4	5
Overall, the Business School professors interacted well with students.						1	2	3	4	5
My professors showed creativity in their teaching methods.						1	2	3	4	5
My professors are at the leading edge of knowledge in their fields.						1	2	3	4	5
I approve of TA's teaching foundation courses.						1	2	3	4	5
My professors were stimulating.						1	2	3	4	5

Resources

Advising

Did you ever use the undergraduate advising office?   Yes   No

    If not, why not?

FIGURE 3.6.1   (continued)

If you answered yes to the question above, please complete the remainder of the questions regarding Advising. If you answered no, please proceed to the following section: Learning Center.

	Strongly Agree (1)	Agree (2)	Neither Agree/Dis. (3)	Disagree (4)	Strongly Disagree (5)				
The advising office played a big role in helping me plan my business curriculum.						1	2	3	4	5
The undergraduate advising office should have more advisors.						1	2	3	4	5
The advisor(s) in the undergraduate advising office was (were) helpful.						1	2	3	4	5
The staff in the advising office was helpful.						1	2	3	4	5
I felt like I was bothering the advisor(s) if I asked him/her a question.						1	2	3	4	5
The advisor(s) in the advising office was (were) concerned about my needs.						1	2	3	4	5
If there were more advisors, I would have used the advising services more often.						1	2	3	4	5
Advice offered by the advising office was not helpful to me.						1	2	3	4	5

Learning Center
Did you ever use The Learning Center?   Yes   No
    If not, why not?

If you answered yes to the question above, please complete the remainder of the questions regarding The Learning Center. If you answered no, please proceed to the following section: Career-Services Facilities/Staff.

	Strongly Agree (1)	Agree (2)	Neither Agree/Dis. (3)	Disagree (4)	Strongly Disagree (5)				
The Learning Center was useful to me.						1	2	3	4	5
The staff at The Learning Center is helpful.						1	2	3	4	5
The Learning Center needs to extend its hours.						1	2	3	4	5

Career-Services Facilities/Staff
Did you ever use the Career-Services office as a resource in your search for full- or part-time employment?   Yes   No
    If not, why not?

If you answered yes to the question above, please complete the remainder of the questions regarding Career-Services Facilities/Staff. If you answered no, please proceed to the following section: Computer Facilities/Staff.

	Strongly Agree (1)	Agree (2)	Neither Agree/Dis. (3)	Disagree (4)	Strongly Disagree (5)				
Overall, the Career-Services office has been a valuable resource in my job search.						1	2	3	4	5
The Career-Services office is/was my main resource used in my search for my job.						1	2	3	4	5
In my opinion, the Career-Services office is understaffed.						1	2	3	4	5
I was pleased with the # of companies interviewing within my major.						1	2	3	4	5
The sign-up process for interviews at the Career-Services office is fair.						1	2	3	4	5
The office provides enough information on how to use the Resume Expert software.						1	2	3	4	5
The Career-Services office offers adequate interview training.						1	2	3	4	5

(continued)

FIGURE 3.6.1   **(continued)**

Computer Facilities/Staff
Did you ever use the Business School's computer facilities?   Yes   No
   If not, why not?

If you answered yes to the question above, please complete the remainder of the questions regarding Computer Facilities/Staff. If you answered no, please proceed to the following section: Library Facilities/Staff.

	Strongly Agree (1)	Agree (2)	Neither Agree/Dis. (3)	Disagree (4)	Strongly Disagree (5)					
The computer room needs to extend its weekend hours.						1	2	3	4	5
The computer room needs to extend its night hours.						1	2	3	4	5
More computers are needed in the computer room.						1	2	3	4	5
More printers are needed in the computer facilities.						1	2	3	4	5
The computer-room staff is helpful.						1	2	3	4	5
A computer was available when I needed to use one.						1	2	3	4	5

Library Facilities/Staff
Did you use the Business School's library facilities?   Yes   No
   If not, why not?

If you answered yes to the question above, please complete the remainder of the questions regarding Library Facilities/Staff. If you answered no, please proceed to the following section—Student Organizations.

	Strongly Agree (1)	Agree (2)	Neither Agree/Dis. (3)	Disagree (4)	Strongly Disagree (5)					
The Library staff is helpful.						1	2	3	4	5
The Library has adequate study space.						1	2	3	4	5

Student Organizations
Were you a member of any Business School student organizations?   Yes   No
   If not, why not?

If you answered yes to the question above, please complete the remainder of the questions regarding Student Organizations. If you answered no, please proceed to the following section—**General.**
How many organizations were you a member of?   1   2   3   more than 3
Did you hold an office?   Yes   No

FIGURE 3.6.1   (continued)

Do you believe the faculty and staff were supportive of the student organizations?   Yes   No   Don't know
What were your reasons for joining?

	Strongly Agree (1)	Agree (2)	Neither Agree/Dis. (3)	Disagree (4)	Strongly Disagree (5)

General

My Business School education has given me a sense of accomplishment.	1	2	3	4	5
The Business School is well respected nationally.	1	2	3	4	5
My undergraduate degree has prepared me well for a successful career in business.	1	2	3	4	5
The caliber of my classmates enhanced my learning.	1	2	3	4	5
The Business School should require more computer courses.	1	2	3	4	5
The copying facilities at the Business School are inadequate.	1	2	3	4	5
My undergraduate experience was disappointing.	1	2	3	4	5
The Business School placed too much emphasis on grades and not enough on learning.	1	2	3	4	5
I felt like a number here at the Business School.	1	2	3	4	5
The Business School should have a mandatory class on ethics for undergraduates.	1	2	3	4	5

Please indicate the extent to which you agree that each of the following factors *positively contributed* to the quality of your overall undergraduate business education:

Class size in major classes	1	2	3	4	5
Class size in required courses	1	2	3	4	5
Group projects	1	2	3	4	5
Case studies	1	2	3	4	5
Multiple-choice exams	1	2	3	4	5
Use of creative thought	1	2	3	4	5
Guest lecturers	1	2	3	4	5
Required classes	1	2	3	4	5
Number of electives you can take	1	2	3	4	5
Number of required computer courses	1	2	3	4	5

Please indicate the extent to which you agree that each of the following core classes *positively contributed* to the quality of your overall undergraduate business education:

Computer Science	1	2	3	4	5
Managerial Acctg.	1	2	3	4	5
Financial Acctg.	1	2	3	4	5
Communications	1	2	3	4	5
Business Law	1	2	3	4	5
Corporate Finance	1	2	3	4	5
Marketing	1	2	3	4	5
Org. Behavior	1	2	3	4	5
Business Statistics	1	2	3	4	5
Operations	1	2	3	4	5
OVERALL	1	2	3	4	5

General Information

Please mark the number corresponding to your gender.   Female   Male
Are you a state resident?   Yes   No
Please check your major(s).

_____ Accounting	_____ Marketing
_____ Actuarial Science	_____ Quantitative Analysis
_____ Diversified	_____ Real Estate
_____ Finance	_____ Risk Management
_____ Information Systems	_____ Transportation and Public Utilities
_____ Management and Human Resources	

(continued)

FIGURE 3.6.1   **(continued)**

Please check your GPA.
_____ 3.5–4.0
_____ 3.0–3.49
_____ 2.5–2.99
_____ 2.0–2.49
During the program (excluding summers), have you been employed?
_____ Employed full-time
_____ Employed part-time
_____ Not employed
What do you plan to do upon graduation?
_____ full-time employment
_____ part-time employment
_____ graduate school
_____ other, please specify _____
If you intend to work full time, please specify if you:
_____ have already accepted a position
_____ are still in the process of interviewing
_____ other, please specify _____

THANK YOU FOR COMPLETING THE SURVEY OF GRADUATING BUSINESS STUDENTS.

Although the survey contained primarily Likert-scale questions, a few open-ended questions were also asked. Specifically, respondents were asked to list the Business School's strengths and weaknesses as well as their reasons for not using the various resource areas. The responses obtained to the question seeking the school's strengths and weaknesses were classified into four major subgroups: classes, reputation, resources, and professors. A sample of the actual verbatim responses are provided in Table 3.6.1.

TABLE 3.6.1   **A Sample of the Survey Responses to Question 1 Regarding Strengths and Weaknesses**

Strengths	Weaknesses
"Breadth of courses and disciplines."	"Not enough real-life applications"
"The increase in group projects was also helpful."	"Core classes tedious."
"Classes in your major are relatively small."	"Too much emphasis on GPA."
"Excellent faculty advising (not undergrad advising)."	"Lack of advisors."
"Good Faculty"	"Lack of support facilities."
"Excellent Profs"	"Awful Undergraduate advising."
"Has a good reputation."	"Classes are too much on theory."
"Required some thought-provoking classes (literature, philosophy)."	"The computer classes are a waste of time."
"Free laser printing in the computer lab."	"Too many unnecessary core requirements that could be used for another class or elective."
"The resources for information gathering are great."	"Too many exams scheduled in the 6th and 12th weeks."
"The options of resources available are great."	"Too many required group projects."
"The competitiveness, quality of students."	"Can't get classes when needed."
"Nice that classes aren't greatly dependent on Fridays (open to work or volunteering)."	"Too few resources for the number of students."
"Clear curriculum of what classes are needed if in Pre-Business or Business—although there are a lot of them, the core classes allow you to touch all majors."	"Students not treated as individuals."
	"Not enough computers."
	"Makes students take core classes in each function of business."
"A well-respected and less costly route to a business undergrad degree than other alternatives available."	"Need more case studies & seminar type classes with fewer students."
"A few good professors that make up for all the bad ones."	"There is too much memorization and not enough practical application of knowledge."
"Some of the professors are terrific and really care about the students."	"Making appointments to see advisors."
	"Professors expect too much."
"National Reputation."	"Computer courses are too technical."

QUESTIONS

1. Considering customer satisfaction as it applies to a university setting, what are some other areas in addition to those identified for this project that may contribute to students' satisfaction/dissatisfaction with their education experience?

2. Does the current questionnaire provide information on students' overall satisfaction with their undergraduate degree program? Explain. What revisions are necessary to this questionnaire to obtain an overall satisfaction rating?

3. Can the School of Business use the results of this study to target the most important areas for improvement? Explain. Identify changes to the questionnaire that would allow the school to target areas based on importance.

4. What are the advantages and disadvantages of using open-ended questions to identify the school's strengths and weaknesses? Taking the responses in Table 3.6.1, what system would you use for coding these responses?

5. Reading through the sample of verbatim responses to Question 1 on the questionnaire, highlight some of the difficulties.

CASE 3.7

CTM Productions (A)[1]

CTM Productions, formerly Children's Theatre of Madison, was formed in 1965 to "produce theater of

_____

[1]The contributions of Sara L. Pitterle to this case are gratefully acknowledged.

the highest quality." CTM's mission is to "ensure that our [CTM's] efforts are inclusive of all the human family, rather than parts of it." In order to measure its present and future achievement of this goal, CTM must learn who its audience actually is.

CTM's research team decided to study the audience of CTM's production *To Kill a Mockingbird*. The study had three major objectives: (1) to develop an audience profile, including demographic and media exposure data; (2) to provide a framework and data-collection instrument for future marketing research; and (3) to supply a list of potential season subscribers. CTM had never undertaken any marketing research before this study, so internal secondary information did not exist. External secondary information provided guidance as to the types of questions to be asked on this type of questionnaire and the appropriate phrasing for such questions. The questionnaire is shown in Figure 3.7.1.

CTM's volunteer ushers distributed the survey at each performance of *To Kill a Mockingbird*. The volunteers gave the survey and a pencil to all adults attending the performances (for the purpose of this survey, adults were defined as anyone 16 years or older). Respondents were instructed to complete the questionnaire and hand it back to the ushers during the intermission. In addition, collection boxes were placed next to all the exits. Although the survey was intended for all adult members of the audience, it is unclear as to whether these instructions were followed at every performance.

CTM Productions held five shows each weekend for three weekends. Surveys were distributed at each of the 15 performances; however, the number of completed surveys varied with the size of the audience for

---

FIGURE 3.7.1   CTM Questionnaire

Introduce Yourself to CTM

Welcome to CTM's production of *To Kill a Mockingbird*. CTM Productions has been around for a long time — since 1965. And in this time we have had over 33,000 people in our audience. People to whom we have never been introduced. Real people like you that presently exist as numbers in our records. Now you have a chance to change your status. Introduce yourself to us by taking two minutes to answer the following questions to help us understand who you really are.

Let's start out with the basics. Your name is_____
and you live at (please include mailing address with ZIP Code)_____

_____

(continued)

FIGURE 3.7.1   (continued)

How many CTM productions have you attended?   [   ] this is my first CTM production

1997–1998 Season	**1996–1997 Season**	**1995–1996 Season**
[ ] season subscriber	[ ] season subscriber	[ ] season subscriber
[ ] *Wind in the Willows*	[ ] *Red Shoes*	[ ] *Beauty and the Beast*
[ ] *A Christmas Carol*	[ ] *A Christmas Carol*	[ ] *A Christmas Carol*
[X] *To Kill a Mockingbird*	[ ] *Anne of Green Gables*	[ ] *I Remember Mama*
[ ] *Babar II* (plan to attend)	[ ] *Narnia*	[ ] *Babar the Elephant*

Who is with you today? (check all that apply)

[ ] myself	[ ] my spouse/partner	[ ] my kids
[ ] adult friend(s)	[ ] unrelated kids	[ ] other families

Who have you attended with in the past? (again, check all that apply)

[ ] myself	[ ] my spouse/partner	[ ] my kids
[ ] adult friend(s)	[ ] unrelated kids	[ ] other families

Have you or any of your family participated in any of these CTM activities? (check all that apply)

[ ] after-school drama classes	[ ] auditions	[ ] have not participated
[ ] summer school	[ ] performances	[ ] did not know I could

How did you find out about our production of **To Kill a Mockingbird**? (check all that apply)

[   ] season brochure   [   ] poster

Read story in:

[ ] *State Journal*	[ ] *Capitol Times*	[ ] *Isthmus*	[ ] other

Saw ad in:

[   ] *State Journal*   [   ] *Capitol Times*   [   ] *Isthmus*   [   ] other
[   ] radio (which station)_____
[   ] television (which station)_____
[   ] magazine (which one)_____
[   ] word of mouth   [   ] other

Did you come to this performance because you knew someone in the cast?   [   ] yes   [   ] no

What other events have you attended in the last six months? (check all that apply)
    With your family or friends:

[ ] sports	[ ] movies	[ ] live musical performances
[ ] museums	[ ] lectures	[ ] other live theatrical performances

FIGURE 3.7.1   (continued)

Alone:

[ ] sports   [ ] movies   [ ] live musical performances
[ ] museums   [ ] lectures   [ ] other live theatrical performances

Your answers to the following demographic questions will help us understand who you are.

Are you a female or male?   [ ] female   [ ] male

Which age category do you belong to?

[ ] 16–20   [ ] 31–40   [ ] 51–60   [ ] 71–80
[ ] 21–30   [ ] 41–50   [ ] 61–70   [ ] 81–100

How did you get here today?

[ ] walked   [ ] car   [ ] bus   [ ] other

From how far away did you come?

[ ] within Madison   [ ] less than 5 miles   [ ] 6–10 miles   [ ] over 10 miles

How long have you lived in the Madison/south-central Wisconsin area?

[ ] do not live here   [ ] just arrived   [ ] 1–3 years   [ ] 4–7 years   [ ] more

What is your highest level of education?

[ ] some high school   [ ] some college   [ ] some graduate school   [ ] more
[ ] high school graduate [ ] college graduate [ ] graduate school graduate

What is your annual household income?

[ ] below $20,000 [ ] $31–40,000 [ ] more than $50,000 [ ] do not wish to reply
[ ] $21–30,000   [ ] $41–50,000 [ ] not sure

Does this represent a dual income household?   [ ] yes   [ ] no

How many people live in your household? **(circle only one, include yourself)**

1   2   3   4   5   6   more

If you have children, how many are in each grade category?

[ ] not in school yet   [ ] 4th–5th grade   [ ] high school   [ ] other
[ ] kindergarten–3rd grade   [ ] 6th–8th grade   [ ] college

Would you like to be on our mailing list to keep informed of CTM activities?   [ ] yes   [ ] no

(continued)

FIGURE 3.7.1   (continued)

Are you a CTM member?   [ ] yes   [ ] no

Now here's your chance to share your thoughts with us.

I wish I had known that CTM _____

I'm glad CTM _____

I wish CTM would _____

I want CTM to know _____

It was a real pleasure meeting you. CTM looks forward to seeing you again very soon.

---

each show. A total of 1,016 usable surveys were collected during the course of the study.

QUESTIONS

1. The CTM research term used secondary data for question types and wording of specific questions. Did the research team use secondary information effectively in this study?

2. Read through the questionnaire shown in Figure 3.7.1. Does the questionnaire provide CTM with the information necessary to meet the stated objectives? Explain.

3. Considering CTM's objectives, does the sampling plan used for the study provide the necessary information? Does the sampling plan bias the results?

CASE 3.8

Calamity-Casualty Insurance Company

Calamity-Casualty is an insurance company located in Dallas, Texas, that deals exclusively with automobile coverage. Its policy offerings include the standard features offered by most insurers, such as collision, comprehensive, emergency road service, medical, and uninsured motorist. The unique aspect of Calamity-Casualty Insurance is that all policies are sold through direct mail. Agents do not make personal calls on clients, and the company does not operate district offices. As a result, Calamity-Casualty's capital/labor requirements are greatly reduced at a substantial cost savings to the company. A great portion of these savings are passed on to the consumer in the form of lower prices (that is, 20 to 25 percent below the average market rate).

The company's strategy of selling automobile insurance by mail at low prices has been very successful. Calamity-Casualty has traditionally been the third largest seller of automobile insurance in the Southwest. During the past five years, the company has consistently achieved an average market share of some 14 percent in the four states it serves: Arizona, New Mexico, Nevada, and Texas. This compares favorably to the 19 percent and 17 percent market shares realized by the two leading firms in the region. However, Calamity-Casualty has never been highly successful in Arizona. The largest market share gained by Calamity-Casualty in Arizona for any one year was 4 percent, which placed the company seventh among firms competing in that state.

The company's poor performance in Arizona greatly concerns Calamity-Casualty's board of executives. Demographic experts estimate that during the next six to ten years, the population in Arizona will increase 10 to 15 percent, the largest projected growth rate of any state in the Southwest. Thus, for Calamity-Casualty to remain a major market force in the area, the company needs to improve its sales performance in Arizona.

TABLE 3.8.1	Calamity-Casualty Marketing Research Questionnaire Items

Risk Aversion
1. It is always better to buy a used car from a dealer than from an individual.
2. Generally speaking, I avoid buying generic drugs at the drugstore.
3. It would be a disaster to be stranded on the road due to a breakdown.
4. It would be important to me to plan a long road trip very carefully and in great detail.
5. I would like to try parachute jumping sometime.
6. Before buying a new product, I would first discuss it with someone who had already used it.
7. Before deciding to see a new movie in a theater, it is important to read the critical reviews.
8. If my car needed even a minor repair, I would first get cost estimates from several garages.

Powerlessness
1. Persons like myself have little chance of protecting our personal interests when they conflict with those of strong pressure groups.
2. A lasting world peace can be achieved by those of us who work toward it.
3. I think each of us can do a great deal to improve world opinion of the United States.
4. This world is run by the few people in power, and there is not much the little guy can do about it.
5. People like me can change the course of world events if we make ourselves heard.

6. More and more, I feel helpless in the face of what's happening in the world today.

Convenience Orientation
1. I like to buy things by mail or catalog because it saves time.
2. I think that it is not worth the extra effort to clip coupons for groceries.
3. I would rather wash my own car than pay to have it washed at a car wash.
4. I would prefer to have an automatic transmission rather than a stick shift in my car.
5. When choosing a bank, I believe that location is the most important factor.
6. When shopping for groceries, I would be willing to drive a longer distance in order to buy at lower prices.

Note: Each item requires one of the following responses:

Responses	Code
S.A.—Strongly Agree	5
A.—Agree	4
N.—Neither Agree nor Disagree	3
D.—Disagree	2
S.D.—Strongly Disagree	1

In response to this matter, Calamity-Casualty sponsored a study that was conducted by the Automobile Insurance Association of America (AIAA), the national association of automobile insurance executives, to determine Arizona residents' attitudes toward and perception of the various insurance companies selling policies in that state. The results of the AIAA research showed that Calamity-Casualty was favorably perceived across most categories measured. Calamity-Casualty received the highest ratings with respect to service, pricing, policy offering, and image. Although these findings were well received by the company's board of executives, they provided little strategic insight into how Calamity-Casualty might increase sales in Arizona.

Because the company was committed to obtaining information useful for developing a more effective Arizona sales campaign, the executive board sought the services of Aminbane, Pedrone, and Associates, a marketing research firm specializing in insurance consulting, to help with the matter. After many discussions between members of the research team

and executives at Calamity-Casualty, it was decided that the most beneficial approach toward designing a more appropriate sales campaign would be to ascertain the psychographic profiles of nonpurchasers and direct-mail purchasers of Calamity-Casualty insurance. This would help the company better understand the personal factors influencing people's decision to respond or not to respond to direct-mail solicitation.

Research Design

To learn more about which psychographic factors are important in describing purchasers of automobile insurance, some exploratory research was undertaken. In-depth interviews were held with two insurance salespersons, who offered various insights on the subject. These experience interviews were followed by a focus group meeting with Arizona residents who had received a direct-mail offer from Calamity-Casualty. Finally, the research team consulted university professors in both psychology and mass communications to uncover other determinants of buyer behavior. Output from these procedures revealed three psychographic factors that could be used to segment purchasers of insurance by mail—namely, risk aversion, powerlessness, and convenience orientation. It was believed that people who were risk averse, had a low sense of powerlessness, and were convenience-oriented would be more favorably disposed toward direct-mail marketing efforts and thus would be more likely to purchase Calamity-Casualty automobile insurance.

METHOD OF DATA COLLECTION

Given these factors of interest, the list of items contained in Table 3.8.1 was generated to form the basis of a questionnaire to be administered to Arizona residents. Two samples of subjects were to be used—one of direct-mail buyers and one of nonbuyers. The research team estimated that 175 subjects would be required from both samples to adequately assess the three constructs. Because a mail questionnaire dealing with psychographic subject matter might have a very low response rate, and because attitude toward direct mail was one of the attributes being measured, a telephone interview was believed to be best suited to the needs at hand.

QUESTIONS

1. Conceptually, what are the constructs *risk aversion, convenience orientation,* and *powerlessness?*

2. Do you think that the sample of items adequately assesses each construct? Can you think of any additional items that could or should be used?

Sample Design and Data Collection

Part 4 is concerned with the actual collection of data needed to answer a problem. Chapter 10 discusses the various types of sampling plans that can be employed to determine the population elements from which the data should be collected; Chapter 11 treats the question of how many of these elements are needed to answer the problem with precision and confidence in the results; and Chapter 12 discusses the many errors that can arise in completing this data-collection task.

10

Sampling Procedures

Once the researcher has clearly specified the problem and developed an appropriate research design and data-collection instrument, the next step in the research process is to select those elements from which the information will be collected. One way to do this would be to collect information from each member of the population of interest by completely canvassing this population. A complete canvass of a population is called a **census**. Another way would be to collect information from a portion of the population by taking a **sample** of elements from the larger group, and, on the basis of the information collected from the subset, to infer something about the larger group. One's ability to make this inference from subset to larger group depends on the method by which the sample of elements was chosen. A major part of this chapter is devoted to the "why" and "how" of taking a sample.

Incidentally, *population* here refers not only to people but also to manufacturing firms, retail or wholesale institutions, or even inanimate objects, such as parts produced in a manufacturing plant. **Target population** is defined as the totality of cases that conform to some designated specifications. The specifications define the elements that belong to the target group and those that are to be excluded. A study aimed at establishing a demographic profile of frozen-pizza eaters requires specifying who is to be considered a frozen-pizza eater. Anyone who has ever eaten a frozen pizza? Those who eat at least one such pizza a month? A week? Those who eat a certain minimum number of frozen pizzas per month? Researchers need to be very explicit in defining the target group of interest and most careful that they have actually sampled the target population and not some other population because an inappropriate or incomplete sampling frame was used.

One might choose a sample to infer something about a population rather than canvassing the population itself for several reasons. First, complete counts on populations of moderate size are very costly. Also, few marketing research studies warrant complete counts, because the information will often be obsolete by the time the census is completed and the information processed. Further, sometimes a census is impossible, such as when testing the life of electric light bulbs. A 100 percent inspection using the bulbs until they burned out would reveal the average bulb life but would leave no product to sell. Finally (and, to novice researchers, surprisingly), one might choose a sample over a census for purposes of accuracy. Censuses involve larger field staffs, which, in turn, introduce greater potential for nonsampling error. This is one reason the Bureau of the Census uses sample surveys to check the accuracy of various censuses. That is correct; samples are used to infer the accuracy of the census.[1]

Required Steps

Figure 10.1 outlines a useful six-step procedure that researchers can follow when drawing a sample of a population. Note that it is first necessary to define the target population or the collection of elements about which the researcher wishes to make an inference. Relevant elements thus are the objects on which measurements are taken. For example, when the preferences of children are involved, researchers have to decide whether the target population to be measured is the kids, their parents, or both:

FIGURE 10.1   **Six-Step Procedure for Drawing a Sample**

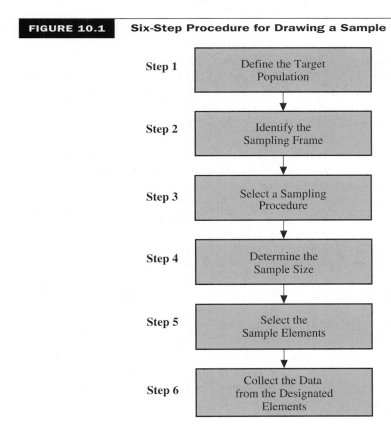

Step 1 — Define the Target Population

Step 2 — Identify the Sampling Frame

Step 3 — Select a Sampling Procedure

Step 4 — Determine the Sample Size

Step 5 — Select the Sample Elements

Step 6 — Collect the Data from the Designated Elements

[1]The fact that sample information is used to gauge the accuracy of the census has embroiled the Census Bureau in a debate about whether census counts should be adjusted on the basis of the sample results. For discussion of the controversy surrounding adjustment, see Haya El Nasser, "Bureau's Goal: Make Census Count," *USA Today* (April 15, 1998), p. 3A; Haya El Nasser, "Concerns With Census Seen in NJ Cities," *USA Today* (November 30, 1998), pp. 17A–18A.

One company tested its slotless road racing sets only with children. Kids loved 'em. But moms said they didn't like the sets because they were teaching children to crash cars, and dads didn't like the fact that the product was made into a toy.

It can work the other way, too. One company introduced a food product with a national ad campaign that starred a rather precocious child. The company tested the campaign only with mothers, who thought it was great. Kids thought the precocious child was obnoxious—and the product, too. End of product.[2]

The researcher must decide whether the target population consists of individuals, households, business firms, other institutions, credit-card transactions, or some other unit. In making this specification, the researcher also has to be careful to specify what units are to be excluded. This means specifying at a minimum both the geographic boundaries and the time period for the study, although additional restrictions are often placed on the elements. When the elements are individuals, for example, the target population may be defined as all those over 18, or females only, or those with a high school education only. A combination of age, sex, education, race, and other restrictions could also be used.

The problem of specifying the geographic boundaries for the target population is sometimes more difficult in international marketing research studies because of the additional complexity an international perspective introduces. For example, urban versus rural areas may be significantly different from each other in various countries. Also, the composition of the population can vary depending on the location within the country. For example, in Chile, the north has a highly centralized Indian population, whereas the south has high concentrations of individuals of European descent.

In general, the simpler the definition of the target population, the higher the incidence and the easier and less costly it is to find the sample.[3] **Incidence** refers to the percentage of the general population that satisfies the criteria defining the target population. Incidence has a direct bearing on the time and cost it takes to complete studies. When incidence is high (that is, most general population elements qualify for the study because only one or very few, easily satisfied criteria are used to screen potential respondents), the cost and time to collect data are minimized. Alternatively, as the number of criteria used to describe what constitutes eligible respondents for the study increases, so does the cost and time necessary to find them. Figure 10.2, for example, shows the percentage of adults who are estimated to participate in various sports. The data in the figure suggest that it would be more difficult and costly to focus a study on people who motorcycle, who are only 3.6 percent of all adults, than people who walk for health, 27.4 percent of all adults. The most important thing in defining the target population is that the researcher is precise in specifying exactly what elements are of interest and what elements are to be excluded. A clear statement of research objectives helps immeasurably in determining the appropriate elements of interest.

---

[2]Cyndee Miller, "Researching Children Isn't Kids' Stuff Anymore," *Marketing News* 24 (September 3, 1990), p. 32.

[3]Seymour Sudman, "Applied Sampling," in Peter H. Rossi, James D. Wright, and Andy B. Anderson, eds., *Handbook of Survey Research* (Orlando: Academic Press, 1983), pp. 145–194. See also "SSI-*LITe*™: *Low Incidence Targeted Sampling*" (Fairfield, CT: Survey Sampling, Inc., 1994).

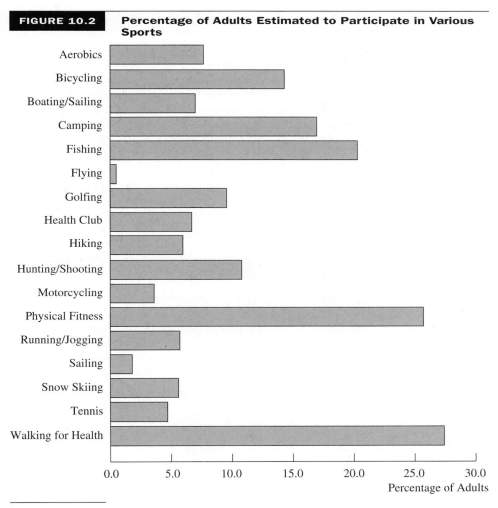

FIGURE 10.2 **Percentage of Adults Estimated to Participate in Various Sports**

Source: Developed from the information in "SSI-*LITe*®: *Low Incidence Targeted Sampling*" (Fairfield, CT: Survey Sampling, Inc., 1994).

The second step in the sample selection process is identifying the **sampling frame,** which is the listing of the elements from which the actual sample will be drawn. A telephone book is an obvious example of a sampling frame, which also illustrates the condition that there is rarely a perfect correspondence between the sampling frame and the target population of interest. Even though the target population may be all households in a particular metropolitan area, the telephone directory provides an inaccurate listing of these households, omitting some without phones and unlisted numbers and double counting others that have multiple listings. One of the researcher's more creative tasks in sampling is developing an appropriate sampling frame when the list of population elements is not readily available. This may mean sampling working blocks of numbers and exchanges, as when random-digit dialing (RDD) is used with telephone surveys because of the inadequacies of directory samples. However, the dramatic increase in the number of working blocks over the last 10 years has made this task more difficult. See Research Realities 10.1. Or it sometimes means sampling geographic areas or institutions and then subsampling within these units when, say, the target population is individuals but a current, accurate list of appropriate individuals is not available.

The third step of selecting a sample procedure is inextricably intertwined with the identification of the sampling frame, because the choice of sampling method depends largely on what the researcher can develop for a sampling frame. A simple random sample, for example, requires that a complete, accurate list of population elements by name or other identification code be available. The rest of this chapter reviews the main types of nonprobability and probability samples employed in marketing research. The connection between sampling frame and sampling method should become obvious from this discussion.

RESEARCH REALITIES 10.1

Changes in the Structure of Telephone Numbers

Since 1986, the estimated number of telephone households in the United States has increased by 14.2 percent, while the number of working residential exchanges has increased by 27.1 percent and the number of working blocks by 182.4 percent. See the chart below. During the same time period, the number of directory-listed households has increased by only 10.4 percent, causing the continuing decline in listed rates.

	1986	1996	Growth
Telephone households	80,900,000	92,366,039	14.2%
Directory-listed households	59,788,590	66,016,760	10.4%
Working residential exchanges	31,530	40,083	27.1%
Working blocks	1,391,237	3,928,200	182.4%

Definition

Block or bank:	the first two digits of the last four digits of the telephone number
Working block:	any block with at least one listed number
Exchange/prefix:	"exchange" designates the city, town, or community in which the number originates. "Prefix" is the 3-digit number assigned to an exchange area. The terms are often used interchangeably.

Technological changes, particularly the explosive growth of cellular and mobile phones, paging equipment, modems, and fax machines, have dramatically increased the demand for telephone numbers. This has not only spurred the introduction of new area codes, but has also produced a reduced density of listed numbers in the working blocks because some of the numbers are dedicated to modems and fax machines.

The new competitive telephone market is also contributing to the declining working block density. Multiple telephone companies are serving smaller markets and are assigned exclusive exchanges. More exchanges are being assigned to more telephone companies, but the working blocks are not being filled out as completely.

What's the significance for sampling? The most obvious change concerns the working phone rate (WPR) of a random-digit dialing (RDD) sample. As the number of listed phones per working block decreases, the probability of selecting a listed number in an RDD sample decreases, which may decrease the WPR. Samples that include metropolitan areas are more likely to be affected by this trend.

Source: "Working Block Density Declines" (Fairfield, CT: Survey Sampling, Inc., 1996).

Step 4 in the sample selection process requires the sample size to be determined. Chapter 11 discusses this question. Step 5 indicates that the researcher needs to choose the elements that will be included in the study. How this is done depends on the type of sample being used, and consequently the discussion of sample selection is woven into the discussion of sampling methods. Finally, the researcher needs to actually collect data from the designated respondents. A great many things can go wrong with this task. These problems are reviewed, and some methods for handling them are discussed, in Chapter 12.

Types of Sampling Plans

Sampling techniques can be divided into the two broad categories of probability and nonprobability samples. **Probability samples** are distinguished by the fact that each population element has a *known, nonzero* chance of being included in the sample. It is not necessary that the probabilities of selection be equal, only that one can specify the probability with which each element of the population will be included in the sample. With **nonprobability samples,** in contrast, there is no way of estimating the probability that any population element will be included in the sample, and thus there is no way of ensuring that the sample is representative of the population. All nonprobability samples rely on personal judgment somewhere in the process, and although these judgment samples may indeed yield good estimates of a population characteristic, they do not permit an objective evaluation of the adequacy of the sample. It is only when the elements have been selected with known probabilities that one is able to evaluate the precision of a sample result.

Samples can also be distinguished by whether they are fixed or sequential. **Fixed samples** imply an *a priori* determination of sample size and the collection of needed information from the designated elements. The question of sample size for fixed samples is discussed in the next chapter. Fixed samples are the most commonly employed types in marketing research and the kind we shall emphasize. Nevertheless, you should be aware that sequential samples can also be taken and that they can be employed with each of the basic sampling plans to be discussed. **Sequential samples** are distinguished by the successive decisions they imply. They aim at answering the research question on the basis of accumulated evidence. If the evidence is not conclusive after a small sample is taken, more observations are made; if still inconclusive, still more population elements are designated for inclusion in the sample, and so on. At each stage a decision is made about whether more information should be collected or whether the evidence is now sufficient to permit a conclusion. The sequential sample allows trends in the data to be evaluated as the data are being collected, and this affords an opportunity to reduce costs when additional observations show diminishing usefulness.

Both probability and nonprobability sampling plans can be further divided by type. Nonprobability samples, for instance, can be classified as convenience, judgment, or quota, whereas probability samples can be simple random, stratified, or cluster, and some of these can be further divided. Figure 10.3 shows the types of samples we shall discuss in this chapter. You should be aware that the basic sample types can be combined into more complex sampling plans. If you understand the basic types, though, you should be able to appreciate the more complex designs.

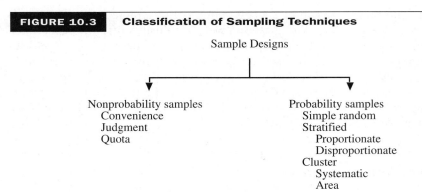

FIGURE 10.3   **Classification of Sampling Techniques**

Sample Designs

Nonprobability samples
   Convenience
   Judgment
   Quota

Probability samples
   Simple random
   Stratified
      Proportionate
      Disproportionate
   Cluster
      Systematic
      Area

Nonprobability Samples

Nonprobability samples involve personal judgment somewhere in the selection process. Sometimes this judgment is imposed by the researcher, and in other cases the selection of population elements to be included is left to individual field workers. The fact that the elements are not selected probabilistically precludes an assessment of "sampling error." Without some knowledge of the error that can be attributed to sampling procedures, we cannot place bounds on the precision of our estimates.

Convenience Samples

Sometimes, **convenience samples** are called *accidental samples* because those composing the sample enter by "accident"—they just happen to be where the information for the study is being collected. Examples of convenience samples abound in our everyday lives. We talk to a few friends, and, on the basis of their reactions, we infer the political sentiment of the country; our local radio station asks people to call in and express their reactions to some controversial issue, and the opinions expressed are interpreted as prevailing sentiment; we ask for volunteers in a research study and use those who come forward.

The problem with convenience samples, of course, is that we have no way of knowing if those included are representative of the target population. And while we might be hesitant to infer that the reactions of a few friends indicate prevailing political sentiment, there does seem to be some temptation to conclude that large samples, even though selected conveniently, are representative. The fallacy of this assumption is illustrated by a personal incident.

One of the local television stations in the city where the author resides conducted a daily public opinion poll several years ago on topics of interest to the local community. The polls were labeled the "Pulse of Madison" and were conducted in the following way: During the six o'clock news every evening, the station would ask a question about some controversial issue to which people could reply with a yes or no. Persons in favor would call one number; persons opposed would call another. The number of viewers calling each number was recorded electronically. Percentages of those in favor and opposed would then be reported on the 10:00 P.M. news. With some 500 to 1,000 people calling in their opinions each night, the local TV commentator seemed to interpret these results as reflecting the true state of opinion in the community.

On one 6:00 P.M. broadcast, the following question was posed: "Do you think the drinking age in Madison should be lowered to 18?" The existing legal limit was 21. Would you believe that almost 4,000 people called in that night and that 78 percent were in favor of lowering the age requirement! Clearly, 4,000 responses in a community of 180,000 people "must be representative!" Wrong. As you may have suspected, certain segments of the population were more vitally interested in the issue than others. Thus, it was no surprise, when discussing the issue in class a few weeks later, to find that students took one-half hour phone shifts on an arranged basis. Each person would call the yes number, hang up, call again, hang up, and so on, until it was the next person's turn. Thus neither the size of the sample nor the proportion favoring the age change was surprising. The sample was simply not representative. Further, increasing its size would not make it so.

The representativeness of a sample must be ensured by the sampling procedure. When participation is voluntary or sample elements are selected because they are convenient, the sampling plan provides no assurance that the sample is representative. Empirical evidence, as a matter of fact, is much to the contrary. Rarely do samples selected on a convenience basis, regardless of size, prove to be representative. Telephone polls using 800 and 900 numbers represent a particularly common example of large, but unrepresentative samples. What is especially unfortunate is that a great many people believe the results of these polls are accurate.

An all-too-common use of convenience samples in international marketing research is to use foreigners from the countries being studied who are currently residing in the country where the study is being conducted (for example, Scandinavians currently residing in the United States). Even though such convenience samples can shed some light on certain country conditions, it must be recognized that these individuals typically represent the elite class, often are already "westernized," and may not be in touch with current developments in their own country. Convenience samples are not recommended for descriptive or causal research. They may be used with exploratory designs in which the emphasis is on generating ideas and insights, but even here the judgment sample seems superior.

Judgment Samples

Judgment samples are often called *purposive samples;* the sample elements are handpicked because it is expected that they can serve the research purpose. Most typically, the sample elements are selected because it is believed that they are representative of the population of interest. One example of a judgment sample is seen every four years at presidential election time, when television viewers are treated to in-depth analyses of the swing communities. These communities are handpicked because they are "representative" in that historically the winner there has been the next president. Thus, by monitoring these pivotal communities, election analysts are able to offer an early prediction of the eventual winner, and even though election analysis and prediction have become much more sophisticated in recent years, the judgment sample of representative communities is still used.

As mentioned, the key feature of judgment sampling is that population elements are purposively selected. This selection may not be made on the basis that they are representative, but rather because they can offer the contributions sought. When the courts rely on expert testimony, they are in a sense using judgment samples, and the same kind of philosophy prevails in creating exploratory designs. When searching for ideas and insights, the researcher is not interested in sampling a cross section of opinion but rather in sampling those who can offer some perspective on the research question.

The **snowball sample** is a judgment sample that is sometimes used to sample special populations.[4] This sample relies on the researcher's ability to locate an initial set of respondents with the desired characteristics. These individuals are then used as informants to identify others with the desired characteristics. Thus, if one were doing a study among the deaf investigating the desirability of various product configurations that would allow deaf people to communicate over telephone lines, one might attempt to initially identify some key people in the deaf community and then ask them for names of other deaf people who might be used in the study. Those initially asked to participate would also be asked for names of others whose cooperation would be solicited. Thus, the sample "snowballs" by getting larger as participants identify still other possible respondents.

As long as the researcher is at the early stages of research when ideas or insights are being sought or when the researcher realizes its limitations, the judgment sample can be used productively. It becomes dangerous, though, when it is employed in descriptive or causal studies and its weaknesses are conveniently forgotten. The Consumer Price Index (CPI) provides a classic example of this. As Sudman points out, "the CPI is in only 56 cities and metropolitan areas selected judgmentally and to some extent on the basis of political pressure. In reality, these cities *represent only themselves* although the index is called the *Consumer Price Index for Urban Wage Earners and Clerical Workers,* and most people believe the index reflects prices everywhere in the United States. Within cities, the selection of retail outlets is done judgmentally, so that the *possible size of sample bias is unknown* (emphasis added)."[5]

Quota Samples

A third type of nonprobability sample is the quota sample. **Quota samples** attempt to ensure that the sample is representative by selecting sample elements in such a way that the proportion of the sample elements possessing a certain characteristic is approximately the same as the proportion of the elements with the characteristic in the population. Consider, for example, an attempt to select a representative sample of undergraduate students on a college campus. If the eventual sample of 500 contained no seniors, one would have serious reservations about the representativeness of the sample and the generalizability of the conclusions beyond the immediate sample group. With a quota sample, the researcher could ensure that seniors would be included and in the same proportion as they occur in the entire undergraduate student body.

---

[4]The technique was originally suggested by Leo A. Goodman, "Snowball Sampling," *Annals of Mathematical Statistics* 32 (1961), pp. 148–170.

[5]Seymour Sudman, *Applied Sampling* (San Francisco: Academic Press, 1976), p. 10. For discussion of the makeup of the CPI, see Christina Duff, "Is the CPI Accurate? Ask the Federal Sleuths Who Get the Numbers," *The Wall Street Journal* (January 16, 1997), pp. A1, A6.

Suppose that a researcher was interested in sampling the undergraduate student body in such a way that the sample would reflect the composition of the student body by class and sex. Suppose further that there were 10,000 undergraduate students in total and that 3,200 were freshmen, 2,600 sophomores, 2,200 juniors, and 2,000 seniors, and further that 7,000 were males and 3,000 females. In a sample of 1,000, the quota sampling plan would require that 320 sample elements be freshmen, 260 sophomores, 220 juniors, and 200 seniors, and further that 700 of the sample elements be male and 300 be female. The researcher would accomplish this by giving each field worker a quota—thus the name *quota sample*—specifying the types of undergraduates he or she is to contact. Thus, one field worker assigned 20 interviews might be instructed to find and collect data from

- 6 freshmen—5 male and 1 female
- 6 sophomores—4 male and 2 female
- 4 juniors—3 male and 1 female
- 4 seniors—2 male and 2 female

Note that the specific sample elements to be used would not be specified by the research plan but would be left to the discretion of the individual field worker. The field worker's personal judgment would govern the choice of specific students to be interviewed. The only requirement would be that the interviewer diligently follow the established quota and interview five male freshmen, one female freshman, and so on.

The quota for this field worker accurately reflects the sex composition of the student population, but it does not completely parallel the class composition; 70 percent (14 of 20) of the field worker's interviews are with males but only 30 percent (6 of 20) are with freshmen, whereas freshmen represent 32 percent of the undergraduate student body. It is not necessary or even usual with a quota sample for the quotas per field worker to accurately mirror the distribution of the control characteristics in the population; usually only the total sample has the same proportions as the target population.

Note finally that quota samples still rely on personal, subjective judgment rather than objective procedures for the selection of sample elements. Here the personal judgment is that of the field worker rather than the designer of the research, as it might be in the case of a judgment sample. This raises the question of whether quota samples can indeed be considered "representative" even though they accurately reflect the target population with respect to the proportion of the sample possessing each control characteristic. Three points need to be made in this regard.

First, the sample could be quite far off with respect to some other important characteristic likely to influence the result. Thus, if the campus study is concerned with racial prejudice existing on campus, it may very well make a difference whether field workers interview students from urban or rural areas. Since a quota for the urban-rural characteristic was not specified, it is unlikely that those participating will accurately reflect this characteristic. The alternative, of course, is to specify quotas for all potentially important characteristics. The problem is that increasing the number of control characteristics makes specifications more complex and makes the location of sample elements more difficult (perhaps even impossible) and certainly more expensive. It is a much more difficult task, assuming that geographic origin and socio-economic status are important characteristics, for a field worker to locate an upper-middle-class male freshman from an urban area than to locate a male freshman.

Second, it is difficult to verify whether a quota sample is indeed representative. Certainly one can check the distribution of characteristics in the sample not used as controls to ascertain whether the distribution parallels that of the target population. However, this type of comparison provides only negative evidence. It can indicate that the sample does not reflect the target population if the distributions on some characteristics are different. If the sample and target population distributions are similar for each of these characteristics, it is still possible for the sample to be vastly different from the target population on some characteristic not explicitly compared.

Finally, interviewers left to their own devices are prone to follow certain practices. They tend to interview their friends in excessive proportion. Because their friends are often similar to themselves, this can introduce bias. The empirical evidence from England, for example, indicates that quota samples are biased (1) toward the accessible, (2) against small households, (3) toward households with children, (4) against workers in manufacturing, (5) against extremes of income, (6) against the less educated, and (7) against low-status individuals.[6] Interviewers who fill their quotas by stopping passersby are likely to concentrate on areas where there are large numbers of potential respondents, such as business districts, railway and airline terminals, and the entrances to large department stores. This practice tends to overrepresent the particular kinds of people that frequent these areas. When home visits are used, interviewers display a propensity for convenience and appearance, concentrating their interviews at certain times of the day so that working people are underrepresented; avoiding upper stories of buildings without elevator service; and selecting corner buildings and avoiding dilapidated ones.

Depending on the subject of the study, all these tendencies have the potential for bias. They may or may not in fact actually bias the result, but it is difficult to correct them when analyzing the data. When the sample elements are selected objectively, on the other hand, researchers have certain tools they can rely on to make the question of whether a particular sample is representative less difficult. In these probability samples, one relies on the sampling procedure and not the composition of the specific sample to solve the problem of representation.

Probability Samples

One can calculate the likelihood that any given population element will be included in a probability sample because the final sample elements are selected objectively by a specific process and not according to the whims of the researcher or field worker. The objective selection of elements, in turn, allows the objective assessment of the reliability of the sample results, something not possible with nonprobability samples regardless of the careful judgment exercised in selecting individuals.

[6]Catherine Marsh and Elinor Scarbrough, "Testing Nine Hypotheses about Quota Sampling," *Journal of the Market Research Society* 32 (October 1990), pp. 485–506. For an example, see Gunter Schweiger, Gerald Haubl, and Geroen Friederes, "Consumers' Evaluations of Products Labeled 'Made in Europe,'" *Marketing & Research Today* 23 (February 1995), pp. 25–34.

TABLE 10.1	**Hypothetical Population**		

Element	Income (Dollars)	Education (Years)	Newspaper Subscription
1 A	5,600	8	X
2 B	6,000	9	Y
3 C	6,400	11	X
4 D	6,800	11	Y
5 E	7,200	11	X
6 F	7,600	12	Y
7 G	8,000	12	X
8 H	8,400	12	Y
9 I	8,800	12	X
10 J	9,200	12	Y
11 K	9,600	13	X
12 L	10,000	13	Y
13 M	10,400	14	X
14 N	10,800	14	Y
15 O	11,200	15	X
16 P	11,600	16	Y
17 Q	12,000	16	X
18 R	12,400	17	Y
19 S	12,800	18	X
20 T	13,200	18	Y

This is not to say that probability samples will always be more representative than nonprobability samples. Far from it. A nonprobability sample may indeed be more representative. What probability samples allow, though, is an assessment of the amount of "sampling error" likely to occur because a sample rather than a census was employed when gathering the data. Nonprobability samples allow the investigator no objective method for evaluating the adequacy of the sample.

Simple Random Sampling

By far the probability samples best known to beginning researchers are **simple random samples,** because they are used to frame the concepts and arguments in beginning statistics courses. Simple random samples are distinguished by the fact that each population element has not only a known but an equal chance of being selected and, further, that every combination of n population elements is a sample possibility and is just as likely to occur as any other combination of n units.

PARENT POPULATION   In discussing the various probability sampling plans and the objective assessment of sampling error that they allow, it will prove useful to explore the notion of sampling distribution in some detail.[7] Consider the hypothetical population of 20 individuals shown in Table 10.1. This population can be described by certain parameters. A **parameter** is simply a characteristic or measure of a parent or target population; it is a fixed quantity that distinguishes one population

---

[7]The concept of a sampling distribution is treated in detail in most introductory statistics texts. The reader who understands the idea of sampling distribution should consider these next few pages an elementary review that will return dividends when discussing the more complex sample designs.

from another. We can calculate a number of parameters to describe this hypothetical population. We could calculate the average income, the dispersion in educational levels, the proportion of the population subscribing to each newspaper, and so on. Note that these quantities are fixed in value. Given a census of this population, we can readily calculate them. Rather than relying on a census, we usually select a sample and use the values calculated from the sample observations to estimate the required population values.

Suppose that our task was one of estimating the average income in this population from a sample of two elements selected randomly. Let μ denote the mean population income and σ^2 the variance of incomes. Both μ and σ are population parameters, one measuring central tendency and the other spread; that is, μ and σ^2 are defined as

$$\mu = \frac{\sum_{i=1}^{N} X_i}{N} = \frac{5,600 + 6,000 + \ldots + 13,200}{20} = 9,400, \text{ and}$$

$$\sigma^2 = \frac{\sum_{i=1}^{N} (X_i - \mu)^2}{N}$$

$$= \frac{(5,600 - 9,400)^2 + (6,000 - 9,400)^2 + \ldots + (13,200 - 9,400)^2}{20}$$

$$= 5,320,000$$

where X_i is the value of the ith observation and N is the number of population elements. Thus, to compute the population mean, we divide the sum of all the values by the number of values making up the sum. To compute the population variance, we calculate the deviation of each value from the mean, square these deviations, sum them, and divide by the number of values making up the sum.

DERIVED POPULATION   It seems logical that our estimates of these population parameters would rest on similar calculations. A **statistic** is a characteristic or measure of a sample. We typically use the similarly calculated statistic to estimate the parameter, but we need to recognize that the value of the statistic depends on the particular sample selected from the parent population under the specified sampling plan. Different samples yield different statistics and different estimates.

Consider the **derived population** of *all* possible distinguishable samples that can be drawn from this parent population under a given sampling plan, which specifies that a sample of Size $n = 2$ is to be drawn by simple random sampling without replacement.[8] Assume, for example, that the information for each element, including its identity, is to be placed on a disk and that these elements are to be placed in an urn and mixed thoroughly. The investigator will reach in the urn, pull out one disk, record the identity and the income of the person and then, without replacing the first disk, will draw a second disk from the urn and record the identity and income. Table 10.2 displays the derived population of all possible samples from fol-

---

[8]The term "sample space" is also used for the concept of derived population. See Martin Frankel, "Sampling Theory," in Rossi, Wright, and Anderson, *Handbook of Survey Research*, pp. 21–67.

TABLE 10.2   Derived Population of All Possible Samples of Size $n = 2$ with Simple Random Selection

k	Sample Identity	Mean	k	Sample Identity	Mean	k	Sample Identity	Mean	k	Sample Identity	Mean
1	AB	5,800	51	CQ	9,200	101	GI	8,400	151	KQ	10,800
2	AC	6,000	52	CR	9,400	102	GJ	8,600	152	KR	11,000
3	AD	6,200	53	CS	9,600	103	GK	8,800	153	KS	11,200
4	AE	6,400	54	CT	9,800	104	GL	9,000	154	KT	11,400
5	AF	6,600	55	DE	7,000	105	GM	9,200	155	LM	10,200
6	AG	6,800	56	DF	7,200	106	GN	9,400	156	LN	10,400
7	AH	7,000	57	DG	7,400	107	GO	9,600	157	LO	10,600
8	AI	7,200	58	DH	7,600	108	GP	9,800	158	LP	10,800
9	AJ	7,400	59	DI	7,800	109	GQ	10,000	159	LQ	11,000
10	AK	7,600	60	DJ	8,000	110	GR	10,200	160	LR	11,200
11	AL	7,800	61	DK	8,200	111	GS	10,400	161	LS	11,400
12	AM	8,000	62	DL	8,400	112	GT	10,600	162	LT	11,600
13	AN	8,200	63	DM	8,600	113	HI	8,600	163	MN	10,600
14	AO	8,400	64	DN	8,800	114	HJ	8,800	164	MO	10,800
15	AP	8,600	65	DO	9,000	115	HK	9,000	165	MP	11,000
16	AQ	8,800	66	DP	9,200	116	HL	9,200	166	MQ	11,200
17	AR	9,000	67	DQ	9,400	117	HM	9,400	167	MR	11,400
18	AS	9,200	68	DR	9,600	118	HN	9,600	168	MS	11,600
19	AT	9,400	69	DS	9,800	119	HO	9,800	169	MT	11,800
20	BC	6,200	70	DT	10,000	120	HP	10,000	170	NO	11,000
21	BD	6,400	71	EF	7,400	121	HQ	10,200	171	NP	11,200
22	BE	6,600	72	EG	7,600	122	HR	10,400	172	NQ	11,400
23	BF	6,800	73	EH	7,800	123	HS	10,600	173	NR	11,600
24	BG	7,000	74	EI	8,000	124	HT	10,800	174	NS	11,800
25	BH	7,200	75	EJ	8,200	125	IJ	9,000	175	NT	12,000
26	BI	7,400	76	EK	8,400	126	IK	9,200	176	OP	11,400
27	BJ	7,600	77	EL	8,600	127	IL	9,400	177	OQ	11,600
28	BK	7,800	78	EM	8,800	128	IM	9,600	178	OR	11,800
29	BL	8,000	79	EN	9,000	129	IN	9,800	179	OS	12,000
30	BM	8,200	80	EO	9,200	130	IO	10,000	180	OT	12,200
31	BN	8,400	81	EP	9,400	131	IP	10,200	181	PQ	11,800
32	BO	8,600	82	EQ	9,600	132	IQ	10,400	182	PR	12,000
33	BP	8,800	83	ER	9,800	133	IR	10,600	183	PS	12,200
34	BQ	9,000	84	ES	10,000	134	IS	10,800	184	PT	12,400
35	BR	9,200	85	ET	10,200	135	IT	11,000	185	QR	12,200
36	BS	9,400	86	FG	7,800	136	JK	9,400	186	QS	12,400
37	BT	9,600	87	FH	8,000	137	JL	9,600	187	QT	12,600
38	CD	6,600	88	FI	8,200	138	JM	9,800	188	RS	12,600
39	CE	6,800	89	FJ	8,400	139	JN	10,000	189	RT	12,800
40	CF	7,000	90	FK	8,600	140	JO	10,200	190	ST	13,000
41	CG	7,200	91	FL	8,800	141	JP	10,400			
42	CH	7,400	92	FM	9,000	142	JQ	10,600			
43	CI	7,600	93	FN	9,200	143	JR	10,800			
44	CJ	7,800	94	FO	9,400	144	JS	11,000			
45	CK	8,000	95	FP	9,600	145	JT	11,200			
46	CL	8,200	96	FQ	9,800	146	KL	9,800			
47	CM	8,400	97	FR	10,000	147	KM	10,000			
48	CN	8,600	98	FS	10,200	148	KN	10,200			
49	CO	8,800	99	FT	10,400	149	KO	10,400			
50	CP	9,000	100	GH	8,200	150	KP	10,600			

ETHICAL DILEMMA 10.1

You are designing an experiment to compare the effectiveness of different types of commercials and need to recruit a large group of subjects of varying ages to watch television for an hour every night for a week. You approach your local church minister and tell her that you will make a donation to the church restoration fund for every member of the congregation who agrees to participate.

- When might incentives be coercive?
- Is it ethical to coerce people to participate in research?
- Will the quality of the data suffer from the coercive recruitment of participants?

---

lowing this procedure. There are 190 possible combinations of the 20 disks. For each combination, one can calculate the sample mean income. Thus, for the sample AB, the sample mean income $\bar{x}_1 = (\$5,600 + \$6,000)/2 = \$5,800$, and, in general,

$$\bar{x}_k = \sum_{i=1}^{n} \frac{X_i}{n}$$

where k refers to the sample number, $\bar{x}$ to the sample average, and n to the sample size. Figure 10.4 displays the estimates of population mean income and the amount of error in each estimate when samples $k = 25, 62, 108, 147,$ and 189 are drawn.

Before discussing the relationship between the sample mean income (a statistic) and population mean income (the parameter to be estimated), a few words are in order about the notion of derived population. First, note that in practice, we do not actually generate the derived population. This would be extremely wasteful of time and data. Rather, all that the practitioner will do is to generate one sample of the needed size. But the researcher will make use of the *concept* "derived population" and the associated notion of sampling distribution in making inferences. We shall see how in just a moment. Second, note that the derived population is defined as the population of all possible distinguishable samples that can be drawn under a *given sampling plan.* Change any part of the sampling plan and the derived population will also change. Thus, when selecting disks, if the researcher is to replace the first disk drawn, the derived population will include the sample possibilities AA, BB, and so on. With samples of size 3 instead of 2, drawn without replacement, ABC is a sample possibility, and there are a number of additional possibilities as well—1,140 versus the 190 with samples of size 2. Change the method of selecting elements by using something other than simple random sampling and the derived population will also change. Finally, note that picking a sample of a given size from a parent population is equivalent to picking a single element (one of the 190 possibilities) out of the derived population. This fact is basic in making statistical inferences.

Sample Mean versus Population Mean   Now consider the relationship between the sample means and the population mean. We wish to make three points. First,

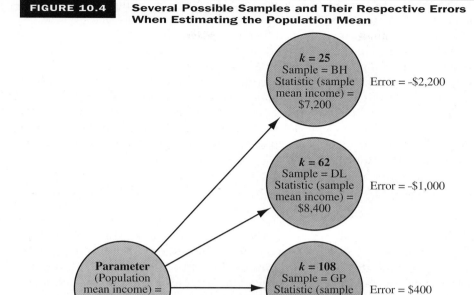

FIGURE 10.4   **Several Possible Samples and Their Respective Errors When Estimating the Population Mean**

suppose that we add up all the sample means in Table 10.2 and divide by the number of samples—in other words, average the averages. By sheer doing, this yields

$$\frac{5{,}800 + 6{,}000 \ldots + 13{,}000}{190} = 9{,}400$$

which is the mean of the population. This is what is meant by an unbiased statistic. A statistic is **unbiased** when its average value equals the population parameter it is supposed to estimate. Note that the fact it is unbiased says nothing about any particular value of the statistic. Even though unbiased, a particular estimate may be very far from the true population value—as for example, if either sample AB or sample ST were selected. In some cases, the true population value may even be *impossible* to achieve with any possible sample even though the statistic is unbiased; this is not true in the example, though, since a number of sample possibilities (for example, AT) yield a sample mean that equals the population average.

Second, consider the spread of these sample estimates and particularly the relationship between this spread of estimates and the dispersion of incomes in the population. We saw previously that the population variance $\sigma^2 = 5,320,000$. We can calculate the *variance of mean incomes* similarly—that is, by taking the deviation of each mean around its overall mean, squaring and summing these deviations, and then dividing by the number of cases:

$$\frac{(5,800 - 9,400)^2 + (6,000 - 9,400)^2 + \ldots + (13,000 - 9,400)^2}{190} = 2,520,000$$

Now note the relationship between σ^2 (the variance or spread of the variable in the original population) and the spread of the estimates in the derived population (call it $\sigma_{\bar{x}}^2$ to denote the variance of means). Instead of direct calculations using the 190 sample estimates, $\sigma_{\bar{x}}^2$ could have also been calculated by the following expression:

$$\sigma_{\bar{x}}^2 = \frac{\sigma^2}{n} \frac{N - n}{N - 1} = \frac{5,320,000}{2} \frac{20 - 2}{20 - 1} = 2,520,000$$

This result is not unique but is true in general, although the expression relating the two variances is typically modified slightly when the sample size is only a small proportion of the population.[9]

Third, consider the distribution of the estimates in contrast to the distribution of the variable in the parent population. Figure 10.5 indicates that the parent population distribution depicted by Panel A is spiked (each of the 20 values occurs once) and is symmetrical about the population mean value of 9,400. The distribution of estimates displayed in Panel B was constructed by placing each of the estimates in categories according to size and then counting the number contained in each category (Table 10.3). Panel B is the traditional histogram discussed in beginning statistics courses and represents the *sampling distribution of the statistic.* Note this: The notion of **sampling distribution** is the single most important notion in statistics; it is the cornerstone of statistical inference procedures. If one knows the sampling distribution for the statistic in question, one is in a position to make an inference about the corresponding population parameter. If, on the other hand, one knows only that a particular sample estimate will vary with repeated sampling and has no information about *how* it will vary, then it will be impossible to devise a measure of the sampling error associated with that estimate. Because the sampling dis-

---

[9]The expression $(N - n)/(N - 1)$ is known as the finite population correction factor. Whenever the sample size is less than 10 percent of the population size, the finite population correction factor is ignored, since $(N - n)/(N - 1)$ is very close to 1 and the more complex form $\sigma_{\bar{x}}^2 = (\sigma^2/n)(N - n)/(N - 1)$ reduces to $\sigma_{\bar{x}}^2 = \sigma^2/n$.

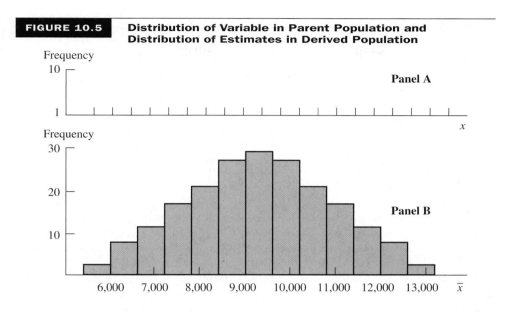

FIGURE 10.5   **Distribution of Variable in Parent Population and Distribution of Estimates in Derived Population**

tribution of an estimate describes how that estimate will vary with repeated sampling, it provides a basis for determining the reliability of the sample estimate. This is why probability sampling plans are so important to statistical inference. With known probabilities of inclusion of any population element in the sample, statisticians are able to derive the sampling distribution of various statistics. Researchers then rely on these distributions—whether they are for a sample mean, sample proportion, sample variance, or some other statistic—in making their inferences from single samples to population values. Note that the distribution of sample means is mound shaped and symmetrical about the population mean with samples of size 2.

TABLE 10.3   **Classification of Estimates by Size**

Sample Mean	Number of Samples
$6,000 or less	2
$6,100 to 6,600	7
$6,700 to 7,200	11
$7,300 to 7,800	16
$7,900 to 8,400	20
$8,500 to 9,000	25
$9,100 to 9,600	28
$9,700 to 10,200	25
$10,300 to 10,800	20
$10,900 to 11,400	16
$11,500 to 12,000	11
$12,100 to 12,600	7
$12,700 or more	2

Recapitulating, we have shown that:

1. The mean of all possible sample means is equal to the population mean.
2. The variance of sample means is related to the population variance by the expression

$$\sigma_{\bar{x}}^2 = \frac{\sigma^2}{n} \frac{N-n}{N-1}$$

3. The distribution of sample means is mound shaped, whereas the population distribution is spiked.

This first result is true in general for simple random sampling. The mean of the sample means is equal to the population mean if sampling is with or without replacement of the elements and sampling is from a finite or infinite parent population. The second result is true only when sampling is from a finite population without replacement. If sampling from an infinite population or when sampling from a finite population with replacement, the simpler expression $\sigma_{\bar{x}}^2 = \sigma^2/n$ holds.

The simpler expression derives from the fact that when the size of the sample is small in *comparison* to the size of the population, the term on the far right in the exact equation for the variance of sample means is approximately equal to one and can be ignored. For many, if not most, problems in marketing, the simpler expression $\sigma_{\bar{x}}^2 = \sigma^2/n$ is used to relate the variance of sample means to the variance of the variable.

Central-Limit Theorem   The third result of a mound-shaped distribution of estimates provides preliminary evidence of the operation of the Central-Limit Theorem. The **Central-Limit Theorem** holds that if simple random samples of size n are drawn from a parent population with mean μ and variance σ^2, then when n is large, the sample mean $\bar{x}$ will be approximately normally distributed with the mean equal to μ and variance equal to σ^2/n. The approximation will become more and more accurate as n becomes larger. Note the impact of this. It means that *regardless* of the shape of the parent population, the distribution of sample means *will be normal* if the sample is large enough. How large is large enough? If the distribution of the variable in the parent population is normal, the means of samples of size $n = 1$ will be normally distributed. If the distribution of the variable is symmetrical but not normal, samples of very small size will produce a distribution in which the means are normally distributed. If the distribution of the variable is highly skewed in the parent population, samples of a larger size will be needed.

The fact remains, however, that the distribution of the statistic, sample mean, can be assumed to be normal only if we work with a sample of sufficient size. We do not need to rely on the assumption that the variable is normally distributed in the parent population to make inferences using the normal curve. Rather, we rely on the Central-Limit Theorem and adjust the sample size according to the population distribution so that the normal curve can be assumed to hold. Fortunately, the normal distribution of the statistic occurs with samples of relatively small size, as Figure 10.6 indicates.

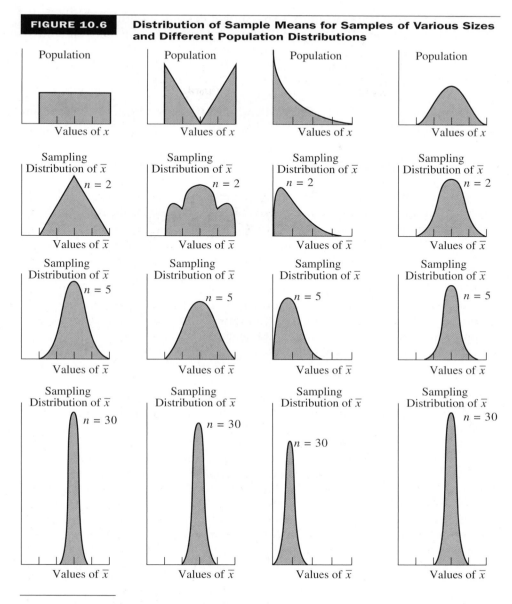

FIGURE 10.6   **Distribution of Sample Means for Samples of Various Sizes and Different Population Distributions**

Source: Ernest Kurnow, Gerald J. Glasser, and Frederick R. Ottman, *Statistics for Business Decisions* (Homewood, IL: Richard D. Irwin, Inc., 1959), pp. 182–183. Copyright 1959, reprinted with permission.

CONFIDENCE INTERVAL ESTIMATES   How does all the preceding information help us in making inferences about the parent population mean? After all, in practice we do not draw all possible samples of a given size but only one, and we use the results obtained in it to infer something about the target group. It all ties together in the following way:

It is known that with any normal distribution, a specific percentage of all observations is within a certain number of standard deviations of the mean, for example,

95 percent of the values are within ± 1.96 standard deviations of the mean. The distribution of sample means is normal if the Central-Limit Theorem holds and thus is no exception. Now, the mean of this sampling distribution is the population mean μ, and its standard deviation is given by the standard error of the mean $\sigma_{\bar{x}} = \sigma/\sqrt{n}$. Therefore, it is true that

- 68.26 percent of the sample means will be within $\pm 1\sigma_{\bar{x}}$ of the population mean,
- 95.45 percent of the sample means will be within $\pm 2\sigma_{\bar{x}}$ of the population mean, and
- 99.73 percent of the sample means will be within $\pm 3\sigma_{\bar{x}}$ of the population mean,

and, in general, that $\mu \pm z\sigma_{\bar{x}}$ will contain some certain proportion of all sample means, depending on the selected value of z. This expression can be rewritten as an inequality relation:

$$\mu - z\sigma_{\bar{x}} \leq \bar{x} \leq \mu + z\sigma_{\bar{x}} \tag{10.1}$$

which is held to be true a certain percentage of the time and which implies that the sample mean will be in the interval formed by adding and subtracting a certain number of standard deviations to the mean value of the distribution. This inequality can be transferred to the equivalent inequality,

$$\bar{x} - z\sigma_{\bar{x}} \leq \mu \leq \bar{x} + z\sigma_{\bar{x}} \tag{10.2}$$

If equation 10.1 was true, say, 95 percent of the time ($z = 1.96$), equation 10.2 is also true 95 percent of the time. *When we make an inference on the basis of a single sample mean, we make use of equation 10.2.*

It is important to note that equation 10.2 says *nothing about the interval constructed from a particular sample as including the population mean.* Rather, the interval addresses the *sampling procedure.* The interval around a single sample mean may or may not contain the true population mean. Our confidence in our inference rests on the property that 95 percent of all the intervals we could construct under that sampling plan would contain the true value. We trust or hope that our sample is one of those 95 out of 100 that does (when we are 95 percent confident) include the true value.[10]

---

[10]The argument expressed here on the interpretation of a confidence interval is the traditional or classical statistics argument, which holds that the parameter being estimated is fixed in value. Thus, it is meaningless to interpret the statement probabilistically, because a given interval will or will not contain the population parameter. Bayesian analysts adopt a different perspective, however. Bayesians hold that it is legitimate to assign personal probabilities to the states of nature, values of the unknown parameter in this case. One can then combine these judgments with sample information to produce posterior probabilities regarding the value of the unknown parameter. The confidence interval formed for a population mean is the same under the two approaches if one adopts the Bayesian assumption that the initial probabilities for each of the possible values of the unknown parameter are equal. The difference in perspectives, though, allows Bayesian analysts to interpret the resulting interval as a probability statement; that is, there is a 95 percent probability that the interval $\bar{x} \pm z\sigma_{\bar{x}}$ contains the true population mean. This interpretation tends to be much more satisfying to decision makers. For a discussion of the difference in the two perspectives, see Frankel, "Sampling Theory."

To illustrate this important point, suppose for the moment that the distribution of sample means of size $n = 2$ for our hypothetical example was normal. Suppose further that by chance the sampling process yielded sample AB, in which the mean income was \$5,800. The 95 percent confidence interval ($z = 1.96$) using equation 10.2 would then be ($\sigma_{\bar{x}} = \sqrt{\sigma_{\bar{x}}^2} = \sqrt{2,520,000} = 1,587$):

$$5,800 - 1.96(1,587) \leq \mu \leq 5,800 + 1.96(1,587) = 2,689 \leq \mu \leq 8,911$$

The confidence interval would *not* include the true (in this case, known) population value, and an inferential error would have been made. The example illustrates that after the sample has been drawn, it is a matter of fact whether or not the particular interval estimate covers the universe mean. Table 10.4 illustrates the outcome pictorially for the first 10 out of the possible 190 samples that could be drawn under the specified sampling plan. Note that only 7 of the 10 intervals contain the true population mean. Confidence in the estimate arises because of the *procedure,* therefore, and not because of a particular estimate. The procedure suggests that with, say, a 95 percent confidence interval, if 100 samples were to be drawn and the sample mean and the confidence interval computed for each, 95 of the constructed intervals would include the true population value. The accuracy of a specific sample is evaluated only by reference to the procedure by which the sample was obtained. A sampling plan that is representative does not guarantee that a particular sample is representative. Statistical inference procedures rest on the representativeness of the sampling plan, and this is why probability samples are so critical to those procedures. Probability samples allow an estimate of the **precision** of the results in terms of how closely the estimates will tend to cluster around the true value. The greater the standard error of the statistic, the more variable the estimates and the less precise the procedure.

If it disturbs you that the confidence level applies to the procedure and not to a particular sample result, you can take refuge in the fact that you can control the level of confidence with which the population value is estimated. Thus, if you do not wish to take the risk that you might have 1 of the 5 sample intervals in 100 that

TABLE 10.4   **Confidence Intervals for First 10 Samples Assuming the Distribution of Sample Means Was Normal**

Sample Number	Sample Identity	Mean	Confidence Interval Lower Limit	Confidence Interval Upper Limit	Pictorial True μ = 9,400
1	AB	5,800	2,689	8,911	
2	AC	6,000	2,889	9,111	
3	AD	6,200	3,089	9,311	
4	AE	6,400	3,289	9,511	
5	AF	6,600	3,489	9,711	
6	AG	6,800	3,689	9,911	
7	AH	7,000	3,889	10,111	
8	AI	7,200	4,089	10,311	
9	AJ	7,400	4,289	10,511	
10	AK	7,600	4,489	10,711	

does not contain the population value, you might employ a 99 percent confidence interval, in which the risk is that only 1 in 100 sample intervals will not contain the population mean. Further, if you are willing to increase the size of the sample, you can increase your confidence and at the same time maintain the precision with which the population value is estimated. This will be explored more fully in the next chapter.

Population Variance Unknown   There is one other, perhaps disturbing, ingredient in our procedure. The confidence interval estimate made use of three values: $\bar{x}$, z, and $\sigma_{\bar{x}}$. Now $\bar{x}$ is computed from the selected sample, and z is specified to produce the desired level of confidence. But what about $\sigma_{\bar{x}}$? It is equal to $\sigma_{\bar{x}} = \sigma/\sqrt{n}$, and thus to calculate it, we need to know the standard deviation of the variable in the population. What do we do if σ is unknown? There is no problem for two reasons. First, variation typically changes much more slowly than level for most variables of interest in marketing. Thus, if the study is a repeat, we can use the previously discovered value for σ. Second, once the sample is selected and the information gathered, we can calculate the sample variance to estimate the population variance. The unbiased sample variance $\hat{s}^2$ is calculated as

$$\hat{s}^2 = \frac{\sum_{i=1}^{n} (X_i - \bar{x})^2}{n - 1}$$

where $\bar{x}$ is the sample mean and n the sample size.[11] To compute the sample variance, then, we first calculate the sample mean. We then calculate the differences between each of our sample values and the sample mean, square them, sum them, and divide the sum by one less than the number of sample observations. The sample variance not only provides an estimate of the population variance, but it can also be used to secure an estimate of the standard error of the mean. When the population variance, σ^2, is known, the standard error of the mean, $\sigma_{\bar{x}}$, is also known because $\sigma_{\bar{x}} = \sigma/\sqrt{n}$. When the population variance is unknown, the standard error of the mean can only be estimated. The estimate is given by $s_{\bar{x}}$, which equals $\hat{s}/\sqrt{n}$. The estimate calculation parallels that for the true value, with the sample standard deviation substituted for the population standard deviation. Thus, if we draw sample AB, with mean of 5,800,

$$\hat{s}^2 = \frac{(5,600 - 5,800)^2 + (6,000 - 5,800)^2}{1} = 80,000$$

---

[11]Division by n, the sample size, is more intuitive because it produces the normal conception of average, which here is the average of the deviations squared. However, the sample variance, when defined as

$$\hat{s}^2 = \frac{\sum_{i=1}^{n} (X_i - \bar{x})^2}{n}$$

produces a biased estimate of the population variance. Thus it is customary to use either the unbiased definition of the sample variance or to generate an estimate of σ^2, denoted by $\hat{\sigma}^2$, by the formula $\hat{\sigma}^2 = [n/(n - 1)]\hat{s}^2$.

thus $\hat{s} = 283$ and $s_{\bar{x}} = \hat{s}/\sqrt{n} = 283/\sqrt{2} = 200$ and the 95 percent confidence interval is now

$$5{,}800 - 1.96(200) \leq \mu \geq 5{,}800 + 1.96(200) = 5{,}408 \leq \mu \leq 6{,}192$$

which is somewhat smaller than before.[12]

Drawing the Simple Random Sample   Although it was useful for illustrating the concepts "derived population" and "sampling distribution," the selection of sample elements from an urn containing all the population elements is not particularly recommended because of its great potential for bias. It is unlikely that the disks would be exactly uniform in size or feel, and slight differences here could affect the likelihood that any single element would be drawn. The national draft during the Vietnam War using a lottery serves as an example. Draft priorities were determined by drawing disks with birth dates stamped on them from a large container in full view of a TV audience. Unfortunately, the dates of the year had initially been poured into the bowl systematically, January first and December last. Although the bowl was then stirred vigorously, December dates tended to be chosen first and January dates last. The procedure was later revised to produce a more random selection process.

The preferred way of drawing a simple random sample is through the use of a table of random numbers. Using a random number table involves the following sequence of steps. First, the elements of the parent population would be numbered serially from 1 to N; for the hypothetical population, the element A would be numbered as 1, B as 2, and so on. Next, the numbers in the table would be treated to have the same number of digits as N. With $N = 20$, two-digit numbers would be used; if N was between 100 and 999, three-digit numbers would be required, and so on. Third, a starting point would be determined randomly. We might simply open the table to some arbitrary place and point to a position on the page with our eyes closed. Since the numbers in a random number table are in fact random (that is, without order), it makes little difference where we begin.[13] Finally, we would proceed in some arbitrary direction (for example, up, down, or across) and select those elements for the sample for which there is a match of serial number and random number.

To illustrate, consider the partial list of random numbers contained in Table 10.5. Since $N = 20$, we need work with only two digits, and therefore we can use the entries in the table as is, instead of having to combine columns to produce numbers covering the range of serial numbers. Suppose that we had previously decided to read down and that our arbitrary start indicated the eleventh row, the fourth column, and specifically the number 77. This number is too high and would be

---

[12]The *t* distribution would strictly be used when σ was unknown. We shall say more about this in Chapter 15.

[13]There are two major errors to avoid when using random number tables: (1) starting at a given place because one knows the distribution of numbers at that place; and (2) discarding a sample because it does not "look right" in some sense and continuing to use random numbers until a "likely looking" sample is selected. Sudman, *Applied Sampling*, p. 165.

TABLE 10.5	Abridged List of Random Numbers

10 09 73 25 33	76 52 01 35 86	34 67 35 48 76	80 95 90 91 17	39 29 27 49 45
37 54 20 48 05	64 89 47 42 96	24 80 52 40 37	20 63 61 04 02	00 82 29 16 65
08 42 26 89 53	19 64 50 93 03	23 20 90 25 60	15 95 33 47 64	35 08 03 36 06
99 01 90 25 29	09 37 67 07 15	38 31 13 11 65	88 67 67 43 97	04 43 62 76 59
12 80 79 99 70	80 15 73 61 47	64 03 23 66 53	98 95 11 68 77	12 17 17 68 33
66 06 57 47 17	34 07 27 68 50	36 69 73 61 70	65 81 33 98 85	11 19 92 91 70
31 06 01 08 05	45 57 18 24 06	35 30 34 26 14	86 79 90 74 39	23 40 30 97 32
85 26 97 76 02	02 05 16 56 92	68 66 57 48 18	73 05 38 52 47	18 62 38 85 79
63 57 33 21 35	05 32 54 70 48	90 55 35 75 48	28 46 82 87 09	83 49 12 56 24
73 79 64 57 53	03 52 96 47 78	35 80 83 42 82	60 93 52 03 44	35 27 38 84 35
98 52 01 77 67	14 90 56 86 07	22 10 94 05 58	60 97 09 34 33	50 50 07 39 98
11 80 50 54 31	39 80 82 77 32	50 72 56 82 48	29 40 52 42 01	52 77 56 78 51
83 45 29 96 34	06 28 89 80 83	13 74 67 00 78	18 47 54 06 10	68 71 17 78 17
88 68 54 02 00	86 50 75 84 01	36 76 66 79 51	90 36 47 64 93	29 60 91 10 62
99 59 46 73 48	87 51 76 49 69	91 82 60 89 28	93 78 56 13 68	23 47 83 41 13
65 48 11 76 74	17 46 85 90 50	58 04 77 69 74	73 03 95 71 86	40 21 81 65 44
80 12 43 56 35	17 72 70 80 15	45 31 82 23 74	21 11 57 82 53	14 38 55 37 63
74 35 09 98 17	77 40 27 72 14	43 23 60 02 10	45 52 16 42 37	96 28 60 26 55
69 91 62 68 03	66 25 22 91 48	36 93 68 72 03	76 62 11 39 90	94 40 05 64 18
09 89 32 05 05	14 22 56 85 14	46 42 75 67 88	96 29 77 88 22	54 38 21 45 98
91 49 91 45 23	68 47 92 76 86	46 16 28 35 54	94 75 08 99 23	37 08 92 00 48
80 33 69 45 98	26 94 03 68 58	70 29 73 41 35	53 14 03 33 40	42 05 08 23 41
44 10 48 19 49	85 15 74 79 54	32 97 92 65 75	57 60 04 08 81	22 22 20 64 13
12 55 07 37 42	11 10 00 20 40	12 86 07 46 97	96 64 48 94 39	28 70 72 58 15
63 60 64 93 29	16 50 53 44 84	40 21 95 25 63	43 65 17 70 82	07 20 73 17 90
61 19 69 04 46	26 45 74 77 74	51 92 43 37 29	65 39 45 95 93	42 58 26 05 27
15 47 44 52 66	95 27 07 99 53	59 36 78 38 48	82 39 61 01 18	33 21 15 94 66
94 55 72 85 73	67 89 75 43 87	54 62 24 44 31	91 19 04 25 92	92 92 74 59 73
42 48 11 62 13	97 34 40 81 21	16 86 84 87 67	03 07 11 20 59	25 70 14 66 70
23 52 37 83 17	73 20 88 98 37	68 93 59 14 16	26 25 22 96 63	05 52 28 25 62
04 49 35 24 94	75 24 63 38 24	45 86 25 10 25	61 96 27 93 35	65 33 71 24 72
00 54 99 76 54	64 05 18 81 59	96 11 96 38 96	54 69 28 23 91	23 28 72 95 29
35 96 31 53 07	26 89 80 93 54	33 35 13 54 62	77 97 45 00 24	90 10 33 93 33
59 80 80 83 91	45 42 72 68 42	83 60 94 97 00	13 02 12 48 92	78 56 52 01 06
46 06 88 52 36	01 39 09 22 86	77 28 14 40 77	93 91 08 36 47	70 61 74 29 41
32 17 90 05 97	87 37 92 52 41	05 56 70 70 07	86 74 31 71 57	85 39 41 18 38
69 43 26 14 06	20 11 74 52 04	15 95 66 00 00	18 74 39 24 23	97 11 89 63 38
19 56 54 14 30	01 75 87 53 79	40 41 92 15 85	66 67 43 68 06	84 96 28 52 07
45 15 51 49 38	19 47 60 72 46	43 66 79 45 43	59 04 79 00 33	20 82 66 95 41
94 86 43 19 94	36 16 81 08 51	34 88 88 15 51	01 54 03 54 56	05 01 45 11 76
98 08 62 48 26	45 24 02 84 04	44 99 90 88 96	39 09 47 34 07	35 44 13 18 80
33 18 51 62 32	41 94 15 09 49	89 43 54 85 81	88 69 54 19 94	37 54 87 30 43
80 95 10 04 06	96 38 27 07 74	20 15 12 33 87	25 01 62 52 98	94 62 46 11 71
79 75 24 91 40	71 96 12 82 96	69 86 10 25 91	74 85 22 05 39	00 38 75 95 79
18 63 33 25 37	98 14 50 65 71	31 01 02 46 74	05 45 56 14 27	77 93 89 19 36
74 02 94 39 02	77 55 73 22 70	97 79 01 71 19	52 52 75 80 21	80 81 45 17 48
54 17 84 56 11	80 99 33 71 43	05 33 51 29 69	56 12 71 92 55	36 04 09 03 24
11 66 44 98 83	52 07 98 48 27	59 38 17 15 39	09 97 33 34 40	88 46 12 33 56
48 32 47 79 28	31 24 96 47 10	02 29 53 68 70	32 30 75 75 46	15 02 00 99 94
69 07 49 41 38	87 63 79 19 76	35 58 40 44 01	10 51 82 16 15	01 84 87 69 38

Source: This table is reproduced from page 1 of The Rand Corporation, *A Million Random Digits with 100,000 Normal Deviates* (New York: The Free Press, 1955). Copyright © 1955 and 1983 by The Rand Corporation. Used by permission.

discarded. The next two numbers would also be discarded, but the fourth entry 02 would be used, because 2 corresponds to one of the serial numbers in the list, element B. The next five numbers would also be passed over as too large, but the number 05 would designate the inclusion of element E. Elements B and E would thus represent the sample of two from whom we would seek information on income.

An alternative strategy would be to use a computer program to generate the random numbers. Although some evidence suggests the numbers generated by computer programs are not as random as is commonly believed, their accuracy is sufficient for most applied marketing research studies, although perhaps not for complex mathematical model building. See Research Realities 10.2.

You should note that a simple random sample requires a serial numbered list of population elements. This means that the identity of each member of the target population must be known. For some populations this is no problem—for example, if the study is to be conducted among *Fortune* magazine's list of the 500 largest corporations in the United States. The list is readily available, and a simple random sample of these firms could be selected easily. For many other target populations of interest, the list of universe elements is much harder to come by (for example, all families living in a particular city), and applied researchers often resort to other sampling schemes.

Stratified Sampling

A **stratified sample** is a probability sample that is distinguished by the following two-step procedure:

1. The parent population is divided into mutually exclusive and exhaustive subsets.
2. A simple random sample of elements is chosen independently from each group or subset.

Note these features. The defining characteristics say nothing about the criterion or criteria that may be used to separate the universe elements into subsets. Admittedly, they will make a difference with respect to the advantages obtained in stratified sampling, but the criteria do not determine whether or not a stratified sample has been drawn. As long as the sample reflects the two-stage process, it is a stratified sample. This argument will be of assistance later when distinguishing cluster samples from stratified samples.

The subsets into which the universe elements are divided are called *strata* or *subpopulations*. Note that the division is mutually exclusive and exhaustive. This means that every population element must be assigned to one and only one stratum and that no population elements are omitted in the assignment procedure. To illustrate the process, assume that we will divide our hypothetical population of Table 10.1 into two strata on the basis of educational level. In particular, suppose that all those with a high school education or less are to be considered as forming one stratum and those with more than a high school education as forming another. Table 10.6 displays the results of this stratification procedure; elements A through J form what is labeled the *first stratum* and elements K through T form the *second stratum*. There is no magic in the choice of two strata. The parent population can be divided

---

RESEARCH REALITIES 10.2

A Problem of Bias in Computer-Generated Random Numbers

When scientists use computers to try to predict complex trends and events, they often apply a type of calculation that requires long series of random numbers. But instructing a computer to produce acceptable random strings of digits is proving maddeningly difficult.

In deciding which team kicks off a football game, the toss of a real coin is random enough to satisfy all concerned. But the cost of even a slightly nonrandom string of electronic coin tosses can be devastating to both practical problem-solving and pure theory, and a new investigation has revealed that nonrandom computer tosses are much more common than many scientists had assumed.

Mathematical "models" designed to predict stock prices, atmospheric warming, airplane skin friction, chemical reactions, epidemics, population growth, the outcome of battles, the locations of oil deposits, and hundreds of other complex matters increasingly depend on a statistical technique called Monte Carlo Simulation, which in turn depends on reliable and inexhaustible sources of random numbers.

Monte Carlo Simulation, named for Monaco's famous gambling casino, can help to mathematically represent very complex interactions in physics, chemistry, engineering, economics, and environmental dynamics. Mathematicians call such a representation a "model," and if a model is accurate enough, it produces the same responses to manipulations that the real thing would do. But Monte Carlo modeling contains a dangerous flaw: if the supposedly random numbers that must be pumped into a simulation actually form some subtle, nonrandom pattern, the entire simulation (and its predictions) may be wrong.

The danger was highlighted in a recent report from Dr. Alan M. Ferrenberg and Dr. D. P. Landau of the University of Georgia at Athens and Dr. Y. Joanna Wong of the IBM Corporation's Supercomputing center at Kingston, New York. In a December 7, 1992, article in the journal *Physical Review Letters,* the scientists showed that five of the most popular computer programs for generating streams of random numbers produced errors when they were used in a simple mathematical model of the behavior of atoms in a magnetic crystal.

The reason for the errors, the scientists found, was that the numbers produced by all five programs were not random at all, despite the fact that they passed several statistical tests for randomness. Beneath their apparent randomness, the sequences actually concealed correlations and patterns, revealed only when the subtle nonrandomness skewed the known properties of the crystal model.

All five of these systems for producing random numbers have long been used by scientists and statisticians with generally satisfactory results, Dr. Ferrenberg said. Major flaws turned up only recently when Dr. Ferrenberg and his colleagues were testing an ultra-powerful network of computers operating in parallel. Unlike ordinary sequential computer operations that execute programs one step at a time, parallel computing systems break up tasks into separate parts, which can be attacked simultaneously, with enormous savings in time. Parallel computers are so much faster and more powerful than the conventional kind that subtle problems in the programs they are executing come to light relatively quickly.

Source: Malcolm W. Browne, "Coin-Tossing Computers Found to Show Subtle Bias," *New York Times* (January 12, 1993), pp. B5–B6.

---

into any number of strata. Two were chosen for purposes of convenience in illustrating the technique.

Stage 2 in the process then requires that a simple random sample be drawn independently *from each* stratum. Suppose that we again work with samples of size 2, formed this time by selecting one element from each stratum. The number of elements from each stratum does not have to be equal, but again the assumption is made simply for exposition purposes. The procedure that would be used to select two elements for the stratified sample would now parallel that for the simple ran-

TABLE 10.6	Stratification of Hypothetical Population by Education

Stratum I Elements	Stratum II Elements
A	K
B	L
C	M
D	N
E	O
F	P
G	Q
H	R
I	S
J	T

dom sample. Within each stratum, the population elements would be serially numbered from 1 to 10. A table of random numbers would be consulted. The first number encountered between 1 and 10 would designate the element from the first stratum. The element from the second stratum could be selected after another independent start or by continuing from the first randomly determined start. In either case it would again be designated by the first encounter with a number between 1 and 10.

DERIVED POPULATION   Although only one sample of size 2 will in fact be selected, let us look briefly at the derived population of all possible samples of size 2 that could be selected under this sampling plan. This derived population, along with the mean of each sample, is displayed in Table 10.7.

Note first that every possible combination of sample elements is no longer a possibility, since every combination of two elements from the same stratum is precluded. There are now only 100 possible sample combinations of elements, whereas with simple random sampling there were 190 possible combinations. In this sense, stratified sampling is always more restrictive than simple random sampling. Note further that every element has an equal chance of being included in the sample—1 in 10—because each can be the single element selected from the stratum. This explains why we specified an additional requirement to define a simple random sample. Although simple random samples provide each element an equal chance of selection, other techniques can also. Thus, equal probability of selection is a necessary but not a sufficient condition for simple random sampling; in addition, each combination of n elements must be a sample possibility and as likely to occur as any other combination of n elements.

SAMPLING DISTRIBUTION   Table 10.8 contains the classification of sample means by size, and Figure 10.7 displays the plot of this sample statistic. Note that in relation to Figure 10.5 for simple random sampling, stratified sampling can produce a more concentrated distribution of estimates. This suggests one reason that we might choose a stratified sample: Stratified samples can produce sample statistics that are more precise or that have smaller error as a result of sampling than simple random samples. With education as a stratification variable, there is a marked reduction in the number of sample means that deviate widely from the population mean.

| TABLE 10.7 | | | Derived Population of All Possible Samples of Size *n* = 2 with Stratified Sampling | | | | | | | | |

k	Sample Identity	Mean	k	Sample Identity	Mean	k	Sample Identity	Mean	k	Sample Identity	Mean
1	AK	7,600	26	CP	9,000	51	FK	8,600	76	HP	10,000
2	AL	7,800	27	CQ	9,200	52	FL	8,800	77	HQ	10,200
3	AM	8,000	28	CR	9,400	53	FM	9,000	78	HR	10,400
4	AN	8,200	29	CS	9,600	54	FN	9,200	79	HS	10,600
5	AO	8,400	30	CT	9,800	55	FO	9,400	80	HT	10,800
6	AP	8,600	31	DK	8,200	56	FP	9,600	81	IK	9,200
7	AQ	8,800	32	DL	8,400	57	FQ	9,800	82	IL	9,400
8	AR	9,000	33	DM	8,600	58	FR	10,000	83	IM	9,600
9	AS	9,200	34	DN	8,800	59	FS	10,200	84	IN	9,800
10	AT	9,400	35	DO	9,000	60	FT	10,400	85	IO	10,000
11	BK	7,800	36	DP	9,200	61	GK	8,800	86	IP	10,200
12	BL	8,000	37	DQ	9,400	62	GL	9,000	87	IQ	10,400
13	BM	8,200	38	DR	9,600	63	GM	9,200	88	IR	10,600
14	BN	8,400	39	DS	9,800	64	GN	9,400	89	IS	10,800
15	BO	8,600	40	DT	10,000	65	GO	9,600	90	IT	11,000
16	BP	8,800	41	EK	8,400	66	GP	9,800	91	JK	9,400
17	BQ	9,000	42	EL	8,600	67	GQ	10,000	92	JL	9,600
18	BR	9,200	43	EM	8,800	68	GR	10,200	93	JM	9,800
19	BS	9,400	44	EN	9,000	69	GS	10,400	94	JN	10,000
20	BT	9,600	45	EO	9,200	70	GT	10,600	95	JO	10,200
21	CK	8,000	46	EP	9,400	71	HK	9,000	96	JP	10,400
22	CL	8,200	47	EQ	9,600	72	HL	9,200	97	JQ	10,600
23	CM	8,400	48	ER	9,800	73	HM	9,400	98	JR	10,800
24	CN	8,600	49	ES	10,000	74	HN	9,600	99	JS	11,000
25	CO	8,800	50	ET	10,200	75	HO	9,800	100	JT	11,200

A second reason for drawing a stratified sample is that stratification allows the investigation of the characteristic of interest for particular subgroups. Thus, by stratifying, one is able to guarantee representation of those with a high school education or less and those with more than a high school education. This can be extremely important when sampling from populations with rare segments. If a manufacturer of diamond rings is conducting a study of sales of the product by social class, for example, it is likely that unless special precautions are taken, the upper class will not be represented at all or will be represented by so few cases as to defy conclusion, because it is estimated to represent only 3 percent of the total popula-

TABLE 10.8	Classification of Sample Means by Size with Stratified Sampling	
	Sample Mean	Number of Samples
	7,300 to 7,800	3
	7,900 to 8,400	12
	8,500 to 9,000	21
	9,100 to 9,600	28
	9,700 to 10,200	21
	10,300 to 10,800	12
	10,900 to 11,400	3

FIGURE 10.7   Distribution of Sample Means with Stratified Sampling

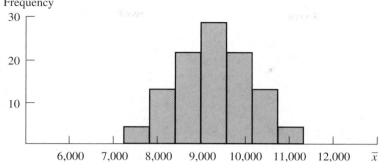

tion. Yet this can be an extremely important segment to the ring manufacturer. It is often true of many populations of interest in marketing that a small subset will account for a large proportion of the behavior of interest (for example, consumption of the product). It then becomes imperative that this subgroup be adequately represented in the sample. Stratified sampling is one way of ensuring adequate representation from each subgroup of interest.

CONFIDENCE INTERVAL ESTIMATE   In establishing a confidence interval with a simple random sample, we saw that we needed three things to complete the confidence interval specifications given by $\bar{x} - zs_{\bar{x}} \leq \mu \leq \bar{x} + zs_{\bar{x}}$:

1. The degree of confidence desired so that a z value can be selected
2. A point estimate of the population mean given by the sample mean $\bar{x}$
3. An estimate of the amount of sampling error associated with the sample mean, which was given by $s_{\bar{x}} = \hat{s}/\sqrt{n}$ when the population variance was unknown

The same three quantities are required for making inferences with a stratified sample. The only difference in the procedure occurs in the way items 2 and 3 are generated. With stratified sampling, the sample estimate of the population mean and the standard error of estimate associated with this statistic are determined by "appropriately weighting" the individual strata results.[14]

What are the appropriate weights? They are related to the stratum population size as compared to the total population size. Consider, for example, because of the need to make one specific point that a sample of size 2 was to be selected from each stratum, producing a total sample of size 4. In particular, suppose that elements B and E were randomly selected from the first stratum and elements N and S from the second stratum. Table 10.9 contains the sample means, sample variances, and estimated standard errors of estimate for each stratum. *These quantities are calculated for each stratum in exactly the same way as they were calculated for the sample as a whole with simple random sampling.*

---

[14]For general discussion of the analysis of data gathered through complex sampling schemes, see Eun Sul Lee, Ronald N. Forthofer, and Ronald J. Lorimar, *Analyzing Complex Survey Data* (Newbury Park, CA: Sage Publications, Inc., 1989).

TABLE 10.9	Sample Means, Sample Variances, and Estimated Standard Errors of Estimate for Each Stratum

Stratum I		Stratum II	
Element	**Income**	**Element**	**Income**
B	6,000	N	10,800
E	7,200	S	12,800

Mean:

$$\bar{x}_1 = \frac{\sum_{i=1}^{n_1} X_i}{n_1} = \frac{6,000 + 7,200}{2} \qquad \bar{x}_2 = \frac{\sum_{i=1}^{n_2} X_i}{n_2} = \frac{10,800 + 12,800}{2}$$

$$= 6,600 \qquad\qquad\qquad = 11,800$$

Variance:

$$\hat{s}_1^{\,2} = \frac{\sum_{i=1}^{n_1} (X_i - \bar{x}_1)^2}{n_1 - 1} \qquad \hat{s}_2^{\,2} = \frac{\sum_{i=1}^{n_2} (X_i - \bar{x}_2)^2}{n_2 - 1}$$

$$= \frac{(6,000 - 6,600)^2 + (7,200 - 6,600)^2}{2 - 1} \qquad = \frac{(10,800 - 11,800)^2 + (12,800 - 11,800)^2}{2 - 1}$$

$$= 720,000 \qquad\qquad\qquad = 2,000,000$$

Standard error of estimate:

$$s_{\bar{x}1} = \frac{\hat{s}_1}{\sqrt{n_1}} = \frac{\sqrt{720,000}}{\sqrt{2}} \qquad s_{\bar{x}2} = \frac{\hat{s}_2}{\sqrt{n_2}} = \frac{\sqrt{2,000,000}}{\sqrt{2}}$$

$$= 600 \qquad\qquad\qquad = 1,000$$

Variance of estimate:

$$s_{\bar{x}1}^{\,2} = 360,000 \qquad\qquad s_{\bar{x}2}^{\,2} = 1,000,000$$

Consider first the combination of strata sample means to produce a point estimate of the population mean. The weights here are the relative proportions of the population in each of the strata, that is,

$$\bar{x}_{st} = \sum_{h=1}^{L} \frac{N_h}{N} \bar{x}_h \qquad\qquad (10.3)$$

where
N_h is the number of elements in the population in stratum h,
N is the total size of the population,
$\bar{x}_h$ is the sample mean for stratum h,
$\bar{x}_{st}$ is the sample mean for a stratified sample,

and where summation is across all L strata. In the Table 10.9 example, $L = 2$; there are 10 elements in each stratum, 20 in all; and the overall point estimate of the population mean is

$$\bar{x}_{st} = \frac{N_1}{N}\,\bar{x}_1 + \frac{N_2}{N}\,\bar{x}_2 = \frac{10}{20}\,(6{,}600) + \frac{10}{20}\,(11{,}800) = 9{,}200$$

The combined standard error of estimate also employs the relative sizes of the strata in the population; however, it is calculated using the relative proportions squared, because the linear combination holds with respect to *variances* and *not* standard deviations. That is, one must compute the variance of the overall estimate and take the square root. The formula for the variance of the estimate is

$$s_{\bar{x}_{st}}^{2} = \sum_{h=1}^{L}\left(\frac{N_h}{N}\right)^2 s_{\bar{x}_h}^{2} \qquad\qquad \textbf{(10.4)}$$

and for the example

$$s_{\bar{x}_{st}}^{2} = \left(\frac{N_1}{N}\right)^2 s_{\bar{x}_1}^{2} + \left(\frac{N_2}{N}\right)^2 s_{\bar{x}_2}^{2} = \left(\frac{10}{20}\right)^2 (360{,}000) + \left(\frac{10}{20}\right)^2 (1{,}000{,}000)$$
$$= 90{,}000 + 250{,}000 = 340{,}000$$

so that

$$s_{\bar{x}_{st}} = \sqrt{340{,}000} = 583$$

The 95 percent confidence interval for this sample would then be

$$\bar{x}_{st} - zs_{\bar{x}_{st}} \le \mu \le \bar{x}_{st} + zs_{\bar{x}_{st}}$$
$$9{,}200 - 1.96(583) \le \mu \le 9{,}200 + 1.96(583)$$
$$8{,}057 \le \mu \le 10{,}343$$

This interval is interpreted as before. The true mean may or may not be in the interval, but since 95 of 100 intervals constructed by this process will contain the true mean, we are 95 percent confident that the true population mean income is between \$8,057 and \$10,343.[15]

Increased Precision of Stratified Samples   We mentioned previously that one reason one might choose a stratified sample is that such samples offer an opportunity for reducing sampling error or increasing precision. When estimating a mean, sampling error is given by the size of $s_{\bar{x}}$; the smaller $s_{\bar{x}}$, the less the sampling error and

---

[15]We are again assuming that the normal distribution applies in making this inference. Although this assumption is not strictly correct in this instance because of the size of the sample taken from each stratum, we are making it to allow more direct comparison with the interval constructed using simple random sampling. In most situations, the normal distribution would hold because the Central-Limit Theorem also applies to the individual strata means, and the linear combination of these means produces a normally distributed $\bar{x}_{st}$.

the more precise the estimate as indicated by the narrower confidence interval associated with a specified degree of confidence.

Consider equation 10.4 again. The total size of the population and the population within each stratum are fixed. The only way for total sampling error to be reduced, therefore, is for the variance of the estimate within each stratum to be made smaller. Now, the variance of the estimate by strata, in turn, depends on the variability of the characteristic within the strata, because $s_{\bar{x}h}^2 = \hat{s}_h^2 / n_h$, where $\hat{s}_h^2$ is the sample variance within the hth stratum and n_h is the size of the sample selected from the hth stratum. Thus, the estimate of the mean can be made more precise to the extent that the population can be partitioned so that there is little variability within each stratum—that is, to the extent the strata can be made internally homogeneous.

A characteristic of interest will display a certain amount of variation in the population. The investigator can do nothing about this total variation because it is a fixed characteristic of the population. But he or she can do something when dividing the elements of the population into strata to increase the precision with which the average value of the characteristic can be estimated. Specifically, the investigator should divide the population into strata so that the elements within any given stratum are as similar in value as possible and the values between any two strata are as disparate as possible. In the limit, if the investigator is successful in partitioning the population so that the elements in each stratum are exactly equal, there will be no error associated with the estimate of the population mean. That is right! The population mean could then be estimated without error because the *variability that exists between strata does not enter into the calculation of the standard error of estimate with stratified sampling.*

One can see this readily in a simple case with a limited number of values. Suppose that in a population of 1,000 elements, 200 had the value 5, 300 had the value 10, and 500 had the value 20. Now, the mean of this population $\mu = 14$ and the variance $\sigma^2 = 39$. If a simple random sample of size $n = 3$ were to be employed to estimate this mean, then the standard error of estimate would be

$$\sigma_{\bar{x}} = \frac{\sigma}{\sqrt{n}} = \frac{\sqrt{39}}{\sqrt{3}} = 3.61$$

and the width of confidence interval would be $\pm z$ times this value 3.61. Suppose, on the other hand, that a researcher employed a stratified sample and was successful in partitioning the total population so that all the elements with a value of 5 on the characteristic were in one stratum, those with the value of 10 were in the second stratum, and those with the value 20 were in the third stratum. To generate a completely precise description of the mean of each stratum, the researcher would then need to take a sample of only one from each stratum. Further, when the investigator combined these individual results into a global estimate of the overall mean, the standard error of the estimate would be zero, because each stratum's standard error of estimate is zero. The population mean value would be determined exactly.

Bases for Stratification   That variation among strata does not enter into the calculation of the standard error of estimate suggests two things. First, it indicates the kinds of criteria that should be used to partition the population. The values assumed by the characteristic will be unknown, for if they were known, there would be no need to take a sample to estimate their mean level. What the investigator attempts to do, therefore, is to partition the population according to one or more criteria that are expected to be related to the characteristic of interest. Thus it was no accident that in the hypothetical example, education was employed to divide the population elements into strata. As Table 10.1 indicates, there is a relation between education level and income level: the more years of school, the higher the income. Newspaper subscriptions, on the other hand, would have made a poor variable for partitioning the population into segments, because there is almost no relation between the paper to which a person subscribes and the individual's income. Whether one selects a "good" or a "bad" variable for partitioning the population does not affect whether or not a stratified sample is selected. It is important in determining whether a good or poor sample is selected, but the two features defining a stratified sample are still (1) the partitioning of the population into subgroups, and (2) the random selection of elements from each subgroup.

Second, the calculation of the standard error of estimate provides some clue to the number of strata that should be employed. Since the standard error of estimate depends only on variability within strata, the various strata should be made as homogeneous as possible. One way of doing this is to employ many very small strata. There are practical limits, however, to the number of strata that should be and are used in actual research studies. First, the creation of additional strata is often expensive in terms of sample design, data collection, and analysis. Second, there is an upper limit to the amount of variation that can be accounted for by any practical stratification. Regardless of the criteria by which the population is partitioned, a certain amount of variation is likely to remain unaccounted for, and the additional strata will serve no productive purpose.

PROPORTIONATE AND DISPROPORTIONATE STRATIFIED SAMPLING   Whether one chooses a stratified sample over a simple random sample depends in part on the trade-off between cost and precision. Although stratified samples typically produce more precise estimates, they also usually cost more than simple random samples. If the decision is made in favor of a stratified sample, the researcher must still decide whether to select a proportionate stratified sample or a disproportionate stratified sample.

With a **proportionate stratified sample,** the number of observations in the total sample is allocated among the strata in proportion to the *relative* number of elements in each stratum in the population. A stratum containing one-fifth of all the population elements would account for one-fifth of the total sample observations and so on. Proportionate sampling was employed in the example; each stratum contained one-half of the population and thus was sampled equally.

One advantage of proportionate allocation is that the investigator needs to know only the relative sizes of each stratum to determine the number of sample observations to select from each stratum with a given sample size.

An alternative allocation scheme, however, can produce still more efficient estimates. **Disproportionate stratified sampling** involves balancing the two criteria of strata size and strata variability. With a fixed sample size, strata exhibiting more variability are sampled more than proportionately to their relative size. Conversely, those strata that are very homogeneous are sampled less than proportionately.

Research Realities 10.3, for example, describes the disproportionate stratified sampling scheme used by ACNielsen to measure market shares of various products.

Although a full discussion of how the sample size for each stratum should be determined would take us too far afield and would be much too technical for our purpose, some feel for the rationale behind disproportionate sampling is useful. Consider at the extreme a stratum with zero variability. Because all the elements are identical in value, a single observation tells all. In contrast, a stratum that is characterized by great variability will require a large number of observations to produce a precise estimate of the stratum mean (recall that $s_{\bar{x}h}^2 = \hat{s}_h^2/n_h$). One can expect greater precision when the various strata are sampled proportionate to the relative

RESEARCH REALITIES 10.3

Disproportionate Stratified Sampling Scheme Used by ACNielsen

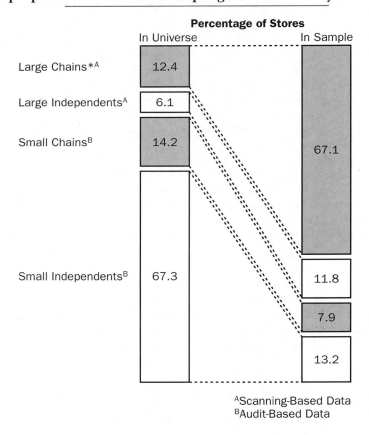

*Scanning-Based Data
*Audit-Based Data

---

*The dividing line between large and small is $2 million per year in sales.

Source: Developed from information supplied by ACNielsen.

variability of the characteristic under study rather than proportionate to their relative size in the population.

A disproportionate stratified sample requires more knowledge about the population of interest than does a proportionate stratified sample. To sample the strata in relation to their variability, one needs knowledge of relative variability. Sampling theory is a peculiar phenomenon in that knowledge begets more knowledge. Disproportionate sampling can produce more efficient estimates than proportionate sampling, but the former method also requires that some estimate of the relative variation within strata be known. One can sometimes anticipate the relative homogeneity likely to exist within a stratum on the basis of past studies and experience. Sometimes the investigator may have to rely on logic and intuition in establishing sample sizes for each stratum. For example, it might reasonably be expected that large retail stores would show greater variation in sales of some product than would small stores. That is one reason that the large stores would be sampled more heavily in the Nielsen Retail Index.

STRATIFIED VERSUS QUOTA SAMPLES   Stratified samples are sometimes confused with quota samples by the inexperienced researcher. There are similarities. Both involve the division of the population into segments and the selection of elements from each segment. However, there is one key difference. Sample elements are selected probabilistically with stratified samples, whereas they are selected judgmentally in quota samples. This has important implications. Because the sample elements are selected probabilistically, stratified samples allow the establishment of the sampling distribution of the statistic in question, which in turn allows confidence interval judgments. Quota samples allow no objective assessment of the degree of sampling error and thus preclude confidence interval estimates and statistical tests of significance.

Cluster Sampling

Cluster sampling involves the following steps: (1) The parent population is divided into mutually exclusive and exhaustive subsets. (2) A random sample of the subsets is selected. If the investigator then uses all the population elements in the selected subsets for the sample, the procedure is one-stage cluster sampling. If, on the other hand, a sample of elements is selected probabilistically from the selected subsets, the procedure is known as two-stage cluster sampling.

Note the similarities and differences between cluster sampling and stratified sampling. Both involve the division of the population into mutually exclusive and exhaustive subgroups, although the criteria used are different. The criteria for dividing the population are not the key in differentiating the techniques. The key ingredient that distinguishes the procedures is that with stratified sampling, a sample of elements is selected *from each subgroup*. With cluster sampling, one chooses a *sample of subgroups*.

Because one chooses a sample of subgroups with cluster sampling, it is desirable for each subgroup to be a small scale model of the population. At the extreme, if the distribution of the characteristic in each subgroup exactly parallels that for the population, one subgroup can tell all. Thus in cluster sampling, the subgroups ideally should be formed to be as heterogeneous as possible. In the hypothetical example, newspaper subscription would be a good basis for forming subgroups for a cluster sample. If all those subscribing to paper X were considered to form one subgroup and all those subscribing to paper Y a second subgroup, one could be relatively safe in randomly selecting either subgroup to estimate the mean income in the population. Although the distribution of incomes within each subgroup is not exactly the same as it is in the population, the range of incomes is such that there would be only a slight error if one were to estimate the mean income and variance of incomes of the population with the elements from either subset.

Admittedly, in practice, clusters are not always formed to be as heterogeneous as possible. Because of the way cluster samples are often drawn, the defined clusters are homogeneous rather than heterogeneous in regard to the characteristic of interest. Beginning researchers display a proclivity for then calling the procedure stratified sampling, since it involves the construction of homogeneous subgroups of population elements. As long as subgroups are selected for investigation randomly, the procedure is cluster sampling, regardless of how the subgroups are formed. Admittedly, homogeneous subgroups produce fewer ideal cluster samples from a statistical efficiency viewpoint than do heterogeneous subgroups.

Statistical efficiency is a relative notion by which sampling plans can be compared. One sampling plan is said to be more statistically efficient than another if, for the same size sample, it produces a smaller standard error of estimate. When the characteristic of interest is the mean, for example, the sampling plan that produces the smallest value of $s_{\bar{x}}$ for a given size sample is most statistically efficient. Cluster samples are typically much less statistically efficient than comparable stratified samples or even simple random samples, because the probable margin of error with a fixed size sample is often greatest with cluster sampling.

Even with its typically lower statistical efficiency, cluster sampling is probably the most widely used sampling procedure in large-scale field surveys, particularly those involving in-home personal interviews. Why? Simply because it is often more *economically efficient* since the cost per observation is less. The economies permit the selection of a larger sample at a smaller cost. Often, so many more observations can be secured for a given cost that the margin of error associated with the estimate is smaller for cluster sampling than it is for stratified sampling with the smaller number of observations. That is, cluster sampling is often more *efficient overall* than the other forms of sampling; although it requires a large sample for the same degree of precision and is thus less statistically efficient, the smaller cost per observation allows samples so much larger that estimates with a smaller standard error can be produced for the same cost.

SYSTEMATIC SAMPLING   The **systematic sample** offers one of the easiest ways of sampling many populations of interest. A systematic sample involves selecting every kth element after a random start.

Consider again the hypothetical population of 20 individuals and suppose that a sample of 5 is to be selected from this population. Number the elements from 1 to 20. With 20 population elements and a sample size of 5, the sampling fraction is $f = n/N = 5/20 = 1/4$, meaning that one element in four will be selected. The sampling interval $i = 1/f$ will be 4. This means that after a random start, every fourth element will be chosen. The random start, which must be some number between 1 and 4 (1 and i in general), is determined from a random number table. Thus, if the random start were 1, the first, fifth, ninth, thirteenth, and seventeenth items would be the sample; if it were 2, the second, sixth, tenth, fourteenth, and eighteenth items would be the sample; and so on.

Systematic sampling is one-stage cluster sampling, because rather than the subgroups being sampled, all the elements in the selected clusters are used. The subgroups or clusters in this case are

Cluster I	A, E, I, M, Q
Cluster II	B, F, J, N, R
Cluster III	C, G, K, O, S
Cluster IV	D, H, L, P, T

One of these clusters is selected randomly for investigation. The random start, of course, determines the cluster that is to be used.

One can readily see the ease with which a systematic sample can be drawn. It is much easier to draw a systematic sample than it is to select a simple random sample of the same size, for example. With a systematic sample one needs to enter the random number table only once. The problem of checking for the duplication of elements, which is cumbersome with simple random samples, does not occur with systematic samples. All the elements are uniquely determined by the selection of the random start.[16]

A systematic sample can often be made more representative than a simple random sample. With our hypothetical population, for example, we are guaranteed representation from the low-income segment and the high-income segment. Regardless of which of the four clusters is chosen, one element must have an income of $6,800 or less; another must have an income of $12,000 or more; and the remaining three elements must have incomes between these two values. A simple random sample of size 5 might or might not include low-income or high-income people.

The same is true when sampling from other populations. Thus, if we are sampling retail stores, we can guarantee representation of both small and large stores by employing a systematic sample, if the stores can be arrayed from smallest to largest according to some criterion such as annual sales or square footage. The ability to guarantee representation from each size segment depends on the availability of knowledge about the size of each store so that the stores can be arrayed from smallest to largest and numbered serially. A simple random sample of stores will probably contain inadequate representation from the large stores, since there are fewer large stores than small stores. Yet the fewer large stores account for a great proportion of all sales.

The degree to which the systematic sample will be more representative than a simple random sample thus depends on the clustering of objects within the list from which the sample will be drawn. The ideal list for a systematic sample will have elements similar in value on the characteristic close together and elements diverse in value spread apart.

---

[16]See J. Michael Brick, Joseph Waksberg, Dale Kulp, and Amy Starer, "Bias in List-Assisted Telephone Samples," *Public Opinion Quarterly* 59 (Summer 1995), pp. 218–235, for discussion of the use of systematic samples in telephone surveys.

There is at least one danger with systematic samples. If there is a natural periodicity in the list of elements, the systematic sample can produce estimates seriously in error. For example, suppose that we have the annual ticket sales of an airline by day and that we wish to analyze these sales in terms of length of trip. To analyze all 365 days may be prohibitively costly, but perhaps the research budget allows the investigation of 52 days of sales. A systematic sample of days using a sampling interval of 7 (365 ÷ 52) would obviously produce some misleading conclusions, because the day's sales will reflect all Monday trips, Friday trips, or Sunday trips, for example.[17] Any other sampling interval will be acceptable, and in general, an enlightened choice of the sampling interval can do much to eliminate the problems associated with natural periodicities in the data. The enlightened choice of sampling interval, of course, depends on knowledge of the phenomenon and nature of the periodicity.

AREA SAMPLING   In every probability sampling plan discussed so far, the investigator needed a list of population elements in order to draw the sample. A list identifying each population element was a necessary requirement for simple random samples, stratified samples, and systematic samples. The latter two procedures also required knowledge about some other characteristic of the population if they were to be designed optimally. For many populations of interest, these detailed lists will be unavailable. Further, it often will prove to be prohibitively costly to construct them. When this condition arises, the cluster sample offers the researcher another distinct benefit—he or she needs only the list of population elements for the selected clusters.

Suppose, for example, that an investigator wished to measure certain characteristics of industrial sales representatives, such as their earnings, attitudes toward the job, hours worked, and so on. It would be extremely difficult (if not impossible) and certainly costly to develop an up-to-date roster listing each industrial sales representative. Yet such a list would be required for a simple random sample. A stratified sample would further require the investigator to possess knowledge about some additional characteristics of each sales representative (for example, education or employer) so that the population could be divided into mutually exclusive and exhaustive subsets. With a cluster sample, on the other hand, one could use companies as sampling units. The investigator would generate a sample of business firms from the population of firms of interest. The business firms would be *primary sampling units* with a **sampling unit** being defined as "that element or set of elements considered for selection in some stage of sampling."[18] The investigator could then get a list of sales representatives working for each of the selected firms—a much

---

[17]Sudman suggests that when the "sampling interval *i* is not a whole number, the easiest solution is to use as the interval the whole number just below or above *i*. Usually, this will result in a selected sample that is only slightly larger or smaller than the initial sample required, and this new sample size will have no noticeable effect on either the accuracy of the results or the budget. For samples in which the interval *i* is small (generally for *i* less than 10), so that the rounding has too great an effect on the sample size, it is possible to add or delete the extra cases . . . it is usually easier to round down in computing *i* so that the sample is larger, and then to delete systematically." Sudman, *Applied Sampling,* p. 54.

[18]Earl R. Babbie, *The Practice of Social Research,* 7th ed. (Belmont, CA: Wadsworth Publishing, 1995), p. 198.

more plausible assignment. If the investigator studied each of the sales representatives in each of the selected firms, it would be one-stage cluster sampling. If the researcher subsampled sales representatives from each company's list, it would be two-stage cluster sampling.

The same principle underlies **area sampling**. Current, accurate lists of population elements are rarely available. Directories of all those living in a city at a particular moment simply do not exist for many cities, and when they do exist, they are obsolete when published; people move, others die, and new households are constantly being formed.[19] Although lists of families are nonexistent, relatively accurate lists of primary sampling units are available in the form of city maps, if the areal divisions of the city serve as the primary sampling units. The details of area sampling are much too complex for our purposes, but an appreciation for the rationale underlying the various approaches can be gathered by considering some of the basic types of area sampling.

One-Stage Area Sampling   Suppose that the investigator is interested in estimating the amount of wine consumed per household in the city of Chicago and how consumption is related to family income. An accurate listing of all households is unavailable for the Chicago area. A phone book when published is already somewhat obsolete, in addition to the other inadequacies previously mentioned. One approach to this problem would be to do the following:

1.   Choose a simple random sample of n city blocks from the population of N blocks.
2.   Determine wine consumption and income for all households in the selected blocks and generalize the sample relationships to the larger population.

The probability of any household being included in the sample can be calculated. It is given simply as n/N, because it equals the probability that the block on which it is located will be selected. Because the probabilities are known, the procedure is indeed probability sampling. Here, though, blocks have been substituted for households when selecting primary sampling units. The substitution is made because the list of blocks in the Chicago area can be developed from city maps. Each block can be identified, and the existence of this universe of blocks permits the calculation of the necessary probabilities.

Because each household on the selected blocks is included in the sample, the procedure is one-stage area sampling. Note that the blocks serve to divide the parent population into mutually exclusive and exhaustive subsets. Note further that the blocks do not serve very well as ideal subsets statistically for cluster samples; households on a given block can be expected to be somewhat similar with respect to

---

[19]R. L. Polk and Company in Taylor, Michigan, publishes some 1,400 directories for most medium-sized cities in the range of 50,000–800,000 people. The directories contain both an alphabetical list of names and businesses and a street address directory of households. Even though the alphabetic list can contain a reasonably large percentage of inaccurate listings at any one time, the address directory is reasonably accurate because it omits new construction only after the directory is published and the directories are revised every two or three years.

their income and wine consumption rather than heterogeneous as desired.[20] On the other hand, the data-collection costs will be very low because of the concentration of households within each block.

Two-Stage Area Sampling The distinguishing feature of the one-stage area sample is that all the households in the selected blocks (or other areas) are enumerated and studied. It is not necessary to employ all items in a selected cluster; the selected areas themselves can be subsampled, and it is often quite advantageous to do so. Two types of two-stage sampling need to be distinguished:

1. Simple, two-stage area sampling
2. Probability-proportional-to-size area sampling

With simple, two-stage area sampling, a certain proportion of second-stage sampling units (for example, households) is selected from each first-stage unit (for example, blocks). Consider a universe of 100 blocks; suppose that there are 20 households per block; assume that a sample of 80 households is required from this total population of 2,000 households. The overall sampling fraction is thus $80/2,000 = 1/25$. There are a number of ways by which the sample can be completed: by (1) selecting 10 blocks and 8 households per block; (2) selecting 8 blocks and 10 households per block; (3) selecting 20 blocks and 4 households per block; or (4) selecting 4 blocks and 20 households per block. The last alternative would, of course, be one-stage area sampling, whereas the first three would be two-stage area sampling.

The probability with which the blocks are selected is called the block or first-stage sampling fraction and is given as the ratio of n_B/N_B, where n_B and N_B are the number of blocks in the sample and in the population, respectively. For the first three schemes illustrated previously, the first-stage sampling fractions would be, in order, 1 in 10, 1 in 12.5, and 1 in 5. The probability with which the households are selected is the household or second-stage sampling fraction. Since there must be a total of 80 households in the sample, the second-stage sampling fraction differs for each alternative. The second-stage sampling fraction is given as $n_{H/B}/N_{H/B}$, where $n_{H/B}$ and $N_{H/B}$ are the number of households per block in the sample and in the population. For sampling scheme 1, the household sampling fraction is calculated to be $8/20 = 2/5$, for scheme 2 it is $10/20 = 1/2$, and for scheme 3 it is $4/20 = 1/5$. Note that the product of the first-stage and second-stage sampling fractions in each case equals the overall sampling fraction of $1/25$.

---

[20]When geographic clustering of rare populations occurs, it can be used to advantage when designing the sample. See, for example, Seymour Sudman, "Efficient Screening Methods for the Sampling of Geographically Clustered Special Populations," *Journal of Marketing Research* 22 (February 1985), pp. 20–29. For other discussions of techniques for sampling rare populations, see Roger Tourangeau and A. Wade Smith, "Finding Subgroups for Surveys," *Public Opinion Quarterly* 49 (Fall 1985), pp. 351–365; Seymour Sudman and Graham Kalton, "New Developments in the Sampling of Special Populations," *Annual Review of Sociology* 12 (1986), pp. 401–429; Seymour Sudman, Monroe G. Sirken, and Charles D. Cowan, "Sampling Rare and Elusive Populations," *Science* 240 (May 20, 1988), pp. 991–996; Leslie Kish, "Taxonomy of Elusive Populations," *Journal of Official Statistics* 7, no. 3 (1991), pp. 339–347; Seymour Sudman and Edward Blair, "Sampling in the 21st Century," *Journal of the Academy of Marketing Science* 27 (Spring 1999), pp. 269–277.

TABLE 10.10	Illustration of Probability-Proportional-to-Size Sampling

Block	Households	Cumulative Number of Households
1	800	800
2	400	1,200
3	200	1,400
4	200	1,600
5	100	1,700
6	100	1,800
7	100	1,900
8	50	1,950
9	25	1,975
10	25	2,000

Which scheme would be preferable? Although we do not want to get into the detailed calculation of what would be optimal, we would like to illustrate the general principle. Economies of data collection dictate that the second-stage sampling fraction should be high. This means that a great many households would be selected from each designated block, as with scheme 2. Statistical efficiency would dictate a small second-stage sampling fraction, because one can expect that the blocks would be relatively homogeneous, and thus it would be desirable to have very few households from any one block. Scheme 3 would be preferred on statistical grounds. Statistical sampling theory would suggest the balancing of these two criteria. There are formulas for this purpose that essentially reflect the cost of data collection and the variability of the characteristic within and between clusters, although a useful rule of thumb is that clusters of three to eight households per block or segment are near optimum for most social science variables.[21]

Simple two-stage area sampling is quite effective when there is approximately the same number of second-stage units per first-stage unit. When the second-stage units are decidedly unequal, simple two-stage area sampling can cause bias in the estimate. Sometimes the number of second-stage units per first-stage unit can be made approximately equal by combining areas. When this option is not available or is cumbersome to implement, probability-proportional-to-size sampling can be employed.

Consider, for example, the data in Table 10.10, and suppose that a sample of 20 elements is to be selected from this population of 2,000 households. With **probability-proportional-to-size sampling,** a *fixed* number of second-stage units is selected from each first-stage unit. After balancing economic and statistical considerations, suppose that the number of second-stage units per first-stage unit is determined to be 10. Two first-stage units must be selected to produce a total sample of 20. The procedure gets its name from the way these first-stage units are selected. The probability of selection is variable because it depends on the size of the first-stage unit. In particular, a table of four-digit random numbers would be consulted. The first two numbers encountered between 1 and 2,000 are employed to indicate the blocks that will be used. All numbers between 1 and 800 indicate the inclusion of

---

[21]Sudman, *Applied Sampling,* p. 81.

block 1, those from 801 to 1,200 indicate block 2, those from 1,201 to 1,400 indicate block 3, and so on.

The probability that any particular household will be included in the sample is equal, since the unequal first-stage selection probabilities are balanced by unequal second-stage selection probabilities. Consider, for example, blocks 1 and 10, the two extremes. The first-stage selection probability for block 1 is $800/2,000 = 1/2.5$, since 800 of the permissible 2,000 random numbers correspond to block 1. In contrast, only 25 of the permissible random numbers (1,976 to 2,000) correspond to block 10, and thus the first-stage sampling fraction for block 10 is $25/2,000 = 1/80$. Because 10 households are to be selected from each block, the second-stage sampling fraction for block 1 is $10/800 = 1/80$, while for block 10 it is $10/25 = 1/2.5$. The products of the first- and second-stage sampling thus compensate, since

$$\frac{800}{2,000} \times \frac{10}{800} = \frac{25}{2,000} \times \frac{10}{25}$$

which is also true for the remaining blocks.

Probability-proportional-to-size sampling is another illustration of how information begets information with applied sampling problems. One can avoid the bias of simple two-stage area sampling and can also produce estimates that are more precise when there is great variation in the number of second-stage units per first-stage unit. The price one pays, of course, is that probability-proportional-to-size sampling requires one to have detailed knowledge about the size of each first-stage unit. This is not quite as high a price as it might be, because the Census Bureau has reported the number of households per block for all cities of over 50,000 in population as well as for many other urbanized areas.[22] Maps are included in each report. Even though they are somewhat obsolete when published, these map and block statistics can be updated. The local electrical utility will have records of connections current to the day and so will the telephone company. In many cases, these statistics will be broken down by blocks.

Combining Sample Types

As you can probably begin to appreciate, sample design is a very detailed subject. Our discussion has concentrated on only a few of the fundamentals and, in particular, the basic types of probability samples. You should be aware that the basic types can be, and are, combined in large-scale field studies to produce some complex designs.

The Gallup poll, for example, is probably one of the best known of all the polls. The sample for the Gallup Poll for each survey "consists of 1,500 adults selected from 320 locations, using area sampling methods. At each location the interviewer is given a map with an indicated starting point and is required to follow a specified direction. At each occupied dwelling unit, the interviewer must attempt to meet sex quotas."[23] Thus, the Gallup Poll uses a combination of area and quota sampling.

---

[22] *United States Census, 2000, Housing: vol. 3, City Blocks,* HC(3)—No. (city number).

[23] Sudman, *Applied Sampling,* p. 71.

It is not uncommon to have several levels of stratification, such as by geographic area and density of population, precede several stages of cluster sampling. You cannot expect to be a sampling expert with the brief exposure to the subject contained here.[24] But you should be able to communicate effectively about sample design and to use the available microcomputer software effectively to select samples. Further, although you may not completely understand, say, why n_1 observations were taken from one stratum and n_2 from another, you should appreciate the basic considerations determining the choice.

Summary

This chapter reviewed the basic types of samples that may be used to infer something about a population. A sample might be preferred to a census on grounds of cost or impossibility of taking a census or because of its greater accuracy.

A practical procedure to use when drawing a sample includes the following steps:

1.   Define the population.
2.   Identify the sampling frame.
3.   Select a sampling procedure.
4.   Determine the sample size.
5.   Select the sample elements.
6.   Collect the data from the designated elements.

Probability samples are distinguished by the fact that every population element has a known, nonzero chance of being included in the sample. With nonprobability samples, the chance of inclusion is not calculable because personal judgment is involved somewhere in the actual selection process. Thus, nonprobability samples do not allow the construction of the sampling distribution of the statistic in question. This, in turn, means that the traditional tools of statistical inference are not legitimately employed with nonprobability samples.

The basic types of nonprobability samples are convenience, judgment, and quota samples. Convenience samples are also known as accidental samples, because those elements included just happen to be at the study site at the right time. Population elements are handpicked to serve a specific purpose with judgment samples, whereas with quota samples, the interviewers personally select subjects with specified characteristics in order to fulfill their quota.

Simple random samples are probability samples in which each population element has an equal chance of being included and every combination of sample elements is just as likely as any other combination of n sample elements. Simple random samples were used to illustrate the basis of statistical inference, in which a parameter (a fixed characteristic of the population) is estimated from a statistic (a characteristic of a sample). The value of the statistic depends on the sample actually selected, since it varies from sample to sample. The derived pop-

---

[24]Those interested in pursuing the subject further should see one of the excellent books on the subject, such as William G. Cochran, *Sampling Techniques*, 3rd ed. (New York: John Wiley, 1977); Morris H. Hansen, William N. Hurwitz, and William G. Madow, *Sample Survey Methods and Theory, Vol. I, Methods and Applications* (New York: John Wiley, 1993); Gary T. Henry, *Practical Sampling* (Thousand Oaks, CA: Sage Publications, Inc., 1990); Leslie Kish, *Survey Sampling* (New York: John Wiley, 1995); Paul S. Levy and Stanley Lemeshow, *Sampling of Populations: Methods and Applications*, 3rd ed. (New York: John Wiley and Sons, Inc., 1999); Richard L. Schaefer, William Mendenhall, and R. Lyman Ott, *Elementary Survey Sampling*, 5th ed. (Belmont, CA: Wadsworth Publishing, 1996); Sharon Lohr, *Sampling: Design and Analysis* (Belmont, CA: Wadsworth Publishing, 1999).

Raphael is investigating conflict development and resolution in channels of distribution. Because of the difficulty of accessing actual channel members, he decides to run an experiment on a convenience sample of undergraduate students. Student samples are tolerated in consumer behavior but have met with more severe criticism in channels research because although a student is also a consumer, a student is not also a channel member. However, determined to present his research endeavor in the best possible light, Raphael ignores the large fraction of art students included in his sample of introductory marketing students and refers to his sample as "business students with an average of three years' work experience in jobs in which bargaining and interpersonal skills were required and developed to a level comparable with most channel members."

• Is it ethical to misrepresent an inappropriate sample as an appropriate sample?

ulation is the set of all possible distinguishable samples that could be drawn from a parent population under a given sampling plan, and the distribution of some sample statistic's values is the sampling distribution of the statistic. The concept of the sampling distribution is the cornerstone of statistical inference, since statistical inferential procedures rely on the sampling distribution of the specific statistic in question. The sampling distributions of a number of statistics of interest to the applied researcher are known from the work of theoretical statisticians.

A stratified sample is a probability sample in which the parent population is divided into mutually exclusive and exhaustive subsets and a sample of elements is drawn from each subset. Stratified samples are typically the most statistically efficient (that is, they have the smallest standard error of estimate for a given size), and they also allow the investigation of the characteristic of interest for particular subgroups within the population. The most statistically efficient stratified samples result when the strata are made as homogeneous as possible. Thus, variables expected to be correlated to the characteristic of interest, and whose values are known, are often employed when establishing the strata. In proportionate stratified sampling, the size of the sample taken from each stratum depends only on the relative size of the stratum in the population, whereas with disproportionate stratified sampling, sample size depends on the variability within the stratum as well.

A cluster sample is a probability sample in which the parent population is divided into mutually exclusive and exhaustive subsets and then a random sample of subsets is selected. If each of the elements within the selected subsets is studied, it is one-stage cluster sampling; if the selected subsets are also subsampled, the procedure represents two-stage cluster sampling. Since only a sample of subsets is selected for analysis, statistical efficiency considerations suggest that the subsets be established to be as heterogeneous as possible. A systematic sample is a form of cluster sample in which every kth element is selected after a randomly determined start.

An area sample is one of the most important types of cluster samples (or any kind of probability sample for that matter) in applied, large-scale studies. Area samples make use of one very desirable feature of cluster samples—one only needs the list of population elements for the selected clusters. By defining areas as clusters and then randomly selecting areas, the investigator needs to develop lists of population elements only for the selected areas. Even here the researcher can use dwelling units and select them systematically. Thus, area samples permit probability samples to be drawn when current lists of population elements are unavailable. In drawing area samples, the researcher typically attempts to balance statistical and economic considerations. Because small areas are basically homogeneous, statistical considerations suggest that a great many areas should be used. However, the economies of data collection dictate that few areas be used and a great many observations be collected within each area.

Many applied sample designs represent combinations of the basic types reviewed here.

Questions

1. What is a census? What is a sample?
2. Is a sample ever preferred to a census? Why?
3. What distinguishes a probability sample from a nonprobability sample?
4. What is a convenience sample?
5. What is a judgment sample?
6. Explain the operation of a quota sample. Why is a quota sample a nonprobability sample? What kinds of comparisons should one make with the data from quota samples to check their representativeness, and what kinds of conclusions can one legitimately draw?
7. What are the distinguishing features of a simple random sample?
8. What is a derived population? How is it distinguished from a parent population?
9. Consider the estimation of a population mean. What is the relation between the mean of the parent population and the mean of the derived population? Between the variance of the parent population and the variance of the derived population?
10. What is the Central-Limit Theorem? What role does it play in making inferences about a population mean?
11. What procedure is followed in constructing a confidence interval for a population mean when the population variance is known? When the population variance is unknown? What does such an interval mean?
12. How should a simple random sample be selected? Describe the procedure.
13. What is a stratified sample? How is a stratified sample selected?
14. Is a stratified sample a probability or nonprobability sample? Why?
15. What principle should be followed in establishing the strata for a stratified sample? Why? How can this principle be implemented in practice?
16. Describe the procedure that is followed in developing a confidence interval estimate for a population mean with a stratified sample. Be specific.
17. Which sampling method typically produces more precise estimates of a population mean—simple random sampling or stratified sampling? Why?
18. What is a proportionate stratified sample? What is a disproportionate stratified sample? What must be known about the parent population to select each?
19. What is a cluster sample? How is a cluster sample selected?
20. What are the similarities and differences between a cluster sample and a stratified sample?
21. What is statistical efficiency? What is economic efficiency? What is overall efficiency?
22. Which sampling method is typically most statistically efficient? Which method is typically most economically efficient? Which method is typically most efficient overall? Why?
23. What is a systematic sample? How are the random start and sampling interval determined with a systematic sample?
24. What are the advantages and disadvantages associated with systematic samples?
25. What is an area sample? Why are area samples used?
26. How does a two-stage area sample differ from a one-stage area sample?
27. Illustrate the selection of a simple, two-stage area sample using hypothetical data of your own choosing.
28. Illustrate probability-proportional-to-size two-stage area sampling using an example of your own choosing.

29.   What information is needed to effectively draw
   a. a simple, two-stage area sample?
   b. a probability-proportional-to-size area sample?

Applications and Problems

1.   For each of the following situations, identify the appropriate target population and sampling frame.
   a. The National Head Injury Foundation Inc. wants to test the effectiveness of a brochure soliciting volunteers for its local chapter in Indianapolis, Indiana.
   b. A regional manufacturer of yogurt selling primarily in the Pacific Northwest wants to test market three new flavors of yogurt.
   c. A national manufacturer wants to assess whether adequate inventories are being held by wholesalers in order to prevent shortages by retailers.
   d. A large wholesaler dealing in electronic office products in Chicago wants to evaluate dealer reaction to a new discount policy.
   e. Your school cafeteria system wants to test a carbonated milk product manufactured in the Food Science department and sold by the cafeteria system.
   f. A local cheese manufacturer wants to assess the satisfaction with a new credit policy offered to mail-order customers.
   g. A regional manufacturer of hog feed wants to conduct an on-farm test of a new type of hog feed in Carroll County, Indiana.

2.   A leisure-wear manufacturer wants to determine consumer preference for several varieties of t-shirts. Respondents will participate in a touch test; that is, they will touch several different t-shirts and then state their preferences. Some aspects of the t-shirts that will be compared are armbands, neckbands, and shirt material. The marketing researcher conducting the study has recommended that the touch tests be conducted by mall intercepts.
   a. What problems, if any, do you see in trying to use the results of this study to estimate the population of consumers who buy t-shirts?
   b. Suggest an alternative to a mall intercept study for determining consumer preferences for t-shirts. Why is this a better method?

3.   A leading film-processing company wishes to investigate the market potential for a new line of digital-processing equipment. Because this is a completely new technology, the company believes that industry leaders might offer insights into the desires of customers and consumers. However, a list of industry leaders does not exist. Discuss possible methods of generating a sampling frame for the influential people in the digital-processing industry.

4.   The My-Size Company, a manufacturer of clothing for large-sized consumers, was in the process of evaluating its product and advertising strategy. Initial efforts consisted of a number of focus-group interviews. Each focus group consisted of 10 to 12 large men and women of different demographic characteristics who were selected by the company's research department using on-the-street observations of physical characteristics.
   a. What type of sampling method was used?
   b. Critically evaluate the method used.

5.   The owners of a popular bed and breakfast inn in Door County, Wisconsin, had noticed a decline in the number of tourists and length of stay during the past three years. An overview of industry trends indicated that the overall tourist trade was expanding and growing rapidly. The managers decided to conduct a study to determine people's attitudes toward the particular activities that were available at the inn. Because they wanted to cause the minimum amount of inconvenience to their guests, the owners devised the following plan. Interview request cards, which were available at the Chamber

of Commerce office, the Visitor Information Center, and three of the more popular restaurants in Sturgeon Bay, indicated the nature of the study and encouraged visitors to participate. Visitors were asked to report to a separate room at either the Chamber of Commerce office or the Visitor Information Center. Personal interviews, lasting 20 minutes, were conducted at these locations.

    a. What type of sampling method was used?

    b. Critically evaluate the method used.

6. A national manufacturer of processed meats was planning to enter the Japanese market. Before the final decision about launching its product, management decided to test market the products in two cities. After reviewing the various cities in terms of external criteria, such as demographics, shopping characteristics, and so on, the research department settled on the cities of Yokohama and Hiroshima.

    a. What type of sampling method was used?

    b. Critically evaluate the method used.

7. The Now-You-See-It-Now-You-Don't Credit Union of Wichita, Kansas, has witnessed a sharp increase in the number of branches it operates and in the company's gross sales and net profit margin in the past five years. Management plans to offer free retirement planning and consultation, a service for which other competing credit unions, banks, and brokerage firms charge a substantial price. To offset the increase in operating expenses, management plans to raise the rates on other services by 7 percent. Before introducing this new service and increasing rates, management decides to do a survey using customers as a sample and employing the method of quota sampling. Your assistance is required in planning the study.

    a. On what variables would you suggest the quotas be based? Why? List the variables with their respective levels.

    b. Management has kept close track of the demographic characteristics of customers during the five-year period and decides that these would be most relevant in identifying the sample elements to be used.

Variable	Level	Percentage of Customers
Age	0–15 years	5%
	16–30 years	30
	31–45 years	30
	46–60 years	15
	61–75 years	15
	76 years or over	5
Sex	Male	42
	Female	58
Income	$0–$9,999	10
	$10,000–$19,999	20
	$20,000–$29,999	30
	$30,000–$39,999	20
	Over $40,000	20

    Based on these three quota variables, indicate the characteristics of a sample of 200 subjects.

    c. Discuss the possible sources of bias with the sampling method.

8. The following table lists the results of one question taken from a survey conducted for Joe's Bar and Grill. The Grill has recently undergone renovations, and with the new look, management has decided to change the menu. They are interested in knowing how well customers like the new menus. Calculate the mean, standard deviation, and confidence interval for menu preference assuming simple random sampling was used.

Respondent	Meal Eaten at Joe's Bar and Grill	Menu Preference on a Five-Point Scale
1	Breakfast	3
2	Breakfast	5
3	Breakfast	4
4	Breakfast	5
5	Breakfast	5
6	Lunch	10
7	Lunch	9
8	Lunch	8
9	Lunch	10
10	Lunch	9
11	Dinner	14
12	Dinner	15
13	Dinner	15
14	Dinner	14
15	Dinner	16

9. The Wisconsin National Bank, headquartered in Milwaukee, Wisconsin, has some 400,000 users of its credit card scattered throughout the state of Wisconsin. The application forms for the credit card ask for the usual information about name, address, phone, income, education, and so on that is typical of such applications. The bank is now very interested in determining if there is any relationship between the uses to which the card is put and the socioeconomic characteristics of the user; for example, is there a difference in the characteristics of those people who use the credit card for major purchases only (for example, appliances) and those who use it for minor as well as major purchases?

   a. Identify the population and sampling frame that would be used by Wisconsin National Bank.
   b. Indicate how you would draw a simple random sample from the sampling frame identified in part a.
   c. Indicate how you would draw a stratified sample from the sampling frame.
   d. Indicate how you would draw a cluster sample from the sampling frame.
   e. Which method would be preferred? Why?

10. Howdy Supermarkets is considering entering the Cleveland market. However, before doing so, management wishes to estimate the average square feet of selling space among potential competitors' stores to plan better the size of the proposed new outlet. A stratified sample of supermarkets in Cleveland produced the following results:

Size	Total Number in City	Number of This Size in Sample	Mean Size of Stores in Sample (sq. ft.)	Standard Deviation of Stores in Sample (sq. ft.)
Small supermarkets	490	24	4,000	2,000
Medium supermarkets	280	14	27,000	4,000
Large supermarkets	40	2	60,000	5,000

   a. Estimate the average-size supermarket in Cleveland. Show your calculations.
   b. Develop a 95 percent confidence interval around this estimate. Show your calculations.
   c. Was a proportionate or a disproportionate stratified sample design used in determining the number of sample observations for each stratum? Explain.

11. A long-distance telephone company wants to investigate the needs of its customers. Propose a stratification scheme for the sample and discuss the benefits of your scheme.

12. Use the table in question 8 to calculate the mean, standard deviation, and confidence interval for menu preference assuming stratified sampling based on the meal eaten was used (that is, the strata were breakfast, lunch, and dinner customers). How do the results obtained from assuming a stratified sampling technique compare with the results you obtained using simple random sampling? Why?

13. Andy Smith, the owner of a local hotel, is interested in assessing customer satisfaction with his hotel. Andy's hotel does not accept reservations. Because all his customers are walk-ins, Andy has no way of knowing how many people will stay in his hotel on any given night. All the hotel guests must check in with the front-desk clerk; due to the small size of the hotel, there is only one check-in terminal. Andy has decided to distribute a survey to every tenth room that checks in.
    a. What type of sampling is to be used?
    b. Critically evaluate this method.

Thorndike Sports Equipment Video Case

1. What does the distribution of racquet weights tell Ted? How is the distribution of weights important to the research question?
2. Does the variation in racquet weights explain the increasing number of complaints?
3. With the distribution information, is Ted able to solve Thorndike's racquet problem?
4. A new machine to keep racquetball racquets a consistent weight is not feasible. What would you do next?
5. With the results of Luke's test, can Thorndike Sports Equipment now claim that its racquets can withstand 240 pounds without breaking? Identify the problems in Luke's research design.
6. If Luke truly feels there is strategic advantage to advertising the resiliency of the Thorndike Graphite Pro racquets, design a test that will provide a valid and reliable answer to how much weight the racquets can withstand before breaking.
7. What are the current legal restrictions on making claims of this sort in advertising copy?

Sample Size

Thus far, our discussion of sampling has concentrated on sample type. Another important consideration is sample size. Unless the researcher is going to use a sequential sample, he or she needs some means of determining the necessary size of the sample before collecting data.

The question of sample size is complex because it depends on (among other things) the type of sample; the statistic in question; the homogeneity of the population; and the time, money, and personnel available for the study. There is no way we can do all these issues justice in one chapter. Rather, our objective will be to illustrate the statistical principles determining sample size, using only simple random samples and a few of the more popular statistics. The reader interested in the determination of sample size for stratified or cluster samples should consult one of the standard references on sampling theory. The reader using a simple random sample to estimate a population variance, for example, should consult an intermediate-level statistics text to determine the proper sample size. The principles will remain the same in each case, but the formulas differ, since they depend on the sampling plan and the statistic in question.

Basic Considerations

It should not be surprising to find that the sampling distribution of the statistic underlies the determination of sample size. Recall that the sampling distribution of the statistic indicates how the sample estimates vary as a function of the particular sample selected. The spread of the sampling distribution thus indicates the error that can be associated with any estimate. For instance, the error associated with the estimation of a population mean by a sample mean was given by the standard error of the mean $\sigma_{\bar{x}} = \sigma/\sqrt{n}$ when the population variance was known, and $s_{\bar{x}} = \hat{s}/\sqrt{n}$ when the population variance was unknown. The first factor that one must consider in estimating sample size, then, is the standard error of the estimate obtained from the known sampling distribution of the statistic.

A second consideration is the precision desired from the estimate. Precision is the size of the estimating interval when the problem is one of estimating a population parameter. For example, a researcher investigating mean income might want the sample estimate to be within ±\$100 of the true population value. This is a more precise estimate than one required to be within ±\$500 of the true value.

A third factor that must be considered is the desired degree of confidence associated with the estimate. There is a trade-off between degree of confidence and

Researchers in the laboratory of a regional food manufacturer recently developed a new dessert topping. This topping was more versatile than those currently on the market because it came in a variety of flavors and thus had more potential uses than a product like Dream Whip, for instance. Although the manufacturer believed that the product had great promise, management also thought it would be necessary to convince the trade of its sales potential in order to get wholesalers and retailers to handle it. The manufacturer consequently decided to test market the product in a couple of areas where it had especially strong distribution. It selected several stores with which it had a long working relationship to carry the product.

During the planned two-month test period, product sales did not begin to compare to sales of other dessert toppings. Feeling that such evidence would make it very difficult to gain distribution, the manufacturer decided to do two things: (1) run the test for a longer period, and (2) increase the number of accounts handling the test product. Four months later, the results were much more convincing and management felt more comfortable in approaching the trade with the test market results.

- Is it ethical to conduct a test market in an area where a firm's distribution or reputation are especially strong?
- Is it ethical not to report this fact to the trade, thereby causing it to misinterpret the market response to the item?
- Is it ethical to increase the size of the sample until one secures a result one wants? What if the argument for increasing sample size was that the product was so novel that two months simply was not enough time for consumers to become sufficiently familiar with it?
- Would it have been more ethical to plan initially for a larger and longer test than to adjust the length and scope of the test on the basis of early results? Why or why not?

degree of precision with a sample of fixed size; one can specify either the degree of confidence or the degree of precision but not both. It is only when sample size is allowed to vary that one can achieve both a specified precision and a specified degree of confidence in the result, and, as a matter of fact, the determination of sample size involves balancing the two considerations against each other.

To illustrate the distinction between confidence and precision, consider a point estimate of a population parameter—say, mean income. A point estimate is a precise estimate in that there are no associated bounds of error; for example, the sample mean indicates that the population mean income is $19,243. This point estimate is also most assuredly wrong, and thus we can have no confidence in it. On the other hand, we can have complete confidence in the following statement: The population mean income is between zero and $1 million. Although we're completely confident about the accuracy of the statement, we must admit that the statement is not particularly helpful, because it tells us next to nothing about mean income. The statement is simply too imprecise to be of value.

Sample Size Determination When Estimating Means

The interrelation of the basic factors affecting the determination of sample size is best illustrated through example. Consider a simple random sample to estimate the mean annual expenditures of licensed fishermen on food and lodging while on fishing trips within a given state.[1] Now, the Central-Limit Theorem suggests that the distribution of sample means will be normal for samples of reasonable size regardless of the distribution of expenditures in the population of fishermen. Consider, then, the sampling distribution of sample means in Figure 11.1 and distinguish two cases: Case I, in which the population variance is known, and Case II, in which the population variance is unknown.

CASE I: POPULATION VARIANCE KNOWN   The population variance might be known from past studies, even though the average expenditures for food and lodging might be unknown, since variation typically changes much more slowly than level.[2] This means that the spread of the distribution given by $\sigma_{\bar{x}}$, as shown in Figure 11.1, is also known up to a proportionality constant, the square root of the sample size, because $\sigma_{\bar{x}} = \sigma/\sqrt{n}$. Thus, we have some idea of the first ingredient in sample size determination, the standard error of estimate.

Suppose that the decision maker desired the estimate to be within $\pm\$25$ of the true population value. Total precision is thus \$50, and half precision (call it H) is \$25. The reason we work with H instead of the full length of the interval is that the normal curve is symmetrical about the true population mean, and it simplifies the calculations to work with only one-half of the curve.

The remaining item that needs to be specified is the degree of confidence desired in the result. Suppose the decision maker further wishes to be 95 percent confident that the interval the researcher constructs will contain the true population mean. This implies that z is approximately equal to 2.[3]

Now we have all we need for determining sample size, because it is known that a number of standard deviations on each side of the mean will include a certain proportion of all observations with a normal curve and, in particular, that two standard deviations will include 95 percent of all observations. In Figure 11.1, each observation is a sample mean; the distribution of these sample means is centered about the population mean, and two standard deviations are $2\sigma_{\bar{x}}$, or $z\sigma_{\bar{x}}$ in the general case. We want our estimate to be no more than \$25 removed from the true pop-

---

[1]The problem would be of interest to the tourist industry, and it also could be of interest to the division of state government concerned with economic development. The problem was chosen because the availability of a list of population elements allows a simple random sample to be selected.

[2]Morris H. Hansen, William N. Hurwitz, and William G. Madow, *Sample Survey Methods and Theory: Vol. 1: Methods and Applications* (New York: John Wiley, 1993). One of the best treatments on securing variance estimates from past data is to be found on pages 450–455.

[3]z more correctly equals 1.96 for a 95 percent confidence interval. The approximation $z = 2$ is used because it simplifies the calculations.

FIGURE 11.1   **Sampling Distribution of Sample Means**

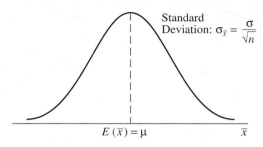

ulation value, so we can simply equate the size of the specified half interval with the number of standard deviations to yield

$$H = z\sigma_{\bar{x}} \tag{11.1}$$

$$= z\frac{\sigma}{\sqrt{n}}$$

This equation can be solved for n, because H and z have been specified and σ is known from past studies. Specifically, n can be shown to be equal to

$$n = \frac{z^2}{H^2}\sigma^2 \tag{11.2}$$

To illustrate, suppose that the historic variation in expenditures on food and lodging as measured by σ was \$100. Then

$$n = \frac{(2)^2}{(25)^2}(100)^2$$

and $n = 64$. Thus, only a relatively small sample needs to be taken to estimate the mean expenditure level when the population standard deviation is \$100 and the allowed precision is \$50.

Note what happens, though, if the estimate must be twice as precise; that is, \$25 is the total width of the desired interval and $H = 12.5$. Substituting in Equation 11.2,

$$n = \frac{(2)^2}{(12.5)^2}(100)^2$$

and $n = 256$. Doubling the precision (halving the total width of the interval) increased the required sample size by a factor of four. This is the basic trade-off between precision and sample size. Whenever precision is increased by a factor c, sample size is increased by a factor c^2. Thus, if the desired precision were \$10 instead of \$50—in other words, the estimate must be five times more precise ($c = 5$)—the sample size would be 1,600 instead of 64 ($c^2 = 25$).

One also pays dearly for increases in the degree of confidence. For example, what if one wished to be 99 percent confident in one's estimate rather than 95 percent confident. Using the integer approximations for z means that $z = 3$ instead of 2 as before. Suppose that $H = 25$ and $\sigma = 100$ as originally. Then

$$n = \frac{(3)^2}{(25)^2}(100)^2$$

and $n = 144$, whereas $n = 64$ when $z = 2$. When z was increased by a factor of d ($d = \frac{3}{2}$ in the example), sample size increased by a factor of d^2 ($d^2 = \frac{9}{4}$ in the example).

The point of all these gyrations is that you should be well aware of the price that must be paid for increased precision and confidence. Although we might constantly strive for very precise estimates in which we can have a great deal of confidence, one can see why applied researchers often learn to live with risky, somewhat imprecise estimates. The degree of precision and lack of confidence that can be tolerated is, of course, a function of the consequences of the decision associated with the result. The more dire the consequences, the more precise and confident the results must be.

CASE II: POPULATION VARIANCE UNKNOWN   The previous examples were all framed employing a known population variance. What happens in the more typical case when the population variance is unknown? The procedure for estimating the sample size is the same except that an estimated value of σ is used in place of the previously known value of σ. Once the sample is selected, however, the variance calculated from the sample is used in place of the originally estimated variance when establishing confidence intervals.

Suppose that there were no past studies on which to base an estimate of σ. How does one then generate an estimate of the population standard deviation? One could do a pilot study.[4] Alternatively, sometimes the variance can be estimated from the conditions surrounding the approach to the problem. Research Realities 11.1, for example, discusses the estimation of the variance when rating scales are used to measure the important variables. Still a third possibility is to take into account the fact that for a normally distributed variable, the range of the variable is approximately equal to plus or minus three standard deviations. Thus, if one can estimate the range of variation, one can estimate the standard deviation by dividing by six. A little *a priori* knowledge of the phenomenon is often enough to estimate the range. If the estimate is in error, the consequence is a confidence interval more or less precise than desired. Let us illustrate:

Certainly some licensed fishermen would spend zero dollars on food and lodging while on fishing trips because they would be making only one-day trips. Some

---

[4]See Raphael Gillett, "Confidence Interval Construction by Stein's Method: A Practical and Economical Approach to Sample Size Determination," *Journal of Marketing Research* 26 (May 1989), pp. 237–240, for discussion of how the pilot study results can be used not only to develop an estimate of the population variance, but also to produce an estimate of the population mean corresponding to the specified confidence level and desired interval size. See also H. Lee, E. Rancourt, and C. E. Sarndal, "Experiments with Variance Estimation from Survey Data with Imputed Values," *Journal of Official Statistics* 10 (1994), pp. 231–243.

RESEARCH REALITIES 11.1

Guidelines for Estimating Variance for Data Obtained Using Rating Scales

Rating scales are doubly-bounded: on a 5-point scale, for instance, responses cannot be less than 1 or greater than 5. This constraint leads to a relationship between the mean and the variance. For example, if a sample mean is 4.6 on a 5-point scale, there must be a large proportion of responses of 5, and it follows that the variance must be relatively small. On the other hand, if the mean is near 3.0, the variance can be potentially much greater. The nature of the relationship between the mean and the variance depends on the number of scale points and on the "shape" of the distribution of responses (for example, approximately normal or symmetrically clustered around some central scale value, or skewed, or uniformly spread among the scale values). By considering the types of distribution shapes typically encountered in practice, it is possible to estimate variances for use in calculating sample size requirements for a given number of scale points.

The table at right lists ranges of variances likely to be encountered for various numbers of scale points. The low end of the range is the approximate variance when data values tend to be concentrated around some middle point of the scale, as in a normal distribution. The high end of the range is the variance that would be obtained if responses were uniformly spread across the scale points. Although it is possible to encounter distributions with larger variances than those listed (such as distributions with modes at both ends of the scale), such data are rare.

In most cases, data obtained using rating scales tend to be more uniformly spread out than in a normal distribution. Hence, to arrive at conservative sample-size estimates (that is, sample sizes that are *at least* large enough to accomplish the stated objectives), it is advisable to use a variance estimate at or near the high end of the range listed.

Number of Scale Points	Typical Range of Variances
4	0.7–1.3
5	1.2–2
6	2–3
7	2.5–4
10	3–7

Source: *Research on Research*, no. 37 (Chicago: Market Facts, Inc., undated).

might also be expected to go on several one-week trips a year. Suppose that 15 days a year were considered typical of the upper limit, and food and lodging expenses were calculated at $30 per day; the total dollar upper limit would be $450. The range would also be 450, and the estimated standard deviation would then be $450/6 = 75$.

With desired precision of ±$25 and a 95 percent confidence interval, the calculation of sample size is now

$$n = \frac{z^2}{H^2}(\text{est. } \sigma)^2$$
$$= \frac{(2)^2}{(25)^2}(75)^2$$

and $n = 36$.

A sample of size 36 would then be selected and the information collected. Suppose that these observations generated a sample mean, $\bar{x} = 35$, and a sample standard deviation, $\hat{s} = 60$. The confidence interval is then, as before,[5]

$$\bar{x} \pm zs_{\bar{x}}$$

or

$$35 \pm 2 \frac{\hat{s}}{\sqrt{n}} = 35 \pm 2 \frac{60}{\sqrt{36}} = 35 \pm 20$$

or

$$15 \leq \mu \leq 55$$

Note what has happened. The desired precision was ±$25; the obtained precision is ±$20. The interval is narrower than planned (a bonus) because we overestimated the population standard deviation as judged by the sample standard deviation. If we had underestimated the standard deviation, the situation would have been reversed, and we would have ended up with a wider confidence interval than desired.

Relative Precision

The preceding examples were all framed employing **absolute precision.** The estimates were to be within plus or minus so many units (dollars). It is also possible to frame the calculations of sample size employing **relative precision,** meaning that precision is expressed relative to level. When level is measured by the mean, relative precision suggests that the estimate should be within plus or minus so many percentage points of the mean regardless of its value. Thus, it may be that an estimate within ±10 percent of the mean is required; if the mean is 50, the interval will be from 45 to 55, whereas if the mean is 100, the interval will be from 90 to 110.

Relative precision presents few new problems for the calculation of sample size. The measure of absolute precision H is simply replaced by the measure of relative precision in Equation 11.1. That is,

$$H = z \frac{\sigma}{\sqrt{n}}$$

is changed to

$$r\mu = z \frac{\sigma}{\sqrt{n}}$$

where r is the measure of relative precision and μ is the unknown parent population mean. This formula can be transformed so that sample size can be read

---

[5]One would more strictly use the t distribution to establish the interval, since the population variance was unknown. The example was framed using the approximate $z = 2$ value for a 95 percent confidence interval so as to better illustrate the consequences of a poor initial estimate of σ.

directly. Simply divide both sides of the equation by $r\mu$ and multiply both sides by n^2 to yield

$$n = \frac{z^2}{r^2}\left(\frac{\sigma}{\mu}\right)^2 \qquad (11.3)$$

Recall from your beginning statistics course that σ/μ is the coefficient of variation C, and thus the formula for sample size reduces to

$$n = \frac{z^2}{r^2}C^2$$

Here z^2 would be known because z is determined by the desired level of confidence, and r^2 would also be known because r is determined by the expressed level of precision. C would have to be estimated. This would entail making a judgment about the size of the population standard deviation relative to the size of the population mean. Again, there might be past studies to guide the judgment. If prior studies are unavailable or prove to be in error, the interval will be wider or narrower to the extent that the estimate of C is larger or smaller than that actually produced by the ratio of the sample standard deviation to the sample mean.

Multiple Objectives

A study is rarely conducted to estimate a single parameter. It is much more typical for a study to involve multiple objectives. Let us assume more realistically, therefore, that the researcher is also interested in estimating the annual mean level of expenditures on tackle and equipment by licensed fishermen and the number of miles traveled in a year on fishing trips. Three means are now to be estimated. Suppose that each is to be estimated with 95 percent confidence and that the desired absolute precision and estimated standard deviation are as given in Table 11.1. Table 11.1 also contains the sample sizes (which were calculated using Equation 11.2) needed to estimate each variable.

The three requirements produce conflicting sample sizes; n should equal 36, 16, or 100, depending on the variable being estimated. The researcher must somehow reconcile these values to come up with a sample size suitable for the study as a

---

TABLE 11.1   **Sample Size Needed to Estimate Each of Three Means**

	Variable		
	Expenditures on Food and Lodging	*Expenditures on Tackle and Equipment*	*Miles Traveled*
Confidence level	95 percent ($z = 2$)	95 percent ($z = 2$)	95 percent ($z = 2$)
Desired precision	±$25	±$10	±100 miles
Estimated standard deviation	±$75	±$20	±500 miles
Required sample size	36	16	100

whole. The most conservative approach would be to choose $n = 100$, the largest value. This would ensure that each variable is estimated with the required precision, assuming that the estimates of the standard deviations are accurate.

If the estimate of miles traveled were less critical than the others, however, the use of a sample of size 100 would waste resources. A preferred approach would be to focus on those variables that are most critical and to select a sample sufficient in size to estimate them with the required precision and confidence. Those variables indicating that a larger sample needed to be taken would then be estimated with either a lower degree of confidence or less precision than planned. Suppose in this case that the expenditure data were most critical and that the analyst, therefore, decided on a sample size of 36. Suppose also that the information from this sample of 36 fishermen produced a sample mean of $\bar{x} = 300$ and a sample standard deviation of $s = 500$ miles traveled. The estimate of the population standard deviation is thus seen to agree with the sample result, so the confidence interval estimate will not be affected by inaccuracies here.

The confidence interval for miles traveled is then calculated as

$$\bar{x} \ \pm zs_{\bar{x}} \ = \ \bar{x} \ \pm z\frac{\hat{s}}{\sqrt{n}} \ = \ 300 \pm 2\frac{500}{\sqrt{36}}$$

or $(133.3 \leq \mu \leq 466.7)$. Whereas the desired precision was ±100 miles, the obtained precision is ±166.7 miles. In order to produce an estimate with the desired precision, the degree of confidence would have to be lowered from its present 95 percent level.

Sample Size Determination When Estimating Proportions

Absolute Precision

The examples considered previously all concern determining sample size to estimate mean values. The population proportion π is often another parameter of interest in marketing. Thus, the researcher might be interested in determining the proportion of licensed fishermen who are from out of state, or from rural areas, or who took at least one overnight trip. This section focuses on the determination of sample size necessary to estimate a population proportion.

At the beginning of this chapter, we suggested that three things were needed to determine sample size: a specified degree of confidence, specified precision, and knowledge of the sampling distribution of the statistic. The first two items are specified to reflect the requirements of the research problem. Precision can again be expressed absolutely or relatively. With percentages, absolute precision means that the estimate will be within plus or minus so many percentage points of the true value, as, for example, within ±5 percentage points of the true value.

The remaining consideration, then, is the sampling distribution of the sample proportion. If the sample elements are selected independently, as can reasonably be assumed if the sample size is small relative to the population size, then the *theoretically correct distribution of the sample proportion is the binomial.* But the binomial

FIGURE 11.2   **Approximate Sampling Distribution of the Sample Proportion**

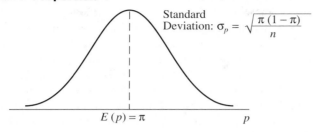

becomes indistinguishable from the normal with large-size samples or when the population proportion is close to one-half.[6] It is *convenient* to use the normal approximation when estimating sample size. After the sample is drawn and the sample proportion determined, the researcher can always fall back on the binomial distribution to determine the confidence interval if the normal approximation proves to be in error.

The distribution of sample proportions is centered on the population proportion (Figure 11.2). The sample proportion is an unbiased estimate of the population proportion. The standard deviation of the normal distribution of sample proportions (that is, the standard error of the proportion, denoted by σ_p) is equal to $\sqrt{\pi(1-\pi)/n}$. Because we are working again with the normal curve, the level of precision is equated to the number of standard deviations the estimate can be removed from the mean value. But now the mean value is the population proportion, while the standard deviation is the standard error of the proportion; that is,

$$H = z\sigma_p \qquad (11.4)$$

Substituting $\sqrt{\pi(1-\pi)/n}$ for σ_p and solving for n yields

$$n = \frac{z^2}{H^2}\,\pi(1-\pi) \qquad (11.5)$$

Let's say that the researcher is interested in estimating the proportion of all fishermen who took at least one overnight fishing trip in the past year. The researcher wants this estimate within ±2 percentage points and he or she wishes to be 95 percent confident in the result. Substitution in Equation 11.5 yields

$$n = \frac{(2)^2}{(0.02)^2}\,\pi(1-\pi)$$

This equation contains two unknowns—the population proportion being estimated and the sample size—and is thus not solvable as it stands. To determine

---

[6]The strict requirement is that $n\pi$ must be above a certain level if the normal curve is to provide a good approximation to the binomial. Some hold that $n\pi$ must be greater than 5, whereas others suggest that the product must be greater than 10.

sample size, the researcher needs to estimate the population proportion. That is right! *The researcher must estimate the very quantity the study is being designed to get at in order to determine sample size.*

This fact is often bewildering and certainly disconcerting to decision makers and beginning researchers alike. Nevertheless, it is true that with proportions, one is forced to make some judgment about the approximate value of the parameter in order to determine sample size. This is another example of how information begets information in sample design. One might use past studies or published data to generate an initial estimate. Alternately, one might conduct a pilot study. In the absence of both these options, one might simply use informed judgment about the probable approximate value of the parameter.

A poor estimate will make the confidence interval more or less precise than desired. Suppose, for example, that the best considered judgment was that 20 percent of all licensed fishermen could be expected to take an overnight fishing trip during the year. Sample size is then calculated to be

$$n = \frac{(2)^2}{(0.02)^2} (0.20)(1 - 0.20)$$

and $n = 1,600$. On receipt of the information from the 1,600 designated fishermen, suppose that the sample proportion p actually turned out to be equal to 0.40. The confidence interval then would be established, employing s_p to estimate the unknown σ_p where $s_p = \sqrt{p(1 - p)/n}$; that is,

$$s_p = \sqrt{\frac{0.40(0.60)}{1,600}} = \sqrt{\frac{0.24}{1,600}} = 0.012$$

The confidence interval is then

$$p \pm z s_p = 0.40 \pm 2(0.012)$$

or

$$0.376 \leq \pi \leq 0.424$$

The interval is wider than desired, since the sample proportion was larger than the estimated population proportion.

Suppose that a wider interval than planned was unacceptable. One way of preventing it is to choose the sample size to reflect the "worst of worlds." Note from the formula that the largest sample size will be obtained when the product $\pi(1 - \pi)$ is greatest, because sample size is directly proportional to this quantity. This product is, in turn, greatest when $\pi = 0.5$, as might be intuitively expected, since if one-half of the population behaves one way and the other half the other way, one would require more evidence for a valid inference than if the situation were more clear-cut and a substantial proportion all behaved in the same way.

In the absence of any other information about the population proportion, then, one can always conservatively assume that π is equal to 0.5. The established confidence interval will simply be more precise to the extent that the sample estimate deviates from the assumed 0.5 value.

Relative Precision

The sample size necessary to estimate a population proportion also can be based on a specification of the relative precision to be provided by the estimate. Relative precision means that the size of the interval will be a function of the value—that is, within a certain percentage of the value regardless of its level. Thus, if the relative precision were to be specified to be within ± 10 percent, this would mean that if the sample proportion were 0.20, the interval would be from 0.18 to 0.22, and if the sample proportion were 0.30, the interval would be from 0.27 to 0.33.

When the interval is specified employing relative precision, the following differences in the calculation of sample size result from the basic formula contained in Equation 11.4. Whereas before

$$H = z\sigma_p$$

now

$$r\pi = z\sigma_p$$

where r is the specified relative precision. The formula can be manipulated to express sample size directly, since

$$r\pi = z\sqrt{\frac{\pi(1-\pi)}{n}}$$

upon substituting the value of σ_p. Simplifying, we obtain

$$n = \frac{z^2}{r^2}\frac{(1-\pi)}{\pi} \tag{11.6}$$

Once again some initial estimate of the population proportion is needed to determine the size of sample necessary to estimate that proportion.

To illustrate the calculation, suppose that the population proportion was estimated to be 0.2, the level of confidence was specified at 95 percent ($z = 2$), and the desired level of relative precision $r = 0.10$. Then

$$n = \frac{(2)^2}{(0.10)^2}\frac{(0.8)}{(0.2)} = 1{,}600$$

After the information is collected from the sample respondents,

$$s_p = \sqrt{p(1-p)/n}$$

would again be used in calculating the confidence interval.

Population Size and Sample Size

Although you may not have noticed it before, consider it now: *The size of the population did not enter into the calculation of the size of sample.* That is right! Except for one slight modification to be discussed shortly, the size of the population has *no direct effect* on the size of the sample.

Although perhaps contrary to your expectations at first, this statement becomes clear when you think it through. When estimating a mean, if all population elements have exactly the same value of the characteristic, then a sample of one is all that is needed to determine the mean. This is true whether there are 1,000, 10,000, or 100,000 elements in the population. The thing that directly affects the size of the sample is the variability of the characteristic in the population. The more variable the characteristic, the larger the sample needed to estimate it with some specified level of precision. This not only makes intuitive sense, but it can be seen directly in the formulas for determining sample size to estimate a population mean; for example, $n = z^2 \sigma^2 / H^2$ with absolute precision and $n = (z^2/r^2)\, C^2$ with relative precision. Thus, population size affects sample size only indirectly through its impact on variability. The larger the population, the greater the *potential* for variation of the characteristic.

It is perhaps less startling to find that population size does not affect sample size when estimating a proportion than when estimating a mean. With a proportion, the determining factor, as we have seen, is the estimated proportion of the population possessing the characteristic; the closer the proportion is to 0.5, the larger the sample that will be needed, regardless of the size of the population. A value of 0.5 signifies greatest variability, because one-half of the population possesses the characteristic and one-half does not.

The slight modification alluded to earlier arises through the finite population correction. We saw previously that many of our results hold when the sample elements are drawn independently of one another. When the sample is small relative to the population, the independence assumption is justified. However, when the sample represents a large portion of the population, the independence assumption is no longer warranted, and the formulas derived under this assumption must be altered accordingly. Thus, for example, we saw in Chapter 10 that the formula for the standard error of the mean was $\sigma_{\bar{x}} = \sigma/\sqrt{n}$ under the independence assumption, whereas it was

$$\sigma_{\bar{x}} = \frac{\sigma}{\sqrt{n}} \sqrt{\frac{N-n}{N-1}}$$

when the sample elements were not independent of one another. The factor $(N-n)/(N-1)$ is the finite population correction factor.

When the estimated sample represents more than 5 percent of the population, the calculated size should be reduced by the finite population correction factor.[7]

---

[7]The 5 percent correction factor is not a hard-and-fast rule. Some contend that the finite population correction factor should be ignored if the sample includes no more than 10 percent of the population. Cochran suggests that the finite population correction can be ignored whenever the "sampling fraction does not exceed 5 percent and for many purposes even if it is as high as 10 percent." William G. Cochran, *Sampling Techniques*, 3rd ed. (New York: John Wiley, 1977), p. 25. See also Richard L. Schaeffer and William Mendenhall, and R. Lyman Ott, *Elementary Survey Sampling*, 5th ed. (Belmont, CA: Wadsworth Publishing Company, 1996). Ignoring the finite population correction will result in overestimating the standard error of estimate.

Thus, for example, if the population contained 100 elements and the calculation of sample size indicated a sample of 20 needed to be taken, fewer than 20 observations would, in fact, be taken to reflect the dependency that existed among the observations. The required sample would be given as $n' = nN/(N + n - 1)$, where n was the originally determined size and n' was the revised size. Thus, with $N = 100$ and $n = 20$, only 17 sample elements would need to be employed.

Other Probability Sampling Plans

So far, the discussions of sample size have been based on simple random samples. You should be aware, though, that there are also formulas for determining sample size when other probability sampling plans are used. The formulas are more complex, to be sure, but the same underlying principles still apply. One still needs a knowledge of the sampling distribution of the statistic in addition to the research specifications regarding level of precision and degree of confidence.

The issue of sample size is compounded, however, by the fact that one now has a number of strata or a number of clusters with which to work. This means that one has to deal with within-strata variability and within- and between-cluster variability in calculating sample size, whereas with simple random sampling, only total population variability entered the picture. As before, the more variable the strata or cluster, the larger the sample that needs to be taken from it, other things being equal. This is precisely the basis for disproportionate stratified sampling discussed in Chapter 10.

Cost must also be equal. Cost did not enter directly into the calculation of sample size with simple random sampling, although it does affect sample size. Perhaps the costs of data collection with a sample of the calculated size would simply exceed the research budget, in which case cost would act to constrain sample size below that indicated by the formulas. Of course, with a simple random sample, one could also base the calculation of sample size directly on cost per observation and the size of the data collection budget. The fact remains, though, that cost per observation did not enter into the formulas for calculating sample size with simple random samples.

With stratified or cluster samples, cost exerts a direct impact. In calculating sample size, one has to allow for unequal costs per observation by strata or by cluster, and in implementing the sample size calculation, one has to have some initial estimate of these costs. The task then becomes one of balancing variability against costs and assessing the trade-off function relating the two. With a stratified sample, for example, one would want to sample most heavily that stratum which was most variable if cost was the same by strata, or which had the lowest cost per observation if the variability was the same within strata. Because the cost per observation or variability probably will not be the same for each stratum, the challenge becomes one of determining sample size by considering the precision likely to result from sampling each stratum at a given rate. Formulas are available for this purpose, as they are for cluster samples. We shall not go into these formulas here, as they are readily available in the standard works on sampling theory and fall largely in the domain of the sampling specialist.[8]

---

[8]See, for example, Cochran, *Sampling Techniques;* Hansen, Hurwitz, and Madow, *Sample Survey Methods;* Leslie Kish, *Survey Sampling* (New York: John Wiley, 1995); Schaeffer and Mendenhall, *Elementary Survey Sampling;* Paul S. Levy and Stanley Lemeshow, *Sampling of Populations: Methods and Applications,* 3rd ed. (New York: John Wiley and Sons, Inc., 1999); Sharon Lohr, *Sampling: Design and Analysis* (Belmont, CA: Wadsworth Publishing, 1999).

You should be aware, though, that when dealing with stratified or cluster samples, cost per observation by subgroup directly enters the calculation of sample size.

You should also know that there are formulas for determining sample size when the problem is one of hypothesis testing and not confidence interval estimation. Once again, the principles are the same, although there are some additional considerations such as the levels of Type I and Type II errors to be tolerated and the issue of whether it is necessary to detect subtle differences or only obvious differences. We shall not deal with these formulas, because they are readily available in standard statistical works and their discussion would take us too far afield.[9]

Using Anticipated Cross Classifications to Determine Sample Size

The discussion thus far has focused on the determination of sample size using only statistical principles, particularly the trade-off between degree of confidence and degree of precision while considering only sampling error. The arguments were framed this way to cast them into bold relief. In applied problems, the size of the sample is also going to be affected by certain practical considerations, such as the total size of the budget for the study and the anticipated cost per observation, the size of the sample that may be needed to convince skeptical executives who do not understand statistical concepts that they indeed can have confidence in the results, and so on. One of the more important practical bases for determining the size of sample that will be needed is the anticipated cross classifications to which the data will be subjected.

Suppose, for example, that in our problem of estimating the proportion of all fishermen who took at least one overnight fishing trip in the past year, we were also interested in assessing whether the likelihood of engaging in this behavior is somehow related to an individual's age and income. Suppose further that the age categories of interest were less than 20, 20–29, 30–39, 40–49, and 50 and over, while the income categories of interest were less than $10,000, $10,000–$19,999, $20,000–$29,999, $30,000–$39,999, and over $40,000. There are thus five age categories and five income categories for which the proportion of fishermen taking an overnight trip would be estimated. Although we might reasonably estimate these proportions for each variable considered separately, we should also recognize that the two variables are interrelated, in that increases in income are typically related to increases in age. To allow for this interdependence, we need to consider the effect of the two variables simultaneously. The way to do this is through a cross-classification table in which age and income jointly define the cells.[10]

Table 11.2, for instance, is a cross-classification table that could be used for the example at hand. Note that this dummy table is complete in all respects except for

---

[9]Computer-based expert systems that rely on artificial intelligence techniques also exist for determining sample size. These systems guide the researcher through a series of questions about the needed degree of confidence, precision, variability, and so on, and, based on the answers, perform the tedious computations concerning the needed sample size. See, for example, Ex-Sample,™ which is available from The Idea Works in Columbia, Missouri.

[10]In Chapter 13, the procedures for setting up and analyzing cross-classification tables so that the proper inferences can be drawn are discussed.

TABLE 11.2	**Number and Proportion of Fishermen Staying Overnight as a Function of Age and Income**				
	Age				
Income	*Less than 20*	*20–29*	*30–39*	*40–49*	*50 and Over*
Less than $10,000					
$10,000–$19,999					
$20,000–$29,999					
$30,000–$39,999					
$40,000 and over					

the numbers that actually go in each of the cells.[11] These would, of course, be determined by the data actually collected on the number and proportion of all those sampled who actually made at least one overnight trip. In the table, 25 cells need estimation. It is unlikely that the decision maker is going to be very comfortable with an estimate of the proportion staying overnight that is based on only a few cases of the phenomenon. Yet even with a sample of, say, 500 fishermen, there is only a potential of 20 cases per cell if the sample is evenly divided with respect to the age and income levels considered. Further, it is very unlikely that the sample would split this way, which would put the researcher in the awkward position of estimating the proportion in a cell engaging in this behavior on the basis of fewer than 20 cases.

One can reverse this argument to estimate how large a sample should be taken. One simply computes the number of cells in the intended cross classifications. It is given by the *product* of the number of levels of the characteristics forming the cross classification. One then allows for the likely distribution of the variables and estimates the sample size so that the important cells can be estimated with a sufficient number of cases to inspire confidence in the results. One rule of thumb is that "the sample should be large enough so that there are 100 or more units in each category of the major breakdowns and a minimum of 20 to 50 in the minor breakdowns."[12] *Major breakdown* refers to the cells in the most critical cross tabulations for the study and *minor breakdown* to the cells in the less important cross classifications. Through all of this, one has to make due allowance for nonresponses, because some individuals designated for inclusion in the sample will be unavailable and others will refuse to participate.[13] The researcher "builds up" the sample, so to speak, from the size of the cross-classification table with due allowance for these considerations.

Perhaps cross classification will not be the basic method used to analyze the data. Perhaps, instead, the main technique will be regression or discriminant analysis or one of the other statistical methods discussed in Part 5. If so, the same arguments for determining sample size apply. That is, one needs a sufficient number of cases to satisfy the requirements of the technique to inspire confidence in the

---

[11]Refer to Chapter 4 for a discussion of the notion of dummy tables and how they should be set up so that they are most productive.

[12]Seymour Sudman, *Applied Sampling* (New York: Academic Press, 1976).

[13]Nonresponse and other nonsampling errors and what can be done about them are discussed in Chapter 12.

A recent discussion between the account manager for an independent research agency and the marketing people for the client left the account manager feeling perplexed. After numerous discussions, the account manager believed that she had a good handle on the client's problem and major concerns. On the basis of this understanding, she had developed a set of dummy tables by which the client's concerns could be investigated. During the most recent meeting, she had presented these to the client. The client had completely accepted the account manager's recommendation about how the data would be viewed; she closed the meeting by asking how large a sample the account manager would recommend and how much the study would cost.

The account manager's anxiety was caused by the fact that she believed from the earlier discussions and some preliminary investigation that two of the seven hypotheses were especially promising. The sample size that was needed to investigate these two hypotheses was almost 60 percent smaller than that needed to address some of the other hypotheses because of the fewer cells in the cross-classification table. The account manager was in a dilemma about whether she should take the safe route and recommend the larger sample size to the client and thereby ensure that all the planned cross-classifications could be completed or whether she should go with her instinct and recommend the smaller sample size and save the client some money.

- What would you recommend that the account manager do?
- Is it ethical for the account manager to recommend the larger sample size when she is fairly certain that the smaller one will provide the answers the client needs? Is it ethical to do the reverse and recommend the smaller sample when there is some risk that the smaller sample will not adequately answer the problem that the firm was hired to solve?
- What are the account manager's responsibilities to the client in a case like this?

results.[14] Different techniques have different sample size requirements, often expressed by the degrees of freedom required for the analysis. Some of these requirements should become obvious when the techniques are discussed. For now, we merely wish to reiterate the important point made earlier when introducing the research process—that the stages are very much related and a decision about one stage can affect all the other stages. Here a decision about stage 5 regarding the

---

[14]See, for example, Sande Milton, "A Sample Size Formula for Multiple Regression Studies," *Public Opinion Quarterly* 50 (Spring 1986), pp. 112–118, for discussion of the procedure for estimating sample size for regression analysis. See also Mark Eakin, Lawrence L. Schkade, and Mary Whiteside, "Optimal Cost Sampling for Decision Making Models with Multiple Regression Models," *Decision Sciences* 20 (Winter 1989), pp. 14–26. Charts are also available for determining the sample size necessary for certain analytical techniques. See Robert Oheh and M. Fox, *Sample Size Choice: Charts for Experiments with Linear Techniques* (New York: Marcel Dekker, Inc., 1991).

RESEARCH REALITIES 11.2

Typical Sample Sizes for Studies of Human and Institutional Populations

Number of Subgroup Analyses	People or Households		Institutions	
	National	*Regional or Special*	*National*	*Regional or Special*
None or few	1,000–1,500	200–500	200–500	50–200
Average	1,500–2,500	500–1,000	500–1,000	200–500
Many	2,500+	1,000+	1,000+	500+

Source: Seymour Sudman, *Applied Sampling* (Orlando, FL: Academic Press, 1976), p. 87.

method of analysis can have an important effect on stage 4, which precedes it, with respect to the size of the sample that should be selected. Thus, the researcher needs to think through the entire research problem, including how the data will be analyzed, before commencing the data-collection process.

Using Historic Evidence to Determine Sample Size

A final method by which an analyst can determine the size of sample to employ is simply to use what others have used for similar studies in the past. Even though this may be different from the optimal size in a given problem, the fact that the contemplated sample size is in line with that used for other similar studies is psychologically comforting, particularly to inexperienced researchers. Research Realities 11.2 summarizes the evidence. It provides a crude yardstick for evaluating the size of sample determined by other means. Note that national studies typically involve larger samples than regional or special studies. Note further that the number of subgroup analyses has a direct effect on sample size.

Summary

In this chapter we reviewed the basic statistical principles involved in determining the size of a sample. The principles were used to develop confidence interval estimates for either a population mean or a population proportion using simple random samples. The examples demonstrated the influence of the sampling distribution of the statistic, the degree of confidence, and the level of precision on sample size. Both absolute and relative precision were discussed. The general conclusion was that sample size must be increased whenever population variability, degree of confidence, or the precision required of the estimate are increased. The size of the parent population does not affect the size of the sample except indirectly, through its impact on variability or through the finite population correction. Sample size can also be determined using the anticipated cross classifications. One simply multiplies the number of cells by the number of observations required in each cell to inspire confidence in the conclusions. A similar argument applies when other data analysis techniques are to be used; the size of the sample must be large enough to satisfy the requirements of the technique.

Questions

1. In determining sample size, what factors must an analyst consider?
2. When estimating a population mean, what is meant by absolute precision? What is meant by relative precision?
3. What is the difference between degree of confidence and degree of precision?
4. Suppose that the population variance is known. How does one then determine the sample size necessary to estimate a population mean with some desired degree of precision and confidence? Given that the sample has been selected, how does one generate the desired confidence interval?
5. How does the procedure in question 4 differ when the population variance is unknown?
6. What effect would relaxing the absolute precision with which a population mean is estimated by 25 percent have on sample size? Decreasing the degree of confidence from 95 percent to 90 percent? ($z = 1.64$)?
7. Suppose that one wanted to estimate a population mean within ± 10 percent at the 95 percent level of confidence. How would one proceed and what quantities would one need to estimate?
8. What is the difference between absolute precision and relative precision in the estimation of a population proportion?
9. Suppose that one wanted to estimate a population proportion within ± 3 percentage points at the 95 percent level of confidence. How would one proceed and what quantities would one need to estimate?
10. Suppose in question 9 that the researcher wanted the estimate to be within ± 3 percent of the population value. What would be the procedure now and what quantities would she or he need to estimate?
11. What happens if the sample proportion is larger than the estimated population proportion used to determine sample size? If it is smaller? What value of the population proportion should be assumed if one wishes to take no chance that the generated interval will be larger than the desired interval?
12. What is the correct procedure for treating multiple study objectives when calculating sample size?
13. How does one determine sample size based on anticipated cross classifications of the data?

Applications and Problems

1. A survey was being designed by the marketing research department of Conner Peripherals, Inc., a large ($2 billion plus) manufacturer of advanced disk drives for portable computers. The general aim was to assess customer satisfaction with the company's disk drives. As part of this general objective, management wanted to measure the average maintenance expenditure per year per computer, the average number of malfunctions or breakdowns per year, and the length of service contracts purchased with new portable computers. Management wanted to be 95 percent confident in the results. Further, the magnitude of the error was not to exceed $\pm\$20$ for maintenance expenditures, ± 1 malfunction, and ± 3 months. The research department noted that although some individuals and businesses would spend nothing on maintenance expenditures per year, others might spend as much as $400. Also, although some portable computers would experience no breakdowns within a year, the maximum expected would be no more than three. Finally, although some portable computers might not be purchased with a service contract, others might be purchased with up to a 36-month contract.

   a. How large a sample would you recommend if each of the three variables is considered separately? Show all your calculations.

b. What size sample would you recommend *overall* given that management thought that accurate knowledge of the expenditure on repairs was most important and the service contract length least important?

c. The survey indicated that the average maintenance expenditure is $100 and the standard deviation is $60. Estimate the confidence interval for the population parameter μ. What can you say about the degree of precision?

2. The management of a major brewery wanted to determine the average number of ounces of beer consumed per resident in the state of Washington. Past trends indicated that the variation in beer consumption (σ) was 4 ounces. A 95 percent confidence level is required, and the error is not to exceed $\pm 1/2$ ounce.

a. What sample size would you recommend? Show your calculations.

b. Management wanted an estimate twice as precise as the initial precision level and an increase in the level of confidence to 99 percent. What sample size would you recommend? Show your calculations. Comment on your results.

3. The director of a state park recreational center wanted to determine the average amount of money that each customer spent traveling to and from the park. On the basis of the findings, the director was planning on raising the entrance fee. The park director noted that visitors living near the center had no travel expenses but that visitors living in other parts of the state or out of state traveled upwards of 250 miles and spent about 24 cents per mile. The director wanted to be 95 percent confident of the findings and did not want the error to exceed ± 50 cents.

a. What sample size should the park director use to determine the average travel expenditure? Show your calculations.

b. After the survey was conducted, the park director found that the average expenditure was $12.00 and the standard deviation was $7.50. Construct a 95 percent confidence interval. What can you say about the level of precision?

4. A large manufacturer of corrugated paper products recently came under severe criticism from various environmentalists for its disposal of industrial effluent and waste. In response, management launched a campaign to counter the bad publicity it was receiving. A study of the effectiveness of the campaign indicated that about 20 percent of the residents of the city were aware of the campaign and the company's position. In conducting the study, a sample of 480 was used and a 95 percent confidence interval was specified. Six months later, it was believed that 40 percent of the residents were aware of the campaign. However, management decided to do another survey and specified a 99 percent confidence level and a margin of error of ± 3 percentage points.

a. What sample size would you recommend for this study? Show all your calculations.

b. After doing the survey, it was found that 35 percent of the population was aware of the campaign. Construct a 99 percent confidence interval for the population parameter.

5. Pac-Trac, Inc., is a large manufacturer of video games. The marketing research department is designing a survey to determine attitudes toward the products. In addition, the percentage of households owning video games and the average usage rate per week are to be determined. The research department wants to be 95 percent confident of the results and does not want the error to exceed ± 3 percentage points for video game ownership and ± 1 hour for average usage rate. Previous reports indicate that about 20 percent of the households own video games and that the average usage rate is 15 hours with a standard deviation of 5 hours.

a. What sample size would you recommend, assuming that only the percentage of households owning video games is to be determined? Show all your calculations.

b. What sample size would you recommend assuming that only the average usage rate per week is to be determined? Show all your calculations.

c. What sample size would you recommend assuming that *both* of the preceding variables are to be determined? Why?

After the survey was conducted, the results indicated that 30 percent of the households own video games and that the average usage rate is 13 hours with a standard deviation of 4.

d. Compute the 95 percent confidence interval for the percentage of individuals owning video games. Comment on the degree of precision.

e. Compute the 95 percent confidence interval for the average usage rate. Comment on the degree of precision.

6. The local bus company in a southwest city of the United States recently started a campaign to encourage people to increase car pooling or use of public transportation. To assess the effectiveness of the campaign, management wanted to do a survey to determine the proportion of people who had adopted the recommended energy-saving measures.

a. What sample size would you recommend if the error is not to exceed ±5 percentage points and the confidence level is to be 90 percent? Show your calculations.

b. The survey indicated that the proportion adopting the measures was 20 percent. Estimate the 90 percent confidence interval. Comment on the level of precision. Show your calculations.

7. A large meat producer recently developed a new brand of hot dogs. The manufacturer wanted to assess the taste preferences of children under the age of seven for its new brand versus its competitor's leading brand. The manufacturer also wanted to assess the average number of hot dogs that a child under seven eats in a month. The director of marketing research wants to be 95 percent confident in the results of the study and does not want the error to exceed 1 percent on any of the estimates. The director believes that 75 percent of children under seven will prefer the new brand to the competitor's leading brand. Past research has shown that children eat approximately five hot dogs each month with a standard deviation of 1.

a. What sample size would you recommend, assuming that only the percentage of children under seven preferring the manufacturer's new brand of hot dogs is to be determined?

b. What sample size would you recommend assuming that the average number of hot dogs consumed by a child under seven is to be determined?

c. The manufacturer decided to use a sample halfway between the two estimates. What is the consequence of doing so?

d. The actual results of the survey showed that 63 percent of children under seven prefer the manufacturer's new brand of hot dogs to the competitor's hot dogs. Compute the 95 percent confidence interval for this point estimate.

e. The actual results of the survey showed that a child under seven eats an average of seven hot dogs in a month with a sample standard deviation of 2. Compute the 95 percent confidence interval for this point estimate.

8. The transit system of a major metropolitan area was interested in determining the average number of miles a commuter drives to work. Past studies have shown that the variation (σ) in commuting distances was 5 miles. The managers of the transit system want to be 95 percent confident in the result and do not want the error to exceed 0.75 mile.

a. What sample size would you recommend?

b. The results of the survey showed that commuters actually drive an average of 20 miles to work with a standard deviation of 10. Compute the 95 percent confidence interval.

c. Compute the 95 percent confidence interval if the mean was found to be 20 miles but the standard deviation was found to be 5 miles.

9. Andy Kendel, the owner of a local record store specializing in disco music from the 1970s, wanted to determine the average age of his customers. Andy estimated a 25-year range from his youngest customer to his oldest customer. He wanted to be 95 percent confident in the results of the survey, and he did not want the error to exceed 9 months.
   a. What sample size would you recommend?
   b. The results of Andy's survey indicated that his customers' average age is 35 with a standard deviation of 15. Construct a 95 percent confidence interval.

10. Mary Scott has just been assigned to do a customer satisfaction study for one of her firm's clients. Mary needs to estimate the sample size required for 95 percent confidence and error not to exceed 5 percent; however, Mary is missing one vital piece of information—the standard error. Suggest to Mary several possible methods of estimating the standard error.

11. Tom Johnson, the owner of a local pizzeria, wanted to conduct a survey to find out local residents' favorite pizza toppings. However, he had only enough funds to have a sample of 100 local residents. Based on the sales of toppings in his pizzeria, Tom expected 40 percent of the residents to like pepperoni the best.
   a. If Tom wanted to be 95 percent confident in the results of this survey, what corresponding level of precision would he be able to achieve?
   b. If Tom instead wanted to not exceed an error rate of 5 percent, what corresponding level of confidence would he be able to achieve?
   c. Relate your results in parts a and b to the concept that one cannot increase both confidence and precision with a fixed sample size.

12. Worldly Travels is a large travel agency located in Indianapolis, Indiana. Management was concerned about its declining leisure travel-tour business. It believed that the profile of those engaging in leisure travel had changed during the past few years. To determine if that was indeed the case, management decided to conduct a survey to determine the profile of the current leisure travel-tour customer. Three variables were identified that required particular attention. Before conducting the survey, the three following dummy tables were developed.

	Age			
Income	18–24	25–34	35–54	55+
0–$9,999				
$10,000–$19,999				
$20,000–$29,999				
$30,000–$39,999				
Over $40,000				

	Education			
Age	Some High School	High School Graduate	Some College	College Graduate
18–24				
25–34				
35–54				
55+				

	Education			
Income	*Some High School*	*High School Graduate*	*Some College*	*College Graduate*
0–$9,999				
$10,000–$19,999				
$20,000–$29,999				
$30,000–$39,999				
Over $40,000				

a. How large a sample would you recommend be taken? Justify your answer.
b. The survey produced the following incomplete table for the variables of age and education. Complete the table on the basis of the assumption that the two characteristics are independent (even though that assumption is wrong). On the basis of the completed table, do you think that an appropriate sample size was used? If yes, why? If not, why not?

	Education				
Age	*Some High School*	*High School Graduate*	*Some College*	*College Graduate*	*Total*
18–24					100
25–34					200
35–54					350
55+					350
Total	200	400	300	100	1,000

13. Jim Stark, managing partner of Askren Monuments in Indianapolis, wants to know consumer attitudes toward the price of markers. Jim wants to be 99 percent confident of the survey results and within a $30 range of error. Customers can spend between $225 and $1,000 on granite markers, depending on size and intricateness of the marker.
   a. What sample size should Jim use to determine the average expenditure on markers? Show your calculations.
   b. After performing the survey, Jim found the average expenditure to be $375, with a standard deviation of $95. Construct Jim's 99 percent confidence interval. What can you say about the level of precision?
   c. If Jim had been willing to accept 90 percent confidence in his results, what sample size would he have needed? What is Jim's 90 percent confidence interval?

12

Collecting the Data: Field Procedures and Nonsampling Errors

The step that follows sample design in the research process is data collection. Data collection entails the use of some kind of field force operating either in the field or from an office, as in a phone, mail, e-mail, or fax survey. This, in turn, raises the questions of selection, training, and control of the field staff. This chapter investigates these issues from the perspective of what can go wrong when conducting a field study. The emphasis will be on those sources of error not previously dealt with. An understanding of the various sources of error in data collection should give much insight into the selection, training, and control questions and should also assist in evaluating the research information on which decisions must be based.

Impact and Importance of Nonsampling Errors

Two basic types of errors arise in research studies: sampling errors and nonsampling errors. The concept of sampling error underlay much of the discussion in Chapters 10 and 11. Basic to that discussion was the concept of the sampling distribution of some statistic, be it the sample mean, sample proportion, or whatever. The sampling distribution arises because of sampling error. The sampling distribution reflects the fact that the different possible samples that could be drawn under the sampling plan will produce different estimates of the parameter. The statistic simply varies from sample to sample because we are sampling only part of the population in each case. **Sampling error,** then, is "the difference between the observed values of a variable and the long-run average of the observed values in repetitions of the measurement."[1] As we saw, sampling errors can be reduced by increasing sample size. The distribution of the sample statistic becomes more and more concentrated about the long-run average value, because the sample statistic is more equal from sample to sample when it is based on a larger number of observations.

    Nonsampling errors reflect the many other kinds of error that arise in research, even when the survey is not based on a sample. They can be random or nonrandom.

---

[1]Frederick Mosteller, "Nonsampling Errors," *Encyclopedia of Social Sciences* (New York: Macmillan, 1968), p. 113. See also the special issue of the *Journal of Official Statistics* 4, no. 3 (1987), edited by Lars Lyberg, which is devoted to nonsampling errors, as well as Elizabeth Hervey Stephen and Beth J. Soldo, "How to Judge the Quality of a Survey," *American Demographics* 12 (April 1990), pp. 42–43; Tom Corlett, "Sampling Errors in Practice," *Journal of the Market Research Society* 38 (October 1996), pp. 307–318.

Nonrandom nonsampling errors are the more troublesome of the two. Random errors produce estimates that vary from the true value; sometimes these estimates are above and sometimes below the true value, but they vary on a random basis. The result is that, in the absence of sampling errors, the sample estimate will equal the population value. Nonrandom nonsampling errors, on the other hand, tend to produce mistakes only in one direction. They tend to bias the sample value away from the population parameter. Nonsampling errors can occur because of errors in conception, logic, interpretation of replies, statistics, or arithmetic; errors in tabulation or coding; or errors in reporting the results. They are so pervasive that they have caused one writer to lament:

> The roster of possible troubles seems only to grow with increasing knowledge. By participating in the work of a specific field, one can, in a few years, work up considerable methodological expertise, much of which has not been and is not likely to be written down. *To attempt to discuss every way a study can go wrong would be a hopeless venture* (emphasis added).[2]

Not only are nonsampling errors pervasive, but they are not as well behaved as sampling errors. Sampling errors decrease with increases in sample size. Nonsampling errors do not necessarily decrease with increases in sample size; they may, in fact, increase. Sampling errors can be estimated if probability sampling procedures are used. The direction, much less the magnitude, of nonsampling errors is often unknown. True, they bias the sample value away from the population parameter, but in many studies it is hard to see whether they cause underestimation or overestimation of the parameter. Nonsampling errors also distort the reliability of sample estimates; the bias resulting from them serves to increase the standard error of estimates of particular statistics to such an extent that the confidence interval estimates turn out to be faulty. Moreover, nonsampling errors become increasingly important relative to sampling errors as sample size increases, and *render meaningless confidence intervals computed by the usual statistical formulas* which take into account only sampling errors.

Nonsampling errors are frequently the most important errors that arise in research. No responses from some targeted for inclusion in a study, and poor responses from others—two types of nonsampling errors—can literally wreak havoc with survey results. In special Census Bureau investigations of their size, nonsampling errors were found to be 10 times the magnitude of sampling errors.[3] This is not an unusual finding. Rather, a consistent finding is that nonsampling error is the major contributor to total survey error, whereas random sampling error has minimal impact.[4] Nonsampling errors can be reduced, but their reduction depends

---

[2]Mosteller, "Nonsampling Errors," p. 113.

[3]W. H. Williams, "How Bad Can 'Good' Data Really Be?" *The American Statistician* 32 (May 1978), p. 61. See also Henry Assael and John Keon, "Nonsampling vs. Sampling Errors in Survey Research," *Journal of Marketing* 46 (Spring 1982), pp. 114–123; Judith T. Lessler and William D. Kalsbeek, *Nonsampling Errors in Surveys* (New York: John Wiley and Sons, Inc., 1992).

[4]See, for example, Ronald Andersen, Judith Kasper, Martin R. Frankel, and Associates, *Total Survey Error* (San Francisco: Jossey-Bass, 1979); Paul B. Biemer, et al., *Measurement Errors in Surveys* (New York: John Wiley and Sons, Inc., 1991).

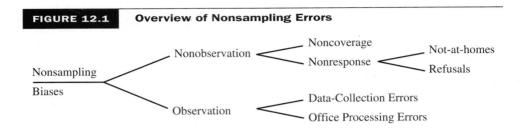

FIGURE 12.1　**Overview of Nonsampling Errors**

on improving method rather than increasing sample size. By understanding the sources of nonsampling errors, the analyst is in a better position to reduce them.

Types of Nonsampling Errors

Figure 12.1 offers a general overview of nonsampling errors. Nonsampling errors are of two basic types—those due to nonobservation or those due to observation. **Nonobservation errors** result from a failure to obtain data from parts of the survey population. Nonobservation errors can happen because part of the population of interest was not included or because some elements designated for inclusion in the sample did not respond.[5] **Observation errors** occur because inaccurate information is secured from the sample elements or because errors are introduced in the processing of the data or in reporting the findings. In many ways, they are more troublesome than nonobservation errors. With nonobservation errors, we at least know we have a problem because of noncoverage or nonresponse. With observation errors, we may not even be aware that a problem exists. The very notion of an observation error rests on the presumption that there is indeed some "true" value for the variable or variables. An observation error, then, is simply the difference between the reported value and the true value. You can readily see that detection of an observation error places the researcher in the awkward position of needing to know the very quantity the study is designed to estimate.

Studies have been specifically designed to estimate the direction and magnitude of data-collection errors. Generally, they have

1. relied on the actual availability of bias-free information, which then served as a validity check;
2. used split-run comparisons in which the respondent received different forms of the same questions, say, so that the person's consistency in responding could be measured; or
3. measured the consistency of replies over time from the same respondent.

These methods, while useful, cannot always be applied in substantive as opposed to method studies, and it becomes difficult to adjust the obtained information for

---

[5]Chapter 13, "Biases and Nonsampling Errors," in the book by Leslie Kish, *Survey Sampling* (New York: John Wiley and Sons, Inc., 1995), is particularly recommended for discussion of the biases arising from nonobservation.

response error. Instead this information is taken at face value. Thus, it is vital that researchers understand the sources of response bias so that they can better anticipate and prevent it.

Noncoverage Errors

Noncoverage denotes failure to include some units, or entire sections, of the defined survey population in the actual operational sampling frame. Because of the actual (though unplanned and usually unknown) zero probability of selection for these units, they are in effect excluded from the survey result. We do *not* refer here to any deliberate and explicit exclusion of sections of a larger population from the survey population. Survey objectives and practical difficulties determine such deliberate exclusions. For example, many surveys of attitudes are confined to adults, deliberately excluding persons under 21 years; residents of institutions are often excluded because of practical survey difficulties. These explicit exclusions differ both in intent and result from noncoverage caused by failures in the procedures. When computing noncoverage rates, members of the deliberately and explicitly excluded sections should not be counted either in the survey population or in the noncoverage. Defining the survey population should be part of the stated *essential survey conditions.*[6]

Noncoverage error is essentially a sampling-frame problem. Researchers realize that the telephone directory, for instance, does not provide a complete sampling frame for most general surveys. Not every family has a phone, and not all those people who have telephones have them listed in the directory. Further, some variation exists between those having and not having phones in terms of some important demographic characteristics. These conditions are compounded for fax surveys of the general population. Although they are not altogether eliminated, they are less of a problem in surveys of businesses or other institutions.

Noncoverage is also a problem in mail and e-mail surveys. The mailing and e-mail lists dictate the sampling frame. If the lists inadequately represent segments of the population, the survey will also suffer from the bias of noncoverage, and rare is the mailing list or list of e-mail addresses that exactly captures the population that the researcher wishes to study.

When the data are to be collected by personal interviews in the home, some form of area sample is typically used to pinpoint respondents. The sampling frame is one of areas and blocks and dwelling units rather than a list of respondents. However, this does not eliminate the incomplete frame problem. Maps of the city may not be totally current, so the newest areas may not have a proper chance of being included in the sample. The instructions to the interviewer may not be sufficiently rigorous. Thus, the direction "Start at the northwest corner of the selected blocks, generate a random start, and take every fifth dwelling unit thereafter" would not be sufficiently precise to handle those blocks, say, with a number of apartment units. The evidence indicates, for example, that lower-income households are avoided when the selection of households is made by the field staff rather than by someone in the home office. Further, interviewers typically select the most accessible individuals within the household, contrary to instructions for random selection. This again means that a portion of the intended population is underrepresented in the study, while the accessible segment is overrepresented.

---

[6]Kish, *Survey Sampling*, p. 528.

ETHICAL DILEMMA 12.1

During the introduction in a telephone interview, interviewers introduce themselves, provide the research company's name, and then assure potential respondents that the client will be unable to link their responses back to them. However, the interviewer notes the respondents' first names and phone numbers on the completed survey so that the supervisor can randomly select a sample of questionnaires for verification. The possibility of a verification call is explained to the respondents.

Once the fieldwork has been completed, the research supplier bundles all the questionnaires and sends them to the client for coding, entry, and analysis. The questionnaires are sent with respondents' names and phone numbers attached.

- Is there a problem with providing the names and phone numbers of respondents to the client company?
- If the client has signed a confidentiality agreement with the field company, is this problem avoided?

There are also sampling-frame problems when personal interviews in shopping malls are used to collect the data. For one thing, there is no list of population elements. Rather, only those people who shop in a particular mall have a chance of being included in the study, and their chances of being included depend on how often they shop there. That is why quota samples are often used in mall-intercept studies.

Noncoverage bias is not eliminated in quota samples, however, whether the interview is conducted in a mall or elsewhere. Rather, the interviewers' flexibility in choosing respondents can introduce substantial noncoverage bias. Interviewers typically underselect in both the high- and low-income classes. This bias is not always discovered, because interviewers also tend to falsify characteristics so that the appropriate number of cases per cell is achieved. Further, the more elaborate and complex the quota sample, the more critical this "forcing" problem becomes. With three or four variables defining the individual cells, the interviewer finds it difficult to locate respondents who have all the prescribed characteristics.

Overcoverage error can also be a source of bias. It can arise because of duplication in the list of sampling units. Units with multiple entries in the sampling frame (for example, families with several phone listings) have a higher probability of being included in the sample than do sampling units with one listing. For most surveys, however, noncoverage is much more common and troublesome.

Noncoverage bias is not a problem in every survey. For some studies, clear, convenient, and complete sampling frames exist. Thus, the department store wanting to conduct a study among its charge-account customers should have little trouble with frame bias. The sampling frame is simply those with charge accounts. There might be some difficulty in distinguishing active accounts from inactive accounts, but this is essentially a definitional problem that should be dictated by the purpose of the study. Similarly, the credit union in a firm should experience little noncoverage bias in conducting a study among its potential clientele. The population of interest here would be the firm's employees, and it could be expected that the list of employees would be current and accurate since it is needed to generate the payroll.

Noncoverage bias raises two questions for the researcher: (1) How pervasive is it likely to be? (2) What can be done to reduce it? One difficulty is that its magnitude can be estimated only by comparing the sample survey results with some outside criterion. The outside criterion can, in turn, be established through an auxiliary quality check of a portion of the results, or it may be available from another reliable and current study, such as the population census. Comparison with the census or another large sample, however, means that the basic sampling units must be similar in terms of operational definitions. The choice of a base, then (for example, dwellings or persons), becomes crucial in effecting such comparisons.

Given that noncoverage bias is likely, what can the researcher do to lessen its effect? The most obvious thing, of course, is to improve the quality of the sampling frame. This may mean taking the time to bring available city maps up to date, or it may mean taking a sample to check the quality and representativeness of a mailing list with respect to a target population. The unlisted number problem common to telephone surveys can be handled by random digit or plus-one dialing, although this will not provide adequate sample representation for those without phones.

There are usually limits to the degree to which an imperfect sampling frame can be improved. Once they are encountered, the researcher's main opportunities for reducing noncoverage bias are through the selection of sampling units and the adjustment of the results, often through weighting subsample results, to account for the remaining imperfections in the frame and sampling procedure. When sampling from lists, for example, three problems are commonly encountered: Both ineligibles and duplicates are included on the list and some members of the target population are excluded. An analyst would first want to update the list, using supplementary sources if possible. Although this would help reduce the third problem, it might do little to correct the problems of ineligibles and duplicates. These problems can be corrected, though. When the sample is drawn, all ineligibles are ignored. There is a great temptation when doing so to substitute the next name on the list. This is incorrect procedure that introduces a bias, because the probability of selection is higher for those elements that follow ineligible listings. Rather, the correct procedure is to draw another element randomly if simple random selection procedures are being used. If systematic sampling procedures are being used, the sampling interval should be adjusted before the fact to allow for the percentage of ineligibles.[7] The problem of duplicates is then handled by adjustment. Specifically, the results are weighted by the inverse of the probability of selection. In a study using a list of car registrations, for example, each contacted respondent would be asked, "How many cars do you own?" The response of someone who said two would be weighted ½, whereas that of someone who said three would be weighted ⅓.[8]

The appropriate sampling and adjustment procedures to account for inadequate sampling frames can become quite technical in complex sample designs and

---

[7]The correct sampling interval is $i = Np/n$, where N is the total size of the list, p is the estimated percentage ineligible, and n is the desired sample size. Seymour Sudman, *Applied Sampling* (New York: Academic Press, 1976), p. 60.

[8]The general adjustment procedure for dealing with the problem of duplicates on a list is to weight sample elements discovered to have been listed k times by $1/k$. Sudman, *Applied Sampling*, p. 63. Most of the standard computer packages for statistically analyzing the data contain mechanisms by which the analyst can specify the weight to be applied to each sample observation.

FIGURE 12.2　**Possible Outcomes When Attempting to Contact Respondents for Telephone Surveys**

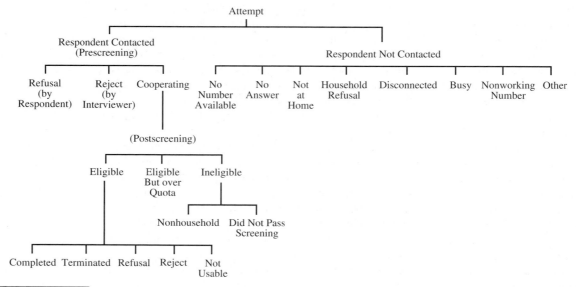

Source: Frederick Wiseman and Philip McDonald, *Toward the Development of Industry Standards for Response and Nonresponse Rates* (Cambridge, MA: Marketing Science Institute, 1980), p. 29. Reprinted with permission.

fall largely in the domain of the sampling specialist. Consequently, we shall not delve into these processes but shall simply note the following:

1. Noncoverage bias is a nonsampling error and is therefore not dealt with in our standard statistical formulas.
2. Noncoverage bias is *not* likely to be eliminated by increasing the sample size.
3. It can be of considerable magnitude.
4. It can be reduced, but not necessarily eliminated, by recognizing its existence, working to improve the sampling frame, and employing a sampling specialist to help reduce, through the sampling procedure, and adjust, through analysis, the remaining frame imperfections.[9]

Nonresponse Errors

Another source of nonobservation bias is **nonresponse error,** which represents a failure to obtain information from some elements of the population that were selected and designated for the sample. One problem in dealing with nonresponse error is simply appreciating all the many things that can go wrong with an attempt to contact a designated respondent. Figure 12.2, for example, depicts the various outcomes of an attempted telephone contact. There is such a bewildering array of

---

[9]Kish, *Survey Sampling*, pp. 530–531, offers a number of suggestions about what can be done to decrease the effect of noncoverage, as well as some general comments regarding the extent of noncoverage bias.

alternatives that even the calculation of a measure of the extent of the nonresponse problem becomes difficult.

Spurred by the concern that the absence of standard, industrywide definitions and methods of calculation for rates of response and nonresponse had prevented an accurate assessment of the potential magnitude of the nonresponse problem, a study was conducted among a sample of members of the Council of American Survey Research Organizations (CASRO) and leading user companies. The study involved mailing questionnaires that displayed actual contact and response data from three different telephone surveys, a telephone directory sample, a random-digit sample, and a list sample. Respondents were asked to calculate the response, contact, completion, and refusal rates for each of the three surveys.[10] The difference in results was rather startling. Panel A of Table 12.1, for example, displays the raw data from the telephone directory sample. Using the very same data, one responding organization reported the response rate as 12 percent while another suggested it was 90 percent. Further, there was little agreement among the other firms. No more than three firms out of forty agreed on any single definition of the response rate, and that occurred with respect to three different definitions. Panel B of Table 12.1 displays the three most frequently used definitions, as well as the definitions producing the minimum and maximum response rates.

Not only does the variation in definitions cause confusion when nonresponse rates are reported for a survey, but it also makes the treatment of the nonresponse error problem more difficult. It becomes hard to discern, for instance, whether a particular method proved to be effective or whether a different definition was responsible for a lower nonresponse error in a particular study. Because of the need to generalize findings in order to improve the practice of survey research, a special CASRO task force developed a definition of response rate that the industry is being encouraged to embrace as the standard definition—namely that[11]

$$\text{Response rate} = \frac{\text{Number of completed interviews with responding units}}{\text{Number of eligible responding units in the sample}}$$

Nonresponse is a problem in any survey in which it occurs, because it raises the question of whether those who did respond are different in some important way from those who did not respond. This is, of course, something we do not know, although study after study has indicated that the assumption that those who did not respond were in fact equal to those who did is risky.

The two main sources of nonresponse bias are not-at-homes and refusals. Nonresponse bias can arise with studies using personal interviews or telephone or mail surveys to secure the data. However, with mail surveys, the not-at-home problem becomes one of nonreceipt of the questionnaire. The questionnaire may simply have been lost in the mail, in which case the nonsampling error could be considered

[10]Frederick Wiseman and Philip McDonald, *Toward the Development of Industry Standards for Response and Nonresponse Rates* (Cambridge, MA: Marketing Science Institute, 1980).

[11]"On the Definition of Response Rates," *CASRO Special Report* (Port Jefferson, NY: The Council of American Survey Research Organizations, 1982). See also M. A. Hidiroglou, J. D. Drew, and G. B. Gray, "A Framework for Measuring and Reducing Nonresponse in Surveys," *Survey Methodology* 19 (1993), pp. 81–94.

TABLE 12.1　**Response Rate Calculations for Telephone Directory Sample**

Panel A: Outcome of Telephone Call

Disconnected/nonworking telephone number	426
Household refusal	153
No answer, busy, not at home	1,757
Interviewer reject (language barrier, hard of hearing, . . .)	187
Respondent refusal	711
Ineligible respondent	366
Termination by respondent	74
Completed interview	501
Total	4,175

Panel B: Most Frequent, Minimum, and Maximum Response Rates

Most frequent:

$$\frac{\text{Household Refusals} + \text{Rejects} + \text{Refusals} + \text{Ineligibles} + \text{Terminations} + \text{Completed Interviews}}{\text{All}} = \qquad (1)$$

$$\frac{153 + 187 + 711 + 366 + 74 + 501}{4{,}175} = 48\%$$

$$\frac{\text{Rejects} + \text{Refusals} + \text{Inegligibles} + \text{Terminations} + \text{Completed Interviews}}{\text{All}} = \qquad (2)$$

$$\frac{187 + 711 + 366 + 74 + 501}{4{,}175} = 44\%$$

$$\frac{\text{Completed Interviews}}{\text{All}} = \frac{501}{4{,}175} = 12\% \qquad (3)$$

Minimum:

$$\frac{\text{Completed Interviews}}{\text{All}} = \frac{501}{4{,}175} = 12\%$$

Maximum:

$$\frac{\text{Refusals} + \text{Ineligibles} + \text{Termination} + \text{Completed Interviews}}{\text{Rejects} + \text{Refusals} + \text{Ineligibles} + \text{Termination} + \text{Completed Interviews}} =$$

$$\frac{711 + 366 + 74 + 501}{187 + 711 + 366 + 74 + 501} = 90\%$$

Source: Frederick Wiseman and Philip McDonald, *Toward the Development of Industry Standards for Response and Nonresponse Rates* (Cambridge, MA: Marketing Science Institute, 1980), pp. 12 and 19. Reprinted with permission. See also M. A. Hidiroglou, J. D. Drew, and G. B. Gray, "A Framework for Measuring and Reducing Nonresponse in Surveys," *Survey Methodology* 19 (1993), pp. 81–94.

random and nonbiasing, or there may be more fundamental reasons for nonreceipt: The addressee may have moved or died. These latter conditions would be a source of systematic nonsampling error.

NOT-AT-HOMES　Replies will not be secured from some designated sampling units because the respondent will not be at home when the interviewer calls. The empirical evidence indicates that there is a long upward trend in the **not-at-homes.** The percentage of not-at-homes depends on the nature of the designated respondent and the time of the call. Married women with young children are more likely to be at home during the day on weekdays than are men, married women without children, or single women. The probability of finding someone at home is also greater for low-income families and for rural families. Seasonal variations, particularly during the holidays, do occur, as do weekday-to-weekend variations. Further, it is much easier to find a "responsible adult" at home than a specified respondent, and thus the choice of the elementary sampling unit is key in the not-at-home problem.

Several things can be done to reduce the incidence of not-at-homes. For example, the interviewer might make an appointment in advance by telephone with the respondent. This approach is particularly valuable in surveys of busy executives, but it may not be justifiable in an ordinary consumer survey. A commonly used technique in the latter instance is the callback, which is particularly effective if the callback (preferably callbacks) is (are) made at a different time than the original call. As a matter of fact, the nonresponse problem due to not-at-homes is so acute and so important to the accuracy of most surveys that one leading expert has suggested that small samples with four to six callbacks are more efficient than large samples without callbacks, unless the percentage of initial response can be increased considerably above normal levels.[12] Some data indicate, for example, that four, five or even more calls are often needed to reach three-fourths of the sample of households.[13]

An alternative to the "straight" callback is the "modified" callback. If the initial contact attempt and first few callbacks were made by an interviewer and a contact was not established, the interviewer might simply leave a self-administered questionnaire with a stamped, self-addressed envelope behind. If the not-at-home is simply a "designated respondent absent" rather than a "nobody-at-home," the interviewer can use the opportunity to inquire about the respondent's hours of availability.

One technique that is sometimes naively suggested for handling the not-at-homes is substituting the neighboring dwelling unit, or, in a telephone survey, calling the next name on the list. This is a very poor way of handling the not-at-home condition. All it does is substitute more at-homes (who may be different from the not-at-homes in a number of important characteristics) for the population segment the researcher is in fact trying to reach. This increases the proportion of at-homes in the sample and, in effect, aggravates the problem instead of solving it.

The proportion of reported not-at-homes is likely to depend on the interviewer and the judgment used in scheduling initial contacts and callbacks. This suggests that one way of reducing not-at-home nonresponse bias is by better interviewer training with particular emphasis on how to schedule callbacks more efficiently.

---

[12]W. Edwards Deming, "On a Probability Mechanism to Attain an Economic Balance between the Resultant Error of Response and the Bias of Nonresponse," *Journal of the American Statistical Association* 48 (December 1953), pp. 766–767. See also Benjamin Lipstein, "In Defense of Small Samples," *Journal of Advertising Research* 15 (February 1975), pp. 33–40; William C. Dunkelburg and George S. Day, "Nonresponse Bias and Callbacks in Sample Surveys," *Journal of Marketing Research* 10 (May 1973), pp. 160–168, a study that provides "evidence on the rate at which sample values converge on their population distribution as the number of callbacks increases;" Lorna Opatow, "Some Thoughts about How Interview Attempts Affect Survey Results," *Journal of Advertising Research* 31 (February/March 1991), pp. RC6–RC9; Thomas Piazza, "Meeting the Challenge of Answering Machines," *Public Opinion Quarterly* 57 (Summer 1993), pp. 219–231.

[13]Robert M. Groves and Robert L. Kahn, *Surveys by Telephone* (New York: Academic Press, 1979), pp. 56–58. See also Paul J. Lavrakas, *Telephone Survey Methods: Sampling, Selection, and Supervision*, 2nd ed. (Thousand Oaks, CA: Sage Publications, 1993).

The fact that interviewer effectiveness affects the number of not-at-homes also suggests one measure by which interviewers can be compared and evaluated. This is the **contact rate** *(K),* defined as the percentage of eligible assignments in which the interviewer makes contact with the designated respondent; that is,

$$K = \frac{\text{Number of eligible sample units contacted}}{\text{Total number of eligible sample units approached}}$$

The contact rate measures the interviewer's persistence. Interviewers can be compared with respect to their contact rate, and corrective measures can often be taken. Those with low contact rates can be checked as to why. Perhaps these interviewers are operating in traditionally high not-at-home areas, such as high-income sections of an urban area. Alternatively, by examining the call reports for time of each call, the trouble may be traced to poor follow-up procedures. This condition would suggest that additional training is necessary, which might then be provided by the field supervisor while the study is still in progress. The contact rate can also be used to evaluate an entire study in terms of the potential nonresponse caused by not-at-homes.

Not-at-home nonresponse bias can also be addressed by statistical adjustment of the results using a scheme developed by Politz and Simmons.[14] Rather than relying on callbacks, their scheme depends on a single attempted contact with each sample member at a randomly determined time. During this contact, the respondent is asked if he or she was home at the time of the interview for the five preceding days. These five answers and the time of the interview provide information on the time the respondent was at home for six different days. The responses from each informant are then weighted by the reciprocal of their self-reported probability of being at home; for example, the answers of a respondent who was home one out of six times would receive a weight of six. The basic rationale is that people who are usually not at home are more difficult to catch for an interview and therefore will tend to be underrepresented in the survey. Consequently, the less a subject reports being at home, the more that subject's responses should be weighted.

REFUSALS In almost every study, some respondents will refuse to participate. In one of the most extensive investigations of the magnitude of the problem, 46 field research companies sponsored a study called "Your Opinion Counts," which involved almost 1.4 million phone and personal interviews. The study indicated that

---

[14]The technique can be used with telephone interviews, although it was designed for personal interviews because of the tremendous expense of personal interview callbacks. Moreover, probing on the phone about when a respondent was home during the last five days can cause mistrust. See Alfred Politz and Willard Simmons, "An Attempt to Get the Not-at-Homes into the Sample Without Callbacks," *Journal of the American Statistical Association* 44 (March 1949), pp. 9–32, for explanation of the technique. For an empirical investigation of the effect of weighting on bias, see James Ward, Bertram Russick, and William Rudelius, "A Test of Reducing Callbacks and Not-At-Home Bias in Personal Interviews by Weighting At-Home Respondents," *Journal of Marketing Research* 22 (February 1985), pp. 66–73. See also I-Fen Lin and Nora Cate Schaeffer, "Using Survey Participants to Estimate the Impact of Nonparticipation," *Public Opinion Quarterly* 59 (Summer 1995), pp. 236–258.

38 percent of the people asked to participate declined to do so, with 86 percent of those refusing to participate before or during the introduction. The rest broke away before the survey was completed.[15] Research Realities 12.1 depicts what is happening to refusal rates in general and presents some of the major reasons respondents give for having refused to participate in surveys.

The rate of **refusals** depends, among other things, on the nature of the respondent, the auspices of the research, the circumstances surrounding the contact, the

---

RESEARCH REALITIES 12.1

Trends in Refusal Rates and Reasons Given for Refusing to Participate

Panel A: Percentage of Those Contacted Who Had Refused to Participate in a Survey in the Past Year

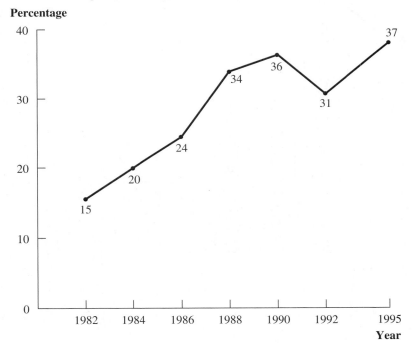

Source: *Respondent Cooperation and Industry Image Survey* (Port Jefferson, NY: The Council for Marketing and Opinion Research, 1996), pp. 36–37.

---

[15] *Your Opinion Counts: 1986 Refusal Rate Study* (Chicago: Marketing Research Association, 1986). See also Erhard Meier, "Response Rate Trends in Britain," *Marketing and Research Today* 19 (June 1991), pp. 120–123; Tom W. Smith, "Trends in Nonresponse Rates," *International Journal of Public Opinion Research* 7 (1995), pp. 157–171.

(continued)

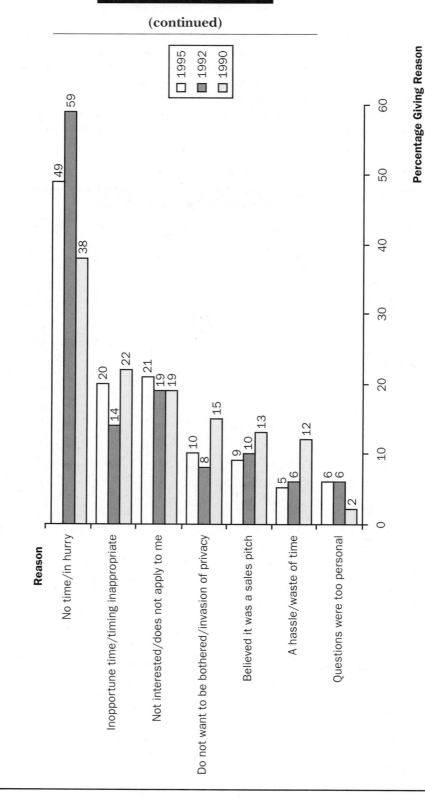

Panel B: Reasons Given for Having Refused to Participate

nature of the subject, and the interviewer. Even the culture of the country can affect the refusal rate. For example, in some cultures (such as Saudi Arabia), it is nearly impossible to interview women. The method used to collect the data also makes a difference. The empirical evidence indicates, for example, that personal interviews are most effective and mail questionnaires least effective in generating response. Telephone interviews are somewhat less successful on average than personal interviews in getting target respondents to cooperate.

Although it is hard to generalize across data-collection techniques about the types of people likely to cooperate in a survey, there does seem to be some tendency for females, nonwhites, those who are less well educated, those who have lower incomes, and those who are older to be more likely to refuse to participate.[16] The auspices of the research can also make a difference in the number of refusals. People not only report differently to different sponsors, but the sponsor can also affect whether or not they report at all. Sometimes the condition surrounding the contact can cause a refusal. A respondent may be too busy or tired or may be sick when contacted and thus refuse to participate. The subject of the research also affects refusal rate. Those who typically respond are those who are most interested in the subject. Also, nonresponse errors tend to increase with the sensitivity of the information being sought. Finally, interviewers themselves can have an important effect on the number of refusals they obtain. Their approach, their manner, and even their own demographic characteristics can affect a respondent's willingness to participate.

What can be done to correct the nonresponse bias introduced when designated respondents refuse their participation? There seem to be three available strategies. One, the initial response rate can be increased. Two, the impact of refusals can be reduced through follow-up. Three, the obtained information can be extrapolated to allow for nonresponse.

INCREASING INITIAL RESPONSE RATE   It would appear that the nature of the respondent is beyond the researcher's control. The problem dictates the target population, and this population is likely to contain households with different educational levels, income levels, cultural and occupational backgrounds, and so forth. The task is not as hopeless as it might seem, though. A model for interviewer-interviewee interaction will be offered when discussing errors of observation. Granted that the nature of the respondent can affect the refusal rate, the interviewee's cooperation can be encouraged by an "appropriate choice" of interviewer. But more on this later.

More traditional methods can also be used to ensure respondents' participation. One thing, of course, is to sell respondents on the value of the research and the importance of their participation. Advance notice may help. Interviewers can be trained in useful approaches. The evidence suggests, for example, that the more information provided about the content and purpose of the survey, the higher the

[16]T. De Maio, "Refusals: Who, Where, and Why," *Public Opinion Quarterly* 44 (Summer 1980), pp. 223–233. See also Jolene M. Strubbe, Jerome B. Kernan, and Thomas J. Grogan, "The Refusal Problem in Telephone Surveys," *Journal of Advertising Research* 26 (June/July 1986), pp. 29–37; Kathy E. Green, "Sociodemographic Factors and Mail Survey Response," *Psychology & Marketing* 13 (March 1996), pp. 171–184.

response rate.[17] Some individuals refuse to participate because they do not wish to be identified with their responses. A guarantee that the replies will be held in confidence (if they truly will be) is often effective in calming such fears.[18] Sometimes money or some other incentive is offered;[19] monetary incentives seem to be most effective in increasing response rates in mail surveys.

Nonresponse attributable to identification of the sponsor can be overcome by hiding the sponsor; this can be accomplished by hiring a professional research organization to conduct the field study. This is one reason companies with established, sophisticated research departments do, in fact, employ research firms to collect data.

The ability to generalize what might happen if a particular inducement technique is used to increase the cooperation rate in a survey is clouded by the fact that the effects are different from survey to survey. When one looks across surveys, the picture becomes somewhat clearer, even though the many review articles do not completely agree on the impact of various response inducement techniques. This is due partially to the articles and time periods included in their reviews.[20] The results of one of the most recent and extensive reviews of mail-survey response involvement techniques are shown in Figure 12.3. The average effect of the facilitation technique is shown by the weighted correlation coefficient across studies where the weights reflect the size of the various samples on which the individual correlations were based. The larger the weighted mean correlation, the more impact the particular facilitation technique has. The results in Figure 12.3 indicate that, on average, the most successful response inducement techniques in mail surveys are the use of

[17]Eleanor Singer, "Informed Consent: Consequences for Response Rate and Response Quality in Social Surveys," *American Sociological Review* 43 (April 1978), pp. 144–162; Eleanor Singer and Martin R. Frankel, "Informed Consent Procedures in Telephone Interviews," *American Sociological Review* 47 (June 1982), pp. 416–427; Robert M. Groves, Robert M. Cialdini, and Mick P. Couper, "Understanding the Decision to Participate in a Survey," *Public Opinion Quarterly* 56 (Winter 1992), pp. 475–495; Terry L. Childers and Steven J. Skinner, "Toward a Conceptualization of Mail Survey Response Behavior," *Psychology & Marketing* 13 (March 1996), pp. 185–209.

[18]For a summary of the empirical evidence of the impact of confidentiality assurances on response, see Eleanor Singer, Dawn R. VonThorn, and Esther R. Miller, "Confidentiality Assurances and Response," *A Quantitative Review of the Experimental Literature* 59 (Spring 1995), pp. 66–77.

[19]Lee Harvey, "Factors Affecting Response Rates to Mailed Questionnaires: A Comprehensive Literature Review," *Journal of the Market Research Society* 29 (July 1987), pp. 341–353; Mike Brennan, "The Effect of a Monetary Incentive on Mail Survey Response Rates: New Data," *Journal of the Market Research Society* 34 (April 1992), pp. 173–177; Jeannine M. James and Richard Bolstein, "Large Monetary Incentives and Their Effect on Mail Survey Response Rates," *Public Opinion Quarterly* 56 (Winter 1992), pp. 442–453; Allan H. Church, "Estimating the Effect of Incentives on Mail Survey Response Rates: A Meta-Analysis," *Public Opinion Quarterly* 57 (Spring 1993), pp. 62–79; Diane K. Willimack, Howard Schuman, Beth-Ellen Pennel, and James M. Lepkowski, "Effects of a Prepaid Nonmonetary Incentive on Response Rates and Response Quality in a Face-to-Face Survey," *Public Opinion Quarterly* 59 (Spring 1995), pp. 78–92.

[20]Leslie Kanuk and Conrad Berenson, "Mail Surveys and Response Rates: A Literature Review," *Journal of Marketing Research* 12 (November 1975), pp. 440–453; T. A. Heberlein and R. A. Baumgartner, "Factors Affecting Response Rates to Mailed Questionnaires: A Quantitative Analysis of the Published Literature," *American Sociological Review* 43 (August 1978), pp. 447–462; Julie Yu and Harris Cooper, "A Quantitative Review of Research Design Effects on Response Rates to Questionnaires," *Journal of Marketing Research* 20 (February 1983), pp. 36–44; Richard J. Fox, Melvin R. Crask, and Jonghoon Kim, "Mail Survey Response Rate: A Meta-Analysis of Selected Techniques for Inducing Response," *Public Opinion Quarterly* 52 (Winter 1989), pp. 467–491; Francis J. Yammarino, Steven J. Skinner, and Terry L. Childers, "Understanding Mail Survey Response Behavior: A Meta-Analysis," *Public Opinion Quarterly* 55 (Winter 1991), pp. 613–639.

FIGURE 12.3   **Impact of Selected Response Inducement Techniques on Mail Survey Response Rates**

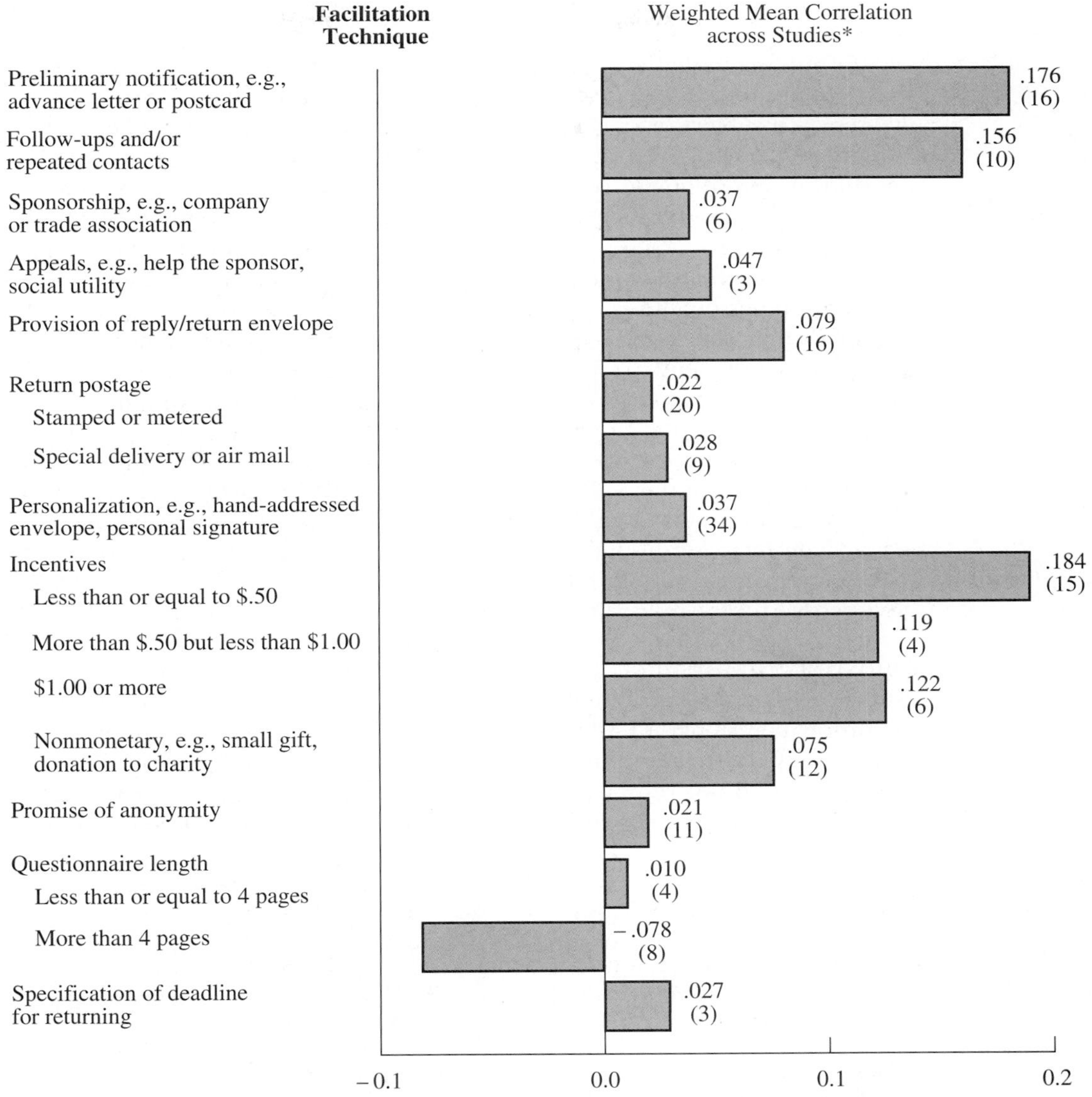

Facilitation
Technique

Weighted Mean Correlation
across Studies*

Facilitation Technique	Weighted Mean Correlation across Studies*
Preliminary notification, e.g., advance letter or postcard	.176 (16)
Follow-ups and/or repeated contacts	.156 (10)
Sponsorship, e.g., company or trade association	.037 (6)
Appeals, e.g., help the sponsor, social utility	.047 (3)
Provision of reply/return envelope	.079 (16)
Return postage — Stamped or metered	.022 (20)
Special delivery or air mail	.028 (9)
Personalization, e.g., hand-addressed envelope, personal signature	.037 (34)
Incentives — Less than or equal to $.50	.184 (15)
More than $.50 but less than $1.00	.119 (4)
$1.00 or more	.122 (6)
Nonmonetary, e.g., small gift, donation to charity	.075 (12)
Promise of anonymity	.021 (11)
Questionnaire length — Less than or equal to 4 pages	.010 (4)
More than 4 pages	−.078 (8)
Specification of deadline for returning	.027 (3)

−0.1   0.0   0.1   0.2

*The numbers shown in brackets indicate the number of correlations on which the average correlation is based.
Source: Developed from the information in Frances J. Yammarino, Steven J. Skinner, and Terry L. Childers, "Understanding Mail Survey Response Behavior: A Meta-Analysis," *Public Opinion Quarterly* 55 (Winter 1991), pp. 613–639. Reprinted with permission University of Chicago Press.

incentives, preliminary notification that the survey is coming, and follow-ups or repeated mailings.

FOLLOW-UP   Because many of the circumstances surrounding a contact are temporary and changeable, this source of bias introduced through refusals can often be reduced. If a respondent declined participation because he or she was busy or sick, a callback at a different time or employing a different approach may be sufficient to secure cooperation. In a mail survey, this may mean a follow-up mailing at a more convenient time. Thus, one means of reducing this source of bias seems to be the training and control of the field staff.

It would seem that very little can be done with the subject of the research as a source of nonresponse bias, since it is dictated by the problem to be solved. A sensitive research subject or one of little interest to the respondents is likely to elicit a high rate of refusals. The researcher should not overlook the opportunity to make the study as interesting as possible, though. This often means that "questions that are interesting but not vital" should be avoided. The development of the measuring instrument thus becomes essential in reducing this source of refusals.

Generally, other than for refusals because of circumstances, callbacks will be less successful in personal interviews and telephone surveys for reducing the incidence of refusals than they are for treating the not-at-home condition. This is not so with mail surveys. Frequently, responses are obtained with the second and third mailings from those who did not respond to earlier mailings. Of course, follow-up in a mail survey requires identification of those not responding earlier. This means that those who did respond need to be identified. However, as we have already seen, respondents who know that they can be identified may refuse to participate. Thus, identification of the respondents, which may serve to decrease one source of nonresponse, may actually increase another. The alternative of sending each mailing to each designated sample member, without screening those who have responded previously, can be expensive for the research organization and frustrating for the respondent.

ADJUSTING THE RESULTS   A third strategy for treating nonresponse bias involves estimating its effects and then adjusting the results.[21] Suppose, for instance, that the problem was one of estimating the mean income for a certain population and that responses were secured from only a portion (p_r) of some designated sample. The proportion not responding could then be denoted p_{nr}. If $\bar{x}_r$ is the mean income of those *responding* and $\bar{x}_{nr}$ the mean income of those *not* *responding*, then the overall mean would be

$$\bar{x} = p_r\bar{x}_r + p_{nr}\bar{x}_{nr}$$

This computation, of course, assumes that $\bar{x}_{nr}$ is known or at least can be estimated. An intensive follow-up of a *sample* of the *nonrespondents* is sometimes used to

[21] *Statistical Adjustment for Nonresponse in Sample Surveys: A Selected Bibliography with Annotations* (Monticello, IL: Vance Bibliographies, 1979); J. Scott Armstrong and Terry S. Overton, "Estimating Nonresponse Bias in Mail Surveys," *Journal of Marketing Research* 14 (August 1977), pp. 396–402; Michael J. O'Neil, "Estimating the Nonresponse Bias Due to Refusals in Telephone Surveys," *Public Opinion Quarterly* 40 (Summer 1976), pp. 218–232; David Elliot and Roger Thomas, "Further Thoughts on Weighting Survey Results to Compensate for Nonresponse," *Survey Methodology Bulletin* 15 (February 1983), pp. 2–11; Juha M. Alho, "Adjusting for Nonresponse Bias Using Logistic Regression," *Biometrika* 77, no. 3 (1990), pp. 617–624; Linda Robinson and Donald Lifton, "Reducing Market Research Costs: Deciding When to Eliminate Expensive Survey Follow-Up," *Journal of the Market Research Society* 33 (October 1991), pp. 301–308; Valentine Uppel and Julian Baim, "Predicting and Correcting Response Rate Problems Using Geodemography," *Marketing Research: A Magazine of Management & Applications* 4 (March 1992), pp. 22–28; R. C. Kessler, P. J. A. Little, and R. M. Groves, "Advances in Strategies for Minimizing and Adjusting for Survey Response," *Epidemiologic Reviews* 17 (1995), pp. 192–204.

generate this estimate. The follow-up may be a modified callback. Although this rarely generates a response from each nonrespondent designated for the follow-up, it does allow a crude adjustment of the initial results. Ignoring the initial nonresponse is equivalent to assuming that $\bar{x}_{nr}$ is equal to $\bar{x}_r$, which is usually incorrect.

A second way by which the adjustment is sometimes made involves keeping track of those responding to the initial contact, the first follow-up, the second follow-up, and so on. The mean of the variable (or other appropriate statistic) is then calculated, and each subgroup is compared to determine whether any statistically significant differences emerge as a function of the difficulty experienced in making contact. If not, the variable mean for the nonrespondents is assumed to be equal to the mean for those responding. If a discernible trend is evident, the trend is extrapolated to allow for nonrespondents. This method is particularly valuable in mail surveys, where it is an easy task to identify those responding to the first mailing, the second mailing, and so on.

Evidence accumulated in past surveys also sometimes serves as the basis of the adjustment for nonresponse. This approach is particularly well suited to organizations that frequently conduct surveys involving similar sampling procedures. While no method of adjustment is perfect, the assumption that nonrespondents are similar to respondents on the characteristic of interest is risky. Yet this is the very assumption we make if no attempt is made to correct for nonresponse.

The preceding discussions all deal with total nonresponse. Item nonresponse, which can also be a problem, occurs when the respondent agrees to the total interview but refuses, or is unable, to answer some specific questions because of the content, form, or sequence of the questions or the amount of work required to produce the requested information. The primary mechanisms for treating these problems lie in the development of the questionnaire and methods for administering it, issues discussed earlier.

Suppose that item nonresponses occur in spite of our best efforts on these tasks. Whether anything can then be done about item nonresponse depends on its magnitude. Here we must distinguish between flagrant item nonresponse and isolated or sporadic nonresponse. If too many questions are left unanswered, the reply becomes unusable, and the treatment, or at least adjustment, is the same as that for a complete nonresponse. On the other hand, if only a few items are left unanswered on any questionnaire, the reply can often be made usable. At the very minimum, the "don't know" and "no answers" can be treated as separate categories when reporting the results. In many ways this is the best strategy, because the little evidence that is available on item nonresponse suggests that the problem is extensive and nonrandom.[22]

---

[22]J. Frances and L. Busch, "What We Know about 'I Don't Knows'," *Public Opinion Quarterly* 39 (Summer 1975), pp. 207–218; Herbert Schuman and Stanley Presser, "The Assessment of 'No Opinion' in Attitude Surveys," in Karl F. Schuessler, ed., *Sociological Methodology 1979* (San Francisco: Jossey-Bass, 1979), pp. 241–275; C. Coombs and L. Coombs, "'Don't Know': Item Ambiguity or Respondent Uncertainty," *Public Opinion Quarterly* 40 (Winter 1976), pp. 497–514; Glenn S. Omura, "Correlates of Item Nonresponse," *Journal of the Market Research Society* 25 (October 1983), pp. 321–330; Richard M. Durand, Hugh J. Guffey, Jr., and John M. Planchon, "An Examination of the Random versus Nonrandom Nature of Item Omissions," *Journal of Marketing Research* 20 (August 1983), pp. 305–313; James H. Leigh and Claude R. Martin, Jr., "'Don't Know' Item Nonresponse in a Telephone Survey: Effects of Question Form and Respondent Characteristics," *Journal of Marketing Research* 24 (November 1987), pp. 418–424.

Alternatively, the information from the missing item or items can sometimes be inferred from other information in the questionnaire.[23] This works if there are other questions on the questionnaire that relate to the same issue. The other questions are checked, and a consistent answer is formulated for the unanswered item. In the absence of such consistency checks, regression analysis is sometimes used. The missing item is treated as the criterion variable, and the functional relationship is established between it and *a priori* related questions through regression analysis for those cases for which the item was answered. The equation is then used to estimate a response for the remaining questionnaires given the information that they contain on the predictor variables. Finally, item nonresponse is handled a third way by substituting the average response for the item of those who did respond. This technique, of course, carries the assumption that those who did not respond to the item are similar to those who did. As we have suggested many times, this assumption may be risky, and, therefore, substituting the average should be done with caution.

Just as the contact rate can be used to compare and evaluate interviewers with respect to not-at-homes, at least two ratios have been suggested for comparing interviewers with respect to refusals: the **response rate R** and the **completeness rate C**. The response rate was discussed previously. It equals the ratio of the number of completed interviews with responding units divided by the number of eligible responding units in the sample. The response rate reflects the interviewer's effectiveness at the door or on the phone.

The completeness rate applies to the individual items in the study. Most typically it will be used to evaluate interviewers with respect to the crucial questions involved in the study (for example, a respondent's income, debt, or asset position), although it can also be used to evaluate the whole contact. The completeness rate simply determines whether or not the response is complete, either in terms of the crucial questions or the whole questionnaire.

Field Errors

Field errors are by far the most prevalent type of observation error. **Field errors** arise after the individual has agreed to participate in a study. Instead of cooperating fully, the individual refuses to answer specific questions or provides a response that somehow differs from what is actually true or correct. Such errors have been referred to, respectively, as errors of omission and errors of commission. It was convenient to discuss errors of omission or item nonresponse in the last section. Now we turn our attention to errors of commission, which are most typically referred to as *response errors*.

---

[23]Graham Kalton, *Compensating for Missing Survey Data* (Ann Arbor: Institute for Social Research, University of Michigan, 1983); R. L. Hinde and R. L. Chambers, "Nonresponse Imputation with Multiple Sources of Nonresponse," *Journal of Official Statistics* 7, no. 2 (1991), pp. 167–179; Otis W. Gilley and Robert P. Leone, "A Two-State Imputation Procedure for Item Nonresponse in Surveys," *Journal of Business Research* 22 (June 1991), pp. 281–291; Paul S. Levy and Stanley Lemeshow, *Sampling of Populations: Methods and Applications,* 3rd ed. (New York: John Wiley and Sons, Inc., 1991), especially Chapter 13.

ETHICAL DILEMMA 12.2

During a telephone survey, the names of respondents who refuse to answer the survey are placed in a special bin. All of these respondents are recontacted 24 hours later and asked again for their answers. The person making these follow-up calls receives special training in converting these refusals to completions. If the respondent refuses again, the interviewer attempts to "sell" the respondent on cooperating in the study. If the respondent remains unwilling to complete the survey, the interviewer terminates the call and notes this as a refusal.

- List the implications arising from increased refusals, as the number of telephone surveys increases.

- List the implications for marketing research if research companies make follow-up calls to refusals the industry standard.

- Should an initial refusal be taken as a refusal? Explain.

When considering response errors, it is useful to keep in mind what needs to occur for respondents to answer questions put to them. First, the respondent needs to understand what is being asked. Second, the individual needs to engage in some cognitive processing to arrive at an answer. That cognitive processing will typically include an assessment of the information needed for an accurate answer, retrieval of the pertinent attitudes, facts, or experiences, and the organization of the retrieved cognitions and the formulation of the response on this basis. Third, the person needs to evaluate the response in terms of its accuracy. Fourth, the subject needs to evaluate the response in terms of other goals he or she might have, such as preserving one's self-image or attempting to please the interviewer. Finally, the subject needs to give the response that results from all this mental processing. Reaching the final step is the object of the survey process. Breakdowns can occur at any of the preceding steps, however, resulting in an inaccurate answer or a response error.

The number of factors that can cause response errors is so large that the factors almost defy categorization. One seemingly useful scheme for dealing with data-collection errors, though, is the **interviewer-interviewee interaction model,** proposed by Kahn and Cannell and shown in Figure 12.4.[24]

The model suggests several things. First, each person brings certain background characteristics and psychological predispositions to the interview. Although some of the background characteristics are readily observable, others are not, nor can the psychological state of the other person be seen. Yet both interviewer and interviewee will form attitudes toward and expectations of the other person on the

---

[24]Robert L. Kahn and Charles L. Cannell, *The Dynamics of Interviewing* (New York: John Wiley, 1957), p. 193. The figure is used by permission of John Wiley & Sons, Inc. See also Floyd J. Fowler, Jr., and Thomas W. Mangione, *Standardized Survey Interviewing: Minimized Interviewer-Related Error* (Thousand Oaks, CA: Sage Publications, Inc., 1989); Wendy Sykes and Martin Collins, "Anatomy of the Survey Interview," *Journal of Official Statistics* 8, no. 3 (1992), pp. 277–291.

FIGURE 12.4   **A Model of Bias in the Interview**

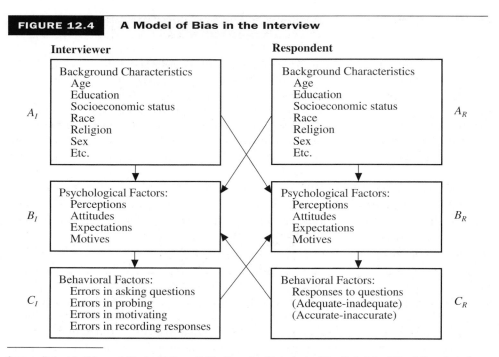

Source: Robert L. Kahn and Charles L. Cannell, *The Dynamics of Interviewing* (New York: John Wiley & Sons, Inc., © 1957), p. 193. Reprinted by permission of John Wiley & Sons, Inc. See also Wendy Sykes and Martin Collins, "Anatomy of the Survey Interview," *Journal of Official Statistics* 8, no. 3 (1992), pp. 277–291.

basis of their initial perceptions. Second, the interview is an interactive process, and both interviewer and interviewee are important determinants of the process. Each party perceives and reacts to the specific behaviors of the other. Note, though, that there is no direct link between the boxes labeled "behavioral factors." Rather, the linkage is more complicated, "involving a behavior on the part of the interviewer or respondent, the perception of this behavior by the other principal in the interview, a cognitive or attitudinal development from that perception, and finally a resultant motivation to behave in a certain way. Only at this point is a behavioral act carried out, which in turn may be perceived and reacted to by the other participant in the interview."[25] The perceptions of this behavior may not be correct, just as the initial perceptions of each party may be in error. Nevertheless, such inferences will inevitably be made as both interviewer and respondent search for cues to help them understand each other and carry out the requirements imposed by the interview situation. In sum, not only do the specific behaviors of each party to the interaction affect the outcome, but so do the background characteristics and psychological predispositions of both interviewer and respondent.

The interviewer-interviewee interaction model is appealing for several reasons. One, it is consistent with the empirical evidence. Two, it offers some valuable insight

---

[25]Kahn and Cannell, *The Dynamics of Interviewing*, p. 194.

on how response errors (as well as nonresponse errors due to refusals) can be potentially reduced. The model partly applies to telephone and mail surveys, thereby further increasing its value. For example, the respondents' perceptions of the background characteristics and behavior of a telephone interviewer are likely to affect the answers he or she provides. The respondent's background is certainly going to affect the person's reported responses. So will the person's suspicions about the true purpose of the study, or the individual's assumption of how confidential his or her responses will truly be. These factors can distort the respondent's answers regardless of the manner used to collect the data, and it is unlikely that these distortions would be random. At any rate, the model suggests certain things that the researcher can do to generate accurate information.

BACKGROUND FACTORS   The empirical evidence is consistent with the supposition that background factors affect reported responses. More particularly, the evidence suggests that better cooperation and more information are obtained when the backgrounds of the interviewer and respondent are similar than when they are different. This is particularly true for readily observable characteristics, such as race, age, and sex, but it applies as well to more unobservable characteristics, such as social class and income.[26] This suggests that it is productive to match the background characteristics of the interviewer and respondent as closely as possible, as the more characteristics the two have in common, the greater the probability of a successful interview.

Unfortunately, the research is somewhat constrained in this regard. Most interviewers are homemakers who use interviewing as a mechanism to supplement their family income. Although the profession also attracts some part-time workers such as students or school teachers, interviewing by no means attracts a balanced demographic cross section of people. Nevertheless, the researcher needs to recognize that the interviewer's background can affect the results, and thus investigators should do what they can to minimize such biases. This may simply mean computing a measure of interviewer variability while analyzing the results. Alternatively, a slight modification of interviewer schedules may be made in a specific project to improve background matches. It certainly seems that recruiting should be aimed at securing interviewers with diverse socioeconomic backgrounds, if other things are equal.

PSYCHOLOGICAL FACTORS   The evidence regarding the impact of psychological factors on responses tends to support the belief that interviewers' opinions, perceptions,

---

[26]Barbara Bailor, Leroy Bailey, and Joyce Stevens, "Measures of Interviewer Bias and Variance," *Journal of Marketing Research* 14 (August 1977), pp. 337–343; Shirley Hatchett and Howard Schuman, "White Respondents and Race-of-Interviewer Effects," *Public Opinion Quarterly* 39 (Winter 1975), pp. 523–528; Patrick R. Cotter, Jeffrey Cohen, and Philip B. Coulter, "Race of Interviewer Effects on Telephone Interviews," *Public Opinion Quarterly* 46 (Summer 1982), pp. 278–284; Robert M. Groves and Nancy H. Fultz, "Gender Effects among Telephone Interviewers in a Study of Economic Attitudes," *Sociological Methods & Research* 14 (August 1985), pp. 31–52; Louis G. Pol and Thomas G. Ponzurick, "Gender of Interviewee/Gender of Respondent Bias in Telephone Surveys," *Applied Marketing Research* 29 (Spring 1989), pp. 9–13; Cynthia Webster, "Hispanic and Anglo-Interviewer and Respondent Ethnicity and Gender: The Impact on Survey Response Quality," *Journal of Marketing Research* 33 (February 1996), pp. 62–72.

expectations, and attitudes affect the responses they receive.[27] Now, certainly, the interviewers' attitudes, opinions, expectations, and so on are going to be conditioned by the interviewers' backgrounds, and since that is something we cannot control, how are we to control for these psychological factors? The primary way is through training. The fact that interviewers will have psychological predispositions is not critical, because these psychological factors are not observed by the respondent. What is critical, however, is that these factors not be allowed to affect interviewers' behavior during the interview and thereby contaminate the response.

Most surveys, therefore, are conducted using a rather rigid set of procedures that interviewers must follow. The instructions should be clear and should be written. Further, they should state the purpose of the study clearly. They should describe the materials to be used, such as questionnaires, maps, time forms, and so on. They should describe how each question should be asked, the kinds of answers that are acceptable, and the kinds and timing of probes that are to be used, if any. The instructions should also specify the number and identity of respondents that interviewers need to contact and the time constraints under which they will be operating. It is also important that the instructions are well organized and unambiguous.

The instructions must be clearly articulated; however, it is even more important that interviewers understand and can follow them. This suggests that practice training sessions will be necessary. It might also be necessary to actually examine the interviewers with respect to study purposes and procedures. Finally, interviewers might also be required to complete the questionnaire so that, if there is a pattern between the interviewers' answers and the answers they get when administering the questionnaire, it can be determined.

BEHAVIORAL FACTORS   The respondents' background, attitudes, motives, expectations, and so on are also potentially biasing. Whether they actually do introduce bias depends on how the interviewer and respondent interact. In other words, the predisposition to bias becomes operative only in behavior.

Unfortunately the evidence indicates that even when the rules are rigid and the questionnaires relatively simple and structured, interviewers do not follow the rules. They thereby introduce bias. In one classic study, 15 college-educated interviewers interviewed the same respondent, who had previously been instructed to give identical answers to all 15.[28] All the interviews were recorded and were later

---

[27]Seymour Sudman, Norman Bradburn, Ed Blair, and Carol Stocking, "Modest Expectations: The Effects of Interviewers' Prior Expectations and Response," *Sociological Methods and Research* 6 (November 1977), pp. 177–182; Eleanor Singer and Luanne Kohnke-Aguirre, "Interviewer Expectation Effects: A Replication and Extension," *Public Opinion Quarterly* 43 (Summer 1979), pp. 245–260; Eleanor Singer, Martin R. Frankel, and Marc B. Glassman, "The Effect of Interviewer Characteristics and Expectations on Response," *Public Opinion Quarterly* 47 (Spring 1983), pp. 68–83; Robert M. Groves and Lou J. Magilavy, "Measuring and Explaining Interviewer Effects in Centralized Telephone Surveys," *Public Opinion Quarterly* 50 (Summer 1986), pp. 251–266; Stanley Presser and Shanyang Zhao, "Attributes of Questions and Interviewers as Correlates of Interviewing Performance," *Public Opinion Quarterly* 56 (Summer 1992), pp. 236–240.

[28]L. L. Guest, "A Study of Interviewer Competence," *International Journal of Opinion and Attitude Research* 1 (March 1947), pp. 17–30. See also P. Davis and A. Scott, "The Effect of Interviewer Variance on Domain Comparisons," *Survey Methodology* 21 (1995), pp. 99–106; Pamela Kiecker and James E. Nelson, "Do Interviewers Follow Telephone Survey Instructions?" *Journal of the Market Research Society* 38 (April 1996), pp. 161–176.

analyzed for the incidence of errors by type and frequency. One of the most startling findings of the study was the sheer number of errors. For example, there were 66 failures to ask supplementary questions when inadequate responses were given, and the number of errors per interviewer varied from 12 to 36. In another study, it was found that "one-third of the . . . interviewers deviated frequently and markedly from their instructions, sometimes failing to explain the key terms or to repeat them as required, sometimes leaving them out altogether, shortening questions, or failing to follow up certain ambiguous answers in the manner required."[29]

At least three interviewer behaviors lead to response bias: (1) errors in asking questions and in probing when additional information is required, (2) errors in recording the answer, and (3) errors due to cheating.

Even though errors in asking questions can arise with any of the basic question types, the problem is particularly acute with open-ended questions where probing follows the initial response. No two interviewers are likely to employ the same probes. The content as well as the timing of the probes may differ. This raises the possibility that the differences in answers may be due to the probes that are used rather than any "true" differences in the position of the respondents.

The manner in which the initial question is phrased can also introduce error. Two of the more common errors here are for interviewers to reword the question to fit their perceptions of what the respondent is capable of understanding or in a way that incorporates their own opinions of what constitutes an appropriate answer. Surprisingly, questions that include alternative answers possess great potential for interviewer bias. This bias occurs because the interviewer places undue emphasis on one of the alternatives in stating the question. Slight changes in tone can change the meaning of the entire question.

One of an interviewer's main tasks is keeping the respondent interested and motivated. At the same time, the interviewer tries to record what the respondent is saying by dutifully writing down the person's answers to open-ended questions or checking the appropriate box with closed questions. These dual, sometimes incompatible, responsibilities can also be a source of error. Interviewers may not correctly "hear" what the respondent is actually saying. This may be because the respondent is inarticulate and the response is garbled or because an interviewer's selective processes are operating. Interviewers may hear what they want to hear and retain what they want to retain. This is a common failing with all of us, and, in spite of interviewer training, recording errors in the interview are all too common.[30] Lest we be too hard on

[29]W. A. Belson, "Increasing the Power of Research to Guide Advertising Decisions," *Journal of Marketing* 29 (April 1965), p. 38. See also Martin Collins and Bob Butcher, "Interviewer and Clustering Effects in an Attitude Survey," *Journal of the Market Research Society* 25 (January 1983), pp. 39–58.

[30]Martin Collins, "Interviewing Variability: A Review of the Problem," *Journal of the Market Research Society* 22 (April 1980), pp. 77–95. For ways of investigating interviewer errors, see Jean Morton-Williams and Wendy Sykes, "The Use of Interaction Coding and Follow-up Interviews to Investigate Comprehension of Survey Questions," *Journal of the Market Research Society* 26 (April 1984), pp. 109–127. See also Jacques Billiet and Geert Loosveldt, "Improvement of the Quality of Responses to Factual Survey Questions by Interviewer Training," *Public Opinion Quarterly* 52 (Summer 1988), pp. 190–211; Floyd J. Fowler, Jr., and Thomas W. Mangione, *Standardized Survey Interviewing* (Thousand Oaks, CA: Sage Publications, Inc., 1989); P. Beatty, "Understanding the Standardized/Nonstandardized Interviewing Controversy," *Journal of Official Statistics* 11 (1995), pp. 147–160.

interviewers, however, we need to recognize that their job is a difficult one. It demands a good deal of ingenuity, creativity, and dogged determination.

Interviewer cheating can also be a source of response error. Cheating may range from the fabrication of a whole interview to the fabrication of one or two answers to make the response complete.

Most commercial research firms validate 10 to 20 percent of the completed interviews through follow-up telephone calls or by sending postcards to a sample of "respondents" to verify that they have in fact been contacted. The validation usually covers such general areas as:

1.   Method of contact—to be sure a personal interview wasn't actually handled on the telephone, for example.

2.   Questions asked—to verify that no important questions, such as qualifying or demographic questions, were skipped.

3.   Exhibits/products shown—to make sure people saw any concept boards or products that they were supposed to see.

4.   Respondent's familiarity with interviewer—to determine that the interviewer did not contact friends or acquaintances.

5.   General reactions to the interview—to check on the general quality of the contact.[31]

Another form of cheating, which is not exactly response error but which has a strong effect on all nonsampling errors, is padding bills. The interviewer may falsify the number of hours worked or the number of miles traveled. The problem is widespread because of the nature of the interviewing situation. The interviewer works without direct supervision in a basically low-paying job. Further, the supervisor's pay is normally geared to the interviewer's charges, so the higher the interviewer's bills, the higher the supervisor's compensation. Bill padding drains resources from other parts of the study and thereby decreases the efficiency (value) of the information because it is obtained at higher cost.

As suggested previously, it is much more difficult to adjust for response errors than for nonresponse errors. Their direction, much less their magnitude, is unknown, because in order to estimate their effects, the true value must be known. The researcher's main hope lies in prevention rather than subsequent adjustment of the results. The various sources of errors themselves suggest preventives. For example, training can help reduce errors in asking questions and recording answers. Similarly, the way interviewers are selected, paid, and controlled could reduce cheating. Overall interviewer performance can be assessed by rating the quality of the work in terms of appropriate characteristics, such as costs, types of errors, ability to follow instructions, and so on. We shall not detail the established procedures

---

[31]Jeffrey L. Pope, *Practical Marketing Research* (New York: American Management Association, 1993), p. 57. See also pages 56–59 for some effective validation questions for getting at these issues.

ETHICAL DILEMMA 12.3

A well-known car agency needed to make a decision about whether or not to import a relatively unknown line of foreign cars to complement its domestic line. To aid in its decision making, the agency contracted a research firm to conduct a study to determine potential consumer interest in and demand for this foreign car line. The results indicated that substantial awareness and interest existed, and consequently the decision was made to take on the new line.

To publicize the new line, a special preview was arranged for interested community members, such as local newspaper and radio people, executives in related automotive industries, filling station and repair shop owners, and leaders of men's and women's clubs. The agency's owners also wanted to invite the survey participants who had expressed an interest in the car; consequently, they asked the research firm to make known to them the respondents' names. The research firm refused to comply with this request, arguing that to do so would be a violation of the respondents' promised anonymity.

- Should the research firm comply with the agency's request?
- Does the car agency have the right to receive the participants' names since it has paid for the research?
- Would it have made a difference if the study had not been one to determine sales potential?
- What are some of the consequences of making the respondents' names known to the car agency?
- If the question had been anticipated before the survey was begun, could the interview structure have avoided the dilemma in which the company and the agency now find themselves?

in this regard, since that would be a book in its own right.[32] For our part we need to recognize the existence of response errors, their sources, and their potentially devastating effect. The interviewer-interviewee interaction model is helpful in visualizing these sources and in indicating methods of prevention.

---

[32]Some useful general sources are: Anderson, Kasper, and Frankel, et al., *Total Survey Error;* Bradburn and Sudman, *Improving Interview Method and Questionnaire Design;* Donald Dillman, *Mail and Telephone Surveys* (New York: John Wiley and Sons, 1978); Paul L. Erdos, *Professional Mail Surveys* (Malabar, FL: Robert E. Kreiger, 1983); Robert Ferber, ed., *Handbook of Marketing Research* (New York: McGraw-Hill, 1974), particularly Section II-B; Robert M. Groves and Robert L. Kahn, *Surveys by Telephone* (New York: Academic Press, 1979); J. Rothman, "Acceptance Checks for Ensuring Quality in Research," *Journal of the Market Research Society* 22 (July 1980), pp. 192–204; James E. Nelson and Pamela L. Kiecker, "Some Causes and Consequences of Interviewer Cheating Behavior," in Stanley Shapiro and A. H. Walle, eds., *Marketing: A Return to the Broader Dimensions* (Chicago: American Marketing Association, 1988), pp. 498–503; Paul Lavrakas, "To Err Is Human," *Market Research: A Magazine of Management & Applications* 8 (Spring 1996), pp. 30–36.

Office Errors

Our problems with nonsampling errors do not end with data collection. Errors can and do arise in the editing, coding, tabulation, and analysis of the data. For the most part, these errors can be reduced, if not eliminated, through the exercise of proper controls in data processing. These questions are discussed in Chapter 13.

Total Error Is Key

By this time we hope that the reader understands the admonition that total error, rather than any single type of error, is the key in designing a research investigation. The admonition particularly applies to sampling error, because there is a general tendency for beginning students of research method to argue for the "largest possible sample." After all, training in statistical method suggests that a large sample is much more likely to produce a statistic close to the population parameter being estimated than a small sample. What the student fails to appreciate, though, is that the argument applies only to sampling error. Increasing the sample size does, in fact, decrease sampling error. It may also increase nonsampling error, however, because the larger sample requires more interviewers, for instance, and this creates additional burdens in selection, training, and control. Further, nonsampling error is a much more insidious and troublesome error than sampling error. Sampling error can be estimated; many forms of nonsampling error cannot. Sampling error can be reduced through more sophisticated sample design or by using a larger sample. The path is clear and relatively well traveled, so the researcher should have little difficulty constraining sampling error within desired bounds. Not so with nonsampling errors. The path is not paved. New sources of nonsampling error are being discovered all the time, and, even though known, many of these sources defy reduction by any automatic procedure. "Improved method" is critical, but what these methods should be is sometimes unknown, although the chapter has attempted to highlight some of the better known sources of nonsampling error and ways of dealing with them.

ETHICAL DILEMMA 12.4

"These new computer-voiced telephone surveys are wonderful!" your friend enthuses over lunch. "Because we don't have to pay telephone interviewers, we can afford to have target numbers automatically redialed until someone answers. Of course, the public finds the computer's voice irritating and the whole notion of being interviewed by a machine rather humiliating. Nevertheless, we can overcome most people's reluctance to participate by repeatedly calling them until they give in and complete the questionnaire."

- Is it ethical to contact respondents repeatedly until they agree to participate in a research study? How many contacts are legitimate?
- If an industry is unable to constrain its members to behave ethically, should the government step in with regulations?
- If the public reacts against this kind of telephone survey, what are the results likely to be for researchers using traditional, more considerate telephone surveys?

TABLE 12.2	Overview of Nonsampling Errors and Some Methods for Handling Them	
Type	*Definition*	*Methods for Handling*
Noncoverage	Failure to include some units or entire sections of the defined survey population in the sampling frame	1. Improve basic sampling frame using other sources. 2. Select sample in such a way as to reduce incidence, such as by ignoring ineligibles on a list. 3. Adjust the results by appropriately weighting the subsample results.
Nonresponse	Failure to obtain information from some elements of the population that were selected for the sample	
Not-at-homes:	Designated respondent is not home when the interviewer calls.	1. Have interviewers make advance appointments. 2. Call back at another time, preferably at a different time of day. 3. Attempt to contact the designated respondent using another approach (for example, use a modified callback).
Refusals:	Respondent refuses to cooperate in the survey.	1. Attempt to convince the respondent of the value of the research and the importance of his or her participation. 2. Provide advance notice that the survey is coming. 3. Guarantee anonymity. 4. Provide an incentive for participating. 5. Hide the identification of the sponsor by using an independent research organization. 6. Try to get a "foot in the door" by getting the respondent to comply with some small task before getting the survey. 7. Use personalized cover letters. 8. Use a follow-up contact at a more convenient time. 9. Avoid interesting-but-not-vital questions. 10. Adjust the results to account for the nonresponse.
Field	Although the individual participates in the study, he or she refuses to answer specific questions or provides incorrect answers to them.	1. Match the background characteristics of the interviewer and respondent as closely as possible. 2. Make sure interviewer instructions are clear and written down. 3. Conduct practice training sessions with interviewers. 4. Examine the interviewers' understanding of the study's purposes and procedures. 5. Have interviewers complete the questionnaire and examine the replies they secure to see if there is any relationship between these answers and their own answers. 6. Verify a sample of each interviewer's interviews.
Office*	Errors that arise when coding, tabulating, or analyzing the data	1. Use field edit to detect the most glaring omissions and inaccuracies in the data. 2. Use a second edit in the office to decide how data-collection instruments containing incomplete answers, obviously wrong answers, and answers that reflect a lack of interest are to be handled. 3. Use closed questions to simplify the coding, but when open-ended questions need to be used, specify the appropriate codes that will be allowed before collecting the data. 4. When open-ended questions are being coded and multiple coders are being used, divide the task by questions and not by data-collection forms. 5. Have each coder code a sample of the other's work to ensure a consistent set of coding criteria is being employed. 6. Follow established conventions; for example, use numeric codes and not letters of the alphabet when coding the data for computer analysis. 7. Prepare a code book that lists the codes for each variable and the categories included in each code. 8. Use appropriate methods to analyze the data.

*Note: Steps that can be taken to reduce the incidence of office errors are discussed in more detail in Chapter 13.

Table 12.2 attempts to summarize what we have been saying about nonsampling errors and how they can be reduced or controlled. The table can be used as a sort of checklist for marketing managers and other users of research to evaluate the quality of the research before making substantive decisions on the basis of the research results. Although not all the methods for handling nonsampling errors will be applicable in every study, a systematic analysis of the research effort using the suggested approaches should provide the proper appreciation for the quality of research information that is obtained.

Summary

This chapter concentrated on the data-collection phase of the research process. The emphasis was on sources of error, because it was thought that an understanding of sources is more fundamental than a how-to-do-it approach. Practitioners need to be aware of the many potential sources of error so that they can better evaluate research proposals and can place research results in a proper perspective. Researchers need an understanding of error sources so that they can design studies with proper controls and allowances.

The main distinction in errors is that between sampling error and nonsampling error. Sampling error represents the difference between the observed values of a variable and the long-run average of the observed values in repetitions of the measurement. Nonsampling errors include everything else. They may arise because of errors in conception, logic, analysis, data gathering, and so forth. They are divided into the two major categories of errors of nonobservation and errors of observation. Errors of nonobservation can, in turn, be divided into errors of noncoverage and errors of nonresponse. Errors of observation can arise while collecting the data or while processing the information collected.

Noncoverage errors are essentially sampling frame problems. The list of population elements is rarely complete. Nonresponse errors reflect a failure to obtain information from certain elements of the population that were designated for inclusion in the sample. They can arise because the designated respondent was not at home or refused to participate. Empirical evidence indicates that the not-at-homes and the refusals often differ from respondents, and thus a systematic bias is introduced when they are excluded.

The interviewer-interviewee interaction model was offered as a useful vehicle for conceptualizing the errors that can arise while collecting the data. This model presents the interview as an interactive process between interviewer and respondent. Each principal brings different background and psychological factors to the interview. These affect each person's behavior and the way he or she perceives the other principal's behavior.

Finally, office errors occur because of weaknesses in the procedures for editing, coding, tabulating, and analyzing the collected data.

The research objective of minimization of total error was reiterated. Total error in conjunction with cost determines the value of any research effort.

Questions

1. Distinguish between sampling error and nonsampling error. Why is the distinction important?
2. What are noncoverage errors? Are they a problem with telephone surveys? How? With mail surveys? How? With personal interview studies? How?
3. How can noncoverage bias be assessed? What can be done to reduce it?
4. What is nonresponse error?
5. What are the basic types of nonresponse error? Are they equally serious for mail, telephone, or personal interview studies? Explain.

6. What can be done to reduce the incidence of not-at-homes in the final sample?

7. What is the contact rate? What role does it play in evaluating the results?

8. What are the typical reasons why designated respondents refuse to participate in a study? What can be done to reduce the incidence of refusals? Do refusals generally introduce random error or systematic biases into studies?

9. What is item nonresponse? What alternatives are available to the researcher for treating item nonresponse?

10. What is the response rate? What is the completeness rate? Is there any relation between the two?

11. What are observation errors? What are the basic types of observation errors?

12. Are observation errors likely to be a more serious or less serious problem than nonobservation errors? Explain.

13. Describe the interviewer-interviewee interaction model, including its basic propositions.

14. What does the interviewer-interviewee interaction model suggest with respect to the background characteristics of interviewers? With respect to their psychological characteristics?

15. What basic types of interviewer behavior can lead to response bias?

16. Explain the statement, "Total error is key."

Applications and Problems

1. Discuss some of the potential problems with each of the following sampling frames. For each potential problem you list, indicate whether it would result in a noncoverage or overcoverage error.
    a. Phone book
    b. Mailing list
    c. Maps

2. Sue Candleshoe, a manager of marketing research at a large over-the-counter drug manufacturer, wanted to investigate consumers' reactions to a recent poisoning scare in one of her brands. She needed the results quickly. However, Sue was familiar with some of the faults of using a phone book for a sampling frame. Recommend another option that would allow Sue to get the results quickly by telephone but would not introduce as much bias as using a phone book. Discuss which biases, if any, your suggested solution might still have.

3. Henry Brown owns a sailboat rental yard located in Sister Bay, Wisconsin. He has been considering altering the services that his business offers to customers. He would like to offer sailboards for rental as well as add a convenience store so that customers could picnic at the state park adjacent to his rental yard. Before making these changes, he has decided to administer a short questionnaire in the store to a random sample of customers. For a period of one month, clerks have been instructed to conduct personal interviews with every fourth customer. Henry gave specific instructions that on no account were customers to be harassed or offended. Identify the major sources of noncoverage and nonresponse errors. Explain.

4. Deal-A-Wheel, a large manufacturer of radial tires located in Pittsburgh, Pennsylvania, was experiencing a problem common to tire manufacturers. The poor performance of the auto industry was having a severe negative impact on the tire industry. To maintain sales and competitive positions, the various manufacturers were offering wholesalers additional credit and discount opportunities. Deal-A-Wheel's management was particularly concerned about wholesaler reaction to a new discount policy they were considering. The first survey the company conducted to explore these reactions was unsatisfactory to top management. Management thought that it was conducted in a haphazard

manner and contained numerous nonsampling errors. Deal-A-Wheel's management decided to conduct another study containing the following changes:

- The sampling frame was defined as a list of 1,000 of the largest wholesalers that stocked Deal-A-Wheel tires, and the sample elements were to be randomly selected from this list.
- A callback technique was to be employed, with the callbacks being made at different times than the original attempted contact.
- The sample size was to be doubled from 200 to 400 respondents.
- The sample elements that were ineligible or refused to cooperate were to be substituted for by the next element from the list.
- An incentive of $1.00 was to be offered to respondents.

Critically evaluate the steps that were being considered to prevent the occurrence of nonsampling errors. Do you think they are appropriate? Be specific.

5. Bingham Seeds is a local, commercial producer of agricultural seed products located in McGraw, New York. Bingham has developed a new variety of field oats that in university field trials has outperformed the industry leaders by 15 to 20 percent during the last three years. Robert Arthur, Bingham's sales and marketing vice president, wants to conduct a survey to determine farmers' interest in the new variety. Robert has contacted a market research agency in Syracuse, New York, to conduct the survey for Bingham Seeds. The research agency has suggested the following study:

- The population is defined as the 100 largest grain crop farms in the United States.
- The sampling frame will be the list of the 400 largest U.S. farms according to *Successful Farming* magazine.
- A telephone survey will be conducted by the agency's interviewing staff, which consists of women and Syracuse University students.
- The next phone number from the list will be used if selected elements are ineligible or refuse to be interviewed.
- Ten questions will be added to the questionnaire for a farm equipment manufacturer.
- In order to keep costs down, the survey will be run without a training session.

Critically evaluate the steps that are being considered by the marketing research agency. Do they control or prevent nonsampling errors? Do you think that they are appropriate? What recommendations would you make to improve the proposed study? Why?

6. Andrew Blake is a new employee at S and S Research. He has just been instructed to write an introduction to a survey for a mail study. Andrew has been told that the survey will evaluate long-distance customers' reasons for calling long distance. He has also been told that the respondents will each receive $20 after the survey has been completed and returned to S and S Research. Andrew is having a difficult time remembering what he should include in an introduction in order to persuade respondents to complete the questionnaire. First, list several persuasive techniques that Andrew should include in his introduction, then write an introduction to this study that you think will increase the response rate.

7. Sharon Klein, the owner of a local furniture-store chain, has recently hired you as her research analyst. Sharon has little experience in research and is expecting you to lead her in the right direction. She wants to conduct a study to determine the buying cycle for living room furniture. Sharon feels that the best approach in conducting this study is to use the largest possible sample that her budget allows. Try to convince Sharon why increasing the sample size may not be the best research strategy. Be sure to include specific strategies on which Sharon might want to spend some of her money rather than spending it all on increasing the sample size.

8. A major publisher of diverse magazines was interested in determining customer satisfaction with three of the company's leading publications: *TrendSetter, BusWhizz,* and *CompuTech.* The three magazines dealt respectively with women's fashions, business

trends, and computer technology developments. Three sampling frames, consisting of lists of subscribers residing in New York, were formulated. Three random samples were to be chosen from these lists. Personal interviews using an unstructured-undisguised questionnaire were to be conducted. The publishing company had a regular pool of interviewers that it called on whenever interviews were to be conducted. The interviewers had varying educational backgrounds, although 95 percent were high school graduates and the remaining 5 percent had some college education. In terms of age and sex, the range varied from 18 years to 45 years, with 70 percent female and 30 percent male. The majority of interviewers were housewives and students. Before conducting a survey, the company sent the necessary information in the mail and asked interviewers to indicate whether they were interested. The questionnaires, addresses, and other detailed information were then sent to those interviewers replying affirmatively. After the interviewer completed his or her quota of interviews, the replies were sent back to the company. The company then mailed the interviewer's remuneration.

a. Using the guidelines in Table 12.2, critically evaluate the selection, training, and instructions given to the field interviewers.

b. Using Kahn and Cannell's model, identify the major sources of bias that would affect the interviews.

Thorndike Sports Equipment Video Case

1. Ted mentions that his grandfather tended to drift off the questionnaire when collecting information. Is this acceptable for interviewers? Why? Why not?

2. If you were hiring interviewers to present this survey to respondents, what type of people would you hire? What would you stress during interviewer briefing sessions?

CASE 4.1

Young Ideas Publishing Company (A)[1]

How does a company go about marketing products to a specified niche of the teenage market? That is the question confronting Linda Halley, co-owner of Young Ideas Publishing Company. Halley is convinced that her unconventional novels for young people would be very attractive to at least a segment of the teenage market. She is unsure, however, about how to reach this "nonconformist" segment of the market.

Background

Three years ago, Halley wrote her first novel, a youth-oriented book (ages 15–18) entitled *Illusions of Summer*. None of the major publishers would publish the book, however, primarily because it dealt with several controversial social and political concerns. Most publishers simply felt that such topics would not be of interest to enough high school teenagers to justify publication, although many agreed that the novel was of publication quality in other respects.

Frustrated in her efforts to publish her novel, Halley and a business partner, Teresa Martinez, decided to form their own publishing company and publish the book themselves. Both believed that teenagers would be interested in social and political topics and would buy the book. Thus, Young Ideas Publishing Company was born. Halley hoped that effective marketing of the books on a local basis by the company might encourage national distributors to alter their positions toward the novel.

When *Illusions of Summer* was released, it was very well received by several literary critics, winning promising reviews and awards. Despite its critical success, however, commercial acceptance has been much harder to find. During the first 24 months after publication, only about 1,500 copies of the book have been sold, mostly through local bookstores and mail order. Most distributors have been unwilling to handle the book because it is not from an established publisher. With few channels through which to market the product, it remains virtually unknown outside of a limited local market.

Even with this poor showing from a commercial standpoint, Halley continued to believe that so-called "nonconformist" teenagers would be willing to buy books of this nature. Accordingly, she wrote and published a second novel, *Ultimate Choices*. Once again, the novel dealt with several controversial issues for teens and social and political concerns; once again, the critics reacted favorably. Initial sales for *Ultimate Choices* have been better than they were for *Illusions of Summer;* currently (two months after publication), about 250 copies have been sold. By talking to clerks in local bookstores, Halley has learned that most of the books are being sold to teenagers.

Nature of the Problem

Although encouraged by the good reviews and increased sales of the second book, Halley and Martinez are concerned about the future of Young Ideas Publishing Company. Even though the company has managed to break even during the past two years by contracting for outside printing jobs, Martinez has indicated that the survival of the company may well depend on the success of the new novel.

Both partners are still convinced that a market exists for the novels. They now recognize, however, that they may not know enough about the teenage market to effectively market the novels. For example, they believe that insights are needed in the following areas:

1. Will high school teenagers specifically select young adult novels, or do they think that these are written for younger teens?

2. Are teenagers interested in social and political issues?

3. Where do high school teenagers usually obtain books for pleasure reading?

4. Do teens purchase books for themselves, or do parents purchase books for them?

5. What types of promotional items do high school teens enjoy most?

6. What advertising media are most effective in reaching teens?

7. How do "nonconformist" teens differ on these issues from other teens?

---

[1]The contributions of Tom J. Brown to the development of this case are gratefully acknowledged.

You have been hired by Young Ideas Publishing Company to develop and implement a research project to investigate these ideas. Resources are limited; Halley would like the results of the research within 60 days.

QUESTIONS

1. Based on the information provided and your knowledge of marketing and marketing research, define the research problem.

2. What is the target population for your study?

3. Discuss your proposed sampling plan, including the implications for the implementation of the project.

CASE 4.2

St. Andrews Medical Center[1]

The Eating Disorders Clinic of the St. Andrews Medical Center has been operating since 1985 to treat patients with anorexia nervosa and bulimia. Anorexia nervosa, often characterized by intense obsession with dieting and weight loss, and bulimia, also known as the "binge and purge syndrome," typically afflict young women between the ages of 14 and 22 years. Both conditions can result in very serious health problems (or even death) if left untreated.

In recent years, the clinic has experienced a dramatic decline in patients, while, officials believe, a competing program offered by City Hospital has continued to grow. The programs are comparable in terms of staffing and cost of treatment. Patients are normally referred to an eating disorders program by their primary care physician or other health-care professional.

Officials at St. Andrews were very concerned about the downward trend in the number of patients being referred to and treated at the Eating Disorders Clinic. Initially, they believed that the decrease might simply be a reflection of a decrease in the prevalence of anorexia nervosa and bulimia in the population. However, a review of the medical literature and discussions with administrators of eating disorders programs from across the country strongly suggested that this was not the case. Furthermore, conversations with the medical director at City Hospital confirmed that the number of cases of the disorders treated by the City Hospital program has continued to increase during recent years.

St. Andrews' officials next turned to the marketing department for the development and implementation of some type of research designed to uncover the reasons behind the decreasing enrollment in the eating disorders program.

Sampling Plan

Because more than 80 percent of the cases treated at the Eating Disorders Clinic are referred to the program by other health-care providers, St. Andrews' marketing staff believed that the research should be directed at these health-care providers. In particular, they wanted to obtain attitudes and opinions about the St. Andrews program specifically and about eating disorders programs in general.

The population for which a sample frame was to be developed included all health-care professionals in the market area of St. Andrews Medical Center who may treat female patients between the ages of 14 and 22 years.

A review of admittance records showed that referrals were most likely to come from primary care practitioners, including physicians in general medicine, family medicine, internal medicine, and gastroenterology. In addition, referrals have been received from pediatricians, obstetricians/gynecologists, psychiatrists, and psychologists. Although the names and addresses of physicians in these specialties were available from several sources, the marketing staff believed that the telephone directory provided the easiest and least expensive listing. The sampling frame thus included all physicians (or psychologists) from each of these specialties and was drawn from the Yellow Pages of the current telephone directory. Table 4.2.1

TABLE 4.2.1	Sampling Frame
Specialty	*No. of Practitioners*
Pediatricians	63
Obstetricians/Gynecologists	63
Psychiatrists	124
Psychologists	128
Primary Care Practitioners*	321
Total	699

---

[1]The contributions of Tom J. Brown to the development of this case are gratefully acknowledged.

*Includes specialists in family medicine, general medicine, internal medicine, and gastroenterology.

provides the breakdown of the number of professionals of each type included in the sampling frame. All health-care providers on the list were to be contacted.

Administration

The marketing department staff decided to conduct a mail survey and constructed a three-page structured questionnaire that was sent to the 699 health-care providers on the list using the addresses obtained from the telephone directory. An appropriate cover letter was also included. Although neither the cover letter nor the questionnaire identified St. Andrews Medical Center as the sponsor of the survey, no attempt was made to disguise the purpose of the survey. In addition to questions related specifically to the St. Andrews' program, the marketing staff included questions about City Hospital's competing program and about eating disorders programs in general.

Of the 699 questionnaires distributed, 56 (8 percent) were returned as undeliverable by the postal service, while 119 were completed and returned by respondents (a 17 percent response rate). Although St. Andrews' officials were displeased with the low response rate—they had anticipated at least a 25 percent return rate—they thought that the data would provide useful information for the management of the Eating Disorders Clinic.

QUESTIONS

1. What is the appropriate target population given the hospital's interest?

2. Evaluate the sampling frame given the target population chosen by the hospital staff. What other sources might exist for use in developing the sampling frame?

3. Evaluate the use of a mail questionnaire for this research.

CASE 4.3
Riverside County Humane Society (B)

The demands on the Riverside County Humane Society (RCHS) had increased rather dramatically over the past several years, while the tax dollars the society received to provide services had remained relatively unchanged. In an effort to halt further decline in the quality of its services and to provide better care for the pets at the center, the Membership Committee of the board of directors began making plans for a member/contributor drive. The organized drive was to be the

first of its kind for the local chapter and the committee members wanted it to be as productive as possible.

As the plans began to evolve, the committee realized that the organization had only scattered bits and pieces of information about its current members. It did have a list of members and contributors for the last five years that had been compiled by the RCHS staff. In addition, it had access to the results of a survey that had been done by a staff member several years previous that focused on member usage of shelter facilities and their opinions of shelter services and programs. However, the organization had only sparse knowledge of the profile of its typical member and contributor, why they belonged or contributed, how long they had been associated with the humane society, how the services of the humane society could be improved, and so on. The committee members believed information on these issues was important to the conduct of a successful membership drive, and thus they commissioned research to secure it.

Initial contacts with other humane society chapters and interviews with some RCHS staff and board members produced a number of hypotheses regarding who is likely to become a member or contributor, why, how much people are likely to give, and so on. The researchers are interested in examining these hypotheses through a mail survey sent to current members and contributors. (See Case 2.2, Riverside County Humane Society (A) for details.)

Sampling Plan

For the last five years, the RCHS had maintained a master list of members and contributors. Contributors were those who had sent a donation to RCHS but had not filled out an official form making them members, which essentially entitled them to receive RCHS's newsletter. The separate list of members contained all those who had expressed interest in membership and who were receiving the newsletter. Both lists were alphabetical. The contributor list included the amount received from each person or business, but not the number of times the person or business gave during the last five years. The member list showed the number of years each organization or person had belonged.

For purposes of the study, all names of businesses or other organizations were deleted and a separate sample was taken from each list. Approximately 1,050 people were on the member list and 300 on the contributor list. The researchers decided to take 120 names from the member list and 50 from the contributor list. They identified those to be sent questionnaires by drawing two random numbers—3 and 5—using a random number table. They then sent questionnaires to the 3rd, 11th, 19th, and so on person on the member list, and the 5th, 11th, 17th, and so on, person on the contributor list.

QUESTIONS

1. What is the sampling frame and is it a good frame for the target population?

2. What type of sample is being used?

3. Can you think of some ways in which the sample could be improved?

CASE 4.4
PartyTime, Inc.[1]

Andrew Todd, chief executive officer of PartyTime, Inc., a manufacturer of specialty paper products, is preparing to make an important decision. In the 14 years since he founded the company, sales and profits have increased over tenfold to all-time highs of $7,000,000 and $1,150,000, respectively, during the current year. Industry analysts predict continued stable growth during the upcoming year. Despite his firm belief in the adage, "If it's not broken, don't fix it," Todd thinks that it might be time for the addition of a new channel of distribution, based on information he has recently received.

About the Company

PartyTime manufactures a variety of specialty paper products that can be grouped into three basic categories: gift wrap (all types), party goods (printed plates, cups, napkins, party favors, and so on), and other paper goods (such as specialty advertising, and calendars). When Todd founded the company, he

---

[1]The contributions of Tom J. Brown to the development of this case are gratefully acknowledged.

purchased and renovated an existing paper mill located in the Pacific Northwest. Today, company headquarters and production facilities remain at the original location. During the heavy production season, the company employs approximately 200 people.

As shown in Table 4.4.1, gift wrap accounts for about 60 percent of revenues (50 percent of profits), and party goods amount to about 30 percent of sales (40 percent of profits). All other paper products sold by the company produce about 10 percent of revenues and an equivalent percentage of profits. Sales of gift wrap and other paper goods have been stable, increasing 3–4% per year during the previous five years. Interestingly (and as Todd is pleased to note), total sales of party goods have been increasing at about a 9 percent annual rate.

The Distribution Decision

Given the profitability of the party-goods line and its substantial sales growth in recent years, Todd is very interested in further increasing sales of specialty party goods. A recent publication of the National Association of Paper and Party Retailers (NAPPR) indicated that industrywide sales of party goods are expected to increase some 10 to 20 percent during the upcoming year. Of particular interest is the projection that sales of party goods through independent party goods (IPG) shops will increase more than 25 percent. Currently, PartyTime party goods are distributed only through mass merchandisers and chain drugstores.

Although sales have been increasing steadily using existing channels, Todd wondered if the time was right to add the IPG channel. Any decision to include the new channel would have to be made early in the year, however, before orders for the holiday season begin arriving (a large percentage of total sales of party goods at the retail level occur during the holiday season).

INDEPENDENT PARTY GOODS (IPG) SHOPS

IPG retailers typically operate small to moderate-sized stores that are often located in malls or strip shopping

TABLE 4.4.1	Current-Year Sales and Profit Breakdown by Category			
Category	*Sales*	*Percentage*	*Profit*	*Percentage*
Gift wrap	$4,302,300	61	$564,700	49
Party goods	2,045,500	29	472,300	41
Other paper goods	705,200	10	115,000	10
Total	$7,053,000	100	$1,152,000	100

centers. The label "independent" indicates that the stores are not owned or franchised by major manufacturers, such as Hallmark. In recent years, the number of IPG shops has grown tremendously, to the point where it is not unusual to have 15 to 20 shops in larger cities. Growth has been particularly strong in California, Florida, the upper Midwest, and the East.

COMPETITIVE ISSUES

Competition within traditional channels of distribution for party goods is intense. Within these channels, PartyTime must compete against major producers, such as C.A. Reed, Beach Products, Unique, Hallmark, and Ambassador. The major competitors within the IPG channel, in contrast, are fewer in number; only AMSCAM, Contempo, and Paper Art serve as primary suppliers. Competition within the IPG channel is thought to be much less intense than that in the traditional channels.

DECEMBER 13   Todd is leaning strongly toward committing the resources necessary to enter the IPG channel and has called a meeting of his managers to discuss the proposed move. He believes that there is room for at least one more supplier, because the competition is less intense than in the traditional distribution channels. In addition, he regards this as an opportunity to further expand the most profitable area of PartyTime's business.

At the meeting, most of PartyTime's managers seem to agree with Todd, although Kim Shinoda, the company's chief accountant, suggests that the company should learn more about IPG retailers before a decision is made. In a memorandum distributed at the meeting, she details the following areas in which more information is needed before a decision is reached:

1. Competitive Products: Are IPG retailers satisfied with current product offerings on the market? Do they receive a satisfactory level of service from the current suppliers?

2. Purchase Criteria: In addition to price and product considerations, what other characteristics of suppliers and product lines do retailers think are important?

3. Supplier Loyalty: To what extent are retailers willing to carry product lines of more than one supplier?

Todd agrees that more information would be useful in making a decision, but he realizes that time con-

straints will force him to make a decision within the next few weeks. Along with his managers, he decides to bring in a marketing research team.

JANUARY 16   The marketing research team is now ready to share the results of the research project with the managers at PartyTime. To implement the research, they had developed an undisguised, semistructured telephone questionnaire designed to obtain the information that Shinoda had suggested.

Officials at PartyTime are particularly interested in the responses of retailers located in those geographic areas in which growth is expected to be strongest over the next year; therefore, a sampling frame was developed using telephone directories in the major cities within these geographic regions. Because many types of stores could conceivably be considered IPG shops, two criteria were established for inclusion in the sampling frame: (1) the shop must devote more than 50 percent of its shelf space to paper and party goods, and (2) the shop must carry products from more than one supplier. A total of 110 shops were identified using the telephone directories. Although attempts were made to contact each of these shops during business hours, only 82 could be reached. Thirty-two of these met the two criteria, and 23 agreed to participate in the interview.

JANUARY 19   Based on the results of the marketing research project and the input of his managers, Todd has decided to increase production of party goods and market these products through the IPG channel.

QUESTIONS

1. Evaluate the research team's development of the sample of store owners. How would you have recommended the research team develop the sampling frame?

2. Do you think that a telephone survey was the best way to collect the needed information?

CASE 4.5
HotStuff Computer Software (B)[1]

Simpson, Edwards and Associates, encouraged by its success with a computer software package for government agencies, is developing a second software product, HotStuff, which is tailored specifically for use in

---

[1]The contributions of Jacqueline C. Hitchon to the development of this case are gratefully acknowledged.

the fire-fighting industry. In the normal course of affairs, fire departments need to handle and store a considerable amount of information: building layouts, hazardous material characteristics and locations, equipment inventories, and so on. Further, although some exploratory research has suggested that some fire departments already owned computers, it was generally recognized that the information-processing needs of the industry made additional computerization a likely probability. Based on preliminary inquiries into the composition of the industry, Simpson, Edwards and Associates decided to restrict its marketing efforts to volunteer fire departments only, at least initially, and planned a national survey to determine the market potential of HotStuff (see Case 2.3 for more background).

Sampling Plan

The key issue in executing a national survey turned on sampling control: how could the research select and contract volunteer fire departments in a reliable, systematic fashion? After much deliberation and a few false starts, Craig Simpson's research staff finally presented him with two cohesive sampling plans.

OPTION 1   The first option that Craig and his staff considered was a mail survey based on a sample drawn from a list of volunteer fire departments nationwide. The National Fire Protection Agency, like other national fire safety organizations, had a comprehensive mailing list of all 30,000 United States fire departments, but it did not distinguish between volunteer and municipal fire departments. Fortunately, the research team discovered a firm that sells listings of population groups. Moreover, the company could provide Craig's team with an exhaustive mailing list of volunteer fire departments, organized by the state in which they are located. The total number of volunteer fire departments included on the recently updated list was almost 20,000, and the cost of sampling names from the list was $40 per 1,000 departments sampled. The names could be drawn according to whatever scheme Simpson, Edwards and Associates preferred.

The research team believed that a viable way to proceed to sample from the list would be to order the 48 states in the United States (excluding Alaska and Hawaii) according to the number of volunteer fire departments in each state. Once the states were ordered from smallest to largest in terms of incidence of volunteer fire departments, a sample could be drawn from all the departments on the list by selecting every *k*th department after a random beginning. If it adopted a

pessimistic perspective, expected only a 20 percent response rate, and were satisfied with only 100 completed surveys, Simpson, Edwards and Associates calculated that it would need to mail 500 questionnaires. With 20,000 population elements and a sample of 500, every 40th volunteer fire station on the list would need to be selected, after a random start between 1 and 40.

OPTION 2   The second sampling plan being considered was founded on information received from the local state fire marshall and on two assumptions. The marshall informed the researchers that most volunteer fire departments were located in communities with populations under 25,000. Based on the assumption that towns with a population under 5,000 would be too small to productively use a computer, the team decided that it should concentrate on two categories of towns: those with populations between 5,000 and 15,000, and those with populations between 15,000 and 25,000. In addition, it seemed logical to assume that volunteer fire departments located near large cities would be more progressive than those in more isolated areas and thus that they would be more likely to own or plan to purchase a computer.

Consistent with the preceding reasoning, the research team also considered drawing a sample in the following way:

Step 1: Randomly select two cities of over 10,000 inhabitants from every state in the continental United States.

Step 2: Randomly select a town of population 5,000–15,000 within 20 miles of one city, and a town of population 15,000–25,000 within 20 miles of the second city.

Step 3: Obtain telephone numbers of the volunteer fire departments in each of the two towns selected in each state from Directory Assistance.

This strategy would provide a sample size of 96 volunteer fire departments from the 48 states. After some discussion, Craig decided to adopt the second option to use in conjunction with a telephone survey.

QUESTIONS

1. What kind of sampling plan was considered for sampling from the mailing list?

2. What kind of sampling plan was actually used to sample volunteer fire departments?

3. Evaluate the sampling plans.

CASE 4.6

International Differences in the Cost of Data

A multinational bank, MNB, was getting interested in measuring customer satisfaction with its consumer banking services and financial products. The managers at MNB Corporate differed in their opinions regarding the form of the optimal customer satisfaction study, for example, survey, focus group, interview, and so on. So as a starting point, MNB commissioned bids from marketing research firms in the United States to describe how they would approach studying their U.S. banking customers. In particular, they asked the bidding firms to offer cost estimates; that is, how many customers could be sampled given the proposed budget of $15,000 for this research project using different techniques.

The bids covered a variety of research methods, which differed in their costs. They considered a personal interview method in which the customer would be intercepted in the bank and asked several questions regarding service and satisfaction. They compared that method to the costs of sending out mail surveys to current customers. Finally, they explored the efficiency of placing small, postcard-sized surveys at each teller station that the banking customer might pick up and complete and return at their leisure.

MNB gathered the marketing research firms' proposals to begin to make a decision of how the bank should approach its customers. In terms of outlay expenses, more postcards could be printed less expensively than surveys sent or interviewers staffing each of the local bank branches. However, in terms of re-

sponse rates, somewhat fewer people turned down the personal interview than who returned the mail survey or postcard survey. Table 4.6.1 presents the comparative estimates for the three different techniques. Clearly the table shows that in the U.S., the postcard technique appears to be the most cost effective. Thus, the bank managers are considering implementing this research tool.

MNB Corporate's second concern is with a few of its satellite locations; in particular the news from abroad is that the Indonesian banking customers are not happy, and MNB wants to understand what is going on. Its first assumption was that the bank should proceed with the postcard methodology to be able to compare the results in Indonesia to those from the States. However, they conducted some preliminary investigations and found the costs of the methods to be quite different. The bank plans to proceed with personal interviews in Indonesia. Consider Tables 4.6.1 and 4.6.2 and answer the questions that follow.

QUESTIONS

1. Under what conditions might it matter that one method is used in one country and another method is used in another?

2. What is the target population under investigation, both in the U.S. and in Indonesia? What are the differences between the sampling frames of each of the three techniques? What customers will each technique miss?

3. What other issues must the bank managers consider in addition to the cost efficiencies of the three methods?

TABLE 4.6.1	The Estimates for the U.S. Samples		
	Interview	*Mail Survey*	*Postcards*
a. research budget	$15,000	$15,000	$15,000
b. cost per contact	$25	$2.50	$.25
c. prospects reached*	2400	6000	60,000
d. response rate	5%	3%	1.5%
e. estimated net sample size (c × d)	120	180	900
f. effective cost per capita (a/e)	$125.00	$83.33	$16.67

---

*For mail and postcard, c = a/b; for interviews, cost is $25 per hour, times a five-hour day, = $125 per day, for each interviewer. Each of 12 interviewers (spread across the area local bank branches) would spend two weeks (10 bank days) approaching and interviewing customers. Each interviewer on each day would target 20 bank customers, on average.

TABLE 4.6.2	The Projections for Indonesia		
	Interview	*Mail Survey*	*Postcards*
a. research budget	$15,000	$15,000	$15,000
b. cost per contact	$12*	$2.50	$0.25
c. prospects reached	5000	6000	60,000
d. response rate	20%*	1.5%*	0.5%
e. estimated net sample size (c × d)	1000	90	300
f. effective cost per capita (a/e)	$15.00	$166.67	$50.00

*These estimates differ from those for conducting the research in the States. Labor costs for interviewing are much less, propensities for customers to acquiesce and be interviewed are much greater, mail surveys are somewhat less efficient because CD-ROM databases on addresses are less accurate, and postcards are an unfamiliar format and are therefore rarely filled out. Given the changes in the interviewing parameters, if the project duration is still two weeks, 25 interviewers can be deployed, so 5,000 customers would be approached.

CASE 4.7
First Federal Bank of Bakersfield

The Equal Credit Opportunity Act, which was passed in 1974, was partially designed to protect women from discriminatory banking practices. It forbade, for example, the use of credit evaluations based on gender or marital status. Although adherence to the law has changed the way many bankers do business, women's perception that there is a bias against them by a particular financial institution often remains unless some specific steps are taken by the institution to counter that perception.

Nearly a dozen "women's banks," that is, banks owned and operated by and for women, opened their doors during the 1980s with the specific purpose of targeting and promoting their services to this otherwise underdeveloped market. Although women's banks currently are evolving into full-service banks serving a wide range of clients, a number of traditional banks are moving in the other direction by attempting to develop services that are targeted specifically toward women. Many of these institutions see such a strategy as a viable way to attract valuable customers and to increase their market share in the short term while gaining a competitive advantage by which they can compete in the long term as the roles of women in the labor force gain in importance. One can find, with even the most cursory examination of the trade press, examples of credit-card advertising that depicts single, affluent, and head-of-the-household female card holders; financial seminar programs for wives of affluent professional men; informational literature that details how newly divorced and separated women can obtain credit; and entire packages of counseling, educational opportunities, and special services for women.

The First Federal Bank of Bakersfield was interested in developing its own program of this kind. The executives were curious about a number of issues. Were women's financial needs being adequately met in the Bakersfield area? What additional financial services would women especially like to have? How do Bakersfield's women feel about banks and bankers? Was First Federal in a good position to take advantage of the needs of women? What channels of communication might be best to reach women who may be interested in the services that First Federal had to offer?

The executives believed that First Federal might have some special advantages if it did try to appeal to women. For one thing, the Bakersfield community seemed to be quite sensitive to the issues being raised by the feminist movement. For another, First Federal was a small, personal bank. The executives thought that women might be more comfortable in dealing with a smaller, more personalized institution and that the bank might not have the traditional "image problem" among women that larger banks might have.

Research Objectives

The bank executives were considering a series of financial seminars that they believed might be particularly attractive to women. The seminars could cover a number of topics, including money management, wills, trusts, estate planning, taxes, insurance, investments, financial services, and establishing a credit rating. The executives were interested in determining women's reactions to each of these potential topics.

They were also interested to know what the best format might be in terms of location, frequency, length of each program, and so on, if there were a high level of interest. Consequently, they decided that the bank should conduct a research study that had the assessment of the financial seminar series as its main objective but that also shed some light on the other issues they had been debating. More specifically, the objectives of the research were as follows:

1. To determine the interest that exists among women in the Bakersfield area for seminars on financial matters.

2. To identify the reasons Bakersfield women would change, or have changed, their banking affiliations.

3. To examine the attitudes of Bakersfield women toward financial institutions and the people who run them.

4. To determine if any correlation could be found between the demographic characteristics of women in the Bakersfield area and the services they might like to have.

5. To analyze the media usage habits of Bakersfield-area women.

Method

The assignment to develop a research strategy by which these objectives could be assessed was given to the bank's internal marketing research department. The department consisted of only five members—Beth Anchurch, the research director, and four project analysts. As Anchurch pondered the assignment, she was concerned about the best way to proceed. She was particularly concerned with the relatively short time period she was given for the project. Top executives thought the seminar idea had promise. If they were right, they wanted to get on with designing and offering the seminars before any of their competitors came up with a similar idea. Thus, they specified that they would like the results of the research department's investigation to be available within 45 to 50 days.

As Anchurch began to contemplate the data collection, she became particularly concerned with whether the study should use mail questionnaires or telephone interviews. She had tentatively ruled out personal interviews because of the short deadline that had been imposed. After several days of contemplating the alternatives, she finally decided that it would be best to collect the information by telephone. Further, she decided that it would be better to hire out the telephone interviewing than to use her four project analysts to make the calls.

Anchurch believed that the multiple objectives of the project required a reasonably large sample of women so that the various characteristics of interest would be sufficiently represented to enable some conclusions to be drawn about the population of Bakersfield as a whole. After pondering the various cross tabulations in which the bank executives would be interested, she finally decided that a sample of 500 to 600 adult women would be sufficient. The sample was to be drawn from the white pages of the Bakersfield telephone directory by the Bakersfield Interviewing Service, the firm that First Federal had hired to complete the interviews.

The sample was to be drawn using a scheme in which two names were selected from each page of the directory, first by selecting two of the four columns on the page at random and then by selecting the fifteenth name in each of the selected columns. The decision to sample names from each page was made so that each interviewer could operate with certain designated pages of the directory, since each was operating independently out of her home.

| TABLE 4.7.1 | Selected Demographic Comparison of Survey Respondents with Bureau of Census Data |

Characteristic/Category	Percentage of Women	
	Survey	Census
Marital Status		
Married	53	42
Single	30	40
Separated	1	2
Widowed	9	9
Divorced	7	7
Age		
18–24	23	23
25–34	30	28
35–44	16	14
45–64	18	21
65+	13	14
Income		
Less than $10,000	9	29
$10,000–$19,999	19	29
$20,000–$50,000	58	36
More than $50,000	2	6
Refused	12	—

The decision to sample every fifteenth name in the selected columns was determined in the following way: First, the directory had 328 pages with four columns of names per page. There were 80 entries per column on average, or approximately 26,240 listings. Using Bureau of the Census data on household composition, it was estimated that 20 percent of all households would be ineligible for the study because they did not contain an adult female resident. This meant that only 20,992 ($0.80 \times 26,240$) of the listings would probably qualify. Since 500 to 600 names were needed, it seemed easiest to select two columns on each page at random and to take the same numbered entry from each column. The interviewer could then simply count or measure down from the top of the column. The number 15 was determined randomly; thus, the fifteenth listing in the randomly selected columns on each page was called. If the household did not answer or if the women of the house refused to participate, the interviewers were instructed to select another number from that column through the use of an abbreviated table of random numbers that each was given. They were to use a similar procedure if the household that was called did not have an adult woman living there.

First Federal decided to operate without callbacks because the interviewing service charged heavily for them. Anchurch did think it would be useful to follow up with a sample of those interviewed to make sure that they indeed had been called, since the interviewers for Bakersfield Interviewing Service operated out of their own homes and it was impossible to supervise them more directly. She did this by selecting at random a handful of the surveys completed by each interviewer. She then had one of her project assistants call that respondent, verify that the interview had taken place, and check the accuracy of the responses of a few of the most important questions. This audit revealed absolutely no instances of interviewer cheating.

The completed interview forms were turned over to First Federal for its own internal analysis. As part of this analysis, the project analyst compared the demographic characteristics of those contacted to the demographic characteristics of the population in the Bakersfield area as reported in the 1990 census. The comparison is shown in Table 4.7.1. The analyst also prepared a summary of the nonresponses and refusals by interviewer. This comparison is shown in Table 4.7.2.

TABLE 4.7.2   Results of Calls by Interviewer

| Interviewer | No. of Nonresponses | | | No. of Refusals | | No. of Completions |
	Line Busy	No Answer	Ineligibles*	Initial	After Partial Completion	
1	7	101	36	15	0	30
2	2	45	13	16	0	30
3	11	71	23	17	7	30
4	14	56	47	35	6	39
5	9	93	10	23	13	30
6	5	102	28	63	14	35
7	6	36	17	16	0	18
8	7	107	23	13	0	30
9	11	106	36	47	0	30
10	10	55	6	35	9	30
11	38	83	48	92	0	30
12	5	22	3	8	0	9
13	23	453	102	65	7	99
14	12	102	27	31	0	19
15	7	173	29	66	0	34
16	2	65	9	33	0	22
Total	169	1,670	457	575	56	515
		1,839			631	

*No adult female resident.

QUESTIONS

1. Compare the advantages and disadvantages of using telephone interviews as compared to personal interviews or mail questionnaires to collect the needed data.

2. Compare the advantages and disadvantages of using in-house staff versus a professional interviewing service to collect the data.

3. Do you think that the telephone directory provided a good sampling frame given the purposes of the study, or would you recommend an alternative sampling frame?

4. What type of sample is being used here? Still using the white pages of the telephone directory as the sampling frame, would you recommend some other sampling scheme? Why or why not?

5. If you were Anchurch, would you be happy with the performance of the Bakersfield Interviewing Service? Why or why not?

CASE 4.8[1]
Digital Euro Music

The music industry is nearing a revolution as consumers are pulling digital recordings off of the Internet. Music is available online through a variety of portals, most of which use a compression software like MP3 to file music in portable sizes to download and play. A handheld device can contain hours of personally selected favorite tunes.

A variety of devices are available for purchase to store and play back the digital, compressed music files. These handheld jukeboxes differ on a number of attributes: price, memory storage, batteries required, whether the LCD provides information on the album title and artist, remaining battery life and storage space, and so forth. Music industry experts claim the sound is not as good as CD-quality sound, but "blind" hearing tests suggest consumers cannot distinguish between a song played directly from a CD versus one that had been compressed, stored, and replayed.

Downloading music is becoming an increasingly popular phenomenon. Currently, approximately one-third to one-half of Internet users have or shortly expect to download music. The confluence of the product sought (that is, music) and the technology by which it is obtained (the Internet) suggests that digital music players would be more popular with younger people, and indeed, teenagers are more likely to be visitors of online music sites than are older people.

Internet music sites are hitting heads with traditional music providers (for example, Sony Music Entertainment) over copyrights and issues of piracy. However, even the big, established music companies acknowledge the digital music future, as all the industry players struggle to sort out what form it will take that will be attractive to consumers and yet protect the current copyrights.

A new wrinkle is that the software and playback devices are entering other markets. The handheld devices are being "pulled" through channels by international customers who have Internet access, and therefore access to the compressed music files, but no devices for playback. Some music industry analysts think the European market will not be a large one for these portable MP3 players because Internet penetration in Europe still somewhat lags that in the States. Others worry that it might become even more popular to circumvent the European taxes. Specifically, Table 4.8.1 contains the Value Added Tax (VAT) for CDs in most of the European countries; the VATs for books are given for comparison. (The VATs for books are lower than those for CDs because a book is considered a purchase of greater cultural status.) Consider these figures and answer the questions that follow.

QUESTIONS

1. If you were determining which European countries to target first, what information would be most useful to you in the table? What information is lacking?

2. How would you sample potential customers from more than one country?

3. If the MP3 music format is newer to Europeans, what kinds of questions would you ask in those countries compared to the questions you would ask of the U.S. consumers?

4. How would you determine whether there might be market potential in Australia, Japan, or Hong Kong?

[1]Information based on euromusic.com, Matthew Graven and Jeremy A. Kaplan, "MP3 to Go," *PC Magazine* (February 8, 2000), pp. 220–221; Martin Peers, "Sony Music," *Wall Street Journal* (April 7, 2000), p. B3.

TABLE 4.8.1

Country	Population (Millions)	Expenditure per Capita (ECU)	Album Units Per Capita	VAT on CDs (%)	VAT on Books (%)
Austria	8.1	38.9	2.7	20	10
Belgium	10.2	30.0	2.0	21	6
Denmark	5.3	45.5	3.4	25	25
Finland	5.1	22.0	2.1	22	0
France	58.6	33.1	2.1	21	6
Germany	81.7	30.6	2.7	16	7
Greece	10.5	9.8	0.8	18	4
Ireland	3.6	26.7	1.8	21	0
Italy	57.6	9.1	1.0	20	4
Netherlands	15.6	34.3	2.4	18	6
Norway	4.4	52.3	3.0	23	0
Portugal	9.9	14.5	1.4	17	5
Spain	39.4	13.4	1.4	16	4
Sweden	8.9	36.8	2.5	25	25
Switzerland	7.1	38.4	3.1	7	0
U.K.	60.0	40.1	3.3	18	0

CASE 4.9
The Dryden Press

The Dryden Press was established in the mid-1960s by Holt, Rinehart and Winston, which had traditionally been a strong social science publisher, as a response to the growth in enrollments that business schools were experiencing and the explosion in enrollments that was predicted they would experience in the future. The venture represented one of the first forays by a traditional nonbusiness text publisher into the college business market. The experiment turned out to be very successful, and The Dryden Press became one of the top six publishers in the business area in sales. Company executives believed that one of the key reasons for Dryden's success was its ability to target books for specific market segments. The company was one of the first to recognize the potential growth in courses in consumer behavior and managerial economics, for example, and introduced the successful texts by Engel, Kollat, and Blackwell in consumer behavior and by Brigham and Pappas in managerial economics in response. Through careful management of the revisions, these books maintained strong market positions more than 25 years after they had been introduced.

The Dryden Press editorial staff tried to maintain a posture of extreme sensitivity to changing market conditions brought about by the publication of new research findings or the changing demands placed on students as a result of changes in the environment and the needs of businesses. The editors made it a point to keep up with these changes so that the company would be prepared with new products when the situation demanded it. This was no small task, because the lead time on a book typically ran from three to four years from the time the author was first signed to a contract to when the book was actually published. It seemed to take most authors almost two years to develop a first draft of a book manuscript. The typical manuscript was then reviewed by a sample of experts in the field. Based on their reactions, most manuscripts would undergo some revision before being placed in production. The production process, which included copyediting the manuscript, setting type, drawing all figures, preparing promotional materials, proofreading, and so on, usually took about a year.

Research Questions and Objectives

So that it would not be caught short if the needs and desires of the market in consumer behavior texts changed, the editorial staff decided to find out the current level of use of the various texts in consumer behavior and the directions in which the market was moving. What were the market shares of the respective texts? What features of the various books were liked and disliked? Did the use of the various texts and the preference for the certain features vary by class of school? Did four-year colleges have different requirements for consumer behavior texts than two-year schools? After a good deal of discussion among the members of the editorial staff, these general concerns were translated into specific research objectives. More specifically, the staff decided to conduct a research investigation that attempted to determine the following:

1. The importance of various topical areas in the teaching of consumer behavior within the next two to five years.

2. The importance and treatment of managerial applications in consumer behavior courses.

3. The level of satisfaction with the textbooks currently in use.

4. The relative market shares of the major consumer behavior textbooks.

5. The degree of switching of texts that goes on in consumer behavior courses from year to year.

6. The importance of various pedagogical aids, such as glossaries, cases, learning objectives, and so on, in the textbook selection decision.

7. The importance of supplementary teaching tools, such as student study guides, overhead transparency masters, or an instructor's manual, among others, in the consumer textbook selection decision.

The editorial staff thought it was important to obtain the needed information from those who were actively teaching consumer behavior courses. The staff also thought it imperative that only one respondent be used from any given school, even though the editors realized that some schools had multiple sections of the consumer behavior course and that different books might be used in different sections. For the most part, however, the editors believed that the same book would be used across sections, though not across courses, in the sense that the introductory courses at the undergraduate and graduate levels would use different books. The editors decided that it would be better to target the questionnaires to one individual at each of the selected institutions and to simply have that person indicate on the questionnaire whether he or she normally taught a graduate or undergraduate course. Dryden could then analyze the responses to determine if any differences could be attributed to the level at which the course was taught.

Method

The editorial staff decided to use a mail questionnaire to collect the data for several reasons. For one thing, the target population was geographically dispersed. Even though it was decided to limit the study only to those actively teaching consumer behavior domestically, that still meant respondents could come from all over the United States, which in turn meant that it could be prohibitive to collect this information by personal interview. At the same time, professors had no standard working schedule. Some might teach in the morning and some in the evening. When they were not teaching, some might work in their offices while others might work elsewhere. This variety of schedules and work conditions required that the questionnaires be available when the professors were inclined to fill them out. Also, the objectives finally decided on allowed the use of a relatively structured and undisguised questionnaire.

The big question facing the Dryden staff was how to draw a sample from the target population of those actively teaching the consumer behavior course, either at the undergraduate or graduate levels. For purposes of the study, "actively teaching" was operationally defined as having taught a consumer behavior course at least once in the last two years or being scheduled to teach one within the next year.

The company was considering drawing the sample from one of two lists that it had at its disposal. One of the lists was an internal list consisting of all those professors whom the salespeople's reports indicated were interested in teaching specific courses, such as financial planning, introductory accounting, marketing management, or consumer behavior. This meant that the salesperson had indicated on his or her reports that the professor was to receive sample copies of all those books in, say, consumer behavior that The Dryden Press published. Most of the entries on the list were developed from salespeople's calls, although some of them arose at the national association meetings at which Dryden displayed its list of titles. Professors would often request sample copies of selected titles at the meetings so that they could review them before making an adoption decision. All requests for complimentary copies were sent for authorization to the salesperson serving the school. By approving the request, the salesperson was aware of the professor's interest and could follow it up in an attempt to get the adoption. Because of how it was developed and used, the internal list paralleled the salesperson territory structure.

Although most salespeople operated within one state and often within only part of a state, some operated across several states. Each salesperson was responsible for all the schools in his or her territory, including the universities with graduate programs, four-year colleges without graduate programs, and two-year institutions. The schools were listed alphabetically by salesperson, and each school had a computer code associated with it, designating its type. Each professor on the list had a set of computer codes associated with the name that identified his or her interest areas.

The alternate list The Dryden Press considered using was the printed membership directory of the Association for Consumer Research (ACR). ACR is an organization formed in the late 1960s that was designed for the pursuit of knowledge in the area of consumer behavior. Its membership is dominated by marketing professors (almost 80 percent of the total), although it also includes interested members from business and government as well as members representing other academic disciplines, such as sociology and psychology. The ACR directory was organized alphabetically by name of the member. Along with each member's name, the directory provided either the office or home address, depending on which the individual preferred to use, and both the office and home phone numbers. While about one-half of the addresses listed only the college at which the individual worked, the other 50 percent also listed the department. There were 64 pages in the directory, and all pages except the last one had 16 names. A small percentage of the addresses were international.

QUESTIONS

1. Given the purposes of the study, how would you recommend a sample be drawn from:
   a. Dryden's internal computer list?
   b. the ACR printed membership directory?
2. Which approach would you recommend and why?

CASE 4.10[1]
Sampling Gambling

Americans spend nearly $50 billion annually on gambling. That expenditure is more than three times the amount spent on going to the movies and theme parks, as alternative means of entertainment. State-run lotteries and casino games are the most popular legal games of chance.

Gambling traditionally held negative connotations, being associated with immoral or even criminal behavior. Critics worry that legalized gambling can encourage compulsive gamblers, that it may encourage people to gamble who can least afford to do so,

and that casinos bring an undesirable element to the surrounding neighborhood.

However, legalized gambling, especially in the form of state lotteries, has largely sanitized the image of gaming behavior. Among people who abstain from gambling, fewer people cite moral or religious objections, instead offering practical reasons: for example, they don't want to spend the money or they don't have the money to spend. Proponents claim casinos create jobs and provide revenue for education that would otherwise be raised by tax hikes.

Secondary data suggest that there is no particular demographic profile of a gambler—people of all walks of life (for example, age and income) enjoy casinos and lotteries. Beyond demographics, the commonly held motivations appear to be a desire to win a large amount of money, and a quick and relatively inexpensive form of entertainment.

The heterogeneity of the demographics of gamblers, and the homogeneity of the motives of gamblers have left some casino managers perplexed as to how the consumer market might be segmented. One hypothesis, based on collective wisdom, is that novice gamblers tend to prefer slot machines because they are simple, whereas more experienced gamblers prefer games like blackjack, baccarat, and craps because they are more strategic in nature. Another frequent assumption is that people who buy lottery tickets are different from people who go to casinos, and that the two types of games satisfy different needs.

The Internet introduces yet another medium in which a consumer might gamble. While the number of gamblers online are far less than those who frequent casinos or lotteries, and online gambling revenues are far less than nonelectronic games (approximately only $2 billion), the online gambling industry is expected to enjoy rapid growth.

If a gaming industry representative were to come to you and say, "I'd like to do some interviews. I want to know more about what kind of games my casino visitors want me to provide. I want to know how much floor space to allot to slots versus blackjack tables. I want to know why they come to any casino, or my casino, rather than to the movies or something. Maybe I should just sell lottery tickets." How would you address the following issues?

QUESTIONS

1. What is the relevant population?
2. What would you recommend in terms of a sampling plan—would you intercept people in (or

[1]For more information, see Kevin Heubusch, "Taking Chances on Casinos," *American Demographics* 19 (May 1997), pp. 35–40.

entering or exiting) casinos? Would you talk to people buying lottery tickets at convenience stores? Would you interview people strolling along in a shopping mall? What sampling frame does each of these locations presume?

3. If you wanted to verify the aforementioned assumptions (for example, that demographics do not matter, or that novice versus experienced gamblers have different game preferences), how would you modify your sampling plan?

4. How would you try to assess objectively whether there are moral or religious concerns against gambling? What kinds of sampling plans would you need to avoid, given the likelihood that they would shape your conclusions pro or con?

CASE 4.11
Canopy of Care (A)1[1]

Canopy of Care is a nonprofit institution that raises money from the public and then allocates the funds to programs run by charitable agencies endeavoring to serve the human-care needs of the community. In this way, it functions as an umbrella or canopy for specialized charities, relieving them in large part of the need to market themselves and solicit donations. The campaign area encompasses a city with a population of half a million and its suburbs. In 1997, for example, Canopy of Care raised almost $17 million, which it distributed to 341 local health and social service programs. An efficient system for giving has been developed with the help of companies and government agencies, which solicit their employees on behalf of Canopy of Care and deduct donations corresponding to the employees' pledges directly out of their wages or salaries.

Despite the relative ease of administration, however, the percentage of solicited employees contributing to Canopy of Care has been decreasing. In 1997, for example, only 50 percent of the employees at companies that agreed to participate contributed. Economic downturns in the area are thought to be partially responsible for the reduction in employee contributions. The manufacturing industry, for example, one of Canopy of Care's largest targets, has recently experienced plant closings leading to employee cutbacks and wage freezes. Although Canopy of Care cannot control the effects of changes in the economy, its officials believe that the agency may be able to com-

pensate for them by becoming more efficient in its approach to potential donors.

Study Objectives

Based on this reasoning, three broad research objectives were developed:

1. To determine why a large percentage of employees in companies solicited by Canopy of Care do not choose to contribute.

2. To assess both the information and attitudes that givers and nongivers in solicited companies have about Canopy of Care.

3. To obtain general information that Canopy of Care can use in better planning its campaigns.

A local marketing research firm was asked to develop a study to investigate these issues.

Data-Collection Procedure

The target population consisted of individuals employed in firms solicited by Canopy of Care. The marketing researcher advised Canopy of Care that it could access the population for research purposes in two principal ways:

a. Sample companies solicited by Canopy of Care, and then select a sample of employees within each selected company from a list of employees provided by the company. Once they were identified, the employees could be surveyed by mail or telephone. Since the desired information could

TABLE 4.11.1   Numbers of Completed and Uncompleted Contracts

Classification	Number of Individuals
Completed contacts	260
Contacts unemployed last year	271
Mid-survey terminations	22
Answering machine contacts	61
Refusals	235
No answers and busy signals	132
Nonworking numbers	419
Businesses contacted	90
Contacts with language/ hearing barrier	13
No adult at home	30
Total dialings	1,533

---

[1]The contributions of Jacqueline C. Hitchon to the development of this case are gratefully acknowledged.

TABLE 4.11.2	Comparison of Household Income	
Income Category	Sample Percentage	1998 Census Percentage
Less than $10,000	12.7	25.7
$10,000–$14,999	17.3	14.3
$15,000–$24,999	31.9	27.8
$25,000–$39,999	26.9	23.0
More than $40,000	11.2	9.2

TABLE 4.11.4	Comparison of Occupation	
Type of Organization	Sample Percentage	1998 Census Percentage
Manufacturing	22.4	28.5
Government	9.9	12.0
Wholesale/Retail	16.5	19.2
Service Industry	51.2	40.3

be obtained through fixed-alternative questions without probing, personal interviews did not seem warranted.

b. Broaden the population of potential respondents to include all adults who were employed in the campaign area. This sample could be accessed by telephone, using plus-one sampling based on the local white-pages telephone directory and screening out unemployed respondents by means of an introductory question about employment. The survey could be administered either by volunteers from Canopy of Care staff or by professional telephone interviewers.

After some deliberation, Canopy of Care selected the second option and decided to employ trained telephone interviewers to conduct the survey, although the budget for the project was very small and the sample size needed to be drastically reduced.

Plus-one dialing was used to generate a random sample that included unlisted numbers. Because of time and budget constraints, callbacks were not made; instead, new numbers were generated and dialed until a valid response was obtained. The telephone interviewers were instructed in the correct manner to administer the survey and were monitored by supervisors both during a pretest and during the actual survey. The research took place between April 21 and April 25, 1998. Calls were placed between the hours of 4:00 P.M. and 9:00 P.M. in order to find a greater number of people at home. A total of 260 completed questionnaires was obtained.

Initial Results

As an initial step in analyzing the results of this survey, the researchers undertook two tasks. First, they examined the statistics on completed and uncompleted contacts (see Table 4.11.1). Second, they compared the demographic profile of their sample with projected census data to evaluate the representativeness of their sample (see Tables 4.11.2, 4.11.3, and 4.11.4).

All in all, the sample demographic profiles were similar to the 1998 population projections with one or two differences. Both the nonwhite and lower-income groups were underrepresented in the sample (Tables 4.11.2 and 4.11.3). Further, all occupational categories were underrepresented except the service category, which appeared to be overrepresented (Table 4.11.4). Nevertheless, the researchers were reasonably happy with these initial results.

TABLE 4.11.3	Comparison of Race	
Racial Classification	Sample Percentage	1998 Census Percentage
White	91.1	82.3
African American	6.5	13.9
Hispanic	0.8	2.4
Asian	0.4	0.8
Native American	1.2	0.6

QUESTIONS

1. What was the response rate?

2. Was the choice of plus-one telephone interviews judicious? Compare its advantages and disadvantages with those of the rejected sampling option.

3. Would you have selected professional interviewers over Canopy of Care volunteers, given the time and budget constraints? Why or why not?

4. Does the evidence indicate that the data-collection effort was of high quality?

PART 5

Analysis and Interpretation of Data

Once data have been collected, emphasis in the research process logically turns to analysis, which amounts to the search for meaning in the collected information. This search involves many questions and several steps. Chapter 13 is a review of the preliminary steps of editing, coding, and tabulating the data. Chapter 14 is a discussion of the main questions that need to be resolved before statistical examination of the data can begin. Chapters 15, 16, and 17 review the statistical techniques that are most useful in the analysis of marketing data: Chapter 15 is a discussion of the procedures appropriate for examining group differences; Chapter 16 examines the assessment of associations; and Chapter 17 covers the multivariate techniques of discriminant analysis, factor analysis, cluster analysis, and multidimensional scaling.

13

Data Analysis: Preliminary Steps

The purpose of analysis is to obtain meaning from the collected data. All previous steps in the research process have been undertaken to support the search for meaning. The specific analytical procedures to be used are closely related to the preceding steps, and the careful analyst will remember this when designing the other steps. The analyst should go so far as to develop dummy tables, indicating how each item of information will be used, before beginning data collection. Thorough preparatory work should reveal undesirable data gaps and should also pinpoint items that are "interesting" but that do not relate to the problem being examined.

The search for meaning can take many forms. However, the preliminary analytical steps of editing, coding, and tabulation are common to most studies. Given their pervasiveness and value, a review of what editing, coding, and tabulation entail and how they are used is desirable.

Editing

The basic purpose of editing is to impose some minimum quality standards on the raw data. Editing involves the inspection and, if necessary, correction of each questionnaire or observation form. Inspection and correction are often done in two stages: the field edit and the central office edit.

Field Edit

The **field edit** is a preliminary edit, designed to detect the most glaring omissions and inaccuracies in the data. It is also useful in helping to control the field force and to clear up its misunderstandings about directions, procedures, specific questions, and so on. For example, in a Roper survey conducted in Ukraine, the field edit revealed that an employee had left the questionnaire with the respondents instead of interviewing them as instructed. The tip-off was the different ways in which the answers were circled.[1]

Ideally, the field edit is done as soon as possible after the questionnaire (or other data-collection form) has been administered, so that problems can be corrected before the interviewing or observation staff is disbanded and while the particular

---

[1]Lourdes Lee Valeriano, "Marketing: Western Firms Poll Eastern Europeans to Discern Tastes of Nascent Consumers," *The Wall Street Journal* (April 27, 1992), p. B1.

RESEARCH REALITIES 13.1

Items Checked in the Field Edit

1. **Completeness:** This check for completeness involves scrutinizing the data form to ensure that no sections or pages were omitted, and it also involves checking individual items. A blank for a specific question could mean that the respondent refused to answer; alternatively, it may simply reflect an oversight on the respondent's part or show that she or he did not know the answer. It may be important for the purposes of the study to know which reason is correct. By contacting the field worker while the interview is fresh in her or his mind, the needed clarification should be provided.

2. **Legibility:** It is impossible to code a questionnaire that cannot be deciphered because the interviewer's handwriting is unintelligible or because abbreviations were used that are not understood by others. It is a simple matter to correct this now, whereas it is often extremely time-consuming later.

3. **Comprehensibility:** Sometimes a recorded response is incomprehensible to all but the field interviewer. By detecting this now, the necessary clarification can be easily provided.

4. **Consistency:** Marked inconsistencies within an interview or observation schedule typically indicate errors in collecting or recording the data and may indicate ambiguity in the instrument or carelessness in its administration. For instance, if a respondent indicated that she or he saw a particular commercial on TV last night on one part of the questionnaire and later indicated that she or he did not watch TV last night, the analyst would indeed be in a dilemma. Such inconsistencies should be detected and corrected in the field edit.

5. **Uniformity:** It is very important that the responses be recorded in uniform units. For instance, if the study is aimed at determining the number of magazines read per week per individual, and the respondent indicates the number of magazines for which she or he has monthly subscriptions, the response base is not uniform, and the result could cause no small amount of confusion in the later stages of analysis. If detected now, perhaps the interviewer can recontact the respondent and get the correct answer.

---

contacts that were the source of trouble are still fresh in the interviewer's or observer's mind. The preliminary edit will more than likely be conducted by a field supervisor. Some of the items that will be checked are described in Research Realities 13.1.

Central Office Edit

The field edit is typically followed by a **central office edit.** This involves more complete and exacting scrutiny and correction of the completed returns. The work calls for the keen eye of a person well versed in the objectives and procedures of the study. To ensure consistency of treatment, it is best if one individual handles all completed instruments. If this is impossible because of length and time considerations, the work can be divided. However, the division should be by parts of the data-collection instruments rather than by respondents. That is, one editor would be concerned with editing Part A of all questionnaires, while the other would edit Part B.

Unlike the field edit, the central office edit depends less on follow-up procedures and more on deciding just what to do with the data. Accurate follow-up is now more difficult because of the time that has elapsed. In deciding what to do with the data, the editor will usually have to decide how data-collection instruments containing incomplete answers, obviously wrong answers, and answers that reflect a lack of interest will be handled. Because such problems are more prevalent with questionnaires than with observational forms, we will discuss these difficulties from that perspective, although the discussion applies generally to all types of data-collection forms.

The study in which all the returned questionnaires are completely filled out is rare. Some will have entire sections omitted; others will reflect sporadic item non-response. The editor's decision on how to handle these incomplete questionnaires depends on the severity of the problem. Questionnaires that omit entire sections are obviously suspect, yet they should not automatically be thrown out. It might be, for example, that the omitted section refers to the influence of the spouse in some major durable purchase and the respondent is not married. This type of reply is certainly usable in spite of the incomplete section. Alternatively, there might not be a logical justification for the large number of questions that were not answered. In this case, the total reply would probably be thrown out, increasing the nonresponse rate for the study. Questionnaires containing only isolated instances of item non-response would be retained, although they might undergo some data cleaning after coding, a subject discussed later in this chapter.

Careful editing of the questionnaire will sometimes show that an answer to a question is obviously incorrect. For example, respondents might be asked for the type of store in which they purchased a camera in one part of the questionnaire and the name of the store in another. If the person responded "department store" whereas the name of the store indicated a discount store, one of the answers is incorrect. The editor may be able to determine which from other information in the questionnaire. Alternatively, the editor may need to establish policies concerning which answer will be treated as correct, if either, when these inconsistencies or other types of inaccuracies arise. These policies will reflect the purposes of the study. As an example, consider the quandary of Susan Hooper, the Eastern Europe marketing director for Pepsi Cola International, who was given results of a survey conducted in Hungary that said drugstores are an outlet for soft drinks. Susan could not take this information at face value for she knew full well that drugstores didn't exist in Hungary and that the information had been forced into a structure developed in the West.[2]

Indications that the completed questionnaire reflects a lack of interest on the part of the subject are sometimes subtle and sometimes obvious. For example, a subject who checked the "5" position on a five-point scale for each of the 40 items in an attitude questionnaire in which some items were expressed negatively and some positively is obviously not taking the study very seriously. An editor would probably throw out such a response. A discerning editor might also be able to pick up more subtle indications of disinterest, such as check marks that are not within the boxes provided, scribbles, spills on the questionnaire, and so on. An editor may not want to throw out these responses, but they should be coded so that it is later possible to run separate tabulations for both questionable instruments and obviously good questionnaires, to see if that makes any difference in the results and conclusions.

---

[2]Ibid.

Coding

Coding is the technical procedure by which raw data are transformed into symbols. Most often the symbols are numerals, because they can be tabulated and counted more easily. The transformation is not automatic, however, but involves judgment on the part of the coder.

The first step in coding is specifying the categories or classes into which the responses are to be placed.[3] There is no magic number of categories. Rather, the number will depend on the research problem being investigated and the specific items used to generate the information. Nevertheless, several rules for specifying the classes can be stated. First, the classes should be mutually exclusive and exhaustive. Every response should logically fall into one and only one category. Multiple responses are legitimate, of course, if the question is, "For what purposes do you use JELL-O?" and the responses include "a dessert item," "an evening snack," "an afternoon snack," and so on. If the question focuses on the person's age, then only one age category is, of course, acceptable, and the code should indicate unequivocally which category.

Coding closed questions and most scaling devices is simple because the coding is established, for all practical purposes, when the data-collection instrument is designed. Respondents then code themselves with their responses, or the interviewer effectively codes them when he or she records the response on the checklist provided.

Coding open-ended questions can be very difficult and is often much more expensive than coding closed questions. The coder has to determine appropriate categories on the basis of answers that are not always anticipated. Because of the freedom allowed respondents, the responses to open-ended questions are often so vague that they are misclassified by coders in spite of the detailed instructions given them.[4]

International studies can create their own special coding problems because different labels may mean different things. For example, a conservative in the former Soviet Union is someone who wishes to adhere to or return to the "old Communism," which in turn might be seen as very left wing in Western countries. Liberal Russians,

---

[3]Some writers would make the specification of categories part of the editing rather than the coding function. Its placement in one or the other function is not nearly as important as the recognition that it is an extremely critical step with important ramifications for the whole research effort.

[4]For an example of the type of detailed instructions that are necessary to code open-ended questions, see Mary Jo Bitner, Bernard H. Booms, and Lois A. Mohr, "Critical Service Encounters: The Employee's Viewpoint," *Journal of Marketing* 58 (October 1994), pp. 95–106. For ideas on how to organize and analyze the information gathered from open-ended questions, see Matthew B. Miles and A. Michael Huberman, *Qualitative Data Analysis: An Expanded Sourcebook,* 2nd ed. (Thousand Oaks, CA: Sage Publications, 1995). To improve the consistency with which similar answers are coded, researchers are turning to computer systems to code open-ended responses. See, for example, Eben A. Weitzman and Matthew B. Miles, *Computer Programs for Qualitative Data Analysis: A Software Sourcebook* (Thousand Oaks, CA: Sage Publications, 1995); Karl Moore, Robert Burbach, and Roger Heeler, "Using Neural Nets to Analyze Qualitative Data," *Marketing Research: A Magazine of Management & Applications* 7 (Winter 1995), pp. 34–39; Mariam Catterall, "Using Computer Programs to Code Qualitative Data," *Marketing Intelligence and Planning* 14, no. 4 (1996), pp. 29–33; Mariam Catterall and Pauline MacLaran, "Using Computer Software for the Analysis of Qualitative Research Data," *Journal of the Market Research Society* 40 (July 1998), pp. 207–222, for discussion of the more popular approaches.

in turn, are the ones who wish to introduce market perspectives into economics and politics, a perspective which usually will be held by conservatives in the West.

The coding of open-ended questions can create the additional problem of inconsistent treatment when the number of questionnaires necessitates the use of several coders. To ensure consistency of treatment, the work should again be divided by task and not by apportioning the questionnaires equally among the coders. The result of allowing coders to concentrate their energies on one or a few questions is that a consistent set of standards is applied to each question. This approach is also more efficient because coders can learn the codes and do not have to consult the code book for each instrument. When several persons do, in fact, code the same question on different batches of questionnaires, it is important that they also code a sample of the others' work to ensure that a consistent set of coding criteria is being employed.[5]

The second step in coding involves assigning code numbers to the classes. For example, sex might be assigned the letters M for male and F for female. Alternatively, the classes could be denoted by 1 for male and 2 for female. Generally, it is better to use numbers than letters to denote the classes. It also is better to treat numerical data in their reported form at this stage rather than collapsing interval or ratio scale data into categories. For example, it is not advisable to code age in years as 1 = under 20, 2 = 20 to 29, 3 = 30 to 39, and so on. This would entail some unnecessary sacrifice of information in the original measurement and can just as easily be done at later stages in the analysis.

When the analysis of data is to be done by computer, it is necessary to code the data so that they can readily be put into the machine. Regardless of how that input will be effected, whether by mark-sense forms, by mouse-activated optical readers, or directly through a keyboard on a terminal, it is helpful to visualize the input in terms of a multiple-column record. Further, it is advisable to follow certain conventions when coding the data:

1. Use only one character per column. Most computer programs cannot read multiple characters per column. When the question allows multiple responses, spread or spray the answers by allowing separate columns in the coding for each answer. Thus, the question on JELL-O usage would dictate that a separate column be provided in the coding form to indicate whether the respondent used it as a dessert item, another column for use as an evening snack, and so on.

2. Use only numeric codes and not letters of the alphabet, special characters such as @, or blanks. Most computer statistical programs have severe difficulty in manipulating anything but numbers.

3. The field or portion of the record assigned to a variable should consist of as many columns as are necessary to capture the variable. Thus, if the variable is

---

[5]For discussion of indices that can be used to investigate coder reliability as well as to determine which questions might prove to be particularly troublesome, see Martin Collins and Graham Kalton, "Coding Verbatim Answers to Open Questions," *Journal of the Market Research Society* 22 (October 1980), pp. 239–247; William D. Perreault, Jr., and Laurence E. Leigh, "Reliability of Nominal Data Based on Qualitative Judgments," *Journal of Marketing Research* 26 (May 1989), pp. 135–148; Marie Adele Hughes and Dennis E. Garrett, "Intercoder Reliability Estimation Approaches in Marketing," *Journal of Marketing Research* 27 (May 1990), pp. 185–195.

such that the 10 codes from 0 to 9 are not sufficient to exhaust the categories, then the analyst should use two columns in the record, which provides 100 codes from 00 through 99. Moreover, no more than one variable should be assigned to any field.

4. Use standard codes for "No information." Thus, all "Don't know" responses might be coded 8, "No answers" as 9, and "Does not apply" as 0. It is best if the same code is used throughout the study for each of these types of "No information."

5. Code in a respondent identification number on each record. This number need not, and typically will not, identify the respondent by name. Rather, the number simply ties the questionnaire to the coded data. This is often useful information in data cleaning. If the questionnaire will not fit on one record, then code the respondent identification number and a sequence number into each record. Column 10 in the first record might then indicate how the respondent answered Question 2, whereas Column 10 in the second record might indicate whether the person is male or female.[6]

The final step in the coding process is to prepare a **codebook.** The codebook contains the general instructions indicating how each item of data was coded. It lists the codes for each variable and the categories included in each code. It further indicates where on the computer record the variable is located, and how the variable should be read—for example, with a decimal point or as a whole number. The latter information is provided by the format specifications. Figure 13A.1 (in Appendix 13A) contains a sample questionnaire, and the codebook for the questionnaire is shown in Table 13A.1.

Tabulation

Tabulation consists simply of counting the number of cases that fall into the various categories. The tabulation may take the form of a simple tabulation or a cross tabulation. **Simple tabulation** involves counting a single variable. It may be repeated for each of the variables in the study, but the tabulation for each variable is independent of the tabulation for the other variables. In **cross tabulation,** two or more of the variables are treated simultaneously; the number of cases that have the joint characteristics are counted (for example, the number of people who bought Campbell's soup at a Kroger store).

The tabulations may be done entirely by hand, entirely by machine, or some by machine and some by hand. Which method is more efficient depends partly on the number of tabulations necessary and partly on the number of cases in each tabulation. The number of tabulations is a direct function of the number of variables, whereas the number of cases is a direct function of the size of the sample. The fewer

---

[6]Philip S. Siedl, "Coding," in Robert Ferber, ed., *Handbook of Marketing Research* (New York: McGraw-Hill, 1974), pp. 2–178 to 2–199. This article provides an excellent overview of the issues that arise in coding data and how they can be handled. See also Linda B. Bourque and Virginia A. Clark, *Processing Data: The Survey Example* (Thousand Oaks, CA: Sage Publications, Inc., 1992).

the number of tabulations required and the smaller the sample, the more attractive hand methods become. However, the attractiveness of either alternative is also highly dependent on the complexity of the tabulations. Complexity increases as the number of variables receiving simultaneous treatment in a cross tabulation increases. Complexity also increases as the number of categories per variable increases.

Although the hand tabulation might be useful in very simple studies involving a few questions and a limited number of responses, most studies rely on computer tabulation using packaged programs. Many such programs are available. Some will calculate summary statistics and plot a histogram of the values, in addition to reporting the number of cases in each category. The basic input to these statistical analyses will be the data array. The data array lists the value of each variable for each sample unit. Each variable occupies a specific place in the record for a sample unit, thereby making it easy to pick off the values for it from all the cases. The location of each variable is given in the codebook. Table 13A.2 in the appendix to this chapter provides an example of a data array, and Table 13A.1 describes what is contained in each column. Note that only one line had to be devoted to each sample unit or observation. If the amount of information sought from each sample unit had been greater, so that it would not fit as a single record, additional lines would have been devoted to each observation. The codebook would still indicate where the information for any particular variable was located.

There are a number of important questions concerning the analysis of data that can be illustrated, using one-way tabulations and cross tabulations as vehicles. Consider, therefore, the data in Table 13.1. Suppose that the data were collected for a study focusing on car ownership, particularly on the following questions:

- What characteristics distinguish families owning two or more cars from families owning one car?

- What are the distinguishing characteristics of those who buy station wagons? Foreign economy cars? Vans?

- Are there differences in the characteristics of families who financed their automobile purchase and those who did not?

Suppose that the data were collected from a probability sample of respondents using mailed questionnaires and that the 100 people to whom the questionnaire was sent all replied. Thus, there are no problems of nonresponse with which to contend.

One-Way Tabulation

The one-way tabulation, in addition to communicating the results of a study, can be used for several other purposes: (1) to determine the degree of item nonresponse, (2) to locate blunders, (3) to locate outliers, (4) to determine the empirical distribution of the variable in question, and (5) to calculate summary statistics. The first three of these are often referred to as "data cleaning."

What to do about item nonresponse is an aggravating problem in most surveys. It seems that some percentage of the survey instruments invariably suffer from item nonresponse. As a matter of fact, the degree of item nonresponse often serves as a useful indicator of the quality of the research. When it is excessive, it calls the whole research effort into question and suggests that a critical examination of the research

TABLE 13.1 Raw Data for Car Ownership Study

Family Ident. No.	(1) Income in Dollars	(2) Number of Members in Family	(3) Education of Household Head in Yrs.	(4) Region Where Live N = North S = South	(5) Lifestyle Orientation L = Liberal C = Conservative	(6) Number of Cars Family Owns	(7) Did Family Finance the Car Purchase?	(8) Does Family Own Station Wagon?	(9) Does Family Own Foreign Economy Car?	(10) Does Family Own Van?	(11) Does Family Own Some Other Kind of Car?
1001	26,800	3	12	N	L	1	N	N	N	Y	N
1002	17,400	4	12	N	L	1	N	N	N	N	Y
1003	14,300	2	10	N	L	1	N	N	N	N	Y
1004	35,400	4	9	N	L	1	N	N	N	N	Y
1005	24,000	3	8	N	L	1	N	N	N	N	Y
1006	17,200	2	12	N	L	1	N	N	Y	N	N
1007	27,000	4	12	N	L	1	N	N	N	N	Y
1008	16,900	3	10	N	L	1	N	N	N	N	Y
1009	26,700	2	12	N	L	1	N	N	N	N	Y
1010	13,800	4	6	N	C	1	Y	N	N	N	Y
1011	34,100	3	8	N	C	1	N	N	N	N	Y
1012	16,300	3	11	N	C	1	N	N	N	N	Y
1013	14,700	2	12	N	C	1	N	N	N	N	Y
1014	25,400	4	12	N	C	1	N	N	N	N	Y
1015	15,400	4	12	N	C	1	N	N	N	N	Y
1016	25,900	3	11	N	C	1	Y	N	N	N	Y
1017	36,300	3	12	N	C	1	Y	N	N	N	Y
1018	27,400	2	12	N	C	2	N	N	N	N	Y
1019	17,300	3	8	N	C	1	N	N	N	N	Y
1020	13,700	2	12	N	C	1	N	N	N	N	Y
1021	26,100	4	12	N	C	1	Y	N	Y	N	N
1022	16,300	3	6	N	C	1	N	N	N	N	Y
1023	33,800	4	8	N	C	1	N	N	N	N	Y
1024	34,400	2	9	N	C	1	Y	N	N	N	Y
1025	15,300	3	12	N	C	1	N	N	N	N	Y
1026	35,900	4	12	N	C	1	N	N	N	N	Y
1027	15,100	2	12	S	L	1	N	N	N	N	Y
1028	17,200	4	10	S	L	1	N	N	N	Y	N
1029	35,400	3	12	S	L	1	N	N	N	N	Y
1030	15,600	3	12	S	L	1	N	N	N	N	Y
1031	24,900	4	11	S	C	1	N	N	N	N	Y
1032	34,800	3	12	S	C	1	N	N	N	Y	N
1033	14,600	3	9	S	C	1	N	N	N	N	Y
1034	23,100	3	12	S	C	1	N	N	N	N	Y
1035	15,900	3	12	S	C	1	N	N	N	Y	N

(continued)

TABLE 13.1 (continued)

Family Ident. No.	(1) Income in Dollars	(2) Number of Members in Family	(3) Education of Household Head in Yrs.	(4) Region Where Live N = North S = South	(5) Lifestyle Orientation L = Liberal C = Conservative	(6) Number of Cars Family Owns	(7) Did Family Finance the Car Purchase?	(8) Does Family Own Station Wagon?	(9) Does Family Own Foreign Economy Car?	(10) Does Family Own Van?	(11) Does Family Own Some Other Kind of Car?
1036	26,700	4	12	S	C	1	N	N	N	N	Y
1037	17,300	4	12	S	C	1	N	N	N	Y	N
1038	37,100	3	12	S	C	1	N	N	N	Y	N
1039	14,000	3	10	S	C	1	N	N	N	N	Y
1040	23,600	3	10	S	C	1	N	N	N	N	Y
1041	16,200	3	12	S	C	1	N	N	N	N	Y
1042	24,100	4	10	S	C	1	N	N	N	Y	N
1043	12,700	2	8	S	L	1	N	N	N	N	Y
1044	26,000	4	13	S	L	2	N	N	N	N	Y
1045	15,400	3	16	N	L	1	N	Y	N	N	N
1046	16,900	4	16	N	L	1	N	Y	Y	N	Y
1047	23,800	6	10	S	C	1	N	Y	N	N	N
1048	37,100	8	16	N	L	2	Y	Y	N	N	Y
1049	16,800	5	15	S	L	2	Y	N	Y	N	N
1050	22,900	5	8	N	C	1	Y	Y	N	N	Y
1051	13,700	6	8	N	L	1	Y	Y	N	N	N
1052	26,800	8	12	S	C	2	N	Y	N	N	Y
1053	16,100	8	12	N	L	2	N	Y	N	N	Y
1054	25,700	6	12	N	C	1	N	N	N	N	Y
1055	38,200	2	12	N	L	1	N	N	N	N	Y
1056	49,800	3	12	N	L	2	Y	N	N	Y	Y
1057	60,400	4	12	N	L	1	N	N	N	N	Y
1058	39,000	2	12	N	L	1	Y	N	N	N	Y
1059	57,600	4	12	N	L	1	N	N	N	N	Y
1060	42,000	3	12	N	L	1	N	N	N	N	Y
1061	38,600	3	12	N	L	1	N	N	N	Y	N
1062	66,400	4	12	N	L	2	Y	N	Y	N	Y
1063	71,200	2	12	N	L	1	N	N	N	N	Y
1064	49,300	4	10	N	C	1	N	N	N	N	Y
1065	37,700	4	10	N	C	1	Y	N	N	N	N
1066	72,400	3	12	N	C	2	N	N	Y	N	Y
1067	88,700	3	12	N	C	1	N	N	N	N	Y
1068	44,200	2	12	S	L	1	Y	N	N	Y	N
1069	55,100	3	12	S	L	2	N	N	N	Y	Y
1070	73,300	4	12	S	L	1	N	N	N	Y	Y
1071	80,200	2	12	S	L	1	Y	N	N	N	Y

1072	39,300	3	10	S	C	2	N	Z	Z	Y	Y
1073	48,200	4	12	S	C	1	Z	Z	Z	N	Y
1074	57,800	2	12	S	C	1	Y	Z	Z	N	Y
1075	38,000	3	10	N	C	1	Y	Y	Y	Y	N
1076	81,300	4	16	N	L	2	N	Z	Z	N	N
1077	96,900	4	16	N	L	1	Z	Z	Z	N	Y
1078	44,700	3	14	N	L	1	Z	Z	Z	N	Y
1079	107,300	3	17	N	L	2	Y	Z	Z	N	Y
1080	38,100	2	13	N	L	1	Z	Z	Z	N	N
1081	304,200	2	14	S	L	1	Z	Z	Z	Y	Y
1082	46,100	3	16	S	L	1	Z	Z	Z	N	Y
1083	49,300	4	13	S	L	9	Z	Z	Z	N	N
1084	160,800	4	16	S	C	1	Z	Z	Z	Y	Z
1085	39,100	2	16	N	L	1	Y	Z	Z	Y	Y
1086	46,400	6	14	N	L	2	Y	Z	Z	N	Y
1087	58,300	5	10	N	L	2	Y	Z	Z	N	Y
1088	47,800	7	10	N	L	2	Y	Z	Z	N	Y
1089	58,000	9	8	N	L	2	Y	Y	Z	Y	Y
1090	69,600	11	12	N	L	2	Y	Y	Y	N	Y
1091	44,200	6	12	N	L	3	Y	Y	Z	Y	Y
1092	62,100	5	10	S	L	2	Y	Y	Y	N	Y
1093	99,000	6	12	S	L	2	Y	Y	Z	Y	Y
1094	53,300	9	12	S	L	2	Y	Y	Y	N	Y
1095	72,200	7	10	N	C	2	Y	Y	Z	N	N
1096	64,700	6	12	S	C	3	Y	Y	Z	Y	N
1097	77,300	6	16	S	L	1	Y	Y	Z	N	Z
1098	116,900	10	18	N	L	2	Y	Y	Y	Y	N
1099	71,200	7	15	S	L	3	N	N	Y	N	Z
1100	103,800	5	16	S	C	1	Y	Y	Y	N	N

objectives and procedures should be undertaken. When it is in bounds, it still demands that decisions be made with respect to what to do about the missing items before analyzing the data. There are several possible strategies:

1. Leave the items blank and report the number as a separate category. While this procedure works well for simple one-way and cross tabulations, it does not work very well at all for some statistical techniques.

2. Eliminate the case with the missing item in analyses using the variable. When using this approach, the analyst must continually report the number of cases on which the analysis is based, because the sample size is not constant across analyses. This approach also ignores the fact that a significant incidence of no information on any item might in itself be insightful; it signals that respondents do not care very deeply about the issue being addressed by the question.

3. Substitute values for the missing items. Typically, the substitution will involve some measure of central tendency, such as the mean, median, or mode. Alternatively, sometimes the analyst attempts to estimate the answer using other information contained in the questionnaire. The substitution of values makes maximum use of the data, since all the reasonably good cases are used. At the same time, it is more work, and it does contain potential for bias. It also raises the question of which statistical technique should be used to generate the estimate.[7]

There is no single "right" answer for how missing items should be handled. It all depends on the purposes of the study, the incidence of missing items, and the methods that will be used to analyze the data.

A **blunder** is simply an error. It can happen during editing, during coding, or when entering the data on the computer. Consider the one-way tabulation of the number of cars owned per family in Table 13.2. A check of the original questionnaire indicates that the family having nine cars had, in fact, one car. The nine is a blunder. The simple one-way tabulation has revealed the error, and it can now be corrected at a very early stage in the analysis with a minimum of difficulty and expense.

An interesting example of the use of the one-way tabulation to locate blunders occurred in a series of articles concerning money laundering that *The Boston Globe* was working on using government-developed data. In this case, the tabulations pro-

---

[7]David W. Stewart, "Filling the Gap: A Review of the Missing Data Problem," unpublished manuscript, provides an excellent review of the literature on the missing data problem, including various methods for eliminating cases and estimating answers. On the basis of this review, Stewart concludes several things: Missing data points should be estimated regardless of whether the data are missing randomly or nonrandomly; for very small amounts of missing data, almost any of the estimation procedures work reasonably well; when larger amounts of data are missing and the average intercorrelation of variables is .20 or less, the substitution of the mean seems to work best; and when the average intercorrelation of the variables exceeds .20, a regression or principal components procedure is the preferred choice when linearity among the variables may be assumed. See also Roderick J. A. Little and Philip J. Smith, "Editing and Imputation for Quantitative Survey Data," *Journal of the American Statistical Association* 82 (March 1987), pp. 58–68; Roderick J. Little and Donald B. Rubin, "The Analysis of Social Science Data with Missing Values," *Sociological Methods and Research* 18 (November 1989), pp. 292–326; Philip L. Roth, "Missing Data: A Conceptual Review for Applied Psychologists," *Personnel Psychology* 47 (Autumn 1994), pp. 537–560; Myunghee Cho Paik, "The Generalized Estimating Equation Approach When Data Are Not Missing Completely," *Journal of the American Statistical Association* 92 (December 1997), pp. 1320–1329.

TABLE 13.2	Cars per Family	
	Number of Cars per Family	Number of Families
	1	74
	2	23
	3	2
	9	1

TABLE 13.3	Cars per Family		
	Number of Cars per Family	Number of Families	Percentage of Families
	1	75	75
	2	23	23
	3	2	2
		100	100

duced large and unexplainable swings in cash transactions in certain cities. "Ultimately, the discrepancies were traced to a clerk in Detroit, who occasionally added five zeros to actual figures to ease boredom."[8]

The number of cases serving as a base for the one-way tabulation in Table 13.2 is 100, and thus the number entries are readily converted to percentages. Conversion will rarely be this easy, but it is good practice to indicate percentages in the table. Percentages facilitate communication, and a more typical presentation of the preceding result, corrected for blunders, is found in Table 13.3. Note that the *percentages are presented to zero decimal places*. Though in this case it is because the sample size was 100, in most cases it would be done *deliberately*. The sample is small, and with small samples one has to be particularly careful not to convey a greater accuracy than the figures can support. They also are easier to read when rounded off. On some occasions the analyst might prefer to report percentages to one decimal place.[9] Rarely, if ever, would they be reported to two decimal places, because this would typically introduce a spurious sense of accuracy and might seriously impair the analysis by lulling the reader into assuming that the data are more accurate than they actually are. The general rule in reporting percentages is: *Unless decimals serve a special purpose, they should be omitted.*

Sometimes the percentages also are presented in parentheses (see Table 13.4) immediately to the right or below the actual count entry in the table. Sometimes only the percentages are presented. In this case it is imperative that the total number of cases on which the percentages are based is provided.

---

[8]Gregory Stricharchuk, "Computer Records Become Powerful Tool for Investigative Reporters and Editors," *The Wall Street Journal* (February 3, 1988), p. 23.

[9]See the classic book by Hans Zeisel, *Say It with Figures*, 5th ed. (New York: Harper & Row, 1968), pp. 16–17, for conditions that would support reporting percentages with decimal-place accuracy.

TABLE 13.4	Income Distribution of Respondents in Car Ownership Study			

Income	*Number of Families*		*Cumulative Number of Families*	
Less than $15,000	8	(8.0)	8	(8.0)
$15,000 to $24,900	25	(25.0)	33	(33.0)
$25,000 to $34,900	15	(15.0)	48	(48.0)
$35,000 to $44,900	18	(18.0)	66	(66.0)
$45,000 to $54,900	8	(8.0)	74	(74.0)
$55,000 to $64,900	8	(8.0)	82	(82.0)
$65,000 to $74,900	7	(7.0)	89	(89.0)
$75,000 to $84,900	3	(3.0)	92	(92.0)
$85,000 to $94,900	1	(1.0)	93	(93.0)
$95,000 to $104,900	3	(3.0)	96	(96.0)
More than $105,000	4	(4.0)	100	(100.0)
Total number of families	100	(100.0)		

The third use of the one-way tabulation is to locate **outliers.** An outlier is not an error. Rather, it is an observation so different in magnitude from the rest of the observations that the analyst chooses to treat it as a special case. This may mean eliminating the observation from the analysis or determining the specific factors that generate this unique observation.[10] Consider, for example, the tabulation of incomes contained in Table 13.4, but ignore the right-hand column for the moment. The tabulation indicates there are only four families with incomes greater than $105,000, and Table 13.1 indicates that only one family had an annual income greater than $161,000, namely Number 1081 with an income of $304,200. This is clearly out of line with the rest of the sample and is properly considered an outlier. What the analyst chooses to do with this observation depends on the objectives of the study. In this case, it is not unreasonable for a family to have such an income, so the observation will be retained in the analysis.

The fourth use of the one-way frequency tabulation is to determine the *empirical distribution* of the characteristic in question. Some analysts ignore the distribution of the variables and automatically calculate summary statistics, such as the mean. Ignoring the distribution of the variables can be a serious mistake. Consider the case of a new sauce product.

> On the average, consumers wanted it neither really hot nor really mild. The mean rating of the test participants was quite close to the middle of the scale, which had "very mild" and "very hot" as its bipolar adjectives. This happened to fit the client's preconceived notion.
>
> However, examination of the distribution of the ratings revealed the existence of a large proportion of consumers who wanted the sauce to be mild and an equally

[10]For discussion of the treatment of outliers, see Terry Clark, "Managing Outliers: Qualitative Issues in the Handling of Extreme Observations in Marketing Research," *Marketing Research: A Magazine of Management & Applications* 1 (June 1989), pp. 31–48; Vic Barnett and Toby Lewis, *Outliers in Statistical Data*, 3rd ed. (New York: John Wiley & Sons, Inc., 1994); William G. Jacoby, *Statistical Graphics for Univariate and Bivariate Data* (Thousand Oaks, CA: Sage Publications, Inc., 1997).

FIGURE 13.1   **Histogram and Frequency Polygon of Incomes of Families in Car Ownership Study**

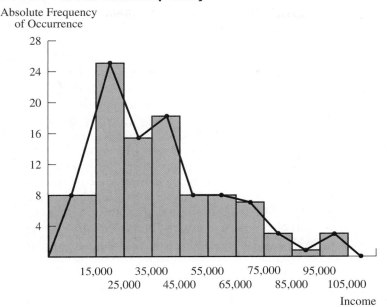

large proportion who wanted it to be hot. Relatively few wanted the in-between product, which would have been suggested by looking at the mean rating alone.[11]

It is always a good idea to get a sense of a variable's distribution before performing any analysis with it.

The distribution of a variable can be visualized through a histogram. A **histogram** is a form of bar chart in which successive values of the variable are placed along the abscissa, or *x*-axis, and the absolute frequency or relative frequency of occurrence of the values is indicated along the *y*-axis, or ordinate. The histogram for the income data in Table 13.4 appears in Figure 13.1, with the incomes over $105,000 omitted because their inclusion would have required an undue extension of the income axis. It is readily apparent that the distribution of incomes is skewed to the right. The actual distribution can be compared to some theoretical distribution to determine whether the data are consistent with some *a priori* model. Further insight into the empirical distribution of income can be obtained by constructing the **frequency polygon.** The frequency polygon is obtained from the histogram by connecting the midpoints of the bars with straight lines. The frequency polygon for incomes is superimposed on the histogram in Figure 13.1.

---

[11]Robert J. Lavidge, "How to Keep Well-Intentioned Research from Misleading New-Product Planners," *Marketing News* 18 (January 6, 1984), p. 8. Some late evidence suggests consumers want their sauces hot. See Kathleen Deveny, "Rival Hot Sauces Are Breathing Fire at Market Leader Tabasco," *The Wall Street Journal* (January 7, 1993), pp. B1, B6.

An alternative way of gaining insight into empirical distribution is through the empirical **cumulative distribution function.** The one-way tabulation is again the source. In this case, though, the number of observations with a value less than or equal to a specified quantity is determined; that is, the cumulative frequencies are generated. Thus, in the right-hand column of Table 13.4, we see that there are eight families with incomes less than $15,000; 33 families (8 + 25) with incomes of $24,900 or less; and 48 families (8 + 25 + 15) with incomes of $34,900 or less. These cumulative frequencies are denoted along the ordinate in Figure 13.2, while the abscissa again contains incomes. The empirical cumulative distribution function is generated by connecting the points representing the given combinations of *x*s (values) and *y*s (cumulative frequencies) with straight lines.

The cumulative distribution function can also be used to determine whether the distribution of observed incomes is consistent with some theoretical or assumed distribution. In addition, it can be used to calculate some of the commonly used measures of location, such as the median, quartiles, and percentiles. These can simply be read from the plot once the cumulative relative frequencies are entered. In our case, the cumulative relative frequencies are equal to the cumulative absolute frequencies divided by 100, since there are 100 cases.

By definition, the sample median is that value at which 50 percent of the values lie below it and 50 percent are above it. To read the sample median from the plot of the cumulative distribution, simply extend a horizontal line from 0.50 on the relative frequency ordinate until it intersects the graph, and then drop a vertical line from the point of intersection to the *x*-axis. The point of intersection with the *x*-axis

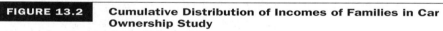

FIGURE 13.2　**Cumulative Distribution of Incomes of Families in Car Ownership Study**

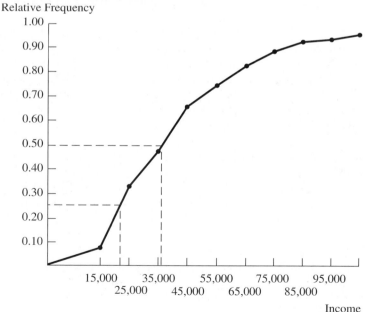

is the approximate sample median. In the case at hand, the sample median equals $35,700. The quality of the approximation could be checked by actually determining the median using the detailed data.

Sample quartiles could be determined in similar fashion. The first sample quartile (also known as the twenty-fifth percentile) is that value at which 25 percent of the observations are below it. This first sample quartile is determined by drawing a horizontal line from 0.25 on the relative frequency ordinate until it intersects the graph, dropping a vertical line from the point of intersection to the horizontal axis, and reading off the value of the first quartile at the point of intersection with the x-axis. The first quartile is thus found to be $21,800. The procedure for the third quartile (seventy-fifth percentile) or any other percentile would be the same as that for the median or first quartile. The only change would be where the horizontal line commenced.

The one-way tabulation is also useful in calculating other summary measures, such as the mode, mean, and standard deviation. The mode, or the most frequently occurring item, can be read directly from the one-way tabulation. Thus, Table 13.3 suggests that most families own one car. The mean, or "average" response, can be calculated from a one-way tabulation by weighting each value by its frequency of occurrence, summing these products, and dividing by the number of cases. The average number of cars per family given the data in Table 13.3 would thus be estimated to be the following:

Value	Frequency	Value × Frequency
1	75	75
2	23	46
3	2	6
	100	127

or

$$\frac{127}{100} = 1.27 \text{ cars per family}$$

The standard deviation provides a measure of spread in the data. It is calculated from the one-way tabulation by taking the deviation of each value from the mean and squaring these deviations. The squared deviations are then multiplied by the frequency with which each occurs, these products are summed, and the sum is divided by one less than the number of cases to yield the sample variance. The square root of the sample variance then yields the sample standard deviation. The calculation of the standard deviation is thus very similar to that for ungrouped data, except that each value is weighted by the frequency with which it occurs. The standard deviation for the data in Table 13.3 is thus calculated to be the following:

Value	Value-Mean	$(Value\text{-}Mean)^2$	Frequency	Frequency Times Difference Squared
1	−0.27	0.0729	75	5.4675
2	0.73	0.5329	23	12.2567
3	1.73	2.9929	2	5.9858
				23.7100

yielding a variance of

$$\frac{23.7100}{99} = 0.2395$$

and a standard deviation of $\sqrt{0.2395} = 0.4894$.

The one-way tabulation as a communication vehicle for the results has not been discussed. The reader needs only to look at Table 13.1 to see how much insight can be gathered about the variable income and then compare that with the insight generated in the one-way tabulation contained in Table 13.4. When one realizes that they also serve as a basic input to the histogram, frequency polygon, and empirical cumulative distribution function, and that they are also used in calculating summary statistics, it is an unwise analyst indeed who does not take the time to develop the one-way tabulations of the variables in the study and to plot the results to get a sense of how they are distributed.[12]

Cross Tabulation

Although the one-way tabulation is useful for examining the variables of the study separately, **cross tabulation** is a most important mechanism for studying the relationships among and between variables. In cross tabulation, the sample is divided into subgroups to learn how the dependent variable varies from subgroup to subgroup. It is clearly the most widely used data analysis technique in marketing research. Some would call it the "bread and butter" of applied research. Most marketing research studies go no farther than cross tabulation, and many of the studies that do use more sophisticated analytical methods still contain cross tabulation as an important component. Thus, the analyst and decision maker both need to understand how cross tabulations are developed and interpreted.

Consider, for example, the question of the relationship, if any, between the number of cars that the family owns and family income. To keep the example simple, suppose that the analyst was interested only in determining if a family with above-average income was more likely than a family with below-average income to own two or more cars. Suppose further that $37,500 was the median income in the population and that this figure was to be used to split the families in the sample into two groups, those with below-average and those with above-average incomes.

Table 13.5 presents the two-way classification of the sample families by income and number of cars. Looking at the marginal totals, we see that 75 families have one car or less, while 25 families have two cars or more. We also see that the sample is not unrepresentative of the population, at least as far as income is concerned: 54 families fall into the lower-than-average income group using the $37,500 cutoff.

Does the number of cars depend on income? It certainly seems so on the basis of Table 13.5, since 19 of the families owning two or more cars are in the upper-income group. Can anything be done to shed additional light on the relationship? The an-

---

[12]Box and whisker plots can also be used to get a sense for the distribution of the variable. They possess the attractive feature of including information about the variable mean, median, 25th and 75th percentiles, and outliers. For discussion of how they are constructed, see "Graphic Displays of Data: Box and Whisker Plots," *Research on Research*, no. 17 (Chicago: Market Facts, Inc., undated).

TABLE 13.5	Family Income and Number of Cars Family Owns		
		Number of Cars	
Income	*1 or None*	*2 or More*	*Total*
Less than $37,500	48	6	54
More than $37,500	27	19	46
Total	75	25	100

swer is *yes. Compute percentages.* Tables 13.6 and 13.7 are mathematically equivalent to Table 13.5 but are based on percentages calculated in different directions: horizontally in Table 13.6 and vertically in Table 13.7. The tables contain quite different messages. Table 13.6 suggests that multiple-car ownership is affected by family income: 41 percent of the families with above-average incomes had two or more automobiles, but only 11 percent of the below-average-income families did so. This is a clear, interesting finding. Table 13.7, on the other hand, conveys a different story. It suggests that 64 percent of those who owned one car had below-average incomes, while only 24 percent of those who owned two or more cars were below average in income. Does this mean that multiple-car ownership paves the way to higher income? Definitely not. Rather, it simply illustrates a fundamental rule of percentage calculations: Always calculate percentages in the direction of the causal factor, or across the effect factor.[13] In this case, income is logically considered to be the cause, or independent variable, and multiple-car ownership to be the effect, or dependent variable. The percentages are correctly calculated, therefore, in the direction of income as in Table 13.6.

One very useful way to think about the direction in which to calculate percentages is to conceptualize the problem in terms of **conditional probability,** or the probability of one event occurring given that another event has occurred or will occur. Thus, the notion of the probability that the family has two or more cars *given* that they are high income makes sense, whereas the notion that the family is high income *given* that they have two or more cars does not.

Although it provides some insight into a dependency relationship, the two-way cross tabulation is not the final answer. Rather, it represents a start. Consider now, for example, the relationship between multiple-car ownership and size of family. Table 13.8 indicates the number of small and large (five or more members) families that possess two or more cars. Now, size of family is logically considered a cause of multiple-car ownership and not vice versa. Thus, the percentages would properly be computed in the *direction of size of family* or *across number of cars.* Table 13.9 presents these percentages and suggests that the number of cars a family owns is affected by the size of the family—77 percent of the large families have two or more cars, while only 10 percent of the small families do.

This result raises the question: Does multiple-car ownership depend on family size or, as previously suggested, on family income? The proper way to answer this

---

[13]See Zeisel, *Say It with Figures,* p. 28, for a slightly modified statement of the percentage-direction–calculation rule, which takes into account the representativeness of the sample.

TABLE 13.6   **Number of Cars by Family Income**

	Number of Cars			
Income	*1 or None*	*2 or More*	*Total*	*Number of Cases*
Less than $37,500	89%	11%	100%	54
More than $37,500	59%	41%	100%	46

TABLE 13.7   **Family Income by Number of Cars**

Income	*1 or None*	*2 or More*
Less than $37,500	64%	24%
More than $37,500	36%	76%
Total	100%	100%
(Number of cases)	(75)	(25)

TABLE 13.8   **Number of Cars and Size of Family**

	Number of Cars		
Size of Family	*1 or None*	*2 or More*	*Total*
4 or less	70	8	78
5 or more	5	17	22
Total	75	25	100

TABLE 13.9   **Number of Cars by Size of Family**

	Number of Cars			
Size of Family	*1 or None*	*2 or More*	*Total*	*Number of Cases*
4 or less	90%	10%	100%	(78)
5 or more	23%	77%	100%	(22)

| TABLE 13.10 | Number of Cars by Income and Size of Family |

Income	Four Members or Less: Number of Cars			Five Members or More: Number of Cars			Total Number of Cars		
	1 or None	2 or More	Total	1 or None	2 or More	Total	1 or None	2 or More	Total
Less than $37,500	44	2	46	4	4	8	48	6	54
More than $37,500	26	6	32	1	13	14	27	19	46
Total	70	8	78	5	17	22	75	25	100

| TABLE 13.11 | Number of Cars by Income and Size of Family |

Income	Four Members or Less: Number of Cars			Five Members or More: Number of Cars			Total Number of Cars		
	1 or None	2 or More	Total	1 or None	2 or More	Total	1 or None	2 or More	Total
Less than $37,500	96%	4%	100% (46)	50%	50%	100% (8)	89%	11%	100% (54)
More than $37,500	81%	19%	100% (32)	7%	93%	100% (14)	59%	41%	100% (46)

question is through the *simultaneous* treatment of income and family size. In effect, the two-way cross-classification table needs to be partitioned and a three-way table of income, family size, and multiple-car ownership formed. One way of doing this is illustrated in Table 13.10. This table is, in one sense, two cross-classification tables of multiple-car ownership versus income—one for small families of four or fewer members and one for large families of five or more members.

Once again we would want to compute percentages in the direction of income within each table. Table 13.11 contains these percentages, which indicate that multiple-car ownership depends on both income and family size. For small families of four or less, 19 percent of those with above-average incomes have two or more cars, while only 4 percent of those with below-average incomes have more than one automobile. For large families, 93 percent of the above-average-income and 50 percent of the below-average-income families have more than one vehicle.

The preceding comparisons highlight the effect of income on multiple-car ownership, holding family size constant. We could also compare the effect of family size on multiple-car ownership, holding income constant. We would still find that each provides a partial explanation for multiple-car ownership. Now, you may have felt a bit uncomfortable with the presentation of the data in Tables 13.10 and 13.11. The information is there to be mined, but perhaps you may have wondered whether it could not have been presented in a more revealing manner. It can, if you are willing to accept a couple of refinements in the manner of presentation. Look specifically at the first row of the first section of Table 13.11, reproducing it as Table 13.12. All the information contained in this table can be condensed into one figure,

TABLE 13.12	Car Ownership for Small, Below-Average-Income Families		

		Number of Cars		
Income		*1 or None*	*2 or More*	*Total*
Less than $37,500		96%	4%	100% (46)

TABLE 13.13	Percentage of Families Owning Two or More Cars by Income and Size of Family		

		Size of Family		
Income		*4 or Less*	*5 or More*	*Total*
Less than $37,500		4%	50%	11%
More than $37,500		19%	93%	41%

4 percent. This is the percentage of small, below-average-income families that have two or more cars. It follows that the complementary percentage, 96 percent, represents those that have one automobile or none.

Table 13.13 shows the rest of the data in Table 13.11 treated in the same way. The entry in each case is the percentage of families in that category that own two or more automobiles. Table 13.13 conveys the same information as Table 13.11, but it delivers the message with much greater clarity. The separate effect of income on multiple-car ownership, holding family size constant, can be determined by reading down the columns, while the effect of family size, holding income constant, can be determined by reading across the rows. Omitting the complementary percentages has helped reveal the structure of the data. Therefore, let us agree to use this form of presentation whenever we attempt to determine the effect of several explanatory variables, considered simultaneously, in the pages that follow.

The original association between number of cars and family income reflected in Table 13.6 is called the **total** (or **zero order**) association between the variables. Table 13.13, which depicts the association between the two variables within categories of family size, is called a *conditional table* that reveals the **conditional association** between the variables. Family size here is a *control variable*. Conditional tables that are developed on the basis of one control variable are called *first-order* conditional tables, those developed using two control variables are called *second-order* conditional tables, and so on.

Which variable has the greater effect on multiple-car ownership—income or family size? A useful method for addressing this question is to calculate the *difference in proportions* as a function of the level of the variable.[14] This can be done for the zero order tables as well as the conditional tables of higher order. Consider again Table

---

[14]See Ottar Hellevik, *Introduction to Causal Analysis: Exploring Survey Data by Crosstabulation*, 2nd ed. (Cambridge, MA: Scandinavian University Press, 1995).

13.6 and concentrate on the effect of income on the probability of the family having multiple cars. The proportion of low-income families that have two or more cars is 0.11, while the proportion of high-income families is 0.41. The probability of having multiple cars is clearly different depending on the family's income; specifically, high income increases the probability of having two or more cars by 0.30 (0.41 − 0.11) over low income. A similar analysis applied to Table 13.9 suggests that the probability of multiple-car ownership is clearly different depending on family size. Whereas 0.10 of the small families have multiple cars, 0.77 of the large families do. Thus, being a large family increases the probability of having two or more cars by 0.67 (0.77 − 0.10) over small families.

To determine whether income or family size has the greater impact, it is necessary to consider the factors simultaneously using a similar analysis. Table 13.13 contains the data that are necessary for this analysis. Let us first consider the effect of income. The proper way to determine income's effect is to hold family size constant, which means in essence that we must investigate the relationship between income and multiple-car ownership for small families and then again for large families. Among small families, having high income increases the probability of having multiple cars by 0.15 (0.19 − 0.04). Among large families, having high income increases the probability of having multiple cars by 0.43 (0.93 − 0.50) compared to low income. The size of the associations between income and multiple-car ownership are different for different family sizes. This means that there is a statistical interaction between the independent variables; to generate a single estimate of the effect of income on car ownership, some kind of average of the separate effects needs to be computed. The appropriate average is a weighted average that takes account of the sizes of the groups on which the individual effects were calculated. There were 78 small families in the sample of 100 cases and 22 large families; the weight for small families is thus 0.78 and for large families 0.22. The weighted average is

$$0.15(0.78) + 0.43(0.22) = 0.21$$

which suggests that, on average, high versus low income increases the probability of owning multiple cars by 0.21.

To investigate the effect of family size, it is necessary to hold income constant or, alternatively, to investigate the impact of family size on multiple-car ownership for low-income families, then for high-income families, and then to generate a weighted average of the two results if they are not the same. Among low-income families, being large increases the probability of having multiple cars by 0.46 (0.50 − 0.04) compared to small families. Among high-income families, large size increases the probability by 0.74 (0.93 − 0.19) versus small size. Since there were 54 low-income families and 46 high-income families, the appropriate weights for weighting the two effects are 0.54 and 0.46, respectively. The calculation yields

$$0.46(0.54) + 0.74(0.46) = 0.59$$

as the estimate of the impact of family size on multiple-car ownership.

Family size has a more pronounced effect on multiple-car ownership than does income. It increases the probability of having two or more cars by 0.59, whereas income increases it by 0.21.

ETHICAL DILEMMA 13.1

After collecting the data for a study that is being repeated with the use of an updated questionnaire, an analyst is instructed to complete the analysis and report for the project. The fieldwork took longer than expected to complete, leaving the analyst with very little time to complete the analysis for the project. So that the project can be completed on time, the analyst follows the analysis plan used for the previous project. For the final report, the analyst decides simply to update the tables from the previous report to reflect the new data and to alter wording only where required by the table information.

- Is it acceptable to charge the new client for a full analysis on this project when the researcher has not completed a full analysis?
- What are the risks associated with this shortcut in data analysis?
- Under the same constraints, what would you have done in this situation?

TABLE 13.14 **Conditions That Can Arise with the Introduction of an Additional Variable into a Cross Tabulation**

	With the Additional Variable	
Initial Conclusion	*Change Conclusion*	*Retain Conclusion*
	I	II
Some relationship	A. Refine explanation	
	B. Reveal spurious explanation	
	C. Provide limiting conditions	
No relationship	III	IV

The previous example highlighted an important application of cross tabulation—the use of an additional variable to refine an initial cross tabulation. In this case, family size was used to refine the relationship between multiple-car ownership and income. This is only one of the many applications of successive cross tabulation of variables, and, in fact, a number of conditions can occur when additional variables are introduced into a cross tabulation, as shown in the various panels of Table 13.14. The two-way tabulation may initially indicate the existence or nonexistence of a relationship between the variables. The introduction of a third variable may occasion no change in the initial conclusion, or it may indicate that a substantial change is in order. We have considered Panel I–A. Let us now turn to an analysis of examples of these alternative conditions.

Panel I: Initial Relationship Is Modified by the Introduction of a Third Variable

CASE I–B: INITIAL RELATIONSHIP IS SPURIOUS   One of the purposes of the automobile purchase study was to determine the kinds of families that purchase specific

TABLE 13.15	Van Ownership by Lifestyle		

	Own Van?		
Lifestyle	*Yes*	*No*	*Total*
Liberal	9 (16%)	46 (84%)	55 (100%)
Conservative	11 (24%)	34 (76%)	45 (100%)

TABLE 13.16	Van Ownership by Lifestyle and Region of Country		

	Region of Country		
Lifestyle	*North*	*South*	*Total*
Liberal	5%	41%	16%
Conservative	5%	43%	24%

kinds of automobiles. Consider vans. It was expected that van ownership would be related to lifestyle and, in particular, that those with a liberal orientation would be more likely to own vans than would those who are conservative by nature. Table 13.15 was constructed, employing the raw data on car ownership in Table 13.1, to test this hypothesis. Contrary to expectation, conservatives are more apt than liberals to own vans; 24 percent of the conservatives but only 16 percent of the liberals in the sample owned vans.

Is there some logical explanation for this unexpected happening? Consider the addition of a third variable, region of the country in which the family resides, to the analysis. A clear picture of the relationship among the three variables considered simultaneously can be developed employing our previously agreed-upon convention; that is, simply report the percentage in each category. The complement, 100 minus the percentage, then indicates the proportion not owning vans.

As Table 13.16 indicates, van ownership is not related to lifestyle. Rather, it depends on the region of the country in which the family resides. When region is held constant, there is no difference in van ownership between liberals and conservatives. Families living in the South are much more likely to own a van than are families who live in the northern states. It just so happens that people in the South tend to be more conservative in their lifestyle than people in the North. The original relationship is, therefore, said to be spurious.

Although it seems counterproductive to calculate the difference in proportions to determine the effect of each variable for each of the potential conditions in Table 13.14, it does seem useful to do it for this case to demonstrate what is meant by a main effect without a statistical interaction. The example is also useful in reinforcing how the difference-in-proportions calculation can be used to isolate the causal relationships that exist in cross-tabulation data. Consider first the zero-order association between van ownership and lifestyle contained in Table 13.15. Being conservative increases the probability of van ownership by 0.08 (0.24 − 0.16) compared to being liberal. Yet Table 13.16 shows that this is a spurious effect that is due to region of the country, since it disappears when region is held constant. Among those living in the North, the partial association between van ownership and lifestyle is 0.00 (0.05 − 0.05). Among those living in the South, there is a slightly higher probability of van ownership among conservatives, namely 0.02 (0.43 − 0.41). This effect is so small that it can be attributed to rounding error, particularly since the proportions were carried only to two decimal places and the number of cases is so small. Regardless of the region of the country in which the family resides, its liberal/conservative orientation has no effect on whether or not it owns a van.

Note to the contrary that the effect of region is pronounced and consistent. Among liberal families, living in the South increases the probability of van ownership by 0.36 (0.41 − 0.05) compared to living in the North. Among conservative families, living in the South increases the probability by 0.38 (0.43 − 0.05). Within rounding error, the effect is the same for families with both philosophical orientations, which means that there is no interaction among the two predictor variables. Rather, there is only a main effect of region on van ownership, and the best estimate of its size is given by either of these estimates or their average.

CASE I–C: LIMITING CONDITIONS ARE REVEALED   Consider now the question of ownership of foreign economy cars. Does it depend on the size of the family? Table 13.17 suggests that it does. *Smaller* families are *less* likely to own a foreign economy car than are larger families! Only 8 percent of the small families but 27 percent of the large families have such automobiles. Can this counterintuitive finding be accounted for?

TABLE 13.17	Foreign Economy Car Ownership by Family Size		
		Own Foreign Economy Car?	
Size of Family	*Yes*	*No*	*Total*
4 or less	6 (8%)	72 (92%)	78 (100%)
More than 4	6 (27%)	16 (73%)	22 (100%)

TABLE 13.18	Foreign Economy Car Ownership by Family Size and Number of Cars		
		Number of Cars	
Size of Family	*1 or None*	*2 or More*	*Total*
4 or less	4%	38%	8%
More than 4	0%	35%	27%

Consider the expansion of this cross classification by adding a variable for the number of cars the family owns. Table 13.18 presents the percentage data, which indicate that it is only when large families have two or more cars that they own a foreign economy car. No large families with one car own such an automobile. The introduction of the third variable has revealed a condition that limits foreign economy car ownership—multiple-car ownership where large families are concerned.

Panel II: Initial Conclusion of a Relationship Is Retained

Consider now the analysis of station wagon ownership based on the data in Table 13.1. *A priori,* it would seem to be related to family size. A case could be made that larger families have a greater need for station wagons than smaller families.

The cross tabulation of these two variables in Table 13.19 suggests that larger families do display a higher propensity to own station wagons: 68 percent of the large families and only 4 percent of the small families own wagons.

Consider, however, whether income might also affect station wagon ownership. As Table 13.20 indicates, income has an effect over and above family size. As one goes from a small to a large family, the propensity to own a station wagon increases. With larger families, though, the increase is larger. Alternatively, if one focuses solely on large families, there is an increase in station wagon ownership from below-average-income to above-average-income families. The initial conclusion is retained: Large families do display a greater tendency to purchase station wagons. Further, the effect of family size on station wagon ownership is much larger than the effect of income.

TABLE 13.19   **Station Wagon Ownership by Family Size**

	Own Station Wagon		
Size of Family	Yes	No	Total
4 or less	3 (4%)	75 (96%)	78 (100%)
More than 4	15 (68%)	7 (32%)	22 (100%)

TABLE 13.20   **Station Wagon Ownership by Family Size and Income**

	Income		
Size of Family	Less than $37,500	More than $37,500	Total
4 or less	4%	3%	4%
More than 4	63%	71%	68%

TABLE 13.21	Financed Car Purchase by Education of Household Head

	Financed Car Purchase		
Education of Household Head	*Yes*	*No*	*Total*
High school or less	24 (30%)	56 (70%)	80 (100%)
Some college	6 (30%)	14 (70%)	20 (100%)

TABLE 13.22	Financed Car Purchase by Education of Household Head and Income

	Income		
Education of Household Head	*Less than $37,500*	*More than $37,500*	*Total*
High school or less	12%	58%	30%
Some college	40%	27%	30%

Panel III: A Relationship Is Established with the Introduction of a Third Variable

Suppose that one purpose of the study was to determine the characteristics of families who financed the purchase of their automobile. Consider the cross tabulation of installment debt compared with education of the household head. Table 13.21 results when the families included in Table 13.1 are classified into one of two educational categories—those with a high school education or less and those with some college training. As is evident, there is no relationship between education and installment debt; the percentage of families with outstanding car debt is 30 percent in each case.

Table 13.22 illustrates the situation when income is also considered in the analysis. For below-average-income families, the presence of installment debt increases with education. For above-average-income families, installment debt decreases with education. The effect of education was obscured in the original analysis because the effects canceled each other. When income is also considered, the relationship of installment debt to education is quite pronounced.

Panel IV: The Conclusion of No Relationship Is Retained with the Addition of a Third Variable

Consider once again the question of station wagon ownership. We have seen previously that it is related to family size. Let us forget this result for a minute and begin the analysis with the question: Is station wagon ownership affected by region of the country in which the family lives? Table 13.23 provides an initial answer. Station

| TABLE 13.23 | Station Wagon Ownership by Region |

	Own Station Wagon		
Region	Yes	No	Total
North	11 (18%)	49 (82%)	60 (100%)
South	7 (18%)	33 (82%)	40 (100%)

| TABLE 13.24 | Station Wagon Ownership by Region and Family Size |

	Size of Family		
Region	4 or Less	More than 4	Total
North	4%	69%	18%
South	3%	67%	18%

wagon ownership does not depend on region; 18 percent of the sample families living in both the North and the South own wagons.

Let us now consider the relationship when family size is again taken into account. Table 13.24 presents the data. Once again the percentages are constant across regions. There is minor variation, but this is due to rounding accuracy. Small families display a low propensity to purchase station wagons, regardless of whether they live in the North or the South. Large families have a high propensity, and this, too, is independent of where they live. The original lack of relationship between station wagon ownership and region of residence is confirmed with the addition of the third variable, family size.

Summary Comments on Cross Tabulation

The previous examples certainly should highlight the tremendous usefulness of cross tabulation as a tool in analysis. We have seen an application in which a third variable helped to uncover a relationship not immediately discernible, as well as applications in which a third variable triggered the modification of conclusions drawn on the basis of a two-variable classification. You may have paused to ask yourself: Why stop with three variables? Would the conclusion change with the addition of a fourth variable? A fifth? Indeed it might. The problem is that one never knows for sure when to stop introducing variables. The conclusion is always susceptible to change with the introduction of the "right" variable or variables. For example, there is currently a great deal of concern about the disappearance of the middle class and what that portends for the United States economically and socially. Yet there is a very real question as to whether the nation's middle class is in fact disappearing. Research Realities 13.2 overviews the concern and highlights what happens when

---

The Disappearance of the Middle Class: Fact or Fancy?

In recent years, there has been a growing and uncritical acceptance of the view that the United States is becoming an increasingly polarized society—with rich and poor growing more numerous, and the middle class becoming an endangered species.

The proponents of this thesis maintain that those developments are the consequence of significant structural changes in our economy and hence will become increasingly aggravated. We are warned that this will eventually have alarming political and social consequences as the middle class—"the glue that holds society together"—continues to wither away.

But this bleak outlook is curiously inconsistent with many of the nation's principal economic indicators. Over the past decade and a half alone, the U.S. economy generated more than 30 million new jobs, an increase of an imposing third in the size of the labor force. Today, close to 80 percent of all working-age men and women are earning a paycheck, up from about 70 percent 20 years ago. Over those years, real per capita income rose at an average annual pace of 1.9 percent—which has added up to almost a 50 percent increase in the real living standards of the average American. Certainly, this is not arithmetic that lends credibility to the notion that the poor are growing poorer, and that the middle class is shrinking.

Precisely how the fortunes of the nation's middle class have changed over the years varies according to which earning brackets are selected to define middle income. But whatever the definition selected, the middle class is clearly not "disappearing." It has, in fact,

been growing—but less rapidly than the nation's total household population and hence has declined in relative importance.

The affluent earning brackets have increased significantly over the years, as millions of families moved up from the middle class. Contributing powerfully to this process has been the growing prevalence of working wives. In fact, over the past two decades, the entire increase in the number of families in the highest fifth of the income scale was accounted for by working-wife families. As of last year, two-thirds of all wives in that bracket brought home a paycheck, up from only one in two 20 years ago.

With millions of families moving from the middle to the affluent brackets, the pertinent issue is why so many households have crowded into the lower brackets. Again, demographic and related social developments provide the answer.

By the early 1970s, the baby-boom generation began to come of age, which made for an extraordinary surge in the number of young adults. That generation has been inclined to marry late. Today, more than two out of every five women aged 20 to 30 are still single, compared with only one in four in 1970. Thus, over the past two decades, the number of husband-wife families in the nation increased by a mere 15 percent, but the number of single-person homes increased by an awesome 90 percent, and young singles by considerably more than that.

Not surprisingly, of the entire increase in the number of households in the lower-income brackets, a large pro-

---

other factors, such as age and marital status, are taken into account. Thus, the analyst is always in the position of "inferring" that a relationship exists. Later research may demonstrate that the inference was incorrect. This is why the accumulation of studies, rather than a single study, supporting a particular relationship is so vital to the advancement of knowledge.

Table 13.25 is an overview of the dilemma that the researcher faces. The true situation is always unknown. If it were known, there would be no need to research it. The analyst may conclude that there is no relationship, or that there is some relationship between two or more variables when in fact there is none or there is some. Only one of these four possibilities in Table 13.25 *necessarily* corresponds to a correct conclusion—when the analyst concludes that there is no relationship and in fact there is no relationship. Two of the other possibilities are necessarily incorrect,

RESEARCH REALITIES 13.2

(continued)

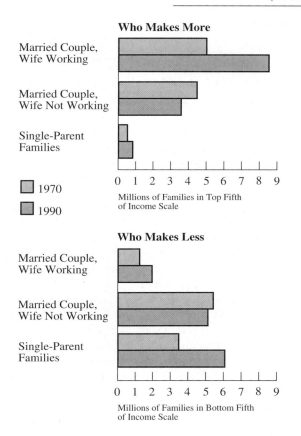

Who Makes More

Married Couple,
Wife Working

Married Couple,
Wife Not Working

Single-Parent
Families

☐ 1970
☐ 1990

0 1 2 3 4 5 6 7 8 9
Millions of Families in Top Fifth
of Income Scale

Who Makes Less

Married Couple,
Wife Working

Married Couple,
Wife Not Working

Single-Parent
Families

0 1 2 3 4 5 6 7 8 9
Millions of Families in Bottom Fifth
of Income Scale

portion was accounted for by single-person households, and because the young are more likely to divorce than those further along in age, the nation also experienced a sharp rise in the number of single-parent families.

Clearly, it's been primarily demographic and social currents, not structural changes in the nation's economy, that have made for some polarization of income in recent years. In fact, over the longer run, we have experienced a continuous upward trend in earnings at all levels of the income scale. Many in the lower brackets moved into the middle, and those in the middle into the upper. Since the mid-1970s, however, while many middle-class homes swelled into the upper-income tiers, the proportion of households with marginal earnings remained stubbornly high. The latter development was not due to a polarization of jobs and wages, as alleged, but principally to the increase in the number of young homes and the rapid growth in the number of single-parent families.

In summary, then, what the proponents of the income-polarization thesis have demonstrated is that the young earn less than at later stages in life, that single-parent families experience financial stress, and that two people working earn more than one.

Source: Fabian Linden, "How We Live," *Across the Board* 27 (December 1990), pp. 9–10. Reprinted with permission of The Conference Board, Inc., New York. For alternate perspectives, see R. C. Longworth and Sharman Stein, "The Unmaking of the Middle Class," *The Chicago Tribune* (August 20, 1995), pp. 1, 14; W. Bradford Fay, "The Fading Post-War Middle Class," *Marketing Research: A Magazine of Management & Applications* 8 (Fall 1996), pp. 47–48.

while one contains the possibility for error. That is, suppose the true situation is one of some relationship between or among the variables. The analyst has reached a correct conclusion *only* if he or she concludes that there is some relationship and has discovered its correct form.

Spurious noncorrelation results whenever the analyst concludes that there is no relationship when, in fact, there is. **Spurious correlation** occurs when the true state of affairs is one of no relationship among the variables, and the analyst concludes that a relationship exists.

Thus, the opportunities for error are great. This necessarily gives rise to a temptation to continue adding variables to the analysis *ad infinitum.* Fortunately, the analyst will be constrained in this regard by theory and by data. Theory will constrain him or her, because certain tabulations simply will not make any sense. The analyst

TABLE 13.25	**The Researcher's Dilemma**	
	True Situation	
Researcher's Conclusion	*No Relationship*	*Some Relationship*
No relationship	Correct decision	Spurious noncorrelation
Some relationship	Spurious correlation	Correct decision if concluded relationship is of proper form

will be constrained by the data in several ways. First, note that he or she will wish to successively add variables to the analysis in the form of higher dimensional cross-classification tables. This can be accomplished only if the analyst has correctly anticipated the tabulations that would be desirable. This is most important. It is too late to say, "If only we had collected information on Variable *X*!" once the analysis has begun. The relationships to be investigated, and thus the cross tabulations that should be appropriate, must be specified before the data are collected. Ideally, the analyst would have constructed dummy tables before beginning to collect the data. The dummy tables would be complete in all respects except for the number of observations falling in each cell. As a practical matter, it is usually impossible to anticipate all the cross tabulations one will want to develop. Nevertheless, careful specification of these tables at problem-definition time can return substantial benefits.

The analyst also is going to be limited by the size of the sample. In the example, since we started with 100 observations, the two-way tables were not particularly troublesome. Yet as soon as we introduced the third variable, cell sizes became extremely small. This occurred even though we treated all variables as dichotomies. Families were either below average or above average in income; they were either small or large; they lived either in the North or in the South, and so on. This was done purposely to simplify the presentation. Yet even here the three-way tabulation offers 8 cells ($2 \times 2 \times 2$) into which the observations may be placed. Assuming an even allocation of the cases to the cells, this allows only 12.5 cases per cell. This is clearly a small number on which to base any kind of conclusion. The problem, of course, would have been compounded if a greater number of levels had been used for any of the variables—for example, if families had been divided into four income groups rather than two—since the number of cells is the product of the number of levels for the variables being considered. For example, four income levels, three educational levels, and four family-size levels would generate a cross-tabulation table with 48 separate cells ($4 \times 3 \times 4$). One would need a much larger sample than 100 to have any confidence in the suggested relationships.

Presenting Tabular Data

Tabular results for commercial marketing-research studies are seldom presented using the tabulation and cross-tabulation procedures discussed so far in this chapter. Rather, the use of banners has become increasingly popular. A **banner** is a series of cross tabulations between a criterion or dependent variable and several (sometimes

ETHICAL DILEMMA 13.2

A manufacturer of aspirin had its marketing research department conduct a national survey among doctors to investigate what common household remedies doctors would be most likely to recommend when treating a patient with a cold. The question asked doctors to pick the one product they would most likely prescribe for their patients from among the choices Advil, Tylenol, aspirin, or none of the above. The distribution of responses was as follows:

Advil	100
Tylenol	100
Aspirin	200
None of the three	600
Total	1,000

The firm used the results of the survey as a basis for an extensive ad campaign that claimed: "In a national survey, doctors recommended aspirin two to one over Advil and Tylenol as the medicine they would most likely recommend to their patients suffering from colds."

- Is the firm's claim legitimate?
- Is it ethical for the firm to omit reporting the number of doctors that expressed no preference?
- What would be the fairest way to state the ad claim? Do you think stating the claim in this way would be as effective as stating it in the way the firm did?

ETHICAL DILEMMA 13.3

Sarah is very happy on the whole with the project that she has just completed for the Crumbly Cookie Company. Most of her hypotheses were supported by the survey data. Two hypotheses did not work out, but she thought that she would just leave them out of the report.

- Is it ethical to omit information that does not tally with your beliefs?
- Can valuable information be lost through the omission?

many) explanatory variables in a single table on a single page. The dependent variable, or phenomenon to be explained, typically serves as the row variable, which is also known as the *stub*. The predictor or explanatory variables serve as the column variables, with each category of these variables serving as a banner point. Table 13.26, for example, shows what the banner format might look like for the car ownership study. Although only two explanatory variables are shown, income and family size, many more could be. The top line in each row of the table indicates the absolute number possessing the characteristic, whereas the second line indicates the percentage.

TABLE 13.26	Banner Format for Car Ownership Data

Question: How Many Cars Does Your Family Own?

	Total Sample	Income		Family Size	
		Less than $37,500	More than $37,500	Four or Less	Five or More
Total	100	54	46	78	22
	100	100	100	100	100
One	75	48	27	70	5
	75	89	59	90	23
Two	23	6	17	8	15
	23	11	37	10	68
Three or more	2	0	2	0	2
	2	0	4	0	9

All percentages have been rounded to zero decimal places in keeping with recommended practice.

Banner tables have several advantages. In the first place, they allow a great amount of information to be conveyed in a very limited space. Second, their display format makes it easy for nonresearch managers to understand. Managers simply need to look at how the responses to the actual questions that were asked are distributed. A difficulty with these tables is that they tend to hide relationships in which it is necessary to consider several variables simultaneously (for example, the joint effect of income and family size on multiple-car ownership). They consequently make it more difficult to probe alternative explanations for what is producing the results. Banners also make it more difficult to detect data errors caused by improper coding or editing. Although popular, they should not be considered as a substitute for careful cross-tabulation analysis but more as an efficient form of data presentation.

Summary

This chapter reviewed the common analysis functions of editing, coding, and tabulation. Editing involves the inspection and correction, if necessary, of each questionnaire or observation form. The field edit, a preliminary edit most often conducted by the field supervisor, is aimed at correcting the most glaring omissions and inaccuracies while the field staff is still intact. The central office edit follows and involves a more careful scrutiny and correction of the completed data-collection instruments. In the central office edit, particular attention is given to such matters as incomplete answers, obviously wrong answers, and answers that reflect a lack of interest.

Coding is the procedure by which data are categorized. It involves the three-step process of (1) specifying the categories or classes into which the responses are to be placed, (2) assigning code numbers to the classes, and (3) preparing a codebook. If the data are to be analyzed by computer, a number of conventions should be followed in assigning the code numbers, including the following:

1.　Use only one character per column.

2.　Use only numeric codes.

3. Assign as many columns as are necessary to capture the variable.

4. Use the same standard codes throughout for "No information."

5. Code in a respondent identification number on each record.

Tabulation consists of counting the number of cases that fall into the various categories. The simple, or one-way, tabulation involves the count for a single variable, whereas cross tabulation involves counting the number of cases that have the characteristics described by two or more variables considered simultaneously. The one-way tabulation is useful for communicating the results of a study, and it can also be employed to locate blunders or errors, to determine the degree of item nonresponse, to locate outliers (observations very different in value from the rest), and to determine the empirical distribution of the variable in question. It also serves as basic input to the calculation of measures such as the mean, median, and standard deviation, which provide a summary picture of the distribution of the variable. Cross tabulation is one of the more useful devices for studying the relationships among and between variables because the results are easily communicated. Further, cross tabulation can provide insight into the nature of a relationship, because the addition of one or more variables to a two-way cross-classification analysis is equivalent to holding each of the variables constant.

A useful method for determining the effect that one variable has on another variable in a cross-tabulation table is to compute the difference in proportions with which the dependent variable occurs as a function of the levels of the independent variable. This can be done for zero order tables as well as conditional tables of higher order. The higher order tables are used to remove the effects of other variables that might be influencing the dependent variable.

In commercial studies, tabular results are often presented using banners, which represent a series of cross tabulations between a dependent variable and several explanatory variables in a single table.

Questions

1. Distinguish among the preliminary data analysis steps of editing, coding, and tabulation.
2. What are the differences in emphasis between a field edit and a central office edit?
3. What should an editor do with incomplete answers? Obviously wrong answers? Answers that reflect a lack of interest?
4. What are the principles that underlie the establishment of categories so that collected data may be properly coded?
5. Suppose that you have a large number of very long questionnaires, making it impossible for one person to handle the entire coding task. How should the work be divided?
6. What is the difference between a one-way tabulation and a cross tabulation? Illustrate through an example.
7. When should you use machine tabulation? Manual tabulation?
8. What are the possible ways for treating item nonresponse? Which strategy would you recommend?
9. What is a blunder?
10. What is an outlier?
11. With how many digits should percentages be reported?
12. What is a histogram? A frequency polygon? What information do they provide?
13. What is the cumulative distribution function? Of what value is it?

14. How is the mean calculated from the one-way tabulation? The standard deviation?
15. What is the proper procedure for investigating the following hypotheses using cross-tabulation analysis?
    a. Consumption of Product X depends on a person's income.
    b. Consumption of Product X depends on a person's education.
    c. Consumption of Product X depends on both.
16. How would you determine whether income or education had the greater effect on the consumption of Product X?
17. Illustrate the procedure from Questions 15 and 16 with data of your own choosing; that is, develop the tables, fill in the assumed numbers, and indicate the conclusions to be drawn from each table.
18. What is meant by the statement: the introduction of an additional variable
    a. refined the original explanation?
    b. revealed a spurious explanation?
    c. provided limiting conditions?
19. How do you explain the condition in which a two-way cross tabulation of Variables X and Y revealed no relationship between X and Y but the introduction of Z revealed a definite relationship between X and Y?
20. What is the researcher's dilemma with respect to cross-tabulation analysis?
21. What constraints operate on researchers that prevent them from adding variables to cross-classification tables *ad infinitum*?
22. What are banners?

Applications and Problems

1. A marketing research supplier has five employees in its coding department. The firm has just received 10,000 completed mail questionnaires. The survey contains 175 questions. How would you recommend that the company handle the editing and coding process? What would you instruct them to look for in the edit, and how would you recommend they handle each of these problems if found?

2. The WITT TV station was conducting research to develop programs that would be well received by the viewing audience and would be considered a dependable source of information. A two-part questionnaire was administered by personal interviews to a panel of 3,000 respondents residing in the city of Chicago. The field and office edits were done simultaneously so that the deadline of May 1 could be met. A senior supervisor, Mr. Z, was placed in charge of the editing tasks and was assisted by two junior supervisors and two field workers. The two field workers were instructed to discard instruments that were illegible or incomplete. Both the junior supervisors were instructed to scrutinize 1,500 of the instruments each for incomplete answers, wrong answers, and responses that indicated a lack of interest. They were instructed to discard instruments that had greater than five incomplete or wrong answers (the questionnaire contained 30 questions). In addition, they were asked to use their judgment in assessing whether the respondent showed a lack of interest, in which case they should also discard the questionnaire.
   a. Critically evaluate the preceding editing tasks. Please be specific.
   b. Make specific recommendations to Mr. D. Witt, the owner of the WITT TV station, about how the editing should be done.

3. Establish response categories and codes for the question, "What do you like about this new brand of cereal?"

4. Code the following responses using your categories and codes.
   a. "$1.50 is a reasonable price to pay for the cereal."
   b. "The raisins and nuts add a nice flavor."
   c. "The sizes of the packages are convenient."

d. "I like the sugar coating on the cereal."

e. "The container does not tear and fall apart easily."

f. "My kids like the cartoons on the back of the package."

g. "It is reasonably priced compared to other brands."

h. "The package is attractive and easy to spot in the store."

i. "I like the price; it is not so low that I doubt the quality and at the same time it is not so high as to be unaffordable."

j. "The crispness and lightness of the cereal improve the taste."

5. Establish response categories and codes for the following question that was asked of a sample of business executives: "In your opinion, which types of companies have not been affected by the present economic climate?"

6. Code the following responses using your categories and codes.

a. *Washington Post*   f. Prentice-Hall   k. Holiday Inns

b. Colgate-Palmolive   g. Hoover   l. Dryden Press

c. Gillette   h. Fabergé   m. Singer

d. Hilton Hotels   i. Marine Midlands Banks   n. Saga

e. Chase Manhattan   j. Zenith Radio   o. Bank America

7. A large manufacturer of electronic components for automobiles recently conducted a study to determine the average value of electronic components per automobile. Personal interviews were conducted with a random sample of 400 respondents. The following information was secured with respect to each subject's "main" vehicle when he or she had more than one.

Average Dollar Value of Electronic Equipment per Automobile

Dollar Value of Electronic Equipment	Number of Automobiles
Less than $50	35
$51 to $100	40
$101 to $150	55
$151 to $200	65
$201 to $250	65
$251 to $300	75
$301 to $350	40
$351 to $400	20
More than $401	5
Total number of automobiles	400

a. Convert the preceding information into percentages.

b. Compute the cumulative absolute frequencies.

c. Compute the cumulative relative frequencies.

d. Prepare a histogram and frequency polygon with the average value of electronic equipment on the x-axis and the absolute frequency on the y-axis.

e. Graph the empirical cumulative distribution function with the average value on the x-axis and the relative frequency on the y-axis.

f. Locate the median, first sample quartile, and third sample quartile on the cumulative distribution function in part e.

g. Calculate the mean, standard deviation, and variance for the frequency distribution. (Hint: Use the midpoint of each class interval and multiply that by the appropriate frequency. For the interval starting at $401, assume the midpoint is 425.5.)

8. An analyst for a leading *Fortune* 500 company demanded that all percentages be reported to one decimal place on graphs being presented to upper management. Several

of the cross-tabulation cells had sample sizes of less than 30. Discuss why you feel it is or is not necessary to record all the percentages to one decimal place.

9. An office-products retailer recently conducted a study. One question asked of those interviewed was the following: "In an average month, how many times does your company purchase office supplies from an office-products retailer?" The following table lists the results of this question. Calculate the mean and standard deviation.

Value	Frequency
0	25
1	10
2	15
3	5
4	20

10. A manufacturer was interested in assessing how children ages four, five, and six play with one of the manufacturer's toys. Each child was asked 15 questions. Following the child's completed interview, the parent was asked the same 15 questions to validate the child's answers. The following table lists the number of responses to selected items from the survey. One hundred interviews were conducted with both the parent and the child. Notice that item response rates varied from question to question. For each question, state at least one method that could be used to attempt to correct for this item nonresponse bias.

Question	Number of Children Responding	Number of Parents Responding
Age of child	95	100
Location of play	80	85
How much the child liked the toy	30	50

11. A large financial institution wanted to know which options were most important to small businesses. The financial institution hypothesized that the options that businesses found to be important would vary as annual sales of the businesses varied. The financial organization set up a cross tabulation to investigate if any changes in importance were occurring between the groups of businesses. The following table lists the number of businesses that reported each of the options as most important. Calculate the percentages. Interpret your calculations.

	Annual Sales	
Option	Under $2 Million	$2 to $10 Million
Checking account	50	30
Mutual fund	10	70
Savings account	40	50

12. A social organization was interested in determining if there were various demographic characteristics that might be related to people's propensity to contribute to charities. The organization was particularly interested in determining whether individuals above age 40 were more likely to contribute larger amounts than individuals below age 40. The average contribution in the population was $1,500, and this figure was used to divide the individuals in the sample into two groups, those who contributed large amounts or more than average versus those who contributed less than average. Table 1 presents a two-way classification of the sample of individuals by contributions and age.

TABLE 1	Personal Contributions and Age

Personal Contribution	Age 39 or Less	40 or More	Total
Less than or equal to $1,500	79	50	129
More than $1,500	11	60	71
Total	90	110	200

In addition, the social organization wanted to determine if contributions depended on income, age, or both. Table 2 presents the simultaneous treatment of age and income. The median income in the population was $38,200, and this figure was used to split the sample into two groups.

a. Does the amount of personal contributions depend on age? Generate the necessary tables to justify your answer.

b. Does the amount of personal contributions depend on age alone? Generate the necessary tables to justify your answer.

c. Present the percentage of contributions that are more than $1,500 by age and income in tabular form. Interpret the table.

13. Suppose that the following exhibit was prepared to present a portion of the results of a national survey aimed at identifying demographic and socioeconomic differences between individuals with published telephone numbers and individuals with nonpublished telephone numbers.

	Published Telephone Numbers	Nonpublished Telephone Numbers
Sex		
Male	43%	40%
Female	57	60
Age		
Under 25	8%	6%
25–34	21	26
35–44	13	27
45–54	14	17
55–64	19	15
65 and Over	25	9
Ethnic Background		
White	95%	87%
Nonwhite (including Hispanic)	5	13
Household Income		
Under $5,000	10%	12%
$5,000–9,999	16	14
$10,000–14,999	15	16
$15,000–19,999	15	16
$20,000–24,999	16	15
$25,000–39,999	18	21
$40,000 or More	10	6

TABLE 2	Personal Contributions by Age and Income

Personal Contributions	Income					
	Less than or Equal to $38,200		More than $38,200		Total	
	Age		Age		Age	
	39 or Less	40 or More	39 or Less	40 or More	39 or Less	40 or More
Less than or equal to $1,500	63	22	16	28	79	50
More than $1,500	7	18	4	42	11	60
Total	70	40	20	70	90	110

a. Describe the type of analysis represented in the exhibit. Is this an appropriate representation of the information on which the exhibit is based? Why or why not?

b. Suppose that the exhibit is based on 4,060 responses; 3,586 respondents indicated that they had a published telephone number and 474 indicated that they did not publish their number. Complete the exhibit below:

	Published Telephone Numbers	Nonpublished Telephone Numbers	Total
	Frequency (%)	Frequency (%)	Frequency (%)
Sex			
Male			
Female			
Age			
Under 25			
25–34			
35–44			
45–54			
55–64			
65 and Over			

	Published Telephone Numbers	Nonpublished Telephone Numbers	Total
	Frequency (%)	Frequency (%)	Frequency (%)
Ethnic Background			
White			
Nonwhite (including Hispanic)			

	Published Telephone Numbers	Nonpublished Telephone Numbers	Total
	Frequency (%)	*Frequency (%)*	*Frequency (%)*
Household Income			
Under $5,000			
$5,000–9,999			
$10,000–14,999			
$15,000–19,999			
$20,000–24,999			
$25,000–39,999			
$40,000 or More			

NFO Applications   NFO Research Inc. (NFO) recently conducted a study of the ground caffeinated coffee market because several of its clients operate in this market. The study was undertaken with several objectives in mind, including the identification of benefits that consumers seek and the comparison of consumer opinions regarding several of the brands offered in the market.

The questionnaire in Figure 8.2 was designed to accomplish these objectives. This questionnaire was mailed to 400 individuals previously identified as consumers of ground caffeinated coffee (personally drinking at least one cup per day). Of those mailed out, 328 were returned; 299 of these were judged to be usable responses.

The data collected from these consumers are stored in a free-field format (space delimited) ASCII file named "coffee.dat" that is available on the data disc. The coding format for the data follows. Missing data are coded −99 for all items and should be disregarded for all analyses. Although the data included are basically the data collected, some items or responses were generated to complete the data set.

Coding Format for NFO Coffee Study

Question Number	Variable (Variable Number)	Coding Specification
—	Questionnaire ID (VAR1)	—
1	Usual Method of Preparation (VAR2)	1 = automatic drip 2 = electric percolator 3 = stove-top percolator 4 = stove-top dripolator

2a	Ever Use:
	  Folgers (VAR3)
	  Hills Bros. (VAR4)
	  Maxwell House Regular (VAR5)
	  Maxwell House Master Blend (VAR6)
	  Yuban (VAR7)
	  Other (VAR8)
		0 = no
		1 = yes

2b	Brand Used Most Often (VAR9)	1 = Folgers 2 = Hills Bros. 3 = Maxwell House Regular 4 = Maxwell House Master Blend 5 = Yuban 6 = Other

2c	On Hand:
	  Folgers (VAR10)
	  Hills Bros. (VAR11)
		0 = no
		1 = yes

(continued)

Question Number	*Variable (Variable Number)*	*Coding Specification*
	Maxwell House Regular (VAR12)	
	Maxwell House Master Blend (VAR13)	
	Yuban (VAR14)	
	Other (VAR15)	
2d	Brand Will Buy Next (VAR16)	1 = Folgers 2 = Hills Bros. 3 = Maxwell House Regular 4 = Maxwell House Master Blend 5 = Yuban 6 = Other
2e	Overall Rating: Folgers (VAR17) Hills Bros. (VAR18) Maxwell House Regular (VAR19) Maxwell House Master Blend (VAR20) Yuban (VAR21) Other (VAR22)	Rating 1–10, where 1 = dislike it extremely 10 = like it extremely
3	Add Nothing (VAR23) Add Dairy Creamer (VAR24) Add Nondairy Creamer (VAR25) Add Sugar (VAR26) Add Artificial Sweetener (VAR27) Add Something Else (VAR28)	0 = no 1 = yes
4	Are You Primary Coffee Purchaser (VAR29)	0 = no 1 = yes
5	Rich Taste (VAR30) Always Fresh (VAR31) Gets Day Off to Good Start (VAR32) Full-Bodied Taste (VAR33) Rich Aroma in the Cup (VAR34) Good Value for the Money (VAR35) Best Coffee in the Morning (VAR36) Rich Aroma in the Can/Bag (VAR37) Smooth Taste (VAR38) Highest Quality Coffee (VAR39) Premium Brand (VAR40) Not Bitter (VAR41) Coffee That Brightens Day Most (VAR42) Costs More Than Other Brands (VAR43) Strong Taste (VAR44) Has No Aftertaste (VAR45) Economy Brand (VAR46) Rich Aroma While Brewing (VAR47) Best Ground Coffee Available (VAR48) Enjoy Drinking with Meal (VAR49) Costs Less Than Other Brands (VAR50)	Importance Ratings, 0–10, where 0 = not at all important 10 = extremely important
6	(see table below)	All variables are rating scales coded 0–10, where 0 = does not describe at all 10 = describes completely

Variable	Folgers Var. No.	Hills Bros. Var. No.	Maxwell House Regular Var. No.	Maxwell House Master Blend Var. No.	Yuban Var. No.
Rich Taste	VAR51	VAR72	VAR93	VAR114	VAR135
Always Fresh	VAR52	VAR73	VAR94	VAR115	VAR136
Good Start	VAR53	VAR74	VAR95	VAR116	VAR137
Full-Bodied Taste	VAR54	VAR75	VAR96	VAR117	VAR138
Rich Aroma/Cup	VAR55	VAR76	VAR97	VAR118	VAR139
Good Value	VAR56	VAR77	VAR98	VAR119	VAR140
Best Coffee in AM	VAR57	VAR78	VAR99	VAR120	VAR141
Rich Aroma/Can	VAR58	VAR79	VAR100	VAR121	VAR142
Smooth Taste	VAR59	VAR80	VAR101	VAR122	VAR143
Highest Quality	VAR60	VAR81	VAR102	VAR123	VAR144
Premium Brand	VAR61	VAR82	VAR103	VAR124	VAR145
Not Bitter	VAR62	VAR83	VAR104	VAR125	VAR146
Brightens Day Most	VAR63	VAR84	VAR105	VAR126	VAR147
Costs More	VAR64	VAR85	VAR106	VAR127	VAR148
Strong Taste	VAR65	VAR86	VAR107	VAR128	VAR149
No Aftertaste	VAR66	VAR87	VAR108	VAR129	VAR150
Economy Brand	VAR67	VAR88	VAR109	VAR130	VAR151
Rich Aroma/Brewing	VAR68	VAR89	VAR110	VAR131	VAR152
Best Available	VAR69	VAR90	VAR111	VAR132	VAR153
Enjoy with Meal	VAR70	VAR91	VAR112	VAR133	VAR154
Costs Less	VAR71	VAR92	VAR113	VAR134	VAR155

Question Number	Variable (Variable Number)	Coding Specification
7a	Gender (VAR156)	1 = male
		2 = female
7b	Age (VAR157)	Actual Age Coded

Because this is a relatively large data file (3,168 bytes), it will probably be useful to conduct the analyses necessary to complete the following application problems using a personal computer with a hard-disk drive or on a mainframe computer.

14. Produce a histogram for the age variable. Does it appear that anything has been obviously miscoded? If so, explain.

15. Produce a histogram for the variable "brand used most often." Determine an estimate of market share for the various brands based on this data set.

16. Cross tabulate "brand used most often" with "age," when the age variable has been recoded into the following categories:

   35 years or less
   36–45 years
   46–59 years
   60 years or more

   Generate percentages as well as frequency counts for each cell. What general conclusions may be drawn based on this information?

17. How is the perceived relationship between "brand used most often" and "age" affected by the addition of a third variable, "sex of the respondent," to the analysis? Explain.

18. Suppose that it is your job to compare Folgers with Maxwell House Regular. Produce a snake diagram profiling these brands on the 21 attributes included in Question 6 of the questionnaire. What do your results indicate?

Thorndike Sports Equipment Video Case

1. If Ted's suggestion to use the sample mean in the body of the print ad were followed, what message would the majority of consumers take away from the advertisement? Why?
2. Would you feel comfortable applying Ted's solution to this problem knowing that a proportion of consumers would believe that their racquet would withstand 230 pounds of pressure? Why or why not?

A P P E N D I X   1 3 A

Contingency Tables and Chi-Squares

In this appendix, we present statistical tests such as the chi-square that enable the marketing researcher to determine whether the pattern observed in frequency data is no more than random fluctuations due to sampling variability or represents something more fundamental. We begin with the chi-square on a single variable computed on a simple one-way tabulation. We then proceed to the chi-square for a two-way cross-classification table. We close with a discussion of logit models.

Chi-Square Test on One Variable

Recall that in Chapter 13, when we were exploring the car ownership data, our examination included the distribution of income for the families in our sample. A question that demographic data are frequently used to address is, "How representative is our sample?" The chi-square statistic can arm the marketing researcher with an answer. Suppose through the use of secondary data, for example, the U.S. Census, you were able to determine the income distribution for your target market (such as your metropolitan area, your area of the country, and your particular head-of-household age focus). The car ownership income data from Table 13.4 are reproduced in the second column of Table 13A.1 for convenience, and the target percentages derived from the secondary data comprise the third column in Table 13A.1. The question of representativeness is directly answered by comparing the data in the sample to the distribution that would be expected if the sample reflected the population.

We'll label the sample data o for "observed" frequency and e for the data you would "expect" if your sample were representative of the target population. Thus, the second and third columns of Table 13A.1 are labeled o_i and e_i respectively, denoting the observed number and expected number of observations that fall in the ith row for each of the r rows of income level. The chi-square is an easy spread-sheet computation. The differences between the observed and expected frequencies are computed $(o_i - e_i)$, and standardized by dividing by $\sqrt{e_i}$ (to compensate for the fact that a difference of, say, 5 is a proportionately smaller error where the base numbers are bigger such as 22) than in the table where the numbers are smaller (for example, 5 or 6). Square those pieces and sum them up, and the calculated χ^2 statistic is defined as follows:

$$\chi^2 = \sum_{i=1}^{r} \frac{(o_i - e_i)^2}{e_i}$$

The chi-square for these data equals 44.188, and by comparing it to a table of critical values, it can be interpreted as big (that is, the observed sample data do not follow the expected distribution) or small (the sample may be "off" from the target but the difference may be attributable to sampling errors). Critical values for the χ^2 can be found in Appendix B in the back of this book using the intersection of an alpha-level and a "degrees of freedom" parameter, which is computed as $(r - 1)$ for χ^2 tests on one-way tables, that is, the number of rows in the table minus one. Our income table has 11 rows, and the critical χ^2 value for 10 degrees of freedom is 18.31. Our χ^2 value exceeds the tabled, critical value, so we reject the "null hypothesis" that our sample resembles the population, and instead conclude that our sample is unlike the general population in terms of its distribution of incomes. (It is rare that a sample exactly resembles a population, and if there had been a good fit on income, another demographic variable might have been skewed. So the marketer must consider the extent to which the differences in income may affect the research questions at hand.)

Standardized Residuals

It might seem that the fourth column in Table 13A.1 was merely a "computational" worksheet column, en route to the final column to be summed, but it also contains valuable information. Whereas the χ^2 indicates, overall, whether the sample reflects

---

TABLE 13A.1   Car Ownership Data: One-Way Chi-Square on Income

Income	o_i: Number of Families	e_i: Target Figures	Standardized Residuals $\dfrac{(o_i - e_i)}{\sqrt{e_i}}$	$\dfrac{(o_i - e_i)^2}{e_i}$
Less than $15,000	8	22	−2.985	8.909
$15,000–$24,900	25	19	1.377	1.895
$25,000–$34,900	15	12	0.866	0.750
$35,000–$44,900	18	18	0.000	0.000
$45,000–$54,900	8	6	0.816	0.667
$55,000–$64,900	8	5	1.342	1.800
$65,000–$74,900	7	6	0.408	0.167
$75,000–$84,900	3	5	−0.894	0.800
$85,000–$94,900	1	5	−1.789	3.200
$95,000–$104,900	3	1.5	1.225	1.500
More than $105,000	4	0.5	4.950	24.500
Total	100	100	$\chi^2 =$	44.188

the population, the numbers in the fourth column are called "standardized residuals," and they indicate, specifically for which income brackets, whether the sample reflects the population or differs from it. Standardized residuals are interpretable, as with z-scores, in that if they exceed 1.96 in magnitude, they are significant.[1]

Note, for example, the comparison on the income bracket of $35,000–44,900, where coincidentally, our sample had exactly the same number of families as would be expected by the target population data. Hence, the residual $(o_i - e_i)$ is zero. Less perfect matches are found in the other rows.

Many of the standardized residuals are positive, indicating that our sample contained more families with incomes in those categories than we would have predicted just knowing the population data. Conversely, the standardized residuals that are negative indicate that our sample contained fewer families with those incomes than we would have expected.

When the standardized residuals do not exceed 1.96, those differences, positive or negative, are attributable to sampling chance. When they exceed 1.96, they are considered to be "real" effects in the sample. For example, the −2.985 indicates that our sample included significantly fewer families with incomes less than $15,000 than the target contains. On the high end of the income scale, the 4.950 indicates that the sample was comprised of significantly more families whose incomes exceed $105,000 than characterizes the target population.

In total, we learn that our sample is somewhat more affluent than the target population. This difference must be factored into any subsequent projections about the rest of the data.

One-way chi-square statistics can be useful in numerous ways. This example used as expected frequencies known population profile data. If the rows instead were manufacturers (such as General Mills or Kraft) or brands in a category (such as Compaq, Dell, or Aerostar), the observed data may be market shares or sales in numbers of units, and the expected frequencies may be the comparable data on the previous selling quarter. Many types of "benchmark" data can be used as the expected frequencies against which to compare one's sample data. Another application of the one-way chi-square is described in the box, Research Realities 13A.1.

Contingency Tables: Chi-Square and Related Indices

We now turn to the analysis of frequencies for variables studied two at a time. In Chapter 13, a number of research questions were raised involving the relationship between auto purchases and family characteristics. A problem frequently encountered in the analysis of nominal data is specifying the nature of the relationship between the variables in the cross classification. Are they independent of each other, or, rather, if you knew one variable such as size of family, could you predict better than just guessing the other, that is, number of cars? Statistical tests of significance were not computed in Chapter 13. Thus, we do not know yet whether the results reflected sample aberrations or true population conditions. The chi-square statistical test for data in contingency tables is ideally suited for investigating these questions.

---

[1]Shelby J. Haberman, "The Analysis of Residuals in Cross-Classified Tables," *Biometrika* 29 (1973), pp. 205–220.

RESEARCH REALITIES 13A.1

It's a Conspiracy!

In the late 1990s, Mars Candy polled children to indicate their favorite colors, whereupon Mars introduced the new M&M color, blue.[1] Subsequent investigation has indicated, however, that the blue M&M may appear less frequently in bags of these chocolates than its nonblue counterparts.

Conduct a study for yourself. Go out and purchase some M&M's, er, data. (Perhaps your dean will offer you research funds to study this phenomenon.) Count the number of each color, and sum those counts. If you found, say, 120 M&M's in the bag, how would you expect those 120 observations to be distributed over the six color categories; that is, what are the expected frequencies?

Compute the χ^2. Overall, what does it indicate? What do the standardized residuals tell you?

Do the answers change if you select Peanut M&M's instead of Plain? Peanut Butter? Almond? What special result do you find for the latter two?[2]

	o_i: Number of M&M's	e_i: Expected Number of M&M's	$\dfrac{(o_i - e_i)}{\sqrt{(e_i)}}$	$\dfrac{(o_i - e_i)^2}{(e_i)}$
Blue				
Brown				
Green				
Orange				
Red				
Yellow				
Total:				$\chi^2 =$

[1] Ronald D. Fricker, Jr., "The Mysterious Case of the Blue M&M's," *Chance* 9 (1996), pp. 19–22.

[2] Statisticians distinguish between a "sampling zero," where you could have observations in that row, but you simply did not (for example, your sample may have been too small), and a "structural zero," where it is not possible to obtain observations in that row. Which do you suppose the zeros are for Peanut Butter and Almond orange M&M's?

TABLE 13A.2   Frequency Data on Car Ownership

	Number of Cars		
Family Size	1 or None	2 or More	Total
4 or less	70	8	78
5 or more	5	17	22
Total	75	25	100

For the chi-square on a two-way table, there is only one null hypothesis:

H_0: the row variable (income) is independent of the column variable (number of cars)

To say two variables are "independent" is also to say they show no association, which is analogous to saying they are not correlated. For example, consider the data in Table 13A.2. If the two variables are not related, then knowing the size of a family would not help predict the number of cars accurately—there is no contingent relationship. If asked to guess the number of cars in a household, one would use the distribution in the sample as a whole (the marginal frequencies of 75 versus 25 tell us the odds of having 0 or 1 car versus 2 or more cars are 3:1). Those proportions would be used as an estimate regardless of family size (that is, for either row). The question before us is whether we can improve our prediction if we take into account family size.

The hypothesis to be tested states that the row variable, A (to use a generic label), is independent of the column variable, B. In Table 13A.2, A would be family size and B, the number of cars the family owns. Moreover, let:

$$
\begin{aligned}
A_1 &= \text{family of 4 or fewer members} \\
A_2 &= \text{family of 5 or more members} \\
B_1 &= \text{family owns 0 or 1 car} \\
B_2 &= \text{family owns 2 or more cars}
\end{aligned}
$$

Recall from your basic statistics class that the probability of two events occurring jointly if those events are independent is simply the product of the likelihood of either occurring: $P(AB) = P(A) \times P(B)$. In the application to contingency tables, if variables A and B are indeed independent, then the probability of occurrence of the event $A_1 B_1$ (a family with 4 or fewer members and 0 or 1 cars) is given as the product of the separate probabilities for A_1 and B_1; that is,

$$
P(A_1 B_1) = P(A_1) P(B_1)
$$

The probability $P(A_1)$ is given by the number of cases possessing the characteristic A_1, that is, n_{A_1} (or the number of small families), over the total number of cases, n. $P(A_1)$ is thus:

$$
\frac{n_{A_1}}{n} = \frac{78}{100}
$$

Similarly, $P(B_1)$ is given by the number of cases having the characteristic B_1, that is, n_{B_1} (or the number of families having 0 or 1 car), over the total sample size, or $P(B_1) = n_{B_1}/n = 75/100$. The joint probability $P(A_1 B_1)$ is:

$$
P(A_1 B_1) = P(A_1) P(B_1) = \left(\frac{78}{100}\right)\left(\frac{75}{100}\right)
$$

Given a total of $n = 100$ cases, the number expected to fall in the cell $A_1 B_1$, e_{11}, is given as the product of the total number of cases and the probability of any one of these cases falling into the $A_1 B_1$ cell; that is,

$$
e_{11} = nP(A_1 B_1) = 100\left(\frac{78}{100}\right)\left(\frac{75}{100}\right)
$$

Note that two of the n's cancel, so the formula for e_{11} reduces to:

$$
\begin{aligned}
e_{11} &= nP(A_1 B_1) = nP(A_1) P(B_1) \\
&= n \frac{n_{A_1}}{n} \frac{n_{B_1}}{n} = \frac{n_{A_1} n_{B_1}}{n} \\
&= \frac{78 \times 75}{100}
\end{aligned}
$$

TABLE 13A.3	Expected Frequencies on Car Ownership Data	
	0 or 1 Cars	*2 or More*
4 or less	58.5	19.5
5 or more	16.5	5.5

Thus, to generate the expected frequencies for each cell, one merely needs to multiply the marginal frequencies and divide by the total. The expected frequencies, all calculated in like manner, are entered in Table 13A.3.

The χ^2 value is calculated over the r rows and c columns, with o_{ij} and e_{ij} denoting the observed and expected number of observations in the (ij)th cell:

$$\chi^2 = \sum_{i=1}^{r} \sum_{j=1}^{c} \frac{(o_{ij} - e_{ij})^2}{e_{ij}}$$

$$= \frac{(70 - 58.5)^2}{58.5} + \frac{(8 - 19.5)^2}{19.5} + \frac{(5 - 16.5)^2}{16.5} + \frac{(17 - 5.5)^2}{5.5}$$

$$= 2.261 + 6.782 + 8.015 + 24.046$$

$$= 41.104$$

The expected frequencies in any row add to the marginal total. This property must be true because of the way the expected frequencies were calculated. There are thus $(c - 1)$ degrees of freedom in a row, where c is the number of columns. Similarly, the expected frequencies in a column must sum to the marginal total and thus there are $(r - 1)$ degrees of freedom per column, where r is the number of rows. The total degrees of freedom (df) in a two-way contingency table are thus given by $(r - 1)(c - 1)$.

In our problem, $df = (2 - 1)(2 - 1) = 1$. Using an $\alpha = 0.05$, the tabled critical value of χ^2 from Appendix B in the back of the book is 3.84. The computed $\chi^2 = 41.104$ thus falls in the critical region. The null hypothesis of independence is rejected. Thus, we conclude that family size is a factor in determining number of cars purchased.

In one form or another, the chi-square test is probably the most widely used test in marketing research, and the serious student is well advised to become familiar with its requirements. Research Realities 13A.2 summarizes them.

Contingency Coefficient

While the χ^2 contingency table test indicates whether two variables are independent, it does not measure the strength of association when they are dependent. The contingency coefficient (C) can be used for this purpose. It is directly related to the χ^2 test, so it can be generated with relatively little additional computational effort:

$$C = \sqrt{\frac{\chi^2}{n + \chi^2}}$$

where n is the sample size and χ^2 is calculated in the normal way.

RESEARCH REALITIES 13A.2

Requirements for the Chi-Square Test

1. The test deals with frequencies. Percentage values need to be converted to counts of the number of cases in each cell.

2. The chi-square distribution, although continuous, is being used to approximate the distribution of a discrete variable. This approximation results in the computed value being proportionately inflated if too many of the expected frequencies are small. It is generally agreed that only a few cells (fewer than 20 percent) should be permitted to have expected frequencies fewer than 5, and none should have expected frequencies fewer than 1. Categories may be meaningfully combined to conform to this rule.

3. Multiple answers per respondent should not be analyzed with chi-square contingency table analysis, because the normal tabled critical values of the chi-square statistic for a specified alpha error no longer apply when more than one cross-tabulation analysis is conducted with the same data. The choices for respondents' answers must comprise exclusive categories (a consumer is classified as one and only one type).

4. Each observation should be independent of the others. The chi-square test would not be appropriate, for example, for analyzing observations on the same individuals in a pretest-posttest experiment.

The calculated χ^2 for the data just described was 41.104. This value is larger than the critical tabled value, so the null hypothesis of independence was rejected. The conclusion that naturally follows—that family size affects the number of cars purchased—is an interesting finding, but it is only part of the story. Although the variables are dependent, what is the strength of the association between them? The contingency coefficient helps answer this question:

$$C = \sqrt{\frac{\chi^2}{n + \chi^2}} = \sqrt{\frac{41.104}{100 + 41.104}} = 0.540$$

Does this value indicate strong or weak association between the variables? We cannot say without comparing the calculated value against its limits. When there is no association between the variables, the contingency coefficient will be zero. Unfortunately, the contingency coefficient does not possess the attractive property of the Pearson product-moment correlation coefficient (to be discussed in greater detail in Chapter 16) of being equal to 1 when the variables are completely dependent or perfectly correlated. Rather, its upper limit is a function of the number of categories. When the number of categories is the same for each variable (that is, $r = c$), the upper limit on the contingency coefficient for two perfectly correlated variables is: $\sqrt{(r - 1)/r}$.

In the example at hand, $r = c = 2$, and thus the upper limit for the contingency coefficient is 0.707. The calculated value, 0.540, is more than halfway between the limits of zero for no association and 0.707 for perfect association, suggesting that there is moderately strong association between size of family and number of cars purchased.

Index of Predictive Association

One of the difficulties associated with the contingency coefficient is interpreting the strength of the association between the variables as judged by the calculated value. For instance, even though we were able to say that there was moderate association between the variables of cross classification, the interpretation was not as straightforward as it would have been if the Pearson correlation coefficient, r, had been calculated. As we shall discuss in Chapter 16, r^2 indicates the proportion of the variance in one variable that is accounted for by covariation in the other, a clear measure of the strength of the association between the variables. The contingency coefficient has no such standard to assist the analyst in interpreting the results. The index of predictive association is "more directly interpretable" in this regard.[2]

Consider once more the data on size of family and car ownership. There is one predictor variable, A (family size) and one criterion variable, B (number of cars in the household), and both had been divided into two classes: A_1 and A_2, and B_1 and B_2. Second, the purpose is to predict the B classification of an object chosen at random; that is, should it be predicted as falling into category B_1, the family owns 0 or 1 car, or B_2, the family owns 2 or more cars. Assume initially that we have no knowledge of the A classification. The best estimate for the randomly chosen object is classification B_1, because 75 percent of all the observations of the B variate fall in this category. Proceeding on this basis, we would make 75 percent of all assignments correctly, since we would assign them all to B_1. Conversely, we would be wrong 25 percent of the time. Suppose now that we know the A classification of the object chosen at random. If the A classification is A_1 (the family is small) the best guess is B_1, since 70 of 78 cases possessing A_1 fall in the B_1 classification. If the A classification is A_2 (the family is large), the best guess is B_2 (17 of 22 cases).

The index of predictive association, $\lambda_{B|A}$, measures the relative decrease in the probability of error by taking account of the A classification in predicting the B classification, over the error of prediction when the A classification is unknown. In the example, $\lambda_{B|A} = 0.48$. The errors in predicting the B classification are reduced by 48 percent by taking account of the A classification. The original classification error rate is 25 percent; these errors drop 12 percent (25 percent times 0.48 equals 12 percent; there would have been 25 misclassifications without knowing A, but with A, only 13 would be misclassified).

The index of predictive association varies from 0 to 1. It is zero if the A variable is of no help in predicting B. It is 1 if the knowledge of the A classification allows the B classification to be predicted perfectly. The index, predicting B from A, is calculated as follows. Let

$n_{.m}$ be the largest marginal frequency among the B classes, and
n_{am} be the largest frequency in the ath row of the table.

[2]The index was originally proposed by Leo A. Goodman and William H. Kruskal, "Measures of Association for Cross-Classifications," *Journal of the American Statistical Association* 49 (December 1954), pp. 732–764. See also Lawrence J. Feick, "Analyzing Marketing Research Data with Association Models," *Journal of Marketing Research* 21 (November 1984), pp. 376–386; Jean Dickinson Gibbons, *Nonparametric Measures of Association* (Thousand Oaks, CA: Sage, 1993), for discussions of a number of other association coefficients that can be used with categorical or nominal data.

Then

$$\lambda_{BIA} = \frac{\sum_a n_{am} - n_{.m}}{n - n_{.m}}$$

where $\sum_a n_{am}$ is taken over all the A classes. For the example, $n = 100$. The largest marginal frequency among the B classes, $n_{.m}$, is 75, corresponding to 0 or 1 cars. If a family has 4 or fewer members, the largest frequency in the first row of the cross-classification table, n_{1m}, is 70; similarly, $n_{2m} = 17$. Thus, the index of predictive association is:

$$\lambda_{BIA} = \frac{(n_{1m} + n_{2m}) - n_{.m}}{n - n_{.m}} = \frac{(70 + 17) - 75}{100 - 75} = 0.48$$

We reduced the errors in predicting B from A, from 25 to 13, a 48 percent improvement. The enhanced predictive accuracy is substantial. Recall also that by using the chi-square test for independence on this contingency table, we had convincingly rejected the notion of independence between the variables.

These findings demonstrate the two important questions in association analysis. First, is there an association between the criterion and predictor variables, or are they independent? Second, if they are dependent, by how much are predictions about the criterion variable improved by taking into account the important predictor variables? The chi-square test and contingency coefficient answer the first question, and the index of predictive association is used to answer the second. The distinction between these two questions is analogous to the difference between correlation and regression, techniques discussed in greater detail in Chapter 16, which analogously seek linear association and prediction, respectively.

Log Linear Models

Log linear models extend the chi-square test to frequency tables of three or more variables.[3] For example, we might explore the relationship between family size, household income, and number of cars, as in Table 13A.4.

---

[3]For more details on log linear models, see Stephen E. Fienberg, *The Analysis of Cross-Classified Categorical Data*, 2nd ed. (Cambridge, MA: The MIT Press, 1980); John J. Kennedy, *Analyzing Qualitative Data: Introductory Log-Linear Analysis for Behavioral Research* (New York: Praeger, 1983); David Knoke and Peter J. Burke, *Log-Linear Models* (Beverly Hills, CA: Sage, 1980); Alfred Demaris, *Logit Modeling: Practical Applications* (Newbury Park, CA: Sage, 1992); John H. Aldrich and Forrest D. Nelson, *Linear Probability, Logit, and Probit Models* (Newbury Park, CA: Sage, 1984); Scott Menard, *Applied Logistic Regression Analysis* (Thousand Oaks, CA: Sage, 1995).

TABLE 13A.4	Car Ownership as a Function of Income and Family Size		
A = family size	B = income	C = 0 or 1 car	2 or more
4 or fewer	less than $37,500	44	2
	more than $37,500	26	6
5 or more	less than $37,500	4	4
	more than $37,500	1	13

Recall that the model of independence between the row variable A and the column variable B in a two-way table was reflected most succinctly in the equation for computing the expected frequencies:

$$e_{ij} = \frac{n_{A_i} n_{B_j}}{n}$$

This equation is multiplicative, which makes the calculus of optimization complicated. If we take the natural logarithm of both sides, the equation simplifies to a "linear" form (that is, terms are added or subtracted) in the "log" scale—hence they are called "log linear" models:

$$\ell n(e_{ij}) = \ell n(n_{A_i}) + \ell n(n_{B_j}) - \ell n(n)$$

Note the first term on the right-hand side of the equation reflects the rows (A_i), the second term reflects the columns (B_j), and the third term, the total sample size.

To facilitate generalization to bigger tables and to more complex models, let us write the parameters simply as "u-terms":[4]

$$\ell n(e_{ij}) = u + u_{A(i)} + u_{B(j)}$$

where

$$u = \frac{1}{rc} \sum_i \sum_j \ell n(e_{ij})$$

$$u_{A(i)} = \frac{1}{c} \sum_j \ell n(e_{ij}) - u$$

$$u_{B(j)} = \frac{1}{r} \sum_i \ell n(e_{ij}) - u$$

---

[4]With constraints, given the degrees of freedom or the fact that the estimates are centered on u, that:

$$\sum_i u_{A(i)} = \sum_j u_{B(j)} = 0$$

The first term is an overall mean of the expected frequencies that looks unusual only because we are working in the natural log scale. The second two terms are also means (for example, the sum over columns, j, divided by the number of columns) "centered around" (subtracting) the overall mean, u. The first term, u, is not typically of substantive interest, but the latter two, $u_{A(i)}$ and $u_{B(j)}$, will reflect the differences among the rows (A), and those among the columns (B).

In our three-dimensional table (13A.3), we add a third variable, C. Now variable A is family size, B is income, and C is the number of cars the family owns. We might wish to test whether there are significant associations between all pairs of variables, A and B, A and C, and B and C. We would write our model as follows:

$$\ell n(e_{ijk}) = u + u_{A(i)} + u_{B(j)} + u_{C(k)} + u_{AB(ij)} + u_{AC(ik)} + u_{BC(jk)}$$

with the first four terms estimated analogously to those for the two-way table in the equations above, and the last three terms which reflect the pairwise associations estimated as follows, for example:[5]

$$u_{12(ij)} = \frac{1}{k} \sum_k \ell n(e_{ijk}) - u_{1(i)} - u_{2(j)} - u$$

Suppose that model fit, but, say, the BC term was not significant; that is, no relationship existed between income and number of cars owned, we might fit a model that is nested within the larger model, maintaining comparable fit, yet improved parsimony, for example:[6]

$$\ell n(e_{ijk}) = u + u_{A(i)} + u_{B(j)} + u_{C(k)} + u_{AB(ij)} + u_{AC(ik)}$$

In this particular example, it is not simply the case that we have three arbitrary variables, and any of them might be related to any of the others. Rather, we have come to think of C, the number of cars, as the dependent variable that might be predicted once we know the family size, A, and the household income, B. Analogous to the difference between the chi-square and the index of predictive association as discussed for the two-way cross tabulation (or, in Chapter 16, the difference between correlation and regression), a log linear model is used to examine associations of any sort, and a "logit" model is used for prediction purposes.

---

[5] Both $u_{A(i)}$ and $u_{B(j)}$ are expressed as deviations around the u, and thus:

$$\sum_i u_{AB(ij)} = \sum_j u_{AB(ij)} = 0$$

Also note, as the tables get bigger or the models more complex, they cannot all be written in analytical form; the iterative proportional fitting or Newton-Raphson algorithm estimation procedures rely upon iterative convergence to proper solutions; cf. Fienberg 1980.

[6] The χ^2 may be computed, but usually one computes: $G^2 = 2 \sum_{i=1}^{r} \sum_{j=1}^{C} o_{ij} \ell n\left(\frac{o_{ij}}{e_{ij}}\right)$, a "badness of fit" index like χ^2 in that both get larger as the data and expected frequencies differ more, and both draw their critical values from chi-square tables, but G^2 has superior statistical properties.

For our data, a logit model poses the question, "Are the odds of having 0 or 1 car versus 2 or more cars different depending on the size and income of the family?" Imagine the model above stated for just the families with 0 or 1 cars ($C = 1$):

$$\ell n(e_{ij1}) = u + u_{A(i)} + u_{B(j)} + u_{C(1)} + u_{AB(ij)} + u_{AC(i1)} + u_{BC(j1)}$$

and comparing it to the model fit to the families that own 2 or more cars ($C = 2$):

$$\ell n(e_{ij2}) = u + u_{A(i)} + u_{B(j)} + u_{C(2)} + u_{AB(ij)} + u_{AC(i2)} + u_{BC(j2)}$$

We might compare the odds directly in a ratio, e_{ij1}/e_{ij2}, or again, given that it is easier to work in the log scale, we would examine the "log odds ratio," also called the "logit," as defined here:

$$\ell n(e_{ij1}/e_{ij2}) = \ell n(e_{ij1}) - \ell n(e_{ij2})$$
$$= u + u_{A(i)} + u_{B(j)} + u_{C(1)} + u_{AB(ij)} + u_{AC(i1)} + u_{BC(j1)}$$
$$- (u + u_{A(i)} + u_{B(j)} + u_{C(2)} + u_{AB(ij)} + u_{AC(i2)} + u_{BC(j2)})$$

Note that several common terms cancel, and algebraically we are left with:

$$(u_{C(1)} - u_{C(2)}) + (u_{AC(i1)} - u_{AC(i2)}) + (u_{BC(j1)} - u_{BC(j2)})$$

In logit models, there are only two levels of the dependent variable (our variable C). And recall that the estimates sum to zero: $u_{C(1)} + u_{C(2)} = 0$. Thus, if $u_{C(1)}$ is some value such as 0.5, then $u_{C(2)}$ will equal -0.5. Thus, the term $(u_{C(1)} - u_{C(2)})$ in the equation above may be restated as $(u_{C(1)} + u_{C(1)})$, or $2 \times u_{C(1)}$. Thus, the equation above simplifies to:

$$2(u_{C(1)} + u_{AC(i1)} + u_{BC(j1)})$$

Note that instead of seven terms in the model, there are only three, all of which involve the dependent variable, C; the first is a logit intercept, the second will reflect the impact of A (family size) on C; and the third will reflect the impact of B (household income) on C.

If we fit this logit model to the data in Table 13A.3, using a statistical computing package such as Sas or Spss, we obtain the following estimates:

$$\ell n(e_{klij}) = -2.18 + 3.56(A_i) + 1.96(B_j)$$

Both predictors are significant (the printouts list standard errors of 0.73 and 0.72 respectively for A and B; the parameter estimates divided by their standard errors yield z-statistics of 4.88 and 2.72). Thus, both family size and household income are significant determinants in predicting the number of cars a family is likely to own. Specifically, both parameters are positive, which indicates that as either predictor increases (larger family or greater income), the likelihood that the family owns 2 or more cars (compared with 0 or 1) increases. We might have suspected as much had we computed a chi-square on the two partial two-way tables, A by C and B by C, but fitting this model to the *A* by *B* by *C* table allows us to estimate each effect of *A* and *B* having controlled for the effect of the other predictor.

In this appendix, we have illustrated log linear models as an extension of the chi-square test to three-dimensional tables, but four, five, or more variables may be cross classified and also modeled using these techniques. The addition of variables naturally allows for more complex modeling. For example, with four variables, there may be associations between *A* and *B,* and *C* and *D,* but perhaps none of the other two-way associations, nor higher-order relationships:

$$\ell n(e_{ijkl}) = u + u_{A(i)} + u_{B(j)} + u_{C(k)} + u_{D(l)} + u_{AB(ij)} + u_{CD(kl)}$$

Log linear modeling, and logit models in particular, are extremely important to the marketing researcher, because they allow the modeling of categorical dependent variables. Brand choice is categorical and of great importance in many marketing decisions systems. We have considered here models for which both the dependent variable and the predictors are categorical. If some of the predictors are continuous variables, models called "logistic regressions" may be fit, using similar logic.

Questions

1. What is the basic question at issue in a chi-square test on a two-way contingency table? What is the null hypothesis for this test? How are the expected frequencies determined?
2. What is the contingency coefficient, and to what types of situations does it apply? How does one determine whether the association between the variables indicated by the calculated value of the contingency coefficient is "strong" or "weak"?
3. What is the index of predictive association? When is it properly used? What is meant by an index of predictive association of $\lambda_{B|A} = 0.750$?
4. How is a log linear model an extension of the χ^2?

Applications and Problems

1. A large publishing house wants to determine if there is an association between newspaper-publication choice and the education level of the customer. A random sample of 400 customers provided the data in Table 1:

TABLE 1   **Education Level versus Newspaper Choice: Observed Frequencies**

	Level of Education			
Newspaper Publication	High School Diploma	Undergraduate Degree	Graduate Degree	Total
A	75	45	5	125
B	35	10	30	75
C	50	35	10	95
D	65	35	5	105
Total	225	125	50	400

a. State the null and alternate hypotheses.
b. Generate the expected frequencies for each cell.
c. Is there an association between newspaper publication choice and level of education at $\alpha = 0.05$? Show your calculations.
d. What is the strength of association as measured by the contingency coefficient between education level and newspaper choice? Show your calculations.

2. A marketing researcher from the publishing company in Problem 1 stated that the best estimate of newspaper choice by a customer chosen at random would be the A publication, since 31.25 percent (125 of 400) customers purchased this publication. The researcher further stated that 68.75 percent of the time the company would be wrong and decided to discard the previous study.
a. How could the predictive accuracy be improved? Show your calculations.
b. The index of predictive association is "more directly interpretable" than the contingency coefficient. Discuss.

A P P E N D I X   1 3 B

Avery Sporting Goods

To provide some hands-on experience to the coding, tabulating, and analysis functions, this appendix and some of the remaining appendices discuss the results of a study on catalog buying. A portion of the data set is included as part of this appendix so that those who are interested can duplicate the analyses to check the results, thereby increasing their understanding of the various analysis techniques. The data are also rich enough to allow interested parties to investigate other questions not addressed in these appendices.

Study Background

The primary purpose of the study was to gain insight into people who are likely to buy from catalogs. Avery's management was stimulated to conduct the study by published research investigating the characteristics of in-home (mail order or catalog) shoppers versus store shoppers. This research had indicated that there were differences in the demographic characteristics of those likely to buy in-home from those likely to buy in a store.[1] These studies had also indicated that those who shop in-home are motivated by convenience. Further, the product "is not necessarily the most important determinant of the success or failure of an in-home sale; prior shopping experience, the quality of the product description, its price, delivery, and guarantee policies also interact to influence the degree of perceived shopping risk."[2] The evidence also indicated that the perceived risk in buying in-home was

---

[1]See Peter L. Gillet, "In Home Shoppers—An Overview," *Journal of Marketing* 40 (October 1976), pp. 81–88; Naveen Donthu and David Gilliland, "Observations: The Infomercial Shopper," *Journal of Advertising Research* 36 (March/April 1996), pp. 69–76, for reviews of the evidence on in-home shopping behavior.

[2]Gillet, "In Home Shoppers," p. 85.

higher than it was with in-store buying. Those who purchased in-home had higher tolerances for perceived risk. Also important was the fact that the degree of risk varied by product. It was highest for high-priced and personalized items.

Background Information

Through the years, Avery Sporting Goods had been one of the leading catalog sellers of sporting equipment in the country. Known for its wide assortment and colorful print displays, the company's catalogs had been very popular with customers and employees, and workers had prided themselves on the high number of orders filled correctly. Still, management was considering expanding company operations by opening retail sporting goods stores. The three stores that the company had recently opened on the east side of Buffalo, New York, had met with tremendous sales success, far surpassing company expectations. Filled with growing optimism, management had developed plans to open three other stores during the next six to eight months in other areas of western New York. However, executives were not sure what to do with the company's catalog sales division.

Although catalog sales had been substantial, the level of growth had begun to taper off. This appeared to be an industry trend, as other sporting equipment enterprises offering catalog sales and services had experienced similar low rates of growth in sales revenues. Although current income from catalog sales was adequate to financially support Avery's plan to develop retail stores, company management had no desire to de-emphasize its catalog operation. In fact, given the catalog's ability to reach a national market at relatively low costs, Avery believed that a large portion of its future success resided in catalog customers. Hence, the company was extremely interested in revitalizing this market segment. As a first step toward the formulation of a long-term strategy for ensuring the continued viability of catalog sales, Avery management decided to have its marketing research department survey a sample of past, present, and potential catalog customers, operationally defined as all those who had been sent catalogs in the past three years, to get a better feel for the catalog market. The issues that were to be addressed included the following:

- Customer perceptions of buying merchandise, in particular sporting equipment, through catalogs
- People's evaluation of Avery's offerings and services
- Characteristics of Avery customers

Randomly sampling individuals from company records and geographic areas served, the questionnaire shown in Figure 13B.1 was mailed to 225 subjects after it was found to work well when pretested on a sample of 25 customers. A three-dollar coupon toward the next item purchased through Avery's catalog was enclosed with each questionnaire; 124 usable surveys were returned, for a 55 percent response rate. The responses to the individual questions were converted to the codes indicated in Table 13B.1. Unanswered questions were coded with a 0 (except for Question 24, in which "blue collar" was coded as 0, and Question 25 in which a 0 is a valid partial response for the subject's years worked). The first three columns of the data listed in Table 13B.2 contain the customer's survey identification number.

The following questions are designed to give the Avery Sporting Goods Company a better idea of people's perceptions of buying sporting goods and other general merchandise through catalogs. Please read each question carefully and indicate your response by putting an X next to the appropriate statement. (Answer each question with a single response.) Thank you for your cooperation in completing the questionnaire.

1. *During the past year, what percentage of the sporting goods you purchased was ordered through a catalog?*

   ____   0 percent   ____   16–20 percent
   ____   1–10 percent   ____   21+ percent
   ____   11–15 percent

2. *How willing are you to purchase merchandise offered through the Avery Sporting Goods catalog?*

   ____ Not at all willing
   ____ Somewhat willing
   ____ Very willing

3. *Have you ever ordered any merchandise from the Avery Sporting Goods catalog?*

   ____ Never
   ____ Ordered before, but not within the last year
   ____ Ordered within the last year

	Not at All Confident	Slightly Confident	Somewhat Confident	Confident	Very Confident
4. *How confident are you that the following sporting goods purchased through a catalog would be of high quality?*					
a. Athletic clothing (shirts, warm-up suits, etc.)	____	____	____	____	____
b. Athletic shoes	____	____	____	____	____
c. Fishing equipment	____	____	____	____	____
d. Balls (basketballs, footballs, etc.)	____	____	____	____	____
e. Skiing equipment	____	____	____	____	____
5. *How confident are you that the following sporting goods would be of high quality if purchased in a retail sporting goods store?*					
a. Athletic clothing (shirts, warm-up suits, etc.)	____	____	____	____	____
b. Athletic shoes	____	____	____	____	____
c. Fishing equipment	____	____	____	____	____
d. Balls (basketballs, footballs, etc.)	____	____	____	____	____
e. Skiing equipment	____	____	____	____	____

6. *Approximately how many items of sporting equipment did you purchase during the past year?*

   ____ 0–1   ____ 6–7
   ____ 2–3   ____ 8 or more
   ____ 4–5

(continued)

FIGURE 13B.1   (continued)

	Strongly Disagree	Disagree	Neither Agree nor Disagree	Agree	Strongly Agree
7. In general, Avery Sporting Goods sells a high-quality line of merchandise.	____	____	____	____	____
8. Avery Sporting Goods carries all of the most popular name brands of sporting equipment.	____	____	____	____	____
9. Avery Sporting Goods has a very high-quality catalog.	____	____	____	____	____
10. The descriptions of the products shown in the Avery catalog are very accurate.	____	____	____	____	____
11. The selection of sporting goods available through the Avery catalog is very broad.	____	____	____	____	____
12. When buying from a catalog, there is a low probability that the merchandise will get lost in the mail.	____	____	____	____	____
13. Before purchasing merchandise through a catalog, people do not need to discuss the product with someone who has already purchased it.	____	____	____	____	____
14. Most catalog merchandising companies can be trusted to deliver the product pictured in the catalog.	____	____	____	____	____
15. I enjoy purchasing merchandise through a catalog because it saves time.	____	____	____	____	____
16. When buying from a catalog, it is not difficult to negotiate the price.	____	____	____	____	____
17. If given a choice, I would purchase merchandise from the catalog company that has the easiest form to fill out.	____	____	____	____	____
18. Merchandise purchased from a catalog is less expensive than merchandise purchased in a retail store.	____	____	____	____	____
19. I prefer ordering merchandise from a catalog because the product is delivered to your door.	____	____	____	____	____
20. Catalogs have lower prices because the company does not have to pay salespeople.	____	____	____	____	____

	Very Unimportant	Unimportant	Neither Important nor Unimportant	Important	Very Important
21. How important are the following factors in your decision to purchase sporting goods through a catalog?					
a. Availability of a toll-free number for placing orders	____	____	____	____	____
b. Availability of quantity discounts	____	____	____	____	____
c. Shipping time	____	____	____	____	____
d. The company's policy on returning merchandise	____	____	____	____	____
e. The provision of a trial period	____	____	____	____	____
f. Number of years the company has been in business	____	____	____	____	____
g. Reputation of the company	____	____	____	____	____
h. Guarantees	____	____	____	____	____
i. Company endorsements by celebrities, sports teams, etc.	____	____	____	____	____

22. In general, do you prefer to do your shopping:

____ in a retail store
____ in a discount outlet store
____ through a catalog
____ over the phone
____ by having salespeople call on you at home

23. What was your approximate before-tax family income during the past year?

____ $0–$14,999   ____ $25,000–$34,999
____ $15,000–$24,999   ____ $35,000–$44,999
                         ____ $45,000 or more

24. Is your current occupation best described as blue collar? ____ **white collar?** ____

25. How long have you been working (in years)? ____

26. What is your current marital status?

____ single   ____ separated
____ married   ____ divorced
                 ____ widowed

27. Are you male? ____ **female?** ____

Column(s)	Question Number	Variable (Variable Number)	Coding Specification
1–3	—	Questionnaire identification number (V1)	—
4	1	Percentage of products purchased through a catalog (V2)	1 = 0 percent 2 = 1–10 percent 3 = 11–15 percent 4 = 16–20 percent 5 = 21+ percent
5	2	Willingness to purchase merchandise from the Avery Sporting Goods catalog (V3)	1 = Unwilling 2 = Somewhat willing 3 = Very willing
6	3	Ever ordered from the Avery Sporting Goods catalog (V4)	1 = Never ordered 2 = Ordered before, but not within the last year 3 = Ordered within the last year
			Coding Specifications 4a–5e 1 = Not at all confident 2 = Slightly confident 3 = Somewhat confident 4 = Confident 5 = Very confident
7	4a	Confidence in buying athletic clothing through a catalog (V5)	
8	4b	Confidence in buying athletic shoes through a catalog (V6)	
9	4c	Confidence in buying fishing equipment through a catalog (V7)	
10	4d	Confidence in buying balls through a catalog (V8)	
11	4e	Confidence in buying skiing equipment through a catalog (V9)	
12	5a	Confidence in buying athletic clothing in a retail store (V10)	
13	5b	Confidence in buying athletic shoes in a retail store (V11)	
14	5c	Confidence in buying fishing equipment in a retail store (V12)	
15	5d	Confidence in buying balls in a retail store (V13)	
16	5e	Confidence in buying skiing equipment in a retail store (V14)	
17	6	Number of sporting equipment items purchased (V15)	1 = 0–1 2 = 2–3 3 = 4–5 4 = 6–7 5 = 8 or more
			Coding Specifications 7–20 1 = Strongly disagree 2 = Disagree 3 = Neither agree nor disagree 4 = Agree 5 = Strongly agree
18	7	Avery sells a high-quality line of merchandise (V16)	
19	8	Avery carries the most popular name brands of sporting equipment (V17)	
20	9	Avery has a high-quality catalog (V18)	
21	10	Descriptions of products in the Avery catalog are accurate (V19)	

Column(s)	Question Number	Variable (Variable Number)	Coding Specification
22	11	Selection of goods available through Avery is very broad (V20)	
23	12	Low probability that merchandise will get lost in the mail (V21)	
24	13	No need to discuss product with someone who has purchased it before buying through a catalog (V22)	
25	14	Can be trusted to deliver product that's pictured in the catalog (V23)	
26	15	Catalog purchasing saves time (V24)	
27	16	Not difficult to negotiate the price (V25)	
28	17	Purchase from catalog with easiest form to fill out (V26)	
29	18	Catalog merchandise is less expensive (V27)	
30	19	Catalogs deliver the product to door (V28)	
31	20	Catalogs have lower prices because the company does not have to pay salespeople (V29)	

Coding Specification 21a–21i
1 = Very unimportant
2 = Unimportant
3 = Neither important nor unimportant
4 = Important
5 = Very important

Column(s)	Question Number	Variable (Variable Number)	Coding Specification
32	21a	Availability of a toll-free number for placing orders (V30)	
33	21b	Availability of quantity discounts (V31)	
34	21c	Shipping time (V32)	
35	21d	Company policy on returning merchandise (V33)	
36	21e	Provision of a trial period (V34)	
37	21f	Number of years company has been in business (V35)	
38	21g	Reputation of the company (V36)	
39	21h	Guarantees (V37)	
40	21i	Company endorsements (V38)	
41	22	Prefer to do shopping (V39)	1 = in a retail store 2 = in a discount outlet store 3 = through a catalog 4 = over the phone 5 = by having salespeople call at home
42	23	Before-tax family income during the past year (V40)	1 = $0–$14,999 2 = $15,000–$24,999 3 = $25,000–$34,999 4 = $35,000–$44,999 5 = $45,000 or more
43	24	Current occupation (V41)	0 = blue collar 1 = white collar
44–45	25	Years worked (V42)	Actual years recorded
46	26	Current marital status (V43)	5 = single 4 = married 3 = separated 2 = divorced 1 = widowed
47	27	Sex (V44)	1 = male 2 = female

Note: Except for variables V1, V41, and V42, zeroes represent nonresponses.

TABLE 13B.2 **Listing of Raw Data**

```
00111155554344434344455544545455445544445311 2551        06311144444543513123134543424244445544425101121
00212144555454535454444545454453242544314212551        06412345533245313122223555555515442433313301421
00341355442453214555545554455555030305042321 4051        06533145555254135321224554545444444444403401231
00432255435543243534541115555552424232433212551        06621155554154535444524435543544540443434212551
00521153554535424544455555545054535555503412551        06741234551543243455512154425214144414341 02551
00613355434524354553443442534244444444402313651        06822355525541235355555555555555555543510 2751
00713144535453545444453443242321444445341511 2451        06951244444254313553344543434444434355432111 2441
00852355435354454354355455525135555553551 45 13651        07013254355254135445444443252324444444435512551
00931235555235555445544535555554243552242321 3651        07113345555543555532555542441414141444444415511531
01013244515534233454444324542422243433311 412551        07213144444545353445444235454543525351 43341 2551
01113535535524555325254535444233333343421 51 2351        07311245355543544355444555454540045552405512551
01223154453355543554325545524344435315156 41        07413345444354444454523535552524334533413112541
01323355555444445555534334225243444242321 41 4051        07513155552355535555533355555555555554511113651
01441153555414553444543355555424442333322 12341        07621344544235455444445555555555454555411112431
01513344442554442555544555555532545535332 21 4051        07723154355235555155534545452544233445213112451
01632255515335554544435322555352554544313212341        07823355544235455555553445555533443344443331 4051
01751344553553455442343414344334444433112551        07921144455324554354554444555454444444441 4212531
01822255345453545444444444453235242040 40 400 41 2451        08052244454355555555444444242413324443415213851
01931155544355554543552432554424040505033412551        08113155453251435355454253535343144252533112551
02033244454325555444444543535333344534325 41 2451        08211254325215452454553454554443234344321113651
02112353545542455555533444554545545445435514041        08312354354543213355543324455243424325311 13651
02213152434555552554532545522334545145315312421        08432234554254513544444554425251553534344021 12441
02313354354321544355541225422554452535253521 3651        08521155545432153355540005451544030504022212441
02413154535351245554445555335525455535525 41 3651        08623255543541235444543425545424435243221 2441
02511354555321235544454335252522545232535 41 2541        08741344444122213435543435251525535443353212531
02622153255521453534445331555454534352511 3211541        08813354335354123444553235543454433543313212551
02721152444354124454543425353524455555412313641        08911255555215355335553335555524343434343421 2441
02821355555333335555544441532534243434322213641        09012153421451232455555544454525454534213651
02921254355235454445534345455550305050 1311 2551        09131211212543252355444245455553535353545 25512542
03012145543542415555442445553224244434 1131 3951        09223312222255541555555334433323553233151112552
03111254123554553355453435442243333443314212551        09311322111344451111214442334424344424413100512
03252255453245315444443232524242434243434212451        09412132211354451231110455454544400435314200922
03311115354421453444454343434355453444535112541        09623121351214553121114445554545445413400512
03432255445354552554443534451514030504015413651        09722232222235555222222534424353353543335511232
03521224554553343554354445554543443545334312541        09851211114554451311222223353425544545514500932
03622313212541541444553244555443433233423212542        09913122111355541123223345554543333343133201232
03711132123543242444454354535233445333444412432        10011323111544331212220003322245324525323003922
03813212343543542545554544555554252525252511213752        10151223222254352111114554525254544444421200412
03912312423543542535555555242525552305230 1 403652        10252211121255551212233425151515554445512200922
04011212423555552355454445553434343414212742        10322222211543542222230005044552020202013201232
04133124123543434445555445455544345334242212742        10431132112354532123211115251515453525513301232
04243321311543542555555222144445525252413 33314052        10541121123444442212140003311330000000004400822
04322311111454351112321544555555553444535413101222        10612351112355432321150002233550000000005400932
04411111222154354111111455335533344455552500412        10732311111244441122225555353535555555555515500927
04513222222235452212124355552523555515352440 0812        10851233211555452311131452515135335434354001032
04613331111454351222223315425252434341 435401222        10921221233545552111112225542522424242334400412
04712321222235451123135553225153355554223200922        11043111123554441231114344515253030303023100922
04823323111545512122232252525245355545313300922        11112322211234551222240005151005355555555111301232
04911112213354231231122225354540 50504012200922        11213131111455451221132125353534343544312200822
05022333324535232111144434543435351 52522100512        11351221122325552112112103515244545454512200522
05111222222555552111324434554453344333332500812        11432111111454541214533555545545555555512201832
05212214112543311112145554543444445354144 00512        11511122225555551241133324554354242313101232
05311124231522445511335523344552555552534100922        11623332224535523211154455444304050504233 00922
05412312321545551122224231425334444243335200922        11742312121435541222214443525153050505023501232
05511322225435521111144542223344332445324004 12        11811223111531552351143245553423222431124501432
05612231112254451222230 0 0550 5 5 500 0505014301232        11923224311555553214123424554454443444242415501232
05711121311533412213345555545434344343244013 32        12043321321354352212334334435454444444415501232
05823111112444441111325455555553555355551500822        12111112451135453421424333525152434452541440 1332
05922312321543541212223555554254 3355553232300922        12222133311545452111115344151544455354533200412
06021222225555552222122225444343324222323500922        12341321312135555512222143421252443434334331501232
06143145355124554111142454534233244423122004 11        12431221311453541355553444445242343530325513652
06213255545453215211113324442333314332234110511
```

One-Way Tabulation

As pointed out in the chapter, one-way tabulation is useful for locating blunders and outliers, for determining the empirical distribution of the variable, and for communicating results. Thus, an analyst would normally construct the one-way tabulations for each variable in the study. This is not done here because of space limitations. Rather, only the one-way tabulation of the percentage of sporting goods purchased from a catalog during the past year is shown in Table 13B.3. This, incidentally, will be a general strategy followed throughout the appendices investigating catalog buying behavior. Even though a number of relationships might be analyzed using a particular technique, only one is used in each case to illustrate the technique.

Table 13B.3 was constructed using the SPSS frequencies program. SPSS is a widely distributed system of computer programs for data management and statistical analysis. It is used whenever possible in the appendices that follow, which analyze the catalog buying data, because of its general availability.

Table 13B.3 indicates that most people receiving Avery catalogs buy only a small portion of their sporting goods through catalogs; 56, or 45 percent, of the respondents bought no sporting goods at all from catalogs in the previous year. Further, more than 83 percent of the catalog recipients satisfied 15 percent or less of their sporting goods purchases through catalogs. Only 8 percent purchased more than 20 percent of their sporting goods through catalogs.

Cross Tabulation

Table 13B.4 is offered as an illustration of the makeup of the two-way tabulation output by SPSS. It depicts the relationship between willingness to purchase merchandise offered through the Avery sporting goods catalog and whether respondents have previously ordered from the catalog. The cross tabulation can be used to assess the extent to which catalog customers are satisfied and are likely to be repeat buyers in the sense that they have ordered before and are willing to order again. The cross tabulation also provides some insight into the size of an untapped market, defined as those who have received Avery catalogs in the past and have not purchased from them but are willing to do so. Because willingness to buy through the Avery Sporting

TABLE 13B.3	One-Way Tabulation Showing Percentage of Sporting Goods Purchased from a Catalog during the Past Year				

Value Label	Value	Frequency	Percent	Valid Percent	Cumulative Percent
0%	1	56	45.2	45.2	45.2
1–10%	2	33	26.6	26.6	71.8
11–15%	3	14	11.3	11.3	83.1
16–20%	4	11	8.9	8.9	91.9
21+%	5	10	8.1	8.1	100.0
Total		124	100.0	100.0	

Valid cases   124   Missing cases   0

TABLE 13B.4	Cross Tabulation of Willingness to Purchase from Avery's Catalog (V3) with Whether Respondent Has Purchased from It Before (V4)

Count Row Percent Column Percent Total Percent	V4	Never Ordered 1	Ordered Before but Not within Past Year 2	Ordered within Past Year 3	Row Total
V3					
Unwilling	1	20	20	10	50
		46.5	51.3	23.8	40.3
Somewhat Willing	2	7	11	17	35
		16.3	28.2	40.5	28.2
Very Willing	3	16	8	15	39
		37.2	20.5	35.7	
Column Total		43	39	42	124
		34.7	31.5	33.9	100.0

A   Raw chi square = 10.997 with 4 degrees of freedom
Significance = 0.027
B   Contingency coefficient = 0.285
C   Lambda (asymmetric) = 0.095 with V3 dependent

Goods catalog is the dependent variable that we are interested in explaining, the percentages are calculated by column. These percentages suggest that the "most willing" group of catalog recipients are those who ordered from Avery within the past year. Over three-fourths of these people (40.5 + 35.7 percent) are somewhat willing or very willing to order from Avery again. At the same time, almost one-fourth of those who bought within the last year are not willing to place another order. This relatively large proportion of potentially dissatisfied customers would certainly deserve further investigation by Avery management.

The column percentages also suggest that there may be a sizable untapped segment of people receiving Avery catalogs who might become customers if the right inducement can be found. Over 50 percent (16.3 + 37.2) of the people who have never placed an order with Avery said that they were willing to place an order.

Note finally the statistics located at the bottom of Table 13B.4, which are output by the SPSS cross-tabulation program. While the program can output a number of measures of association, the three that are highlighted for our purposes are the chi-squared statistic, the contingency coefficient, and the index of predictive association, which are labeled *A, B,* and *C,* respectively, and which are described in Appendix 13A. Their interpretations, which you will appreciate after reading that appendix, are as follows:

A.   The chi-square value of $\chi^2 = 10.997$ with 4 degrees of freedom is significant at the .027 level. This indicates that the null hypothesis of independence between the two variables should be rejected in favor of the alternative that willingness to purchase from Avery's catalog is a function of having purchased from it before.

B   The contingency coefficient value of $C = .285$ suggests that there is only moderate association between the variables, given that the maximum value for C in a table with three rows and three columns is .816.

C   The index of predictive association $\lambda_{3.4} = .095$ indicates that errors in predicting Variable 3 (willingness to purchase through Avery's catalog) are only reduced by 9.5 percent by taking account of Variable 4 (whether or not the respondent has ordered from the Avery catalog before). This again suggests that, although statistically significant, the strength of the relationship between the two variables is low.

14

Data Analysis: Basic Questions

Chapter 13 discussed the preliminary data analysis steps of editing, coding, and tabulating. The chapter was intended to convey the importance and potential value of these preliminary procedures, which are common to almost all research studies. Some studies stop with tabulation and cross tabulation. Many involve additional analyses, though, particularly the search for statistical significance. A recurring problem in this search is the determination of the appropriate statistical procedure. This chapter will highlight the basic considerations that dictate a choice of method.

Choice of Analysis Technique: An Example

The considerations that underlie a choice of analysis method and the interpretation of the results are best demonstrated through example. Assume that the following hypothetical study was completed by a consumer products firm that manufactures the dishwashing liquid Sheen. The study was designed to determine homemakers' perceptions of the gentleness of Sheen and its nearest competitor, Glitter. Assume that the study used a scientifically determined probability sample and that the data were collected by administering a rating scale to each respondent. The respondents were specifically asked to locate each brand on a five-point mildness scale with the following descriptors, according to how they thought the brand affected their hands:

- Very rough (VR)
- Rough (R)
- Neither rough nor gentle (N)
- Mild (M)
- Very mild (VM)

The basic considerations underlying the choice of method can be easily illustrated using a small sample, so assume that the analysis was to be based on the 10 responses contained in Table 14.1, which also contains some alternative ways of analyzing the data. Not all these methods are correct, nor are all the conclusions that can be drawn from the data. As a matter of fact, it is the purpose of this section to demonstrate how the conclusion depends on the method. There is no problem in most studies in deciding "What ways *can* the analysis be done?" There is an acute problem in deciding the question "What way *should* the analysis be conducted?"

TABLE 14.1	Homemakers' Perceptions of Dishwashing Liquids

					Respondent Scores for Each Brand under Method						
	Perception of		*A*		*B*		*C*		*D*		*E*
	VR R N M VM		*-2 -1 0 1 2*		*1 2 3 4 5*		*5 4 3 2 1*		*-1 0 1*		*Higher-Rated*
Respondent	*S*	*G*	*S*	*G*	*S*	*G*	*S*	*G*	*S*	*G*	*Alternative**
1	VM	VM	2	2	5	5	1	1	1	1	T
2	M	VM	1	2	4	5	2	1	1	1	G
3	N	VM	0	2	3	5	3	1	0	1	G
4	M	VM	1	2	4	5	2	1	1	1	G
5	M	VM	1	2	4	5	2	1	1	1	G
6	M	VM	1	2	4	5	2	1	1	1	G
7	M	M	1	1	4	4	2	2	1	1	T
8	M	R	1	-1	4	2	2	4	1	-1	S
9	N	R	0	-1	3	2	3	4	0	-1	S
10	N	M	0	1	3	4	3	2	0	1	G
Sums			8	12	38	42	22	18	7	6	
Averages			0.8	1.2	3.8	4.2	2.2	1.8	0.7	0.6	

*A "T" indicates a tie, in that both brands received the same rating.

The methods reported in Table 14.1 vary according to how values (numbers) were assigned to each of the scale locations. Consider Method A, for instance. Underlying Method A is the assumption that mildness is desirable and roughness undesirable in dishwashing liquids. Thus, if the respondent believed that the dishwashing soap was very mild on one's hands, that response received a positive score of +2. A response of "very rough" received a negative score of −2, a response of "rough" a score of −1, and so on. The scores are totaled and averaged at the bottom of Table 14.1.

Look at the average scores for Method A: Sheen had an average score of 0.8, and Glitter had an average score of 1.2. Both soaps are thus "mild." Now let us search for the milder product, looking at the average score differences between the products and converting them to a percentage mildness difference. With Sheen as the comparative yardstick, we find that

$$\frac{\bar{x}_G - \bar{x}_S}{\bar{x}_S} (100) = \frac{1.2 - 0.8}{0.8} (100) = 50 \text{ percent}$$

and the conclusion is that Glitter is 50 percent milder on the hands. With Glitter as the basis of comparison, the result is

$$\frac{\bar{x}_G - \bar{x}_S}{\bar{x}_G} (100) = \frac{1.2 - 0.8}{1.2} (100) = 33 \text{ percent}$$

and the conclusion is that Glitter is 33 percent milder on the hands. Similar calculations underlie each of the comparisons reflected in Table 14.1 except for Method E, the conclusions for which are summarized in Table 14.2. Methods B and C, for example, employ assignments of numbers to response categories similar to those used in Method A, except that Method B uses all positive numbers, with "very mild" receiving a score of 5. Method C reverses the scoring so that a score of 5 represents a "very rough" evaluation. Method D assigns negative values to "rough" evaluations and positive values to "mild" evaluations, but the "rough" and "very rough" evaluations receive the same score (-1), as do the "mild" and "very mild" evaluations ($+1$). Method E, in contrast, does not rely on average scores for all respondents but focuses on the alternative rated higher by each respondent. In particular, the conclusions in Method E reflect the facts that Respondents 1 and 7 perceived Glitter and Sheen to be of equal mildness, six of the ten respondents perceived Glitter as milder, and two perceived Sheen as milder.

The right-hand column of Table 14.2 suggests a number of conclusions about which is the preferred detergent. Which of these conflicting statements is correct and why? The answer is the last one, corresponding to Method E, and the reasons are intimately associated with the considerations that dictate the choice of analysis method. These considerations include the type of data, the research design, and the assumptions underlying the test statistic.

Before discussing these considerations, let us show why the last statement is correct and, in the process, reveal some of the caveats associated with these data. First, some analysts would hold that the response categories reflect ordinal measurements, in that the difference between "very rough" and "rough" is not the same as

TABLE 14.2   Comparison of Dishwashing Liquids

Method	Base in Comparison	Calculation	Conclusion
A	Sheen	$\dfrac{\bar{x}_G - \bar{x}_S}{\bar{x}_S}(100) = \dfrac{1.2 - 0.8}{0.8}(100) = 50.0\%$	Glitter is 50% milder on the hands.
	Glitter	$\dfrac{\bar{x}_G - \bar{x}_S}{\bar{x}_G}(100) = \dfrac{1.2 - 0.8}{1.2}(100) = 33.3\%$	Glitter is 33% milder on the hands.
B	Sheen	$\dfrac{\bar{x}_G - \bar{x}_S}{\bar{x}_S}(100) = \dfrac{4.2 - 3.8}{3.8}(100) = 10.5\%$	Glitter is 11% milder on the hands.
	Glitter	$\dfrac{\bar{x}_G - \bar{x}_S}{\bar{x}_G}(100) = \dfrac{4.2 - 3.8}{4.2}(100) = 9.5\%$	Glitter is 10% milder on the hands.
C	Sheen	$\dfrac{\bar{x}_S - \bar{x}_G}{\bar{x}_S}(100) = \dfrac{2.2 - 1.8}{2.2}(100) = 18.2\%$	Glitter is 18% milder on the hands.
	Glitter	$\dfrac{\bar{x}_S - \bar{x}_G}{\bar{x}_G}(100) = \dfrac{2.2 - 1.8}{1.8}(100) = 22.2\%$	Glitter is 22% milder on the hands.
D	Sheen	$\dfrac{\bar{x}_S - \bar{x}_G}{\bar{x}_S}(100) = \dfrac{0.7 - 0.6}{0.7}(100) = 14.3\%$	Sheen is 14% milder on the hands.
	Glitter	$\dfrac{\bar{x}_S - \bar{x}_G}{\bar{x}_G}(100) = \dfrac{0.7 - 0.6}{0.6}(100) = 16.7\%$	Sheen is 17% milder on the hands.
E	. . . .		60% of the respondents thought Glitter was milder on the hands, while 20% thought Sheen was milder.

ETHICAL DILEMMA 14.1

A beer producer conducted a study to determine whether consumers perceive an actual or a psychological difference in the taste of beer. As part of the experiment, each subject was asked to taste three unmarked cans of beer and to order them according to preference. Although subjects were led to believe that the three cans of beer were different beers, the participants discovered when the beers were unmasked that the three cans were, in fact, the same beer. A fair proportion of participants had stated that the three beers tasted quite different.

- It is argued that such an experiment may induce stress in some participants inasmuch as it may lead them to doubt their competence as shoppers. Comment on this argument.
- Should the investigator offer some sort of psychic support (such as debriefing) upon completion of the experiment to counteract any possible negative effects?
- Under what conditions might debriefing be problematic?

---

the difference between "rough" and "neither rough nor gentle." Further, we saw previously that the assignment of scale values is completely arbitrary with order data as long as the order relationships are preserved, but that the calculation of means is misleading. Thus, these analysts would argue that Methods A to D are inappropriate, *not because of the values that were assigned to the categories but rather because the values were averaged.*

Second, even if the data had interval properties, Methods A to D would still be incorrect for two reasons. First, the comparisons in Table 14.2 involve absolute magnitudes, because each difference is compared to a mean and the result is interpreted as a certain percentage of the mean. Such comparisons are inappropriate unless the variables have a natural zero. The comparisons involving Methods A through D would be meaningful, then, if the variables were on a ratio scale but not when the zero position is so arbitrary, as it is in the rating scales. Further, the evaluations of Sheen and Glitter are not independent and cannot be treated as such statistically. Instead, they represent multiple responses from the same individual. They are related or dependent samples, and the appropriate procedure involves an analysis of the difference in the evaluations per individual. Method E is the only procedure that correctly deals with these differences.

Third, the conclusion was that "60 percent of the people thought Glitter was milder on the hands." The question has not been raised about whether this is a statistically significant result. The question of statistical significance involves the size of the sample employed to generate the percentage. In this case, the result is not significant. Yet if 60 out of 100 people thought that Glitter was milder on the hands than Sheen, the result would be statistically significant, although the percentage "preferring" Glitter would remain the same. Sample size is an important barometer in determining whether a research finding is due to chance or represents an underlying condition in the population.

Basic Considerations

The example has highlighted some of the considerations involved in the choice of analysis method. One useful classification of these considerations is that the appropriate technique depends on the type of data, the research design, and the assumptions underlying the test statistic and its related consideration, the power of the test.

Type of Data

The level at which attributes can be measured was discussed earlier. At that time it was pointed out that a useful classification involves nominal, ordinal, interval, and ratio scales of measurement. Consider again some of the main differences in the application of these scales. The nominal scale is used when categorizing objects. A letter or numeral is assigned to each category so that each number represents a distinct category. For instance, if individuals are to be classified by sex, the numbers 1 and 2 serve equally as well as the letters M and F for denoting males and females. The nominal scale remains undistorted under a one-to-one substitution of the numerals. Thus, the number 2 could be used to denote males and the number 1 to denote females without a loss of information. The mean and median are not appropriate measures of central tendency. The appropriate measure of central tendency is the mode. Only it remains unchanged under a one-to-one substitution of the numerals. Thus, if there are more females than males, the mode describes the category "female" regardless of whether we choose to call it 1, 2, or F.

The ordinal scale represents a higher level of measurement than the nominal because the numerals assigned reflect order as well as serve to identify the objects. For example, we might want to classify students into three categories, such as good, average, and poor. We might simply choose to call the categories A, B, and C. Alternatively, we might use the numbers 1 = good, 2 = average, and 3 = poor, or perhaps the reverse, in which good = 3 and poor = 1. The schemes are equally fruitful as long as the numeral assignment is understood by all. The structure of an ordinal scale is undistorted by any one-to-one substitution that preserves the order, since only order is implied by the assignment of numerals. The median and the mode are now both legitimate measures of central tendency.

The assignment of numerals to objects using an interval scale conveys information about the magnitude of the differences between the objects. We can determine how much more one category is than another. We *cannot*, however, *compare the ratio of absolute magnitudes* of the objects; for example, A is five times larger than B. All comparisons must be made using differences between objects. The reason is that the interval scale contains an arbitrary zero. An interval scale is undistorted under linear transformations—that is, transformations of the form $y = b + cx$. The effect of this transformation is to shift the origin b units and multiply the unit of measurement by c, as in going from a Fahrenheit scale to a centigrade scale. The mean, the median, and the mode are all appropriate measures of central tendency.

The ratio scale is similar to the interval scale except that it has a natural zero point. Thus, it makes sense to say that A is twice as heavy or twice as tall as B, since both of the scales possess a natural zero. The ratio scale is undistorted under proportionate or scalar transformations—that is, transformations of the form $y = cx$. The effect of such a transformation is to change the scale of measurement by the factor c. The conversion of feet to inches is an example; c in this case would equal 12. All statistics appropriate for the interval scale are also appropriate for a ratio scale.

The analyst has to be very careful in interpreting numerical relationships to properly reflect the properties of the measurement scale. The user of information has to be equally cautious. Consider the following hypothetical ad claim, which is not too different from what one sees on television and in magazines:

> New Lustre gets your clothes 20 percent brighter and you need 50 percent less detergent compared to old Lustre. Furthermore, even for linens you can use water temperatures 30 percent lower than that required for old Lustre.

Probably, the "brighter" claim in this ad is based on homemakers' reactions to clothes washed with old Lustre. It is also likely that these perceptions were determined by having the respondents complete "dingy" to "bright" rating scales. Suppose, indeed, that a seven-point scale was employed and that old Lustre received an average score of five and new Lustre an average score of six; thus, the 20 percent brighter claim results from the calculation

$$\frac{\overline{x}_{new} - \overline{x}_{old}}{\overline{x}_{old}} (100) = \frac{6 - 5}{5} (100) = 20 \text{ percent}$$

The use of adjective scales like this highlights the disagreement between those who insist that most marketing measurements reflect ordinal measurement and those who argue that such scales can be treated as interval measures. There is some evidence to support each position. On the one hand, several empirical studies have demonstrated that descriptors that might appear to the scale developer to reflect equal increments of the characteristic are often not interpreted that way by those responding.[1] Research Realities 14.1, for example, depicts how sensitive the distribution of responses can be to the descriptors used to label the various categories. Of the two versions of each questionnaire that were administered to different samples of respondents, the main difference in each case was how the second highest and middle positions on the scales were described. Yet, the percentage responding "good" was different, as was the total distribution of the responses for the two versions in each case. The evidence also indicates that it is possible to develop questions in which the descriptors do reflect equal increments of the characteristic by the proper choice of descriptors—that is, by carefully choosing descriptors on the basis of their scale positions. The descriptors "remarkably good," "good," "neutral," "reasonably poor," and "extremely poor" could be used, for example, to approximate

---

[1]James H. Myers and W. Gregory Warner, "Semantic Properties of Selected Evaluation Adjectives," *Journal of Marketing Research* 5 (November 1968), pp. 409–412; Paul E. Spector, "Choosing Response Categories for Summated Rating Scales," *Journal of Applied Psychology* 61 (September 1976), pp. 374–375; Melvin R. Crask and Richard J. Fox, "An Exploration of the Interval Properties of Three Commonly Used Marketing Research Scales: A Magnitude Estimation Approach," *Journal of the Market Research Society* 29 (July 1987), pp. 317–339. See also Madhubalen Viswanathan, Mark Bergen, Shantanu Dutta, and Terry Childers, "Does a Single Response Category in a Scale Completely Capture a Response?" *Psychology & Marketing* 13 (August 1996), pp. 457–479.

RESEARCH REALITIES 14.1

It Depends on How It's Asked

Panel A: How would you rate the quality of your telephone service? Would you say it's (read scale)?

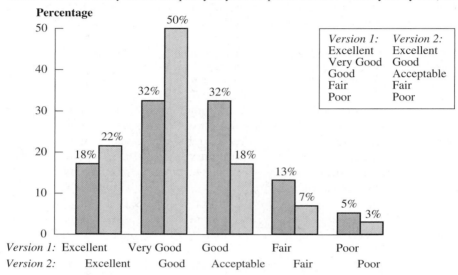

Panel B: How would you rate the service of the U.S. Postal Service? Would you say it's (read scale)?

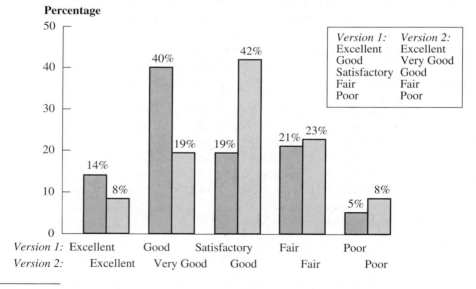

Source: Omar J. Bendikas, "A Lot Depends on How It's Asked," *Telenation Reports* (Summer 1987), p. 4; and Lisa Lainer, "It All Depends on How It's Asked," *Telenation Reports* (Spring 1988), p. 2, for the examples in Panels A and B, respectively.

a five-point interval scale. While the debate rages, a reasonably balanced argument suggests the following:

1.   It is very safe, and certainly productive, to treat the total score summed over a number of items as an interval scale.

2.   It is sometimes safe to treat individual items as interval scales, such as when specific steps have been taken to ensure the intervality of the response categories.

3.   It is always legitimate to treat the scale as ordinal when neither Condition 1 nor 2 is satisfied. Suppose that Condition 3 applied to the "dingy" to "bright" rating scale so that the descriptors anchoring the categories did not reflect equal increments of "brightness." The calculation and comparison of the difference in means would then be suspect.

Suppose, on the other hand, that appropriate procedures were employed, that the evaluation scale did reflect interval measurement, and that the calculation of means was appropriate. The "brighter" claim would still be in error, and for the same reason that the temperature claim is also probably erroneous. More likely than not, the temperature claim would be based on the fact that whereas old Lustre required 200°F water to be effective, new Lustre requires only 140°F water; that is, new Lustre can operate effectively with temperatures 30 percent lower, since:

$$\frac{200 - 140}{200} (100) = 30 \text{ percent}$$

We have previously seen, however, that the Fahrenheit scale is an interval scale because it possesses an arbitrary zero and that the calculation of ratios with such scales is meaningless. To see the folly in this exercise, simply convert the 200°F and 140°F temperatures to their centigrade equivalents of 93.3°C and 60.0°C, respectively. Now you can use 36 percent lower temperatures with new Lustre. The same argument applies to the brightness comparison. Unless the "dingy" to "bright" scale was ratio, it would be incorrect to divide the difference in mean ratings for the two formulations by the original rating.

Thus, only one of the three ad claims is probably legitimate—the claim that 50 percent less detergent is needed with new Lustre. The scale here is of the ratio variety, and if one uses, say, ½ cup of new Lustre whereas one used 1 cup of old Lustre, then indeed one needs 50 percent less detergent. This is not to say that the claims could not be supported with data. For instance, the temperature claim follows if all measurements were made on a Kelvin scale, which possesses an absolute zero. Similarly, the brightness claim would follow if measurements were made using the integrating sphere.[2] The brightness claim does not follow, though, from the aggregation of consumer perceptions.

---

[2]The integrating sphere measures the amount of light reflected from an object placed in the sphere. Black objects do not reflect any of the light directed at them, while white objects reflect 100 percent of the light directed into the sphere. See, for instance, K. S. Gibson, *Spectrophotometry*, National Bureau of Standards, Circular Number 484 (1949).

An understanding of the level of measurement underlying data is crucial to proper interpretation. Incidentally, this comment is equally valid for day-to-day living. For instance, the other night on the news, a meteorologist reported that the month of December was 38 percent colder than normal. The statement was based on the fact that, although the average mean temperature in December is 40°F, this past December it was 25°F, or 38 percent colder. In fact, using the proper Kelvin scale, it was only 3 percent colder than normal.

Research Design

A second consideration that affects the choice of analysis technique is the research design used to generate the data. Some of the more important questions the analyst has to face involve the dependency of observations, the number of observations per object, the number of groups being analyzed, and the control exercised over the variables of interest. Consider several hypothetical cases.

SAMPLE INDEPENDENCE   Consider first the question of dependent or independent samples. Without worrying at this point about the details of the research design (and whether it was good or poor), suppose that you were interested in determining the effectiveness of a mailed brochure. Suppose, too, that the measure of effectiveness was attitudes toward a product, that the scale used to measure attitudes was interval, and in particular that the research design was

$$X \quad O_1$$
$$O_2$$

where O_1 represents the attitudes of those who received the brochure and O_2 the attitudes of those who did not receive the brochure. In this case, the samples are independent. The O_2 measures do not depend on the O_1 measures. An appropriate test of significance would allow for the independence of the samples. In this case, the t test for the difference in two means would be appropriate.[3]

Consider another research design that could be diagrammed thus:

$$O_1 \quad X \quad O_2$$

There are again two sets of observations, O_1 and O_2. Now, however, they are made on the same individuals, before and after receiving the brochure. The measurements are not independent, and a t test of the difference between two means is inappropriate. The observations must be analyzed in pairs. The focus is on differences in attitudes per individual before and after exposure to the brochure. A paired difference test for statistical significance should be used in this case.[4]

NUMBER OF GROUPS   Consider next the question of number of groups being compared. Suppose that you were interested in the relative effectiveness of two different brochures and you decided to explore the question through a controlled

---

[3] The t test for the difference in means is discussed in Chapter 15.

[4] The paired difference statistical test is discussed in Chapter 15.

experiment. In the experiment, some respondents receive X_1, others get X_2, and a third group receives neither. The design can be diagrammed:

$$X_1 \qquad O_1$$
$$X_2 \qquad O_2$$
$$O_3$$

This design parallels that for the single brochure, except for the addition of the alternative brochure X_2. Now, however, there are three groups (two experimental and one control) whereas previously there were two (one experimental and one control). The t test for the difference in two means is no longer applicable; the problem is best handled through analysis-of-variance procedures.[5]

NUMBER OF VARIABLES   Let us return to the one-brochure design to illustrate how the number of measurements per object affects the analysis procedure. Previously we have used attitudes toward the advertised product as the measure of effectiveness of the brochure; specifically, we contrasted the attitudes of the "receivers" with those of the "nonreceivers." Suppose that we believe this attitude to be a legitimate measure of effectiveness, but the sales impact of the brochure must also be considered. That is, we now wish to contrast the "exposed" and "unexposed" groups not only in terms of their differences in attitude but also in terms of the sales of the product to each group. The design has not changed. It is still diagrammed

$$X \qquad O_1$$
$$O_2$$

only now O_1 and O_2 represent measures of both sales and attitudes.

Of course, one way to proceed would be to test separately for the differences in attitudes and the differences in sales to the two groups. What happens, though, if the two groups differ only slightly on each criterion so that neither of the univariate tests detects a significant difference? Would we conclude that the brochure had no impact even though the average attitude score and average sales were higher for the experimental group? Or do we conclude that the small, nonsignificant differences, taken together, indicate a real difference? On the other hand, let's say that the individual tests are statistically significant but inconsistent; that is, one result is more favorable to the control group and the other to the experimental group. Do we take the favorable and unfavorable results at their face value, or do we take the position that one of them represents a Type I error and in reality is attributable to chance?[6] To answer this question (and it becomes much more conceptually difficult as the number of measurements per object increases), we need to have some means of looking at the differences among groups when several characteristics are considered simultaneously. This type of problem is handled using multivariate statistical procedures.

---

[5]Analysis of variance is discussed in the appendix to Chapter 15.

[6]Type I error is discussed in the appendix to this chapter.

VARIABLE CONTROL   Another important question in analysis involves the control of variables that can affect the result. Return to the one-brochure design

$$X \quad O_1$$
$$O_2$$

in which the emphasis is on the differences in attitudes between the two groups. One variable that would certainly seem to determine attitudes is previous usage of the product. If so, in the experimental design, the analyst would like to control for prior usage to minimize its effect. A good way of doing this would be to make the experimental and control groups equal with respect to prior usage by matching, by randomization, or by some combination of these approaches. If this control procedure is followed, the t test for analyzing the difference in two means can legitimately be employed. If the control is not affected but attitudes do depend on prior use of the product, the conclusions produced using the t test will be in error to the extent that the two groups differ in their previous use of the product. One way to adjust for these differences is by allowing prior use to be a covariate—that is, by regressing attitudes on use and adjusting the attitude scores represented by O_1 and O_2 by the resulting regression equation. The adjusted scores for the experimental and control groups would then be compared.

Assumptions Underlying Test Statistic

Also underlying the choice of a statistical method of analysis is a consideration of the assumptions supporting the various test statistics. Examine once again (you will be glad to know, for the last time) the test for the differences in attitudes toward the product of those who received the brochure and those who did not. The t test for the difference in two means was deemed appropriate for this analysis. Therefore, let us look at the assumptions implicit in the choice of this statistical test.

The samples are assumed to have been drawn independently of each other. Further, it is assumed that the individuals composing the experimental group come from a population with unknown mean μ_1 and unknown variance σ_1^2, that those in the control group come from a population with unknown mean μ_2 and unknown variance σ_2^2, and that attitudes toward the product are *normally distributed* in each of these populations. It is also assumed that the variances of the two populations are equal—that is, $\sigma_1^2 = \sigma_2^2$; thus, a pooled estimator for the overall variance is warranted.[7] In sum, the assumptions

1.   are independent samples;
2.   have normal distribution of the characteristic of interest in each population; and
3.   have equal variances in the two populations.

---

[7]The assumption of equality of variances is not mandatory. When the variances cannot be assumed to be equal, though, the "proper procedure" is shrouded in controversy. There is a vast statistical literature on this condition, which is known as the Behrens-Fisher problem.

The t test is more sensitive to certain violations of these assumptions than others. For example, it still works well with respect to violations of the normality assumption but is quite sensitive to violations of the equal-variance assumption. When the violation is "too severe," the conclusions drawn are inappropriate. Yet it is surprising how little attention is paid to these underlying conditions in published research. At least little mention is made of the tests used to verify that the assumptions were satisfied. This is surprising in view of the availability of such checks. For instance, the independent-samples assumption can be checked by analyzing the sampling plan employed. The normality assumption can be investigated through a χ^2 goodness-of-fit test or Kolmogorov-Smirnov test, and the equality of the variances can be examined through an F test for homogeneity of variances.[8]

This is not the time or the place to discuss how such analyses would be conducted, nor to criticize the t test for differences in two means. Our purpose is simply to illustrate the basic fact that statistical tests depend on certain assumptions for their validity. If the assumptions are not met, analysts can do several things. Perhaps the assumptions can be satisfied through some transformation (for example, change from actual units to log units). If not, analysts can perhaps choose a different test statistic that employs different assumptions. Perhaps they might even employ a distribution-free statistical test.[9] In any case, careful analysts will not neglect the assumptions that underlie the technique, nor will they blindly assume that all the conditions for a valid test are satisfied. Analysts will be too concerned about the correctness of the results to neglect a check of assumptions.

Overview of Statistical Procedures

In the previous section, some of the more important considerations in the choice of analytic technique were highlighted. Perhaps the section raised more questions than answers. This section will introduce some of the answers by overviewing the statistical techniques discussed in Chapters 15 to 17. Such an overview must necessarily be brief. However, it should serve to direct you to the section or sections that discuss the techniques appropriate for a given problem. Figures 14.1 and 14.2 should assist in this regard. The figures illustrate the sequence of questions an

---

[8]The chi-square goodness-of-fit test and the Kolmogorov-Smirnov test are discussed in Chapter 15. Most introductory statistics books discuss the F test for the equality of variances.

[9]A *distribution-free statistical test* is one that involves minimal assumptions. The somewhat misleading nomenclature *nonparametric test* is often used interchangeably to distinguish such techniques from the *parametric tests*. The parametric tests include such tests as the t, z, or F and typically involve a greater number of and more rigorous assumptions. The nonparametric label is inappropriate for distribution-free tests because the researcher does, in fact, try to generate statements about population parameters with these tests. The emphasis is still on parameters, although the specific parameter in question may change; for example, the median rather than the mean is used as the measure of central tendency. For discussion of some of the more popular nonparametric tests, see Jean D. Gibbons, *Nonparametric Statistics: An Introduction* (Thousand Oaks, CA: Sage Publications, Inc., 1992); Jean D. Gibbons, *Nonparametric Measures of Association* (Thousand Oaks, CA: Sage Publications, Inc., 1993); Myles Hollander and Douglas A. Wolfe, *Nonparametric Statistical Methods*, 2nd ed. (New York: John Wiley, 1998); W. J. Conover, *Practical Nonparametric Statistics*, 3rd ed. (New York: John Wiley, 1998).

FIGURE 14.1 Flow Diagram for Choosing a Univariate Statistical Test

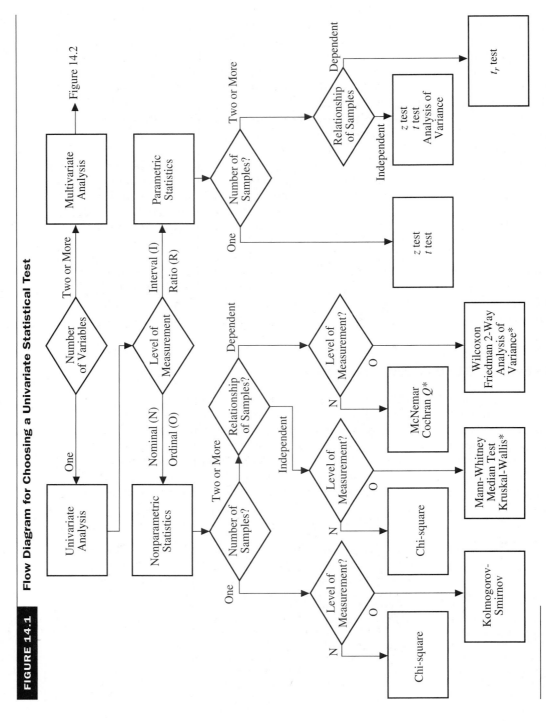

*These tests are not discussed in this book, although they are useful for some problems in marketing research.

FIGURE 14.2 Flow Diagram for Choosing a Multivariate Statistical Test

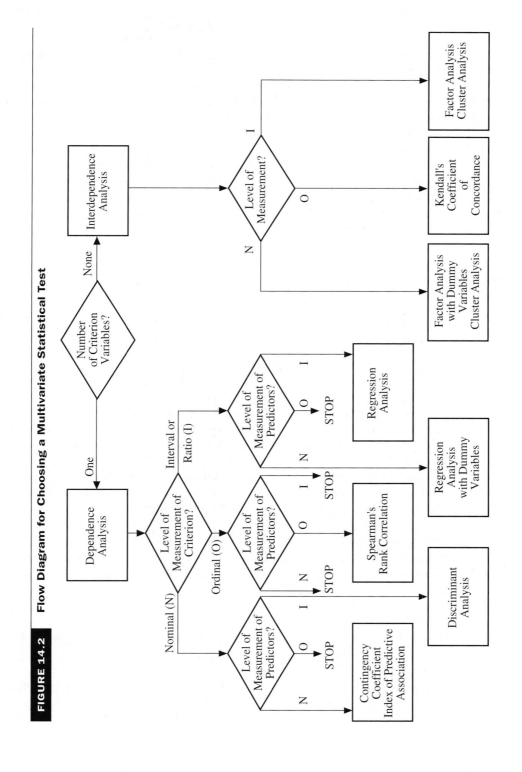

ETHICAL DILEMMA 14.2

A member of your research staff has submitted the results of an experiment to you, and you note with pleasure that all the hypotheses are fulfilled at $p \le 0.05$. The fact that they are all fulfilled at exactly $p \le 0.05$ eventually arouses your suspicions, however. When challenged, your staff member happily explains: "Oh, yes, I rounded down some 0.06s and 0.07s. Do you remember how you explained to me that measurement is by convention? And how $p \le 0.05$ is an arbitrary number selected to be significant by general agreement, although it is not very logical to have $p \le 0.05$ be significant but $p \le 0.06$ be insignificant? Well, I agree that it's not logical, so I decided that p levels close to 0.05 could be rounded to 0.05 without any harm being done."

- Is your researcher's position reasonable?
- If you do not agree with a standard, does that mean that you can cheat to meet it?

---

analyst needs to ask and answer in order to determine the appropriate statistical technique.[10]

The most important task in preparing to run the maze of statistical methods is deciding whether the problem is of a univariate or multivariate nature. The problem is **univariate** if there is a single measurement of each of the n sample objects, or if there are several measurements of each of the n observations but each variable is to be analyzed in isolation. In a **multivariate** problem, there are two or more measures of each observation (for example, number of new accounts generated and total sales by salesperson), and the variables are to be analyzed simultaneously. Given that there are multiple measures per sample observation, we find ourselves dealing with two distinct emphases: the search for differences and the investigation of association. The search for group differences is the multivariate extension of much univariate analysis. These techniques are not discussed in this book,[11] although techniques for investigating association are.

Univariate Analysis

Figure 14.1 overviews the subsequent decisions that must be made given that the problem is univariate. Let us review several of the questions that an analyst can ask in deciding among the procedures.

A useful first question involves the level of measurement of the data. Is the variable nominal, ordinal, interval, or ratio scaled? If it is nominal or ordinal, distribution-free (nonparametric) statistical procedures are appropriate. If the data

---

[10]Computer programs are available that guide analysts through a sequence of decisions to the proper choice of statistical technique. See, for example, *Statistical Navigator Professional.*™

[11]See P. J. Rulon and W. D. Brooks, "On Statistical Tests of Group Differences," in Dean K. Whittla, ed., *Handbook of Measurement and Assessment in Behavioral Sciences* (Reading, MA: Addison-Wesley, 1968), pp. 60–99, for a succinct overview of the issues and procedures.

are either interval or ratio scaled, the variable is metric, and parametric procedures apply. Actually, from a *statistical theory perspective,* the level of measurement is *not* important when selecting techniques. As Lord said so elegantly almost 50 years ago, "The numbers do not know where they come from"[12]—meaning that statistical techniques do not "know" what the level of measurement of the input data is. Rather, it is the *assumptions* that are key in determining whether a particular statistical technique is appropriate for analyzing a particular set of data. If the assumptions are satisfied, or if the statistical technique is robust (works well anyway) to violations of the assumptions, the technique can be used.

Although scale of measurement *may not be important* from a *statistical theory perspective,* it is *important* from a *measurement theory perspective.* In this sense, it is important that the numbers assigned be meaningful given the attributes of concern, that we are careful in interpreting what the numbers imply with respect to the "amount of the attribute" possessed by the object, and that we take care in how we manipulate the numbers when generating meaning from the data. Further, it is difficult even to address the topic of how to choose a statistical test without considering the level of measurement, because the level of measurement often provides important clues about statistical assumptions. In sum, level of measurement provides a useful heuristic or map for getting an analyst in the right ball-park. Consequently, the heuristic is employed to organize the discussion on choosing a statistical test, although one needs to be conscious of the fact that it may be perfectly appropriate to apply a parametric test, say, to data that are only ordinal.[13]

The analyst must then determine whether a single sample or multiple samples are involved. A hypothesis about the mean income of residents of Chicago is a single-sample analysis. If we were interested in determining how the mean income of Chicago residents compares with that of New York City residents, two independent samples are involved—that is, the population of Chicago and the population of New York City. Suppose that we were interested in comparing the mean income in Chicago now with the mean income five years ago; again, two samples are involved. Whether the samples are dependent or independent depends on the specifics of the sampling procedure employed. Let's assume that the recent sample was selected without considering the sample five years ago. The samples are then

---

[12]F. M. Lord, "On the Statistical Treatment of Football Numbers," *American Psychologist* 8 (1953), p. 751. While Lord was one of the first to contradict Stevens' assertion that his four levels of measurement had important implications for choosing statistical techniques, a number of authors later made the same point. Gaito points out, for example, that "Scale properties do not enter into any of the mathematical requirements for the various statistical procedures. I have not known of any mathematical statistician who agreed with the Stevens' misconception. A number have indicated in print that this suggestion is erroneous." John Gaito, "Measurement Scales and Statistics: Resurgence of an Old Misconception," *Psychological Bulletin* 87 (1980), p. 564. See also J. Paul Peter and Peter A. Dacin, "Measurement Scales, Permissible Statistics, and Marketing Research," in Terry L. Childers and Scott B. MacKenzie, eds., *Marketing Theory and Applications,* vol. 2 (Chicago: American Marketing Association, 1991), pp. 275–283.

[13]The product moment correlation coefficient, for example, has been found to be quite robust to violations of the "continuous variable" assumption on which it is based. Thus, it can be used to assess the degree of association between two variables when the data are intervally scaled or ordinally scaled, or even when one or both of the variables are dichotomies. See, for example, Donald G. Morrison, "Regression with Discrete Random Variables: The Effect on R^2," *Journal of Marketing Research* 9 (August 1972), pp. 338–340; Jum Nunnally and Ira H. Bernstein, *Psychometric Theory,* 3rd ed. (New York: McGraw-Hill, 1994), especially pp. 114–158.

independent. Suppose, instead, that the study's emphasis was one of determining the income changes that occurred among the families composing the first sample. The samples are then dependent; the latest income measurements are related to the earlier incomes, and those statistical methods that treat dependent samples should be used.

Suppose that we are interested in how average income and average educational levels compare in Chicago and New York City. Now there are two (multiple) measures—income and education—for two independent samples—residents of Chicago and New York City. One of the multivariate tests for group differences could be used.

Multivariate Analysis

As was stated previously, multivariate procedures are distinguished by the fact that each of n sample observations bears the value of p different variates. The p variate condition means that additional considerations must be dealt with in choosing from among available procedures. One of these considerations, previously mentioned, was the investigation of association and the determination of group differences, and this latter condition was categorized with univariate techniques. The following discussion will, therefore, emphasize association.

Two considerations dictate a choice of technique here: the type of scale used in making the measurements and the role the individual variables will play in the specific model being discussed. The most common distinction is the one between independent (antecedent or predictor) variables and dependent (consequent or criterion) variables. The distinction suggests a division of the subject into two parts: dependence and interdependence. In dependence analysis, one (or more) of the variables is selected to serve as a dependent or criterion variable, and the analyst seeks to investigate how it depends on the other variables. In interdependence analysis, none of the variables is selected as special in the sense of serving as a dependent or criterion variable. Rather, the emphasis in the analysis is on the relationships among the whole set of variables as a set.

Unfortunately, these dual considerations of scale and role of each variable interact to generate a somewhat complex classification scheme. The problem is particularly acute because a great many variables may be involved, and they may represent different levels of measurement. One has to simultaneously entertain the following questions in order to determine the appropriate method:

1. Are one or more of the variables to be singled out for separate treatment as dependent or criterion variables? If so, how many and what level of measurement do they reflect?

2. How many independent variables are there? What level of measurement does each of these variables reflect?

Figure 14.2 illustrates the sequence of decisions involved in the choice of multivariate statistical techniques. The techniques were chosen because they represent the most useful procedures for the marketing research analyst, although all cases to which they are applicable are not shown in the figure. For instance, one could convert nominal or ordinal variables to dummy variables and then run a multivariate regression analysis.[14] The figure is designed to clearly indicate the types of problems for which multivariate techniques of association are appropriate. Chapters 15 through 17 and their associated appendices should place flesh on the skeleton so that you will be able to picture some of the modifications that are possible.

Note in the figure that technique is highly dependent on the number and scaling of the variables. Change either of these and the technique typically changes. For instance, consider factor analysis and multiple regression analysis. In multiple regression analysis, one of the variables is singled out for special treatment as a criterion variable, and the relationship between the single criterion variable and the predictor variables is investigated. If the emphasis were on determining the relationships that exist among all the variables considered at once, the problem would be dealt with using factor analysis procedures.

Similarly, suppose that the variable singled out as the criterion variable reflected a nominal scale of measurement involving two categories (for example, purchase of Product A or B). It would then be appropriate to use linear discriminant analysis rather than multivariate regression.

Summary

The basic considerations involved in choosing a statistical method with which to analyze the collected data were discussed in this chapter. Scale of measurement, the research design, and the assumptions underlying the test statistic all affect this choice.

When considering the scale of measurement, an analyst must be careful to distinguish between ideas of measurement theory and statistical theory. The origin of the numbers is important from the standpoint of the interpretation of the results. That is, from a measurement theory perspective, it makes a difference whether the level of measurement is nominal, ordinal, interval, or ratio. The level of measurement does not make a difference from a statistical theory perspective, however. The key in dictating a choice of technique in that case is the assumptions underlying the technique. The assumptions should be satisfied or the technique should be robust to violations of the assumptions at issue if the technique is to be used to analyze the data. Even here, though, scale of measurement provides a useful heuristic for identifying statistical techniques for which the assumptions are likely to be satisfied.

Several questions in the research design affect choice of method, including the independence of the sample observations, the number of groups, the number of variables, and the control exercised over those variables likely to affect the results.

In choosing from among the many available tests, the analyst needs to ask a number of questions, the first of which is whether the problem is univariate or multivariate. If univariate, the next questions are whether the variable reflects nonmetric or metric measurement, whether a single sample or multiple samples are involved, and, if multiple, whether the samples are dependent or independent.

In multivariate analysis, there are two or more variables to be analyzed simultaneously. If one (or more) of these variables is considered a criterion variable that is to be related to some other variables, the problem is one of dependence analysis. If we are solely concerned with the relationships within and among the set of variables considered together, the problem is one of interdependence analysis. The role of each variable in the analysis and the level of measurement reflected by each variable interact to produce a complex classification scheme of multivariate techniques.

---

[14]Dummy variables are discussed in Chapter 16.

Questions

1. What basic considerations underlie the choice of a statistical test? Explain.
2. What are the basic levels of measurement? How does the type of data affect the choice of a statistical test?
3. Discuss the difference between independent and dependent samples, and indicate how sample independence/dependence affects the choice of a statistical test.
4. Discuss the difference between one-, two-, and three-group analyses, and indicate how the number of groups affects the choice of a statistical test.
5. Discuss the difference between a univariate analysis and a multivariate analysis. What are the problems inherent in treating a multivariate problem as a number of univariate problems?
6. What is the distinction between a multivariate test of group differences and a multivariate test of the association among the variables?
7. Discuss the difference between dependence and interdependence analysis.

Applications and Problems

1. Evaluate the two following hypothetical advertising claims. Do you think the claims are legitimate?
   a. "Con-Air gives you twice as much satisfaction while traveling—at a price 50 percent lower than other major airlines."
   b. "In blind taste tests, the majority of people preferred our beer twice as much as any other major brand of beer. Is it any wonder we sell one and one-half times more beer than our nearest competitor?"
2. Discuss whether the use of adjective scales reflects ordinal or interval measurement.
3. Discuss the importance of the level of measurement from a statistical theory perspective and a measurement theory perspective.
4. The Tobacco Institute wanted to test the effectiveness of two booklets that discuss the issue of whether advertising causes children to start smoking. A random sample of 1,200 was selected from a mailing list of 10,000 people. The sample was randomly divided into three groups of size 400 each; one group received one version of the booklet, the second received the other version, and the third group received neither booklet. One week later the attitudes of all three groups about whether advertising causes children to smoke were measured on an interval scale.
   a. Present the experimental design in diagrammatic form.
   b. What analysis technique would you recommend? Why?
5. A large national chain of department stores wanted to test the effectiveness of a promotional display for a new brand of household appliances. Fifty stores were randomly selected from a total of 263 stores. The sample of 50 stores was randomly divided into two groups of 25 stores each. Only one group used the promotional display. For three weeks, sales of the new brand of appliances were monitored for both groups.
   a. Present the experimental design in diagrammatic form.
   b. What analysis technique would you recommend? Why?
6. A medium-sized life insurance company was concerned about its poor public image resulting from a major lawsuit. The public relations department designed a 20-page bulletin that was to be mailed to all existing and prospective clients and shareholders in order to allay any negative feelings that might have resulted from the bad publicity. Prior to incurring the expenses of the complete mailing, the department randomly selected 300 clients and shareholders and mailed the 20-page bulletin to them. Attitudes toward the company were measured on an interval scale before and after sending the bulletin. However, top management was dissatisfied with this experiment and requested that another random sample of 500 clients and shareholders be generated. This sample was

to be randomly divided into two groups of 250 respondents each. The bulletin was to be mailed to one group of respondents. Attitudes toward the company were to be measured for both groups on an interval scale two weeks after mailing the bulletin.
   a. Present the experimental designs in diagrammatic form.
   b. What analysis technique would you recommend for each? Why?

7. A large national automobile manufacturer wanted to relate sales of its latest models by area to the demographic composition of each area as measured by such variables as average income, average size of household, average age of head of household, and so on.
   a. Is this dependence or interdependence analysis? Why?
   b. Are there any criterion or predictor variables? If so, what are they? Identify the level of measurement of each.
   c. On the basis of the preceding information, what multivariate procedure would you recommend?

8. A medium-sized department store wanted to determine its customers' attitudes, opinions, interests, and so on using a five-point Likert scale.
   a. Is this dependence or interdependence analysis? Why?
   b. Are there any criterion or predictor variables? If so, what are they? Identify the level of measurement of each.
   c. On the basis of the preceding information, what multivariate procedure would you recommend?

9. A large soft-drink manufacturer conducted a survey to determine customers' likes and dislikes about a new diet soft drink. The "lightness" of the soft drink was perceived as being one of the three most important soft-drink attributes. The "low calorie" attribute was not ranked as high as "lightness." The company was wondering if most consumers believed that low calorie content of the soft drink was associated with lightness.
   a. Is this dependence or interdependence analysis? Why?
   b. Are there any criterion or predictor variables? If so, what are they? Identify the level of measurement of each.
   c. On the basis of the preceding information, what multivariate procedure would you recommend?

10. Discuss the advantages of Design a over Design b. Does Design a also have advantages over Design c? Explain.
   a. O_1 X_1 O_2
        O_3 O_4
   b. O_1 X_1 O_2
   c. X_1 O_1
                    O_2

11. A survey asked users of a new deodorant product how satisfied they were with the product's performance using the following scale:

Very Satisfied	Satisfied	Neither Satisfied nor Dissatisfied	Dissatisfied	Very Dissatisfied
1	2	3	4	5

A research analyst noticed an interesting difference between male and female respondents. The mean satisfaction score for this product was 30 percent higher for women than men. Given the scale, is this a valid calculation? What are valid calculations? Can any comparison between men and women be made with these data?

12. A political opinion poll was conducted concerning the performance of two presidential candidates. Two hundred respondents were asked to rate Candidates A and B on a seven-point scale. In summarizing the results, a pooled sample t test was used to show that significant differences existed in the mean scores at $p \leq 0.05$ for Candidates A and B.

Discuss whether the *t* test is an appropriate test to use in this circumstance. Have any of the underlying assumptions of the test been violated in this example?

13. On a product-tracking survey, the following three categories were used to capture consumers' knowledge and trial of different products: "Never heard of the product," "Heard of the product but have never bought the product," and "Have bought the product." These categories were coded 1, 3, 6. The research team leader changed the codes to 1, 2, 3 so that the scores reflected equal intervals. Explain why the team leader's correction is unnecessary and unwarranted.

14. With the introduction of grocery-store scanners, elaborate marketing experiments can be run in the field. For example, a company wanting to test the effects of a new advertising campaign on its breakfast cereal sales designed the following test to determine which campaign was the most effective. Six cities were chosen for this experiment. In three cities, viewers saw the new advertisement, and in the other three cities, viewers continued to see the traditional advertising campaign.

a. Present the experimental design in diagrammatic form.

b. What analysis technique would you recommend? What assumptions underlie the recommended test?

c. Given the company's research objective, discuss alternative designs.

15. The following figure shows the satisfaction scores obtained from a survey on a new car model. Looking at the plot, can the *t* test be used to check for statistically significant differences in the satisfaction scores between these two groups? Explain.

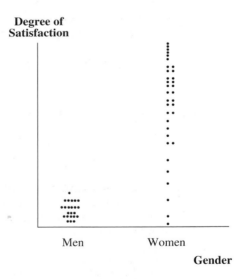

Degree of Satisfaction

Men   Women

Gender

Thorndike Sports Equipment Video Case

1. What are the benefits of sponsoring a player in the racquetball tournament?

2. Is it possible to quantify the benefits received from sponsoring a player in the racquetball tournament?

3. Is it possible to measure the exposure Thorndike receives from sponsoring a player in this racquetball tournament?

4. What other promotions would allow Thorndike to fully capitalize on the racquetball tournament as a marketing opportunity? Along with your proposals for promotions, design means of tracking the exposure that resulted from these promotions.

A P P E N D I X   1 4 A

Hypothesis Testing

Many procedures discussed in the next few chapters are used to test specific hypotheses. Therefore, it seems useful to review some basic concepts that underlie hypothesis testing in classical statistical theory, such as framing the null hypothesis or setting the risk of error in making a wrong decision, as well as the general steps involved in testing the hypothesis.[1]

Null Hypothesis

One simple fact underlies the statistical test of a hypothesis: A hypothesis may be rejected but can never be accepted except tentatively, because further evidence may prove it wrong. In other words, one rejects the hypothesis or does not reject the hypothesis on the basis of the evidence at hand. It is wrong to conclude, though, that since the hypothesis was not rejected, it can necessarily be accepted as valid.

A naive qualitative example should illustrate the issue.[2] Let's say we are testing the hypothesis that "John Doe is a poor man." We observe that Doe dines in cheap restaurants, lives in the slum area of the city in a run-down building, wears worn and tattered clothes, and so on. Although his behavior is certainly consistent with that of a poor man, we cannot "accept" the hypothesis that he is poor. It is possible that Doe may, in fact, be rich but extremely tight in his spending. We can continue gathering information about him, but for the moment we must decide not to reject the hypothesis. One single observation, for example, that indicates he has a six-figure bank account or that he owns 100,000 shares of AT&T stock would allow the immediate rejection of the hypothesis and the conclusion that "John Doe is rich."

Thus, researchers need to recognize that in the absence of perfect information (such as is the case when sampling), the best they can do is form hypotheses or conjectures about what is true. Further, their conclusions about these conjectures can be wrong, and thus there is always some probability of error in accepting any hypothesis. Statistical parlance holds that researchers commit a Type I error when they reject a true null hypothesis and thereby accept the alternative; they commit a Type II error when they do not reject a false null hypothesis, which they should given that it is false. The null hypothesis is *assumed to be true* for the purpose of the test. Such an assumption is used to generate knowledge about how the various sample estimates produced under the sampling plan might vary. Further, researchers need to be aware that Type I errors can be specified to be no more than some specific amount (that is, ≤ 0.05), whereas Type II errors are functions.[3]

---

[1]With respect to hypothesis testing, Bayesian statistical theory assumes a different posture than classical statistics. Because classical statistical-significance testing procedures are more commonly used in marketing research, only the basic elements underlying classical statistical theory are presented here.

[2]The author expresses his appreciation to Dr. B. Venkatesh of The Burke Institute for suggesting this example to illustrate the rationale behind the framing of hypotheses.

[3]We will have more to say about Type I and Type II errors later.

The upshot of these considerations is that the researcher needs to frame the null hypothesis in such a way that its rejection leads to the acceptance of the desired conclusion—that is, the statement or condition that the researcher wishes to verify. For example, suppose that a firm was considering introducing a new product if it could be expected to secure more than 10 percent of the market. The proper way to frame the hypotheses then would be

$$H_0: \pi \leq 0.10$$
$$H_a: \pi > 0.10$$

If the evidence leads to the rejection of H_0, the researcher would then be able to "accept" the alternative—that the product could be expected to secure more than 10 percent of the market—and the product would be introduced, since such a result would have been unlikely to occur if the null was indeed true. If H_0 cannot be rejected, though, the product should not be introduced unless more evidence to the contrary becomes available. The example as framed involves the use of a "one-tailed" statistical test; the alternate hypothesis is expressed directionally—that is, as being greater than 0.10. The one-tailed test is most commonly used in marketing research, although there are research problems that warrant a "two-tailed" test. For example, the market share achieved by the new formulation of Product X is no different from that achieved by the old formulation, which was 10 percent. A two-tailed test would be expressed as

$$H_0: \pi = 0.10$$
$$H_a: \pi \neq 0.10$$

No direction is implied with the alternate hypothesis; the proportion is simply expressed as not being equal to 0.10.

The one-tailed test is more commonly used than the two-tailed test in marketing research for two reasons. First, there is typically some preferred direction to the outcome—for example, the greater the market share, the higher the product quality, or the lower the expenses, the better. The two-tailed alternative is used when there is no preferred direction in the outcome or when the research is meant to demonstrate the existence of a difference but not its direction. Second, the one-tailed test, when it is appropriate, is more powerful statistically than the two-tailed alternative.

Types of Errors

Because the result of statistically testing a null hypothesis would be to reject it or not reject it, two types of errors may occur. First, the null hypothesis may be rejected when it is true. Second, it may not be rejected when it is false and, therefore, should be rejected. These two errors are, respectively, termed **Type I error** and **Type II error** (or **α error and β error,** which are the probabilities associated with their occurrence). The two types of errors are not complementary, in that $\alpha + \beta \neq 1$.

To illustrate each type of error and to demonstrate that they are not complementary, consider a judicial analogy.[4] Under U.S. criminal law, a person is innocent

---

[4]R. W. Jastram, *Elements of Statistical Inference* (Berkeley, CA: Book Company, 1947), p. 44.

until proven guilty. Therefore, the judge and jury are always testing the hypothesis of innocence. The defendant may, in fact, be either innocent or guilty, but based on the evidence, the court may reach either verdict regardless of the true situation. Table 14A.1 displays the possibilities. If the defendant is innocent and the jury finds the person innocent, or if the defendant is guilty and the jury finds him or her guilty, the jury has made a correct decision. If, however, the defendant truly is innocent and the jury finds the person guilty, or if the defendant is guilty and the jury finds him or her not guilty, they have made an error. The jury must decide one way or the other, and thus the probabilities of the jury's decision must sum vertically to 1. If we let α represent the probability of incorrectly finding the person guilty when he or she is innocent, then $1 - \alpha$ must be the probability of correctly finding him or her not guilty. Similarly, β and $1 - \beta$ represent the probabilities of findings of innocence and guilt when the person is guilty. It is intuitively obvious that $\alpha + \beta$ is not equal to 1, although later discussion will indicate that β must increase when α is reduced if other things remain the same. Because our society generally holds that finding an innocent person guilty is more serious than finding a guilty person not guilty, α error is reduced as much as possible in our legal system by requiring proof of guilt "beyond a reasonable doubt."

Table 14A.2 contains the analogous research situation. Just as the defendant's true status is unknown to the jury, the true situation regarding the null hypothesis is unknown to the researcher. The researcher's dilemma parallels that of the jury in that he or she has limited information with which to work. Suppose that the null hypothesis is true. If the researcher concludes it is false, he or she has made a Type I error. The significance level associated with a statistical test indicates the probability with which this error may be made. Because sample information will always be somewhat incomplete, there will always be some α error. The only way it can be

TABLE 14A.1   Judicial Analogy Illustrating Decision Error

	True Situation: Defendant Is	
Verdict	*Innocent*	*Guilty*
Not Guilty	Correct decision: probability = $1 - \alpha$	Error: probability = β
Guilty	Error: probability = α	Correct decision: probability = $1 - \beta$

TABLE 14A.2   Types of Errors in Hypothesis Testing

	True Situation: Null Hypothesis Is	
Research Conclusion	*True*	*False*
Do not reject H_0	Correct decision Confidence level probability = $1 - \alpha$	Error: Type II Probability = β
Reject H_0	Error: Type I Significance level probability = α	Correct decision Power of test probability = $1 - \beta$

avoided is by never rejecting the null hypothesis (never finding anyone guilty, in the judicial analogy). The *confidence level* of a statistical test is $1 - \alpha$, and the more confident we want to be of a statistical result, the lower we must set α error. The **power** associated with a statistical test is the probability of correctly rejecting a false null hypothesis. One-tailed tests are more powerful than two-tailed tests because, for the same α error, they are simply more likely to lead to a rejection of a false null hypothesis. β error represents the probability of not rejecting a false null hypothesis. There is no unique value associated with β error.

Procedure

The relationship between the two types of errors is best illustrated through example, and the example would be most productive if developed following the general format of hypothesis testing. Research Realities 14A.1 overviews the typical sequence of

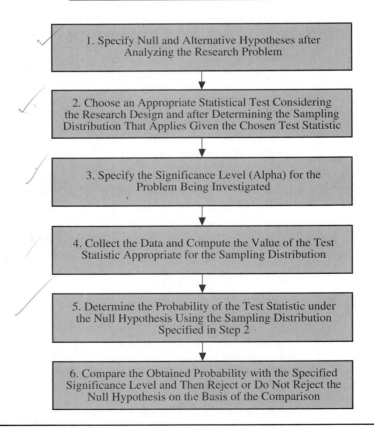

RESEARCH REALITIES 14A.1

Typical Hypothesis Testing Procedure

1. Specify Null and Alternative Hypotheses after Analyzing the Research Problem

2. Choose an Appropriate Statistical Test Considering the Research Design and after Determining the Sampling Distribution That Applies Given the Chosen Test Statistic

3. Specify the Significance Level (Alpha) for the Problem Being Investigated

4. Collect the Data and Compute the Value of the Test Statistic Appropriate for the Sampling Distribution

5. Determine the Probability of the Test Statistic under the Null Hypothesis Using the Sampling Distribution Specified in Step 2

6. Compare the Obtained Probability with the Specified Significance Level and Then Reject or Do Not Reject the Null Hypothesis on the Basis of the Comparison

steps that is followed. Assume the problem is indeed one of investigating the potential for a new product and the research involves the preferences of consumers. Suppose that, in the judgment of management, the product should not be introduced unless at least 20 percent of the population could be expected to prefer it and that the research calls for 625 respondents to be interviewed for their preferences.

STEP 1   The null and alternate hypotheses would be

$$H_0\text{:}\pi \leq 0.20$$
$$H_a\text{:}\pi > 0.20$$

The hypotheses are framed so that if the null hypothesis is rejected, the product should be introduced.

STEP 2   The appropriate sample statistic is the sample proportion, and the distribution of all possible sample proportions under the sampling plan is based on the assumption that the null hypothesis is true. Although the distribution of sample proportions is theoretically binomially distributed, the large sample size permits the use of the normal approximation.[5] The z test therefore applies. The z statistic in this case equals

$$z = \frac{p - \pi}{\sigma_p}$$

where p is the sample proportion preferring the product and σ_p is the standard error of the proportion, or the standard deviation of the distribution of sample ps. In turn, σ_p equals

$$\sqrt{\frac{\pi(1 - \pi)}{n}} = \sqrt{\frac{0.20(0.80)}{625}} = 0.0160$$

where n is the sample size. Note this peculiarity of proportions. As soon as we have hypothesized a population value, we have said something about the standard error of the estimate. The proportion is the most clear-cut case of "known variance," since the variance is specified automatically with an assumed π. The researcher thus knows all the values for calculating z except p before ever taking the sample and further knows *a priori* the distribution to which the calculated statistic will be related. This is true in general, and the researcher should have these conditions clearly in mind before taking the sample.

---

[5]The binomial distribution tends toward the normal distribution for a fixed π as sample size increases. The tendency is most rapid when $\pi = 0.5$. With sufficiently large samples, normal probabilities may be used to approximate binomial probabilities with πs in this range. As π departs from 0.5 in either direction, the normal approximation becomes less adequate, although it is generally held that the normal approximation may be used safely if the smaller of $n\pi$ or $n(1 - \pi)$ is 10 or more. If this condition is not satisfied, binomial probabilities can either be calculated directly or found in tables that are readily available. In the example, $n\pi = 625(0.2) = 125$, and $n(1 - \pi) = 500$, and thus there is little question about the adequacy of the normal approximation to binomial probabilities.

STEP 3   The researcher selects a significance level (α) using the following reasoning. In this situation, α error is the probability of rejecting H_0 and concluding that $\pi > 0.2$, when in reality $\pi \leq 0.2$. This conclusion will lead the company to market the new product. However, because the venture will only be profitable if $\pi > 0.2$, a wrong decision to market would be financially unprofitable and possibly disastrous. The probability of Type I error should, therefore, be minimized as much as possible. The researcher recognizes, though, that the probability of a Type II error increases as α is decreased, other things being equal. Type II error in this case implies concluding that $\pi \leq 0.2$ when in fact $\pi > 0.2$, which in turn suggests that the company would table the decision to introduce the product when it could be profitable. The opportunity loss from making such an error could be quite serious. Although, as explained later, the researcher does not know what β would be, he or she knows that α and β are interrelated and that an extremely low value of α (say, $\alpha = 0.01$ or 0.001) would produce intolerable β errors. Therefore, the researcher decides on an α level of 0.05 as an acceptable compromise.[6]

STEP 4   Since Step 4 involves the computation of the test statistic, it can be completed only after the sample is drawn and the information collected. Suppose 140 of the 625 sample respondents preferred the product. The sample proportion is thus $p = 140/625 = 0.224$. The basic question that needs to be answered is conceptually simple: "Is this value of p too large to have occurred by chance from a population with π assumed to be equal to 0.2?" or, in other words, "What is the probability of getting $p = 0.224$ when $\pi = 0.2$?"

$$z = \frac{p - \pi}{\sigma_p} = \frac{0.224 - 0.20}{0.0160} = 1.500$$

STEP 5   The probability of occurrence of a z value of 1.500 can be found from standard tabled values of areas under the normal curve. (See Appendix A at the end of the book.) Figure 14A.1 shows the procedure. The shaded area between $-\infty$ and

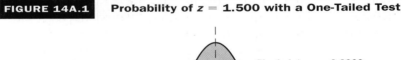

FIGURE 14A.1   **Probability of $z = 1.500$ with a One-Tailed Test**

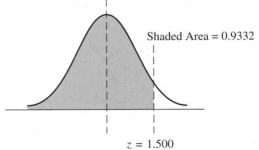

Shaded Area = 0.9332

$z = 1.500$

---

[6]We shall have more to say about the choice of $\alpha = 0.05$ and its interpretation after we have introduced the notion of power.

1.500 equals 0.9332; this means that the area to the right of $z = 1.500$ is $1.000 - 0.9332$, or 0.0668. This is the probability of securing a z value of 1.500 under a true situation of $\pi = 0.2$.

STEP 6   Since the calculated probability of occurrence is higher than the specified significance level of $\alpha = 0.05$, the null hypothesis is not rejected. The product would not be introduced because, although the evidence is in the right direction, it is not sufficient to conclude beyond "any reasonable doubt" that $\pi > 0.2$. If the decision maker had been able to tolerate a 10 percent chance of committing a Type I error, the null hypothesis would have been rejected and the product marketed, since the probability of getting a sample $p = 0.224$ when the true $\pi = 0.20$ is, as we have seen, 0.0668.

Power

The example illustrates the importance of correctly specifying the risk of error. If a 10 percent chance of an α error were tolerable and the researcher specified $\alpha = 0.05$, a potentially profitable opportunity would have been bypassed. The choice of the proper significance level involves weighing the costs associated with the two types of error—unfortunately a procedure that most researchers ignore, choosing out of habit $\alpha = 0.10$ or 0.05. Perhaps this lapse is due to the difficulty encountered in specifying β error, or Type II error.[7]

The difficulty arises because β error is not a constant. Recall that it is the probability of not rejecting a false null hypothesis. Therefore, the probability of committing a Type II error depends on the size of the difference between the *true,* but unknown, population value and the value *assumed to be true* under the null hypothesis. Other things being equal, we would prefer a test that minimized such errors. Alternatively, since the power of a test equals $1 - \beta$, we would prefer the test with the greatest power so that we would have the best chance of rejecting a false null hypothesis.[8] Clearly, our ability to do this depends on how false H_0 truly is. It could be just a little bit false or way off the mark, and the probability of an incorrect conclusion would certainly be higher in the first case. The difference between the assumed value under the null hypothesis and the true, but unknown, value is known as the effect size. As intuition suggests, large effects are easier to distinguish than small effects.

---

[7]See Robert Hooke, *How to Tell the Liars from the Statisticians* (New York: Dekker, 1983), for several interesting analogies highlighting the trade-offs between Type I and Type II errors.

[8]See Alan G. Sawyer and A. Dwayne Ball, "Statistical Power and Effect Size in Marketing Research," *Journal of Marketing Research* 18 (August 1981), pp. 275–290, for a persuasive argument about why marketing researchers need to pay more attention to power in their research designs. The article also offers some suggestions on how to improve statistical power. For general discussions, see Jacob Cohen, *Statistical Power Analysis for the Behavioral Sciences,* 2nd ed. (Hillsdale, NJ: Lawrence Erlbaum and Associates, 1988); M. W. Lipsey, *Design Sensitivity: Statistical Power for Experimental Research* (Thousand Oaks, CA: Sage Publications, Inc., 1990); Kevin R. Murphy and Brett Myors, *Statistical Power Analysis: A Simple and General Model for Traditional and Modern Hypothesis Tests* (Hillsdale, NJ: Lawrence Erlbaum and Associates, 1998).

Consider again the hypotheses

$$H_0: \pi \leq 0.20$$
$$H_a: \pi > 0.20$$

where $\sigma_p = 0.0160$ and $\alpha = 0.05$, as before. Any calculated z value greater than 1.645 will cause us to reject this hypothesis, since this is the z value that cuts off 5 percent of the normal curve. The z value can be equated to the *critical* sample proportion through the formula

$$z = \frac{p - \pi}{\sigma_p}$$

$$1.645 = \frac{p - 0.20}{0.0160}$$

or $p = 0.2263$. Thus, any sample proportion greater than $p = 0.2263$ will lead to the rejection of the null hypothesis that $\pi \leq 0.2$. This means that if 142 or more $[0.2263(625) = 141.4]$ of the sample respondents prefer the new product, the null hypothesis will be rejected and the product introduced, while if 141 or less of the sample respondents prefer it, the null hypothesis will not be rejected and the new product will not be introduced.

The likelihood of a sample proportion of $p = 0.2263$ is much greater for certain values of π than for others. Suppose, for instance, that the true but unknown value of π was 0.22. The sampling distribution of the sample proportions is again normal, but now it is centered about 0.22. The probability of obtaining the critical sample proportion $p = 0.2263$ under this condition is found again from the normal curve table, where[9]

$$z = \frac{p - \pi}{\sigma_p} = \frac{0.2263 - 0.22}{0.0166} = 0.380$$

The shaded area between $-\infty$ and $z = 0.380$ is given in Appendix A at the end of the book as 0.6480, and thus the area to the right of $z = 0.380$ is equal to $1.000 - 0.6480 = 0.3520$ (see Panel B in Figure 14A.2). This is the probability that a value as large or larger than $p = 0.2263$ would be obtained if the true population proportion was $\pi = 0.22$. It is also the power of the test in that, if π is truly equal to 0.22, the null hypothesis is false and 0.3520 is the probability that the null will be rejected. Conversely, the probability that $p < 0.2263$ equals $1 - 0.3520 = 0.6480$, which is β error. The null hypothesis is false and yet the false null hypothesis is not rejected for any sample proportions $p < 0.2263$.

Suppose that the true population condition was $\pi = 0.21$ instead of $\pi = 0.22$, and the null hypothesis was again $H_0: \pi \leq 0.20$. Since the null hypothesis is less false in this second case, we would expect power to be lower and the risk of β error to be higher because the null hypothesis is less likely to be rejected. Let us see if that is indeed the case. The z value corresponding to the critical $p = 0.2263$ is 1.000. Power

---

[9]Note that σ_p is now $\sqrt{0.22(0.78)/625} = 0.0166$, because a different specification of π implies a different standard error of estimate.

given by the area to the right of $z = 1.000$ is 0.1587 (the β error is 0.8413), and the expected result does obtain. (See Figure 14A.2, Panel C.)

Consider one final value, true $\pi = 0.25$. The null hypothesis of $\pi = 0.20$ would be way off the mark in this case, and we would expect there would be only a small chance that it would not be rejected and a Type II error would be committed. The calculations are displayed in Figure 14A.2, Panel D; $z = -1.368$, and the area to the right of $z = -1.368$ is 0.9144. The probability of β error is 0.0856, and the *a priori* expectation is confirmed.

Table 14A.3 contains the power of the test for other selected population states, and Figure 14A.3 shows these values graphically.

Figure 14A.3 is essentially the power curve for the hypothesis

$$H_0: \pi \leq 0.20$$
$$H_a: \pi > 0.20$$

and it confirms that the farther away the true π from the hypothesized value in the direction indicated by the alternate hypothesis, the higher the power. Note that power is not defined for the hypothesized value because if the true value in fact equals the hypothesized value, a β error cannot be committed.

Because power is a function rather than a single value, the researcher attempting to balance Type I and Type II errors logically needs to ask how false the null hypothesis is likely to be and to establish the decision rule accordingly. The way to control both errors within predetermined bounds for a given size effect is to vary the sample size.[10] The need to specify all three items—α error (or degree of confidence), β error (or power), and the size of the effect it is necessary to detect—possibly explains why so many researchers content themselves with the specification of Type I or α error and allow β error to fall where it may. The failure to even worry about, much less explicitly take into account, the power of the statistical test represents one of the fundamental problems with the classical statistics hypothesis-testing approach as it is commonly practiced in marketing research. Moreover, Type II errors are often more costly than Type I errors. Another common problem is the misinterpretation of what a "statistically significant result" really means. There are several common misinterpretations.[11]

One of the most frequent misinterpretations is to view a p value as representing the probability that the results occurred because of sampling error. Thus, the commonly used $p = 0.05$ is taken to mean that there is a probability of only 0.05 that the results were caused by chance and thus there must be something fundamental causing them. In actuality, a p value of 0.05 means that *if* (and this is a big if) the null hypothesis is indeed true as assumed, the odds are only 1 in 20 of getting a sample result of the magnitude that was observed. Unfortunately, there is no way in classical statistical significance testing to determine whether the null hypothesis is true.

---

[10]See Helena Chumura Kraemer and Sue Thiemann, *How Many Subjects?* (Thousand Oaks, CA: Sage Publications, Inc., 1987), for discussion of the use of power to determine sample size.

[11]For an excellent discussion of some of the most common misinterpretations of classical significance tests and some recommendations on how to surmount the problems, see Alan G. Sawyer and J. Paul Peter, "The Significance of Statistical Significance Tests in Marketing Research," *Journal of Marketing Research* 20 (May 1983), pp. 122–133; Jacob Cohen, "Things I Have Learned (So Far)," *American Psychologist* 45 (December 1990), pp. 1304–1312; Jacob Cohen, "The Earth Is Round ($p < .05$)," *American Psychologist* 49 (December 1994), pp. 997–1003.

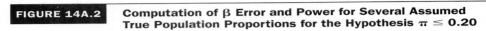

FIGURE 14A.2   **Computation of β Error and Power for Several Assumed True Population Proportions for the Hypothesis π ≤ 0.20**

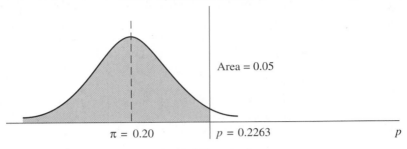

Area = 0.05

$\pi = 0.20$ $p = 0.2263$ p

Panel A: Critical Proportion under Null Hypothesis

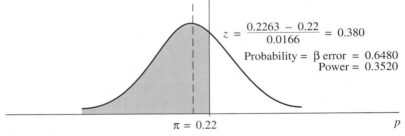

$z = \dfrac{0.2263 - 0.22}{0.0166} = 0.380$

Probability = β error = 0.6480
Power = 0.3520

$\pi = 0.22$ p

Panel B: Probability of Realizing Critical Proportion When $\pi = 0.22$, Which Means Null Hypothesis Is False

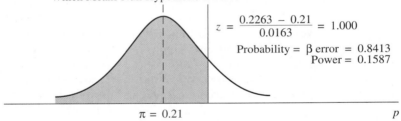

$z = \dfrac{0.2263 - 0.21}{0.0163} = 1.000$

Probability = β error = 0.8413
Power = 0.1587

$\pi = 0.21$ p

Panel C: Probability of Realizing Critical Proportion When $\pi = 0.21$, Which Means Null Hypothesis Is False

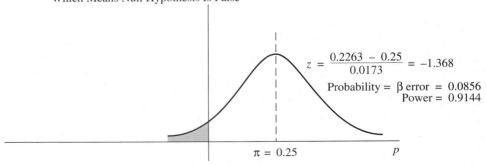

$z = \dfrac{0.2263 - 0.25}{0.0173} = -1.368$

Probability = β error = 0.0856
Power = 0.9144

$\pi = 0.25$ p

Panel D: Probability of Realizing Critical Proportion When $\pi = 0.25$, Which Means Null Hypothesis Is False

| TABLE 14A.3 | β Error and Power for Different Assumed True Values of π and the Hypotheses $H_0: \pi \le 0.20$ and $H_a: \pi > 0.20$ |

Value of π	Probability of Type II or β Error	Power of the Test: $1 - \beta$
0.20	$(0.950) = 1 - \alpha$	$(0.05) = \alpha$
0.21	0.8413	0.1587
0.22	0.6480	0.3520
0.23	0.4133	0.5867
0.24	0.2133	0.7867
0.25	0.0856	0.9144
0.26	0.0273	0.9727
0.27	0.0069	0.9931
0.28	0.0014	0.9986
0.29	0.0005	0.9995
0.30	0.0000	1.0000

A *p* value reached by classical methods is not a summary of the data. Nor does the *p* value attached to a result tell how strong or dependable the particular result is. . . . Writers and readers are all too likely to read .05 as *p(H/E)* "the probability that the Hypothesis is true, given the Evidence." As textbooks on statistics reiterate almost in vain, *p* is *p(E/H)*, the probability that this Evidence would arise if the (null) hypothesis is true.[12]

Another common misinterpretation is to equate statistical significance with practical significance. Many fail to realize that a difference can be of practical importance and not statistically significant if the power of the test is weak. Conversely, a result may be of no practical importance, even if highly significant, if the sample size is very large.

A third frequent misinterpretation is to hold that the α or *p* level chosen is in some way related to the probability that the research hypothesis captured in the alternative hypothesis is true. Most typically, this probability is taken as the complement of the α level. Thus, a *p* value of 0.05 is interpreted to mean that its complement, $1 - 0.05 = 0.95$, is the probability that the research hypothesis is true. "Related to this misinterpretation is the practice of interpreting *p* values as a measure of the degree of validity of research results, that is, a *p* value such as *p* < .0001 is 'highly statistically significant' or 'highly significant' and therefore much more valid than a *p* value of, say, 0.05."[13] Both of these related interpretations are wrong.

The only logical conclusion that can be drawn when a null hypothesis is rejected at some predetermined *p* level is that sampling error is an unlikely explanation of the results *given* that the null hypothesis is true. In many ways that is not saying very much, because, as was argued previously, the null hypothesis is set up to be

---

[12]Lee J. Cronbach and R. E. Snow, *Aptitudes and Instructional Methods: A Handbook for Research on Interactions* (New York: Irvington, 1977), p. 52.

[13]Sawyer and Peter, "The Significance," p. 123. For other useful discussions of what statistical tests of significance mean, see Mick Alt and Malcolm Brighton, "Analyzing Data or Telling Stories?" *Journal of the Market Research Society* 23 (October 1981), pp. 209–219; Siu L. Chow, *Statistical Significance: Rationale, Validity, and Utility* (Thousand Oaks, CA: Sage Publications, Inc., 1996).

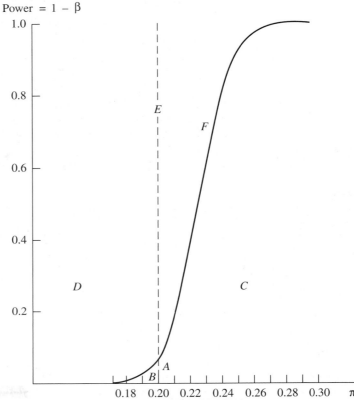

FIGURE 14A.3   **Power Function for Data in Table 14A.3**

Probability of Rejecting H_0: $\pi \leq 0.20$

Power = $1 - \beta$

A—Type I error; true null hypothesis is rejected; significance level.
B—Type I error; true null hypothesis is rejected.
C—No error; false null hypothesis is rejected.
D—No error; true null hypothesis is not rejected.
E—No error; true null hypothesis is not rejected; confidence level.
F—Type II error; false null hypothesis is not rejected.

false. The null, as typically stated, holds that there is no relationship between two certain variables, say, or that the groups are equal with respect to some particular variable. Yet, we do not really believe that. Rather, we investigate the relationship between variables because we believe there is some association between them, and we contrast the groups because we believe they are different with respect to the variable. Further, we can control our ability to reject the null hypothesis simply by the power we build into the statistical test, primarily through the size of the sample used to test it. "Given sufficiently high statistical power, one would expect virtually *always* to conclude the exact null hypothesis is false."[14]

---

[14]Sawyer and Peter, "The Significance," p. 125.

Marketing researchers then need to be wary when interpreting the results of their hypothesis testing procedures so that they do not mislead themselves and others. They constantly need to keep in mind both types of errors that are possible to make. Further, they need to make certain that they do not misinterpret what a test of significance reveals. It represents no more than a test against the null hypothesis. One useful way of avoiding misinterpretation is to calculate confidence intervals when possible, because this gives decision makers a much better feel for how much faith they can have in the results. A test of significance is very much a yes-no situation: either the sample result is statistically significant or it is not. In contrast, "the confidence interval not only gives a yes or no answer, but also, by its width, gives an indication of whether the answer should be whispered or shouted."[15] Although not every test of significance can be put in the form of a confidence interval estimate, many of them can, and it is advisable to do so when the opportunity arises.[16]

Questions
1. Comment on the statement: "A hypothesis can never be accepted, only rejected." Is the statement true? Why or why not?
2. What is the basic scientific proposition that guides the framing of hypotheses? Illustrate the principle with a research question of your own choosing.
3. When is a two-tailed test preferred to a one-tailed test, and vice versa?
4. What is a Type I error? What is a Type II error? What is the relationship between these two types of error?
5. What is meant by the statistical notion of power?
6. Illustrate the steps involved in the statistical testing of hypotheses with your own example.
7. Explain the comment, "The farther away the true population parameter is from the hypothesized population value in the direction indicated by the alternate hypothesis, the higher the power." Is power not a constant? Why?
8. Using your own example, construct the power function.
9. What does it mean when the null hypothesis is rejected at the $\alpha = 0.10$ level?

Applications and Problems
1. Assume that the brand manager of a medium-sized manufacturer of consumer products decides to introduce a new brand of breakfast cereal if the company can initially acquire 1.5 percent of the market. The following hypotheses are to be tested:

$$H_0: \pi \leq 0.015$$
$$H_a: \pi > 0.015$$

---

[15]Mary G. Natrella, "The Relation between Confidence Intervals and Tests of Significance," *American Statistician* 14 (1960), p. 22. See also G. R. Dawling and P. K. Walsh, "Estimating and Reporting Confidence Intervals for Market and Opinion Research," *European Research* 13 (July 1985), pp. 130–133; Charles Cowan, "Testing versus Description: Confidence Intervals and Hypothesis Testing," *Marketing Research: A Magazine of Management & Application* 2 (September 1990), pp. 59–61.

[16]For an excellent discussion of the relationship between tests of significance and confidence interval estimates, see Natrella, "The Relation between Confidence Intervals," pp. 20–22, 33.

Explain and discuss the Type I and Type II errors that could occur while testing these hypotheses. What are the implications for the company?

2. Discuss the danger of specifying Type I or α error and allowing β error to fall where it may.

3. Bentley Foods, Inc., a large manufacturer of frozen foods, has developed a new line of frozen pizza. Management has agreed to begin producing and marketing the new line if at least 15 percent of the population would prefer the pizza over other frozen pizzas currently available. To determine preferences, a sample of 1,000 consumers was obtained; 172 indicated that they would prefer the new product over existing brands.
   a. State the null and alternative hypotheses.
   b. Compute the standard error of the proportion.
   c. Calculate the z statistic. What is the probability of obtaining this value of the z statistic if the null hypothesis is true?
   d. The research manager for Bentley Foods is comfortable using the 0.05 significance level. Should the null hypothesis be rejected?
   e. At this significance level, what is the critical sample proportion?

4. A computer company is considering a nationwide introduction of a new type of personal computer. In order to test whether the product would be successful, the company is contemplating a nationwide survey to assess people's intentions to purchase the new model instead of existing models. The research team has framed the hypotheses as follows:

$$H_0: \pi_N \leq \pi_O$$
$$H_a: \pi_N > \pi_O$$

where N and O refer to the new and old models, respectively. If people do not prefer the new model, introducing it would be extremely costly for the company. Under this scenario, does the research team need to be more concerned about a Type I or Type II error? What should α be set at to minimize the company's risk?

5. A research team tested new batteries to see if they lasted significantly longer than the company's existing battery. Traditionally, all experiments have been run at $\alpha = 0.05$. After testing 100 old batteries as well as 100 new batteries, the mean life for the new battery was found to be greater than that of the old, at $\alpha = .05$ significance level; however, a new analyst became greatly excited when it was discovered that the difference was significant at $\alpha = 0.001$. He commented, "This product is much better than we thought; the difference is highly significant!"
   a. Is this a correct interpretation of the test results? Explain.
   b. Is it appropriate for the research team to announce that the difference in mean life is significant at $\alpha = 0.001$ instead of $\alpha = 0.05$?

6. Before analyzing a set of scores, a researcher decides to test whether the assumption of a normal distribution is appropriate for the data. When testing to verify assumptions, does the researcher need to be more concerned about Type I or Type II error? What should α be set at under these circumstances?

15

Data Analysis: Examination of Differences

A question that arises regularly in the analysis of research data is, "Are the research results statistically significant? Could the result have occurred by chance because only a sample of the population was contacted, or does it indicate an underlying condition in the population?" To answer, we use some kind of test of statistical significance.

This chapter reviews some of the more important tests for examining the statistical significance of differences. The difference at issue might be between some sample result and some expected population value, or it might be between two or more sample results. The intent is to indicate the types of tests that are available and the types of problems to which they apply. The first part of the chapter reviews the χ^2 goodness-of-fit test, which is especially useful with nominal data, and the second part reviews the Kolmogorov-Smirnov test, which is useful with ordinal data. The latter sections focus on the parametric tests that are applicable when examining differences in means or proportions.

Goodness of Fit

In a number of marketing situations, it is necessary to determine whether some observed pattern of frequencies corresponds to an "expected" pattern. Consider a breakfast food manufacturer who has recently developed a new cereal called Score. The cereal will be packaged in the three standard sizes: small, large, and family size. The manufacturer's past experience suggests that for every one small package, three of the large and two of the family size are also sold. The manufacturer wishes to see if this same tendency would hold with this new cereal, since a change in consumption patterns could have important production implications. Therefore, the manufacturer decides to conduct a market test to determine the relative frequencies with which the various sizes would be purchased.

Suppose that, in an appropriate test market over a one-week period, 1,200 boxes of the new cereal were sold and that the distribution of sales by size was as follows:

	Number Buying		
Small	*Large*	*Family*	*Total*
240	575	385	1,200

Does this preliminary evidence indicate that the firm should expect a change in the purchase patterns of the various sized packages with Score?

This is the type of problem for which the **chi-square goodness-of-fit test** is ideally suited. The variable of interest has been broken into k mutually exclusive categories ($k = 3$ in the example), and each observation logically falls into one of the k classes or cells. The trials (purchases) are independent, and the sample size is large.

All that is necessary to employ the test is to calculate the *expected* number of cases that would fall in each category and to compare that with the *observed* number actually falling in the category using the statistic

$$\chi^2 = \sum_{i=1}^{k} \frac{[O_i - E_i]^2}{E_i}$$

where
O_i is the observed number of cases falling in the ith category;
E_i is the expected number of cases falling in the ith category; and
k is the number of categories.

The expected number falling into a category is generated from the null hypothesis that the composition of sales of Score by package size would follow the manufacturer's normal sales; that is, for every small package, three large and two family sizes would be sold. In terms of proportions, $\pi_1 = 1/(1 + 3 + 2) = \frac{1}{6}$, $\pi_2 = \frac{3}{6}$, and $\pi_3 = \frac{2}{6}$. Thus the expected sales would be $E_1 = n\pi_1 = 1,200(\frac{1}{6}) = 200$ of the small size, $E_2 = n\pi_2 = 1,200(\frac{3}{6}) = 600$ of the large size, and $E_3 = n\pi_3 = 1,200(\frac{2}{6}) = 400$ of the family size. The appropriate χ^2 statistic is computed as

$$\chi^2 = \frac{(240 - 200)^2}{200} + \frac{(575 - 600)^2}{600} + \frac{(385 - 400)^2}{400} = 9.60$$

The chi-square distribution is one of the statistical distributions that is completely determined by its degrees of freedom ν. The mean of the chi-square distribution is equal to the number of degrees of freedom ν, and its variance is equal to 2ν. For large values of ν, the chi-square distribution is approximately normally distributed.

In the example, the number of degrees of freedom is one less than the number of categories k; that is, $\nu = k - 1 = 2$. This is because the sum of the differences between the observed and expected frequencies is zero. Both the expected and observed frequencies must sum to the total number of cases. Given any $k - 1$ differences, the remaining difference is thus fixed, and this results in the loss of one degree of freedom.

Suppose that the researcher has chosen a significance level of $\alpha = 0.05$ for this test. The tabled value of χ^2 for two degrees of freedom and $\alpha = 0.05$ is 5.99. (see Appendix B at the end of the book). Since the calculated value ($\chi^2 = 9.60$) is larger, the conclusion is that the sample result would be unlikely to occur by chance alone. Rather, the preliminary market test results suggest that sales of Score will follow a different pattern than is typical. The null hypothesis of sales in the ratio of $1:3:2$ is rejected.

ETHICAL DILEMMA 15.1

A marketing researcher is perplexed at the results of his experiment—they do not tally at all with his *a priori* hypotheses. He immediately starts hunting through the literature for alternative hypotheses that will account for the findings. Halfway through the stack of journal articles on his desk, he stops reading and leans back in his chair with a whistle of relief. "Thank goodness! That idea fits my findings pretty well." He reaches for a pad of paper to write his final report, in which his new hypothesis is presented *a priori* and is neatly upheld in the experiment.

- Is it ethical to select the first explanation that fits the existing data without considering all alternative explanations *and* without further testing?

- Is it ethical to present a *post hoc* explanation as an *a priori* hypothesis?

- How often, in fact, are theories abandoned in the face of disconfirming evidence?

The chi-square test just outlined is an approximate test.[1] The approximation is relatively good if, as a rule of thumb, the *expected* number of cases in each category is five or more, although this value can be as low as one for some situations.[2]

The previous example illustrated the use of the chi-square distribution to test a null hypothesis concerning k population proportions, $\pi_1, \pi_2, \ldots, \pi_k$. The proportions were needed to generate the expected number of cases in each of the k categories. Viewed in this light, the test of a single proportion discussed when reviewing the logic of hypothesis testing in the appendix to Chapter 14 is a special case; in the goodness-of-fit test, the single parameter π is replaced by the k parameters $\pi_1, \pi_2, \ldots, \pi_k$.

Another use of the chi-square goodness-of-fit test is in determining whether a population distribution has a particular form. For instance, we might be interested in finding out whether a sample distribution of scores might have arisen from a normal distribution of scores. To investigate, we could construct the sample frequency histogram. The intervals would correspond to the k cells of the goodness-of-fit test. The observed cell frequencies would be the number of observations falling in each interval. The expected cell frequencies would be the number falling in each interval, if indeed the sample came from a normal distribution with mean μ and

---

[1]The correct distribution to test the hypothesis is the hypergeometric. The hypergeometric distribution, however, is unwieldy for anything but very small samples. The chi-square distribution approximates the hypergeometric for large sample sizes. For a discussion of this point, as well as the other conditions surrounding a goodness-of-fit test, see Jean D. Gibbons, *Nonparametric Statistics: An Introduction* (Thousand Oaks, CA: Sage Publications, 1992); Myles Hollander and Douglas A. Wolfe, *Nonparametric Statistical Methods*, 2nd ed. (New York: John Wiley, 1998); W. J. Conover, *Practical Nonparametric Statistics*, 3rd ed. (New York: John Wiley, 1998).

[2]W. G. Cochran, "The χ^2 Test of Goodness of Fit," *Annuals of Mathematical Statistics* 23 (1952), pp. 315–345.

variance σ^2. If the population mean and variance were unknown, the sample mean and variance could be used as estimates. This would result in the loss of two additional degrees of freedom, but the basic test procedure would remain unchanged.

Kolmogorov-Smirnov Test

The **Kolmogorov-Smirnov test** is similar to the chi-square goodness-of-fit test because it uses a comparison between observed and expected frequencies to determine whether observed results are in accord with a stated null hypothesis. But the Kolmogorov-Smirnov test takes advantage of the ordinal nature of the data.

Consider, for example, a manufacturer of cosmetics who is testing four different shades of a foundation compound—very light, light, medium, and dark. The company has hired a marketing research firm to determine whether any distinct preference exists toward either extreme. If so, the company will manufacture only the preferred shades. Otherwise, it is planning to market all shades. Suppose that in a sample of 100, 50 persons preferred the "very light" shade, 30 the "light" shade, 15 the "medium" shade, and 5 the "dark" shade. Do these results indicate some kind of preference?

Since shade represents a natural ordering, the Kolmogorov-Smirnov test can be used to test the preference hypothesis. The test involves specifying the cumulative distribution function that would occur under the null hypothesis and comparing that with the observed cumulative distribution function. The point at which the two functions show the maximum deviation is determined, and the value of this deviation is the test statistic.

The null hypothesis for the cosmetic manufacturer would be that there is no preference for the various shades. Thus, it would be expected that 25 percent of the sample would prefer each shade. The cumulative distribution function resulting from this assumption is presented as the last column of Table 15.1.

Kolmogorov-Smirnov D, which is equal to the *absolute value of the maximum deviation* between the observed cumulative proportion and the theoretical cumulative proportion, is $0.80 - 0.50 = 0.30$. If the researcher chooses an $\alpha = 0.05$, the critical value of D for large samples is given by $1.36/\sqrt{n}$, where n is the sample size. In our case, the critical value is 0.136. Calculated D exceeds the critical value, and thus the null hypothesis of no preference among shades is rejected. The data indicate a statistically significant preference for the lighter shades.

TABLE 15.1	**Observed and Theoretical Cumulative Distributions of Foundation Compound Preference**				
Shade	*Observed Number*	*Observed Proportion*	*Observed Cumulative Proportion*	*Theoretical Proportion*	*Theoretical Cumulative Proportion*
Very light	50	0.50	0.50	0.25	0.25
Light	30	0.30	0.80	0.25	0.50
Medium	15	0.15	0.95	0.25	0.75
Dark	5	0.05	1.00	0.25	1.00

The careful reader will have noticed that the hypothesis of no preference could also have been tested with the chi-square goodness-of-fit test. When the data are ordinal, though, the Kolmogorov-Smirnov test is the preferred procedure. It is more powerful than chi-square in almost all cases, is easier to compute, and does not require a certain minimum expected frequency in each cell as the chi-square test does.

The Kolmogorov-Smirnov test can also be used to determine whether two independent samples have been drawn from the same population or from populations with the same distribution. An example would be a manufacturer interested in determining whether consumer preference among sizes for a new brand of laundry detergent was the same as for the old brand. To apply the test, we would simply need to create a cumulative frequency distribution for each sample of observations using the same intervals. The test statistic would be the value of the maximum deviation between the two observed cumulative frequencies.

Hypotheses about One Mean

A recurring problem in marketing research studies is the need to make some statement about the parent population mean. Recall that the distribution of sample means is normal, with the mean of the sample means equal to the population mean and the variance of the sample means, $\sigma_{\bar{x}}^2$, equal to the population variance divided by the sample size—that is, $\sigma_{\bar{x}}^2 = \sigma/n$. Thus, it should not be surprising to find that the appropriate statistic for testing a hypothesis about a mean when the population variance is *known* is

$$z = \frac{\bar{x} - \mu}{\sigma_{\bar{x}}}$$

where
$\bar{x}$ is the sample mean;
μ is the population mean; and
$\sigma_{\bar{x}}$ is the standard error of the mean, which is equal to $\sigma/\sqrt{n}$, where n is the sample size.

The z statistic is appropriate if the sample comes from a normal population, or if the variable is not normally distributed in the population but the sample is large enough for the Central-Limit Theorem to be operative. What happens, though, in the more realistic case in which the population variance is *unknown*?

When the parent population variance is unknown, then, of course, the standard error of the mean, $\sigma_{\bar{x}}$, is unknown since it is equal to $\sigma/\sqrt{n}$. The standard error of the mean must then be estimated from the sample data. The estimate is $s_{\bar{x}} = \hat{s}/\sqrt{n}$, where $\hat{s}$ is the unbiased sample standard deviation; that is,

$$\hat{s} = \sqrt{\frac{\sum_{i=1}^{n}(X_i - \bar{x})^2}{n - 1}}$$

The test statistic now becomes $(\bar{x} - \mu)/s_{\bar{x}}$, which is t distributed with $n - 1$ degrees of freedom if the conditions for the t test are satisfied.

To use the *t* statistic appropriately for making inferences about the mean, two basic questions need to be answered:

- Is the distribution of the variable in the parent population normal or is it asymmetrical?
- Is the sample size large or small?

If the variable of interest is normally distributed in the parent population, then the test statistic $(\bar{x} - \mu)/s_{\bar{x}}$ is *t* distributed with $n - 1$ degrees of freedom. This is true whether the sample size is large or small. For small samples, we actually use *t* with $n - 1$ degrees of freedom when making an inference. Although *t* with $n - 1$ degrees of freedom is also the theoretically correct distribution for large *n*, the distribution approaches and becomes indistinguishable from the normal distribution for samples of 30 or more observations. The test statistic $(\bar{x} - \mu)/s_{\bar{x}}$ is therefore referred to a table of normal deviates when making inferences with large samples. Note, though, that this is because the theoretically correct *t* distribution (since σ is unknown) has become indistinguishable from the normal curve, which is somewhat easier to use.

What happens if the variable is not normally distributed in the parent population when σ is unknown? If the distribution of the variable is symmetrical or displays only moderate skew, there is no problem. The *t* test is quite robust to departures from normality. However, if the variable is highly skewed in the parent population, the appropriate procedure depends on the sample size. If the sample is small, the *t* test is inappropriate. Either the variable has to be transformed so that it is normally distributed, or one of the distribution-free statistical tests must be used. If the sample is large, the normal curve could be used for making the inference, provided that the two following assumptions are satisfied:

1. The sample size is large enough so that the sample mean $\bar{x}$ is normally distributed because of the operation of the Central-Limit Theorem. The greater the degree of asymmetry in the distribution of the variable, the larger the sample size needed to satisfy this assumption.
2. The sample standard deviation $\hat{s}$ is a close estimate of the parent population standard deviation σ. The higher the degree of variability in the parent population, the larger the size of the sample that is needed to justify this assumption.

Research Realities 15.1 summarizes the situation for making inferences about a mean for known and unknown σ and normally distributed and asymmetrical parent population distributions.

To illustrate the application of the *t* test, consider a supermarket chain investigating the desirability of adding a new product to the shelves of its associated stores. Suppose that 100 units must be sold per week in each store for the item to be sufficiently profitable to warrant handling it in lieu of the many products competing for the limited shelf space. The research department decides to investigate the item's turnover by putting it in a random sample of 10 stores for a limited period of time. Suppose that the average sales per store per week are as shown in Table 15.2.

RESEARCH REALITIES 15.1

Testing Hypotheses about a Single Mean

	σ *Known*	σ *Unknown*
Distribution of variable in parent population is normal or symmetrical.	Small *n:* Use $z = \dfrac{\bar{x} - \mu}{\sigma_{\bar{x}}}$ Large *n:* Use $z = \dfrac{\bar{x} - \mu}{\sigma_{\bar{x}}}$	Small *n:* Use $t = \dfrac{\bar{x} - \mu}{s_{\bar{x}}}$ where $s_{\bar{x}} = \hat{s}/\sqrt{n}$ and $\hat{s} = \sqrt{\dfrac{\sum_{i=1}^{n}(X_i - \bar{x})^2}{n - 1}}$ and refer to *t* table for $n - 1$ degrees of freedom. Large *n:* Since the *t* distribution approaches the normal as *n* increases, use $z = \dfrac{\bar{x} - \mu}{s_{\bar{x}}}$ for $n > 30$.
Distribution of variable in parent population is asymmetrical.	Small *n:* There is no theory to support the parametric test. Either one must transform the variate so that it is normally distributed and then use the *z* test, or one must use a distribution-free statistical test. Large *n:* If the sample is large enough so that the Central-Limit Theorem is operative, use $z = \dfrac{\bar{x} - \mu}{\sigma_{\bar{x}}}$	Small *n:* There is no theory to support the parametric test. Either one must transform the variate so that it is normally distributed and then use the *t* test, or one must use a distribution-free statistical test. Large *n:* If sample is large enough so that 1. the Central-Limit Theorem is operative and 2. $\hat{s}$ is a close estimate of σ, use $z = \dfrac{\bar{x} - \mu}{s_{\bar{x}}}$

TABLE 15.2   **Store Sales of Trial Product per Week**

Store i	Sales X_i	Store i	Sales X_i
1	86	6	93
2	97	7	132
3	114	8	116
4	108	9	105
5	123	10	120

Since the variance of sales per store is unknown and has to be estimated, the t test is the correct parametric test if the distribution of sales is normal. The normality assumption seems reasonable and could be checked using one of the goodness-of-fit tests. The little sales evidence that is available does not indicate any real asymmetry, so let us assume that the normality assumption is satisfied.

A one-tailed test is appropriate, because it is only when the sales per store per week are at least 100 that the product will be introduced on a national scale. The null and alternate hypotheses are

$$H_0 : \mu \leq 100$$
$$H_a : \mu > 100$$

Assume that the significance level is to be $\alpha = 0.05$. From the data in Table 15.2,

$$\bar{x} = \frac{\sum\limits_{i=1}^{n} X_i}{n} = 109.4$$

and

$$\hat{s} = \sqrt{\frac{\sum\limits_{i=1}^{n} (X_i - \bar{x})^2}{(n-1)}} = 14.40$$

Therefore, the standard error of the mean $s_{\bar{x}} = \hat{s}/\sqrt{n} = 4.55$. Calculations yield

$$t = \frac{\bar{x} - \mu}{s_{\bar{x}}} = \frac{109.4 - 100}{4.55} = 2.07$$

Critical t as read from the t table with $\nu = n - 1 = 9$ degrees of freedom is 1.833 ($\alpha = 0.05$). (See Appendix C at the end of the book.) It is unlikely that the calculated value would have occurred by chance if the sales per store in the population were indeed less than or equal to 100 units per week.

Some insight into the sales per store per week that might be expected if the product were introduced on a national scale can be achieved by calculating the confidence interval. The appropriate formula is $\bar{x} \pm ts_{\bar{x}}$. For a 95 percent confidence interval and 9 degrees of freedom, $t = 1.833$, as we have already seen. The 95 percent confidence interval is thus $109.4 \pm (1.833)(4.55)$, or 109.4 ± 8.3, or, alternatively, $101.1 \le \mu \le 117.7$.

Suppose that the product were placed in 50 stores and that the sample mean and standard deviation were the same; that is, $\bar{x} = 109.4 = 109.4$ and $\hat{s} = 14.40$. The test statistic would now be $z = 4.62$, which would be referred to a normal table since the t is indistinguishable from the normal for samples of this size. Calculated z is greater than critical $z = 1.645$ for $\alpha = 0.05$, and, as expected, the same conclusion is warranted. The evidence is stronger now because of the larger sample of stores; the product could be expected to sell at a rate greater than 100 units per store per week.

The effect of the larger sample and the opportunity it provides to use the normal curve can also be seen in the smaller confidence interval that the larger sample produces. When the normal curve rather than t distribution applies, the formula $\bar{x} \pm ts_{\bar{x}}$, for calculating the confidence interval changes to $\bar{x} \pm zs_{\bar{x}}$, where the appropriate z value is read from the normal-curve table. Since for a 95 percent confidence interval $z = 1.645$, the interval is $109.4 \pm (1.645)(4.55)$, or 109.4 ± 7.5, which yields the estimate $101.9 \le \mu \le 116.9$, a slightly narrower interval than that produced when 10 stores instead of 50 were in the sample.

Hypotheses about Two Means

Consider testing a hypothesis about the difference between two population means. An example is a nationwide consumer survey that was sponsored by the National Restaurant Association. The study gathered demographic data and data about preferences for takeout foods. The results showed that patrons at gourmet coffee shops have an average household income of $48,520, compared with a mean of $47,660 for all customers of takeout establishments.[3] A relevant question is whether the two means are significantly different; that is, are coffee shop customers richer than others who buy takeout, or could the observed difference be due to sampling?

The methodology for testing a hypothesis about two means will vary according to whether the samples are independent or related. Assuming that the samples are independent, three cases are to be considered:

- The two parent population variances are known.
- The parent population variances are unknown but can be assumed equal.
- The parent population variances are unknown and cannot be assumed equal.

After exploring these alternatives, we will see how to test a hypothesis about two means when the samples are related.

VARIANCES ARE KNOWN   Experience has shown that the population variance usually changes much more slowly than the population mean. This means that the "old" variance can often be used as the "known" population variance for studies that are being repeated. For example, we may have annually checked the per capita soft-

[3]"Coffee-Bar Patrons Are a Richer Blend: Study," *Supermarket News* (October 26, 1998), p. 27.

drink consumption of people living in different regions of the United States. If we were now to test a hypothesis about the differences in per capita consumption of a new soft drink, we could use the previously determined variances as known variances for our new soft drink. Consider that our problem is indeed one of determining whether any differences exist between Northerners and Southerners in their consumption of a new soft drink that our company has recently introduced, called Spark. Further, past data indicate that per capita variation in the consumption of soft drinks is 10 ounces per day for Northerners and 14 ounces per day for Southerners as measured by the standard deviation; that is, $\sigma_N = 10$ and $\sigma_S = 14$.

The null hypothesis is that there is no difference between Northerners and Southerners in their consumption of Spark ($H_0 : \mu_N = \mu_S$), whereas the alternate hypothesis is that there is a difference ($H_a : \mu_N \neq \mu_S$). It so happens that if $\bar{x}_N$ and $\bar{x}_S$, the sample means, are normally distributed random variables, their sum or difference is also normally distributed. The two sample means could be normally distributed because per capita consumption is normally distributed in each region or because the two samples are large enough that the Central-Limit Theorem is operative. In either case, the test statistic is

$$z = \frac{(\bar{x}_1 - \bar{x}_2) - (\mu_1 - \mu_2)}{\sigma_{\bar{x}_1 - \bar{x}_2}}$$

where
$\bar{x}_1$ is the sample mean for the first (Northern) sample;
$\bar{x}_2$ is the sample mean for the second (Southern) sample;
μ_1 and μ_2 are the unknown population means for the Northern and Southern samples;
and
$\sigma_{\bar{x}_1 - \bar{x}_2}$ is the standard error of estimate for the difference in means and is equal to $\sqrt{\sigma_{\bar{x}_1}^2 + \sigma_{\bar{x}_2}^2}$ where, in turn, $\sigma_{\bar{x}_1}^2 = \sigma_1^2/n_1$ and $\sigma_{\bar{x}_2}^2 = \sigma_2^2/n_2$.

Now, σ_1^2 and σ_2^2 are the "known" population variances of $\sigma_1^2 = (10)^2 = 100$ and $\sigma_2^2 = (14)^2 = 196$. Suppose that a random sample of 100 people from the North and South, respectively, was taken and that $\bar{x}_1 = 20$ ounces per day and $\bar{x}_2 = 25$ ounces per day. Does this result indicate a real difference in consumption rates? The standard error of estimate is

$$\sigma_{\bar{x}_1 - \bar{x}_2} = \sqrt{\frac{100}{100} + \frac{196}{100}} = \sqrt{2.96} = 1.720$$

and the calculated z is

$$z = \frac{(20 - 25) - (\mu_N - \mu_S)}{1.720} = \frac{-5 - 0}{1.720} = -2.906$$

Calculated z exceeds the critical tabled value of -1.96 for $\alpha = 0.05$, and the null hypothesis is rejected. There is a statistically significant difference in the per capita consumption of Spark by Northerners and Southerners.

The confidence interval for the difference in the two means is given by the formula

$$(\bar{x}_1 - \bar{x}_2) \pm z\sigma_{\bar{x}_1 - \bar{x}_2}$$

For a 95 percent confidence interval, $z = 1.96$, and the interval estimate of the difference in consumption of Spark by the two groups is $-5 \pm (1.96)(1.720) = -5 \pm 3.4$. Northerners on average are estimated to drink 1.6 to 8.4 ounces less of Spark per day than Southerners.

VARIANCES ARE UNKNOWN   When the two parent population variances are unknown, the standard error of the test statistic $\sigma_{\bar{x}_1 - \bar{x}_2}$ is also unknown, since $\sigma_{\bar{x}_1}$ and $\sigma_{\bar{x}_2}$ are unknown and have to be estimated. As was true with one sample, the sample standard deviations are used to estimate the population standard deviations:

$$\hat{s}_1^{\,2} = \frac{\sum_{i=1}^{n_1} (X_{i1} - \bar{x}_2)^2}{(n_1 - 1)}$$

is used to estimate $\sigma_1^{\,2}$ and

$$\hat{s}_2^{\,2} = \frac{\sum_{i=1}^{n_2} (X_{i2} - \bar{x}_2)^2}{(n_2 - 1)}$$

is used to estimate $\sigma_2^{\,2}$. Thus, the estimates of the standard error of the means become $s_{\bar{x}_1} = \hat{s}_1/\sqrt{n_1}$ and $s_{\bar{x}_2} = \hat{s}_2/\sqrt{n_2}$. The general estimate of $\sigma_{\bar{x}_1 - \bar{x}_2}$ is then

$$s_{\bar{x}_1 - \bar{x}_2} = \sqrt{s_{\bar{x}_1}^{\,2} + s_{\bar{x}_2}^{\,2}} = \sqrt{\frac{\hat{s}_1^{\,2}}{n_1} + \frac{\hat{s}_2^{\,2}}{n_2}}$$

Although unknown, if the two parent population variances *can be assumed to be equal*, a better estimate of the common population variance can be generated by *pooling* the samples to calculate

$$\hat{s}^2 = \frac{\sum_{i=1}^{n_1} (X_{i1} - \bar{x}_1)^2 + \sum_{i=1}^{n_2} (X_{i2} - \bar{x}_2)^2}{n_1 + n_2 - 2}$$

where $\hat{s}^2$ is the pooled sample variance used to estimate the common population variance. In this case the estimated standard error of the test statistic $s_{\bar{x}_1 - \bar{x}_2}$ reduces to

$$s_{\bar{x}_1 - \bar{x}_2} = \sqrt{\frac{\hat{s}_1^{\,2}}{n_1} + \frac{\hat{s}_2^{\,2}}{n_2}} = \sqrt{\frac{\hat{s}^2}{n_1} + \frac{\hat{s}^2}{n_2}} = \sqrt{\hat{s}^2\left(\frac{1}{n_1} + \frac{1}{n_2}\right)}$$

If the distribution of the variable in each population can further be assumed to be normal, the appropriate test statistic is

$$t = \frac{(\bar{x}_1 - \bar{x}_2) - (\mu_1 - \mu_2)}{s_{\bar{x}_1 - \bar{x}_2}}$$

which is t distributed with $\nu = n_1 + n_2 - 2$ degrees of freedom.

Let's say, for example, that a manufacturer of floor waxes has recently developed a new wax. The company is considering designs for two different containers for the wax, one plastic and one metal. The company decides to make the final determination on the basis of a limited sales test in which the plastic containers are introduced in a random sample of 10 stores and the metal containers are introduced in an *independent* random sample of 10 stores. The test results are contained in Table 15.3.

$$\text{Calculated } t = \frac{(\bar{x}_1 - \bar{x}_2) - (\mu_1 - \mu_2)}{s_{\bar{x}_1 - \bar{x}_2}}$$

$$= \frac{(403.0 - 390.3) - (0)}{8.15} = 1.56$$

This value is referred to a t table for $\nu = n_1 + n_2 - 2 = 18$ degrees of freedom. The test is two-tailed because the null hypothesis is that the containers were equal; there was no *a priori* statement that one was expected to sell better than the other. For $\alpha = 0.05$, say, and 18 degrees of freedom, critical $t = 2.101$. (One needs to look in the column headed $1 - \alpha = 0.975$ rather than 0.95 in Appendix C at the end of the text, because this is a two-tailed test.) Since calculated t is less than critical t, the null hypothesis of no difference would not be rejected. The sample data do *not* indicate that the plastic container could be expected to outsell the metal container in the total population, even though it did so in this limited experiment.

The example again demonstrates the importance of explicitly determining the statistical significance level by appropriately balancing Type I and Type II errors. Here α error was arbitrarily set equal to 0.05. This led to nonrejection of the null hypothesis and the conclusion that the plastic container would not be expected to outsell the metal container in the total population. Yet if the decision maker had been able to tolerate an α error of, say, 0.20, just the opposite conclusion would

| TABLE 15.3 | Store Sales of Floor Wax in Units |

Store	Plastic Container	Metal Container	Store	Plastic Container	Metal Container
1	432	365	6	380	372
2	360	405	7	422	378
3	397	396	8	406	410
4	408	390	9	400	383
5	417	404	10	408	400

have been warranted, since interpolating in the table in Appendix C for 18 degrees of freedom indicates that the probability of getting calculated $t = 1.56$ under an assumption of no difference in the population means is approximately 15 percent. Assuming that the production and other costs associated with each container were the same, it would clearly seem that the final packaging decision should favor the plastic container. If the production and other costs were not the same, these costs should clearly be reflected in the statistical decision rule.[4]

One of the assumptions underlying the previous procedure was that the variances in sales of the plastic and metal containers were equal in the population. The assumption could be checked using an F test for the equality of variances, and indeed, the sample evidence does not contradict the assumption.[5] Suppose, though, that the assumption was not justified. Then the pooling of the variances is also no longer warranted, and the estimated standard error of the test statistic becomes

$$s_{\bar{x}_1 - \bar{x}_2} = \sqrt{\frac{\hat{s}_1^2}{n_1} + \frac{\hat{s}_2^2}{n_2}}$$

instead of

$$s_{\bar{x}_1 - \bar{x}_2} = \hat{s}^2\left(\frac{1}{n_1} + \frac{1}{n_2}\right)$$

A real question now arises about the appropriate degrees of freedom for the test statistic. A large amount of controversial literature deals with this condition, known as the Behrens-Fisher problem. One suggested approach is the Aspin-Welch test, in which the degrees of freedom is a kind of weighted average of the degrees of freedom in each of the independent samples.[6] If the samples are both large so that $\hat{s}_1^2$ and $\hat{s}_2^2$ provide good estimates of their respective population variances σ_1^2 and σ_2^2, then the problem becomes less acute, as the normal z statistic can be used to examine the hypothesis.

The preceding discussion assumed that the samples are independent and that the variable of interest is normally distributed in each of the parent populations. The normality assumption was again necessary to justify the use of the t distribution. What happens, though, if the variable is not normally distributed or the samples are not independent? The lower half of Research Realities 15.2 summarizes the

---

[4]The Bayesian posture would be to introduce the plastic container even with the obtained sample results if the opportunity costs associated with each alternative were the same. If they were not the same, then the Bayesian approach would incorporate these costs directly into the decision rule regarding which container should be produced.

[5]Most introductory statistics books detail the procedure for testing the equality of two parent population variances. See, for example, Ronald C. Serlin and Leonard A. Marascuillo, *Statistical Methods for the Social and Behavioral Sciences* (New York: W. H. Freeman & Company, 1995); William L. Hays, *Statistics*, 5th ed. (Austin, TX: Holt, Rinehart, and Winston, 1997); Warren Chase and Fred Brown, *General Statistics*, 4th ed. (New York: John Wiley, 2000).

[6]See Acheson J. Duncan, *Quality Control and Industrial Statistics*, rev. ed. (Burr Ridge, IL: Richard D. Irwin, 1959), pp. 476–478, for one of the better discussions of the Aspin-Welch test. See also Samuel Kotz and Norman L. Johnson, *Encyclopedia of Statistical Sciences*, vol. 9 (New York: John Wiley, 1988), pp. 586–589, for discussion of some of the alternatives that have been proposed for handling the problem.

Testing Hypotheses about the Difference in Two Means

σ's *Known*	σ's *Unknown*

Distribution of variables in parent populations is normal or symmetrical.

Small n:

Use $z = \dfrac{(\bar{x}_1 - \bar{x}_2) - (\mu_1 - \mu_2)}{\sigma_{\bar{x}_1 - \bar{x}_2}}$

where $\sigma_{\bar{x}_1 - \bar{x}_2} = \sqrt{\dfrac{\sigma_1^2}{n_1} + \dfrac{\sigma_2^2}{n_2}}$

Small n: Can you assume $\sigma_1 = \sigma_2$?
1. Yes: Use pooled variance t test where

$$t = \frac{(\bar{x}_1 - \bar{x}_2) - (\mu_1 - \mu_2)}{s_{\bar{x}_1 - \bar{x}_2}}$$

and

$$s_{\bar{x}_1 - \bar{x}_2} =$$

$$\sqrt{\frac{\displaystyle\sum_{i=1}^{n_1}(X_{i1} - \bar{x}_1)^2 + \sum_{i=1}^{n_2}(X_{i2} - \bar{x}_2)^2}{n_1 + n_2 - 2}\left(\frac{1}{n_1} + \frac{1}{n_2}\right)}$$

with $(n_1 + n_2 - 2)$ degrees of freedom.
2. No: Approach is shrouded in controversy. Might use Aspin-Welch test.

Large n:

Use $z = \dfrac{(\bar{x}_1 - \bar{x}_2) - (\mu_2 - \mu_2)}{\sigma_{\bar{x}_1 - \bar{x}_2}}$

Large n:

Use $z = \dfrac{(\bar{x}_1 - \bar{x}_2) - (\mu_1 - \mu_2)}{s_{\bar{x}_1 - \bar{x}_2}}$

and use pooled variance if variances can be assumed to be equal and unpooled variance if equality assumption is not warranted.

Distribution of variables in parent populations is asymmetrical.

Small n: There is no theory to support the parametric test. Either one must transform the variates so that they are normally distributed and then use the z test, or one must use a distribution-free statistical test.

Large n: If the individual samples are large enough so that the Central-Limit Theorem is operative for them separately, it will also apply to their sum or difference. Use

$$z = \frac{(\bar{x}_1 - \bar{x}_2) - (\mu_2 - \mu_2)}{\sigma_{\bar{x}_1 - \bar{x}_2}}$$

Small n: There is no theory to support the parametric test. Either one must transform the variates so that they are normally distributed and then use the t test, or one must use a distribution-free statistical test.

Large n: One must assume that n_1 and n_2 are large enough so that the Central-Limit Theorem applies to the individual sample means. Then it can also be assumed to apply to their sum or difference. Use

$$z = \frac{(\bar{x}_1 - \bar{x}_2) - (\mu_1 - \mu_2)}{s_{\bar{x}_1 - \bar{x}_2}}$$

employing a pooled variance if the unknown parent population variances can be assumed to be equal and unpooled variance if the equality assumption is not warranted.

approach for nonnormal parent distributions for known and unknown σ, and the next section treats the case of dependent samples.

SAMPLES ARE RELATED   A manufacturer of camping equipment wanted to study consumer color preferences for a sleeping bag it had recently developed. The bag was of medium quality and price. Traditionally, the high-quality, high-priced sleeping bags used by serious campers and backpackers came in earth colors, such as green and brown. Previous research indicated that the low-quality, low-priced sleeping bags were frequently purchased for children, for use at slumber parties. The vivid colors were preferred by this market segment, with bright reds and oranges leading the way. Production capacity restrictions would not allow the company to produce both sets of colors. To make the comparison, the company selected a random sample of five stores into which it introduced bags of both types. The sales per store are indicated in Table 15.4. Do the data present sufficient evidence to indicate a difference in the average sales for the different colored bags?

An analysis of the data indicates a difference in the two means of $(\bar{x}_1 - \bar{x}_2) = (50.2 - 45.2) = 5.0$. This is a rather small difference, considering the variability in sales that exists across the five stores. Further, application of the procedures of the last section suggests that the difference is not statistically significant. The pooled estimate of the common variance is

$$\hat{s}^2 = \frac{\sum_{i=1}^{n_1} (X_{i1} - \bar{x}_1)^2 + \sum_{i=1}^{n_2} (X_{i2} - \bar{x}_2)^2}{n_1 + n_2 - 2}$$

$$= \frac{1,512.8 + 1,222.8}{8} = 341.95$$

and

$$s_{\bar{x}_1 - \bar{x}_2} = \sqrt{\hat{s}^2\left(\frac{1}{n_1} + \frac{1}{n_2}\right)} = \sqrt{341.95\left(\frac{1}{5} + \frac{1}{5}\right)} = 11.70$$

Calculated t is thus

$$t = \frac{(\bar{x}_1 - \bar{x}_2) - (\mu_1 - \mu_2)}{s_{\bar{x}1 - \bar{x}2}} = \frac{(50.2 - 45.2) - 0}{11.70} = 0.427$$

| TABLE 15.4 | Per-Store Sales of Sleeping Bags |

Store	Bright Colors	Earth Colors
1	64	56
2	72	66
3	43	39
4	22	20
5	50	45

which is less than the critical value $t = 2.306$ found in the table for $\alpha = 0.05$ and $v = n_1 + n_2 - 2 = 8$ degrees of freedom. The null hypothesis of no difference in sales of the two types of colors cannot be rejected on the basis of the sample data.

But wait a minute! A closer look at the data indicates a marked inconsistency with this conclusion. The bright-colored sleeping bags outsold the earth-colored ones in each store, and, indeed, an analysis of the per-store differences (the procedure is detailed below) indicates that there is a statistically significant difference in the sales of the two bags. The reason for the seeming difference in conclusions (the difference is not significant versus it is significant) arises because the t test for the difference in two means is *not appropriate* for the problem. The difference-in-means test assumes that the samples are independent. These samples are not. Sales of bright-colored and earth-colored bags are definitely related, since they are both found in the same stores. Note how this example differs from the floor wax example, in which the metal containers were placed in one sample of stores and the plastic containers were located in an independent sample of stores. We need a procedure that takes into account the fact that the observations are related.

The appropriate procedure is the t test for related samples. The procedure is as follows. Define a new variable d_i, where d_i is the difference between sales of the bright-colored bags and the earth-colored bags for the ith store. Thus,

$$
\begin{aligned}
d_1 &= 64 - 56 = 8 \\
d_2 &= 72 - 66 = 6 \\
d_3 &= 43 - 39 = 4 \\
d_4 &= 22 - 20 = 2 \\
d_5 &= 50 - 45 = 5
\end{aligned}
$$

Now calculate the mean difference

$$
\bar{d} = \frac{\sum_{i=1}^{n} d_i}{n} = \frac{8 + 6 + 4 + 2 + 5}{5} = 5.0
$$

and the standard error of the difference

$$
s_d = \sqrt{\frac{\sum_{i=1}^{n} (d_i - \bar{d})^2}{n - 1}} = \sqrt{\frac{20}{4}} = 2.24
$$

The test statistic is

$$
t = \frac{\bar{d} - D}{s_d / \sqrt{n}}
$$

where D is the difference that is expected under the null hypothesis. Since there is no *a priori* reason why one color would be expected to sell better than the other, the appropriate null hypothesis is that there is no difference, while the alternate hypothesis is that there is:

$$H_0{:}D = 0$$
$$H_a{:}D \neq 0$$

Calculated t is thus

$$t = \frac{5.0 - 0}{2.24/\sqrt{5}} = 5.0$$

This value is referred to a t table for $\nu = $ (number of differences $- 1$) degrees of freedom; in this case, there are five paired differences, and thus $\nu = 4$. Critical t for $\nu = 4$ and $\alpha = 0.05$ is 2.776, and, therefore, the hypothesis of no difference is rejected. The sample evidence indicates that the bright-colored sleeping bags are likely to outsell the earth-colored ones.

An estimate of how much sales per store of the vivid-colored sleeping bags would exceed those of the earth-colored bags can be calculated from the confidence interval formula $\bar{d} \pm t(s_d/\sqrt{n})$. The 95 percent confidence interval is $5.0 \pm (2.776)(2.24/\sqrt{5}) = 5.0 \pm 2.8$, suggesting that sales of the vivid-colored bags would be in the range of 2.2 to 7.8 bags greater per store on average.

Hypotheses about Two Proportions

The appendix to Chapter 14 reviewed the essential nature of hypothesis testing, employing as an example the testing of a hypothesis about a single population proportion. In this section, we want to illustrate the procedure for testing for the difference between two population proportions.[7] An example of where this would arise is the Mail Monitor survey, which tracks consumer responses to direct-mail offers of credit cards. Each quarter, Mail Monitor determines what percentage of consumers in the sample responded to such a mailing, and it compares those percentages from quarter to quarter. For example, in a recent report, Mail Monitor announced that the credit card response rate had fallen to 0.6 percent, a record low in 10 years of the study.[8] Was this rate truly the lowest level

---

[7]The tests for population proportions are logically considered with nominal data because they apply in situations in which the variable being studied can be divided into those cases *possessing* the characteristic and those cases *lacking* it, and the emphasis is on the number or proportion of cases falling into each category. Marketing examples abound: "prefer A" versus "do not prefer A"; "buy" versus "do not buy"; "brand loyal" versus "not brand loyal"; "sales representatives meeting quota" versus "sales representatives not meeting quota." The test for the significance of the difference between two proportions is treated here because the hypothesis is examined using the z test, and the procedure relies on an "automatic pooled sample variance" estimate. It was thought that these concepts would be better appreciated after the discussion of the test of means rather than before.

[8]BAIGlobal, "Credit Card Response Rate at Record Low for 1999's Second Quarter," September 1999. (Downloaded from the company's Web site, www.baiglobal.com. Mail Monitor is a service provided by BAIGlobal.)

of consumer response in a decade, or could the results be attributable to sampling error?

The test for the difference between two population proportions is basically a large sample problem. The samples from each population must be large enough so that the normal approximation to the exact binomial distribution of sample proportions can be used. As a practical matter, this means that np and nq should be greater than 10 for each sample, where p is the proportion of "successes" and q is the proportion of "failures" in the sample, and n is the sample size.

To illustrate, consider a cosmetics manufacturer that was interested in comparing male college students and nonstudents in terms of their use of hair spray. Random samples of 100 male students and 100 male nonstudents in Austin, Texas, were selected, and their use of hair spray during the last three months was determined. Suppose that 30 students and 20 nonstudents had used hair spray within this period. Does this evidence indicate that a significantly higher percentage of college students than nonstudents use hair spray?

Because we are interested in determining whether the two parent population proportions are different, the null hypothesis is that they are the same; that is,

$$H_0{:}\pi_1 = \pi_2$$
$$H_a{:}\pi_1 \neq \pi_2$$

where Population 1 is the population of college students, and Population 2 is the population of nonstudents. The sample proportions are $p_1 = 0.30$ and $p_2 = 0.20$, and, therefore, $n_1 p_1 = 30$, $n_1 q_1 = 70$, $n_2 p_2 = 20$, $n_2 q_2 = 80$, and the normal approximation to the binomial distribution can be used. The test statistic is

$$z = \frac{(p_1 - p_2) - (\pi_1 - \pi_2)}{\sigma_{p_1 - p_2}}$$

where $\sigma_{p_1 - p_2}$ is the standard error of the difference in the two sample proportions. The one question that still remains in the calculation of z is what does $\sigma_{p_1 - p_2}$ equal?

A general statistical result that is useful for understanding the calculation of $\sigma_{p_1 - p_2}$ is that the *variance of the sum or difference of two independent random variables is equal to the sum of the individual variances.* For a single proportion, the variance is $\pi(1 - \pi)/n$, and thus the variance of the difference is

$$\sigma^2_{p_1 - p_2} = \sigma^2_{p_1} + \sigma^2_{p_2} = \frac{\pi_1(1 - \pi_1)}{n_1} + \frac{\pi_2(1 - \pi_2)}{n_2}$$

Note that the variance of the difference is given in terms of the two unknown population proportions π_1 and π_2. Although unknown, the two population proportions have been assumed to be equal, and thus we have a "natural" case of a *pooled variance* estimate; $s^2_{p_1 - p_2}$ is logically used to estimate $\sigma^2_{p_1 - p_2}$, where

$$s^2_{p_1 - p_2} = pq\left(\frac{1}{n_1} + \frac{1}{n_2}\right)$$

and

$$p = \frac{\text{Total number of successes in the two samples}}{\text{Total number of observations in the two samples}}$$

$$q = 1 - p$$

For the example

$$p = \frac{30 + 20}{100 + 100} = \frac{50}{200} = 0.25$$

$$s^2_{p_1 - p_2} = (0.25)\ (0.75) \left(\frac{1}{100} + \frac{1}{100}\right) = 0.00375$$

and

$$s_{p_1 - p_2} = 0.061$$

calculated z is found as follows:

$$z = \frac{(0.30 - 0.20) - (0)}{0.061} = \frac{0.10}{0.061} = 1.64$$

whereas critical $z = 1.96$ for $\alpha = 0.05$. The sample evidence does not indicate that there is a difference in the proportion of college students and nonstudents using hair spray.

The 95 percent confidence interval calculated by the formula $(p_1 - p_2) \pm z s_{p_1 - p_2}$, which is $(0.30 - 0.20) \pm 1.96\ (0.061) = 0.10 \pm 0.12$, yields a similar conclusion. The interval includes zero, suggesting that there is no difference in the proportions of males using hair spray in the two groups.

ETHICAL DILEMMA 15.2

A field experiment was conducted to determine the most effective advertising appeal for an immunization program for a serious flu epidemic, one in which people had a chance of dying if they contracted the flu. The control communities received no appeal at all, whereas the experimental communities received varying appeals in different strengths. An analysis of the differences in the proportion of people with respiratory problems getting immunization shots clearly indicated the level of advertising that would be most cost effective for a national campaign.

- Is it ethical to withhold benefits (that is, knowledge of an immunization program) from participants in the control group?
- What participant rights are being violated?
- How can this research be justified? Do the long-term benefits of the research outweigh the costs?

Summary

Several statistical tests that are useful to marketing researchers for examining differences were discussed in this chapter. The difference at issue might be between some sample result and some expected population value or between two sample results.

The chi-square goodness-of-fit test is appropriate when a nominally scaled variable falls naturally into two or more categories and the analyst wants to determine whether the observed number of cases in each cell corresponds to the expected number.

The Kolmogorov-Smirnov test is the ordinal counterpart to the chi-square goodness-of-fit test in that it focuses on the comparison of observed and expected frequencies. It can be employed to test whether a set of observations could have come from some theoretical population distribution, such as a normal distribution, or whether two independent samples could have come from the same population distribution.

In testing a hypothesis about a single mean, the z test is appropriate if the variance is known, whereas the t test applies with unknown variance. A similar situation arises in the analysis of two means from independent samples. If the variances are known, the z test is used. If the variances are unknown but assumed to be equal, a t test using a pooled sample variance estimate applies. If unknown and probably unequal, there is controversy surrounding the correct procedure. If the samples are related instead of independent, the t test for paired differences is appropriate.

The test of the equality of proportions from two independent samples involves a "natural" pooling of the sample variances. The z test applies.

Questions

1. What is the basic use of a chi-square goodness-of-fit test? How is the value of the test statistic calculated? How are the expected frequencies determined?
2. If the data are ordinal and the analyst wishes to determine whether the observed frequencies correspond to some expected pattern, what statistical test is appropriate? What is the basic procedure to follow in implementing this test?
3. What is the appropriate test statistic for making inferences about a population mean when the population variance is known? When the population variance is unknown? Suppose that the population variance is unknown, but the sample is large. What is the appropriate procedure then?
4. Suppose one is testing for the statistical significance of the observed difference between the sample means from two independent samples. What is the appropriate procedure when the two parent population variances are
   a. known?
   b. unknown but can be assumed to be equal?
   c. unknown and cannot be assumed to be equal?
   What conditions must occur in each case regarding the distribution of the variable?
5. Would your response to Question 4 change if the samples were related? Explain.
6. How do you test whether two parent population proportions differ?

Applications and Problems

1. A large publishing house recently conducted a survey to assess the reading habits of teenagers. The company publishes four magazines specifically tailored to suit the interests of teenagers. Management hypothesized that there were no differences in the preferences for the magazines. A sample of 1,600 teenagers interviewed in the city of Buffalo, New York, indicated the following preferences for the four magazines.

Publication	*Frequency of Preference*
1. Rock-Town	350
2. Rappin'	500
3. Teen-Tips	450
4. R.A.D.	300
Total	1,600

Management needs your expertise to determine whether there are differences in teenager preferences for the magazines.

a. State the null and alternate hypotheses.

b. How many degrees of freedom are there?

c. What is the chi-square critical table value at the 5 percent significance level?

d. What is the calculated χ^2 value? Show all your calculations.

e. Should the null hypothesis be rejected or not? Explain.

2. Moon Shine Company is a medium-sized manufacturer of shampoo. In recent years, the company has increased the number of product variations of Moon Shine shampoo from three to five to increase its market share. Management conducted a survey to compare sales of Moon Shine shampoo with sales of Sun Shine and Star Shine, the brand's two major competitors. A sample of 1,800 housewives indicated the following frequencies with respect to most recent shampoo purchased:

Shampoo	Number Buying
1. Moon Shine	425
2. Sun Shine	1,175
3. Star Shine	200
Total	1,800

Past experience had indicated that three times as many households preferred Sun Shine to Moon Shine and that, in turn, twice as many households preferred Moon Shine to Star Shine. Management wants to determine if the historic tendency still holds, considering that Moon Shine Company has increased the range of shampoos available.

a. State the null and alternate hypotheses.

b. How many degrees of freedom are there?

c. What is the chi-square critical table value at the 5 percent level?

d. What is the calculated χ^2 value? Show all your calculations.

e. Should the null hypothesis be rejected or not? Explain.

3. A manufacturer of music cassettes wants to test four different cassettes varying in tape length: 30 minutes, 60 minutes, 90 minutes, and 120 minutes. The company has hired you to determine whether customers show any distinct preference toward either extreme. If there is a preference toward any extreme, the company would manufacture only cassettes of the preferred length; otherwise, the company is planning to market cassettes of all four lengths. A sample of 1,000 customers indicated the following preferences.

Tape Length	Frequency of Preference
30 minutes	150
60 minutes	250
90 minutes	425
120 minutes	175
Total	1,000

a. State the null and alternate hypotheses.

b. Compute Kolmogorov-Smirnov D by completing the following table.

Tape Length	Observed Number	Observed Proportion	Observed Cumulative Proportion	Theoretical Proportion	Theoretical Cumulative Proportion
30 min.					
60 min.					
90 min.					
120 min.					

    c. Compute the critical value of D at $\alpha = 0.05$. Show your calculations.

    d. Would you reject the null hypothesis? Explain.

    e. What are the implications for management?

    f. Explain why the Kolmogorov-Smirnov test would be used in this situation.

4. A medium-sized manufacturer of paper products was planning to introduce a new line of tissues, hand towels, and toilet paper. However, management had stipulated that the new products should be introduced only if average monthly purchases per household were $2.50 or more. The product was market tested and the diaries of the 100 panel households living in the test market area were checked. They indicated that average monthly purchases were $3.10 per household with a standard deviation of $0.50. Management is wondering what decision it should make and has asked for your recommendation.

    a. State the null and alternate hypotheses.

    b. Is the sample size considered large or small?

    c. Which test should be used? Why?

    d. At the 5 percent level of significance, would you reject the null hypothesis? Support your answer with the necessary calculations.

5. The president of a chain of department stores had promised the managers of the various stores a bonus of 8 percent if the average monthly sales per store increased $300,000 or more. A random sample of 12 stores yielded the following sales increases:

Store	Sales Increase	Store	Sales Increase
1	$320,000	7	$380,000
2	$230,000	8	$280,000
3	$400,000	9	$420,000
4	$450,000	10	$360,000
5	$280,000	11	$440,000
6	$320,000	12	$320,000

The president is wondering whether this random sample of stores indicates that the population of stores has reached the goal. (Assume that the distribution of the variable in the parent population is normal.)

    a. State the null and alternate hypotheses.

    b. Is the sample size considered small or large?

    c. Which test should be used? Why?

    d. Would you reject the null hypothesis at the 5 percent level of significance? Support your conclusion with the necessary calculations.

6. Ruby Gem is the owner of two jewelry stores located in Los Angeles and San Francisco. During the past year, the San Francisco store spent a considerable amount on in-store displays compared to the Los Angeles store. Ruby Gem wants to determine if the in-store displays resulted in increased sales. The average sales for a sample of 100 days for the San Francisco and Los Angeles stores were $21.8 million and $15.3 million, respectively. (Past experience has shown that $\sigma_{SF} = 8$ and $\sigma_{LA} = 9$, where σ_{SF} is the standard deviation

in sales for the San Francisco store and σ_{LA} is the standard deviation for the Los Angeles store.)

a. State the null and alternate hypotheses.

b. What test would you use? Why?

c. What is the calculated value of the test statistic? Show your calculations.

d. What is the critical tabled value at the 5 percent significance level?

e. Would you reject the null hypothesis? Explain.

f. What can Ruby Gem conclude?

7. Travel Time Company, a large travel agency located in Baltimore, Maryland, wanted to study consumer preferences for its package tours to the East. For the past five years, Travel Time had offered two similarly priced package tours to the East that differed only in the places included in the tour. A random sample of five months' purchases from the past five years was selected. The number of consumers that purchased the tours during these five months is as follows:

Month	Packaged Tour I	Packaged Tour II
1	90	100
2	70	60
3	120	80
4	110	90
5	60	80

The management of Travel Time needs your assistance to determine whether there is a difference in preferences for the two tours.

a. State the null and alternate hypotheses.

b. What test would you use? Why?

c. What is the calculated value of the test statistic? Show your calculations.

d. What is the critical tabled value at the 5 percent significance level?

e. Would you reject the null hypothesis? Explain.

f. What can the management of Travel Time Company conclude about preferences for the two tours?

8. A manufacturer of exercise equipment for health clubs is interested in comparing usage of exercise equipment at health clubs by men and women. Random samples of 250 women and 250 men in Oklahoma City were selected and the usage of health club facilities was determined. The results indicated that 87 men and 51 women from the samples had been to a health club and had used exercise equipment at least once during the previous six weeks. The manufacturer is interested in determining whether or not this evidence indicates that a significantly higher percentage of men than women use exercise equipment at health clubs.

a. State the null and alternate hypotheses.

b. Which test would you use? Why?

c. Calculate the test statistic. Show all your calculations.

d. Assuming that $\alpha = 0.05$, can you conclude that a higher proportion of men use exercise equipment at health clubs? Since the discovery that a larger proportion of women than men use such equipment would be just as important a finding, use a two-tailed test.

e. Construct a 90 percent confidence interval for the difference between the proportion of men and the proportion of women using exercise equipment at health clubs. What conclusions can you draw from the confidence interval?

9. A local charity wanted to run an advertisement encouraging people to donate their old winter coats to the organization to redistribute to the city's homeless people. The charity is able to obtain some free commercial time on both local TV and radio sta-

tions. However, the charity wants to use the medium that provides the greatest recall. A short pilot was conducted to test whether there was a difference in recall between spots run on the radio and those on TV. The table that follows provides the results.

	Radio	TV
Number of people who were able to recall the charity's commercials	25	29
Number of people who did not recall the charity's commercials	50	46
Total number of people surveyed	75	75

   a. State the null and alternate hypotheses for the test.
   b. At $\alpha = 0.10$, use an appropriate test and interpret the results for the charity.
   c. If the research objective had been to determine whether TV advertisements resulted in greater recall, do the null and alternative hypotheses change? State and test the new hypotheses. Do the results change?

10. A large manufacturer of healthful snacks wants to test whether the sales of a health-food snack bar follow the same pattern with respect to package size in both Los Angeles and New York. The company has equal distribution in both cities and sells the following package sizes: packages of 6 bars, packages of 8 bars, packages of 12 bars, and econo-packs of 24 bars. In Los Angeles, sales of these package types are in the following ratio: 3:1:2:5. In New York during the same period, 4,880 bars are sold; specifically, sales for the four package types are as follows: 1,500, 475, 925, 1,980.
   a. State the null and alternative hypotheses for the test.
   b. What is the appropriate test in this situation? How many degrees of freedom are there? At $\alpha = 0.05$, can the null hypothesis be rejected?

11. The Spazi Italian food company is considering introducing a new extra-spicy spaghetti sauce. Before introducing the new sauce, however, the company wants to test it against its major competitor's spicy sauce. In a mall test, shoppers were stopped at random and asked to taste the two sauces. Shoppers were then asked to rate the sauces on a scale of 1 to 10, with 1 being awful and 10 being excellent. The table that follows shows the ratings given to the two sauces by 10 shoppers.

Shopper	Spazi's Sauce	Other Sauce	Shopper	Spazi's Sauce	Other Sauce
1	1	7	6	8	10
2	7	10	7	10	7
3	5	7	8	2	8
4	6	10	9	3	8
5	2	9	10	9	10

   a. What is the appropriate test to use for analyzing these scores? Explain.
   b. At $\alpha = 0.05$, is there a significant difference in ratings for these two sauces?
   c. Is this an appropriate design to use for this situation? Explain. What are alternative designs that may be more appropriate for this situation?
   d. After looking at Spazi's scores, do you think that additional research is warranted? Why?

Refer to the NFO Research, Inc., coffee study described on pages 611–613 in Chapter 13 for the next two problems.

12. Compare the overall ratings (from Question 2) of Folgers and Yuban. Is there a difference in the ratings for the two brands of coffee ($\alpha = 0.05$)? If so, which brand is rated more highly?

13. Compute a "taste" index score on the following features of Question 6 for Maxwell House Regular: rich taste, always fresh, full-bodied taste, smooth taste, not bitter, has no aftertaste. Is there a difference in this overall score for individuals who add nothing to their coffee versus those who do add something ($\alpha = 0.05$)?

A P P E N D I X   1 5 A

Analysis of Variance

In Chapter 15, we used the example of packaging floor wax in plastic and metal containers to examine that statistical test of the difference in two population means. Let us now reconsider the data of Table 15.3 to demonstrate an alternate approach to the problem. Known as the **analysis of variance (ANOVA),** it has the distinct advantage of being applicable when more than two means are being compared. Although ANOVA would not normally be applied when there are only two means, it is best illustrated using a familiar example.

Although not necessary for this simple example, a little additional notation at this time will pay dividends when more complex examples are introduced. Therefore, let: x_{ij} = the ith observation on the jth treatment or group. There are two treatments in the example: $j = 1$ refers to plastic containers and $j = 2$ to metal containers. For each treatment there are 10 stores. Thus, for the first treatment $X_{11} = 432$, $X_{21} = 360, \ldots, X_{10,1} = 408$ and for the second treatment $X_{12} = 365$, $X_{22} = 405$, and $X_{10,2} = 400$.

n_j = the number of observations on the jth treatment; $n_1 = 10$ and $n_2 = 10$.
n = the total number of observations in all treatments combined: $n = n_1 + n_2 = 20$.
$\bar{x}_{\cdot j}$ = the mean of the jth treatment:

$$\bar{x}_j = \frac{\sum\limits_{i=1}^{n_j} X_{ij}}{n}$$

Thus,

$$\bar{x}_{\cdot 1} = \frac{432 + 360 + \ldots + 408}{10} = 403.0$$

and

$$\bar{x}_{\cdot 2} = \frac{365 + 405 + \ldots + 400}{10} = 390.3$$

$x_{\cdot\cdot}$ = the grand mean of all n observations:

$$x_{\cdot\cdot} = \frac{\sum\limits_{j=1}^{2} \sum\limits_{i=1}^{n_j} X_{ij}}{n}$$

$$= \frac{432 + \ldots + 408 + 365 + \ldots + 400}{20} = 396.7$$

Now, one can conceptualize the deviation of any sales figure from the overall mean as consisting of two components—a deviation due to the fact that it is a plastic or metal container and a deviation due to variation in the sales of each type of container from store to store (that is, a deviation around the mean sales of that type of container). Conceptually,

$$(X_{ij} - \bar{x}_{..}) = (\bar{x}_{.j} - \bar{x}_{..}) + (X_{ij} - x_{.j})$$

The first difference on the right-hand side is called a treatment or between-group difference, and the second is called a within-group difference.

The basic idea underlying the analysis of variance is that the parent population variance can be estimated from the sample in several ways, and comparisons among these estimates can tell us a great deal about the population. Recall that the null hypothesis was that the two parent population means were equal; that is, $\mu_1 = \mu_2$. If the null hypothesis is true, then, except for sampling error, the following three estimates of the population variance should be equal:

1. The *total variation*, computed by comparing each of the 20 sales figures with the grand mean

2. The *between-group variation*, computed by comparing each of the two treatment means with the grand mean

3. The *within-group variation*, computed by comparing each of the individual sales figures with the mean of its own group

If, however, the hypothesis is not true and there is a difference in the means, then the between-group variation should produce a higher estimate than the within-group variation, which only considers the variation within groups and is independent of differences between groups.

These three separate estimates of the population variation are computed in the following way when there are k treatments or groups.

1. Total variation—sum of squares total SS_T:

$$SS_T = \sum_{j=1}^{k} \sum_{i=1}^{n_j} (X_{ij} - \bar{x}_{..})^2$$
$$= (432 - 396.7)^2 + \ldots + (408 - 396.7)^2$$
$$+ (365 - 396.7)^2 + \ldots + (400 - 396.7)^2$$

The difference between *each observation* and the *grand mean* is determined; the differences are squared and then summed.

2. Between-group variation—sum of squares between groups SS_B:

$$SS_B = \sum_{j=1}^{k} n_j(\bar{x}_{.j} - \bar{x}_{..})^2$$
$$= 10(403.0 - 396.7)^2 + 10(390.3 - 396.7)^2$$

The difference between each *group mean* and the *overall mean* is determined, the difference is squared, each squared difference is weighted by the number of observations making up the group, and the results are summed.

3.   Within-group variation—sum of squares within groups SS_W:

$$SS_W = \sum_{j=1}^{k} \sum_{i=1}^{n_j} (X_{ij} - \bar{x}_{.j})^2$$
$$= (432 - 403.0)^2 + \ldots + (408 - 403.0)^2$$
$$+ (365 - 390.3)^2 + \ldots + (400 - 390.3)^2$$

The difference between *each observation* and its *group mean* is determined; the differences are squared and then summed.

Let us take a closer look at the behavior of these three sources of variation. First, SS_T measures the overall variation of the n observations. The more variable the n observations, the larger SS_T becomes. Second, SS_B reflects the total variability of the means. The more nearly alike the k means are, the smaller SS_B becomes. If they differ greatly, SS_B will be large. Third, SS_W measures the amount of variation within each column or treatment. If there is little variation among the observations making up a group, SS_W is small. When there is great variability, SS_W is large.

It can be shown that $SS_T = SS_B + SS_W$ and that each of these sums of squares, when divided by the *appropriate number of degrees of freedom,* generates a mean square, which is essentially an unbiased estimate of the population variance.[1] Further, if the null hypothesis of no difference among population means is true, they are all estimates of the same variance and should not differ more than would be expected because of chance. If the variance between groups is significantly greater than the variance within groups, the hypothesis of equality of population means will be rejected.

In other words, we can view the variance within groups as a measure of the amount of variation in sales of containers that may be expected on the basis of chance. It is the *error variance* or *chance variance.* The between-group variance reflects error variance *plus* any group-to-group differences occasioned by differences in popularity of the two containers. Therefore, if it is found to be significantly larger than the within-group variance, this difference may be attributed to group-to-group variation, and the hypothesis of equality of means is discredited.

But what are these degrees of freedom? The total number of degrees of freedom is equal to $n - 1$, since there is only a single constraint $\bar{x}_{..}$ in the computation of SS_T. For the within-group sum of squares, there are n observations and k constraints, one constraint for each treatment mean. Hence, the degrees of freedom for the within-group sum of squares equals $n - k$. There are k values, one corresponding to each treatment mean, in the calculation of SS_B, and there is one constraint imposed by $\bar{x}_{..}$; hence the degrees of freedom for the between-group sum of squares is $k - 1$.

---

[1]See Geoffrey Keppel, *Design and Analysis: A Researcher's Handbook,* 3rd ed. (Englewood Cliffs, NJ: Prentice-Hall, 1991) for the derivation. See also Richard Harris, *An Analysis of Variance Primer* (Itasca, IL: F. E. Peacock Publishers, 1994). For a more complete discussion of the various designs discussed in this appendix, see B. J. Winer, Donald R. Brown, and Kenneth M. Michels, *Statistical Principles in Experimental Design,* 3rd ed. (New York: McGraw Hill, 1991).

The separate estimates of the population variance or the associated mean squares are

$$MS_T = \frac{SS_T}{df_T} = \frac{SS_T}{n-1}$$

$$MS_B = \frac{SS_B}{df_B} = \frac{SS_B}{k-1}$$

$$MS_W = \frac{SS_W}{df_W} = \frac{SS_W}{n-k}$$

The mean squares computed from the sample data are estimates of the true mean squares. The true mean squares are, in turn, given by the expected values of the corresponding sample mean squares. Given that the samples are independent, the population variances are equal, and the variable is normally distributed in the parent population, it can be shown that these expected values, E, are

$$E(MS_W) = \sigma^2 = \text{Error variance or chance variance}$$

and

$$E(MS_B) = \sigma^2 + \text{Treatment effect}$$

The ratio $E(MS_B)/E(MS_W)$ will equal 1 if there is no treatment effect. It will be greater than 1 if there is a difference in the sample means. Because the two expected values are not known, the sample mean squares are used instead to yield the ratio

$$\frac{MS_B}{MS_W} = F$$

which follows the F distribution. Unlike the t or χ^2 distributions, the F distribution depends on two degrees of freedom: one corresponding to the mean square in the numerator and one corresponding to the mean square in the denominator. Since MS_B and MS_W are only sample estimates of the true variances, one should not expect the ratio MS_B/MS_W to be exactly 1 when the treatment effect is zero, and one should not immediately conclude that there is a difference among the group means when the ratio is greater than 1. Rather, given a significance level and the respective degrees of freedom for the numerator and denominator, a critical value of F may be read from standard tables. The critical value indicates the magnitude of the ratio that can occur because of random sampling fluctuations, even when there is no difference in the group means; that is, $E(MS_B)/E(MS_W) = 1$. The entire analysis is conveniently handled in an analysis-of-variance table.

Table 15A.1 is the analysis-of-variance table for the plastic and metal container sales data. The calculated F value is referred to an F table for 1 and 18 degrees of freedom (see Appendix D at the end of the book). Using the same α as before, $\alpha = 0.05$, critical F is found to be 4.41, and again the sample evidence is not sufficient to reject the hypothesis of the equality of the two means. This should not be surprising, since it can be shown that when the comparison is between two means (the

TABLE 15A.1	Analysis of Variance of Sales of Plastic versus Metal Containers			
Source of Variation	*Sum of Squares*	*Degrees of Freedom*	*Mean Square*	*F Ratio*
Between group	806.5	1	806.5	2.43
Within group	5,978.1	18	332.1	
Total	6,784.6	19		

degrees of freedom in the numerator of the F ratio are then $v_1 = k - 1 = 1$), $F = t^2 = (1.56)^2 = 2.43$.[2] Both tests are identical in this special case, and if one test does not indicate a significant difference between the two means, neither will the other.

The plastic and metal container sales example is the simplest type of what is known as a **completely randomized design,** since there were only two treatments. The distinguishing feature of the completely randomized design is that experimental treatments are assigned to the stores on a random basis. In this case, the container types were assigned to the stores at random, with no attempt to match stores or make the test units equal in any way.

An alternative statement of the hypothesis of equality of means can be generated from the model of a completely randomized design. The model statement has the added advantage of facilitating discussion when more complex models are introduced. The model for a completely randomized design is

$$X_{ij} = \mu + \tau_j + \epsilon_{ij}$$

This means that an observation, X_{ij}, is conceived of as being made up of three components: the overall mean μ; the effect of the jth treatment, τ_j; and the random error associated with the ith observation on the jth treatment, ϵ_{ij}. The null hypothesis of equality of population means is equivalent to the hypothesis that the treatment effects are all zero, since $\mu_1 = \mu_2$ implies that $\tau_1 = \mu_1 - \mu_2 = 0$. The alternate hypothesis, when there are k treatments, is that at least one of the treatment effects is not zero; this is equivalent to the statement that at least one mean differs from the others. The symbolic statement of the hypotheses is

$$H_0: \tau_j = 0 \quad \text{for all } j = 1, \ldots, k$$
$$H_a: \tau_j \neq 0 \quad \text{for at least one } j \text{ where } j = 1, \ldots, k$$

The assumptions underlying the model and the test are that the samples are independent, the variable is normally distributed, and the variance is the same for each treatment. The last assumption is necessary to justify the pooling of variances and, in this respect, is similar to the t test for two means.

---

[2]It can be shown mathematically that if a random variable is t distributed with v degrees of freedom, then t^2 is F distributed with $v_1 = 1$, $v_2 = v$ degrees of freedom; that is, if $t \sim t_v$, then $t^2 \sim F_{1,v}$.

Randomized Blocks

The reader can readily appreciate the difficulty that can arise in the preceding situation if, by chance, the stores selected to handle one type of container were, say, systematically larger than the stores chosen to distribute the other type. If a significant difference had been observed, it could have been because the plastic container was sold in the large stores, which have greater sales potential because they have more traffic.

When, in fact, there is one source of extraneous variation distorting the results of an experiment, a **randomized-block design** can be employed. This design involves the grouping of "similar" test units into blocks and the random assignment of treatments to test units in each block. Similarity is determined by matching the test units on the expected extraneous source of variation (for example, store size in the container example). The hope is that the units within each block will be more alike than units selected completely at random. Since the differences between blocks can be taken into account in the variance analysis, for the same number of observations the error mean square should be smaller than it would be if a completely randomized design had been used. Therefore, the test should be more efficient.

Consider, for example, an investigation of the effectiveness of alternative sales representatives' call-frequency plans made by a manufacturer that sells primarily to industrial distributors. There are three plans: A, B, and C. The plans differ in the frequency with which the various sized accounts are called on, and the manufacturer is interested in determining which of the three would produce the most sales. The firm employs some 500 sales representatives. Rather than choose one of the schemes arbitrarily, it was believed that it would be worthwhile to employ each on a trial basis before making a decision. The firm's management selected a sample of 30 sales representatives who were to try the new call plans. Management was concerned that differences in sales ability might affect the results of the test. Consequently, it decided to match the sales representatives in terms of their ability, employing their past sales as the matching criterion. Thus, 10 blocks with three sales representatives having relatively equal sales records within a block were formed, resulting in a randomized-block design.

The sales that resulted are given in Table 15A.2. The model that underlies the randomized-block experiment is given by[3]

$$X_{ij} = \mu + \tau_j + \beta_i + \epsilon_{ij}$$

where
X_{ij} is the ith observation (ith block) on the jth treatment;
μ is the overall mean;
τ_j is the effect attributable to the jth treatment or call plan, $j = 1, 2, \ldots, k$;
β_i is the effect attributable to the ith block, $i = 1, 2, \ldots, r$; and
ϵ_{ij} is the random error associated with the ith observation on the jth treatment.

---

[3]The example is an illustration of a mixed model. The treatments are fixed; only the three call plans being investigated are of interest. The test units are a random sample from the population of sales representatives, and thus a random-effects model would apply. The combination of fixed treatments and the random sample of test units creates the conditions for a mixed model.

TABLE 15A.2	Sales Generated by Various Call Plans (in thousands of dollars)						

	Plan				*Plan*		
Block	*A*	*B*	*C*	*Block*	*A*	*B*	*C*
1	42	51	43	6	29	35	30
2	36	35	36	7	52	50	54
3	40	52	44	8	46	49	44
4	38	47	42	9	40	44	40
5	32	38	36	10	38	36	35

The assumptions are that a random sample of Size 1 is drawn from each of the kr (k treatments times r blocks) populations; X is normally distributed in each of the kr populations; the variance of each is the same; and the block and treatment effects are additive. Except for the last assumption, these are the same assumptions that were made in the completely randomized design. But now there are kr populations, whereas there were k populations with the completely randomized design.

Let $j = 1$ be Call Plan A, $j = 2$ Call Plan B, and $j = 3$ Call Plan C. The average sales under each call plan are

$$\bar{x}_{.1} = \frac{\sum_{i=1}^{r} X_{i1}}{r} = \frac{42 + 36 + \ldots + 38}{10} = 39.3$$

$$\bar{x}_{.2} = \frac{\sum_{i=1}^{r} X_{i2}}{r} = \frac{51 + 35 + \ldots + 36}{10} = 43.7$$

$$\bar{x}_{.3} = \frac{\sum_{i=1}^{r} X_{i3}}{r} = \frac{43 + 36 + \ldots + 35}{10} = 40.4$$

while the overall mean is

$$\bar{x}_{..} = \sum_{j=1}^{k} \sum_{i=1}^{r} \frac{X_{ij}}{n} = \frac{(42 + \ldots + 38) + (51 + \ldots + 36) + (43 + \ldots + 35)}{30} = 41.1$$

In addition to the total, treatment, and error sum of squares, the sum of squares corresponding to blocks must now be computed. The block means are helpful in determining this sum of squares. They are given by the formula

$$\bar{x}_{i.} = \frac{\sum_{j=1}^{k} X_{ij}}{k}$$

where $\bar{x}_{i.}$ refers to the mean of the ith block. Thus, for the first block, $i = 1$,

$$\bar{x}_{1.} = \frac{\sum_{j=1}^{k} X_{1j}}{k} = \frac{(42 + 51 + 43)}{3} = 45.3$$

The remaining block means, which are calculated similarly, are

$$\bar{x}_{2.} = 35.7 \qquad \bar{x}_{5.} = 35.3 \qquad \bar{x}_{8.} = 46.3$$
$$\bar{x}_{3.} = 45.3 \qquad \bar{x}_{6.} = 31.3 \qquad \bar{x}_{9.} = 41.3$$
$$\bar{x}_{4.} = 42.3 \qquad \bar{x}_{7.} = 52.0 \qquad \bar{x}_{10.} = 36.3$$

The sums of squares are

$$SS_T = \sum_{j=1}^{k} \sum_{i=1}^{r} (X_{ij} - \bar{x}_{..})^2$$
$$= (42 - 41.1)^2 + (36 - 41.1)^2 + \ldots + (35 - 41.1)^2$$
$$= 1{,}333.5$$

$$SS_{TR} = \sum_{j=1}^{k} r(\bar{x}_{.j} - \bar{x}_{..})^2$$
$$= 10(39.3 - 41.1)^2 + 10(43.7 - 41.1)^2 + 10(40.4 - 41.1)^2$$
$$= 104.9$$

$$SS_B = \sum_{i=1}^{r} k(\bar{x}_{i.} - \bar{x}_{..})^2$$
$$= 3(45.3 - 41.1)^2 + 3(35.7 - 41.1)^2 + \ldots + 3(36.3 - 41.1)^2$$
$$= 1{,}093.5$$

$$SS_E = SS_T - SS_{TR} - SS_B = 1{,}333.5 - 104.9 - 1{,}093.5$$
$$= 135.1$$

As mentioned, the model underlying the randomized-block design suggests that any sample response can be written as the sum of four additive factors: (1) the overall mean, (2) the effect of the jth treatment, (3) the effect of the ith block, and (4) the error term. It may happen that the effect of an individual treatment will vary according to the type of test unit to which it is applied; for example, Call Plan A works best for the better sales representatives, whereas Call Plan B works better for the average sales representatives. Interaction between the treatment and the blocks is said to be present when this condition occurs, and the additive model is no longer applicable. The reasonableness of the additivity assumption can be checked with Tukey's test for nonadditivity.[4] If the additivity assumption is rejected, the interpretation of the results becomes difficult, because it is then hard to say which call plan is best.

The additivity assumption is not rejected in the sample at hand. Table 15A.3 is the analysis-of-variance table for the applicable linear model. There are now two F ratios of interest—one corresponding to blocks and one corresponding to treatments. Calculated F for the treatment mean square is 6.98; critical F for $\alpha = 0.05$

---

[4]See Keppel, *Design and Analysis*, pp. 155–156, for a discussion of and calculation formulas for Tukey's test of nonadditivity. For discussion of the handling of nonadditivity or interactions, see U. N. Umesh, Robert A. Peterson, Michelle McCann-Nelson, and Rajiv Vaidyanathan, "Type IV Error in Marketing Research: The Investigation of ANOVA Interactions," *Journal of the Academy of Marketing Science* 24 (Winter 1996), pp. 17–26.

TABLE 15A.3	Analysis of Variance of Randomized-Block Design Investigating Sales Call Plans			
Source of Variation	Sum of Squares	Degrees of Freedom	Mean Square	F Ratio
Blocks	1,093.5	$(r - 1) = 9$	121.50	16.18
Treatments	104.9	$(k - 1) = 2$	52.45	6.98
Error	135.1	$(r - 1)(k - 1) = 18$	7.51	
Total	1,333.5	$rk - 1 = 29$		

and $v_1 = 2$ and $v_2 = 18$ is 3.55. Calculated F exceeds critical F, and the null hypothesis of equal means is rejected. There is a difference in the effectiveness of at least one of the call plans. Call Plan B, in particular, produces significantly better sales.[5]

Calculated F for the block effect is 16.18. Critical F for $\alpha = 0.05$ and $v_1 = 9$ and $v_2 = 18$ is 2.46. Since calculated F exceeds critical F, the block variation is statistically significant. This means that the grouping of sales representatives according to ability before assigning the call plans has eliminated a source of variation in the results. The blocking was indeed worthwhile. The randomized-block design was more efficient than a completely randomized design would have been.

Latin Square

The **Latin-square design** is appropriate when two extraneous factors can cause serious distortion in the results. Suppose in the previous example that we wanted to conduct the investigation not only with sales representatives of different ability but also among sales representatives having different sized territories. Suppose, in fact, that we had divided the sales representatives into three classes on the basis of ability—outstanding, good, and average—and the territories into three classes—large, average, and small. There are thus nine different conditions with which to cope. One way of proceeding would be to use randomized blocks and test each of the three call plans under each of the nine conditions. This would require a sample of 27 sales representatives. An alternate approach would be to try each call plan only once with each size territory and each level of ability. This would require a sample of only nine test units or sales representatives. The primary gain in this case would be administrative control. In other cases, there may be cost advantages associated with the use of fewer test units. The interesting point is that if differences in territory size do indeed have an effect, the Latin-square design with nine test units could be as efficient as the randomized-block design with many more test units.

The Latin-square design requires that the number of categories for each of the extraneous variables we wish to control be equal to the number of treatments. With

---

[5]If the null hypothesis of equality of means is rejected, then it is reasonable to look for the means or other possible linear contrasts that are responsible. For discussion of the tests for determining which means are statistically significantly different, see Keppel, *Design and Analysis,* pp. 144–156.

three call plans to investigate, it was no accident that we divided the sales representatives into three ability levels and the territories into three size categories. The
Latin-square design also requires that the treatments be randomly assigned to the
resulting categories. This is typically accomplished by selecting one of the published squares at random and then randomizing the rows, columns, and treatments
using this square.[6]

As an example of the analysis of a Latin square, consider the supermarket chain
interested in the effect of an in-store promotion on sales of its private-label cola.
Suppose that the three promotional plans being considered were

- A—no promotion
- B—free samples with demonstrator
- C—special end display

and that the company decided to run a controlled experiment to test the effectiveness of the choices. The company's management was concerned that the timing of the experiment could affect the results because of changes in weather and
also that the size of the store might influence the outcome. Since there are two potentially serious distorting factors, a Latin-square design is appropriate. Further,
since there are three treatments, there also must be three categories for each extraneous variable. Let the stores, therefore, be divided into three size classes—1, 2,
and 3—and assume that one had been selected at random from each class. Let the
time for the experiment also be broken into three segments, and suppose that
randomization of rows, columns, and treatments yielded the 3×3 design reported
in Table 15A.4.

The underlying model for a Latin-square design is

$$X_{ijk} = \mu + \alpha_i + \beta_j + \tau_k + \epsilon_{ijk}$$

where
X_{ijk} is the result when the kth treatment is applied to cell ij;
μ is the overall mean;
α is the effect attributable to the ith block (say, time period), $i = 1, 2, \ldots, r$;
β_j is the effect attributable to the jth block (say, store size), $j = 1, 2, \ldots, r$;
τ_k is the effect attributable to the kth treatment (promotional plan), $k = 1, \ldots,$
r; and
ϵ_{ijk} is the random error associated with the ijk observation.

We have already remarked that the number of categories for each of the extraneous variables must equal the number of treatments in a Latin-square experiment.
Thus, the ranges of i, j, and k are all the same, 1 to r in the general case and 1 to 3
in the example at hand. There are now r^2 populations—r populations for each

---

[6]See R. A. Fisher and F. Yates, *Statistical Tables* (Edinburgh: Oliver and Boyd, 1948) for Latin squares from
4×4 to 12×12.

TABLE 15A.4	Latin-Square Design and Results for Experiment on Effect of Promotion on Cola Sales

	Design				*Sales*		
	Store				*Store*		
Time Period	*1*	*2*	*3*		*1*	*2*	*3*
1	B	C	A		69	63	72
2	C	A	B		63	63	72
3	A	B	C		48	66	51

Time Period (rows)   **Mean Sales**

1

$$\bar{x}_{1..} = \sum_{j,k=1}^{3} \frac{X_{1jk}}{3} = \frac{69 + 63 + 72}{3} = 68.0$$

2

$$\bar{x}_{2..} = \sum_{j,k=1}^{3} \frac{X_{2jk}}{3} = \frac{63 + 63 + 72}{3} = 66.0$$

3

$$\bar{x}_{3..} = \sum_{j,k=1}^{3} \frac{X_{3jk}}{3} = \frac{48 + 66 + 51}{3} = 55.0$$

Store (columns)

1

$$\bar{x}_{.1.} = \sum_{i,k=1}^{3} \frac{X_{i1k}}{3} = \frac{69 + 63 + 48}{3} = 60.0$$

2

$$\bar{x}_{.2.} = \sum_{i,k=1}^{3} \frac{X_{i2k}}{3} = \frac{63 + 63 + 66}{3} = 64.0$$

3

$$\bar{x}_{.3.} = \sum_{i,k=1}^{3} \frac{X_{i3k}}{3} = \frac{72 + 72 + 51}{3} = 65.0$$

Treatment

A

$$\bar{x}_{..1} = \sum_{i,j=1}^{3} \frac{X_{ij1}}{3} = \frac{48 + 63 + 72}{3} = 61.0$$

B

$$\bar{x}_{..2} = \sum_{i,j=1}^{3} \frac{X_{ij2}}{3} = \frac{69 + 72 + 66}{3} = 69.0$$

C

$$\bar{x}_{..3} = \sum_{i,j=1}^{3} \frac{X_{ij3}}{3} = \frac{63 + 63 + 51}{3} = 59.0$$

Overall

$$\bar{x}_{...} = \sum_{i,j=1}^{3} \frac{X_{ijk}}{9} = \frac{(69 + 63 + \ldots + 51)}{9} = 63.0$$

blocking factor or $r \times r$ populations in all. The assumptions of the Latin-square experiment are that a random sample of Size 1 is drawn from each of the r^2 populations; X is normally distributed in each of the r^2 populations; the variance of each of the r^2 populations is the same; and the row, column, and treatment effects are additive. These are the same assumptions made in the randomized-block design, with two minor modifications: (1) There are r^2 populations, whereas there are rk populations in the randomized-block design; (2) there is an additional additive effect, resulting from the second blocking factor.

The null hypothesis in a Latin-square experiment is that the means are equal or that sales are the same under the three treatments. This is equivalent to testing the hypothesis

$$H_0: \tau_k = 0 \text{ for } k = 1, 2, 3$$

$$H_a: \text{not all the } \tau_k \text{ are zero}$$

The sales reported in Table 15A.4 resulted from the experiment. The overall mean and the mean sales for each time period, store, and treatment must be determined so that the sums of the squares can be calculated. These means are presented in the lower portion of Table 15A.4, where it is understood that i, j, k are summed over the proper values. The various sums of squares are

$$SS_T = \sum_{i=1}^{r} \sum_{j=1}^{r} (X_{ijk} - \bar{x}_{...})^2$$
$$= (69 - 63)^2 + (63 - 63)^2 + \ldots + (51 - 63)^2 = 576$$

$$SS_R = r \sum_{i=1}^{r} (\bar{x}_{i..} - \bar{x}_{...})^2$$
$$= 3[(68 - 63)^2 + (66 - 63)^2 + (55 - 63)^2] = 294$$

$$SS_C = r \sum_{j=1}^{r} (\bar{x}_{.j.} - \bar{x}_{...})^2$$
$$= 3[(60 - 63)^2 + (64 - 63)^2 + (65 - 63)^2] = 42$$

$$SS_{TR} = r \sum_{k=1}^{r} (\bar{x}_{..k} - \bar{x}_{...})^2$$
$$= 3[(61 - 63)^2 + (69 - 63)^2 + (59 - 63)^2] = 168$$

$$SS_E = SS_T - SS_R - SS_C - SS_{TR}$$
$$= 576 - 294 - 42 - 168 = 72$$

Table 15A.5 contains the resulting mean squares and F ratios. Assuming that $\alpha = 0.05$, critical F for $v_1 = 2$ and $v_2 = 2$ is 19.0. None of the calculated F ratios is statistically significant. The hypothesis of equal means is not rejected. The sample evidence does not indicate that the promotions significantly affected sales nor that stores or time periods significantly affected the results.

| TABLE 15A.5 | Analysis-of-Variance Table for Latin-Square Experiment on Effect of Promotion of Cola Sales |

Source of Variation	Sum of Squares	Degrees of Freedom	Mean Square	F Ratio
Rows (time periods)	294	$r - 1 = 2$	147	4.083
Columns (stores)	42	$r - 1 = 2$	21	0.583
Treatments	168	$r - 1 = 2$	84	2.333
Error	72	$(r - 1)(r - 2) = 2$	36	
Total	576	$r^2 - 1 = 8$		

Factorial Designs

So far we have considered designs that involve only one experimental variable, although it may have had multiple levels (for example, three different call plans). It is often desirable to investigate the effects of two or more factors in the same experiment. For instance, it might be desirable to investigate the sales impact of the shape as well as the construction material of containers for floor wax. Suppose that in addition to packaging a new floor wax in metal or plastic containers, two shapes, A and B, were being considered for the containers. Package shape and package type would both be called factors. There would be two different levels of each factor, four different treatments in all since they can be used in combination, and a factorial design would be used. A **factorial design** is one in which the effects of two or more independent treatment variables are considered simultaneously.

There are three very good reasons why one might want to use a factorial design.[7] First, it allows the interaction of the factors to be studied. The plastic container might sell better in Shape A, whereas the metal container might sell better in Shape B. This type of effect can only be investigated if the factors are considered simultaneously. Second, a factorial design allows a saving of time and effort, because all the observations are employed to study the effects of each of the factors. Suppose that separate experiments were conducted, one to study the effect of container type and another to study the effect of container shape. Some of the observations would yield information about type and some about shape. By combining the two factors in one experiment, all the observations bear on both factors. "Hence one two-factor experiment is more economical than two one-factor experiments."[8] Third, the conclusions reached have broader application, since each

---

[7]William C. Guenther, *Analysis of Variance* (Englewood Cliffs, NJ: Prentice-Hall, 1964), pp. 99–100; John Neter, Michael H. Kutner, William Wasserman, and Chris Nachtsheim, *Applied Linear Statistical Models*, 4th ed. (New York: McGraw-Hill/Irwin, 1996), Chapter 19.

[8]Guenther, *Analysis of Variance*, p. 100. For examples of factorial experiments in marketing, see Paul M. Herr, Frank R. Kardes, and John Kim, "Effects of Word-of-Mouth and Product Attribute Information on Persuasion: An Accessibility-Diagnosticity Perspective," *Journal of Consumer Research* 17 (March 1991), pp. 454–462; Syed Saad Andaleeb, "An Experimental Investigation of Satisfaction and Commitment in Marketing Channels: The Role of Trust and Dependence," *Journal of Retailing* 72 (Spring 1996), pp. 77–93.

factor is studied with varying combinations of the other factors.[9] This result is much more useful than it would be if everything else had been held constant.

The factorial design may be used with any of the single-factor designs previously discussed—completely randomized, randomized block, and Latin square. The underlying model changes, as does the analysis-of-variance table, but the principle remains the same. Consequently, let us illustrate the method with the simplest case, a completely randomized design.

Consider again the sales representatives' call plan example. Suppose that the company's managers were thinking of revising both the method and frequency of customer contact by supplementing sales representatives' personal contacts with office telephone contacts. Two phone contact plans, which differed in the frequency with which customers were contacted, were being considered. Call the telephone contact Plan A and the personal contact Plan B, and consider the 2×3 factorial experiment in which each of the two levels of A occurs with each of the three levels of B to yield six treatments. Suppose that the treatments were randomly assigned to each of five sales representatives. Thus, there would be five replications for each treatment.

	Personal Call Plan		
Telephone Call Plan	B_1	B_2	B_3
A_1	A_1B_1	A_1B_2	A_1B_3
A_2	A_2B_1	A_2B_2	A_2B_3

Suppose that the results were as contained in Table 15A.6. Let:

α_i = the effect of the ith level of the A factor (telephone call plan), $i = 1, \ldots, a$;

β_j = the effect of the jth level of the B factor (personal call plan), $j = 1, \ldots, b$;

$(\alpha\beta)_{ij}$ = the effect of the ith level of the A factor and jth level of the B factor;

X_{ijk} = the kth observation on the ith level of the A factor and the jth level of the B factor;

μ = the grand mean; and

ϵ_{ijk} = the error associated with the kth observation on the ith level of A and jth level of B.

---

[9]One can often use select combinations of factor levels rather than every possible combination, which greatly simplifies the experiment. See Charles W. Holland and David W. Cravens, "Fractional Factorial Experimental Designs in Marketing Research," *Journal of Marketing Research* 10 (August 1973), pp. 270–276. See also Raghu N. Kacker and Kwock-Leung Tsui, "Interaction Graphs: Graphical Aids for Planning Experiments," *Journal of Quality Technology* 22 (January 1990), pp. 1–14, for discussion of graphical aids to plan fractional factorial experiments. For examples of the use of fractional factorials, see Paul D. Berger and Gerald E. Smith, "The Effect of Direct Mail Framing Strategies and Segmentation Variables on University Fundraising Performance," *Journal of Direct Marketing* 11 (Winter 1997), pp. 30–43; Gerald E. Smith and Paul D. Berger, "Different Message-Framing for Different Response Marketing Goals: Choice Versus Attitude Formation," *Journal of Interactive Marketing* 12 (Spring 1998), pp. 33–48.

| TABLE 15A.6 | Sales Generated by Various Personal and Telephone Call Plans | | | | |

Telephone Call Plan	*Personal Call Plan*			Total	Mean
	B_1	B_2	B_3		
A₁	42	51	43	691	46.1
	40	52	44		
	52	50	54		
	46	49	44		
	40	44	40		
A₂	36	35	36	543	36.2
	38	47	42		
	32	38	36		
	29	35	30		
	38	36	35		
Total	393	437	404	1,234	41.1
Mean	39.3	43.7	40.4		

Cell	A_1B_1	A_1B_2	A_1B_3	A_2B_1	A_2B_2	A_2B_3
Total	220	246	225	173	191	179
Mean	44.0	49.2	45.0	34.6	38.2	35.8

The underlying model for this completely randomized design suggests that any observation X_{ijk} can be written as the sum of the grand mean, treatment effects, and an error term; that is,

$$X_{ijk} = \mu + \alpha_i + \beta_j + (\alpha\beta)_{ij} + \epsilon_{ijk}$$

The assumptions are the same as for a completely randomized design except there are now $r = ab$ populations, whereas in the completely randomized design there were k populations—one for each treatment. Otherwise, though, it is still assumed that the distribution of the variable in each of the populations is normal and that the populations have the same variance.

There are three main hypotheses, all of which essentially state that the treatment effects are zero (the cell means are equal). The alternate hypotheses are that at least some of the cell means differ. The hypotheses can be written as follows:

$$H_0^{(1)}: \alpha_i = 0 \quad i = 1, \ldots, a$$

$$H_a^{(1)}: \text{not all } \alpha_i \text{ are zero}$$

$$H_0^{(2)}: \beta_j = 0 \quad j = 1, \ldots, b$$

$$H_a^{(2)}: \text{not all } \beta_j \text{ are zero}$$

$$H_0^{(3)}: (\alpha\beta)_{ij} = 0 \quad i = 1, \ldots, a \quad j = 1, \ldots, b$$

$$H_a^{(3)}: \text{not all } (\alpha\beta)_{ij} \text{ are zero}$$

The first two hypotheses state that there are no differences caused, respectively, by the levels of the A and B factors; the third says that the effects caused by Factors A and B are additive. To test these hypotheses, the following sums of squares are needed ($n = 5$ replications):

$$SS_T = \sum_{i=1}^{a} \sum_{j=1}^{b} \sum_{k=1}^{n} (X_{ijk} - \bar{x}_{...})^2$$

$$= (42 - 41.1)^2 + (40 - 41.1)^2 + \ldots + (35 - 41.1)^2$$

$$= 1{,}333.5$$

$$SS_{TR} = n \sum_{i=1}^{a} \sum_{j=1}^{b} (\bar{x}_{ij.} - \bar{x}_{...})^2$$

$$= 5[(44.0 - 41.1)^2 + (49.2 - 41.1)^2 + (45.0 - 41.1)^2$$

$$+ (34.6 - 41.1)^2 + (38.2 - 41.1)^2 + (35.8 - 41.1)^2]$$

$$= 839.9$$

$$SS_A = bn \sum_{i=1}^{a} (\bar{x}_{i..} - \bar{x}_{...})^2$$

$$= 3 (5) [(46.1 - 41.1)^2 + (36.2 - 41.1)^2] = 735.1$$

$$SS_B = an \sum_{j=1}^{b} (\bar{x}_{.j.} - \bar{x}_{...})^2$$

$$= 2 (5) [(39.3 - 41.1)^2 + (43.7 - 41.1)^2 + (40.4 - 41.1)^2]$$

$$= 104.8$$

$$S_{AB} = SS_{TR} - SS_A - SS_B$$

$$= 839.9 - 735.1 - 104.8 = 0.0$$

$$S_E = SS_T - SS_{TR}$$

$$= 1.333.5 - 839.9 = 493.6$$

Table 15A.7 contains the various mean squares and F ratios. Consider the interaction term first. Calculated F is zero. Critical F for $\alpha = 0.05$ and $v_1 = 2$, $v_2 = 24$ is 3.40. Calculated F is less than critical F, and the null hypothesis is not rejected. The effects are additive. The effectiveness of the telephone call plan is not dependent on the personal sales call plan, and vice versa. Consider next the effectiveness of the sales representative personal call plan. Calculated F is again less than critical F, and the null hypothesis of equality of means is not rejected. The data do not indicate that there is any difference in the effectiveness of the three personal call plans.

TABLE 15A.7	Analysis-of-Variance Table for 2 × 3 Factorial Experiment of Telephone and Personal Call Plans

Source of Variation	Sum of Squares	Degrees of Freedom	Mean Square	F Ratio
A (telephone)	735.1	$(a-1)=1$	735.1	35.86
B (personal)	104.8	$(b-1)=2$	52.4	2.56
AB (interaction)	0.0	$(a-1)(b-1)=2$	0.0	0.00
Error	493.6	$ab(n-1)=24$	20.5	
Total	1,333.5	$abn-1=29$		

Consider finally the telephone call plan. Calculated F is 35.86. Critical F for $v_1=1$, $v_2=24$ and $\alpha=0.05$ is 4.26. Since calculated F exceeds critical F, the null hypothesis is rejected. There is a difference in effectiveness of the two telephone call plans. An examination of the cell means in Table 15A.6 indicates that telephone call Plan A_1 is much better than Plan A_2. If the company were to make a change, this would be the plan it would adopt.

Suppose that the interaction term had tested significantly. We would not have bothered to check for the significance of the A and B factors by themselves. Rather, we would have looked for the best combination of a telephone call plan with a personal call plan, because a significant interaction term would have indicated that the effects were not additive; a significant interaction term would have implied that the effects of A were different for some levels of B or vice versa.

Questions

1. What is the basic idea underlying the analysis-of-variance procedure? In general, how are these sources of variation computed? What is the basic statistic used to test for the differences among means in analysis of variance?
2. When is a randomized-block design preferred over a completely randomized design? How does the underlying model change? How do the calculations change?
3. When is a Latin square the preferred experimental design? What is its basic nature? What is the underlying model for a Latin-square design? What is the basic test procedure?
4. When is a factorial design appropriate? What is the basic model of a completely randomized factorial design? What sums of squares are calculated? What are the basic comparisons among the various mean squares?

Applications and Problems

1. Mr. Z, the advertising manager of a medium-sized manufacturer of rug and room deodorizers, has developed three preliminary advertising campaigns for the company's line of deodorizers. The three campaigns are tested in an independent sample of 24 cities across the United States, and the sales in each city are monitored. (Note: (1) cities are

randomly assigned to each treatment or campaign, and (2) the 24 cities are comparable in terms of various socioeconomic and demographic variables.) The results of this test market are as follows:

Sales (in thousands of dollars)

City	Advertising Campaign 1	City	Advertising Campaign 2	City	Advertising Campaign 3
1	10	9	9	17	12
2	6	10	7	18	10
3	8	11	6	19	8
4	12	12	10	20	13
5	6	13	6	21	11
6	8	14	4	22	10
7	9	15	5	23	9
8	7	16	5	24	7

Mr. Z wants to determine if there is a difference in sales as a result of the three advertising campaigns. He requires your assistance in analyzing the preceding information.

a. State the null and alternate hypotheses.

b. What statistical test is appropriate in this situation? Identify the assumptions underlying the test of the hypotheses.

c. Compute the grand mean and the mean of the jth treatment ($j = 1, 2, 3$). Show your calculations.

d. Compute the total variation (the sum of squares total). Show your calculations.

e. Compute the between-group variation (sum of squares between groups). Show your calculations.

f. Compute the within-group variation (sum of squares within groups). Show your calculations.

g. What are the degrees of freedom associated with each of these sums of squares?

h. Compute the mean squares associated with each of the sums of squares. Show your calculations.

i. Complete the following analysis-of-variance table.

Source of Variation	Sum of Squares	Degrees of Freedom	Mean Square	F Ratio
Between-group				
Within-group				
Total				

j. Discuss your findings on the basis of preceding calculations. (Note: Assume that $\alpha = 0.05$ to find the critical F value.)

2. The training coordinator of a *Fortune* 500 company is considering different training approaches for a course to be offered the following year for new managers in entry-level positions. The course is intended to teach managers with no technical background the basic electrical engineering skills necessary to understand the company's products. The coordinator believes that the course can be offered in two ways: the traditional lecture format, in which an instructor provides the necessary information to the new managers with minimal interaction between the instructor and the managers; and the group

discussion format, in which interaction between the managers and the instructor is encouraged.

In addition, the training coordinator is considering two types of instructional materials for the new course—one using a standard electrical engineering textbook, and one using a series of workbooks, or training modules.

To determine how the course should be conducted and what materials to use to maximize the amount of information learned by new managers, the coordinator has decided to conduct a simple experiment using 20 new managers who were scheduled to take the course. Based on experience and college coursework and grades, there were no obvious differences among the 20 managers. Using a factorial design, the 20 managers were randomly assigned to one of four training groups. Managers in the first group were taught using a standard lecture format and a current electrical engineering textbook. A second group also used a textbook, but sessions were held using the group discussion format. The third group used a series of workbooks rather than a textbook and was taught by the instructor in the lecture format. Finally, the fourth group also used the workbooks, but it was taught in the group discussion format. The same instructor was used for each of the four experimental groups.

At the conclusion of the course, the managers were given a comprehensive test to determine how much of the material each retained from the coursework. The training coordinator plans to use this information to determine how the new course should be implemented in the future. The test scores for each of the participants are as follows:

Group 1: *Lecture-Textbook*	*Group 2:* *Discussion-Textbook*	*Group 3:* *Lecture-Workbook*	*Group 4:* *Discussion-Workbook*
62	74	84	94
78	86	72	84
86	76	72	88
64	88	66	78
70	84	88	86

a. State the null and alternate hypotheses.
b. Complete the following table:

Source of *Variation*	*Sum of* *Squares*	*Degrees of* *Freedom*	*Mean* *Square*	*F Ratio*
A (instruction format)				
B (instruction materials)				
AB (interaction)				
Error				
Total				

c. What recommendations can you make based on the findings of the experiment? (Note: Assume that $\alpha = 0.05$ to find the critical F value.)

3. What are the underlying assumptions for the ANOVA model? Which assumption is necessary to allow the pooling of variances? What happens if this assumption is violated and the variances are still pooled?

4. A beverage company is testing different point-of-purchase displays. The marketing manager selects 12 stores in a market area and assigns them at random to the following treatment conditions: Control group (no change in display), end-of-aisle display, and store shelf flyer with tear-away coupon. The manager will measure the sales occurring in each

treatment condition and analyze the figures using ANOVA. The sales for each store are shown in the following table:

Control Stores (No change)				Experimental Group I (End-of-aisle display)				Experimental Group II (Shelf display with coupon)			
6	14	19	17	18	11	20	23	7	11	18	10

a. List the sources of variation for this test. What are the corresponding degrees of freedom for each source?

b. Considering the underlying assumptions for ANOVA, which of these assumptions may be violated? Is there a more appropriate design for this experiment? Discuss the advantages and disadvantages of your proposed design.

c. Assume that all assumptions are valid for the experiment. Using the data, perform a one-way analysis of variance. What is the calculated F statistic? At $\alpha = 0.05$, can we reject the null hypothesis of no difference in sales between the treatment groups?

Refer to the NFO Research, Inc., coffee study described on pages 671–674 in Chapter 13 or the next problem.

5. Is there a difference in the importance rating of the attribute "premium brand" for people who prefer the various brands ($\alpha = .05$)? Conduct an analysis of variance using the importance rating as the dependent variable to determine your answer.

A P P E N D I X   1 5 B

Analysis of Catalog-Buying Data

Differences in Means

One question of major interest in the catalog-buying study (Appendix 13A) is the amount of confidence people have when purchasing products from a catalog. The CATCON "catalog confidence" index was formed to address this question. The CATCON index is the summed score for the responses to Questions 4a through 4e in the survey.

Table 15B.1 investigates whether the CATCON index depends on the person's sex. The table indicates that the mean score for males is higher than that for females. The difference is also statistically significant, indicating that males are more confident than females when buying from catalogs. The variance in CATCON scores is the same for males and females, suggesting that it is better to use the pooled sample variance when checking the statistical significance of the difference in the two means.

Paired Difference Test

To investigate whether there was a difference in confidence when purchasing sporting goods from retail stores rather than from catalogs, a second index was formed to go along with the CATCON index just described. Called RETCON for

TABLE 15B.1	Difference in Means for CATCON Index between Males and Females

| | | | | | *t-test for Equality of Means* | | |
Variable/ Group	*Number of Cases*	*Mean*	*Standard Deviation*	*Standard Error*	*t Value*	*Degrees of Freedom*	*2-Tail Probability*
CATCON							
1. Males	65	21.462	2.001	0.248	33.87	121	0.000
2. Females	58	9.224	2.000	0.263			

TABLE 15B.2	Paired Difference Test for the CATCON and RETCON Indices

Variable/ Group	*Number of Cases*	*Mean*	*Standard Deviation*	*Standard Error*	*(Difference) Mean*	*Standard Deviation*	*Standard Error*	*t Value*	*Degrees of Freedom*	*2-Tail Probability*
CATCON	124	15.605	6.494	0.583	-3.790	8.402	0.755	-5.02	123	0.000
RETCON		19.395	3.154	0.283						

"retail store confidence," this index was formed by summing the numerical responses to Questions 5a through 5e in the survey. Note that each of these questions involving retail stores has an exact parallel for purchases made through a catalog. Thus, it makes sense to look at the difference in the two summed scores for each person, a comparison contained in Table 15B.2. The comparison indicates that there is indeed a statistically significant difference in the two summed scores. Subjects are more confident when buying sporting goods from retailers as compared to buying from catalogs, at least with respect to the five items contained in the questionnaire.

Analysis of Variance

Table 15B.3 contains the analysis investigating whether the CATCON index varies as a function of the number of sporting goods items purchased in the past year. The analysis-of-variance table indicates that the differences among the cell means are statistically significant; there is less than 1 chance in 1,000 that the differences in mean squares would have been as large as they were under the null hypothesis of no differences in the CATCON index as a function of the number of sporting goods items purchased in the past year. The cell means in the lower portion of the table suggest that as the number of items purchased goes up, so does the CATCON index.

TABLE 15B.3   **Analysis of Variance of CATCON Index as a Function of Number of Sporting Goods Items (V15) Purchased in Past Year**

Source of Variation	Sum of Squares	DF	Mean Square	F	Significance of F
Between Groups	4320.278	4	1080.069	148.183	.0000
Within Groups	867.359	119	7.289		
Total	5187.637	123			

	V15	N	Mean	Standard Deviation
	1	29	7.76	1.35
	2	27	11.26	3.32
	3	18	17.44	4.03
	4	15	20.87	2.39
	5	35	22.26	2.25
Total		124	15.61	6.49

16

Data Analysis: Investigation of Association

In a good deal of data analysis, marketing researchers will be concerned with testing the significance of differences obtained under various research conditions. It may have been a difference between a sample result and an assumed population condition, or between two or more sample results. In other circumstances, the researcher has the different assignment of determining whether there is any association between two or more variables and, if so, the strength and functional form of the relationship.

Typically, we try to predict the value of one variable (for example, consumption of a specific product by a family) on the basis of one or more other variables (for example, income and number of family members). Prediction, or forecasting, is a crucial element of business planning and marketing strategy; some aspects of a consumer or marketplace can serve as predictors or leading indicators of consumer or market behavior. If we can understand the antecedents (for example, consumers' attitudes), we can understand, predict, and perhaps even change the consequences (such as consumers' purchase behaviors). The variable being predicted is called the dependent, or criterion, variable. The variables that form the basis of the prediction are called the independent, or predictor, variables.

Simple Regression and Correlation Analysis

Regression and correlation analysis are terms referring to techniques for studying the relationship between two or more variables. Although the two terms are often used interchangeably, the purposes are different. **Correlation analysis** involves measuring the closeness of the relationship between two or more variables; it considers the joint variation of two measures. **Regression analysis** refers to the techniques used to derive an equation that relates the criterion variable to one or more predictor variables; it considers the distribution of the criterion variable, when one or more predictor variables are held fixed at various levels.[1] It is perfectly legitimate to

---

[1] Although the regression model theoretically applies to fixed levels of the predictor variables (Xs), it can also be shown to apply when the Xs themselves are random variables, assuming that certain conditions are satisfied. See Michael H. Kutner, Christopher J. Nachtschiem, William Wasserman, and John Neter, *Applied Linear Statistical Models*, 4th ed. (Burr Ridge, IL: Irwin, 1996); Thomas H. Wonnacott and Ronald J. Wonnacott, *Regression: A Second Course on Statistics* (Malabar, FL: Krieger, 1986), pp. 49–50. See also Edward W. Frees, *Data Analysis Using Regression Models: The Business Perspective* (Englewood Cliffs, NJ: Prentice-Hall, 1995); Terry E. Dielman, *Applied Regression Analysis for Business and Economics*, 2nd ed. (Belmont, CA: Wadsworth, 1996) for discussion of the use of regression analysis in business.

measure the closeness of the relationship between variables without deriving an estimating equation. Similarly, one can perform a regression analysis without investigating the correlation. But, since it is common to do both, the body of techniques is usually referred to as either regression or correlation analysis.

Before introducing simple correlation analysis, a comment on the distinction between correlation and causation is in order. The use of the terms dependent (criterion) and independent (predictor) variables to describe the measures in correlation analysis stems from the mathematical functional relationship between the variates and is in no way related to dependence of one variable on another in a causal sense. Nothing in correlation analysis, or any other mathematical procedure, can be used to establish causality. All these procedures can do is measure the nature and degree of association or covariation between variables. Statements of causality must be based on underlying knowledge and theories about the phenomena under investigation, not the mathematics.[2] Research Realities 16.1, for example, highlights what Lawrence Gibson, former director of marketing research at General Mills, has to say about the important role of theory in directing marketing inquiry.

The subject of regression and correlation analysis is best discussed through example. Consider the national manufacturer of a ballpoint pen, Click, which is interested in investigating the effectiveness of the firm's marketing efforts.[3] The company uses regional wholesalers to distribute Click and supplements its efforts with company sales representatives and spot TV advertising. It intends to use annual territory sales as its measure of effectiveness. These data and information on the number of sales representatives serving a territory are readily available in company records. The other characteristics to which the company wants to relate sales—TV spot advertising and wholesaler efficiency—are more difficult to determine. Obtaining information on TV spot advertising in a territory requires analysis of advertising schedules and a study of area coverage by channel to determine which areas each broadcast could be considered to be reaching. Wholesaler efficiency requires rating the wholesalers on a number of criteria and aggregating the ratings into an overall measure of wholesaler efficiency, where 4 = outstanding, 3 = good, 2 = average, and 1 = poor. Because of the time and expense required to generate these advertising and distribution characteristics, the company has decided to carry out its analysis employing only a sample of sales territories. The data for a simple random sample of 40 territories are contained in Table 16.1.

The effect of each of the marketing-mix variables on sales can be investigated in several ways. One way is simply to plot sales as a function of each of the variables. Figure 16.1 contains these plots, which are called scatter diagrams. Panel A suggests that sales increase as the number of TV spots per month increases. Panel B suggests that sales increase as the number of sales representatives serving the territory increases. Finally, Panel C suggests little relationship exists between sales in a territory and the efficiency of the wholesaler serving the territory. Panels A and B further suggest that the relationship between sales and each of the predictor variables could

---

[2]See the classic little book by Darrell Huff, *How to Lie with Statistics* (New York: Norton, 1954), pp. 87–99, for a discussion of this point using some rather humorous anecdotes.

[3]Many of the results contained in the discussion were determined by computer and thus may differ slightly from those generated using hand calculations because of the rounding errors associated with the latter method.

RESEARCH REALITIES 16.1

Role of Theory in Directing Marketing Inquiry

If marketing researchers want to acquire true marketing "knowledge," they should devote more time and effort to developing and validating marketing theories, according to Lawrence D. Gibson, director of marketing research, General Mills, Inc., Minneapolis.

"There's a funny notion around that theories are vague, ephemeral, and useless, and data are nice, hard, real things. And that somehow knowledge is associated with facts and data. This is nonsense.

"Knowledge is an interrelated set of validated theories and established facts, not just facts. In marketing, we are profoundly ignorant of what we're doing because we're woefully short on theory while we're drowning in data."

Deploring the lack of validated marketing theories and overabundance of marketing "facts," Gibson quoted the scientist R. B. Braithwaite. "The world is not made up of empirical facts with the addition of the laws of nature. What we call the laws of nature are simply theories, the conceptual devices by which we organize our empirical knowledge and predict the future."

And he quoted Albert Einstein: "The grand aim of all science is to cover the maximum number of empirical facts, by logical deduction, into the smallest number of axioms, axioms which represent that remainder which is not comprehended."

In other words, Gibson said, "the axioms and theories are not our knowledge, they are our ignorance. They're part of the problem we assume away." A theory, he said, is how "scientists choose to organize their knowledge and perceptions of the world. Theories are pretty well laid out, simplistic, general, have predicted usefulness, and fit the facts.

"Theory is basic to what data you choose to collect," he said, "You can't observe all the veins of all the leaves of all the branches of all the trees of all the forests in the world. You've got to choose what facts you choose to observe, and you're going to be guided in some sense by some kind of theory.

"And when you turn around to use the data, you're also going to be guided by theory. It will have a profound effect on what you do."

This shows up in the way researchers go about analyzing different kinds of data. For example, when working with observational data, people simply don't realize the weak theoretical ground on which they stand. They wander around the data, happily and merrily, trying to find out what makes sense.

"Perhaps you've seen some fairly typical versions of this. The creative analyst looks at the data and the survey and they don't make sense. 'Make sense' means the findings are congenial to his prior judgment. But the world isn't working the way he thought it was supposed to be working.

"So he cross-tabs by big cities vs. little cities. Still doesn't make sense. But he is very creative, and observes there are more outer-directed people in big cities than in little cities, so he now cross-tabs by inner-directed vs. outer-directed by city size, and—lo and behold—he finds out he was right all along!"

"Now, obviously, as long as you keep analyzing when you don't like what you see, and stop analyzing when you do like what you see, the world always will look to you the way it's supposed to look. You'll never learn anything."

Source: Larry Gibson, "Marketing Research Needs Validated Theories," *Marketing News* 17 (January 21, 1983), p. 14. Reprinted with permission from *Marketing News,* published by the American Marketing Association. For an example of the danger associated with continuing to analyze data when "you don't like what you see," see Ralph T. King, Jr., "The Tale of a Dream, a Drug and Data Dredging," *The Wall Street Journal* (February 7, 1995), pp. B1, B6.

be adequately captured with a straight line. One way to generate the relationship between sales and either TV spots or number of sales representatives would be to "eyeball" it; that is, one could draw a straight line through the points in the graphs. Such a line would represent the line of "average" relationship. It would indicate the average value of the criterion variable, sales, for given values of either of the predictor variables, TV spots, or number of sales representatives. One could then enter the graph with, say, the number of TV spots in a territory and read off the average

TABLE 16.1	Territory Data for Click Ballpoint Pens			
Territory	Sales (in thousands) Y	Advertising (TV spots per month) X_1	Number of Sales Representatives X_2	Wholesaler Efficiency Index X_3
005	260.3	5	3	4
019	286.1	7	5	2
033	279.4	6	3	3
039	410.8	9	4	4
061	438.2	12	6	1
082	315.3	8	3	4
091	565.1	11	7	3
101	570.0	16	8	2
115	426.1	13	4	3
118	315.0	7	3	4
133	403.6	10	6	1
149	220.5	4	4	1
162	343.6	9	4	3
164	644.6	17	8	4
178	520.4	19	7	2
187	329.5	9	3	2
189	426.0	11	6	4
205	343.2	8	3	3
222	450.4	13	5	4
237	421.8	14	5	2
242	245.6	7	4	4
251	503.3	16	6	3
260	375.7	9	5	3
266	265.5	5	3	3
279	620.6	18	6	4
298	450.5	18	5	3
306	270.1	5	3	2
332	368.0	7	6	2
347	556.1	12	7	1
358	570.0	13	6	4
362	318.5	8	4	3
370	260.2	6	3	2
391	667.0	16	8	2
408	618.3	19	8	2
412	525.3	17	7	4
430	332.2	10	4	3
442	393.2	12	5	3
467	283.5	8	3	3
471	376.2	10	5	4
488	481.8	12	5	2

level of sales expected in the territory. The difficulty with the graphic approach is that two analysts might generate different lines to describe the relationship, which raises the question of which line is more correct or fits the data better.

An alternative approach is to mathematically fit a line to the data. The general equation of a straight line is $Y = \alpha + \beta X$, where α is the Y intercept and β is the slope coefficient. In the case of sales Y and TV spots X_1, the equation could be written as $Y = \alpha_1 + \beta_1 X_1$. For the relationship between sales Y and number of sales representatives X_2, it could be written as $Y = \alpha_2 + \beta_2 X_2$, where the subscripts indicate the predictor variable being considered. As written, each of these models is a

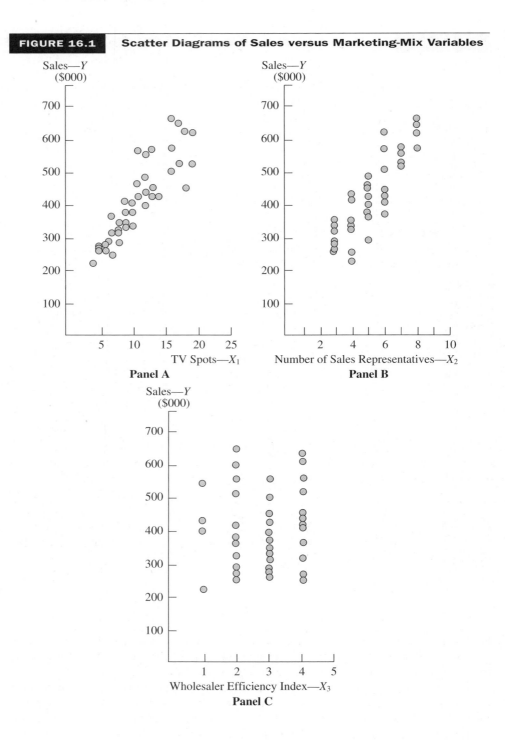

FIGURE 16.1 **Scatter Diagrams of Sales versus Marketing-Mix Variables**

Panel A

Panel B

Panel C

deterministic model. When a value of the predictor variable is substituted in the equation with specified α and β, a unique value for Y is determined and no allowance is made for error.

When investigating social science phenomena (for example, consumer behavior), there is rarely, if ever, zero error. Thus, in place of the deterministic model, we might substitute a probabilistic model and make some assumptions about the error. For example, let us work with the relationship between sales and the number of TV spots and consider the model:

$$Y_i = \alpha_1 + \beta_1 X_{i1} + \epsilon_i$$

where
Y_i is the level of sales in the ith territory,
X_{i1} is the level of advertising in the ith territory, and
ϵ_i is the error associated with the ith observation.

This form of the model is used for regression analysis. The error term is part and parcel of the model. It represents a failure to include all possible determining factors of sales in the model, the fact that there is an unpredictable element in human behavior, and the condition that there are errors of measurement.[4] The probabilistic model allows for the fact that the Y value is not uniquely determined for a given X_i value. Rather, all that is determined for a given X_i value is the "average value" of Y. Individual values can be expected to fluctuate above and below this average.

The mathematical solution for finding the line of "best fit" for the probabilistic model requires that some assumptions be made about the distribution of the error term. The line of best fit could be defined in several ways. The typical way is in terms of the line that minimizes the sum of the deviations squared about the line (the least-squares solution). Consider Figure 16.2, and suppose that the line drawn in the figure is the estimated equation. Employing a caret to indicate an estimated value, the error for the ith observation is the difference between the actual Y value, Y_i, and the estimated Y value, $\hat{Y}_i$; that is, $e_i = Y_i - \hat{Y}_i$. The least-squares solution is based on the principle that the sum of these squared errors should be made as small as possible; that is,

$$\sum_i^n e_i^2$$

should be minimized. The sample estimates $\hat{\alpha}_1$ and $\hat{\beta}_1$ of the true population parameters α_1 and β_1 are determined so that this condition is satisfied.

---

[4] Strictly speaking, the regression model requires that errors of measurement be associated only with the criterion variable and that the predictor variables be measured without error. See Wonnacott and Wonnacott, *Regression,* pp. 293–299, for a discussion of the problems and solutions when the predictor variables also have an error component.

FIGURE 16.2   **Relationship between *Y* and *X₁* in the Probabilistic Model**

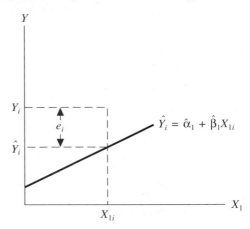

Three simplifying assumptions are made about the error term in the least-squares solution:

1.   The mean or average value of the disturbance term is zero.
2.   The variance of the disturbance term is constant and is independent of the values of the predictor variable.
3.   The values of the error term are independent of one another.

Given these assumptions, the sample estimates of the intercept and slope population parameters, α and β in the general case, can be shown to be:[5]

$$\hat{\alpha} = \bar{y} - \hat{\beta}\bar{x}$$

$$\hat{\beta} = \frac{n\sum_{i=1}^{n}(X_i - \bar{x})(Y_i - \bar{y})}{nS_x^2} = \frac{n\sum_{i=1}^{n}X_iY_i - \left(\sum_{i=1}^{n}X_i\right)\left(\sum_{i=1}^{n}Y_i\right)}{n\left(\sum_{i=1}^{n}X_i^2\right) - \left(\sum_{i=1}^{n}X_i\right)}$$

where

$$\bar{y} = \sum_{i=1}^{n}\frac{Y_i}{n} \text{ and } \bar{x} = \sum_{i=1}^{n}\frac{X_i}{n}$$

Thus, one needs various sums, sums of squares, and sums of cross products to generate the least-squares estimates.

---

[5]See Kutner, Nachtschiem, Wasserman, and Neter, *Applied Linear Statistical Models*, for the derivation. For discussion of the assumptions and whether they are satisfied, see William D. Berry, *Understanding Regression Assumptions* (Thousand Oaks, CA: Sage, 1993).

Predicting sales Y from the number of TV spots per month X_1, use the data provided in Table 16.1 to confirm that

$$\sum_{i=1}^{40} Y_i = 260.3 + 286.1 + \ldots = 16{,}451.5$$

$$\sum_{i=1}^{40} X_{i1} = (5 + 7 + \ldots + 12) = 436.0$$

$$\sum_{i=1}^{40} X_{i1} Y_i = 5(260.3) + 7(286.1) + \ldots + 12(481.8) = 197{,}634$$

$$\sum_{i=1}^{40} X_{i1}^2 = (5)^2 + (7)^2 + \ldots + (12)^2 = 5{,}476$$

$$\bar{y} = \frac{\sum_{i=1}^{40} Y_i}{n} = 16{,}451.5/40 = 411.3$$

$$\bar{x} = \frac{\sum_{i=1}^{40} X_{i1}}{n} = 436/40 = 10.9$$

Therefore,

$$\hat{\beta}_1 = \frac{n \sum_{i=1}^{n} X_{i1} Y_i - \left(\sum_{i=1}^{n} X_{i1} \right) \left(\sum_{i=1}^{n} Y_i \right)}{n \left(\sum_{i=1}^{n} X_{i1}^2 \right) - \left(\sum_{i=1}^{n} X_{i1} \right)^2}$$

$$= \frac{40(197{,}634) - (436)(16{,}451.5)}{40(5{,}476) - (436)^2} = 25.3$$

$$\hat{\alpha} = \bar{y} - \hat{\beta}_1 \bar{x}_1 = 411.3 - (25.3)(10.9) = 135.4$$

The equation is plotted in Figure 16.3. The slope of the line is given by β_1. The value 25.3 of $\hat{\beta}_1$ suggests that sales increase by \$25,300 for every unit increase in TV spots. As mentioned previously, this is an estimate of the true population condition based on our particular sample of 40 observations. A different sample would most assuredly generate a different estimate. Further, we have not yet asked whether this is a statistically significant result or whether it could have occurred by chance. Nevertheless, it is a most vital item of information that helps in determining whether advertising expense is worth the estimated return. The estimate of the intercept parameter is $\hat{\alpha}_1 = 135.4$; this value indicates where the line crosses the Y axis because it represents the estimated value of Y when the predictor variable equals zero.

Standard Error of Estimate

An examination of Figure 16.3 shows that, although the line seems to fit the points fairly well, some deviation still occurs in the points about the line. The size of these deviations measures the accuracy of the prediction, or the goodness of the fit, and a

FIGURE 16.3   Plot of Equation Relating Sales to TV Spots

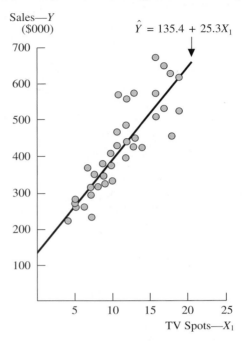

numerical measure of the variation of the points about the line may be computed in much the same way as we compute the standard deviation of a frequency distribution. Just as the sample mean is an estimate of the true parent population mean, the line given by $Y_i = \hat{\alpha}_1 + \hat{\beta}_1 X_{i1} + e_i$ is an estimate of the true regression line $Y_i = \alpha_1 + \beta_1 X_{i1} + \epsilon_i$. Consider the variance of the random error ϵ around the true line of regression; that is, σ_ϵ^2 or $\sigma_{Y/X}^2$. When the population variance σ^2 is unknown, an unbiased estimate is given by

$$\hat{s}^2 = \frac{\sum_{i=1}^{n} (X_i - \bar{x})^2}{(n-1)}$$

Similarly, let $s_{Y/X}^2$ be an unbiased estimate of $\sigma_{Y/X}^2$. Now it can be shown that

$$s_{Y/X}^2 = \frac{\sum_{i=1}^{n} e_i^2}{(n-2)} = \frac{\sum_{i=1}^{n} (Y_i - \hat{Y}_i)^2}{(n-2)}$$

is an unbiased estimator of $\sigma_{Y/X}^2$, where Y_i and $\hat{Y}_i$ are, respectively, the observed and estimated values of Y for the ith observation. The square root of the quantity $s_{Y/X}$ is often called the **standard error of estimate,** although the term standard deviation from regression is more meaningful.

FIGURE 16.4   **Rectangular Distribution of Error Term**

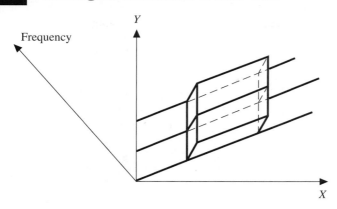

The interpretation of the standard error of estimate parallels that for the standard deviation. Consider any X_{i1} value. The standard error of estimate means that for any such value of TV spots X_{i1}, Y_i (sales) tends to be distributed about the corresponding $\hat{Y}_i$ value—the point on the line—with a standard deviation equal to the standard error of estimate. Further, the variation about the line is the same throughout the entire length of the line. The point on the line (the arithmetic mean) changes as X_{i1} changes, but the distribution of Y_i values around the line does not change with changes in the number of TV spots. Figure 16.4 depicts the situation under the assumption that the error term is rectangularly distributed, for example.[6] Note that the assumption of constant $s_{Y/X}$, irrespective of the value of X_{i1}, produces parallel bands around the regression line.

The smaller the standard error of estimate, the better the line fits the data (the *closer the data points lie to the line*). For the line relating sales to TV spots, it is $s_{Y/X} = 59.6$.

Inferences about the Slope Coefficient

The slope coefficient, $\hat{\beta}_1 = 25.3$, has not yet been tested to see whether the effect of advertising on sales is significantly greater than zero, or if the effect was due to chance. To deal with that question requires an additional assumption—namely, that the errors are normally distributed. (However, before proceeding, let us emphasize that the least-squares estimators of the parent population parameters are *b*lue; that is, they are the *b*est, *l*inear, *u*nbiased *e*stimators of the true population parameters regardless of the distribution of the error term. All that is necessary is that the previous assumptions be satisfied. This is the remarkable result of the Gauss-Markov theorem. It is only if we wish to make statistical inferences about the regression coefficients that the assumption of normally distributed errors is required.)

---

[6]This assumption will be modified shortly to that of normally distributed errors. It is made this way now in order to make more vivid the fact that the assumption of normally distributed errors is only necessary if statistical inferences are to be made about the coefficients.

It can be shown that if the ϵ_i are normally distributed random variables, then $\hat{\beta}_1$ is also normally distributed. In other words, if we were to take repeated samples from our population of sales territories and calculate a $\hat{\beta}_1$ for each sample, the distribution of these estimates would be normal and *centered* on the *true population* parameter β_1. Further, the variance of the distribution of $\hat{\beta}_1$s can be shown to be equal to

$$\sigma_{\beta_1}^2 = \frac{\sigma_{Y/X_1}^2}{\sum_{i=1}^{n}(X_{i1}-\bar{x}_1)^2}$$

Because the population $\sigma_{Y/X}^2$ is unknown, $\sigma_{\hat{\beta}_1}^2$ is also unknown and has to be estimated. The estimate is generated by substituting the standard error of estimate $s_{Y/X}$ for $\sigma_{Y/X}$:

$$s_{\hat{\beta}_1}^2 = \frac{s_{Y/X_1}^2}{\sum_{i=1}^{n}(X_{i1}-\bar{x}_1)^2}$$

The null hypothesis we will test is that no linear relationship exists between the variables, whereas the alternate hypothesis is that a linear relationship does exist; that is,

$$H_0: \beta_1 = 0$$
$$H_a: \beta_1 \neq 0$$

The test statistic is $t = (\hat{\beta}_1 - \beta_1)/s_{\hat{\beta}_1}$, which is t distributed with $n-2$ degrees of freedom. In the example,

$$s_{\hat{\beta}_1}^2 = \frac{(59.6)}{(723.6)} = 4.91$$

$$S_{\hat{\beta}_1} = \sqrt{4.91} = 2.22$$

$$t = \frac{(25.3 - 0)}{2.22} = 11.4$$

For a 0.05 level of significance, the tabled t value for $n - 2 = 38$ degrees of freedom is 2.02. Our calculated t exceeds critical t, so the null hypothesis is rejected; $\hat{\beta}_1$ is sufficiently different from zero to warrant the assumption of a linear relationship between sales and TV spots. This conclusion does not mean that the true relationship between sales and TV spots is necessarily linear, only that the evidence indicates that Y (sales) changes as X_1 (TV spots) changes and that we may obtain a better prediction of Y using X_1 and the linear equation than if we simply ignored X_1 (for example, perhaps the relationship between X_1 and Y is linear only in the range of the number of TV sports we measured).

What if the null hypothesis is not rejected? As we have noted, β_1 is the slope of the assumed line over the region of observation and indicates the linear change in Y

for a one-unit change in X_1. If we do not reject the null hypothesis that β_1 equals zero, it *does not mean* that Y and X_1 are unrelated. There are two possibilities. First, we may simply be committing a Type II error by not rejecting a false null hypothesis. Second, it is possible that Y and X_1 might be strongly related in some curvilinear manner, and we have simply chosen the wrong model to describe the physical situation.

Prediction of Y

Having established that the regression is not attributable to chance, let us use it to predict sales from given values of TV spots. Two cases must be considered:

1. Predicting the average value of Y for a given X_1
2. Predicting an individual value of Y for a given X_1

Let us consider these cases in order.

For a given X_1 value, say, X_{01}, the Y value predicted by the regression equation is the average value of Y given X_1. Thus, in a territory with 10 TV spots per month, the expected sales $\hat{Y}_0$ are

$$\hat{Y}_0 = \hat{\alpha}_1 + \hat{\beta}_1 X_{01} = 135.4 + 25.3(10) = 388.4$$

This is an unbiased estimate of the true *average* value of sales to be expected when there are indeed 10 TV spots per month in a territory. Individual territories may, of course, exhibit sales above or below the average, just as there are observations above and below the prediction line. $\hat{Y}_0$ may not exactly equal Y_0, the population mean it is estimating for the given X_1 value, so it would seem useful to place bounds of error on the estimate.

To determine the bounds of error, it is necessary to know the variance of the distribution of Y_0 given X_{01}. This variance can be estimated as

$$s_{\hat{Y}_0/X_{01}}^2 = s_{Y/X_1}^2 \left[\frac{1}{n} + \frac{(X_{01} - \bar{x}_1)^2}{\sum_{i=1}^{n} (X_{i1} - \bar{x}_1)^2} \right]$$

Note that this variance depends on the particular X_1 value in question. When X_1 equals the mean of the $X_1 s$, the variance is smallest, because $(X_{01} - \bar{X}_1)$ is then equal to zero. As X_1 moves away from the mean, the variance increases. For 10 TV spots per day,

$$s_{\hat{Y}_0/X_{01}}^2 = (59.6)^2 \left[\frac{1}{40} + \frac{(10 - 10.9)^2}{723.6} \right] = 92.8$$

The confidence interval for the estimate is given by

$$\hat{Y}_0 \pm t s_{\hat{Y}_0/X_{01}}$$

where t is the tabled t value for the assumed level of significance and $n - 2$ degrees of freedom. We have already mentioned that for a 0.05 level of significance and 38 degrees of freedom, $t = 2.02$. Thus, the confidence interval for the average value of sales when there are 10 TV spots per month is

$$388.4 \pm 2.02\sqrt{92.8} = 388.4 \pm 19.5$$

Although the preceding equation enables us to predict the average level of sales for all sales territories with 10 TV spots per month, we might want to predict the sales that could be expected in some particular territory. This prediction contains an additional element of error, the amount by which the particular territory could be expected to deviate from the average. Thus, the error in predicting a specific value will be larger than that for predicting the average value. Specifically, it equals

$$s_{Y_0/X_{01}}^2 = s_{Y/X_1}^2 \left[1 + \frac{1}{n} + \frac{(X_{01} - \bar{x}_1)^2}{\sum_{i=1}^{n} (X_{i1} - \bar{x}_1)^2} \right]$$

where the caret is removed from Y_0 to indicate that we are now talking about a specific value of Y_0 rather than an average value. Note that $s_{Y_0/X_{01}}^2$ also equals $s_{Y_0/X_{01}}^2 + s_{Y/X_1}^2$. This alternate expression shows why the confidence interval is wider when the prediction involves a specific value of Y_0 instead of the average value. The second term in this expression, s_{Y/X_1}^2, represents the estimated amount by which the particular value deviates from the average value. For 10 TV spots per month,

$$s_{Y_0/X_{01}}^2 = (59.6)^2 \left[1 + \frac{1}{40} + \frac{(10 - 10.9)^2}{723.6} \right] = 3,645$$

and the confidence interval is

$$Y_0 \pm ts_{Y_0/X_{01}} = 388.4 \pm 2.02\sqrt{3,645} = 388.4 \pm 122.0$$

Note that the bounds of error are much wider when a particular Y value is being predicted.

Even though the regression equation can be used to develop predictions about the average or likely value of Y for a given X, those doing so must be mindful of the dangers in all such predictions. It is particularly risky to predict outside of the range of values on which the equation was developed (that is, "extrapolation"). (Check Research Realities 16.2 for Mark Twain's view on the matter!)

Correlation Coefficient

So far we have been concerned with the functional relationship of Y to X. Suppose that we were also concerned with the *strength of the linear relationship* between Y and X. This concern leads to the notion of the correlation coefficient.

Two additional assumptions are made when discussing the correlation model. First, X_i is also assumed to be a random variable. A sample observation yields both an

---

RESEARCH REALITIES 16.2

Life on the Mississippi—742 Years from Now

Mark Twain may not have been a statistician, and he may not have had the aid of a computer, but he knew enough about the tricks numbers can play to write this little spoof for those who would predict "logical" outcomes based on past data.

"In the space of one hundred and seventy-six years the Lower Mississippi has shortened itself two hundred and forty-two miles. This is an average of a trifle over one mile and a third per year. Therefore, any calm person, who is not blind or idiotic, can see that in the Old Oölitic Silurian Period, just a million years ago next November, the Lower Mississippi River was upward of one million three hundred thousand miles long, and stuck out over the Gulf of Mexico like a fishing-rod. And by the same token any person can see that seven hundred and forty-two years from now the Lower Mississippi will be only a mile and three-quarters long, and Cairo and New Orleans will have joined their streets together, and be plodding comfortably along under a single mayor and a mutual board of aldermen. There is something fascinating about science. One gets such wholesale returns of conjecture out of such a trifling investment of fact."

Source: Mark Twain, *Life on the Mississippi*.

FIGURE 16.5   **Scatter of Points for Sample of *n* Observations**

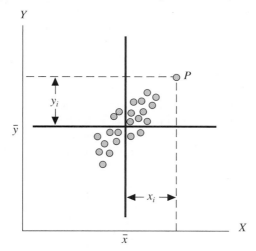

X_i and Y_i value. Second, it is assumed that the observations come from a bivariate normal distribution, which implies that the X and Y variables are normally distributed.

Now consider the drawing of a sample of n observations from a bivariate normal distribution. Let ρ represent the strength of the linear association between the two variables in the parent population. Let r represent the sample estimate of ρ. Assume that the sample of n observations yielded the scatter of points shown in Figure 16.5, and consider the division of the figure into the four quadrants formed by erecting perpendicular axes at $\bar{x}$ and $\bar{y}$.

Consider the deviations from these bisectors. Take any point P with coordinates (X_i, Y_i) and define the deviations:

$$x_i = X_i - \bar{x}$$
$$y_i = Y_i - \bar{y}$$

where the small letters indicate deviations around a mean. It is clear from an inspection of Figure 16.5 that the product $x_i y_i$ is:

- positive for all points in Quadrant I,
- negative for all points in Quadrant II,
- positive for all points in Quadrant III, and
- negative for all points in Quadrant IV.

Hence, it would seem that the quantity $\Sigma_i x_i y_i$ could be used as a measure of the linear association between X and Y, for:

- if the association is positive, most of the data points will lie in Quadrants I and III, and $\Sigma_i x_i y_i$ will tend to be positive;
- if the association is negative, most of the data points will lie in Quadrants II and IV, and $\Sigma_i x_i y_i$ will tend to be negative; and
- if no relation exists between X and Y, the points will be scattered over all four quadrants and $\Sigma_i x_i y_i$ will be near zero.

The quantity $\Sigma_i x_i y_i$ has two defects, however, as a measure of linear association between X and Y. First, it can be increased arbitrarily by increasing the sample size. Second, it can also be arbitrarily influenced by changing the units of measurement for either X or Y or both (for example, by changing feet to meters). These defects can be removed by making the measure of the strength of linear association a dimensionless quantity and dividing by n. The result is the Pearson product-moment correlation coefficient:

$$r = \frac{\sum_{i=1}^{n} (X_i - \bar{x})(Y_i - \bar{y})}{ns_x s_y} = \frac{\sum_{i=1}^{n} x_i y_i}{ns_x s_y}$$

where s_X is the standard deviation of the X variable and s_Y is the standard deviation of the Y variable. The correlation coefficient computed from the sample data is an estimate of the parent population parameter ρ, and part of the job of the researcher is to use r to test hypotheses about ρ. It is unnecessary to do so for the example at hand, because the test of the null hypothesis H_0: $\rho = 0$ is equivalent to the test of the null hypothesis H_0: $\beta_1 = 0$. (Note the identity in the numerator of this equation for r and the earlier equation for β_1.) We have already performed the latter test, so we know that the sample evidence leads to the rejection of the hypothesis that there is no linear relationship between sales and TV spots; that is, it leads to the rejection of H_0: $\rho = 0$.

The product-moment coefficient of correlation may vary from -1 to $+1$. Perfect positive correlation, where an increase in X determines exactly an increase in Y, yields a coefficient of $+1$. Perfect negative correlation, where an increase in X determines exactly a decrease in Y, yields a coefficient of -1. Figure 16.6 depicts these situations and several other scatter diagrams and their resulting correlation coefficients. An examination of these diagrams will provide some appreciation of the size of the correlation coefficient associated with a particular degree of scatter. The square of the correlation coefficient is the **coefficient of determination.** By some algebraic manipulation, it can be shown to be equal to

$$r^2 = 1 - \frac{s^2_{X/Y}}{s^2_Y}$$

FIGURE 16.6   **Sample Scatter Diagrams and Associated Correlation Coefficients**

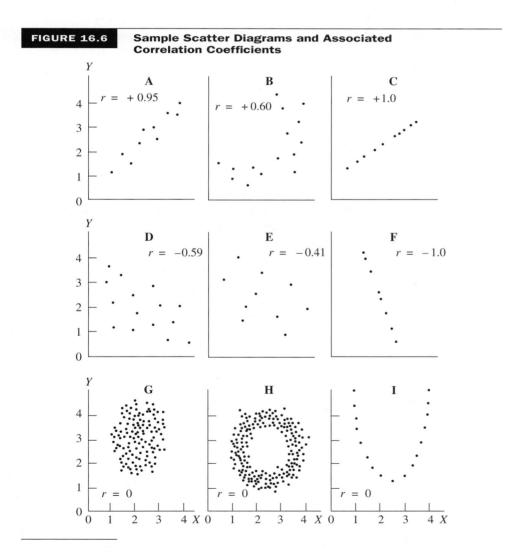

Source: Ronald E. Frank, Alfred A. Kuehn, and William F. Massy, *Quantitative Techniques in Marketing Analysis* (Burr Ridge, IL: Irwin, 1962), p. 71. Copyright 1962, reprinted with permission.

In the absence of the predictor variable, our best estimate of the criterion variable would be the sample mean, $\bar{y}$. If low variability in sales from territory to territory existed, the sample mean would be a good estimate of the expected sales in any territory. High variability would render it a poor estimate, however. Thus, the variance in sales s_Y^2 is a measure of the "badness" of such an estimating procedure. The introduction of the predictor X might produce an improvement in the territory sales estimates. It depends on how well the equation fits the data. Since $s_{Y/X}^2$ measures the scatter of the points about the regression line, $s_{Y/X}^2$ can be considered a measure of the "badness" of an estimating procedure that takes account of X. If $s_{Y/X}^2$ is small in relation to s_Y^2, then X can be said to have substantially improved the predictions of the criterion variable, sales. Conversely, if $s_{Y/X}^2$ is approximately equal to s_Y^2, then X can be considered not to have helped improve the predictions of Y. Thus, the ratio $s_{Y/X}^2/s_Y^2$ can be considered to be the ratio of variation left unexplained by the regression line divided by the total variation; that is,

$$r^2 = \frac{1 - (\text{unexplained variation})}{(\text{total variation})}$$

The right side of the equation can be combined in a single fraction to yield

$$r^2 = \frac{(\text{total variation} - \text{unexplained variation})}{(\text{total variation})}$$

ETHICAL DILEMMA 16.1

Imagine that the analyst you recently hired for your firm's marketing research department was given the responsibility of developing a method by which market potential for the firm's products could be estimated by small geographic areas. The analyst gathered as much secondary data as he could. He then ran a series of regression analyses using the firm's sales as the criterion and the demographic factors as predictors. He realized that several of the predictors were highly correlated (for example, average income in the area and average educational level), but he chose to ignore this fact when presenting the results to management.

- What is the consequence when the predictors in a regression equation are highly correlated?

- Is a research analyst ethically obliged to learn all he or she can about a particular technique before applying it to a problem in order to avoid incorrectly interpreting the results?

- Is a research analyst ethically obliged to advise those involved to be cautious in interpreting results because of violations of the assumptions in the method used to produce the results?

- What are the researcher's responsibilities if management has no interest in the technical details by which the results are achieved?

Total variation minus unexplained variation leaves "explained variation," or the variation in Y that is accounted for or explained by the introduction of X. Thus, the coefficient of determination can be considered to equal

$$r^2 = \frac{\text{(explained variation)}}{\text{(total variation)}}$$

where it is understood that total variation is measured by the variance in Y. For the sales and TV spot example, $r^2 = 0.77$. This means that 77 percent of the variation in sales from territory to territory is accounted for, or can be explained, by the variation in TV spot advertising across territories. Thus, we can do a better job of estimating sales in a territory if we take account of TV spots than if we neglect this advertising effort.

Multiple-Regression Analysis

So far we have considered only two variables in our analysis: sales and TV spot advertising. We now want to deal with the introduction of additional variables by considering multiple-regression analysis. The purposes will remain the same. We still want to construct an equation that will enable us to estimate values of the criterion variable, but now doing so from given values of *several* predictor variables. And we still wish to measure the closeness of the estimated relationship. Our objective in introducing additional variables is basic—to improve our predictions of the criterion variable.

Revised Nomenclature

A more formal, revised notational framework is valuable for discussing multiple-regression analysis. Consider the general regression model with three predictor variables. The regression equation is

$$Y = \alpha + \beta_1 X_1 + \beta_2 X_2 + \beta_3 X_3 + \epsilon$$

which is a simplified statement of the more elaborate and precise equation

$$Y_{(123)} = \alpha_{(123)} + \beta_{Y1.23} X_1 + \beta_{Y2.13} X_2 + \beta_{Y3.12} X_3 + \epsilon_{(123)}$$

In this more precise system:

$Y_{(123)}$ is the value of Y that is estimated from the regression equation, in which Y is the criterion variable and X_1, X_2, and X_3 are the predictor variables.

$\alpha_{(123)}$ is the intercept parameter in the multiple-regression equation, in which Y is the criterion variable and X_1, X_2, and X_3 are the predictor variables.

$\beta_{Y1.23}$ is the coefficient of X_1 in the regression equation, in which Y is the criterion variable and X_1, X_2, and X_3 are the predictor variables. It is called the **coefficient of partial (or net) regression.** Note the subscripts. The two subscripts to the left of the decimal point are called primary subscripts. The first identifies the criterion variable, and the second identifies the predictor variable of which this β value is the coefficient. There are always two primary subscripts. The two subscripts to the right of the decimal point are called secondary subscripts. They indicate which other predictor variables are in the regression equation. The number of secondary subscripts varies from zero for simple regression to any number $k - 1$, where there are k predictor variables in the problem. In this case, the model contains three predictor variables $(k - 3)$, and there are two secondary subscripts throughout.

$\beta_{Y1.23}$ is called the partial regression coefficient because it reflects the impact of X_1 on Y, having partialled out, or statistically controlled for the predictors, X_2 and X_3.

$\epsilon_{(123)}$ is the error associated with the prediction of Y when X_1, X_2, and X_3 are the predictor variables.

When the identity of the variables is clear, it is common practice to use the simplified statement of the model. The more elaborate statement is helpful, though, in interpreting the solution to the regression problem.

Multicollinearity Assumption

The assumptions that we made about the error term for the simple regression model also apply to the multiple-regression equation. The multiple-regression model also requires the additional assumption that the predictor variables are not correlated among themselves. When the levels of the predictor variables can be set by the researcher, the assumption is easily satisfied. When the observations result from a survey rather than an experiment, the assumption is often violated because many variables of interest in marketing vary together. For instance, higher incomes are typically associated with higher education levels. Thus, the prediction of purchase behavior employing both income and education would violate the assumption that the predictor variables are independent of one another. **Multicollinearity** is said to be present in a multiple-regression problem when the predictor variables are correlated among themselves.

Coefficients of Partial Regression

Consider the introduction of number of sales representatives into our problem of predicting territory sales. We could investigate the two-variable relationship between sales and the number of sales representatives. This would involve, of course, the calculation of the simple-regression equation relating sales to number of sales representatives. The calculations would parallel those for the sales and TV spot relationship. Alternatively, we could consider the simultaneous influence of TV spots and number of sales representatives on sales using multiple-regression analysis. If we assume that that is indeed the research problem, the regression model would be written

$$Y_{(12)} = \alpha_{(12)} + \beta_{Y1.2}X_1 + \beta_{Y2.1}X_2 + \epsilon_{(12)}$$

indicating that the criterion variable, sales in a territory, is to be predicted employing two predictor variables, X_1 (TV spots per month) and X_2 (number of sales representatives).

Once again the parameters of the model could be estimated from sample data employing least-squares procedures. Let us again distinguish the sample estimates from the true, but unknown, population values by using a caret to denote an estimated value. Let us not worry about the formulas for calculating the regression coefficients. They typically will be calculated on a computer anyway and can be found in almost any introductory statistics book. The marketing analyst's need is how to interpret the results provided by the computer.

For this problem, the equation turns out to be

$$\hat{Y} = \hat{\alpha}_{(12)} + \hat{\beta}_{Y1.2}X_1 + \hat{\beta}_{Y2.1}X_2 = 69.3 + 14.2X_1 + 37.5X_2$$

This regression equation may be used to estimate the level of sales to be expected in a territory, given the number of TV spots and the number of sales representatives serving the territory. Like any other least-squares equation, the line (a plane in this case because three dimensions are involved) fits the points in such a way that the sum of the deviations about the line is zero. In other words, if sales for each of the 40 sales territories were to be estimated from this equation, the positive and negative deviations about the line would exactly balance.

The level at which the plane intercepts the Y axis is given by $\hat{\alpha}_{(12)} = 69.3$. Consider now the coefficients of partial regression, $\hat{\beta}_{Y1.2}$ and $\hat{\beta}_{Y2.1}$. *Assuming that the multicollinearity assumption is satisfied,* these coefficients of partial regression can be interpreted as the *average change* in the criterion variable associated with a *unit change* in the appropriate predictor variable while holding the other predictor variable constant. Thus, assuming that there is no multicollinearity, $\hat{\beta}_{Y1.2} = 14.2$ indicates that on the average, an increase of \$14,200 in sales can be expected with each additional TV spot in the territory if the number of sales representatives is not changed. Similarly, $\hat{\beta}_{Y2.1} = 37.5$ suggests that each additional sales representative in a territory can be expected to produce \$37,500 in sales, on the average, if the number of TV spots is held constant.

In simple-regression analysis, we tested the significance of the regression equation by examining the significance of the slope coefficient employing the t test. Calculated t was 11.4 for the sales and TV spot relationship. The significance of the regression could also have been checked with an F test. In the case of a two-variable regression, calculated F is equal to calculated t squared; that is, $F = t^2 = (11.4)^2 = 130.6$. In general, calculated F is equal to the ratio of the mean square due to regression to the mean square due to residuals. In simple regression, the calculated F value would be referred to an F table for 1 and $n - 2$ degrees of freedom. The conclusion would be exactly equivalent to that derived by testing the significance of the slope coefficient employing the t test.

In the multiple-regression case, it is *mandatory that the significance of the overall regression* be examined using an F test. The appropriate degrees of freedom are k and $n - k - 1$, where there are k predictor variables. Critical F for 2 and $40 - 2 - 1 = 37$ degrees of freedom and a 0.05 level of significance is 3.25. Calculated F for the regression relating sales to TV spots and the number of sales representatives is 128.1. Since calculated F exceeds critical F, the null hypothesis of no relationship is rejected. A statistically significant linear relationship exists between sales and the predictor variables (number of TV spots and number of sales representatives).

The slope coefficients can also be tested individually for their statistical significance in a multiple-regression problem, given that the overall function is significant. The t test is again used, although the validity of the procedure is highly dependent on whether there exists multicollinearity in the data. If the data are highly multicollinear, there will be a tendency to commit Type II errors; that is, many of the predictor variables will be judged as not being related to the criterion variable when in fact they are. It is even possible to have a high R^2 value and to conclude that the overall regression is statistically significant but that none of the coefficients are significant. The difficulty with the t tests for the significance of the individual slope coefficients arises because the standard error of estimate of the least-squares coefficients, s_{bi}, increases as the dependence among the predictor variables increases. And, of course, as the denominator of calculated t gets larger, t itself decreases, occasioning the conclusion of no relationship between the criterion variable and the predictor variable in question.

Is multicollinearity a problem in our example? Consider again the simple regression of sales on TV spots; $\hat{\beta}_1$ ($\hat{\beta}_{Y1}$ in our more formal notational system) was equal to 25.3. Thus, when the number of sales representatives in a territory was not considered, the average change in sales associated with an additional TV spot was $25,300. Yet when the number of sales representatives is considered, the average change in sales associated with an additional TV spot was $14,200 ($\hat{\beta}_{Y1.2} = 14.2$). Part of the sales effect that we were attributing to TV spots was in fact due to the number of sales representatives in the territory. We were thus overstating the effect of the TV spot advertising because of the way decisions have historically been made in the company. Specifically, those territories with the greater number of sales representatives also received more TV advertising support (or vice versa). Perhaps this was logical, because they contained a larger proportion of the consuming public. Nevertheless, the fact that the two predictor variables are not independent (the coefficient of simple correlation between TV spots and number of sales representatives is 0.78) has caused a violation of the assumption of independent predictors. Multicollinearity is present within this data set.

A multicollinear condition *reduces the efficiency* of the estimates for the regression parameters: the amount of information about the effect of each predictor variable on the criterion variable declines as the correlation among the predictor variables increases. The reduction in efficiency can easily be seen in the limiting case as the correlation between the predictor variables approaches 1 for a 2-predictor model. Such a situation is depicted in Figure 16.7, where it is assumed that a perfect linear relationship exists between the two predictor variables, TV spots, and number of sales representatives, and also that a strong linear relationship exists between the criterion variable sales and TV spots. Consider the change in sales from $75,000 to $100,000. This change is associated with a change in the number of TV spots from three to four. This change in TV spots is also associated with a change in the number of sales representatives from four to five. What is the effect of a TV spot on sales? Can we say it is $100 - 75 = 25$, or $25,000? Most assuredly not, for historically a sales representative has been added to a territory whenever the number of TV spots has been increased by one (or vice versa). The number of TV spots and sales representatives varies in direct proportion, and it is impossible to distinguish their separate influences on sales—that is, their influence when the other predictor variable is held constant.

FIGURE 16.7 **Hypothetical Relationship between Sales and TV Spots and between TV Spots and Number of Sales Representatives**

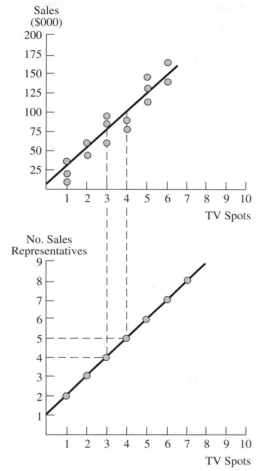

Very little meaning can be attached to the coefficients of partial regression when multicollinearity is present, as it is in our example. The "normal" interpretation of the coefficients of partial regression as "the average change in the criterion variable associated with a unit change in the appropriate predictor variable while holding the other predictor variables constant" simply does not hold.[7] The equation may be quite useful for prediction, assuming that conditions are stable; it still may be used to predict sales in the various territories for given levels of TV spots and number of sales representatives if the historical relationship between sales and each of the predictor variables, and between or among the predictor variables

---

[7]See Douglas C. Montgomery and Elizabeth A. Peck, *Introduction to Linear Regression Analysis*, 2nd ed. (New York: Wiley, 1992); Thomas P. Ryan, *Modern Regression Methods* (New York: Wiley, 1996).

themselves, is expected to continue.[8] The partial-regression coefficients should not be used, though, as the basis for making marketing strategy decisions when significant multicollinearity is present.[9]

Coefficients of Multiple Correlation and Determination

One item of considerable importance in simple-regression analysis was the measure of the closeness of the relationship between the criterion and predictor variables. The coefficient of correlation and its square, the coefficient of multiple determination, were used for this purpose. In multiple regression, there are similar coefficients for the identical purpose.

The coefficient of multiple correlation is formally denoted by $R_{Y.123}$, where the primary subscript identifies the criterion variable and the secondary subscripts identify the predictor variables. When the variables entering into the relationship are obvious, the abbreviated form, R, is used. The **coefficient of multiple determination** is denoted formally by $R^2_{Y.123}$ and informally by R^2. It represents the proportion of variation in the criterion variable that is accounted for by the covariation in the predictor variables. In the investigation of the relationship between sales and TV spots and number of sales representatives, $R^2_{Y.12} = 0.874$. This means that 87.4 percent of the variation in sales is associated with variation in TV spots and number of sales representatives. The introduction of the number of sales representatives has improved the fit of the regression line; 87.4 percent of the variation in sales is accounted for by the two-predictor variable model, whereas only 77.5 percent was accounted for by the one-predictor model. The square root of this quantity, $R_{Y.12} = 0.935$, is the **coefficient of multiple correlation.** It is always expressed as a positive number. (Thus, while r ranges from -1 to $+1$, and r^2 from 0 to 1, both R and R^2 range from 0 to 1.)

---

[8]There are some things that the analyst faced with multicollinear data can do. See R. R. Hocking, "Developments in Linear Regression Methodology: 1959–1982," *Technometrics* 25 (August 1983), pp. 219–230, for a discussion of the problem and some alternative ways of handling it. See also Charlotte H. Mason and William D. Perreault, Jr., "Collinearity, Power, and Interpretation of Multiple Regression Analysis," *Journal of Marketing Research* 28 (August 1991), pp. 268–280; Peter Kennedy, *A Guide to Econometrics*, 4th ed. (Cambridge, MA: The MIT Press, 1998); George C. S. Wang, "How to Handle Multicollinearity in Regression Modeling," *Journal of Business Forecasting* 15 (Spring 1996), pp. 23–27. A common solution is to "factor analyze" the variables, and form subscales among the factors, or groups of the more highly inter-correlated variables, for example, described in Terry Grapentine, "Managing Multicollinearity," *Marketing Research* 9 (1997), pp. 11–21.

[9]Another interpretation danger in the example that was not discussed. It is reasonable to assume that both the number of sales representatives serving a territory and the number of TV spots per month were both determined on the basis of territorial potential. If this is the case, the implied causality is reversed or at least confused; instead of the number of sales representatives and number of TV spots determining sales, sales in a sense (potential sales anyway) determine the former quantities, and they in turn could be expected to affect realized sales. If this scenario holds, the coefficient-estimating procedure needs to take into account the two-way "causation" among the variables. See Wonnacott, *Regression*, pp. 284–292, for a discussion of the problems and the logic underlying the estimation of simultaneous equation systems.

Coefficients of Partial Correlation

Two additional quantities must be considered when interpreting the results of a multiple-regression analysis that were not present in simple-regression analysis: the coefficient of partial correlation and its square, the coefficient of partial determination.

Recall that in the simple-regression analysis relating sales Y to TV spots X_1, the coefficient of simple determination could be written

$$r_{Y.1}^2 = \frac{1 - \text{(unexplained variation)}}{\text{(total variation)}}$$

and the unexplained variation was given by the square of standard error of estimate, $s_{Y.1}^2$, since the standard error of estimate measures the variation in the criterion variable that was unaccounted for by the predictor variable X_1. Total variation, of course, was given by the variance in the criterion variable s_Y^2. Thus,

$$r_{Y.1}^2 = 1 - \frac{s_{Y.1}^2}{s_Y^2}$$

The last term in this formula is the ratio of the variation *remaining* in the criterion variable, after taking account of the predictor variable X_1, to the total variation in the criterion variable. It measures the *relative degree* to which the association between the two variables can be used to provide information about the criterion variable.

Now consider the multiple-regression case with two predictor variables, X_1 and X_2. Denote the standard error of estimate by $s_{Y.12}$ and its square by $s_{Y.12}^2$. The standard error of estimate measures the variation *still remaining* in the criterion variable Y after the two predictor variables X_1 and X_2 have been taken into account. Since $s_{Y.1}^2$ measures the variation in the criterion variable that remains after the first predictor variable has been taken into account, the ratio $s_{Y.12}^2/s_{Y.1}^2$ can be interpreted as measuring the relative degree to which the association among the three variables Y, X_1, and X_2 provides information about Y over and above that provided by the association between the criterion variable and the first predictor variable alone. In other words, the ratio $s_{Y.12}^2/s_{Y.1}^2$ measures the *relative degree* to which X_2 adds to the knowledge about Y after X_1 has already been fully utilized. The ratio is the basis for the **coefficient of partial determination,** which in the sales (Y) versus TV spots (X_1) and number of sales representatives (X_2) example is

$$r_{Y2.1}^2 = 1 - \frac{s_{Y.1}^2}{s_Y^2} = 1 - \frac{(45.2)^2}{(59.6)^2} = 1 - 0.576 = 0.424$$

This result means that 42.4 percent of the variation in sales that is not associated with TV spots is incrementally associated with the number of sales representatives. Alternatively, the errors made in estimating sales from TV spots are, as measured by the variance, reduced by 42.4 percent when the number of sales representatives X_2 is added to X_1 as an additional predictor variable. The square root of the coefficient of partial determination is the **coefficient of partial correlation.**

In our example there were two predictors. Thus, we defined the coefficient of partial determination for the number of sales representatives X_2 as $r_{Y2.1}^2$. We could similarly define a coefficient of partial determination for TV spots. It would be denoted as $r_{Y1.2}^2$, and it would represent the percentage of the variation in sales not associated with X_2 that is incrementally associated with X_1; this latter coefficient would show the incremental contribution of X_1 after the association between Y and X_2 had already been considered.

When there are more than two predictors, we could define many more coefficients of partial determination. Each would have two primary subscripts indicating the criterion variable and the newly added predictor variable. There could be a great many secondary subscripts, as they always indicate which predictor variables have already been considered. Thus, if we had three predictor variables, we could calculate $r_{Y2.1}$, $r_{Y3.1}$, $r_{Y1.2}$, $r_{Y3.2}$, $r_{Y1.3}$, and $r_{Y2.3}$. These would all be *first-order* partial correlation coefficients, because they have one secondary subscript indicating that one other predictor variable is taken into account. We could also calculate $r_{Y1.23}$, $r_{Y2.13}$, and $r_{Y3.12}$. These are all *second-order* partial correlation coefficients. Each has two secondary subscripts, indicating that the incremental contribution of the variable is being considered after two other predictor variables have already been taken into account. Simple correlation coefficients, of course, have no secondary coefficients; they are, therefore, often referred to as zero-order partial correlation coefficients.

Variable Transformations

Thus far, we have focused on regressions that model linear relationships among variables. The scope of the regression model and its applicability may be expanded by transforming variables.

A variable transformation is simply a change in the scale in which the given variable is expressed. Consider the model

$$Y = \alpha X_1^{\beta_1} X_2^{\beta_2} X_3^{\beta_3} \epsilon$$

in which the relationships are assumed to be multiplicative. At first glance, it seems that it would be impossible to estimate the parameters α, β_1, β_2, β_3 using our normal least-squares procedures. However, consider the model

$$W = \alpha' + \beta_1 Z_1 + \beta_2 Z_2 + \beta_3 Z_3 + \epsilon'$$

This model is linear, so it can be fitted by the standard least-squares procedures, and it is exactly equivalent to our multiplicative model if we simply let

$$
\begin{aligned}
W &= \ln Y & Z_2 &= \ln X_2 \\
\alpha' &= \ln \alpha & Z_3 &= \ln X_3 \\
Z_1 &= \ln X_1 & \epsilon' &= \ln \epsilon
\end{aligned}
$$

Thus, we have converted a nonlinear model to a linear model using variable transformations. To solve for the parameters of our multiplicative model, we

ETHICAL DILEMMA 16.2

Sarah was absolutely convinced that there was a relationship between the firm's product sales to a household and the household's total disposable personal income. Consequently, she was very disappointed when her first pass through the diary panel data that she had convinced her superior to purchase revealed virtually no relationship between household purchases of the product and household income in the simple regression of one on the other. A series of additional passes in which a variety of transformations were tried proved equally disappointing. Finally, Sarah decided to break the income variable into classes through a series of dummy variables. When she regressed household purchases of the product against the income categories, she found a very irregular but strong relationship as measured by R^2. Purchases rose as income increased up to $25,000, then decreased as income went from $25,000 to $59,999, increased again for income between $60,000 and $104,999, and seemed to be unaffected by incomes greater than $105,000.

- How would you evaluate Sarah's approach?
- Do you think it is good procedure to continue searching data for support for a hypothesis that you absolutely believe is true, or would you recommend a single pass through the data with the procedure that *a priori* you thought was best?
- What are Sarah's ethical responsibilities when reporting the results of her analysis? Is she obliged to discuss all the analyses she ran, or is it satisfactory for her to report only the results of the dummy variable regression?

---

simply: (1) take the natural log of Y and each of the Xs; (2) solve the resulting equation by the normal least-squares procedures; (3) take the antilog of α' (raise e to α' power) to derive an estimate of α; and (4) read the values of the β_i, because they are the same in both models.

This transformation to natural logarithms involved the transformation of both the criterion and predictor variables. It is also possible to change the scale of either the criterion or predictor variables. Transformations to the exponential and logarithmic are some of the most useful, because they serve to relax the constraints imposed by the assumptions that[10] the relationship between the criterion variable and the predictor variables is linear and additive, and that the errors are homoscedastic (that is, constant for all values of the predictors).

In the section that follows, we discuss Dummy Variables. They offer another form of transformation, to allow for nonlinear relationships, and categorical or rank-order variables in regression problems.

---

[10]See Ronald E. Frank, "Use of Transformations," *Journal of Marketing Research* 3 (August 1966), pp. 247–253, for a discussion of these conditions and how the proper transformation can serve to fulfill them. See also Richard A. Johnson and Dean W. Wichern, *Applied Multivariate Statistical Analysis*, 4th ed. (Upper Saddle River, NJ: Prentice-Hall, 1998).

Dummy Variables

The analysis in the sales data in Table 16.1 is still not complete. No attention has yet been given to the effect of distribution on sales, particularly as measured by the wholesaler efficiency index. One way of considering the effect of wholesaler efficiency on sales would be to introduce the index directly; that is, the X_3 value for each observation would simply be the value recorded in the last column of Table 16.1. Letting X_3 represent the wholesaler efficiency index, the multiple-regression equation would be:

$$Y = \alpha + \beta_1 X_1 + \beta_2 X_2 + \beta_3 X_3 + \epsilon$$

The least-squares estimate of β_3 in this equation turns out to be $\hat{\beta}_3 = 11.5$. Note what this number implies if the predictor variables are independent. It means that the estimated average change in sales is $11,500 for each unit change in the wholesaler efficiency index. This means that a fair distributor could be expected to sell $11,500 more on the average than a poor one; a good one could be expected to average $11,500 more than a fair one; and an excellent one could be expected to sell $11,500 more on the average than a good one. The sales increments are assumed to be constant for each change in wholesaler rating. The implication is that the wholesaler efficiency index is an interval-scaled variable and that the difference between a poor and a fair wholesaler is the same as the difference between a fair one and a good one. This is a questionable assumption with an index that reflects ratings.

An alternative way of proceeding would be to convert the index into a set of dummy variables or, more appropriately, binary variables. A binary variable is one that takes on one of two values, 0 or 1. Binary variables are very flexible; they can provide a numerical representation for attributes or characteristics that are not essentially quantitative. For example, one could introduce gender into a regression equation using the dummy variable X_i, where

$X_i = 0$ if the person is female
$X_i = 1$ if the person is male

The technique is readily extended to handle multichotomous as well as dichotomous classifications. For instance, suppose that one wanted to introduce the variable social class into a regression equation, and there were three distinct class levels: upper, middle, and lower class. This could be handled using two dummy variables, say, X_1 and X_2, where

	X_1	X_2
• if a person belongs to the upper class	1	0
• if a person belongs to the middle class	0	1
• if a person belongs to the lower class	0	0

Given that alternative coding schemes could be used (for example, X_1 to denote middle class and X_2 to denote lower class), it is important that the analyst interpreting the output from a regression employing dummy variables pays close attention to the coding of the variables. It should be clear that an m category classification is capable of unambiguous representation by a set of $m-1$ binary variables and that an mth binary would be entirely superfluous. As a matter of fact, the use of m variables to code an m-way classification variable would render most regression programs inoperative.

Suppose that we were to employ three dummy variables to represent the four-category wholesaler efficiency index in the Click ballpoint pen example and that

	X_3	X_4	X_5
• if a wholesaler is poor	0	0	0
• if a wholesaler is fair	1	0	0
• if a wholesaler is good	0	1	0
• if a wholesaler is excellent	0	0	1

The regression model is

$$Y = \alpha + \beta_1 X_1 + \beta_2 X_2 + \beta_3 X_3 + \beta_4 X_4 + \beta_5 X_5 + \epsilon$$

The least-squares estimates of the wholesaler efficiency parameters are[11]

$$\hat{\beta}_3 = 9.2 \qquad \hat{\beta}_4 = 20.3 \qquad \hat{\beta}_5 = 33.3$$

These coefficients indicate that on the average, a fair wholesaler could be expected to sell \$9,200 more than a poor one, a good wholesaler could be expected to sell \$20,300 more than a poor one, and an excellent wholesaler could sell \$33,300 more than a poor one. Note that all these coefficients are interpreted with respect to the baseline which has the codes of {0, 0, 0} ("poor" in this case).[12]

The analyst who wants to determine the difference in sales effectiveness between other classifications must look at coefficient differences. Thus, if the researcher wanted to calculate the estimated difference in expected sales from a good wholesaler and a fair wholesaler, the appropriate difference would be $\hat{\beta}_4 - \hat{\beta}_3 = 20.3 - 9.2 = 11.1$ thousand dollars (\$11,100). Similarly, an excellent wholesaler could be expected on the average to sell $\hat{\beta}_5 - \hat{\beta}_{43} = 33.3 - 20.3 = 13.0$ thousand dollars (\$13,000) more than a good one.

The use of dummy variables indicates that the relationship between sales and the wholesaler efficiency index is not linear as was assumed when the index was introduced as a single interval-scaled variable. Instead of an across-the-board increase of \$11,500 with each rating change, the respective increases are 9.2 (\$9,200) from poor to fair, 11.1 (\$11,100) from fair to good, and 13.0 (\$13,000) from good to excellent.

---

[11]The data were artificially created employing specified parameter values and a random error term in a linear equation. The parameters were actually $\beta_3 = 2.0$, $\beta_4 = 22.0$, and $\beta_5 = 32.0$.

[12]For a useful discussion of some alternative ways to code dummy variables and the different insights that can be provided by the various alternatives, see Jacob Cohen and Patricia Cohen, *Applied Multiple Regression/Correlation Analysis for the Behavioral Sciences,* 2nd ed. (Mahwah, NJ: Erlbaum, 1983), pp. 181–222; Melissa A. Hardy, *Regression with Dummy Variables* (Thousand Oaks, CA: Sage, 1993).

Conjoint Analysis

A very special implementation of a dummy variable regression is **conjoint analysis,** or conjoint measurement, which relies on the ability of respondents to make judgments about stimuli. The stimuli represent some predetermined combinations of attributes, and respondents are asked to make judgments about their preference for these various attribute combinations. The basic aim is to determine the features respondents most prefer. Respondents might use, for example, such attributes as miles per gallon, seating capacity, price, length of warranty, and so on in making judgments about which automobile they prefer. Yet, if asked to do so directly, many respondents might find it very difficult to state which attributes they were using and how they were combining them to form overall judgments. Conjoint analysis estimates how much each of the attributes is valued on the basis of the choices respondents make among product concepts that are varied in systematic ways. In essence, respondents' value systems are inferred from their behaviors as reflected in their choices rather than from self reports about how important each of the various attributes is to them.

The word *conjoint* has to do with the notion that the relative values of things considered jointly can be measured when they might not be measurable if taken one at a time. Quite often respondents are asked to express the relative value to them of various alternatives by ordering the alternatives from most desirable to least desirable. The attempt in a conjoint analysis solution, then, is to assign values to the levels of each of the attributes so that the resulting values or utilities predict as well as possible the consumer's input judgments.

Example

Suppose that we were considering introducing a new coffee maker and wished to assess how consumers evaluated the following levels of each of these product attributes:

- Capacity—4, 8, and 10 cups
- Price—$28, $32, and $38
- Brewing time—3, 6, 9, and 12 minutes

For all three of these attributes, most consumers would probably prefer either the most or least of each property—the largest capacity maker, the shortest brewing time, at the lowest price. Unfortunately, life is not that simple. The larger coffee maker will cost more to manufacture; faster brewing means a larger heating element for the same pot capacity, which also raises the cost; a larger-capacity maker with no change in the heating element will require increased brewing time. In sum, a consumer is going to have to trade off some of one feature to secure more of another. The manufacturer is interested in determining how consumers value these specific attributes. Is low price most valued, or are consumers willing to pay a higher price to secure some of the other features? At what price should the coffee maker go to market, and with what other attributes?

To answer these questions, we might form all possible combinations of these product attributes, 36 combinations in all, and describe each coffee maker on an index card (or a separate computer screen). We would then ask a respondent to order these product descriptions from least desirable (rank = 1) to most desirable (rank = 36), with higher numbers reflecting greater preference. The respondent could be instructed, for example, to sort the cards first into four categories, labeled "very undesirable," "somewhat undesirable," "somewhat desirable," and "very desirable" and then, after completing the sorting task, to order the cards in each category from least to most desirable. Suppose that the ordering contained in Table 16.2 resulted from this process.

Note several things about these entries. First, as we anticipated, the respondent preferred least the $38 maker with 4-cup capacity and 12 minutes brewing time (rank = 1) and preferred most the 10-cup maker with 3 minutes brewing time priced at $28 (rank = 36). Second, if the respondent cannot have her first choice, she is willing to "suffer" with a longer brewing time so that she could still get the 10-cup maker for $28 (rank = 35). She is not willing to suffer too much, though, as reflected by her third choice (rank = 34). Rather, she is willing to pay a little more to secure the faster 3-minute brewing time rather than having to endure an even slower 9-minute brewing time. In effect, she is willing to trade off price for brewing time.

The type of question that conjoint analysis attempts to answer is: What are the individual's utilities for price, brewing time, and pot capacity in determining her choices?

Procedure

Several analytical procedures are used to determine an individual's utilities for each of several product attributes in a conjoint analysis. Some techniques depend on the availability of somewhat esoteric software. In these programs, the computer begins with random starting values for the utility estimates (or "part-worth functions") and iteratively converges in modifying those utility estimates until they predict the consumer's preferences within some tolerable margin of error.

However, increasingly, dummy variable regressions are being used to estimate the components of a conjoint analysis. The consumer's preferences (for example, the judgments of 1 through 36) would form the dependent variable, and dummy variables representing the attributes (such as price) would comprise the predictors. The advantages of the dummy variable regression approach include:

- The wide availability of regression software
- The wide understanding and accessibility of regression as a model
- Demonstrable robustness and comparable results of the dummy variable approach compared to alternative, more sophisticated approaches[13]

---

[13]For more detail on conjoint analysis, see Jordan J. Louviere, *Analyzing Decision Making: Metric Conjoint Analysis* (Thousand Oaks, CA: Sage, 1988). For a comparison of currently popular conjoint programs, see the review by Frank J. Carmone and C. M. Schaffer, *Journal of Marketing Research* 32 (February 1995), pp. 113–120. For empirical comparisons of several popular estimation techniques, see Franklin Acito and Arun K. Jain, "Evaluation of Conjoint Analysis Results: A Comparison of Methods," *Journal of Marketing Research* 17 (February 1980), pp. 106–112; and Marco Vriens, Michel Wedel, and Tom Wilms, "Metric Conjoint Segmentation Methods: A Monte Carlo Comparison," *Journal of Marketing Research* 33 (February 1996), 73–85. For more sophisticated models still, see Rinus Haaijer, Michel Wedel, Marco Vriens, and Tom Wansbeek, "Utility Covariances and Context Effects in Conjoint MNP Models," *Marketing Science* 17 (1998), pp. 236–252.

To demonstrate, suppose we create dummy variables for each of the attributes:

$X_1 = 1$ if brewing time = 6 minutes
$X_2 = 1$ if brewing time = 9 minutes
$X_3 = 1$ if brewing time = 12 minutes
$Y_1 = 1$ if capacity = 8 cups
$Y_2 = 1$ if capacity = 10 cups
$Z_1 = 1$ if price = \$32
$Z_2 = 1$ if price = \$38

and fit a regression model to the preference judgments:

$$\text{Predicted Preference} = \beta_1 X_1 + \beta_2 X_2 + \beta_3 X_3 + \beta_4 Y_1 + \beta_5 Y_2 + \beta_6 Z_1 + \beta_7 Z_2$$

The beta weights can serve to instruct us as to the consumer's utilities of the attributes. If an attribute did not matter, the beta estimate would be zero (that is, changing the feature would have no impact on the predicted preference rating). The larger the beta, the more utility the attribute has—the more the consumer cares about it.

For example, fitting a regression to the data in Table 16.2 yields the following estimates:

$$\text{Predicted Preference} = -0.06 X_1 - 0.28 X_2 - 0.59 X_3 + 0.53 Y_1 + 0.86 Y_2$$
$$- 0.09 Z_1 - 0.36 Z_2$$

That is, we have obtained the following utilities for each level of these attributes:

Brewing Time		Capacity		Price	
3 minutes	0	4 cups	0	\$28	0
6 minutes	−0.06	8 cups	0.53	\$32	−0.09
9 minutes	−0.28	10 cups	0.86	\$38	−0.36
12 minutes	−0.59				

Most often, a simple additive function is used so that the utility of any combination of features is simply the sum of the utilities of the attribute levels making up the combination. Thus, a 10-cup, 9-minute brewing time, \$32 pot would have a utility of 0.49 (0.49 = 0.86 −0.28 −0.09). The utilities for each of the other alternatives are shown in Table 16.3.

These utilities may be plotted against the original judgments to see how well the estimated utilities anticipate the consumer's overall preferences. A measure of the goodness of prediction can be obtained by computing the correlation between the original judgments (the data in Table 16.2) and the predicted utilities (the values in Table 16.3). For these data, the utilities have captured well the preference structure of the consumer, $r = 0.99$.

In addition, the utility estimates themselves may be plotted to examine whether the relationships between the levels of each attribute and the utility consumers place on the levels are linear or nonmonotonic. The utility estimates for capacity and price look approximately linear; thus, more cups are better than fewer, and less expensive is better than more expensive. Brewing time is slightly quadratic—as wait-

TABLE 16.2   **Respondent Ordering of Various Product Descriptions**

| | *4 cups* | | | *8 cups* | | | *10 cups* | | |
				Capacity					
Price	$28	$32	$38	$28	$32	$38	$28	$32	$38
Brewing Time									
3 minutes	17	15	6	30	26	24	36	34	28
6 minutes	16	12	5	29	25	22	35	33	27
9 minutes	9	8	3	21	20	8	32	31	23
12 minutes	4	2	1	14	13	7	19	18	11

TABLE 16.3   **Utilities for the Feature Combinations Given the Assumed Values**

| | *4 cups* | | | *8 cups* | | | *10 cups* | | |
				Capacity					
Price	$28	$32	$38	$28	$32	$38	$28	$32	$38
Brewing Time									
3 minutes	0.00	−0.09	−0.36	0.53	0.44	0.17	0.86	0.77	0.50
6 minutes	−0.06	−0.15	−0.42	0.47	0.38	0.11	0.80	0.71	0.44
9 minutes	−0.28	−0.37	−0.64	0.25	0.16	−0.11	0.58	0.49	0.22
12 minutes	−0.59	−0.68	−0.95	−0.06	−0.15	−0.42	0.27	0.18	−0.09

ing time increases, utility drops off faster; thus, a seemingly benign decision to go to market with a brewing time of 12 minutes versus 9 will lose more potential customers than the analogous decision of going to market with 9 minutes versus 6.

These utilities can be used to determine the relative importance of each of these attributes by examining the range of utilities between the highest- and lowest-rated levels of the attribute. The rationale is that, if all levels of, say, price have the same utility to an individual, then we would say that price is unimportant to the person or that the person was price insensitive. Conversely, if different levels of price produce widely differing utilities, the individual is sensitive to the levels, implying the attribute is important. In interpreting these importance values, one has to remain cognizant that they depend on the range of the attributes used to structure the stimuli. Thus, if price levels of $28, $38, and $48 were used instead of $28, $32, and $38, the differences in utilities for the various price levels would have been greater, suggesting that price was relatively more important to the individual than other attributes. Given the attribute levels used, capacity is most important and price is least important to the subject.

The real payoff from conjoint analysis comes from the fact that one can use the results to identify the optimal levels and importance of each attribute in structuring a new-product offering. Further, by aggregating consumers who have similar preferences or utility functions, products can be designed that come closer to satisfying particular market segments. Thus, conjoint analysis is quite useful at the concept-evaluation stage of the product-development process.[14]

Key Decisions

The example illustrates a conjoint analysis study, but it is a simple example, and does not convey a proper appreciation for the many decisions analysts typically have to make to conduct a conjoint study. Figure 16.8 highlights the more critical decision points.[15]

SELECT ATTRIBUTES   The first step in the process involves deciding on the attributes to be used when constructing the stimuli. These will stem primarily from the purpose of the investigation, but the analyst will have some discretion in this regard. When choosing, analysts should be guided by the principles that the attributes used should be both actionable and important to individuals. Actionable attributes are those that the company can do something about; that is, it has the technology or resources to make the changes that might be indicated by consumer preferences. Important attributes are those that actually affect consumer choice, as determined by managerial judgment or exploratory research. In any single conjoint study, only a handful of all the attributes that could be used will be used, so it is important that they be selected with care. When the number of attributes that need to be varied exceed reasonable limits with respect to data-collection problems, a series of conjoint studies can be conducted. The number of attributes actually used in a typical conjoint analysis study averages six or seven.

DETERMINE ATTRIBUTE LEVELS   Step 2 in the process involves specifying the actual levels for each attribute. The number of levels for each attribute has a direct bearing on the number of stimuli respondents will be asked to judge and consequently on the burden placed on each consumer. In general, we would like to minimize that burden (both for the goodwill of interacting with that consumer as well as to try to maximize the quality of the data that the consumer does give us). At the same time, we would like to end up with good estimates of the utility of each

---

[14]See Paul E. Green, J. Douglas Carroll, and Stephen M. Goldberg, "A General Approach to Product Design Optimization via Conjoint Analysis," *Journal of Marketing* 45 (Summer 1981), pp. 17–37, for discussions of the use of conjoint analysis in product design. For examples, see Jonathan Weiner, "Consumer Electronics Marketer Uses a Conjoint Approach to Configure Its New Product and Set the Right Price," *Marketing Research: A Magazine of Management & Applications* 6 (Summer 1994), pp. 7–11; Amy Ostrom and Dawn Iacobucci, "Consumer Trade-Offs and the Evaluation of Services," *Journal of Marketing* 59 (January 1995), pp. 17–28.

[15]The articles by Paul E. Green and V. Srinivasan, "Conjoint Analysis in Consumer Research: Issues and Outlook," *Journal of Consumer Research* 5 (September 1978), pp. 103–123, and Joseph Curry, "After the Basics," *Marketing Research* 9 (1997), pp. 6–11, discuss a number of issues in the implementation of conjoint analysis. The articles by Paul E. Green and V. Srinivasan, "Conjoint Analysis in Marketing: New Developments with Implications for Research and Practice," *Journal of Marketing* 54 (October 1990), pp. 3–19; J. Douglas Carroll and Paul E. Green, "Psychometric Methods in Marketing Research: Part I, Conjoint Analysis," *Journal of Marketing Research* 32 (November 1995), pp. 385–391, provide a perspective on the development and role of conjoint analysis in marketing research.

FIGURE 16.8	Key Decisions When Conducting a Conjoint Analysis

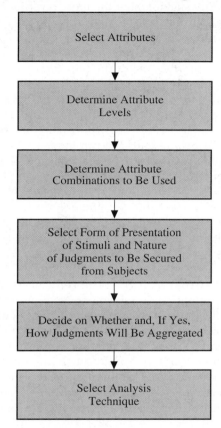

Select Attributes

↓

Determine Attribute Levels

↓

Determine Attribute Combinations to Be Used

↓

Select Form of Presentation of Stimuli and Nature of Judgments to Be Secured from Subjects

↓

Decide on Whether and, If Yes, How Judgments Will Be Aggregated

↓

Select Analysis Technique

attribute level. Our ability to generate good estimates requires that the number of stimuli be relatively large versus the number of parameters that need to be estimated, and the number of parameters in turn depends on the preference model being embraced. Is the model linear in the sense that more or less of the attribute can be expected to be most desired, or is it nonlinear in a systematic way, or could there be a nonsystematic relationship between preference and attribute levels? Most subjects may prefer the lowest price or the highest quality when choosing a ballpoint pen, suggesting a linear relationship between their utilities and the attribute levels. At the same time, many may prefer a medium point to a fine or broad point, suggesting that a smooth nonlinear relationship may be appropriate. The nonlinear model requires the estimation of more parameters than the linear model, and, other things being equal, we would like more stimuli when estimating it than when estimating the parameters of the linear model. An irregular and nonsystematic relationship between utilities and attribute levels would require even more stimuli for good estimation.

When creating stimuli for a conjoint judgment task, analysts also need to be aware that there is a relationship between the number of levels used to measure an attribute and the inferred importance of the attribute to the respondent. Specifically, the empirical evidence suggests that the more levels one uses for an attribute, the more important the attribute is estimated to be in a conjoint analysis.[16] While analysts might want to include more levels for those attributes expected to produce nonlinear versus linear utility functions, they also need to be aware of the erroneous conclusion this can produce about the importance of each of the attributes.

Another factor that affects the choice of attribute levels is their effect on consumer choice. Using levels that are similar to those in existence increases respondents' believability in the task and the validity of their preference judgments. Using attribute levels that are outside the range normally encountered decreases the believability of the task for respondents but can increase the accuracy by which the parameters can be estimated statistically. Similarly, decreasing the intercorrelations among the attributes being varied (such as by combining a very low price with very high quality) decreases the believability of the options for respondents but also increases the accuracy with which the parameters can be estimated. The general recommendation seems to be to make the ranges for the various attributes somewhat larger than what is normally found but not so large as to make the options unbelievable.

DETERMINE ATTRIBUTE COMBINATIONS   The third major decision analysts have to make to conduct a conjoint analysis involves deciding on the specific combinations of attributes that will be used—that is, what the full set of stimuli will look like. In our example, only three attributes were considered, but the respondent was required to make 36 judgments. Since the number of possible combinations is given by the product of the number of levels of the attributes, one can readily appreciate what happens to the judgment task if the number of attributes or the number of levels for any attribute is increased. Can we reasonably expect a respondent, for example, to provide meaningful judgments if there are five attributes at three levels each (not an unusual case) requiring $3 \times 3 \times 3 \times 3 \times 3 = 3^5 = 243$ rank-order judgments? In such a situation, analysts might be tempted to reduce the number of attributes that are varied (for example, 3^4) or the number of levels (2^5) at which attributes are set. An alternative scheme is to use only select combinations of the attributes. For example, it is possible to use orthogonal designs to select a subset of the total number of stimuli if the analyst is willing to assume that there are no interactions among the attributes.[17] That is, a person's utility for various width tips on a ballpoint pen, for example, is independent of the person's utility for various

---

[16]Dick R. Wittink, Lakshman Krishnamurthi, and David J. Reibstein, "The Effect of Differences in the Number of Attribute Levels on Conjoint Results," *Marketing Letters* 1, no. 2 (1990), pp. 113–129; Jan-Benedict E. M. Steenkamp and Dick R. Wittink, "The Metric Quality of Full-Profile Judgments and the Number-of-Attribute-Levels Effect in Conjoint Analysis," *International Journal of Research in Marketing* 11 (June 1994), pp. 275–286.

[17]The use of orthogonal designs to select combinations of the stimuli can produce significant economies in the number of stimuli that respondents need to evaluate. See Sidney Addleman, "Orthogonal Main-Effect Plans for Asymmetrical Factorial Experiments," *Technometrics* 4 (February 1962), pp. 21–46, which is an excellent general source on orthogonal designs. See also William F. Kuhfield, Randall D. Tobias, and Mark Garrett, "Efficient Experimental Design with Marketing Research Applications," *Journal of Marketing Research* 31 (November 1994), pp. 545–557, which discuss the notions involved more from the perspective of designing choice experiments.

prices. The orthogonal array of stimuli can also be augmented to include combinations of particular interest.

The example used the full-profile approach to collect the judgments; that is, all possible combinations of each of the attributes resulted in its own stimulus. One can simplify the judgment task by using a trade-off matrix to structure the stimuli instead of the full-profile approach. The trade-off matrix, or pair-wise procedure, treats two attributes at a time but considers all possible pairs. Thus, in the example, the subject would be asked to indicate preference between each combination of brewing time and price, brewing time and capacity, and price and capacity by independently completing each of the matrices contained in Figure 16.9.

It is typically easier for subjects to supply pair-wise judgments than full-profile judgments. On the other hand, typically, more pair-wise judgments are required, and one runs a danger of missing some important trade-offs among attributes when the pair-wise approach to data collection is used. There can also be a potential loss in realism when only two attributes are considered at a time, because respondents are then forced to make some implicit assumptions about the levels of the other attributes not explicitly varied. As Panel A in Research Realities 16.3 indicates, the full-profile approach is more popular than the pair-wise approach in practice.

Another approach is that of paired comparisons. An advantage of the paired-comparison approach is that it allows one to check how consistent respondents are in their judgments. Thus, unmotivated or uninterested respondents (that is, those whose answers display a great deal of inconsistency, which suggests that the respondents are not taking the task seriously) can be removed from the analysis. Respondents simply indicate which stimulus in each pair they prefer and by how much. Figure 16.10, for example, depicts one pair of coffee makers.

Increasingly, any of these data collection approaches are being administered via computer, which produces several advantages:

- The judgments requested from a respondent can be made individual-specific, in that different attributes and different attribute levels can be used for each consumer/segment. Thus, respondents can be interviewed in detail about only those attribute levels that would be acceptable to them and about only those attributes that they regard as relatively important.

- The number of judgments required from an individual can be reduced because the parameters can be estimated iteratively, as soon as a sufficient number of judgments are obtained. Further, the number and kind of additional judgments required from a respondent can be structured to provide the most incremental

---

FIGURE 16.9   **Pair-wise Approach to Data Collection in Conjoint Analysis**

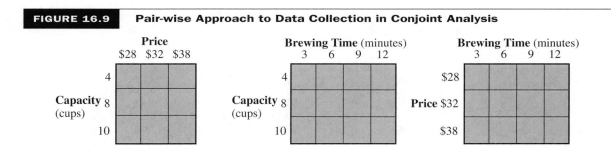

RESEARCH REALITIES 16.3

Relative Frequency of Usage of Various Techniques in Conjoint Analysis

	*Percentage of Projects on Which Used**		
	Europe	*United States*	
	1986–1991	*1981–1985*	*1971–1980*
Panel A: Data Collection Methods			
Full profile (concept evaluation)	66**	61	56
Paired comparisons	4	10	NR
Two factors at a time (trade-off matrices)	15	6	27
Combination of the preceding methods	5	10	14
Panel B: Methods of Presenting Stimuli			
Verbal descriptions	75	NR	50
Paragraph descriptions	3	NR	20
Pictorial descriptions	9	NR	19
Actual products	6	NR	7
Panel C: Nature of the Judgments			
Preference	68	NR	33
Liking	4	NR	10
Intention to buy	18	NR	54
Panel D: Nature of Task			
Rank order	22	36	45
Paired comparison	5	9	11
Rating scale	70	49	34
Total number of projects (100%)	956	1,062	698

*The percentages within each panel do not always add to 100; not all categories are included because of the changing nature of the survey instrument.

**Includes both the full profile percentage (24) and the adaptive conjoint analysis percentages (42).

NR = Not Reported.

Sources: Developed from the tables in Philippe Cattin and Dick R. Wittink, "Commercial Use of Conjoint Analysis: A Survey," *Journal of Marketing* 56 (Summer 1982), pp. 44–53; Dick R. Wittink and Philippe Cattin, "Commercial Use of Conjoint Analysis: An Update," *Journal of Marketing* 53 (July 1989), pp. 91–96; Dick R. Wittink, Marco Vriens, and Wim Burhenne, "Commercial Use of Conjoint Analysis in Europe: Results and Critical Reflections," *International Journal of Research in Marketing* 11 (January 1994), pp. 41–52.

information, taking into account what is already known about the respondent's utilities.

- Results can be shown to respondents immediately at the end of the exercise. They can be given the opportunity to comment on how realistically the estimates seem to mirror their preferences. The results can also be given to management more quickly.[18]

---

[18]For more detailed discussion of the advantages of computer administration of the conjoint task, see Richard M. Johnson, *Adaptive Conjoint Analysis* (Ketchum, ID: Sawtooth Software, 1987); Manoj K. Agarwal and Paul E. Green, "Adaptive Conjoint Analysis versus Self-Explicated Models: Some Empirical Results," *International Journal of Research in Marketing* 8 (June 1991), pp. 141–146.

FIGURE 16.10   **Computer-Administered Paired-Comparison Choice**

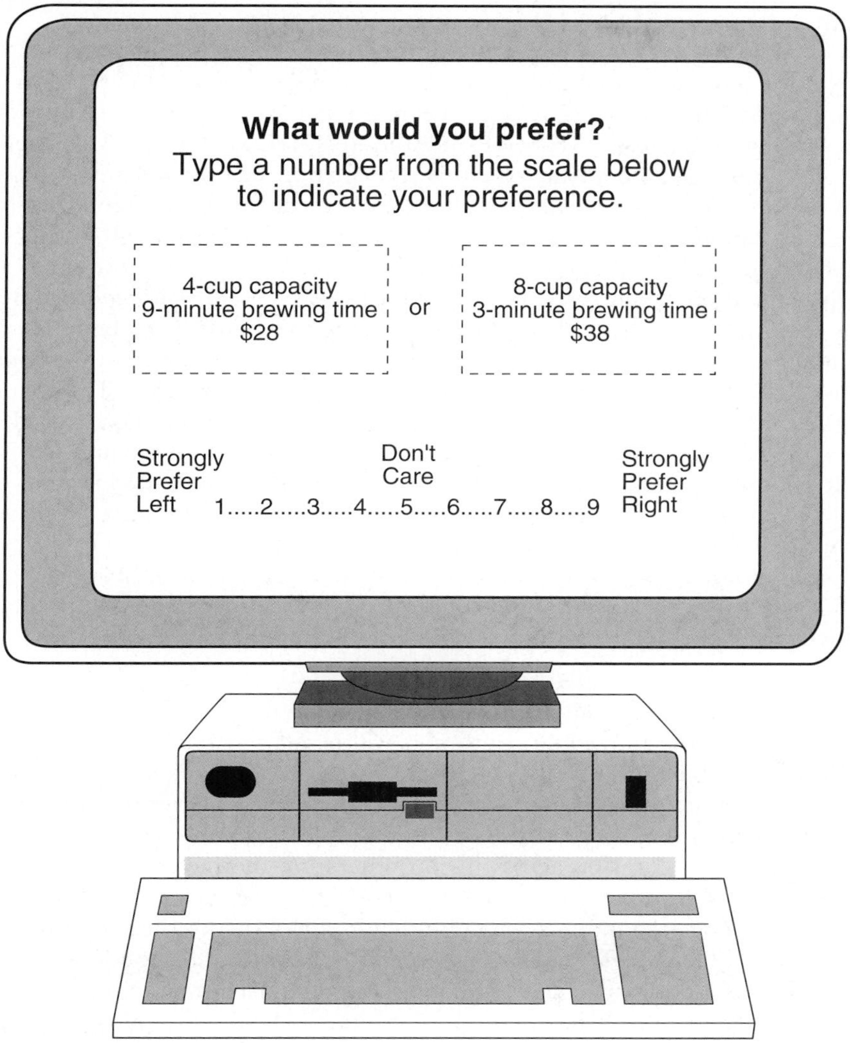

What would you prefer?
Type a number from the scale below
to indicate your preference.

4-cup capacity		8-cup capacity
9-minute brewing time	or	3-minute brewing time
$28		$38

Strongly   Don't   Strongly
Prefer   Care   Prefer
Left   1.....2.....3.....4.....5.....6.....7.....8.....9   Right

SELECT FORM OF PRESENTATION OF STIMULI AND NATURE OF JUDGMENTS   Step 4 in the process involves selecting the form of presentation of the stimuli and the nature of the judgments to be secured from subjects. The full-profile approach has used variations and combinations of three basic approaches—verbal description, paragraph description, and pictorial representation. Verbal description relies on presenting the cues in list form, typically one stimulus per card, much as was assumed in the coffee-maker example. Paragraph description operates just as the name implies; a paragraph is used to describe each stimulus. Pictorial description relies on some kind of visual prop or three-dimensional model. When visual aids are used, they are typically used in combination with verbal descriptions. As Panel B of Research Realities 16.3 indicates, verbal descriptions are the most frequently encountered in practice.

Related to the issue of the form of presentation of the stimuli is the issue of the nature of the judgments that will be secured from respondents. The two most common approaches measure respondents' preferences for each alternative or their intention to buy each alternative. See Panel C in Research Realities 16.3. In the earliest applications of conjoint analysis, this information was secured most often by asking respondents to rank-order the alternatives according to preference or intention to buy. Rating scales have recently become more popular, though, for securing the needed judgments. Some of the main reasons advanced by those using rank-order judgments are their ease of use by subjects, ease of administration, and a desire to keep the judgment task as close as possible to a consumer's behavior while actually shopping. Those using rating scales believe that they are less time consuming, more convenient for respondents to use, and easier to analyze. The nature of the task is different in the two schemes. When the rank-order method is used, consumers are asked to make relative judgments with respect to their preference for one alternative over another. When the rating method is used, the judgments are typically made independently; that is, consumers are asked to indicate their degree of liking of each stimulus by checking the appropriate location along the preference or intention-to-buy scale as the alternative is presented. As Panel D of Research Realities 16.3 indicates, rank order originally was the preferred procedure, but the use of rating scales has now surpassed it in popularity.

DECIDE ON AGGREGATION OF JUDGMENTS   Step 5 in the process involves deciding if the responses from individual consumers will be aggregated and, if so, how? Although it is possible to derive the utilities for each level of each attribute at the individual level, much as we did in the example, individual-level results are very difficult for marketing managers to use for developing marketing strategy. The other extreme is to pool the results across all consumers and then to estimate one overall utility function. This option fails to recognize any heterogeneity in preference that might exist among respondents, which in turn reduces the predictive power of the model. The middle ground is to form segments or groups of respondents in such a way that the model will have both predictive power and clear marketing strategy implications for managers. The question, of course, is how these groups should be formed.[19] Typically segments are formed that are homogeneous with respect to the benefits that the respondents want from the product or service. Operationally, this goal often translates into estimating utilities for the individual-level models and then clustering respondents into groups that are homogeneous with respect to the utilities assigned to the various levels of the individual attributes.

---

[19]For additional discussion of the aggregation issue, see William L. Moore, "Levels of Aggregation in Conjoint Analysis: An Empirical Comparison," *Journal of Marketing Research* 17 (November 1980), pp. 516–523; Marco Vriens, Michel Wedel, and Tom Wilms, "Metric Conjoint Segmentation Methods: A Monte Carlo Comparison," *Journal of Marketing Research* 33 (February 1996), pp. 73–85.

An attractive feature of conjoint analysis is that it allows market share predictions for selected product alternatives. For example, a common choice rule is the first-choice rule, which assumes that each respondent chooses the object with the highest predicted preference. Given the estimated utilities for each level of each attribute, the analyst can investigate which of several product options being considered is likely to appeal most to respondents and what may also be the share of preference for each of the other options. The analyst can also attempt to link consumers' utilities with their personal characteristics—for example, do high-income households have a higher utility for after-the-sale service than low-income households?[20] Research Realities 16.4, for example, describes how marketing researchers used conjoint analysis to help design the EZPass system for New York and New Jersey.

SELECT ANALYSIS TECHNIQUE   Step 6 in the execution of a conjoint analysis study involves selecting the technique by which the input data will be analyzed. The choice depends in part on the type of preference model embraced and the method that was used to secure the input judgments. When linear or smooth nonlinear models are hypothesized to capture preference, a parameter estimation model like regression can be used to estimate the functions. When an irregular model is assumed, utilities need to be estimated for each level of each attribute, using, for example, dummy variables in regression, as described in the example, or a related technique like the analysis of variance.[21] When rank-order data have been obtained, the assumption of a linear relationship may be dubious, so a nonmetric, monotonic regression model may be substituted to estimate the utilities.

GENERAL COMMENTS   It is only after the analyst has made decisions about each of the steps listed in Figure 16.8 that he or she is in a position to actually collect data for a conjoint analysis study. Unfortunately, beginning researchers have a propensity to hurry into the data-collection task. Interrelationships among the many decisions need to be made, and rushing into the data-collection effort before the interrelated choices are all spelled out can only result in suboptimizing some of the choices. For example, one technique that has become popular in recent years is obtaining conjoint responses to a limited set (usually three to nine) of full profiles drawn from a larger master set and combining that information with other information that respondents directly provide about the relative importance to them of each of the attributes and which levels of each attribute they prefer. Called hybrid models, the essential purpose is to combine the simplicity of the self-explicated

---

[20]See, for example, Saul Sands and Kenneth Warwick, "What Product Benefits to Offer to Whom: An Application of Conjoint Segmentation," *California Management Review* 24 (Fall 1981), pp. 69–74; Paul E. Green and Abba M. Krieger, "Segmenting Markets with Conjoint Analysis," *Journal of Marketing* 55 (October 1991), pp. 20–31; Greg M. Allenby and James L. Ginter, "Using Extremes to Design Products and Segment Markets," *Journal of Marketing Research* 32 (November 1995), pp. 392–403; and Eric J. Johnson, Robert J. Meyer, Bruce G. S. Hardie, and Paul Anderson, "Watching Customers Decide," *Marketing Research* 9 (1997), 32–37.

[21]Analysis of variance is described in Appendix 15A.

RESEARCH REALITIES 16.4

Using Conjoint Analysis to Assess Consumer Response to a New Tollway Technology

Several years ago, a task force comprised of seven transportation agencies in New York and New Jersey commissioned a study to understand their commuters' likely reaction to and adoption of EZPass. EZPass is a form of electronic toll collection. Electronic toll systems work through high frequency radio waves that are transmitted from a small "tag" or transponder mounted on a vehicle's inside windshield to an antenna in a toll booth lane as the vehicle proceeds through the lane. The information transmitted identifies the vehicle number, and the toll is debited from the owner's account.

Electronic toll collection systems have enjoyed great success in Texas, Louisiana, and Florida, where drivers extol the benefits of not needing to stop to manually pay the tolls (the vehicle can proceed through the lane up to 40 m.p.h.). As a result, traffic congestion culminating near the toll booths is greatly alleviated. In addition, drivers need not fumble for change, and fleet operators need not advance cash to their drivers nor worry about cash reimbursements.

With such encouraging results as secondary data, the New York and New Jersey transportation groups were planning on following suit and implementing such a system. However, an electronic toll system could be designed with a variety of features, and marketing researchers were brought in to distill those features that commuters cared about the most, and determine what the optimal system might look like.

Thus, a study was designed to pretest "consumers' acceptance of and preference for a different way of paying tolls at roadways, bridges, and tunnels." A conjoint study was considered best suited to address these questions.

Different methodologies of data collection were considered for the conjoint. Providing "verbal descriptions" of the EZPass system (and then requesting ratings from the commuters) was deemed inadequate because the system was too complex and novel to express clearly in a written statement. Ideally, the researchers would have liked to set up a "demonstration toll plaza," but product trial on this scale was of course considered impractical. Researchers ultimately elected to send a videotape that contained an 11-minute "infomercial," which described the system, demonstrated its use, and explained how traffic flow would be improved, as had been experienced at other systems throughout the United States.

After viewing the video that described the general EZPass system, commuters would be asked to judge their preferences among specific variants on the system. With much consultation, the researchers were able to whittle down the number of attributes thought to be important (by the commissioning agencies) to these seven:

1. How many facilities would the user need to open an EZPass account with, and therefore, how many periodic invoices would the user receive?

2. How and where would a user apply and pay for a new EZPass account?

3. How many lanes would be available for EZPass at a typical toll plaza and how would they be controlled?

4. Would the EZPass tag be transferable to different vehicles?

5. What would be the acquisition cost (if any) for EZPass and would there be a periodic service charge?

6. What would the toll price be with EZPass?

7. What other uses, if any, such as parking at local airports or purchasing gasoline, would commuters find valuable for EZPass?

A subset of 49 of the possible configurations of these features formed the product descriptions used in the study. Each commuter would be asked to rate 7 of these 49 plus another "control" option (to enable comparison across the samples).

Next, sampling was considered. Each of the seven sponsoring agencies wanted data from representatives of their commuting regions. In addition, it was thought prudent to survey some commuters who regularly used several specific facilities (for example,

RESEARCH REALITIES 16.4

(continued)

the George Washington Bridge, the Holland and Lincoln tunnels, and the three Staten Island bridges). Altogether, 13 sectors were delineated, and 250 commuters were sampled from each group.

Random-digit dialing was used to solicit cooperation. Households indicating that they would participate were sent a videotape and survey. The survey responses were conveyed over the phone, either to an 800-phone number printed on the survey, or by the researchers calling the commuters' home phone number again at a later date. Researchers recruited 6,500 commuters, and obtained responses from 3,369, for a rather high response rate of 52 percent.

Conjoint analysis indicated commuters' clear prioritization among the features, as indicated in Table 1. The number of lanes and their control was the most important feature (21 percent). The New York and New Jersey agencies had anticipated that commuters would be concerned about the acquisition cost but were surprised to see that it was of only moderate importance (15 percent). Commuters did care about the price of the toll (18 percent), however. Commuters

showed little concern for the multiple uses for the device (4 percent).

In addition to yielding diagnostic information as to what features are more important than others, marketing researchers were also able to provide information on which levels of each feature were deemed most desirable. For example, for the feature of acquisitions costs, the researchers had explored four levels. They derived utilities from the conjoint analysis that represented commuters' preferences for each level of this factor, as illustrated in Table 2. These results indicated that the first option was most desirable, the fourth option least desirable, and commuters were indifferent between their second and third choices.

The overall conjoint results demonstrated which features should be emphasized and which could be de-emphasized in the design of the electronic toll system. System designers also studied the utilities of each of the features to provide the attribute that commuters most wanted. Finally, the marketing researchers also used the conjoint results as input to a series of simulations to forecast demand and usage of the system during its first year.

TABLE 1

Feature of EZPass System	Importance (in percent)
How many lanes would be available and how would they be controlled?	21
Price of the toll with EZPass	18
How and where a user would apply and pay for a new EZPass account	17
The acquisition cost for EZPass and any periodic service charges	15
Number of EZPass accounts necessary/number of periodic invoices received	13
Would the EZPass tag be transferable to different vehicles?	12
Other potential uses for the EZPass tag	4

TABLE 2

Implementation Level of Acquisition Costs	Utility
$10 deposit + $15 yearly service charge	0.68
$2 per month service charge	0.48
$10 charge + $1.50 per month service charge	0.43
$40 credit card charge if tag not returned + $20 annual fee	0.10

Source: Terry G. Vavra, Paul E. Green, and Abba M. Krieger, "Evaluating EZPass: Using Conjoint Analysis to Assess Consumer Response to a New Tollway Technology," *Marketing Research* 11 (Summer 1999), pp. 5–13

approach to attribute measurement with the greater generality of conjoint models.[22]

One can see that vital marketing questions in product design are being addressed by conjoint analysis. Further, the technique is not restricted to product evaluations. It can be used whenever one is making a choice among multiattribute alternatives. With multiattribute alternatives, one typically does not have the option of having more of everything that is desirable and less of everything that is not desirable. Instead, most decisions involve trading off part of something in order to get more of something else. Conjoint analysis attempts to mirror the trade-offs a consumer is willing to make. The modeling is rather straightforward, and the payoff (the results) is highly informative, making conjoint among the more popular of marketing research tools. It is most often used for product design and concept evaluation, in applications such as: airlines, credit cards, pantyhose, pharmaceuticals, and highway EZPass systems.[23] Conjoint studies are also used regularly as an aid in pricing decisions, market segmentation questions, or advertising decisions. Conjoint analysis has also been used for making distribution decisions, evaluating vendors, determining the rewards that salespeople value, and determining consumer preferences for attributes of health organizations, among other things.

Summary

This chapter examined the question of association or covariation between variables when one of the variables is considered a criterion variable. Simple regression and correlation analysis is the primary statistical device for analyzing the association between a single predictor and a single criterion variable. This model allows the estimation of a functional equation relating the variables as well as an estimate of the strength of the association between them. Some of the more useful outputs from a simple regression analysis are the following:

1. The functional equation, which allows the prediction of the criterion variable for assumed values of the predictor variable

2. The standard error of estimate, which provides an absolute measure of the lack of fit of the equation to the data

3. The coefficient of determination, which provides a relative assessment of the goodness of fit of the equation

4. The slope coefficient, which indicates how much the criterion variable changes, on the average, per unit of change in the predictor variable

---

[22]For an exposition of hybrid models and a review of their comparative performance in cross-validation tests, see Paul E. Green, "Hybrid Models for Conjoint Analysis: An Expository Review," *Journal of Marketing Research* 21 (May 1984), pp. 155–169; Michael J. Dorsch and R. Kenneth Teas, "A Test of the Convergent Validity of Self-Explicated and Decompositional Conjoint Measurement," *Journal of the Academy of Marketing Science* 20 (Winter 1992), pp. 37–48; V. Srinivasan and Chan Su Park, "Surprising Robustness of the Self-Explicated Approach to Customer Preference Structure Measurement," *Journal of Marketing Research* 34 (May 1997), 286–291. For empirical investigations of the quality of conjoint analysis results, see Thomas W. Leigh, David B. MacKay, and John O. Summers, "Reliability and Validity of Conjoint Analysis and Self-Explicated Weights: A Comparison," *Journal of Marketing Research* 21 (November 1984), pp. 456–462.

[23]Paul E. Green, Abba M. Krieger, and Terry G. Vavra, "Evaluating New Products," *Marketing Research* 9 (1997), pp. 12–21; Terry G. Vavra, Paul E. Green, and Abba M. Krieger, "Evaluating EZPass," *Marketing Research* 11 (1999), pp. 5–13.

The regression model is readily extended to incorporate multiple predictor variables to estimate a single criterion variable. If the predictor variables are not correlated among themselves, each partial regression coefficient indicates the average change in the criterion variable per unit change in the predictor variable in question, holding the other predictor variables constant. If the predictor variables are correlated among themselves, little substantive meaning can be attached to the slope coefficients, although the regression equation often can still be used successfully to predict values of the criterion variable for assumed values of the predictor variables. The coefficient of multiple determination measures the proportion of the variation in the criterion variable accounted for or explained by all the predictor variables. The coefficient of partial determination measures the relative degree to which a given variable adds to our knowledge of the criterion variable over and above that provided by other predictor variables. Variable transformations increase the scope of the regression model, because they allow certain nonlinear relationships to be considered, and dummy or binary variables allow the introduction of nominal variables in the regression equation. Conjoint analysis may be viewed as a special application of dummy variable regression, and it is an extremely powerful marketing tool for the planning of product development.

Questions

1. What is the basic nature of the distinction between tests for group differences and tests to investigate association?
2. What is the difference between regression analysis and correlation analysis?
3. What is the difference between a correlation between two variables and an X^2 for a cross-tabulation of two variables? What type of variables are analyzed in each case?
4. What is the difference between a deterministic model and a probabilistic model? Which type of model underlies regression analysis? Explain.
5. What assumptions are made about the error term in the least-squares solution to the regression problem? What is the effect of the assumption; that is, what is the Gauss-Markov theorem? When the analyst wishes to make an inference about a regression population parameter, what additional assumption is necessary?
6. What is the standard error of estimate?
7. Suppose that an analyst wished to make an inference about the slope coefficient in a regression model. What is the appropriate procedure? What does it mean if the null hypothesis is rejected? If it is not rejected?
8. What is the correlation coefficient, and what does it measure? What is the coefficient of determination, and what does it measure?
9. What is a coefficient of partial or net regression, and what does it measure? What condition must occur for the usual interpretation to apply? What happens if this condition is not satisfied?
10. What is the coefficient of multiple determination?
11. What is a coefficient of partial determination? What does it measure?
12. What is a variable transformation? Why is it employed?
13. What is a dummy variable? When is it used? How is it interpreted?
14. What is a conjoint analysis? When is it used?

Applications and Problems

1. The quality of public school education has become a major political issue. In many states, dissatisfied parents are voting for school-choice legislation that allows them to use public money to send their children to the school they deem most appropriate. Under some school-choice legislation, parents can even choose to send their children

to private schools and pay only the difference between the amount charged by the private school and the amount it would have cost to send the child to a public school.

One local school district in which parents were calling for school-choice reform hired a marketing research company to assess customer satisfaction and relate this satisfaction to demographic variables. The school district had hypothesized that satisfaction was related to income levels, with those earning more money being more dissatisfied with the public school system. The research company found that income explained only 10 percent of the total variance in school satisfaction; thus, the company stated that no relationship existed between income and school satisfaction. Given the analysis described, is this a valid conclusion for the research company to make? Why?

2. A cereal manufacturer believes that there is an association between cereal sales and the number of facings the cereal has on each store's shelves. Eight stores were surveyed to test this hypothesis. The data are as follows:

Facings	Sales
5	45
6	50
6	52
7	53
5	44
7	57
6	49
8	56

a. Is there an association between shelf facings and sales?
b. Based on these data, is it appropriate to state that increased shelf facings produce additional sales? Why or why not?
c. What other variables can you think of that may help predict cereal sales?

3. The Brite-Lite Bottling Company, which provides glass bottles to various soft-drink manufacturers, has the following information pertaining to the number of cases per shipment, size of cartons, and the corresponding transportation cost:

Number of Cases per Shipment (in hundreds)	Size of Carton (in cubic inches)	Transportation Costs (in dollars)
15	12	200
22	16	260
35	20	310
43	24	360
58	28	420
65	32	480
73	36	540
82	40	630
85	44	710
98	48	730

The marketing manager is interested in studying the relationship between the number of cases per shipment and the transportation costs. Your assistance is required in performing a simple regression analysis.

a. Plot the transportation costs as a function of the number of cases per shipment.
b. Interpret the scatter diagram.
c. Calculate the coefficients $\hat{\alpha}$ and $\hat{\beta}$, develop the regression equation, interpret the coefficients.

d. Calculate the standard error of estimate and interpret it.
e. Compute the t value with n-2 degrees of freedom with the use of the following formula for the square root of the variance of the distribution of βs:

$$s_{\hat{\beta}_1} = \sqrt{\frac{s_{Y/X}^2}{\sum_{i=1}^{10}(X_i - \bar{x})^2}}$$

$$t = \frac{\hat{\beta}_1 - \beta_1}{s_{\hat{\beta}_1}}$$

where β is assumed to be zero under the null hypothesis of no relationship; that is:

$$H_0: \beta_1 = 0$$
$$H_a: \beta_1 \neq 0$$

f. What is the tabled t value at a 0.05 significance level?
g. What can you conclude about the relationship between transportation costs and number of cases shipped?
h. The marketing manager wants to estimate the transportation costs for 18 cases.
   i. Use the regression model to derive the average value of Y_0.
   ii. Provide a confidence interval for the estimate.

4. The marketing manager of Brite-Lite Company wanted to determine if there was an association between the size of carton and the transportation cost per shipment. (The company followed a policy of including the same-sized cartons for any particular shipment.) Refer to the previous question for information on the transportation costs per shipment and size of carton.
   a. Calculate the correlation coefficient and interpret it.
   b. Determine the coefficient of determination and interpret it.

5. The marketing manager of Brite-Lite Company is considering multiple regression analysis with number of cartons per shipment and size of cartons as predictor variables and transportation costs as the criterion variable. The manager has devised the following regression equation:

$$\hat{Y} = \hat{\alpha}_{(12)} + \hat{\beta}_{Y1.2}X_1 + \hat{\beta}_{Y2.1}X_2 = -41.44 - 3.95X_1 + 24.44X_2$$

where X_1 is the number of cartons per shipment and X_2 is the size of the carton.
   a. Interpret $\hat{\alpha}_{(12)}, \hat{\beta}_{Y1.2}$, and $\hat{\beta}_{Y2.1}$.
   b. Is multiple regression appropriate in this situation? If yes, why? If no, why not?

6. An analyst for a large shoe manufacturer had developed a formal linear regression model to predict sales of the firm's 122 retail stores located in different selling areas in the United States.
   The model is:

$$Y_{(123)} = \alpha_{(123)} + \beta_{1.23}X_1 + \beta_{2.13}X_2 + \beta_{3.12}X_3$$

where
X_1 = population in surrounding area in thousands;
X_2 = marginal propensity to consume;
X_3 = median personal income in surrounding area in thousands of dollars; and
Y = sales in thousands of dollars.

Some empirical results were as follows:

Variable	Regression Coefficient	Standard Errors
X_1	$\hat{\beta}_{1.23} = 0.49$	0.24
X_2	$\hat{\beta}_{2.13} = -0.40$	95
X_3	$\hat{\beta}_{3.12} = 225$	105
$R^2 = 0.47$	$\hat{\alpha} = -40$	225

a. Interpret each of the regression coefficients.
b. Are X_1, X_2, and X_3 significant at the 0.05 level? Show your calculations.
c. Which independent variable seems to be the most significant predictor?
d. Provide an interpretation of the R_2 value.
e. The marketing research department of the shoe manufacturer wants to include an index that indicates whether the service in each store is poor, fair, or good. The coding scheme is as follows:

$$1 = \text{poor service} \qquad 2 = \text{fair service} \qquad 3 = \text{good service}$$

   i. Indicate how you would transform this index so that it could be included in the model. Be specific.
   ii. Write out the regression model including the transformation that you developed.
   iii. Suppose that two of the parameters for the index are 4.6 and 10.3. Interpret these values in light of the scheme you adopted.

7. Carol Lynne and K. C. Lee are leaders of a popular local country and western band. Each week during the summer, the band played an outdoor concert at a different park located in the city. Advertising for the concerts consisted of handbills posted around the city on public billboards, at supermarkets, and so on. During some weeks, Carol, K. C., and the other band members were able to distribute many handbills; during other weeks, fewer were distributed. Similarly, many people attended some concerts, and only a few attended others. At the end of the summer, the band wanted to know if there was any relationship between the number of handbills that were distributed and the number of people attending its concerts. Following are the approximate number of handbills distributed each week along with the number of people attending that week's concert:

Number of Handbills	Number of People
900	625
550	400
750	450
300	200
600	500
1,000	650
400	375
325	350
675	400
200	200
500	500
150	125
500	300
700	550
600	400

a. Develop and interpret a scatter diagram showing number of people as a function of number of handbills.

b. Calculate the coefficients $\hat{\alpha}$ and $\hat{\beta}$, and develop the regression equation using a statistical software package.

c. Interpret the coefficients and $\hat{\alpha}$ and $\hat{\beta}$. Be specific about the meaning of the terms in this situation.

d. What is the standard error of estimate, and what is its interpretation in this situation?

e. What is the t value associated with $\hat{\beta}$? Is this value significant at the 0.05 level? If so, what can be concluded about the relationship between the number of handbills distributed and the number of people attending the concerts?

f. How much of the variance in the number of people attending the concerts can be explained by the number of handbills delivered?

g. What are some other factors that might be included in a multiple regression model to explain the number of people attending the concerts?

8. Occasionally, business periodicals publish charts of CEO pay, along with indicators of corporate performance. The following data were sampled from pp. 106–108, the "Office Equipment and Computers" industry section of the article, "Executive Pay," in the April 19, 1999 issue of *BusinessWeek*. Use the corporate performance indicators (sales in millions of dollars, and return on earning) to predict the CEO salary and bonus package (in thousands of dollars). After obtaining the regression coefficient estimates, plug the actual company performance numbers into the equation, to obtain the predicted CEO salary figures.

a. Which CEOs are overcompensated? Which are undervalued?

b. If you were one of the CEOs identified as having been overcompensated, how might you argue that a regression model has limitations in this application?

Company Name	Sales (millions of dollars)	ROE (%)	CEO compensation	Company Name	Sales (millions of dollars)	ROE (%)	CEO compensation
America Online	3305.0	17.5	1177	Microsoft	16660.0	29.3	542
Apple Computer	6073.0	23.4	0	Novell	1117.7	7.7	1222
Cisco Systems	9988.7	14.9	891	Oracle	7966.4	36.0	1530
Compaq Computers	31169.0	−24.2	4479	Sabre Group	2306.0	25.0	1004
Ebay	47.4	2.8	247	Seagate Technology	6604.0	−1.1	764
Gateway 2000	7467.9	25.8	1800	Sun Micro-systems	10517.6	21.5	1698
Hewlett-Packard	47182.0	17.0	1911	3Com	5571.7	10.2	818
IBM	81667.0	34.3	9387	Unisys	7208.4	289.2	4333
Intuit	717.2	0	1006	Xerox	19449.0	11.1	5676

9. The management of HotSiteTravel Company decided to introduce new vacation packages. However, the management was uncertain about the price and destination to introduce. The marketing research department decided to use conjoint analysis to

determine the level of each attribute that would come closest to satisfying consumers. The following levels of each of the product attributes were used:

Price	$499/week	$799/week	$1299/week
Destination	Cancun	Miami	San Diego

A respondent's rank ordering of the various product descriptions are noted here (1 is least preferred, 9 is most preferred):

		Destination	
Price	*Cancun*	*Miami*	*San Diego*
$499	4	1	2
$799	6	5	3
$1299	9	8	7

The regression assigned the following utilities:

Price	*Utility*	*Destination*	*Utility*
$499	0	Cancun	0.6
$799	0.43	Miami	0.2
$1299	1.03	San Diego	0.1

a. Calculate the utilities for all 9 travel package combinations.
b. Plot the original input judgments against the derived utilities from (a). Discuss your findings.
c. How might you characterize a segment that prefers the $499 price? The $1299 price?
d. Would you expect a linear utility function for price? For destination?

10. Imagine you've completed your recruiting, and you have six job offers from which to choose: Job A is on the West Coast and it pays $200,000; B is on the West Coast paying $50,000; C is in the Midwest paying $200,000; D is in the Midwest paying $50,000; E is East Coast at $200,000; F is East Coast at $50,000.

a. Which job do you prefer? If you cannot take your first choice job, what attribute are you willing to trade off for the other?
b. If you compared your answers to your friends', do you think salary preferences will tend to be linear? Will location?

A P P E N D I X   1 6 A

Nonparametric Measures of Association

Chapter 16 focused on the product-moment correlation as the measure of association. Although the correlation coefficient was originally developed to deal with continuous variables, it has proved to be quite robust to scale type and can handle variables that are ordinal or dichotomous as well as those that are interval.[1] It is, therefore, a rather general measure of association although it is not universally applicable. Appendix 13A presented some alternate measures of association which are

---

[1] Jum Nunnally and Ira H. Bernstein, *Psychometric Theory*, 3rd ed. (New York: McGraw-Hill, 1994), especially pp. 114–158. For an empirical comparison of how various correlation coefficients perform with rating scale data, see Emin Babakus and Carl E. Ferguson, Jr., "On Choosing the Appropriate Measure of Association When Analyzing Rating Scale Data," *Journal of the Academy of Marketing Science* 16 (Spring 1988), pp. 95–102.

more appropriate for nominal data and cross-tabs, namely, the chi-square, the contingency coefficient, the index of predictive association, and log linear models. In this appendix, we treat two indices that are analogous to product-moment correlation coefficients, but are better suited for the analysis of rank-order data, namely, Spearman's rank-order correlation coefficient and the coefficient of concordance.

Spearman's Rank Correlation Coefficient

One of the best known coefficients of association for rank-order data is **Spearman's rank correlation coefficient,** denoted r_s. The coefficient is appropriate when there are two variables per object, both of which are measured on an ordinal scale so that the objects may be ranked in two ordered series.

Suppose, for instance, that a company wished to determine whether there was any association between the overall performance of a distributor and the distributor's level of service. Many measures of overall performance can be used: sales, market share, sales growth, profit, and so on. The company's management thought that no single measure adequately defined distributor performance but that overall performance was a composite of all these measures. Thus, the marketing research department was assigned the task of developing an index of performance that effectively incorporated all these characteristics. The department was also assigned the responsibility of evaluating each distributor in terms of the service provided. This evaluation was to be based on customer complaints, customer compliments, service turnaround records, and so on. The research department believed that the indices it developed to measure these characteristics could be employed to rank-order the distributors in terms of overall performance and service.

Table 16A.1 contains the ranks of the company's 15 distributors with respect to each of the performance criteria. One way to determine whether there is any

TABLE 16A.1	Distributor Performance			
Distributor	Service Ranking X_i	Overall Performance Ranking Y_i	Ranking Difference $d_i = X_i - Y_i$	Difference Squared d_i^2
1	6	8	-2	4
2	2	4	-2	4
3	13	12	$+1$	1
4	1	2	-1	1
5	7	10	-3	9
6	4	5	-1	1
7	11	9	$+2$	4
8	15	13	$+2$	4
9	3	1	$+2$	4
10	9	6	$+3$	9
11	12	14	-2	4
12	5	3	$+2$	4
13	14	15	-1	1
14	8	7	$+1$	1
15	10	11	-1	1
				$\Sigma d_i^2 = 52$

association between service and overall performance would be to look at the differences in ranks based on each of the two variables. Let X_i be the rank of the ith distributor in terms of service and Y_i be the rank of the ith distributor with regard to overall performance. Further, let $d_i = X_i - Y_i$ be the difference in rankings for the ith distributor. Now, if the rankings on the two variables are exactly the same, each d_i will be zero. If there is some discrepancy in ranks, some of the d_is will not be zero. Further, the greater the discrepancy, the larger some of the d_is would be. Thus, one way of looking at the association between the variables would be to examine the sum of the d_is. The difficulty with this measure is that some of the negative d_is would cancel some of the positive ones. To circumvent this difficulty, the differences are squared in calculating the Spearman rank-order correlation coefficient. The calculation formula is[2]

$$r_s = 1 - \frac{6 \sum_{i=1}^{n} d_i^2}{n(n^2 - 1)}$$

In the example at hand, $\Sigma_i d_i^2 = 52$, and

$$r_s = 1 - \frac{6(52)}{15(15^2 - 1)} = 1 - \frac{312}{3{,}360} = 0.907$$

Now the null hypothesis for the example would be that there is no association between service level and overall distributor performance, whereas the alternate hypothesis would suggest that there is a relationship. The null hypothesis that $\rho_s = 0$ can be tested by referring directly to tables of critical values of r_s or, when the number of sample objects is greater than 10, by calculating the t statistic,

$$t = r_s \sqrt{\frac{n - 2}{1 - r_s^2}}$$

which is referred to a t table for $n-2$ degrees of freedom. Calculated t is

$$t = 0.907 \sqrt{\frac{15 - 2}{1 - (0.907)^2}} = 7.77$$

while critical t for $\alpha = 0.05$ and 13 degrees of freedom is 2.16. Calculated t exceeds critical t, and the null hypothesis of no relationship is rejected. Overall distributor performance is related to service level. The upper limit for the Spearman rank correlation coefficient is one, since if there were perfect agreement in the ranks, $\Sigma_i d_i^2$ would be zero. Thus, the relationship is significant and relatively strong.

---

[2] See Sidney Siegel and N. John Castellan, Jr., *Nonparametric Statistics for the Behavioral Sciences,* 2nd ed. (Boston: McGraw-Hill, 1988); W. J. Conover, *Practical Nonparametric Statistics,* 3rd ed. (New York: Wiley, 1998). An alternate measure of rank correlation is provided by Kendall's tau coefficient. See Maurice G. Kendall and Jean D. Gibbons, *Rank Correlation Methods,* 5th ed. (New York: Oxford University Press, 1990); Peter Sprent, *Applied Nonparametric Statistical Methods,* 2nd ed. (New York: Chapman and Hall, Inc., 1993).

Coefficient of Concordance

So far, we have been concerned with the correlation between two sets of rankings of n objects. There has been an X and Y measure in the form of ranks for each object. In some cases, we will want to analyze the association among three or more rankings of n objects or individuals. When there are k sets of rankings, Kendall's coefficient of concordance (W) can be employed to examine the association among the k variables.

One particularly important use of the coefficient of concordance is in examining interjudge reliability. Consider the computer equipment manufacturer interested in evaluating its domestic sales branch managers. Many criteria could be used: Sales from the branch office, sales in relation to the branch's potential, sales growth, and sales representative turnover are just a few. It was believed that different executives in the company would place different emphasis on the various criteria and that a consensus about how the criteria should be weighted would be hard to achieve. It was decided, therefore, that the vice president in charge of marketing, the general sales manager, and the marketing research department should all attempt to rank the 10 branch managers from best to worst. Table 16A.2 contains these rankings. The company wished to determine whether there was agreement among these rankings.

The right-hand column of Table 16A.2 contains the sum of ranks assigned to each branch manager. If *perfect agreement* existed among the three rankings, the sum of ranks, R_i, for the top-rated branch manager would be $1 + 1 + 1 = k$, where $k = 3$. The second-rated branch manager would have sum of ranks $2 + 2 + 2 = 2k$, and the nth-rated branch manager would have sum of ranks $n + n + n + nk$. Thus, when there is perfect agreement among the k sets of rankings, the R_i would be k, $2k$, $3k$, . . . , nk. If there is little agreement among the k rankings, the R_i would be approximately equal. Thus, the degree of agreement among the k rankings could be measured by the variance of the n sums of ranks; the greater the agreement, the larger the variance in the n sums would be.

TABLE 16A.2   Branch Manager Rankings

Branch Manager	Vice President, Marketing	General Sales Manager	Marketing Research Department	Sum of Ranks R_i
A	4	4	5	13
B	3	2	2	7
C	9	10	10	29
D	10	9	9	28
E	2	3	3	8
F	1	1	1	3
G	6	5	4	15
H	8	7	7	22
I	5	6	6	17
J	7	8	8	23

The **coefficient of concordance** (W) is a function of the variance in the sums of ranks. It is calculated in the following way. First, the sum of the R_i for each of the n rows is determined. Second, the average R_i, $\bar{R}$, is calculated by dividing the sum of the R_i by the number of objects. Third, the sum of the squared deviations is determined; call this quantity s, where

$$s = \sum_i (R_i - \bar{R})^2$$

The coefficient of concordance is then computed as

$$W = \frac{s}{\dfrac{1}{12}\, k^2(n^3 - n)}$$

The denominator of the coefficient represents the maximum possible variation in sums of ranks if perfect agreement in the rankings were achieved. The numerator, of course, reflects the actual variation in ranks. The larger the ratio, the greater the agreement among the evaluations. For our data,

$$\bar{R} = \frac{(13 + 7 + \ldots + 23)}{10} = \frac{165}{10} = 16.5$$

$$s = (13 - 16.5)^2 + (7 - 16.5)^2 + \ldots + (23 - 16.5)^2 = 720.5$$

and

$$\left(\frac{1}{12}\right)k^2(n^3 - n) = \left(\frac{1}{12}\right)(3)^2(10^3 - 10) = 742.5$$

Thus,

$$W = \frac{(720.5)}{(742.5)} = 0.970$$

The significance of W can be examined by using special tables when the number of objects being ranked is small, in particular when $n \leq 7$. When there are more than seven objects, the coefficient of concordance is approximately chi-square distributed where $\chi^2 = k(n-1)W$ with $n-1$ degrees of freedom. The null hypothesis is that there is no agreement among the rankings, and the alternate hypothesis is that there is some agreement. For an assumed $\alpha = 0.05$, critical χ^2 for 9 degrees of freedom is 16.92, whereas calculated X^2 is

$$X^2 = k(n - 1)W = 3(9)(0.970) = 26.2$$

Calculated X^2 exceeds critical χ^2, and the null hypothesis of no agreement is rejected; there is agreement. Further, the agreement is good, as is evidenced by the calculated coefficient of concordance. The limits of W are zero with no agreement and one with perfect agreement among the ranks. The calculated value of W of 0.970 suggests that although the agreement in the ranks is not perfect, it is certainly good. The marketing vice president, the general sales manager, and the marketing research department are applying essentially the same standards in ranking the branch managers.

Kendall has suggested that the best estimate of the true ranking of n objects is provided by the order of the various sums of ranks, R_i, when W is significant.[3] Thus, the best estimate of the true ranking of the sales managers is that F is doing the best job and B the next best job, and that C is doing the poorest job.

Questions

1. What is the Spearman rank correlation coefficient? To what types of situations does it apply? How is it calculated and interpreted?
2. What is the coefficient of concordance? When is it used? What is the rationale underlying its computation?

Applications and Problems

1. Katherine Martin is the newly hired marketing director for the Alpine Bottling Company (ABC). ABC produces a premium line of soft-drink products made with all-natural ingredients. ABC soft drinks are typically about 20 percent more expensive than other soft drinks, including the industry leaders.

Convinced that ABC soft drinks would appeal to a large segment of the market (beyond just the health-conscious consumers) if moved into nationwide distribution, Martin decided that the best way to introduce the product would be to show that it tastes better than other soft drinks. This could be accomplished by using the "blind taste test" approach and showing the results in ABC's television advertising. Before proceeding, however, she decided to conduct a very limited taste test to get a rough idea of how ABC ranked with other soft drinks. Five subjects each sampled eight brands of soft drinks, including one of the ABC products and the industry leaders. None of the soft drinks was identified. The subjects then ranked the eight soft drinks according to their taste preferences (the most preferred was given a ranking of 1). The results of this limited test are as follows:

Brand	Subject				
	1	2	3	4	5
ABC Brand	2	3	1	1	1
Brand A	7	8	7	6	7
Brand B	3	2	3	2	3
Brand C	5	5	5	5	6
Brand D	8	7	8	8	8
Brand E	1	1	2	3	2
Brand F	6	6	6	7	5
Brand G	4	4	4	4	4

a. Calculate the coefficient of concordance to determine the five subjects' degree of agreement with respect to their taste preferences.

---

[3]Kendall, *Rank Correlation Methods*, p. 87.

  b. Assuming a 0.05 significance level, is there evidence of agreement among the subjects?
  c. What is the best estimate of the true ranking of the soft drinks based on this analysis?
  d. What are the managerial implications for Martin?
2. When should one use the coefficient of concordance instead of Spearman's rank correlation coefficient? What is the null hypothesis for this test? What are the limits of this test and what do these limits mean?

A P P E N D I X   1 6 B

Analysis of Catalog-Buying Data

Simple Regression

One of the questions of concern was the attitude of catalog recipients toward buying from Avery Sporting Goods and whether that attitude was related in any way to the person's demographic characteristics. To address this issue, an "attitude toward Avery" index, called ATTAVRY, was formed from the responses to Questions 7 through 11 of the questionnaire (the questionnaire appears in Appendix 13A). ATTAVRY was formed in such a way that higher scores implied more favorable attitudes about buying from Avery. The responses to the five questions were summed to produce the ATTAVRY score for each subject.

Table 16B.1 investigates whether the ATTAVRY index varies as a function of the person's occupation. Recall that blue-collar workers were coded as 0 and white-collar workers as 1. Instead of the t value discussed in the text, the statistical significance of the equation is assessed in the program using analysis-of-variance techniques discussed in Appendix 15A. The calculated F value of 374.512 is statistically

TABLE 16B.1	Simple Regression Analysis of ATTAVRY Index versus Occupation

Dependent Variable: ATTAVRY, Predictor: V41 = Occupation

		Analysis of Variance	DF	Sum of Squares	Mean Square	F	Significance
Multiple R	0.869	Regression	1	4071.174	4071.174	374.512	0.000
R square	0.754	Residual	122	1326.213	10.871		
Adjusted R square	0.752						
Standard error	3.297						

Variables in the Equation					
Variable	B	Beta	Standard Error B	t	Significance
V41	11.534	0.869	0.596	19.352	0.000
(Constant)	9.727				

significant at the 0.01 level, since the tabled F value for 1 and 122 degrees of freedom is approximately 2.75. The relationship is also practically significant. The adjusted R^2 value of 0.752 indicates that approximately 75 percent of the variation in the ATTAVRY index can be accounted for or explained by the variation in occupation. A positive relationship exists between the two variables ($B = 11.534$); white-collar workers have more favorable attitudes toward Avery than blue-collar workers.

Multiple Regression

In an attempt to determine if the ATTAVRY index was related to other demographic characteristics, a multiple-regression analysis was conducted in which the ATTAVRY index was regressed on how long the catalog recipient had worked and the person's marital status in addition to the person's occupation. Since marital status was categorical, it was necessary to convert it to a series of dummy variables before proceeding. More specifically, the five marital status categories were converted to four dummy variables with the following equivalences using SPSS's recode ability.

V43	Implying	D2	D3	D4	D5
1	Widowed	0	0	0	0
2	Divorced	1	0	0	0
3	Separated	0	1	0	0
4	Married	0	0	1	0
5	Single	0	0	0	1

Table 16B.2 contains the output. Note first that the overall regression equation is statistically significant; the calculated F value of 277.036 compares with a tabled

TABLE 16B.2   Multiple-Regression Analysis of ATTAVRY Index versus Several Demographic Characteristics

Dependent Variable: ATTAVRY

		Analysis of Variance	DF	Sum of Squares	Mean Square	F	Significance
Multiple R	0.967	Regression	6	5042.459	840.410	277.036	0.000
R square	0.934	Residual	117	354.928	3.034		
Adjusted R square	0.931						
Standard error	1.742						

Variables in the Equation

Variable	B	Standard Error B	Beta	t	Significance
V41	3.753	0.600	0.283	6.252	0.000
V42	0.213	0.029	0.368	7.458	0.000
D2	2.851	0.627	0.165	4.546	0.000
D3	4.387	0.646	0.267	6.788	0.000
D4	7.006	0.948	0.391	7.390	0.000
D5	7.577	0.935	0.550	8.101	0.000
(Constant)	4.491	0.502		8.945	0.000

F value of approximately 1.82 for 6 and 117 degrees of freedom for $\alpha = 0.01$. Further, the variables as a set account for 93 percent of the variation in the ATTAVRY index as witnessed by the adjusted R^2 value of 0.931.

The results also provide an interesting opportunity to interpret a dummy variable coding. Note that the respective values for the dummy variables D2 through D5 referring to the marital status categories are

$$D2 = 2.851$$
$$D3 = 4.387$$
$$D4 = 7.006$$
$$D5 = 7.577$$

The four positive values all indicate that in comparison to the null state (defined as widowed), divorced, separated, married, and single people all have more favorable attitudes toward Avery. The D2 value indicates that there is an increase in the ATTAVRY index of 2.85 on average if the person is divorced rather than widowed. The differential resulting from comparisons with other than widowed people is found by looking at appropriate differences in the dummy variable values. Thus, for example, married people have an ATTAVRY index approximately 2.62 higher on average than separated people, since D4 − D3 = 2.619.

17

Multivariate Data Analysis: Discriminant Analysis, Factor Analysis, Cluster Analysis, and Multidimensional Scaling

In this chapter, we present the four multivariate statistical techniques that have proven to be the most popular multivariate tools for marketing researchers: (1) discriminant analysis, (2) factor analysis, (3) cluster analysis, and (4) multidimensional scaling. In Appendix 17A, we also describe briefly several additional multivariate models: structural equations, correspondence analysis, neural networks, and social networks analysis, to illustrate still further the great variety of questions that may be asked, and answered, by marketing researchers using multivariate statistical methods. We introduce each technique by describing the kinds of problems the method is ideal to solve.

Discriminant Analysis

Many marketing problems involve the investigation of group differences. Two or more groups are compared and the question is one of determining whether the groups differ from one another and, if so, how. For example, we might be interested in determining the characteristics that differentiate the following:

- Light and heavy users of the product
- Purchasers of our brand and those of competing brands
- Customers who patronize an every-day-low-pricing retail outlet and those who patronize high-end, service-oriented ones
- Good, mediocre, and poor sales representatives
- Good and poor loan risks

Suppose that the comparisons between any of these groups were to be made along demographic-socioeconomic lines. One way to proceed would be to calculate the mean income, age, education level, and so on to determine the profiles for each group. Comparing the groups on one variable at a time would be interesting and informative. We would become more familiar with the data, and we would begin to form hypotheses about how the groups are different. However, such a univariate analysis would not indicate the relative importance of each variable in distinguishing the groups nor their respective impacts when used in combination. Furthermore, the variables are likely to be at least somewhat correlated, which implies that the tests of one variable to the next are not independent, and that the variables contain somewhat redundant information that may be leveraged better jointly.

Suppose, for example, that we were investigating the characteristics that distinguish light from heavy investors of our mutual funds. If the groups showed a difference with respect to mean income levels, it is also likely that they would show a difference with respect to educational levels, because these two variables are fairly highly correlated. Yet if we were interested in segmenting the market using income and education, we would be interested in the total effect of the two variables in combination, not their separate effects. Further, we would be interested in determining which of the variables was more important or had the greater impact (for example, like comparing the size of betas in multiple regression). In essence, we need a mechanism that allows us to consider the variables simultaneously to take into account their interrelationship and partially overlapping information.

One alternative is to construct a linear combination of the variables (that is, a weighted sum) in such a way that this newly created function will optimally discriminate among the groups. We can then assess how the groups differ with respect to this new linear combination score, and we can also look at the relative weights assigned to each of the variables when forming the linear combination to get some idea as to their relative importance.

Discriminant analysis is the method by which such linear combinations are determined.[1] When two groups are being compared, one linear combination, or discriminant function, results. When the technique is applied to the analysis of three or more groups (for example, light, medium, and heavy users), several discriminant functions can result.[2]

Two-Group Case

We will begin with the simpler case of two groups, and later in the chapter we will extend the logic to three or more groups. In addition, to facilitate learning the purposes and results of discriminant analyses, we will present the approach in the context of an example.

A manufacturing firm that relied upon a large sales force conducted a "new account" sales contest among its salespeople in an attempt to increase the number of distributors handling the firm's products. The contest ran for three months. Each salesperson was assigned a quota for the number of new accounts he or she was expected to generate in that period. The quotas were determined by the sales analysis

---

[1] R. A. Fisher, "The Use of Multiple Measurements in Taxonomic Problems," *Annuals of Eugenics* 8 (1936), pp. 376–386.

[2] The extension is customarily attributed to Rao, although it seems to have been accomplished by several researchers working independently. See J. G. Bryan, "A Method for the Exact Determination of the Characteristic Equation and Latent Vectors of a Matrix with Applications to the Discriminant Function for More Than Two Groups," unpublished doctoral dissertation, Harvard University, 1950; C. P. Rao, "The Utilization of Multiple Measurements in Problems of Biological Classification, *Journal of the Royal Statistical Society, Series B,* 10 (1948), pp. 159–193; J. W. Tukey, "Dyadic Anova, An Analysis of Variance for Vectors," *Human Biology* 21 (1949), pp. 65–110.

department, which had historic data on the penetration of different industry segments (based on NAICS codes) and the number of accounts of each type that were not current customers in each sales territory. All salespeople who had 15 or more new accounts place an order during the contest period received an all-expense-paid vacation for two to Hawaii. Salespeople who had at least five new accounts place an order received a lesser prize—an HDTV. Those converting fewer than five new accounts received nothing. As it turned out, 15 salespeople won the grand prize and another 15 the consolation prize, while a third of the salespeople won nothing.[3] The sales analysis department was interested in determining what salesperson activities made a difference in terms of whether a salesperson was a prizewinner or not.

One can proceed with the analysis in a number of ways. The sales department could compare those who were grand prize winners against the others. Alternatively, it might compare those who won any kind of prize against those who won nothing. It might compare each group against each of the other two. To begin with a simple demonstration of a two-group discriminant analysis, let us determine what activities tended to have the greatest impact on whether a salesperson won a grand prize or only a consolation prize. We will take up the question of what activities tend to discriminate among all three groups later.

Table 17.1 contains the data that the sales analysis department collected on each salesperson's new account activities. One way to proceed would be to plot the salespeople according to their activities while maintaining the identity of the group to which each salesperson belongs. Figure 17.1 contains several such plots comparing the grand prize and consolation prize winners. Consider Panel A, which displays the plot of the percentage of calls for which the salesperson had advance appointments against the total number of calls the salesperson made on new accounts. Panel A indicates that, in general, both of these variables were positively related to success, because the more calls on new accounts the salesperson made and the greater the percentage of advance appointments, the more likely the salesperson was to be a grand prize winner than a consolation prize winner. There were exceptions, though. Some consolation prize winners made more calls on new accounts than did grand prize winners. Similarly, some grand prize winners made a smaller percentage of advance appointments than did consolation prize winners. Overall, however, the mean number of calls on new accounts and the mean percentage with advance appointments were higher for grand prize winners as compared to consolation prize winners. A similar type of analysis, conducted with respect to Panels B and C of Figure 17.1, indicates that grand prize winners made more telephone calls to prospects and called on more new accounts on average than did consolation prize winners.

The graphical approach for determining which activities seemed to make the most difference in terms of whether a salesperson won a grand prize or consolation prize is intuitively insightful, but it has its limitations. In the first place, it is difficult and time consuming to anticipate and then construct all the graphs that might be useful in a given situation. Even for our four-variable example, Figure 17.1 contains

---

[3]The contest had a number of the ingredients that are generally recommended for sales contests, including a specific objective, a theme, and a reasonable percentage of contest winners. See Gilbert A. Churchill, Jr., Neil M. Ford, and Orville C. Walker, Jr., *Sales Force Management*, 5th ed. (Burr Ridge, IL: Irwin, 1997), pp. 507–512, for a general discussion of the purposes and structure of sales contests.

TABLE 17.1   Discriminant Analysis Example: Salespeople's New Account Activities

		Number of Calls on New Accounts X_1	Percentage of Calls with Advance Appointments X_2	Telephone Calls Made to Prospects X_3	Number of New Accounts Visited X_4
Grand Prize Winner (W)					
1	RMB	130	62	148	42
2	ALB	122	70	186	4
3	BCC	89	68	171	32
4	JJC	104	58	135	40
5	EDC	116	40	160	36
6	WPD	100	65	151	30
7	RHH	85	66	183	42
8	BEK	113	59	130	25
9	DAK	108	52	163	41
10	JJN	116	48	154	48
11	MYS	99	57	188	32
12	PJS	78	70	190	40
13	CET	106	61	157	38
14	LLV	94	58	173	29
15	LMW	98	64	137	36
	Mean	103.9	59.9	161.7	37.0
Consolation Prize Winner (C)					
1	JGB	105	39	155	45
2	RAB	86	60	140	33
3	HAF	64	48	132	36
4	PPD	104	36	119	29
5	BCE	102	53	143	41
6	ASG	73	62	128	30
7	WLH	94	51	152	36
8	LHL	59	64	130	28
9	RJL	84	31	102	32
10	WFM	91	47	96	35
11	JRP	83	40	87	30
12	EJS	95	42	114	28
13	VES	68	52	123	26
14	HMT	101	51	98	24
15	BMT	89	39	117	33
	Mean	86.5	47.7	122.4	32.4
Unsuccessful Salespeople (U)					
1	RBB	80	23	69	32
2	GEB	47	42	74	33
3	ADC	26	37	132	20
4	JFC	94	24	68	26
5	LDE	57	32	94	23
6	JFH	38	41	83	28
7	JCH	29	52	96	22
8	RPF	48	24	73	26
9	APL	57	36	82	28
10	HAL	39	37	98	21
11	ERM	51	38	117	24
12	WRR	40	42	112	22
13	JTS	64	21	67	29
14	JMV	35	32	78	25
15	HEY	51	29	81	26
	Mean	50.4	34.0	88.3	25.7
Overall					
Mean		80.3	47.2	124.1	31.7
Standard Deviation		15.91	8.97	19.99	5.37

FIGURE 17.1	**Discriminant Analysis: Scatter Plots of Selected Two-Variable Combinations**

X_2—Percentage of Calls with Advance Appointments

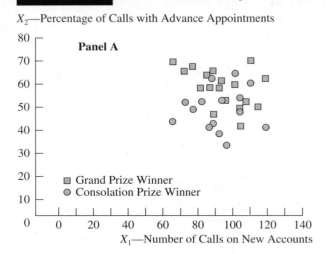

X_3—Telephone Calls Made to Prospects

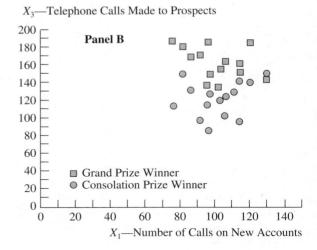

X_4—Number of New Accounts Visited

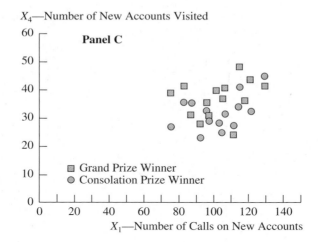

only three of the six possible combinations of the variables from which separate graphs could be constructed when the variables are taken two at a time.[4] Although we might consider more variables at one time to reduce the number of potential graphs, higher dimensional graphs become difficult to interpret. At the same time, two-dimensional graphs are limited in the amount of information they convey, since

---

[4]The number of possible two-way graphs is given by the standard combinatorial formula:

$$C\frac{m}{2} = \frac{m!}{(m-2)!2!} = \frac{m(m-1)}{2}$$

where m is the number of variables.

they allow us to consider only two independent variables at once. What is needed is a mechanism that allows us to assess the effect of each factor, taking into account the factors' partially overlapping information.

DETERMINING THE COEFFICIENTS   One effective way to determine which variables discriminate between the two types of contest winners is to build an index that separates the two groups on the basis of their values on the measured characteristics. The index would be a linear combination of number of calls on new accounts X_1, percentage of calls with advance appointments X_2, telephone calls made to prospects X_3, and number of new accounts visited X_4:

$$Y = v_1 X_1 + v_2 X_2 + v_3 X_3 + v_4 X_4$$

where v_1, v_2, v_3, and v_4 are the weights indicating the importance of each X in helping the researcher differentiate prize-winning groups. Note the equation form of the linear combination, or weighted sum. It is said to be a "combination" because the information contained in the four X variables is being combined in some manner to create a single new score, Y. It is said to be "linear" because once the Xs are multiplied by their importance weights, the terms are simply added together (or subtracted if a v is negative, but there are no terms such as $v_1 X_1 \times v_2 X_2$, say).

Given values for v_1 through v_4, we can readily calculate a Y or index score for each of the 30 prize winners. The question is how to derive values for v_1 through v_4?

In discriminant analysis, the weights are derived so that the variation in Y scores (that is, the new index) between the two groups is as large as possible, while the variation in Y scores within the groups is as small as possible. That is, the weights are derived so that the ratio of between-group differences to within-group differences is maximized. This makes the groups as distinct as possible with respect to the new index scores.

The operation of the index score is seen most easily in the two-variable case, so let us consider for the moment only the two predictors, "number of calls on new accounts" (X_1) and "percentage of calls with advance appointments" (X_2). Given values for v_1 and v_2, we can calculate an index score for each of the 30 prizewinners using the linear combination

$$Y = v_1 X_1 + v_2 X_2$$

It turns out that the values for v_1 and v_2 that maximize the ratio of the between-group to within-group variation with respect to the new index scores are $v_1 = 0.064$ and $v_2 = 0.106$; that is, the linear combination

$$Y = 0.064X_1 + 0.106X_2$$

Not only can we calculate each salesperson's score on the new index, but we can graph what is happening, because most algebraic concepts (for example, a linear combination of variables) have geometric counterparts (such as a new axis in the plot). We begin with Panel A of Figure 17.1, and draw the axis from the origin to the coordinates (0.064, 0.106), which are the v-weights. The plot is scaled from 0 to 140 on X_1 and 0 to 80 on X_2, so it is more convenient to extend the line from the origin to

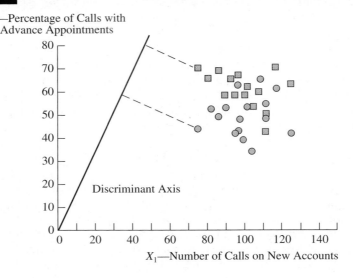

| FIGURE 17.2 | **Discriminant Analysis: Scatter Plot Containing New Axis** |

some multiple of the v-weights, for example, to the coordinates (64, 106). Figure 17.2 contains the new axis that represents the linear combination. (Note the axis will not necessarily go through the scatterplot, as we expect for regression lines.) Now, take each person's data point and "project" it onto the new axis; that is, draw a line from each data point to the new axis in such a way that the drawn line is perpendicular to the axis. These projections represent the Y scores that we have computed using the discriminant analysis equation. What had been a two-dimensional scatterplot (X_1 versus X_2) is now simplified to a frequency distribution of all the scores onto the one-dimensional line (Y). Once all the data points have been projected onto the discriminant axis, note that most of the consolation prize winners would be lower on the new dimension than most of the grand prize winners. The distinction is not perfect (some grand prize winners overlap with some consolation prize winners), but given that the v-weights were determined in a manner to optimally separate the groups, there are no other v-weights, or no other orientation of that axis in the two-dimensional plot, that could yield better discrimination between the groups.[5]

Using the index score we created through the discriminant analysis model, we can now classify each salesperson as a grand prize winner or a consolation prize winner. If the salesperson's index score is closer to the mean of the grand prize winners' index scores, we would classify him or her as a grand prize winner, and vice versa.

---

[5]Once the axis representing the linear combination is located (by drawing the vector from the origin to the coordinates of the v-weights (0.064, 0.106, or as stated, some multiple such as 64 and 106), there is also a relationship between the correlations between the variables and the new linear combination, and cosines of angles between the original X_1 and X_2 dimensions and the new axis. Specifically, the weights assigned each of the variables, when divided by the square root of the sum of the squared weights, equals the cosine of the angle between each of the variables and the new axis: $(0.064)^2 + (0.106)^2 = 0.015$, and $\sqrt{0.015} = 0.122$. Since $0.064/0.122 = 0.525$, the angle θ between the X_1 and the new discriminant axis is given by $\cos \theta = 0.525$, or $\theta = 58°$.

As an aside, let us note that the basic approach in discriminant analysis is similar to that of regression analysis. In each case, the analyst uses a weighted linear combination of independent variables to predict a dependent variable. In regression analysis, the dependent variable is continuous (for example, interval scaled). In discriminant analysis, the dependent variable is dichotomous or multichotomous, depicting group membership. (These qualities also make the analysis similar to logit models and logistic regressions, as discussed in the appendix to Chapter 13.) In fact, one can transform a two-group discriminant analysis problem into a regression problem by using a dummy code for the dependent variable (for example, $Y = 0$ if a consolation prize winner and $Y = 1$ if a grand prize winner). The resulting regression coefficients will be proportional to those obtained using standard discriminant analysis procedures.

Let us return to the more complex, original four-variable problem. The discriminant weights are $v_1 = 0.058$, $v_2 = 0.063$, $v_3 = 0.034$, and $v_4 = -0.032$, so the linear combination that maximally differentiates between the groups is[6]

$$Y = 0.058X_1 + 0.063X_2 + 0.034X_3 - 0.032X_4$$

The function presents the weights to be applied to X_1 through X_4 so that the distribution of Y scores will show the largest separation (or, distinguish most clearly) between grand prize and consolation prize winners (compared to any other possible linear combination that could have been formed). These Y scores are known as discriminant scores, and they are presented for our sample in Table 17.2. Note that the discriminant scores of grand prize winners are similar in magnitude, as are those of consolation prize winners, and that the two sets of scores are rather different from each other. The members within the groups are as much alike as possible on these generated scores, and the groups themselves are as different as possible on these generated scores.

Note what we have done. We have taken a four-variable problem (the groups compared on four measures of a salesperson's new account activities) and have reduced it to a much simpler, univariate problem by forming a linear combination of X_1 through X_4. We now need to compare only the discriminant scores of the groups (Y) rather than comparing the groups on all four variables (X_1 through X_4). Further, we are secure in the knowledge that the groups are as different as possible with respect to these discriminant scores. But how does that help us in determining how grand prize winners differ from consolation prize winners in terms of their new account activities? Further, how does that help the sales analysis department isolate those factors that were most critical to salespeople's success? In effect, what can we do with this discriminant function now that we have it? These questions are answered by:

- interpreting the discriminant function (Y), and
- using it to classify individuals in groups.

---

[6]The weights are given by the eigenvector in the solution of the equation: $(W^{-1}B - \lambda I)v = 0$, where W is the pooled within-sample variance-covariance matrix and B is the between-group, sum-of-squares, cross-products matrix.

TABLE 17.2	Discriminant Analysis Example: Calculated Discriminant Scores for Grand Prize and Consolation Prize Winners Using the Discriminant Function: $Y = 0.058X_1 + 0.063X_2 + 0.034X_3 - 0.032X_4$

		X_1	X_2	X_3	X_4	Y
Grand Prize Winners						
1	RMB	130	62	148	42	15.2
2	ALB	122	70	186	44	16.5
3	BCC	89	68	171	32	14.3
4	JJC	104	58	135	40	13.0
5	EDC	116	40	160	36	13.6
6	WPD	100	65	151	30	14.1
7	RHH	85	66	183	42	14.0
8	BEK	113	59	130	25	13.9
9	DAK	108	52	163	41	13.8
10	JJN	116	48	154	48	13.5
11	MYS	99	57	188	32	14.8
12	PJS	78	70	190	40	14.2
13	CET	106	61	157	38	14.2
14	LLV	94	58	173	29	14.1
15	LMW	98	64	137	36	13.3
	Mean	103.9	59.9	161.7	37.0	
Consolation Prize Winners						
1	JGB	105	39	155	45	12.4
2	RAB	86	60	140	33	12.5
3	HAF	64	48	132	36	10.1
4	PPD	104	36	119	29	11.4
5	BCE	102	53	143	41	12.8
6	ASG	73	62	128	30	11.6
7	WLH	94	51	152	36	12.7
8	LHL	59	64	130	28	11.0
9	RJL	84	31	102	32	9.3
10	WFM	91	47	96	35	10.4
11	JRP	83	40	87	30	9.4
12	EJS	95	42	114	28	11.2
13	VES	68	52	123	26	10.6
14	HMT	101	51	98	24	11.7
15	BMT	89	39	117	33	10.6
	Mean	86.5	47.7	122.4	32.4	

INTERPRETING THE DISCRIMINANT FUNCTION   We first verify that the discriminant function is statistically significant, that is, that a reliable differentiation of the groups exists. (If the function is not significant, interpretation of the function would be meaningless because the estimates would differ only due to sampling error.) Most statistical computing packages routinely print F statistics for *Mahalanobis's* D^2 statistics (a squared distance measure similar to Euclidian distance which measures the distance from each salesperson to the group mean while allowing for correlated axes and different measurement units for the variables).[7] In our

---

[7]See William R. Dillon and Matthew Goldstein, *Multivariate Analysis: Methods and Applications* (New York: Wiley, 1984), pp. 366–369, for the details of how the significance of a discriminant function can be tested. See also Geoffrey J. McLachlan, *Discriminant Analysis and Statistical Pattern Recognition* (New York: Wiley, 1992); Carl J. Huberty, *Applied Discriminant Analysis* (New York: Wiley, 1994).

example, the discriminant function is statistically significant, so the interpretation of the function can proceed.

DISCRIMINANT COEFFICIENTS Discriminant coefficients are interpreted in much the same way as regression coefficients, in that each coefficient reflects the relative contribution of a unit change of each of the independent variables on the discriminant function. A small coefficient means that a one-unit change in that particular variable produces a small change in the discriminant function score, and a larger coefficient, a larger change in Y. Like regression coefficients, discriminant coefficients are affected by the scale of the independent variables. That is, the original function $Y = 0.058X_1 + 0.063X_2 + 0.034X_3 - 0.032X_4$ contains the weights to be applied to the variables in raw-score scales.

The problem with this is that if the unit of measurement for one or more variables were to be changed—for example, variable X_2 reflecting calls with advance appointments was measured as a proportion (a decimal) rather than as a percentage (a whole number)—the discriminant function would also change. To remove arbitrary scale-of-measurement effects, the discriminant weights that would be applied to the predictors in standardized form are employed when comparing the contributions of the individual variables. The relative magnitudes of these standardized weights are determined by multiplying each raw score weight by the standard deviation of that variable. Define v_k^* as the standardized weight; v_k^* is related to the raw-score weight v_k by the formula

$$v_k^* = v_k s_k$$

where s_k is the pooled sample standard deviation of the kth variable. Considering our grand and consolation prize winners, we pool over only the two prize groups, to obtain the pooled sample standard deviations for the four variables: $s_1 = 16.76$, $s_2 = 10.89$, $s_3 = 28.16$, and $s_4 = 6.33$. Therefore:

$$v_1^* = v_1 s_1 = 0.058(16.76) = 0.972$$
$$v_2^* = v_2 s_2 = 0.063(10.89) = 0.686$$
$$v_3^* = v_3 s_3 = 0.034(28.16) = 0.957$$
$$v_4^* = v_4 s_4 = -0.032(6.33) = -0.203$$

The absolute size of the standardized weights can be compared to determine the relative contribution of the variables. They indicate that the variables "number of calls on new accounts" (X_1) and "telephone calls made to prospects" (X_3) are the most important and that "number of new accounts visited" (X_4) is the least important in differentiating grand prize from consolation prize winners. Further, variables X_1 through X_3 exert a positive effect because the greater the number of calls, the higher the percentage of calls with advance appointments, and the greater the number of telephone calls made to prospects, the more likely it is the salesperson was a grand prize instead of a consolation prize winner. In contrast, the number of new accounts the salesperson visited (X_4) has a negative impact on the likelihood that the representative was a grand prize winner.

The standardized weights agree with what intuition might suggest about the importance of the variables when there is relatively little correlation among the predictors. For example, one common intuitive assessment of the relative importance of the variables in distinguishing between the groups is a comparison of their means. Large differences in the means on a particular variable suggest that the variable is an important discriminator between the groups, and smaller mean differences suggest that the variable will not help us understand much about how the groups differ. When little correlation exists among the predictors, the relative size of the coefficients in the discriminant function will yield the same ranking of importance of each variable in discriminating between the groups as ranking the size of their proportionatal mean differences. When there is correlation among the predictors (that is, the problem of multicollinearity, as discussed in Chapter 16), the ordering is not necessarily the same; and, in fact, the coefficients in the discriminant function need to be interpreted with more caution. Just as in regression analysis, a small standardized weight may mean either that the variable is irrelevant in discriminating between the groups or, alternatively, that its effect has been partialed out of the relationship because of the high degree of multicollinearity in the data.

DISCRIMINANT LOADINGS   Also used to assess the importance of the variables in discriminating between groups, a discriminant loading gives the simple pair-wise correlation between the variable (X_1 through X_4) and the discriminant score (Y).[8] These correlations or loadings follow:

$$\begin{array}{ll} \text{Between } Y \text{ and } X_1: & 0.627 \\ \text{Between } Y \text{ and } X_2: & 0.679 \\ \text{Between } Y \text{ and } X_3: & 0.847 \\ \text{Between } Y \text{ and } X_4: & 0.441 \end{array}$$

The loadings suggest that variable X_3 (reflecting the telephone calls made to prospects), is now the most important and that variable X_4 (number of new accounts visited), is still the least important in discriminating between grand prize and consolation prize winners. The difference in the ordering of the variables in comparison to the standardized weights is due to the correlations among the predictors. As with any correlation coefficient, the squared discriminant loadings (such as r^2) indicate the amount of variance that the discriminant score (Y) shares with the variable (the Xs).

In sum, three quantities are typically used to assess the relative importance of variables in discriminating between groups: (1) the mean differences of the groups on each variable, (2) the standardized discriminant function coefficients, and (3) the discriminant loadings. All three will produce similar conclusions about the relative importance of the variables in discriminating between the groups when little intercorrelation exists among the predictors. When multicollinearity is a problem, their conclusions will differ, and the same caveats that apply when interpreting the coefficients in a regression analysis when the predictors are correlated apply here.

CLASSIFYING INDIVIDUALS USING THE DISCRIMINANT FUNCTION   To assist in interpretation, we could also calculate the mean discriminant score for each group. To do this, we substitute the mean values of the variables for each group into the

---

[8]We will have more to say about loadings later in this chapter when discussing factor analysis.

calculated discriminant function. For the grand prize winners, $\bar{x}_1 = 103.9$, $\bar{x}_2 = 59.9$, $\bar{x}_3 = 161.7$, and $\bar{x}_4 = 37.0$, and thus the mean discriminant score for grand prize winners, $\bar{Y}_W$, is

$$\bar{Y}_W = v_1\bar{x}_1 + v_2\bar{x}_2 + v_3\bar{x}_3 + v_4\bar{x}_4$$
$$= 0.058(103.9) + 0.063(59.9) + 0.034(161.7) - 0.032(37.0) = 14.2$$

For consolation prize winners, $\bar{x}_1 = 86.5$, $\bar{x}_2 = 47.7$, $\bar{x}_3 = 122.4$, and $\bar{x}_4 = 32.4$, and the mean discriminant score, $\bar{Y}_C$, is similarly calculated as

$$\bar{Y}_C = 0.058(86.5) + 0.063(47.7) + 0.034(122.4) - 0.032(32.4) = 11.2$$

This calculation indicates that on the average, grand prize winners have higher discriminant scores on Y than consolation prize winners. (The same result would be obtained if the discriminant scores in Table 17.2 had been averaged.)

We have established that the discriminant function provides statistically reliable differentiation for these data. Let us now determine whether it provides meaningful and practical differentiation between the two groups. We will apply the discriminant function to each individual to predict the person's score and, on the basis of that score, classify the salesperson as a grand prize or consolation prize winner. We will then compare this prediction with the individual's known actual classification to determine whether the function provides meaningful discrimination, in accurately representing each individual's prize status. We have already calculated the discriminant scores, so let us create a predicted classification for each sample member using the simple decision rule: If a salesperson's discriminant score is closer to the mean score for grand prize winners than for consolation prize winners, we will classify the salesperson as a grand prize winner; otherwise, we will classify him or her as a consolation prize winner. An alternative, but equivalent, procedure is to compute the score that divides the mean discriminant scores. This "cutting score" is then used to assign objects to groups in the following way: If the individual's score is above the cutting score, classify the salesperson as a grand prize winner; if it is below, classify the salesperson as a consolation prize winner. When the groups are equal in size, the cutting score, Y_{cs}, is given as the simple average of the mean discriminant scores for the groups—that is, by the calculation

$$Y_{cs} = (\bar{Y}_W + \bar{Y}_C)/2 = (14.2 + 11.2)/2 = 12.7$$

When the groups are not equal, the formula needs to be modified to take the size of each group into account. The appropriate formula is then

$$Y_{cs} = \frac{n_2\bar{Y}_1 + n_1\bar{Y}_2}{n_1 + n_2}$$

where $\bar{Y}_1$ and $\bar{Y}_2$ are the mean discriminant scores and n_1 and n_2 the sizes of Groups 1 and 2, respectively.[9]

---

[9]See Joseph F. Hair, Jr., Rolph E. Anderson, Ronald L. Tatham, and William C. Black, *Multivariate Data Analysis with Readings,* 5th ed. (New York: Macmillan, 1998), p. 266, for a discussion of optimal cutting scores when the groups are not equal in size.

Either decision rule essentially defines the group to which the individual is most similar. Applying this rule predicts the classifications contained in the right-hand column of Table 17.3. Table 17.4 contains the predicted classifications as the columns, and the known, actual classifications as the rows. We can use this table to assess the accuracy of the predictive classification decision rule. The entries on the diagonal represent the hit rate, or the proportion of people who have been correctly classified, P_{cc}:

$$P_{cc} = (15 + 13)/(30) = 28/30 = 0.933$$

TABLE 17.3		Discriminant Analysis Example: Predicted Group Membership Using the Simple Classification Rule		

	Discriminant Score Y_i	Differences from Mean of		Predicted Group Membership
		First Group $Y_i - \bar{Y}_W = Y_i - 14.2$	Second Group $Y_i - \bar{Y}_C = Y_i - 11.2$	
Grand Prize Winners (W)				
1	15.2	1.0	4.0	W
2	16.5	2.3	5.3	W
3	14.3	0.1	3.1	W
4	13.0	−1.2	1.8	W
5	13.6	−0.6	2.4	W
6	14.1	−0.1	2.9	W
7	14.0	−0.2	2.8	W
8	13.9	−0.3	2.7	W
9	13.8	−0.4	2.6	W
10	13.5	−0.7	2.3	W
11	14.8	0.6	3.6	W
12	14.2	0.0	3.0	W
13	14.2	0.0	3.0	W
14	14.1	−0.1	2.9	W
15	13.3	−0.9	2.1	W
Consolation Prize Winners (C)				
1	12.4	−1.8	1.2	C
2	12.5	−1.7	1.3	C
3	10.1	−4.1	−1.1	C
4	11.4	−2.8	0.2	C
5	12.8	−1.4	1.6	W
6	11.6	−2.6	0.4	C
7	12.7	−1.5	1.5	W*
8	11.0	−3.2	−0.2	C
9	9.3	−4.9	−1.9	C
10	10.4	−3.8	−0.8	C
11	9.4	−4.8	−1.8	C
12	11.2	−3.0	0.0	C
13	10.6	−3.6	−0.6	C
14	11.7	−2.5	0.5	C
15	10.6	−3.6	−0.6	C

*The assignments were actually carried out using more significant digits in the calculations of discriminant scores. While the calculations to one decimal place suggest this case is equidistant from the two group means, it actually is slightly closer to the mean for the grand prize winners.

TABLE 17.4   **Discriminant Analysis Example: Matrix of Actual vs. Predicted Group Membership**

	Predicted Classification		
Actual Classification	Grand Prize Winner	Consolation Prize Winner	Total
Grand prize winner	15	0	15
Consolation prize winner	2	13	15

Approximately 93 percent of the salespeople are correctly classified as grand prize or consolation prize winners on the basis of their new account activities.

ASSESSING CLASSIFICATION ACCURACY   A question that logically arises with any hit rate is assessing how good it is. One would probably argue for our example that a 93 percent hit rate is very good, given that one would expect only a 50 percent hit rate by chance alone, considering that the sample of salespeople had as many consolation as grand prize winners. How would you assess the hit rate, though, if the two groups were not equal in size? Suppose that in a sample of 100 salespeople, 20 won grand prizes and 80 won consolation prizes, which could easily be the case if the quota requirements for the grand prize were changed. What then is a good hit rate? At least two criteria can be used: the maximum chance criterion and the proportional chance criterion.[10]

The **maximum chance criterion** holds that any object chosen at random should be classified as belonging to the larger group, because that will maximize the proportion of cases correctly classified. In the sample of 100, we would thus classify anyone chosen at random as a consolation prize winner, because that would make 80 percent of the classifications correct.

The maximum chance classification rule is not very helpful from a marketing viewpoint, though, because we wish to identify the two types of winners. Thus, we would like to classify some salespeople chosen at random as grand prize winners and thereby defy the *a priori* odds. In such instances, we use the proportional chance criterion, C_{pro}, as the standard of evaluation:

$$C_{pro} = \alpha^2 + (1 - \alpha)^2$$

where
α = the proportion of individuals in Group 1
$1 - \alpha$ = the proportion of individuals in Group 2

If the sample of 100 contained 20 grand prize winners (Group 1) and 80 consolation prize winners (Group 2), the proportional chance criterion would equal

[10]Donald G. Morrison, "On the Interpretation of Discriminant Analysis," *Journal of Marketing Research* 6 (May 1969), pp. 156–163. For a general discussion of the issues surrounding linear discriminant analysis and linear classification analysis, as well as an extensive bibliography, see Carl J. Huberty, "Issues in the Use and Interpretation of Discriminant Analysis," *Psychological Bulletin* 95 (1984), pp. 156–171.

$C_{\text{pro}} = (0.20)^2 + (0.80)^2 = 0.68$. Thus, a classification accuracy of, say, 85 percent through the use of the discriminant function would represent a good improvement over chance alone ($C_{\text{pro}} = 0.68$), but 85 percent classification accuracy would not look very impressive against the maximum chance criterion (0.80). When the two groups are equal in size, as they are in the original example, the proportional chance criterion equals the maximum chance criterion (that is, $C_{\text{pro}} = 0.5^2 + (1 - 0.5)^2 = 0.25 + 0.25 = 0.5$).

A couple of comments must be made about the original classification procedure summarized in Table 17.4. First, there is an upward bias in the procedure because the proportion of correct hits is somewhat overstated.[11] This upward bias results because the same data that were used to develop the discriminant model are also used to test the model. Since the criterion used to fit the model generates an equation that is derived to be statistically optimal, the actual predictive accuracy of the model should be tested on a new sample of data. Given that it is costly and time consuming to collect more data, usually what discriminant analysts do is to split the original sample of observations into two subsamples. One subsample, called the analysis sample, is used to develop the equation, while the other, called the holdout sample, is employed to examine how well the equation predicts group membership.[12]

Second, the particular decision rule we used to classify grand prize and consolation prize winners will minimize the costs of misclassification (that is, it will be optimal) when: (1) the costs of misclassifying a grand prize winner as a consolation prize winner, and vice versa, are equal; (2) the *a priori* probabilities of winning each prize are equal; and (3) the distribution of the variables in the two populations is multivariate normal with equal and known covariance matrices. When these conditions are not satisfied, the decision rule for classifying objects must be revised.[13]

Three-Group Case

Let us now consider discriminant analysis for $k \geq 3$ groups. The biggest change that occurs when we move beyond two groups is that there can be more than one

---

[11] R. E. Frank, W. F. Massy, and D. G. Morrison, "Bias in Multiple Discriminant Analysis," *Journal of Marketing Research* 2 (August 1965), pp. 250–258. See also Robert A. Eisenbeis, "Pitfalls in the Application of Discriminant Analysis in Business, Finance, and Economics," *Journal of Finance* 23 (June 1977), pp. 875–900, for a general discussion of the problems encountered in applying discriminant analysis to business problems.

[12] With small samples, one often cannot afford the luxury of setting aside some of the observations for later use because all the data are needed to develop the equation. In such instances, one can systematically delete one case in turn from a sample of size n and fit the equation to each of the remaining $n - 1$ observations. The process, which is repeated n times with each observation left out in turn, provides useful estimates of the coefficients and prediction accuracy of the equation. See Melvin R. Crask and William D. Perreault, Jr., "Validation of Discriminant Analysis in Marketing Research," *Journal of Marketing Research* 14 (February 1977), pp. 60–68, for details of the procedure, which is technically called "jackknifing the estimates." See also Jun Shao, Dongsheng Tu, and K. Krickeberg, *The Jackknife and Bootstrap* (New York: Springer Verlag, 1995); Michael R. Chernick, *Bootstrap Methods: A Practitioner's Guide* (New York: Wiley, 1999).

[13] For general discussions about the accuracy of the classification rules under various conditions, see Dillon and Goldstein, *Multivariate Analysis*, pp. 392–393; B. Efron, "Estimating the Error Rate of a Prediction Rule: Improvement and Cross-Validation," *Journal of the American Statistical Association* 78 (1983), pp. 316–331.

discriminant function.[14] As a matter of fact, when there are k groups and p variables, the maximum number of discriminant functions will be given by the following rules:

- If there are more variables p than groups k (the typical case), there will be at most $k - 1$ discriminant functions.

- If the number of variables p is less than the number of groups k, there will be no more than p discriminant functions.

In either case, the number of statistically significant discriminant functions is usually less than the maximum number possible. It depends on whether the extracted functions provide "meaningful differentiation" among the objects forming the groups.

Consider again the sample of salespeople and their success in securing new accounts. This time, though, consider all three groups (grand prize winners, consolation prize winners, and sales people who won nothing). Since the number of groups ($k = 3$) is less than the number of variables ($p = 4$), the number of discriminant functions that can be derived is $k - 1 = 2$.

The two discriminant functions turn out to be

$$Y_1 = 0.064X_1 + 0.079X_2 + 0.027X_3 - 0.002X_4$$
$$Y_2 = 2.036X_1 - 0.037X_2 + 0.041X_3 - 0.003X_4$$

The functions have the following interpretation: Of all the linear combinations of the four variables that could be developed, the linear combination given by the first function provides maximum separation among the three groups. Maximum separation is understood, of course, to be defined on the basis of discriminant scores; the salespeople within a group are very similar with respect to their Y_1 scores, while the salespeople in different groups have very dissimilar Y_1 scores. Given the first linear combination, the second function provides maximum separation among all possible linear combinations that were uncorrelated with (that is, so as not to be redundant with) the first set of scores. Thus, the second function provides maximum separation on a contingent set of scores, provided that they are uncorrelated with the first set of scores; that is, $r_{Y1,Y2} = 0$.

CLASSIFYING RESPONDENTS   We check the statistical significance of these functions before trying to use them to classify salespeople,[15] and find that only the first func-

---

[14]There are two variations in discriminant analysis when there are more than two groups: the classical and simultaneous approaches. The classical approach generates one classification function for each group that maximize the likelihood of correct classifications of the members of the group. It produces $g(g - 1)/2$ discriminant functions (where g is the number of groups) to separate each pair of groups. The simultaneous approach (also known as the canonical approach) is emphasized here. For a very readable discussion of the differences between the two approaches, see Donald R. Lehmann, *Market Research and Analysis*, 3rd ed. (Burr Ridge, IL: Irwin, 1989), pp. 769–770.

[15]See Dillon and Goldstein, *Multivariate Analysis*, pp. 400–406, for a discussion of how to test the statistical significance of each of the discriminant functions that can be generated where there are more than two groups.

tion is significant. Thus, we will develop a classification rule that depends only on it. The rule is an extension of the one previously described; that is, we assign salespeople to the group to which their discriminant score is closest. This rule requires that the mean discriminant scores be known for each group. They can be generated by substituting the means of the four variables for each group in the discriminant function.

$$\text{Grand prizewinner: } \overline{Y}_W = 0.064(103.9) + 0.079(59.9) + 0.027(161.7) - 0.002(37.0)$$
$$= 15.67$$
$$\text{Consolation prize winner: } \overline{Y}_C = 0.064(86.5) + 0.079(47.7) + 0.027(122.4) - 0.002(32.4)$$
$$= 12.54$$
$$\text{Unsuccessful salesperson: } \overline{Y}_U = 0.064(50.4) + 0.079(34.0) + 0.027(88.3) - 0.002(25.7)$$
$$= 9.58$$

The cutting scores $(15.67 + 12.54)/2 = 14.11$ and $(12.54 + 9.58)/2 = 11.06$ bisect the difference in mean scores between grand prize and consolation prize winners, and between consolation prize winners and unsuccessful salespeople, respective. Thus, any salesperson with a score less than 11.06 would be considered an unsuccessful contest competitor, those with discriminant scores greater than 14.11 would be considered grand prize winners, and those with scores between 11.06 and 14.11 would be considered consolation prize winners. The scores and predicted classification of each of the 45 salespeople are contained in Table 17.5. Table 17.6 contains the matrix of predicted versus actual classifications. The performance of this procedure is quite good; the hit rate says 91.1 percent of the salespeople are predicted correctly, against the chance criterion of 33 percent. The incorrect predictions involve consolation prize winners (two of whom are predicted to be grand prize winners and two of whom are predicted to be unsuccessful in the sales contest), so we might say that, perhaps not surprisingly, the function is particularly

---

TABLE 17.5   **Discriminant Scores for Each Salesperson and Predicted Group Membership Using the Function** $Y = 0.064X_1 + 0.079X_2 + 0.027X_3 - 0.002X_4$

	Person	Score	Prediction*		Person	Score	Prediction		Person	Score	Prediction
1	RMB	17.25	W	1	JGB	14.00	C	1	RBB	8.80	U
2	ALB	18.40	W	2	RAB	14.06	C	2	GEB	8.32	U
3	BCC	15.73	W	3	HAF	11.47	C	3	ADC	8.18	U
4	JJC	14.91	W	4	PPD	12.74	C	4	JFC	9.76	U
5	EDC	14.94	W	5	BCE	14.60	W	5	LDE	8.73	U
6	WPD	15.66	W	6	ASG	13.06	C	6	JFH	7.92	U
7	RHH	15.63	W	7	WLH	14.18	W	7	JCH	8.58	U
8	BEK	15.45	W	8	LHL	12.38	C	8	RPF	6.94	U
9	DAK	15.45	W	9	RJL	10.59	U	9	APL	8.71	U
10	JJN	15.39	W	10	WFM	12.14	C	10	HAL	8.08	U
11	MYS	15.97	W	11	JRP	10.83	U	11	ERM	9.45	U
12	PJS	15.69	W	12	EJS	12.50	C	12	WRR	8.93	U
13	CET	15.88	W	13	VES	11.81	C	13	JTS	7.56	U
14	LLV	15.32	W	14	HMT	13.17	C	14	JMV	6.88	U
15	LMW	15.06	W	15	BMT	11.95	C	15	HEY	7.75	U

*W, grand prize winners; C, consolation prize winners; U, unsuccessful salespeople.

TABLE 17.6	Discriminant Analysis Example: Matrix of Predicted vs. Actual Classifications

| | *Predicted Classification* | | | |
Actual Classification	*Grand Prize Winner*	*Consolation Prize Winner*	*Unsuccessful Salesperson*	*Total*
Grand Prize Winner	15	0	0	15
Consolation Prize Winner	2	11	2	15
Unsuccessful Salesperson	0	0	15	15

effective in discriminating between the extremes: the grand prize winners and those who did not win anything.

KEY VARIABLES   To determine the key new-account activities that differentiated salespeople's performance, we cannot use the raw-score coefficients but we must generate the standardized coefficients to negate the effect of the units with which we measure the variables. The standardized weights are

$$v_1{}^* = v_1 s_1 = 0.064(15.91) = 1.018$$
$$v_2{}^* = v_2 s_2 = 0.079(8.97) = 0.709$$
$$v_3{}^* = v_3 s_3 = 0.027(19.99) = 0.540$$
$$v_4{}^* = v_4 s_4 = -0.002(5.37) = -0.011$$

Number of calls on new accounts, X_1, is the most important variable in differentiating among the levels of success in the sales contest, while the number of new accounts visited, X_4, is the least important. However, the relative importance of each predictor should be interpreted with a degree of caution, because there is some correlation among the predictors.

Marketing Applications

Discriminant analysis has been used for a variety of marketing problems. For example, it has been used to determine those characteristics that distinguish the listening audiences of various radio stations, to differentiate among different types of automobile buyers, to predict adopters and nonadopters of new products, to relate purchase behavior to advertising exposure, to determine the relationship between personality variables and the consumer decision choice process, to discriminate between those who save their money at commercial banks and those who choose savings and loan institutions, to assess the differences in importance of various attributes where the same products are being purchased in different countries, and to determine the factors that supermarket buyers use in deciding whether to stock a new product. See Research Realities 17.1 for more in-depth examples. The main "take away" on "When do I use discriminant analysis?" is this: Discriminant analysis is applicable when the marketing researcher has data on customers who fall into groups, and the information on the customers can be used to understand how the members in one group differ from those in another.

RESEARCH REALITIES 17.1

More Applications of Discriminant Analysis

1. Why do some international firms enjoy success in the U.S. while others do not? Marketing researchers conducted a telephone survey of nearly 100 marketing vice presidents or presidents of international (European or Japanese) industrial products firms that had established a manufacturing presence in the U.S. during the last 30 years.

Firms were considered to be "successful" if they had achieved at least 5 percent market share in the U.S., and were classified as "underachieving" with less.

The results of a discriminant analysis revealed the main ingredients of the successful firms to be:

- A larger percentage of senior managers in the U.S. firm who were U.S. nationals

- A greater commitment to research and development

- A willingness to tailor product design to local taste

Other factors that were tested did not matter; neither mode of entry into the U.S. (acquiring or building a facility) nor competitive pricing were predictive in discriminating between successful firms and unsuccessful ones.

2. Some consumers use the Internet as an important source of logistical information for travel arrangements; others do not. Marketing researchers surveyed more than 5,000 consumers to try to understand the difference between the user and nonuser groups. Using discriminant analysis, they found that people who are likely to use the Internet in their travel planning are more likely to be college-educated owners of computers, younger than 45, with larger average daily travel expenditures than people who did not use the Internet in their travel planning. Furthermore, e-planners were also more likely to collect more information about their destination city before their trip than nonusers.

Sources: Zoher E. Shipchandler and James S. Moore, "Factors Influencing Foreign Firm Performance in the U.S. Market," *American Business Review* 18 (January 2000), pp. 62–68; Mark A. Bonn, H. Leslie Furr, and Alex M. Susskind, "Predicting a Behavioral Profile for Pleasure Travelers on the Basis of Internet Use," *Journal of Travel Research* 37 (May 1999), pp. 333–340. For still more examples, see James J. Vanecko and Andrew W. Russo, "Spinning Data into Gold," *Direct Marketing* 62 (November 1999), pp. 26–30; Stephen J. O'Connor, Hanh Q. Trinh, and Richard M. Shewchuk, "Perceptual Gaps in Understanding Patient Expectations for Health Care Service Quality," *Health Care Management Review* 25 (Spring 2000), pp. 7–23; Betty J. Parker and Richard E. Plank, "A Uses and Gratifications Perspective on the Internet as a New Information Source," *American Business Review* 18 (June 2000), pp. 43–49.

Factor Analysis

The remaining three multivariate models in this chapter—factor analysis, cluster analysis, and multidimensional scaling—are different from discriminant analysis in that none of the three methods poses research questions in which we try to predict one variable (such as group membership in discriminant analysis) by other variables. Rather, these techniques are referred to as tools for "interdependence analysis," in that all the variables have equal status, and none is singled out for special treatment as a criterion variable. The three models pose different variations on the question, "How are these p variables interrelated?"

Factor analysis addresses a number of goals. It is one of the more popular "analysis of interdependence" techniques because one of its goals is usually referred to as "data reduction." That is, factor analysis is often used to simplify the marketing researcher's job of data analysis. It does so by taking advantage of the overlapping information contained in the correlations among p variables, extracting the core

ETHICAL DILEMMA 17.1

A marketing research consultant was asked to address a local business group to discuss some of the research methods currently being used in the field. To make the presentation more meaningful, the consultant recounted the details of some recent studies undertaken by her firm. The consultant was particularly explicit in recounting how her company had used multidimensional scaling at various times to develop perceptual maps and cluster analysis to identify clients' customer segments. As a consequence of such detail, most of the audience had sufficient information with which to identify the clients for whom the research was conducted.

- What are the clients' rights?
- Is there a tacit agreement between the researcher and clients to uphold the confidentiality of the clients' studies?
- Should the consultant have obtained the clients' consent before revealing the nature of their studies?
- What are the consequences of such a presentation for the client?
- What might be some of the consequences for the researcher and her firm?

information down to just a few "factors." For example, Table 17.7 shows two sets of correlations among $p = 9$ variables. Note that none of the nine variables is labeled as a dependent variable to be predicted by the others, as would be the case in regression or discriminant analysis; in a factor analysis, we will focus on the whole matrix of interrelationships.

The correlations depicted in Panel A suggest that the nine variables might be reduced down to two factors. Variables 1 through 4 seem to go together and variables 5 through 9 also seem to covary because the pair-wise correlations between the variables in each set are relatively high. The two sets of variables seem to behave differently, though, because the correlations between 1–4 and 5–9 are rather low. (If all the pairs of correlations were high, we would reduce the nine variables down to a single underlying factor.) In contrast, Panel B suggests that three factors underlie the nine variables; that is, variables 1–3, 4–6, and 7–9 covary or behave similarly.

To conduct a factor analysis, we need to translate that conceptual understanding of factor analysis into a more mathematical one. Mathematically, a factor is simply a linear combination of variables, chosen to capture the "essence" of the data. Since this can be done in various ways, the term *factor analysis* applies to a body of techniques, which are differentiated in terms of how the weights in the linear combinations are determined.[16]

---

[16]Dawn Iacobucci, "Classic Factor Analysis," in Richard Bagozzi, ed., *Principles of Marketing Research* (Cambridge, MA: Blackwell, 1994), pp. 279–316; also see the two succinct volumes by J. Kim and C. W. Mueller, *Introduction to Factor Analysis and Factor Analysis* (Beverly Hills, CA: Sage, 1978) and Norman Cliff, *Analyzing Multivariate Data* (San Diego: Harcourt Brace Jovanovich, 1987).

TABLE 17.7	**Factor Analysis Example: Two Hypothetical Sets of Correlations among Nine Variables**

Variable

Panel A Variable	1	2	3	4	5	6	7	8	9
1	1.00								
2	.96	1.00							
3	.94	.88	1.00						
4	.91	.95	.89	1.00					
5	.05	.09	.08	.10	1.00				
6	.12	.04	.03	.11	.92	1.00			
7	.07	.14	.06	.03	.86	.91	1.00		
8	.10	.12	.08	.04	.94	.95	.88	1.00	
9	.08	.11	.06	.13	.97	.87	.91	.90	1.00

Variable

Panel B Variable	1	2	3	4	5	6	7	8	9
1	1.00								
2	.92	1.00							
3	.95	.98	1.00						
4	.07	.13	.02	1.00					
5	.09	.05	.11	.95	1.00				
6	.06	.09	.07	.90	.89	1.00			
7	.10	.08	.10	.08	.14	.10	1.00		
8	.05	.07	.09	.09	.06	.12	.94	1.00	
9	.13	.04	.08	.13	.09	.06	.91	.92	1.00

The purposes of factor analysis are actually two: data reduction and substantive interpretation. We have already seen that the first purpose emphasizes summarizing the important information in a set of observed variables by a new, smaller set of factors expressing that which is common among the original variables. The second purpose concerns the identification of the factors or constructs that underlie the observed variables.

Consider a company with a large sales force. Suppose the company were interested in isolating the personality traits that lead to successful sales. There are many ways to measure the performance of a salesperson, for example, sales growth, profitability of sales, new account sales and so on. The company wants its salespeople to be good at all these things, not just one, so looking at any single measure would seem inadequate. On the other hand, salespeople who are good at generating sales of one kind are often also good at generating sales of another; that is, we would expect these three performance measures to be correlated. Thus, the company decided to employ several measures. To prepare the data, to compensate for potential differences caused by differences in sales territory, the company converted each sales representative's performance on each of these variables to an index where 100 indicates "average." Table 17.8 contains the data for a sample of 50 sales reps.

TABLE 17.8	Factor Analysis Example: Sales Performance Data for Sample of Sales Representatives		

Sales Representative	Sales Growth X_1	Sales Profitability X_2	New Account Sales X_3
1	93.0	96.0	97.8
2	88.8	91.8	96.8
3	95.0	100.3	99.0
4	101.3	103.8	106.8
5	102.0	107.8	103.0
6	95.8	97.5	99.3
7	95.5	99.5	99.0
8	110.8	122.0	115.3
9	102.8	108.3	103.8
10	106.8	120.5	102.0
11	103.3	109.8	104.0
12	99.5	111.8	100.3
13	103.5	112.5	107.0
14	99.5	105.5	102.3
15	100.0	107.0	102.8
16	81.5	93.5	95.0
17	101.3	105.3	102.8
18	103.3	110.8	103.5
19	95.3	104.3	103.0
20	99.5	105.3	106.3
21	88.5	95.3	95.8
22	99.3	115.0	104.3
23	87.5	92.5	95.8
24	105.3	114.0	105.3
25	107.0	121.0	109.0
26	93.3	102.0	97.8
27	106.8	118.0	107.3
28	106.8	120.0	104.8
29	92.3	90.8	99.8
30	106.3	121.0	104.5
31	106.0	119.5	110.5
32	88.3	92.8	96.8
33	96.0	103.3	100.5
34	94.3	94.5	99.0
35	106.5	121.5	110.5
36	106.5	115.5	107.0
37	92.0	99.5	103.5
38	102.0	99.8	103.3
39	108.3	122.3	108.5
40	106.8	119.0	106.8
41	102.5	109.3	103.8
42	92.5	102.5	99.3
43	102.8	113.8	106.8
44	83.3	87.3	96.3
45	94.8	101.8	99.8
46	103.5	112.0	110.8
47	89.5	96.0	97.3
48	84.3	89.8	94.3
49	104.3	109.5	106.5
50	106.0	118.5	105.0

TABLE 17.9	**Factor Analysis: Simple Pairwise Correlations among the Performance Measures**		
	X_1	X_2	X_3
X_1	1.000		
X_2	0.926	1.000	
X_3	0.884	0.843	1.000

Summarizing Data

Consider the first purpose of factor analysis—summarizing the important information contained in the data by a fewer number of factors. The question is, what is "important information." Two kinds of information are typically highlighted: the variance of each variable (the measure of variability of the variable across customers), and the correlation between variables (a measure of covariation of variables across customers). Most factor analyses are implemented using standardized variables because in many problems, the raw variables reflect widely differing units of measurement.[17] By standardizing the variables (to mean zero and unit standard deviation), the effect of units of measurement on the final solution is removed. (In our case, standardization would not be necessary because the variables are measured in the same units. Because standardization is common, however, let us discuss the issues that follow with standardized data.)

Table 17.9 contains the pairs of correlations among the variables, and Table 17.10 is the *factor-loading matrix* that results from performing a *principal components analysis (PCA)* on the data. The factor-loading matrix is one of the key outputs of a factor analytic solution, so let us closely examine the entries in Table 17.10.

FACTOR LOADINGS   Consider first the individual row/column entries. These are the correlations between the variables and the factors. For example, 0.976, the entry in the first row and first column, represents the correlation between the first variable and the first factor; 0.083 is the correlation between the first variable and the second factor; 0.961 is the correlation between the second variable and first factor, and so on. These correlations are called factor loadings. When we examine the table of loadings, we find that all three variables load heavily on (correlate highly with) Factor F_1.

---

[17]The researcher need not actually standardize the variables—the first step of a factor analysis in any of the widely available statistical computing packages, for example, SAS, SPSS, SYSTAT, is to take in the variables you specify and compute the matrix of intercorrelations. Recall the equation for a correlation between two variables X and Y:

$$r_{xy} = \sum_{i=1}^{n} \frac{(X_i - \overline{X})(Y_i - \overline{Y})}{n s_X s_Y}$$

In this equation, the data X_i and Y_i are automatically adjusted to standard scores when the means are subtracted and the standard deviations divided.

| TABLE 17.10 | Factor Analysis: Factor Loading Matrix |

	Factor		
Variable	F_1	F_2	F_3
	1	2	3
1	0.976	0.083	−0.203
2	0.961	0.232	0.151
3	0.945	−0.321	0.056
Sum of Squares	2.769	0.164	0.067

Given that these numbers are correlations, if we square them, we obtain the proportion of variation in the variable that is accounted for by the factor. Thus,

$$(0.976)^2 = 0.952$$
$$(0.961)^2 = 0.924$$
$$(0.945)^2 = 0.894$$

are the proportions of variance in variables 1, 2, and 3, respectively, accounted for by the first factor. Thus, note that with just a single factor, we have very nearly represented the entire variance of each of the three variables (the 1.00s on the diagonal in the correlation matrix in Table 17.9).

We might also test to see how well our single factor captures the correlations among the three variables. We use the factor analysis model to represent the covariability of two variables in the following manner. The variables are the rows in Table 17.10, and the model's prediction of the correlation between any two variables is obtained by multiplying the factor loadings of the two variables, one factor at a time, and then summing up the products over the factors. Thus, consider the sum of the products of the respective column entries of rows 1 and 2 of Table 17.10. The sum of the products is

$$(0.976)(0.961) + (0.083)(0.232) + (-0.203)(0.151) = 0.926$$

which reproduces exactly the original correlation, r_{12}, between variables 1 and 2 displayed in Table 17.9. Any of the correlations in Table 17.9 can be regenerated exactly if the number of factors extracted equals the number of original variables input. The general calculation formula is

$$r_{jl} = \sum_{k=1}^{3} a_{jk} a_{lk}$$

where j and l denote the original variables, k denotes the factor, and a_{jk} is the loading or correlation between the jth variable and kth factor (that is, the entry in the jth row and kth column of Table 17.10). While we have fit our data well, note that in doing so, we have not achieved the parsimonious goal of "data reduction"—we began with three variables, and we now have three factors. Thus, we usually extract fewer factors than we had variables to begin with.

What happens when fewer factors are used? The model no longer reproduces the pair-wise correlations exactly; rather, they are only estimated (however, the estimates are often quite good). The estimate is given by the same formula, but now the summation is from 1 to m, where m denotes the number of factors being considered $(m < p)$. For one-factor $(m = 1)$, the estimated correlation between variables 1 and 2 $(j = 1, l = 2)$ is

$$r_{12} = \sum_{k=1}^{l} a_{1k}a_{2k} = (0.976)(0.961) = 0.937$$

This estimate is actually quite close to the true value of 0.926. The other estimates are

$$\hat{r}_{13} = (0.973)(0.945) = 0.922 \quad \text{and} \quad \hat{r}_{23} = (0.961)(0.945) = 0.908$$

compared to actual values of 0.884 and 0.843, respectively. These estimates are quite good.

This example, showing the results for the extremes of one versus three factors, demonstrates the natural tension in factor analysis—the more factors that are extracted, the better the data are represented. However, the fewer the factors extracted, the easier it is to work with the results, interpret them, and communicate them.[18] Is one factor sufficient, or is more than one factor needed to summarize the data adequately? To answer this question, it is helpful to realize that in a principal components solution, the m newly formed components (or factors) are uncorrelated. This means that the proportion of variance accounted for by m factors is simply the sum of the proportions accounted for by each factor. Take two factors, for example. The proportion of the variation in each variable accounted for by a two-factor solution is

$$\text{Variable 1: } (0.976)^2 + (0.083)^2 = 0.959$$
$$\text{Variable 2: } (0.961)^2 + (0.232)^2 = 0.977$$
$$\text{Variable 3: } (0.945)^2 + (-0.321)^2 = 0.997$$

COMMUNALITIES   These values, which express the proportion of the variance of the variables extracted by m factors, are called the communalities of the variables and are typically denoted as h_j^2 (for variable j). Thus, we see that two factors account for 95.9 percent $(= h_1^2)$ of the variation in X_1, 97.7 percent $(= h_2^2)$ of the variation in X_2, and 99.7 percent $(= h_3^2)$ of the variation in X_3. The two-factor model does a remarkable job in accounting for the variability within the data. Variable 1 is most poorly captured, but even for it, 95.9 percent of its total variability

---

[18]The trade-off is found in most statistical modeling. For example, in a multiple regression, the prediction will be better—the R^2 higher—with more predictors. However, the model is easier to understand, and easier to express to marketing research clients, with fewer predictors.

is captured by the first two factors in the principal components solution. This result raises the question of whether it would be wise to retain two factors as the "proper" factor-analytic solution.

Although no definitive answer can be given, the column totals in Table 17.10 can assist the analyst in making a decision. As mentioned, the row/column entries represent the correlations between the variables and the factors, and their squares represent the proportions of variation in each variable explained by the factor. Thus, the sum of the squares in a column will provide a measure of the amount of variation accounted for by the factor representing the column. Take Column 1, for example:

$$(0.976)^2 + (0.961)^2 + (0.945)^2 = 2.769,$$

the column total. The three variables are all standardized to unit variance, so the total variance equals 3. Thus, the proportion of total variance that is accounted for by the first factor is $2.769/3 = 92.3$ percent. The first two factors account for $(2.769 + 0.164)/3 = 0.978$, or 97.8 percent of the total variance. The second factor accounts for 5.5 percent of the total variance in the three variables. It seems that in the interest of scientific parsimony, a one-factor solution would suffice; the addition of the second factor provides only a small gain in explained variation. (The argument is one of diminishing returns—does the second factor explain enough additional variance that it is worth retaining it?)

CONCEPTUAL BASIS OF PRINCIPAL COMPONENTS ANALYSIS (PCA)   The objective of a PCA is to transform a set of interrelated variables into a set of uncorrelated linear combinations of these variables. Each linear combination (or component) accounts for a decreasing proportion of the variance in the original variables, subject to the condition that each linear combination is uncorrelated (geometrically at right angles) to all previous linear combinations.

The physical analogy of a watermelon should help in understanding the conceptual basis of PCA. The watermelon has three basic dimensions; call them length, width, and height, and conceive of them as being at right angles to one another. Further, let length always refer to the longest dimension, width to the next longest dimension that is perpendicular to the length axis, and height to the axis perpendicular to the length and width axes. Now, the total size of the watermelon can be indicated by specifying its length, width, and height. Would fewer dimensions provide a reasonably accurate estimate of its size? It all depends on the shape of the watermelon. Suppose that the watermelon was raised near a nuclear reactor and it grew to be very long and narrow, much like a cigar. Then clearly its size would be fairly accurately indicated by simply specifying its length. If the melon was long and wide but rather flat, like an oblong deep-dish pizza, two dimensions would be needed to accurately portray its size. Finally, if it was your good old-fashioned, normal watermelon—long, wide, and high—three dimensions would be needed to describe its size.

The principal components correspond to the axes of the watermelon in this three-dimensional problem. Now consider the sales performance data. Each sales representative has three scores, one for each of the performance criteria. The scores could thus be plotted in 3-D space (in which the coordinates would be the reported values for X_1, X_2, and X_3). The task in PCA is to produce a set of uncorrelated composite scores that measure what the variables have in common, trying to do so getting as much "bang for the buck" (that is, accounting for the most variance in the first extracted components). The first component corresponds to the principal axis of the ellipsoid in three space (the length of the watermelon). Of all the linear combinations that could be formed, it explains the maximum variation contained in the original variables. Whether it adequately captures the important information contained in the data depends on the shape of the concentration of the swarm of points. If the plot of the data results in a cigar-shaped figure, one factor is enough. If not, more than one factor is needed to summarize the data. The second principal component would be chosen so that it accounts for the maximum variation left unexplained, consistent with the condition that it is uncorrelated with the first component (the width of the watermelon). Thus, a PCA reveals how several measures can be combined and reduced down to a single measure, the first component, that nevertheless yields an understanding of how objects vary along this single new dimension. The variation accounted for by each additional component indicates when several independent dimensions or components are needed to adequately define the domain under investigation.

DETERMINING THE NUMBER OF FACTORS   With the watermelon analogy in mind, we can proceed to one of the more important decisions in factor analysis—determining the number of factors necessary to account for the variation in the data. Returning to the sales performance data, the determination is fairly straightforward. Recall from Table 17.10 that the first factor explained 92 percent of the variance, and that the second factor explained only 5 percent more. Thus, we would conclude that one factor effectively summarizes the important information in the data.

Sometimes more factors are required. To illustrate, we will turn to a study that was conducted to compare the images of various department stores in a city. The data were collected using a semantic differential scale, including the items in Figure 17.3. (The negative or undesirable descriptor sometimes appears on the left and sometimes on the right, so the scoring was reversed for those variables where the negative descriptor appeared on the right so that higher scores always reflect more desirable amounts of the property.) Table 17.11 shows the correlations among the responses to these items. A PCA was conducted, and the amount of variation accounted for by each factor is presented in Table 17.12. We can use this more complex example to illustrate the selection of the number of factors.

A number of rules have been advanced for deciding how many factors to retain for a factor analytic solution. Two of the most popular are (1) the latent roots criterion and (2) the scree test.[19]

The **latent roots** criterion holds that the amount of variation explained by each factor must be greater than 1. The rationale is that the variation in each variable is

---

[19]For a discussion of these criteria and others, see Iacobucci, "Classic Factor Analysis," and Kim and Mueller, *Introduction to Factor Analysis* and *Factor Analysis*. If the data can be assumed to be multivariate normal in distribution, maximum likelihood estimation procedures may be used (for example, through Proc Factor in SAS). Maximum likelihood factor loadings would be estimated, and hypotheses about the number of appropriate factors could be tested statistically. See D. N. Lawley and A. E. Maxwell, *Factor Analysis as a Statistical Method* (New York: American Elsevier, 1971); Alexander Basilevsky, *Statistical Factor Analysis and Related Methods: Theory and Applications* (New York: Wiley, 1994).

FIGURE 17.3   Portion of Items Used to Measure Department-Store Image

1. Convenient place to shop	:____:____:____:____:____:____:____:	Inconvenient place to shop
2. Fast checkout	:____:____:____:____:____:____:____:	Slow checkout
3. Store is clean	:____:____:____:____:____:____:____:	Store is dirty
4. Store is not well organized	:____:____:____:____:____:____:____:	Store is well organized
5. Store is messy, cluttered	:____:____:____:____:____:____:____:	Store is neat, uncluttered
6. Convenient store hours	:____:____:____:____:____:____:____:	Inconvenient store hours
7. Store is far from home, school, or work	:____:____:____:____:____:____:____:	Store is close to home, school, or work
8. Store has bad atmosphere	:____:____:____:____:____:____:____:	Store has good atmosphere
9. Attractive decor inside	:____:____:____:____:____:____:____:	Unattractive decor inside
10. Store is spacious	:____:____:____:____:____:____:____:	Store is crowded

TABLE 17.11   Factor Analysis: Correlations among Items in Department-Store Image Survey

					Question or Variable					
Variable	X_1	X_2	X_3	X_4	X_5	X_6	X_7	X_8	X_9	X_{10}
X_1	1.00	0.79	0.41	0.26	0.12	0.89	0.87	0.37	0.32.	0.18
X_2	0.79	1.00	0.32	0.21	0.20	0.90	0.83	0.31	0.35	0.23
X_3	0.41	0.32	1.00	0.80	0.76	0.34	0.40	0.82	0.78	0.72
X_4	0.26	0.21	0.80	1.00	0.75	0.30	0.28	0.78	0.81	0.80
X_5	0.12	0.20	0.76	0.75	1.00	0.11	0.23	0.74	0.77	0.83
X_6	0.89	0.90	0.34	0.30	0.11	1.00	0.78	0.30	0.39	0.16
X_7	0.87	0.83	0.40	0.28	0.23	0.78	1.00	0.29	0.26	0.17
X_8	0.37	0.31	0.82	0.78	0.74	0.30	0.29	1.00	0.82	0.78
X_9	0.32	0.35	0.78	0.81	0.77	0.39	0.26	0.82	1.00	0.77
X_{10}	0.18	0.23	0.72	0.80	0.83	0.16	0.17	0.78	0.77	1.00

TABLE 17.12   Factor Analysis: Amount of Variance Explained per Factor

Factor	Variance Explained
1	5.725
2	2.761
3	0.366
4	0.357
5	0.243
6	0.212
7	0.132
8	0.123
9	0.079
10	0.001

1.0 after the variable has been standardized, and a factor should account for at least that much variation to be considered useful from a data summarization perspective. Since there are two factors with latent roots greater than 1, the latent roots criterion would suggest a two-factor solution for the department-store image data.

The **scree test** plots the latent roots against the number of factors, in their order of extraction, as in Figure 17.4. Note how the curve drops sharply at first and then levels off as it approaches the horizontal axis. This is often the case in such plots, and the method actually gets its name because of the resemblance of the plot to a side view of a mountain. The high value(s) at the left-top represents the peak of the mountain, the drop in values represents the mountain face, and at the foot of the mountain, there will be a fairly straight line approaching horizontal, where rocks that have fallen off the mountain have piled up. The pile of rocks are called *scree*. The last "real" factor is considered to be that point before the scree begins. In the example, the scree or straight line begins at Factor 3, thus the scree plot criterion suggests that a two-factor solution will be sufficient to capture the store image data.

How much of the total variation in the data is explained by the two-factor solution? The total variance of the 10 variables when standardized is 10. The first component accounts for $5.725/10 = 57.3$ percent, and the second component accounts for $2.761/10 = 27.6$ percent. The two components together account for 84.9 percent of the total variation in the 10 variables. (Note that the potential third factor would explain only an additional 3.66 percent of the variance, an amount not deemed worthy to pursue—it is just noise, or scree.)

FIGURE 17.4   **Variance Explained by Each Factor or Latent Root**

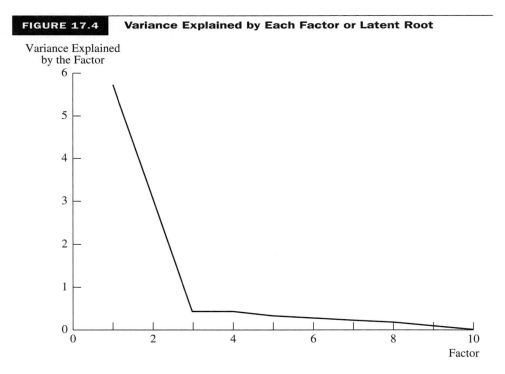

TABLE 17.13	Unrotated Factor-Loading Matrix for Department-Store Image Data Using Two Principal Components

	Factor		
Variable	1	2	Communality
1	0.633	0.707	0.900
2	0.621	0.695	0.869
3	0.872	−0.241	0.819
4	0.833	−0.366	0.828
5	0.774	−0.469	0.818
6	0.626	0.719	0.908
7	0.619	0.683	0.850
8	0.859	−0.303	0.829
9	0.865	−0.293	0.835
10	0.790	−0.454	0.831
Eigenvalue	5.725	2.761	

In addition to examining how much variance among the 10 variables is explained by the 2 factors, we can also investigate the communalities of each of the separate variables; that is, how much of the variation in each variable is accounted for by the two-factor solution? The factor-loading matrix is contained in Table 17.13, and the communalities are in the right-hand column. They were obtained, as we have described, by squaring each factor loading and adding the results across factors. Thus, for variable 1, the communality is

$$(0.633)^2 + (0.707)^2 = 0.900$$

and it is similarly derived for the other variables. The information contained in each of the variables is captured rather nicely by the two-factor solution. Variable 5 is most poorly captured, but even so, 81.8 percent of its variation is reflected by the first two factors.

Substantive Interpretation

Thus far, we have seen how principal components analysis provides a useful tool from the standpoint of data reduction. We have not yet said much about interpretation. That is, we wish to identify the construct(s) that underlie the observed variables. The problem is captured in Figure 17.5. This figure depicts the model where two factors are assumed to have given rise to the five measures. Recall from your basic statistics class that "correlation does not imply causation"; that is, X_1 and X_2 may be correlated because X_1 causes X_2, X_2 causes X_1, or some other cause is common to both X_1 and X_2. The factor analysis model posits the last scenario—that a common factor gives rise to both X_1 and X_2, thereby producing the observed correlation between the variables. The idea is that these variables share a factor in common that reflects some underlying, unobserved construct or constructs. After we have determined how many factors seem to explain the data, we will want to determine what those factors or underlying constructs are. Substantive interpretation in factor analysis focuses on isolating and identifying the factors.

| **FIGURE 17.5** | **Search for Substantive Interpretation in a Factor Analysis Solution** |

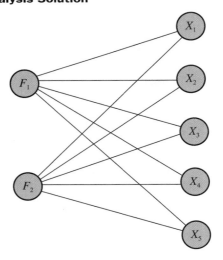

Recall that the sales performance data was fairly straightforward—one factor effectively summarized the important information in the data. Thus, it poses little problem for substantive interpretation. A factor score could be calculated for each sales representative using this "general performance" factor, and the sales representatives could then be ranked according to these factor scores. The "best"-performing sales representative would have the highest score and the "worst" sales representative the lowest score.

Rarely is a factor solution so tidy—even the store image data are slightly more complex. In these more complicated situations (essentially any time there are two or more factors), it is useful to "rotate" the initial factor solution to facilitate substantive interpretation.

ROTATING THE FACTORS What are the factors in the store image data? Their interpretation from the loadings matrix in Table 17.13 is somewhat obscure. All 10 variables correlate highly with or load heavily on the first factor. Variables 1, 2, 6, and 7 also have high positive loadings on the second factor. Figure 17.6 shows a plot of the loadings (using the two factors as the axes and the loadings as coordinates), which suggests that the variables do cluster somewhat in two spaces. Variables 1, 2, 6, and 7 occupy the same general location, and variables 3, 4, 5, 8, 9, and 10 also occupy the same general two-space location. That some variables share a common location raises the question of whether the original factor axes can be rotated to a new orientation to facilitate interpretation of the factors. There is no question of whether the axes can be rotated; they can be mathematically, since an axis rotation simply amounts to forming linear combinations of the factors (essentially a new linear combination of the original variables). The key question is: How should these new linear combinations be selected to best facilitate interpretation?

FIGURE 17.6   **Scatter Diagram Using Correlations between Variables and Factors as Coordinates**

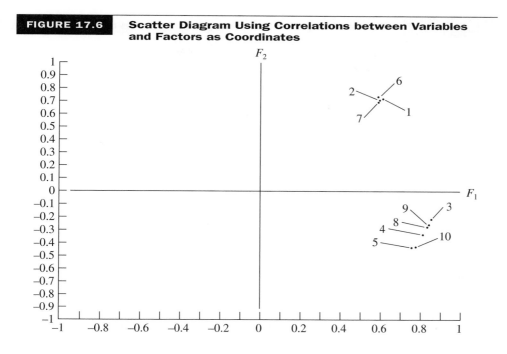

Several alternatives have been proposed by which the new linear combinations can be formed. Just about all these methods attempt to produce loadings that are close to either 0 or 1, because such loadings show more clearly what things go together and, in this sense, are more interpretable. When a variable is uncorrelated with a factor (that is, the loading is near zero, or less than 0.3 in magnitude), we can dismiss the variable as not being useful in interpreting the factor. Conversely, when a variable is more highly correlated (that is, the loading is nearer 1, or, say, greater than 0.5), we rely on that variable to help us interpret and understand the factor. Different rotation methods differ in the criterion that is satisfied when these modified loadings are produced.[20] For example, both orthogonal and oblique rotations have been proposed. Orthogonal rotations are also called rigid or angle-preserving rotations, because they preserve the right angles that exist among the factor axes. Oblique rotations do not, which means that the factors themselves can be correlated.

Figure 17.7 displays the "varimax" orthogonal rotation of the original axes. Varimax attempts to simplify the factor loadings; that is, force them to be near 0 or 1. Varimax is a robust and simple procedure that typically enhances the

---

[20]The earliest axes rotations in factor analysis were done graphically by hand and were aimed at satisfying the five criteria of "simple structure" that Thurstone proposed. Factor rotations are a standard, simple step in computing packages today, which results in greater objectivity of solutions (than the former "eyeball" methods) and which allows for the analysis of more complex problems. See L. L. Thurstone, *Multiple Factor Analysis* (Chicago: University of Chicago Press, 1947) or Harry H. Harman, *Modern Factor Analysis*, 3rd ed. (Chicago: University of Chicago Press, 1976) for the rationale of simple structure.

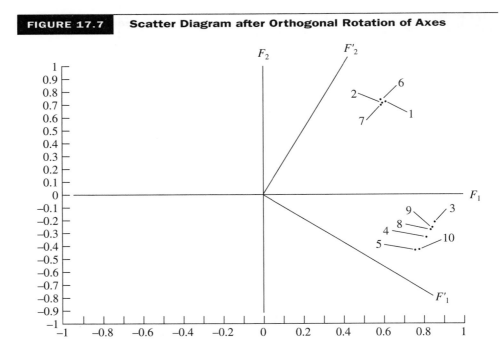

FIGURE 17.7   **Scatter Diagram after Orthogonal Rotation of Axes**

interpretability of factors, and it is consequently the most popular orthogonal rotation scheme.[21] In the figure, the original axes are labeled F_1 and F_2, and the rotated axes are labeled F'_1 and F'_2.

Note in Figure 17.7 that each of the new axes seems to be purer than the original axes. That is, whereas the variables had high loadings—as represented by the magnitude of the vertical projections—on both of the original factor axes, they seem to have high loadings on either one or the other of the new axes but not both. Table 17.14 presents the "rotated factor loadings," which are the magnitudes of these vertical projections, or the correlations of the variables with the new factors.

NAMING THE FACTORS   What are these factors? In order to name them, it is useful to see which variables go with each factor and to name the factors accordingly. The following process is useful for this purpose.

1. Begin with the first variable and first factor in the rotated factor-loading matrix and move horizontally from left to right looking for the highest loading. Circle that loading. Repeat this procedure for each of the other variables in turn.

---

[21]Among oblique rotations, the algorithm "promax" programmed in Proc Factor in SAS performs best, and "direct oblimin" in SPSS is next best. Oblique rotations tend to pass the axes through groups of points without regard to the angles separating the axes. For a brief discussion of the criteria that the major oblique rotations attempt to satisfy, see Dillon and Goldstein, *Multivariate Analysis*, pp. 91–95.

| TABLE 17.14 | Factor-Loading Matrix for Department-Store Image Data after Orthogonal Rotation of Two Principal Components Using Varimax |

	Factor		
Variable	1	2	Communality
1	0.150	0.937	0.900
2	0.147	0.920	0.869
3	0.864	0.269	0.819
4	0.899	0.142	0.828
5	0.904	0.024	0.818
6	0.138	0.943	0.908
7	0.151	0.909	0.850
8	0.886	0.209	0.829
9	0.887	0.221	0.835
10	0.910	0.045	0.831
Eigenvalue	4.859	3.628	

2. Examine each of the circled loadings and assess its "significance." The significance of any loading can be judged using either statistical or practical criteria. Statistical criteria mean that the loading is statistically significant at some specified alpha level, typically 0.05. This means that for samples of less than 100, the loading would have to be greater than 0.30 to be considered statistically significant. The practical significance criterion means that the factor must account for a certain percentage of the variation in the variable. In this regard, a loading of 0.30 means that the factor accounts for 9 percent of the variation in the variable. Typically, the cutoff for saying that the loading is significant is somewhere in the neighborhood of 0.30 or 0.35.

3. Underline the other significant loadings using the criteria decided on in Step 2.

4. Examine the loading matrix and identify all those variables that do not have significant loadings on any factor. It is to be hoped that every variable will load on some factor, but if there is a variable that does not, the analyst has two options: (1) interpret the solution as it is and simply ignore those variables without any large loading, or (2) critically evaluate each of the variables that do not load significantly on any factor. This evaluation would be in terms of the variable's overall contribution to the research as well as its communality index. If a variable is of minor importance to the study's objective and it has a low communality index, the analyst may decide to eliminate the variable and derive a new factor solution with that nonloading variable eliminated.

5. Focus on the significant loadings, and attempt to name the factors on the basis of what the variables loading significantly on a given factor seem to have in common. Variables that have significant loadings on more than one factor complicate the naming task and are also candidates for elimination, depending on the purpose of the study as well as on whether the mixed pattern of

loadings makes sense or indicates there are fundamental problems with the variable or item.[22]

It turns out that when these steps are applied to the loadings in Table 17.13, each variable loads significantly on one and only one factor. Specifically, variables 3, 4, 5, 8, 9, and 10 load only on Factor 1, whereas variables 1, 2, 6, and 7 load only on Factor 2. An examination of the wording of the individual items suggests that Factor 1 is a "store atmosphere" factor; it addresses the issue of whether the store is clean, organized, spacious, and in general has a nice atmosphere. Factor 2 reflects whether the store is a convenient place to shop because of its hours, its location, and the speed of the checkouts. Therefore, we would probably want to call it a "convenience" factor. Instead of describing differences in department stores using the 10 original variables, considerable economy is gained by describing these differences in terms of the two derived factors. For these data, we have achieved "data reduction" and "substantive interpretation!"

Note that the rotation of a factor solution is contemplated for one reason and one reason only—to facilitate the isolation and identification of the factors underlying a set of observed variables. The rotation does not help explain additional variance. If two factors were originally needed to capture the important information in the data, two factors will also be needed after the rotation, if information is not to be discarded. To see this, one simply has to compare Tables 17.13 and 17.14. First, note that the communality for each variable is the same after rotation as it was before. The contribution of each factor in accounting for the variation in each variable has changed, but the total explained variation has not. For variable 1, the communality before rotation was $(0.633)^2 + (0.707)^2 = 0.900$, while after rotation it is $(0.150)^2 + (0.937)^2 = 0.900$, still the same. However, whereas before rotation the second factor accounted for 50.0 percent of the total variation in variable 1, after rotation it accounts for 87.8 percent of this variation. The contributions of the factors have simply been altered, although no additional variation has been accounted for. The same holds true for the contribution of factors to total explained variation. The total remains constant, although the contribution of each factor in explaining this total variation changes. The variance explained is simply reapportioned across the factors differently. Initially, the contribution of the first factor was $5.725/10 = 57.3$ percent and the second was $2.761/10 = 27.6$ percent, for a total of 84.9 percent. After rotation, the contribution of the first factor is $4.859/10 = 48.6$ percent and the second is $3.628/10 = 36.3$ percent, so the total remains the same. Once again, rotation is undertaken for the sole purpose of naming the underlying factors. No additional variance is accounted for in any variable, nor in the variables as a set.

The Key Decisions

We had stated that factor analysis represents a body of techniques for studying the interrelation among a set of variables. The method used to analyze both the sales

---

[22]Although a discussion of the criteria that are used to judge whether an item is a bad or garbage item would take us too far afield, readers should be aware that the criteria are intimately bound up in the psychometric processes that one uses to develop measures of constructs. For a discussion of these processes, see Gilbert A. Churchill, Jr., "A Paradigm for Developing Better Measures of Marketing Constructs," *Journal of Marketing Research* 16 (February 1979), pp. 64–73; Anne Anastasi and Susana Urbina, *Psychological Testing*, 7th ed. (Upper Saddle River, NJ: Prentice Hall, 1996).

performance data and the store image data was based on a rather specific assumed underlying model—in particular, the principal components model, which posits

$$z_j = W_{j1}F_1 + W_{j2}F_2 + \ldots + W_{jm}F_m, \qquad j = 1, 2, \ldots, p$$

That is, it was assumed that any of the p performance variables could be perfectly described by a set of m common factors. Many factor analysts would argue that this model could be enhanced. In particular, we might suspect that it is unreasonable to expect all the variance of a variable to be summarized by common factors only; a fraction would seem to be unique. Thus, although income and assets are both manifestations of the underlying trait of "being rich," for example, they are not one and the same.

When these conditions are expected to arise, an alternative model is often suggested:

$$\begin{aligned}
z_1 &= W_{11}F_1 + W_{12}F_2 + \ldots + W_{1m}F_m + d_1 V_1 \\
z_2 &= W_{21}F_1 + W_{22}F_2 + \ldots + W_{2m}F_m + d_2 V_2 \\
z_p &= W_{p1}F_1 + W_{p2}F_2 + \ldots + W_{pm}F_m + d_p V_p
\end{aligned}$$

This model looks similar to the principal components model given previously, except for the additional $d_j V_j$ terms. In this model, each variable is described linearly in terms of m common factors and a factor unique to the particular observed variable. This is the classical model for factor analysis, and it involves a different approach for its solution.

The distinction between the classical model and the principal components model can be best appreciated by again referring to the sales performance data. If we had used all three principal components and their loadings displayed in Table 17.10, we would have been able to reproduce exactly the value of each variable for each of the 50 observations contained in Table 17.8; alternatively, we would have been able to account for all the variation in each variable. Viewed from the vantage point of the variable-by-variable correlation matrix, we would have been able to generate the ones in the diagonal of the correlation matrix from Table 17.9.

By comparison, under the assumption of the classical factor model, the correlations between variables are reproduced by means of the common factor coefficients alone. Thus, if the estimated correlations closely approximate the observed correlations, the diagonal elements in the correlation matrix must also be reproduced from the common factor portion of the classical model. The diagonal of a correlation matrix contains 1.0s, so the classical factor model could not possibly apply. There is no way in which a variable could be considered to have a unique portion and yet have it reproduced exactly by common factors only. Now, if numbers approximating communalities (measuring what the variable has in common with other variables) are placed in the diagonal of the matrix of observed correlations, the factor solution will involve both common and unique factors. Of course, this raises the question of how these communalities are to be estimated.

GENERATING COMMUNALITY ESTIMATES   At least three popular approaches are used for securing communality estimates. One approach uses the results from a PCA. That is, the correlation matrix with 1s in the diagonal is analyzed using the principal components model. The communalities for each variable estimated by the PCA solution would be entered into the diagonal of the correlation matrix, and this matrix would then be factor analyzed.

A second alternative makes use of the multiple-regression model. Each variable is regressed on all of the other variables in the analysis, and the resulting R^2s are determined. The diagonal of the correlation matrix is replaced by these squared multiple correlations before the correlation matrix is factor analyzed. This technique has been demonstrated to work well; it is widely available and often the default in the major statistical computing packages.

A third alternative is to determine the largest absolute value of the correlation of the variable with any other variable in the analysis by examining the off-diagonal elements in the correlation matrix. This value is placed on the diagonal before the correlation matrix is factor analyzed.

Note that all three of these schemes attempt to assess what the variable in question has in common with the other variables in the analysis. Even though the initial communality estimates may be quite different, all three schemes tend to produce similar solutions for large sample sizes, and moderate to large numbers of variables.

DECISION ITEMS   Not only must factor analysts make decisions about what values to enter into the diagonal of the correlation matrix, they also need to make decisions about other issues as well. Figure 17.8 outlines the sequence of decisions that need to be made. We have already discussed the content of some of these decisions, but let us briefly review the essential questions that need to be addressed at each stage in the process.

1.   Should factor analysis be applied to the data? First, factor analysis does not work well if any, or certainly if many, of the variables are binary. Rating scales

---

FIGURE 17.8   **Key Decisions When Factor Analyzing Data**

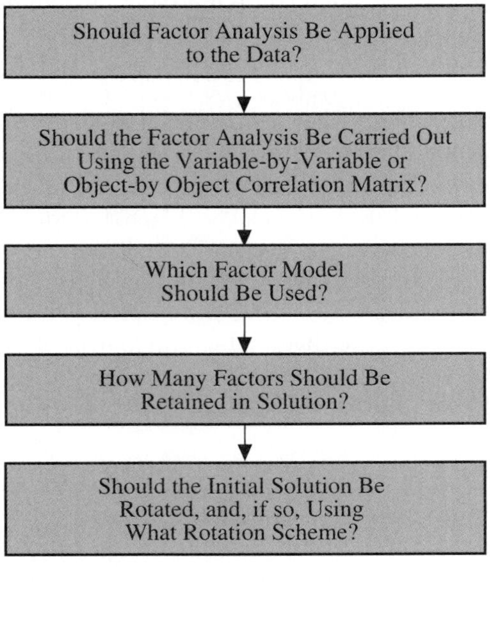

Should Factor Analysis Be Applied
to the Data?

Should the Factor Analysis Be Carried Out
Using the Variable-by-Variable or
Object-by Object Correlation Matrix?

Which Factor Model
Should Be Used?

How Many Factors Should Be
Retained in Solution?

Should the Initial Solution Be
Rotated, and, if so, Using
What Rotation Scheme?

generally work fine. Second, it is probably wise to examine the correlation matrix and plot the latent roots to determine whether a factor analysis is likely to prove fruitful. Factor analysis is concerned with the homogeneity of items, which means that some of the values in the correlation matrix should be large, indicating that they go together. A pattern of low correlations throughout the matrix indicates a heterogeneous set of items and suggests that the matrix may be inappropriate for factoring. The plot of the latent roots or eigenvalues should indicate a sharp break. If the plot of the original, unrotated roots results in a continuous, unbroken line, factoring may be inappropriate. These conditions often go together.

2. Should the factor analysis be carried out using the variable-by-variable or object-by-object correlation matrix? Typically, the variable-by-variable correlation matrix is analyzed because most studies aim at determining which variables go together. That is not the only alternative. The object-by-object matrix can also be analyzed, and there are other options as well.

3. Which factor model would be used? We have discussed the principal components model and the factor model, in which 1s and communalities, respectively, are placed in the diagonal of the correlation matrix before it is analyzed. Suppose that the analyst decides on the factor model to allow for the unique components in the variables. The question then becomes one of deciding which of the many factor models to use, as there are a number of choices. Most of the popular statistical packages have a default option that selects one of the more robust alternatives when a choice is not specified.

4. How many factors should be retained in the solution? We have discussed some of the main criteria that can be used to decide on the proper number of factors. The latent roots and scree criteria generally work well, although not always perfectly, and analysts may be uncertain about how many factors they should retain. When too few factors are retained and carried into rotation, the factor output can be very difficult to interpret. When too few factors are carried into rotation, the variance in each variable is forced on too few factors, resulting in a number of midsize loadings rather than loadings near 0 and 1. This, of course, makes interpretation much more difficult. When too many factors are carried into rotation, some factors come out capturing the variance of a single variable or, at most, two variables. This result is counter to the whole notion underlying factor analysis, which suggests that a factor is a latent variable reflecting what a number of observed variables have in common (a "factor" with a single variable loading on it seems not to have identified variables with anything in common). In general, though, the empirical evidence suggests that overfactoring by one or two factors has fewer severe consequences for the final solution than does taking too few factors into rotation.

5. Should the initial solution be rotated, and if so, using what rotation scheme? Often different rotation schemes largely converge in what they reflect about the data. However, even if they highlight slightly different properties in the data, it is useful to keep in mind that all rotations are equivalent from a statistical point of view. They differ only in how they distribute the variation accounted for across the factors, which, of course, is what is used to name the factors. Thus, performing several rotations and examining the results to see

---

RESEARCH REALITIES 17.2

Factors That Make Commercials Likeable

If you like an ad, will you buy the product? According to a study conducted by Ogilvy Mather, when people like a commercial, they are twice as likely to be persuaded by it as people who simply feel neutral toward the ad.

What makes a commercial likeable? Does it need to be entertaining to be liked? Or are consumers content with the more subtle pleasures evoked by a sentimental or nostalgic approach? What role does creativity play? Do clever treatments of old topics make people like the advertising more?

To answer these questions, the Ogilvy Center for Research and Development tackled the problem of what makes a likeable commercial. Researchers studied a representative sample of 80 prime-time commercials using a nationwide sample of target market consumers. The researchers located consumers who had seen the commercials in their own homes and asked them to describe what they had seen, using a well-researched advertising checklist. The consumers were then asked how much they liked each commercial, using a five-point scale that ranged from "liked a lot" to "disliked a lot." Every respondent rated an average of five commercials, and, on average, each commercial was rated by 133 viewers.

To get people to systematically describe the commercials that they had seen, the research team at

Ogilvy had them describe the commercials using the following list of adjectives:

Amusing	Irritating
Appealing	Lively
Believable	Original
Clever	Phony
Confusing	Pointless
Convincing	Seen a Lot
Dull	Sensitive
Easy to Forget	Silly
Effective	True to Life
Familiar	Warm
Fast Moving	Well Done
Gentle	Worn Out
Imaginative	Worth Remembering
Informative	

The researchers then used factor analysis to reduce this long list of adjectives to a more manageable set of summary ratings. They found that 26 of the adjectives clustered nicely into five distinct category groupings.

For example, if people used the word "clever" to describe a commercial, they were also likely to say that the same commercial was imaginative, amusing, and original. The factor analysis allowed the researchers to combine these adjectives, along with "silly" and "not

---

which rotation produced the "most interpretable" structure is often a productive analysis strategy. The right rotation can be very revealing of the underlying structure in the data.

Marketing Applications

In marketing, factor analysis historically has been employed to "purify" scale items by isolating and then eliminating those items that do not seem to belong with the rest of the items, as well as to name the factors captured by the measures.[23] Research Realities 17.2, for example, discusses the use of factor analysis by the Ogilvy Center for Research and Development to isolate the features that make commer-

---

[23]The emphasis on factor analysis in scale development is particularly evident in the semantic differential scales. See the original book describing the development of the semantic differential technique by Charles E. Osgood, George J. Suci, and Percy H. Tannenbaum, *The Measurement of Meaning* (Urbana, IL: University of Illinois Press, 1957).

RESEARCH REALITIES 17.2

(continued)

dull," into a summary category that measured ingenuity. The five summary categories were as follows:

Ingenuity	Clever, Imaginative, Amusing, Original, Silly, (not) Dull
Meaningful	Worth Remembering, Effective, (not) Pointless, (not) Easy to Forget, True to Life, Believable, Convincing, Informative
Energy	Lively, Fast Moving, Appealing, Well Done
Rubs Wrong Way	Seen a Lot, Worn Out, Irritating, Familiar, Phony
Warmth	Gentle, Warm, Sensitive

Now that the researchers at Ogilvy had a way to summarize people's descriptions of what they saw, they sought to relate this to how well the people liked what they saw. The researchers attempted, by means of multiple-regression analysis, to determine which of the five summary labels (or combinations of labels) was most related to commercial liking. Specifically, they regressed the liking scores on the five dimension scores.

The analysis revealed that consumers best liked the commercials that seemed relevant and meaningful to their lives. An energetic and lively execution also contributed to liking, although it was less important than how meaningful the commercial was to consumers. Ingenuity and whether the commercial rubbed people the wrong way were much less important to commercial liking.

Strangely enough, whether or not a commercial was perceived as being warm had little effect on how well the commercial was liked. The glaring exception to this finding was that advertisements featuring animals consistently ranked tops in terms of likeability and warmth.

The researchers point out that their findings apply differently to different categories of products. Growing evidence suggests that the relationship between liking and persuasion is strongest in low-involvement categories, such as fast-moving consumer goods, for which the emotional component of persuasion is proportionately more important than the deliberate consideration of product attributes.

Sources: "What Makes a Likeable Commercial?" *Viewpoint* 19 (March/April 1987), pp. 32–35; Alexander L. Biel and Carol A. Bridgewater, "Attributes of Likeable Television Commercials," *Journal of Advertising Research* 30 (June/July 1990), pp. 38–44.

cials likeable. Factor analysis has been used in lifestyle and psychographic research problems to develop consumer profiles reflecting people's attitudes, activities, interests, opinions, perceptions, and preferences to better predict their consumption and purchase behavior. It also has been used in marketing to ascertain the key attributes that determine customer preferences for particular products or organizations, to assess a company's image, to isolate those dimensions of printed advertisements that most affect readership, to develop a measure by which the job satisfaction of industrial sales representatives can be assessed, and to screen variables before performing a regression analysis to eliminate or at least reduce the problems of correlated predictors. See Research Realities 17.3 for more in-depth examples. The bottom line on "When do I use factor analysis?" is this: Factor analysis is useful when a survey contains multiple correlated measures that may be measuring a common underlying construct. This model extracts few factors from many variables and yet retains most of the "important information." As a result, it helps the marketing researcher simplify the task at hand.

RESEARCH REALITIES 17.3

More Applications of Factor Analysis

1. Tens of billions of dollars are spent annually by corporations sponsoring sporting events—are they getting their money's worth? Does sponsorship enhance the sports fans' attitude to the company and its products?

Two hundred Australians completed 7-point scales measuring these attitudes. Using factor analysis, six factors resulted from the initial 25 items: personal liking for the event (for example, measured by ratings scales like, "I am a strong supporter of this event"; "I enjoy following coverage of this event"); perceived status of the sponsored event (for example, "This is a significant sporting event"; "This event is important for where I live"); sponsor-event fit (for example, "There is a logical connection between the event and the sponsor"; "The image of the event and the sponsor are similar"); attitude toward the sponsor (such as, "good-bad"; "like-dislike"); sincerity of the sponsor (for example, "This sponsor would likely have the best interests of the sport at heart"); ubiquity of the sponsor (such as, "It is very common to see this company sponsoring sports events"; "This company sponsors many different sports").

These six factors were then used in two multiple regressions to predict ratings of favorability toward the sponsor, and the willingness to consider using the sponsor's products, respectively. A positive attitude toward the sponsor, a good sponsor-event fit, and a perception of the sincerity of the sponsor all enhanced both the favorability toward the sponsor and the likelihood of purchasing the sponsor's products. In addition, personal liking for the event enhanced likelihood of purchase, and perceived ubiquity of the sponsor decreased likelihood of purchase. The status of the event helped enhance favorability judgments.

2. Tourism is crucial to Hong Kong's economy, and shopping comprises 50 percent of tourist expenditures. Surveys inquiring into the factors important to shopping were obtained from 220 tourists in Hong Kong.

Marketing researchers used factor analysis to derive four shopping factors from 15 measured attributes: quality of tangibles (for example, "lighting and physical setting of shops"; "window display"; "open hours of shops"); staff service quality (such as, "language ability of sales staff"; "attitude of sales staff"); product value (for example, "price of product"; "value for the money"); and product reliability (such as, "product is reliable").

These factors were used in a multiple regression to predict tourists' levels of satisfaction with their Hong Kong shopping experiences. Staff service quality had the biggest effect on their customer satisfaction, followed by product value and reliability.

3. Factor analysis has been used to develop scales of service quality in the health care setting. Researchers anticipated that consumers' evaluations of quality may be a function of three factors: "search" attributes (that is, those that can be evaluated upon looking at the product or service), "experience" attributes (those that can be evaluated only after some trial and consumption), and "credence" attributes (those whose evaluations are difficult even after consumption).

Their hypotheses were supported: three factors were identified from 14 items: The first factor looked like their search factor: measured by "attractive interior"; "accepts insurance"; "complete range of service"; "specialists available"; and "current medical equipment." The second factor resembled experiential qualities: measured by variables, "clarity of admission procedures"; "privacy"; "hospital accessibility"; "amount of personal attention received"; and "visitation policies." The third factor was comprised of the features that would be difficult for a patient to evaluate, and was considered to be the credence factor, measured by variables "nurse's competence"; "quality of emergency care"; "physician's competence"; and "use of current medical procedures."

Sources: Richard Speed and Peter Thompson, "Determinants of Sports Sponsorship Response," *Journal of the Academy of Marketing Science* 28 (Spring 2000), pp. 226–238; Vincent C. S. Heung and Eliza Cheng, "Assessing Tourists' Satisfaction with Shopping in the Hong Kong Special Administrative Region of China," *Journal of Travel Research* 38 (May 2000), pp. 396–404; Donald J. Shemwell and Ugur Yavas, "Measuring Service Quality in Hospitals," *Journal of Marketing Theory and Practice* 7 (Summer 1999), pp. 65–75.

ETHICAL DILEMMA 17.2

Clark was feeling very smug. He had just completed the analysis and writeup of a study that involved respondents' completing a lengthy attitude scale about such things as their need for security, their attitudes toward life insurance, their willingness to assume risk, how vulnerable they feel to life's unexpected events, and similar constructs. The purpose of the investigation was to determine if those people purchasing his firm's products could somehow be differentiated from those purchasing competitors' products on the basis of the attitude profiles. He analyzed the responses to discover which items belonged to which constructs. This involved a series of iterations.

After Clark had purified the items and felt comfortable with the results, he formed a total score for each construct for each respondent by summing the responses to the items making up that construct. He used the total scores thus generated as independent variables in a discriminant analysis in which "brand purchased" served as the criterion. The results clearly indicated that the attitude profile of those purchasing his firm's insurance differed from that of people purchasing competitors' products and, further, that some of the differences lent themselves to actionable strategies by which the firm might increase its share.

Clark's smugness began to dissipate, however, when a chance conversation with one of his old college buddies caused him to wonder if he had not made a mistake. His college friend pointed out that, according to the accepted rules of thumb for factor analysis, Clark did not have a large enough sample in terms of the number of respondents versus the number of items. Consequently, his factor analysis results might be quite unstable.

- What should Clark do? If he admits his error now to his boss, his boss might think less highly of him, particularly since Clark was hired into the marketing research department partially on the basis of his statistical skills. However, not reporting it could cause those in his firm to place more confidence in the results than they should.

- What are Clark's ethical responsibilities?

- Would the ethical problem be different if Clark knew of the requirement and intentionally overlooked it, knew it but inadvertently forgot it, or never learned it in the first place?

Cluster Analysis

In marketing there is keen interest in developing useful ways of classifying objects. Very often the objects to be classified are customers—if you hear "segmentation," you should think "cluster analysis." A firm segmenting its market is seeking to group potential customers into homogeneous groups that are large enough to be profitably cultivated. The segmentation base could involve many characteristics, ranging from the commonly used socioeconomic bases to buyer behavior and psychological bases. One thing is sure: The segmentation would be based on numerous factors and not simply on one or two variables. This, of course, raises a problem for the researcher—how to identify natural groupings of the customers given the multivariate nature of the data. To segment them on a single variable would be an oversimplification, but how should the multiple variables be combined? Cluster analysis offers the researcher a solution. It is designed to deal with how objects should be assigned to groups so that there will be as much similarity within groups, and difference among groups, as possible.[24]

One of the more important uses of cluster analysis has been in identifying aggregates of consumers who behave similarly. By determining the areas where they live and the demographics of those areas from census data, geodemographic segments of the population can be formed. Research Realities 17.4, for example, lists the 12 major groups, the subgroups forming each group, and a few features of some selected subgroups in the Claritas Prizm system. We tend to live near people who are similar to us, and at the same time, our clusters can be found in several geographic locations. For example, the "Towns and Gowns" lifestyle, which includes disproportionately high rentals of foreign videos and online services, and low usage of coupons and dry-cleaners, is similar whether the clustered customers are in Boulder, Colorado; Berkeley, California or Gainesville, Florida. Even internationally, the "hip singles in America's 'Bohemian Mix' lifestyle have more in common with their counterparts in England's 'Studio Singles' cluster than with working class neighborhoods down the street. Both groups tend to buy imported food, hang out at bars and coffee shops, and dislike fast-food chains." The rich people living in "Blue Blood Estates" in the U.S. are like the Canadian "Establishment" in that residents "live in sprawling mansions, drive luxury imports, belong to nearby country clubs, . . . and hire outsiders to do everything from cooking and gardening to interior decorating and child care."[25] (For more on geodemographic data, see Chapter 6.)

A related problem that marketing researchers might face that cluster analysis can help solve is the problem of test-marketing products, prices, promotional campaigns, and so on. Similar cities must be selected (for example, to assign one city as the test market, and the other city to serve as a control) so that the results obtained are not attributable to differences in market areas. But how does one determine which cities are alike? To keep things simple, consider the situation when similarity is assessed on the basis of only two city characteristics—population and median income. To prepare the data for clustering, the variables are first standardized, because they are usually measured on quite different scales. Without standardization, the groups would change if the measurement units were altered; for example, population specified as a number of thousands of people instead of simply number of people. Table 17.15 contains the standardized income and population scores for 15 test cities that a firm is considering grouping into like categories.

---

[24]Recall that for discriminant analysis, there were *a priori* groups, and we were trying to understand the group differences using variables measured on the individuals in those groups. For cluster analysis, we have the obverse problem; we are trying to use information on consumers to form groups.

[25]Michael J. Weiss, *The Clustered World: How We Live, What We Buy, and What It All Means About Who We Are* (Boston: Little, Brown and Co, 2000), pp. 240, 305–306.

RESEARCH REALITIES 17.4

Characteristics of Selected Subgroups in Prizm Lifestyle Clusters

Major Group	Subgroups	Demographic Description	Lifestyle/Media/ Financial Preferences
Suburban Elite	Blue-Blood Estates Money and Brains **Furs & Station Wagons**	New-money families in suburbs, upwardly mobile white collar, college grads, age 35–54	Own a CD player All-news radio 3+ stock transactions/yr
Affluentials	**Pools and Patios** Two More Rungs Young Influentials	Upper-middle income, two-income empty nesters, age 45–64, in upscale suburbs	Foreign cruise Epicurean magazines $5,000+ mutual funds
Greenbelt Families	Young Suburbia **Blue-Chip Blues**	Upper-middle income, traditional suburban families, age 25–44, mixed white/blue collar, single-family houses	Go fishing Watch headline news Interest-bearing checking accounts
The Urban Gentry	Urban Gold Coast Bohemian Mix Black Enterprise **New Beginnings**	Lower-middle income families and singles, age 25–34, low-level white collar and clerical	Jog/run AOR/prog radio Have first mortgage
The Exurban Boom	God's Country **New Homesteaders** Towns & Gowns	Lower-middle income, town-dwelling, young families, age 18–34, some college, blue/white collar	Ride motorcycles MOR/nostalgia radio Veterans life insurance
Suburban Elders	**Levittown, U.S.A.** Gray Power Rank and File	Middle-income, suburban, (older couples) age 55–65, tract housing, two income, high school education	Belong to a union Golden oldies radio Christmas Club account
Satellite Blues	Blue-Collar Nursery **Middle America** Coalburg & Corntown	Lower-middle income, mid-size town families, age 45–64, blue collar, single-unit housing	Woodworking Fishing/hunt magazines Christmas Club account
Mid-City Mix	New Melting Pot Old Yankee Rows Emergent Minorities **Single City Blues**	Low income, urban singles, age 18–34, some college, mixed blue and white collar	Contribute to public radio Jazz radio Non-interest-bearing checking accounts

The bold subgroup is the largest subgroup in its major group.
For more information, see Prizm Lifestyle Cluster System (Alexandria, VA: Claritas, Inc., 1992).

	Cluster Analysis Example: Key Characteristics of Cities to Be Grouped Expressed in Standardized Units	
TABLE 17.15		

City	Income X_1	Population X_2
A	1.14	1.72
B	−1.25	−1.17
C	1.62	0.89
D	1.64	1.35
E	0.55	0.10
F	−0.94	−1.25
G	0.89	1.32
H	−0.87	−0.63
I	−0.44	−0.07
J	0.08	−0.55
K	−0.18	0.62
L	−1.29	−0.86
M	−1.07	−1.38
N	−0.09	0.02
O	0.21	−0.11

A simple, subjective way of grouping objects is to plot the results and make a visual assignment. Figure 17.9 uses the two variables of income and population as axes. The scatterplot suggests that there are three distinct clusters in the data:

- Cluster 1, consisting of Cities {A, C, D, G}
- Cluster 2, consisting of Cities {E, I, J, K, N, O}
- Cluster 3, consisting of Cities {B, F, H, L, M}

The visual assignment procedure worked in this example because there were only two dimensions and the natural groupings were pretty clear. However, the cities might be grouped on potentially many characteristics, and graphical display becomes more difficult as the number of dimensions increases. It would be useful to have a way of incorporating the higher dimensionality. Furthermore, it would be useful to have a more objective measure of "similarity" or "likeness" to use as a basis to form the clusters.

Euclidean Distance to Measure Similarity

One measure that would capture the closeness of two objects in a scatterplot is the Euclidean distance between the points representing those objects. In the two-dimensional figure, the distance between, say, Cities A and C would be calculated:

$$d_{A,C} = \sqrt{(X_{C1} - X_{A1})^2 + (X_{C2} - X_{A2})^2}$$

where X_{C1}, for example, represents the coordinate of City C on the first dimension, median income. This distance is

$$d_{A,C} = \sqrt{(1.62 - 1.14)^2 + (0.89 - 1.72)^2} = 0.959$$

If, in addition to having income and population variables on the cities, we also had a variable that captured, say, literacy rates, we would effectively have a three-

FIGURE 17.9   **Cluster Analysis Example: Two-Dimensional Plot of City Characteristics**

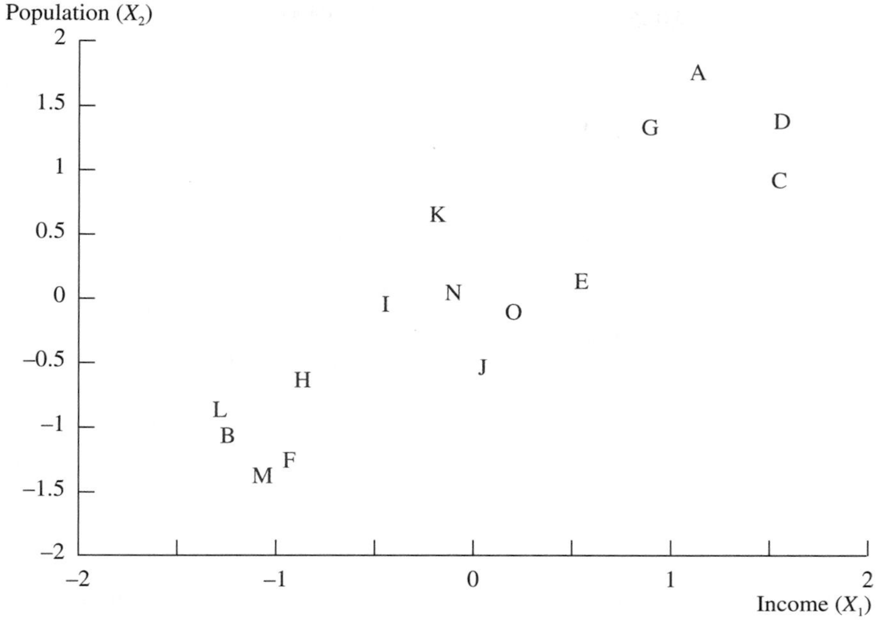

dimensional problem. Three dimensions is only a little trickier to visualize in plots than two, but the expression for the Euclidian distance is even more easily extended:

$$d_{A,C} = \sqrt{(X_{C1} - X_{A1})^2 + (X_{C2} - X_{A2})^2 + (X_{C3} - X_{A3})^2}$$

and generally, for any two objects, i and j:

$$d_{ij} = \sqrt{\sum_{k=1}^{3} (X_{ik} - X_{jk})^2}$$

(The generalization to n dimensions to account for n characteristics should be apparent; the summation is simply taken from $k = 1$ to n.)

The "distance" between all 15 cities is presented in Table 17.16. (These Euclidian distances capture psychological dissimilarity or distance; they are not geographical "distances" between cities.) Note that distance is an inverse measure of similarity because the larger the distance, the farther apart the objects. The matrix of distances also makes it clear why cluster analysis is highly dependent on computers.[26] In this relatively simple example involving 15 objects, there were $15(14)/2 = 105$ distances that needed computing. In the general case of n objects, there would be

---

[26]The growth in the popularity of cluster analysis paralleled the early growth in computer installations. The major stimulus was the classic book by R. Sokal and P. Sneath, *Principles of Numerical Taxonomy* (San Francisco: W. H. Freeman, 1963). The literature on cluster analysis virtually exploded after its publication and continues to show dramatic annual increases even now.

| TABLE 17.16 | Cluster Analysis: Distance between Cities *i* and *j* in Two-Space | | | | | | |

				$j =$			
	1	*2*	*3*	*4*	*5*	*6*	*7*
i =	*A*	*B*	*C*	*D*	*E*	*F*	*G*
1. (A)	0.000						
2. (B)	3.750	0.000					
3. (C)	0.959	3.533	0.000				
4. (D)	0.622	3.834	0.460	0.000			
5. (E)	1.724	2.203	1.330	1.658	0.000		
6. (F)	3.626	0.320	3.337	3.663	2.011	0.000	
7. (G)	0.472	3.283	0.847	0.751	1.266	3.155	0.000
8. (H)	3.092	0.660	2.917	3.197	1.597	0.624	2.627
9. (I)	2.388	1.366	2.273	2.518	1.004	1.282	1.924
10. (J)	2.505	1.467	2.108	2.458	0.802	1.237	2.038
11. (K)	1.718	2.085	1.820	1.961	0.896	2.019	1.279
12. (L)	3.544	0.313	3.396	3.670	2.075	0.524	3.083
13. (M)	3.807	0.277	3.520	3.847	2.194	0.184	3.336
14. (N)	2.098	1.662	1.919	2.182	0.645	1.528	1.628
15. (O)	2.053	1.804	1.729	2.044	0.400	1.619	1.583

$n(n-1)/2$ separate distances. In addition, the clusters are not as readily apparent as when the data were presented in a simple two-dimensional graph. The question is, how should we proceed in specifying clusters?

Clustering Methods

A number of methods have been suggested for forming groups of objects. There are *linkage, nodal,* and *factor* procedures,[27] and variations within each method. The objective underlying each method is the same—to assign objects to groups so that there will be as much similarity within groups and as much difference between groups as possible. Unfortunately, the different methods can produce widely divergent results with the same data set, and none of the methods is as yet accepted as the "best" under all circumstances. The research analyst must, therefore, be familiar with the various methods to exercise caution in choosing the method that is most compatible with the research project's goals.

LINKAGE METHODS   Various linkage methods have been advanced.[28] We shall discuss the single-linkage method in some detail, because an understanding of this

---

[27]For an alternative seven-category classification, see Mark S. Aldenderfer and Roger K. Blashfield, *Cluster Analysis* (Thousand Oaks, CA: Sage, 1984); also see Brian S. Everitt, Cluster Analysis, 3rd ed. (New York: Halsted Press, 1993); Juan E. Mezzich and Herbert Solomon, *Taxonomy and Behavioral Science: Comparative Performance of Grouping Methods* (New York: Academic Press, 1980).

[28]For useful introductions to the subject, see Aldenderfer and Blashfield, *Cluster Analysis;* M. Lorr, *Cluster Analysis for the Social Sciences* (San Francisco: Jossey-Bass, 1983); Phipps Arabie and Lawrence Hubert, "Cluster Analysis in Marketing Research," in Richard P. Bagozzi, ed., *Advanced Methods of Marketing Research* (Cambridge, MA: Blackwell Publishers, 1994), pp. 160–189; John A. Hartigan, *Cluster Analysis* (New York: Wiley, 1975); Phipps Arabie, Lawrence J. Hubert, G. De Soete, eds., *Clustering and Classifcation* (New York: World Scientific, 1996).

TABLE 17.16	(continued)

| | | | | $j =$ | | | |
8 H	9 I	10 J	11 K	12 L	13 M	14 N	15 O
0.000							
0.706	0.000						
0.953	0.708	0.000					
1.428	0.737	1.199	0.000				
0.479	1.160	1.405	1.850	0.000			
0.776	1.454	1.418	2.189	0.565	0.000		
1.015	0.361	0.595	0.607	1.488	1.709	0.000	
1.199	0.651	0.459	0.828	1.677	1.803	0.327	0.000

method is the key to understanding the other linkage procedures, such as complete linkage and average linkage.

Single Linkage   Single-linkage computer programs operate in the following way: First, the similarity values are arrayed from most to least similar. Then, those objects with the highest similarity (or smallest distance) coefficients are clustered together. The threshold of how similar two objects must be before being joined is systematically lowered, and the union of objects at each similarity value is recorded. The union of two objects (that is, the admission of an object into a cluster, or the merging of two clusters) is by the criterion of "single linkage." This means that if the similarity level in question is, say, 0.20, a single link of an object at that level with any member of a cluster would enable the object to join the cluster. Similarly, any pair of objects (one in each of two clusters) related at the criterion level will make their clusters join.

Let us begin, for example, with all the similarity values less than 1.000 in Table 17.16. When arrayed from most similar to least similar, the tabulation in Table 17.17 results. The highest reported similarity value (or the smallest distance) is 0.184, the distance between F and M. Starting at a distance of zero, the first computer iteration would be to this value, and objects F and M would be joined to form a cluster. The next table entry is 0.277, the distance between objects B and M. Consider what happens at this second computer iteration value.

Since M has already been joined to F at the first iteration, the situation can be diagrammed as follows:

TABLE 17.17	Cluster Analysis: All Distances Less Than 1.000 Arrayed in Increasing Order of Dissimilarity				
Distance Level	**City Pairs**	**Distance Level**	**City Pairs**	**Distance Level**	**City Pairs**
0.184	FM	0.524	FL	0.737	IK
0.277	BM	0.565	LM	0.751	DG
0.313	BL	0.595	JN	0.776	HM
0.320	BF	0.607	KN	0.802	EJ
0.327	NO	0.622	AD	0.828	KO
0.361	IN	0.624	FH	0.847	CG
0.400	EO	0.645	EN	0.896	EK
0.459	JO	0.651	IO	0.953	HJ
0.460	CD	0.660	BH	0.959	AC
0.472	AG	0.706	HI		
0.479	HL	0.708	IJ		

Will B be allowed to join the cluster consisting of the elements F and M? The answer is yes under the criterion of single linkage. Even though the distance from B to F is higher (0.320), that does not matter under the criterion of single linkage. Rather, the one link between B and M that satisfies the criterion value is sufficient to allow B to join F and M to form the larger group BFM. The next iteration would be to the similarity value 0.313, representing the distance between B and L. Would L be allowed to join the group BFM at this iteration value? Again, the answer would be yes under the criterion of single linkage; even though the distances between F and L (0.524), and L and M (0.565) are both greater than the criterion value at this iteration (0.313), that would not matter under the criterion of single linkage. Next, since BFL and M are already joined, nothing further happens at the similarity value 0.320 (corresponding to B and F). At the value 0.327, however, N joins O, and I joins this new pair at the iteration value 0.361 to form the larger group INO. E and J are subsequently admitted to this cluster of objects at the iteration values 0.400 and 0.459, respectively. The process would continue to cluster together objects and clusters until, after the 15th iteration corresponding to a distance of 0.607, the situation would look like this:

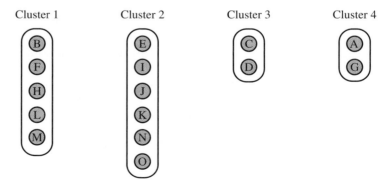

At this point, none of the variables would still be in clusters by themselves. When will the clusters themselves join to form larger groupings? According to the criterion of single linkage, the clusters will join when the distance between any pair of objects in the distinct clusters equals the iteration distance value. Consider, for example, the situation between Clusters 3 and 4, which can be diagrammed as follows:

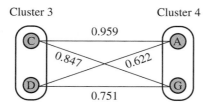

At an iteration value of 0.622, Cluster 3 will be joined with Cluster 4, because the single bond between A and D satisfies the criterion. Note that although the clusters are joined because of the single bond between two members of the respective clusters, some of the members within the newly formed cluster are much farther removed (or very different) from one another; for example, the distance from A to C is 0.959 and the distance from C to G is 0.847, approximately 1.5 times larger than the merging distance. Single linkage thus frequently produces *chaining*, that is, long, straggling groups, yielding solutions that are not particularly helpful to the researcher.

Cluster analysis results are often presented in the form of a *dendrogram*, a "tree" figure that indicates the groups of objects formed at various similarity (distance) levels. The dendrogram for the city data employing the single linkage method is shown in Figure 17.10.

Objects A through O are shown at the top. As we saw, the class FM forms first ($d_{FM} = 0.184$); B is admitted to this cluster at a distance iteration value of 0.277; and

FIGURE 17.10   **Cluster Analysis Example: Dendrogram of City Data Using Single Linkage**

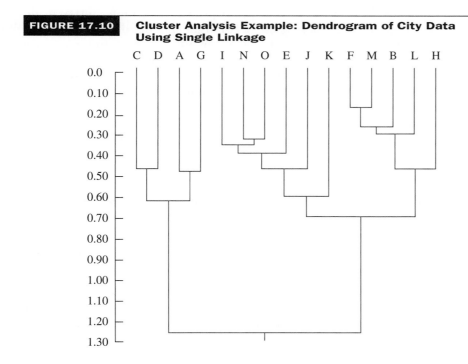

so on. These unions and the values at which they occur (now called the "fusion" co-efficients) are shown on the horizontal axis in the figure. What are the natural groupings in the data? It all depends on what similarity level one is using. At a distance level of 0.50, there are five separate classes, reading from left to right:

- Group 1—CD
- Group 2—AG
- Group 3—INOEJ
- Group 4—K
- Group 5—FMBLH

If instead a distance level of 0.65 is to be used, there are three clusters:

- Group 1—CDAG
- Group 2—INOEJK
- Group 3—FMBLH

Finally, if one selects a distance level of 0.80, there are only two groups:

- Group 1—CDAG
- Group 2—INOEJKFMBLH

Many researchers would probably select a cutoff distance of 0.65, because the two-dimensional portrayal of the data suggests that there are three natural groupings. With p variables, the decision concerning the proper cutoff value must be made without such a visual referent, making the decision much more difficult. The purpose of the analysis would assist the analyst in making the choice. If the researcher simply needed two cities that were very much alike, he or she might use a more stringent criterion level, such as 0.35 to obtain groups with quite homogeneous cities (that is, one group consisting of the pair of cities N and O and the other group consisting of the four cities F, M, B, and L). If the analyst needed a larger number of similar test-market cities, he or she would use a more relaxed similarity coefficient, such as 0.65, which would produce three groups of four, six, and five members.

An alternative way of deciding the number of clusters is to plot the number of clusters against the fusion coefficients. Note, for example, that at a value of 0.184 in the figure, where objects F and M join, there are 14 groups. At the value of 0.277, where objects F, M, and B join, there are 13 groups, and so on. These fusion values and number of groups serve as the coordinates for the two points farthest to the left in Figure 17.11.

The idea is to use a fusion plot in much the same way as the plot of eigenvalues is used in factor analysis. The researcher looks for large jumps in the fusion coefficient, indicating that two relatively dissimilar clusters have been merged, which suggests that the number of clusters before the merger is the most probable solution. Alternatively, the researcher can look to see where the curve flattens out, which suggests that no new information is portrayed by the subsequent mergers of the clusters that would follow. Note that in Figure 17.11 the curve flattens at two points, once when

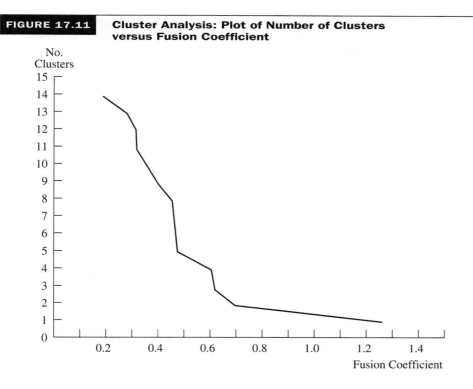

FIGURE 17.11   **Cluster Analysis: Plot of Number of Clusters versus Fusion Coefficient**

going from five to four clusters and once when going from two clusters to one, imply-ing that five or two clusters exist in the data. The incremental change in the fusion coefficient also suggests either five or two clusters are in the data, since there is a sub-stantial jump in the value of the coefficient between five and four and between two and one clusters. As the example indicates, these rules of thumb for determining the number of clusters can be helpful, but they sometimes produce ambiguous results.

Complete Linkage   In the complete linkage method, an object joining a cluster at a certain similarity coefficient must be that close or closer to every member of the cluster. Thus, single bonds with just one member of the cluster would not be suffi-cient to effect the juncture. This would seem to be a fierce condition, with larger groups forming only when the criterion level is lowered considerably. And as a re-sult, complete linkage has a tendency to produce very tight, compact clusters. The fact that the cluster solutions are so well-defined makes complete link clustering among the more useful and popular of clustering techniques.

Consider again the group ADGC. This group will eventually form under the complete linkage criterion, but consider how. The respective distances are:

	A	*C*	*D*	*G*
A	0.000			
C	0.959	0.000		
D	0.622	0.460	0.000	
G	0.472	0.847	0.751	0.000

At a value of 0.460, objects C and D join, and at 0.472, A and G join. When will the two groups join? Under the criterion of complete linkage, they will come together only when all the linkages among the objects in the two groups satisfy the criterion level. In other words, the largest distance (or most dissimilar) among the objects in the groups controls the union. This means that the two groups will not join to form the larger cluster until the iteration distance value 0.959 is reached. This largest distance, between object A in the one group and object C in the other, ensures that all the other distances also satisfy the criterion (that is, if 0.959 is "close enough," then surely so are 0.622, 0.847, and 0.751).

Average Linkage   The average-linkage method is an approach intermediate to single and complete linkage. As the name implies, an object will join a cluster when the average of all similarities between the object and the members of the cluster are above the given level for linkage to occur. The average-linkage method involves some (simple) calculations: as soon as a new cluster forms, these average distances or similarities must be calculated anew. For example, once C joins with D at the level 0.460, the matrix above would be recalculated to reflect the cluster:

	A	*CD*	*G*
A	0.000		
CD	0.7905	0.000	
G	0.472	0.7990	0.000

where $0.7905 = (0.959 + 0.622)/2$ and $0.7990 = (0.847 + 0.751)/2$, the average of A with C and D, and the average of G with C and D. In this smaller 3×3 matrix, it should be clear that in the next step, A would join G at the 0.472 level. The matrix of similarities would again be updated:

	A G	*CD*
AG	0.000	
CD	0.7948	0.000

where $0.7948 = (0.7905 + 0.7990)/2$, the average of CD with A and with G. These computations may not seem like much, especially for our small example of 15 (and here, 4) objects, but remember that cluster analysis is frequently used to segment customers—sometimes hundreds of thousands of them.

Although more computer-intensive in terms of calculations, empirical evidence indicates that the average-linkage method generally works well. For example, in simulation studies where there are "known" cluster configurations, average link recovers the results cleanly. It seems to exhibit the advantage of complete link (fairly tight clusters) without the disadvantage of the very rigorous criterion that all objects must be sufficiently similar. Because it performs so well empirically, it is probably the most popular of the cluster linkage techniques.

The linkage methods are all considered hierarchical clustering methods. That is, a hierarchy of groupings is formed as the criterion similarity value is altered; if objects C and D cluster together when there are five clusters, they will also be together in the same cluster, perhaps with additional objects, when there are four clusters, and so on. The dendrogram captures the resulting hierarchy—an object cannot break out of a cluster once it has been subsumed into the cluster.

Nodal Methods   Another class of clustering method involves selecting an object that will serve as focal objects, or "nodes" for clusters. The remaining objects are then allocated to each cluster on the basis of their similarity to the focal object(s). The basic operation of the nodal methods can be illustrated by the following scheme:

- Choose as nodes those objects that have the least similarity or greatest distance between each other.
- Consider these two objects as extremes, polar nodes, and allocate all remaining objects to one or the other cluster based on their similarity to the polar nodes.
- Split the two resulting clusters in the same way. Continue the process until the collection of objects is split into its original members.

In the city example, Cities D and M are most dissimilar ($d_{DM} = 3.847$), and thus they would be considered as the nodes for the two clusters. Each of the remaining objects would then be allocated to each cluster on the basis of the shortest distance to either D or M. Thus, the first iteration would form these clusters:

- Group 1—DACEGK
- Group 2—MBFHIJLNO

Next, in Group 1, the least similar cities are D and K ($d_{DK} = 1.961$), so they would be considered new nodes, and the remaining objects in Group 1 would be allocated to each of the new clusters on the basis of their distances to these new nodes. Those new groups would be:

- Group 1A—DACG
- Group 1B—KE

Similarly, Group 2 would be divided (using B and J as new nodes) to yield:

- Group 2A—BFHLM
- Group 2B—JINO

At each stage, the cluster analyst could check to see if the resulting subgroups should be retained, or combined back together, based on, say, some average measure of similarity between the objects within and among subgroups.

An alternative nodal clustering method employs a *prime* node. The prime node is the most "prototypical" object—that is, the object that has characteristics closest to the average characteristics for all the objects. Because the data have been standardized, the average median income and average population for the 15 cities are zero. City N is most typical (its values on both variables are closest to zero, the standardized mean), so it would be considered the prime node, and the clustering would begin around it. Cities would be added to this cluster one at a time. After each addition, a measure of the resulting homogeneity of the cluster would be determined. When the measure of homogeneity (for example, the average-within-cluster distance) took a large jump in value, the "natural" limits of the cluster would be considered to have been exceeded, and the last object added to the cluster would be removed. The proper solution would be considered to be the previous stage in the iterative clustering.

After this primary cluster were determined, it would be removed from the analysis. A new prototype object would be determined from the remaining objects, and the process would be repeated. The procedure would continue until all the objects had joined clusters or until only a few isolated objects remained. (They could be left alone, or they could be attached to whatever clusters that they seemed to fit best.) The nodal methods are also known as "iterative partitioning methods" because of the way they work; they begin with some initial partition of the data and subsequently change these assignments.

The use of polar nodes or a prime node represents just two of the many alternatives that have been proposed for effecting an initial partition of the objects. Two other alternatives are to specify "seed points" by picking certain objects to serve as group centroids or even to randomly assign objects to one of a prespecified number of clusters (for example, three).[29] Regardless of how the initial assignment of objects to groups is determined, the next step is to calculate the centroids (group means) of each cluster and then to reallocate each data point to the cluster that is nearest. After all reassignments are made, the centroids of the new clusters are computed, and the process is repeated until no reassignments occur. Thus, iterative partitioning methods make more than one pass through the data, which usually results in good solutions, even if the initial partition was poor.

Currently, the most popular partitioning method is the "*k*-means" approach, which requires that the number of clusters, *k*, be specified in advance and that *k* starting points be determined by purposively selecting certain objects to serve as nodes, randomly, or by some other means.[30] In the first pass through the data, each object is assigned to one of the *k* starting points according to which starting point it is most similar or closest to. Then (1) the mean or centroid for each group is calculated and (2) the objects are reassigned on the basis of the mean to which they are closest, and these two steps are repeated until no objects are reclassified. Research Realities 17.5 visually demonstrates the operation of the *k*-means approach; while the example suggests *k*-means can recover quickly from a poor specification of starting points, that is not always true—it depends on how clearly separated the groups are.

FACTOR ANALYSIS   A third major way of attacking the clustering problem is actually through applying factor analysis. When we presented the factor analytic technique, we focused on its usual use, the search for latent dimensions of the variables by determining which variables go together or measure common characteristics.

---

[29]For a very readable discussion of some of the main options when using iterative partitioning methods, see Aldenderfer and Blashfield, *Cluster Analysis,* especially pp. 45–49.

[30]For more on *k*-means clustering, see Anil Chaturvedit, J. Douglas Carroll, Paul E. Green, and John A. Rotondo, "A Feature-Based Approach to Market Segmentation via Overlapping K-Centroids Clustering," *Journal of Marketing Research* 34 (Aug. 1977), pp. 370–377; Frank J. Carmone, Jr., Ali Kara, and Sarah Maxwell, "HINoV: A New Model to Improve Market Segment Definition by Identifying Noisy Variables," *Journal of Marketing Research* 36 (Nov. 1999), pp. 501–509.

RESEARCH REALITIES 17.5

Operation of the *k*-Means Method of Cluster Analysis

Suppose that the two swarms of *x* characters in Figure A were two clusters of points in a two-dimensional plot awaiting discovery. If we want to find the two-cluster solution, we first pick two starting points. As a random choice, suppose that the starting points are at the A and B in the point swarm on the right.

Figure A

```
    xxxxx                      xxxxx
  xxxxxxxxx                   xxxxxxxxx
xxxxxxxxxxxxx               xxxxAxxxxxxx
xxxxxxxxxxxxxxx            xxxxxxxxxxxxxxx
xxxxxxxxxxxxx             xxxxxxxxxBxx
 xxxxxxxxxxx               xxxxxxxxxxx
  xxxxxxx                   xxxxxxx
```

We measure the distance of each *x* to starting points A and B, classifying each *x* into the group associated with the closer of those two. In Figure B, each point is identified with an *x* or a *y*, depending on whether it is closer to A or B.

Figure B

```
    xxxxx                      xxxxx
  xxxxxxxxx                   xxxxxxxxx
xxxxxxxxxxxxx               xxxxAxxxxyyyy
xxxxxxxxxxxxxxx            xxxxxxxyyyyyyy
xxxxxxxxxxxxx             xxxxyyyyByy
 xxxxxxxxxxx               xxxyyyyyy
  xxxxxxx                   xyyyyyy
```

Notice that only the lower right side of the right-hand swarm in Figure C is closer to B than A. Now we compute the averages, or "centers of gravity" of all the *x* points and all the *y* points. We indicate those by labels A and B in Figure C.

Figure C

```
    xxxxx                      xxxxx
  xxxxxxxxx                   xxxxxxxxy
xxxxxxxxxxxxx               xxxxxxxxxxyyyy
xxxxxxxxxxxxxxxA            xxxxxxyyyyyyyy
 xxxxxxxxxxxxx              xxxxxyyyByy
 xxxxxxxxxxx                xxxyyyyyy
  xxxxxxx                    xyyyyyy
```

In Figure D we have reclassified each point according to whether it is closer to the new A or the B.

Figure D

```
    xxxxx                      yyyyy
  xxxxxxxxx                   xyyyyyyyy
xxxxxxxxxxxxx               xyyyyyyyyyyy
xxxxxxxxxxxxxxxA            xxyyyyyyyyyyyy
xxxxxxxxxxxxx              xyyyyyyyByyy
 xxxxxxxxxxx               yyyyyyyyy
  xxxxxxx                   yyyyyyy
```

Notice that only a few points in the right-hand swarm are still closer to the A than the B. Again, we compute the averages of the points now classified as *x* and those classified as *y*, indicating those positions by A and B in Figure E.

Figure E

```
    xxxxx                      yyyyy
  xxxxxxxxx                   xyyyyyyyy
xxxxxxxxxxxxx               xyyyyyyyyyyy
xxxxxxxxAxxxxx             xxyyyyyyByyyyyy
xxxxxxxxxxxxx              xyyyyyyyyyyy
 xxxxxxxxxxx               yyyyyyyyy
  xxxxxxx                   yyyyyyy
```

Finally, we would classify as *x* all the points closer to A and classify as *y* all points closer to B. Because all points on the left would now be identified as *x* and all on the right identified as *y*, the continuation of this process would result in no further reclassification of points.

This process would have converged even more quickly if our starting points had not been chosen so poorly. For example, if one point had been in the swarm on the left and the other in the swarm on the right, convergence might have been immediate.

Source: Richard M. Johnson, *Convergent Cluster Analysis System* (Ketchum, ID: Sawtooth Software, 1988), pp. 7–8. Printed with permission.

TABLE 17.18	Cluster Analysis: Object-by-Object Raw-Score Cross-Product Matrix

				j:			
	1	*2*	*3*	*4*	*5*	*6*	*7*
i:	*A*	*B*	*C*	*D*	*E*	*F*	*G*
1.	4.252						
2.	−3.434	2.932					
3.	3.371	−3.065	3.413				
4.	4.186	−3.626	3.849	4.500			
5.	0.809	−0.813	0.987	1.044	0.316		
6.	−3.218	2.634	−2.626	−3.221	−0.647	2.443	
7.	3.284	−2.654	2.608	3.236	0.626	−2.487	2.537
8.	−2.083	1.832	−1.976	−2.283	−0.548	1.609	−1.611
9.	−0.626	0.636	−0.777	−0.818	−0.250	0.502	−0.485
10.	−0.848	0.538	−0.355	−0.607	−0.013	0.610	−0.653
11.	0.861	−0.501	0.262	0.546	−0.033	−0.609	0.663
12.	−2.950	2.621	−2.856	−3.274	−0.803	2.285	−2.281
13.	−3.595	2.952	−2.956	−3.615	−0.733	2.732	−2.778
14.	−0.064	0.087	−0.127	−0.117	−0.048	0.056	−0.050
15.	0.056	−0.139	0.247	0.200	0.105	−0.063	0.044

In using factor analysis to cluster objects, we simply attempt to determine which objects (rather than which variables) logically belong together. This "object-by-object" factor analysis is often called *Q analysis* or *inverse factor analysis.*[31]

Consider again the distance matrix contained in Table 17.16. It had been obtained by computing the distances between the observations (here they were cities, but they could have been customers), and summing over the variables (here they were "income" and "population" but they could be "customer satisfaction," "indices of loyalty," "propensity for price sensitivity," "number of children in household," and so on). It has been demonstrated that a distance matrix can be factored and that doing so is equivalent to factoring the "raw-score cross-products."[32] Thus, the starting point for this analysis is the cross-products matrix computed between observations (cities, customers) across objects (variables), as presented in Table 17.18.[33]

---

[31]Variable-by-variable and object-by-object are just two types of factor analysis. See R. B. Cattell, "The Three Basic Factor Analytic Research Designs—Their Interrelationships and Derivatives," *Psychological Bulletin* 49 (1952), pp. 449–520.

[32]Jum C. Nunnally, "The Analysis of Profile Data," *Psychological Bulletin* 59 (1962), 313–319.

[33]The entries in Table 17.18, these so-called raw-score cross-products, were obtained in the following way: Call the data in Table 17.15 the raw scores matrix, $X = (X_{ik})$, where X_{ik} represents the score of the ith city on the kth variable ($i = 1, 2, . . . ,15$ and $k = 1, 2$). From the matrix sums of cross-products $S = (S_{ij})$, where:

$$S_{ij} = \sum_{k=1}^{2} X_{ik} X_{jk}$$

Thus, for $i = 1$ (city A) and $j = 2$ (city B),

$$S_{12} = \sum_{k=1}^{2} X_{1k} X_{2k} = X_{11} X_{21} + X_{12} X_{22} = (1.14)(-1.25) + (1.72)(-1.17) = -3.434$$

The remaining entries in the object-by-object, cross-product matrix reported in Table 17.18 were computed in similar fashion.

TABLE 17.18	(continued)

| | | | | *j:* | | | | |
8 H	9 I	10 J	11 K	12 L	13 M	14 N	15 O
1.163							
0.430	0.199						
0.276	0.005	0.305					
−0.237	0.033	−0.352	0.413				
1.672	0.630	0.367	−0.304	2.407			
1.807	0.570	0.672	−0.668	2.568	3.056		
0.065	0.038	−0.020	0.030	0.098	0.065	0.009	
−0.116	−0.085	0.076	−0.104	−0.180	−0.076	−0.022	0.056

This cross-products matrix can be factored using any of the usual methods. Let us determine what happens when the principal components procedure is used. The sum of the diagonal elements in Table 17.18 yields the total variability in the data, which is 28.0. By again comparing the variance explained by each factor with this total variance, we are in a position to estimate the number of factors that are needed to satisfactorily recover the data. It turns out that two factors are needed to summarize all the variance in the data; and 95 percent of the variance is accounted for by the first factor alone. Thus, it would seem that the objects could be clustered along a single dimension. (This should not be surprising when you recall the conceptual basis of principal components analysis and apply it to the two-dimensional plot of the data contained in Figure 17.9. The first component is simply the major axis of the ellipse generated by this scatter of points extending from the southwest to the northeast quadrant of the graph.)

The resulting factor loadings on this one factor are presented in Table 17.19. There seem to be three levels of magnitude: high positive values, near-zero values, and high negative values. The use of these values would suggest the clusters

- Cluster 1—ACDG
- Cluster 2—EIJKNO
- Cluster 3—BFHLM

These are the clusters that we visually distinguished from the scatter of cities in Figure 17.9. This tidy result is not generally to be expected but occurs simply because the objects were aligned rather nicely along the southwest-northeast diagonal of the figure.

Note that, as in this example, the number of clusters (three) was not determined by the number of factors (one). The pattern of loadings determines both the number of clusters and which objects belong to which cluster.

	TABLE 17.19		Cluster Analysis: Factor Loadings on First Factor		

Object	Loading	Object	Loading
A	2.02	I	−0.36
B	−1.71	J	−0.33
C	1.77	K	0.31
D	2.11	L	−1.52
E	0.46	M	−1.73
F	−1.55	N	−0.05
G	1.56	O	0.07
H	−1.06	L	−6.5

	FIGURE 17.12		Key Decisions When Cluster Analyzing Data

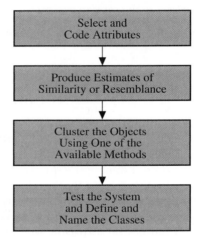

Select and
Code Attributes

↓

Produce Estimates of
Similarity or Resemblance

↓

Cluster the Objects
Using One of the
Available Methods

↓

Test the System
and Define and
Name the Classes

Key Decisions

The discussion so far may suggest that to use cluster analysis, the analyst must make one key decision: which clustering method to use. This is not the case. We had kept the presentation simple to bring the basic objective of cluster analysis into bold relief. It is time to introduce additional complications.

To perform a cluster analysis, it is necessary to make decisions concerning each of the four stages depicted in Figure 17.12. The discussion so far has concentrated on Stage 3 in that process. Let us now look at each of the other stages in turn.

SELECT AND CODE ATTRIBUTES   Stage 1 focuses on the related questions "Which attributes will we use to generate the clusters?" and "How are these attributes to be coded?" The example assumed that income and population were the characteristics of importance in defining similar test cities. These are both ratio-scaled variables, and no additional coding other than standardization was necessary before generating Euclidean distances to assess similarity. However, had we changed the city characteristics used to define similarity, the clusters might well have changed.

The literature does not provide a great deal of guidance with regard to selecting attributes. Yet the choice of variables used to cluster the objects is one of the most critical decisions analysts make. The best advice seems to be to choose those variables that make sense conceptually rather than using any and all variables simply because they are convenient or accessible.

When coding the attributes, it is necessary to keep their basic nature in mind. Some of them may be continuous in nature (for example, income), whereas others may be categorical (such as geography). For example, we could have classified the cities by whether they were located in the southern half of the United States or the northern half.

The basic problem is to select the variables that best represent the concept of similarity for the given study. Ideally, some explicitly stated theory, or say assumptions based on prior brand-account knowledge, would provide the basis for a rational choice of the variables to be used in the study. The importance of using theory to guide the choice of variables should not be underestimated. The temptation to succumb to a naive empiricism in the use of cluster analysis is very strong, since the technique is ostensibly designed to produce "objective" groupings of entities. By "naive empiricism" we mean the collection and subsequent analysis of as many variables as possible in hope that the "structure" will emerge if only enough data are obtained.

Not only is it sometimes difficult to make the choice of attributes, but the weights that are to be given to each attribute when producing estimates of similarity can also prove troublesome. Again, theory should guide the choice. When theory has little to say on the subject, the prevailing sentiment is to consider all the attributes of equal importance and to weight them equally when producing estimates of similarity.

PRODUCE ESTIMATES OF SIMILARITY OR RESEMBLANCE The estimates of similarity that are used to specify the closeness of the objects also depend on the level of measurement used to capture the attributes. There was little question in our example about the measures. Both income and population were ratio scaled, and it was natural to define similarity employing Euclidean distance. Consider now a situation in which the analyst's interest is in grouping people into similar groups, as in a market segmentation study, where a number of variables would be nominally or ordinally scaled (for example, marital status, ethnic background, religious preference, stage in the life cycle). Such variables raise the question of what kind of index of similarity should be used as input to the cluster algorithm. Are they to be binary (0 = absence, 1 = presence of an attribute), or matching coefficients (for example, two customers are more similar if they both subscribe to *Sports Illustrated*), or are the coefficients to reflect categories (for example, someone in the household subscribes to theater, opera, or orchestra series performances), and so on?

Given the input variables, the analyst has several decisions to make to produce the similarity indices. The decisions are in large part dictated by the scale quality of the measures. If the input measures reflect cardinal measurement (that is, whole numbers), the analyst's most basic decision is whether to use a distance function or a correlation coefficient to capture resemblance. Further, if the researcher chooses a distance function, should it be Euclidean distance, as in the example, or should it be city-block distance, or even perhaps Mahalanobis distance?[34] Euclidean distance is clearly the most popular, yet one of the problems with it is that it is not "scale invariant." That is, the relative ordering of the objects in terms of their similarity can be affected by a simple change in the scale by which one or more of the variables are measured. For example, we could measure income in dollars or in thousands of dollars and that can affect the ordering of the similarity coefficients if the data are not first standardized (to mean zero and standard deviation one). In general, we prefer that the similarity coefficients are not sensitive to the units in which we choose to measure variables. While standardization is one way to remove that sensitivity, standardization carries its own costs, because it can reduce the differences between groups on those variables that may very well be the best discriminators of group differences.[35] The standardization issue is far from settled. The best advice is to decide the standardization issue on a case-by-case basis. If the units in which the variables are measured are roughly of the same magnitude, it might be best not to standardize them. If the variables are measured on widely differing units, standardization is needed to prevent the variables measured in larger units from dominating the cluster solution.[36]

What if the data are dichotomous or multichotomous (more than two categories)? Rather than using distance or product-moment correlations to measure resemblance, some kind of matching coefficient is called for. A matching coefficient will represent the number of characteristics on which two objects match in relation to the number of comparisons made. However, this simple notion begs the question of what kind of matches should count: Positive matches? Negative matches? Both kinds?

To illustrate the fundamental dilemma concerning what types of matches to emphasize, consider the hypothetical data for three objects contained in Panel A of Table 17.20. Each object has been measured on 10 attributes; a 1 indicates that the object possesses the attribute and a 0 indicates that it does not. The attributes could represent any number of features of the objects. Suppose, for example, that the attributes indicate which of 10 magazines these three people read, and we wish to calculate the similarity of reading habits for each of the people-pairs AB, AC, and BC. A 1–1 indicates that both people in the pair read the same magazine and represents a positive match; a 0–0 indicates that neither person reads that particular magazine and represents a negative match; a 1–0 means that the first person reads it but the second does not, whereas a 0–1 indicates the opposite, implying a mismatch in reading habits in both cases. Panel B of Table 17.20 summarizes the information contained in Panel A concerning the number of positive matches, negative matches, and mismatches for each of the three possible pairs of the three objects.

---

[34]Morrison suggests that Mahalanobis distance is best, because it allows for correlations among the variables and also provides for explicit rather than implicit variable weighting by the investigator. An example of implicit weighting is when, say, four highly correlated variables are used, among others, to compute the similarity indices, the effect is the same as using only one of those variables with a weight four times greater than the other variables. Donald G. Morrison, "Measurement Problems in Cluster Analysis," *Management Science* 13 (August 1967), pp. 755–780.

[35]For a discussion of the issues involved in standardization, see Everett, *Cluster Analysis*.

[36]Glenn W. Milligan and Martha C. Cooper, "A Study of Standardization of Variables in Cluster Analysis," *Journal of Classification* 4, no. 2 (1988), pp. 181–204.

TABLE 17.20   **Cluster Analysis: Some Alternative Similarity Coefficients**

A. Attributes Possessed by Each Object

					Attributes					
Object	1	2	3	4	5	6	7	8	9	10
A	1	0	0	0	1	0	0	1	1	1
B	0	1	0	0	1	0	0	1	0	0
C	0	0	1	0	0	1	0	1	1	0

B. Summary of the Number of Positive Matches, Negative Matches, and Mismatches

	Object Pairs		
	AB	AC	BC
Number of positive matches (a)	2	2	1
Number of negative matches (b)	4	3	4
Number of mismatches (c)	4	5	5

C. Similarity of the Various Pairs Using Alternative Similarity Coefficients

Coefficient	Object Pair	Value
1. $\dfrac{a}{(a + b + c)}$	AB	.200
	AC	.200
	BC	.100
2. $\dfrac{a}{(a + b)}$	AB	.333
	AC	.400
	BC	.250
3. $\dfrac{a}{(a + c)}$	AB	.333
	AC	.286
	BC	.167
4. $\dfrac{(a + c)}{(a + b + c)}$	AB	.600
	AC	.700
	BC	.600
5. $\dfrac{c}{(a + b)}$	AB	.667
	AC	1.000
	BC	1.000

Panel C of Table 17.20 illustrates the computation of several possible similarity coefficients.[37] Formula C1 expresses similarity as a function of the ratio of {the number of positive matches} versus {the total number of attributes on which the objects were measured}. Formula C2 also emphasizes positive matches, but it is based on the ratio of {the number of positive matches} to {the number of total matches, both positive and negative}. Mismatches do not explicitly count in C2. Formula C3

[37]Many coefficients have been proposed for assessing the similarity of objects. A detailed discussion is found in Sokal and Sneath, *Numerical Taxonomy*. See also H. Clifford and W. Stephenson, *An Introduction to Numerical Taxonomy* (New York: Academic Press, 1975); Lorr, *Cluster Analysis for the Social Sciences*.

compares {the number of positive matches} to {the number of positive matches plus the number of mismatches}; it explicitly deemphasizes negative matches while considering mismatches. Formula C4 also explicitly considers mismatches; it compares {the number of positive matches plus the number of mismatches} to {the total number of comparisons that are made between the objects}. Formula C5 looks at {the number of features on which the objects are different} versus {the number on which they are the same}.

As indicated, the essential difference among the formulas is how they handle the different kinds of matches and the mismatches. A case could be made for any one of them when deciding which people have more similar reading habits. We could argue that it is the magazines that two people both read that determines whether they have similar reading habits and thereby choose a coefficient that emphasizes positive matches. Alternatively, we could argue that it is important to note that neither one reads, say, *Sports Illustrated,* and could thereby choose to emphasize negative matches as well. Or, we could argue that because one of the respondents reads *Sports Illustrated* while the other does not indicates something important about the similarity of their reading habits, and we would therefore want to give some weight to mismatches, though perhaps not as much as to positive or negative matches.

The five sample coefficients reflect these types of considerations. The important thing to note about these coefficients is that they produce different orderings in terms of the similarity of the three objects. Coefficient C1 indicates that object pairs AB and AC are the most similar. Coefficient C2 suggests that object pair AC is more similar than AB, and that, in turn, is more similar than BC. A different ordering of similarity is produced by coefficient C3. Whereas for the first three coefficients, BC is always less similar than either of the other two pairs, that is not the case with coefficients C4 and C5; with C4, BC is tied with AB for being the least similar, and with C5, BC is tied with AC for being the most similar. In sum, with as few as three objects, the ordering of the pairs in terms of their similarity is affected by the emphasis that is given to positive and negative matches and mismatches. The situation is simply exaggerated when more objects are grouped. Further, there is no answer as to which emphasis is inherently correct. It all depends on the objectives of the study.

The most popular of the five coefficients highlighted in Table 17.20 are coefficients C1 and C3. Coefficient C1 is known as the *simple matching coefficient,* whereas C3 is known as *Jaccards' coefficient.* Both emphasize the importance of positive matches.

Another problem can arise when determining similarity indices when the attributes reflect different levels of measurement. If they are all interval- or ratio-scaled variables, the correlation coefficient or a distance measure can be, and typically is, used. If they are all categorical, some sort of matching coefficient can be calculated to describe how similar they are. When the variables are mixed, the situation is more difficult. Should the continuous variables be converted to categorical variables so that a matching coefficient can be calculated, or should they be left as is? If they are left as is, how are the two types of measures to be combined?

One coefficient that is particularly attractive for this purpose is Gower's coefficient of similarity, which is capable of handling binary (such as gender), multicategory (such as religious preference), and quantitative (for example, age) characteristics. The coefficient is calculated by the formula

$$S_{ij} = \frac{\sum_{k=1}^{m} w_k s_{ijk}}{\sum_{k=1}^{m} w_k}$$

where S_{ij} is the overall similarity of objects i and j, s_{ijk} is the similarity of objects i and j on the kth characteristic and there are m characteristics in all. The value s_{ijk} must be greater than or equal to 0 and less than or equal to 1. With qualitative characters, it is 1 when there is a match and 0 with a mismatch. With quantitative characters $s_{ijk} = (|X_{ik} - X_{jk}|/R_k)$, where X_{ik} and X_{jk} are the values of character k for the ith and jth objects, respectively, and R_k is the range of character k in the sample, w_k is the weight attached to the kth character.

Note that the coefficient allows the analyst to specify which of the two types of matches to count with respect to any attribute. The analyst simply sets w_k to 1 if the comparison is to count and 0 if not. Further, the coefficient allows the analyst to weight certain attributes more than others. For example, in Panel A of Table 17.20, say the first five attributes represent readership of business magazines and the last five refer to general-interest magazines such as *Time* and *Newsweek*. And supposing we are trying to cluster executives in terms of their reading of business literature, we might want to weight the positive matches more than the negative ones. The situation can be diagrammed as follows:

Object	1	2	3	4	5	6	7	8	9	10
					Attribute					
A	1	0	0	0	1	0	0	1	1	1
B	0	1	0	0	1	0	0	1	0	0
s_{ijk}	0	0	1	1	1	1	1	1	0	0
w_k	2	2	2	2	2	1	1	1	1	1

This suggests that the overall similarity of executives A and B is

$$S_{AB} = \frac{2(0) + 2(0) + 2(1) + 2(1) + 2(1) + 1(1) + 1(1) + 1(1) + 1(0) + 1(0)}{2 + 2 + 2 + 2 + 2 + 1 + 1 + 1 + 1 + 1}$$

$$= \frac{9}{15}$$

$$= 0.600$$

To illustrate the computation of Gower's coefficient for quantitative characteristics, consider the city data again. For City A, income has a value of 1.14 and population a value of 1.72. For City E, income has a value of 0.55 and population a value of 0.10. The range of population values across all cases is 3.10, and the range for income values is 2.93. The similarity of objects $A(i = 1)$ and $E(j = 5)$ in terms of income $(k = 1)$ would be $s_{151} = (|1.14 - 0.55|/2.93) = 0.201$, whereas in terms of population $(k = 2)$ it would be $s_{152} = (|1.72 - 0.10|/3.10) = 0.526$. Assuming that we wanted to weight income and population equally, the overall similarity of objects A and E would be:

$$S_{AE} = \frac{1(0.201) + 1(0.526)}{1 + 1} = 0.364$$

As these two example illustrate, Gower's coefficient offers the analyst a great deal of flexibility in generating similarity values, which is one of the primary reasons for its popularity.

CLUSTER THE OBJECTS USING ONE OF THE AVAILABLE METHODS   We have already discussed the issue of clustering methods at some length and have only a few comments to add. All the methods are based on heuristics that seem logical at face value, but are backed up by little statistical theory.[38] The empirical evidence available as to which is best is based on the ability of various methods to recover known configurations in computer-simulation studies. It suggests that the factor-based procedures generally work poorly. The hierarchical methods work somewhat better, but tend to have problems when the data contain a high level of error. One problem with them is that what appear to be trivial decisions made early in the clustering tend to have large effects on the final outcome because only one pass is made through the data. The multiple-pass partitioning methods work best, particularly *k*-means. However, this method's performance depends on the use of fairly accurate starting points.[39]

Thus, analysts need to display the proper caution when interpreting cluster analysis output. Equally important, analysts need to recognize that all the methods have the same aim. They should not be thought of as mutually exclusive alternatives but as complementary procedures to get at the same objective. Sometimes they can be productively used in combination. For example, one way of getting the seed points for a *k*-means approach is to use average linkage and the resulting dendrogram to determine both the number of clusters and which objects to use as the starting points for each cluster.

TEST THE SYSTEM AND DEFINE AND NAME THE CLUSTERS   Given the set of derived clusters, the big remaining question concerns what they mean. Do the groups reflect some natural or compelling structures in the data, or do they simply represent

---

[38]For an empirical examination of some of the things that can affect the reliability of a clustering methods, see G. Ray Funkhouser, "A Note on the Reliability of Certain Clustering Algorithms," *Journal of Marketing Research* 20 (February 1983), pp. 99–102. For a summary of some of the main attempts to generate statistical criteria by which the results of a cluster analysis can be assessed, see Dillon and Goldstein, *Multivariate Analysis,* pp. 202–205. For a demonstration of how one can test whether given clusters differ significantly from clusters that are randomly determined, see T. D. Klastorin, "Assessing Cluster Analysis Results," *Journal of Marketing Research* 20 (February 1983), pp. 92–98.

[39]One strategy for minimizing the problem of accurate starting points is to replicate the analysis using different starting points. See, for example, Kristiaan Helsen and Paul E. Green, "A Computational Study of Replicated Clustering with an Application to Market Segmentation," *Decision Sciences* 22 (November/December 1991), pp. 1124–1141. See also Anul Chaturvedi, J. Douglas Carroll, Paul E. Green, and John A. Rotondo, "A Feature-Based Approach to Market Segmentation via Overlapping K-Centroids Clustering," *Journal of Marketing Research* 34 (August 1997), pp. 370–377, which discusses the use of *k*-means when overlapping clusters are allowed.

artifacts of the method? To address this issue, analysts have to examine and test the solution and then name the clusters.

The system test focuses on whether the results offer a reasonable summary of the similarity, correlation, or distance matrix. First, are the individual clusters sufficiently homogeneous? Some measure of average similarity is typically useful in this regard.[40] Second, is the system as a whole consistent with the input similarities? Suppose that one of the linkage methods was used to generate object groupings. A dendrogram would result. Now, for each pair of objects, the *fusion coefficient* (also known as the *cophenetic value,* or the *amalgamation coefficient*), could be read from the dendrogram. If the dendrogram represented perfectly all the information in the similarity matrix, the fusion value for each pair of objects would exactly equal the input similarity value. They will not be equal in practice, of course, because the union of any two objects is affected by their links with the other objects. Consider again, as an example, the application of the single linkage method to the city data. A comparison of the actual distances between objects F, M, and H as read from the distance matrix in Table 17.16 and the distances where the objects joined as read from the dendrogram indicates the following differences:

Object Pair	Actual Distance	Distance When Joined
FM	0.184	0.184
FH	0.624	0.479
MH	0.776	0.479

A similar comparison could be made for each of the other 225 pairs of objects, and then some measure of goodness of fit (for example, a correlation) between the actual values with the obtained values could be calculated.[41]

Both of these approaches for testing cluster solutions are commonly found in the literature, but methodologists working in the area usually recommend a cross-validation test of the reliability of the cluster solution across data sets. This typically involves splitting the data into at least two subsets and assessing whether the same clusters are produced when the different portions of the data set are analyzed.

Another alternative that is used less often but has much to recommend it is to perform significance tests comparing the clusters on variables that were not used to generate the cluster solution. For example, we could compare our 15 cities in terms of the average age of the population. Those cities in the same cluster should be similar, or approximately equal in terms of average age, whereas those cities in different clusters should be different.

If the resulting clusters are acceptable, the analyst must then describe and name them. The researcher's description will typically center on those variables that determine membership in a given class rather than membership in other classes. The example produced: (1) a large-size, high-income cluster, (2) a medium-size,

---

[40]Milligan compared the performance of 30 measures that have been proposed for assessing the internal consistency of clusters. See Glenn W. Milligan, "A Monte Carlo Study of Thirty Internal Measures for Cluster Analysis," *Psychometrika* 46 (1981), pp. 187–199. Also see James N. Breckenridge, "Validating Cluster Analysis," *Multivariate Behavioral Research* 35, no. 2 (2000), pp. 261–284.

[41]Aldenderfer and Blashfield, *Cluster Analysis,* p. 65. See pages 62–74 of this book for an excellent discussion of the various alternatives that are used to test the quality of a cluster solution.

More Applications of Cluster Analysis

1. Managers of Real Estate Investment Trusts and other investors are increasingly comparing their property returns against the benchmark measure of revenue per available room (revpar) because this index combines changes in occupancy and average daily rates (that is, revpar = [avg. daily rate] × [no. occupied rooms] / [total no. available rooms]).

In a recent study, nearly 60 metropolitan areas in the U.S. were cluster analyzed on the basis of their revpar scores. The clusters were interpreted as a function both of these scores (for example, large or small scores, fast or slow growth determined as change from last year, and so on), as well as other known qualities of the cities in each cluster.

Cluster 1 consisted of large, mature business centers primarily on the east or west coasts, mostly served by major airport hubs (for example, Boston; Charlotte, NC; Chicago; Newark; Philadelphia; Los Angeles; San Francisco). Cluster 2 consisted of smaller markets that were growing faster, many of which depended on port (ship or plane) and international trade (for example, Greensboro, NC; Indianapolis; Miami; Norfolk, VA; Oakland, CA.; Sacramento, CA; St. Louis; Washington, D.C.). Cluster 3 contained several top tourist destinations whose growth can be weak in the presence of global (such as U.S. or recent Asian and Latin American) financial crises (for example, New York; Las Vegas; Orlando, West Palm, and Fort Lauderdale, FL; Honolulu). Cluster 4 was comprised of several fast-growing markets that are emerging as important high-tech and information-technology business centers (for example, Atlanta; Austin, TX; Dallas, Raleigh, NC; Phoenix; San Diego).

2. A booming application area for cluster analysis is the problem of "recommendation agents" on the Internet. When you visit Amazon.com (among

many other providers), a list of books or other products are suggested to you. These recommendations are a function of cluster analyses.

Internet providers store huge matrices (hundreds of thousands of customers as rows and their inventory of SKUs as columns). When consumer j purchases book k, the jth, kth element in the matrix becomes a "1" rather than the previous "0." Two consumers are indexed as similar if they have purchased a number of books in common. Once a consumer has been identified as similar to a segment of other customers, the segment's portfolio of purchase histories become sources of recommendations (for example, "Purchasers of this book also tended to buy these books. . . .").

3. MasterCard International and Symmetrical Resources are hooking up to cluster consumers. They have plans to sample from a panel of more than 650,000 consumers whose buying habits have been recorded in more than 30 categories, including department store shopping, apparel retail, catalogers, and travel. Cluster analysis will allow for the identification of gross clusters (for example, 25- to 35-year-old women who shop at upscale department stores) and finer gradations within (such as who also read fashion magazines and listen to top-40 radio stations on their commutes to work).

Sources: Mark Gallagher and Asieh Mansour, "An Analysis of Hotel Real Estate Market Dynamics," *Journal of Real Estate Research* 19 (January 2000), pp. 133–164; Dawn Iacobucci, Phipps Arabie, and Anand Bodapati, "Recommendation Agents on the Internet," *Journal of Interactive Marketing* 14 (2000), pp. 2–11; Jennifer Lach, "In the (Credit) Cards," *American Demographics* 21 (April 1999), p. 43. Also see Steven H. Cohen and Venkatram Ramawamy, "Latent Segmentation Models," *Marketing Research* 10 (Summer 1998), pp. 15–21.

middle-income cluster, and (3) a small-size, low-income cluster of cities. In most cases, the names may not be so obvious, but this task is often a fun, creative one for marketers (recall the labels in Research Realities 17.4, for example, "Pools and Patios," "Young Suburbia," "New Homesteaders," and so on).

Marketing Applications

The example of forming homogeneous groups of cities that we used to demonstrate the purpose and logic of cluster analysis reflects a pervasive marketing problem. The problem of determining clusters of similar objects is a real one in accurately assessing the impact of marketing manipulations. For many kinds of experimental manipulations, we must be sure that the groups of objects being manipulated were equal at some prior time. Thus, when market-testing products, advertisements, or packages, it is important that the test cities used be similar so that the results cannot be attributed to idiosyncratic differences in the cities.

The number of applications of cluster analysis in marketing continues to increase.[42] For example, it has been used to sort householders' demand patterns for electricity, to group customers according to the product benefits they seek or according to their lifestyle, to group TV programs into similar types on the basis of viewers' reports, to group other kinds of media in terms of the similarity of audiences to which they appeal, to develop homogeneous configurations of census tracts, to construct market segments, to group personality profiles, to group brands and products on the basis of how similar to competitors' products they are perceived to be and also how they serve as substitutes in use, to determine spheres of opinion leadership, and to assess the similarity of world markets. For more examples, see Research Realities 17.6. The question of "When do I use cluster analysis?" is easily answered: Cluster analysis is an extremely useful statistical tool to help the marketing researcher identify groups of similar things; for example, brands, products, and, most frequently, people in segmentation studies.

Multidimensional Scaling and Perceptual Mapping

If factor analysis has mostly been used to help refine the questions on a survey, and cluster analysis has been mostly used to segment the consumers who respond to the survey, multidimensional scaling has been used primarily to capture consumers' perceptions of brands through the creation of *perceptual maps*. **Multidimensional scaling (MDS)** is a technique to measure and represent people's perceptions about various objects—products, brands, stores, or other elements. In its constant quest for a differential advantage, the firm must correctly position its products against competitive offerings. To do this, managers need to identify the following:

1. The number of dimensions consumers use to distinguish products and the competition

2. The names of these dimensions

---

[42]For reviews of the applications of cluster analysis in marketing, see Girish Punj and David W. Stewart, "Cluster Analysis in Marketing Research," *Journal of Marketing Research* 20 (May 1983), pp. 134–148; Arabie and Hubert, "Cluster Analysis in Marketing Research."

RESEARCH REALITIES 17.7

Positioning of Selected Toy Departments and Stores

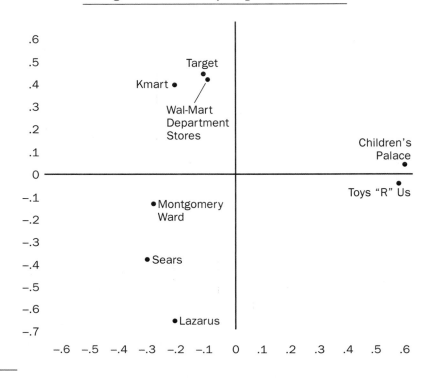

Sources: Arthur J. Adams and Stuart Van Auken, "Observations: A New Approach to Measuring Product Category Membership," *Journal of Advertising Research* 35 (September/October 1995), pp. 73–79.

3. The positioning of existing products along these dimensions
4. The location where consumers prefer a product to be on the dimensions[43]

One way in which managers can grasp the positioning of their brand versus competing brands is through the study of perceptual maps. In a perceptual map, each product or brand occupies a specific point on the map. Brands that are similar lie close together, and those that are different lie far apart. Perceptual maps provide managers with meaningful pictures of how their brands compare to other products and brands. Research Realities 17.7, for example, depicts the situation among toy stores and toy departments. Perceptual maps can be created in several ways. As

[43]Glen L. Urban and John R. Hauser, *Design and Marketing of New Products*, 2nd ed. (Englewood Cliffs, NJ: Prentice-Hall, 1993). For discussion of the usefulness of various techniques for answering these questions, see Michael D. Johnson and Elania J. Hudson, "On the Perceived Usefulness of Scaling Techniques in Market Analysis," *Psychology & Marketing* 13 (October 1996), pp. 653–675.

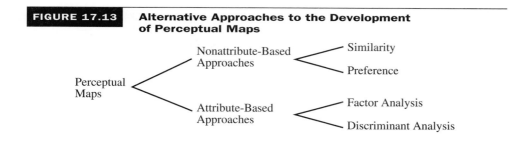

FIGURE 17.13   Alternative Approaches to the Development of Perceptual Maps

Figure 17.13 indicates, they can be created using nonattribute-based or attribute-based approaches. We begin with the nonattribute-based approach.

Survey items that ask a consumer to rate some object (such as brand or product) on several attributes are extremely common. The "nonattribute-based" approach to MDS requires different data. Customers are asked to make judgments about the similarities among objects (for example, brands). When making these similarity judgments, people are free to use the characteristics that matter most to them. The analyst attempts to locate the objects in a multidimensional space in which the number of dimensions corresponds to the number of characteristics the individual used in forming the judgments.[44]

Example

MDS might be most easily illustrated by example. Imagine that we wish to develop a multidimensional map to characterize the perceived relationships among a set of cameras. Label the brands or camera models A, B, C, D, E, F, G, H, I, and J. In designing a multidimensional scaling, it is worth considering the range of perceived similarity of the objects of study. For example, are certain models seen to be alike while others are viewed as being very dissimilar? Are they all alike? All dissimilar? Just how close are they perceived to be in psychological space? The notion of psychological proximity plays a central role in the technique of multidimensional scaling, and the technique is sometimes referred to as the *analysis of proximities data.*[45]

Suppose that we were to ask a single respondent for perceptions of the similarities among the 10 cameras by asking for his or her judgments about all possible pairs of cameras. For instance, we might form all possible pairs of the 10 cameras—45 pairs in all. We could then place a picture or a description of each pair of cameras on a separate card and ask the individual to rank the cards by increasing dissimilarity of the camera pairs using whatever criteria he or she normally uses to distinguish cameras. Initially the individual could be instructed to sort the cards into four piles, for example, with the piles labeled extremely similar, somewhat similar, somewhat dissimilar, and extremely dissimilar. After placing each of the 45 cards in one of the piles, the

[44]MDS techniques vary on whether they require interval- or ratio-scaled data ("metric" MDS) or allow rank-level data ("nonmetric" MDS).

[45]Psychological proximity may be defined on the basis of the psychological distance between the perceptions of two objects or between a person's preference and perception of an object, resulting in the scaling of similarities and preferences, respectively.

| TABLE 17.21 | | | | MDS: Respondent Similarity Judgments | | | | | |

| | | | | | Camera | | | | | |
Camera	A	B	C	D	E	F	G	H	I	J
A										
B	28									
C	5	29								
D	24	21	17							
E	32	1	26	18						
F	37	3	34	25	4					
G	31	36	22	7	35	41				
H	27	43	20	13	42	45	9			
I	16	40	23	12	39	44	10	6		
J	7	30	2	15	33	38	19	14	11	

individual would then be asked to order those within each pile from most similar to least similar. Suppose Table 17.21 resulted from this process. The table indicates that the respondent perceived Cameras B and E as the most similar, Cameras C and J as the next most similar, and Cameras F and H as the least similar.

Given the ranking contained in the table, at least three questions of concern arise: (1) How many dimensions underlie this respondent's judgments about the similarity-dissimilarity of the 10 cameras? (2) What does the configuration—the map—look like? That is, which cameras are perceived as most similar and which are perceived as most dissimilar when they are all considered simultaneously? (3) What attributes is the individual using in making his or her judgments?

Multidimensional scaling can be used to generate answers to the first two questions. The identification of the attributes underlying the judgments (the third question) requires the collection of additional information or an intuitive assessment on the part of someone connected with the research, as we shall describe.[46]

Conceptual Operation of Computer Programs

Many computer programs can perform a multidimensional scaling analysis, although most owe their existence to the early work done by Shepard.[47] Fundamentally, the programs operate by finding the "best" fit in several dimensions, where quality of fit is determined by how well the distance between the points matches the input judgments. Thus, if the distances between the points in a two-dimensional configuration, say, when ordered for smallest to largest perfectly matched the order of the

---

[46]Nonmetric MDS take ordinal input data and, using monotonic regressions, indicate the dimensionality and shape of the configuration (that is, the map) needed to reflect the perceived proximities among the objects. Metric models of MDS take rating scale data as input (that is, assumed to be interval-level) and relate the model-derived distances to the input dissimilarity judgments through a more restrictive, linear relationship.

[47]Roger N. Shepard, "The Analysis of Proximities: Multidimensional Scaling with an Unknown Distance Function, I," *Psychometrika* 27 (June 1962), pp. 125–140, and "The Analysis of Proximities: Multidimensional Scaling with an Unknown Distance Function, II," *Psychometrika* 27 (September 1962), pp. 219–246.

input judgments of similarity, the fit would be perfect. To the extent the ordering of the distances is inconsistent with the judged similarities, the fit is imperfect.

The computer programs operate by starting with an arbitrary configuration in each of several dimensions (1-D, 2-D, 3-D, and so on). Given the arbitrary configuration, they move the points or objects around in systematic fashion using a series of iterations to improve the fit until that is no longer possible, at which time they stop. In essence, they determine the best fit for each dimensionality and report how good or bad the fit is.

The number of dimensions that are appropriate for one's data and that should be interpreted and communicated is determined by looking at the quality of fit in each dimension, recognizing that it is easier to get a better fit in more dimensions because there is more latitude in how the points can be moved.[48] The basic aim is to find the lowest dimensionality in which the fit is good, that is, where the ordered distances between the objects "closely match" the similarity judgments.

Example Solution

Figure 17.14 displays the computer-determined two-space solution for the rank-order data of Table 17.21. As the figure shows, the cameras are seen to be relatively heterogeneous, although Cameras B, E, and F appear similar to the respondent, and Cameras A, C, and J seem to form another cluster. One can immediately see how a picture like this could help a firm or product manager quickly identify the company's or product's major competitors, as well as how the picture could be used to formulate a repositioning strategy.

Why two dimensions? As mentioned, the basic objective in MDS is to find the lowest dimensional space solution in which there is good correspondence between the input judgments and the distances between the objects. As suggested, the lower space solutions will rarely provide a perfect fit. Rather, it is to be expected that some differences will always exist between the rank orders of the plotted distances and the rank orders of the judged similarities. Thus, one can compute a measure of the lack of fit for each dimension. The lower the lack-of-fit index, the better the computer configuration matches the original configuration.

Different MDS programs report different lack-of-fit indices.[49] The particular configuration displayed in Figure 17.14 was developed using Kruskal's "stress" for its lack-of-fit index.[50] Figure 17.15 displays the plot of the stress value as a function of the number of dimensions employed to represent the solution. The fit in 1-D is fair-to-poor using Kruskal's evaluations.[51]

---

[48]When the number of objects or stimuli is small (fewer than seven or eight), it is relatively easy to get a "good fit" in three dimensions or fewer. However, when the number of objects being compared gets beyond 10, one will not get a "good fit" in a few dimensions unless the model has validity.

[49]Multidimensional scaling programs are discussed and compared in A. P. M. Coxon, *The User's Guide to Multidimensional Scaling* (London: Heinemann Educational Books, 1982). Also see Ingwer Borg and Patrick Groenen, *Modern Multidimensional Scaling* (New York: Springer, 1997).

[50]Kruskal's stress is the most commonly used measure for lack of fit. See J. B. Kruskal, "Multidimensional Scaling by Optimizing Goodness of Fit to a Nonmetric Hypothesis," *Psychometrika* 29 (March 1964), pp. 1–27.

[51]Kruskal 1964, p. 3. These descriptions of what is "good" stress depend on the use of Formula 1 to calculate stress.

FIGURE 17.14   **Multidimensional Scaling Map of Similarity Judgments for Table 17.21**

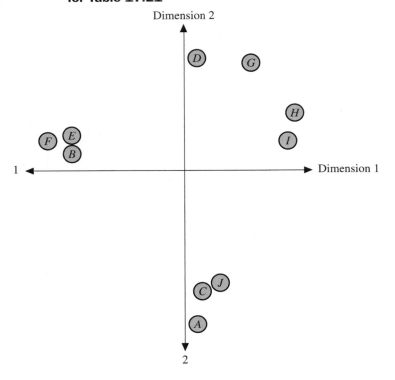

FIGURE 17.15   **Stress Index for Camera Similarity Judgments**

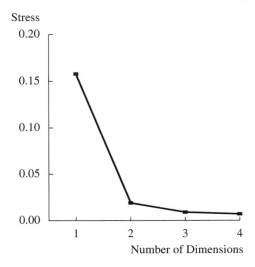

Stress	Goodness of Fit
20.0%	Poor
10.0%	Fair
5.0%	Good
2.5%	Excellent
0.0%	Perfect

The fit in 2-D appears adequate enough, though, to conclude that the two-space solution is appropriate. The stress value of 0.019 is excellent, and there is an elbow in the stress function. The elbow indicates that goodness of fit substantially improves with an increase in the number of dimensions from one to two, but only improves slightly as the number of dimensions is increased to three or even to four. The two-space solution seems most consistent with the objective of minimum dimensionality, because it reproduces the original rankings just as efficiently as do the three- and four-space solutions.[52]

Accepting the two-space solution as adequately capturing the individual's similarity judgments is one thing; naming the dimensions that serve as a basis for these judgments is quite another, and this output is not provided by the computer program. Rather, the names of the dimensions are supplied by someone associated with the research effort.[53]

Several approaches can be used. First, the individual can be asked to evaluate the objects (that is, the cameras) in terms of several defined attributes, such as automatic flash, automatic focus, brand name, price, and so on. The researcher then correlates the attribute scale scores for each object with the coordinates for each object in the plot. In this scheme, the size of the respective correlation coefficients between attributes and dimensions is used to attach labels. Another approach is to have the manager or researcher interpret the dimensions using his or her own experience and the visual configuration of points. Still a third approach is to attempt to relate the dimensions to physical characteristics of the cameras, such as physical size or price.

Suppose that the dimensions were named using one of these schemes, and that dimension 1 turned out to be a "good value" dimension while dimension 2 turned out to be an "easy to use" dimension. Suppose also that you are the manager for Brand J. The perceptual map in Figure 17.14 indicates that your brand is perceived as being difficult to use and only an average value by our single respondent. If a

---

[52]This stress plot should remind you of the "scree plot" in factor analysis (or the fusion coefficient plot in cluster analysis). These plots are used to help the analyst determine the number of factors or dimensions to retain in the model. In both cases, the diagnostic sought is the "break" or "elbow" in the curve. The difference is that in factor analysis, a "variance explained" (or "goodness" of fit) index is being plotted, hence the number of factors to retain is the number that precede the break (1 in this case, if it were a plot of latent roots), because the next, small number indicates that little is added with the additional factor. For MDS, "stress" (that is, a "badness" of fit index) is plotted, so the number of dimension to keep is the number that follow the break (2 in Figure 17.15), because the addition of that dimension is what reduces the badness of fit to something reasonable.

[53]Once again, the analogy to naming factors in factor analysis should be clear. In factor analysis, we examine the variables that load (correlate) high on a factor to infer what that factor is capturing. In MDS, we will compare the brands at the left-most and right-most of the map (and then, top versus bottom, and so on) to try to determine what they have in common and how they differ, in order to deduce a sensible name for the dimension.

large enough number of respondents felt this way, and you are suffering market share problems, it might behoove you to examine how value, and especially ease-of-use, can be increased.

Even though the example demonstrates only the placement of stimuli (that is, cameras), it also is possible to locate preferences in the same geometric space. For example, the individual's "ideal" camera is a hypothetical camera possessing just the perfect combination of the two attributes, ease of use and value. The individual's ideal point is located from the preference data that he or she supplies. Once again, the objective is to locate the ideal so that the distance between the customer's ideal and each of the objects corresponds as closely as possible to the stated preferences for the objects.

Key Decisions

The example provides some appreciation for the conceptual underpinnings of MDS analysis, but once again, an analyst must make a number of decisions (see Figure 17.16). The first decision is to specify the set of products or brands that will be considered. Although they will be partly determined by the purpose of the study, they will not be completely specified by it, and analysts will have some discretion in choosing products or brands to use. When exercising this discretion, analysts need to recognize that the dimensions that appear in the perceptual map will be a direct function of the stimulus set that was used to collect the judgments.[54] For example, suppose that a study was being conducted to determine respondents' perceptions of various soft drinks. If no unsweetened or low-calorie soft drinks were included in the stimulus set, this very important dimension would not appear in the results. To avoid such a risk, analysts may be tempted to include every conceivable product or brand in the stimulus set. This strategy, though, can place such a burden on respondents that their answers may be meaningless.

The burden on respondents is going to depend partly on the number of judgments each has to make and partly on the difficulty of each judgment. Both of these issues, in turn, depend on how the similarity judgments are to be obtained.[55] Under each alternative are two main alternatives and a number of options. The two major options are "direct" or "indirect" similarity judgments, two terms that are relatively self-explanatory. The direct methods rely on data-collection mechanisms in which respondents compare stimuli using whatever criteria they desire and, on the basis of that comparison, state which of the stimuli are most similar, least similar, and so on (as we have been discussing). All possible pairs of the brands being evaluated could be evaluated, ranked from most to least similar. Alternatively, a brand could be

---

[54]Naresh K. Malhotra, "Validity and Structural Reliability of Multidimensional Scaling," *Journal of Marketing Research* 24 (May 1987), pp. 164–173. See also Jan-Benedict E. M. Steenkamp and Hans C. M. van Trijp, "Task Experience and Validity in Perceptual Mapping: A Comparison of Two Consumer-Adaptive Techniques," *International Journal of Research in Marketing* 13 (July 1996), pp. 265–276.

[55]For discussion of some of the main ways by which similarity judgments can be collected, see Mark L. Davison, *Multidimensional Scaling* (New York: Wiley, 1983); S. S. Schiffman, M. L. Reynolds, and F. W. Young, *Introduction to Multidimensional Scaling* (New York: Academic Press, 1981). For an empirical comparison of the impact of the method on respondents, see Tammo H. A. Bijmolt and Michel Wedel, "The Effects of Alternative Methods of Collecting Similarity Data for Multidimensional Scaling," *International Journal of Research in Marketing* 12 (November 1995), pp. 363–371.

FIGURE 17.16   **Key Decisions When Conducting a Multidimensional Scaling Analysis**

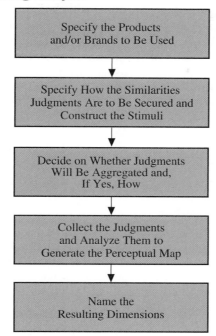

singled out as a focal brand, and respondents could be asked to rank-order each of the other brands in terms of their similarity to the focal brand. Each brand would then serve as the focal brand in turn. There are a number of alternative ways of collecting these judgments, but they all have one thing in common: The respondents are asked to judge directly how similar the various alternatives are using criteria that they choose. (The indirect methods operate differently—these are the "attribute-based" approaches that we will describe in the section that follows.)

The third decision analysts have to make is whether the judgments of individual respondents will be aggregated so that group perceptual maps can be developed or whether individual maps will be generated. The problem with individual maps is that they would be numerous, even for a modest sample size (for example, 100 MDS maps, one for each sample member), so it becomes very difficult for the marketing manager to use to develop marketing strategy. Managers typically look at marketing planning questions in terms of segments, not individuals. Yet, as soon as the segment issue is raised, the question becomes one of deciding how the individual judgments will be aggregated. Is it likely that individuals used the same number of criteria when evaluating the various brands? Even if they used the same number, are the criteria themselves likely to be the same? If they are not, what criteria should be used to group respondents? One popular algorithm, **INDSCAL** (for *INDividual differences SCALing*), assumes that everyone uses the same criteria to judge the similarity of objects, but that they weight the dimensions differently when forming their judgments.[56] So, in the cameras example, "value" would be "weighted more" for some people, and "ease of use" would be more important to others.

Step 4 in Figure 17.16 involves the actual collection of the judgments and their processing. The processing involves two steps: First, an initial configuration must be determined for each of the dimensions. Different programs use different routines to generate an initial solution. Second, the points must be moved around until the fit is the best it can be in that dimensionality, using the criterion under which the program operates. The output of this analysis is the stress index, or measures of fit alluded to earlier, which analysts use to decide on the most appropriate number of dimensions.

The last decision analysts have to make when conducting an MDS involves labeling the dimensions. As suggested before, several procedures are used to help name the dimensions. The practical fact, though, is that difficulty in naming the dimensions (or the somewhat subjective nature of doing so) is one of management's major concerns with MDS.

Attribute-Based Approaches

The attribute-based approaches obtain "indirect" measures of customers' perceptions of similarities between objects. Instead of asking for a direct rating of similarity, for which respondents select their own criteria to compare the alternatives, they are asked to make the more standard rating of evaluating each brand on a number of attributes (or they could be asked to check which brands possess each of a given list of attributes). The attributes rating scales (for example, semantic differential or Likert scales) are chosen by the research team putting together the survey, prespecifying the features or criteria for the respondents. For example, rather than asking, "How similar are cameras A and B?" we would ask, for example, "How easy to use is camera A?" "How easy to use is camera B?" "How good is the value of camera A?" and "How good is the value of camera B?".

A measure of similarity is then calculated for each pair of brands (that is, usually the correlation between the ratings of the brands). These derived similarity indices are subsequently analyzed using typically either factor or discriminant analysis to identify the key dimensions that consumers use to distinguish the objects.

One advantage of the attribute-based approaches to the development of perceptual maps is that they do make the naming of dimensions easier. They also seem to be easier for respondents to use.[57]

---

[56]For an overview of some marketing studies that have used various algorithms, see Tammo H. A. Bijmolt and Michel Wedel, "A Comparison of Multidimensional Scaling Methods for Perceptual Mapping," *Journal of Marketing Research* 36 (May 1999), pp. 277–285. For a review of algorithms generally available on microcomputers, including INDSCAL, see Paul E. Green, Frank J. Carmone, Jr., and Scott M. Smith, *Multidimensional Scaling: Concepts and Applications* (Boston: Allyn and Bacon, 1989) and Phipps Arabie, Douglas Carroll, and Wayne S. DeSarbo, *Three-Way Scaling and Clustering* (Newbury Park, CA: Sage, 1987).

[57]For general discussions on the use of attribute-based approaches for developing perceptual maps, see John R. Hauser and Frank S. Koppelman, "Alternative Perceptual Mapping Techniques: Relative Accuracy and Usefulness," *Journal of Marketing Research* 16 (November 1979), pp. 495–506; Joel Huber and Morris B. Holbrook, "Using Attribute Ratings for Product Positioning: Some Distinctions among Compositional Approaches," *Journal of Marketing Research* 16 (November 1979), pp. 507–516; William R. Dillon, Donald G. Frederick, and Vanchai Tangpanichdee, "Decision Issues in Building Perceptual Product Spaces with Multiattribute Rating Data," *Journal of Consumer Research* 12 (June 1985), pp. 47–63.

The emphasis in discriminant analysis is on determining the combinations of attributes that best discriminate between the objects or brands. The dependent measures are the products rated, and the predictor variables are the attribute ratings. The analysis is typically run across groups of respondents to find a common structure. The dimensions are named by examining the weights of the attributes that make up a discriminant dimension or by computing the correlations between the attributes and each of the discriminant scores.

Factor analysis relies on the assumption that there are only a few basic dimensions that underlie the attribute ratings. It examines the correlations among the attributes to identify these basic dimensions. The correlations are typically computed across brands and groups of consumers. The dimensions usually are named by examining the factor loadings, which represent the correlations between each attribute and each factor.

Comparison of Approaches

The advantages of the attribute-based versus the nonattribute-based approaches to multidimensional scaling analysis are summarized in Table 17.22. Most of the nonattribute-based applications in marketing use similarity judgments. Similarity measurement has the advantage of not depending on a predefined attribute set. This is a two-edged sword. Although it allows respondents to use only those dimensions

TABLE 17.22   MDS: Comparison of the Nonattribute- and Attribute-Based Approaches for Developing Perceptual Maps

Technique	Respondent Measures	Advantages	Disadvantages
Non-attribute-based similarity judgments	Judged similarity of various products or brands	+ Does not depend on a predefined attribute set + Allows respondents to use their normal criteria when judging objects + Allows for condition that perception of the whole may not be simply the sum of the perceptions of the parts	− Difficult to name dimensions − Difficult to determine if, and how, the judgments of individual respondents should be combined − Criteria that respondents use depend on the stimuli being compared − Requires special programs − Provides oversimplified view of perceptions when few objects are used
Attribute-based discriminant or factor analysis	Ratings on various products or brands on pre-specified attributes	+ Facilitates naming the dimensions + Easier to cluster respondents into groups with similar perceptions + Easy to use + Computer programs more readily available	− Requires a relatively complete set of attributes − Rests on assumption that overall perception of a stimulus is made of the individuals' reactions to the attributes being rated

that they normally use in making judgments among objects, it creates difficulties in naming the dimensions. Further, different consumers can use different dimensions, and one then has to grapple with how best to combine consumers when forming maps. Constructing a separate map for each individual is prohibitively costly. Aggregating all the responses and then developing one map distorts reality because it implies a homogeneity in perceptions that probably does not exist. The middle ground of grouping consumers into segments raises the whole issue of how the aggregation should be effected. Even individual consumers have been known to vary the criteria they are using when making a series of judgments, indicating that the criteria depend on the products or brands in the immediate stimulus set. The fact that the criteria can change as a series of similarity judgments are made makes an already difficult problem of naming the dimensions even harder. One has to be especially careful when using the similarity-based programs if the number of objects being judged is less than eight, as it is then very easy to secure an oversimplified picture of the competitive environment.

As previously mentioned, the attribute-based approaches facilitate naming the dimensions, and they also make it easier to cluster respondents into groups with similar perceptions. These methods presume, however, that the list of attributes used to secure the ratings are relatively accurate and complete. They contain the implicit assumption that a person's perception or evaluation of a stimulus is some combination of the individual's reactions to the attributes being rated. Yet, people may not perceive or evaluate objects in terms of underlying attributes, but as a whole that is not decomposable in terms of separate attributes. Or, the analyst may simply overlook the inclusion of an attribute that the customer considers important.

Regardless of the approach taken, the appeal of multidimensional scaling analysis lies in the maps produced by the technique. MDS is well-suited for strategic competitive analysis, product life-cycle analysis, market segmentation, vendor evaluation, the evaluation of advertisements, test marketing, sales representative and store image research, brand-switching research, and attitude scaling. For more examples of the use of MDS, see Research Realities 17.8. The answer to the question, "When do I use multidimensional scaling?" is basically: Whenever you wish to obtain a map of customer perceptions and preferences. These maps can be used to provide insight into some very basic questions about markets, including the following:[58]

1.   The salient product attributes perceived by buyers in the market
2.   The combination of attributes buyers most prefer

---

[58]For more information on MDS, see J. Douglas Carroll and Paul E. Green, "Psychometric Methods in Marketing Research: Part II, Multidimensional Scaling," *Journal of Marketing Research* 34 (May 1997), pp. 193–204; Wayne S. DeSarbo, Martin R. Young, and Arvind Rangaswamy, "A Parametric Multidimensional Unfolding Procedure for Incomplete Nonmetric Preference/Choice Set Data in Marketing Research," *Journal of Marketing Research* 34 (November 1997), pp. 499–516; Indrajit Sinha and Wayne S. DeSarbo, "An Integrated Approach Toward the Spatial Modeling of Perceived Customer Value," *Journal of Marketing Research* 35 (May 1998), pp. 236–249.

RESEARCH REALITIES 17.8

More Applications of Multidimensional Scaling

1. Destination image is an important element in attracting international travelers. In a recent study, U.S. and Taiwanese segments provided ratings of their perceptions of Canada. The participants compared nine photos depicting scenes such as a mountain lake with a canoe; a whitewater river scene, a sunset over a lake, a hotel with a golf course, hay bales on a field, mountains and wildflowers, restaurants, and campers.

   Respondents judged the pair-wise similarities among these nine photos, and then rated each photo on a number of attributes (for example, attractive-unattractive, simple-complex, smooth-rough, man-made-natural, exciting-peaceful, and so on). MDS was used to obtain a perceptual map for the U.S. participants and another for the Taiwan sample. The attribute ratings were used to help interpret the dimensions in the two perceptual maps.

   Both the Taiwan and U.S. maps yielded the dimensions of: 1) The presence or absence of water. This dimension was further interpreted as being symbolic of relaxation, solitude, and spirituality. 2) Scenes that were smooth and man-made (for example, hotel) compared to those that were natural. This dimension was subsequently labeled a "comfort" factor. In addition, the Taiwan map yielded a third dimension: 3) The presence or absence of mountains and rough terrain, which was labeled a "wilderness" dimension.

2. Selecting television programs that are likely to reach one's target audience so as to spend one's advertising budget effectively is a fundamental question in media planning. A recent study compared the Nielsen's National TV Index for each of 91 TV shows (essentially all prime-time programs, and selected daytime and late-night shows) in each of 10 viewer segments as determined by automobile ownership (for example, compact cars, luxury cars, SUVs, and compact trucks) among 14,488 consumers.

   Two TV shows were computed to be highly similar if a great deal of overlap occurred in an audience member watching both shows. Cluster analysis was then superimposed on the MDS map to find groups of programs and segments of automobile owners.

   Researchers found automobile owners to be more heterogeneous than they had anticipated. For example, two top TV shows popular among compact car owners were "The Practice" and "Party of Five," but these TV shows belonged in different program clusters. Compact car ownership is also popular among enthusiasts of "Drew Carey," and people who watch "Drew Carey" also tend to watch "Dateline NBC Friday," but "Dateline" viewers do not tend to own compact cars. Clearly car ownership is only one characteristic of a TV viewer; people who share that characteristic may differ on many others.

   Sources: Kelly J. MacKay and Daniel R. Fesenmaier, "An Exploration of Cross-Cultural Destination Image Assessment," *Journal of Travel Research* 38 (May 2000), pp. 417–423; Henry Assael and David F. Poltrack, "Relating Products to TV Program Clusters," *Journal of Advertising Research* 39 (March/April 1999), pp. 41–52.

---

3. The products that are viewed as substitutes and those that are differentiated from one another

4. The viable segments that exist in a market

5. Those "holes" in a market that can support a new-product venture

Summary

Four analysis techniques that are useful in the solution of marketing research problems were reviewed in this chapter. The techniques are all multivariate in that they involve the analysis of multiple (p) measures. Discriminant analysis treats the p measures in a dependency relationship (some variables are used to predict another), whereas factor analysis, cluster analysis, and multidimensional scaling involve the examination of interdependencies among the variables.[59]

Discriminant analysis shows the relationship between a dichotomous or multichotomous criterion variable and a set of p predictor variables. The emphasis is on determining the variables that are most important in discriminating among the objects falling into the various classes of the criterion variable. With a number of predictor variables and a multichotomous criterion variable, several discriminant functions may be derived. Not all these functions will necessarily be statistically significant, however. The discriminant function or functions can also be used to predict the classification of new objects.

Factor analysis examines the interdependence among all p variables. The emphasis is on isolating the factors that are common to the interrelated manifest variables to summarize the important information in the data and assist in interpreting it. The initial factor solution and the choice of the number of factors to be retained are key in accomplishing the first task, whereas the rotation of the initial solution is important for accomplishing the latter.

Cluster analysis searches for the natural groupings among objects described by p variables. It places together the objects that are similar in terms of the p variables. Their similarity is properly captured with a coefficient reflecting the scale of measurement that underlies the variables. The analyst has many choices in this regard, as well as with respect to the clustering algorithm that will be used to generate the groupings.

Multidimensional scaling is a technique to obtain perceptual maps. The input data are typically direct similarity judgments that reflect comparisons between pairs of objects like brands. The MDS model seeks to represent the objects as points in a map so that similar objects are close in space, and different objects are farther apart in space. The number of dimensions is determined by examining "stress" indices, and the labeling of the dimensions can be subjective or can be assisted through the use of additional ratings data and regression.

Questions

1. How does the purpose of discriminant analysis differ from that of regression analysis?
2. What basic criterion is satisfied in determining the weights for a discriminant function?
3. Just as in regression analysis, discriminant analysis has two basic purposes: prediction or classification and structural interpretation. How are both of these purposes achieved with the discriminant model?
4. Suppose that more than two groups are to be discriminated. How many discriminant functions will there be?
5. Describe the basic purpose of factor analysis. What is meant by variability recovery and covariability recovery?
6. What is a factor-loading table? What do the individual entries measure? How does the table help to determine the "appropriate" number of factors?
7. What is the basic principle that underlies the principal components procedure?

---

[59]For more information on multivariate statistical techniques, see Laurence G. Grimm and Paul R. Yarnold, eds., *Reading and Understanding Multivariate Statistics* (Washington, D.C.: APA, 1995); Narayan C. Giri, *Multivariate Statistical Analysis* (New York: Marcel Dekker, 1996); Alvin C. Rencher, *Methods of Multivariate Analysis* (New York: Wiley, 1995); Alvin C. Rencher, *Multivariate Statistical Inference and Applications* (New York: Wiley, 1998); Barbara G. Tabachnick and Linda S. Fidell, *Using Multivariate Statistics,* 3rd ed. (New York: Harper Collins, 1996); Howard Tinsley and Steven Brown, eds., *Handbook of Applied Multivariate Statistics and Mathematical Modeling* (San Diego, CA: Academic Press, 2000); and J. Douglas Carroll, Paul E. Green, and Anil Chaturvedi, *Mathematical Tools for Applied Multivariate Analysis* (San Diego, CA: Academic Press, 1997).

8. What is the "substantive interpretation" question in factor analysis? How is such interpretation typically facilitated?

9. What is the essence of the communality question in factor analysis? What is the effect of the communality issue?

10. What is the basic purpose of cluster analysis?

11. Explain the differences among the linkage procedures, nodal procedures, and factor procedures in cluster analysis.

12. What is the difference between complete link and average link cluster analysis?

13. What is a dendrogram? How might its fusion coefficients be used?

14. What is MDS good for? What kind of data are required to do a MDS analysis?

15. How does one determine the number of dimensions that are optimal for a given data set? How are the dimensions interpreted?

Applications and Problems

1. The management of a large chain of grocery stores is thinking about opening several chains, "south of the border," in Mexico. The manager wants to determine how national-brand shoppers and private-label shoppers differed with respect to income and the size of household. Personal interviews with a random sample of national-brand shoppers and private-label shoppers generated the following data:

	Annual Income (thousands of dollars) X_1	Household Size (number of persons) X_2
National-Brand Shoppers		
1	16.8	3.0
2	21.4	2.0
3	17.3	4.0
4	18.4	1.0
5	23.2	2.0
6	21.1	5.0
7	14.5	4.0
8	18.9	1.0
9	17.8	2.0
10	19.3	1.0
Private-Label Shoppers		
1	17.3	4.0
2	15.4	3.0
3	14.3	4.0
4	14.5	5.0
5	17.4	2.0
6	16.7	6.0
7	13.9	7.0
8	12.4	7.0
9	15.3	6.0
10	13.3	4.0

A discriminant analysis of the data resulted in the following discriminant function:

$$Y = 0.333X_1 - 0.315X_2$$

a. What criterion was satisfied in deriving these weights?
b. Use the discriminant function to derive the discriminant scores (Y) for each shopper.
c. What do the discriminant scores indicate?
d. Compute the pooled standard deviation for X_1 and X_2. (Hint: Refer to Chapter 15 for the formula of the pooled standard deviation.)
e. Convert the original weights of the discriminant function to standardized weights.
f. Interpret the discriminant function by evaluating the standardized weights.
g. Compute the mean values of the variables for each group.
h. Compute the mean discriminant scores for each group. Interpret them.
i. Compute the cutting score.
j. For each shopper (i), next to the discriminant score (Y_i), compute $Y_i - \bar{Y}_1$ and $Y_i - \bar{Y}_2$. Determine which difference is smaller for each shopper, and in so doing, predict their group membership.
k. Create the table of predicted versus actual classifications. Compute the hit rate or the proportion correctly classified. Assess the goodness of the hit rate by computing the proportional chance criterion. Interpret your results.
l. Suppose that the management wanted to classify two individuals according to whether they were national-brand shoppers or private-label shoppers. The characteristics are as follows:

Individual I	*Individual II*
X_1—annual income, $18,300	X_1—annual income, $21,000
X_2—household size, 4 persons	X_2—household size, 7 persons

How should management classify these individuals? Show your calculations.

3. When is factor analysis an appropriate technique? What do the eigenvalues (or latent roots) tell you about the amount of variance explained by each factor? How can this be used to determine the number of factors retained in the final solution? Should an analyst ever keep a factor with an eigenvalue less than 1? Explain.
4. In a rotated factor solution, what is the implication if an item has significant loadings on more than one factor?
5. What is the purpose behind rotating the factors?
6. Prefertronics, Inc., is a medium-sized manufacturer of electronic toys. The vice president of sales has asked Bill Jurkowski, a product manager, to conduct a marketing research study to determine the key attributes that contribute to consumer preferences for the firm's products. Jurkowski had interviewers conduct personal interviews with a random sample of 100 customers. The respondents were asked to rate Prefertronics' toys on four attributes (expensive-inexpensive, safe-unsafe, educational-uneducational, and good quality-poor quality) using a seven-point semantic differential scale. Jurkowski conducted a principal components analysis with the standardized scores, which resulted in the following factor-loading matrix. Jurkowski needs your help in analyzing this information.

The factor-loading matrix was as follows:

| | Factors | | | |
Variable	1	2	3	4
X_1	0.812	0.567	0.121	0.070
X_2	0.532	−0.743	0.321	0.249
X_3	0.708	−0.640	0.205	0.217
X_4	0.773	0.630	0.018	0.078

where

X_1 = expensive-inexpensive
X_2 = safe-unsafe
X_3 = educational-uneducational
X_4 = good quality-poor quality

a. What are the individual row/column entries called, and what do they indicate?
b. What does the entry in the 2nd row and 1st column indicate?
c. What is the proportion of variation in each of the four variables that is accounted for by Factor 1? Show your calculations.
d. What is the proportion of variation in each of the four variables that is accounted for by Factor 2? Show your calculations.
e. The following table is a partially completed correlation matrix derived from the preceding factor-loading matrix. Complete the original correlation matrix using all four of the factors. Hint: Use the formula:

$$r_{jl} = \sum_k a_{jk} a_{lk}$$

Simple Pair-wise Correlations among the Attributes
(computed from four factors)

	X_1	X_2	X_3	X_4
X_1	1.000			
X_2	0.067	1.000		
X_3			1.000	
X_4			0.165	1.000

f. For comparison, complete the following correlation matrix using only the first and second factors to estimate the correlations. Comment on your results.

Simple Pair-wise Correlations among the Attributes
(computed from two factors)

	X_1	X_2	X_3	X_4
X_1	1.000			
X_2		1.000		
X_3			1.000	
X_4				1.000

g. Compute the communalities of the four variables using the first and second factors. Show your calculations. Comment on your results.

h. Compute the proportion of the total variation in the data that is accounted for by each of the four factors. Show your calculations. Comment on your results.

i. On the basis of the preceding computations, discuss how well two factors compared to four factors reproduced the variability and covariability of the variables.

j. Construct a scatter diagram using the correlations between the variables and the first and second factors as coordinates of the points.

k. On the basis of the scatter diagram, would you recommend that the factors be rotated? If yes, why? If no, why not?

l. Assume that the factors were rotated. Provide an interpretation of the factors.

m. Assume that the original factor solution was rotated. Explain the following statement: "The contribution of each factor in accounting for the variation in the respective variables has changed; however, the total variation accounted for by the factors has remained constant."

7. A company has decided to cluster respondents based on the four product characteristics that customers have chosen as most important from a list of 18 characteristics. If the research analyst finds that a particular product characteristic is important for all customers, how should the analyst proceed? Justify your answer.

8. In the example above, how should the research team proceed if cluster membership changes substantially based on the algorithm being used?

9. Adstar, Inc., is a large-sized advertising agency located in New York City. The marketing research manager wants to identify the market segments for one of the agency's clients, a manufacturer of caffeine-free soft drinks, so that an effective advertising campaign can be developed. The manufacturer believes that the product would appeal to high-income families with large households. The marketing research manager has collected information from a probability sample of 500 regular purchasers of the caffeine-free soft drink. The manager has decided to use cluster analysis but is not familiar with the technique. Information pertaining to a sample of 10 regular purchasers is given to you. The following table contains the standardized scores for income and household size for the sample of 10 respondents.

| | *Average Ratings on Attributes Expressed in Standardized Units* | |
| | *Income* | *Household Size* |
Respondents	X_1	X_2
1	−2.75	−2.50
2	3.00	3.00
3	2.50	2.75
4	−1.75	−2.25
5	4.00	3.50
6	−3.50	−2.75
7	2.75	3.25
8	−2.25	−2.50
9	3.50	2.50
10	−3.00	−3.25

a. Plot the individual scores in two dimensions using the two variables as axes. What does the plot suggest?

b. Determine the similarity of each pair of respondents by computing the Euclidean distance between them.

c. Use the single linkage clustering method to develop the clusters. Consider the similarity values less than 1.00 (from part b), and array the distances from most similar to least similar.

d. What clusters exist after the fourth iteration (distance levels of approximately 0.70)?

e. What clusters exist after the eighth iteration (distance levels of approximately 1.12)?

f. Construct a dendrogram for similarity values up to approximately 0.56. Interpret the dendrogram.

g. Suppose that the complete linkage method of clustering is used; indicate at what distance level the results will be the same as part e.

10. Kay Sealey is the news director for KASI-TV, the local NBC affiliate for a large southwestern city. Sealey believes that the most important quality of an on-air news broadcaster is credibility in the eyes of the viewer. Accordingly, surveys are taken every six months that attempt to evaluate the credibility of the news broadcasters who appear on the local news programs. The following figure shows one of the survey instruments used by the station to measure the credibility of a newscaster:

Evaluate the anchorperson on the news broadcast that you reviewed by completing the following series of scales. Place a check mark on the scale position that most nearly matches your feelings about this anchorperson. For example, if you thought that this anchorperson was extremely likeable, you would place a check mark in the blank nearest "likeable" (in this case, the far left blank).

a.	likeable	__	__	__	__	__	__	__	not likeable
b.	knowledgeable	__	__	__	__	__	__	__	not knowledgeable
c.	unattractive	__	__	__	__	__	__	__	attractive
d.	intelligent	__	__	__	__	__	__	__	not intelligent
e.	not similar to you	__	__	__	__	__	__	__	similar to you
f.	good looking	__	__	__	__	__	__	__	bad looking
g.	unexciting	__	__	__	__	__	__	__	exciting
h.	confident	__	__	__	__	__	__	__	not confident
i.	friendly	__	__	__	__	__	__	__	not friendly
j.	not believable	__	__	__	__	__	__	__	believable
k.	expert	__	__	__	__	__	__	__	not expert
l.	ugly	__	__	__	__	__	__	__	beautiful
m.	don't identify with	__	__	__	__	__	__	__	identify with
n.	competent	__	__	__	__	__	__	__	not competent
o.	active	__	__	__	__	__	__	__	passive
p.	irritating	__	__	__	__	__	__	__	not irritating
q.	not trustworthy	__	__	__	__	__	__	__	trustworthy
r.	dull	__	__	__	__	__	__	__	interesting
s.	not sincere	__	__	__	__	__	__	__	sincere

Suppose that this questionnaire were administered to a sample of 50 people after they had watched a videotape of a nightly news broadcast that featured the specific broadcaster. The following table contains the responses of the 50 people surveyed:

Items

a	b	c	d	e	f	g	h	i	j	k	l	m	n	o	p	q	r	s
1	2	5	3	3	3	4	3	3	6	3	4	4	3	3	6	6	5	6
1	4	6	3	1	2	4	2	2	6	2	5	7	1	3	5	6	5	5
5	6	5	5	5	5	6	3	3	5	6	4	3	6	2	1	2	2	2
2	2	5	2	4	3	4	3	3	5	3	5	5	3	3	3	5	5	5

(continued)

Items

a	b	c	d	e	f	g	h	i	j	k	l	m	n	o	p	q	r	s
2	2	6	2	1	2	6	1	1	6	1	6	5	2	1	7	6	5	6
4	5	3	3	2	5	2	2	2	4	5	4	4	3	2	3	5	2	6
3	3	5	5	2	3	5	2	2	4	3	5	2	3	3	5	5	5	6
1	1	6	1	5	2	5	1	2	7	2	5	6	1	1	7	7	6	7
5	4	3	3	1	5	4	2	2	6	3	4	3	3	6	6	6	4	6
3	3	5	1	4	2	4	1	1	7	4	4	6	1	1	7	7	7	7
3	3	5	4	3	3	4	2	4	5	4	5	4	4	3	3	4	4	5
2	5	6	4	4	3	3	5	2	1	6	5	4	5	3	3	2	4	1
3	5	2	4	1	6	3	3	4	4	5	3	3	4	3	5	4	2	3
3	3	6	2	4	2	4	2	4	5	2	5	4	3	2	6	5	4	4
2	3	6	3	4	3	6	2	2	6	4	5	4	2	2	6	5	5	5
5	4	4	3	2	4	2	3	3	4	5	4	2	4	4	1	4	3	4
3	3	4	4	3	4	4	3	3	4	4	4	3	4	3	4	5	3	4
5	3	3	6	1	3	4	1	1	2	2	4	2	2	2	3	5	3	6
2	3	6	2	1	3	5	1	1	3	5	4	2	1	1	6	5	5	3
2	2	5	2	3	3	4	2	3	6	4	4	4	2	2	3	5	3	4
3	6	1	5	1	7	2	4	1	7	7	2	1	5	4	1	4	1	6
2	2	6	2	4	3	6	2	3	6	4	5	4	2	2	5	6	6	6
2	2	6	3	6	2	5	2	2	6	3	6	6	2	2	6	6	6	6
2	2	4	2	4	4	6	1	1	6	2	4	4	2	4	6	6	6	6
3	3	4	3	4	4	3	4	2	6	4	4	4	2	3	4	5	5	5
3	3	6	3	5	2	6	4	2	4	3	5	4	3	1	3	4	5	4
5	4	5	3	3	3	2	3	4	2	5	5	2	4	4	3	4	2	1
2	4	5	4	4	3	4	4	3	4	5	5	4	3	3	6	5	4	4
3	5	7	5	2	2	2	2	3	2	6	6	1	5	5	4	2	3	1
2	3	2	3	4	2	5	2	2	6	3	5	5	3	2	6	6	5	6
3	3	5	4	3	4	4	3	3	4	5	4	4	4	3	5	5	4	5
2	2	6	2	4	2	7	1	1	5	2	6	4	2	1	6	5	6	6
1	1	6	1	6	1	6	1	1	7	4	5	6	1	1	7	6	6	7
2	3	6	5	5	2	4	6	2	6	4	5	5	2	2	6	5	4	6
2	3	5	2	1	2	1	3	2	4	6	5	2	2	6	2	4	2	5
2	3	5	4	2	4	6	6	2	6	4	5	4	2	3	6	5	5	5
4	4	4	4	2	3	3	2	3	4	4	5	4	3	2	3	4	3	2
4	5	4	4	2	4	3	3	4	3	4	4	2	3	5	3	3	4	2
3	2	3	2	3	2	4	1	3	7	1	5	4	6	3	3	7	4	5
4	5	7	5	3	2	4	2	2	6	4	4	5	3	4	4	4	3	4
3	3	4	3	1	4	5	2	2	6	4	4	3	2	2	4	6	4	6
2	4	5	5	4	5	3	3	3	5	5	5	4	3	3	5	4	5	5
4	3	4	3	4	4	3	2	5	4	4	4	2	3	5	5	4	5	5
3	2	4	2	2	4	3	1	1	5	6	4	3	2	2	5	4	4	5
2	2	6	3	4	2	4	2	2	6	4	6	4	2	2	6	4	6	6
4	3	3	3	2	4	4	1	2	5	4	4	2	3	5	4	4	3	4
2	3	6	3	4	2	6	2	2	5	4	5	5	3	2	5	5	5	3
5	4	5	4	3	3	3	3	2	4	6	4	3	5	2	2	4	4	3
2	2	5	2	4	3	5	1	1	6	2	5	7	1	2	6	7	6	7
2	2	6	2	4	2	4	1	1	7	2	5	4	1	4	7	7	6	6

Note: For each item in the survey, the responses are coded 1–7, with 1 representing the left-most position on the scale and 7 representing the right-most position. Items a, b, d, f, h, i, k, n, and o must be reverse-scaled before any analysis is attempted.

a. Discuss the possible reasons for the use of factor analysis with these data.
b. Produce a correlation matrix for the 19 variables (scale items). Does it appear that factor analysis would be appropriate for these data?
c. Do a principal components analysis (with rotation if necessary for interpretation) using these data. How many factors should be retained? What is the percentage of variance accounted for by each factor?
d. Interpret the factors.

11. Assume that you are a staff researcher for a manufacturer of three nationally branded breakfast cereals. The research and development department has formulated a new type of cereal that the company has decided to introduce under a new brand name. The product manager for the breakfast cereal line has expressed concern that the new brand, unless it is carefully positioned, may cannibalize sales of the firm's current brands. You have been assigned to provide research-based information that will assist management in properly positioning the new brand to minimize the possibility of cannibalization. What method of analysis should you employ and why? Given your choice of method, what are some fundamental decisions that you must make?

12. Crystal Clear Beverage Company, a medium-sized manufacturer of bottled water, wanted to expand its line of clear beverages by the introduction of a clear cola. Five major brands served the market. The marketing research department decided to use multidimensional scaling to determine the viable "holes" in the market. Perceptions of the similarities among the five brands resulted in the following similarity judgments.

	Respondent Similarity Judgments				
Brand	A	B	C	D	E
A		5	9	10	8
B			1	2	7
C				6	4
D					3
E					

The coordinates of the brands (determined by the computer model) in two-space for the preceding rank-order data follows:

	Dimension 1	Dimension 2
A	−0.80	0.30
B	−0.60	0.25
C	−0.75	−0.20
D	−0.50	−0.18
E	−0.60	−0.39
Ideal	−0.55	0.50

a. Plot the brands and the ideal point.
b. How are the distances between the objects ordered?
   The stress value, as a function of the number of dimensions employed, is shown in the following table:

No. of Dimensions	Stress
1	0.110
2	0.105
3	0.100
4	0.095

    c. Plot the stress values.

    d. Do you think that the similarity judgments between the brands can be captured by one dimension? Give three reasons to support your decision.

    e. The marketing research department has identified dimension 2 as "price." How would you advise management to position its brand?

13. Refer back to Figure 17.14 in the chapter. Suppose that objects A–J represent 10 fast-food restaurants in a city, each of which is attempting to attract the same market segment. Dimension 1 represents the perceived price of a meal, and Dimension 2 represents the perceived quality of service. Further suppose that an ideal fast-food restaurant would feature very high-quality service and moderate to moderately high prices and that restaurant G is in exactly such a position on the map.

    a. Using this information, briefly describe restaurants F and E and give managerial implications for these restaurants.

    b. Briefly describe and provide managerial implications for restaurant J.

    c. Briefly describe and provide managerial implications for restaurant D.

A P P E N D I X   1 7 A

More Multivariate Statistical Techniques

Multivariate models are constantly proliferating—some methods come and go while others prove to be sufficiently useful to the marketing researcher that they are adopted and demonstrate staying power. In this appendix, we describe four such techniques—correspondence analysis, structural equations modeling, neural networks, and social networks—relatively more modern than the classic techniques described in Chapter 17, but like them, so useful that they should be added to the marketing researcher's ever-expanding analytical repertoire.

Correspondence Analysis

Correspondence Analysis (CA) produces results that look much like MDS. A perceptual map is obtained in which the interpoint distances are interpreted to represent the similarities between the objects (for example, brands). CA differs from MDS in two ways: First, the data requirements are flexible; for example, the data can be rating scales (as in MDS) or frequencies (for example, number of consumers who checked a brand as their favorite from a list). Second, in addition to the map containing points representing objects, CA also allows points to represent attributes of those objects and attributes of the respondents.

For example, Figure 17A.1 contains the results of a correspondence analysis in which marketing researchers were studying the character of Web sites as a marketing tool, compared to extant media.[1] The various media (for example, Web, radio,

---

[1]This example is based loosely on Elain K. F. Leong, Xueli Huang, and Paul-John Stanners, "Comparing the Effectiveness of the Web Site with Traditional Media," *Journal of Advertising Research* 38 (September/October 1998), pp. 44–51. For more examples, see Terrence V. O'Brien, "Correspondence Analysis," *Marketing Research* 5 (Fall 1993), pp. 54–56; Thomas W. Whipple, "Mapping Focus Group Data," *Marketing Research* 6 (Winter 1994), pp. 16–21; Dawn Iacobucci and Amy Ostrom, "Commercial and Interpersonal Relationships," *International Journal of Research in Marketing* 13 (1996), pp. 53–72.

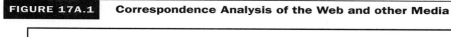

FIGURE 17A.1   **Correspondence Analysis of the Web and other Media**

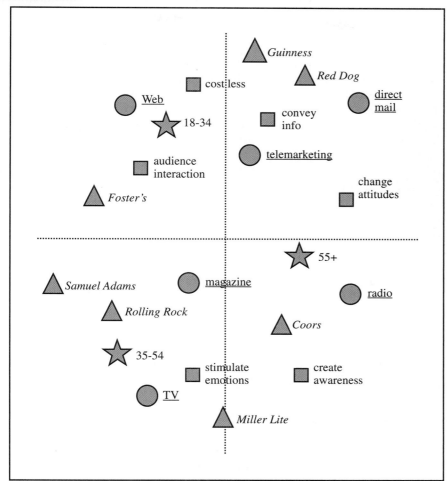

Key: 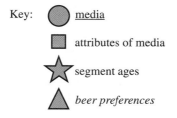 media

attributes of media

segment ages

beer preferences

telemarketing) were the objects; they are plotted close together if they were perceived to be similar, as per MDS. In addition, there are attributes of the media plotted (such as stimulate emotions, audience involvement), as well as attributes of the respondents (segment age groups, favorite beers).

The points representing the attributes of the media help interpret the configuration and the dimensions; the closer a medium exists to one of the attribute ratings, the more that attribute is descriptive of that medium. For example, Web sites share two qualities of telemarketing: both cost relatively little to reach their target markets, and they both involve interactions with the target audience members. Both of these media are different from TV and radio in being more about conveying information and less about stimulating emotions, creating awareness, or attempting to change attitudes.

The points representing the attributes of people can help segment consumers, and illustrate more richly their lifestyles and the images that are likely to appeal to them when trying to reach them. For example, the youngest segment enjoys the Web, and drinks Foster's, Guinness, and Red Dog. The oldest segment in the sample enjoys radio and magazines and prefers Coors.

The essential objective of correspondence analysis is to represent everything as a Euclidean distance—the similarities between the objects, the extent to which different attributes describe those objects, and segments of consumers prefer those objects. The same distance formula is used as in cluster analysis or MDS (for $k = 2$ dimensions):

$$d_{ij} = \sqrt{\sum_{k=1}^{2} (X_{ik} - X_{jk})^2}$$

where d_{ij} represents the distances between any two points in the map. For MDS, the distances would be computed among 6 objects—the 6 media. For CA, the distances would be computed among 22 entities: the 6 media, the 6 attributes, the 3 segment age groups, and the 7 beer brands. References to learn more about correspondence analysis abound, and procedures for fitting the CA model are increasingly accessible in statistical computing packages (for example, SAS, SPSS).[2]

Structural Equations Models

A structural equations model (SEM) is somewhat like a multiple regression in that several variables are used to predict another variable. SEMs are more complex than regressions, however, in that they may be comprised of many layers of variables and their interrelationships. Thus, a variable that is being predicted by one set of variables may in turn help to predict yet another. Variables that are being predicted are

---

[2]For good expository treatments of CA, see J. Douglas Carroll, Paul E. Green, and C. M. Schaffer, "Comparing Interpoint Distances in Correspondence Analysis," *Journal of Marketing Research* 24 (1987), pp. 445–450. Donna L. Hoffman and George R. Franke, "Correspondence Analysis: Graphical Representation of Categorical Data in Marketing Research," *Journal of Marketing Research* 23 (August 1986), pp. 213–227; Susan C. Weller and A. Kimball Romney, *Metric Scaling: Correspondence Analysis* (Thousand Oaks, CA: Sage, 1990); Henry S. Lynn and Charles E. McCullogh, "Using PCA and Correspondence Analysis for Estimation in Latent Variable Models," *Journal of the American Statistical Association* 95 (June 2000), pp. 561–572.

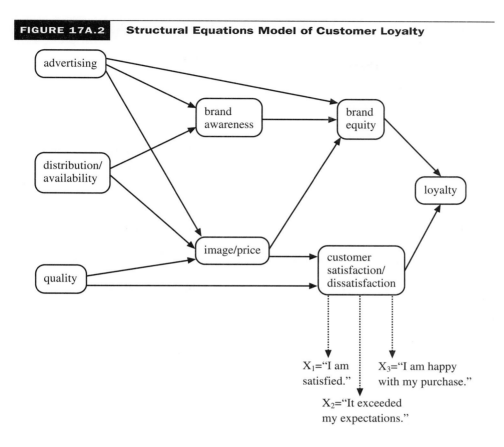

FIGURE 17A.2   Structural Equations Model of Customer Loyalty

known as **dependent variables** (as in regression) or **endogenous variables.** Variables that are not predicted, but predict others are referred to as **exogenous variables.**

For example, in Figure 17A.2, a structural equations model for customer loyalty is depicted.[3] Ultimately, the marketing researchers wish to understand loyalty, which they posit as a direct function of brand equity and customer satisfaction. They expect brand equity to be a function, in turn, of advertising, brand awareness and image or price. In an indirect manner, then, loyalty is a function of advertising, brand awareness, and image—through brand equity.

If we were to try to fit the model in Figure 17A.2 via regression, we would state the following direct relationships and run five regressions:

loyalty $= b_1$ brand equity $+ b_2$ customer satisfaction
brand equity $= c_1$ advertising $+ c_2$ brand awareness $+ c_3$ image/price
customer satisfaction $= d_1$ image/price $+ d_2$ quality

[3]For more examples of SEM, see William R. Dillon, John B. White, Vithala R. Rao, and Doug Filak, "'Good Science': Using Structural Equation Models to Decipher Complex Customer Relationships," *Marketing Research* 9 (Winter 1997), pp. 22–31; Boonghee Yoo, Naveen Donthu, and Sungho Lee, "An Examination of Selected Marketing Mix Elements and Brand Equity," *Journal of the Academy of Marketing Science* 28 (Spring 2000), pp. 195–211; Jacob K. Eskildsen, Jens J. Dahlgaard, and Anders Norgaard, "The Impact of Creativity and Learning on Business Excellence," *Total Quality Management* 10 (July 1999), pp. S523–S530.

$$\text{brand awareness} = e_1 \text{ advertising} + e_2 \text{ distribution}$$
$$\text{image/price} = f_1 \text{ advertising} + f_2 \text{ distribution} + f_3 \text{ quality}$$

The advantage of SEM over running a series of regressions is that these components of the larger model are fit simultaneously, so the researcher can test at once all the interrelationships, and direct and indirect paths, statistically controlling for all the others.

In the example, as these equations indicate, no variables are used to predict advertising, distribution, or quality, so they comprise the set of exogenous variables. The others are endogenous. Brand awareness, brand equity, image/price, and customer satisfaction may also be referred to as mediators, in that they establish indirect links from some variables to others.

Another advantage of SEM over regression is that it incorporates factor analysis to take advantage of the correlations among variables tapping a common construct. In the figure, this element of SEM is depicted only for the construct of customer satisfaction (to keep the figure simple). There it is noted that customer satisfaction was measured by three indicator variables, X_1 ("I am satisfied"), X_2 ("It exceeded my expectations"), and X_3 ("I am happy with my purchase"). If these three variables had been used to predict loyalty, without first acknowledging that they share an underlying construct, their intercorrelations would have caused problematic multicollinearity. In SEM, their intercorrelations are first leveraged advantageously to identify the underlying factors, and then the factors are used to predict the other endogenous constructs.

There are many good references on structural equations models.[4] The software to fit these models are only beginning to be incorporated into the larger statistical packages (for example, SAS), but the stand alone packages (such as Lisrel and Eqs) are readily available.[5]

Neural Networks

Neural networks derive from models of expert systems, where the "neural" descriptor captures the idea that these models are rough analogs of the brain. Each neuron in the brain receives inputs from other neurons, which it combines in some manner to create a resulting output signal that it subsequently passes along to other neurons. Regardless of the model's origin, or whether researchers currently believe that a network model truly describes neural functioning, network techniques have exploded as powerful and flexible analytical tools.

---

[4]For example, see Barbara M. Byrne, *Structural Equation Modeling with Lisrel, Prelis, and Simplis: Basic Concepts, Applications, and Programming* (Mahwah, NJ: Erlbaum, 1998); E. Kevin Kelloway, *Using Lisrel for Structural Equations Models* (Thousand Oaks, CA: Sage, 1998); Rick H. Holye, ed., *Structural Equation Models: Concepts, Issues, and Applications* (Thousand Oaks, CA: Sage, 1995); Rex B. Kline, *Principles and Practice of Structural Equations Models* (New York: Guildford Press, 1998); Kenneth A. Bollen and J. Scott Long, eds., *Testing Structural Equation Models* (Newbury Park, CA: Sage, 1993).

[5]The two leading software packages for SEMs are Lisrel, available from Scientific Software International (see ssicentral.com) and Eqs, from Multivariate Software, Inc. (see mvsoft.com).

In their use as statistical tools, neural networks are comprised of three types of layers: an input layer, an output layer, and a hidden layer. To explain neural networks in terms of familiar models—regression, or, now, structural equations—we would say the input layer consists of the predictor variables and the output layer, the dependent variable. Neural networks modelers call the variables, **nodes.**

As an example, consider the network model depicted in Figure 17A.3. In this figure, the marketing researchers are using neural nets to try to assist them in their go/no-go decision in launching a product line in China. There are three input nodes: how the product did locally in concept testing, how it fared at in-home use testing, and the marketing research department's forecasts of likely market share.

The hidden layer is also comprised of nodes. These nodes are functions that translate the inputs into the output. The inputs to one hidden node are weighted and combined and then sent along to the next layer. Note that the neural net in Figure 17A.3 would be functioning like a regression if the following conditions were true: (1) there was no second, hidden node (labeled "function 2"); (2) there were no links to or from it; and (3) the weights going from the three input layer nodes to the hidden layer node were betas and the combination was linear. This neural net is more complicated than a regression because of that second hidden node. Furthermore, neural nets are different from regressions, in general, in that weights may be selected to optimize other criteria, and the inputs may be combined in a function that is nonlinear. For example, an input variable of market share is continuous, more is better, and it may well contribute to the go/no-go decision. However, coupled with that, many firms operate with the criterion that the achieved market share

FIGURE 17A.3   Neural Networks Model of Product Introduction

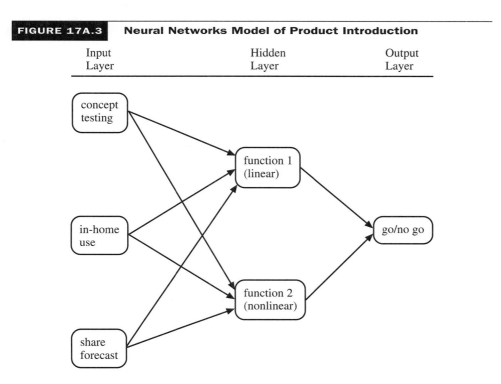

would have to be "at least" some number to deem going to market worthwhile. Hence, a threshold or step function might be useful supplemental information in this go/no-go model.

In addition, neural network modelers speak of a network model *learning* the relationship among the variables. What learning means for an algorithm is convergence and cross-validation. Specifically, a "training" data set is introduced to the neural network model, which seeks to optimize the model predictions to fit the data by trying weights and functions, and updating iteratively to improve the fit. Then, when the weights and nodal functions have been estimated on the training data, the hold-out sample of data is input to see how well the model fits in the cross-validation, which is used to further refine the model parameters and specifications.

Many introductions to neural networks exist.[6] They are gaining popularity because they are so flexible; for example, the functions at the nodes need not be so restrictive as "linear," and very few assumptions are made about the data (such as ordinal or interval) or distributions (data do not need to be multivariate normally distributed). As a result of this flexibility, the models are also found to be quite robust—there are no distributional assumptions to be violated, and the data can be relatively messy. The only major drawback is that these techniques, like many nonparametric (that is, flexible, nondistributional) methods, require large databases. Increasingly, of course, many applications include large databases. Thus, these tools seem to be a good answer to many contemporary database problems. In particular, neural networks have been used in business applications like credit approval, predicting bankruptcy, and stock market simulations, to name a few. Marketers are currently exploring their usefulness to data-mining and other applications with large databases.[7]

Social Networks

While "social networks" might sounds like "neural networks," the two methods have little in common. A social network is a body of techniques that facilitate the description of relationships. The relationships exist between **actors.** In marketing, actors can be organizations, departments within organizations, or people. For example, networks have been used in marketing to study power conflicts among distribution channel members, communication links between departments within an organization, and the dynamic exchange between two people negotiating, such as a buyer and seller in a market exchange, or a husband and wife in a consumer purchase.

---

[6]For helpful introductions, see Lane H. Mann, "Gaining Global Insights: Using Neural Networks for Marketing Research Can Give You Access to Uncharted Territories," *Marketing Research* 9 (Summer 1997), pp. 25–30; Efraim Turban and Jay E. Aronson, Chapter 17: "Neural Computing: The Basics," and Chapter 18: "Neural Computing Applications," in *Decision Support Systems and Intelligent Systems,* 5th ed. (Upper Saddle River, NJ: Prentice Hall, 1998), pp. 649–719.

[7]For more examples of neural nets, see Richard A. Briesch and Dawn Iacobucci, "Using Neural Networks to Compare Theoretical Models: An Application to Persuasive Communications," *Proceedings of the Winter Educators' Conference* (Chicago: AMA, 1995), pp. 177–184; Jaymeen R. Shah and Mirza B. Murtaza, "A Neural Network Based Clustering Procedure for Bankruptcy Prediction," *American Business Review* 18 (June 2000), pp. 80–86; Peter Hackl and Anders H. Westlund, "On Structural Equation Modeling for Customer Satisfaction Measurement," *Total Quality Management* 11 (July 2000), pp. 4–6.

As an example, consider the network depicted in Figure 17A.4. This network shows the flow of information among four marketing representatives of a high-tech firm, three engineers, and two computer scientists. The actors in the network are depicted by the labels, "M1" (first marketer), M2 (second marketer), E1 (first engineer), and so on.

The communication relationships that exist among these nine actors are depicted by the arrows linking them. Note that most of the communications are represented by bidirectional arrows, meaning that the flow of information goes in both directions. However, a few arrows are unidirectional, representing that CS1 (or CS2) shares information with CS2 (or M3), but information is not returned reciprocally. These asymmetric ties may be sensible if, say, CS2 worked for CS1, and CS1 was merely keeping CS2 informed of the firm's developments. Note also that the "strength of ties" can be captured with, say, the bold lines between M2 and M4, and between E2 and E3. These bold lines indicate that the communication ties in these two dyads are even stronger than those among the other people in the network.

Network data may be collected in a variety of ways. Each of these nine people might be asked, "How often do you talk with employee X about your work projects?" where each of the eight remaining network members' names would appear as "X" in turn. The relation might be asked more specifically, "How often do you ask for advice from X?" or "How often do you share data with X?" The relation might

FIGURE 17A.4   Interdepartmental Communications Network

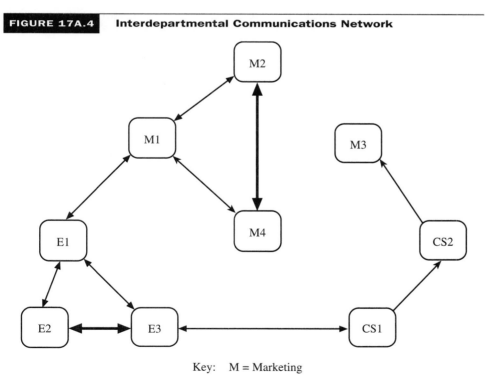

Key: M = Marketing

E = Engineering

CS = Computer science

convey content beyond communication, for example, "How much do you respect X?" "Would your position in the company be enhanced if X were laid off in a downsizing?" or "Do you and your family socialize with X and X's family?" and so forth. Data might also be observational, for example, noting the number of e-mails in the company system that are sent from M1 to M2 and back again. Network researchers have also clocked social interaction time (for example, around the water cooler, or visits by one person to another's office).

The diagrams of network connections are often enlightening in themselves. For example, this particular figure might indicate some problem for person M3, a marketing person who gets information only through the CS2 person, and not as a function of communication with others in the marketing department.

Beyond graphing the relationships, it is also important to analyze them more systematically. The relationship between actors i and j are recorded in a matrix, where the (ith, jth) element is a "1" if actor i sends an e-mail, say, to j, and "0" if actor i does not, and the (jth, ith) element in the matrix is a "1" if actor j sends an e-mail to actor i, and "0" if j does not. These matrices are then analyzed to identify certain qualities of the relationship structures. For example, actors E3 and CS1, and E1 and M1 would be considered actors with high "centrality," because if their respective links were broken, communication would not flow throughout the entire network. For information to pass from M4 to M3, say, these two particular links must remain intact. The centrality of an actor is one indication of the actor's importance in the network—without these key actors, the structure of the network would change substantially. If, on the other hand, actor M2 or E2 were removed from the network, the flow of communication would remain largely unchanged in the organization—other actors would make up for their loss, so these "less central" actors are less important to the network.

Subgroups are also a focus of network analysis. The members M1, M2, and M4, and the engineers, form two "cliques," groups of actors who are all interconnected amongst themselves. Cliques can be beneficial, as in this setting of sharing information. Cliques in other applications can be troublesome, for example, as in coalition formation and negotiation disputes. Whether a quality of a network (centrality, cliques, and so on) is good or bad depends on the setting and the content of the relationships being represented in the network.

More information about network data and their analyses can be found in several good sources.[8] Modeling social networks will continue to increase in importance as marketers come to realize their full potential.[9]

---

[8]For more information on social networks, see David Knoke and James H. Kuklinski, *Social Network Analysis* (Beverly Hills, CA: Sage, 1982); Dawn Iacobucci, ed., *Networks in Marketing* (Thousand Oaks, CA: Sage 1996); John Scott, *Social Network Analysis* (Newbury Park, CA: Sage, 1991); Nitin Nohria and Robert G. Eccles, eds., *Networks and Organizations* (Boston: Harvard Business School Press, 1992).

[9]For more examples using social networks, see R. Bruce Money, "International Multilateral Negotiations and Social Networks," *Journal of International Business Studies* 29 (1998), pp. 695–710; Priti Pradhan Shah, "Network Destruction: The Structural Implications of Downsizing," *Academy of Management Journal* 43 (February 2000), pp. 101–112; Morten T. Hansen, "The Search-Transfer Problem: The Role of Weak Ties in Sharing Knowledge Across Organization Subunits," *Administrative Science Quarterly* 44 (March 1999), pp. 82–111; Marc-David L. Seidel, Jeffrey T. Polzer, and Katherine J. Stewart, "Friends in High Places: The Effects of Social Networks on Discrimination in Salary Negotiations," *Administrative Science Quarterly* 45 (March 2000), pp. 1–24.

A P P E N D I X   1 7 B

Analysis of Catalog-Buying Data

Discriminant Analysis

A question of interest in the Avery Sporting Goods study (found in Appendix 13A) was to catalog recipients' feelings toward the breadth of the Avery line. To address this question, two groups were formed from Question 11, "The selection of sporting goods available through the Avery catalog is very broad." Those agreeing or strongly agreeing with this statement were placed in one group, labeled as those perceiving Avery as having a broad product line. Those strongly disagreeing, disagreeing, or neither agreeing nor disagreeing with the statement were placed in the other group, labeled as those perceiving Avery to have a narrow product line.

Table 17B.1 contains the results of the discriminant analysis that relates group membership to the same demographic characteristics used in the multiple-regression analysis with the ATTAVRY index—namely, the individual's occupation, years worked, and marital status. In addition, the gender of the respondent (V44) was included as an additional predictor variable, with females recoded to 1 (use the SPSS RECODE command), and males to 0.

The calculated chi-square value of 133.46 is significant at the 0.001 level, suggesting that these demographic variables can discriminate between those who think Avery has a broad product line and those who think Avery's line is narrow. Note the discriminant function that states the following:

$$
\begin{aligned}
Y = \ & 0.502 \times \text{V41 (if white collar)} \\
& 0.085 \times \text{V42 (years worked)} \\
-\,& 0.042 \times \text{V44 (if female)} \\
& 0.959 \times \text{D5 (if single)} \\
& 0.752 \times \text{D4 (if married)} \\
& 0.468 \times \text{D3 (if separated)} \\
& 0.139 \times \text{D2 (if divorced)}
\end{aligned}
$$

where Y is the discriminant score. This function, of course, is constructed in such a way that it maximally discriminates between the two groups. The group centroid for those who think Avery has a broad product line is 1.237, while the group centroid for those who believe that Avery has a narrow product line is -1.657.

Note from the matrix in Table 17B.2 that there were actually 53 people in Group 1 and 71 in Group 2. Using the discriminant function, 48 of the 53 belonging to Group 1 would be predicted to belong there and 65 of the 71 belonging to Group 2 would be predicted to belong there. The overall classification accuracy is approximately 91 percent. Because the proportional chance or C_{pro} criterion is

$$
\begin{aligned}
C_{\text{pro}} &= \alpha^2 + (1 - \alpha)^2 \\
&= (71/124)^2 + (53/124)^2 = 0.328 + 0.182 = 0.511
\end{aligned}
$$

there is approximately a 40 percent (91–51) improvement in prediction accuracy through the use of the discriminant function.

TABLE 17B.1	**Discriminant Analysis of Those Believing Avery's Product Line Is Narrow or Broad as a Function of Demographic Characteristics**

Number of Cases by Group

	Number of Cases	
V20	*Unweighted*	*Weighted*
1	53	53.0
2	71	71.0
Total	124	124.0

Canonical Discriminant Function

Minimum number of functions .1
Minimum cumulative percent of variance 100.0
Maximum significance of Wilks' lambda 1.0000
Prior probability for each group is 0.500

Canonical Discriminant Functions

Function	Eigenvalue	Percent of Variance	Cumulative Percent	Canonical Correlation
1	2.084	100.0	100.0	0.822

After Function	Wilks' Lambda	Chi-squared	DF	Significance
0	0.324	133.46	7	0.000

Standardized Canonical Discriminant Function Coefficients

	Function 1
V41	0.502
V42	0.085
V44	−0.042
D5	0.959
D4	0.752
D3	0.468
D2	0.139

Canonical Discriminant Functions Evaluated at Groups' Means (Group Centroids)

Group	Function 1
1	−1.657
2	1.237

TABLE 17B.2	Matrix of Predicted vs. Actual Classifications			

			Predicted Group Membership	
Actual Group	Number of Cases		1	2
Group 1	53		48 (90.6%)	5 (9.4%)
Group 2	71		6 (8.5%)	65 (91.5%)

Percent of "grouped" cases correctly classified: 91.13%

Factor Analysis

Another question of interest in the Avery study is whether people's attitudes toward buying from catalogs is a unidimensional trait or whether it has dimensions to it, just like a person's arithmetic ability is a composite of the individual's addition, subtraction, multiplication, and division abilities. To explore this issue, the responses to Questions 12 through 20, which all deal with what might happen when ordering from catalogs, were factor analyzed.

Table 17B.3 contains the results. Principal components analysis was used to generate the initial solution. The eigenvalues suggested that a three-factor solution was appropriate. Consequently, three factors were rotated using the varimax criterion. The communality for each of the variables is high. Further, close to 72 percent of the total variation in the data is explained by the three-factor solution. The factors are, of course, named by looking at the variation in the variables accounted for by each factor. Panel C of Table 17B.3 suggests, for example, that Factor 2 does a particularly good job of accounting for the variation in variables 24, 26, and 28; Factor 1 for the variation in variables 21, 22, and 23; and Factor 3 for the variation in variables 25, 27, and 29. Variables 24, 26, and 28 all address the convenience of ordering through catalogs, and thus Factor 2 might be called a convenience factor or dimension. Similarly, Factor 1 might be labeled a riskiness factor and Factor 3 an economy factor.

Cluster Analysis

The responses to Question 21 concern the importance of the various services or features when purchasing through catalogs. These responses were cluster analyzed to determine if the various features go together in the sense that there are such things as convenience features, risk-reducing features, and so on. The average linkage method was used.

The squared Euclidean distances between the variables are shown in Panel A of Table 17B.4, while Panel B contains the dendrogram resulting from the analysis. A

| TABLE 17B.3 | Factor Analysis of Attitude Statements Concerning Buying from Catalogs |

Panel A: Initial Factor Analysis Solution

Variable	Estimated Commonality	Factor	Eigenvalue	Percentage of Variance	Cumulative Percentage
V21	1.000	1	2.964	32.9	32.9
V22	1.000	2	2.120	23.6	56.5
V23	1.000	3	1.390	15.4	71.9
V24	1.000	4	0.662	7.4	79.3
V25	1.000	5	0.612	6.8	86.1
V26	1.000	6	0.465	4.5	90.6
V27	1.000	7	0.350	3.9	94.5
V28	1.000	8	0.272	3.0	97.5
V29	1.000	9	0.226	2.5	100.0

Panel B: Factor Loadings before Rotation

Variable	Factor 1	Factor 2	Factor 3	Communality
V21	0.778	0.153	−0.419	0.804
V22	0.801	0.201	−0.270	0.756
V23	0.792	0.223	−0.398	0.836
V24	−0.022	0.721	0.183	0.553
V25	0.552	0.021	0.569	0.628
V26	−0.021	0.875	0.136	0.784
V27	0.708	−0.280	0.381	0.724
V28	−0.136	0.760	0.277	0.673
V29	0.514	−0.258	0.621	0.717

Panel C: Varimax Rotated Factor Matrix

Variable	Factor 1	Factor 2	Factor 3	Communality
V21	0.891	−0.030	0.096	0.804
V22	0.840	0.058	0.217	0.756
V23	0.907	0.042	0.107	0.836
V24	0.044	0.742	−0.013	0.553
V25	0.140	0.149	0.766	0.628
V26	0.106	0.876	−0.080	0.784
V27	0.302	−0.203	0.770	0.724
V28	−0.090	0.815	−0.013	0.673
V29	0.019	−0.099	0.842	0.717

TABLE 17B.4	Cluster Analysis of Importance Features

Panel A: Squared Euclidean Distances

Variable	V30	V31	V32	V33	V34	V35	V36	V37
V31	354							
V32	203	385						
V33	462	160	349					
V34	191	475	194	485				
V35	425	159	378	143	476			
V36	109	463	180	507	182	500		
V37	410	100	349	120	477	117	477	
V38	654	598	669	724	885	673	723	670

Panel B: Dendrogram

Variable	Description	Coefficient (0 100 200 300 400 500 600 700)
V31	Quantity discount	
V37	Guarantees	
V35	Years in business	
V33	Return policy	
V30	Toll-free number	
V36	Company reputation	
V34	Trial period	
V32	Shipping time	
V38	Endorsements	

glance at this diagram reveals that the nine variables might best be divided into three clusters:

Cluster 1	Cluster 2	Cluster 3
Quantity discounts	Toll-free number	Endorsements
Guarantees	Company reputation	
Years in business	Trial period	
Return policy	Shipping time	

The researcher would then undertake the more subjective task of naming the three clusters.

CASE 5.1
Wisconsin Power & Light[1] (C)

In response to the current consumer trend toward increased environmental sensitivity, Wisconsin Power & Light (WP&L) adopted several high-visibility environmental initiatives. These environmental programs fell under the BuySmart umbrella of WP&L's Demand-Side Management Programs and were intended to foster the conservation of energy among WP&L's residential, commercial, and industrial customers. Examples of specific programs include: Appliance Rebates, Energy Analysis, Weatherization Help, and the Home Energy Improvement Loan (HEIL) program. All previous marketing research and information gathering focused primarily on issues from the customers' perspective, such as an evaluation of net program impacts in terms of energy and demand savings and an estimation of the levels of free ridership (individuals who would have undertaken the conservation actions promoted by the program, even if no program in place). In addition, a study has been designed and is currently being conducted to evaluate and identify customer attitudes and opinions concerning the design, implementation, features, and delivery of the residential programs. Having examined the consumer perspective, WP&L's next objective is to focus on obtaining information from other participants in the programs, namely employees and lenders.

WP&L's immediate research focus is to undertake a study of the HEIL program of the BuySmart umbrella. The HEIL program was designed to make low-interest-rate financing available to residential gas and electric WP&L customers for conservation and weatherization measures. The low-interest guaranteed loans are delivered through WP&L account representatives in conjunction with participating financial institutions and trade allies. The procedures for obtaining a loan begin with an energy audit of the interested customer's residence to determine the appropriate conservation measures. Once the customer decides on which measures to have installed, the WP&L representative assists in arranging low-interest-rate financing through one of the participating local banking institutions. At the completion of the projects, WP&L representatives conduct an inspection of the work by checking a random sample of participants. Conservation measures eligible under the HEIL program include the installation of natural gas furnaces/boilers, automatic vent dampers, intermittent ignition devices, heat pumps, and heat pump water heaters. Eligible structural improvements include the addition of attic/wall/basement insulation, storm windows and doors, sillbox insulation, window weather-stripping, and caulking.

Purpose

The primary goal of the current study is to identify ways of improving the HEIL program from the lenders' point of view. Specifically, the following issues need to be addressed:

- Identify the lenders' motivation for participating in the program.
- Determine how lenders get their information regarding various changes/updates in the program.
- Identify how lenders promote the program.
- Assess the current program with respect to administrative and program features.
- Determine the type of credit analysis conducted by the lenders.
- Identify ways of minimizing the default rate from the lenders' point of view.
- Assess the lenders' commitment to the program.
- Identify lenders' opinions of the overall program.
- Identify if the reason for loan inactivity in some lending institutions is due to lack of a customer base.

Methodology

WP&L decided to use a telephone survey of participating lending institutions to collect the data for its study. WP&L referenced two lists of lending institutions, which were supplied by their residential marketing staff, to select the sample for the survey. A total of 124 participating lending institutions was identified with the lists. However, it was found that one of the

---

[1]The contributions of Kavita Maini and Paul Metz to the development of this case are gratefully acknowledged, as is the permission of Wisconsin Power & Light to use the material included.

lists was shorter than the other by 15 names. Specifically, the names of some of the branches of major banks were not enumerated on one of the lists. Nevertheless, all 124 institutions, including the 15 discrepant ones, were included in the pool of names from which the sample was drawn.

The sample pool was stratified into three groups based on loan activity in the 1998 calendar year. The groups fell out as follows:

Group	Number of Lenders	Loan Activity, 1998
1	44	0 loans
2	40	1–7 loans
3	40	8–54 loans

The final sample for the survey consisted of 20 systematically chosen lenders from Groups 2 and 3, and 10 randomly chosen institutions from Group 1. The 40 institutions selected from among Groups 2 and 3 formed the sample base in which WP&L was most interested (this was because each of these 40 institutions demonstrated loan activity in the past year). Consequently, WP&L used a systematic selection procedure for this key group to ensure that the sample represented the population and to improve the statistical efficiency of the sample. The sample size ($n = 40$) was based on judgment. The 10 randomly selected institutions from Group 1 were chosen primarily to explore the hypothesized reasons for zero-loan activity. These 10 zero-loan lenders received a shortened version of the telephone survey that focused only on their lack of activity.

All the districts within WP&L's service territory were notified two weeks in advance that a survey would be conducted. A survey was designed to address

---

TABLE 5.1.1   Verbatim Responses Regarding the Benefits Conveyed to Lenders by Participation in the HEIL Program

1. We acquire a new loan customer. The customer likes the fact that the loan is guaranteed.
2. It's good public relations to be associated with WP&L. Also, we have nothing to lose on it. It is a risk-free program.
3. It fulfills the CRA (Credit Reinvestment Act) requirement.
4. We got some new customers. People from other towns cannot get into the HEIL program from their bank.
5. We make some money through the buydown.
6. We have access to more services and can therefore cross-sell other services. We stay competitive this way. It's also good PR to be associated with WP&L.
7. We provide another service to the customer. It helps us to stay competitive.
8. We improve on customer service by providing an additional service. It helps us stay competitive.
9. We can provide another service. We have also built customer contact a lot more.
10. We earn interest income. Customers look on us more favorably because this program is really good.
11. We got some new customers. In addition, the HEIL program helps us make more loans, which is helping us to make revenue.
12. We get money out of the interest buydowns.
13. Another service to provide our customers.
14. It is an added service that enriches our offerings. People come back for other loans.
15. It fulfills CRA. Also, good public relations to be associated with WP&L.
16. It fulfills CRA. Also, more loans implies more income for the bank and a higher proportion can be reinvested back into the community.
17. Another service to provide our customers.
18. It fulfills CRA.
19. Another service to provide for our customers.
20. Good public relations.
21. We can provide another service to our customers.
22. We got some new customers.
23. It's good for our customers.
24. No benefits anymore. There are so many restrictions. There should be more types of options.
25. We are in it for the CRA.
26. We can provide another service to our customers.
27. No benefits because too many good options are excluded.
28. It fulfills the CRA requirement. We are providing the customers a service that has very good rates.
29. We got some new customers.
30. Financially, we get more money by lending without the program.
31. We provide another service to our customers.
32. We are in it for the CRA.
33. We get money through the buydowns.
34. We gain new customers.
35. Good public relations.
36. We provide another service and it allows us to help people who really need the loan.
37. We provide another service to our clients and community.
38. It helps us provide another service to our clients and community.
39. We don't have a high enough volume to be able to say that there has been a benefit.
40. We provide another service to our customers.

the research objectives and included both closed and open-ended questions. The survey was pretested and modified before final administration. All interviewing was conducted over a one-week period by a project manager and research assistant, both employees of WP&L's marketing department.

One of the open-ended questions in the survey asked lenders to identify the benefits gained by participating in the HEIL program. The actual wording of the question follows:

Q.6 Does your bank benefit in any way by participating in this program?   1 Yes   2 No
Q.7 Would you please explain your answer?

Data from this question, it was hypothesized, could be used to address several of the aforementioned research objectives. First, the responses would provide qualitative insights into the lenders' motivation for participating in the program. Second, they would help explain lenders' level of commitment to the program as well as help identify reasons why banks promote (or fail to promote) the HEIL program. Finally, the benefits cited could provide WP&L with an understanding of the lenders' overall opinion of the program. Table 5.1.1 contains a list of the verbatim responses to this open-ended question.

QUESTIONS

1. Synthesize the verbatim responses by developing a set of codes and then grouping them into categories that would help WP&L understand the perceived benefits of the HEIL program.

2. What advantages does the researcher gain by coding open-ended data?

3. What recommendations would you make to WP&L about the HEIL program based on what the open-ended data suggest?

CASE 5.2
Star Equipment (A)[1]

Star Equipment is a Fortune 500 company that manufactures technologically advanced equipment for a variety of applications. Star Equipment's office-products division is one of the three largest manufacturers of office equipment in the world. Traditionally, its largest competitor in the office-equipment cate-

gory has been Vetra—a domestic manufacturer of advanced office equipment. However, beginning in the 1980s and continuing into the 1990s, Calt, a large foreign manufacturer of office equipment, achieved major gains in the U.S. market. Star also faces significant competition from a number of smaller, specialized office-equipment manufacturers.

For Star Equipment's office-products division to remain profitable with the increased competition, division managers outlined four strategies to promote sales: (1) identify key accounts for Star's office products, (2) examine the purchase decision process within these key accounts, (3) determine the critical vendor services sought by these accounts, and (4) assess the performance of Star and its two main competitors on these critical characteristics.

Research Method

Star's marketing research team designed a two-stage research project involving both secondary and primary research to gather the information identified in the four strategies. The first stage of the project involved exhaustive secondary research along with internal and external depth interviews to identify the vendor attributes important to office-equipment customers. Thirteen vendor characteristics were identified as being of some importance to customers.

The thirteen characteristics were incorporated in a survey in which respondents were asked to select the four most- and four least-important characteristics. Respondents were also asked to rate the vendors considered for their company's most recent office-equipment purchase on each of the attributes. Since Star was interested primarily in its own performance ratings along with its two major competitors, Calt and Vetra, these three vendors were explicitly specified in Question 3 in the survey; an "other" column was provided to capture the ratings of smaller vendors that may have been considered.

The survey in Figure 5.2.1 was mailed to 812 respondents who were either considering an office-equipment purchase or had purchased this type of equipment within the last two years. The sample was drawn from the customer lists of both Star and its office-equipment dealers. A $10 incentive was used to encourage responses. The research sponsor was not identified, and data collection was coordinated through an independent research-supply firm. Three hundred usable surveys were returned from the initial mailing. Figure 5.2.2 displays the coding of the questionnaires.

[1]The contributions of Sara L. Pitterle to this case are gratefully acknowledged.

FIGURE 5.2.1   **Star Office Equipment Questionnaire**

Q1. Thinking specifically about your most recent equipment purchase decision, list all the vendors considered in this decision. By vendor we mean companies that manufacture the equipment.

_____	7–8
_____	9–10
_____	11–12
_____	13–14

Q2. Listed below are vendor characteristics that could be used to make a decision about which equipment to purchase. Thinking about your most recent purchase decision:
A. Check (✔) the four (4) most important vendor characteristics in your purchase decision.
B. Check (✔) the four (4) least important vendor characteristics in your purchase decision.

Vendor Characteristics	A Most Important (Check 4)	B Least Important (Check 4)
a. Vendor values a long-term relationship and works to meet my organization's unique needs...........................	01 ☐ 15–16/	01 ☐ 23–24/
b. My relationships with the vendor's sales and support representatives are easy and productive...........................	02 ☐ 17–18/	02 ☐ 25–26/
c. Vendor enables my organization to have a smooth decision process..............	03 ☐ 19–20/	03 ☐ 27–28/
d. The vendor establishes fair pricing policies for products and services........	04 ☐ 21–22/	04 ☐ 29–30/
e. The vendor's service organization is responsive to my organization's needs ...	05 ☐	05 ☐
f. The vendor offers an extensive line of reliable products meeting the needs of my organization	06 ☐	06 ☐
g. The vendor's solutions enable my organization to use people, space, and resources efficiently	07 ☐	07 ☐
h. The vendor offers software to increase the productivity and satisfaction of my department and employees	08 ☐	08 ☐
i. Vendor's products are easy to use	09 ☐	09 ☐
j. The vendor's solutions help my business grow	10 ☐	10 ☐
k. The vendor's solutions give me the ability to offer quick response to my customers' needs	11 ☐	11 ☐

(continued)

FIGURE 5.2.1   (continued)

Vendor Characteristics	A Most Important (Check 4)	B Least Important (Check 4)
l. The vendor provides my company with solutions that protect the safety and legality of information	12 ☐	12 ☐
m. The vendor provides my firm with technological advantages today that can be leveraged to meet our future requirements	13 ☐	13 ☐

Q3. Using the following scale, write the number (in each box) that best describes how well each of the vendors fulfilled your expectations during your <u>most recent purchase</u> decision.

1 = *Completely* *Fulfilled*	*2 =* *Somewhat* *Fulfilled*	*3 =* *Neither* *Fulfilled* *nor Unfulfilled*	*4 =* *Somewhat* *Unfulfilled*	*5 =* *Not at All* *Fulfilled*	*0 =* *Not* *Appropriate*

Vendor Characteristics	Calt	Star	Vetra	Other
a. Vendor values a long-term relationship and works to meet my organization's unique needs	☐ 31/	☐ 44/	☐ 57/	☐ 70/
b. My relationships with the vendor's sales and support representatives are easy and productive	☐ 32/	☐ 45/	☐ 58/	☐ 71/
c. Vendor enables my organization to have a smooth decision process	☐ 33/	☐ 46/	☐ 59/	☐ 72/
d. The vendor establishes fair pricing policies for products and services . . .	☐ 34/	☐ 47/	☐ 60/	☐ 73/
e. The vendor's service organization is responsive to my organization's needs	☐ 35/	☐ 48/	☐ 61/	☐ 74/
f. The vendor offers an extensive line of reliable products meeting the needs of my organization	☐ 36/	☐ 49/	☐ 62/	☐ 75/
g. The vendor's solutions enable my organization to use people, space, and resources efficiently	☐ 37/	☐ 50/	☐ 63/	☐ 76/
h. The vendor offers software to increase the productivity and satisfaction of my department and employees	☐ 38/	☐ 51/	☐ 64/	☐ 77/
i. Vendor's products are easy to use	☐ 39/	☐ 52/	☐ 65/	☐ 78/
j. The vendor's solutions help my business grow	☐ 40/	☐ 53/	☐ 66/	☐ 79/

FIGURE 5.2.1   (continued)

Vendor Characteristics	Calt	Star	Vetra	Other
k. The vendor's solutions give me the ability to offer quick response to my customers' needs...................	☐ 41/	☐ 54/	☐ 67/	☐ 80/
l. The vendor provides my company with solutions that protect the safety and legality of information.........	☐ 42/	☐ 55/	☐ 68/	☐ 81/
m. The vendor provides my firm with technological advantages today that can be leveraged to meet our future requirements......................	☐ 43/	☐ 56/	☐ 69/	☐ 82/

Q4. How often do you acquire new equipment?

1☐ Less than 1 year   3☐ 3 years to less than 6 years   83/
2☐ 1 year to less than 3 years   4☐ 6 years or more

Q5. From whom do you acquire your equipment? (Check all that apply.)

1☐ Directly from manufacturers   3☐ Broker   84–87/
2☐ Dealer   4☐ Other (Specify):_____

Q6. From whom do you acquire your supplies and software? (Check all that apply.)

1☐ Manufacturer   6☐ Small storefront   88–98/
2☐ Mail order   7☐ Super stores
3☐ Contract dealer   8☐ Warehouse club
4☐ Buying group   9☐ Dealer
5☐ Supplies merchant   10☐ Other (Specify):_____

Q7. What are the reasons for using these suppliers and software? (Check all that apply.)

1☐ Reputation of supplier   5☐ Recommendation   99–106/
2☐ Product-quality   6☐ Delivery time
3☐ Product-performance/yield   7☐ Price
4☐ Ease of ordering   8☐ Other (Specify):_____

Q8. Do you purchase, rent, and/or lease your equipment? (Check all that apply.)

1☐ Purchase   3☐ Lease   107–110/
2☐ Rent   4☐ Other (Specify):_____

Q9. Which of the following best describes where these types of purchase decisions are made in your company?

1☐ At corporate headquarters for all locations   111/
2☐ At each company location or branch office
3☐ Departmental level within each location
4☐ My company has only one office or location
5☐ Other (specify):_____

The Sample

Star was able to identify the primary office-equipment manufacturer for each of the 300 respondents. This information is contained in Table 5.2.1. Table 5.2.2 lists the equipment vendors considered by these respondents for their most recent equipment purchase. Table 5.2.3 summarizes the variables chosen as Most Important and Least Important by the respondents.

QUESTIONS

1. Star wants the questionnaire in Figure 5.2.1 to be completed by the person responsible for purchasing office equipment. Is a mail survey the most appropriate way to reach these people? Why or why not?

2. Was conducting secondary research followed by depth interviews an appropriate means of

FIGURE 5.2.2	Coding Format for Star Office Equipment Questionnaire
Columns	**Contents**
1–5	Respondent identification number
6	Current primary equipment manufacturer for respondent: precoded, not a survey question.
	Manufacturers:
	1 = Star
	2 = Vetra
	3 = Calt
	4 = Snap
	5 = Reggies
	Q1. Vendors considered in *most recent* purchase
7–8	Vendor 1 (See vendor code list below)
9–10	Vendor 2
11–12	Vendor 3
13–14	Vendor 4
	Vendor codes:
	1 = Calt
	2 = Star
	3 = Reggies
	4 = Snap
	5 = Vetra
	94 = No selection made
	95 = Other vendor
	98 = Don't know
15–22	Q2. Four most important vendor characteristics (See Questionnaire for definition of codes 01–13)
23–30	Q2. Four least important vendor characteristics (See Questionnaire for definition of codes 01–13)
31	Q3a, Calt rating of how well vendor fulfilled expectations (See Questionnaire for definition of characteristics a–m and scale values)
32	Q3b
33	Q3c
34	Q3d
35	Q3e
36	Q3f
37	Q3g
38	Q3h
39	Q3i

FIGURE 5.2.2	(continued)
Columns	**Contents**
40	Q3j
41	Q3k
42	Q3l
43	Q3m
44	Q3a, Star rating of how well vendor fulfilled expectations
	(See Questionnaire for definition of characteristics a – m and scale values)
45	Q3b
46	Q3c
47	Q3d
48	Q3e
49	Q3f
50	Q3g
51	Q3h
52	Q3i
53	Q3j
54	Q3k
55	Q3l
56	Q3m
57	Q3a, Vetra rating of how well vendor fulfilled expectations
	(See Questionnaire for definition of characteristics a–m and scale values)
58	Q3b
59	Q3c
60	Q3d
61	Q3e
62	Q3f
63	Q3g
64	Q3h
65	Q3i
66	Q3j
67	Q3k
68	Q3l
69	Q3m
70	Q3a, "Other vendor" rating of how well the vendor fulfilled expectations
	(See Questionnaire for definition of characteristics a–m and scale values)
71	Q3b
72	Q3c
73	Q3d
74	Q3e
75	Q3f
76	Q3g
77	Q3h
78	Q3i
79	Q3j
80	Q3k
81	Q3l
82	Q3m
83	Q4. How often do you purchase this equipment?

(continued)

FIGURE 5.2.2	(continued)
Columns	**Contents**
84	Q5. Acquire equipment from manufacturers
85	from dealers
86	from brokers
87	from other
88–96	Q6. Where acquire supplies
	1 = Manufacturer
	2 = Mail order
	3 = Contract dealer
	4 = Buying group
	5 = Supplies merchant
	6 = Small storefront
	7 = Super stores
	8 = Warehouse club
	9 = Dealer
97–98	10 = Other
99–106	Q7. Reasons use suppliers
	1 = Reputation of supplier
	2 = Product-quality
	3 = Product-performance/yield
	4 = Ease of ordering
	5 = Recommendation
	6 = Delivery time
	7 = Price
	8 = Other
107	Q8. Purchase equipment
108	Rent equipment
109	Lease equipment
110	Other
111	Q9. Where purchase decisions made

generating the primary vendor characteristics for this survey? Why or why not?

3. Read each of the 13 vendor-characteristic statements carefully. Are these statements appropriate for a mail survey? Are there particular statements that may pose problems for respondents? Why?

4. Star's sample for this study was generated from its own sales lists and those of its dealers. Did the use of these lists as sampling frames lead to a biased sample? Explain.

5. Using the questionnaire and coding format provided in Figures 5.2.1 and 5.2.2, how many variables are necessary to capture completely the responses to Questions 6 and 7? Identify the problems that may arise from this particular coding format.

6. Using data supplied on the computer disk, generate one-way tabulations for Survey Questions 6 and 7 (columns 88–106). How can these frequencies be explained? Is there a better way of coding these questions to avoid these types of problems?

7. Can the data in columns 88–106 still be used in this analysis? Justify your decision.

8. Star's research team wants to group respondents based on the similarity of attributes chosen as either important or not important. Thus, Question 2 is critical to the success of this project. Looking at Table 5.2.3, did respondents answer this question correctly? What should be done with those cases that are incorrect? Justify your answer.

9. How would you recode the data from Question 3 to facilitate interpretation? How would you handle the 0 ("Not Appropriate") ratings in this question?

TABLE 5.2.1	Primary Manufacturers

Manufacturer	Frequency	% Sample
Vetra	98	33
Star	87	29
Calt	61	20
Snap	32	11
Reggies	22	7

TABLE 5.2.2	Vendors Considered in Most Recent Equipment Purchase

Manufacturer	Frequency	% Sample
Vetra	166	55
Star	109	36
Calt	109	36
Other Vendors	97	32
Snap	57	19
Reggies	46	15

TABLE 5.2.3	Attributes Chosen as Most and Least Important

	Most Important							Least Important
Attribute	1	2	3	4	1	2	3	4
a	183	0	0	0	33	0	0	0
b	48	75	0	0	44	8	0	0
c	8	13	5	0	110	32	3	0
d	37	101	40	2	4	7	0	0
e	12	71	104	26	1	5	1	1
f	2	16	47	29	26	35	12	0
g	4	6	16	5	37	62	21	1
h	1	10	30	21	9	29	25	8
i	2	3	31	102	4	10	16	4
j	3	2	11	23	13	49	45	5
k	0	3	9	24	4	37	54	11
l	0	0	6	1	0	7	91	130
m	0	0	0	62	0	0	3	104
Total	300	300	299	295	285	281	271	264

CASE 5.3
Canopy of Care (B)[1]

Canopy of Care is a nonprofit organization that solicits donations on behalf of various local charities, thereby relieving them of the need to market themselves and raise funds on an individual basis (see Canopy of Care [A] for more details). Fundraising is accomplished with the cooperation of local businesses and government agencies, who approach their employees on behalf of Canopy of Care and, given employee pledges, deduct donations directly out of their wages and salaries.

Recent statistics have shown that only 50 percent of the employees in participating companies agree to contribute. With economic conditions in the

[1]The contributions of Jacqueline C. Hitchon to the development of this case are gratefully acknowledged.

community deteriorating, Canopy of Care officials believe that their approach to potential donors needs to be more effective. To determine why solicited employees do not contribute, they decided to investigate differences in knowledge and attitudes about Canopy of Care between givers and nongivers. A marketing research firm was hired to tackle the problem, and, based on interviews with Canopy of Care personnel and a review of secondary sources, the following ideas were developed to guide the research:

1. The manner in which a firm conducts its Canopy of Care campaign may negatively affect employee giving. Employee reactions to the following issues could be important in this regard:
   a. Employees are pressured to contribute by management.
   b. Firms participate in Canopy of Care campaigns to enhance their image.
   c. Employees would like to be more involved with their firms' Canopy of Care campaigns.
   d. Employees think that the union should be involved in Canopy of Care campaigns.
2. Employees who have inaccurate information about Canopy of Care's functions and activities are less likely to give. Influential knowledge factors could be the following:
   a. Employees think that Canopy of Care receives government funding.
   b. Employees don't know about the donor option program.
   c. Employees of firms conducting Canopy of Care campaigns have more accurate knowledge about Canopy of Care.

3. Employees who have negative attitudes toward and perceptions about Canopy of Care are less likely to give. Key negative attitudes and perceptions could include the following:
   a. Canopy of Care is inefficient.
   b. Canopy of Care programs are not useful to employees in general.
   c. Canopy of Care funds programs that do not aid an employee and his or her family.
   d. Canopy of Care helps only the poor.

Method

The previously outlined issues were addressed by means of a questionnaire (see Figure 5.3.1). Because lists of employees might be considered confidential by many businesses, it was decided that the research population would be broadened from employees of companies solicited by Canopy of Care to all adult employees in the area. The white pages in the local telephone book could then be used as the sampling frame. Accordingly, professional interviewers were hired to complete the telephone survey using Plus-One dialing. Because the target population was employed adults, the majority of whom are working away from home during the day, phone calls were placed during evening hours.

QUESTIONS

1. Which items in the questionnaire correspond to each of the issues guiding the research?
2. How would you propose to analyze the data to investigate these issues? Be specific.

FIGURE 5.3.1   **Canopy of Care Telephone Survey**

Name of interviewer _____

(Interviewer — fill out for each person:)

First name _____
Time called _____
Date _____
Sex of respondent   M   or   F   {Do not ask}
Telephone # _____

Hello, my name is _____

{If a child answers, ask:} *Could I please speak to someone over 16 who is employed?*

FIGURE 5.3.1   (continued)

I am conducting a survey for Canopy of Care. I'd appreciate it if you would answer a few questions. I will not be soliciting donations.

1. *Which of the programs funded by Canopy of Care do you feel is the most important?*_____

2. *Have you been employed in the last year?*   Y   or   N

{If No, stop questionnaire.}

3. *Does your employer conduct a Canopy of Care campaign?*   Y   or   N

{If No, go to question #8.}

4. *How would you describe your company's attitude toward employee giving? Would you say:* **{Read a–c.}**
   a.   The company is against employee giving.
   b.   The company is neutral to the entire issue.
   c.   The company encourages employee giving.
   d.   Don't know.

5. *For the following statements, please indicate whether you Agree, have No opinion, or Disagree.*

   The company should support Canopy of Care.   A,   N,   D
   Pressure is put on me to contribute.   A,   N,   D
   The Canopy of Care fund drive should be run by the company's   A,   N,   D
     executives.
   The company wants to contribute in order to help its image.   A,   N,   D
   More employees at all levels should be involved in the Canopy   A,   N,   D
     of Care fund and its fund drive.
   Unions should not be involved in the Canopy of Care fund drive.   A,   N,   D
   Canopy of Care should solicit people at home.   A,   N,   D

6. *Please answer the following question Yes or No.*
   Did you, personally, give money to Canopy of Care last year?   Y   or   N

{If Yes, go to #8.}

7. *We are interested in why people do not contribute. The following is a list of answers others have given. Please tell me which, if any, apply to you.*

{Read each and ask for a yes or a no.}

   a.   _____   Someone else in my household had already contributed.
   b.   _____   I did not have the money at the time.
   c.   _____   I gave to other charities.

(continued)

FIGURE 5.3.1   (continued)

---

    d. ____ I volunteered my services to Canopy of Care instead of contributing
            money.

    e. ____ I volunteered my services to other charities instead of contributing to
            Canopy of Care.

    f. ____ I did not give because Canopy of Care spends its money inefficiently.

    g. ____ None of the above.

8. *To how many different charities do you think Canopy of Care gives money?*

{Interviewer — Circle the appropriate response.}

    a. 0–20
    b. 21–40
    c. 41–80
    d. 81–100
    e. More than 100
    f. Don't know.

9. *For the following statements, please indicate whether you Agree, have No opinion, Disagree, or Don't Know.*

The programs funded by Canopy of Care are useful.	A, N, D, DK
The government should be responsible for the type of services Canopy of Care agencies provide.	A, N, D, DK
Canopy of Care programs are not useful to me or my family.	A, N, D, DK
Canopy of Care agencies help only the poor.	A, N, D, DK
Canopy of Care receives government funding.	A, N, D, DK
Canopy of Care can be viewed as a kind of insurance policy for everyone.	A, N, D, DK
Canopy of Care funds programs it should not support.	A, N, D, DK

10. *Respond True or False — You can specify which charity your money goes to when donating to Canopy of Care.*   T   or   F   or   DK

{If False, or Don't Know, go to #12.}

11. *Again, True or False — The money donated really goes to the specific charity picked.*   T   or   F   or   DK

12. *I'm going to read to you a list that includes a number of organizations. Please tell me which of these groups, if any, you contributed to last year.*

{Interviewer — please read the list, and check the appropriate spaces.}

____ American Cancer Society
____ Red Cross
____ American Heart Association
____ March of Dimes

FIGURE 5.3.1   **(continued)**

_____ Easter Seals
_____ Multiple Sclerosis
_____ Salvation Army
_____ MACC Fund
_____ UPAF (United Performing Arts Funds)
_____ Other
_____ Did not contribute

13. How many employees are there in the firm for which you work?

{Interviewer — Circle the appropriate response.}

   a.   Fewer than 100 employees
   b.   100 to 500 employees
   c.   More than 500 employees
   d.   Don't know

14. For what type of organization do you work?

{Interviewer — please read the list.}

   a.   Manufacturing
   b.   Government
   c.   Wholesale/retail
   d.   Service industry — includes trades and professions
   e.   Other

15. Are you employed full-time?   Y   or   N

16. In your present company, are you in a managerial position?   Y   or   N

17. Do you presently belong to a union?   Y   or   N

18. How long have you lived in the area?
   a.   Less than 1 year
   b.   1 year up to 3 years
   c.   3 years up to 5 years
   d.   More than 5 years

19. How many children do you have at home?
   a.   None
   b.   One
   c.   Two
   d.   Three
   e.   More than three

(continued)

FIGURE 5.3.1   (continued)

20. *What is your marital status?*
    a. Married
    b. Single — never married
    c. Separated
    d. Divorced
    e. Widowed
    f. Other

21. *What is your zip code?*_____

22. *What is your race?* {**Read list.**}
    a. White
    b. African-American
    c. Hispanic
    d. Native American
    e. Asian
    f. Other_____

23. *Please stop me when I come to the category that contains your age.*
    a. 16–24
    b. 25–34
    c. 35–49
    d. 50 and over

24. *Stop me when we get to your annual personal income level before taxes.*
    a. Less than $10,000
    b. $10,000 to under $15,000
    c. $15,000 to under $25,000
    d. $25,000 to under $40,000
    e. More than $40,000

CASE 5.4

CTM Productions (B)[1]

CTM Productions, formerly Children's Theatre of Madison, was formed in 1965 to "produce theater of the highest quality." CTM's mission is to ensure that the theatre's efforts are inclusive of the entire family. For CTM to fulfill its role in the community, the organization must identify its present audience in terms of demographic, psychographic, and media-exposure characteristics.

The research team decided to study the audience of CTM's production *To Kill a Mockingbird.* The study had three major objectives: (1) to develop an audience profile, including demographic and media-exposure data; (2) to provide a framework and data-collection instrument for future marketing research; and (3) to supply a list of potential season subscribers.

CTM had never undertaken marketing research prior to this study, so internal secondary information about previous audiences did not exist. External secondary information provided guidance as to the types of questions to be asked in a survey and the appropriate phrasing of these questions. The questionnaire is shown in Figure 1 of CTM Productions (A) in Case 3.7.

CTM's volunteer ushers distributed the survey at each of the 15 performances of *To Kill a Mockingbird.*

[1]The contributions of Sara L. Pitterle to this case are gratefully acknowledged.

The number of completed surveys for each show varied with the size of the audience for that show. A total of 1,016 usable surveys were collected during the course of the study. The data coding scheme for the survey is shown in Figure 5.4.1. The research team wants to analyze the data to understand the profile of CTM audiences in general as well as how the audience profiles vary among different performances of the same production.

QUESTIONS

1. Discuss the implications for CTM's marketing team if there are significant differences in the demographic profiles of those people attending the afternoon versus the evening shows.

2. Generate *a priori* hypotheses about the demographic profiles for the *To Kill a Mockingbird* performances. Identify the cross tabulations necessary to test your hypotheses. Explain why these particular cross tabulations are necessary.

3. Using data provided on the computer disk, run one-way tabulations on this data. Discuss the general findings from these tabulations.

4. Run the cross tabulations that you chose. What recommendations would you make to CTM based on these tables? Are the recommendations actionable? Explain.

5. What are the limitations of these profiles? Explain.

FIGURE 5.4.1	Coding Format for CTM Productions Questionnaire

Column(s)	Question Number	Variable	Coding Specification
1	—	Weekend of performance	1 = First weekend
			2 = Second weekend
			3 = Third weekend
2	—	Day and time of performance	1 = Friday, 7:30 P.M.
			2 = Saturday, 3:30 P.M.
			3 = Saturday, 7:30 P.M.
			4 = Sunday, 1:00 P.M.
			5 = Sunday, 3:30 P.M.
3–4	—	Performance in production	1 = Weekend 1, Show 1
			2 = Weekend 1, Show 2
			3 = Weekend 1, Show 3
			4 = Weekend 1, Show 4
			5 = Weekend 1, Show 5
			6 = Weekend 2, Show 1
			7 = Weekend 2, Show 2
			8 = Weekend 2, Show 3
			9 = Weekend 2, Show 4
			10 = Weekend 2, Show 5
			11 = Weekend 3, Show 1
			12 = Weekend 3, Show 2
			13 = Weekend 3, Show 3
			14 = Weekend 3, Show 4
			15 = Weekend 3, Show 5
5–7	1	Zip code — last three digits	999 = No response
			000 = Outside of 53XXX
			XXX = other digit combos
8	2a	Attending first CTM production	1 = Yes, box checked
			2 = No, box checked
9–22		Past Attendance of CTM productions	Questions 2b–2o
9	2b	Season subscriber 97/98	1 = Yes, box checked
10	2c	*Wind in the Willows*	2 = No, box checked

(continued)

FIGURE 5.4.1   (continued)

Column(s)	Question Number	Variable	Coding Specification
11	2d	*A Christmas Carol* 97	
12	2e	*Babar II* — Plan to attend	
13	2f	Season subscriber 96/97	
14	2g	*Red Shoes*	
15	2h	*A Christmas Carol* 96	
16	2i	*Anne of Green Gables*	
17	2j	*Narnia*	
18	2k	Season subscriber 95/96	
19	2l	*Beauty and the Beast*	
20	2m	*A Christmas Carol* 95	
21	2n	*I Remember Mama*	
22	2o	*Babar the Elephant*	
23–28		Who attending with today	Questions 3a–3f
23	3a	By myself	1 = Yes, box checked
24	3b	Adult friends	2 = No, box checked
25	3c	Partner/spouse	9 = All blank = No response
26	3d	Unrelated kids	
27	3e	My kids	
28	3f	Other families	
29–34		Who attended with in past	Questions 4a–4f
29	4a	By myself	1 = Yes, box checked
30	4b	Adult friends	2 = No, box checked
31	4c	Partner/spouse	9 = All blank = No response
32	4d	Unrelated kids	
33	4e	My kids	
34	4f	Other families	
35–40		CTM activity participation	Questions 5a–5f
35		After-school drama classes	1 = Yes, box checked
36		Summer school	2 = No, box checked
37		Auditions	9 = All blank = No response
38		Performances	
39		Have not participated	
40		Did not know I could	
41–55		Media Exposure for *To Kill a Mockingbird*	Questions 6a–6o
41	6a	Season brochure	1 = Yes, box checked
42	6b	Poster	2 = No, box checked
43	6c	*State Journal* story	9 = All blank = No response
44	6d	*Capital Times* story	
45	6e	*Isthmus* story	
46	6f	Other story	
47	6g	*State Journal* ad	
48	6h	*Capital Times* ad	
49	6i	*Isthmus* ad	
50	6j	Other ad	
51	6k	Radio	

FIGURE 5.4.1	**(continued)**		

Column(s)	Question Number	Variable	Coding Specification
52	6l	Television	
53	6m	Magazine	
54	6n	Word of mouth	
55	6o	Other media/exposure	
56	7	Attending because knew cast member	1 = Yes; 2 = No; 9 = No response
57–62		Events attended in the last 6 months	Questions 8a–8f
57	8a	Sports	1 = Yes, box checked
58	8b	Museums	2 = No, box checked
59	8c	Movies	9 = All blank = No response
60	8d	Lectures	
61	8e	Live musical performances	
62	8f	Other live theatrical performances	
63	9	Gender of survey respondent	1 = Female; 0 = Male; 9 = No response
64	10	Age category of respondent	1 = 16–20 6 = 61–70 2 = 21–30 7 = 71–80 3 = 31–40 8 = 81–100 4 = 41–50 9 = No response 5 = 51–60
65	11	Method of transport to performance	1 = Walk 4 = Other 2 = Car 9 = No response 3 = Bus
66	12	Distance traveled to performance	1 = Within Madison 2 = Less than 5 miles 3 = 6–10 miles 4 = Over 10 miles 9 = No response
67	13	Time lived in Madison/SC Wis.	1 = Do not live here 2 = Just arrived 3 = 1–3 years 4 = 4–7 years 5 = More 9 = No response
68	14	Level of education	1 = Some high school 2 = High school graduate 3 = Some college 4 = College graduate 5 = Some graduate school 6 = Graduate school graduate 7 = More 9 = No response
69	15	Annual household income	1 = Below $20,000 2 = $21–$30,000 3 = $31–$40,000

(continued)

FIGURE 5.4.1		(continued)	
Column(s)	Question Number	Variable	Coding Specification
			4 = $41–$50,000
			5 = More than $50,000
			6 = Not sure
			7 = Do not wish to reply
			9 = No response
70	16	Dual-income household	1 = Yes; 2 = No; 9 = No response
71	17	Number of people in household	1 = 1 (person) 5 = 5
			2 = 2 6 = 6
			3 = 3 7 = More
			4 = 4 9 = No response
72–78		Number children in grade categories	Questions 18a–18g
72	18a	Not in school yet	1, 2, . . . = Yes, # = Quantity
73	18b	Kindergarten–3rd grade	0 = None, box not checked
74	18c	4th–5th grade	9 = All blank = No response
75	18d	6th–8th grade	
76	18e	High school	
77	18f	College	
78	18g	Other	
79	19	Like to be on mailing list?	1 = Yes; 0 = No; 9 = No response
80	20	CTM member	1 = Yes; 0 = No; 9 = No response

CASE 5.5
Young Ideas Publishing Company (B)[1]

Young Ideas Publishing Company was founded three years ago by Linda Halley and her business partner, Teresa Martinez. Thus far, the company has published two novels, *Illusions of Summer* and *Ultimate Choices,* both written by Halley. The novels address several controversial social and political topics and are targeted toward high-school teenagers (ages 15 to 18 years). Both books have received critical praise but have not fared well commercially. Distributors have been unwilling to carry the books, believing that no real market demand exists for novels of this type. Halley, however, maintains that her novels would appeal to teens, particularly "nonconformist" teens—by her definition, teens who take an interest in social and political issues.

In an effort to generate insights into the local teen market, Halley has retained the services of a young marketing researcher. A research project has been designed to focus on the potential demand for the product among teens as well as potential marketing-mix elements. A questionnaire has been designed and administered to 166 teens in the target age group. A portion of the questionnaire is shown in Figure 5.5.1; note that a scale to measure the nonconformity construct is included.

QUESTIONS

1. Items 13 through 25 in Figure 5.5.1 attempt to measure nonconformity. Define "nonconformity" based on these items. How well do these items tap into the construct? What other items could (or should) have been included?

2. Analyze the data provided on the compter disk using cross-tabulations or other analyses. Summarize your findings and make recommendations. Include descriptions of the student market in general, the most likely student market for books of this nature (if one exists), and the "nonconformist" student market.

[1]The contributions of Tom J. Brown to the development of this case are gratefully acknowledged.

FIGURE 5.5.1   **Partial Questionnaire/Coding**

The following is a portion of a questionnaire administered to teens ages 15 to 18 years. The questionnaire was designed to gather information and opinions pertaining to reading habits, subject matter preferences, and related issues.

NOTE: Nonresponses were coded as "9" or "99."

For the first group of questions, respondents were asked to check the appropriate box.

1. *On average, how many books do you read for pleasure outside of school in one month?*
   - ☐ Less than one
   - ☐ One
   - ☐ Two
   - ☐ Three
   - ☐ Four
   - ☐ Five
   - ☐ Six
   - ☐ I never read any.

2. *In the last 12 months, where have you usually gotten the books you have read for pleasure?*
   - ☐ I never read any.
   - ☐ Public library
   - ☐ School library
   - ☐ Home
   - ☐ Borrow from another person
   - ☐ Book store
   - ☐ Store other than book store
   - ☐ Book club
   - ☐ Mail order other than book club
   - ☐ Receive as gifts
   - ☐ Other

3. *On average, what would you pay for a new paperback book?*
   - ☐ Less than $3.00
   - ☐ $3.00 to $3.99
   - ☐ $4.00 to $4.99
   - ☐ $5.00 to $5.99
   - ☐ $6.00 to $6.99
   - ☐ $7.00 to $7.99
   - ☐ $8.00 or more

In the following section, the teens were asked to judge the importance of various features of books in their decision process of purchasing a book.

	Very Important	Somewhat Important	Neither Important nor Unimportant	Somewhat Unimportant	Very Unimportant
4. *The story description*	☐	☐	☐	☐	☐

(continued)

FIGURE 5.5.1   (continued)

	Very Important	Somewhat Important	Neither Important nor Unimportant	Somewhat Unimportant	Very Unimportant
5. *The author*	☐	☐	☐	☐	☐
6. *The price*	☐	☐	☐	☐	☐

Next, respondents were asked to circle the appropriate number corresponding to how likely they were to read books within various subject-matter categories.

	Extremely Likely			Neither Likely nor Unlikely			Extremely Unlikely
7. *Science fiction*	1	2	3	4	5	6	7
8. *Humor/comedy*	1	2	3	4	5	6	7
9. *Mystery/suspense*	1	2	3	4	5	6	7
10. *Political*	1	2	3	4	5	6	7
11. *Romance*	1	2	3	4	5	6	7
12. *Social issues/problems*	1	2	3	4	5	6	7

To determine the degree to which a teen was "nonconformist," he/she was asked to indicate his/her level of agreement with each of the following statements.

	Strongly Agree	Agree	Disagree	Strongly Disagree
13. *When I make decisions, I like to get other people's opinions.*	1	2	3	4
14. *I would lead a demonstration for a social cause if I felt strongly about it.*	1	2	3	4
15. *I fit in well with society.*	1	2	3	4

FIGURE 5.5.1   (continued)

	Strongly Agree	Agree	Disagree	Strongly Disagree
16. *I respect the opinions of most adults.*	1	2	3	4
17. *I like to try to change society.*	1	2	3	4
18. *It's important to me that I fit in well with other students my age.*	1	2	3	4
19. *I would participate in a local/national campaign to promote a candidate who represented my views.*	1	2	3	4
20. *My lifestyle is different than most students my own age.*	1	2	3	4
21. *I keep up with current events.*	1	2	3	4
22. *I don't like to call attention to myself.*	1	2	3	4
23. *If I feel strongly about something, I need to make my statement even if my friends disagree.*	1	2	3	4
24. *I try to avoid conflict with my parents.*	1	2	3	4
25. *Keeping up with the trends is important to me.*	1	2	3	4

Finally, two of the classification questions from the questionnaire are presented.

26. *What is your age?* _____ *years old.*
    [actual age was coded]

27. *Are you male or female?*
    ☐ Male
    ☐ Female

CASE 5.6

E-Food and the Online Grocery Competition (C)

Ashley Sims, the MBA student who is thinking about starting an online grocery, has some click-stream data to analyze. She recruited 10 volunteers for her study as they left a local grocery retail store. At a mutually convenient time, each participant came to the local library and sat before Sims's computer, where they were told to try using the system as if they were really going to shop for groceries. Upon completion, Sims asked them what they thought of the whole process. Figure 5.6.1 contains click-streams from four of these consumers.

QUESTIONS

1. What do you learn upon examination of the click-streams? How does consumer 1 think? 2? 3? What do you suppose is going on with consumer 4?

2. Could you reproduce the layout of the screens—where the various buttons (for example, "sort by price," "sort by nutritional value") are located, using these data? (Keep in mind that a boxed area on which a user clicks takes up several spaces in all directions, and that most users' clicks are not precisely in the center of the buttons.)

3. What do you suppose long time intervals between clicks mean? What assumptions are you making?

4. What recommendations would you make to Sims about designing her online grocery software, based on what these click-stream data suggest?

FIGURE 5.6.1   Click-Stream Data from Online Grocery Consumers*

Consumer 1: <11:29:42:03; 50:49; welcome scrn> <11:31:05:23; 50:19; search scrn> <11:31:48:10; 49:47; i= 'coke'> <11:32:52:00; 85:31; sort-by-size> <11:34:02:03; 84:61; sort-by-nutrition> <11:37:12:59; 83:77; sort-by-price> <11:37:44:09; 83:76; sort-by-price> <11:38:29:42; 85:44; sort-by-brand> <11:40:33:13; 90:81; buy-2,cocacola, 6-12zcans,$2.99,notonsale> <11:41:47:53; 10:13; returntosearch> <11:42:42:52; 50:49; i= 'pretzels'> <11:42:57:12; 50:50; o= 'notfound'> <11:43:14:51; 50:49; i='pretzels'> <11:43:22:33; 84:49; noinput> <11:43:42:03; 84:45; sort-by-brand> <11:44:12:15; 92:67; buy-1,roldgold,15oz,$1.99,onsale> <11:44:47:13; 10:15; returntosearch> <11:46:02:02; 50:51; i='snickers'> <11:46:24:03; 85:31; sort-by-size> <11:46:54:12; 89:85; buy-3,bigsnickers,3.7oz,$.95,notonsale> <11:47:41:42; 95:05; checkout>

Consumer 2: <14:39:12:13; 50:47 welcome scrn> <14:39:28:23; 50:42; personal-list> <14:40:10:49; 10:89; i='2'> <14:40:52:38; 90:88; buy-2,lettuce,head,$1.39,notonsale> <14:41:42:07; 89:86; buy-1,deanskimmilk,.5gal,$2.09,notonsale> <14:42:09:10; 11:82; i='3'> <14:42:29:42; 90:81; buy-3,lrgdelicapples,$1.29/lb,notonsale> <14:43:13:13; 10:60; i='1'> <14:43:19:53; 91:61; buy-1,ryebread,slcd,1lb,$2.29,notonsale> <14:44:14:42; 94:06; checkout>

Consumer 3: <08:23:09:42; 50:49; welcome scrn> <08:23:17:43; 50:20; search scrn> <08:23:58:10; 50:49; i='mustard'> <08:24:11:01; 85:75; sort-by-price> <08:24:52:53; 89:61; buy-1,smlFrnchylwmustard,8oz.,$.95,onsale> <08:25:27:23; 09:10; returntosearch> <08:26:32:00; 50:48; i= 'buns'> <08:27:11:12; 10:15; returntosearch> <08:27:49:21; 49:50; i='hotdog buns'> <08:29:18:51; 90:05; buy-1,htdgbuns,8ct,$2.19,onsale> <08:33:11:12; 94:05; checkout>

Consumer 4: <16:53:22:01; 50:50; welcome scrn> <16:55:31:55; 50:49; welcome scrn> <16:57:44:19; 50:62; browse> <17:02:22:50; 95:95; helpscroll> <17:13:42:33; 14:75; browse-frozen> <17:17:59:22; 35:65; browse-icecream> <17:23:45:49; 94:91; noinput> <17:24:18:09:42; 94:95; helpscroll> <17:30:10:27; 76:15; browse-icespecialties> <17:32:41:03; 94:96; helpscroll> <17:35:12:02; 50:90; i= 'buy 1 icecream'> <17:37:07:42; 50:10; o= 'cannotexec'> <17:39:50:15; 95:06; checkout>

---

*Click-stream data can be stored in different formats. This format contains the essential information: each click is stored between < and >. The first piece of information depicted in the click-stream data unit is the PC internal time recorder in hours, minutes, seconds, and 60ths of seconds. The second piece of information is the location on the screen upon which the user clicked. The pixel coordinates offer the most precise measurement of location, but for ease of interpretation, those coordinates have been translated to units ranging from 0 to 100, with the first coordinate denoting the relative placement of the click from left (0) to right (100), and the second coordinate denoting bottom (0) to top (100) of the screen. The final piece of information is the http, the exact location in internet space of where the click sends the user. For the purposes of this analysis, the data have already been preprocessed, so as to interpret those internet locations. For example, rather than an apparently meaningless-looking location of www.onlinefood.com/1445.html, the data are represented as: softdrink/CocaCola/sort-size-by-value (that is, the "onlinefood.com" is constant since all these clicks are in its subdomain, and the content of the html is provided). In the content stream, o = output (something the computer displays) and i = input (something the user enters).

CASE 5.7

Transitional Housing, Inc. (B)[1]

Transitional Housing Inc. (THI) is a nonprofit organization located in Madison, Wisconsin. THI provides assistance to homeless and very low-income individuals and families in finding emergency shelter, food, employment, transitional housing, and affordable apartment housing (see Case 1.2, Transitional Housing, Inc. [A], for more details). As part of its planning,

the board of directors of THI was interested in finding ways to improve the organization's services. It decided to assemble a task force to evaluate THI's current facilities and services, and to determine what future facilities and services it should provide.

Methodology

The task force was assembled in February 2001. After evaluating external information on the homeless situation in Dane County and internal information on THI, the task force submitted a proposal to the board outlining their methodology and time frame (see Figure 5.7.1). The proposal consisted of three surveys,

---

[1]The contributions of Monika Wingate to the development of this case are gratefully acknowledged.

FIGURE 5.7.1	**Research Proposal to Transitional Housing**

Purpose and Limits of the Project
THI is interested in knowing how services provided enable them to meet community needs and if the services are aiding the clients in their struggle to "get out of the loop." Specifically, Transitional Housing, Inc. (THI), would like to address the following questions:

1. What are the needs of the homeless community?
2. Are current services meeting the homeless community's needs?
3. How could the homeless community's needs better be met?

As discussed in earlier meetings, this project will focus on the services provided by the Drop-In Shelter and the Hospitality House, as it is used in conjunction with the Drop-In Shelter.

Data Sources and Research Methodology
The primary source of data collection will be through the use of a questionnaire. Focus groups will be conducted in order to facilitate development of the questions asked of the target populations. Secondary data collection sources will be: statistics on the current homeless population in Dane County, and internal information provided by THI, such as statistics of the guest services and previous/simultaneous studies conducted by THI.

   The target population to be surveyed are current guests (at the Drop-In Shelter and Hospitality House), staff, volunteers, and previous guests of the Drop-In Shelter or Hospitality House who are currently in Transitional Housing. Sample sizes for the target population will be determined as follows:

- The current guest sample will be based on the number of guests staying at the Drop-In Shelter on two separate nights.
- The staff and volunteers sample sizes will be based on the number of years of service to the organization and will be adjusted for sample population mortality.
- The previous guests sample will be taken from the actual number of guests currently in one of the Transitional Housing facilities who were previous guests of the Drop-In Shelter and/or Hospitality House.

These groups were chosen because they are representative of the population who use THI services and who administer them.

Estimate of Time and Personnel Requirements
The study will be conducted by the five research team members. Additional personnel may be required for administration of the questionnaire. They will be recruited from the THI volunteer base not included in the sample population. The projected time frame for the project is listed below:

- Focus groups and questionnaire development: 4–5 weeks
- Sample selection: 1 week
- Administration of the survey: 3–4 weeks
- Analysis of data and presentation to agency: 2 weeks

FIGURE 5.7.2   **Quesionnaires**

Guest Questionnaire

PHYSICAL FACILITIES OF THE DROP-IN SHELTER:

The following questions relate to potential future facilities of the Drop-In Shelter. Please circle the number which most closely represents your opinion of the need for the following facilities.

	Definitely Needed	Needed	Neutral	Not Needed	Definitely Not Needed
1. Personal Storage Areas	1	2	3	4	5
2. Study Areas	1	2	3	4	5
3. Library	1	2	3	4	5
4. Separate Areas for Guests with Contagious Diseases (e.g., flu, cold, etc.)	1	2	3	4	5
5. Wheelchair Accessibility	1	2	3	4	5

6. Often there is limited funding, and choices on where to spend these funds must be made. Please rank the following items in order of importance using 1 through 5 (1 being most important and 5 being least important). Please use each number only once.
   _____ Personal Storage Areas
   _____ Study Areas
   _____ Library
   _____ Separate Areas for Guests with Contagious Diseases
   _____ Wheelchair Accessibility
7. If the option existed for you to stay in a room by yourself for the night, what is the most that you would be willing (and able) to pay for this room? Would you be willing to pay . . . (CHECK HIGHEST AMOUNT YOU WOULD BE WILLING TO PAY)
   _____ $2–$3 per night
   _____ $4–$5 per night
   _____ $6–$8 per night
   _____ More than $8 per night
   _____ I would not be willing to pay for my own room (skip to question 10)
8. If the option existed for you to stay in a room by yourself for the night, what is the farthest you would be willing to walk from the Capitol?
   _____ under 1 block
   _____ 1–2 blocks
   _____ 3–4 blocks
   _____ 5–6 blocks
   _____ 7–8 blocks

If the option existed for you to stay in a room by yourself for the night, the following list of features are items that might be included in such a facility. On a scale of 1 to 5, where 1 is "very important" and 5 is "not at all important," please rate the need for the following facilities.

	Very Important	Somewhat Important	Neutral	Not Very Important	Not at All Important
9. Personal storage areas in the room	1	2	3	4	5
10. Cafeteria/food service	1	2	3	4	5
11. Private bathroom	1	2	3	4	5

12. What other features, if any, do you think should be included in this type of facility?
_____
_____
_____

13. Would you be willing to pay for personal storage facilities at the Drop-In Shelter if they were available?
   _____ Yes
   _____ No

FIGURE 5.7.2   **(continued)**

SERVICES AT THE DROP-IN SHELTER

The questions in this section of the survey relate to the services available to guests of the Drop-In Shelter. The first section relates to services that are already provided at the Drop-In Shelter. The second section relates to potential services that may be provided at the Drop-In Shelter in the future.

Current Services

14. I find the social worker at the Drop-In Shelter helpful.

Strongly Agree	Agree	Neutral	Disagree	Strongly Disagree
1	2	3	4	5

15. There are enough social workers available to meet the guests' needs.

Strongly Agree	Agree	Neutral	Disagree	Strongly Disagree
1	2	3	4	5

   IF GUEST ANSWERS WITH A 4 OR 5: How many social workers do you think would be better?_____

16. How do you think the counseling services could be improved, if at all, to better serve the needs of the Drop-In Shelter guests?

   _____
   _____
   _____

17. I find the medical services at the Drop-In Shelter useful.

Strongly Agree	Agree	Neutral	Disagree	Strongly Disagree
1	2	3	4	5

18. There are enough staff people available for the medical services to meet the guests' needs.

Strongly Agree	Agree	Neutral	Disagree	Strongly Disagree
1	2	3	4	5

19. How do you think the medical services could be improved, if at all, to better serve the needs of the Drop-In Shelter guests?

   _____
   _____
   _____

20. There are enough staff people available for the legal services to meet the guests' needs.

Strongly Agree	Agree	Neutral	Disagree	Strongly Disagree
1	2	3	4	5

21. How do you think the legal services could be improved, if at all, to better serve the needs of the Drop-In Shelter guests?

   _____
   _____
   _____

22. One Mental Health worker (like Axel) is enough to meet the guests' needs.

Strongly Agree	Agree	Neutral	Disagree	Strongly Disagree
1	2	3	4	5

23. How do you think the mental health services could be improved, if at all, to better serve the needs of the Drop-In Shelter guests?

   _____
   _____
   _____

24. There are enough volunteers available to meet the guests' needs.

Strongly Agree	Agree	Neutral	Disagree	Strongly Disagree
1	2	3	4	5

(continued)

FIGURE 5.7.2   (continued)

Potential Future Services

The following questions relate to potential future services of the Drop-In Shelter. Please circle the number which most closely represents your opinion of the need for the following services.

	Definitely Needed	Needed	Neutral	Not Needed	Definitely Not Needed
25. On-Duty Drug and Alcohol Counselor	1	2	3	4	5
26. Dental Services	1	2	3	4	5
27. Optical Services	1	2	3	4	5
28. Tutors for Guests	1	2	3	4	5
29. Assistance with Social Service Agencies	1	2	3	4	5
30. Seasonal clothing	1	2	3	4	5
31. Interview clothing	1	2	3	4	5
32. Haircuts	1	2	3	4	5

33. Are there any services that are offered during the day by the Hospitality House that you would like offered at the Drop-In Shelter at night?

_____
_____
_____

34. What other services do you think should be offered at the Drop-In Shelter?

_____
_____
_____

DEMOGRAPHICS SECTION:

35. On average, how many times a week do you stay at the Drop-In Shelter?
_____ once a week or less
_____ 2–3 times a week
_____ 4–5 times a week
_____ 6–7 times a week

36. Which months during the year do you usually stay at the Drop-In Shelter? (CHECK ALL THAT APPLY)

_____ January	_____ July
_____ February	_____ August
_____ March	_____ September
_____ April	_____ October
_____ May	_____ November
_____ June	_____ December

37. On average, how many times a week do you visit the Hospitality House?
_____ I don't use the Hospitality House
_____ Only once per week
_____ 2–3 times a week
_____ 4–5 times a week
_____ 6–7 times a week

38. If you do not use the Hospitality House when you stay at the Drop-In Shelter, why not?
(DO NOT READ LIST; CHECK ALL THAT APPLY)
_____ Not Applicable, I use the HH.
_____ Too crowded / I don't feel safe.
_____ Too far.
_____ Don't like staff.
_____ Don't feel it meets my service needs.
_____ Don't want to participate in clean-up.
_____ Not open on weekends.
_____ Don't know about Hospitality House.
_____ Other _____

FIGURE 5.7.2   (continued)

Volunteer Questionnaire

Questions 1–6 are identical to Guest Questions 1–6
Questions 7–27 are identical to Guest Questions 14–34

DEMOGRAPHICS SECTION:

28. How many years have you been a volunteer at the Drop-In Shelter?
_____ This is my first night volunteering at the Drop-In Shelter.
_____ 1 year or less
_____ 2–3 years

29. On average, how often do you volunteer at the Drop-In Shelter?
_____ At least once a month
_____ 4 times a year
_____ 2 times a year
_____ Once a year
_____ Less than once a year

30. How did you initially come to volunteer at the Drop-In Shelter?
_____ Church group
_____ Work group
_____ Mandatory community service for a university class
_____ Mandatory community service for some other reason
_____ Personal interest
_____ Other

31. What volunteer shift do you normally work?
_____ Breakfast
_____ 8pm to midnight
_____ midnight to 4 am

Staff Questionnaire

Questions 1–6 are identical to Guest Questions 1–6
Questions 7–27 are identical to Guest Questions 14–34

DEMOGRAPHICS SECTION:

28. How long have you worked for Transitional Housing, Inc.?
_____ Less than 1 year
_____ 1–2 years
_____ 3–4 years
_____ 5 or more years

29. At which THI facility do you work?
_____ Hospitality House
_____ Drop-In Shelter

30. Are you a full-time or part-time employee?
_____ Full-time
_____ Part-time

FIGURE 5.7.3   **THI Coding Scheme**

Column(s)	Question #	Contents
1–3	N/A	Questionnaire I.D. #
4	N/A	Type: 1 - Guest
		2 - Volunteer
		3 - Staff
5	1	Personal Storage
6	2	Study Areas
	3	Library
8	4	Separate Areas for Guests with
7		Contagious Diseases
9	5	Wheelchair Accessibility
10	6a	Personal Storage
11	6b	Study Areas
12	6c	Library
13	6d	Separate Areas
14	6e	Wheelchair Accessibility
15	7 (G14)	Social Worker Helpful
16	8a (G15a)	Enough Social Workers
17	8b (G15b)	How Many Social Workers
18–19, 20–21	9 (G16)	Counseling Services Improved OPEN-ENDED
(2 ideas)		01 - Make guests aware of counseling services
		02 - More individual - one-on-one (case) interaction
		03 - Should give referrals
		04 - More structured and enforced rules
		05 - Better trained/new staff
		06 - More AODA counseling
		07 - Be available more often
		08 - Job opportunities advice
		09 - More time with social workers
		10 - Better help with handicapped/special needs
		11 - Other
22	10 (G17)	Medical Services Helpful
23	11 (G18)	Enough Medical Staff
24–25, 26–27	12 (G19)	Medical Services Improved OPEN-ENDED
(2 ideas)		01 - Services offered more often
		02 - Better trained people or "real" doctors/nurses
		03 - More medicine available
		04 - Offer dental care
		05 - Offer eye doctor services
		06 - Better equipment and/or facilities (clinic)
		07 - Keep medical records of guests
		08 - Get rid of it—use other existing programs
		09 - Offer medical tests (TB, etc.)
		10 - Offer more staff—more doctors
		11 - More emphasis on preventive medicine
		12 - Other
28	13 (G20)	Enough Staff—Legal Services
29, 30	14 (G21)	Legal Services Improved OPEN-ENDED
(2 ideas)		1 - Longer appointments—more time with lawyers
		2 - More staff (lawyers) available
		3 - Offered more nights (accessibility)
		4 - Schedule lawyers ahead of time by appt.
		5 - Give guests info about legal rights, rental, etc.
		6 - Other
31	15 (G22)	One Mental Health Worker Is Enough

FIGURE 5.7.3   **(continued)**

Column(s)	Question #	Contents

32, 33
(2 ideas)
	16 (G23)	Mental Health Services Improved OPEN-ENDED
		    1 - Awareness (communicate availability to guests)
		    2 - Offer classes
		    3 - Network with existing agencies (referrals)
		    4 - More staff (one-female; one-male)
		    5 - Separate the mentally ill
		    6 - More individual counseling
		    7 - More hours of service
		    8 - More structured rules at Drop-In
		    9 - Other

34	17 (G24)	Enough Volunteers Available
35	18 (G25)	On-Duty Drug & Alcohol Counselor
36	19 (G26)	Dental Services
37	20 (G27)	Optical Services
38	21 (G28)	Tutors for Guests
39	22 (G29)	Assistance with Social Service Agencies
40	23 (G30)	Seasonal Clothing
41	24 (G31)	Interview Clothing
42	25 (G32)	Haircuts

43–44, 45–46,
47–48
(Maximum 3 ideas)
	26 (G33)	Any services offered at Hospitality House that
		could be offered? (OPEN-ENDED)
		    01 - Doesn't use Hospitality House/Unaware
		    02 - Counseling services
		    03 - Job listings
		    04 - Telephone and/or long distance
		    05 - Drug/alcohol referrals
		    06 - More staff available
		    07 - Newspaper
		    08 - Computer/typewriter access
		    09 - Mailboxes
		    10 - Bus tickets/transportation
		    11 - Rental/housing lists
		    12 - Activities/game room
		    13 - Cooking facilities
		    14 - Nothing/should use Hospitality House
		    15 - Other

49–50, 51–52,
53–54, 55–56
(Maximum: 4 ideas)
	27 (G34)	What Other Services Should Be Offered?
		    01 - More laundry facilities (& ironing board)
		    02 - Daily newspaper
		    03 - More counseling services
		    04 - More showers/sinks
		    05 - Additional entertainment
		    06 - Bible study
		    07 - Answering/message service
		    08 - Telephone
		    09 - Chiropractor
		    10 - Better ventilation
		    11 - More beds
		    12 - Drug/alcohol treatment
		    13 - Better food & more variety
		    14 - Enforce rules (drinking)
		    15 - Extended shelter hours in winter
		    16 - VCR/movies/stereo
		    17 - Offer Bible counseling/priests
		    18 - Skills training/jobs
		    19 - Check for weapons
		    20 - Transportation (bus passes)
		    21 - More blankets
		    22 - More staff (more accommodating staff)
		    23 - Mailing address/mail service
		    24 - Other

(continued)

FIGURE 5.7.3   **(continued)**

Column(s)	Question #	Contents

GUEST-ONLY QUESTIONS: (For volunteer & staff, put spaces in)

57	G7	Own Room by Yourself Willing to Pay
58	G8	Own Room—Farthest Willing to Walk
59	G9	Personal Storage
60	G10	Cafeteria/Food Service
61	G11	Private Bathroom
62–63, 64–65	G12	What other features should be included? OPEN-ENDED
(2 ideas)		

        01 - Warm blankets
        02 - A good bed
        03 - TV
        04 - Radio/stereo
        05 - Kitchenette
        06 - Telephone
        07 - Social room
        08 - Separate smoking room
        09 - Laundry facilities
        10 - Job training courses
        11 - Games/entertainment
        12 - Counseling services (all types)
        13 - Workout facilities/gym
        14 - Good ventilation
        15 - Refrigerator
        16 - First aid
        17 - Rules/policies enforcement
        18 - Other

66	G13	Would you be willing to pay for personal storage facilities ... ?
67	G35	On average, how many times a week do you stay ... ?
68–69, 70–71,	G36	Which months during the year?
72–73, 74–75		
76–77, 78–79		
ROW 2: 1–2,		
3–4, 5–6, 7–8,		
9–10, 11–12		
(12 possible months)		

        01 - January   07 - July
        02 - February   08 - August
        03 - March   09 - September
        04 - April   10 - October
        05 - May   11 - November
        06 - June   12 - December

ROW 2:

13	G37	On average, how many times a week do you visit HH?
14–15, 16–17	G38	If you do not use HH, why not?
(2 ideas)		

        01 - N/A; I use HH
        02 - Too crowded
        03 - Don't feel safe
        04 - Don't like staff
        05 - Don't feel meets service needs
        06 - Don't want to take part in clean-up
        07 - Not open on weekends
        08 - Don't know about HH
        09 - Busy doing other things
        10 - Should have area for sleeping
        11 - Too far away
        12 - Too noisy
        13 - Other

VOLUNTEER-ONLY QUESTIONS: (For guests & staff, put in spaces)

18	V28	How many years have you been a volunteer?
19	V29	On average, how often ...
20	V30	How did you initially come to volunteer at the Drop-In?
21	V31	What volunteer shift do you work?

STAFF-ONLY QUESTIONS: (For guests & volunteers, put in spaces)

22	S28	How long have you worked for?
23	S29	At which THI facility ... ?
24	S30	Are you full-time/part-time?

conducted on the organization's paid staff, volunteers, and guests (the homeless staying at THI or using its facilities/services).

Given the exploratory nature of the research project, the task force decided to use a nonprobability convenience sample for guests and volunteers, and a census for the small number of staff members. Three separate questionnaires were used, with volunteers and staff being surveyed using self-administered questionnaires and guests being surveyed using structured in-person interviews.

Questionnaire

The initial research done by the task force suggested several areas of interest, including the need for adding staff members and services at the drop-in shelter, and the addition of personal sleeping and storage areas for guests. However, to create more directed questions, separate focus groups were conducted with staff, volunteers, and guests. Individual survey questions were based on the focus group responses.

The final questionnaire was broken out into four sections: physical facilities, current services, potential future services, and demographics (Figure 5.7.2). Most questions for the three surveys were identical. Exceptions included demographic questions that were unique for guests, staff, and volunteers, and physical facilities questions that were applicable only to guests.

Both closed- and open-ended questions were asked to all three groups. After all the questionnaires were complete, open-ended responses were evaluated to determine representative categories. A coding sheet was then created to facilitate data entry (see Figure 5.7.3). A total of 68 guests, 33 volunteers, and 11 staff members completed questionnaires. Two of the volunteer surveys were discarded due to incomplete responses. The raw data are contained in file THI.dat.

QUESTIONS

1. One of the research objectives was to determine what new services are needed by the homeless men. Which survey questions best address this research objective? Why?

2. Using the data provided on the computer disk, run one-way tabulations on the survey questions you recommended in Question 1. Discuss the general findings from these tabulations.

3. Using the data provided on the computer disk, run cross tabulations on the survey questions you recommended in Question 1 against the type of respondent. Are there significant differences among guests, volunteers, and staff? If yes, what are the implications for THI's board of directors?

4. What recommendations would you make to THI based on your findings? Why?

CASE 5.8

Internet Advertising and Your Brain (B)

Recall your responsibilities as the key marketing person for a relatively new Internet company that offers travel packages for "extreme sports." Given that the majority of customers are young men, and that young men are disproportionately online, it was thought that purchasing Internet banner ads at popular sites would be a cost-efficient way of encouraging these thrill-seekers and potential buyers to click through your banner ad at the host site, sending them onto your site to, it was hoped, learn about and eventually purchase an extreme sports vacation adventure.

As marketing guru, you had created two ads, a "beauty" ad (which was colorful and big on graphics) and an "info" ad (less splashy, more writing and detail). You tested both of these ads in a left-screen position and a right-screen position because of the research you had found which led you to expect that the beauty ad might do better at the left, so as to be processed by the right-brain hemisphere, which handles pictures better. Analogously, the info ad might do better at the right, to be processed by the left brain, which deals with verbal, detailed information better.

You've obtained the click-through data from your banner advertisement Web hosts, in proportion to the traffic to their site who did not click through your banner onto your site. The results are presented below in an analysis of variance table format. Some of the information is missing—you will need to fill it in before proceeding to answer the questions below. (The critical F-value for each test is 4.00.)

The incomplete analysis of variance table of results follows:

Source	SS	df	MS	F
Banner Type	18.4	1	?	?
Banner Placement	13.3	1	?	?
Type × Placement	?	1	?	?
Error	670.1	?	?	?
Total	756.0	99	?	?

The mean number of click-throughs for each combination of ad banner type (beauty or info) and ad banner placement (left or right) follow:

Banner Type

Banner Placement	Beauty	Info	Marginal Means
Right	152.5	175.4	163.9
Left	182.5	144.6	163.5
Marginal Means	167.5	160.0	

QUESTIONS

1. Fill in the analysis of variance table of results.

2. What effects are "significant" (that is, you can reject the null hypothesis)? What is going on in these data?

3. Which banner type (beauty/info) and which banner location (left/right) would you choose? Why? Can you make the choices (type and location) independently?

4. Were your initial guesses about the beauty/info and left/right combinations right?

5. What strategic questions might supplement your interpretation of the data?

CASE 5.9

A Picture is Worth a Megabyte of Words: Census Data and Trends in Lifestyle Purchases

While it is always dangerous to make generalizations about people and their consumption behaviors, it is helpful to the marketer to have an aggregate sense of what people tend to buy as a function of some of their demographic characteristics. For example, household expenditures on furniture might be higher for younger people as they begin to set up house, and decline as the house is established. With a fact like this in hand, and extrapolations of the likely sizes, and timing, of baby-booms and baby-busts, a furniture manufacturer could use this trend information to project market sizes, and to modify the product line (for example, bean bag chairs for college students, finer wood and upholstered furniture for older, wealthier consumers).

The data that follow were extracted from the Bureau of Labor Statistics[1] and reflect expenditures on various goods and services categories, broken down by the census age groups. Within each purchase category (the columns), the data have been calibrated so that a score of "100" means the age group (the row) spends about the average on that category. Numbers that exceed 100 mean that the age group spends more on that category of purchases than the other age groups, and numbers that are less than 100 mean that age group spends less than other age groups. For example, people younger than 25 years old and those 65 years old or older spend less on food; people between the ages of 35–44 and 45–54 spend more. People aged 25–34 and 55–64 spend about the "average." Use these data to answer the questions that follow.

---

[1]For example, see "The New Consumer Paradigm," *American Demographics* (April 1999), pp. 50–58.

Age (in years)	Total Spending	Food	Women's Apparel	Furniture	Computers	Health Care	Entertainment	Travel
<25	59	74	62	55	60	30	62	47
25–34	99	101	85	105	98	67	109	81
35–44	129	134	119	147	119	96	141	98
45–54	130	128	145	126	161	111	123	143
55–64	105	101	120	107	103	122	95	136
65–74	77	69	87	64	55	149	73	102
75+	50	39	49	19	15	141	26	53

QUESTIONS

1. If you wanted to know whether expenditures on furniture and computers were correlated, why might the actual computation of a correlation coefficient be inappropriate, or at least not very compelling?

2. Plot these data with the age categories as the horizontal axis, and the different columns as profiles depicting the peaks and valleys of expenditures with age.

   a. Plot total spending by age and overlay that plot with the plots of food by age and women's apparel by age. What is the pattern of spending on these apparent basic necessities?

b. Overlay the plots for furniture, computers, and health care by age. Generally speaking, what target age groups will you be aiming for if you are Scandinavian Design? Dell? A hospital network or health and life insurance company?

c. Overlay the plot for entertainment expenditures by age with the plot for travel by age. How do we tend to amuse ourselves as younger versus older people?

d. Finally, use whichever variables interest you and whatever plotting format you think will lend insight to creatively discover any other phenomenon in the data.

CASE 5.10
Star Equipment (B)[1]

Star Equipment is a Fortune 500 company manufacturing technologically advanced equipment for numerous purposes. Star's office-products division is one of the three largest manufacturers of office equipment in the world. Traditionally, its largest competitors in this area have been Vetra and Calt. However, Star has also been facing significant competition in

---

[1]The contributions of Sara L. Pitterle to this case are gratefully acknowledged.

recent years from a number of other smaller, specialized office-equipment manufacturers.

To ensure its future competitiveness, Star's office-products division managers developed a four-stage plan to promote sales: (1) identify key accounts for Star's office products, (2) examine the purchase decision process within these key accounts, (3) determine the critical vendor services sought by these accounts, and (4) assess the performance of Star and its two main competitors on these characteristics.

Research Method

Star's marketing research team designed a two-stage research project involving both secondary and primary research to gather the information identified in the four strategies. The first stage of the project involved exhaustive secondary research along with internal and external depth interviews to identify the vendor attributes important to office-equipment customers. Thirteen vendor characteristics were identified as being of some importance to customers.

The 13 characteristics were incorporated in a survey in which respondents were asked to select the four most- and four least-important characteristics. Respondents were also asked to rate the vendors considered for their company's most recent office-equipment purchase on each of the attributes. Since Star was interested primarily in its own performance ratings along with its two major competitors, Calt and Vetra, these three vendors were explicitly specified in Question 3 in the survey; an "other" column was

---

TABLE 5.10.1   Attributes Chosen as Most and Least Important

Attribute	Most Important				Least Important			
	1	2	3	4	1	2	3	4
a	183	0	0	0	33	0	0	0
b	48	75	0	0	44	8	0	0
c	8	13	5	0	110	32	3	0
d	37	101	40	2	4	7	0	0
e	12	71	104	26	1	5	1	1
f	2	16	47	29	26	35	12	0
g	4	6	16	5	37	62	21	1
h	1	10	30	21	9	29	25	8
i	2	3	31	102	4	10	16	4
j	3	2	11	23	13	49	45	5
k	0	3	9	24	4	37	54	11
l	0	0	6	1	0	7	91	130
m	0	0	0	62	0	0	3	104

FIGURE 5.10.1   **Primary Vendor Characteristics**

Q2. Listed below are vendor characteristics that could be used to make a decision about which equipment to purchase. Thinking about your most recent purchase decision:
A. Check (✔) the four (4) most important vendor characteristics in your purchase decision.
B. Check (✔) the four (4) least important vendor characteristics in your purchase decision.

Vendor Characteristics	A Most Important (Check 4)	B Least Important (Check 4)
a. Vendor values a long-term relationship and works to meet my organization's unique needs	01 ☐ 15–16/	01 ☐ 23–24/
b. My relationships with the vendor's sales and support representatives are easy and productive	02 ☐ 17–18/	02 ☐ 25–26/
c. Vendor enables my organization to have a smooth decision process	03 ☐ 19–20/	03 ☐ 27–28/
d. The vendor establishes fair pricing policies for products and services	04 ☐ 21–22/	04 ☐ 29–30/
e. The vendor's service organization is responsive to my organization's needs	05 ☐	05 ☐
f. The vendor offers an extensive line of reliable products meeting the needs of my organization	06 ☐	06 ☐
g. The vendor's solutions enable my organization to use people, space, and resources efficiently	07 ☐	07 ☐
h. The vendor offers software to increase the productivity and satisfaction of my department and employees	08 ☐	08 ☐
i. Vendor's products are easy to use	09 ☐	09 ☐
j. The vendor's solutions help my business grow	10 ☐	10 ☐
k. The vendor's solutions give me the ability to offer quick response to my customers' needs	11 ☐	11 ☐
l. The vendor provides my company with solutions that protect the safety and legality of information	12 ☐	12 ☐
m. The vendor provides my firm with technological advantages today that can be leveraged to meet our future requirements	13 ☐	13 ☐

provided to capture the ratings of smaller vendors that may have been considered. (See Case 5.2, Star Equipment [A], for additional background information and initial results.)

Segmentation Based on Importance Scores

Star planned to use cluster analysis to group together those respondents who chose similar vendor characteristics as being most and least important. Specifically, the analysts planned to treat the four characteristics in Question 2 chosen as most important by each respondent as a set and the four characteristics chosen as least important as another set. The remaining five characteristics were to be considered a set of neutral attributes. Table 5.10.1 shows the frequency tables for the attributes chosen as least and most important in Question 2. The actual question is shown in Figure 5.10.1. (See Star Equipment [A] for the complete questionnaire.)

After forming clusters based on the importance ratings given to the vendor characteristics by survey respondents, the research team planned to analyze cluster membership to determine Star's performance ratings as well as the demographic characteristics of the respondents within each cluster. The results of this analysis were to be used to identify clusters of opportunities for Star as well as clusters in which Star's competitors appear to have an advantage.

QUESTIONS

1. Is cluster analysis the most appropriate technique to use to meet the objectives of this project? What other analyses may prove helpful in this situation?

2. How must the data be recoded to be appropriate for cluster analysis? How many new variables are necessary to recode the data from survey Question 2 so that it can be used in cluster analysis?

3. Using data provided on the computer disk, perform a cluster analysis aimed at determining the appropriate number of customer groupings based on the importance of characteristics. Justify your choice of clusters.

4. How do the obtained clusters differ? In which clusters does Star Equipment dominate? In which clusters do Vetra and/or Calt dominate? What general recommendations would you make to Star Equipment based on this analysis?

CASE 5.11
Fabhus Inc.

Fabhus Inc., a manufacturer of prefabricated homes located in Atlanta, Georgia, had experienced steady, sometimes spectacular, growth since its founding in the early 1950s. By the mid-1990s, however, things were not so rosy. Sales fell off 8 percent from 1995 to 1996 and another 6 percent from 1996 to 1997, in spite of a very attractive interest-rate environment for home building.

In an attempt to offset the decline in sales, company management decided to use marketing research to get a better perspective on their customers and more effectively target their marketing efforts. After much discussion, the members of the executive committee finally determined that the following questions would be important to address in this research effort.

1. What is the demographic profile of the typical Fabhus customer?

2. What initially attracts these customers to a Fabhus home?

3. Do Fabhus home customers consider other factory-built homes when making their purchase decision?

4. Are Fabhus customers satisfied with their homes? If they are not, what particular features are dissatisfactory?

Method

The research firm that was called in on the project suggested conducting a mail survey of past owners. Preliminary discussions with management revealed that Fabhus had the greatest market penetration near its factory. As one moved farther from the factory, the share of the total new housing business that went to Fabhus declined. The company suspected that this might result from the higher prices of the units due to shipping charges. Fabhus relied on a zone-price system in which prices were based on the product delivered at the construction site.

Local dealers actually supervised construction. Each dealer had pricing latitude and could charge more or less than Fabhus's suggested list price. Individual dealers were responsible for seeing that customers were satisfied with their Fabhus home, although Fabhus also had a toll-free number that customers could call if they were not satisfied with the way their dealer handled the construction or if they had problems moving in.

Considering the potential impact distance and dealers might have, the research team thought it was important to sample purchasers in the various zones as well as customers of the various dealers. Since Fabhus's records of houses sold were kept by zone and by date sold within zone, sample respondents were selected in the following way. First, the registration cards per zone were counted. Second, the sample size per zone was determined so that the number of respondents per zone was proportionate to the number of homes sold in the zones. Third, a sample interval, k, was chosen for each zone, a random start between 1 and k was generated, and every kth record was selected. The mail questionnaire shown in Figure 5.11.1 was sent to the 423 households selected.

A cover letter informing Fabhus's customers of the general purpose of the survey accompanied the questionnaire, and a new one-dollar bill was included with each survey as an incentive to respond. Further, the anonymity of the respondents was guaranteed by enclosing a self-addressed, postage-paid postcard in the survey. Respondents were asked to mail the postcard when they mailed their survey. All of those who had not returned their postcards in two weeks were sent a notice reminding them that their survey had not been returned. The combination of incentives, guaranteed anonymity, and follow-up prompted the return of 342 questionnaires for an overall response rate of 81 percent.

FIGURE 5.11.1   Factory-Built Home Owners Survey

1. *How did you first learn of the factory-built home that you bought? (check one, please)*
   - [ ] Friend or relative
   - [ ] Another customer
   - [ ] Realtor
   - [ ] Model home
   - [ ] Yellow pages
   - [ ] National magazine
   - [ ] Direct mail
   - [ ] Newspaper
   - [ ] Radio
   - [ ] TV
   - [ ] Don't remember
   - [ ] Other_____ (please specify)

2. *Did you own the land your home is on before you first visited your home builder?*
   - [ ] Yes
   - [ ] No

3. *How long have you lived in your home?* _____ years

4. *Where did you live before purchasing your factory-built home? (please check one)*
   - [ ] Rented a house, apartment, or mobile home
   - [ ] Owned a mobile home
   - [ ] Owned a conventionally built home
   - [ ] Owned another factory-built home
   - [ ] Other_____ (please specify)

5. *Please rate your overall level of satisfaction with your home. (please check one)*
   - [ ] Very satisfied
   - [ ] Somewhat satisfied
   - [ ] Somewhat dissatisfied
   - [ ] Very dissatisfied

FIGURE 5.11.1   (continued)

6. *How important to you were each of the following considerations in purchasing your factory-built home? (please check a box for each item)*

Considerations	Extremely Important	Important	Slightly Important	Not Important
Investment value	☐	☐	☐	☐
Quality	☐	☐	☐	☐
Price	☐	☐	☐	☐
Energy features	☐	☐	☐	☐
Dealer	☐	☐	☐	☐
Exterior style	☐	☐	☐	☐
Floor plan	☐	☐	☐	☐
Interior features	☐	☐	☐	☐
Delivery schedule	☐	☐	☐	☐

7. *Below, please list any other homes you looked at before purchasing the home you chose. Please state the reason you did not purchase the other home.*

Name of Home	Factory-Built?	Reason for Not Purchasing
_____	☐ Yes ☐ No	_____
_____	☐ Yes ☐ No	_____
_____	☐ Yes ☐ No	_____
_____	☐ Yes ☐ No	_____

Now we would like you to please tell us about yourself and your family.

8. *How many children do you have living at home?* _____ children

9. *What is the age of the head of your household? (check one, please)*
   ☐ Under 20   ☐ 35–44   ☐ 55–64
   ☐ 20–24   ☐ 45–54   ☐ 65 or over
   ☐ 25–34

10. *What is the occupation of the head of the household? (check one, please)*
    ☐ Professional or official   ☐ Labor or machine operator
    ☐ Technical or manager   ☐ Foreman
    ☐ Proprietor   ☐ Service worker
    ☐ Farmer   ☐ Retired
    ☐ Craftsperson   ☐ Other_____
    ☐ Clerical or sales   (please specify)

(continued)

FIGURE 5.11.1   (continued)

11. **Which of the following categories includes your family's total annual income? (check one, please)**

☐ Less than $20,000   ☐ $50,000–$59,999
☐ $20,001–$29,999   ☐ $60,000–$69,999
☐ $30,000–$39,999   ☐ $70,000–$79,999
☐ $40,000–$49,999   ☐ $80,000 or over

12. **Is the spouse of the head of the household employed? (check one, please)**

☐ Spouse employed full-time
☐ Spouse employed part-time
☐ Spouse not employed
☐ Not married

One final question:

13. **Would you recommend your particular factory-built home to someone interested in building a new home?**

☐ Yes   ☐ No

Thank you very much for completing this survey.
Your help in this study is greatly appreciated.

A complete list of the data is available on the computer disk.

QUESTIONS

1. Using the data provided on the computer disk and analytic techniques of your own choosing, address as best you can the objectives that prompted the research effort in the first place.

2. Do you think the research design was adequate for the problems posed? Why or why not?

CASE 5.12
Como Western Bank[1]

Como Western Bank is one of several commercial lending institutions located in the Colorado community of Brentwood Hills. The bank maintains four branch offices with one branch each located in the

---

[1]The contributions of David M. Szymanski to the development of this case are gratefully acknowledged.

east, west, north, and south districts of town. Its main office is located in downtown Brentwood Hills.

During the past decade, changes in the banking industry in Brentwood Hills have paralleled those taking place nationally, in that the environment has become increasingly complex and competitive. Deregulation, technological innovation, and changing interest rates have all made it difficult for banks to attract and keep customers. Local banks must now compete with insurance companies, multiservice investment firms, and even the government for clients. As a result, lending institutions are focusing increased attention on meeting consumer needs and developing strategies to increase their client base. Como Western is no exception.

A 1982 study of commercial banking in Brentwood Hills showed Como Western to have an above-average proportion of older households, long-time residents of the community, and middle-income persons as customers. The bank appeared to be less successful in attracting younger households, college graduates, and new residents of Brentwood Hills. In addition, the study found noncustomers of Como Western to have a weak image of the bank, even though

FIGURE 5.12.1 **Como Western Bank Customer Questionnaire**

Please have the person who normally does the banking for your household fill out this questionnaire. The following information will be strictly confidential and is used ONLY for statistical analysis.

1. How many years have you been banking at the Como Western Bank?
   _____ years

2. Why did you choose to bank at Como Western Bank?
   _____
   _____
   _____

3. How often do you use the following to do your banking?

	Sometimes	Almost Always	Never
Lobby	_____	_____	_____
TYME machine	_____	_____	_____
Drive-up	_____	_____	_____
Walk-up	_____	_____	_____
Bank-by-mail	_____	_____	_____
Telephone	_____	_____	_____

4. The following is a list of GENERAL banking services. If you believe a service is available at Como Western Bank, please check whether you use the service. Otherwise, check if you believe a service is not available or if you are not certain.

	Available Used	Available Not Used	Not Available	Not Certain
Regular Checking	_____	_____	_____	_____
Regular Savings	_____	_____	_____	_____
Partnership Savings	_____	_____	_____	_____
NOW Account	_____	_____	_____	_____
Repurchase Agreement	_____	_____	_____	_____
IRA	_____	_____	_____	_____
Certificate of Deposit	_____	_____	_____	_____
U.S. Savings Bond	_____	_____	_____	_____
Personal Loan	_____	_____	_____	_____
Auto Loan	_____	_____	_____	_____
Mortgage Loan/Home Improvement Loan	_____	_____	_____	_____

5. How important are the following to you in selecting and staying with a bank? For each item, please place an X in the box which indicates the level of importance you assign to that item. For example, with the first item, "Close to my shopping areas," an X under "Extremely Important" means the item is extremely important to you in selecting and staying with a bank.

	Extremely Important	Very Important	Somewhat Important	Not Important But Desirable	Unimportant
Close to my shopping areas	_____	_____	_____	_____	_____
Close to home	_____	_____	_____	_____	_____
Close to work	_____	_____	_____	_____	_____
Makes few errors	_____	_____	_____	_____	_____
Friendly tellers	_____	_____	_____	_____	_____
Leader with new services	_____	_____	_____	_____	_____
Availability of personal loans	_____	_____	_____	_____	_____
Low service charges	_____	_____	_____	_____	_____
Convenient parking	_____	_____	_____	_____	_____
Charges low rates for loans	_____	_____	_____	_____	_____
Convenient hours	_____	_____	_____	_____	_____
Is a large bank	_____	_____	_____	_____	_____
Handles my complaints well	_____	_____	_____	_____	_____
Pays high interest on savings	_____	_____	_____	_____	_____
Has a wide variety of services	_____	_____	_____	_____	_____
Fast service	_____	_____	_____	_____	_____
Gives me enough information	_____	_____	_____	_____	_____
Friendly personnel	_____	_____	_____	_____	_____
Concerned about the community	_____	_____	_____	_____	_____
Modern	_____	_____	_____	_____	_____

(continued)

FIGURE 5.12.1   **(continued)**

6a. Please rate the Como Western Bank on the following PAIRS of characteristics. Make an X in the box which you feel best describes the Como Western Bank. In the first item, for example, an X on the LEFT side under "Very Descriptive" means that you feel the bank is very close to your shopping areas. An X under "Very Descriptive" on the RIGHT side of the scale means you feel the bank is very far from the areas where you do your shopping.

The Como Western Bank:

	Very Descriptive	Somewhat Descriptive	Neither	Somewhat Descriptive	Very Descriptive	
Is close to my shopping areas	___	___	___	___	___	Is far from my shopping areas
Is close to home	___	___	___	___	___	Is far from home
Is close to work	___	___	___	___	___	Is far from work
Makes a lot of errors	___	___	___	___	___	Makes few errors
Has friendly tellers	___	___	___	___	___	Has unfriendly tellers
Is a leader with new services	___	___	___	___	___	Is a follower with new services
Has personal loans available	___	___	___	___	___	Does not have personal loans available
Has low service charges	___	___	___	___	___	Has high service charges
Has inconvenient parking	___	___	___	___	___	Has convenient parking
Charges high rates for loans	___	___	___	___	___	Charges low rates for loans
Has convenient hours	___	___	___	___	___	Has inconvenient hours
Is large	___	___	___	___	___	Is small
Handles my complaints poorly	___	___	___	___	___	Handles my complaints well
Pays high interest on savings	___	___	___	___	___	Pays low interest on savings
Offers a wide variety of services	___	___	___	___	___	Offers limited services
Gives fast service	___	___	___	___	___	Gives slow service
Gives me enough information	___	___	___	___	___	Does not give me enough information
Has unfriendly personnel	___	___	___	___	___	Has friendly personnel
Is concerned about the community	___	___	___	___	___	Is not concerned about the community
Is old-fashioned	___	___	___	___	___	Is modern

6b. Since there are many financial institutions in the Brentwood Hills area, we are interested in knowing whether you feel the Como Western Bank is above average or below average. Using the scales from question 6a, mark an O on each line where you think other financial institutions as a whole rate.

7. Which of the following services would you use if they were offered at the Como Western Bank?

Discount brokerage	___	Financial counseling	___
Insurance	___	Travel service	___
Tax preparation	___	In-home banking (Using personal computers)	___

Branch bank if it were located:

East ___   West ___   North ___   South ___

FIGURE 5.12.1 (continued)

8. The following is a list of SPECIAL banking services. If you believe a service is available at the Como Western Bank, please check whether you use or do not use the service. Otherwise check if you believe a service is not available or if you are not certain.

	Available Used	Available Not Used	Not Available	Not Certain
Safe deposit	___	___	___	___
VISA/MASTERCARD	___	___	___	___
Priority Service for Seniors	___	___	___	___
24-Hour Depository	___	___	___	___
Overdraft Protection	___	___	___	___
Investment Management	___	___	___	___
Notary Public	___	___	___	___
Estate and Financial Planning	___	___	___	___
Trust Services	___	___	___	___
Utility Payments	___	___	___	___
Traveler's Cheques	___	___	___	___
Foreign Currency Exchange	___	___	___	___
TYME Card	___	___	___	___
Telephone Transfer	___	___	___	___
Wire Transfer	___	___	___	___
Direct Deposit	___	___	___	___
U.S. Treasury Bills and Notes	___	___	___	___

9. How do you obtain your local banking and financial information? (Please check all that apply.)

Newspaper ___   Friends ___
Television ___   Magazines ___
Radio ___   Bank Newsletter ___
Bank Personnel ___   Bank Statement Stuffers ___
  Other (please write in) ___

10. Is the information you obtain from the above sources sufficient?
Yes ___ No ___
If No, why not? _____

11. Do you maintain accounts with other financial institutions (savings & loan, credit union, other bank, etc.)?
Yes ___ No ___
—If Yes, please answer the next two questions (11a & 11b) before going on.
—If No, go on to question 12.

11a. Which services do you use at other financial institutions?

Checking Account ___   U.S. Treasury Bills and Notes ___
Regular Savings ___   Safe Deposit Box ___
Certificate of Deposit ___   Personal Loan ___
Repurchase Agreement ___   Mortgage Loan ___
IRA ___   Auto Loan ___
VISA/MASTERCARD ___   Other (please write in) ___
Trust Services ___
Money Market Funds ___
Stocks and Bonds ___

11b. Why do you use services at other financial institutions rather than the Como Western Bank?
_____

12. Would you recommend the Como Western Bank to a friend?
Yes ___ No ___ Don't Know ___

13. Overall, how do you rate the service you have received from the Como Western Bank?

Excellent	Good	Acceptable	Poor	Unacceptable
___	___	___	___	___

(continued)

FIGURE 5.12.1   **(continued)**

14. Do you have any comments about or suggested changes for the Como Western Bank?

    _____

    _____

    _____

15. Please check your sex and marital status.

    Male _____   Single _____   Widowed _____

    Female _____   Married _____   Divorced/Separated _____

16. How many dependents do you have in your household?

    0 _____   1–2 _____   3–5 _____   6 or more _____

17. Are you the primary wage earner in your household?

    Yes _____   No _____

18. Please check your age and the highest level of education you reached. (If applicable, please check your spouse's age and highest level of education.)

Age	Self	Spouse	Education	Self	Spouse
Under 18	_____	_____	Grade School	_____	_____
18–21	_____	_____	Some High School	_____	_____
22–30	_____	_____	High School Graduate	_____	_____
31–40	_____	_____	Vocational/Technical	_____	_____
41–50	_____	_____	Attended College	_____	_____
51–64	_____	_____	College Graduate	_____	_____
65 or over	_____	_____	Post-Graduate Study	_____	_____

19. Please check the occupation which best applies to you. (If applicable, please check your spouse's occupation.)

	Self	Spouse		Self	Spouse
Professional/Technical	_____	_____	Craftsman	_____	_____
Farmer	_____	_____	Serviceworker	_____	_____
Manager, Administrator	_____	_____	Laborer	_____	_____
Proprietor	_____	_____	Retired	_____	_____
Clerical	_____	_____	Student	_____	_____
Sales	_____	_____	Not Currently Working	_____	_____

20. Please check the estimated total household income before taxes in 1997.

    $0–19,999 _____ $40,000–49,999 _____ $70,000–79,999 _____

    $20,000–29,999 _____ $50,000–59,999 _____ $80,000 or more _____

    $30,000–39,999 _____ $60,000–69,999 _____

21. How many people in your household work outside the home?_____

22. How many years have you lived in the Brentwood Hills area?

    Less than 1 year _____   6–10 years _____

    1–3 years _____   more than 10 years _____

    4–5 years _____

Thank you for taking the time to complete this questionnaire.

FIGURE 5.12.2	Coding Form

Record 1

Columns	Description (Question)	Coding
1–3	Subject ID	
4–5	Years banking at Como Western (#1)	
6	Reason for choosing Como Western (#2)	1 = location
		2 = convenience
		3 = recommendation/reputation
		4 = previous contact
		5 = quality of service
		6 = free checking
		7 = variety of accounts
		8 = loan
		9 = other reasons
	Frequency with which services are used (#3)	1 = sometimes
		2 = almost always
		3 = never
7	Lobby	
8	TYME Machine	
9	Drive-up	
10	Walk-up	
11	Bank-by-mail	
12	Telephone	
	Use of services (#4)	1 = available/used
		2 = available/not used
		3 = not available
		4 = not certain
13	Regular checking	
14	Regular savings	
15	Partnership savings	
16	NOW account	
17	Repurchase agreement	
18	IRA	
19	Certificate of deposit	
20	U.S. Savings Bond	
21	Personal loan	
22	Auto loan	
23	Mortgage/home improvement loan	
	Importance of various features (#5)	1 = extremely important
		2 = very important
		3 = somewhat important
		4 = not important but desirable
		5 = unimportant
24	Close to my shopping areas	
25	Close to home	
26	Close to work	
27	Makes few errors	
28	Friendly tellers	
29	Leader with new services	
30	Availability of personal loans	
31	Low service charges	
32	Convenient parking	
33	Charges low rates for loans	
34	Convenient hours	

(continued)

FIGURE 5.12.2   **(continued)**

Record 1

Columns	*Description (Question)*	*Coding*
35	Is a large bank	
36	Handles my complaints well	
37	Pays high interest on savings	
38	Has a wide variety of services	
39	Fast service	
40	Gives me enough information	
41	Friendly personnel	
42	Concerned about the community	
43	Modern	

Rating of Como on various features (#6A)

1 = very descriptive
2 = somewhat descriptive
3 = neither
4 = somewhat descriptive
5 = very descriptive

44	Close to my shopping areas/far from my shopping areas	
45	Close to home/far from home	
46	Close to work/far from work	
47	Makes a lot of errors/makes few errors	
48	Friendly tellers/unfriendly tellers	
49	A leader with new services/a follower with new services	
50	Personal loans available/personal loans not available	
51	Low service charges/high service charges	
52	Inconvenient parking/convenient parking	
53	Charges high rates for loans/charges low rates for loans	
54	Convenient hours/inconvenient hours	
55	Large/small	
56	Handles my complaints poorly/handles my complaints well	
57	Pays high interest on savings/pays low interest on savings	
58	Wide variety of services/limited services	
59	Fast service/slow service	
60	Gives me enough information/does not give me enough information	
61	Unfriendly personnel/friendly personnel	
62	Concerned about the community/not concerned about the community	
63	Old-fashioned/modern	

Services that would be used if available (#7)   1 = yes; 2 = no

64	Discount brokerage	
65	Insurance	
66	Tax preparation	
67	Financial counseling	
68	Travel service	
69	In-home banking	
70	East side branch	
71	West side branch	
72	North side branch	
73	South side branch	

FIGURE 5.12.2   (continued)

<table>
<tr><td colspan="3">Record 2</td></tr>
<tr><td>Columns</td><td>Description (Question)</td><td>Coding</td></tr>
<tr><td>1–3</td><td>Subject ID
Use of special services at Como Western (#8)</td><td>1 = available/used
2 = available/not used
3 = not available
4 = not certain</td></tr>
<tr><td>4</td><td>Safe deposit</td><td></td></tr>
<tr><td>5</td><td>VISA/MASTERCARD</td><td></td></tr>
<tr><td>6</td><td>Priority service for seniors</td><td></td></tr>
<tr><td>7</td><td>24-hour depository</td><td></td></tr>
<tr><td>8</td><td>Overdraft protection</td><td></td></tr>
<tr><td>9</td><td>Investment management</td><td></td></tr>
<tr><td>10</td><td>Notary public</td><td></td></tr>
<tr><td>11</td><td>Estate and financial planning</td><td></td></tr>
<tr><td>12</td><td>Trust services</td><td></td></tr>
<tr><td>13</td><td>Utility payments</td><td></td></tr>
<tr><td>14</td><td>Traveler's cheques</td><td></td></tr>
<tr><td>15</td><td>Foreign currency exchange</td><td></td></tr>
<tr><td>16</td><td>TYME card</td><td></td></tr>
<tr><td>17</td><td>Telephone transfer</td><td></td></tr>
<tr><td>18</td><td>Wire transfer</td><td></td></tr>
<tr><td>19</td><td>Direct deposit</td><td></td></tr>
<tr><td>20</td><td>U.S. Treasury Bills and Notes</td><td></td></tr>
<tr><td></td><td>Source of local banking and financial information (#9)</td><td>1 = use
2 = do not use</td></tr>
<tr><td>21</td><td>Newspaper</td><td></td></tr>
<tr><td>22</td><td>Television</td><td></td></tr>
<tr><td>23</td><td>Radio</td><td></td></tr>
<tr><td>24</td><td>Bank personnel</td><td></td></tr>
<tr><td>25</td><td>Friends</td><td></td></tr>
<tr><td>26</td><td>Magazines</td><td></td></tr>
<tr><td>27</td><td>Bank newsletter</td><td></td></tr>
<tr><td>28</td><td>Bank statement stuffers</td><td></td></tr>
<tr><td>29</td><td>Other</td><td></td></tr>
<tr><td>30</td><td>Is information sufficient (#10)</td><td>1 = yes; 2 = no</td></tr>
<tr><td>31</td><td>Maintain accounts with other financial institutions (#11)</td><td>1 = yes; 2 = no</td></tr>
<tr><td></td><td>Services used at other institutions (#11a)</td><td>1 = use; 2 = do not use</td></tr>
<tr><td>32</td><td>Checking account</td><td></td></tr>
<tr><td>33</td><td>Regular savings</td><td></td></tr>
<tr><td>34</td><td>Certificate of Deposit</td><td></td></tr>
<tr><td>35</td><td>Repurchase agreement</td><td></td></tr>
<tr><td>36</td><td>IRA</td><td></td></tr>
<tr><td>37</td><td>VISA/MASTERCARD</td><td></td></tr>
<tr><td>38</td><td>Trust services</td><td></td></tr>
<tr><td>39</td><td>Money market funds</td><td></td></tr>
<tr><td>40</td><td>Stocks and bonds</td><td></td></tr>
<tr><td>41</td><td>U.S. Treasury bills and notes</td><td></td></tr>
<tr><td>42</td><td>Safe deposit box</td><td></td></tr>
<tr><td>43</td><td>Personal loan</td><td></td></tr>
<tr><td>44</td><td>Mortgage loan</td><td></td></tr>
<tr><td>45</td><td>Auto loan</td><td></td></tr>
<tr><td>46</td><td>Other</td><td></td></tr>
</table>

(continued)

FIGURE 5.12.2　(continued)

Record 2

Columns	Description (Question)	Coding
47–48	Why use services at other institutions (#11b)	1 = branch location 2 = convenience 3 = already had account 4 = special services unavailable 5 = charges/balance 6 = savings interest rates 7 = low loan rates 8 = loan availability 9 = risk diversification 10 = service quality 11 = need separate accounts 12 = other
49	Recommend Como to a friend (#12)	1 = yes; 2 = no; 3 = don't know
50	Quality of service overall (#13)	1 = excellent 2 = good 3 = acceptable 4 = poor 5 = unacceptable
51–52	Comments and suggested changes (#14)	1 = branches 2 = personnel 3 = service charge 4 = hours 5 = general-negative 6 = error rate 7 = general-favorable 8 = neutral 9 = other
53	Sex (#15)	1 = male; 2 = female
54	Marital status (#15)	1 = single 2 = married 3 = widowed 4 = divorced/separated
55	Number of dependents (#16)	1 = none 2 = 1–2 3 = 3–5 4 = 6 or more
56	Primary wage earner (#17)	1 = yes; 2 = no
57;58	Age of self; age of spouse (#18)	1 = under 18 2 = 18–21 3 = 22–30 4 = 31–40 5 = 41–50 6 = 51–64 7 = 65 or over

FIGURE 5.12.2   (continued)

		Record 2	

Columns	Description (Question)	Coding
59;60	Education of self; education of spouse (#18)	1 = grade school 2 = some high school
61–62; 63–64	Occupation of self; occupation of spouse (#19)	1 = professional technical 2 = farmer 3 = manager/administrator 4 = proprietor 5 = clerical 6 = sales 7 = craftsman 8 = serviceworker 9 = laborer 10 = retired 11 = student 12 = not currently working
65	Estimated household income (#20)	1 = $0–$19,999 2 = $20,000–$29,999 3 = $30,000–$39,999 4 = $40,000–$49,999 5 = $50,000–$59,999 6 = $60,000–$69,999 7 = $70,000–$79,999 8 = $80,000 or more
66	Number of people working outside home (#21)	1 = 0 2 = 1 3 = 2 4 = 3 or more
67	Years lived in area (#22)	1 = less than 1 2 = 1–3 3 = 4–5 4 = 6–10 5 = more than 10

customers held a very positive image. Bank officials sensed that these results typified the current situation as well. However, because the officials were in the process of developing a comprehensive marketing plan, they desired more up-to-date and detailed information to aid in formulating an appropriate marketing strategy. Therefore, bank officials contracted with the Mestousis Research Agency to study current bank customers. This small, local agency was led by its founder, Mike Mestousis, and Kathy Rendina, who served as the principal investigator on most projects. In addition, it employed six clerical people. The objectives of the study given to the Mestousis Agency were: (1) to determine the demographic profiles of present bank customers; (2) to determine customer awareness, use, and overall perception of current bank services; and (3) to identify new bank services desired by customers.

Research Method

The Mestousis Agency proposed and the bank's directors agreed that the study should be conducted in two phases. The first phase was designed to increase the research team's familiarity with Como Western's current clientele and service offerings. Several methods of inquiry were used. They included personal interviews with customers, bank employees, and members of the bank's board of directors, as well as a literature search of studies relating to the banking industry. Based on information gathered through these procedures, a questionnaire was developed to be used in the second portion of the project.

Because the information being sought was general yet personal in nature, the mail survey was deemed appropriate for data-collection purposes. To encourage a high response rate, the bank president wrote a cover letter describing the research objectives and importance of responding, which was mailed with each questionnaire, along with a stamped, self-addressed envelope. Furthermore, those who returned the questionnaire became eligible to participate in a drawing to win one of five $50 bills. To ensure anonymity, the name and address of the respondent was to be sealed in a separate envelope, which was supplied, and returned with the questionnaire.

The questionnaire shown in Figure 5.12.1 was also designed to encourage high response. The instructions made it clear that the information would be held in strict confidence, and the more sensitive questions were asked last. In addition, the questionnaire was extensively pretested using bank customers of various ages and backgrounds.

Several weeks before the questionnaire was mailed, customers were notified by means of the bank's newsletter of the possibility that they would be receiving the questionnaire.

Sampling Plan

The relevant population for the study was defined as all noncommercial customers of Como Western Bank who lived in Brentwood Hills and who were not employees of the bank. The total number of customers meeting these requirements was 10,300. A printout of bank customers revealed that bank records list customers in blocks according to zip codes.

The researchers were of the opinion that 500 survey responses were required to adequately perform the analysis. Anticipating a 30 to 35 percent response rate, 1,500 to 1,600 surveys needed to be mailed. Given 10,300 population elements and the estimated sample size of 1,600, the researchers decided to send a questionnaire to one of every six names on the list. They generated the first name randomly using a table of random numbers. It was the fourth name on the list. They consequently sent questionnaires to the fourth, tenth, sixteenth, and so on names on the list. In all, 1,547 questionnaires were sent and 673 were returned for a response rate of approximately 44 percent. Figure 5.12.2 displays the coding form while the raw data are contained in file COMOWEST.DAT.

QUESTIONS

1. Evaluate the general research design.

2. Evaluate the sampling plan.

3. What do the results suggest with respect to the following?
   a. The demographic characteristics of Como Western's customers.
   b. Customer awareness, use, and perceptions of the various services provided by Como Western.
   c. The relationship, if any, between age and income of the respondents and their overall evaluation of the services provided by Como Western.

4. What new services, if any, should Como Western offer?

The Research Report

Part 6 consists of one chapter and an epilogue. The chapter discusses one of the most important parts of the entire research process, the research report. The research report often becomes the standard by which the research effort is assessed. Chapter 18 deals with the criteria a research report should satisfy and the form a research report can follow so that it contributes positively to the research effort. The chapter also discusses oral reports and some of the graphic means that can be used to communicate important findings more forcefully. The epilogue ties together the parts of the research process. It reinforces the points made earlier that the steps in the research process are highly interrelated and that a decision made at one stage has implications for the others as well.

CHAPTER 18

The Research Report

A frustrated executive of a large corporation recently remarked that he is convinced reports are devices by which the informed ensure that the uninformed remain that way.[1]

To avoid creating the kind of reports that the executive was thinking of requires considerable skill and attention to detail. If length were the criterion of a chapter's importance, there would be an inverse relationship between this chapter and the criterion. The chapter is short, but its subject is vital to the success of the research effort. Regardless of the sophistication displayed in other portions of the research process, the project is a failure if the research report fails. Empirical evidence indicates, for example, that the research report is one of the five most important variables affecting the use of research information.[2] The preceding research steps determine the content. The research report provides the form, and since the report is all that many executives will see of the project, it becomes the yardstick for evaluation. The writer must ensure that the report informs without misinforming.

The report must tell readers what they need and wish to know. Typically, executives are interested in results and must be convinced of the usefulness of the findings. They must be able to act on the report while recognizing the caveats entailed in the results. This means that they must sufficiently appreciate the method to recognize its weaknesses and bounds of error. The researcher must convey the limitations and necessary details of the method to allow this appreciation. However, the researcher must do it in a way that is understandable and useful, and this is often easier said than done.

---

[1]William J. Gallagher, *Report Writing for Management* (Reading, MA: Addison-Wesley, 1969), p. 1. Much of this introductory section is also taken from this excellent book. See also Pnenna Sageev, *Helping Researchers Write, So Managers Can Understand*, 2nd ed. (Columbus, OH: Battelle Press, 1995); Carol M. Lehman and Debbie D. Du Frene, *Himstreet and Baty's Business Communications*, 12th ed. (Cincinnati, OH: Southwestern Publishing Company, 1999).

[2]The other variables are the extent of interaction that researchers have with managers, the research objectives, the degree of surprise in the results, and the stage of the product or service in its life cycle. See Rohit Deshpande and Gerald Zaltman, "A Comparison of Factors Affecting Researcher and Manager Perceptions of Market Research Use," *Journal of Marketing Research* 21 (February 1984), pp. 32–38. The understandability of the research report also affects managers' trust in it and that, in turn, affects what they do with the information. See, for example, Christine Moorman, Rohit Deshpande, and Gerald Zaltman, "Factors Affecting Trust in Market Research Relationships," *Journal of Marketing* 57 (January 1993), pp. 81–101; Kent Grayson and Tim Ambler, "The Dark Side of Long-Term Relationships in Marketing Services," *Journal of Marketing Research* 36 (February 1999), pp. 132–141.

This chapter, which is designed to assist the researcher in this regard, is divided into four main sections: (1) the criteria by which research reports are evaluated, (2) the parts and forms of the written research report, (3) the oral report, and (4) some graphic means of presenting the results.

Fundamental Criteria of Research Reports

Research reports are evaluated by one fundamental criterion—communication with the reader. The "iron law" of marketing research holds that "people would rather live with a problem they cannot solve than accept a solution they cannot understand."[3] The reader is not only the reason that the report is prepared but also the standard by which its success is measured. This means, purely and simply, that the report must be tailor-made for the reader or readers, with due regard for their technical sophistication, interest in the subject area, the circumstances under which they will read the report, and the use they will make of it.

The technical sophistication of the readers determines their capacity for understanding methodological decisions, such as experimental design, measurement device, sampling plan, analysis technique, and so on. Readers with little technical sophistication will probably be offended by the use of unexplained technical jargon. "The readers of your reports are busy people, and very few of them can balance a research report, a cup of coffee, and a dictionary at one time."[4] Unexplained jargon may even make such persons suspicious of the report writer. Researchers must be particularly sensitive to this, because, being technical people, they may fail to realize that they are using technical language and terms.

The readers' capacity establishes the technical upper limit of the report, while their interest, circumstances, and intended use restrict its level. These factors delineate individual preferences, and such preferences must be considered by the report writer.

> Some executives demand a minimum report; they want only the results—not a discussion of how the results were obtained. Others want considerable information on the research methods used in the study. Many executives place a premium on brevity, while others demand complete discussion. Some are interested only in the statistical results and not in the researcher's conclusions and recommendations.
>
> Thus, *the audience determines the type of report.* Researchers must make every effort to acquaint themselves with the *specific preferences of their audiences.* They should not consider these preferences as unalterable, but *any deviations from them should be made with reason and not from ignorance!* (emphasis added)[5]

---

[3]Walter B. Wentz, *Marketing Research: Management, Method, and Cases,* 2nd ed. (New York: Harper & Row, 1979), p. 61. See also Edward P. Bailey and Philip A. Powell, *The Practical Writer,* 6th ed. (Orlando, FL: Harcourt Brace College Publishers, 1994).

[4]Stewart Henderson Britt, "The Communication of Your Research Findings," in Robert Ferber, ed., *Handbook of Marketing Research* (New York: McGraw-Hill, 1974), pp. 1–90. See also Edward R. Steinberg, ed., *Plain Language: Principles and Practice* (Detroit: Wayne State University Press, 1992).

[5]Harper W. Boyd, Jr., Ralph Westfall, and Stanley F. Stasch, *Marketing Research: Text and Cases,* 7th ed. (Burr Ridge, IL: Richard D. Irwin, 1989), p. 657.

The report writer's difficulties in tailoring the report are often compounded by the existence of several audiences. The marketing vice president might have a different technical capacity and level of interest than the manager responsible for the product discussed in the report. There is no easy solution to this problem of "many masters." The researcher has to recognize the potential differences that may arise and must often use a great deal of ingenuity to reconcile them. This sometimes may require the preparation of several reports, each designed for a specific audience, although it is customary to satisfy the conflicting demands with one report containing both technical and nontechnical sections for different readers.

Writing Criteria

Certain specific criteria that the report should satisfy enhance the likelihood that it will indeed communicate with the reader. In particular, the report should be complete, accurate, clear, and concise.[6] These criteria are intimately related. A clear report is an accurate report. For purposes of exposition, though, it helps to discuss the criteria as if they were distinct.

COMPLETENESS   A report is complete when it provides all the information readers need in language they understand. This means that the writer must continually ask whether every question in the original assignment has been addressed. What alternatives were examined? What was found? An incomplete report implies that supplementary reports, which are annoying and delay action, will be forthcoming.

The report may be incomplete because it is too brief or too long. The writer may omit necessary definitions and short explanations. Alternatively, the report may be heavy because it is lengthy but not profound. Report writers tend not to waste collected information. However, presenting information outside the interest of the intended readers may distract them from the main issues. If the report is big, it may discourage readers from even attempting to digest its contents. Readers' interests and abilities thus determine what clarification should be added and what findings should be omitted. In general, the amount of detail should be proportionate to the amount of direct control users can exercise over the areas under discussion.

ACCURACY   The previous steps in the research process are not the only determinants of accuracy. They are vital, to be sure, for a report cannot be accurate when the basic input is inaccurate. But even with accurate input, the research report may generate inaccuracies because of carelessness in handling the data, illogical reasoning, or inept phrasing.[7] Thus, accuracy is another writing criterion. Table 18.1 illustrates some examples of sources of inaccuracy in report writing.

An excellent example of inept phrasing and its consequences is provided in Research Realities 18.1 by the experience of Jock Elliott, the chairman emeritus of

---

[6]Gallagher, *Report Writing*, p. 78.

[7]See Gallagher, *Report Writing*, pp. 80–83, for a number of examples that display some of the inaccuracies that may arise. The examples are particularly interesting because they have been extracted from actual company reports.

TABLE 18.1	Some Examples of Sources of Inaccuracy in Report Writing

A. Simple Errors in Addition or Subtraction

"In the United States, 14 percent of the population has an elementary school education or less, 51 percent has attended or graduated from high school, and 16 percent has attended college."

An oversight such as this (14 + 51 + 16 do not equal 100 percent) can be easily corrected by the author, but not so easily by the reader because he or she may not know if one or more of the percentage values is incorrect or if a category might have been left out of the tally.

B. Confusion between Percentages and Percentage Points

"The company's profits as a percentage of sales were 6.0 percent in 1995 and 8.0 percent in 2000. Therefore, they increased only 2.0 percent in five years."

In this example, the increase is, of course, 2.0 percentage points, or 33 percent.

C. Inaccuracy Caused by Grammatical Errors

"The reduction in the government's price supports for dairy products has reduced farm income $600 million to $800 million per year."

To express a range of reduction, the author should have written: "The reduction in the government's price supports for dairy products has reduced farm income by between $600 million and $800 million per year."

D. Confused Terminology Resulting in Fallacious Conclusion

"The Jones's household and annual income increased from $10,000 in 1970 to $30,000 in 2000, thereby tripling the family's purchasing power."

Although the Jones's household annual income may have tripled in the 30 years, the family's purchasing power certainly did not, as the cost of living, as measured by the consumer price index, more than tripled in the same period.

the Ogilvy & Mather advertising agency. Elliott makes no bones about the importance of being able to write well in order to advance in a career. "As you sail along on your career, bad writing acts as a sea anchor, pulling you back, good writing as a spinnaker, pulling you ahead."[8]

Examples of inept phrasing abound, often permeating our daily lives. Inaccuracies also arise because of grammatical errors in punctuation, spelling, tense, subject and verb agreement, and so on.[9]

CLARITY   Clarity is probably violated more than any other principle of good writing. Clear and logical thinking and precise expression produce clarity. When the underlying logic is fuzzy or the presentation imprecise, readers have difficulty understanding what they read. They may be forced to guess, in which case the

---

[8]Jock Elliott, "How Hard It Is to Write Easily," *Viewpoint: The Ogilvy & Mather Magazine* 2 (1980), p. 18.

[9]Gallagher, *Report Writing*, Chapter 10, "Reviewing for Accuracy: Grammar," pp. 156–177, has examples of how these inaccuracies can confuse and misinform.

RESEARCH REALITIES 18.1

An Example of Inept Phrasing and Its Consequences

Last month I got a letter from a vice president of a major management consulting firm. Let me read you two paragraphs. The first:

"Recently, the companies of our Marketing Services Group were purchased by one of the largest consumer research firms in the U.S. While this move well fits the basic business purpose and focus of the acquired MSG units, it is personally restrictive. I will rather choose to expand my management opportunities with a career move into industry."

What he meant was: The deal works fine for my company, but not so fine for me. I'm looking for another job.

Second paragraph:

"The base of managerial and technical accomplishment reflected in my enclosed resumé may suggest an opportunity to meet a management need for one of your clients. Certainly my experience promises a most productive pace to understand the demands and details of any new situation I would choose."

What he meant was: As you can see in my resumé, I've had a lot of good experience. I am a quick study. Do you think any of your clients might be interested in me?

At least, that's what I think he meant.

This fellow's letter reveals him as pompous. He may not be pompous. He may only be a terrible writer. But I haven't the interest or time to find out which. There are so many people looking for jobs who *don't* sound pompous.

Bad writing done him in—with me, at any rate.

Source: Jock Elliott, "How Hard It Is to Write Easily," *Viewpoint: The Ogilvy & Mather Magazine* 2 (1980), p. 18. Reprinted with permission. The use of jargon and imprecise expression has become so commonplace that computer programs that analyze grammar readability and sentence structure and suggest alternative wordings have been developed to deal with it. Microsoft Office 97, for example, contains a grammar checker as do many of the most popular word-processing programs. See Stephen H. Wildstrom, "Good Help Gets Easier to Find," *Business Week* (February 10, 1997), p. 21.

---

corollary to Murphy's law applies. "If the reader is offered the slightest opportunity to misunderstand, he probably will."[10]

It is easy to say that the report should be clear, but it is much more difficult to develop such a report. It is essential that the organization of the report is clear.[11] For this to happen, you must know what you want to say. Make an outline of your major points. Order the points logically and place the supporting details in their proper position. Tell the reader where you are going and then do what you said you were going to do. Use short paragraphs and short sentences. Don't mumble; once you have decided what to say, come out and say it. Choose your words carefully. See Research Realities 18.2 for some specific suggestions when choosing words. Don't expect to get it right the first time; expect to rewrite it several times. When rewriting, try to reduce the length by half. That forces you to simplify and remove the clutter. It also forces you to think about every word and its purpose. Jock Elliott has some pointed comments on writing clearly:

> Our written and spoken words reflect what we are. If our words are brilliant, precise, well ordered and human, then that is how we are seen.

---

[10]Gallagher, *Report Writing*, p. 83.

[11]Kenneth Roman and Joel Raphaelson, *Writing That Works* (New York: Harper & Row, 1981). This book gives some excellent advice on how to write more effective reports, memos, letters, and speeches. See also Simon Mort, *Professional Report Writing* (Brookfield, VT: Ashgate Publishing Company, 1995). The little book by William Strunk, Jr., and E. B. White, *The Elements of Style,* 3rd ed. (New York: Macmillan, 1979), is a classic on how to write clearly.

RESEARCH REALITIES 18.2

Some Suggestions When Choosing Words for Marketing Research Reports

1. *Use short words.* Always use short words in preference to long words that mean the same thing.

Use This	Not This
Now	Currently
Start	Initiate
Show	Indicate
Finish	Finalize
Use	Utilize
Place	Position

2. *Avoid vague modifiers.* Avoid lazy adjectives and adverbs and use vigorous ones. Lazy modifiers are so overused in some contexts that they have become clichés. Select only those adjectives and adverbs that make your meaning more precise.

Lazy Modifiers	Vigorous Modifiers
Very good	Short meeting
Awfully nice	Crisp presentation
Basically accurate	Baffling instructions
Great success	Tiny raise
Richly deserved	Moist handshake
Vitally important	Lucid recommendation

3. *Use specific, concrete language.* Avoid technical jargon. There is always a simple, down-to-earth word that says the same thing as the show-off fad word or the vague abstraction.

Jargon	Down-to-Earth English
Implement	Carry out
Viable	Practical, workable
Net net	Conclusion
Suboptimal	Less than ideal
Proactive	Active
Bottom line	Outcome

4. *Write simply and naturally—the way you talk.* Use only those words, phrases, and sentences that you might actually say to your reader if you were face-to-face. If you wouldn't say it, if it doesn't sound like you, don't write it.

Stiff	Natural
The reasons are fourfold	There are four reasons
Importantly	The important point is
Visitation	Visit

5. *Strike out words you don't need.* Certain commonly used expressions contain redundant phrasing. Cut out the extra words.

Don't Write	Write
Advance plan	Plan
Take action	Act
Study in depth	Study
Consensus of opinion	Consensus
Until such time as	Until
The overall plan	The plan

Source: Excerpts on pages 7, 9, 10, and 15 from *Writing That Works* by Kenneth Roman and Joel Raphaelson. Copyright © 1981 by Kenneth Roman and Joel Raphaelson. Reprinted by permission of Harper & Row Publishers, Inc.

When you write, you must constantly ask yourself: What am I trying to say? If you do this religiously, you will be surprised at how often you don't know what you are trying to say.

You have to *think* before you start every sentence, and you have to *think* about every word.

Then you must look at what you have written and ask: Have I said it? Is it clear to someone encountering the subject for the first time? If it's not, it is because some fuzz has worked its way into the machinery. The clear writer is a person clearheaded enough to see this stuff for what it is: fuzz.

It is not easy to write a simple declarative sentence. Here is one way to do it. Think what you want to say. Write your sentence. Then strip it of all adverbs and adjectives. Reduce the sentence to its skeleton. Let the verbs and nouns do the work.

If your skeleton sentence does not express your thought precisely, you've got the wrong verb or noun. Dig for the right one. Nouns and verbs carry the guns in good writing; adjectives and adverbs are decorative camp followers.[12]

CONCISENESS   Although the report must be complete, it must also be concise. This means that the writer must be selective about what is included. The researcher must avoid trying to impress the reader with all that has been found. If something does not pertain directly to the subject, it should be omitted. The writer must also avoid lengthy discussions of commonly known methods.

Even if the material is appropriate, conciseness can still be violated by writing style. This commonly occurs when the writer is groping for the phrases and words that capture an idea. Instead of finally coming to terms with the idea, the writer writes around it, restating it several times in different ways, hoping that repetition will overcome poor expression. Concise writing, in contrast, is effective because "it makes maximum use of every word . . . no word in a concise discussion can be removed without impairing or destroying the function of the whole composition. . . . To be concise is to express a thought completely and clearly in the fewest words possible."[13]

One helpful technique for ensuring that the report is concise is reading the draft aloud. This points out sections that should be pruned or rewritten:

Silent reading allows him [the writer] to skim over the familiar material and thus impose an artificial rapidity and structural simplicity on something that is in reality dense and tangled. The eye can grow accustomed to the appearance of a sentence, but it is much more difficult for the tongue, lips, and jaw to deal with what the eye might accept readily.[14]

Form of the Report

The organization of the report influences all the criteria of report writing. Good organization cannot guarantee clarity, conciseness, accuracy, and completeness, but poor organization can preclude them. There is no single, acceptable organization for a report. The form chosen depends on the audience. The following format is flexible enough to allow the inclusion or exclusion of elements to satisfy particular needs.

1. Title page
2. Table of contents
3. Summary
   a. Introduction
   b. Results
   c. Conclusions
   d. Recommendations

---

[12]Elliott, "How Hard It Is to Write Easily," pp. 18–19.

[13]Gallagher, *Report Writing*, p. 87.

[14]Ibid., p. 84.

ETHICAL DILEMMA 18.1

As a member of an independent research team, it is your job to write the final report for a client. One of your colleagues whispers to you in passing, "Make it sound very technical. Lots of long words and jargon—you know the sort of thing. We want to make it clear that we earned our money on this one."

- Is it ethical to obscure the substance of a report beneath complex language?
- Will some clients be impressed by words that they do not fully understand?

---

4. Introduction
5. Body
   a. Methodology
   b. Results
   c. Limitations
6. Conclusions and recommendations
7. Appendix
   a. Copies of data-collection forms
   b. Detailed calculations supporting sample size, test statistics, and so on
   c. Tables not included in the body
   d. Bibliography

Title Page

The title page indicates the subject of the report, the name of the organization for which the report is made, the name of the organization submitting it, and the date. If the report is internal, the names of organizations or companies are replaced by those of individuals. Those for whom the report is intended are listed on the title page, as are the departments or people preparing the report. It is advisable to list those who should receive a confidential report with intended limited distribution.

Table of Contents

The table of contents lists, in order of appearance, the divisions and subdivisions of the report with page references. In short reports, the table of contents may simply contain the main headings. It will also typically include lists of tables and figures and the pages on which they can be found. For most reports, exhibits will be labeled as either tables or figures, with maps, diagrams, and graphs falling into the latter category.

Summary

The summary is the *most important* part of the report. It is its heart and core. Many executives will read only the summary. Others will read more, but even they will use the summary as a guide to those questions about which they would like more information.

The true summary is not an abstract of the whole report in which everything is restated in condensed form; neither is it a simple restatement of the subject, nor a brief statement of the significant results and conclusions. A true summary gives the high points of the entire body of the report. Properly written, the summary saves busy executives' time without sacrificing their understanding. A good test of a summary is self-sufficiency. Can it stand on its own, or does it collapse without the full report?

A good summary contains the necessary background information, as well as the important results and conclusions. Whether or not it contains recommendations is determined to an extent by the reader. Some managers prefer that the writer suggest appropriate action, while others prefer to draw their own conclusions on the basis of the evidence contained in the study. Although the good summary contains the necessary information, it will rarely be broken down through the use of headings and subheadings. The summary that requires such subdivisions is probably too long.

The introduction in the summary provides the reader with minimal background to appreciate the study's results, conclusions, and recommendations. The introduction should state who authorized the research and for what purpose and should explicitly outline the problem(s) or hypotheses that guided the research. The problems as stated here should also guide the remainder of the report. No subject should be treated in the report if it is not anticipated here.

The results presented in the summary must agree, of course, with those in the body of the report, but only the key findings should be presented here. It is useful to include one or several findings to each problem or objective.

Conclusions and recommendations are not the same. A conclusion is an opinion based on the results. It is a statement of what we know and what it means. A recommendation is a suggestion for appropriate future action. Conclusions should be included in the summary section. The writer is in a better position to base conclusions on the evidence than are the readers, as the writer is more familiar with the methods used to generate and analyze the data. The writer is at fault if conclusions are omitted and readers are allowed to draw their own.

Recommendations, though, are another matter. Some managers simply prefer to determine the appropriate courses of action themselves and do not want the writer to offer recommendations. Others hold that the writer, being closest to the research, is in the best position to suggest a course of action. For example, the Lipton Company has the philosophy that it is the responsibility of the marketing research people to interpret the findings. As Dolph von Arx, while serving as executive vice president, commented, "We feel strongly that our market research people must go beyond reporting the facts. We want them to tell us what *they* think the facts mean—both in terms of conclusions, and, if possible, indicated actions. Those who are responsible for making the decisions may or may not accept those conclusions or recommendations, but we want this input from our market research people."[15]

---

[15]Dolph von Arx, "The Many Faces of Market Research," paper delivered at meeting of the Association of National Advertisers, Inc., New York, April 3, 1985. See also Arthur Shapiro, "Downsizing and Its Effect on Corporate Marketing Research," *Marketing Research: A Magazine of Management & Applications* 2 (December 1990), pp. 56–59; Michelle Wirth Fellman, "Qualitative Research Must Anticipate Technology Changes," *Marketing News* 32 (December 7, 1998), pp. 1–4.

The Lipton Company's philosophy is consistent with recent trends in the industry. Increasingly, marketing researchers are being asked to interpret the findings in terms of what they mean to the business and to make recommendations as to appropriate courses of action.

Introduction

Whereas in the summary the readers' interests are taken into account, in the introduction their education and experience are considered. The introduction provides background information that readers need in order to appreciate the discussion in the body of the report. Some form of introduction is almost always necessary. Its length and detail, however, depend on the readers' familiarity with the subject, the approach to it, and the treatment of it.[16] As a rule, the report with wide distribution will require a more extensive introduction than a report for a narrow audience.

The introduction often defines unfamiliar terms or terms that are used in a specific way in the report. For instance, in a study of market penetration of a new product, the introduction might be used to define the market. What products and companies were considered "competitors" in calculating the new product's market share?

The introduction may provide some pertinent history. What similar studies have been conducted? What findings did they produce? What circumstances precipitated the present study? How were its scope and emphasis determined? Clearly, if readers are familiar with the history of this project and related research or the circumstances that inspired the current research, these items can be omitted. A report going to executives with only tangential interest in the particular product or service dealt with would probably have to include them.

The introduction should state the specific objectives of the research. If the project was part of a larger, overall project, this should be mentioned. Each of the subproblems or hypotheses should be explicitly stated. After reading the introduction, readers should know exactly what the report concerns and what it omits. They should appreciate the overall problem and how the subproblems relate to it. They should be aware of the relationship between this study and other related work. And they should appreciate the need for the study and its importance. Through all of this, the introduction should serve to win the readers' confidence and dispel any prejudices they may have.

Body

The details of the research are contained in the body of the report. This includes details of method, results, and limitations.

One of the hardest portions of the report to write is that giving the details of the method. The writer has a real dilemma here. Sufficient information must be presented so that readers can appreciate the research design, data-collection methods, sample procedures, and analysis techniques that were used without being bored or overwhelmed. However, technical jargon, which is often a succinct way of communicating a complex idea, should be omitted, because many in the audience will not understand it.

---

[16]Gallagher, *Report Writing*, p. 54.

Readers must be told whether the design was exploratory, descriptive, or causal as well as why the particular design was chosen. What are its merits in terms of the problem at hand? Readers should also be told whether the results are based on secondary or primary data. If primary, were they based on observation or questionnaire? And if the latter, were the questionnaires administered in person or by mail, e-mail, or telephone? Again, it is important to mention why the particular method was chosen. What were its perceived advantages over alternative schemes? This may mean *briefly* discussing the perceived weaknesses of the other data-collection schemes that were considered.

Sampling is a technical subject, and the writer cannot hope to convey all the nuances of the sampling plan in the body of the report but must be selective in this regard. At the minimum, the researcher should answer the following questions:

1. How was the population defined? What were the geographical, age, gender, or other bounds?

2. What sampling units were employed? Were they business organizations or business executives? Were they dwelling units, households, or individuals within a household? Why were these particular sampling units chosen?

3. How was the list of sampling units generated? Did this produce any weaknesses? Why was this method used?

4. Were any difficulties experienced in contacting designated sample elements? How were these difficulties overcome, and was bias introduced in the process?

5. Was a probability or nonprobability sampling plan employed? Why? How was the sample actually selected? How large a sample was selected? Why was this size sample chosen?

Readers need to understand at least three things pertaining to the sample: What was done? How was it done? Why was it done?

Little can be said about the method of analysis when discussing research methods, since the results tend to show what has been done in this regard. It often is quite useful, though, to discuss the method in general before detailing the results. Thus, if statistical significance was established through chi-square analysis, the writer might provide the general rationale and calculation procedure for the chi-square statistic, as well as the assumptions surrounding this test and how well the data supported the assumptions. This enables readers to divorce what was found from how it was determined. This can not only help their understanding but also prevent repetition. The procedure is outlined with its key components once and for all, and the results are then simply reported in terms of these components.

The results are the findings of the study, and their detailed presentation, with supporting tables and figures, will consume the bulk of the report. The results need to address the specific problems posed, and they must be presented with some logical structure.[17] The first requirement suggests that information that is interesting

---

[17]Some of the many structures and the conditions under which they can be used are contained in Jessamon Dawe, *Writing Business and Economic Papers: Theses and Dissertations* (Totowa, NJ: Littlefield, Adams, 1975), pp. 75–86. See also David Morris and Satish Chandra, *Guidelines for Writing a Research Report* (Chicago: American Marketing Association, 1992).

but irrelevant to the specific problems guiding the research be omitted. The second requirement suggests that the tables and figures should not be a random collection but should reflect some psychological ordering.[18] This may be by subproblem, geographic region, time, or other criterion that served to structure the investigation. Tables and figures should be used liberally when presenting the results. Whereas the tables in the appendix are complex and detailed, and apply to a number of problems, the tables in the body of the report should be simple summaries of this information. Each table should address only a single problem, and should be especially constructed to shed maximum light on this problem. Researchers should do several things to accomplish this, including the following:

1. Order the columns or rows of the table by the marginal averages or some other measure of size. If there are many similar tables, keep the same order in each one.

2. Put the figures to be compared into columns rather than rows, and, if possible, put the larger numbers at the top of the columns.

3. Round the numbers to two effective digits.

4. Give brief verbal summaries of each table that guide the reader to the main patterns and exceptions.[19]

Figure 18.1 shows how these guidelines can yield better tables. The figures should also address one and only one subproblem. Further, they should be chosen carefully for the type of message they can most effectively convey (but more on their choice later).

Although it would be nice to conduct the "perfect" study, this goal is unrealistic. Every study has its limitations. The researcher knows what these limitations are and should not try to hide them from the readers. An open, frank admission of the study's limitations can actually increase rather than diminish (as is sometimes feared) the readers' opinion of the quality of the research. If some limitations are not stated and readers discover them, they may begin to question the whole report and assume a much more skeptical, critical posture than they would if the limitations were explicitly stated. Stating them also allows the writer to discuss whether, and by how much, the limitations might bias the results. Their exclusion and later discovery allows readers to draw their own conclusions in this regard.

When discussing the limitations, the writer should provide some idea of the research's accuracy. Specifically, the sources of nonsampling error and the suspected direction of their biases should be discussed. This often means that the researcher

---

[18]See Gallagher, *Report Writing*, pp. 50–68, for a discussion of the psychological order of things in research reports.

[19]See A. S. C. Ehrenberg, "Rudiments of Numeracy," *Journal of the Royal Statistical Society*, Series A, 140 (1977), pp. 277–297, and A. S. C. Ehrenberg, "The Problem of Numeracy," *American Statistician* 35 (May 1981), pp. 67–71, for particularly informative discussions using examples of how adherence to these principles can dramatically improve readers' abilities to comprehend the information being presented in tables. For a general discussion of the problem of numeracy in interpreting economic data, see Ingrid H. Rima, ed., *Measurement, Quantification, and Economic Analysis: Numeracy in Economics* (New York: Routledge, 1995).

FIGURE 18.1   **Guidelines for Producing Better Tables**

Table A displays some sales figures for a product being sold in ten U.S. cities. At first glance it seems fairly laid out, but look again. How would you summarize the information in the table to someone over the phone?

TABLE A   **Quarterly Sales of Product Y in Ten Cities**

City	*Sales in Thousands of Dollars*			
	Quarter 1	*Quarter 2*	*Quarter 3*	*Quarter 4*
Atlanta	540.4	507.6	528.4	833.2
Chattanooga	68.9	64.0	55.4	64.5
Des Moines	65.7	61.1	52.9	61.5
Hartford	61.1	71.5	59.0	70.5
Indianapolis	153.2	162.8	122.8	185.7
Los Angeles	700.2	660.3	580.8	662.7
Miami	553.6	517.2	446.0	672.4
Omaha	78.3	72.8	63.0	73.3
Phoenix	196.8	227.6	198.5	235.2
San Antonio	168.2	179.3	166.9	207.1

The table seems to be a jumble when looked at more carefully. It appears that no thought was given to communicating what the numbers really mean. The main difficulty is that the cities for which the numbers are given are listed alphabetically. There is no apparent pattern in each column. Now look at the same information as presented in Table B.

TABLE B   **Quarterly Sales of Product Y in Ten Cities Ordered by Population Size (Rounded and with Averages)**

City	*Quarter 1*	*Quarter 2*	*Quarter 3*	*Quarter 4*	*Average*
Los Angeles	700	660	580	660	650
Miami	550	520	450	670	550
Atlanta	540	510	530	830	620
Phoenix	200	230	200	240	220
San Antonio	170	180	170	210	180
Indianapolis	150	160	120	190	160
Hartford	60	70	60	70	70
Omaha	80	70	60	70	70
Chattanooga	70	60	60	60	60
Des Moines	70	60	50	60	60
Average	260	250	230	310	260

Note how ordering the information by following these steps improves the table's readability:

- Order the columns or rows of the table by the marginal averages or some other measure of size. In this case, the cities are ordered by the size of the populations.
- Round the numbers to two effective digits.
- Give brief verbal summaries of each table that guide the reader to the main patterns and exceptions.

Table B's heading informs the reader that the cities are ordered by population size. Having this information and examining the table as it's now laid out, we can begin to see major patterns emerge: the bigger the cities, the higher the sales, as might be expected. The single exception is Atlanta, where sales are relatively high given its population.

Trends over time are also easier to see. Although not typical, the column averages help us see that sales in each city were relatively steady quarter by quarter, but that they were lower in Quarter 3 and higher in Quarter 4. We can also see that the 4th quarter increases were largest in Miami and Atlanta.

The difference between Tables A and B is the difference between a good table and a poor one. In a good table, the patterns and exceptions should be obvious at a glance, at least once one knows what they are.

Next time you have trouble reading a table, ask yourself if the information could be better ordered. The fault may not be in your ability to comprehend the information but in the table itself.

Source: Adapted from A. S. C. Ehrenberg, "The Problem of Numeracy," *The American Statistician* 35 (May 1981), pp. 67–71.

must provide some limits by which the results were distorted as a result of these inaccuracies. Readers should be informed about how far the results can be generalized. To what populations can they be expected to apply? If the study was done in Miami, readers should be warned not to generalize the results to the southern states or to all the states. The writer should provide the proper caveats for readers and not allow them to discover the weaknesses themselves. However, *the writer should not overstate the limitations either but should assume a balanced perspective.*

Conclusions and Recommendations

The results precipitate the conclusions and recommendations. In this section, the writer shows the step-by-step development of the conclusions and states them in greater detail than in the summary. There should be a conclusion for each study objective or problem. As one book puts it, "readers should be able to read the objectives, turn to the conclusions section, and find specific conclusions relative to each objective."[20] If the study does not provide evidence sufficient to draw a conclusion about a problem, this should be explicitly stated.

Researchers need to be careful that the conclusions drawn reflect an unbiased interpretation of the data. (See Research Realities 18.3.) Researchers' recommendations should follow the conclusions. In developing the recommendations, researchers need to focus on the value of the information that has been gathered. They need to interpret this information in terms of what it means for the business. One of the best ways of doing this is by offering specific recommendations as to the appropriate courses of action—along with reasons why—given the evidence. While not all managers want the researcher's recommendations, many do, and the researcher needs to be prepared to offer and support them.

ETHICAL DILEMMA 18.2

A colleague confides in you: "I've just run a survey for a restaurant owner who is planning to open a catering service for parties, weddings, and the like. He wanted to know the best way to advertise the new service. In the questionnaire, I asked respondents where they would expect to see advertisements for catering facilities, and the most common source was the newspaper. I now realize that my question only established where people are usually exposed to relevant ads, not where they would like to see relevant ads or where they could most productively be exposed to an ad. All we know is where other caterers advertise! Yet I'm sure my client will interpret my findings as meaning that the newspaper is the most effective media vehicle. Should I make the limitations of the research explicit?"

- What are the costs of making the limitations of the research explicit?
- What are the costs of not doing so?
- Isn't promoting the correct use of the research one of the researcher's prime obligations?

---

[20]Boyd, Westfall, and Stasch, *Marketing Research,* p. 663.

RESEARCH REALITIES 18.3

Are American Students Really Lost in Math and Science?

A 1989 government-funded study concluded that American students ranked last or near the bottom in an international comparison of mathematics and science skills. Politicians, educators, and journalists expressed concerns about continued American competitiveness in the international marketplace. The U.S. school system seemed to be lagging behind in preparing students for global competition.

However, research experts have questioned the validity of the international comparisons. "I find it scary when I look at a magazine and see a graph ranking countries with virtually no explanatory material," said David Robitaille, a researcher at the University of British Columbia. "The graph makes it look like the Japanese system is wonderful and the U.S. system is the pits. The actual facts are much more complicated."

International comparisons have routinely been made since the 1960s. Students in selected countries take tests designed to find out which country has the best system of education. The overall goal is to improve the effectiveness of schools. But as soon as the results are published, people start comparing results of the participating countries.

"Countries have different emphases in different areas so they produce different profiles of achievement," according to Richard Wolfe, a Canadian researcher. Consider the question of curriculum. In Hungary, students before the eighth grade study math more extensively than do students in other countries. It should come as no surprise that Hungary scored higher than the United States in math for 13-year-olds. This does not necessarily lead directly to the conclusion that Hungarians teach math more effectively than Americans.

The weighting of the elements of the test also affects the results. The 1989 study placed particular emphasis on numbers and operations, two areas that are not stressed in Great Britain. The British stress logic in the study of math. However, the 1989 study placed little weight on the logic section of the test. Not surprisingly, British students did not place well in the math category.

Sampling can also affect the validity of comparisons. In Hungary, about half of its 12th graders take advanced math. In Great Britain only 6 percent of its 12th graders, mostly the math whizzes, do the same. Comparing the results of Hungary's 50 percent with Britain's elite 6 percent is not fair. Ranked near the top in eighth-grade math because of its curriculum, Hungary falls to apparent mediocrity by the 12th grade, largely due to the belief that advanced math should be taught to more than just the select few.

Other factors that can affect the comparisons include cultural differences, educational system setup, and teaching patterns. So where does this leave the United States? "The public perception that the U.S. is falling behind in science and mathematics . . . is based on a narrow criterion that has serious methodological deficiencies," wrote Iris Rotberg, an education specialist with the National Science Foundation, in a recent *Phi Delta Kappan* article. "Clearly, we have problems in science and mathematics education. But the bottom line is not so grim as the current rhetoric would have us believe."

Source: Malcolm Gladwell, "U.S. Education Gap Called Overstated," *The Washington Post* (November 1, 1991), p. A1. © 1991 The Washington Post. Reprinted with permission.

Appendix

The appendix contains material that is too complex, too detailed, too specialized, or not absolutely necessary for the text. The appendix will typically contain as an exhibit a copy of the questionnaire or observation form used to collect the data. It will also contain any maps used to draw the sample, as well as any detailed calculations used to support the determination of the sample size and sample design. The appendix may include detailed calculations of test statistics and will often include detailed tables from which the summary tables in the body of the report are generated. The writer should recognize that the appendix will be read by only the most technically competent and interested reader. Therefore, the writer should not put material in the appendix if its omission from the body of the report would create gaps in the presentation.

Table 18.2 can serve as a checklist of items to include in reports. The checklist reflects the guidelines that have been developed to evaluate research that is to be put to a public purpose. Public-purpose research can affect the interests of people and organizations who have had no part in its design, execution, or funding. Consequently, the criteria on which it is evaluated tend to be stricter than those applied to research done for private use. Still, the general issues and questions serve as useful criteria by which all research reports can be judged.

The Oral Report

In addition to the written report, most marketing research investigations require one or more oral reports. Frequently, they require interim reports regarding progress. Almost always they require a formal oral report at the conclusion of the study. The principles surrounding the preparation and delivery of the oral report parallel those for the written report.

That means report preparers and presenters need to realize that many listeners will not truly understand the technical ramifications involved in research and certainly will not be able to judge whether the research done is "quality research." However, they can judge whether the research was presented in a professional, confidence-inspiring manner or in a disorganized, uninformed one. A quality presentation can disguise poor research, but quality research cannot improve a poor presentation.

Preparing the Oral Report

The first imperative is to know the audience. What is its technical level of sophistication? What is its members' involvement in the project? Their interest? Once again, oral reports being delivered to those who are heavily involved or have a high degree of technical sophistication can contain more detail than reports to those only tangentially involved or interested. In general, it is better to err on the side of too little technical detail than too much. Executives want to hear and see what the information means to them as managers of marketing activities. What do the data suggest in terms of marketing actions? They can ask for the necessary clarification about the technical details if they want it.

Another important consideration is the organization of the presentation. There are two popular forms. Both begin by stating the general purpose of the study and the specific objectives that were addressed. They differ in terms of when the conclusions are introduced. In the most popular structure, the conclusions are introduced after all the evidence supporting a particular course of action is presented. This allows the presenter to build a logical case in sequential fashion. By progressively disclosing the facts, the presenter has the opportunity to deal with audience concerns and biases as they arise and thus can lead them to the conclusion that the case builds.

The alternative structure involves presenting the conclusions immediately after the purpose and main objectives. The structure tends to involve managers immediately in the findings. It not only gets them thinking about what actions are called for given the results but also sensitizes them to paying attention to the evidence supporting the conclusions. It places them in the desirable position of wanting to evaluate

TABLE 18.2	Checklist for Evaluating Research Reports

A. Origin: What Is Behind the Research

Does the report identify the organizations, discussion, or departments that initiated and paid for the research?

Is there a statement of the purpose of the research that says clearly what it was meant to accomplish?

Are the organizations that designed and conducted the research identified?

B. Design: The Concept and the Plan

Is there a full, nontechnical description of the research design?

Is the design consistent with the stated purpose for which the research was conducted?

Is the design evenhanded? That is, is it free of leading questions and other biases?

Have precautions been taken to avoid sequence or timing bias or other factors that might prejudice or distort the findings?

Does it address questions that respondents are capable of answering?

Is there a precise statement of the universe or population that the research is meant to represent?

Does the sampling frame fairly represent the population under study?

Does the report specify the kind of sample used and clearly describe the method of sample selection?

Does the report describe the plan for the analysis of the data?

Are copies of all questionnaire forms, field and sampling instructions, and other study materials available in the appendix or on file?

C. Execution: Collecting and Handling the Information

Does the report describe the data-collection and data-processing procedures?

Is there an objective report on the care with which the data were collected?

What procedures were used to minimize bias and ensure the quality of the information collected?

D. Stability: Sample Size and Reliability

Was the sample large enough to provide stable findings?

Are sampling error limits shown if they can be computed?

Are methods of calculating the sampling error described, or, if the error cannot be computed, is this stated and explained?

Does the treatment of sampling error limits make clear that they do not cover nonsampling error?

For the major findings, are the reported error tolerances based on direct analysis of the variability of the collected data?

E. Applicability: Generalizing the Findings

Does the report specify when the data were collected?

Does the report say clearly whether its findings do or do not apply beyond the direct source of the data?

Is it clear who is underrepresented by the research, or not represented at all?

If the research has limited application, is there a statement covering who or what it represents and the times or conditions under which it applies?

F. Meaning: Interpretations and Conclusions

Are the measurements described in simple and direct language?

Does it make logical sense to use such measurements for the purpose to which they are being put?

Are the actual findings clearly differentiated from the interpretation of the findings?

Have rigorous objectivity and sound judgment been exercised in interpreting the research findings?

G. Candor: Open Reporting and Disclosure

Is there a full and forthright disclosure of how the research was done?

Has the research been fairly presented?

Source: Adapted from *Guidelines for the Public Use of Market and Opinion Research*, © 1981 by the Advertising Research Foundation. Adapted with permission.

the strength of the evidence supporting an action, because they know beforehand the conclusions that were drawn from it. The structure a presenter decides to use should depend on what is preferred within the corporate culture as well as the presenter's own comfort level with each organizational form. In either case, the evidence supporting the conclusions must be presented systematically, and the conclusions drawn must be consistent with the evidence.

A third important consideration for effective delivery of the oral report is the use of appropriate visual aids. Flip charts, transparencies, slides, and even chalkboards can all be used to advantage. Their use depends on the size of the group and the physical facilities in which the meeting is held. Regardless of which type of visual is used, make sure that it can be read easily by those in the back of the room. Some other principles of effective visual-aid design are listed in Table 18.3.

Delivering the Oral Report

Honor the time limit set for the meeting. Use only a portion of the time set aside for the formal presentation, no more than a third to a half. At the same time, don't rush the presentation of the information. Remember that the audience is hearing it for the first time. Reserve the remaining time for questions and discussion. One of the unique benefits of the oral presentation is that it allows interaction. Use this potential benefit to advantage to clear up points of confusion and to highlight points deserving special emphasis. Adapt the presentation so that there is enough time to both present and discuss the most critical findings.

Finally, use the time-honored principles of public speaking when delivering the message. Keep the presentation simple and uncluttered so that the audience does not have to mentally backtrack to think about what has been said. When writing out

---

TABLE 18.3	Ten Tips for Preparing Effective Presentation Visuals

Keep it simple. Deliver complex ideas in a manner that your audience can understand. Present one point per slide, with as few words and lines as possible.

Use lots of slides as you talk, rather than lots of talk per slide. Less is more when you are speaking.

Use one minute per visual. Slides and overheads should make their impact quickly; then move on. No more than 10 words per slide.

Highlight significant points. Bullets work for black and white transparencies; slides are better suited for color and graphics.

Use a graphic on every page. One is usually enough. Take advantage of "white space," and don't overcrowd.

Build complexity. If you have a complicated concept to communicate, start with the ground level and use three or four slides to complete the picture.

Be careful with color. Color can add interest and emphasis. It can also detract if used without planning. Plan your color scheme and use it faithfully throughout.

Prepare copies of overheads or slides. Hand them to the audience before or after your presentation. If people have to take notes, they won't be watching or listening closely.

Number your pages. You will have a better reference for discussion or a question-and-answer period.

Make visuals easy to read. Use large, legible typefaces. You can use up to three sizes of type, but use only one or two typefaces. Bold and italics can be used freely for emphasis. With slides, use light type against a dark background.

Source: Colleen Paul, "You're in Show Biz! 10 Tips for Presenters," *Micro Monitor* 6 (May 1989), pp. 12–13. See also Joline Morrison and Doug Vogel, "The Impacts of Presentation Visuals on Persuasion," *Information and Management* 33 (January 12, 1998), pp. 125–135.

the presentation, choose simple words and sentences that are naturally spoken and expressed in your usual vocabulary.[21]

Graphic Presentation of the Results

The old adage that "a picture is worth a thousand words" is equally true for business reports. A picture, called a graphic illustration in the case of the research report, can indeed be worth a thousand words when it is appropriate and a good design form is selected. When inappropriate or poorly designed, such a presentation may actually detract from the value of the written or oral research report. In this section, therefore, we wish to briefly review when graphics are appropriate and to discuss the use of some of the more popular forms.[22]

As used here, graphic illustration refers to the presentation of quantities in graph form. Effective graphic presentation means more than merely converting a set of numbers into a drawing.

> It means presenting a picture that will give the reader an accurate understanding of a particular set of "figure" information: a picture of the comparisons or relationships that he would otherwise have to search for—and perhaps fail to see. And if well done, it will give him this understanding more quickly, more forcefully, more completely, and more accurately than could be done in any other way.[23]

Graphic presentation is not the only way to present quantitative information, nor is it always the best. Text and tables can also be used. Graphics should be used only when they serve the purpose better than these other modes. Textual material is generally the most useful in explaining, interpreting, and evaluating results, whereas tables are particularly good for providing emphasis and vivid demonstrations of important findings. Since some readers tend to shy away from graphic presentation because it is "too technical," it should be used with discretion and designed with care.

---

[21]A number of excellent books are available on making effective oral presentations. See, for example, Dorothy Sarnoff, *Make the Most of Your Best: A Complete Program for Presenting Yourself and Your Ideas with Confidence and Authority* (Garden City, NY: Doubleday, 1983); Sonya Hamlin, *How to Talk So People Listen: The Real Key to Job Success* (New York: Harper & Row, 1988); Jan D'Arcy, *Technically Speaking: Proven Ways to Make Your Next Presentation a Success* (New York: AMACOM, 1992); Rudolph F. Verderber, *The Challenge of Effective Speaking*, 10th ed. (Belmont, CA: Wadsworth, 1997).

[22]The presentation by no means includes all the graph forms that could be used, just some of the more common ones. Those interested in more detail should see Mary E. Spear, *Practical Charting Techniques* (New York: McGraw-Hill, 1969); Edward R. Tufte, *The Visual Display of Quantitative Information* (Cheshire, CT: Graphics Press, 1983); Edward R. Tufte, *Envisioning Information* (Cheshire, CT: Graphics Press, 1991).

[23]American Management Association, *Making the Most of Charts: An ABC of Graphic Presentation,* Management Bulletin 28 (New York: American Telephone and Telegraph Company, 1960). See also J. M. Chambers, W. J. Cleveland, B. Kleiner, and P. A. Tukey, *Graphical Methods for Data Analysis* (Boston: Duxbury Press, 1983); William S. Cleveland, *The Elements of Graphing Data*, 2nd ed. (New York: Chapman & Hall, 1993).

FIGURE 18.2   **Pie Chart Showing Personal Consumption Expenditures by Major Category for 1999**

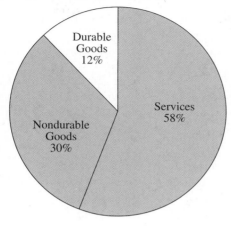

Graphic presentation used to be expensive and often delayed the presentation of reports because the visuals had to be drawn by graphic artists. Computer graphics changed that. The development of computer software for graphically portraying the results of a study now makes the preparation of visuals fast and inexpensive. There is no longer any excuse for not using appropriately chosen graphics to emphasize the points being studied.

There are three basic kinds of graphics: charts that show how much, maps that show where, and diagrams that show how. Charts are generally the most useful of the three types for research reports, and diagrams the least.[24] The following sections discuss a few of the more common chart types and maps.

Pie Chart

Probably one of the more familiar charts, the **pie chart** is simply a circle divided into sections, with each section representing a portion of the total. Since the sections are presented as part of a whole, the pie chart is particularly effective for depicting relative size or emphasizing static comparisons. Figure 18.2 uses the data from Table 18.4, for instance, to show the breakdown of personal consumption expenditures by major category for 1999. The conclusion is obvious. Expenditures for services account for the largest proportion of total consumption expenditures. Further, expenditures for services and nondurable goods completely dwarf expenditures for durable goods.

---

[24]Although some general comments are offered about the usefulness of the various types, the serious reader will want to examine the empirical evidence that has been gathered regarding which form communicates best. See, for example, Jacques Bertin, *Graphics and Graphic Information Processing* (New York: Walter de Gruyter, 1981). The graphics portion of the SYSTAT statistical package for microcomputers, SYGRAPH, has useful suggestions concerning the best ways to structure graphs so that they communicate accurately. The suggestions are based on the evidence regarding visual processing of information. See Leland Wilkinson, *SYGRAPH* (Evanston, IL: Systat, Inc., 1990), especially pp. 38–61.

TABLE 18.4	Personal Consumption Expenditures for 1984-1999 (billions of dollars)			
Year	*Total Personal Consumption Expenditures*	*Durable Goods*	*Nondurable Goods*	*Services*
1984	2492.3	325.1	883.6	1283.6
1985	2704.8	361.1	927.6	1416.1
1986	2892.7	398.7	957.2	1536.8
1987	3094.5	416.7	1014.0	1663.8
1988	3349.7	451.0	1081.1	1817.6
1989	3954.8	472.8	1163.8	1958.1
1990	3839.3	476.5	1245.3	2117.5
1991	3975.1	455.2	1277.6	2242.3
1992	4219.8	488.5	1321.8	2409.4
1993	4459.2	530.2	1370.7	2558.4
1994	4717.0	579.5	1428.4	2709.1
1995	4953.9	611.0	1473.6	2869.2
1996	5215.7	643.3	1539.2	3033.2
1997	5493.7	673.0	1600.6	3220.1
1998	5848.6	698.2	1708.9	3441.5
1999	6257.3	758.6	1843.1	3655.6

Figure 18.2 has three slices, and the interpretation is obvious. With finer consumption classes, a greater number of sections would have been required, and although more information would have been conveyed, emphasis would have been lost. As a rule of thumb, no more than six slices should be generated; the division of the pie should start at the 12 o'clock position; the sections should be arrayed clockwise in decreasing order of magnitude; and the percentages should be provided on the graph.[25]

Line Chart

The pie chart is a one-scale chart, which is why its best use is for static comparisons of the phenomena at a point in time. The **line chart** is a two-dimensional chart that is particularly useful in depicting dynamic relationships, such as time-series fluctuations of one or more series. For example, Figure 18.3, produced from the data in Table 18.5, shows the fluctuations in retail sales of domestic and imported cars during the period 1984–1997.

The line chart is probably the most commonly used chart. It is typically constructed on graph paper with the *x*-axis representing time and the **y**-axis representing values of the variable or variables. When more than one variable is presented, it is recommended that the lines for different items be distinctive in color or form (dots and dashes in suitable combinations) with identification of the different forms given in a legend.

---

[25]Jessamon Dawe and William Jackson Lord, Jr., *Functional Business Communication,* 3rd ed. (Englewood Cliffs, NJ: Prentice-Hall, 1983). See also Gene Zelazny, *Say It With Charts: The Executive's Guide to Visual Communication,* 3rd ed. (Burr Ridge, IL: Irwin Professional Publishing, 1996).

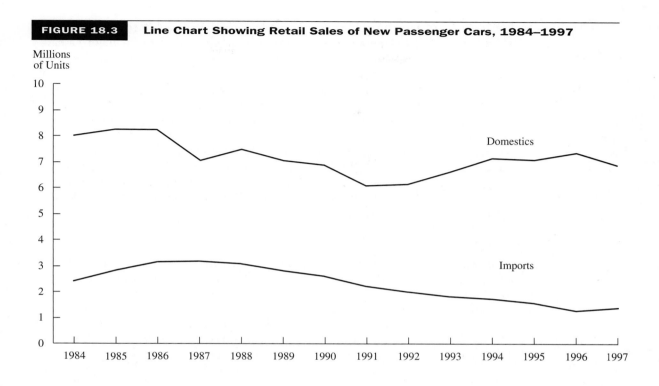

FIGURE 18.3   Line Chart Showing Retail Sales of New Passenger Cars, 1984–1997

TABLE 18.5   Retail Sales of New Cars for 1984–1997 (millions of units)

Year	Total	Domestics	Imports
1984	10.4	8.0	2.4
1985	11.0	8.2	2.8
1986	11.4	8.2	3.2
1987	10.3	7.1	3.2
1988	10.6	7.5	3.1
1989	9.9	7.1	2.8
1990	9.5	6.9	2.6
1991	8.4	6.1	2.3
1992	8.2	6.2	2.0
1993	8.4	6.6	1.8
1994	8.9	7.2	1.7
1995	8.7	7.1	1.6
1996	8.7	7.4	1.3
1997	8.3	6.9	1.4

Stratum Chart

In some ways, the **stratum chart** is a dynamic pie chart, because it can be used to show relative emphasis by sector (for example, quantity consumed by user class) and change in relative emphasis over time. The stratum chart consists of a set of line charts whose quantities are aggregated (or a total that is disaggregated). It is also called a stacked line chart. For example, Figure 18.4 (again resulting from the data in Table 18.4) shows personal consumption expenditures by major category for the period 1984–1999. The lowest line shows the expenditures just for services; the second lowest line shows the total expenditures for services *plus* nondurable goods. Personal consumption expenditures for nondurable goods are thus shown by the area between the two lines. So it is with the remaining areas. We would need 23 pie charts to capture the same information, and the message would not be as obvious.

The *x*-axis typically represents time in the stratum chart, and the *y*-axis again captures the value of the variables. The use of color or distinctive cross-hatching is strongly recommended to distinguish the various components in the stratum chart. As was true for the pie chart, the number of components distinguished in a stratum chart should not exceed six.

Bar Chart

The **bar chart** can be either a one-scale or two-scale chart. This feature, plus the many other variations that it permits, probably accounts for its wide use. Figure 18.5, for example, is a one-scale chart. It also shows personal consumption expenditures by major category at a single point in time. Figure 18.5 presents the same information as Figure 18.2 but is, in at least one respect, more revealing; it not only offers some appreciation of the relative expenditures by major category, but it also indicates the magnitude of the expenditures by category. Readers could, of course, generate this information from the pie chart, but it would involve some calculation on their part.

Figure 18.6 is a two-scale bar chart. It uses the data contained in Table 18.5 and shows total automobile sales for the period 1988–1997. The *y*-axis represents quantity, and the *x*-axis shows time.

Figures 18.5 and 18.6 should illustrate the fact that the bar chart can be drawn either vertically or horizontally. When emphasis is on the change in the variable through time, the vertical form is preferred, with the *x*-axis as the time axis. When time is not a variable, either the vertical or horizontal form is used.

Bar Chart Variations

As previously suggested, great variation is possible with bar charts. One variation is to convert the charts to **pictograms.** Instead of using the length of the bar to capture quantity, amounts are shown by piles of dollars for income, pictures of cars for automobile production, people in a row for population, and so on. This can be a needed change of pace if there are a number of graphs in the report.[26]

A variation of the basic bar chart—the grouped bar chart—can be used to capture the change in two or more series through time. Figure 18.7, for example, shows the change in consumption expenditures by the three major categories for the period 1990–1999. Just as distinctive symbols are effective in distinguishing the separate series in a line chart, distinctive coloring or cross-hatching is equally helpful in a grouped bar chart.

---

[26]Pictograms are especially susceptible to perceptual distortions. Report users have to be especially careful when reading them so that they are not led to incorrect conclusions.

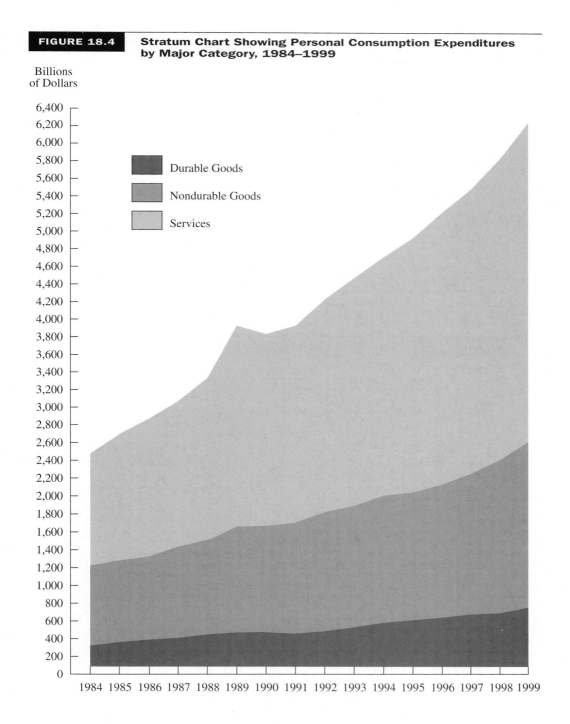

FIGURE 18.4   **Stratum Chart Showing Personal Consumption Expenditures by Major Category, 1984–1999**

Billions
of Dollars

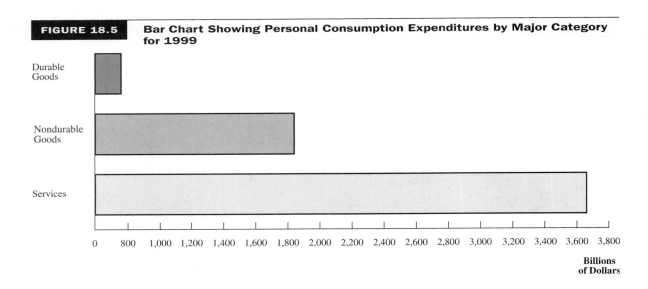

FIGURE 18.5 **Bar Chart Showing Personal Consumption Expenditures by Major Category for 1999**

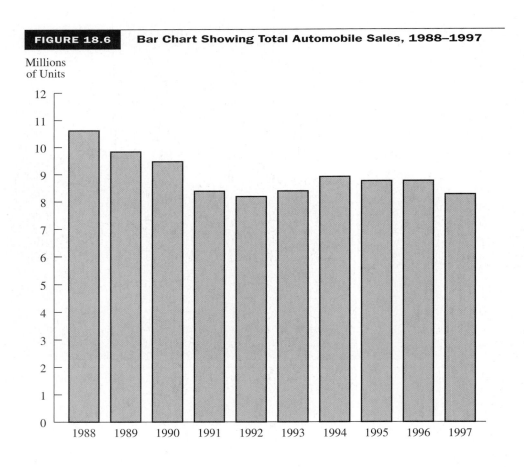

FIGURE 18.6 **Bar Chart Showing Total Automobile Sales, 1988–1997**

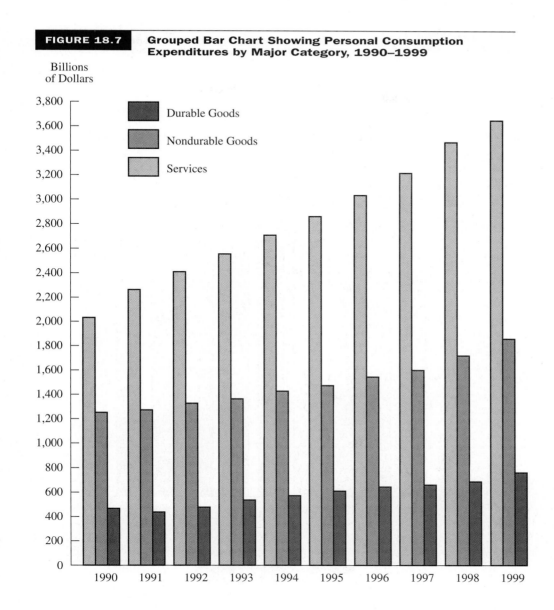

FIGURE 18.7   **Grouped Bar Chart Showing Personal Consumption Expenditures by Major Category, 1990–1999**

There is also a bar chart equivalent to the stratum chart—the divided bar chart or stacked bar chart. Its construction and interpretation are similar to those for the stratum chart. Figure 18.8, for example, is a divided or stacked bar chart showing personal consumption expenditures by major category. It shows both total and relative expenditures through time. It, too, makes use of distinctive cross-hatching for each component.

Maps

Maps focus attention on geographic areas. When used for the geographic display of quantitative or statistical information, they are usually called data maps.

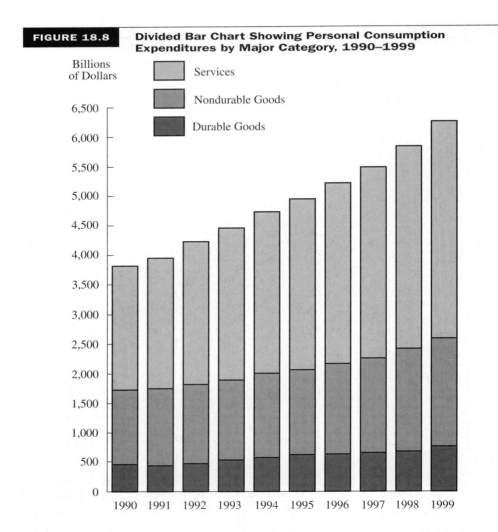

FIGURE 18.8   **Divided Bar Chart Showing Personal Consumption Expenditures by Major Category, 1990–1999**

Billings of Dollars

- Services
- Nondurable Goods
- Durable Goods

ETHICAL DILEMMA 18.3

You are writing the final report for top management to make the case that your new advertising campaign has increased sales dramatically in trial areas. Your conceptual arguments on behalf of the new campaign are very convincing, but although there has been a consistent rise in sales in trial areas, the bar charts look rather disappointing: 61,500 units the first month, 61,670 units the next, 61,820 the next. . . . Why, the increase is barely visible! Then you notice how much more exciting your results would look if the *y*-axis were broken above the origin so that the plots started at 50,000 units.

- Where does salesmanship stop and deception start?

| FIGURE 18.9 | Data Map Showing Growth in Employment, 1982–1991 |

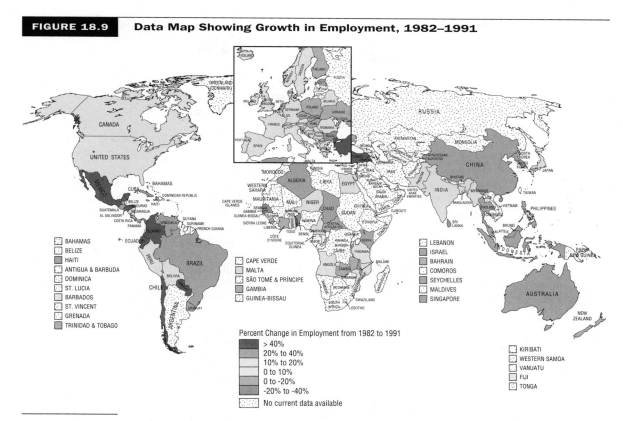

Source: Michael R. Czinkota, Ikka A. Ronkainen, and Michael H. Moffett, *International Business,* 3rd ed. (Fort Worth, TX: The Dryden Press, 1994), p. 366.

Data maps are especially suited to the presentation of rates, ratios, and frequency-distribution data by areas. In constructing data maps, the quantity of interest is typically broken into groups, and cross-hatching, shading, or color is used to display the numerical group in which each area belongs. In general, it is helpful to keep the group intervals approximately equal and to use a limited number of shadings, four to seven and certainly no more than ten. Moreover, the shadings should run progressively from light to dark, and all areas should have some shading. Leaving an area blank or white tends to weaken its importance. For example, Figure 18.9 shows how employment, a sign of economic vitality, grew over a 10-year period in various countries.

Summary

The research report was discussed in this chapter. Four points were emphasized: the criteria for evaluating research reports, the elements of a written research report, the delivery of an oral report, and the graphic presentation of results.

The fundamental criterion for the development of every research report is communication with the audience. The readers' interests, capabilities, and circumstances determine what goes in the report, what is left out, and how the information included in the report is presented. The other criteria that need to be kept in mind in preparing the report are the following:

1. **Completeness**—does it provide all the information readers need in a language they understand?
2. **Accuracy**—is the reasoning logical and the information correct?
3. **Clarity**—is the phrasing precise?
4. **Conciseness**—is the writing crisp and direct?

There is no standard form for a research report since this, too, depends on the readers' preferences. Nonetheless, a standard report form that can be adapted to suit specific preferences was offered. It included a title page, table of contents, summary, introduction, body, conclusions and recommendations, and appendix. The main items contained in each section were highlighted.

The first rule when preparing an oral report is also to know the audience. It is useful to begin an oral report by stating the general purpose of the study and the specific objectives. The remainder of the presentation needs to systematically build on the evidence so that logical conclusions are drawn. It is better to present too little detail in an oral report than too much. Visual aids used in an oral report should be easily understood and easily seen by those in the back of the room. The time limit set for the meeting should always be honored, and only a portion of the allotted time should be used for the formal presentation. The remainder should be set aside for questions and discussion. The words and sentences used in the oral report should be natural sounding and simple, reflecting the presenter's usual vocabulary.

Graphic presentation is often the best way to communicate those findings that require emphasis. Three main forms are the pie chart, the line chart, and the bar chart. The pie chart is a one-scale chart that is particularly effective in communicating a static comparison. The bar chart can be either a one-scale chart or a two-scale chart, while all the other types are basically two-scale charts. The two-scale chart can show the relationship between two variables and is often used when one of the variables is time, in which case time is captured on the *x*-axis.

Questions

1. What is the fundamental report criterion? Explain.
2. What is meant by the report criteria of completeness, accuracy, clarity, and conciseness?
3. On the one hand, it is argued that the research report must be complete and, on the other, that it must be concise. Are these two objectives incompatible? If so, how do you reconcile them?
4. What is the essential content of each of the following parts of the research report?
   a. title page
   b. table of contents
   c. summary
   d. introduction
   e. body
   f. conclusions and recommendations
   g. appendix
5. What are the key considerations in preparing an oral report?
6. What is a pie chart? For what kinds of information is it particularly effective?
7. What is a line chart? For what kinds of information is it generally employed?
8. What is a stratum chart? For what kinds of information is it particularly appropriate?
9. What is a bar chart? For what kinds of problems is it effective?

10.   What is a pictogram?
11.   What is a grouped bar chart? When is it used?

Applications and Problems

1.   Many marketing research professionals would argue that the summary is the most important part of the research report. Describe the information that should be contained in the summary and why it is so important.

2.   The owner of a medium-sized home building center specializing in custom-designed and do-it-yourself kitchen supplies asked the I & J Consulting firm to prepare a customer profile report for the kitchen design segment of the home improvement market. Evaluate the following sections of the report.

> The customer market for the company can be defined as the do-it-yourself and kitchen design segments. A brief profile of each follows.
>
> The do-it-yourself (DIY) market consists of individuals in the 25–45 age group living in a single dwelling. DIY customers are predominantly male, although an increasing number of females are becoming active DIY customers. The typical DIY customer has an income in excess of $20,000 and the median income is $22,100 with a standard deviation of 86. The DIY customer has an increasing amount of leisure time, is strongly value and convenience conscious, and displays an increasing desire for self-gratification.
>
> The mean age of the custom-kitchen design customer segment is 41.26, and the annual income is in the range of $25,000 to $35,000. The median income is $29,000 with a standard deviation of 73. Custom-kitchen design customers usually live in a single dwelling. The wife is more influential and is the prime decision maker about kitchen designs and cabinets.

3.   The executive director of the Cortland Chamber of Commerce asked the marketing research class of the community college located nearby to prepare a research report on members' attitudes toward the service offerings of the chamber. Evaluate the completeness of the executive summary portion of their report, which follows.

> To provide a foundation for a comprehensive marketing plan, the Cortland Chamber of Commerce (CCC) undertook a membership survey in November 1998. Eighty-four usable surveys were returned from a stratified proportionate sampling plan of 172 CCC members.
>
> Results showed that members were familiar with all of the services except National Safety Council materials and employers manuals. Newsletters were found to be the most often used as well as the most important service offered by CCC. Government regulation and mandated employee benefits were thought to be the most threatening issues facing businesses, according to the survey results. Over half of all members responding felt favorably toward 11 statements about CCC services.

4.   Discuss the difference between conclusions and recommendations in research reports.

5.   Your marketing research firm is preparing the final written report on a research project commissioned by a major manufacturer of water ski equipment. One objective of the project was to investigate seasonal variations in sales, both on an aggregate basis and by each of the company's sales regions individually. Your client is particularly interested in the width of the range between maximum and minimum seasonal sales. The following table was submitted by one of your junior analysts. Critique the table and prepare a revision suitable for inclusion in your report.

Seasonal Variations in Sales (thousands of dollars)

Sales Region	Spring	Summer	Fall	Winter
Northeast	120.10	140.59	50.90	30.00
East-Central	118.80	142.70	61.70	25.20
Southeast	142.00	151.80	134.20	100.10
Midwest	100.20	139.42	42.90	20.00
South-Central	80.77	101.00	90.42	78.20
Plains	95.60	120.60	38.50	19.90
Southwest	105.40	110.50	101.60	92.10
Pacific	180.70	202.41	171.54	145.60

6. The management of the Canco Company, a manufacturer of metal cans, presents you with the following information.

THE CANCO COMPANY

Comparative Profit and Loss Statement, Fiscal Years 1996–2000

	1996	1997	1998	1999	2000
Net sales	$40,000,000	$45,000,000	$48,000,000	$53,000,000	$55,000,000
Cost and expenses					
Cost of goods sold (COGS)	$28,000,000	$32,850,000	$33,600,000	$39,750,000	$40,150,000
Selling and administrative expenses	4,000,000	4,500,000	4,800,000	5,300,000	5,500,000
Depreciation	1,200,000	1,350,000	1,440,000	1,590,000	1,650,000
Interest	800,000	900,000	960,000	1,060,000	1,100,000
	$34,000,000	$39,600,000	$40,800,000	$47,700,000	$48,400,000
Profits from operations	6,000,000	5,400,000	7,200,000	5,300,000	6,600,000
Estimated taxes	$ 2,400,000	$ 2,160,000	$ 2,880,000	$ 2,120,000	$ 2,640,000
Net profits	$ 3,600,000	$ 3,240,000	$ 4,320,000	$ 3,180,000	$ 3,960,000

a. Management has asked that you develop a visual aid to present the company's distribution of sales revenues in 2000.
b. You are asked to develop a visual aid that would compare the change in the net profit level to the change in the net sales level.
c. The management of Canco Company wants you to develop a visual aid that will present the following expenses (excluding COGS) over the five-year period: selling and administrative expenses, depreciation, and interest expenses.
d. The management has the following sales data relating to the company's two major competitors:

	1996	1997	1998	1999	2000
The We-Can Co.	$35,000,000	$40,000,000	$42,000,000	$45,000,000	$48,000,000
The You-Can Co.	$41,000,000	$43,000,000	$45,000,000	$46,000,000	$48,000,000

You are required to prepare a visual aid to facilitate the comparison of Canco Company's sales performance with that of its major competitors.

The subject of marketing research can be approached in several ways. The perspective used in this book is primarily a *project emphasis*. We have focused on the definition of a problem and the research needed to answer it. Initially, the whole research process may have appeared to be a number of disconnected bits and pieces because of the necessity of separating it into logical components so that the design issues that arose at each stage could be highlighted. As mentioned early in the book, however, the research process is anything but a set of disconnected parts. All the steps are highly interrelated, and a decision made at one stage has implications for the others as well. To remind us how this integration functions, the research process and some of the key decisions that must be made are reviewed in this epilogue.

A research project should not be conceived as the end in itself. Projects arise because managerial problems need solving. The problems themselves may concern the identification of market opportunities, the evaluation of alternative courses of action, or control of marketing operations. Because these activities, in turn, are the essence of the managerial function, research activity can also be viewed from the broader perspective of the firm's marketing intelligence system. Chapter 2, therefore, focused on the nature and present status of the supply of marketing intelligence.

Marketing research was defined as the function that links the consumer, customer, and public to the marketer through information—information used to identify and define marketing opportunities and problems; generate, refine, and evaluate marketing actions; monitor marketing performance; and improve our understanding of marketing as a process. Addressing these issues involves the systematic gathering, recording, and analyzing of data. These tasks are logically viewed as a sequence called the research process, consisting of the following steps:

1. Formulate the problem
2. Determine the research design
3. Design data-collection methods and forms
4. Design the sample and collect the data
5. Analyze and interpret the data
6. Prepare the research report

The decision problem logically comes first. It dictates the research problem and the design of the project. However, the transition from problem to project is not an automatic one. There is a good deal of iteration from problem specification to tentative research design to problem respecification to modified research design and back again. This is natural, and one of the researcher's more important roles involves helping to define and redefine the problem so that it can be researched and, more important, so that it answers the decision maker's problem. Although this might appear to be simple in principle, the task can be formidable, because it requires a clear specification of objectives, alternatives, and environmental constraints and influences. The decision maker may not readily provide these, and it is up to the researcher to dig them out in order to design effective research.

Perhaps research is not even necessary. If the decision maker's views are so strongly held that no amount of information might change them, the research will be wasted. It is up to the researcher to determine this before rather than after conducting the research. This often entails asking "what if" questions: What if consumer reaction to the product concept is overwhelmingly favorable? What if it is unfavorable? What if it is only slightly favorable? If the decision maker indicates that the same decision will be made in each case, there are other objectives that have not been explicitly stated. This is a critical finding. Every research project should have one or more objectives, and one should not proceed to other steps in the process until these can be explicitly stated.

Here it is also important to ask whether the contemplated benefits of the research exceed the expected costs. It is a mistake to assume that simply because something might change as a result of the research, the research is called for. It may be that the likelihood of finding something that might warrant a change in the decision is so remote that the research still would be wasted. Researchers constantly need to ask: Why should this research be conducted? What could we possibly find out that we do not already know? Will the expected benefits from the research exceed its costs? If the answers indicate research, then the question logically turns to: What kind?

If the problem cannot be formulated as some specific "if-then" conjectural relationship, exploratory research is in order. The primary purpose of exploratory research is to gather ideas and insights into the phenomenon. The output of an exploratory study will *not* be answers but more specific questions or statements of tentative relationships. The search for insights demands a flexible research design. Structured questionnaires or probability sampling plans are not used in exploratory research, because the emphasis is not on gathering summary statistics but on gaining insight into the problem. The personal interview is much more appropriate than the telephone interview, and that, in turn, is more appropriate than a mail survey, since the unstructured question is most useful in the experience survey. Interviewees should be handpicked because they can provide the wanted information; thus, a convenience or judgment sample is very much in order here, whereas it would be completely out of place in descriptive or causal research. Focus groups can be productive for gaining important insights. A survey of the literature and an analysis of selected cases can also be used to advantage in exploratory research, particularly if the researcher assumes the correct posture of seeking rather than finding. The analysis of sharp contrasts or striking features in published data or selected cases is particularly productive of tentative explanations for the occurrence of the phenomenon.

Given that the exploratory effort has generated one or more specific hypotheses to be investigated, the next research thrust would logically be descriptive or causal research. The design actually selected would depend on the conviction with which the tentative explanation is held to be *the* explanation and the feasibility and cost of conducting an experiment. While experiments typically provide more convincing proof of causal relationships, they also usually cost more than descriptive designs. This is one reason descriptive designs are the most commonly employed type in marketing research.

Whereas exploratory designs are flexible, descriptive designs are rigid. Descriptive designs demand a clear specification of the who, what, when, where, how, and why of the research before data collection begins. They generally employ structured questionnaires or scales because these forms provide advantages in coding and tabulating. In descriptive designs, the emphasis is on generating an accurate picture of the relationships between and among variables. Probability sampling plans are desirable, but if the sample is to be drawn using nonprobabilistic methods, it is important that a quota sample be used. Descriptive studies typically rely heavily on cross-tabulation analysis or other means of investigating the association among variables, such as regression analysis or discriminant analysis, although the emphasis can also be on the search for differences. The great majority of descriptive studies are cross-sectional, although some do use longitudinal information.

Experiments are the best means we have for making inferences about cause-and-effect relationships, because, if designed properly, they provide the most compelling evidence about concomitant variation, time order of occurrence of variables, and elimination of other factors. A key feature of the experiment is that the researcher is able to control who will be exposed to the experimental stimulus (the presumed cause). This allows the researcher to establish the prior equality of groups by randomization, either with or without matching, which in turn allows the adjustment of the results to eliminate many contaminating influences.

Sampling plays little role in experiments other than in selecting objects that are to be assigned randomly to the treatment conditions. Because the emphasis is on testing a specific relationship, causal designs demand a clear specification of what is to be measured and how it is to be measured. Structured data-collection instruments should be used, and, although structured questionnaires and scales are often employed, experiments also rely heavily on the observational mode of data collection because of the typically more objective, more accurate information obtained this way. The major thrust in the analysis of experimental results is a test for differences between those exposed to the experimental stimulus and those not exposed; the analysis-of-variance procedure is most often employed, although other techniques (for example, the t test for the difference in means of independent or correlated samples) are used as well.

The previous paragraphs should indicate how intimately the steps are interrelated. In particular, it should be noted how the basic nature of the research design implies various things in terms of the structure of the data-collection form, design of the sample, and collection and analysis of the data. A decision about appropriate research design does not completely determine the latter considerations, of course, but simply suggests their basic nature. The analyst still has to determine the specific format. For example, is the structured questionnaire to be disguised or undisguised? Is the probability sample to be simple, stratified, or cluster? How large a sample is needed? These questions, too, will be determined in large part by the way the research question is framed, although the ingenuity displayed by the designer of the research will determine their final form. The researcher will have to balance the various sources of error that can arise in the process when determining this final form. In effecting this balance, the researcher must be concerned with assessing and minimizing total error; this often means assuming additional error in one of the parts of the process so that total error can be diminished.

APPENDIX A Cumulative Standard Unit Normal Distribution

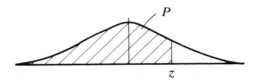

Values of P corresponding to Z for the normal curve. Z is the standard normal variable. The value of P for $-Z$ equals one minus the value of P for $+Z$ (e.g., the P for -1.62 equals $1 - .9474 = .0526$).

Z	.00	.01	.02	.03	.04	.05	.06	.07	.08	.09
.0	.5000	.5040	.5080	.5120	.5160	.5199	.5239	.5279	.5319	.5359
.1	.5398	.5438	.5478	.5517	.5557	.5596	.5636	.5675	.5714	.5753
.2	.5793	.5832	.5871	.5910	.5948	.5987	.6026	.6064	.6103	.6141
.3	.6179	.6217	.6255	.6293	.6331	.6368	.6406	.6443	.6480	.6517
.4	.6554	.6591	.6628	.6664	.6700	.6736	.6772	.6808	.6844	.6879
.5	.6915	.6950	.6985	.7019	.7054	.7088	.7123	.7157	.7190	.7224
.6	.7257	.7291	.7324	.7357	.7389	.7422	.7454	.7486	.7517	.7549
.7	.7580	.7611	.7642	.7673	.7704	.7734	.7764	.7794	.7823	.7852
.8	.7881	.7910	.7939	.7967	.7995	.8023	.8051	.8078	.8106	.8133
.9	.8159	.8186	.8212	.8238	.8264	.8289	.8315	.8340	.8365	.8389
1.0	.8413	.8438	.8461	.8485	.8508	.8531	.8554	.8577	.8599	.8621
1.1	.8643	.8665	.8686	.8708	.8729	.8749	.8770	.8790	.8810	.8830
1.2	.8849	.8869	.8888	.8907	.8925	.8944	.8962	.8980	.8997	.9015
1.3	.9032	.9049	.9066	.9082	.9099	.9115	.9131	.9147	.9162	.9177
1.4	.9192	.9207	.9222	.9236	.9251	.9265	.9279	.9292	.9306	.9319
1.5	.9332	.9345	.9357	.9370	.9382	.9394	.9406	.9418	.9429	.9441
1.6	.9452	.9463	.9474	.9484	.9495	.9505	.9515	.9525	.9535	.9545
1.7	.9554	.9564	.9573	.9582	.9591	.9599	.9608	.9616	.9625	.9633
1.8	.9641	.9649	.9656	.9664	.9671	.9678	.9686	.9693	.9699	.9706
1.9	.9713	.9719	.9726	.9732	.9738	.9744	.9750	.9756	.9761	.9767
2.0	.9772	.9778	.9783	.9788	.9793	.9798	.9803	.9808	.9812	.9817
2.1	.9821	.9826	.9830	.9834	.9838	.9842	.9846	.9850	.9854	.9857
2.2	.9861	.9864	.9868	.9871	.9875	.9878	.9881	.9884	.9887	.9890
2.3	.9893	.9896	.9898	.9901	.9904	.9906	.9909	.9911	.9913	.9916
2.4	.9918	.9920	.9922	.9925	.9927	.9929	.9931	.9932	.9934	.9936
2.5	.9938	.9940	.9941	.9943	.9945	.9946	.9948	.9949	.9951	.9952
2.6	.9953	.9955	.9956	.9957	.9959	.9960	.9961	.9962	.9963	.9964
2.7	.9965	.9966	.9967	.9968	.9969	.9970	.9971	.9972	.9973	.9974
2.8	.9974	.9975	.9976	.9977	.9977	.9978	.9979	.9979	.9980	.9981
2.9	.9981	.9982	.9982	.9983	.9984	.9984	.9985	.9985	.9986	.9986
3.0	.9987	.9987	.9987	.9988	.9988	.9989	.9989	.9989	.9990	.9990
3.1	.9990	.9991	.9991	.9991	.9992	.9992	.9992	.9992	.9993	.9993
3.2	.9993	.9993	.9994	.9994	.9994	.9994	.9994	.9995	.9995	.9995
3.3	.9995	.9995	.9995	.9996	.9996	.9996	.9996	.9996	.9996	.9997
3.4	.9997	.9997	.9997	.9997	.9997	.9997	.9997	.9997	.9997	.9998

Source: Appendix A from *Analyzing Multivariate Data* by Paul E. Green, copyright © 1978 by The Dryden Press. Reprinted by permission of the publisher.

APPENDIX B Selected Percentiles of the χ^2 Distribution

Values of χ^2 corresponding to P

ν	$\chi^2_{.005}$	$\chi^2_{.01}$	$\chi^2_{.025}$	$\chi^2_{.05}$	$\chi^2_{.10}$	$\chi^2_{.90}$	$\chi^2_{.95}$	$\chi^2_{.975}$	$\chi^2_{.99}$	$\chi^2_{.995}$
1	.000039	.00016	.0098	.0039	.0158	2.71	3.84	5.02	6.63	7.88
2	.0100	.0201	.0506	.1026	.2107	4.61	5.99	7.38	9.21	10.60
3	.0717	.115	.216	.352	.584	6.25	7.81	9.35	11.34	12.84
4	.207	.297	.484	.711	1.064	7.78	9.49	11.14	13.28	14.86
5	.412	.554	.831	1.15	1.61	9.24	11.07	12.83	15.09	16.75
6	.676	.872	1.24	1.64	2.20	10.64	12.59	14.45	16.81	18.55
7	.989	1.24	1.69	2.17	2.83	12.02	14.07	16.01	18.48	20.28
8	1.34	1.65	2.18	2.73	3.49	13.36	15.51	17.53	20.09	21.96
9	1.73	2.09	2.70	3.33	4.17	14.68	16.92	19.02	21.67	23.59
10	2.16	2.56	3.25	3.94	4.87	15.99	18.31	20.48	23.21	25.19
11	2.60	3.05	3.82	4.57	5.58	17.28	19.68	21.92	24.73	26.76
12	3.07	3.57	4.40	5.23	6.30	18.55	21.03	23.34	26.22	28.30
13	3.57	4.11	5.01	5.89	7.04	19.81	22.36	24.74	27.69	29.82
14	4.07	4.66	5.63	6.57	7.79	21.06	23.68	26.12	29.14	31.32
15	4.60	5.23	6.26	7.26	8.55	22.31	25.00	27.49	30.58	32.80
16	5.14	5.81	6.91	7.96	9.31	23.54	26.30	28.85	32.00	34.27
18	6.26	7.01	8.23	9.39	10.86	25.99	28.87	31.53	34.81	37.16
20	7.43	8.26	9.59	10.85	12.44	28.41	31.41	34.17	37.57	40.00
24	9.89	10.86	12.40	13.85	15.66	33.20	36.42	39.36	42.98	45.56
30	13.79	14.95	16.79	18.49	20.60	40.26	43.77	46.98	50.89	53.67
40	20.71	22.16	24.43	26.51	29.05	51.81	55.76	59.34	63.69	66.77
60	35.53	37.48	40.48	43.19	46.46	74.40	79.08	83.30	88.38	91.95
120	83.85	86.92	91.58	95.70	100.62	140.23	146.57	152.21	158.95	163.64

Source: Adapted with permission from *Introduction to Statistical Analysis*, 2nd ed., by W. J. Dixon and F. J. Massey, Jr., McGraw-Hill Book Company, Inc., copyright 1957.

APPENDIX C   Upper Percentiles of the _t_ Distribution

ν \ 1−α	.75	.90	.95	.975	.99	.995	.9995
1	1.000	3.078	6.314	12.706	31.821	63.657	636.619
2	.816	1.886	2.920	4.303	6.965	9.925	31.598
3	.765	1.638	2.353	3.182	4.541	5.841	12.941
4	.741	1.533	2.132	2.776	3.747	4.604	8.610
5	.727	1.476	2.015	2.571	3.365	4.032	6.859
6	.718	1.440	1.943	2.447	3.143	3.707	5.959
7	.711	1.415	1.895	2.365	2.998	3.499	5.405
8	.706	1.397	1.860	2.306	2.896	3.355	5.041
9	.703	1.383	1.833	2.262	2.821	3.250	4.781
10	.700	1.372	1.812	2.228	2.764	3.169	4.587
11	.697	1.363	1.796	2.201	2.718	3.106	4.437
12	.695	1.356	1.782	2.179	2.681	3.055	4.318
13	.694	1.350	1.771	2.160	2.650	3.012	4.221
14	.692	1.345	1.761	2.145	2.624	2.977	4.140
15	.691	1.341	1.753	2.131	2.602	2.947	4.073
16	.690	1.337	1.746	2.120	2.583	2.921	4.015
17	.689	1.333	1.740	2.110	2.567	2.898	3.965
18	.688	1.330	1.734	2.101	2.552	2.878	3.922
19	.688	1.328	1.729	2.093	2.339	2.861	3.883
20	.687	1.325	1.725	2.086	2.528	2.845	3.850
21	.686	1.323	1.721	2.080	2.518	2.831	3.819
22	.686	1.321	1.717	2.074	2.508	2.819	3.792
23	.685	1.319	1.714	2.069	2.500	2.807	3.767
24	.685	1.318	1.711	2.064	2.492	2.797	3.745
25	.684	1.316	1.708	2.060	2.485	2.787	3.725
26	.684	1.315	1.706	2.056	2.479	2.779	3.707
27	.684	1.314	1.703	2.052	2.473	2.771	3.690
28	.683	1.313	1.701	2.048	2.467	2.763	3.674
29	.683	1.311	1.699	2.045	2.462	2.756	3.659
30	.683	1.310	1.697	2.042	2.457	2.750	3.646
40	.681	1.303	1.684	2.021	2.423	2.704	3.551
60	.679	1.296	1.671	2.000	2.390	2.660	3.460
120	.677	1.289	1.658	1.980	2.358	2.617	3.373
∞	.674	1.282	1.645	1.960	2.326	2.576	3.291

ν = degrees of freedom

Source: Table taken from Table III of Fisher and Yates: _Statistical Tables for Biological, Agricultural and Medical Research_, 6th ed., 1974, published by Longman Group UK Ltd., London (previously published by Oliver and Boyd Ltd., Edinburgh) and by permission of the authors and publishers.

APPENDIX D   Selected Percentiles of the F Distribution

$F_{.90(\nu_1, \nu_2)}$ $\alpha = 0.1$

ν_1 = degrees of freedom for numerator

ν_2 \ ν_1	1	2	3	4	5	6	7	8	9	10	12	15	20	24	30	40	60	120	∞
1	39.86	49.50	53.59	55.83	57.24	58.20	58.91	59.44	59.86	60.19	60.71	61.22	61.74	62.00	62.26	62.53	62.79	63.06	63.33
2	8.53	9.00	9.16	9.24	9.29	9.33	9.35	9.37	9.38	9.39	9.41	9.42	9.44	9.45	9.46	9.47	9.47	9.48	9.49
3	5.54	5.46	5.39	5.34	5.31	5.28	5.27	5.25	5.24	5.23	5.22	5.20	5.18	5.18	5.17	5.16	5.15	5.14	5.13
4	4.54	4.32	4.19	4.11	4.05	4.01	3.98	3.95	3.94	3.92	3.90	3.87	3.84	3.83	3.82	3.80	3.79	3.78	3.76
5	4.06	3.78	3.62	3.52	3.45	3.40	3.37	3.34	3.32	3.30	3.27	3.24	3.21	3.19	3.17	3.16	3.14	3.12	3.10
6	3.78	3.46	3.29	3.18	3.11	3.05	3.01	2.98	2.96	2.94	2.90	2.87	2.84	2.82	2.80	2.78	2.76	2.74	2.72
7	3.59	3.26	3.07	2.96	2.88	2.83	2.78	2.75	2.72	2.70	2.67	2.63	2.59	2.58	2.56	2.54	2.51	2.49	2.47
8	3.46	3.11	2.92	2.81	2.73	2.67	2.62	2.59	2.56	2.54	2.50	2.46	2.42	2.40	2.38	2.36	2.34	2.32	2.29
9	3.36	3.01	2.81	2.69	2.61	2.55	2.51	2.47	2.44	2.42	2.38	2.34	2.30	2.28	2.25	2.23	2.21	2.18	2.16
10	3.29	2.92	2.73	2.61	2.52	2.46	2.41	2.38	2.35	2.32	2.28	2.24	2.20	2.18	2.16	2.13	2.11	2.08	2.06
11	3.23	2.86	2.66	2.54	2.45	2.39	2.34	2.30	2.27	2.25	2.21	2.17	2.12	2.10	2.08	2.05	2.03	2.00	1.97
12	3.18	2.81	2.61	2.48	2.39	2.33	2.28	2.24	2.21	2.19	2.15	2.10	2.06	2.04	2.01	1.99	1.96	1.93	1.90
13	3.14	2.76	2.56	2.43	2.35	2.28	2.23	2.20	2.16	2.14	2.10	2.05	2.01	1.98	1.96	1.93	1.90	1.88	1.85
14	3.10	2.73	2.52	2.39	2.31	2.24	2.19	2.15	2.12	2.10	2.05	2.01	1.96	1.94	1.91	1.89	1.86	1.83	1.80
15	3.07	2.70	2.49	2.36	2.27	2.21	2.16	2.12	2.09	2.06	2.02	1.97	1.92	1.90	1.87	1.85	1.82	1.79	1.76
16	3.05	2.67	2.46	2.33	2.24	2.18	2.13	2.09	2.06	2.03	1.99	1.94	1.89	1.87	1.84	1.81	1.78	1.75	1.72
17	3.03	2.64	2.44	2.31	2.22	2.15	2.10	2.06	2.03	2.00	1.96	1.91	1.86	1.84	1.81	1.78	1.75	1.72	1.69
18	3.01	2.62	2.42	2.29	2.20	2.13	2.08	2.04	2.00	1.98	1.93	1.89	1.84	1.81	1.78	1.75	1.72	1.69	1.66
19	2.99	2.61	2.40	2.27	2.18	2.11	2.06	2.02	1.98	1.96	1.91	1.86	1.81	1.79	1.76	1.73	1.70	1.67	1.63
20	2.97	2.59	2.38	2.25	2.16	2.09	2.04	2.00	1.96	1.94	1.89	1.84	1.79	1.77	1.74	1.71	1.68	1.64	1.61
21	2.96	2.57	2.36	2.23	2.14	2.08	2.02	1.98	1.95	1.92	1.87	1.83	1.78	1.75	1.72	1.69	1.66	1.62	1.59
22	2.95	2.56	2.35	2.22	2.13	2.06	2.01	1.97	1.93	1.90	1.86	1.81	1.76	1.73	1.70	1.67	1.64	1.60	1.57
23	2.94	2.55	2.34	2.21	2.11	2.05	1.99	1.95	1.92	1.89	1.84	1.80	1.74	1.72	1.69	1.66	1.62	1.59	1.55
24	2.93	2.54	2.33	2.19	2.10	2.04	1.98	1.94	1.91	1.88	1.83	1.78	1.73	1.70	1.67	1.64	1.61	1.57	1.53
25	2.92	2.53	2.32	2.18	2.09	2.02	1.97	1.93	1.89	1.87	1.82	1.77	1.72	1.69	1.66	1.63	1.59	1.56	1.52
26	2.91	2.52	2.31	2.17	2.08	2.01	1.96	1.92	1.88	1.86	1.81	1.76	1.71	1.68	1.65	1.61	1.58	1.54	1.50
27	2.90	2.51	2.30	2.17	2.07	2.00	1.95	1.91	1.87	1.85	1.80	1.75	1.70	1.67	1.64	1.60	1.57	1.53	1.49
28	2.89	2.50	2.29	2.16	2.06	2.00	1.94	1.90	1.87	1.84	1.79	1.74	1.69	1.66	1.63	1.59	1.56	1.52	1.48
29	2.89	2.50	2.28	2.15	2.06	1.99	1.93	1.89	1.86	1.83	1.78	1.73	1.68	1.65	1.62	1.58	1.55	1.51	1.47
30	2.88	2.49	2.28	2.14	2.05	1.98	1.93	1.88	1.85	1.82	1.77	1.72	1.67	1.64	1.61	1.57	1.54	1.50	1.46
40	2.84	2.44	2.23	2.09	2.00	1.93	1.87	1.83	1.79	1.76	1.71	1.66	1.61	1.57	1.54	1.51	1.47	1.42	1.38
60	2.79	2.39	2.18	2.04	1.95	1.87	1.82	1.77	1.74	1.71	1.66	1.60	1.54	1.51	1.48	1.44	1.40	1.35	1.29
120	2.75	2.35	2.13	1.99	1.90	1.82	1.77	1.72	1.68	1.65	1.60	1.55	1.48	1.45	1.41	1.37	1.32	1.26	1.19
∞	2.71	2.30	2.08	1.94	1.85	1.77	1.72	1.67	1.63	1.60	1.55	1.49	1.42	1.38	1.34	1.30	1.24	1.17	1.00

ν_2 = degrees of freedom for denominator

APPENDIX D continued

$$F_{.95}(\nu_1, \nu_2) \qquad \alpha = 0.05$$

ν_1 = degrees of freedom for numerator

ν_2 = degrees of freedom for denominator

ν_2 \ ν_1	1	2	3	4	5	6	7	8	9	10	12	15	20	24	30	40	60	120	∞
1	161.4	199.5	215.7	224.6	230.2	234.0	236.8	238.9	240.5	241.9	243.9	245.9	248.0	249.1	250.1	251.1	252.2	253.3	254.3
2	18.51	19.00	19.16	19.25	19.30	19.33	19.35	19.37	19.38	19.40	19.41	19.43	19.45	19.45	19.46	19.47	19.48	19.49	19.50
3	10.13	9.55	9.28	9.12	9.01	8.94	8.89	8.85	8.81	8.79	8.74	8.70	8.66	8.64	8.62	8.59	8.57	8.55	8.53
4	7.71	6.94	6.59	6.39	6.26	6.16	6.09	6.04	6.00	5.96	5.91	5.86	5.80	5.77	5.75	5.72	5.69	5.66	5.63
5	6.61	5.79	5.41	5.19	5.05	4.95	4.88	4.82	4.77	4.74	4.68	4.62	4.56	4.53	4.50	4.46	4.43	4.40	4.36
6	5.99	5.14	4.76	4.53	4.39	4.28	4.21	4.15	4.10	4.06	4.00	3.94	3.87	3.84	3.81	3.77	3.74	3.70	3.67
7	5.59	4.74	4.35	4.12	3.97	3.87	3.79	3.73	3.68	3.64	3.57	3.51	3.44	3.41	3.38	3.34	3.30	3.27	3.23
8	5.32	4.46	4.07	3.84	3.69	3.58	3.50	3.44	3.39	3.35	3.28	3.22	3.15	3.12	3.08	3.04	3.01	2.97	2.93
9	5.12	4.26	3.86	3.63	3.48	3.37	3.29	3.23	3.18	3.14	3.07	3.01	2.94	2.90	2.86	2.83	2.79	2.75	2.71
10	4.96	4.10	3.71	3.48	3.33	3.22	3.14	3.07	3.02	2.98	2.91	2.85	2.77	2.74	2.70	2.66	2.62	2.58	2.54
11	4.84	3.98	3.59	3.36	3.20	3.09	3.01	2.95	2.90	2.85	2.79	2.72	2.65	2.61	2.57	2.53	2.49	2.45	2.40
12	4.75	3.89	3.49	3.26	3.11	3.00	2.91	2.85	2.80	2.75	2.69	2.62	2.54	2.51	2.47	2.43	2.38	2.34	2.30
13	4.67	3.81	3.41	3.18	3.03	2.92	2.83	2.77	2.71	2.67	2.60	2.53	2.46	2.42	2.38	2.34	2.30	2.25	2.21
14	4.60	3.74	3.34	3.11	2.96	2.85	2.76	2.70	2.65	2.60	2.53	2.46	2.39	2.35	2.31	2.27	2.22	2.18	2.13
15	4.54	3.68	3.29	3.06	2.90	2.79	2.71	2.64	2.59	2.54	2.48	2.40	2.33	2.29	2.25	2.20	2.16	2.11	2.07
16	4.49	3.63	3.24	3.01	2.85	2.74	2.66	2.59	2.54	2.49	2.42	2.35	2.28	2.24	2.19	2.15	2.11	2.06	2.01
17	4.45	3.59	3.20	2.96	2.81	2.70	2.61	2.55	2.49	2.45	2.38	2.31	2.23	2.19	2.15	2.10	2.06	2.01	1.96
18	4.41	3.55	3.16	2.93	2.77	2.66	2.58	2.51	2.46	2.41	2.34	2.27	2.19	2.15	2.11	2.06	2.02	1.97	1.92
19	4.38	3.52	3.13	2.90	2.74	2.63	2.54	2.48	2.42	2.38	2.31	2.23	2.16	2.11	2.07	2.03	1.98	1.93	1.88
20	4.35	3.49	3.10	2.87	2.71	2.60	2.51	2.45	2.39	2.35	2.28	2.20	2.12	2.08	2.04	1.99	1.95	1.90	1.84
21	4.32	3.47	3.07	2.84	2.68	2.57	2.49	2.42	2.37	2.32	2.25	2.18	2.10	2.05	2.01	1.96	1.92	1.87	1.81
22	4.30	3.44	3.05	2.82	2.66	2.55	2.46	2.40	2.34	2.30	2.23	2.15	2.07	2.03	1.98	1.94	1.89	1.84	1.78
23	4.28	3.42	3.03	2.80	2.64	2.53	2.44	2.37	2.32	2.27	2.20	2.13	2.05	2.01	1.96	1.91	1.86	1.81	1.76
24	4.26	3.40	3.01	2.78	2.62	2.51	2.42	2.36	2.30	2.25	2.18	2.11	2.03	1.98	1.94	1.89	1.84	1.79	1.73
25	4.24	3.39	2.99	2.76	2.60	2.49	2.40	2.34	2.28	2.24	2.16	2.09	2.01	1.96	1.92	1.87	1.82	1.77	1.71
26	4.23	3.37	2.98	2.74	2.59	2.47	2.39	2.32	2.27	2.22	2.15	2.07	1.99	1.95	1.90	1.85	1.80	1.75	1.69
27	4.21	3.35	2.96	2.73	2.57	2.46	2.37	2.31	2.25	2.20	2.13	2.06	1.97	1.93	1.88	1.84	1.79	1.73	1.67
28	4.20	3.34	2.95	2.71	2.56	2.45	2.36	2.29	2.24	2.19	2.12	2.04	1.96	1.91	1.87	1.82	1.77	1.71	1.65
29	4.18	3.33	2.93	2.70	2.55	2.43	2.35	2.28	2.22	2.18	2.10	2.03	1.94	1.90	1.85	1.81	1.75	1.70	1.64
30	4.17	3.32	2.92	2.69	2.53	2.42	2.33	2.27	2.21	2.16	2.09	2.01	1.93	1.89	1.84	1.79	1.74	1.68	1.62
40	4.08	3.23	2.84	2.61	2.45	2.34	2.25	2.18	2.12	2.08	2.00	1.92	1.84	1.79	1.74	1.69	1.64	1.58	1.51
60	4.00	3.15	2.76	2.53	2.37	2.25	2.17	2.10	2.04	1.99	1.92	1.84	1.75	1.70	1.65	1.59	1.53	1.47	1.39
120	3.92	3.07	2.68	2.45	2.29	2.17	2.09	2.02	1.96	1.91	1.83	1.75	1.66	1.61	1.55	1.50	1.43	1.35	1.25
∞	3.84	3.00	2.60	2.37	2.21	2.10	2.01	1.94	1.88	1.83	1.75	1.67	1.57	1.52	1.46	1.39	1.32	1.22	1.00

APPENDIX D *continued*

$$F_{975}(v_1, v_2) \qquad \alpha = 0.025$$

v_1 = degrees of freedom for numerator

v_2 = degrees of freedom for denominator

v_2 \ v_1	1	2	3	4	5	6	7	8	9	10	12	15	20	24	30	40	60	120	∞
1	647.8	799.5	864.2	899.6	921.8	937.1	948.2	956.7	963.3	968.6	976.7	984.9	993.1	997.2	1001	1006	1010	1014	1018
2	38.51	39.00	39.17	39.25	39.30	39.33	39.36	39.37	39.39	39.40	39.41	39.43	39.45	39.46	39.46	39.47	39.48	39.49	39.50
3	17.44	16.04	15.44	15.10	14.88	14.73	14.62	14.54	14.47	14.42	14.34	14.25	14.17	14.12	14.08	14.04	13.99	13.95	13.90
4	12.22	10.65	9.98	9.60	9.36	9.20	9.07	8.98	8.90	8.84	8.75	8.66	8.56	8.51	8.46	8.41	8.36	8.31	8.26
5	10.01	8.43	7.76	7.39	7.15	6.98	6.85	6.76	6.68	6.62	6.52	6.43	6.33	6.28	6.23	6.18	6.12	6.07	6.02
6	8.81	7.26	6.60	6.23	5.99	5.82	5.70	5.60	5.52	5.46	5.37	5.27	5.17	5.12	5.07	5.01	4.96	4.90	4.85
7	8.07	6.54	5.89	5.52	5.29	5.12	4.99	4.90	4.82	4.76	4.67	4.57	4.47	4.42	4.36	4.31	4.25	4.20	4.14
8	7.57	6.06	5.42	5.05	4.82	4.65	4.53	4.43	4.36	4.30	4.20	4.10	4.00	3.95	3.89	3.84	3.78	3.73	3.67
9	7.21	5.71	5.08	4.72	4.48	4.32	4.20	4.10	4.03	3.96	3.87	3.77	3.67	3.61	3.56	3.51	3.45	3.39	3.33
10	6.94	5.46	4.83	4.47	4.24	4.07	3.95	3.85	3.78	3.72	3.62	3.52	3.42	3.37	3.31	3.26	3.20	3.14	3.08
11	6.72	5.26	4.63	4.28	4.04	3.88	3.76	3.66	3.59	3.53	3.43	3.33	3.23	3.17	3.12	3.06	3.00	2.94	2.88
12	6.55	5.10	4.47	4.12	3.89	3.73	3.61	3.51	3.44	3.37	3.28	3.18	3.07	3.02	2.96	2.91	2.85	2.79	2.72
13	6.41	4.97	4.35	4.00	3.77	3.60	3.48	3.39	3.31	3.25	3.15	3.05	2.95	2.89	2.84	2.78	2.72	2.66	2.60
14	6.30	4.86	4.24	3.89	3.66	3.50	3.38	3.29	3.21	3.15	3.05	2.95	2.84	2.79	2.73	2.67	2.61	2.55	2.49
15	6.20	4.77	4.15	3.80	3.58	3.41	3.29	3.20	3.12	3.06	2.96	2.86	2.76	2.70	2.64	2.59	2.52	2.46	2.40
16	6.12	4.69	4.08	3.73	3.50	3.34	3.22	3.12	3.05	2.99	2.89	2.79	2.68	2.63	2.57	2.51	2.45	2.38	2.32
17	6.04	4.62	4.01	3.66	3.44	3.28	3.16	3.06	2.98	2.92	2.82	2.72	2.62	2.56	2.50	2.44	2.38	2.32	2.25
18	5.98	4.56	3.95	3.61	3.38	3.22	3.10	3.01	2.93	2.87	2.77	2.67	2.56	2.50	2.44	2.38	2.32	2.26	2.19
19	5.92	4.51	3.90	3.56	3.33	3.17	3.05	2.96	2.88	2.82	2.72	2.62	2.51	2.45	2.39	2.33	2.27	2.20	2.13
20	5.87	4.46	3.86	3.51	3.29	3.13	3.01	2.91	2.84	2.77	2.68	2.57	2.46	2.41	2.35	2.29	2.22	2.16	2.09
21	5.83	4.42	3.82	3.48	3.25	3.09	2.97	2.87	2.80	2.73	2.64	2.53	2.42	2.37	2.31	2.25	2.18	2.11	2.04
22	5.79	4.38	3.78	3.44	3.22	3.05	2.93	2.84	2.76	2.70	2.60	2.50	2.39	2.33	2.27	2.21	2.14	2.08	2.00
23	5.75	4.35	3.75	3.41	3.18	3.02	2.90	2.81	2.73	2.67	2.57	2.47	2.36	2.30	2.24	2.18	2.11	2.04	1.97
24	5.72	4.32	3.72	3.38	3.15	2.99	2.87	2.78	2.70	2.64	2.54	2.44	2.33	2.27	2.21	2.15	2.08	2.01	1.94
25	5.69	4.29	3.69	3.35	3.13	2.97	2.85	2.75	2.68	2.61	2.51	2.41	2.30	2.24	2.18	2.12	2.05	1.98	1.91
26	5.66	4.27	3.67	3.33	3.10	2.94	2.82	2.73	2.65	2.59	2.49	2.39	2.28	2.22	2.16	2.09	2.03	1.95	1.88
27	5.63	4.24	3.65	3.31	3.08	2.92	2.80	2.71	2.63	2.57	2.47	2.36	2.25	2.19	2.13	2.07	2.00	1.93	1.85
28	5.61	4.22	3.63	3.29	3.06	2.90	2.78	2.69	2.61	2.55	2.45	2.34	2.23	2.17	2.11	2.05	1.98	1.91	1.83
29	5.59	4.20	3.61	3.27	3.04	2.88	2.76	2.67	2.59	2.53	2.43	2.32	2.21	2.15	2.09	2.03	1.96	1.89	1.81
30	5.57	4.18	3.59	3.25	3.03	2.87	2.75	2.65	2.57	2.51	2.41	2.31	2.20	2.14	2.07	2.01	1.94	1.87	1.79
40	5.42	4.05	3.46	3.13	2.90	2.74	2.62	2.53	2.45	2.39	2.29	2.18	2.07	2.01	1.94	1.88	1.80	1.72	1.64
60	5.29	3.93	3.34	3.01	2.79	2.63	2.51	2.41	2.33	2.27	2.17	2.06	1.94	1.88	1.82	1.74	1.67	1.58	1.48
120	5.15	3.80	3.23	2.89	2.67	2.52	2.39	2.30	2.22	2.16	2.05	1.94	1.82	1.76	1.69	1.61	1.53	1.43	1.31
∞	5.02	3.69	3.12	2.79	2.57	2.41	2.29	2.19	2.11	2.05	1.94	1.83	1.71	1.64	1.57	1.48	1.39	1.27	1.00

APPENDIX D *continued*

$$F_{.99}(\nu_1, \nu_2) \qquad \alpha = 0.01$$

ν_1 = degrees of freedom for numerator

ν_2	1	2	3	4	5	6	7	8	9	10	12	15	20	24	30	40	60	120	∞
1	4052	4999.5	5403	5625	5764	5859	5928	5982	6022	6056	6106	6157	6209	6235	6261	6287	6313	6339	6366
2	98.50	99.00	99.17	99.25	99.30	99.33	99.36	99.37	99.39	99.40	99.42	99.43	99.45	99.46	99.47	99.47	99.48	99.49	99.50
3	34.12	30.82	29.46	28.71	28.24	27.91	27.67	27.49	27.35	27.23	27.05	26.87	26.69	26.60	26.50	26.41	26.32	26.22	26.13
4	21.20	18.00	16.69	15.98	15.52	15.21	14.98	14.80	14.66	14.55	14.37	14.20	14.02	13.93	13.84	13.75	13.65	13.56	13.46
5	16.26	13.27	12.06	11.39	10.97	10.67	10.46	10.29	10.16	10.05	9.89	9.72	9.55	9.47	9.38	9.29	9.20	9.11	9.02
6	13.75	10.92	9.78	9.15	8.75	8.47	8.26	8.10	7.98	7.87	7.72	7.56	7.40	7.31	7.23	7.14	7.06	6.97	6.88
7	12.25	9.55	8.45	7.85	7.46	7.19	6.99	6.84	6.72	6.62	6.47	6.31	6.16	6.07	5.99	5.91	5.82	5.74	5.65
8	11.26	8.65	7.59	7.01	6.63	6.37	6.18	6.03	5.91	5.81	5.67	5.52	5.36	5.28	5.20	5.12	5.03	4.95	4.86
9	10.56	8.02	6.99	6.42	6.06	5.80	5.61	5.47	5.35	5.26	5.11	4.96	4.81	4.73	4.65	4.57	4.48	4.40	4.31
10	10.04	7.56	6.55	5.99	5.64	5.39	5.20	5.06	4.94	4.85	4.71	4.56	4.41	4.33	4.25	4.17	4.08	4.00	3.91
11	9.65	7.21	6.22	5.67	5.32	5.07	4.89	4.74	4.63	4.54	4.40	4.25	4.10	4.02	3.94	3.86	3.78	3.69	3.60
12	9.33	6.93	5.95	5.41	5.06	4.82	4.64	4.50	4.39	4.30	4.16	4.01	3.86	3.78	3.70	3.62	3.54	3.45	3.36
13	9.07	6.70	5.74	5.21	4.86	4.62	4.44	4.30	4.19	4.10	3.96	3.82	3.66	3.59	3.51	3.43	3.34	3.25	3.17
14	8.86	6.51	5.56	5.04	4.69	4.46	4.28	4.14	4.03	3.94	3.80	3.66	3.51	3.43	3.35	3.27	3.18	3.09	3.00
15	8.68	6.36	5.42	4.89	4.56	4.32	4.14	4.00	3.89	3.80	3.67	3.52	3.37	3.29	3.21	3.13	3.05	2.96	2.87
16	8.53	6.23	5.29	4.77	4.44	4.20	4.03	3.89	3.78	3.69	3.55	3.41	3.26	3.18	3.10	3.02	2.93	2.84	2.75
17	8.40	6.11	5.18	4.67	4.34	4.10	3.93	3.79	3.68	3.59	3.46	3.31	3.16	3.08	3.00	2.92	2.83	2.75	2.65
18	8.29	6.01	5.09	4.58	4.25	4.01	3.84	3.71	3.60	3.51	3.37	3.23	3.08	3.00	2.92	2.84	2.75	2.66	2.57
19	8.18	5.93	5.01	4.50	4.17	3.94	3.77	3.63	3.52	3.43	3.30	3.15	3.00	2.92	2.84	2.76	2.67	2.58	2.49
20	8.10	5.85	4.94	4.43	4.10	3.87	3.70	3.56	3.46	3.37	3.23	3.09	2.94	2.86	2.78	2.69	2.61	2.52	2.42
21	8.02	5.78	4.87	4.37	4.04	3.81	3.64	3.51	3.40	3.31	3.17	3.03	2.88	2.80	2.72	2.64	2.55	2.46	2.36
22	7.95	5.72	4.82	4.31	3.99	3.76	3.59	3.45	3.35	3.26	3.12	2.98	2.83	2.75	2.67	2.58	2.50	2.40	2.31
23	7.88	5.66	4.76	4.26	3.94	3.71	3.54	3.41	3.30	3.21	3.07	2.93	2.78	2.70	2.62	2.54	2.45	2.35	2.26
24	7.82	5.61	4.72	4.22	3.90	3.67	3.50	3.36	3.26	3.17	3.03	2.89	2.74	2.66	2.58	2.49	2.40	2.31	2.21
25	7.77	5.57	4.68	4.18	3.85	3.63	3.46	3.32	3.22	3.13	2.99	2.85	2.70	2.62	2.54	2.45	2.36	2.27	2.17
26	7.72	5.53	4.64	4.14	3.82	3.59	3.42	3.29	3.18	3.09	2.96	2.81	2.66	2.58	2.50	2.42	2.33	2.23	2.13
27	7.68	5.49	4.60	4.11	3.78	3.56	3.39	3.26	3.15	3.06	2.93	2.78	2.63	2.55	2.47	2.38	2.29	2.20	2.10
28	7.64	5.45	4.57	4.07	3.75	3.53	3.36	3.23	3.12	3.03	2.90	2.75	2.60	2.52	2.44	2.35	2.26	2.17	2.06
29	7.60	5.42	4.54	4.04	3.73	3.50	3.33	3.20	3.09	3.00	2.87	2.73	2.57	2.49	2.41	2.33	2.23	2.14	2.03
30	7.56	5.39	4.51	4.02	3.70	3.47	3.30	3.17	3.07	2.98	2.84	2.70	2.55	2.47	2.39	2.30	2.21	2.11	2.01
40	7.31	5.18	4.31	3.83	3.51	3.29	3.12	2.99	2.89	2.80	2.66	2.52	2.37	2.29	2.20	2.11	2.02	1.92	1.80
60	7.08	4.98	4.13	3.65	3.34	3.12	2.95	2.82	2.72	2.63	2.50	2.35	2.20	2.12	2.03	1.94	1.84	1.73	1.60
120	6.85	4.79	3.95	3.48	3.17	2.96	2.79	2.66	2.56	2.47	2.34	2.19	2.03	1.95	1.86	1.76	1.66	1.53	1.38
∞	6.63	4.61	3.78	3.32	3.02	2.80	2.64	2.51	2.41	2.32	2.18	2.04	1.88	1.79	1.70	1.59	1.47	1.32	1.00

ν_2 = degrees of freedom for denominator

Source: Adapted from *Biometrika Tables for Statisticians*, Vol. 1 (2nd ed.), edited by E. S. Pearson and H. O. Hartley, 1958. Reproduced by permission of the Biometrika Trustees, the Imperial College of Science and Technology, London, England.

GLOSSARY

absolute precision   Degree of precision in an estimate of a parameter expressed as within plus or minus so many units.

accuracy   Criterion used to evaluate a research report according to whether the reasoning in the report is logical and the information correct.

administrative control   Term applied to studies relying on questionnaires and referring to the speed, cost, and control of the replies afforded by the mode of administration.

analysis of selected cases   Intensive study of selected examples of the phenomenon of interest.

analysis of variance (ANOVA)   Statistical test employed with interval data to determine if $k(k \geq 2)$ samples came from populations with equal means.

area sampling   Form of cluster sampling in which areas (for example, census tracts, blocks) serve as the primary sampling units. The population is divided into mutually exclusive and exhaustive areas using maps, and a random sample of areas is selected. If all the households in the selected areas are used in the study, it is one-stage area sampling. If the areas themselves are subsampled with respect to households, the procedure is two-stage area sampling.

attitudes/opinions   Some preference, liking, or conviction regarding a specific object or idea; a predisposition to act.

awareness/knowledge   Insight into or understanding of facts about some object or phenomenon.

banner   A series of cross-tabulations between a criterion, or dependent, variable and several (sometimes many) explanatory variables in a single table.

bar chart   Chart in which the relative lengths of the bars show relative amounts of variables or objects.

Bayes' rule   Formal mechanism for revising prior probabilities in the light of new information.

Bayesian probability   Probability based on a person's subjective or personal judgments and experience.

behavior   What subjects have done or are doing.

benchmarking   The comparison of one's data (for example, customers' reception of service quality) to an industry standard, or best-practices.

blunder   Error that arises when editing, coding, entering, or tabulating the data.

brain wave research   Research technique that assesses the stimuli that subjects find arousing or interesting by using electrodes fitted to the subject's head that monitor the electrical impulses emitted by the brain.

branching questions   A technique used to direct respondents to different places in a questionnaire based on their response to the question at hand.

brand-switching matrix   Two-way table that indicates which brands a sample of people purchased in one period and which brands they purchased in a subsequent period, thus highlighting the switches occurring among and between brands as well as the number of persons that purchased the same brand in both periods.

causal research   Research design in which the major emphasis is on determining a cause-and-effect relationship.

census   A complete canvass of a population.

Central-Limit Theorem   Theorem that holds that if simple random samples of size n are drawn from a parent population with mean μ and variance σ^2, then when n is large, the sample mean $\bar{x}$ will be approximately normally distributed with the mean equal to μ and variance equal to σ^2/n. The approximation will become more and more accurate as n becomes larger.

central office edit   Thorough and exacting scrutiny and correction of completed data collection forms, including a decision about what to do with the data.

971

chi-square goodness-of-fit test   Statistical test to determine whether some observed pattern of frequencies corresponds to an expected pattern.

clarity   Criterion used to evaluate a research report; specifically, whether the phrasing in the report is precise.

classical probability   Probability determined by the relative frequency with which an event occurs when an experiment is repeated under controlled conditions.

cluster analysis   Body of techniques concerned with developing natural groupings of objects based on the relationships of the p variables describing the objects.

cluster sample   A probability sample distinguished by a two-step procedure in which (1) the parent population is divided into mutually exclusive and exhaustive subsets, and (2) a random sample of subsets is selected. If the investigator then uses all of the population elements in the selected subsets for the sample, the procedure is one-stage cluster sampling; if a sample of elements is selected probabilistically from the subsets, the procedure is two-stage cluster sampling.

codebook   A document that describes each variable, gives it a code name, and identifies its location in the record.

coding   Technical procedure by which data are categorized; it involves specifying the alternative categories or classes into which the responses are to be placed

and assigning code numbers to the classes.

coefficient alpha   A statistic that summarizes the extent to which a set of k-items making up a measure intercorrelate or go together; the square root of coefficient alpha is the estimated correlation of the k-item test with errorless true scores.

coefficient of concordance   Statistic used with ordinal data to measure the extent of association among $k(k \geq 2)$ variables.

coefficient of determination   Term used in regression analysis to refer to the relative proportion of the total variation in the criterion variable that can be explained or accounted for by the fitted regression equation.

coefficient of multiple correlation   In multiple-regression analysis, the square root of the coefficient of multiple determination.

coefficient of multiple determination   In multiple-regression analysis, the proportion of variation in the criterion variable that is accounted for by the covariation in the predictor variables.

coefficient of partial correlation   In multiple-regression analysis, the square root of the coefficient of partial determination.

coefficient of partial determination   Quantity that results from a multiple-regression analysis, which indicates the proportion of variation in the criterion variable not accounted for by the earlier variables that is accounted for by adding a new variable into the regression equation.

coefficient of partial (or net) regression   Quantity resulting from a multiple-regression analysis, which indicates the average change in the criterion variable per unit change in a predictor variable, holding all other predictor variables constant; the interpretation applies only when the predictor variables are independent, as required for a valid application of the multiple-regression model.

cohort   The aggregate of individuals who experience the same event within the same time interval.

communality   Quantity resulting from a factor analysis that expresses the proportion of the variance of a variable extracted by m factors, where m can vary from one to the total number of variables; the communalities help determine how many factors should be retained in a solution.

communication   Method of data collection involving questioning of respondents to secure the desired information using a data collection instrument called a questionnaire.

comparative rating scale   Scale requiring subjects to make their ratings as a series of relative judgments or comparisons rather than as independent assessments.

completely randomized design   Experimental design in which the experimental treatments are assigned to the test units completely at random.

completeness   Criterion used to evaluate a research report; specifically, whether the report provides all the information readers need in a language they understand.

completeness rate (*C*)
Measure used to evaluate and compare interviewers in terms of their ability to secure needed information from contacted respondents; the completeness rate measures the proportion of complete contacts by interviewer.

computer-assisted interviewing (CAI) The conducting of surveys using computers to manage the sequence of questions in which the answers are recorded electronically through the use of a keyboard.

conciseness Criterion used to evaluate a research report; specifically, whether the writing in the report is crisp and direct.

conditional association
Association existing between two variables when the levels of one or more other variables are considered in the analysis; the other variables are called control variables.

conditional probability
Probability that Event A will occur when it is known whether another Event B has occurred or not.

confusion matrix Device used in discriminant analysis to assess the adequacy of the discriminant function or functions; the confusion matrix is essentially a cross-classification table, in which the variables of cross classification are the actual group membership categories and the predicted group membership categories, and the entries are the number of observations falling into each cell.

conjoint analysis Technique in which respondents' utilities or valuations of attributes are inferred from the preferences they express for various combinations of these attributes.

constant sum method A type of comparative rating scale in which an individual is instructed to divide some given sum among two or more attributes on the basis of their importance to him or her.

constitutive (conceptual) definition Definition in which a given construct is defined in terms of other constructs in the set, sometimes in the form of an equation that expresses the relationship among them.

construct validity Approach to validating a measure by determining what construct, concept, or trait the instrument is in fact measuring.

contact rate (*K*) Measure used to evaluate and compare the effectiveness of interviewers in making contact with designated respondents. K = number of sample units contacted/total number of sample units approached.

content validity Approach to validating a measure by determining the adequacy with which the domain of the characteristic is captured by the measure; it is sometimes called face validity.

contingency coefficient
Statistic used to measure the extent of association between two nominally scaled attributes.

contingency table Statistical test employing the χ^2 statistic that is used to determine whether the variables in a cross-classification analysis are independent.

controlled test market A market in which an entire marketing test program is conducted by an outside service. Also called a forced distribution test market.

convenience sample
Nonprobability sample, sometimes called an accidental sample, because those included in the sample enter by accident, in that they just happen to be where the study is being conducted when it is being conducted.

convergent validity
Confirmation of the existence of a construct determined by the correlations exhibited by independent measures of the construct.

cophenetic value Level at which a pair of objects or classes are actually linked in cluster analyses.

correlation analysis Statistical technique used to measure the closeness of the linear relationship between two or more intervally scaled variables.

cross-sectional study
Investigation involving a sample of elements selected from the population of interest at a single point in time.

cross tabulation Count of the number of cases that fall into each of several categories when the categories are based on two or more variables considered simultaneously.

cumulative distribution function
Function that shows the number of cases having a value less than or equal to a specified quantity; the function is generated by connecting the points representing the given combinations of *X*s (values) and *Y*s (cumulative frequencies) with straight lines.

cutting score Term used in discriminant analysis to indicate the score that divides the groups in terms of their respective discriminant scores; if the object's score is above the cutting score, the object is assigned to one group, whereas if its score is below the cutting score, it is assigned to the other group.

data system The part of a decision support system that includes the processes used to capture and the methods used to store data coming from a number of external and internal sources.

decision support system (DSS) A coordinated collection of data, system tools, and techniques with supporting software and hardware by which an organization gathers and interprets relevant information from business and the environment and turns it into a basis for marketing action.

decision tree Decision flow diagram in which the problem is structured in chronological order, typically with small squares indicating decision forks and small circles indicating chance forks.

dendrogram Treelike device employed to interpret the output of a cluster analysis that indicates the groups of objects forming at various similarity levels.

deontology An ethical or moral reasoning framework that focuses on the welfare of the individual and that uses means, intentions, and features of the act itself in judging its ethicality; sometimes referred to as the rights or entitlements model.

depth interview Unstructured personal interview in which the interviewer attempts to get subjects to talk freely and to express their true feelings.

derived population Population of all possible distinguishable samples that could be drawn from a parent population under a specific sampling plan.

descriptive research Research design in which the major emphasis is on determining the frequency with which something occurs or the extent to which two variables covary.

dialog system The part of a decision support system that permits users to explore the data bases by employing the system models to produce reports that satisfy their particular information needs. Also called language systems.

dichotomous question Fixed-alternative question in which respondents are asked to indicate which of two alternative responses most closely corresponds to their position on a subject.

discriminant analysis Statistical technique employed to model the relationship between a dichotomous or multichotomous criterion variable and a set of p predictor variables.

discriminant validity Criterion imposed on a measure of a construct requiring that it not correlate too highly with measures from which it is supposed to differ.

disguise Amount of knowledge about the purpose of a study communicated to the respondent by the data collection method. An undisguised questionnaire, for example, is one in which the purpose of the research is obvious from the questions posed, whereas a disguised questionnaire attempts to hide the purpose of the study.

disproportionate stratified sampling Stratified sample in which the individual strata or subsets are sampled in relation to both their size and their variability; strata exhibiting more variability are sampled more than proportionately to their relative size, while those that are very homogeneous are sampled less than proportionately.

domain sampling model A measurement model that holds that the true score of a characteristic is obtained when all of the items in the domain are used to capture it. Since only a sample of items is typically used, a primary source of measurement error is the inadequate sampling of the domain of relevant items; to the extent that the sample of items correlates with true scores, it is good.

double-barreled question A question that calls for two responses and thereby creates confusion for the respondent.

dummy table Table that contains a title and headings to denote the categories to be used for each variable making up the table to categorize the data when it is collected.

dummy (or binary) variable Variable that is given one of two values, 0 or 1, and that is used to provide a numerical representation for attributes or characteristics that are not essentially quantitative.

editing Inspection and correction, if necessary, of each questionnaire or observation form.

electronic test market   Market or geographic area in which a firm tracks purchases made by specific households that are part of its panel, using identification cards held by panel members and the electronic recording of the products they purchase using scanners.

element   Term used in sampling to refer to the objects on which measurements are to be taken, such as individuals, households, business firms, or other institutions.

equal-appearing intervals   Self-report technique for attitude measurement in which subjects are asked to indicate those statements in a larger list of statements (typically 20 to 22) with which they agree and disagree; subjects' attitude scores are the average score of the scale values of the statements with which they agree.

equivalence   Measure of reliability that is applied to both single instruments and measurement situations. When applied to instruments, the equivalence measure of reliability is the internal consistency or internal homogeneity of the set of items forming the scale; when applied to measurement situations, the equivalence measure of reliability focuses on whether different observers or different instruments used to measure the same individuals or objects at the same point in time yield consistent results.

ethics   A concern with the development of moral standards by which situations can be judged; applies to all situations in which there can be actual or potential harm of any kind (for example, economic, physical, or mental) to an individual or group.

expected value   Value resulting from multiplying each consequence by the probability of that consequence occurring and summing the products.

expected value of perfect information   Difference between the expected value under certainty and the expected value of the optimal act under uncertainty.

expected value of a research procedure   Value determined by multiplying the probability of obtaining the kth research result by the expected value of the preferred decision given the kth research result and summing the products.

expected value under certainty   Value derived by multiplying the consequence associated with the optimal act under each possible state of nature by the probability associated with that state of nature and summing the products.

experience survey   Interviews with people knowledgeable about the general subject being investigated.

experiment   Scientific investigation in which an investigator manipulates and controls one or more independent variables and observes the dependent variable for variation concomitant to the manipulation of the independent variables.

experimental design   Research investigation in which the investigator has direct control over at least one independent variable and manipulates at least one independent variable.

experimental mortality   Experimental condition in which test units are lost during the course of an experiment.

exploratory research   Research design in which the major emphasis is on gaining ideas and insights; it is particularly helpful in breaking broad, vague problem statements into smaller, more precise subproblem statements.

external data   Data that originate outside the organization for which the research is being done.

external validity   One criterion by which an experiment is evaluated; the extent to which the observed experimental effect can be generalized to other populations and settings.

eye camera   Camera used to study eye movements while the subject reads advertising copy.

factor   Linear combination of variables.

factor analysis   Body of techniques concerned with the study of interrelationships among a set of variables, none of which is given the special status of a criterion variable.

factor loading   Quantity that results from a factor analysis and that indicates the correlation between a variable and a factor.

factorial design   Experimental design that is used when the effects of two or more variables are being studied simultaneously; each level of each factor is used with each level of each other factor.

field edit   Preliminary edit, typically conducted by a field supervisor, that is designed to detect the most glaring omissions and inaccuracies in a completed data collection instrument.

field error   Nonsampling error that arises during the actual collection of the data.

field experiment   Research study in a realistic situation in which one or more independent variables are manipulated by the experimenter under as carefully controlled conditions as the situation will permit.

field survey   Survey research conducted in realistic situations (e.g., shopping mall, home).

fixed-alternative questions Questions in which the responses are limited to stated alternatives.

fixed sample   Sample for which size is determined *a priori* and needed information is collected from the designated elements.

focus group   Personal interview conducted among a small number of individuals simultaneously; the interview relies more on group discussion than on directed questions to generate data.

frequency polygon   Figure obtained from a histogram by connecting the midpoints of the bars of the histogram with straight lines.

full profile   An approach to collecting respondents' judgments in a conjoint analysis in which each stimulus is made up of a combination of each of the attributes.

funnel approach   An approach to question sequencing that gets its name from its shape, starting with broad questions and progressively narrowing the scope.

fusion coefficients   In linkage cluster analysis, the numerical

values at which various cases merge to form clusters. Also called amalgamation coefficients, they can be read directly from a dendrogram.

galvanometer   Device used to measure the emotion induced by exposure to a particular stimulus by recording changes in the electrical resistance of the skin associated with the minute degree of sweating that accompanies emotional arousal; in marketing research, the stimulus is often specific advertising copy.

geodemography   The availability of demographic consumer behavior and lifestyle data by arbitrary geographic boundaries that are typically quite small.

goodness of fit   Statistical test employing χ^2 to determine whether some observed pattern of frequencies corresponds to an expected pattern. *See also* chi-square goodness of fit.

graphic rating scale   Scale in which individuals indicate their ratings of an attribute by placing a check at the appropriate point on a line that runs from one extreme of the attribute to the other.

halo effect   Problem that arises in data collection when there is carryover from one judgment to another.

histogram   Form of bar chart on which the values of the variable are placed along the X axis, or abscissa, and the absolute frequency or relative frequency of occurrence of the values is indicated along the Y axis, or ordinate.

history   Specific events external to an experiment but occurring

at the same time that may affect the criterion or response variable.

hit rate   Measure used to assess the results of a discriminant analysis by measuring the proportion of the objects that were correctly classified by the discriminant function(s) in the group to which they actually belong.

hypothesis   A statement that specifies how two or more measurable variables are related.

implicit alternative   An alternative answer to a question that is not expressed in the options.

implied assumption   A problem that occurs when a question is not framed to explicitly state the consequences; thus, it elicits different responses from individuals who *assume* different consequences.

incidence   The percentage of the general population that satisfies the criteria defining the target population.

index of predictive association A statistic used to measure the extent of association between two nominally scaled attributes.

information control   Term applied to studies using questionnaires and concerning the amount and accuracy of the information that can be obtained from respondents.

instrument variation   Any and all changes in the measuring device used in an experiment that might account for differences in two or more measurements.

intention   Anticipated or planned future behavior.

interdependence analysis Problem in multivariate analysis to determine the relationship of a set of variates among themselves; no one variate is selected as special in the sense of the dependent variable.

internal data   Data that originate within the organization for which the research is being done.

internal validity   One criterion by which an experiment is evaluated; the criterion focuses on obtaining evidence demonstrating that the variation in the criterion variable was the result of exposure to the treatment or experimental variable.

interval scale   Measurement in which the assigned numbers legitimately allow the comparison of the size of the differences among and between members.

interviewer-interviewee interaction model   Model that attempts to describe how an interviewer and a respondent could be expected to respond to each other during the course of an interview; it is helpful in suggesting techniques by which response errors can be potentially reduced.

item nonresponse   Source of nonsampling error that arises when a respondent agrees to an interview but refuses or is unable to answer specific questions.

itemized rating scale   Scale in which individuals must indicate their ratings of an attribute or object by selecting one from among a limited number of categories that best describes their attitude toward the attribute or object.

judgment sample Nonprobability sample that is

often called a purposive sample; the sample elements are handpicked because they are expected to serve the research purpose.

***k*-means**   One of the nodal or partitioning methods for cluster analysis; the technique revolves around the selection of k starting points and the assignment of each element to the starting point to which it is most similar. After all points are assigned, the mean or centroid for each group is determined. Then the objects are reassigned on the basis of which mean they are closest to, and the process of computing new centroids and reassigning points is repeated until no objects are reclassified.

Kolmogorov-Smirnov test Statistical test employed with ordinal data to determine whether some observed pattern of frequencies corresponds to some expected pattern; also tests whether two independent samples have been drawn from the same population or from populations with the same distribution.

laboratory experiment Research investigation in which investigators create a situation with exact conditions in order to control some variables and manipulate others.

Latin-square design Experimental design in which (1) the number of categories for each extraneous variable we wish to control is equal to the number of treatments, and (2) each treatment is randomly assigned to categories according to a specific pattern. The Latin-square design is appropriate when two extraneous factors are to be explicitly controlled.

leading question   A question framed to give the respondent a clue about how he or she should answer.

line chart   Two-dimensional chart constructed on graph paper in which the X axis represents one variable (typically time) and the Y axis represents another variable.

literature search   Search of statistics, trade journal articles, other articles, magazines, newspapers, and books for data or insight into the problem at hand.

longitudinal study   Investigation involving a fixed sample of elements that is measured repeatedly through time.

mail questionnaire Questionnaire administered by mail to designated respondents with an accompanying cover letter to be returned by mail by the subject to the research organization.

mall intercept   A method of data collection in which interviewers in a shopping mall stop a sample of those passing by to ask them if they would be willing to participate in a research study; those who agree are typically taken to any interviewing facility that has been set up in the mall, where the interview is conducted.

market test   Controlled experiment, done in a limited but carefully selected sector of the marketplace; its aim is to predict the sales or profit consequences, either in absolute or relative terms, of one or more proposed marketing actions.

marketing information system (MIS)   Set of procedures and methods for the regular, planned collection, analysis, and presentation of information for use in making marketing decisions.

marketing research   Function linking the consumer to the marketer through information used to identify and define marketing opportunities and problems; generate, refine, and evaluate marketing actions; monitor marketing performance; and improve understanding of marketing as a process.

maturation   Processes operating within the test units in an experiment as a function of the passage of time *per se*.

maximum chance criterion Decision rule used in discriminant analysis to develop a comparison yardstick for assessing the predictive accuracy of the discriminant function: the maximum chance criterion holds that an object chosen at random should be classified as belonging to the largest size group.

MDS   See multidimensional scaling (MDS)

measurement   Rules for assigning numbers to objects to represent quantities of attributes.

method variance   The variation in scores attributable to the method of data collection.

model system   The part of a decision support system that includes all the routines that allow the user to manipulate the data in order to conduct the kind of analysis the individual desires.

motive   Need, want, drive, wish, desire, or impulse, or any inner state that energizes, activates, or moves and that directs or channels behavior toward goals.

multichotomous question Fixed-alternative question in which respondents are asked to choose the alternative that most closely corresponds to their position on the subject.

multicollinearity   Condition said to be present in a multiple-regression analysis when the predictor variables are not independent as required but are correlated among themselves.

multidimensional scaling (MDS) Approach to measurement in which people's perceptions of the similarity of objects and their preferences among the objects are measured, and these relationships are plotted in a multidimensional space.

multivariate   Problem of analysis in which there are two or more measures of each of n sample objects, and the variables are to be analyzed simultaneously.

nominal scale   Measurement in which numbers are simply assigned to objects or classes of objects solely for the purpose of identification.

noncoverage error Nonsampling error that arises because of a failure to include some units or entire sections of the defined survey population in the actual sampling frame.

nonobservation error Nonsampling error that arises because of nonresponse from some elements designated for inclusion in the sample.

nonparametric tests   Class of statistical tests, also known as distribution-free tests, that are applicable when the data reflect nominal or ordinal measurement or when the data reflect interval measurement but the

assumptions required for the appropriate parametric test are not satisfied.

nonprobability sample   Sample that relies on personal judgment somewhere in the element-selection process and therefore prohibits estimating the probability that any population element will be included in the sample. *See also* quota sample.

nonresponse error Nonsampling error that represents a failure to obtain information from some elements of the population that were selected and designated for the sample.

nonsampling errors   Errors that arise in research that are not due to sampling; nonsampling errors can occur because of errors in conception, logic, misinterpretation of replies, statistics, and arithmetic; errors in tabulating or coding; or errors in reporting the results.

not-at-home   Source of nonsampling error that arises when replies are not secured from some designated sampling units because the respondents are not at home when the interviewer calls.

observation   Method of data collection in which the situation of interest is watched and the relevant facts, actions, or behaviors are recorded.

observation error   Nonsampling error that arises because inaccurate information is secured from the sample elements or because errors are introduced in processing the data or in reporting the findings.

office error   Nonsampling error that arises in the processing of the data because of errors in editing, coding, entering, tabulating, or some other part of the analysis.

omnibus panel Panel in which the information collected from the participating panel members varies from study to study.

open-ended question Question characterized by the condition that respondents are free to reply in their own words rather than being limited to choosing from among a set of alternatives.

operational definition Definition of a construct that describes the operations to be carried out in order for the construct to be measured empirically.

ordinal scale Measurement in which numbers are assigned to data on the basis of some order (for example, more than, greater than) of the objects.

outlier Observation so different in magnitude from the rest of the observations that the analyst chooses to treat it as a special case.

overcoverage error Nonsampling error that arises because of the duplication of elements in the list of sampling units.

paired comparison A data collection procedure in which respondents indicate which item in each pair of items is preferred; when used in conjoint analysis, the items in each pair represent predetermined combinations of attributes.

pair-wise procedure Method by which pairs of stimuli (e.g., print ads, brands) are presented to be compared, as when asking consumers, "Which do you prefer?"

panel (omnibus) Fixed sample of respondents who are measured repeatedly over time but on variables that change from measurement to measurement.

panel (true) Fixed sample of respondents who are measured repeatedly over time with respect to the same variables.

parameter Fixed characteristic or measure of a parent or target population.

parametric tests Class of statistical tests used when the variable(s) is (are) measured on at least an interval scale.

part-worth function Function that describes the relationship between the perceived utilities associated with various levels of an attribute and the objective or physical levels of the attributes (for example, utilities associated with various prices).

payoff table Table containing three elements: alternatives, states of nature, and consequences of each alternative under each state of nature.

people meter A device used to measure when a TV is on, to what channel it is tuned, and who in the household is watching it. Each member in a household is assigned a viewing number, which the individual is supposed to enter into the people meter whenever the set is turned on, the channel is switched, or the person enters or leaves the room.

performance of objective tasks Method of assessing attitudes that rests on the presumption that a subject's performance of a specific assigned task (for example, memorizing a number of facts) will depend on the person's attitude.

personal interview Direct, face-to-face conversation between a representative of the research organization (the interviewer) and a respondent, or interviewee.

personal (or subjective) probability See Bayesian probability.

personality Normal patterns of behavior exhibited by an individual; the attributes, traits, and mannerisms that distinguish one individual from another.

physiological reaction technique Method of assessing attitudes in which the researcher, by electrical or mechanical means, monitors the subject's response to the controlled introduction of some stimuli.

pictogram Bar chart in which pictures represent amounts—for example, piles of dollars for income, pictures of cars for automobile production, people in a row for population.

pie chart Circle, representing a total quantity, divided into sectors, with each sector showing the size of the segment in relation to that total.

plus-one sampling Technique used in studies employing telephone interviews in which a single randomly determined digit is added to numbers selected from the telephone directory.

population See target population.

power Function associated with a statistical test indicating the probability of correctly rejecting a false null hypothesis.

pragmatic validity Approach to validation of a measure based on the usefulness of the measuring instrument as a predictor of some other characteristic or behavior of the individual; it is sometimes called predictive validity or criterion-related validity.

precision Desired size of the estimating interval when the problem is one of estimating a population parameter; the notion of degree of precision is useful in determining sample size.

pretest Use of a questionnaire (observation form) on a trial basis in a small pilot study to determine how well the questionnaire (observation form) works.

primary data Information collected specifically for the purpose of the investigation at hand.

primary source Originating source of secondary data.

probability-proportional-to-size sampling Form of cluster sampling in which a fixed number of second-stage units is selected from each first-stage cluster. The probabilities associated with the selection of each cluster are, in turn, variable because they are directly related to the relative sizes of each cluster.

probability sample Sample in which each population element has a known, nonzero chance of being included in the sample.

projective technique A method of questioning respondents using a vague stimulus that respondents are asked to describe, expand on, or build a structure around; the basic assumption is that an individual's organization of the relatively unstructured stimulus is indicative of the person's basic

perceptions of the phenomenon and reactions to it.

proportional chance criterion Decision rule used in discriminant analysis to develop a comparison yardstick for assessing the predictive accuracy of the discriminant function; the proportional chance criterion holds that the percentage of objects likely to be classified correctly by chance alone equals $\alpha^2 + (1 - \alpha)^2$, where α equals the proportion of objects in Group 1 and $1 - \alpha$ equals the proportion of objects in Group 2.

proportionate stratified sampling Stratified sample in which the number of observations in the total sample is allocated among the strata in proportion to the relative number of elements in each stratum in the population.

psychographic analysis Technique that investigates how people live, what interests them, and what they like; it is also called lifestyle or AIO analysis, because it relies on a number of statements about a person's *A*ctivities, *I*nterests, and *O*pinions.

Q-sort technique General methodology for gathering data and processing the collected information. The subjects are assigned the task of sorting various statements by placing a specific number of statements in each sorting category; the emphases are on determining the relative ranking of stimuli by individuals and deriving clusters of individuals who display similar preference orderings of stimuli.

quota sample Nonprobability sample chosen in such a way that the proportion of sample elements possessing a certain characteristic is approximately the same as the proportion of

the elements with the characteristic in the population; each field worker is assigned a quota that specifies the characteristics of the people he or she is to contact.

random-digit dialing (RDD) Technique used in studies employing telephone interviews in which the numbers to be called are randomly generated.

random error Error in measurement due to the transient aspects of the person or measurement situation.

randomized-block design Experimental design in which (1) the test units are divided into blocks or homogeneous groups using some external criterion, and (2) the objects in each block are randomly assigned to treatment conditions. The randomized-block design is typically employed when there is one extraneous influence to be explicitly controlled.

randomized-response model Interviewing technique in which potentially embarrassing and relatively innocuous questions are paired, and the question the respondent answers is randomly determined.

ratio scale Measurement that has a natural or absolute zero and that therefore allows the comparison of absolute magnitudes of the numbers.

recall loss A type of error caused by a respondent forgetting that an event happened at all.

refusals Nonsampling error that arises because some designated respondents refuse to participate in the study.

regression analysis Statistical technique used to derive an equation that relates a single criterion variable to one or more predictor variables.

relative precision Degree of precision desired in an estimate of a parameter as expressed relative to the level of the estimate of the parameter.

reliability Similarity of results provided by independent but comparable measures of the same object, trait, or construct.

research design Framework or plan for a study that guides the collection and analysis of the data.

research process Sequence of steps in the design and implementation of a research study, including problem formulation, determination of sources of information and research design, determination of data collection method and design of data collection forms, design of the sample and collection of the data, analysis and interpretation of the data, and the research report.

response latency The amount of time a respondent deliberates before answering a question.

response rate (R) Measure used to evaluate and compare interviewers in terms of their ability to induce contacted respondents to participate in the study; R = number of interviews/number of contacts.

sample Selection of a subset of elements from a larger group objects.

sample survey Cross-ctional study in which the sample is selected to be representative of the target population and in which the emphasis is on the generation of summary statistics such as averages and percentages. Also called a field survey.

sampling control Term applied to studies relying on questionnaires and concerning the researcher's dual abilities to direct the inquiry to a designated respondent and to secure the desired cooperation from that respondent.

sampling distribution Distribution of values of some statistic calculated for each possible distinguishable sample that could be drawn from a parent population under a specific sampling plan.

sampling error Difference between the observed values of a variable and the long-run average of the observed values in repetitions of the measurement.

sampling frame List of sampling units from which a sample will be drawn; the list could consist of geographic areas, institutions, individuals, other units.

sampling units Nonoverlapping colle   on. elements from the evice that

scanner Elec imprinted automaticall ct Codes (UPC) Universal t is pulled across as the er, looks up the price in the ched computer, and amtly prints the price of the em on the cash register tape.

secondary data Statistics not gathered for the immediate study at hand but for some other purpose.

secondary source Source of secondary data that did not originate the data but secured them from another source.

selection bias Contaminating influence in an experiment

occurring when there is no way of certifying that groups of test units were equivalent at some previous time.

self report Method of assessing attitudes in which individuals are asked directly for their beliefs about or feelings toward an object or class of objects.

semantic differential Self-report technique for attitude measurement in which subjects are asked to check which cell between a set of bipolar adjectives or phrases best describes their feelings the object.

sentence compl at Questionnair to complete number of s that come to subjects with t **bias** Distortion in mi wers to some questions on estionnaire because the eplies are not independently arrived at but are conditioned by responses to other questions; the problem is particularly acute in mail questionnaires because the respondent can see the whole questionnaire.

sequential sample Sample formed on the basis of a series of successive decisions. If the evidence is not conclusive after a small sample is taken, more observations are taken; if still inconclusive after these additional observations, still more observations are taken. At each stage, a decision is made about whether more information should be collected or whether the evidence is sufficient to draw a conclusion.

simple random sample Probability sample in which each population element has a known and equal chance of being included in the sample and in which every combination of n population elements is a sample possibility and is just as likely to occur as any other combination of n units.

simple tabulation　Count of the number of cases that fall into ch category when the ories are based on one

test marketing　Test hom ne by firms in market or consumers'

snake diag e to a full-scale called becaus e product. connects with str m (so average responses to that semantic differential she thereby depicting the pro. the object or objects being evaluated. Also called *profile plo*.

snowball sample　Judgment sample that relies on the researcher's ability to locate an initial set of respondents with the desired characteristics; these individuals are then used as informants to identify still others with the desired characteristics.

Spearman's rank correlation coefficient (r_s)　A statistic employed with ordinal data to measure the extent of association between two variables.

Split ballot　A technique used to combat response bias in which one phrasing is used for a question in one-half of the questionnaires while an alternative phrasing is used in the other one-half of the questionnaires.

spurious correlation　Condition that arises when there is no relationship between two

variables but the analyst concludes that a relationship exists.

spurious noncorrelation
Condition that arises when the analyst concludes that there is no relationship between two variables but, in fact, there is.

stability　A technique for assessing the reliability of a measure by measuring the same objects or individuals at two different points in time and then correlating the scores; the procedure is known as test–retest reliability assessment.

standard error of estimate
Term used in regression analysis to refer to the absolute amount of variation in the criterion variable that is left unexplained or unaccounted for by the fitted regression equation.

standard test market　A market which companies sell their cts through normal **St** tion channels.

techn e　Self-report measure attitude responden which the indicate how a ked to of a number of st ly each describes the object ts

statistic　Characteristi rest. measure of a sample.

statistical efficiency　Measure used to compare sampling plans; one sampling plan is said to be superior (more statistically efficient) to another if, for the same size sample, it produces a smaller standard error of estimate.

statistical regression
Tendency of extreme cases of a phenomenon to move toward a more central position during the course of an experiment.

storytelling　Questionnaire method of data collection relying on a picture stimulus such as a cartoon, photograph, or drawing, about which the subject is asked to tell a story.

stratified sample　Probability sample that is distinguished by the two-step procedure in which (1) the parent population is divided into mutually exclusive and exhaustive subsets, and (2) a simple random sample of elements is chosen independently from each group or subset.

stratum chart　Set of line charts in which quantities are aggregated or a total is disaggregated so that the distance between two lines represents the amount of some variable.

stress　Measure of the "badness of fit" of a configuration determined by multidimensional scaling analysis when compared to the original input data.

structure　Degree of standardization imposed on the data collection instrument. A highly structured questionnaire, for example, is one in which the questions to be asked and the responses permitted subjects are completely predetermined; a highly unstructured questionnaire is one in which the questions to be asked are only loosely predetermined and pondents are free to respond i ir own words and in any way see fit.

summa ratings　Self-report technique attitude measurement which the subjects are aske to indicate their degree of agr ment or disagreement with ea of a number of statements; a subject's attitude score is the total obtained by summing the scale values assigned to each category checked.

syndicated research
Information collected on a regular basis that is then sold to interested clients (for example, Nielsen Retail Index).

systematic error   Error in measurement that is also known as constant error, since it affects the measurement in a systematic way.

systematic sample   Probability sample in which every kth element in the population is designated for inclusion in the sample after a random start.

tabulation   Procedure by which the number of cases that fall into each of a number of categories are counted.

tachistoscope   Device that provides the researcher timing control over a visual stimulus; in marketing research, the visual stimulus is often a specific advertisement.

target population   Totality of cases that conforms to some designated specifications.

teleology   An ethical or moral reasoning framework that focuses on the net consequences that an action may have. If the net benefits minus all costs are positive, the act is morally acceptable; if the net result is negative, the act is not morally acceptable.

telephone interview   Telephone conversation between a representative of the research organization, the interviewer, and a respondent or interviewee.

telescoping error   A type of error resulting from the fact that most people remember an event as having occurred more recently than in fact is the case.

testing effect   Contaminating effect in an experiment occurring because the process of experimentation itself affected the observed response. The *main testing effect* refers to the impact of a prior observation on a later observation, whereas the *interactive testing effect* refers to the condition when a prior measurement affects the test unit's response to the experimental variable.

Thematic Apperception Test (TAT)   Copyrighted series of pictures about which the subject is asked to tell stories.

total association   Association existing between the variables without regard to the levels of any other variables; also called the zero-order association between the variables.

trade-off matrix   A method of structuring the stimuli that respondents evaluate in a conjoint analysis that treats two attributes at a time but considers all possible pairs; also known as the pair-wise procedure.

turnover table   *See* brand-switching matrix.

Type I error   Rejection of a null hypothesis when it is true; also known as α error.

Type II error   Failure to reject a null hypothesis when it is false; also known as β error.

unbiased   Used to describe a statistic when the average value of the statistic equals the population parameter it is supposed to estimate.

univariate   Problem of analysis in which there is a single measurement on each of n sample objects or there are several measurements on each of the n observations, but each variable is to be analyzed in isolation.

utilitarianism   The most well-known branch of teleological ethics; the utilitarian perspective holds that the correct course of action is the one that promotes the greatest good for the greatest number and that all acts for which the net benefits exceed the net costs are morally acceptable.

validity   Term applied to measuring instruments reflecting the extent to which differences in scores on the measurement reflect true differences among individuals, groups, or situations in the characteristic that it seeks to measure, or reflect true differences in the same individual, group, or situation from one occasion to another, rather than constant or random errors.

variable transformation
Change in scale in which a variable is expressed.

varimax   Angle-preserving rotation of a factor-analytic solution done to facilitate substantive interpretation of the factors.

voice-pitch analysis   Type of analysis that examines changes in the relative frequency of the human voice that accompany emotional arousal.

word association
Questionnaire containing a list of words to which respondents are instructed to reply with the first word that comes to mind.

zero-order association   *See* total association.

Subject Index

Company Index

Author Index